Financial Accounting and Reporting

A Global Perspective

Third Edition

Hervé Stolowy, ...

SOUTH-WESTERN
CENGAGE Learning

Australia • Brazil • Japan • Korea • ... • United States

SOUTH-WESTERN
CENGAGE Learning

**Financial Accounting and Reporting:
A Global Perspective, Third Edition**
Hervé Stolowy, Michel J. Lebas and Yuan Ding

Publishing Director: Linden Harris

Publisher: Stephen Wellings

Development Editor: Annabel Ainscow

Content Project Editor: Alison Cooke

Manufacturing Manager: Jane Glendening

Production Controller: Tom Relf

Marketing Manager: Amanda Cheung

Typesetter: KnowledgeWorks Global, India

Cover design: Adam Renvoize

Text design: Design Deluxe

For product information and technology assistance,
contact **emea.info@cengage.com**.

For permission to use material from this text or product,
and for permission queries,
email **clsuk.permissions@cengage.com**.

The Author has asserted the right under the Copyright, Designs and Patents Act 1988 to be identified as Author of this Work.

This work is adapted from Financial Accounting and Reporting, 2nd Edition, published by Thompson Learning, a division of Cengage Learning, Inc. © 2006

British Library Cataloguing-in-Publication Data
A catalogue record for this book is available from the British Library.

ISBN: 978-1-4080-2113-2

Cengage Learning EMEA
Cheriton House, North Way, Andover, Hampshire. SP10 5BE. United Kingdom

Cengage Learning products are represented in Canada by Nelson Education Ltd.
For your lifelong learning solutions, visit
www.cengage.co.uk
Purchase your next print book, e-book or e-chapter at
www.cengagebrain.com

Printed by Seng Lee Press, Singapore
2 3 4 5 6 7 8 9 10 – 13 12 11

Dedication

To Nicole, Natacha, and Audrey
For their indefatigable renewed support and immense and lasting patience.

To my wife Michael Adler and to Alfie
Each one, in her or his way, provided their support, loving encouragement and the serenity required by this project.

To Xiaowei and Dale
For giving me the serenity and optimism essential for being an effective teacher and productive researcher.

Brief Contents

Contents

Part 2 Major Accounting Topics **171**

13 Business Combinations 503

14 Statement of Cash Flows Construction 541

Part 3 Financial Statement Analysis **573**

15 Balance Sheet Analysis 575

16 Income Statement Analysis 603

List of Real Companies Referenced

Sanofi-Aventis	France	Chapter 3, 8
Sauer-Danfoss	USA	Chapter 9
Saurer	Switzerland	Chapter 9
SEB	France	Chapter 9
Securitas	Sweden	Chapter 8
Shenzhen Expressway Limited	China	Chapter 14
Siemens	Germany	Chapters 6, 9, 18
Sinopec	China	Chapters 12, 15,17, 18
Skis Rossignol	France	Chapter 3
Sony Corporation	Japan	Chapters 9, 10, 12, 18
Sprint	USA	Chapter 13
Stern-Stewart & Co.	USA	Chapter 18
Stora Enso	Finland	Chapters 2, 10, 12 , 13, 14
Sulzer	Switzerland	Chapters 10, 12
Taylor Nelson Sofres	UK	Chapter 9
TCL	China	Chapter 10
TDA Armaments SAS	France	Chapter 13
TeleChoice International	Singapore	Chapter 18
Telefònica	Spain	Chapters 4, 9
Tesco Group	UK	Chapter 12
Tesco UK	UK	Chapter 12
Thales	France	Chapter 12
Thales Air Systems SA	France	Chapter 13
Thales ATM GmbH	Germany	Chapter 13
Thales Australia	Australia	Chapter 13
Toray Industries	Japan	Chapters 9, 10, 11, 12, 18
Total	France	Chapter 15
Toyota Motor Corp.	Japan	Chapters 9, 18
Trigano	France	Chapter 5
TSS	Denmark	Chapter 8
UBS	Switzerland	Chapter 6
ULMA Construccion Polska SA	Poland	Chapter 18
Unilever	UK/Netherlands	Chapter 9
United Internet	Germany	Chapter 12
Vimpel Communications (VimPelCom)	Russia	Chapters 8, 15
Vivendi	France	Chapters 16, 17
Vivendi Universal	France	Chapters 16, 17
Volkswagen	Germany	Chapter 18
Volvo Group	Sweden	Chapters 8, 9, 11
Waitrose	UK	Chapter 12
Wal-mart Group	USA	Chapters 2, 12
Washington Mutual	USA	Chapter 13
Weyerhauser	USA	Chapters 7, 10, 12
Wyeth	USA	Chapter 13
Yahoo!	USA	Chapter 10
Youngor	China	Chapter 10

About the Authors

Hervé Stolowy is Professor of Accounting at HEC Paris (Jouy-en-Josas, France). He holds a degree in business administration (ESCP – Paris Graduate School of Management), a master's degree in private law (Université Paris-Val de Marne), a BA in Russian and American studies (Université Paris-Sorbonne), a PhD in financial accounting (Université Paris-Panthéon-Sorbonne) and an *'habilitation à diriger des recherches'* (which certifies him as a qualified doctoral dissertation adviser). He is a certified *'expert comptable'* (French equivalent of a chartered accountant or certified public accountant).

He has authored and co-authored 10 books, chapters in 15 collective works and published over 75 articles in academic and applied journals, such as *Abacus, Accounting Auditing & Accountability Journal, Accounting, Organizations and Society, Advances in International Accounting, Comptabilité – Contrôle – Audit, European Accounting Review, Finance – Contrôle – Stratégie, The International Journal of Accounting, Issues in Accounting Education, Journal of Accounting and Public Policy, Les Echos*, the *Review of Accounting and Finance*, the *Revue de Droit Comptable* and the *Revue Française de Comptabilité*.

Professor Stolowy's research and teaching interests span financial and international accounting, and focus most specifically on IFRS/IAS, intangibles, accounts manipulation, and design and use of statement of cash flows. He is a member of the Association Francophone de Comptabilité (AFC), the European Accounting Association (EAA), the American Accounting Association (AAA), and Canadian Academic Accounting Association (CAAA). He is past president of AFC and current co-editor of *Comptabilité – Contrôle – Audit*. He has been a member of the Standards Advice Review Group [SARG] created to advise the [European] Commission on the objectivity and neutrality of the European Financial Reporting Advisory Group's (EFRAG's) opinions.

Hervé Stolowy teaches financial accounting and financial statement analysis in the different graduate programs of HEC Paris (HEC-MBA Program and HEC Master of Science in Management – *Grande Ecole*). He also teaches in the HEC doctoral program (research in financial accounting).

Michel J. Lebas is Emeritus Professor of Management Accounting and Management Control at HEC Paris. He was educated both in France (HEC) and in the United States (Tuck School at Dartmouth College and Stanford University Graduate School of Business). After a brief career as an economic analyst for a US multinational company in Boston, and later as a staff consultant in the New York office of then Price Waterhouse, he joined the academic profession while maintaining an active freelance consulting practice. He is now a freelance consultant and executive education trainer, working for multinational companies and various international executive MBA programs in Europe, Asia, North America and Africa.

Professor Lebas' field of research and consulting concentrates on advanced practices in management accounting and performance management systems. He is one of the academic research associates in the Beyond Budgeting Round Table Program; from July 1992 to July 2000 he represented the *French Ordre des Experts Comptables* and the *Compagnie des Commissaires aux Comptes* on the then 'Financial and Management Accounting Committee' (FMAC) (currently 'Accountant in Business Committee') of the

International Federation of Accountants (IFAC). He is the founder, and was, from 1992 until 1996, co-editor of the management accounting section of the *Revue Française de Comptabilité*. His publications, in addition to this textbook, include chapters in major international collective works, co-authorship/editorship of a *Glossary of Accounting English*, co-authorship of a *Management Accounting Glossary*, as well as a French language management accounting textbook. He co-authored a CAM-I monograph on *Best Practices in World Class Organizations* with Ken Euske and C.J. McNair. His numerous articles have been published in many academic and professional journals including *Administración de Empresas, Cahiers Français, De Accountant, Les Echos, European Accounting Review, European Management Journal, The Financial Times, International Journal of Production Economics, Journal of Management Studies, Management Accounting Research, Performances Humaines et Techniques, Problemi di Gestione, Revue Française de Comptabilité, Revue Française de Gestion Industrielle, Sviluppo & Organizzazione, Travail*, and in the publications of IFAC.

Professor Lebas has been Associate Dean for Academic Affairs of the HEC *Grande Ecole* (1986–1989). He holds or has held visiting appointments at the Aarhus Business School, SDA Bocconi in Milan, the Fletcher School of Law and Diplomacy at Tufts University, INSEAD, the Mediterranean School of Business in Tunis, the Darden Graduate School of Business at the University of Virginia, and at the Foster School of Business of the University of Washington. Michel Lebas is a member of the Association Francophone de Comptabilité, the American Accounting Association, and the Institute of Management Accountants.

Yuan Ding is Professor of Accounting at China Europe International Business School (CEIBS). Prior to joining CEIBS, he was a tenured faculty member at HEC Paris, France. He received his PhD in Accounting from the Université Montesquieu (Bordeaux IV), France. He also holds a Master's in Enterprise Administration from the Université de Poitiers, France.

Professor Ding's research has been published in *Accounting, Organizations and Society, Journal of Accounting and Public Policy, European Accounting Review, Abacus, The International Journal of Accounting, Review of Accounting and Finance, Advances in International Accounting, Issues in Accounting Education, Managerial Finance, Journal of Business Venturing, Management International Review, Corporate Governance: An International Review, International Journal of Disclosure and Governance* and several leading French academic journals.

Professor Ding is the Academic Deputy President of the Research Centre of Complex Data analysis of Beihang University, Beijing, China. He is a member of the European Accounting Association, the Association Francophone de Comptabilité and the American Accounting Association. He is Editorial Board Member of *China Journal of Accounting Research, Global Perspectives on Accounting Education Journal, The International Journal of Accounting, Journal of Accounting and Public Policy, Research in Accounting in Emerging Economies*. His current research is focused on intangibles, international accounting harmonization, earnings management, analyst forecasts, corporate governance issues, and accounting reform in China.

Professor Ding lectures in financial accounting, financial statement analysis, international accounting and corporate governance in Master's of Science in Management, MBA, EMBA and PhD programs in Europe and in China. He designed and delivered in-company special and open executive education programs in China and in Europe. At CEIBS, he co-founded the first CFO open program in China in 2005 and is involved in many top executive programs co-organized with Harvard, Wharton, INSEAD, New York University, London School of Economics, IESE and HEC Paris. He frequently provides consulting services for many multinational and Chinese companies in the areas of financial communication, corporate governance, cost control system design, investment and M&A. He also serves on the Board of Directors of several major Chinese listed firms and financial institutions.

The author team is a reflection of the spirit and the tone of the text. Hervé Stolowy and Yuan Ding bring the accounting and reporting practitioner/researcher and external financial analyst viewpoint, while Michel Lebas brings the internal and managerial pre-occupations in the design of information systems and the interpretation of accounting information. Currently living and working in three different continents (Europe, America and Asia), the team brings a unique combined global vision on current accounting issues and their management implication.

Preface

This third edition is published at a time of both turmoil and hope for financial accounting:

- Turmoil, which follows the financial scandals and the economic crisis that started in mid 2008.
- Turmoil, since that storm challenged both accounting rules and practices.
- Hope, because these rules and practices held fast, and helped the boat stay the course, despite showing some potential weak points (mainly around the concept of fair value).
- Hope, because the importance of good accounting and reporting is now more evident than ever. Had many of the disabled firms actually followed best accounting practices, had shareholders showed some common-sense and less gullibility, and had managers indulged in less greed, much of the misery created around the world would not have taken place – even if accounting alone could not have prevented some form of crisis.
- Hope because the convergence between IFRS (the standards on which this book is mainly based) and US GAAP seems to be gaining traction again at the time of this writing, following a fast track forward until the crisis, and many ups and downs since.
- Hope because the field of accounting, despite being over 3,800 years old, is now more alive and full of youthful vitality than ever, and is still developing to serve the needs of businesses and investors.

Increasing numbers of people, students and executives, see the usefulness of gaining an ability to read and understand financial statements, and rely on trained, qualified professionals to produce them.

This third edition acknowledges the turmoil described above, and offers tools to comfort and reinforce hope, in line with the harmonization of best practice, and respecting local cultural differences.

A book to meet changing student and faculty expectations

The success of the first two editions of this award-winning textbook confirmed that the authors' original point of view remains correct: most students in business or management around the world want and need, regardless of their career plans, to understand how accounting figures and documents are produced in order to better decode them, and extract their information content for decision-making.

The profile of executive, graduate and undergraduate business students studying the programs which the authors teach has become increasingly international, either because programs have developed without reference to borders, or because executive trainees, students and faculty show increasing worldwide mobility.

To these students as to most managers, English is the *lingua franca* of business. More and more business programs are being taught in part or completely in 'International English', regardless of the location of their venue.

Most students or executive program participants in our target audience know their career is already, or will be, in an international context, i.e., neither where they grew up, nor where they were educated.

The composition of the team of authors reflects this quasi supra-nationality of accounting. Hervé Stolowy, based in France, brings a European viewpoint, Michel J. Lebas, based in the US, teaches and consults on three continents, and Yuan Ding, based in China, teaches and consults in Asia and Europe. All three authors teach in international programs, each one its own mini melting pot of cultures, of educational backgrounds, of diverse previous experiences, of a variety of firms from industrial, commercial or service sectors, of different professional responsibilities, and of individual career or professional objectives.

The book is written first and foremost for all managers and students of management, rather than future or existing professional accountants. However, these will always find the user orientation of the book a source of enlightenment and improvement to their own practice. The richness of the Web-based appendices and supplements extends the reach of the book to include advanced accounting students and make it a life-long reference tool, regardless of career evolutions.

Students and managers want and need, within a context of continuous learning, to be trained to appreciate, understand and analyze a variety of Financial Accounting and Reporting issues from a theoretical, universal and generic point of view. They know the principles and tools they will have mastered through this textbook will allow them to adapt and apply their understanding of accounting and reporting to any local circumstances they will face. The authors' choice has been to provide much real-world case data from a variety of contexts (industrial, commercial, distribution or services), variety of firm size (from the single proprietorship to the multinational corporation), or variety of countries of operation (within Europe, Asia, America or Africa). These real-world cases are analyzed and used in illustrations in the chapters or are the basis for well-focused and progressive assignments. The book's content of principles, practices, tools and techniques can be immediately applied to the rich and complex environment where our readers currently work, and will work.

A book based on three simultaneous perspectives

The authors conceived their work to enable the teaching of Financial Accounting and Reporting to a non-specialist audience, with the following three perspectives in mind:

- First, it definitely takes a *user-orientation* position throughout, whether it is when explaining principles and their implications for quality information, usable by decision-makers, or in the practice of analyzing financial statements.

- Second, it provides an *a-national* approach: the issues are explained as natural business and common-sense problems, with multiple possible solutions and positions. As much as is possible, all likely solutions are examined with their own logic and pros and cons. The accounting language is presented as a natural language rather than as esoteric jargon, reserved for the few and the brave. Accounting issues are created by business needs, and by the ever-increasing, and evolving, globalization of the economy. They transcend local politics and economic upturns or downturns.

- Third, it takes on an *international point of view*. Although unabashedly based on IFRS principles and rules, the authors are aware of, and fully acknowledge and explain, the implications of the different positions other regulators may have taken on relevant issues. Our choice simply reflects the growing harmonization and convergence between local rules and regulations and the leading international providers of principles, rules and regulations.

Target audience for this text

This textbook is designed primarily:

- For business and management graduate students, essentially MBA students, following their course of studies in institutions where knowledge of a single (national) accounting system is recognized as being insufficient preparation for the world in which the graduates will work.

- For junior or senior undergraduate business students with minimal business experience.

- For non-financial business executives, from any background or experience, who originate from functions distant from financial techniques and information and who wish to understand the financial performance of the entities they interact with and be able to decode their reporting to the outside world.

- For intermediate courses on Financial Statement Analysis, Financial Reporting or International Accounting, when supplementing the text with the full power of the appendices on the dedicated website.

Our approach derives from the characteristics of our target audience

The approach is based on the following ideas:

- As mentioned above, we adopted a *user*, rather than a preparer perspective. Our choice results from our deeply held belief that business 'students' (graduate, senior undergraduate, or executive trainees), regardless of the area of specialization they have selected, or the career(s) they will embrace over their lifetime, will be, first and foremost, and on a regular basis, users of financial statements.

  Whether they will use accounting and financial information as internal managers or executives, or as external users (investors, credit analysts, etc.) they will need to interpret accounting data to be able to communicate and decide.

  Their knowledge of the preparation of accounting and reporting numbers need only encompass enough comprehension of key principles to prevent the user being at the mercy of the information preparer. An old Chinese proverb says: 'If you want to build a bridge, ask the river'. If a manager wants to make the right decision about a business, he or she would do well to listen to what the firm says about itself, and how it reports on its performance or its cash flow.

  The book's target audience is a mix of specialists and non-specialists. While helping non-specialists become skillful in financial information understanding and use, our approach opens a new perspective for specialists to review, from the user viewpoint, the information they prepare and rethink their financial communication strategy to more effectively satisfy the users' needs.

- The book is based on real-world examples and illustrations. It incorporates a profusion of extracts from the annual reports of well-known firms and excerpts from the financial press. Some of these elements of annual reports are commented on in detail, in order to prepare the students for reading and interpreting annual reports and articles in the financial press.

- Rather than providing a regulatory (technical) solution to a (simple or complex) reporting or measurement issue, we have chosen to first examine the economic logic of the problem, and second to identify generic possible solutions and what impact each might have on a company's or decision-maker's decisions. Accounting rules, regulations and practices result from well-reasoned arguments, which are dissected, when appropriate, in the chapters.

■ Throughout the book and whenever appropriate, we cite and explain the latest International Accounting Standards Board (IASB) standards (i.e., IFRS/IAS). We strongly believe that, in many situations, the IASB recommendations, with the leeway and flexibility they contain, offer a good *a-national* approach, but we do not hesitate to highlight the areas where the debate is still open, or where we feel in disagreement, with aspects of a currently 'recommended' solution, always taking the point of view of the user. We take into account all sources of good accounting principles and practices: the IASB (which produces IFRS), the US-based Financial Accounting Standards Board (which produces SFAS), the Financial Market regulators such as IOSCO (International Organization of Securities Commissions) or the US SEC (Securities and Exchange Commission) and their national or regional partners or equivalents.

■ The body of each chapter is supplemented by five parts: (1) Key points, (2) Review problems with detailed analysis and solutions, (3) Assignments, including multiple-choice questions on the key points, (4) References and (5) Further reading.

■ A Glossary of key terms is provided at the end of the book, as well as a full index.

■ At their first appearance, the terms included in the Glossary are highlighted in the text as bold and underlined.

■ All chapters are supplemented on the dedicated book website by appendices that deal with particularly technical issues or special cases.

■ The authors have written this text with the intention of showing that quality accounting reports are essential to decision-makers. The ability to read and understand accounting statements is as essential to managers as their ability to read newspapers, magazines, and books, or to attend professional conferences. Good accounting, like good journalism, follows rules and is limited only by professionalism, culture, ethics and tradition. The talent of the accountant, like that of the journalist, rests in his or her ability to choose the right descriptors that will give a true and fair view of events and of their implications. Accounting describes the economic reality of enterprises by using a dedicated language. We hope, with this book, to help demystify the world of financial reporting.

A few practical considerations

■ As the choice of currency unit has no bearing on the logic of our arguments or presentation, and in keeping with our *a-national* editorial choice and the current practice of the IASB, throughout the book we use a generic Currency Unit (or CU). The exception is when we refer to real-life examples when the original currency is always used.

■ All assignments based on actual business organizations are identified, in the name of the assignment, with an asterisk next to the name of the company to highlight the 'real-world' origin of the assignment.

■ In some tables, based on real-world examples, the use of parentheses is equivalent to a negative sign, as it is a common practice in many countries.

■ Tables and figures are numbered by chapter. Those in appendices are referred to with a letter A added after the number.

Supplementary support materials for students and teachers

Supplementary support material is available for both students and instructors and teachers on the book's dedicated website at the following address: http://www.cengage.co.uk/stolowy3

For students

- Excel files for selected assignments.
- Appendices for each chapter.
- Multilingual glossary of accounting terms (English, French, German, Italian, Spanish).

For instructors and teachers

- PowerPoint slides of the figures, tables and text summary corresponding to each chapter.
- Solutions to the end-of-chapter assignments:
  - Word files containing complete solutions. The authors have written special notes to the instructor, indicating frequently-made mistakes and alternative acceptable solutions when applicable.
  - Excel files with all detailed calculations when useful.
  - PowerPoint slides of the solutions for class use when appropriate.
- Additional assignments and their solution (Word and Excel files).

The supplementary material may be found on the Internet at the following password protected address: http://www.cengage.co.uk/ stolowy3

New features of the third edition

In addition to updating the second edition throughout for the latest developments in the IFRS program and bringing the IAS up-to-date (and quoting the relevant FASB pronouncements, when useful), and using the most recently available company financial statements at the time of writing, the third edition also offers:

- New and updated real-life examples from companies operating in a range of countries throughout the world, with a large development of cases about businesses headquartered in Asia.
- Conformity with current IFRS/IAS (as at the Fall of 2009).
- Extensive developments on fair value in Chapter 10.
- Financial analysis sections in almost all chapters before those specifically dedicated to financial statement analysis.
- Enrichment and development of old Chapter 15 on financial statement analysis into four better-focused chapters.
- Ample developments in Chapter 18 on governance and ethics.
- Vastly expanded level of detail within the many new review problems at the end of each chapter.
- Expanded glossary of key terms added at the end of the book
- More and updated exercises and case material at the end of each chapter.
- Multiple-choice questions in all chapter assignments.
- Further streamlining and simplification of bookkeeping (preparer technology) issues in Chapter 4.
- An enriched provision of materials on the faculty website, which instructors can share, as needed, with their students.

Acknowledgments

Stephen Wellings, our publisher for this third edition at Cengage, followed in the foot-steps of Jennifer Pegg (at Thomson Learning) for the first edition and Patrick (Pat) Bond (Thomson Learning and Cengage) for the second edition. He provided us with caring support and showed the same constructive and positive attitude and professionalism as his predecessors.

Our appreciation also goes to all the staff at Cengage who have assisted Annabel M. Ainscow, development editor, and Alison E. Cooke, content project editor, with the creation of this book. Annabel must be particularly acknowledged for her diplomacy and patience, which allowed her to firmly prod and encourage the authors, with great effectiveness, while giving them the space needed to meet deadlines, without sacrificing quality. A fine balancing act we appreciated and are grateful for.

Our very special appreciation goes to Claire Martin, our copy editor, whose flexibility, intelligence and understanding has been essential to our meeting our deadlines, and hopefully to the quality of the book, even if we assume full responsibility for any remaining lack of clarity or error.

Anonymous reviewers and adopters of the previous editions played a significant role in shaping the third edition. Their constructive comments helped us narrow down or focus our views and, we believe, improve the pedagogical approach in this third edition. They 'kept us honest' by telling us where our pet topics had led to outsized sections or had led us to overlook some critical issue. Adopters and reviewers helped us create what we feel is now a better-balanced text. Some of these evaluators who also often helped us in the design of the previous editions, have agreed to lose their anonymity and we gladly acknowledge in person these friends and kindred souls:

Ignace de Beelde, University of Gent
Begoñia Giner Inchausti, University of Valencia
Phil Cahill, Ecole de Management de Normandie
Axel Haller, University of Regensburg
Agnieszka Herdan, University of Greenwich
Paul Jennings, University of Winchester
Ann Jorissen, University of Antwerp
Josephine Maltby, University of Sheffield
Jan Marton, University of Gothenberg
Pat Sucher, Royal Holloway College, University of London
Anne Ullathorne, University of Birmingham
Charles P. van Wymeersch, University of Namur
Peter Walton, ESSEC
Stefano Zambon, University of Ferrara

Our students, and users from all over the world, have often been our toughest evaluators. They have challenged, criticized and commented on the previous editions of this book. Our greatest appreciation goes to these truly international students for their patience and tolerance with our occasional remaining areas of shadow and weaknesses and for their generally constructive comments.

We wish to recognize Michael Erkens, our research assistant on this edition, whose initiative, energy and patience helped update the financial reports we use, and helped us identify other interesting cases. We also want to acknowledge Nils Clotteau and Sophie Marmousez, our research assistants on the previous editions, who helped us build a sound base on which we have kept building. Our students and assistants' work has allowed us to create this more focused, better balanced and updated third edition.

The multilingual glossary (available on the instructor's section of the website) is a collective work and we are pleased to acknowledge our co-authors: Eva Eberhartinger (Professor of Tax Management, Department of Finance, Accounting and Statistics, WU Vienna University of Economics and Business, Austria), José Antonio Gonzalo (Professor of Accounting and Financial Economics, Department of Managerial Science, University of Alcalá, Spain), and Stefano Zambon (Professor of Business Economics, Faculty of Economics, University of Ferrara, Italy).

Lastly but certainly not the least, we wish to thank Georges Langlois who has translated and adapted both this edition and the second one for the French speaking markets. Translation is a very unforgiving test for the authors, as any lack of clarity becomes perfectly obvious once the sentences need to be translated, even by a brilliantly competent translator/adaptor. Georges' almost real time comments and questions helped us clarify our English text, correct errors and made sure we remained on the straight and narrow of both our objectives and accounting theory.

We warmly thank all these contributors for the generosity of their time and intelligence.

The authors, nonetheless, assume full responsibility for the ideas expressed and for any errors or omissions.

We will appreciate any and all comments from readers and users.

Hervé Stolowy, Paris, France
Michel J. Lebas, Seattle, USA
Yuan Ding, Shanghai, China
December 2009

Contacts:
stolowy@hec.fr
lebas@uw.edu
dyuan@ceibs.edu

Walk Through Tour

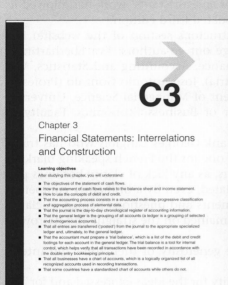

Chapter opening page
◀ Learning objectives set out concisely what is to be learned in the chapter, and ultimately link in to the Key points at the end of the chapter.

Introductory text expands on the learning objectives and shows how the chapter fits in with other chapters. This helps readers to put the chapter in context and see the 'big picture'.

Key terms
▲ Basic definitions and clarification of key terms are given in a glossary section at the end of the book.

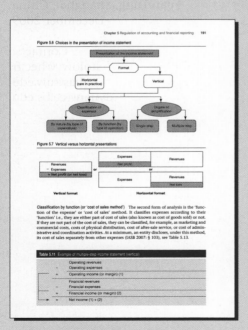

Diagrams and figures
▲ These are exceptionally clear to help the reader conceptualise abstract ideas such as income statement formats. Tables clearly present financial statements in an accessible format.

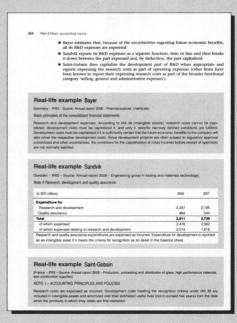

Real-life examples
▲ Extracts from the financial statements of companies from around the world help bring the learning points to life

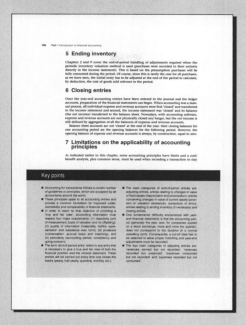

Key points
▲ Key points conclude the chapter and highlight the core learning points covered. They link in to the learning objectives introduced at the start of the chapter. They are a useful reminder for a reader who is reviewing the chapter.

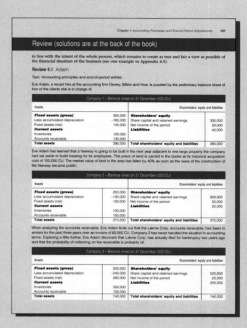

Review
▲ The Review section at the end of the chapter contains questions, the solutions to which are found at the back of the book. Readers are encouraged to attempt the questions without first looking at the solutions.

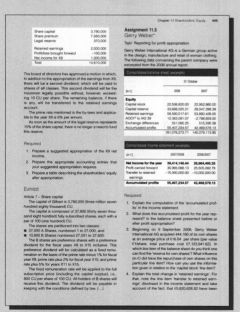

Assignments
▲ The numerous Assignments test a range of issues covered in the chapter. Solutions are provided on the companion website and are available only to lecturers adopting the book.

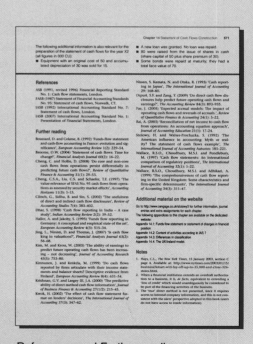

References and Further reading
▲ These provide directions to further sources of information

Companion website

Visit the *Financial Accounting and Reporting* companion website at
http://www.cengage.co.uk/stolowy3
to find valuable teaching and learning material including:

For students
■ Appendices for each chapter
■ Excel files for selected assignments
■ Multilingual glossary

For lecturers
■ A secure, password-protected site with teaching material
■ PowerPoint slides to be used in your lectures
■ Solutions to all assignments as Word files and, when appropriate, as Excel files
■ Additional assignments with solutions (Word files and, when appropriate, Excel files)
■ ExamView - Using hundreds of questions created specifically for this textbook, this test bank and test generator allows lecturers to create tests easily.

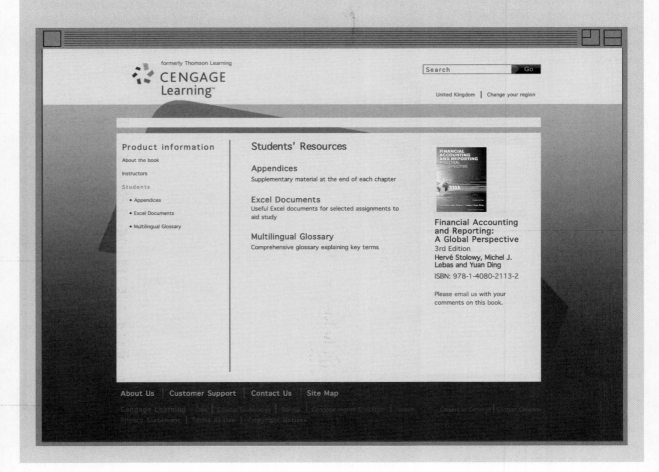

P1

Part 1

Introduction to Financial Accounting

C1

Chapter 1
Accounting: The Language of Business

Learning objectives

After studying this chapter, you will understand:

- That accounting is a language that helps understand and model business activity.
- What accounting, financial accounting and managerial accounting represent.
- That financial accounting is, in practice, a process.
- That reporting on the financial condition of the firm through financial statements is the end-product of this process.
- That different users, with possibly different objectives, are interested in financial accounting information.
- How basic transactions are recorded and impact financial statements.
- What are the characteristics and roles of each financial statement.
- That accounting, historically, is a very old decision-making tool.

Accounting is inseparable from **business** and management. In this book on **accounting** and reporting, we will be discussing business issues and decisions from the point of view of both management and investors. 'Accounting is the language of business' is a frequently heard expression. Let us see what is behind what has, by now, become a banal expression.

1 A model of business activity

Business is about action (transformation of resources) and involves transactions between several people (Robinson Crusoe, alone on his island, may have had 'undertakings', but could not have had a 'business').

Business involves suppliers and customers, but also a variety of people, each bringing to the business a specialized skill set that will be used in the enterprise's transformation process.

Business is about transforming resources into something else (product or service, tangible or intangible) aimed at meeting customers' expectations. The market offering by the producer is its 'value proposition' (functionalities, availability, durability, etc. of the product or service). Creating and delivering the value proposition consumes resources. The customer who chooses to acquire the value proposition will hand over some of their resources to the producer. The purpose (and requirement for survival) of business is that the resources acquired from sales exceed the resources consumed, i.e., that it creates 'profit'.

Each skill set provided by individuals or groups of individuals (marketing, research and development [R&D] and engineering, purchasing, manufacturing, selling, hiring, coordinating, managing, measuring, etc.) contributes to the transformation process of resources into making available, and delivering effectively, a product or service value proposition to a (solvent) customer base.

Business decisions involve how resources will be acquired, allocated to each skill set and utilized (i.e., transformed) to 'serve' customers. All decisions in an enterprise are therefore built on a *representation* of the transformation process that includes a description of the role of each skill set. Each firm has its own vision of its transformation process (and therefore about its allocation of resources): it is its specific strategy. The strategy of Scania Trucks (Johnson and Bröms, 2000) is, for example, still different from that of Volvo Trucks. Both firms try to provide customers with the ability to find the truck that serves their specific needs as perfectly as possible. They have however opted for very different business processes. Scania opted, more than 30 years ago, for a modular design of its products that allows great possibilities for customization while limiting complexity at the manufacturing level, at the expense of a large investment in upfront research for flexibility and compatibility. Meanwhile, Volvo Trucks, having grown largely through external acquisition of international manufacturers, has a rich product offering coming from a much more complex transformation process to create a market offering which is about as rich as Scania's. Both enterprises are among the leaders in their markets and accounting must be able to compare them. Accounting must, therefore, be generic enough to be applicable to a variety of situations and business models.

A generic representation of the activity of any business is shown in Figure 1.1 as a '**cash pump**' cycle. In this cycle, resources are transformed into a value proposition, physically 'packaged' as goods or services delivered to customers. These, in turn, exchange cash (or other resources equivalent to cash) for said goods, and that cash is, in due course, used for the acquisition of additional resources. The 'cash pump' cycle is essentially endless, as long as the enterprise can acquire resources and continues giving satisfaction to customers (at least better than competitors) and receives more cash from customers than it must give to all suppliers (including labor and capital providers) that allow the transformation cycle to continue to take place.

This cycle needs to be monitored by the managers of the firm. Every transaction (between suppliers and the enterprise or between the enterprise and its customers, but also inside the transformation process) needs to be recorded in order to serve as a basis for analysis over time (for example: does the enterprise need more or fewer resources than during the previous period in order to find a customer or create a new product or service?) and comparatively to competitors (does the enterprise require more resources than its competitors to find a reliable supplier of a resource or to keep human talent inside the firm?).

Figure 1.1   The generic business model is a 'cash pump' cycle

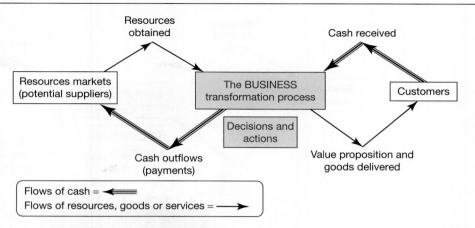

The only way for the various managers and actors in the firm (actors operating the 'cash pump') to be able to analyze transactions and take any action required to maintain the competitiveness of the firm is to agree on shared rules for describing transactions so they can communicate with one another. In other words, they need to share a language with its vocabulary, grammar and syntax to describe events and transactions that need to be examined in order to manage the 'cash pump'. That language is called accounting.

2 Accounting: A language for business

Accounting is a specialized language that has the specificity of being able to:

- Describe a state or a result (such as: 'the sales revenue obtained from customers in the month of October amounted to 12 million Currency Units [CU]').

- Describe the events (purposeful mobilization of resources) that led to that result (such as: 'An advertising campaign worth 750,000 CU was run on TV in the first week of October; market share increased by 10% between October 1 and October 31; prices were reduced by 5% on October 1 from what they had been since last year; additional customers were acquired, etc.').

- Provide a rank ordering of results allowing evaluators of accounting signals to be able to say 'This result – be it for a time period, or for a market, or for a responsibility center – is better (or worse) than that result'.

Figure 1.1 must therefore be amended to show that accounting is needed to support decision-making. Figure 1.2 illustrates such amendment.

Accounting records every event of an economic nature that flows through the 'cash pump' or business cycle. Accounting records economic variables principally using monetary units. It can, however, also describe non-financial parameters as in a physical balance of the weight of materials consumed, which, in a well-managed organization, must be equal to the weight of finished goods plus that of waste.[1]

The thin solid blue lines refer to internally generated accounting data and information, while the dotted blue lines refer to data and information, used in accounting but emanating from either suppliers or customers.

Accounting is an integral part of the life of business. It is as inseparable from business activity as the shadow is to the illuminated object. Accounting helps managers know what

Figure 1.2 Accounting describes – and is linked to – every part of the activity of the firm

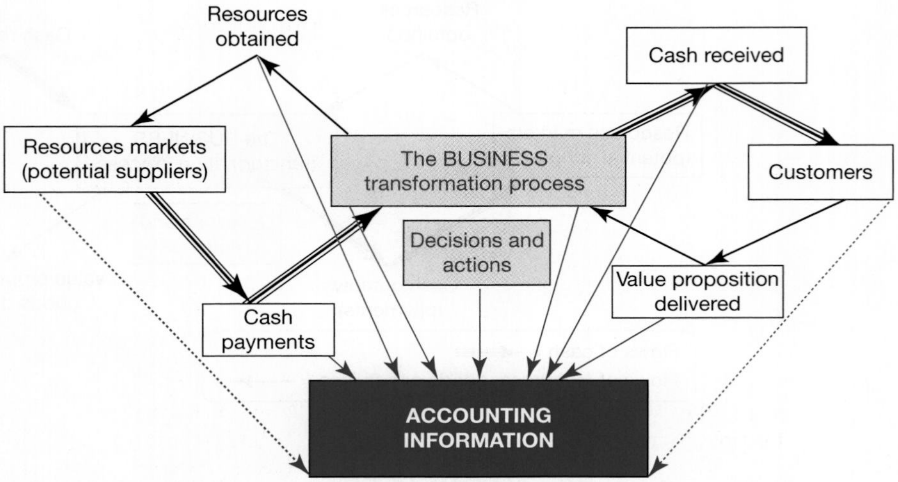

The thin solid blue lines refer to internally generated accounting data and information, while the dotted blue lines refer to data and information, used in accounting but emanating from either suppliers or customers.

was done so they can modify their future actions in order for the future to yield results that either are as coherent or more coherent with their intent and objective.

However the reader will remember that the title of this book is Financial Accounting and **Reporting**. Why also reporting?

2.1 Business creates an agency relationship that calls for reporting

Business is about delegation:

■ Delegation from the capital providers to the managers in charge of creating wealth with the capital they were awarded; and

■ Delegation within the organization to specialized managers (responsible for skill-set pools) to work in a coordinated and coherent way to create wealth (among other things for capital providers, but also for other participants in the business process).

Delegation means control: was the devolution and autonomy granted used appropriately? Control requires that **information** be provided about what the 'delegatee' (or agent) did and what results were achieved. The flow of information, allowing control by the 'delegator' (or principal), is called reporting.

Reporting is accounting for what the subordinate or delegatee has done with the resources she or he has received from her or his superior or principal. A 'report' may document effort, or results, or both. If 'effort' (on the part of the agent) is reported, accounting will be detailed and will provide the values of those parameters needed to describe the business processes transforming resources into a value proposition and its delivery. Reporting on effort will be strictly internal and business-specific (we will call it 'managerial accounting'). If, on the contrary, only 'results' are reported, the report may be generic since the questions from **users** of financial information are essentially the same regardless of the nature of the business (this type of report will be the focus of this text and is part of what we call 'financial accounting'). The questions (or informational wants or needs) – are essentially about three topics:

■ whether the business has created value for capital providers (current or potential), i.e., a comparatively positive return on investment, given a certain level of risk, and will continue to do so at what kind of rate of growth,

■ whether current and past actions increase or decrease the level of risk the firm is facing, and

■ whether the resources the business controls make its operations viable for the future, and for how long (this question being of prime importance for employees, customers and suppliers, among many stakeholders[2] in the business).

2.1.1 Reporting to capital providers

The 'cash pump' cycle described in Figure 1.1 is not completely operational. Like any pump, this one too must be primed. How can the business acquire resources to feed its transformation process unless there is already some cash in the enterprise before it starts to operate? Suppliers might extend credit to prime the pump, but the operating (transformation) cycle might be much longer than the duration of the credit the suppliers are willing to extend.

There must be capital providers who provide initial financial resources that will be used to prime the transformation cycle. The business manager is therefore the agent of the capital provider: she or he has received the mandate to use the capital to earn a positive return within acceptable risk-taking practices. In some cases the entrepreneur/manager and the capital provider might be one and the same person but, as we will see later, it is essential to distinguish the business' activities from those engaged in *privately* by the individuals who are either providing capital or are the operators of the transformation process.

Since the providers of capital are not, in a capitalistic system, doing so without the motive of earning a return on their investment, it is normal for a business to report on what they used the funds for and what output and outcome was obtained from their application to the transformation process, i.e., what wealth was created.

There are two kinds of capital providers:

■ Those known as **shareholders** in the case of an incorporated business who (a) are investing capital for an unspecified term, (b) are willing to assume or share, directly or vicariously, the risks of the business in exchange for a variable but hopefully large return, and (c) are participating in decision-making, directly or through the Board of Directors representing them.

■ Those known as **lenders** who (a) are not willing to assume much of the risks of the business and (b) want a guaranteed return on their provision of funds within (c) a specified short-, medium- or long-term horizon.

Each category of funds provider has specific needs in terms of reporting, which the accounting information system will need to satisfy. Lenders are mainly interested in being kept informed about the ability of the business to reimburse the money it has borrowed by the due date. The emphasis is therefore on the cash generation potential of the firm.

Shareholders, by way of contrast, are interested in two types of information: on the one hand, from a fiduciary point of view, shareholders want to know periodically what the firm they have invested in owns or controls (and what their share of ownership is) and be sure that appropriate controls are in place to avoid inappropriate disbursement of resources (we call the accounting report that serves this purpose the **balance sheet** or **statement of financial position**); on the other hand they are interested in knowing how much residual wealth was created in the transformation process that they can claim as theirs (we call the accounting report that serves this purpose the **income statement** or **profit and loss account**).

In addition, both lenders and capital providers are interested in knowing more about the plans of the business and the dynamics of the evolution of the relevant and specifically defined 'cash pump'.

Figure 1.2 can now be enriched again to recognize the complexity of all processes behind the life of an enterprise. Figure 1.3 reflects, in addition to the representation of the business cycle (the 'cash pump'), the fact that an initial flow of capital is essential to

Figure 1.3 Flow of funds and flows of information (accounting and reporting) between a business and its funds providers

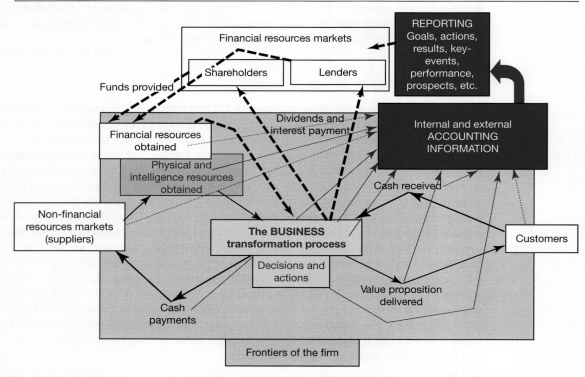

The solid lines indicate the flow of resources within the business cycle, while the bold black dotted lines indicate the flow of resources linked to the relations between the business and its funds providers. Accounting information is another 'resource' that flows between parties. As in Figure 1.2 the thin dotted blue lines reflect the fact accounting information contains additional data about customers and suppliers.

start the value creation cycle (transformation process) and that **capital providers need to be rewarded** by either dividends or **interest** payment, and require they be provided with information (reporting) about how well the business is functioning. Since accounting reflects all economic transactions, it is the key medium of communication inside the firm as well as with its partners or **stakeholders**, including capital providers and lenders among the many we list in endnote 2.

2.1.2 Reporting to business 'partners'

Although, technically, the firm is not an agent of employees, customers or suppliers (the firm has not received a mandate from them), it is normal, if the relationships with these actors are to be durable, that they be kept informed since they are *de facto* 'partners' in the future success of the firm. All others who need to evaluate the risks of a business and the likelihood of its survival will use, for that purpose, accounting reports that were originally prepared mainly for capital providers. These other users will do so by surmising the business model and looking at telltale ratios or metrics describing the 'health' of the 'cash pump' process both in terms of efficiency and relevance, but also in terms of security of provision of funds by capital providers (we call this **'financial statement analysis'** and Chapters 15 to 18 are devoted entirely to such activity).

2.1.3 Reporting to superiors and peers

Accounting describes transactions linked to – and results of – actions and decisions. It is normal (and convenient, since the information already has been captured to satisfy capital providers) that a superior uses accounting information to verify the subordinate discharged her or his responsibility appropriately. If the superior is only interested in results, information in a format similar to the one used to report to capital providers might prove to be sufficient (financial accounting is 'results oriented'), while, if the superior is interested in evaluating the effort of the subordinate, she or he might be interested in the detailed steps undertaken by the subordinate in fulfilling her or his mission. In this case the accounting report will be more process oriented and will be called, as already mentioned, 'managerial accounting'.

2.2 Accounting is a living language

As we have seen, accounting describes what actors in the transformation process of the firm do. The process of the 'cash pump' is one of value creation. Business makes sense only if more resources, in the broad sense of the term resources, i.e., financial and non-financial, are created as the outcome of the transformation process than were consumed in its course.

The process of doing business changes over time (the application of the generic 'cash pump' changes continuously) in order to adapt to innovations and the evolution of competitive pressures. Business relationships are affected by technology. For example, the introduction of the Internet has greatly modified the way the transformation process is organized. Web-based market places and speed of communication change the relationships between enterprises, suppliers and customers. Similarly, new issues appear with the evolution of society. For example, 75 years ago, few businesses paid significant attention to the possible creation of a retirement income for their former employees. New business issues are born every day that accounting must be able to describe as an enrichment of what was previously provided. The reality that accounting describes is alive and evolving continuously. The accounting language must therefore be very strong and flexible and rest on solid principles that will allow that flexibility.

Accounting is a language and its 'words' are symbols that reflect a certain view of the world. Just like our everyday language evolves continuously, accounting must be able to adapt to the needs of the time.

Accounting is a very special language in that the way it describes the world of business affects the timing or recognition and measurement of wealth creation. To give a brief example, when one buys a machine, one could offset the purchase cost against the revenue generated by the use of the machine during the first year (a procedure called 'cash accounting') or one could consider that the machine will be useful to generate sales over several years and therefore one would offset, in the first year, only a part of the cost of the machine ('depreciating' the machine over its useful life, a part of what we call **'accrual accounting'**). Clearly, the choice between these two approaches will affect greatly the perceived timing of the wealth created through the use of the machine to serve customers. Accounting is so important for the smooth operation of a society that few countries have allowed its evolution to go unchecked.

Language is essential to the operation of any organized society. Cardinal de Richelieu, Prime Minister to the French King, Louis XIII, founded in 1635 the *Académie Française* to create, standardize and regulate the French language. His decision was both political and economical. It was, of course, part of a process to unify the kingdom (there were over 25 main local languages or dialects spoken in the kingdom) and facilitate its government but, also, to facilitate inter-regional trade (there is no easy business transaction if the two parties do not speak a relatively common language). In a process similar to the unique case of the French attempt at standardizing their language, accounting standards-setting bodies have been created in many countries to define (regulate) the terms of this special language to facilitate measurement of wealth creation and therefore open exchanges and facilitate the support financial markets provide to the development of businesses.

Today, regulation of the accounting language is carried out at the global level because businesses trade globally, and financial markets also span the globe (see Chapter 5).

2.3 Accounting is a language with some maneuvering room

Accounting, because of the variety of requirements placed on its applicability and evolution, remains, by necessity, built on very broad generic principles. This leaves some room for customizing to the specific needs of businesses, or classes of users of accounting information, the representations it creates. The accounting language must be able to describe any business activity. It must allow any user to shape their opinion about an economic entity by looking at the entity's financial statements. These statements are the 'end product' of the accounting process.

The users' opinions and decision-making are built on several aspects of a business entity's potential: financial situation through the balance sheet, sales performance and efficiency in its consumption of resources for the generation of sales through the income statement, and cash generation through the statement of cash flows.

Financial statements allow users to take very concrete decisions such as whether to invest or not in the business entity, to acquire additional resources for the entity, to give, or receive, credit terms for settling accounts between customers, or suppliers, and the business entity, to grant, or seek, or not, a loan, to provide the basis for calculation of taxation of business entities by tax authorities, etc.

Since there are different yet perfectly legitimate[3] ways of describing the same reality, especially the timing of recognition of profit, the choice of an accounting 'solution' (embodiment of principles into practice) will impact the perception financial markets and funds-providers hold about a business enterprise.

The stakes are high in communicating fairly and effectively the value created and the value creation potential of the business segments a firm manages. Practitioners, managers and the media have even coined the expression 'accounting strategy' to reflect the fact that there is 'wiggle room' in describing a given reality. An accounting strategy means that, sometimes, when needed (in theory to better serve the users), one can alter the accounting representation to achieve better the purpose of communicating at that time. Clearly that maneuvering space has to be regulated. Although room exists for variations in measurement, timing and classification of a given reality, over the long run the results are always the same, but the decisions of the users of accounting information may have been affected in the meantime. Some **accounting changes** are also required by regulation. Some quotes illustrate this point.

> FamilyMart Co. announced that group net profit fell 16% year on year to 3.9 billion yen in the March–May quarter. This was the first time for the Japanese convenience store operator to book impairment charges on a quarterly basis; previously they were booked only twice a year. Without this accounting change, earnings would have been 1.2–1.3 billion yen higher, according to the firm.
>
> (Source: Factiva database, adapted from Nikkei Report, 6 July 2009)

Here the change in accounting method is related to the periodicity of recording of impairment charges (expenses), a concept which will be more fully covered in Chapters 7 and 8. In short, an impairment charge is the recognition of the reduction in value of an asset, either intangible, tangible or financial.

> Electronic Arts (EA), a California-based firm specializing in video games, announced that its 2007 third-quarter profit drop reflected the company's shift of $231 million in sales into deferred revenue to comply with accounting rules for products that include a service as part of their offerings. Many EA games now offer additional services, such as multiplayer capabilities, over the Internet. Without that accounting change and other items, EA said it would have earned $290 million in the holiday quarter compared with $201 million in the year-earlier period.
>
> (Adapted from Nick Wingfield, *The Wall Street Journal*, 1 February 2009, J, B5)

This example illustrates the concept of revenue recognition (see Chapter 6). If a sale of a product also includes a service, which should be delivered after the sale, the portion of the sale corresponding to this service should, then, be deferred (hence the concept of 'deferred revenue') to be matched with (recognized at the same time as) the actual delivery of the service. Apparently, the company used to consider the invoiced amount for the whole package (sale of the product + future service) as sales revenue at the time of invoicing.

> British mining company Rio Tinto's earnings could swing by million of dollars when it issues its first set of results under IFRS[4] later this year. Rio Tinto has operations in Africa, Europe, the Americas, Australasia and the Pacific Rim and is exposed to fluctuations in exchange rates because of its geographic spread and the link between commodity prices and currency values. New reporting standards will change how foreign-exchange gains on debt and derivatives are dealt with, which will have a significant impact on how the mining multinational manages the risk of foreign-exchange variations.
>
> (Adapted from Nicholas Neveling, *Accountancy Age*, 11 February 2005)

> LAN Airlines, the Chilean international air carrier, announced as a preliminary estimate that the impact of the adoption of IFRS will result in a 4.3% decline in the company's shareholders' equity (share capital and non-distributed earnings – see Chapters 2 and 11) as of 31 December 2007. This represents a US$42 million reduction and as a result adjusted shareholders' equity will amount to US$946 million.
>
> (Source: Factiva database, adapted from *Business Wire*, 30 September 2008)

The Rio Tinto example illustrates the impact of the implementation of one new International Financial Reporting Standard (IFRS), a topic covered later in Chapter 5, while the LAN Airlines example illustrates the changing of the whole coding system. In the latter case, the change may be perceived as detrimental to the immediate apparent profitability, but it is mainly a modification in the rules guiding the timing of recognition of expenses and revenues and possibly a change in the rules concerning the recognition of certain elements of the commitments of the firm. Whether switching from one standard of reporting to another or from a whole framework to another, for example from local **GAAP** (Generally Accepted Accounting Principles – see later in the chapter) to IFRS, the change most of the time has a real impact on the reported income of a firm (or its shareholders' equity, i.e., the book value of their claim on the firm's assets). However, the directionality of the impact cannot be specified *ex ante*. The apparent paradox that switching to IFRS appears to have a short-term impact that may appear to be either positive or negative to the unprepared user can easily be explained: the set of standards and topics covered in the IFRS is extremely wide. Depending on the topic covered, the impact on companies' accounts can vary widely, depending on the standard that used to be followed and the firm's circumstances. However, in the long run, the impact is generally negligible since it mainly reflects differences in timing of recognition of full effects of transactions.

These examples also illustrate that accounting is not just a blind application of mechanical or deterministic rules. This is why the field has drawn so much interest for so long: within a limited set of rules and principles the language of accounting is there to serve the users by giving the most useful, true and fair description of a sometimes ambiguous reality (especially when it comes to the timing of the recognition of expenses and revenues).

This chapter defines financial accounting, introduces the various users of financial information and describes some elements of the accounting process. The following part revisits the distinction we briefly touched on in the introduction between reporting issues to shareholders and to third parties (financial accounting) and issues of efficiency in the use of resources (managerial accounting), before presenting the qualitative characteristics of useful financial statements.

Accounting is almost as old as human economic activity. We therefore provide a short overview of the history and evolution of accounting over the years. Accounting, being the language of business, is, like art, an open language. An artist can use a variety of techniques to create a representation (portrait, for example) of the reality of her or his 'model'. However, unlike art, accounting, because it must be universal, will follow a socially-accepted set of rules of representation of reality. These rules evolve over time, just like those of painting or sculpture, with technological advances and changes in social and societal values.

3 Definition of financial accounting

3.1 Accounting

Accounting is about information for decision-making (i.e., more than just data) about the economic and financial aspects of the life of an enterprise. It comprises three facets:

1. To count is to measure and quantify.
2. To account for something is to acknowledge its existence and describe it.
3. To be accountable is to explain what one has done and take responsibility for the consequences.

Accounting, by carrying out the first two facets, contributes to the third. It is thus an essential part of reporting. Accounting is, of course, a method of counting and measuring; it makes transactions and their consequences 'real' (we cannot discuss what we cannot measure, as Lord Kelvin[5] said). Accounting is a system of acknowledgement of the socially defined parameters describing the economic life of an enterprise, be it 'for' or 'not-for' profit. By describing the economic reality of actions and consequences in a firm's life, accounting becomes a tool for accountability and reporting. What is reported is the basis of analyses for decision-making.

Broadly speaking, accounting information is an essential decision-support tool. Most decisions in a business are about resource planning, resource acquisition and resource allocation and usage in order to fulfill the firm's strategic intent (see, for example, Lebas 1999: 54). These decisions are based on financial and non-financial (i.e., operational) information.

Such information is the output of an ongoing process of identifying, capturing, managing, analyzing, interpreting and distributing data describing the economic activity of the firm.

Accounting has two key missions:

- To facilitate value creation by supporting resource acquisition, allocation and usage decision-making. Value can be reduced to economic wealth if one refers only to shareholders who are looking for a financial return on their investment. However, we will keep using the term 'value' because it refers to the broader concept of being 'better off' for a variety of stakeholders whose utility preference functions may not be expressed solely in economic or monetary terms.

- To measure and report to stakeholders the amount of value created during a given period.

Although accounting is a complete discipline, this duality of missions has traditionally led to separating it in two (though closely interactive) subclasses on the basis of the different users who have access to its output:

- The first is called managerial accounting. It deals with a rather detailed account of how resources (which may include non-financial resources such as employee or customer loyalty or ability to create a network of resource providers) are acquired, managed and used in the various business processes constituting the firm and is thus of particular interest to managers inside the firm.

- The second one is called regulated, legacy or financial accounting. It is the focus of this text. It is aimed at reporting, in a somewhat aggregated way, the economic performance of the firm to essential external users such as shareholders, bankers, creditors, customers, unions, tax authorities, etc. Financial accounting focuses on the financial or monetary aspects of performance. Since its output will be used by outside investors and stakeholders to allocate their own resources, accounting information is a social good and therefore is generally regulated, as mentioned earlier, so that all classes of users receive, in a timely fashion, signals of equivalent significance.

As we will see later, such a distinction between the accounting subclasses is somewhat artificial and often causes debates as to where the frontier should be placed between them.

3.2 Financial accounting

Financial accounting is a **process** of description of the various events that take place in the life of a firm. These events are essentially **transactions** between the firm and outside partners (suppliers of resources and customers of the firm's output). The description of each elemental transaction is **materialized** by source documents that contain both financial and non-financial elements to allow a **valuation** of that transaction. These are **recorded**, classified and **analyzed** so as to allow for the **periodic** creation of synthetic reports called **financial statements**. These generally comprise an income statement, a balance sheet, notes and, in most countries, a statement of cash flows. Financial statements are established periodically. It is traditional to create these synthetic documents at least once every year, generally around a date when sales activity is the slowest (and, logically, inventories are at their lowest).

The origin of the annual nature of financial statements can probably be traced back to the cycle of nature as it applies to economic undertakings such as hunting or farming. After the harvest was completed, the farmer calculated the amount of wealth created before it could be distributed between the various stakeholders according to the contract binding the partners (owner of the land and provider of the labor-force that created the harvest) in such formats as sharecropping (shared risks, alas not always in the fairest of ways), farming (the landowner takes no risk since she or he will receive a rent from the operator of the agricultural business) or salaried labor force (the landowner takes all the business risks). It was traditional to 'close the books' on the harvest at the end of the production cycle, i.e., at the end of the year (in the Northern Hemisphere). Therefore many countries have retained a preference for a civil 'year-end' closing. However, in businesses such as retail sales, home electronics, toys or gifts sales, and many more, a civil year-end closing would not make much sense as that is a period of boom. It would be more logical to close the books (i.e., prepare the synthetic financial statements) when business is slack, inventories are low and the wealth or value created by the business cycle is pretty well definitively acquired. For example, a toy retailer might logically choose to have a year-end in February or March. A toy retailer expects few returns more than two months after the year-end boom sales. The topic of the choice of a closing date is developed further in Appendix 1.1.

From the above definition of financial accounting several keywords merit attention.

- **Process**: The method of describing events and transactions and collecting the descriptors is organized by what is called the accounting process. It is a set of rules and practices, supported by dedicated hardware and software, and coordinated through the activities of a variety of people, extending well beyond the staff of the accounting department, such as procurement, payroll, inventory managers, materials handling, etc.

- **Transactions** include such events as the acquisition of resources, selling the firm's output, securing work space through the signing of a lease, payment of the monthly rent, obtaining a loan from a financial institution, etc. Financial accounting only recognizes transactions that have or will have monetary implications, i.e., which will result in an exchange of cash at some point. However, rules that govern financial accounting create certain exceptions such as depreciation in which the cash transaction (acquisition of the fixed assets) takes place before the recognition of the 'value creation event' (recognition of the consumption of the value creation potential of a piece of equipment or an asset), see Chapters 2 and 7.

■ **Materialization of transactions**: Each transaction is materialized by a concrete document (invoice, bank statement, voucher, receipt, secure instructions given by electronic communication, etc.). If a transaction is not documented, the accountant cannot recognize it and record it. For example, if a business were to acquire a resource without a corresponding invoice or pay a worker without some record of it, it would be impossible to record it.

■ **Analysis of transactions** consists in defining the category or class each transaction belongs to, so they may be aggregated into homogeneous classes. This step in the accounting process (described in Chapter 3) is often manual, with the possibility of human errors and inconsistencies. This classification and aggregation tends, however, to be replaced or supplemented by automated procedures, for example by the definition of barcodes placed on types of documents corresponding to certain transactions, or by linking software such as the accounting recording and invoicing software so that transactions are automatically recorded in the appropriate category, or by using some form of artificial intelligence to indicate to an operator, on the basis of partial information about the transaction, either a suggested logical class or, on the contrary, indicate incoherence in the selected classification of part of the transaction.

■ **Recording** is generally carried out on a regular periodic basis (most frequently, daily), and in chronological order. This may explain why the record of these transactions is called the **journal**, from the root 'jour', in French, meaning 'day' (see Chapter 3).

■ **Valuation** consists in attaching to the transaction the monetary amount that will be recorded. It is often easy to know the monetary value of a transaction when it is backed by an invoice, but the choice of the amount is, often, a more subjective decision as, for example, in the case of an exchange of non-cash assets, or in the recording in the acquirer's books of the purchase price of an acquired business that is comprised of both physical assets and such 'intangible' assets as a 'loyal' clientele (the monetary value of which is dependent on what the acquirer will do after the acquisition).

■ **Financial statements** also called 'accounts' or '<u>**annual accounts**</u>': They provide a synthesis of the performance of the firm in terms of wealth or 'value' creation. The balance sheet describes the 'stock' of resources of the firm at one point in time and the claims on that stock. The income statement describes how, and how much, wealth or value was created between two 'balance sheet' dates. Notes to the statements explain choices made by the firm and give more details about some transactions. The statement of cash flows describes the cash situation, and how it changed during the period.

■ **Periodicity** of financial statements, also called 'frequency of reporting', has been generally agreed to be at least one calendar year (IAS 1, IASB 2007: § 36), but these can be established for any period duration, if it is useful for decision-makers.

4 Users of financial accounting

4.1 Presentation of the various users

Financial accounting reflects the economic activity of the firm. Its purpose is to allow users to understand its situation in comprehensive and synthetic ways. It produces information for managers as well as for third-party stakeholders. Financial accounting is also often used in establishing tax obligations and is therefore subject to regulation and control by tax authorities. Creditors expect from financial accounting that it will help them better understand the profitability of the firm, as well as its ability to generate cash in the future to repay its lenders. Customers, suppliers and employees alike look to financial accounting for information about the ongoing nature of the business: their questions bear on whether the firm is a 'going concern'. As we can see, there are many users of financial accounting (see also endnote 2). Each group has, by definition, different needs and expectations from the others.

However, the first user of financial accounting information should be seen as the firm itself. Managers need to have a synthetic view of their collective performance (they are, after all, the 'ship's captains' in the high seas).

It is impossible to create a hierarchy of users. Any rank-ordering would be context- and culture-specific. Figure 1.4 illustrates a generic list of potential financial accounting users and is not meant to carry any idea of rank ordering.

The diversity of needs of the different users is analyzed in further detail in Table 1.1[6] that illustrates how each class of users may employ financial statements for their own purposes.

While all the information needs of these users cannot conceivably be met by only one set of financial statements, there are needs that are common to all users. As investors are providers of risk capital to the enterprise, the provision of financial statements that meet their needs and expectations will also likely meet many or most of the needs of other users who are interested in estimating risks and potential rewards attached to the operations of a given enterprise (see Conceptual framework, IASB 1989: § 10).

Limited liability companies must periodically file financial statements with a regulatory organization such as the Registrar in the UK, the Commercial Register in Spain or the

Figure 1.4 A set of financial accounting users

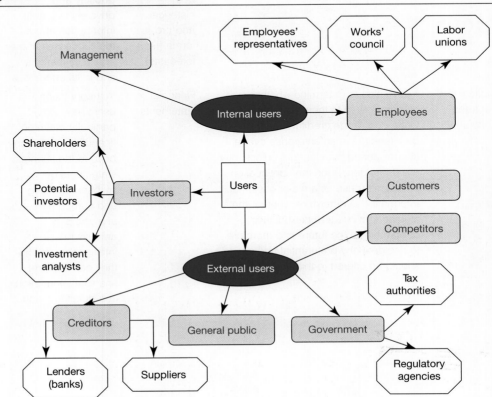

Table 1.1 Users and their different needs

Users	Needs	Accounting source-documents	Accessible information (accounting and other)	Delay to obtain information
Management	Information to plan, make strategic- and resource-allocation decisions and control	Transaction documents, financial statements	Total access, from source documents to financial statements	Information is accessible on an ongoing basis. Its availability depends on the organization itself
Shareholders/investors	Are concerned with the risk inherent in, and return provided by, their investments: ■ Information to help them determine whether they should buy, hold or sell ■ Information to assess the ability of the enterprise to pay dividends	Financial statements	Financial statements plus additional publicly available information about the successes of the firm in its markets and in its operations	The date on which the financial statements must be made available before the general assembly is regulated in each and every country. The trend is towards earlier publication
Bankers, lenders	Information to determine whether their loans, and the interest attached to them, will be paid when due	Financial statements, both historical and pro forma (i.e., forecasts)	Financial statements plus additional publicly and privately available information about the successes of the firm in its markets and in its operations	A business will produce any additional *ad hoc* documents whenever it needs to raise funds from banks or on the market
Suppliers and other trade creditors	Information to determine whether amounts owed to them will be paid when due. Trade creditors are likely to be interested in an enterprise over a shorter period than lenders unless they are dependent upon the continuation of the enterprise as a major customer. Information to determine whether the studied firm offers better business opportunity in the future and therefore to decide if any preferential treatments should be offered to this particular firm	Financial statements	In theory these users have no particular claim on financial information beyond the financial statements but by benchmarking and comparative analysis plus an organized intelligence watch, they can interpret financial information in a detailed manner	Case by case

(continued)

Table 1.1 (*continued*)

Users	Needs	Accounting source-documents	Accessible information (accounting and other)	Delay to obtain information
Customers	Information about the going concern nature of an enterprise, especially when they have a long-term involvement with, or are dependent on, the enterprise. Customers are especially interested in evaluating the viability of the firm as an ongoing supplier for service after sales and/or for future orders	Financial statements	Just like suppliers, customers will ask information directly and cross-reference it to be able to have leading signals indicating possible opportunities or problems	Case by case
Competitors	To compare relative performance	Financial statements	Competitive analysis will be the output of large databases of financial statements, cross-referenced with business intelligence and a good understanding of the economic sector	Case by case, as a function of the amount of resources dedicated to information gathering
Employees	Information about the stability and profitability of their employers. Information to assess the ability of the enterprise to provide remuneration, retirement benefits and employment opportunities	Financial statements	Access is regulated through legislation in every country	Case by case moderated by local legislation
Government, regulatory agencies, tax authorities	Are interested in resource allocation and, therefore, want to know about the activities of enterprises. Also use information in decisions to stimulate the economy, to determine taxation policies and assessments. Also use some or all the information in the calculation of national economic statistics	Financial statements, often recast in a pre-defined tax-based format possibly following different rules	On a recurring basis the tax-formatted financial statements plus, in the case of a tax audit, access to all source documents	Each country has specific rules. For example, in the UK, most companies are required to pay corporation tax nine months and a day after the end of an accounting period
General public	Enterprises affect members of the public individually and collectively. For example, enterprises may make a substantial contribution to the local economy in many ways, including the number of people they employ and their patronage of local suppliers. Financial statements may assist the public by providing information about the trends and recent developments in the prosperity of the enterprise and the range of its activities	Financial statements	Regulated access	Case by case

Commercial Courts in France. Such filings are required in each European Union member country for the protection of third parties. The European Union reinforced such an obligation by the 1st (9 March 1968) and 4th Directives (25 July 1978). The EU Directive No. 90-605 (8 November 1990) essentially extends to all incorporated businesses, whatever their form of incorporation, the requirement to file financial statements.

4.2 Financial reporting standards: how to satisfy the users' needs

The obligation to serve the various (and numerous) users of financial statements, mentioned in the previous section, requires that financial information be the result of a *unique* coding of events and transactions. For that reason, within each country, local regulations issue generally accepted accounting principles (GAAP)[7] that are called **accounting standards** or **financial reporting standards** (see endnote 4). Accounting standards are authoritative statements of how particular types of transactions and other events should be recorded and reflected in financial statements. These standards include specific principles, bases, conventions, rules and practices necessary to capture the data and prepare the financial statements. The concept of financial reporting standards and their evolution on an international basis is developed in Chapter 5.

5 Introduction to the accounting process

An illustration will show how the need for accounting arises from a simple set of transactions between persons or corporations and how the accounting process is created to monitor and record these transactions.

Let us assume we are at the end of the fifteenth century in Venice. Costas, a young merchant of Greek origin, wants to become rich and powerful. A quick survey of his environment leads him to the conclusion that the most effective way for him to achieve his objective is to trade with the Orient. His family have endowed him with some 120 gold ducats. In order not to mix his own 'estate' with the risky venture he is considering, Costas, as an individual, creates a separate entity he calls 'Venture Costas', or VC for short. Costas decides to invest 100 of his ducats in this entity (VC or the Venture). Costas, as the sole investor in this business venture, holds claim to all the profit the Venture might create **in the future**. He is a 100% owner or 'shareholder'.

However, if profit is to be created, this initial capital of 100 ducats is not enough to buy and commission a ship to start trading with the Orient. Such an activity would require about 1,000 ducats. Thus Costas, now as the *manager* of the Venture, visits a Florentine banker who agrees to lend the Venture the 900 additional ducats it needs for the acquisition and outfitting of a ship. The loan will be for not more than five years and will carry an annual compound interest rate of 10% (compounded in that, for example, if the loan duration is greater than one year, the unpaid interests of the first year due on the principal will themselves bear interest in the future years, and so on). The interest is to be paid in one lump sum on the date of the return of the ship or at the end of the five-year term, when the principal must be reimbursed, whichever comes first.

The Venture must record that it has entered into two obligations: it has agreed to refund the money it received from the banker (the principal of the loan) not later than five years from now, and it has agreed to pay a compound interest charge of 10% a year for as many years as the money will be borrowed. In a blank notebook or diary, let us call it a 'journal', Costas, as manager of VC, records the commitment the Venture has made. If VC were to 'take stock' of its wealth at that moment, it would show on one side the cash it holds (the original 100 ducats provided by Costas, the individual, plus the cash received from the banker), and it also would record the debt commitment that, if – and when – the loan was called by the bank, would diminish the wealth of the venture.

Essentially, VC's 'net situation' (value of resources minus debt to others than shareholders) has evolved this way:

- Situation before the loan from the banker: Wealth or 'net worth' = 100 ducats.
- Situation after the loan is received from the banker: Wealth = 100 ducats plus 900 ducats received minus a debt of 900 ducats = 100 ducats.

Borrowing, in itself, does not create wealth. It is what the money will be used for that, eventually, creates wealth.

The 'wealth account' (balance sheet or statement of financial position) of the Venture at this stage is presented in Table 1.2.

Accounting alone (i.e., recording) does not create wealth.[8] It only keeps track of what the economic entity (Venture Costas in this example) does with its resources and what claims (so far, only from the lender and from the investor) exist, at any point in time, on the resources of the business. The owner's (investor's or capitalist's) claim is equal, at any moment, to the net worth of the enterprise, i.e., the sum of the resources minus the claims from the lender(s). Since the Venture has done nothing so far to create wealth (there has been neither 'productive transformation' activity, nor trading of output with third parties), the claim of Costas, the individual, is still equal to the 100 gold ducats he invested in the business.

Costas (as the manager of VC) then uses the cash resource (1,000 ducats) to buy a good ship, outfit it, staff it, and load its hold with cargo and merchandise the captain of the ship will trade in the Orient (actually the 'Near Orient' or Middle East, at the Eastern end of the Mediterranean, at the end of the overland 'Silk Road' from China). Venture Costas' wealth has not changed. Cash has simply been changed into tangible goods. If VC were operating in a perfect market, whether it holds cash or merchandise should not make any difference. Both are resources that VC, as an economic entity, can and will use to try to create future economic benefits, i.e., wealth.

The VC 'wealth account' once the expedition is about ready to depart reads like Table 1.3.

Since VC owns goods, a ship and cash worth 1,000 ducats in total but owes 900 ducats, its net wealth (or net worth) is still only 100 ducats. Not only does Table 1.3 show VC's net worth, it also lists all that the venture owns, structured in different classes or categories. Such a document is of great importance for 'controlling' the efforts of the captain (Venture Costas' representative or agent) in his efforts to create more wealth. It can also be used to verify that no pilferage takes place (internal control). At any time, Costas, or someone else, can verify the physical existence of what the venture owns.

The fact that Costas was able to select a good captain, a good crew, and a solid ship is very important: the likelihood of success rests on the quality of the captain and his or her crew. Costas' worth (as an individual), not only represents the reality of what he owns (he is the sole proprietor of VC), but that ownership represents a potential profit to come if and when the ship returns and is sold along with its cargo for more than VC owes the banker. His hope and intention is that the captain of his venture will bring back more than just one ship. He has encouraged him or her to behave as a privateer, capture as

Table 1.2 VC's 'Wealth account' at step 1

Venture Costas owns		Venture Costas owes	
Cash in hand (100 + 900)	1,000 ducats	Owed to banker	900 ducats
Total	1,000 ducats	Total	900 ducats
		'Net worth' of Venture Costas (conceptually, it is 'owed' by VC to Costas, the individual capitalist)	100 ducats

Table 1.3 'Wealth account' after step 2

Venture Costas owns		Venture Costas owes	
Cash in hand (petty cash)	10 ducats	Owed to banker	900 ducats
Cash in the hands of the captain for sailors' future wages and operating expenses	150 ducats		
Inventory of food and supplies on board	330 ducats		
Inventory of merchandise to be traded	350 ducats		
Ship and equipment	160 ducats		
Total	1,000 ducats	Total	900 ducats
		'Net worth' of Venture Costas	100 ducats

many 'enemy' ships as possible and place them under his (her) control. Costas is looking forward to the success of the VC expedition.

Costas is assuming it will take four years before the ship can be expected to return, hopefully loaded with more valuable merchandise than it sailed out with. Costas needs resources to live on while the venture runs its course. He realizes that not only has he handed over most of his cash to the Venture, but, also, he is not even entirely confident in its success (business is risky). He wants to obtain more cash to live on (as an individual) and hedge his bet (i.e., diversify his risks). He therefore seeks partners who are willing to share the risks and the returns of his planned 'expedition'. He finds a wealthy friend who agrees Costas has bought a solid ship and hired an excellent and entrepreneurial captain who is likely to return with valuable goods. This friend buys, in exchange for 500 ducats in cash paid to Costas, the person, a half 'share' of the rights and claims Costas (as an individual) holds over the Venture: i.e., half of the net worth today, which includes the right to receive 50% of the possible profit realized if and when the ship returns. Essentially Costas (individual) sold privately a state conditional claim (50% of future profits or losses, whatever they will be) for 500 ducats, thus reducing his own claim on future profits from 100% to 50%.

The wealth of the Venture remains at 100 ducats, although the wealth of Costas, the individual, has been modified by his receiving 500 ducats in cash. The fundamental advantage of having created Venture Costas is that the 'shares' (i.e., unit claims on future profits) can be sold privately by 'shareholders'. Such a sale has no impact on the situation of the Venture itself. Costas' claim on the future profit of the Venture has been reduced to 50% while it used to be 100% before his private transaction with his friend. Costas' personal wealth before the sale of a half of his share was 20 ducats [120 (received from his parents) – 100] in hand – he had handed over most of his cash wealth to the Venture – plus a 100% claim on the profits of VC.

His personal wealth after the private sale of a 50% interest in the venture is now 520 ducats in hand [120 – 100 + 500] plus an only 50% interest in the future profits of VC. Costas traded his rights to 100% of an uncertain reward (future profits or losses) for 500 ducats in hand plus only 50% of the uncertain future reward. He has diversified his risk but reduced the possible high return he would eventually claim from the venture when it is concluded.

The wealth account of VC, integrating the fact Costas sold half his personal contingent claim on future profit, is summarized in Table 1.4. As the reader can see, the sale of Costas' half-interest in VC is completely external to the Venture itself. It is a private matter

Table 1.4 'Wealth account' of VC after step 3

Venture Costas owns		Venture Costas owes	
Cash in hand	10 ducats	Owed to banker	900 ducats
Cash given to the captain for wages and operating expenses	150 ducats		
Inventory of food and supplies	330 ducats		
Inventory of merchandise to be traded	350 ducats		
Ship and equipment	160 ducats		
Total of resources (1)	1,000 ducats	Total owed to third parties (2)	900 ducats
		'Net worth' of the venture (1) – (2)	100 ducats
		Share of 'net worth' held by Costas	50%
		Share held by friend	50%

between the two partners, both now 'shareholders'. The only element recorded is that, if the venture were to be liquidated or earn profit, there are now two equal claimants on the net worth or profit, where there was only one before.

It can be noticed that, although the 'share' holders hold a claim on the resources, their claim is recorded separately from the amount payable to the banker. Although the shareholders (Costas and his friend) certainly hope to recover their investment, it will not be by reimbursement, but by sharing first in the profit of the venture and second, in case of liquidation, in the market value of the resources liquidated. Since businesses are mainly intended to last for a long time (they are 'going concerns'), their liquidation is not a major preoccupation. Accounting stresses the fact that each 'share' holder has a right over future profits (or losses) proportionate to the number of shares they hold. The 500 ducats the friend paid was part of the net worth of Costas, the individual, not part of the venture's net worth. The change in the ownership structure of the venture does not create wealth for the venture.[9] If we were to look at the immediate or instantaneous net worth accruing to each shareholder, it would be half of the net worth of the venture or 50 ducats each. The friend essentially bought from Costas for 500 ducats what is, immediately and at first glance, worth only 50 ducats; however, the acquisition also includes a claim on future returns to be obtained in the next few years. The friend paid 450 gold ducats more than the 'book value' of what he holds because he thinks future returns will be greater than the 'premium' he paid (here that premium is 450 ducats). The amount paid to obtain a share has nothing to do with the claim on resources or future profits the holder has acquired: each share has the same claim, regardless of its market value (we will see in Chapter 11 there are some deviations from this principle).

Costas' **personal** wealth is now 520 ducats plus a claim of only 50% on the future profit of the venture. The Venture is a separate entity from Costas as a person. It is essential in accounting to know exactly the perimeter of the economic entity of which one speaks. From now on, we will speak only of the Venture as the relevant economic entity.

We can record the situation for the 'sailing/trading expedition' by saying the Venture 'owns or controls' physical or tangible resources (or 'assets') in the amount of 1,000 ducats[10] and owes 900 ducats. The net worth of the Venture to date (and at any point in the future until the contract between Costas and his partner is ended) is to be distributed half to his partner and half to him. When the ship returns, hopefully within the time frame originally intended, the merchandise the ship (ships) carries (carry) will be sold. Any profit will be calculated after the interest on the loan has been paid to the banker, and any bonuses have been paid to the captain and the crew, etc., i.e., all operating expenses of the venture have been offset against the venture's revenues.

Let us assume that, after only four years or she the captain of VC's expedition brings back three ships (the original ship plus two more he or she, commandeered in the high seas), and that the merchandise they hold is sold and brings-in 10,008 ducats in cash.

Given the great success of the expedition,[11] Costas decides to grant a bonus of 1000 ducats to the captain and his or her crew, over and above the agreed-upon salary of 150 ducats.

The banker also considers the Venture a success, and thinks highly of its manager. He/she offers VC the possibility to extend the term of the loan, at the same interest rate, if he and his shareholder friend decide to continue their business venture, even in another line of trade. The banker, therefore, accepts that the principal of the loan be repaid at a later date (to be renegotiated, and which will be after the end of our story). However, of course, the Venture must pay the 418 ducats of interest that have accrued over the four years on the principal of the loan (interest rate = 10% → $900 \times 1.10^4 - 900 = 417.69$, which we choose to round up to 418 ducats, for the sake of simplicity). The interest is a consumption of the resources of the Venture and is, as such, what we call an expense.

Costas, with the approval of his shareholder friend, decides to continue the Venture and not dissolve or liquidate the business. However, the shareholders decide to shift the venture's focus towards a less risky business. They plan to reorient their efforts and talents towards agricultural production, a more predictable, although still risky, business in their view. Since the Venture no longer needs the ships, the three vessels are sold. This will give Costas, manager of the Venture, a very clear vision of the liquidities the Venture can invest in acquiring a large farm and its equipments.

The original ship suffered wear and tear during its four years at sea. The loss, due to wear and tear, in future benefits-generating potential is called '**depreciation**'. This concept will be developed further in Chapters 2 and 7. At this stage in the book we have no other way to estimate the loss of value of the ship than by comparing its original market value of 160 ducats to its current market value, which happens to be 100 ducats. Thus an operating expense, which we will later call a 'depreciation expense', amounting to 60 ducats (i.e., 160 minus 100) must be recognized to acknowledge that (a) the business would not have been able to operate without the ship, and (b) the very use of the ship caused its loss of value.

If the venture had continued its activities in the 'shipping + privateering + trading' business, the ship would have been kept on the books of VC at its 'net value' of 160 minus 60 i.e., 100 ducats. However, since the Venture plans to change completely the nature of its business, it sells its three ships. We record as expenses both the depreciation of 60 ducats and the residual net book value of the used original ship (i.e., 100 ducats or 160 minus 60) since the ship is liquidated. We, *de facto*, and in two steps, expense the totality of its original cost of 160 ducats. On the other hand we recognize, as revenue, 100 ducats received for the sale of the ship. The other two ships were captured by the privateering captain and thus we have no explicit cost or historical value for them (we can assume their historical value is zero). The other two ships are sold respectively for 75 and 125 ducats.

In order to summarize the elements related to the expedition and its 'final outcome' for the period (the full four years), we prepare Table 1.5, called report of the business activity or 'income statement'.

The positive elements creating wealth are called 'revenues' and the negative ones consuming (destroying) wealth or resources are called 'expenses'. The difference between the revenues and the expenses represents the income generated (or the wealth created) by the business.

The ending cash balance is computed in Table 1.6.

Table 1.6 can be rearranged in the format shown in Table 1.7, distinguishing the three sources and uses of cash: operations, investing and financing.

Table 1.5 Report on the activity of the Venture Costas for the four years of its activity

Revenues	
Revenue from the sale of merchandise	10,008
Revenue from the sale of the ships (100 + 75 +125)	300
Total revenues	10,308
Expenses	
Wages and expenses (as planned)	−150
Bonus paid to the captain and crew	−1,000
Consumption of initial inventory of 'food and supplies'	−330
Consumption of the initial inventory of 'merchandise to be traded'	−350
Interest expense paid to banker	−418
Consumption of the original ship (depreciation)	−60
Net book value of original ship after wear and tear	−100
Consumption of the two additional ships (these were captured and therefore have no cost)	0
Total expenses	−2,408
Income	7,900

Table 1.6 Ending cash balance

Beginning cash balance (1)	0
Receipts	
Capital contribution by Costas	100
Amount received from the banker	900
Sales of merchandise	10,008
Sale of ships	300
Total receipts (2)	11,308
Payments or disbursements	
Different payments (cash for wages and operating expenses, inventory, food, ship)	−990
Payment of bonus to captain and crew	−1,000
Interest expense paid	−418
Total payments (3)	−2,408
Ending cash balance (4) = (1) + (2) + (3)	8,900
Cash flow generated during the period (5) = (2) + (3)	8,900

Table 1.7 offers an analytical view of the cash flow generation. The net cash flow is divided into three sections: (1) operations (including the interest expense, because the

Table 1.7 Statement of cash flows

Beginning cash balance (1)	0
Operating cash flows	
Sales of merchandise	10,008
Different payments (cash for wages and operating expenses, inventory, food) (excluding the ship)	–830
Payment of bonus to captain and crew	–1,000
Interest expense	–418
Total operating cash flows (cash from operations) (2)	*7,760*
Investing cash flows	
Acquisition of one ship	–160
Sale of ships	300
Total investing cash flows (cash from investing) (3)	*140*
Financing cash flows	
Capital contribution by Costas	100
Amount received from the banker	900
Total financing cash flows (cash from financing) (4)	*1,000*
Cash flow generated during the period (5) = [(2) + (3) + (4)]	8,900
Ending cash balance (1) + (5)	8,900

operating cash flow includes all elements related to wealth creation and destruction), (2) investments (here, we have the purchase and sale of the ships) and (3) financing. This table, named 'statement of cash flows' will be studied in more detail in Chapters 3, 14 and 17.

We can also see the evolution of the 'wealth account' in Table 1.8.

Compared to the original net worth of 100 ducats, the net worth of VC has increased by 7,900 ducats (8,000 – 100). This difference represents the increase, over the period, of the wealth of the Venture. We call it profit (if it had been a reduction on wealth, we would have called it a loss).

Table 1.8 'Wealth account' after step 4 (return of the expedition)

Venture Costas owns		Venture Costas owes	
Cash in hand (see Tables 1.6 and 1.7)	8,900 ducats	Owed to banker	900 ducats
Total resources (1)	8,900 ducats	Total owed to third parties (2)	900 ducats
		Net 'worth' of the venture (1) – (2)	8,900 – 900 = 8,000 ducats
		Percentage of the net worth owned by Costas himself	50%
		Percentage of the net worth owned by the shareholder friend	50%

Since we are not looking at the accounts of the Venture Costas over its complete life cycle (it plans to continue to live on, even if under a different business model), net worth and ending cash balance do not show the same amount. It would be extremely unusual, in the real world, to be able to look at the complete life cycle of any business venture. Most businesses are created in the belief of their ongoing nature, without any specified predetermined liquidation date (a business venture with a specified date of 'birth' and date of 'end' is generally called a 'campaign' or 'project', not an enterprise or a business). Thus, in general, and as shown in the VC example, cash on hand and net worth have no reason to ever be the same (more on this in Chapters 2 and 3).

The profit earned during the period (7,900) could be distributed as 'dividends' to the 'shareholders' Costas and his friend (not to exceed one half to each of 7,900 ducats), or retained, in total or in part, in the Venture (hence the term of '**retained earnings**'). Profit can be retained, partially or completely, in order to finance future operations. Since VC intends to start a new operation in agriculture, the shareholders know that they need to have a significant amount of available funds to acquire a good property (and 'prime the cash pump'). Since VC has the cash on hand, by not distributing it, the Venture could avoid having to borrow additional money to finance its growth and development in farming. If we assume that a good farm and its equipment can be bought for about 5,000 ducats and a cushion of 600 ducats would be required to prime the pump, not all the cash would be required for the ongoing business activity, VC could still be able to distribute a significant dividend to its two shareholders without endangering its ability to be a 'going concern'. This way Costas (the individual share-holder) could receive a cash dividend of 1,150 ducats ($[7,900 - 5,600 = 2,300] \times 1/2$) (and his friend the same amount), without endangering the business's capability to prosper. The concepts of profit and retained earnings will be further developed in Chapters 2 and 11.

Was the investment a good one? Costas received a return on his investment of $(1/2 *7,900)/100 = 3,950/100 = 3,950\%$ over four years (i.e., over 150% per year[12]), while his friend got a return on investment of $(1/2*7,900)/500 = 3,950/500 = 790\%$ over four years (i.e., approximately 68% per year[13]). Whether Costas' talent at setting up a merchant marine expedition will transfer to his intended farming activity is not clear and should be a matter for discussion between Costas and his friend and, also, with the banker.

In this short story, we have shown the need to:

- Record the financial position or the condition of an economic entity called the Venture. We have called this a 'statement of financial position' or 'balance sheet' and we established one at the beginning (see Table 1.2), one at the end (see Table 1.8) and two in between (see Tables 1.3 and 1.4).

- Acknowledge the business entity is separate from its shareholders.

- Record the composition of the resources of the business entity at any time.

- Record the proportional rights of each shareholder to share in future profit or losses.

- Establish the baseline against which wealth creation will be calculated.

- Establish rules about how wealth created will be calculated before it can be shared.

- Establish a synthetic document recording how much value was created by the economic activity of the Venture (the income statement).

- Understand how the captain (a manager, i.e., an agent acting on behalf of the two co-owners of the Venture) came to have three fully loaded ships upon her or his return so as to allow VC's management (presumably Costas himself, as the initiator of this and potentially future ventures) to learn about patterns of how the expedition could have been run more efficiently or where additional resources would have facilitated the process of wealth creation. Looking at a 'journal' in which the captain would have recorded every transaction that took place during the four years of the 'campaign' would be very helpful for this purpose.

■ Provide proof of the success of the past business model to secure, if needed, more funds from bankers or from other potential partners for a continuation or expansion of the Venture. However, the results only pertain to the past business model and little can be extrapolated about the potential success of a different business model.

We can also notice that:

■ The income of the period and the cash flow of the period are not the same. This situation is not exceptional. It happens because some cash inflows are not revenues. For example, in the case of VC, the loan received from the banker is not revenue but debt (i.e., not an increase in shareholders' wealth resulting from operations). Such a situation is common for most businesses as the timing of revenues and expenses and of cash inflows and outflows are generally different if one spans a period of a year or less. Most businesses are conceived as 'going concerns', that, theoretically, and if well managed, should never cease their activity. The relationship between profit and cash in an ongoing business will be studied in more detail in Chapters 3 and 14.

■ The profit computed directly from the activity of a venture is equal to the change in net wealth. This situation is no coincidence, as we will show in Chapter 2.

Accounting encompasses the whole process of recording, analyzing and reporting relevant information, whether with the intention of helping settle the claims at the end of the business venture or for a better understanding, and thus better management of, the business processes leading to wealth creation.

6 Financial accounting and managerial accounting

As mentioned earlier, accounting is separated between financial (external reporting) and managerial (internal) components to reflect the distinction between the users, either mainly external or mainly internal.

Managerial accounting deals with the informational needs of decision-makers inside the firm. It therefore deals with complex issues such as detailed product cost or business-process cost analyses or the diffusion of information inside the firm to create a mobilization of the energies of all members of personnel and staff. It spans a wide range of fields from cost issues to management of performance including anticipatory management, motivation and commitment building, and the analysis of deviations from plans.

Financial accounting and managerial accounting use the same basic information (economic events occurring with the purpose of creating current or future economic benefits) for different purposes. They cannot describe events in different ways. Simply put, financial accounting tends to be a 'recording' of historical events and reports it in aggregated ways, while managerial accounting uses the same information, kept at a higher level of details and structured differently, to forecast future situations through a fine modeling of business processes. In the end, both types of information processing should (and do) lead to the very same *ex post* measure of the amount of wealth created in a given period.

Aside from being linked at the beginning (one single and unique basic record of the same event serves as input for both) and at the end (one single income statement), financial and managerial accounting are also linked during the data analysis processes itself in that the costing aspect of managerial accounting, although used primarily for product and customer portfolio management is also used, by financial accounting, for the valuation of inventories of finished or semi-finished goods, and of work-in-progress. Table 1.9 below presents some key differences between financial accounting and managerial accounting.

Table 1.9 Differences between managerial and financial accounting

	Managerial accounting	Financial accounting
Purpose	Understand how value is created in detail so as to assist internal decisions	Measure the performance of the firm as a whole and report it to relevant decision-makers
Principal users of the output	Managers and decision-makers at all levels inside the firm and within responsibility delegation	Senior management of the firm, but, originally, intended mainly for external users who look at the firm as a whole: investors, banks, customers, personnel, etc.
Regulatory context	None in most industries (government contract costing is regulated in most countries), but focus on continuous progress in a philosophy of balancing costs and benefits	Financial accounting information is a social good and is therefore regulated at least by the bodies regulating financial markets, by tax authorities and by the profession itself in a spirit of giving a true and fair view of the situation of the firm. Although the cost benefit approach is not mentioned in regulations, it is common sense to expect that managers should never produce data or information at a cost that exceeds its expected benefits from 'better' decision-making
Behavioral implications	Aimed at mobilizing energies inside the firm by the distribution of the appropriate information after *ad hoc* analyses	Does not attempt to influence behavior and, even on the contrary, tries to be as fair as possible to all parties involved
Time frame	Oriented toward anticipation (based on fine modeling of internal and market-linked business processes) and analysis of deviations between anticipated and observed results	An objective record of what was actually realized, thus mainly oriented towards the past (comparison of periods allows extrapolation)
Time horizon	Flexible and continuous. Information is collected on any time period deemed interesting to the decision-maker	Financial statements must be made available at predetermined fixed intervals
Orientation	Detailed units of analysis such as: business processes, functions, knowledge sets, customer markets, customer types, products, resources markets, etc.	A process of systematic aggregation of records of discrete, simple and elemental events to create categories of like transactions and create, *in fine,* financial statements that give a synthetic view of the situation of the firm on a given date
Fineness	Accent is placed on interactions and on the operation of business models: can be finely partitioned as needed	Aggregate and *ex post facto* vision
Frontiers	Defined by the usefulness of the data: importance of commercial, strategic, behavioral, economic aspects in decision-making aspects. It is totally normal in managerial accounting to extend the analysis beyond the legal borders of the entity	Often defined and constrained by the regulatory and legal context, financial accounting records transactions within the legal (or otherwise specified) perimeter of the entity and between the legal entity and third parties

It is very important to remember that there is only one discipline called accounting. Although each approach deals with a specific angle of analysis, in the end both must be reconciled to give the same figure for the increase in the net worth, i.e., the amount of wealth created during a given period.

7 Qualitative characteristics of useful financial statements

According to the **IASB** (Conceptual framework, 1989: § 24), the qualitative characteristics of useful financial statements are 'the attributes that make the information provided in financial statements relevant to users'. Figure 1.5 highlights the characteristics of useful financial information and the constraints it must satisfy.

The four principal qualitative characteristics are understandability, **relevance**, **reliability** and comparability. They drive a series of principles guiding recording practices that ensure these four characteristics can be met.

7.1 Understandability

The information provided in financial statements should be readily understandable by users. For this purpose, users are assumed to have a reasonable knowledge of generic business processes (as for example those shown in Figures 1.1 to 1.3) and economic activities and accounting. They should also have a willingness to study the information with reasonable diligence.

7.2 Relevance

7.2.1 Definition

Relevance refers to the decision-making process of users. Information is relevant when it has the potential to influence the economic decisions of users by helping them evaluate past, present or future events and either confirming, or correcting, past evaluations.

Figure 1.5 Useful information

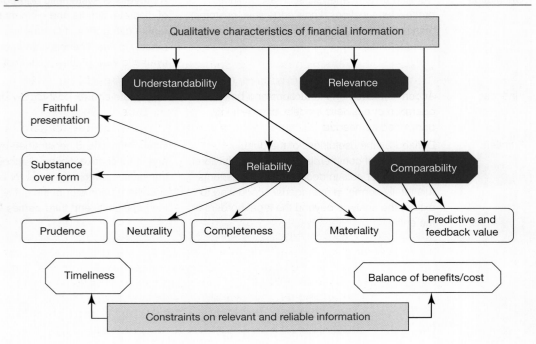

7.2.2 Link with materiality

The relevance of information is affected by its nature and materiality. Information is material if its omission or misstatement could influence the economic decisions of users taken on the basis of the financial statements. Materiality depends on the size of the item or of a possible error, judged in the particular circumstances of its omission or misstatement. Materiality is often related to as 'materiality level' or 'materiality threshold', i.e. the amount an estimate or a figure can change before the decision of the user is affected. Materiality is often decision-specific.

Concretely, financial statements may contain approximations and minor errors not worth fixing in the spirit of a cost/benefit balance. It is of no consequence as long as their 'materiality' places them under a threshold of significance (i.e., is not likely to affect the decisions of the users). With the speed of decision-making and the size of the stakes of the decisions in the 'new economy' (an information and knowledge-based economy has little hysteresis and a business turnaround can happen in no time[14]), issues of materiality have become extremely relevant and are often discussed in the press and, more and more often, in court cases: weak signals can be leading indicators – or forerunners – of significant shifts in opportunities or problems.

7.3 Reliability

To be useful, information should also be 'reliable, in that financial statements:

1. represent faithfully the financial position, financial performance and cash flows of the entity;
2. reflect the economic substance of transactions, other events and conditions, and not merely the legal form;
3. are neutral, i.e., free from bias;
4. are prudent; and
5. are complete in all material respects' (IAS 8, IASB 2003: § 10).

We could add a sixth qualifier to have reliability (see comparability below): the same transaction is always recorded in the same and only way, regardless of its timing or who does the recording.

These aspects will be developed in Chapter 4.

7.4 Comparability

Users must be able to compare the financial statements of an entity through time in order to identify trends in its financial position and performance. Hence, the measurement and display of the financial effect of like transactions and other events must be carried out in a consistent way throughout an entity and over time.

Users also would like to be able to compare the financial statements of different enterprises in order to evaluate their relative financial position, performance and changes in financial position. However, comparability is often in contradiction with the requirement of relevance. The need to choose a common coding process (between firms) for like events may lead to the choice of a 'lowest common denominator', i.e., a very 'coarse' description of events or their consequences through which, in the end, very little is learned. For example, without reporting by segment of business (i.e., by types of markets or technology) in a complex firm (and most medium- or larger-sized firms are complex), total revenue measures may be misleading because revenues from a booming but narrow market may hide, temporarily, the declining revenues from one larger market that is dying. Total revenue is difficult to exploit and compare unless more than the bare minimum is reported. If left to their own devices, each management team would probably be inclined to code events in a way they feel gives the 'best' description of the very strategic view they hold of their firm's business processes and results.

The debate about the pros and cons of common coding of events and common presentation of accounts between firms is never closed. Following World War II, France opted for a common presentation and imposed a constraining chart of accounts on all businesses (see Chapter 3). This is not the case in most of Europe, although Spain and Belgium also have a somewhat standardized chart of accounts, or in the rest of the world.

Given that entities generally do not follow exactly the same format as other firms in the same sector, there is a need for an informational arbitraging business, provided, generally, as a sellable service by analysts, stockbrokers, banks, consulting firms or semi-governmental agencies that use sophisticated models and additional information to recast financial statements into industry-specific formats fitting the business model applicable to a particular industrial sector.

7.5 Predictive and feedback value

Accounting information is useful both to account for what was done and for anticipating what decisions will be taken or modified, if any.

It is, therefore, important to remember that the rules and principles such as understandability, relevance, comparability, prudence, neutrality, completeness, materiality, etc. need to be subjected to the filter that, in the end, information is useful only if it helps understand the past (and particularly how agents have discharged their responsibility), and predict the future (by extrapolation or other more sophisticated models).

7.6 Constraints on useful information

7.6.1 Timeliness

If there is undue delay in the reporting of information, it may lose its relevance. Management may need to balance the relative merits of timely reporting (including the cost of the information technology and processes allowing such timely reporting) and of the provision of reliable information to decision-makers. Balancing timeliness and relevance is a day-to-day issue for all businesses. Timely information is expensive, but missing a strategic opportunity may be even more expensive. The old issue is 'Better approximate but timely information than untimely but very exact information'. Which is best: A timely but approximate or not reliable piece of information or a reliable and precise but not timely piece of information? Each management team has its own set of ad hoc answers.

7.6.2 Benefits/cost relation

Given we said the purpose of a business is to create more resources that it consumes, the benefits derived from any piece of information should exceed the cost of providing it.

7.7 Balance between qualitative characteristics

In practice, a balancing, or trade-off, between qualitative characteristics is often necessary. Generally, the aim is to achieve an appropriate balance among the characteristics in order to meet the objective of financial statements. The relative importance of the characteristics in different cases is a matter of professional judgment.

8 History of accounting: from Sumer to Luca Pacioli

Accounting is not the 'new kid on the block'. Some historians (Colasse and Lesage 2007: 24) assert that marks found on bones dating as far back as 20,000 or 30,000 years ago were a form of accounting, recording claims of various tribe members on the result of hunting expeditions.

Let us see how modern accounting originated from before the time of the Hammurabi Code in the times of ancient Sumer (Hammurabi[15] ruled Babylon from 1795 to 1750 BCE[16]) to the founding work of Fra Luca Pacioli (1494) that recorded the accounting practices of Venetian merchants (based on the earlier practices of Florentine bankers, themselves adapted from those of earlier Arab merchants) and allowed the development of modern accounting.[17]

8.1 Sumerian times

The origins of accounting are often traced to the times of Sumer, in Mesopotamia, starting in the fourth millennium BCE. The Sumerian civilization pre-dates that of ancient Egypt by a few centuries. Archeological explorations in the region between the Tigris and Euphrates rivers have unearthed innumerable vestiges of accounting documents recorded on stone or clay tablets. The very fragility of the material was the guarantee of the security of the record because any attempt at falsification would have caused its destruction. The efforts to protect these tablets were commensurate with the likely desire to uphold the contracted commitment and the corresponding counting.

As far back as the third millennium BCE, during the Ur Dynasty, accounting entries became both more complex and precise. All features of a modern account were recorded on clay tablets: nature of objects being transacted, names of the parties to the contract, quantities of goods and their equivalent value in other goods or currency. Some tablets even carry over the balance of the previous period, separate increases from decreases, and also show the end of period balance.

In some cases, rules were 'discovered' that required use of materials such as stone, more sturdy than clay, to record official or sacred accounts or statements. One such example is the Hammurabi Code, which dates back to the eighteenth century BCE. This 'document' reflects societal rules in Babylon. This text, essentially about contracts and family law, contains notions of accounting and management that refer to an agency contract. This implies that the agent keep clear accounts or, more likely, that some specified transactions be recorded in the form of accounts (bookkeeping). Accounting, then and since, has always been placed in an agency context: the issues are (a) to define the increase in wealth (profit) resulting from transactions carried by the agent (manager) in the name of the principal (owner); (b) provide the basis for sharing wealth created between the principal, the agents, and other stakeholders; and (c) keep a record of who owns or has control over what, and who owes what to whom.

Surprisingly, this first 'accounting civilization' seems to have left little further traces when the cuneiform language[18] it used was supplanted by the 'more efficient' Aramaic and Phoenician languages and writing techniques. Whether this is due to an unlikely abandonment of the principles of accounting, or more likely to a change in physical support or to wars, which left no archeological archives, is an intriguing question that remains open today.

8.2 Accounting in Egypt

Accounting was well developed in ancient Egypt. Scribes had a simplified script (less complex than hieroglyphics) dedicated to home and business economics. They were required to know both arithmetic and bookkeeping. They kept their records on papyrus, a lighter and more flexible but more vulnerable medium than stone or clay tablets. Transactions were registered first in draft form before being copied carefully in 'definitive' chronological records. From time to time, and at least once a year, chronological records were summarized in synthetic documents. Accounts had all the characteristics of 'universal accounts': name of the account, date and amount of the transaction. Receipts were distinguished from disbursements. From 300 BCE, Egyptians, who by then had become a part of the Greek cultural universe, adopted the Greek language and practices in banking. These include account-to-account transfers, which are an essential step in the development of modern accounting as they provide a way to add to or subtract from any account without actually going through a cash transaction.

8.3 Accounting in Greece

Greek accounting was, as already mentioned, very advanced. Some historians believe that temples were the first organizations to need accounting (and incidentally to play the role of bankers). Exactly as was the case in ancient Babylon (In Hammurabi's code, temples explicitly have a role as a 'bank of seeds') or in Egypt, offerings to the gods were recorded on marble or limestone tablets. Independently of temple accounting, Greek bankers kept thorough accounts. The complexity of the banking network led to the development of accounting control systems, the predecessors of auditing. As far back as 300 BCE, Athens had an audit court comprised of ten 'logists'[19] who had the responsibility of controlling accounts. The set of practices, including completeness of records, thorough controls and existence of public records, and accountability, obvious signs of democracy, seems to have vanished with its demise.

8.4 Accounting in Rome

In Rome, each family was in fact an economic entity with its own production and trading systems. This was a much broader concept than the nuclear family of the twenty-first century CE and included all parents from all generations, plus uncles, aunts and their offspring as well as a multitude of servants and slaves. The concept has endured in the Italian accounting and management tradition called Economia Aziendale.[20] Keeping books was the responsibility of the head of the household (*pater familias*) as it is the responsibility today of a person heading an entity. According to Cicero (143–106 BCE), who described the set of books kept in his time, the main document was the *Codex Accepti et Expansi* or journal of receipts and payments. Entries were first recorded in a draft before being organized in the *Codex*. The *Codex Rationum* was the permanent document with value of proof. It was the predecessor of what we now call the **general ledger** (see Chapter 3). The demise of the Roman civilization caused the disappearance of this body of accounting knowledge.

8.5 Accounting in the Middle Ages

Although the so-called Barbarians overran and destroyed the western part of the Roman Empire early on, the eastern part of the empire, including Greece, Constantinople and the Middle East remained untouched for a while. The Greek accounting expertise was preserved in the Byzantine Empire. The development of the Arab civilization and its intense trading activity capitalized on the accounting knowledge of the territories it conquered, and developed it even further by incorporating refinements derived from mathematics and astronomy.

It is not clear whether the western European merchants learned from their Byzantine and Arab partners or whether they actually rediscovered administrative and accounting practices. The fact is accounting underwent a rebirth in western Europe, mainly in northern Italy, the Netherlands and Flanders as early as the thirteenth century.

Whether merchants formed large, multi-establishment 'companies' (the predecessors of our multinational corporations), or dealt through mercantile or commissioned agents, they needed rigorous accounting. Accounting recorded transactions, wealth created and its transfer between establishments. This allowed agents to be (or made them be) accountable for their activity. The development of international trade, of capitalistic companies (separation between the providers of capital and the actual decision-making with the intent of growing wealth), and of agency contracts is probably the major cause of the slow re-emergence of accounting in the Middle Ages. The extended period of resurgence has known three sequential phases: memorial, single entry and double entry bookkeeping.

8.5.1 Memorial

The 'memorial' is essentially a journal recording a business entity's transactions on a daily basis without any attempt at regrouping transactions of similar nature. It is essentially the same rudimentary practice that was predominant in early antiquity.

8.5.2 Single entry bookkeeping

Single entry bookkeeping is a significant improvement to the simplistic memorial method. The growing complexity of the operations of medieval merchants led to the partitioning of the memorial into separate accounts of similar nature, such as purchases, payment to labor, sales to a given customer, etc. Each type of transaction within or between establishments or with third parties is recorded in its own coherent specialized table keeping track of all relevant specific events, thus forming an account.

8.5.3 Double entry bookkeeping

Double entry bookkeeping marks the birth of modern accounting. Each transaction is recorded by entries in two accounts: one entry 'credits'[21] one account and the other one 'debits'[22] another one. The earliest record of double entry bookkeeping is found in the books of the *Massari* (treasurers of the city state of Genoa) around 1340 CE. However, it is the Franciscan monk, Luca Pacioli, who formalized and extensively described these procedures in his 1494 mathematics text entitled *Summa de arithmetica, geometria, proportioni et proportionalita*. Incidentally, his purpose in inserting a chapter on accounting in his book was not to write a business text, but to illustrate one way of handling the concept of 'zero' which had been lost to western European mathematicians (although not to Arabic ones, but the western European merchants and the Arabic ones were not exactly on 'friendly terms' at the time …). In effect, the fundamental equation of accounting 'debits = credits' or 'resources held = financing (i.e., obligations to outside parties + shareholders' claims)' shows that, if this is true, the balance has to be zero, i.e., 'nothing', a very difficult concept to apprehend at the time. It was especially important for accountants to be able to show, for example, a debt had been paid back, or extinguished, and that the borrower, in fact, owed 'nothing', but the record of both the debt and its payment should not have been lost in the recording of the settlement. This was done easily by simultaneously reducing cash (a resource) and reducing the debt account where the borrower's debt was recorded (thus, eliminating the debt). In Chapter 3, we will see that accountants use specialized words (credit and debit) to describe the increase or decrease of a resource account, or the opposite direction for an account representing an obligation to pay a third party or shareholders. Modern accounting was born with Luca Pacioli, and this text will deal only with double entry bookkeeping and with the accounting that derives from such practice. We will however use the terms debit and credit as little as possible since this text is written mainly for students of management and not for accountants.

Key points

- Accounting is a language that allows any person interested in the economic life of a business to communicate with others having the same interests about the past, present and future of that business as an economic entity.
- Broadly speaking, accounting information is an essential decision-support tool. Most decisions in a business are about resource planning, acquisition, and resource allocation and usage in order to fulfill the firm's strategic intent.
- Accounting information is the output of an ongoing process of identifying, capturing, managing, analyzing,

interpreting and distributing data and information describing the economic transactions of the firm.
- Accounting is inseparable from and necessary to any business activity. It allows any user to shape their opinion about the economic aspects of an economic entity by looking at its financial statements.
- Financial statements are the synthetic 'final product' of the accounting business process. These generally include an income statement, a balance sheet, notes (which explain choices made by the firm and provide more detail regarding some complex or critical transactions) and, in most countries, a statement of cash flows.

- Financial statements are established periodically and it is traditional to create these synthetic documents at least once every civil or fiscal year, generally around a date when the sales activity is expected to be the least intense in the year.
- The various (and numerous) users of financial statements need to understand the financial information in the same way. For that reason, within each country, local regulations issue generally accepted accounting principles (GAAP) that are called accounting standards or financial reporting standards which include specific principles, bases, conventions, rules and practices necessary to prepare the financial statements.

- Accounting is separated between financial (external reporting) and managerial components to reflect the distinction between the decision needs of users, either mainly external or mainly internal.
- Financial statements relevant to users meet four criteria: understandability, relevance, reliability and comparability.
- Accounting is both rooted in a long historical tradition and continuously updated to reflect the need of enterprises and investors.
- Accounting matches all aspects of transactions, i.e., recognizes and records them in the same time frame, not necessarily when cash changes hands.

Review (solutions are at the back of the book)

Review 1.1 Multiple-choice questions

Select the right answer (only one answer is possible, unless otherwise indicated).

1. In general, financial statements are comprised of the following documents (several possible answers)

- (a) Statement of financial position or Balance sheet
- (b) Statement of cash flows
- (c) Notes to financial statements
- (d) Income statement
- (e) Value added statement
- (f) Value created statement

2. Only events with a monetary implication (potential impact on the cash situation) must be recorded in financial accounting

- (a) True
- (b) False

3. Financial accounting offers the great advantage of being completely objective and thus leaves no room for subjectivity in decision-making

- (a) True
- (b) False

4. Bookkeeping is a subset of …

- (a) Management accounting
- (b) Financial accounting
- (c) Auditing

Review 1.2 Discussion questions

1. Why do decision-makers use accounting information and for what purpose?

2. Why have standards of reporting emerged that constrain the way events are recorded in accounting?

3. What distinguishes financial accounting and reporting from managerial accounting?

Assignments

Assignment 1.1
Multiple-choice questions

Select the right answer (only one answer is possible, unless otherwise indicated).

1. The objectives of financial reporting for a business entity are based on which elements?
   (a) Generally Accepted Accounting Principles.
   (b) The need of users.
   (c) The need for managers to be accountable to owners.
   (d) The principles of prudence and conservatism.
   (e) Tax policies formulated by the tax authorities of the country.

2. Which of the following statements best describes the purpose of financial reporting? (Explain why you chose your answer and why you rejected the others.)
   (a) Provide a listing of an entity's resources and obligations.
   (b) Provide an estimate of future cash flows on the basis of past cash flows.
   (c) Provide an estimate of the market value of the entity.
   (d) Provide a fair description of how wealth was created in the past as a basis for estimating future wealth creation.

3. The operating cycle of a business is defined by:
   (a) Tax authorities.
   (b) Seasons.
   (c) The time it takes for cash consumed (or committed) to acquire resources to be returned to cash through sales and payment by customer (cash to cash cycle).
   (d) Each industry trade association.

4. For a manufacturing firm, the choice of reporting date (date at which the books are 'closed' and the balance sheet, income statement and statement of cash flows are established) is based largely on:
   (a) Tax constraints.
   (b) Time at which the inventory of finished goods is at its lowest.
   (c) The timing of the major vacation period for most of the personnel and staff.
   (d) The availability of time for the accountants.

5. In the following list of qualitative characteristics of an accounting signal, choose the two that seem to you to be the most important ones (explain your choice):
   (a) Verifiable
   (b) Fair and true
   (c) Precise
   (d) Relevant
   (e) Unambiguous
   (f) Reliable
   (g) Consistent
   (h) Comparable
   (i) Neutral
   (j) Material
   (k) Conservative
   (l) Timely

6. An accounting piece of data is considered 'material' if (explain your choice):
   (a) It refers to raw materials.
   (b) It is relevant to the decisions considered.
   (c) It is more than a previously defined percentage of net income.
   (d) It refers to transactions that are critical in the customer-oriented supply chain.
   (e) Its nature and magnitude have the potential of changing the decision of a user in a given context.
   (f) It is declared to be so by the tax authorities.
   (g) It exceeds a previously defined amount.

Assignment 1.2
Discussion questions

1. Should managers of a firm (i.e., decision-makers who are inside the business entity) be considered to be part of the population of 'users' of financial accounting?

2. Are there possible conflicts of interests between the various users of financial information?

3. How can a decision-maker obtain a copy of a firm's financial statements if the latter does not make them public (for example, statements of an unlisted business or of a closely held competitor)? Identify concrete examples in a given country.

4. Why are suppliers and customers interested in studying the financial statements of a company?

5. What sources of information on a business' economic situation, other than financial statements, are available to the general public?

Assignment 1.3
Xenakis

Topic: Statement of financial position

Xenakis, a young Greek person, arrives on the first day of summer in Byblos, a Phoenician port city. His parents, respectable rich merchants in Athens, have sent him on a 'world' journey to discover himself and learn about business. They have given him some material goods and a little money. Xenakis brings these goods and some of the cash to a venture he sets up for the purpose of trading. This business venture is called Venture Xenakis.

When he arrives in Byblos for a planned ten-day stay, Venture Xenakis' wealth is as follows:

- 6 gold flatware pieces, worth 50 drachmas each on the Athens market
- 10 crystal glassware pieces, worth 15 drachmas each on the Athens market
- 102 drachmas in cash (down from the 150 drachmas he left home with – his sea passage had cost him 48 drachmas).

As soon as he sets foot on land, he rents a room at the Cedar Inn. The innkeeper offers full room and board for 10 days for one drachma a day. Once settled in, Xenakis goes out looking for the Phoenician merchants his parents have recommended to him. As he ambles along the narrow streets and sunny piazzas, he reminisces about the basic rule his tutor had taught him: 'keep a detailed account of all operations and transactions you engage in'.

Xenakis meets a tableware merchant who agrees to buy all of Xenakis' 6 pieces of golden flatware for 70 drachmas each. Next, Xenakis sells his crystal pieces for 25 drachmas each to a glass merchant. He buys, for 45 drachmas each, a dozen amphorae of assorted spices. He also buys two pieces of silk fabric for 90 drachmas each. Very happy with his transactions, he then buys, for 50 drachmas in cash, his return fare to Piraeus (the port of Athens). As soon as he is back in Athens he sells, at the locally accepted prices, all the merchandise he has brought back:

- 60 drachmas per amphora of spices,
- 120 drachmas per silk piece.

Required

1. Describe Venture Xenakis' 'net worth' on the day of his departure from Athens for Byblos.

2. How much cash does the Venture Xenakis have after he sells all his merchandise after his return to Athens?

3. Compute the income generated by the Venture Xenakis on his round trip.

4. Describe the Venture Xenakis' 'net worth' after his return to Athens.

Assignment 1.4
Theodorakis

Topic: Users of financial information

Required

Identify at least five classes of users (including at least one not-for-profit organization) of financial information about a given business (specify clearly the characteristics of the business you chose) and list on what specific aspects of the life of the business (including short- and long-term if necessary) each class of users might like to be informed. Show whether accounting, as described in the chapter, is likely to satisfy these classes of users. If you feel accounting statements do not provide all the relevant information needed, elaborate on at least three legitimate reasons why accounting information falls short of expectation of this or these classes of users.

Assignment 1.5
Horn of Abundance

Topic: Users of financial information and investors

The following list contains data or information that might be provided about a business.

1. List of managers and directors.

2. Compensation package of directors and managers.

3. List of major competitors by markets and by product groups.

4. Allocation of responsibility in the business.

5. Age distribution pyramid of employees and managers.

6. Result of labor union elections in the various establishments of the business.

7. Social climate in each department of the business.

8. Financial statements (balance sheet, income statement, notes, statement of cash flows)

9. Map of the layout of the plant and the warehouse.

10. Location, size and staffing of all points of sale.

11. Evolution of sales of each key product group over the past three years.

12. Age distribution of products (products still sold today that were launched one, two, or three years ago or more).

13. Number of employees.

14. Distribution of shares ownership (with major shareholders and percentage they own as well as percentage of total shares traded in a normal month).

15. Details of the loans received (amounts and reimbursement schedule).

16. Cost of capital (weighted current average cost of capital).

17. Opportunities for investments in the business and their expected rate of return.

18. Major capital investment projects approved over the last three years.

19. Partition of assets between owned and leased.

20. Percentage of completion of investment projects started in the last three years.

21. Outside expert report on the technological and physical obsolescence of assets owned by the business.

22. Details on the incentive plans implemented in this business (including stock options).

23. Evolution of the share price of the business on the NYSE Euronext Stock markets over the past three years (including a comparison with other firms in the same economic sector).

24. Description of the sales technology and techniques used in each of the markets in which the products are sold.

25. Amount spent on acquiring new customers and creating demand (marketing, advertising, promotion and sales expenses).

26. Tax filings for the past three years and amount of taxes still owed.

27. Cash or liquid assets position.

28. Description of key customers with length of relationship and evolution of percentage each represents in the business' total sales.

29. Opinion of the senior management team about how they see the future of the firm and its markets.

30. Amounts spent on R&D, structured by types of research.

31. Evolution of the duration of R&D projects until success or abandonment and percentage of successful projects in the last 10 years.

32. Percentage of sales (per product group) carried out in currencies other than that of the home country

of the business. Percentage of total physical volume of sales that is exported.

33. Existence, details and status of any court litigation against the business or which the business has originated against others.

34. A summary of the history of the business.

35. By-laws or articles of incorporation.

36. Existence, value and relevance of proprietary technology owned by the business (own research or purchased?).

37. Percentage of total expenses spent on humanitarian or not-for-profit activities (and the list of these activities).

38. Environmental report by an external independent agency evaluating the effect of the business on noise, air and water quality as well as the health environment of both workers and citizens in a ten-kilometer radius around the plant.

39. Statistics of the work-related injuries and deaths over the past ten years.

40. Partnership agreements with suppliers and customers.

41. List of subsidiaries and affiliates.

42. Percentage of employees (structured by homogeneous classes) connected effectively via a broadband intranet/internet system.

Required

From the list above select the 10 most important items you feel an investor might want to find, for her or his analysis and review, in a business' annual report. Explain why you selected these and rejected the others. Examine whether the items you wish to provide investors originate in the accounting or in other information systems. If they do not originate in the accounting systems, explain which aspect of accounting regulation or practice may explain why these items have been excluded from the traditional reach of accounting.

Assignment 1.6
Kalomiris Construction

Topic: Useful information

Kalomiris Construction, Inc. is a locally very important construction company listed in a regional stock exchange. Its main market is building single-family homes, either for individuals or for developers. At the end of X2, it announces that the full year's profit will, in all likelihood, exceed that of X1 by a third, but that the net value of orders for later delivery (orders received minus orders delivered = order book or backlog) is down 40%. It also reports that its net cash has been depleted by 50% from figures at the beginning of the year.

Required

What content of the financial statements of Kalomiris Construction for this year and the previous three years would the following parties be interested in and what actions might they take on the basis of these data and information?

- current stockholders,
- potential investors,
- creditors,
- customers having a contract with Kalomiris Construction,
- tax authorities,
- bankers,
- regional association of real estate developers,
- national associations of suppliers of lumber and construction materials,
- regional government,
- industrial council (representing all employees of Kalomiris Construction).

Assignment 1.7
Nikopoulos

Topic: Book value versus market value

Elisabeth Rossiter, the single proprietor of Nikopoulos, Inc., a successful manufacturer of advanced microchips for computer gaming consoles, is seeking new long-term capital to finance the growth of her business. The net worth of the company to date is 500,000 CU.

Required

You are considering buying a twenty percent stake in the company. Why might you be willing to offer Elisabeth more than 100,000 CU for such an investment?

References

Chatfield, M. and Vangermersch, R. (eds) (1996) *The History of Accounting, an International Encyclopedia*, New York and London: Garland Publishing.

Colasse, B. and Lesage, C. (2007) *Comptabilité générale*, 10th edn, Paris: Economica.

Degos, J.G. (1998) *Histoire de la comptabilité, Que-sais-je?* no. 3398, Paris: PUF.

Fiore, P. (2009) Fiori Successione Zappa: Controversia Tra la Grecia e la Romania, Bibliobazaar/Bibliolife (online publisher).

IASB (1989) Framework for the Preparation and Presentation of Financial Statement, London.

IASB (2003) International Accounting Standard, No.8: Accounting policies, changes in accounting estimates and errors, London.

IASB (2007) International Accounting Standard No. 1, Presentation of Financial Statements, London.

Johnson, H.T. and Bröms, A. (2000) *Profit Beyond Measure*, New York: The Free Press.

Lebas, M.J. (ed.) (1999) *Management Accounting Glossary*, Paris: ECM and London: CIMA.

Mattesich, R. (2008) *Two Hundred Years of Accounting Research: An International Survey of Personalities, Ideas and Publications*, New York: Routledge.

Further reading

Aiken, M. and Lu, W. (1998) 'The evolution of book-keeping in China: Integrating historical trends with western influences', *Abacus* 34(2): 220–42.

Additional material on the website

Go to http://www.cengage.co.uk/stolowy3 for further information, journal entries and extra assignments for each chapter.

The following appendix to this chapter is also available on the dedicated website:

Appendix 1.1: The reporting period.

Notes

1. See for example, Carmona, S., Ezzamel, M. and Gutierrez, F. (1997) Control and cost accounting practices in the Spanish Royal Tobacco Factory, *Accounting, Organizations and Society*, 22(5): 411–46, for a description of an early use of physical balance in a Spanish plant in 1773.

2. Stakeholders are any party that has an interest, i.e., a 'stake' in the outcome and output resulting from the activity of an enterprise. They include a variety of parties. A far from exhaustive list may include the following stakeholders in addition to the obvious capital providers which, in the western economies, tend to be seen as the major stakeholders (see also Figure 1.4 and Table 1.1):

   - Employees whose interest is in the long-term stability of their employment and/or in the ability for the firm to maintain the employability of its personnel (i.e., stability of employment outside the firm as well as inside the firm).
   - Customers who want to be certain their supplier will be able to serve them in the future. This is both a question of security and of efficiency because finding a good supplier is expensive.
   - Suppliers whose interest is to have a long-lasting buyer for their output. (It is costly to find a good customer.)
   - Health and environmental protection authorities, as the economic activity of the enterprise can impact on

the health of employees, of the community surrounding the plants, of the community of users of the output, and their environment now and in the future, etc.

- Government authorities who are looking at the effect of the economic activity of the firm on the country's balance of payment (net importer or net exporter) or employment level.

- Social watchdog organizations looking for the enforcement of evolving societal values like 'no child labor' or 'no prisoner labor', 'no discrimination in employment, or sourcing or selling', etc.

3. A German and a North American user may not require that the same reality, for example income, be couched in the same format and terms. The German user of accounting information, coming from a culture where business, banks and labor unions are quite intermingled, may tend to have a long-term view of business and probably would support wholeheartedly an accounting language that would smooth-over peaks and valleys in the reporting and timing of value creation. Her or his North American counterpart, coming from a culture of rapid movement and short-term investment decisions where 'a dollar today is always better than a dollar tomorrow', might, on the other hand, be more short-term minded and might support an accounting language that would be as reactive as possible and would not allow smoothing of good or bad events or news.

4. IFRS = International Financial Reporting Standard, published by the IASB. The two main bodies establishing accounting standards are the International Accounting Standards Board (IASB) and the Financial Accounting Standards Board (FASB), the latter being recognized mainly in the United States and their sphere of influence. See more on this in Chapter 5.

5. Lord Kelvin (Sir William T. Kelvin) (1824–1907): 'To measure is to know'. 'If you cannot measure it, you cannot improve it'.

6. For *investors, lenders, suppliers, customers, employees, government* and the *general public* the needs listed in Table 1.1 are adapted from the IASB conceptual framework (1989: § 9).

7. The AICPA (American Institute of Certified Public Accountants) in its APB Statement No. 4 'Basic Concepts and Accounting Principles Underlying Financial Statements of Business Enterprises' (New York, 1970) defines a GAAP as encompassing 'conventions, rules and procedures necessary to define accepted accounting practice at a particular time. It includes not only broad guidelines of general application but also detailed practices and procedures. Those conventions, rules and procedures provide a standard by which to measure financial presentations'. Every country, every culture or society creates its own GAAP, adapted to its tradition, principles, values and practices.

8. But wealth and wealth creation cannot be measured unless assets, obligations and transactions are recorded and 'accounts' drawn.

9. Here the capital or endowment of the venture was not modified by the private sale of shares. We will see in Chapter 11 how a business can issue shares and increase its capital.

10. Note that the 'market value' of the captain and his crew are not valued as resources in the accounts, as they are free to leave whenever they want and the venture neither controls nor owns them.

11. And also because of the honesty of the captain that is attested by an examination of the log or journal he or she kept of his periodic authorization of payments, trades and transactions.

12. $(3{,}950\%)^{1/4} = 2.5$, i.e., 150% (approximately).

13. $(790\%)^{1/4} = 1.68$, i.e., 68% (approximately).

14. See for example the fate of Nokia, still leader in volume of sales in cell phones with about 41% of global market share in 2009, but unable to counteract the success of Apple, Blackberry or Google in the area of so called 'smart phones' (despite having been the leader in technology, too early for the market). The loss of value of the shares of Apple after the burst of the bubble in October 2008 was almost erased by the end of the summer of 2009, while those of Nokia keep stagnating and slipping and have not recovered any of their lost luster. In this economy leadership is gained and lost quickly and can be regained as easily as it can be lost.

15. For a review of the literature on Hammurabi's code, see: http://www.fordham.edu/halsall/ancient/hamcode.html.

16. CE = Common Era (BCE = Before Common Era). When one says the Vancouver Winter Olympic Games took place in 2010, one uses the 'Common Era Calendar'. Numerous other calendars exist that are as valid as the one 'commonly' used. Throughout the book, we will refer only to the Common Era calendar, since it is the one used in most financial reporting and by financial markets.

17. This section draws heavily, with permission of the author, on Degos (1998). This short abstract is however our entire responsibility. The reader can also refer to Chatfield and Vangermersch (1996).

18. Cuneiform refers to a scripture based on a combination of wedge-shaped marks resembling 'little nails', thus its name from the Latin *cuneus* or nail.

19. The 'logists' were selected by random drawing from the 500 members of the *Boulé*, or parliament (50 representatives per tribe) to audit the accounts of the elected city-state officials at the end of their mandate.

20. See for example the work of Gino Zappa, La determinazione del reddito nelle imprese commerciali. I valori di conto in relazione alla formazione dei bilanci, Roma, 1920–1929. Bilanci di imprese commerciali. Note e commenti, Milano, 1923. More easily accessible works on the contributions of Zappa are Fiore (2009) and Mattesich (2008).

21. Credit comes from the Latin *credere* or to believe or to trust (see Chapter 3).

22. Debit comes from the Latin *debere* or to owe (see Chapter 3).

C2

Chapter 2
Introduction to Financial Statements

Learning objectives

After studying this chapter, you will understand:

- That financial statements comprise, at least, the statement of financial position or balance sheet, the income statement and the notes to both of these (explaining assumptions, principles or detailing aggregated figures).
- How these financial statements are defined and constructed.
- That the statement of financial position or balance sheet is a detailed representation of the 'business equation' (resources to operate the business = financing received from various stakeholders). It is the fundamental building block of accounting.
- That the equilibrium (or balance) in this equation must always be respected when recording any transaction.
- What double-entry accounting is.
- How the income statement is derived from the basic business equation and is interlaced with the evolution of the balance sheet between two dates.
- What the concept of depreciation represents.
- How purchases of goods (merchandise, raw materials and finished products) are recorded.
- How transactions involving inventories are recorded, during the year and at year-end.
- How profit is appropriated, i.e., divided between dividends (distributed to shareholders) and retained earnings (kept in the business, as a *de facto* increase in the financial investment of shareholders).
- How a basic financial statements analysis can be performed by comparing statements over time (trend analysis), or by using the internal structure of the statements (common-size analysis) and by using a few ratios.

We have seen in the previous chapter that **financial statements** are one of the key 'outputs' of the financial accounting process. They form the reporting package and are comprised of several documents:

■ The statement of financial position or balance sheet, the income statement and notes to these documents (common to all countries' accounting standards).

■ One or more of the following: a statement of cash flows (also called cash flow statement or funds flow statement – developed in Chapters 3, 14 and 17), a statement of retained earnings (developed in Chapter 11) and a statement of changes in equity, required in some, but not all countries (developed in Chapter 11).

This chapter introduces the two main documents: balance sheet or statement of financial position and **income statement**. In doing so, we introduce the 'basic business equation' also known as the 'balance sheet equation' or 'accounting equation'. We also introduce important concepts, which are developed in later chapters, such as **depreciation**, inventory valuation and profit appropriation.

1 Statement of financial position or balance sheet

As any good sailor knows, a business' manager (captain or pilot) needs to know the ship's position at any given time in order to decide on the next course of action (i.e., action required in order to achieve its destination). For a business, it means how to obtain, allocate and use its resources and create value for its owners (its objective or 'destination'). A manager or an investor therefore needs to know what the business' resources are, and what the firm's obligations to third parties are.

The very term **balance sheet** (called statement of financial position in IFRS/IAS) contains a message about its format. It is a set of two lists: resources on one side (also called **assets**) and obligations to external parties on the other side (liabilities to creditors and the 'net worth', conceptually owed, by the firm as a separate entity, to shareholders or owners). The totals of the two lists, expressed in monetary terms as we have stated in Chapter 1, must be equal, i.e., the two lists must be balanced.

In languages other than English, the term used for balance sheet emphasizes more the *status* of the firm's position at a particular point in time, rather than the *balancing* aspect of the statement. For example *Bilanz* in German or *bilan* in French imply drawing a statement of up-to-date information – rather like a photo – but the idea of equilibrium between resources and obligations is not explicitly present in the term. The International Accounting Standard No. 1 (IAS 1, 2007) has adopted the term '**statement of financial position**' in lieu of the traditional 'balance sheet'. We will use the two terms as being totally substitutable.

This statement shows the accounting 'net worth' of a business at a given point in time by offsetting resources and obligations to third parties (i.e., other than shareholders). As we will see on many occasions throughout the book, the accounting net worth has little relationship to the market value of the firm: the net worth is the historical record of the excess of resources created by the business over the resources consumed; it looks backwards, whereas the market value of a firm is based on its potential of future **net value** creation. The statement of financial position is the document that allows a netting of what the firm possesses or controls, i.e., its resources to engage in the fulfillment of its 'strategic intent' to create value, and what it owes, i.e., what obligations it has contracted in order to obtain these resources.

The obligations side is generally separated into two parts: the *liabilities* and the *shareholders' equity*. **Liabilities** represent what is owed (with certainty) to third parties that are not participants in the ownership of the business (and therefore are not sharing the risks taken by the business venture). The **equity** (or 'net worth') is what remains, at one point in time, when resources (assets) are offset against the external obligations (liabilities).

Shareholders' equity represents the obligation the firm has towards its shareholders or, conversely, it is the claim the owners of the business collectively hold over the firm's current 'net worth' and potential future wealth. Each shareholder's claim is proportional to his or her contribution to the capital. Since (a) the amount of equity is conditional on the success of the business, and (b) the shareholders are committed to supporting the business without any specified deadline, the nature of the shareholders' claim is different from that of the lenders. It is, thus, recorded separately.

The 'business equation' or 'balance sheet equation' is therefore as follows:

> Resources (or assets) = Obligations to third parties (liabilities) *plus* Shareholders' equity (shareholders' claim)
>
> or
>
> Assets *minus* Liabilities = Net assets = Shareholders' equity (or 'net worth')

We prefer to qualify this equation as the 'business equation' rather than calling it 'balance sheet equation' because it anchors accounting in the domain of business modeling, i.e., the identification and reporting of a dynamic set of relationships, flows and stocks of resources which, when appropriately engaged and coordinated, create value for the owners.

The balance sheet is a table that records in detail all resources and all obligations that have definite monetary implications and for which an amount can be determined without ambiguity.

A balance sheet is a snapshot[1] of the status of the financial position of a business entity at a given point in time. It focuses on the composition of its financial position (see Figure 2.1 and Table 2.1).

The lists of obligations and resources can be structured either in increasing or decreasing order of liquidity. Although the rank ordering of resources and obligations in terms of relative liquidity does not change anything of substance in the situation of the firm, the behavioral implications may be meaningful in the sense that what appears on the top of a list is often considered, at least in the western world, to be the most important item(s). If the firm wishes to focus the attention of the reader on its potential for future value creation, management may prefer to show buildings, machinery and inventories on the top of the list of assets. If, on the contrary, a business wishes to communicate its ability to pay its short-term obligations, it might choose to present its cash balance and marketable securities at the top of the list of assets, and short-term liabilities at the top of the list of liabilities.

One important element to keep in mind is that, for reasons of logic, the rank ordering preference must apply homogeneously to both assets, on the one hand, and liabilities and shareholders' equity, on the other.

Figure 2.1 Financial position

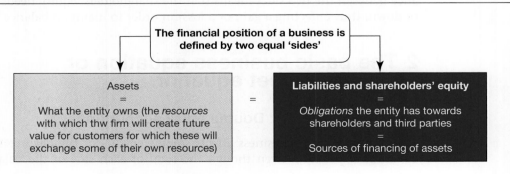

Table 2.1 Balance sheet or Statement of financial position (Continental European presentation)

000 Currency Units or CU*

ASSETS		SHAREHOLDERS' EQUITY AND LIABILITIES	
Land and equipment	200	Shareholders' equity	400
Inventories	150		
Accounts receivable	100		
Cash	50	Liabilities	100
Total	**500**	**Total**	**500**

Note: * As indicated in the Preface, the choice of the currency unit has no bearing on the logic of our presentation. We will specify the actual currency only when presenting real cases.

Table 2.2 Balance sheet (North American presentation)

000 CU

ASSETS		LIABILITIES AND SHAREHOLDERS' EQUITY	
Cash	50	Liabilities	100
Accounts receivable	100		
Inventories	150		
Land and equipment	200	Shareholders' equity	400
Total	**500**	**Total**	**500**

Continental European tradition tends to favor reporting first the 'stock' of assets (long-term resources), thus emphasizing the long-term potential of the business; on the other hand the North American tradition tends to favor reporting first the data that help understand the short-term survival potential of the firm, i.e., resources are listed in decreasing order of liquidity.

In Table 2.1, assets are ordered from least liquid to most liquid ('increasing liquidity') and liabilities are presented with longer term liabilities first and shorter term last (increasing degree of maturity). Some firms, mainly in the United States and Canada, use the reverse order (see Table 2.2).

Chapter 5, partly devoted to the format of financial statements, will explore further the pros and cons of each presentation. At this point, the way the balance sheet is presented is not important in itself. Whatever the order of the various elements, what matters is that both sides be balanced and that the equilibrium of the **basic business equation** be respected when recording transactions. Any transaction that apparently creates an imbalance between the two sides means that the shareholders' equity needs to be adjusted (up or down, thus reflecting a gain or a loss) in order to maintain balance.

2 The basic business equation or balance sheet equation

2.1 Basic principle: Double entry accounting

Any transaction in a business affects some elements of the balance sheet or statement of financial position. Even though the total of each side of the balance sheet may be modified, the net effect of the transaction is that a perfect balance between the two sides will always remain. This principle is part of the very foundation of modern accounting.

The recording of each transaction impacts the basic equation in at least two opposite ways that will keep the equation balanced. This system is known as '**double entry accounting**'.

The double impact of transactions (double entry) can take place in any of three possible combinations:

(a) between assets only (such as 'reduce cash and increase inventory of goods for sale', for example, when purchasing goods in a retail business); or

(b) between liabilities only (such as a portion of a long-term debt becomes current or payable, due to the passage of time); or

(c) it can involve both sides of the balance sheet (first example: a seasonal loan-increase increments both cash on the assets side and short-term liabilities on the other; second example: reduce cash and reduce accounts payable when the business settles a debt-payable to a supplier).

2.2 Terminology

2.2.1 Assets

An **asset** is a 'resource controlled by an entity as a result of past events and from which future economic benefits are expected to flow to the entity' (Conceptual framework, IASB 1989: § 49).

As shown in Tables 2.1 and 2.2 and further illustrated in Figure 2.2, assets are divided into several subcategories. First, assets are traditionally separated between non-current and current assets. As a brief overview, we can define **non-current assets** as resources not supposed to be sold or potentially consumed in their entirety in the normal operating cycle, or resources not supposed to be realized (sold or transformed into cash) within twelve months after the reporting period. **Current assets** are defined in a symmetric way: resources related to the normal operating cycle or resources to be sold or potentially consumed in their entirety within twelve months after the reporting period, or cash (see IAS 1, IASB 2007, § 66).

Non-current assets are in turn subdivided into tangible assets (resources tangible in nature such as property, plant and equipment), intangible assets (resources intangible in nature such as trademarks, patents or software) and financial assets (e.g., shares or bonds

Figure 2.2 Main categories of assets

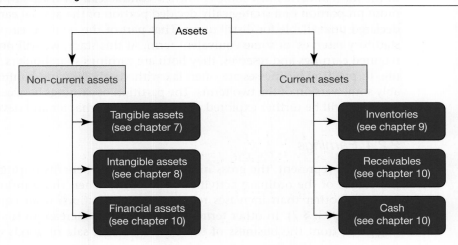

of another business or the representation of medium or long-term credit extended to a third party business). Current assets include three main categories: inventories held at the end of the reporting period (**merchandise** for resale, **raw materials**, parts and components for transformation or assembly and production, work in progress; or finished 'products'); receivables (e.g., accounts receivable due to a sale on credit); and cash.

2.2.2 Liabilities

A **liability** is a 'present obligation of the entity arising from past events, the settlement of which is expected to result in an outflow from the entity [at an agreed upon date] of resources embodying economic benefits' (IASB 1989: § 49).

2.2.3 Shareholders' equity or equity capital

Equity is a claim, a right or an interest one has over some 'net worth'. Equity, taken globally, represents the claim of all shareholders. Equity is generally represented by some form of 'shares' indicating how much of the total claim accrues to each of the parties comprising the group of shareholders.

Equity is defined (IASB 1989: § 49) as 'the residual interest in the assets of the entity after deducting all its liabilities':

Assets − Liabilities = Shareholders' equity (or net worth)

Shareholders' equity is itself composed of two components, identical in nature (they represent claims shareholders have over the firm's 'net worth'), but not in their origin. They are 'share capital' and 'retained earnings'.

Share capital is the historical value of the contributions to the firm shareholders have made in the beginning and during the life of the firm by making external resources available to the firm and handing over control over these resources (cash, effort or ideas, physical assets, etc.) to the business entity.

Retained earnings represent that part of the value created through the firm's operations that shareholders have chosen not to take out of the firm as dividends. It is a *de facto* increase in their contribution to the ongoing activity of the firm. Unlike share capital, which remains constant until shareholders decide to increase it, retained earnings is an account that fluctuates each period with the accumulation of the results of the operations of the firm (profit or loss) and the decisions of shareholders to withdraw the wealth created in the form of dividends. Some countries' commercial- or fiscal-law mandates that a minimum proportion or a strategically decided portion of the annual earnings of a business be declared unavailable for distribution. That part of the retained earnings is called 'legal or statutory reserves' or some equivalent term. At this stage, we will not distinguish between retained earnings and reserves: they both are earnings shareholders 'agreed' not to distribute. In practice, businesses are often lax with vocabulary and confuse or use interchangeably some version of the two terms. The partition of earnings between dividends and other purposes will be further explored at the end of this chapter and developed in Chapter 11.

2.2.4 Earnings

Revenues represent 'the gross inflow of economic benefits during the period arising in the course of the ordinary activities of an entity when those inflows result in increases in equity, other than increases relating to contributions from equity participants' (IAS 18, IASB 1993: § 7). In other terms, revenues are an increase in shareholders' equity that originates from the business of the firm such as a sale of goods or services or interest received from short-term investments: revenues generally balance the increase they create in shareholders' equity by increases in cash or in accounts receivable.

Expenses represent 'decreases in economic benefits during the accounting period in the form of outflows or depletion of assets or incurrence of liabilities that result in decreases in equity, other than those relating to distributions to equity participants' (IASB 1989: § 70). Expenses originate from activities of the firm such as purchase of services from an outside source, payment of salaries or remuneration to employees, payment of rent for the use of certain physical facilities, wear and tear on equipment, royalties for the right to use someone else's idea, etc. In other words, expenses result from the consumption of resources, and represent a decrease in shareholders' equity that originates from carrying out the business of the company.

Earnings (or **net income,** or **period earnings**) are thus the net difference between the resources **created** by the economic activity of the business (total revenues) and the resources **consumed** in operating the firm (total expenses). They represent the profit or loss of a period. In essence, earnings are the net increase (profit) or decrease (loss) of the shareholders' equity, i.e., the value created or destroyed through the activity of the business. The following equation applies:

Earnings (net income) (for period t)
=
Shareholders' equity (at the end of period t)
minus
Shareholders' equity (at the beginning of period t)
(All things being otherwise equal)

The net income is generally calculated in a separate and subsidiary account called 'Income Statement' (abbreviated as I/S) (mostly used in the US accounting terminology) or '**Profit and Loss Account**' (abbreviated as P&L) (mostly used by firms using the British accounting terminology).[2] This special account or statement will be further developed later in this chapter. The income statement allows managers to follow revenues and expenses separately without measuring changes in shareholders' equity after each transaction. The balance of the income statement (or P&L) is the net income, i.e., the amount that describes the net effect of one period's activity on the shareholders' equity.

2.3 Transactions

The operation of the basic business equation is illustrated throughout the chapter by looking sequentially and chronologically at several illustrative transactions pertaining to a single business, a firm called Verdi. Although the limited transactions of our examples cover a short period of time, we will consider these transactions are the only ones taking place during the accounting period X1, supposed, for the sake of simplicity, to be equal to a year. Any transaction, not explicitly completed according to the text, is considered still 'open' at the end of the period (year).

As a convention, we have chosen to follow the rank ordering of items on the balance sheet where the most liquid items are listed first, and the least liquid are listed last. It is important to remind the reader at this point that the rank ordering preferences have no impact on the output of accounting.

Transaction 1 – Initial investment by shareholders   Stefania, an English professor, and her life partner Stefano, a graphic-design artist, decide to create a public relations and communications agency on 1 January X1. The financial resources they choose to invest in their business venture amount, in total, to 150 CU. They create their business (an incorporated company) with a capital contribution of 150 CU in cash. It is agreed between them that Stefania will contribute three-fifths of the initial capital and thus will receive 90 shares with a nominal par value of 1 CU. Stefano will contribute the remaining two-fifths and thus will receive 60 shares with the same par value. They choose to name their business venture 'Verdi' and open a bank **account**[3] in that name. Each shareholder transfers the agreed upon amount of cash into the bank account.

Once in Verdi's bank account, the funds belong to neither Stefania nor Stefano. They are now part of the 'net worth' of Verdi (here, cash at bank = net worth, since no other transaction has taken place and no value has been created). Stefania holds a claim of three-fifths over that 'net worth', while Stefano holds a claim of two-fifths. The net worth amount will change over time with the activity of the business, but the percentage of claim held by each of the shareholders over the net worth will not change over time, unless one of them increases or decreases (with the approval of the other), his or her contribution to the capital of the firm.

The personal 'net worth' of the 'shareholders' is always distinct from that of the business in which they have invested. Various legal structures exist that reinforce the separation of 'net worth' of the entity from that of the individual shareholders – limited liability companies for example – or weaken the separation – self-employed or unincorporated entrepreneur, for example. These legal structures will be covered in more detail in Chapter 11.

Figure 2.3 illustrates the effect of the company's creation as a separate economic entity on the basic equation.

The transaction results in an increase by the same amount (from zero to 150) in both assets (cash) and shareholders' equity. Investments by shareholders do not represent revenues and are excluded from the determination of net income. 'Cash' and 'share capital' will be set up as individual 'accounts' so as to allow the tracing of the many transactions that will impact their balance in the normal course of the life of the agency.

The equilibrium of the business equation is respected because the 'assets' side equals the 'liabilities plus equity' side. Equity will, in time, and as we will see later in this chapter, become more complex. For example, shareholders might choose to reinvest part or all of the income of the period, i.e., add to the capital they initially brought in. Shareholders' equity (or net worth) will eventually be equal to share capital, plus income from previous years reinvested by shareholders (retained earnings and/or reserves), plus income of the most recently concluded period.

The net income for the period (from before the creation of Verdi to the acknowledgment of the receipt of initial capital and opening of the bank account) is zero since this transaction created neither value nor wealth (wealth or value is only created through transactions with customers) and neither value nor wealth was destroyed (value is destroyed by consumption of resources or assets).

Income corresponds to a period of time, while the balance sheet (or statement of financial position) corresponds to an instant in time. Net income is calculated at the end of a period of any duration and reflects all transactions that took place during that period. Conceptually, income (or change in shareholders' equity) could be calculated for each transaction but it would be very cumbersome to do so. Net income is generally required to be reported to shareholders at least once a year, for the previous year, but management

Figure 2.3 Transaction 1

	Assets	=	Liabilities	+	Shareholders' equity (SE)	
	Cash		Financial debt		Share capital	Details of SE transaction
Transaction (1)	+ 150				+ 150	Initial investment

and, increasingly, other users and financial markets, require more frequent reporting of net income so as to help managers, users and investors alike evaluate the performance trend on which a given firm operates. Managers will be interested in adjusting the course of action they have selected, on the basis of the confrontation between expected and observed results and also on the basis of their perceived evolution of the external competitive conditions under which the firm operates. Shareholders meanwhile will essentially use the information to review their investment decision: Should I stay invested in this firm or should I sell and invest in another opportunity?

Transaction 2 – Verdi obtains a loan   Early in January X1, Verdi obtains a 60 CU loan from its bank (it could be from any financial institution – the nature of the lender has no bearing on our accounting for the transaction). The principal of the loan is deposited in Verdi's bank account. The contract specifies interest, at the rate of 6 and 2/3 percent per period, shall be paid at the end of each period, on the principal remaining at the beginning of the period.

When Verdi contracts the loan, it actually takes on an obligation to repay 60 CU in the future, and also the obligation to pay interest on the principal outstanding. Since obtaining the loan increases Verdi's external obligations, we record an increase of liabilities by 60 CU (interest is not due until the end of the period, thus only the principal will be recorded at this date). Of course, the counterbalancing event (double entry accounting) is that the cash balance is increased by the same amount. Since we have increased both sides of the equation, the impact on equity is zero. Borrowing in itself does not create nor destroy value or wealth; at least not until we consider the passage of time and the fact we will have to pay interest (recognizing interest expense reduces cash or creates another obligation to pay in the future).

At the end of the period, interest becomes due and thus payable. At the time when interest payable is recognized, it will reduce shareholders' equity while, after its effective payment resulting in a cash decrease, the interest payable will be canceled as a liability. In other words, interest is an expense as defined earlier. We will not, however, record the interest expense at this stage since we have opted for a chronological sequence of transactions and the interest will only be paid on the last day of the period.

This borrowing transaction will increase both the cash and the liabilities of Verdi Company as recorded in Figure 2.4.

Figure 2.4 shows the cumulative effect of the previous transactions, the specific effect of the current transaction and the cumulative effect of all transactions. After this transaction, net income is still zero. No value was created by the simple acquisition of additional funding.

Transaction 3 – Purchase of equipment in exchange for liquidity   In the first half of January X1 Verdi acquires some equipment: a fast computer, a high quality color printer and art and

Figure 2.4 Transaction 2

	Assets	=	Liabilities	+	Shareholders' equity (SE)
	Cash		Financial debt		Share capital
Beginning balance	150				150
Transaction (2)	+ 60		+ 60		
Ending balance	210	=	60	+	150

210   210

page-setting software worth 100 CU in total and, for an additional 25 CU, a second computer plus a small black and white printer. The latter equipment will only be used for the administration of the business. These resources, or assets, have been acquired for a total cost of 125 CU. The supplier is paid for this purchase with a check drawn on Verdi's bank account.

This equipment and software will be used in the future to create (or contribute to the creation of) services that will be sold to customers in keeping with the chosen strategy. Such equipment has the potential for creating future streams of revenues (i.e., economic benefits). It is now a resource of the business, i.e., an asset.

An interesting question is the definition of the 'value' at which the resources will be recognized in Verdi's statement of financial position or balance sheet. The need to keep the 'business equation' in balance gives us the answer: since the equipment and software originally cost 125 CU (the amount of cash, another resource, that was consumed), the assets will be valued at their invoiced price (or cost of acquisition, also known as **historical cost**). The substitution of a resource for another does not, in itself, create (or destroy) value or wealth: value creation (value destruction) happens only when there is increase (decrease) in the equity the shareholders have in the business. Clearly a resource substitution does not, in itself, create (nor consume) value. Even if the asset substitution modifies the potential of future value creation, the 'prudence rule' calls for ignoring the modification until the use of the new resource actually generates additional resources through the sale of the output of the consumption of the resources.

The acquired equipment and software increases Verdi's assets by 125 CU and simultaneously, because of the immediate payment to the supplier, the bank account is decreased by 125 CU and thus the event 'acquisition of equipment' has the following net effect: $(+125) + (-125) = 0$, i.e., no effect on total assets, and, logically, on equity. The business has neither gained nor lost wealth or value due to this investment in equipment and software.

However, this will not be the case in the future, as two sequences of events will normally take place: (a) a stream of revenues will derive (directly or indirectly) from the sales generated by the use of the equipment, i.e., additional resources will be created; and (b) the equipment will be consumed, i.e., its future ability to create resources will be diminished through use and thus its value in the list of resources of the firm will have to be decreased. Thus, in the future, the *net* effect of the use of the equipment will be either a creation of resources (resources created exceed resources consumed) – that is to create profit, or a net consumption of resources (resources consumed exceed resources created) – which is called a loss.

In summary, the asset acquisition transaction results in an equal increase and decrease in total assets and does not change the magnitude of total assets, liabilities or shareholders' equity of Verdi Company. Figure 2.5 shows that this transaction only changed the composition of the company's assets by increasing equipment and decreasing cash.

Figure 2.5 Transaction 3

	Assets			=	Liabilities	+	Shareholders' equity (SE)
	Cash	+	Equipment		Financial debt		Share capital
Beginning balance	210				60		150
Transaction (3)	– 125		+ 125				
Ending balance	85	+	125	=	60	+	150

Assets: 210

Liabilities + SE: 210

Transaction 4 – Services rendered   Sheila Burns, a retailer, approaches Verdi on 14 May and contracts for a public relations campaign to be carried out throughout June around the opening of a new store. After discussion about the content and format of the campaign, Sheila Burns agrees she will pay 250 CU for the service Verdi will render. She also agrees to pay the full amount 30 days after she receives the invoice, which will be sent after the public relations campaign has been implemented. Therefore, she agrees to pay the full amount no later than 31 July. Verdi has thus engaged in a transaction that will generate sales revenue of 250 CU, which will be recognizable on 1 July, when Verdi invoices Sheila (to recognize a revenue – or an expense – is to record it formally and officially in the accounts that will serve in preparing the financial statements). The likelihood that Sheila will actually give the promised cash is extremely high and we can anticipate the future cash inflow. Simply, Verdi will recognize the 250 CU sales revenue, when the invoice is mailed, as 'potential cash' under the name of **accounts receivable**. It is not really cash, but represents a claim on Sheila Burns that Verdi will exercise on 31 July. In fact, such a claim could be sold for cash now (at a discount of course, because of the time value of money – see this concept in Chapter 12), just like any other resource.

Booking the order is not a transaction recorded in accounting since neither resources nor liabilities or net worth are affected until the service has been rendered.

The invoicing transaction, by creating the accounts receivable entry, will create an increase in the resources side of the business equation. There must be a counterbalancing entry, which will either be an increase in the equity component of the 'net worth' (which will be called earnings or income or net income), or a reduction in other resources. It could even be a combination of both (as we will see after Transaction 6).

At this stage, in this simplistic example, let us assume, for the time being, there are no costs attached to the actual execution of the public relations campaign. The net effect on the balance sheet, after invoicing, is that, on the left-hand side, the claim on the customer (accounts receivable) has increased by 250 CU (increase in assets: the account receivable is a resource that could be exchanged for cash or transformed to create different or more resources) while on the right-hand side, equity has increased by the same amount (liabilities were not affected).

Revenues increase shareholders' equity. Because the 'sale of services' is not, in this case, for cash, assets other than cash will increase: this was done through the recognition of the accounts receivable. Revenues are included in the determination of earnings/net income (see Figure 2.6).

To understand the effect of all transactions on equity, one must separate the shareholders' equity into two parts:

(a) 'share capital' which recognizes the initial amount brought-in by the investors (two investors or shareholders in Verdi's case); and

(b) 'earnings' which record the net cumulative effect on equity of any and all transactions.

Figure 2.6 Transaction 4

	Assets			= Liabilities +	Shareholders' equity (SE)		
	Cash +	Equipment +	Accounts receivable	Financial debt	Share capital +	Earnings	Detail of SE transaction
Beginning balance	85	125		60	150		
Transaction (4)			250			250	Service revenue
Ending balance	85 +	125 +	250 =	60 +	150 +	250	

460

460

Earnings are in fact the property of the owners of the firm (shareholders). If they choose not to withdraw the earnings over which they have a claim, these earnings become 'retained earnings' (i.e., retained in the business to allow it to conserve its resources pool – especially cash – and allow the shareholders to increase their stake in the firm while supporting its ability to grow).

- *Remark 1*: Shareholders' equity increased by 250 CU. Because we have (for the time being) assumed there were no costs attached to the creation of the revenues, the sale is plainly an increase in the shareholders' equity. This is so because the accounts receivable have increased the left-hand side of the balance sheet but there is no counterpart other than 'sales revenue', which is, in fact, a subsidiary account of shareholders' equity (revenues minus costs equals income or increase – or decrease – in shareholders' equity). When net additional resources enter the financial position of the firm without resources being decreased or new obligations created to third parties, value is created.

- *Remark 2*: The balance sheet remains balanced (the equilibrium is maintained by recognizing the income).

- *Remark 3*: The cash position has not been modified because the customer has not paid yet. This sale was on credit, and this fact is reflected in the 'accounts receivable' account. Such an account is clearly an asset (or a resource) since Verdi has a legal claim on Sheila Burns to request payment and can even go to court to collect if Sheila Burns were to fail to pay on the due date.

Transaction 5 – Receipt of cash in settlement of the accounts receivable   When, on 31 July, Sheila Burns sends a check to pay 180 of her 250 CU debt to Verdi, this check is immediately deposited in Verdi's bank account. The claim is only partially settled.

As was the case in Transaction 3, this transaction results in an equal increase and decrease in assets and does not change the total assets, liabilities and shareholders' equity of Verdi Company. It only changes the composition of the company's assets by increasing cash and decreasing accounts receivable. However, the accounts receivable transaction related to the transaction between Sheila Burns and Verdi is not entirely completed, there remains some accounts payable in Verdi's books. The new balances are as shown in Figure 2.7.

As the 180 CU actual payment of the revenue has already been 'earned' (included as part of the 250 CU in Transaction 4), it cannot increase shareholders' equity a second time. The new balance of accounts receivable (here it is 70 CU, since the original balance was 250 and the customer paid 180) represents the amount which still remains to be collected. Cash payment of a receivable or of a debt does not create value (i.e., does not modify shareholders' equity).

Figure 2.7 Transaction 5

	Assets			= Liabilities +	Shareholders' equity (SE)		
	Cash +	Equipment +	Accounts receivable	Financial debt	Share capital	+	Earnings
Beginning balance	85	125	250	60	150		
Transaction (5)	180		– 180				250
Ending balance	265 +	125 +	70 =	60 +	150	+	250

460

460

Transaction 6 – Expenses either in cash or on account   Let us now relax the assumption we made earlier that no resources had been consumed to create the service sold to Sheila Burns. In order to carry out the public relations campaign mentioned in Transaction 4, Verdi had to pay wages to two employees for a total amount of 101 CU, including social contributions and fringe benefits (a disc jockey, specialized in new-store openings and in-store commercial promotions, for 56 CU and an accountant for 45 CU). The payment of 101 CU is carried out by writing checks to the various persons and public agencies, but is treated here, for the sake of simplicity, as one single transaction. In addition, the lending institution withdraws from the bank balance, at the end of the period, the interest accrued which amounts to 4 CU. Lastly, Verdi had contracted with an advertising agency for a targeted advertisement campaign to promote its own business to potential customers. The campaign has now been fully carried out. Verdi has received the invoice for this service in the amount of 85 CU. This invoice is due within 60 days of receipt.

Services purchased from suppliers, or work realized by employees, are not free of charge. They are the foundation of claims by these parties on the resources of the enterprise. The recognition of these claims creates what we have called expenses (i.e., consumption of resources). When the claims will eventually be settled (extinguished), it will be by transferring cash to the relevant parties. The conclusion of these transactions will reduce Verdi's cash account balance (i.e., reduce resources).

When a claim by a supplier is not settled immediately for cash, it is first recognized under the name '**accounts payable**' (a debt owed by Verdi) before finally being settled through a transfer of cash, at a later date, to the creditors – supplier and employees in this case.

For example, Verdi Company has consumed 85 CU worth of resources to acquire and consume external services from a supplier (this consumption is called 'external expenses' since Verdi benefited from a service that used resources that belong to the supplier, i.e., were 'external' to Verdi's resources). That amount has a direct impact on equity. Even if the invoice will be paid in two installments, for example an initial payment of 80 on the due date in X1 and the remaining 5 early in X2, the way the claim is settled has no impact on equity (see Transaction 7 for details).

When the financial institution lent money to Verdi, it was expecting both repayment of the principal (the nominal amount lent or principal) and the periodic payment of interest on any remaining balance on the loan at scheduled intervals. The **interest** represents the fee paid for having the right to use money that belongs to the bank. That 'rental fee' will be settled by giving up (consuming) resources (cash) in favor of the bank. Interest is, as mentioned above, an expense and will be recognized on the agreed upon anniversary dates. This is called a 'financial expense'.

> An expense is the recognition of a consumption of resources creating a claim on current or future cash (with the exception of depreciation, which reflects the consumption of the productive potential of an existing long-term asset already acquired, whether for cash or on credit – see more on depreciation later in this chapter).
>
> An expense is equivalent to a reduction in the equity of the business.

The way the bank's claim will be settled (now or later) does not affect the equity of the firm. The interest expense is a reduction in the equity of Verdi, i.e., an expense. However, if Verdi were to repay all or part of the principal of the loan, this transaction would have no impact on equity because there would be a simultaneous reduction of cash, on the assets side, and of the debt payable, on the liabilities side (see transaction 8 below).

Figure 2.8 Transaction 6

	Assets			=	Liabilities		+	Shareholders' equity (SE)		
	Cash	+ Equipment	+ Accounts receivable		Accounts payable	+ Financial debt		Share capital	+ Earnings	Detail of SE transaction
Beginning balance	265	125	70			60		150	250	
Transaction (6)	−101								−101	Salaries expense
	−4								−4	Interest expense
					85				−85	External expense
Ending balance	160 +	125 +	70	=	85	+ 60	+	150 +	60	

355

355

To sum up:

- Any expense (with the very important exception of depreciation) will eventually be settled in cash.

- The recognition of any expense (settled in cash or not) causes a reduction in equity in a way symmetrical to the recognition of revenue, which, as we have seen, causes an increase in the equity of the firm (see, for example, Transaction 4).

- The way the expense will actually be settled does not affect equity.

The effect of these three transactions on the basic equation is shown in Figure 2.8.

Transaction 7 below shows how the settlement of a delayed claim affects the statement of financial position or balance sheet. The three types of expenses listed above are completely consumed in the course of Verdi's activity. It confirms the common wisdom that it is generally necessary to consume resources in order to create revenues. For example, in Old Dutch the saying goes: *De cost gaet for de baet* or 'the cost is what "gets" – i.e., drives – the [sales] revenue'.

Both expenses and revenues affect equity (earnings). It might be interesting to regroup expenses by homogeneous type so as to gain a better understanding of how the business model of the firm actually creates wealth or value. Here, we distinguished expenses by their nature (operational or financial) but we will see below and with more details in Chapter 5 that they could also usefully be regrouped by functions (purposes such as meeting demand, creating demand or administering the firm) or destinations (be they products or services, customers, markets, or even departments). The expense classification is secondary to understanding the impact of the expenses on earnings and shareholders' equity.

Transaction 7 – Settlement of accounts payable   Verdi only settles 80 out of the 85 CU supplier's claim (accounts payable) on the due date. The remaining 5 CU will be settled at a later date in early X2. The supplier's invoice has been previously recorded (see Transaction 6) as an account payable. This payment will decrease both assets (cash) and liabilities (accounts payable). The effect of this transaction on the equation is illustrated in Figure 2.9.

When 80 CU are paid in cash to the supplier, there is simultaneously a reduction of the asset side of the basic equation and a reduction of the claim amount recognized in the accounts payable on the right-hand (liabilities) side. Thus, since both sides are decreased by exactly the same amount, there is no impact on equity. The fact that an amount of 5 CU remains unsettled simply means we have to recognize it as a residual claim to be

Figure 2.9 Transaction 7

	Assets			=	Liabilities			+	Shareholders' equity (SE)		
	Cash +	Equipment +	Accounts receivable	=	Accounts payable	+	Financial debt	+	Share capital	+	Earnings
Beginning balance	160 +	125 +	70	=	85	+	60	+	150	+	60
Transaction (7)	−80				−80						
Ending balance	80 +	125 +	70	=	5	+	60	+	150	+	60

275   275

settled in the future (no later than early X2, if we want to remain on good terms with this supplier).

No value was created nor destroyed by this operation. The impact on equity was already recorded in Transaction 6 and cannot be recorded a second time.

Transaction 8 – Repayment of a debt   Verdi partially reimburses the lender by returning 12 CU out of the loan principal of 60:

■ The assets side will be reduced by 12 (reduction of cash),
■ Debt is also, simultaneously, reduced by 12 CU.

By reimbursing part of its debt, Verdi did not create value. It neither gained nor lost wealth! Since the reimbursement affects simultaneously both the assets and liabilities sides by the same amount, there is no impact on equity.

Here we see an important limitation of accounting. Although the statement that Verdi neither gained nor lost wealth is arithmetically (and accounting-wise) perfectly correct, the 'leverage effect' would lead us to think otherwise. Hopefully, the business could have used, as an alternative, the cash used in the reimbursement of part of the principal of the loan to generate a sale activity that might have yielded a return that could have exceeded the interest expense avoided through the early reimbursement of the loan principal. Thus, if the firm had had opportunities that could have yielded more income or earnings than the avoided interest rate on the same amount of resources (12 CU), it should not have reimbursed the principal early. Reimbursing early, when more profitable alternative uses of cash exist, deprives the shareholders of potential future earnings, therefore making them lose an opportunity to earn more wealth. If, on the contrary, no such opportunity had existed, it was definitely best for the shareholders to have Verdi reimburse the bank for part of the principal on the loan because the interest expense avoided is greater than the earnings that would have been generated through the use of these resources. When no 'more profitable' alternative use of cash exists, early reimbursement of a debt actually avoids future expenses and is therefore equivalent to a (future or potential) creation of wealth. Accounting, however, will not recognize these possible opportunities because they are not known with certainty.

Accounting is essentially prudent and only recognizes, or considers, elements that are certain and for which the amount is known, i.e., that are historical (or contractually defined) or not set in an uncertain (state conditional) future.

Transaction 8 is very close in nature to the previous one: decrease in assets (cash) and decrease in liabilities (financial debt). Figure 2.10 illustrates the effect of this transaction on the business equation.

Summary   A summary of the eight transactions affecting Verdi Company is presented in Figure 2.11.

After all these transactions have been recorded, the synthetic statement of financial position (balance sheet) appears as shown in Table 2.3.

Figure 2.10 Transaction 8

	Assets			=	Liabilities			+	Shareholders' equity (SE)		
	Cash	+ Equipment +	Accounts receivable	=	Accounts payable	+	Financial debt	+	Share capital	+	Retained Earnings
Beginning balance	80 +	125 +	70	=	5	+	60	+	150	+	60
Transaction (8)	−12						−12				
Ending balance	68 +	125 +	70	=	5	+	48	+	150	+	60

263   =   263

Figure 2.11 Summary table

	Assets			=	Liabilities		+	Shareholders' equity (SE)		
Transaction	Cash +	Equipment +	Accounts receivable	= Accounts payable	+ Financial debt	+	Share capital	+ Earnings	Detail of SE transaction
(1)	+150						+150		Initial investment
(2)	+60				+60				
(3)	−125	+125							
(4)			+250					+250	Service revenue
(5)	+180		−180						
(6)	−101							−101	Salaries expense
(6)	−4							−4	Interest expense
(6)				85				−85	External expense
(7)	−80			−80					
(8)	−12				−12				
Ending balance	68 +	125 +	70	= 5	+ 48	+	150 +	60	

263   =   263

Table 2.3 Balance sheet on 31 December X1

ASSETS		EQUITY AND LIABILITIES		
Fixed assets		**Shareholders' equity**		210
Equipment	125	Capital	150	
		Earnings (net income)	60	
Current assets		**Liabilities**		
Accounts receivable	70	Financial debt		48
Cash at bank	68	Accounts payable		5
Total assets	263	**Total equity and liabilities**		263

Conclusion – some key points   The previous transactions illustrate the following points.

1. *Both sides of the business equation must always be balanced with one another.*
2. *Each transaction must be analyzed specifically to identify its possible impact on shareholders' equity.*
3. *All transactions that create or consume value (i.e., create profit or loss) ultimately impact the '(retained) earnings' account, a subsidiary account of shareholders' equity in a way that can be described by the following formula:*

> (Beginning [retained] earnings balance) + (Profit or loss from the period) − (Dividends) =
> (Ending [retained] earnings balance)

In our example, since there have been no dividends paid, and we only looked at the first year of operations, the change in the amount of the retained earnings at the end of a period is equal to the net income of that period (here it is + 60 CU).

Since income belongs to the shareholders, part, or all of it, can be distributed in the form of dividends. Income (or loss) for a period is only reflective of what happened during that period. If the shareholders decide to withdraw some of the wealth created (either this period or during previous periods), it is their right and therefore the ending balance of the earnings retained in any balance sheet (accumulating in the retained earnings account) is given by the formula above.

The **retained earnings** account (sometimes, and often abusively, due mainly to errors in translation, called **reserves**) reflects the cumulated effect of the earnings the shareholders have chosen not to withdraw from the business.

4. *What creates income?*

There was no income (impact on shareholders' equity that results from business operations) until Transaction 4 (sale of services). This transaction was the first operation in our illustrative sequence that created profit (i.e., affected positively the shareholders' equity) and therefore, ultimately, affected the retained earnings account. Any transaction that affects either assets and/or liabilities (excluding shareholders' equity, of course) in uneven or unbalanced ways affects earnings (the balance of all transactions is what we call net income). Any transaction that only affects assets and/or liabilities in even or balanced ways is not a source of value creation. Only transactions with outside customers are susceptible to create revenues, and transactions with outside customers always require the consumption of resources, i.e., consume or destroy 'value'.

Income is the difference between the value created in customer-based transactions and the value destroyed by consuming resources to serve customers.

5. *Net income is different from cash*

Since our example only looked at the first period of existence of Verdi, and no dividend payment has been decided, the net income of the period and the retained earnings show, by definition, identical amounts, namely + 60 CU. The cash balance (in the bank) went from 0 CU (beginning of the story) to + 68, i.e., a fluctuation of plus 68 CU. The variation in the cash balance is in no way directly connected to the magnitude of the income of the period. Two main explanations for the difference can be proposed at this stage (a third one – depreciation – will be added later).

■ Some transactions only have an impact on the bank's cash balance and not on earnings: e.g., Transaction 2 (obtaining a loan) and Transaction 3 (acquisition of an asset or equipment).

■ The fact that some sales lead to extending credit to customers (and conversely some acquisitions of resources lead to credit being extended by the supplier) creates a situation in which the earnings account is modified when the transaction takes place and not when it is finally settled through payment from the customer or to the supplier. This was the case in Transaction 4 (sale of services) in which earnings were increased but not the cash account. Similarly, Transaction 6 (purchasing resources or services from an outside supplier) generated a reduction in earnings without modifying the bank balance at the same moment.

The timing difference between cash and profit is crucial, especially in a fast-growing business. Let us build a simple example to illustrate the situation. Assume there is a business whose sales double each period. Expenses are 80% of revenues. Customers pay two periods after the sales take place and suppliers require payment within one period after the delivery. The resources are acquired in the same period when the sales take place (see Table 2.4).

We have here a business which is clearly extremely profitable, but for which the cash situation is dramatically dangerous and probably will lead to bankruptcy unless something is done, such as obtaining more starting cash (upfront capital or borrowing), changing the credit terms given to customers (not always possible for a start-up business), or obtaining better credit terms from the suppliers (here again, not an easy task for a small and young enterprise). Many fast-growing businesses actually go bankrupt because they cannot generate enough long-term capital to provide stable resources to keep the firm alive through this fast growth phase.

The statement of cash flows (see Chapters 3, 14 and 17) describes in detail the relationship between the income and cash situation.

6. *The order in which items are listed on the balance sheet is not random*

Each national or enterprise culture lists items in a sequential order that matches their value system. Chapter 5 shows that some countries go as far as defining a standard rank order. One of the reputed advantages of a normalized rank ordering is that it facilitates comparability of financial statements between comparable enterprises. The opposite is, of course, that comparability is useless if it is obtained at the detriment of the quality and descriptive flexibility of accounting. Most multinational companies have imposed on their subsidiaries, all over the globe, the obligation to report (to the parent) in similar formats (regardless of the locally required format) and also to use the same definition of terms so as to facilitate the comparative evaluation of the value creation potential of each subsidiary by senior management in the headquarters. Similarly, financial analysts and investment advisors are interested in homogeneous reporting so as to facilitate their task of identifying superior performers in an industrial sector.

Table 2.4 Cash versus profit

Period	1	2	3	4	5	6	7
Sales	10	20	40	80	160	320	640
Expenses	8	16	32	64	128	256	512
Profit	**2**	**4**	**8**	**16**	**32**	**64**	**128**
Opening cash	0	0	−8	−14	−26	−50	−98
Cash inflow	0	0	10	20	40	80	160
Cash outflow	0	8	16	32	64	128	256
Ending cash	**0**	**−8**	**−14**	**−26**	**−50**	**−98**	**−194**

2.4 Typical transactions

Table 2.5 below lists some typical transactions and their impact on assets, liabilities and shareholders' equity. This table is in no way exhaustive and we have deliberately focused on the most common transactions. However, it aims to show that the knowledge of a relatively limited number of transactions allows one to understand the impact (on the elements of the business equation) of almost any 'ordinary' transaction realized by a firm.

Table 2.5 Impact of most common transactions

Example	Assets	=	Liabilities	+	Shareholders' equity
Creation of the company by capital contribution	+				+ C
Purchase of equipment for cash	+ and −				
Purchase of equipment on credit	+		+		
Sales revenue for cash or on account	+				+ E
Collection of accounts receivable	+ and −				
Expense for cash	−				− E
Expense on account			+		− E
Payment of a liability (e.g., accounts payable)	−		−		
Obtaining a loan (recording of a debt)	+		+		
Repayment of a debt	−		−		
Conversion of a debt into share capital			−		+ C
Reduction of capital (repayment of the capital)	−				− C

Note: The shareholders' equity account is separated between: C = capital and E = earnings

3 Income statement (or I/S or profit and loss account, also known as P&L statement, or simply P&L)

In the previous section, revenues and expenses generated by each transaction were recorded through their impact on shareholders' equity and, more specifically, on the '[retained] earnings' account. This choice was made to show the fundamental mechanism of the business equation. The number of transactions in the life of a business is, however, so large that it would be extremely cumbersome to record each change individually in the [retained] earnings account or to handle the revenues and expenses accounts as a subsidiary account of shareholders' equity in the balance sheet. Dealing with each transaction individually as it affects equity would also make it difficult to carry out analyses of transactions to understand the business model of value creation during the period. Remember that the balance of retained earnings reflects the cumulated impact of all transactions – including distribution of income to shareholders – since the firm was created.

In practice, transactions will be recorded in specific accounts opened only for a given period of time. These accounts will form the 'income statement'. This statement is also known as 'profit and loss account', 'profit and loss statement', 'P&L' or 'I/S'. For purposes of simplicity, we will use the terms 'income statement' or 'I/S' throughout the book.

The accounts composing the income statement allow us to analyze the processes through which income of the period was created, and thus how [retained] earnings will be modified. For each period, only the income statement's net balance at the end of the period (i.e., net income of the period) will be transferred to the balance sheet account (as part of the shareholders' equity, pending decision by shareholders of dividend payment or incorporation in the retained earnings). The income statement will be the record of what happened during the period that caused the observed income (profit or loss). This separate record of actions can be subjected to analysis so as to identify which decisions can be modified to create even more profit for the next period.

The statement of financial position or the balance sheet will remain a 'snapshot' of the financial position of the firm while the income statement will record the dynamics of how such position changed during a period of time. In a way, if the balance sheet is a snapshot, the income statement is like the 'film' of the 'activity' of the business during a given period that explains how the beginning balance sheet became the ending balance sheet.

Some key terms have been introduced here:

- **Activity**: this term refers to both the service, industrial or commercial sector in which a business operates, and the level of intensity of its transactions (level of activity). The term activity refers to what the firm does. The income statement reflects the activity of the firm. It gives a view of how it went from one balance sheet to the next. The income statement, therefore, does not give the financial position (or a record of the 'net worth' of the firm). It provides a view of what the firm did during the period. It records the consumption of resources and the creation of revenues. Resources used can be short-lived, as would be the case for salaries, supplies, energy, etc., or can be **long-lived** such as tangible or physical assets (land, buildings, machinery, fixtures, office equipment, etc.) or intangible assets (e.g., patents). In the case of long-lived assets, what is recorded as a resource consumption is the reduction of their potential to create future economic benefits due to usage (wear and tear, obsolescence, etc.) during the period.

- **During a given period**: the income statement is a recapitulation of all transactions linked to serving customers (creating demand, satisfying demand and administering the process) during a given period of time called 'accounting period' as defined in Chapter 1.

The income statement allows managers and accounting information users to track revenues (conventionally placed on the right-hand side of the I/S account, to mimic the fact that revenues are equivalent to an increase in shareholders' equity) and the expenses or costs (conventionally placed on the left-hand side).

The income statement is a temporary account that will be 'closed' at the end of the period by the transfer of its balance to the shareholders' equity and ultimately to the 'retained earnings' account on the balance sheet. If revenues are greater than expenses, there is profit, i.e., an increase in shareholders' equity. Income (difference between revenues and expenses, whether positive [profit], or negative [loss]) is the amount required to balance both sides of the income statement. Thus, when closing the income statement at the end of the period, 'profit' will appear on the left-hand side of the income statement, and the counterbalancing entry will be the recognition of the increase in the shareholders' equity, on the right-hand side of the balance sheet. If there had been a loss (expenses exceed revenues), the loss would have appeared on the right-hand side of the income statement and the counterbalancing entry, at closing, would have been a reduction of shareholders' equity. Such reduction, conceptually on the left-hand side of the balance sheet, would appear as a negative impact on shareholders' equity.

This co-temporal recognition of related revenues and expenses, called the **accrual principle**, is essential for financial statements to be useful. This principle means that revenue (expense) is recorded in the income statement at the time of the transaction that causes it, and not at the time of the cash inflow (for a revenue) or outflow (for an expense). Both managers and outside information users can read directly from the income statement (established on an accrual basis) how much of the business' resources must be mobilized to create revenues. By comparing several successive periods, these users can also see whether the 'productivity' of the business' resources is improving or deteriorating (due to any combination of quality of management, changes in competitive conditions, relevance of value offering to customers, etc.).

3.1 Business equation and income statement

Figure 2.12 illustrates the link between the basic business (balance sheet or accounting) equation and the income statement.

3.2 Elements of the income statement

3.2.1 Revenues

Revenue is an influx of economic resources for the firm, coming from third parties and whose origin is generally a commercial transaction. Revenue is always an increase in shareholders' equity.

The ultimate purpose of an enterprise is to create profit so as to give a positive return to (or increase the wealth of) its shareholders. The way an enterprise creates profit is by satisfying its customers. The **sales** revenue (or sales turnover) is the metric that reflects how successful the firm is at creating and delivering a customer value proposition at any given point. Note that the concept of value offering or value proposition includes provision of goods or services as well as rental of facilities, technologies or goods. The concept of rental revenue recognition is of increasing interest in the 'new economy' and will be further explored in Chapter 6. The rate of growth of the sales revenue is an even better indicator of the appreciation by the customers of the firm's value proposition or value

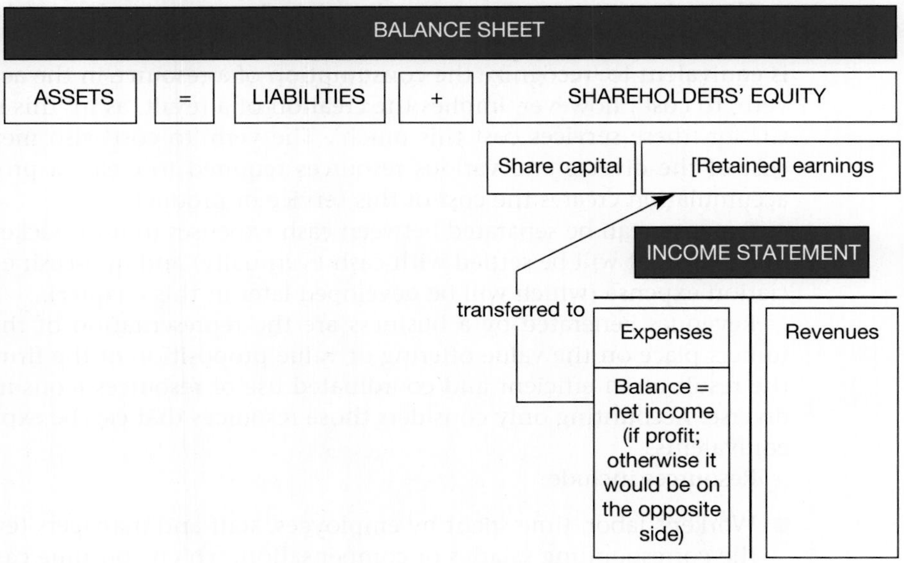

Figure 2.12 Link between the balance sheet and the income statement

offering than the absolute value of the sales revenue, as is shown in Chapter 16. Sales are measured in accounting by the recording of some form of invoice, which is the material proof of the existence of the transaction (including in electronic format).

Accounting records a sale assuming that the customer will pay the invoice on the agreed upon date. It is therefore critical to understand that 'revenue' and 'receipt of funds' are very different. The actual receipt of funds may happen (1) earlier than when the revenue is recognized (as in the case of a down payment); (2) simultaneously with the revenue recognition (as in the case of a cash sale); or (3) later than the revenue recognition (as in the case of a credit sale or sale 'on account').

Revenues may also come from a financial investment made by the firm (interest or return on investment). For example if a retailer receives cash from a customer 30 days before the supplier must be paid, the retailer can invest the cash received for 30 days and earn additional revenue on the sale in the form of interest revenue. Retail distributors (such as Walmart, Carrefour, H&M, and many others) are known to rely in part on this time lag to generate financial revenue or avoid borrowings (the consequences of the latter action are hard to evaluate in financial terms – for Walmart in 2009, the float was about 400 billion dollars for over 30 days, i.e. an opportunity of at least $1 billion in earnings or interest avoided, or about 8% of net profit), which often represents a not negligible share of their net income (for Walmart, in 2009, actual interest earned was over 2% of profit) and thus allows them to keep trading margins at a low level (see further developments in Chapter 16).

3.2.2 Expenses

An expense is a consumption of resources, i.e., a reduction in shareholders' equity. The term 'cost' refers to the amount of value exchanged with a third party to acquire control over a resource and, by extension, the total value of resources (singly or collectively) consumed when the object, product or service is created through the consumption of said resources.

For example, if producing a product (or service) ready to be sold consumes 3 components (components are acquired for 100 CU per batch of 20 units – i.e., 5 CU per component) and 1.5 hour of labor (labor costs 20 CU per hour), and requires support costs (overhead costs) of 14 CU per unit, the cost of the product is 59 CU ($3 \times 5 + 1.5 \times 20 + 14$). So as to not complicate a vocabulary, which, in practice, is not completely stabilized, we will use the terms 'cost' and 'expense' as synonyms in this text.

However, it is important to realize that the corresponding verbs, 'to expense' and 'to cost', are not equivalent. The verb 'to expense' is dynamic and active in its meaning. It is equivalent to 'recognize the consumption of a resource in the accounting process'. The verb 'to cost', however, implies the creation of a result, as in 'this resource costs so many CU' or 'these services cost this much'. The verb 'to cost' also means to accumulate the cost of the diverse and various resources required to create a product or a service; this accumulation creates the cost of this service or product.

Expenses can be separated between cash expenses (out-of-pocket expenses or expenses on credit that will be settled with cash eventually) and non-cash expenses such as depreciation expense (which will be developed later in this chapter).

Revenues generated by a business are the representation of the exchange value customers place on the value offering or value proposition of the firm. The value offering is the result of an efficient and coordinated use of resources (consumption). Resources are diverse. Accounting only considers those resources that can be expressed in terms of cash equivalents.

Resources include:

- Workers' labor, time spent by employees, staff and managers (evaluated financially by the corresponding salaries or compensation, which consume cash),

- Supplies or services provided by third parties (they eventually consume cash directly, or indirectly, if bartered),
- Information and information technology systems support (often separated from 'resources provided by third parties' because of their strategic importance in the competitive position of the firm),
- Raw materials, components and products for sale (manufacturing or producing a service consumes, among other resources, part of the inventory of components or materials which was purchased for cash, and eventually cash will be spent for replenishing the inventories to the level strategically decided),
- Property, plant and equipment (often abbreviated PPE or PP&E), such as buildings, machinery, computers, telephone systems, commercial facilities.

On its date of acquisition, the value of an asset is presumably equal to at least the net present value of the future cash flows it will generate for the acquirer. Expensing a fixed asset (depreciation) recognizes the fact that usage and obsolescence reduce future cash flows and thus the value of the asset.

One critical issue in revenues and expenses recognition is their '**matching**' in the proper time period. The matching principle, derived from the accrual principle, stipulates that when revenues are recorded, all expenses that contributed to the generation of these revenues should be reported in the same period.

Implementing this principle is not always easy. For example, resource consumption for research and development, for acquiring customers, for developing a market, or for promoting a new product may not take place in the same period as the revenue that will result from these cash outlays and/or resource consumption. Accounting will pay great attention to the 'matching' of related revenues and expenses. An income statement will attempt to show side-by-side the revenues and the expenses corresponding to the same business activity for a given period. Matching will be further addressed in Chapter 4.

3.2.3 Income or 'bottom line'

Every year (or at the end of any 'accounting period'), the balance between all revenues and expenses is drawn. This is done by balancing out all of the increases and decreases in shareholders' equity that resulted from normal business operations. As mentioned before, the difference between revenues and expenses is called [net] income.

If revenues are greater than expenses, shareholders' equity records a net increase and income is called profit. If, however, revenues of the period are not sufficient to cover expenses, it means shareholders' equity has been reduced during the period, and income is then a loss.

The profit or the loss appears as the last line (bottom line) of the two lists of revenues and expenses, when the income statement is presented vertically (see below). Thus it has become colloquially acceptable to refer to a period's profit or loss as the period's 'bottom line'.

In summary, during any given period we have the following equation:

Revenues − Expenses = Income (profit or loss)

3.3 Application to Verdi

During the year X1, Verdi Company has recognized net sales or net revenue of 250 CU. This means it has produced invoices in the amount of 250 CU. It has concurrently consumed resources (services and supplies) that outside suppliers invoiced to Verdi for a total amount of 85. In addition Verdi consumed the labor force of its employees and incurred for such consumption an expense of 101 CU (salaries and fringe and social benefits). Lastly, Verdi was able to generate the 250 CU of revenue because it had been able to use its resources, including some which have been financed through the acquisition of financial debt. The interest expense of 4 CU is thus a relevant cost that must be matched against the revenue of 250 CU.

We chose deliberately, at this stage, to ignore the cost of consuming fixed assets. This 'omission' will be corrected in section 4.2 below.

The operations of Verdi Company, so far, are summarized in Table 2.6.

During X1, Verdi's business activities have created a profit of 60 CU (before income tax). In the statement, revenues and expenses have been presented in a vertical list (vertical format) and the income is truly the 'bottom line' (see above).

The business transactions could also have been shown as a subset of the shareholders' equity account, i.e., using the convention of showing increases in shareholders' equity on the right-hand side and decreases on the left-hand side. Such a format is known as the horizontal format and is illustrated in Table 2.7.

In this format of the income statement, 'profit' appears to be in the same column as expenses or costs. It is simply the result of the fact the net income is the balance of revenues minus expenses and would be written as a way to update the shareholders' equity account (see Figure 2.13).

Of course, if there had been a loss (i.e., expenses exceed revenues), the net income would have been shown on the right-hand side of the income statement because the counterpart would have been a decrease in shareholders' equity.

In the Verdi example, expenses have been, so far, listed '**by nature**', simply summarizing transactions of a similar nature, without any other calculations besides simple additions. Some countries, such as the United States and Canada, have chosen to present

Table 2.6 Income statement of Verdi Company for accounting year X1 (vertical format [by nature])

Total revenues		**250**
Sales	250	
Total expenses		**190**
Services and supplies	85	
Personnel expenses	101	
Interest expenses	4	
Income (revenues − expenses)		**+ 60**

Table 2.7 Income statement for the year X1 (horizontal format [by nature])

Expenses		Revenues	
Purchases and external expenses	85	Sales	250
Personnel expenses	101		
Interest expenses	4		
Profit	*60*		
Total	250	**Total**	250

Figure 2.13 Link between profit and shareholders' equity

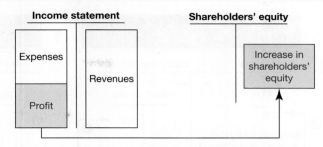

expenses by grouping them further **by function**. In their model, expenses are shown in 'blocks' groupings, expenses having the same purpose or function such as cost of sales or **cost of goods sold**, cost of acquiring and servicing customers, general and administrative expenses, etc. (i.e., implicitly, the detailed 'nature' of these expenses is considered less useful for the decider than the purpose for which the aggregated resources were consumed).

The functional approach distinguishes at least four categories of cost groupings by functions: 'cost of goods sold', 'cost of selling' (which, most of the time, includes commercial and marketing costs as well as the costs of delivering the goods or services), 'cost of administering' the firm and 'cost of financing'. The functional approach will be further developed in Chapter 5, which is partly devoted to the format of financial statements. At this point, the format of presentation of the income statement is not important for our purpose. However, Table 2.8 presents the Verdi income statement for the period X1 by function in a vertical format, the horizontal format being almost never used when expenses are organized by function.

3.4 Impact of transactions on financial statements

So far, we have recorded transactions, one by one, by applying the basic business equation (Assets = Liabilities + Shareholders' equity). We will now focus on the transactions that impact the financial statements as a (temporary) stand-alone document. The income statement will no longer be considered being a subpart of shareholders' equity **at each step**, but will be linked to the balance sheet **only at the end of the period** (see Figure 2.14). This will thus create the income statement as a document that records all transactions (the recording process creates an archive of all transactions for further analysis if needed) and only the ending balance (of the income statement) will be carried over to the balance sheet as a modification to shareholders' equity.

Table 2.8 Income statement for period X1 (vertical format [by function])

Sales	250
Cost of sales [personnel expense related to the disc jockey]	−56
Gross margin	194
Selling expenses (advertising campaign)	−85
General and administrative expenses [personnel expense related to the accountant]	−45
Operating profit	64
Interest expense	−4
Profit	60

Figure 2.14 Impact on financial statements

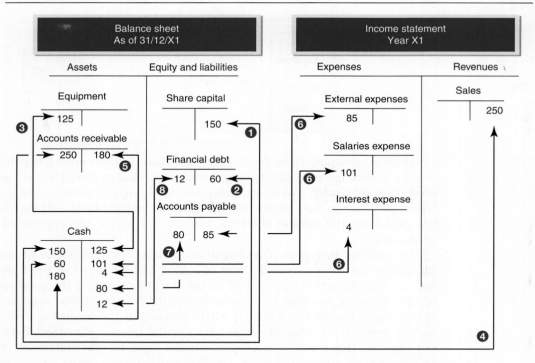

From now on, we will use this **T-account** based format to illustrate the handling of transactions.

T-accounts operate like miniature versions of the basic business equation (Assets = Liabilities plus Shareholders' Equity). Since assets are on the left-hand side of the equal sign in the business equation, an increase in assets will be shown on the left side of the corresponding T-account and, conversely, a decrease in assets will be shown on the right-hand side of the appropriate T-account. Since liabilities and shareholders' equity are on the right-hand side of the equal sign in the business equation, an increase in liabilities or shareholders' equity will be entered on the right-hand side of the corresponding T-account, while a reduction in liabilities or shareholders' equity will be entered on the left-hand side of the appropriate T-account.

The same line of reasoning applies to T-accounts used in the income statement. Since revenues increase shareholders' equity, they will be shown on the right-hand side of an income statement related T-account and conversely, any expense, i.e., a reduction in shareholders' equity, will be entered on the left-hand side of the appropriate income statement related T-account. A reduction of revenues (such as a discount on the catalog price) and a reduction of expenses will be entered on the side opposed to the one used for an increase: on the left for a reduction of revenues and on the right for a reduction of expenses.

The double arrows linking elements of a record imply that the two or more elements connected cannot be separated. The set of transactions records will always be balanced by definition.

3.5 Balance sheet and value creation

Appendix 2.1 illustrates how the change between two balance sheets can be related to value creation.

4 Depreciation

4.1 Principle

In order to fulfill its mission of creating value for shareholders by providing value to customers (in the form of goods or services), a business needs to invest in *permanent* 'means of production'. The term 'production' is to be taken here in its largest sense and includes activities such as procurement, inventorying, preparation, manufacturing or fabricating, delivering, selling or supervising. The operational term, here, is 'permanent'. These resources can be in the form of buildings, plants, machinery, warehouses, retail facilities, fixtures, computers, software, vehicles, distribution systems, etc. Most of these assets have a useful life that exceeds the duration of the accounting period. They are called 'fixed assets' to distinguish them from the 'current assets', which are acquired and consumed within the duration of the operating cycle or the accounting period (whichever is the shortest).

Fixed assets gradually lose value (they lose their potential to create future economic benefits, i.e., sellable goods or services) due to usage, aging or obsolescence. They must be replaced periodically to maintain the value creation ability of the business. The loss of value of such a 'fixed' asset due to any of the previously mentioned causes is considered as a cost since it is an actual 'consumption' of an asset. The firm could not have carried on its activity if these 'fixed' resources had not been available to support, facilitate and sustain the business. The consumption of a fixed asset is called '**depreciation expense**' since it reflects the gradual loss of value of this asset.

Depreciation leads to a process of adjusting (downwards) the **book value** (i.e., net value) of an asset by recognizing it as consumed in a way that does not completely eliminate the resource. It would have been a violation of the matching principle to recognize the full value of the equipment as being consumed in the very period when it was acquired since benefits will continue in the future years to derive from owning the asset. Verdi knew their equipment would create a flow of revenues for several periods.

Depreciation is the procedure that allows a business to match revenues and fixed asset (resource) consumption, when the asset will benefit several periods. Rather than trying to estimate the actual consumption of the fixed assets in the creation of revenues of a period, always difficult to determine, the original depreciable value of the asset is allocated according to pre-agreed rules over the productive life of the asset. Generally, the depreciable value of a fixed asset includes the cost of acquisition and installation, minus the future resale value – if the latter can be estimated. IAS 16 (IASB 2003: § 6) defines depreciation as 'the systematic allocation of the depreciable amount of an asset over its useful [productive] life' (see further developments in Chapter 7).

Carrying amount (often called 'book value' or 'net value' in practice) is 'the amount at which an asset is recognized after deducting any accumulated depreciation and accumulated impairment losses' (IAS 16: § 6).

In many cases, the **accumulated depreciation** expense of any fixed asset will eventually be equal to the amount initially paid to acquire it and bring it into the productive stream. The fixed asset will then be recorded as 'fully depreciated' and have a zero book (or net) value (see more on this in Chapter 7), but the 'no offsetting' principle will require that a fully depreciated asset, until it is disposed of, remains listed in the balance sheet at its historical cost of acquisition minus the accumulated depreciation. The two amounts offsetting each other, the statement of financial position actually reflects the fact the asset is valued, in the books, at zero. If an asset is fully depreciated but still operational, no further depreciation expense pertaining to this asset can be charged to the income statement.

A **depreciation expense** is recognized every year (or period) in the income statement just as supplies or salary expenses are. Depreciation, however, will be recognized only at the end of each period, not each time the asset is used.

4.2 Application to Verdi

Verdi had acquired fixed assets at the beginning of the period for 125 CU (a computer, a color printer and an art and page-setting software for its 'productive' activity, and a second computer and printer for the administration of the firm). Let us assume these assets have an expected useful life of five years (i.e., they will be able to contribute to the generation of economic benefits for five years). This means that, in five years, they will be worthless and will no longer be productive assets. Verdi will have consumed the fixed assets completely over five years. If we choose a simple approach, we may recognize that these fixed assets lose 20% of their original value every year. We will see in Chapter 7 that methods other than this '**straight-line**' approach (proportional to the passage of time) are possible. The choice of method however, although it modifies the timing of recognition of the depreciation expense, does not modify the principle of depreciation: all outputs created by using a fixed asset must bear a part of the cost of the depreciation of the asset.

In Verdi's case, the depreciation expense for the year is thus 25 CU. At the end of the first period, the book (or net) value of these fixed assets would now be 125 minus 25 or 100. The yearly depreciation expense of 25 CU is an expense we have not yet considered in the period X1 income statement. It will be offset against revenues to help determine the income for the period. Thus, for the next four years, an annual expense of 25 CU (because we have chosen the straight-line method of depreciation) will also be recognized in the annual income statement to acknowledge the consumption of the productive capacity, regardless of the level of activity. At the end of the five years, the book (net) value of the equipment will effectively be zero. In theory the equipment will have to be replaced at the end of the five-year period if the exhaustion of the value creation potential of the asset is also physical, in addition to being financial. As long as the assets are not physically disposed of, their value will be listed on two, not netted, lines 'cost of acquisition 125 CU' minus 'accumulated depreciation 125 CU', thus effectively showing a net value of zero.

An 'improved', i.e., more complete, representation of the situation of Verdi Company appears as Figure 2.15. It is important to notice that the balance sheet reports 'accumulated depreciation' while the income statement reports the 'depreciation expense' of the

Figure 2.15 Recording the depreciation

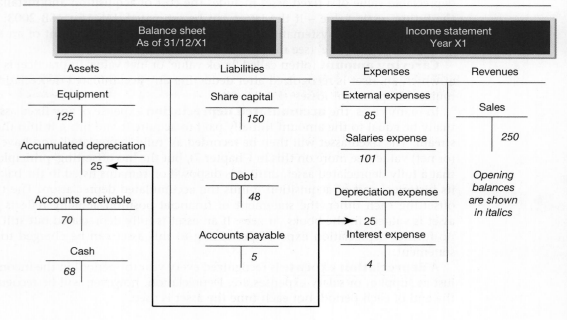

period. Since we have only one period of activity the two amounts are (exceptionally) identical, but it must be clear that, as early as period two, the two balances will no longer be identical: accumulated depreciation (in the balance sheet) is the sum of the depreciation expenses (in the successive income statements) of each of the consecutive years or periods during which the depreciable asset is detained.

The balance sheet (assuming no other transactions) is adjusted as shown in Table 2.9. The income statement is also modified (see Tables 2.10 and 2.11).

Table 2.9 Balance sheet after depreciation

Assets				Balance sheet as of 31 December X1	Equity and liabilities
Equipment	Gross value	125	100	Shareholders' equity	
	– Acc. depreciation	25		Capital	150
Accounts receivable			70	Earnings	35
Cash			68	Liabilities	
				Debt	48
				Accounts payable	5
Total assets			238	**Total liabilities**	238

Table 2.10 Horizontal income statement [by nature] after depreciation

Expenses		Income statement for the period ending 31 December X1	Revenues
External expenses (services purchased from third parties)	85	Sales	250
Salaries expense	101		
Depreciation expense	25		
Interest expense	4		
Profit	**35**		
	250		250

Table 2.11 Vertical income statement [by nature] for the period ending 31 December X1

Revenues	
Sales	250
Total revenues	250
Expenses	
External expenses	85
Salaries expense	101
Depreciation expense	25
Interest expense	4
Total expenses	215
Income (revenues – expenses)	35

Table 2.12 Vertical income statement [by function] for the period ending 31 December X1		
Sales		250
Salaries expense (disc jockey)	−56	
Depreciation expense (technical equipment)	−20	
Cost of sales (or cost of goods sold)		−76
Gross margin		174
Selling expenses (advertising campaign)		−85
Salaries expense (accountant)	−45	
Depreciation expense (administrative equipment)	−5	
General and administrative expenses		−50
Operating profit		39
Interest expense		−4
Profit		35

Table 2.12 presents the income statement reported by function. We need to allocate the depreciation expense to each function. In Verdi's example, the depreciation of the equipment used for production (100 CU/5 = 20 CU) will be included in the cost of sales (or cost of goods sold) while the depreciation of the computer used for the administration (25 CU/5 = 5 CU) will be recorded in the general and administrative expenses.

5 Consumption of resources and inventory valuation

We will introduce the subject only briefly here as it is further developed in Chapter 9. In the Verdi example, the concept of inventory was not needed since Verdi sold a service that could not be stored for sale at a later date. Further, we assumed that no preparation work had been incurred during the accounting period for public relations campaigns ordered by customers that would be implemented in the following accounting period. Thus we were in the simple (and generally rare) situation in which all expenses and revenues could be physically, and without ambiguity, matched in the same period.

Expenses reflect consumed resources. Assume that during X1, reproduction company X has consumed supplies and services for an amount of 80 CU. Supplies (paper, toner, etc.) must be purchased before their consumption, and it is probably best to have on hand some '**inventory**' of such supplies so as to never run out (which might mean a lost opportunity to serve a customer who would not be willing to wait). The two physical flows, purchases and consumption, are not synchronous and the role of an inventory is to serve as a buffer against incidents in the supply chain, so that stock-outs do not occur. It is most common, even in a world of 'just in time' to have on hand, at any time, some consumable resources physically stored ahead of consumption. Therefore, at the end of the accounting period, there is an inventory of resources to be evaluated and recorded in the balance sheet on the asset side. This inventory is derived from the following two equations:

> *In the case of a retail or wholesale business (no transformation) or*
> *of an intermediate workshop in a manufacturing plant:*
>
> Beginning inventory + Acquired consumable resources = Resources available for consumption
> Resources available for consumption − Resources consumed = Ending inventory
>
> *In the case of a manufacturing firm and for finished products (FP):*
> Beginning inventory + Cost of finished goods manufactured = Finished products available for sale
> Finished products available for sale − Cost of finished products sold = Ending inventory of FP

Let us illustrate the impact of inventories on the financial statements through the case illustration of Puccini & Co, an umbrella manufacturer.

5.1 Goods purchased for resale (merchandise) or for use in a transformation process (raw materials, parts and consumables)

Assume that Puccini & Co. acquires, with cash of 100 CU, the raw materials (for example, fabric), parts (such as mechanical parts, baleens or handles) and consumables (such as thread or screws and rivets) necessary for the manufacturing of umbrellas. We will call these 'components' materials in the development below. During the accounting period, Puccini & Co. consumed only 80 CU worth of materials. It, therefore, still holds 20 CU worth of parts, materials and consumables at the end of the period.

Two different approaches exist for recording this situation. The first one (called 'perpetual inventory system') creates a record each time goods (materials, parts or consumables) are consumed in order to satisfy customer orders (i.e., each time resources are withdrawn from inventory). The second one (known as 'periodic inventory system') calculates the total consumption at the end of the period by measuring what remains on hand (i.e., knowing the ending balance, the beginning balance and purchases or additions, the consumption can be deducted).

5.1.1 Method 1 – Purchases recorded as inventory in the balance sheet (perpetual system)

In this method, withdrawals from inventory or consumption to satisfy customers are recorded as they occur. The parts and materials purchased are considered to enter first in the inventory of Puccini & Co. before they can be withdrawn and consumed. Therefore a purchase corresponds to an increase in the 'inventory' account on the asset side of the balance sheet and either a decrease in cash or an increase in payables. When parts and materials are required for the manufacturing of umbrellas (probably on several occasions during the period), the plant manager (or the retail store manager, if we had not been in a manufacturing context) issues a requisition order and the goods (parts and materials, here) are withdrawn from inventory. Their value will be recognized each time a withdrawal takes place, as both an expense (consumption of a resource) and a reduction of the asset amount listed under the heading 'inventory'. The total of all withdrawals will be either (a) recognized under the name of 'cost of merchandise sold' if there is only a resale without transformation; or (b) considered as a component of the 'cost of goods manufactured' (and, eventually, of 'cost of goods sold' as products manufactured are sold).

We can summarize this process very simply:

	Beginning inventory
Plus	Purchases (sum of all invoices of the period)
Minus	*Consumption or withdrawals (sum of all recorded material or merchandise requisitions)*
Equals	Ending inventory (which can be validated by a physical stocktaking, i.e., counting what really and physically exists in the inventory)

Figure 2.16 Impact on financial statements – Year X1

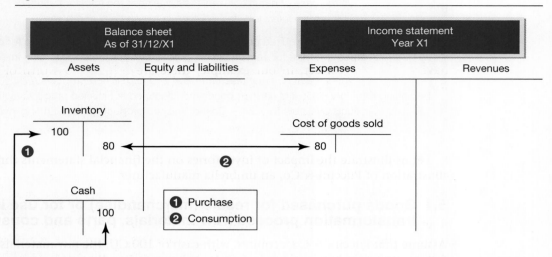

In X1, a period in which there was no beginning inventory, the impact of inventories carried under this first method on the financial statements, is as shown in Figure 2.16. Here we assume that production takes place after the customers orders have been received and thus the consumption of parts and materials can flow directly to the 'cost of goods sold' since there is no need for a finished goods inventory.

The impact on the basic business equation is shown in Appendix 2.2.

Suppose that during X2, Puccini & Co. purchases supplies for an amount of 200 CU. The value of the 'supplies available' for consumption in the normal operations of the firm is 200 *plus* the existing beginning inventory of 20, which means a total available for use worth 220 CU. Consumption (i.e., sum of the withdrawals) during X2 equals 211 CU. As a consequence, the ending inventory (computed by difference) is 9 (i.e., [20 + 200 − 211]). The impact on the financial statements is shown in Figure 2.17.

5.1.2 Method 2 – Purchases are recorded as an expense in the income statement (Periodic system)

This approach, instead of assuming all materials or parts acquired for future production are held in an inventory account before being consumed, makes the simplifying hypothesis that all that is purchased (100 CU worth in Puccini & Co.'s case) is meant to be

Figure 2.17 Impact on financial statements – Year X2

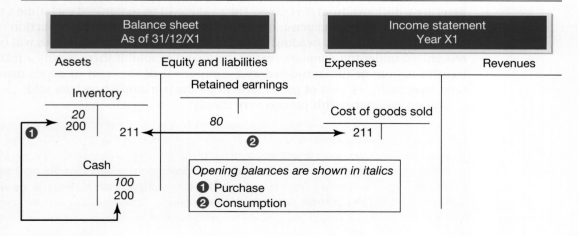

consumed in the current period (either through resale or consumed in the manufacturing process) and is therefore considered to be expensed immediately for the full amount at the time of purchase.

At the end of the period, when Puccini & Co. orders a physical stocktaking, it will observe that the hypothesis of exhaustive consumption of materials and parts may not have been quite correct. In our example, there are still 20 CU worth of goods left in inventory at the end of the period. Expenses (consumption of parts and materials) have, therefore, been 'overestimated' because of our simplifying hypothesis. Expenses must be adjusted *ex post* to recognize (the matching principle strikes again) only that part of the 'materials and parts' that have been consumed so as to match them against revenues from sales.

This second method is very simple to apply and was, before computers and Enterprise Resource Planning (ERP) systems, relatively less expensive than the perpetual inventory-based approach (here, there is no need for record keeping of withdrawals from inventory during the period), but it does not give the same control over consumption or the same fineness of information which managers and external users of information may want to have in their resource allocation decision. Computerization, the generalization of ERP systems, the common use of barcodes, or the emerging Radio Frequency Identification of articles, tends to make the periodic system approach obsolete since it has become rather economical today, save for the smallest retail businesses, to record every movement of goods, materials or parts. However, physical stocktaking (inventory counting) is still a necessity, generally once a year, in order to validate the quality of the computerized recording process of withdrawals and detect and prevent pilferage and human (or software) errors.

When we assume resources purchased are consumed in the period of acquisition, the equation defining the relation between beginning and ending inventories is modified. Instead of the ending inventory being the unknown, it is the consumption of materials which is the unknown. The equation becomes:

	Beginning inventory
Plus	Purchases (sum of all invoices of the period)
Equals	Available for consumption to satisfy customers
Minus	*Ending inventory (which results from a physical stocktaking)*
Equals	Consumption

At the end of the period, the physical stocktaking carried out shows the final inventory to be worth 20 CU (physical quantities multiplied by the unit purchase cost of the items found in inventory). The amount recorded as an expense must therefore be adjusted so as to reflect the correct value for the consumption of materials and parts. We create an 'ending inventory account' which takes on the value of 20 CU. If we want to use a crude physical illustration of what happens in the periodic method, the inventory is taken out of the 'plant' (the income statement), where it was 'temporarily' stored (under the name of expense) and stored in a 'warehouse' (the inventory account in the balance sheet).

Figure 2.18 illustrates how accounting records the transaction under this approach. The impact of inventories on the financial statements is as follows (since there is no impact on liabilities, they can be ignored).

To further understand the entries recorded in the income statement, let us see what happens the following year. During the following year, purchases are 200 CU and the final inventory measured by stocktaking at the end of the year is estimated to be worth 9 CU.

The beginning inventory (BI) (ending inventory of the previous period) was worth 20 CU. The ending inventory (EI) is valued at 9 CU. The accounting **change in inventory** is therefore +11 (i.e., BI − EI, or 20 − 9), and the cost of materials consumed to satisfy customers is the full 200 purchased plus the reduction of inventory, or 200 + 11 = 211 CU.

Figure 2.18 Impact on financial statements – Year X1

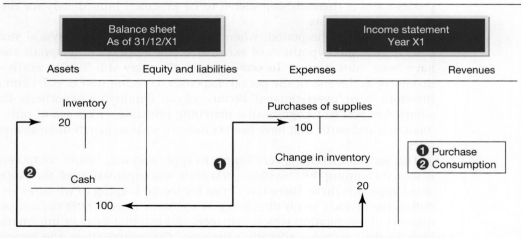

Note: In this example, we have made the hypothesis that purchases have an immediate impact on income and that the consumption is adjusted ex post via a physical inventory taking. We have seen above, and we will also see in greater details in Chapter 9 that the perpetual inventory valuation is an alternate method.

	Purchases	200
Plus	Beginning inventory	20
Equals	*Supplies available for use*	*220*
Minus	Ending inventory	−9
Equals	Total consumed supplies	211

Accountants define 'variations in inventory level' or 'changes in inventory' of raw materials, supplies and merchandise as the difference [beginning inventory (BI) minus ending inventory (EI)]. By convention, the change in inventory level of purchased goods (raw materials, supplies and merchandise) is always shown on the expenses side of the income statement (see further developments on finished products below and in Chapter 9).

The impact of inventory on the financial statements for X2 appears in Figure 2.19.

Figure 2.19 Impact on financial statements – Year X2

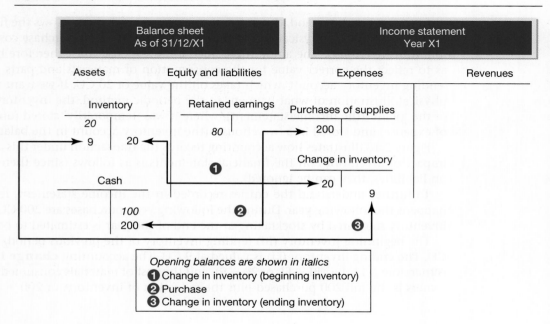

The example was simplified in that purchases were assumed to have been paid for in cash (they could have been purchased 'on account', thus impacting accounts payable).

If the ending inventory has a larger value than that of the beginning inventory, the change in inventory is negative, by our convention. This means that some of the resources incurred during the period have been devoted not to the creation and delivery of the value proposition, but to the creation of an increased inventory. Incidentally, an increased inventory can be a good thing when it prepares the firm better to meet a growing demand with short response time. In this (continental European) approach the current expenses recognized on the left-hand side of the income statement include all purchases, creating a 'change in inventory' account that reduces (or increases) the expenses of the period so that the balance is equal to the costs that need to be matched with revenues. The way of calculating the 'change in inventory' as 'BI − EI' adjusts the accounts automatically to recognize the amount of materials (or components or parts) expenses that matches the revenues, regardless of when these were acquired.

Intuitively (more logically, maybe?), we could have written:

> Consumption = Purchases *minus* Increase (or *plus* Decrease) in inventories
>
> where increase and decrease are defined as the difference [ending minus beginning inventories] which leads us to define consumption as being equal to purchases minus [ending inventory − beginning inventory].

The choice between the perpetual and periodic inventory methods depends on the tradition of each country and on the resources and needs of each enterprise. The two methods give exactly the same results in a non-inflationary world. If there are frequent and multiple purchases and there is serious inflation applying to the resources purchased, under the perpetual method the cost of resources consumed may better reflect the current prices of the resources.

> The main difference between the two methods is the reporting of one account ('cost of goods sold') versus two accounts ('purchases' and 'change in inventory') in the income statement. Thus it is a question of fineness of information in the income statement and that is an issue which affects the users.

> It is worth noting that despite their using the perpetual inventory system for their ERP-based management of physical flows in their business, a large part of continental European businesses still present their financial statements as if they were using the periodic approach. Our observation of practices in financial markets is that they seem to encourage the perpetual inventory method (cost of goods sold is a quantity that is more and more expected to appear directly in the income statement), so as to have direct access to the **gross margin** ratio. This probably means the end of the periodic approach in the near future for most listed companies.

5.2 Inventory of goods manufactured

The main objective of Puccini & Co. is to manufacture and sell umbrellas. It could also offer a service of maintenance and repairs on its umbrellas. Service cannot, by definition, be stored. At the end of any period Puccini & Co. may, however, have the following types of inventories:

- Inventory of finished umbrellas, ready for sale.
- Inventory of semi-finished umbrellas. For example the mechanical parts of the umbrella may be assembled and the fabric cut and sewn in two different workshops before

final assembly in a third workshop. Each workshop may create an inventory of partially finished umbrellas or umbrella subsystems (they are called semi-finished goods).

■ Work in progress (umbrellas or subsystems that are still being worked on – i.e., not yet available for transfer to the next stage of production – when the period ends). They are neither finished nor semi-finished, but somewhere in-between. In industries where the transformation process is very long (such as law firms, construction, ship building or aircraft manufacturing or assembly), this inventory may be very significant and its correct evaluation may be essential to the estimation of the income of the period (to stay in line with the matching principle).

■ 'Inventory' of development projects (R&D, engineering of new custom products, development of new machinery by the manufacturing personnel themselves, etc.).

For all these 'inventories', the logic of valuation is absolutely similar to the one followed above for raw materials, goods, merchandise or parts and components for consumption or resale. Instead of being consumed to satisfy customers' request directly, raw materials, parts and consumables are first used in a production process and then the finished products are made available to customers and are, hopefully, sold.

Figure 2.20 illustrates the complete process.

In each box the same equation applies: Beginning inventory plus new 'entries' minus 'Withdrawals' equals 'Ending inventory'.

Logically, given that there are two methods for inventory accounting, there are two different but perfectly compatible income statement presentations, as illustrated in Figure 2.21.

If the income statement is prepared according to the perpetual method for inventory recording, the users will only have available the cost of goods sold and the selling, general, and administrative expenses, which might or might not be reported in some detail. However, inventory levels will only be found by looking at the balance sheet.

If, on the contrary, the periodic method of recording inventories is followed, the income statement will, in principle, provide more details, in that both purchases and inventories will be provided. Some companies, particularly in Germany, report one line 'Materials consumed', which represents the netting of purchases of raw materials and of the change in inventory of raw materials, whereas the change in inventory of finished products is displayed in the revenues side of the income statement. These cases, even if they indicate the probable use of the periodic method, show that some businesses feel the need to disclose only one line of expenses for the consumption of materials and rely on the balance sheet to provide the complementary information that could more fully enlighten the users.

Figure 2.20 The process of inventory accounting

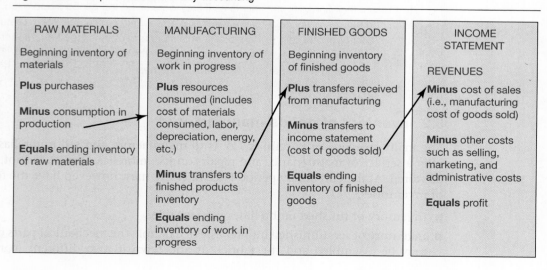

Figure 2.21 Income statement and inventory

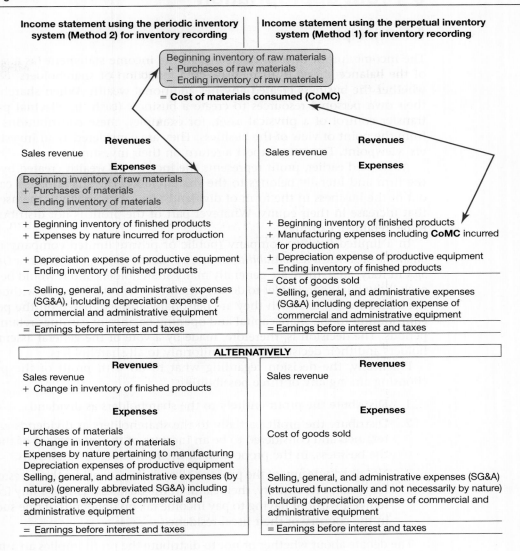

Regardless of the method, any change in inventory is automatically reported, either by (a) a one-line item (the cost of goods consumed); (b) by reporting purchases and the net change in inventory; or (c) by providing the three components that define the balance, i.e., purchases and beginning and ending inventories. In recent years, the choice appears to have been limited to the first two positions, thus relegating in any case the absolute value of inventories to the balance sheet.

Whether or not to report the balance of the change in inventory in the income statement is a question of choice and of uses of the financial statement. It may appear interesting to some users to be able to find a measure of the evolution of inventories over the period (i.e., a measure of the preparedness of the firm for subsequent periods) in the income statement, next to information pertaining to the profitability of current sales. Others may find the information redundant since ending and beginning inventories are in the balance sheet. What matters is that either the perpetual or the periodic approaches provide a good matching of expenses with revenues. The income for the period is, of course, the same, regardless of the method used (in a non-inflationary world).

6 Profit appropriation

6.1 Principle

The income (profit or loss) calculated in the income statement (as a subsidiary account of the balance sheet) is an increase or a reduction of shareholders' equity and reflects whether the business created any net additional wealth. When shareholders contribute their own personal resources to create a business (cash, intellectual property, effort, or transfer control of a physical asset, for example), these contributions form the capital from the point of view of the business. They are considered as an investment (shareholders' viewpoint. The latter expect a return on their investment.

As we said earlier, profit represents the increase in wealth created by the operation of the firm and literally belongs to the shareholders. The shareholders can choose to take out of the business in the form of dividends, i.e., appropriate to themselves all or part of that increase in their equity. Whatever part of the profit is not distributed is considered to be 'retained' earnings.

In a limited liability company (public or private limited company in the UK, *société anonyme* or *société à responsabilité limitée*, in France, *Aktiengesellschaft* or *GmbH* in Germany, *SpA* in Italy, etc.), there are generally many shareholders and it would be difficult to allow each individual shareholder to decide whether or not they wish to withdraw their share of the added wealth to which they are personally entitled, based on the percentage of their contribution to the share capital and opening balance of earnings retained from previous periods. The decision is, therefore, made by a vote of the general assembly of the shareholders and their decision applies uniformly to all shareholders.

Practically, the decision regarding what to do with profit of the period consists in choosing among any of three possibilities:

1. Distribute the profit entirely to the shareholders as dividends.
2. Distribute the profit partially to the shareholders as dividends and the balance is retained and considered to be an increase of the investment of the shareholders in the business, in the proportion of their previous contributions.
3. Not distribute any of the profit at all and, thus, consider the investors (shareholders) reinvest, in its entirety, their claim in the business. This is a way for shareholders to reinvest without having to pay income tax on dividends, if one such tax is imposed in the country of their fiscal residence.

The debate about whether or not to distribute the profit implies an arbitration between tax rules on income, individual needs of shareholders for cash income (and the opportunities they have to privately earn a return on that cash by investing it elsewhere) and the medium- to long-term interest of the firm. When dividends are paid out, there is a reduction of shareholders' equity, and a simultaneous reduction in cash. If the drain on the cash of the firm is too high, it may create a serious limitation to the ability of the firm to pursue its operations (remember that profit and cash flow are often disconnected – see Table 2.4). The issue is generally to balance any partition of the profit of the firm between owners and the firm itself (retained earnings) in such a way that the shareholders receive enough cash for their needs, and the firm is not drained of cash, which is the fuel for its smooth operation and growth (and thus avoids having to borrow, which is always costly).

After the shareholders have approved the terms of distribution, the part of the profit that will be paid out as dividends is first recognized as a short-term debt to shareholders (dividends payable). When the dividend is actually paid out, the debt is cancelled and cash is reduced appropriately.

The profit retained in the business is aggregated to the shareholders' equity but remains, often for legal or regulatory reasons, distinct from the strictly defined 'capital'. Profit retained in the business is called either 'retained earnings' (for example in the

United States or in Canada) or 'reserves' (this is often the case in the Nordic countries, Germany, France or the UK).

It should be clear that retained earnings (or reserves) are in no way equivalent to available cash. Since income and cash are disconnected through the accrual process, i.e., credit terms and different timings of revenue flows and expense flows, a business can be in a situation where there is a lot of profit (and potentially a large addition to the retained earnings) but a negative cash position (see Tables 2.4 and 2.13).

The topic of **profit appropriation** will be further developed in Chapter 11 and reporting for retained earnings and reserves is presented in Appendix 2.3.

6.2 Application to Verdi

The shareholders of Verdi Company observe their business results during the recently closed accounting period and determine that they made a profit of 35 CU (after depreciation and we ignore taxes, for the time being). They decide to award themselves a dividend of 3 CU or, in other words, they decide to keep in the business 32 CU (of a profit amounting to 35 CU) as retained earnings. In fact, this is equivalent to their reinvesting that same amount into the business, with the significant personal tax advantage that since the amount reinvested was never distributed, the shareholders will not be individually taxed on the investment income they now choose to reinvest. The shareholders' decision to pay a dividend will be recorded by recognizing the immediate liability to the shareholders under the name of 'dividends payable'. The impact on cash, however, will not take place until the actual payout takes place (here, we can assume it will take place in the early part of period X2).

The transaction of 'declaring dividends' results in a decrease in retained earnings and creation of a liability for the same amount. On the date of payment, this liability account is cancelled and cash is decreased. We show below the impact on the basic financial statements. Because the intermediate step using the 'dividends payable' account is not necessary for the understanding of profit appropriation, we don't disclose it in Figure 2.22. For the sake of simplification, we have also ignored the tax implications in the above illustration. In the 'real world', before recording it on the balance sheet, income would first have been subject to taxation according to the rules of the country where Verdi is operating.

Figure 2.22 Recording of profit appropriation

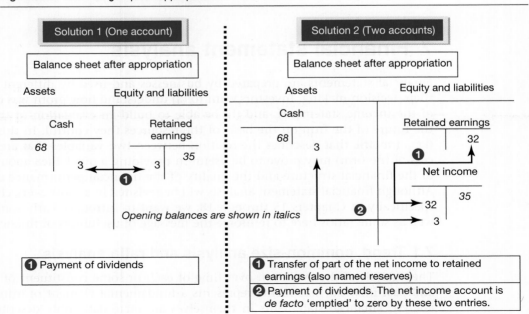

Depending on the country or the company, retained earnings can be reported in two different ways (for more details, see Appendix 2.3).

6.3 Cash, profit and reserves

At the risk of repeating ourselves, we must emphasize the fact that the terms 'retained earnings' and, even more so, 'reserves' prove to be misleading at times to students (and executives alike) who do not fully grasp the accrual principle, i.e., the distinction between profit and cash balance. As was shown earlier, and in Table 2.4 especially, a business can be very profitable but be extremely cash poor, or the converse can be true as illustrated in Table 2.13 for a business whose unprofitable sales double each period. For each currency unit of revenue the cost is 1.1 CU. However, the customers pay immediately but the business does not have to pay the supplier(s) until two periods after the cash sale was realized.

We can see from this illustration that the business is a cash generating machine although it is actually 'losing money' on every sale. In Table 2.13, if we ignore that the cash generated could be invested profitably (which could yield a substantial return – but in no way enough to compensate the operating loss), the business is literally destroying the capital provided by its shareholders. Losses are reducing equity and if the business were to keep on going under these conditions, the capital could be entirely destroyed as negative retained earnings are created. Negative retained earnings are no more equivalent to a cash shortage than retained earnings or (positive) 'reserves' are equivalent to available cash.

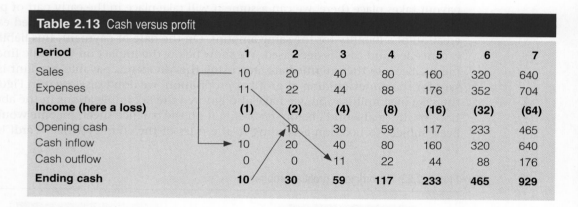

Table 2.13 Cash versus profit							
Period	**1**	**2**	**3**	**4**	**5**	**6**	**7**
Sales	10	20	40	80	160	320	640
Expenses	11	22	44	88	176	352	704
Income (here a loss)	**(1)**	**(2)**	**(4)**	**(8)**	**(16)**	**(32)**	**(64)**
Opening cash	0	10	30	59	117	233	465
Cash inflow	10	20	40	80	160	320	640
Cash outflow	0	0	11	22	44	88	176
Ending cash	**10**	**30**	**59**	**117**	**233**	**465**	**929**

7 Financial statement analysis

Financial statements are prepared by businesses and used by different stakeholders in their decision-making. Investors want to (a) understand how profit was created (analysis of the income statement), and (b) be able to build an evaluation of the prognosis for the future of the firm on the basis of the resources they control. In this context, ratios (i.e., a metric that describes the relation between two variables that are key to the success of the firm) may prove to be useful in providing a quick idea about the soundness of the financial structure and the quality of the financial performance of the company. Although financial statement analysis will be revisited in almost every chapter and more specifically in Chapters 15 through 18, we want to introduce early some basic tools as well as some ratios here to reinforce the message of usefulness of financial statements.

7.1 Trend, common-size analysis and ratio analysis

The analysis of the evolution over time of each or some constituent of a firm's current and past financial statements represents a fundamental element of information for the analyst. Financial statements in themselves are mere data, only describing facts. Their analysis creates information on the basis of which the analysts or users can base their recommendations or decisions.

The comparison of financial statements over time is known as '**trend analysis**'. This comparison is carried line item by line item (in absolute values and/or in percentages) against the like value in a base-year (often the previous year). If the percentage change approach is used, the base-year item amount (asset, liability, sales revenue, cost, etc.) is used as an index with a conventional base-value of 100. Other periods are then measured against that index.

Common-size analysis, on the other hand, focuses on the structure of the financial statements. It can be used in combination with a trend analysis to visualize the evolution of the structure of one or more statements over time. Common sizing involves restating each balance sheet, income statement, and/or statement of cash flows by presenting each line item as a proportion of a base figure (conventionally indexed as 100, thus the proportion is expressed as a percentage). Such restated statements are said to have been 'common sized' and are 'common-size statements'. The base figure is generally total assets (or total equity and liabilities) for the balance sheet, net sales for the income statement, and cash flow from operating activities for a statement of cash flows. Both trend and common-size analyses will be further developed in Chapters 15, 16 and 17.

Ratio analysis focuses on the comparison of two elements of the financial statements. A ratio is the quotient of two quantities and, to be meaningful, assumes there is a relationship between these two quantities. Unlike trend analysis and common-sized analysis, which focus only on statements in their entirety (statement of financial position, income statement or statement of cash flows), ratio analysis may measure assumed relationships between quantities within one or between statements.

7.2 Financial situation ratios

7.2.1 Short-term liquidity ratios

The following ratios assess the firm's ability to finance its day-to-day operations and to pay its liabilities as they fall due.

> **Current ratio** = Current assets/Current liabilities (also called amounts falling due within one year)

The current ratio shows the firm's ability to pay its current liabilities from its current assets, i.e., the probability that a slowdown in the economy or in the operating cycle will place the firm in a difficult liquidity position.

> **Cash ratio** = (Cash + Marketable securities)/Current liabilities

The objective of the cash ratio is to evidence the firm's ability to pay its current liabilities from its cash and cash equivalents (i.e., the ability of the firm to cover its short-term obligations even without having to wait until the end of the operating cycle).

7.2.2 Management ratios

> **Average collection period** =
> [(Accounts receivable Year 2 + Accounts receivable Year 1)/2 × 365]/Sales revenue

The average length of time to collect accounts receivable is an important indicator relating to the management of receivables but also a metric describing part of the operating cycle. The longer the collection period, the longer the cash to cash cycle. The longer the operating cash to cash cycle is, the more long-term financing the firm needs.

Inventory turnover =
Cost of merchandise sold/[(Beginning inventory of merchandise + ending inventory of merchandise)/2]l

or

Cost of raw materials consumed/[(Beginning inventory of raw materials + ending inventory of raw materials)/2]

or

Cost of finished products sold/[(Beginning inventory of finished products + ending inventory of finished products)/2]

or

Cost of goods sold (COGS)/[(Beginning inventory + ending inventory)/2]

with:

- Cost of merchandise sold = Beginning inventory of merchandise + Purchases of merchandise − Ending inventory of merchandise
- Cost of raw materials consumed = Beginning inventory of raw materials + Purchases of raw materials − Ending inventory of raw materials
- Cost of finished products sold = Beginning inventory of finished products + Cost of finished products manufactured − Ending inventory of finished products

This metric is defined as the number of times the inventory 'turns' during the accounting period. The shorter the operating cycle, the higher the turnover. Several methods of computation are provided above, depending on the nature of information available in the income statement.

7.2.3 Long-term solvency ratio

This ratio indicates the firm's ability to cover its long-term liabilities (eventually by selling its assets).

Long-term debt to equity ratio = Long-term debt/equity

This metric is often used to describe the degree of **financial leverage**. A firm that has a large equity to debt ratio is said to be 'overcapitalized' or 'underleveraged'. A firm that has a very small equity and large debt is called 'undercapitalized' or 'highly leveraged'.

If two, nearly equivalent, firms differ only on their value of this debt to equity ratio, the one with the highest leverage will provide the better return to their shareholders (interest expense is not proportional to sales revenue but to the level of indebtedness, all things being equal). But, of course, that firm is also the one that takes a higher risk because it has more external debt than the lesser leveraged firm. If a firm is too leveraged, loan and debt providers may feel the situation is risky for lenders and thus may charge a higher rate of interest than they would have otherwise. The interest expense that arises from the long-term debt may place the highly leveraged firm in a difficult position in terms of profitability. Overleveraged firms are generally undercapitalized and must dedicate an often undue proportion of their cash flow to meeting their interest expense, thus depriving the firm of the possibility of investing in developing products or markets.

Conversely, overcapitalized firms may not avail themselves of the opportunity of using borrowed capital effectively. External capital is generally obtained at a cost that is lower than the cost of shareholder capital (shareholders expect dividends plus capital gains as their return, plus the issuance of new shares can be a costly operation). As long as the business invests in projects that return more than the cost of financing through debt, the shareholders receive wealth without having had to provide the incremental capital. The level of leverage appropriate for a business is a question beyond the scope of this textbook. Each managerial team, under the oversight of the board of directors, will decide on the level of leverage they feel suits best the interests of their shareholders.

Many large retailers are undercapitalized. They rely on the float offered by their suppliers (thanks to the rapid turnover of their retail inventory and cash sales) for long-term funding, while the source of funds is actually very short-term. As long as their business is in expansion or, at worse, stable and their bargaining power vis-à-vis their suppliers remains high, the float keeps growing or stays even and is statistically 'long-term', but if there is a downturn for any reason, the payables must be covered on time and there may not be enough revenue to cover what was essentially a short-term debt. We will revisit this situation when we will look at the concept of working capital in Chapter 15.

7.3 Profitability ratios

Profitability ratios reflect the firm's ability to generate profit.

> **Return on sales (net profit margin)** = Net income/Sales

This ratio computes the percentage of each sales revenue currency unit that contributes to net income. It can be used internally to compare markets or customers, and externally to compare the firm with others in the same sector (with approximately the same risk and opportunities environment, if the comparison is to be meaningful).

> **Return on shareholders' equity (ROE)** = Net income/Average equity[4]
> (or Earnings before interest and tax (EBIT)/Average equity)

This ratio emphasizes the return to shareholders, i.e., the profit generated during a period on the capital invested by the shareholders. The 'or' in the definition does not mean that the concepts are strictly equivalent but that there are two alternative ways to compute the ROE. Each definition provides a different ratio but these are close in terms of informational content.

> **Return on capital employed** or **ROCE** (also called **Return on investment**
> or **ROI**) = Earnings before interest and tax (EBIT)/Capital employed
> (Where 'capital employed' is: 'Average long-term liabilities + Average equity').
> Alternatively, ROI is calculated as Net income /Capital employed.

This ratio measures the wealth created on long-term invested funds, regardless of the leverage ratio of the firm.

> **Return on assets (ROA)** = Net income/[(Assets Year 2 + Assets Year 1)/2]

This ratio measures the firm's ability to use its assets to create profits.

Key points

- Financial statements include a minimum set of documents: balance sheet or statement of financial position, income statement and notes. Additionally, they may comprise a statement of cash flows and a statement of changes in equity.
- A balance sheet is a set of two lists: resources on one side (also called assets) and obligations to external parties on the other side (liabilities to creditors and residual interest due to the shareholders or owners). The two lists must be equal in total value, i.e., balanced.
- Shareholders' equity represents (depending on the point of view, internal or external), the obligation the firm has towards its shareholders, or the claim the owners of the business have collectively over the firm's current 'net worth' and potential future wealth.
- The statement of financial position or balance sheet can be represented by an equation: Assets (resources) = Liabilities (obligations to third parties) + Equity (claims of shareholders).
- An asset is a resource controlled by an entity as a result of past events and from which future economic benefits are expected to flow to the enterprise.
- A liability is a present obligation of the entity arising from past events. Its settlement is expected to result in an outflow from the enterprise of resources generating economic benefits.
- The income statement summarizes the processes through which income of the period was created and, thus, how retained earnings have been modified.

- Revenues represent an increase in shareholders' equity that originates from the business of the company such as a sale of goods or services or interest received from short-term investment.
- Expenses are decreases in shareholders' equity that originate from the business of the company such as services purchased, salaries paid to the employees, rent paid for the use of certain physical facilities, wear and tear on equipment, etc.
- Depreciation is the recognition of the consumption of a fixed asset in the course of carrying out the firm's business. It is an expense.
- Net income for a period is, thus, the difference between total revenues and total expenses recorded during that period. Net income, if positive, is called profit, and, if negative, is called loss. Net income belongs to the shareholders.
- Retained earnings represent that part of the value created through the firm's operations (profit) that shareholders have chosen not to take out of the firm as dividends.
- Net income is different from cash due to the accrual rules of recognition that separate the booking of a transaction from its eventual settlement in cash.
- Profit appropriation is the decision taken by the shareholders to distribute entirely, partially or not to distribute, the profit of the year.
- Financial statement analysis is a value-adding process to the simple presentation of financial statements. It relies largely on tools such as trend analysis, common-size analysis and ratios.

Review (solutions are at the back of the book)

Review 2.1 Vivaldi Company (1)

Topic: Transactions and the business equation

Vivaldi Company is a retailer. During the year X1 it carried out the following transactions:

a   Creation of the business and provision by shareholders of tangible assets in the amount of 40 CU and of cash for 60 CU.

b   Purchase of merchandise for resale: 40 CU (on account).

c   Advertising expense: 7 CU (on account).

d   Sale of merchandise to customers (on account): 120 CU. The purchase price of the merchandise that was sold is 30 CU.

e   Personnel expenses for the period: salaries 30 CU, social charges and fringe benefits 15 CU (the latter will be paid out in cash during the next period).

f   Miscellaneous business taxes: 20 CU (will be paid cash during the next period).

g   Cash received from customers (who had bought on account): 60 CU.

h   Payment to the merchandise suppliers: 35 CU.

i   Payment of salaries: 30 CU.

j   The assets brought as a capital contribution when the business was created are expected to have a useful life of 10 years. The loss of value of the asset is expected to be the same each year for 10 years.

k   The purchase value of the merchandise on hand at the end of the year (ending inventory) is 10 CU.

Required

1. Show the impact of each event on the basic business equation (recording the purchase of merchandise in expenses).

2. Prepare the year-end balance sheet reflecting the events listed in (a) to (k) above.

3. Prepare the income statement for the period reflecting the events listed in (a) to (k) above.

Review 2.2 Vivaldi Company (2)

Topic: Transactions and impact on the financial statements

Refer to the Vivaldi (1) exercise above.

Required

Record the transactions in the appropriate accounts.

Review 2.3 Albinoni Company

Topic: Transactions and the business equation

Albinoni Company is a retailer. During one accounting period, it carried out the following transactions:

1. Creation of the business and provision by shareholders of a piece of equipment for the amount of 80 CU, and of cash for 30 CU.

2. A loan was received from the banker: 200 CU.

3. Miscellaneous business taxes: 40 CU (paid cash during the period).

4. Purchase of merchandise for resale: 50 CU (on account).

5. Legal fees: 10 CU (cash outflow during the period).

6. Personnel expenses for the period: salaries and social charges: 30 CU (paid cash during the period).

7. Sale of merchandise to customers: 80 CU (on account) and 20 CU (cash sales). The merchandise that was sold had been purchased for 40 CU.

8. Payment to the merchandise suppliers: 30 CU.

9. Cash received from customers: 70 CU.

10. The assets brought as a capital contribution when the business was created are expected to have a useful life of four years. The loss of value of the asset is expected to be the same each year for four years.

11. The value of the merchandise on hand at the end of the year (ending inventory) is 10 CU.

Required

Show the impact of each event on the balance sheet equation. You have the following choices:

1. To record the purchases of merchandise as inventory ('perpetual inventory system') or
2. To record theses purchases as expenses ('periodic inventory system'). Please mention clearly your choice.

Use the format presented in Appendix 1.

Appendix 1

Please identify your choice of inventory carrying method:
Purchases recorded as inventory ('Perpetual inventory system') or Purchases recorded as expenses ('Periodic inventory system')

	Assets				=	Liabilities		+ Shareholders' equity (SE)
	+	+	+	+	=	+	+	+	Details of SE transactions
(1)								
(2)								
(3)								
(4)								
(5)								
(6)								
(7)								
(8)								
(9)								
(10)								
(11)								
End Balance								

Assignments

Assignment 2.1
Multiple-choice questions

Select the right answer (only one possible answer unless otherwise stated).

1. Raw materials and merchandise purchased can be included in (two alternative answers)

   (a) Cash
   (b) Expenses
   (c) Fixed assets
   (d) Current assets
   (e) None of these

2. Obtaining a long-term debt affects which of the following accounts

   (a) Operating liabilities
   (b) Financial liabilities
   (c) Shareholders' equity
   (d) Retained earnings
   (e) None of these

3. Land, buildings, furniture and computers are included in

   (a) Current assets
   (b) Fixed assets
   (c) Cash
   (d) Inventory
   (e) None of these

4. The document reporting all the expenses and revenues for a given period is the

(a) Statement of financial position
(b) Statement of cash flows
(c) Income statement
(d) Balance sheet
(e) Notes to financial statements
(f) Statement of changes in equity
(g) None of these

5. A balance sheet is presented

(a) Only after profit appropriation
(b) Only before profit appropriation
(c) Before and after profit appropriation
(d) None of these

6. An income statement is presented

(a) Only after profit appropriation
(b) Only before profit appropriation
(c) Always before and after profit appropriation
(d) None of these

7. Advance payments received from customers are included in

(a) Revenues
(b) Assets
(c) Liabilities
(d) Shareholders' equity
(e) Expenses
(f) None of these

8. Advance payments to suppliers are included in

(a) Revenues
(b) Assets
(c) Liabilities
(d) Shareholders' equity
(e) Expenses
(f) None of these

9. The depreciation recorded in the balance sheet includes

(a) Accumulated depreciation for past years
(b) Depreciation for the current year
(c) Both
(d) None of these

10. An example of an item that is not a current asset is

(a) Accounts receivable
(b) Inventory
(c) Equipment
(d) Cash
(f) None of these

Assignment 2.2
Vivaldi Company (3)

Topic: Transactions and the business equation

Please refer to Review 2.1 Vivaldi Company (1) above.

Required

1. Show the impact of each event on the accounting equation (recording the purchases of merchandise in inventory in the balance sheet).

2. Prepare the year-end balance sheet reflecting the events listed in (a) to (k) above.

3. Prepare the income statement for the period reflecting the events listed in (a) to (k) above.

Assignment 2.3
Busoni Company

Topic: Transactions and the financial statements

Busoni Company is a wholesaler. During one accounting period, it carried out the following transactions

1. Creation of the business and provision by shareholders of a piece of equipment in the amount of 100 CU, and of cash for 40 CU.

2. Merchandise for resale were purchased: 60 CU (on account).

3. A debt was received from the banker: 100 CU.

4. Personnel expenses were incurred for the period: salaries and social charges: 35 CU (paid cash).

5. Merchandise was sold to customers: 50 CU (on account) and 40 CU (paid cash). The merchandise that was sold had been purchased for 38 CU.

6. Cash was received from customers: 42 CU.

7. Merchandise suppliers were given a partial payment: 55 CU.

8. The assets brought as a capital contribution when the business was created are expected to have a useful life of five years. The loss of value of the asset is expected to be the same each year.

9. The value of the merchandise on hand at the end of the year (ending inventory) is 22 CU.

Required

Show the impact of each event on the financial statements with T-Accounts. You have the following choices:

1. To record the purchases of merchandise as inventory ('perpetual inventory system'), or

2. To record these purchases as expenses ('periodic inventory system'). Please mention clearly your choice.

Use the following structure.

Balance sheet		Income statement	
Assets	Equity and liabilities	Expenses	Revenues

Assignment 2.4
Corelli Company (1)

Topic: Classification of accounts

Corelli Company provides below a list (in alphabetical order) of all the accounts it uses (far left column). For each line you are provided five choices of families of accounts to which the account listed on the left can be related.

Required

Indicate by a checkmark in the appropriate column to which account family each account is related. It should be noted that the accounts should be related to one column only (one 'family'), because one account is only one part of a double entry.

	Assets	Shareholders' equity	Liabilities	Revenues	Expenses
Accounts payable					
Accounts receivable					
Administrative expense					
Advance payments received from customers					
Advance payments to suppliers					
Buildings					
Cash at bank					
Cash in hand					
Computing equipment					
Financial debts					
Income tax expense					
Income tax payable					
Industrial equipment					
Insurance expense					
Interest expense					
Interest revenue					
Loans					
Marketable securities					
Repair and maintenance expense					
Salaries payable					
Salary expense					
Sales of merchandise					
Selling expense					
Share capital					
Social security payable					

Assignment 2.5
Corelli Company (2)

Topic: Classification of accounts

Corelli Company provides below a listing (in alphabetical order) of all the accounts it uses (far left column). For each line you are provided five choices of families of accounts to which the account listed on the left can be related.

Required

Indicate by a checkmark in the appropriate column to which account family or families each account is related. It should be noted that the accounts should be related to one column only (one 'family'), because one account is only one part of a double entry.

	Assets	Shareholders' equity	Liabilities	Revenues	Expenses
Accumulated depreciation					
Cost of goods sold					
Finished products					
Merchandise					
Purchases of merchandise					
Purchases of supplies					
Raw materials					
Reserves					
Retained earnings					

Assignment 2.6
adidas Group*

Topic: Financial statement analysis

For over 80 years, the adidas Group has been part of the world of sports on every level, delivering state-of-the-art sports footwear, apparel and accessories.[5] Today, the adidas Group, headquartered in Germany, is a global leader in the sporting goods industry and offers a broad portfolio of products. Products from the adidas Group are available in virtually every country of the world. The group describes its strategy as simple: *continuously strengthen its brands and products to improve its competitive position and financial performance.*

The adidas Group has divided its operating activities by major brands into three segments:

adidas	Footwear, apparel, and hardware such as bags and balls

Reebok	Footwear, apparel and hardware
TaylorMade-adidas Golf	Golf equipment: metalwoods, irons, putters, golf balls, footwear, apparel and accessories

Effective 31 December 2008, the adidas Group employed 38,982 people.

From its annual reports 2005 through 2008, we extracted the following balance sheets and income statements, which have been prepared in accordance with International Financial Reporting Standards (IFRS), as adopted by the European Union, and the additional requirements of German commercial law pursuant to § 315a section 1 HGB.

Consolidated balance sheet (IFRS)				
31 December	2008 € in millions	2007 € in millions	2006 € in millions	2005 € in millions
Cash and cash equivalents	244	295	311	1,525
Short-term financial assets	141	86	36	61
Accounts receivable	1,624	1,459	1,415	965
Inventories	1,995	1,629	1,607	1,230
Income tax receivables	110	60	84	49
Other current assets	789	529	413	537
Assets classified as held for sale	31	80	59	0
Total current assets	**4,934**	**4,138**	**3,925**	**4,367**
Property, plant and equipment	886	702	689	424
Goodwill	1,499	1,436	1,516	436
Trademarks	1,390	1,291	1,454	15
Other intangible assets	204	194	223	76
Long-term financial assets	96	103	106	114
Deferred tax assets	344	315	332	195
Other non-current assets	180	147	134	123
Total non-current assets	**4,599**	**4,188**	**4,454**	**1,383**
Total assets	**9,533**	**8,326**	**8,379**	**5,750**

31 December	2008 € in millions	2007 € in millions	2006 € in millions	2005 € in millions
Short-term borrowings	797	186		
Accounts payable	1,218	849	752	684
Income taxes	321	285	283	283
Accrued liabilities and provisions	1,008	1,025	921	566
Other current liabilities	295	266	232	190
Liabilities classified as held for sale	6	4	4	0
Total current liabilities	**3,645**	**2,615**	**2,192**	**1,723**
Long-term borrowings	1,776	1,960	2,578	1,035
Pensions and similar obligations	132	124	134	148
Deferred tax liabilities	463	450	522	42
Non-current accrued liabilities and provisions	65	73	74	67
Other non-current liabilities	52	69	43	23
Total non-current liabilities	**2,488**	**2,676**	**3,351**	**1,315**
Share capital	194	204	204	130
Reserves	−10	161	425	700
Retained earnings	3,202	2,658	2,199	1,854
Shareholders' equity	**3,386**	**3,023**	**2,828**	**2,684**
Minority interests	14	11	8	28
Total equity	**3,400**	**3,034**	**2,836**	**2,712**
Total liabilities and equity	**9,533**	**8,325**	**8,379**	**5,750**

Consolidated income statement (IFRS)					
Year ending 31 December	2008 € in millions	2007 € in millions	2006 € in millions	2005 € in millions	Signs
Net sales	10,799	10,299	10,084	6,636	+
Cost of sales	5,543	5,417	5,589	3,439	−
Gross profit	5,256	4,882	4,495	3,197	=
Royalties and commissions income	89	102	90	47	+
Other operating income	103	80	55	36	+
Other operating expenses	4,378	4,115	3,759	2,573	−
Operating profit	1,070	949	881	707	=
Financial income	37	36	39	42	+
Financial expenses	203	170	197	94	−
Income before taxes	904	815	723	655	=
Income taxes	260	260	227	221	
Income from discontinued operations, net of tax				−44	+/−
Net income	644	555	496	390	=

N.B. The column with the signs '+', '−' and '=' has been added by the authors, in order to facilitate the understanding of the different steps in the calculation of the net income.

From the notes to the financial statements, we obtain for the following information:

- 'Note 11 Goodwill – Goodwill[6] primarily relates to the Group's acquisitions of the Reebok and TaylorMade businesses as well as recent and previous acquisitions of subsidiaries in the United States, Australia / New Zealand, Netherlands / Belgium and Italy'.
- 'Note 12 Trademarks and other intangible assets', indicates that the 'trademarks' are also related to acquisitions by the Group.

Required

1. Prepare the common-size income statements (i.e., all figures as percentage of net sales).

2. Whenever possible, compute the ratios which have been introduced at the end of the chapter for the years 2005 through 2008.

3. Analyze the financial situation and performance of the adidas Group on the basis of these ratios and the common-size income statements.

Please notice that minority interests[7] are often included in equity in the computation of ratios based on this concept.

Assignment 2.7
Stora Enso*

Topic: Financial statement analysis

Stora Enso is a Finnish integrated global paper producer. Its sales have been relatively stable over the past five years. The group had in 2008 some 29,000 employees in more than 85 production facilities in over 35 countries worldwide. The operations of Stora Enso and its subsidiaries are organized into business areas: magazine paper, newsprint and book paper, fine paper, consumer board, industrial packaging, wood products, and other, the latter comprising wood supply and supporting activities such as energy and head office, together with other corporate functions. From its annual reports 2005 through 2008, we extracted the following balance sheets and income statements, which have been prepared in accordance with International Financial Reporting Standards.

Consolidated balance sheet				
As at 31 December **€ millions**	**2008**	**2007**	**2006**	**2005**
Assets				
Fixed assets and non-current investments				
Goodwill	207.6	502.7	906.8	961.8
Other intangible fixed assets	77.5	159.1	170.4	194.1
Property, plant and equipment	5,413.7	6,476.7	9,153.6	9,936.8
	5,698.8	7,138.5	10,230.8	11,092.7
Biological assets	133.6	88.7	111.5	76.8
Emission rights	67.0	5.2	98.1	43.7
Investment in associated companies	1,042.5	1,154.5	805.2	719.9
Available-for-sale: interest-bearing securities	154.9	161.8	41.2	211.6
Available-for-sale: unlisted shares	954.3	1,260.8	794.3	403.6
Non-current loan receivables	130.3	126.5	149.2	127.6
Deferred tax assets	74.5	63.7	53.5	72.2
Other non-current assets	16.2	22.6	61.1	28.3
	8,272.1	**10,022.3**	**12,344.9**	**12,776.4**
Current assets				
Inventories	1,693.6	1,992.6	2,019.5	2,150.5
Tax receivables	25.0	34.3	66.6	85.3
Short-term operative receivables	1,583.2	2,063.1	2,156.6	2,186.2
Interest-bearing receivables	251.1	227.8	185.5	280.9
Cash and cash equivalents	415.8	970.7	609.0	351.4
	3,968.7	**5,288.5**	**5,037.2**	**5,054.3**
Total assets	**12,240.8**	**15,310.8**	**17,382.1**	**17,830.7**
Equity and liabilities				
Equity attributable to parent company shareholders				
Share capital	1,342.2	1,342.2	1,342.2	1,382.1
Share premium (reclassified)	2,037.5	2,037.5	2,039.9	545.9
Reserve fund	238.9	238.9	238.9	238.9
Treasury shares	−10.2	−10.2	−10.5	−259.9
Other comprehensive income	334.0	960.4	735.6	468.0
Cumulative translation adjustment	−443.8	−115.6	−132.0	−127.1
Retained earnings (restated)	2,768.8	3,355.1	3,118.0	5,083.3
Net (loss)/profit for the period	−673.4	−214.7	585.0	−111.1
	5,594.0	**7,593.6**	**7,917.1**	**7,220.1**
Minority interests	56.5	71.9	103.5	93.6
Total equity	**5,650.5**	**7,665.5**	**8,020.6**	**7,313.7**
Non-current liabilities				
Post-employment benefit provisions	299.0	327.3	763.1	888.3
Other provisions	202.3	135.9	308.3	142.6
Deferred tax liabilities	277.5	582.0	793.0	866.0
Non-current debt	3,007.8	3,354.8	4,081.0	4,353.9
Other non-current operative liabilities (restated)	28.5	52.7	76.2	204.7
	3,815.1	**4,452.7**	**6,021.6**	**6,455.5**
Current liabilities				
Current portion of non-current debt	437.4	513.1	630.2	385.0
Interest-bearing liabilities	587.7	482.2	217.3	1,114.8
Bank overdrafts	43.2	91.4	299.4	201.9
Current operative liabilities	1,602.1	1,971.3	1,992.5	2,003.6
Tax liabilities	104.8	134.6	200.5	356.2
	2,775.2	**3,192.6**	**3,339.9**	**4,061.5**
Total equity and liabilities	**12,240.8**	**15,310.8**	**17,382.1**	**17,830.7**

Consolidated income statement				
	2008 € millions	2007 € millions	2006 € millions	2005 € millions
Continuing operations				
Sales	**11,028.8**	**11,848.5**	**11,460.4**	**11,342.7**
Other operating income	120.2	88.4	360.0	79.0
Changes in inventories of finished goods and work in progress	−78.1	81.0	−14.3	55.9
Change in net value of biological assets	−18.2	7.5	−2.2	−6.7
Materials and services	−6,815.7	−7,051.5	−6,371.9	−6,499.7
Freight and sales commissions	−1,127.1	−1,133.9	−1,193.2	−1,089.3
Personnel expenses	−1,669.1	−1,712.9	−1,728.1	−1,820.0
Other operating expenses	−752.6	−761.9	−846.5	−921.2
Share of results in associated companies	7.6	341.3	88.0	67.1
Depreciation, amortization and impairment charges	−1,422.4	−1,529.6	−1,043.8	−998.5
Operating (loss)/profit	**−726.6**	**176.9**	**708.4**	**209.3**
Financial income	356.7	161.9	274.1	238.6
Financial expense	−523.9	−318.6	−289.0	−343.5
(Loss)/profit before tax	**−893.8**	**20.2**	**693.5**	**104.4**
Income tax	214.8	−7.4	−6.2	−28.7
Net (loss)/profit for the year from continuing operations	**−679.0**	**12.8**	**687.3**	**75.7**
Discontinued operations: profit/(loss) after tax for the year	**4.3**	**−225.2**	**−98.1**	**−183.1**
Net (loss)/profit for the year from total operations	**−674.7**	**−212.4**	**589.2**	**−107.4**
Attributable to:				
Equity holders of the parent company	−673.4	−214.7	585.0	−111.1
Minority interests net (loss)/profit for the year	−1.3	2.3	4.2	3.7
	−674.7	−212.4	589.2	−107.4

Required

1. Prepare the common-size income statements (i.e., all figures in percentage of net sales).

2. Whenever possible, compute the ratios which have been introduced at the end of the chapter for the years 2005 through 2008.

3. Analyze the financial situation and performance of the Stora Enso Group on the basis of these ratios and the common-size income statement.

Please notice that minority interests (see endnote 7) are often included in equity in the computation of ratios based on this concept.

References

IASB (1989) Framework for the Preparation and Presentation of Financial Statements, in International Financial Reporting Standards (bound volume, annual edition), London.

IASB (1993) International Accounting Standard No. 18, Revenue, London.

IASB (2003) International Accounting Standard No. 16, Property, Plant and Equipment, London.

IASB (2007) International Accounting Standard No. 1, Presentation of Financial Statements, London.

Additional material on the website

Go to http://www.cengage.co.uk/stolowy3 for further information, journal entries and extra assignments for each chapter.

The following appendices to this chapter are available on the dedicated website:

Appendix 2.1: Balance sheet and value creation

Appendix 2.2: Reporting for retained earnings and reserves

Appendix 2.3: Recording of inventory – Impact on the basic business equation

Notes

1. The snapshot however represents the picture only at its 'historical' value. For example, a piece of land will be shown at its purchase price, even if events, subsequent to the purchase, may have modified the potential resale value of the land. If, for example, the development of a shopping area next to the plot has increased its value, such a change in value will not be recorded in the accounts. Accounting must be credible without ambiguity or debate. Since the value of a resource (exchange or resale value, potential to create sellable objects or services in the future) changes continuously, accounting practitioners have chosen long ago to prefer reliability over accuracy and use only historical costs.

2. It should be noted that the expression 'P&L' is also used in a North American environment where the term 'Income statement' is the official name of the document. 'P&L' is then simply an alternative way to refer to the 'income statement'.

3. Each transaction amount is recorded in an 'account', i.e., a table with several columns that classifies entries describing the transaction between increases or decreases. There is an account for every type of resource or obligation, and therefore for revenues and expenses (cash, capital, accounts payable, etc.). By convention, accounts are often presented in the form of a T (thus the term T-Account), separating movements in homogeneous categories on either side of the vertical bar of the T (see further illustrations in Chapter 3). Here, the T-account in Verdi's books recording the cash deposited at the bank is called 'cash' or 'cash at bank' and all transactions involving the checkbook pertaining to this account will be recorded in that T-account (or file in a computer-based accounting system).

4. Average equity = (Beginning shareholders' equity + Ending shareholders' equity)/2.

5. This brief presentation is based on the following website: http://www.adidas-group.com/en/ourgroup/our_business/default.aspx. Last accessed: 15 December 2009.

6. Goodwill primarily relates to the premium an acquirer pays over the market-adjusted value of the assets of an acquired firm. Goodwill is more precisely analyzed in Chapters 8 and 13.

7. Also called 'non-controlling interests', they represent the equity in a subsidiary not attributable, directly or indirectly, to a parent company. This item will be presented in a more detailed manner in Chapter 13, devoted to consolidation.

C3

Chapter 3
Financial Statements: Interrelations and Construction

Learning objectives

After studying this chapter, you will understand:

- The objectives of the statement of cash flows.
- How the statement of cash flows relates to the balance sheet and income statement.
- How to use the concepts of debit and credit.
- That the accounting process consists in a structured multi-step progressive classification and aggregation process of elemental data.
- That the journal is the day-to-day chronological register of accounting information.
- That the general ledger is the grouping of all accounts (a ledger is a grouping of selected and homogeneous accounts).
- That all entries are transferred ('posted') from the journal to the appropriate specialized ledger and, ultimately, to the general ledger.
- That the accountant must prepare a 'trial balance', which is a list of the debit and credit footings for each account in the general ledger. The trial balance is a tool for internal control, which helps verify that all transactions have been recorded in accordance with the double entry bookkeeping principle.
- That all businesses have a chart of accounts, which is a logically organized list of all recognized accounts used in recording transactions.
- That some countries have a standardized chart of accounts while others do not.

In the first two chapters we briefly introduced two of the main documents called financial statements that are part of the financial information-set. These documents describe the financial situation of the firm and the value creation process. The accounting information contained in the **balance sheet**, the **income statement**, and the notes to financial statements (the latter will be developed in Chapter 5) is essential for decision-makers and all stakeholders. These three documents are the minimum reporting required by a large majority of countries. Most countries add a requirement that a statement of cash flows (see below and Chapters 14 and 17) and/or a statement of changes in shareholders' equity (see Chapter 11) be also provided, so that investors, shareholders and other accounting information users be well informed about the situation of a business.

In its International Accounting Standard No. 1 (IASB 2007: § 10), the International Accounting Standards Board (IASB) offers a definition of **financial statements** by stating that 'a complete set of financial statements comprises:

(a) a statement of financial position as at the end of the period;

(b) a statement of comprehensive income for the period;

(c) a statement of changes in equity for the period;

(d) a statement of cash flows for the period;

(e) notes, comprising a summary of significant accounting policies and other explanatory information; and

(f) a statement of financial position as at the beginning of the earliest comparative period when an entity applies an accounting policy retrospectively or makes a retrospective restatement of items in its financial statements, or when it reclassifies items in its financial statements.'

The same paragraph of IAS 1 adds an important element: 'an entity may use titles for the statements other than those used in this Standard'. Thus, the new title of 'statement of financial position' can be replaced by the traditional 'balance sheet'. The same applies to the 'statement of comprehensive income' which continues to be called, in practice, 'income statement'.

The purpose of this chapter is to, first briefly introduce the statement of cash flows, which will be fully developed in Chapters 14 (preparation) and 17 (analysis). Secondly it is to illustrate how the three financial statements are interconnected. Incidentally, we will also develop further the two core components of financial statements (balance sheet and income statement). Finally, this chapter will develop the practical steps in the construction of financial statements (professionals tend to say 'production of financial statements' and we will use this term throughout the book).

1 Statement of cash flows

Although the **statement of cash flows** is not a required component of financial statements in some countries, our position is that it constitutes an essential document for understanding the economic financial life of a business. The vision given through both balance sheet and income statement may appear to be limited because:

1. The balance sheet offers only a static vision of the financial position and fails to disclose the movements of funds related to operations, investment (preparing the future) and financing (how were external funds obtained or modified).

2. The income statement, especially because it is based on the matching principle and its corollary, the accrual approach (concept introduced in Chapter 1 and developed below in 1.1), fails to show the importance of cash in the operation of the firm. As illustrated in Chapter 2, cash and profit can give vastly different signals of the consequences of the transactions a business engaged in during a given period.

Figure 3.1 Example of an operating cycle

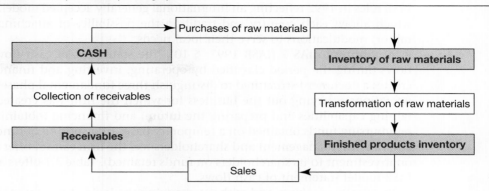

As the saying goes: 'cash is king'. Cash is the blood of any organization as shown in Figure 3.1 above (a simplified version of the cash pump diagram seen in Chapter 1), which describes a basic operating cycle. Current assets are shown in blue boxes.

Neither the balance sheet nor the income statement emphasizes the dynamics of cash flowing in and out of the business. Comparing two consecutive balance sheets certainly allows the user to calculate the net change in cash position. However that is not sufficient to understand **how** this change happened. Operations bring-in and take-out cash, but (a) this happens with delays linked to credit terms on both the revenue and the cost sides; and (b) plenty of other events affect the cash balance, such as additional cash contributions by shareholders, payment of dividends, acquisition or disposal of fixed assets, acquisition or granting of rights to operate specific technologies, etc. All these events need to be understood before the full meaning of the ending cash balance can be understood. Where did cash come from and what was it used for are the two key questions the statement of cash flows addresses.

We will only present here a brief outline of this statement and Chapter 14 will give us the opportunity to explore this document further in terms of preparation, while Chapter 17 will deal with the analysis of the statement of cash flows. We will emphasize here the relations between the three documents: balance sheet, income statement and statement of cash flows.

1.1 Accrual basis of accounting

The need for the statement of cash flows arises from the choice made of the **accrual** approach for the recognition of revenues and expenses. IAS 1 (IASB 2007: § 27) states: 'an entity shall prepare its financial statements, except for cash flow information, under the **accrual basis** of accounting'. Under this method, transactions and events are recognized when they occur (and not as cash or its equivalent is received or paid) and they are recognized in the accounting records and reported in the financial statements of the periods to which they relate. Such a principle distinguishes modern accounting from cash basis accounting in which transactions and events are recorded at the time of the flow of cash they trigger. Accrual accounting creates a timing difference between recognition of revenues or expenses and their cash implications. The statement of cash flows explains this timing difference.

1.2 Evolution

After many years of diversity of orientation and presentation, the statement of cash flows has become a relatively standardized document. The requirement to publish one has spread rapidly since the mid-eighties. Canada was first in requiring a statement of cash flows in 1985, followed by the USA (1987), France (1988), and the UK (1991). Most importantly, the statement of cash flows became part of the standard reporting package required under IASB rules in 1992 reflecting an international generally accepted model. It offers a template, which allows each country and tradition the possibility of attaching some specific (but minor) modifications to serve their local needs.

According to IAS 7 (IASB 1992: § 10), 'the statement of cash flows shall report cash flows during the period classified by operating, investing and financing activities'. This creates a document structured to distinguish three fundamental phases of life in an entity: operations (carrying out the business for which the firm was created), investing (maintaining capabilities and preparing the future) and financing (obtaining funds if needed, reimbursing funds obtained on a temporary basis, or disposing of funds if an excess exists and the firm management and shareholders feel the firm cannot offer a satisfactory return on investment to its shareholders on funds retained). Table 3.1 offers an illustration of the IASB model statement of cash flows.

Practically speaking, and without changing the logic of the approach, the statement of cash flows can start with the opening cash balance and conclude with the closing balance. Then, using the same figures as above, we can present the statement of cash flows for the period as illustrated below (see Table 3.2).

1.3 Links between balance sheet, income statement and statement of cash flows

The balance sheet, the income statement and the statement of cash flows are totally linked as is shown in Figure 3.2. They form a closed system in which everything that happens in the life of the business is recorded so that the user of accounting information can understand very well how value was created (income statement) and how the liquidity of the firm (availability of cash) has been affected by operations and decisions during the period

Table 3.1 Illustrative statement of cash flows

Cash flows from operating activities		
Cash received from customers		80
Cash paid to suppliers and employees		−30
Net cash from operating activities	*(1)*	*50*
Cash flows from investing activities		
Purchase of property, plant and equipment		−15
Proceeds from sale of equipment		5
Net cash used in investing activities	*(2)*	*−10*
Cash flows from financing activities		
Proceeds from issuance of share capital		35
Proceeds from long-term borrowings		10
Dividends paid		−20
Net cash from financing activities	*(3)*	*25*
Net increase in cash and cash equivalents	**(4) = (1) + (2) + (3)**	**65**
Cash and cash equivalents at beginning of year	(5)	5
Cash and cash equivalents at end of year	(6)	70
Change in cash	**(7) = (6) − (5)**	**65**
Control	**(4) = (7)**	

Table 3.2 Statement of cash flows — alternative presentation

Cash and cash equivalents at beginning of year	(1)	5
Net cash from operating activities	(2)	50
Net cash used in investing activities	(3)	−10
Net cash from financing activities	(4)	25
Cash and cash equivalents at end of year	(5) = (1) + (2) + (3) + (4)	70

Figure 3.2 Link between balance sheet, income statement and statement of cash flows

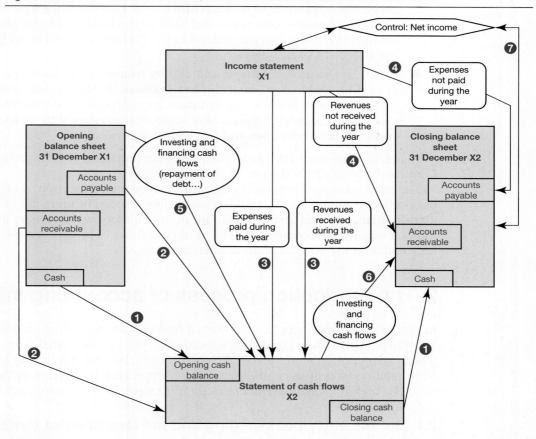

(statement of cash flows). The balance sheet records the situation that is the outcome of the previously mentioned transactions recorded in the other two documents of the financial statements.

Each key relation is explored in further detail below. (Each number refers to Figure 3.2.)

■ The cash balance in the opening balance sheet is the opening cash balance in the statement of cash flows. This transfer from the balance sheet is not a flow of cash *per se* but only an accounting entry that is used to start the statement of cash flows. The same line of reasoning will be used to transfer back the closing cash balance in the statement of cash flows to the closing balance sheet.

■ Revenues and expenses of the previous year that were not collected or paid during that year (and recorded as accounts receivable or accounts payable) will, in principle, be collected or paid during the current year. They will impact on the statement of cash flows.

■ The income statement impact on the statement of cash flows is through those revenues and expenses collected or paid during the year.

■ Conversely, if revenues and expenses of the current period are not collected or paid during this period, they will, in all likelihood, be collected or paid in the following period. They are recognized as part of the receivables and payables balances in the closing balance sheet.

■ Items in the opening balance sheet that are connected to investment or financing may also have an impact on the statement of cash flows. For example, repaying all or part of the principal of a debt will generate a cash outflow, whereas proceeds from the sale of a fixed asset will create a cash inflow.

■ Some investing or financing cash flows will also impact on the closing balance sheet. The acquisition of new machines, or of a license to use a patent, are cash out-flows; the flotation of a new bond issue or the issuance of new share capital lead, on the other hand, to cash inflows in the business and will as such be recorded in the statement of cash flows.

■ When the income statement and closing balance sheet have been prepared, it is critical to double-check that the **net income** (in the income statement) and the increase in shareholders' equity before appropriation of dividends (in the balance sheet) show identical figures. This is the closing relation to make sure the system was truly comprehensive and is therefore 'balanced'.

Figure 3.2 is illustrated through quantified examples in the Review problems 'Beethoven Company (1) and (2)' at the end of the chapter.

The set of relations illustrated in Figure 3.2 can be used either from an historical (*ex post*) perspective in reports to shareholders and external users, or more importantly, it can be used by managers and analysts alike in an anticipatory way (*ex ante*) in preparing pro forma, budgeted or forecasted statement of cash flows to be used for decision-making or for simulating the effect on cash of alternative decisions.

2 The production process of accounting information

In order to establish financial statements a business needs to set up an organized account-ing system. This system consists in a multi-stage process, illustrated here. The accounting process relies not only on the use of technical tools, but requires human intervention and interpretation (mainly in classifying the recording of each transaction in the proper catego-ries). The importance of the human factor must never be underestimated in accounting.

2.1 Double entry bookkeeping and the recording of transactions

2.1.1 Accounts

Chapter 2 provided a direct illustration of the impact of economic transactions on the balance sheet, or on both balance sheet and income statement. Business organizations deal with very large numbers of transactions, and some degree of systematic organization quickly becomes necessary to avoid chaos and to provide the ability for users of account-ing information to understand how the business works.

Each balance sheet or income statement item or line may undergo thousands or even millions of modifications (entries) during an accounting period. At one extreme end of the spectrum, for example, Walmart, the US-based largest retail chain in the world, declared in 2009 it served over 200 million customers per week, employed 2.1 million persons, and sourced its products from tens of thousands of suppliers, an activity which gener-ates hundreds of millions of accounting entries per month. Each transaction represents a modification of the appropriate specialized accounts that are subdivisions, according to the type of transaction, of balance sheet and income statement items. At year-end, only the net summary positions of the accounts, known as their 'balance', are used in establishing the balance sheet and income statement. Only appropriate balances are reported as too much detail would make the accounting signals incomprehensible or overwhelming and, therefore, useless. For example, in a statement of cash flows, the detailed cash remuneration of each individual employee is not needed. Only the aggregated line 'cash paid to employees' might be reported to shareholders. The Human Resources manager, however, might want to separate that aggregated amount between various categories of employees since these partial balances would be of use to his or her decision-making.

In the Verdi Co. example, discussed in Chapter 2 (Figures 2.3 to 2.11), the company's cash on 1 January X1, before the incorporation of the Company, was 0 CU. This initial amount (or opening balance) underwent several modifications (entries) following transactions either raising this amount (+390) or lowering it (−322), such that the year-end cash showed a positive balance of 68. This last figure (see Table 3.3) is reported in the balance sheet assets on 31 December X1: the cash balance is one of the components of the financial position of Verdi Co. at the end of the accounting period (see Chapter 2, Table 2.3).

2.1.2 The concept of debit and credit

Basic principles   Since the concepts of increases and decreases to monetary amounts in the accounts can be confusing, the respective sides must be clearly defined. *By convention*, the left-hand side of a T-account is called the debit side, and the right-hand side the credit side. Thus, the 'cash' account (an asset account) increases on the debit side and decreases on the credit side. The initial positive amount is a debit balance. Similarly, a 'debt' account (part of shareholders' equity and liabilities) increases on the credit side (the right-hand side), and decreases on the debit side (the left-hand side). The balance of this account, when the borrowing is not totally repaid, is thus a credit balance.

In general, the asset side of the balance sheet is designed to summarize balance sheet accounts with debit balances, while the shareholders' equity and liabilities side contains the balance sheet accounts with credit balances. Since the balance sheet is always balanced, it means the total of debit balances (the assets) equals the total of credit balances (shareholders' equity and liabilities). Expense accounts function similarly to asset accounts, while revenue accounts function in the same way as shareholders' equity and liabilities.

A schematic presentation of these rules is shown in Figure 3.3, using the basic business equation.

Table 3.3 Cash account of Verdi Co.

Cash account			
Cash inflows		Cash outflows	
Beginning balance	0	Cash payment on equipment	125
Capital contribution	150	Cash payment to employees	101
Cash receipt on debt	60	Cash payment on interest	4
Cash receipt from customers	180	Cash payment to suppliers	80
		Cash repayment of debt	12
		Total cash outflows	322
Total cash inflows	390	Ending balance[1]	68

Note: We have not specified what sort of 'cash' this account covers. Cash inflows and outflows refer, at this stage, indiscriminately to either cash in hand or cash at bank (or totally liquid assets in deposit at some financial institution).

Figure 3.3 Basic business equation and concepts of debit and credit

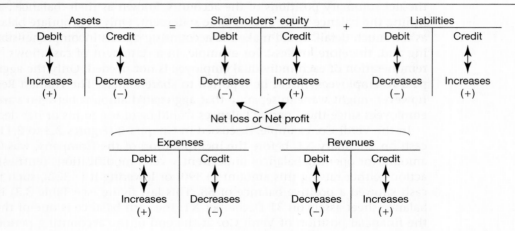

It is important to note that the terms '**debit**' and '**credit**' correspond to the left-hand and right-hand sides. They are not synonymous with 'increase' and 'decrease'. To understand the meaning of debit and credit for accounts recording expenses and revenues, suffice it to remember that revenues increase shareholders' equity, but expenses reduce it. For this reason, revenue accounts 'behave' in a way similar to that of shareholders' equity accounts (credit = increase, and debit = decrease), while, for expense accounts, the opposite applies.

Figure 3.3 also shows that net income is the difference between revenues and expenses, and becomes a component of shareholders' equity (retained earnings).

Origins of the concept   To understand the concepts of debit and credit, we must go back to the origin of the terms. According to Vlaemminck (1979: 63) among others, they 'are derived from the Latin words used in the middle-ages 'debet' (verb *debere*: to owe) and 'credit' (verb *credere*: to lend or to trust)'. The terms debit and credit refer to the other party's position in relation to the business. In other words, a debit means a claim *of the business* on something (equipment, inventory or a promise to pay by a customer), while a credit reflects a claim of a third party *on the business*.

As an illustration, let us use the example of a sale of merchandise on credit by Romulus to his brother Remus for 100 CU. This transaction will be recorded in Figure 3.4.

In Romulus' books the sale, worth 100 CU, is recorded on the credit side (Romulus is potentially getting richer, subject to Romulus incurring costs to procure and sell what he

Figure 3.4 Debit and credit

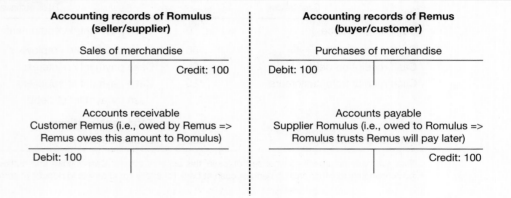

sold to Remus and which are not considered in the recording of this transaction). This is recorded by recognizing the counterbalancing entry, a debit to accounts receivable called 'customer Remus' which shows that Romulus holds a claim of 100 CU over Remus. This entry in Romulus' books shows that (a) a potential enrichment of Romulus' shareholders has been created for 100 CU on the credit side of the 'sales' account, and (b) a claim of Romulus' business on Remus (reflecting the fact the cash or equivalent resources will be transferred at a later date) is created as a debit to the accounts receivable. In a mirror image, the same amount is recorded on the credit side of the 'supplier' account in Remus' books, because the supplier, Romulus, trusts his buyer Remus.

By extension of this principle, the terms debit and credit are used to position the effects of any transaction, even those that do not involve a third party, such as the recognition of a depreciation expense, even though we can hardly, in the case of depreciation, say the old meanings of 'owes us', or 'trusts us' apply.

Confusion with banking vocabulary The way banks use the terms debit and credit should not become a source of confusion. Banks use the terms to mean the opposite of what a business records. The first operation by Verdi Co. (setting up the company by means of a capital contribution of 150 CU) consisted in the business opening a bank account with an original deposit of 150 CU. In Verdi Co.'s books, the amount of 150 is recorded on the debit side of the **cash account** named 'Bank of Venice'. However, the bank records the same amount as a credit to the Verdi Co.'s account, because from the bank's point of view, Verdi Co. is showing its trust by depositing its money, and thus, for the bank, the figure represents a credit (Figure 3.5). In fact, the bank owes the money to Verdi Co, it is not its own; it can and will make it bear fruit, but the depositor can withdraw the deposit, either partially or completely, at any time he or she desires. The Verdi Co. account at the bank and the account 'Bank of Venice' in Verdi Co.'s books are 'mirror accounts'.

We have often observed that when students of accounting use the terms debit and credit, they first think of their own bank statements, and thus adopt the bank's point of view. In fact, a bank statement is an extract from the individual's account, in the financial institution's accounts, and not the opposite. Another approach, based on the concepts of 'use' and 'source' is possible and presented in Appendix 3.1.

Figure 3.6 summarizes these basic rules in a diagram form.

Figure 3.5 Debit and credit from a bank's perspective

Accounting records of Verdi Company		Accounting records of Bank of Venice	
Cash at bank (Bank of Venice)		Verdi Co.	
D	C	D	C
Debit: 150			Credit: 150

Figure 3.6 Basic rules for debit and credit

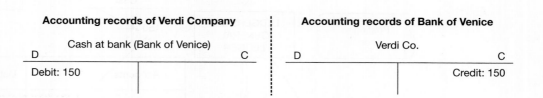

Assets or expenses	
Debit	Credit
Left	Right
Increase	Decrease

Shareholders' equity, liabilities or revenues	
Debit	Credit
Left	Right
Decrease	Increase

In the end, the reader should use the vocabulary he or she finds most helpful. The most important thing is to translate the true impact of the transactions recorded on the position of the firm in an understandable and consistent way, regardless of the specific set of words used.

2.2 The accounting process

2.2.1 Description of the process

Double entry bookkeeping is entirely based on a fundamental idea: each individual accounting transaction has two sides, which are always balanced. In accounting for cash, for example, double entry describes on the one hand the reasons why money has been received (or paid out), and on the other, which account (cash at bank or cash in hand) was increased (or decreased).

On one hand, for practical reasons evoked earlier, it would be impossible to report the full effect of every transaction on the shareholders' equity. On the other hand, in order to leave a clear audit trail (i.e., a possibility of *ex post* verification), all transactions must be recorded. The accounting process consists in a structured multi-step progressive aggregation of elemental data, which is designed to be both exhaustive and efficient. It is illustrated in Figure 3.7.

Each accounting transaction is materialized by a 'supporting **document**'. This document serves as the basis for an entry in a **journal**. The journal provides a chronological list of all transactions. The next step is to distribute the effects of events between special-

Figure 3.7 Accounting process/accounting system

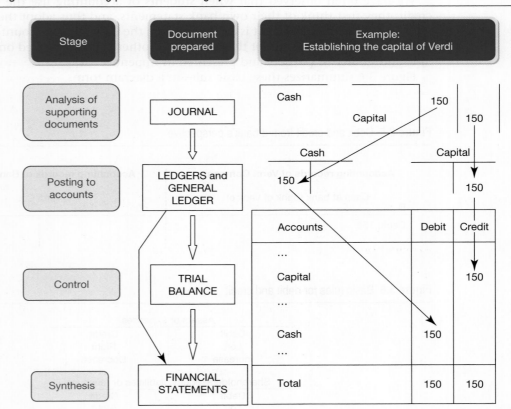

ized **ledger** accounts where they can be accumulated in homogenous classes of nature and type of transaction. The ledger balances (net sum of a class of effect of transactions) will in turn be aggregated in the two main components of the **financial statements** (balance sheet, income statement).

2.2.2 Documents

The 'supporting documents' or 'source documents' can take a variety of formats: invoices, records of written checks, cancelled checks, insurance premium receipts, contracts, tax and social security filings, etc. Supporting documents are not necessary on paper, more and more, thanks to the existence of secure electronic transactions, many transactions supporting documents are dematerialized. The data describing the transaction are recorded in the accounts. In some cases such as the consumption of a physical or intellectual asset i.e., depreciation and amortization (see Chapters 7 and 8), the establishment of provisions for known or unknown risks (see Chapter 12), or for adjusting entries (see Chapter 4), no specific document exists, and the transaction is classified as 'miscellaneous' or time-based.

The accountant should verify that each source document specifically and unambiguously pertains to the business in whose accounts it will be recorded. This question is essential because of the need to clearly distinguish between the business entity (or a legal entity) and individual shareholders or employees (sometimes a problematic distinction in the case of a sole proprietorship – see Chapter 11). Recording personal expenses, unrelated to the company's business and objectives, is a misappropriation of company assets and a fraud, which is disallowed by legal and/or tax authorities and may give rise to litigation.

2.2.3 Journal

As its name implies, the journal is the day-to-day chronological register of accounting information found in the source documents of all allowable transactions. The journal is often referred to as the 'record of prime entry' or the 'book of original entry', since it is the first formal phase in the accounting process, frequently called 'journalizing'. The information recorded in the journal must be sufficiently detailed to provide management with the possibility of analyses required both for ongoing management needs and for complying with the legal obligations pertaining to the annual financial statements.

Bookkeeping entries for the eight transactions of Verdi Co. (see Chapter 2) are shown in Table 3.4 following the standardized form adopted when the journal is maintained as one centralized register.

Since the journal's actual format depends on the computer software used, the following explanations concerning Table 3.4 may be useful:

■ In practice, the first two columns (or computer fields or zones) are used to record the code numbers of the accounts debited and credited – each account has its own alphanumeric code name or account 'number'. The principles of account numbers and charts of accounts will be discussed later in this chapter. This book does not use account numbers. We have, however, kept the two columns, to indicate the impact of each account on the financial statements. This decision was made because of its pedagogical value, and because it provides a constant reminder of the link between the accounts and the financial statements, even at the journal stage.

Table 3.4 Verdi Co. Journal

			(1)	Establishing capital payment		
BS (A+)		Cash			150	
	BS (L+)			Capital		150
			(2)	Borrowing from Bank of Venice		
BS (A+)		Cash			60	
	BS (L+)			Financial debt		60
			(3)	Purchasing equipment		
BS (A+)		Equipment			125	
	BS (A−)			Cash		125
			(4)	Sale to customer Sheila Burns		
BS (A+)		Accounts receivable			250	
	IS (R+)			Service revenue		250
			(5)	Partial settlement of accounts receivable by customer Burns		
BS (A+)		Cash			180	
	BS (A−)			Accounts receivable		180
			(6)	Payment of workers remuneration		
IS (E+)		Payroll expenses			101	
	BS (A−)			Cash		101
				Payment of interest on debt (Bank of Venice)		
IS (E+)		Interest expense			4	
	BS (A−)			Cash		4
				Purchases of services		
IS (E+)		External expense			85	
	BS (L+)			Accounts payable		85
			(7)	Partial settlement of accounts payable		
BS (L−)		Accounts payable			80	
	BS (A−)			Cash		80
			(8)	Partial reimbursement of debt principal		
BS (L−)		Financial debt			12	
	BS (A−)			Cash		12
					1,047	1,047

The abbreviations used in Table 3.4 are as follows:

BS	Balance sheet
IS	Income statement
A+	Increase in assets
A−	Decrease in assets
L+	Increase in shareholders' equity and liabilities
L−	Decrease in shareholders' equity and liabilities
R+	Increase in revenues
R−	Decrease in revenues
E+	Increase in expenses
E−	Decrease in expenses

- The two central columns in the journal are used for the names of the accounts debited or credited. By convention, the debited account(s) is (are) recorded first, to the left on the upper line, while the credited account(s) is (are) shown to the right on a line below (one single transaction may require that more than two accounts be used).

- The last two columns in the journal (one for debits and one for credits) show the amounts relevant to the entry.

Each transaction is described in words that allow the reader to understand the nature of the transaction and to identify the source document(s) (often numbered sequentially). The date of each transaction is also indicated in each entry, even if here, in this very simple illustration, we chose to omit the dates for reasons of simplicity.

The debit and credit columns must be totaled (the action of creating the total of a column is called 'footing'), and the absolute equality of the totals shows (and allows the accountant to verify) that double entry rules have been properly applied (the action of verifying the equality of the two totals is called 'cross footing'). At this stage, no error, not even a difference of one hundredth of a currency unit, can be tolerated. A difference between the totals of two columns would signal an error in recording since, for each entry, debits must equal credits.

The journal recording only recognizes the existence of the elements of the transaction. The subsequent steps will organize, classify and aggregate the data in significant groupings (as on the balance sheet, for example) allowing comparison with prior information from the same firm, or with industry benchmarks. This is done in ledgers.

2.2.4 Ledger

Any set of homogeneously defined accounts used in a business is called a **ledger**[2] or **specialized ledger**. For example, all accounts pertaining to sourcing transactions 'on credit' constitute, collectively, the payables ledger. A ledger is a classification category or the book in which it is recorded. It contains all the details of the relevant side of the journal entries and provides an ending balance, which is the net sum of all entries in this category.

The **general ledger** is the sum of all specialized numbered ledgers, each regrouping one relevant aspect of transactions (as defined by management in their quest for information assisting them in the effective and efficient running of the business – cash, purchases, sales, salaries, etc.). A specialized ledger is generally an 'intermediate' database, allowing the manager to analyze in detail that category of transactions. For example, the payables ledger will allow the management team to analyze their relationships with all or some categories of suppliers. The data recorded in the journal are integrally transcribed in the specialized ledgers and, ultimately, in the general ledger, still in chronological order in their category. Ledgers do not create data, they are the repository of data. Ledgers, however, reveal the informational content of data by creating (and archiving) meaningful aggregates. The advantage of a ledger is that, even if its current balance is zero (for example, its previous balance was – or all its transactions were – transferred to the general ledger), all its historical content is still available for further analysis if needed.

The process of transferring entries from the journal to the ledger is called '**posting**'. Each account debited or credited in the journal is thus transferred as a debit or credit of the relevant account in the general ledger and the specialized ledgers. Posting is a purely mechanical task, with no analysis required. Indeed, one of the first advantages of dedicated accounting software is that they automate this task, saving businesses considerable time and eliminating errors (see the later section on 'trial balance' below for further discussion of errors).

The above-described system transfers balances from the specialized ledgers to accounts in the general ledger. For example, all the individual accounts receivable (from the specialized ledger 'receivables' or 'customers') are transferred to a general (aggregated) account entitled 'accounts receivable' in the general ledger. However, with the ease of electronic database management, most modern accounting software have preserved the intent of unbending rigorousness offered by the process we described and freed themselves from practices dating back to manual bookkeeping by simplifying the actual data manipulation. The specialized ledgers are not 'transferred' to the general ledger but simply added, in a single 'ledger-like' database where all accounts are recorded, whether they would have been detailed or not in a specialized ledger (e.g., share capital, fixed assets, etc. do not always give rise to specialized ledgers in a traditional recording system and any transaction affecting them would be recorded directly in the general ledger). In this case, the large database can be considered the 'ledger' since it includes the traditional general ledger and all individual accounts appearing in the different specialized ledgers. If managers need a specialized analysis that would have required data from a specialized ledger, they simply extract the information they need from the ledger database. The process is simpler, but the logic is the same as the one used in the basic (essentially manual) system we described.

Table 3.5 shows Verdi Co.'s general ledger where each account (here the situation is extremely simplified) is listed according to their position in the financial statements.

2.2.5 Trial balance

Principle   Before establishing the financial statements, the accountant will prepare a '**trial balance**', which is simply a list of the debit and credit entries and footings for each account in the general ledger. The object of this exercise is to check that the sum of all the debit entries or balances is equal to the sum of all the credit entries or balances. In other words, it is the verification that 'total debits' = 'total credits'.

The format of the trial balance varies from one business (or software) to another. Table 3.6 illustrates a model of trial balance, using the Verdi Co. data.

Accounts are nearly always listed in the order of the company's account codes. To simplify matters, our example follows the order used in the financial statements of Verdi, i.e., asset accounts first, followed by equity and liabilities accounts in the upper portion of Table 3.6, expenses accounts and revenues accounts are listed sequentially in the lower part of the table.

The trial balance is used to verify two fundamental equations:

$$\text{Sum of debit entries} = \text{Sum of credit entries}$$
$$\text{Sum of debit balances} = \text{Sum of credit balances}$$

The initial purpose of the trial balance was a straightforward arithmetical verification. Above all, it was used to check that the amounts in the journal had been correctly manually copied (posted) into the ledger, and that the double entry rules had been applied properly. Today, thanks to the use of computer software, both the above equations are (fortunately) always mechanically verified. And yet – perhaps surprisingly – the trial balance is still established, for, essentially, the following two reasons:

1. It is a useful instrument in auditing accounts, since the trial balance reveals potential errors (accounts with an 'abnormal' type of balance, for instance a capital account with a debit balance or an equipment account with a credit balance – Table 3.7 lists 'normal' balances), and anomalies (for instance, balances that are higher or lower than usual, or than during a previous relevant period, accounts missing or wrongly included, etc.).

2. It provides a simple determination of the net profit/loss without having to establish a balance sheet or income statement. Whatever the system of codes attributed to the accounts, the trial balance generally comprises two distinct parts (as in Table 3.6): balance sheet accounts, followed by income statement accounts.

Table 3.5 Verdi Co.'s Ledgers

Balance sheet
(On the last day of accounting period X1)

| Assets | | | | Shareholders' equity and liabilities | | |

D	Equipment	C
125 (3)		
D balance = 125		

D	Capital	C
	150 (1)	
	C balance = 150	

D	Accounts receivable	C
250 (4)	180 (5)	
D balance = 70		

D	Financial debt	C
12 (8)	60 (2)	
	C balance = 48	

D	Cash	C
150 (1)	125 (3)	
60 (2)	101 (6)	
180 (5)	4 (6)	
390	80 (7)	
	12 (8)	
	322	
D balance = 68		

D	Accounts payable	C
80 (7)	85 (6)	
	C balance = 5	

Income statement
(For the accounting period X1)

| Expenses | | | | Revenues | | |

D	External expenses	C
85 (6)		
D balance = 85		

D	Sales	C
	250 (4)	
	C balance = 250	

D	Payroll expense	C
101 (6)		
D balance = 101		

D	Interest expense	C
4 (6)		
D balance = 4		

Numbers in parentheses next to the entry refer to the transaction number in the journal (see Table 3.4).
D = debit and C = credit.

Notes

1. For transactions with customers and suppliers, one account alone (a 'collective' or 'general' account) is not enough. These accounts must be subdivided into one account per customer and per supplier, and all individual customer and supplier accounts taken together form, respectively, the accounts receivable and accounts payable specialized ledgers (also called special or subsidiary ledgers).

2. The totals of each column of an account are called 'footings'. The difference between the debit footing and the credit footing is called the balance of the account.

3. For learning purposes, we chose to record transactions directly in T-accounts. Doing this has the advantage of providing a clear view of the impact of a transaction on each account.

4. In the summary of balance sheet accounts:
   - The total of debit balances (D) is 125 + 70 + 68 = 263
   - The total of credit balances (C) is 150 + 48 + 5 = 203
   - Therefore, since the total of debit balances and the total of credit balances must be equal, the 'shortfall' of 60, on the equity and liabilities side, must, by construction, correspond to the net income of the period.

5. In the summary of the income statement accounts:
   - The total of debit balances (D) is 85 + 101 + 4 = 190
   - The total of credit balances (C) is 250.
   - There is thus a positive net income of 60, which is by definition identical to the income found through the summary of the balance sheet debits and credits.

6. As expected, the amount (net profit/loss) to be added to the shareholders' equity is the same regardless of whether one uses the balance sheet or the income statement approach. It was easy in our example to calculate the net profit/loss both ways because very few accounts were involved. When a business' accounts comprise thousands of individual accounts, the transcription of their balances in the trial balance is the primary tool of internal control.

Table 3.6 Verdi Co. Trial balance

	Accounts	Entries		Balances	
		Debit	Credit	Debit	Credit
Balance sheet	Equipment	125		125	
	Accounts receivable	250	180	70	
	Cash	390	322	68	
	Capital		150		150
	Financial debt	12	60		48
	Accounts payable	80	85		5
Income statement	External expenses	85		85	
	Payroll expenses	101		101	
	Interest expense	4		4	
	Sales		250		250
	Total	1,047	1,047	453	453

Table 3.7 Examples of 'normal' account balances (This list is in no way exhaustive)

Accounts	Debit	Credit
Assets	**x**	
Set up expenses	x	
Land	x	
Plant, machinery or office equipment	x	
Accumulated depreciation of plant, machinery or office equipment		x
Investments	x	
Provision for depreciation of investments		x
Deposits and guarantees	x	
Merchandise inventories (inventories of goods acquired for resale)	x	
Provision for depreciation of merchandise		x
Accounts receivable	x	
Doubtful accounts receivable	x	
Provision for doubtful accounts receivable		x
Advance payments made to suppliers	x	
Income tax receivable	x	
Prepaid rent	x	
Cash at bank	x	
Cash in hand	x	
Shareholders' equity		
Share capital		x
Retained earnings (or reserves)		x
Losses brought forward	x	
Profits brought forward		x

Table 3.7 *(Continued)*

Liabilities		**x**
Long-term debt or bonds		x
Short-term debt or bonds payable		x
Bank overdrafts		x
Accounts payable		x
Advance payments received from customers		x
Salaries payable		x
Revenues		**x**
Sales of merchandise (goods purchased for resale)		x
Sales of finished products		x
Changes in finished (manufactured) products inventories (two possible normal balances)	x	x
Other trade revenues		x
Financial income		x
Exceptional revenues (or extraordinary revenue items)		x
Expenses	**x**	
Purchases of merchandise	x	
Change in merchandise inventory (two possible normal balances)	x	x
Purchases of raw materials (RM), parts and components (P&C)	x	
Change in RM, P&C inventories (two possible normal balances)	x	x
Cost of goods sold	x	
Selling and marketing expenses	x	
General and administrative expenses	x	
R&D expense	x	
External services – electricity, utilities	x	
Insurance and other services	x	
Miscellaneous payroll taxes	x	
Wages and salaries	x	
License fees	x	
Financial expense and interest	x	
Exceptional expenses (or extraordinary expense items)	x	

The following equations permit a rapid calculation of the income of the period:

Using only Balance sheet accounts:
'Sum of debit balances' minus 'Sum of credit balances' = Net income
Using only Income statement accounts:
'Sum of credit balances' minus 'Sum of debit balances' = Net income.

Table 3.6 was structured in this way. The net profit/loss is thus determined as follows:

Using only Balance sheet accounts: Debit balances − Credit balances = 263 − 203 = 60
Using only Income statement accounts: Credit balances − Debit balances = 250 − 190 = 60.

Figure 3.7 above showed, with a thin arrow, that the trial balance could, technically, be bypassed in the preparation of the financial statements, thus allowing the accountant to go directly from the ledgers to the financial statements. However, such a solution is not recommended because it sidesteps the essential internal control usage of the trial balance. Even if arithmetic errors are now technically impossible with the use of computers, the trial balance still will be used effectively to detect errors of entry or of logic in the choice of accounts used, which could be revealed, for example, by the unexpected algebraic sign of an account balance. The normal directionality of account balances is illustrated below (see also Appendix 3.2).

Trial balance errors Appendix 3.2 provides some explanations regarding errors which might be found in a trial balance.

2.2.6 Financial statements

The establishment of the financial statements is the final stage of the accounting process. We have already discussed financial statements, principally in section 1 above. Some operations are undertaken specifically to establish the year-end financial statements. These are known as 'end-of-period entries', and are discussed in Chapter 4.

Going back to the example of Verdi Co., we have a balance sheet on 31 December X1 (see Table 2.3 in Chapter 2) that summarizes the debit balances on the asset side (excess of debits over credits) and the credit balances on the liabilities side (excess of credits over debits) and an income statement for the accounting period X1 (see Tables 2.6 through 2.8 in Chapter 2).

As we have seen, thanks to the double entry system, it is possible to establish both the balance sheet and the income statement at the same time. The balance sheet registers the profit of 60 CU, and the income statement explains how it was obtained.

3 Organization of the accounting system: The chart of accounts

The accounts kept by a business serve three essential purposes:

1. They constitute legal evidence, and as such, must be easily accessible to controllers (e.g., tax inspectors or auditors) and comply with laws and regulations.

2. They are instruments for business management. For example, the accounts payable should tell, with accuracy and timeliness, how much the company owes each of its suppliers; or the accounts receivable should reflect how much is owed by each of its customers, etc.

3. They are a source of management information. The accounting process, and the accounts that comprise it, allow reports on value creation (or subsets thereof, such as sales by market segment or costs by nature) at any desired interval, including the minimum legally required annual financial statements.

To be effective, the organization of the accounting system must therefore strike the best balance between these objectives or constraints, and the related operating costs. Appendix 3.3 provides some developments on the organization of the accounting system, in terms of timing, specialized journals and computer software. It also describes the accounting function within the company.

Accounting systems usually include a **chart of accounts**: a pre-established, logically organized list of all recognized (and authorized) accounts used in recording all transactions the firm can engage in. A chart of accounts generally assigns a unique code to each account.

3.1 Principles

As indicated earlier, each account must be identified by a name or, most frequently, by a code. Several coding methods are possible, mainly: Alphabetical, Numerical and Alphanumerical. Each account's unique code is necessary for quick reference in processing transactions to the accounts, and is absolutely vital for computer-based information technology (IT) systems.

Alphabetical coding appears, at first glance, to be the simplest to use: no numbers to remember, and only the names of the accounts to know, generally in natural language. But in practice, it is not necessarily such a good solution, because:

■ It proved in the past to be complicated for programming IT systems;

■ It may prove to be time-consuming to enter the full name of an account, unless the name is given a shortcut name, a double-edged sword which may make matters more complex again;

■ Each account must have a specific name, and no variants (such as spelling errors or unspecified abbreviations) can be recognized. The practical difficulties associated with natural language codes have made pure alphabetical coding rather uncommon.

For these reasons, account codes are almost always numerical or alphanumerical. For example, 'accounts receivable' might be coded 142, and account '142Soprano' (a subsidiary account of account 142 referring to customer Soprano) would be used to record sales transactions with the Soprano Family businesses, whereas '142Tessitura' would be used to record sales transactions with Tessitura Inc.

In general, charts of accounts are based on a hierarchical classification, in which key classes or groups of accounts are first identified, and then subdivided as the need requires. There can be as many subclasses or nested subdivisions as the company requires. Figure 3.8 illustrates one possible chart of accounts.

3.2 Standardized chart of accounts

In countries including Belgium, France, Portugal, Spain and many African countries, the overall structure of the accounts code is laid down nationally, whilst in other countries the choice of structure is left entirely up to company management (e.g., Italy, the Netherlands, Switzerland, the UK and the US).

3.3 The importance of account codes

As stated above, some countries (but in no way a majority) have a standardized chart of accounts, while most other countries let the company decide on its own chart. Although the debate over standardization of charts of accounts is not a fundamental issue, the proponents of national standardized charts argue that:

Figure 3.8 A possible chart of accounts

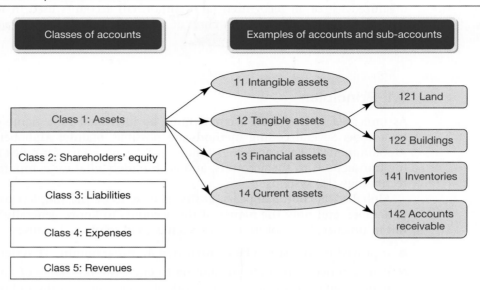

- it facilitates the mobility of qualified accountants since all firms use the same basic account structure;
- it reduces the cost of designing accounting software packages;
- it facilitates intercompany comparability of published accounts.

The internal logic of a hierarchical numbering of accounts allows an immediate understanding of the nature and role of an account, often in a clearer way than words might. For example, an account called 'fees' can be unclear as it may refer either to fees received or to fees paid. If the account is numbered '4xxx-Fees' (using the basic chart of accounts introduced in Figure 3.8) it is clearly fees paid, while if the code is '5yyy-Fees', it unambiguously refers to fees received. The numerical part of the account allows for further decomposition into subsidiary accounts when needed. Any large organization with multiple establishments, plants and/or subsidiaries is sooner or later forced to create its own internal standardized chart of accounts (applicable throughout the world) to allow managerial discussions and facilitate consolidation (regrouping of subsidiaries' financial positions, cash flows, and income into the parent company accounts).

The list of codes chosen either nationally or by any one firm has no intrinsic meaning and no classification is superior to any other. What matters is that the users understand the reasons for the choices made. We deliberately chose, in this book, to de-emphasize the use of codes in referring to accounts since there is no international standardization of charts of account.

Key points

- The statement of cash flows records all the transactions affecting cash during the period. It reflects the effects of timing differences existing between the recognition of revenues and expenses and their impact on cash. It excludes any transaction affecting the income statement only.
- In order to prepare its financial statements, a business needs to set up an organized accounting process supported by an accounting system made up of a set of accounts and of pre defined rules of assignment of the effects of transactions to these accounts.
- By convention, the left-hand side of any account is called the debit side, and the right-hand side the credit side.
- Each accounting transaction has its origin in a source document.

- The source document serves as the basis for making a descriptive entry in a journal.
- The journal provides a chronological list of the transactions. After journalizing accounting entries, they are posted in the specialized ledgers and the general ledger where the components of the description of the transaction are structured by nature and/or type of transaction.
- The general ledger is the preliminary step to the establishment of the two main financial statements (balance sheet and income statement).
- Detailed individual accounts entries are grouped together and replaced by the balance of the aggregated account, and recapitulated in the trial balance.
- All companies use a chart of accounts, i.e., a predetermined structured list of accepted account codes.

Review (solutions are at the back of the book)

Review 3.1 Beethoven Company (1)

Topic: Link between balance sheet, income statement and statement of cash flows (Income statement by nature)

Beethoven Company, a limited liability company that was incorporated in X1, has a commercial activity. It buys and sells books and CDs devoted to the learning of foreign languages. (The founder of the company speaks at least 10 languages fluently.)

The balance sheet as at 31 December X1 is presented below.

Balance sheet as at 31 December X1 (in 000 CU)			
Assets		Shareholders' equity and liabilities	
Fixed assets		*Shareholders' equity*	
Equipment (net value)	800	Capital	710
		Accumulated retained earnings	300
		Net income for X1[a]	216
Current assets		*Liabilities*	
Merchandise inventory	150	Financial debt	110
Accounts receivable[b]	400	Accounts payable[c]	120
Cash at bank	250	Income tax payable[c]	144
Total	1,600	Total	1,600

[a] To be appropriated in X2: one third will be distributed.

[b] To be received in X2.

[c] To be paid in X2.

The following budgeted activities are envisaged for the year X2 (in 000 CU):

1. Sales budget: 1,600 (1,400 in cash will be received from customers during the year)

2. Purchases budget (merchandise): 510 (400 will be paid cash to suppliers during the year)

3. Planned merchandise-ending inventory: 130

4. Finance budget: repayment of financial debt for 80

5. Salaries and social expenses budget: 430 (entirely paid before the end of the year)

6. Advertising expenses budget: 250 (entirely paid before the end of the year)

7. Miscellaneous taxes budget (other than income tax): 120 (entirely paid before the end of the year)

8. Additional fixed assets will be purchased: 300 (entirely paid before the end of the year)

9. Budgeted depreciation expense: 40

The income tax rate is 40%. (taxes are paid in the year following that for which the income is calculated)

Required

Prepare the following documents: balance sheet, income statement and cash flow budget (forecasted statement of cash flows) for the year X2.

Review 3.2 Beethoven Company (2)

Topic: Link between balance sheet, income statement, and statement of cash flows (Income statement by function).

Required

Referring to Review 3.1 Beethoven Company (1), prepare the three documents: balance sheet, income statement, and cash flow budget (forecasted statement of cash flows) for the year X2 integrating the following additional information: salaries and social expenses budget (430, paid during the year) is split between 300 for sales persons and 130 for administration staff.

The income statement will be presented by function. For the sake of simplicity, because we are dealing with a multi-period situation, we choose, rather than entering into cost accounting discussions, to consider, in this exercise, that all depreciation is charged to the income statement as a single item after all other operating expenses.

All figures are in 000 CU unless otherwise specified.

Review 3.3 Grieg Company (1)

Topic: The accounting process: from the journal to the financial statements (purchases of merchandise are recorded first in inventory)

The Grieg Company was incorporated on 1 January X1. Grieg had five holders of share capital. The following events occurred during January X1.

1. The company was incorporated. Common shareholders invested a total of 10,000 CU cash.

2. Equipment valued at 1,200 CU was acquired for cash.

3. Merchandise inventory was purchased on credit for 9,000 CU.

4. Cash was borrowed from a bank, 500 CU.

5. Merchandise carried in inventory at a cost of 7,000 CU was sold for 11,000 CU (cash for 6,000 CU and on credit for 5,000 CU).

6. Collection of the above accounts receivable, 4,000 CU.

7. Payment of accounts payable, 8,000 CU (see transaction 3).

8. Depreciation expense of 120 CU was recognized.

Required

1. Prepare an analysis of Grieg Company's transactions and record the entries in the journal, *assuming that the purchases of merchandise are first recorded in inventory* (see Chapter 2).

2. Post the entries to the ledger, entering your postings by transaction number.

3. Prepare a trial balance, as of 31 January X1.

4. Prepare a balance sheet as of 31 January X1, and an income statement for the month of January.

Review 3.4 Grieg Company (2)

Topic: The accounting process: from the journal to the financial statements (purchases of merchandise are first recorded in the income statement)

The Grieg Company was incorporated on 1 January X1. Grieg had five holders of share capital.

Required

1. Prepare an analysis of Grieg Company's transactions (see Review 3.3) and record the entries in the journal, *assuming that the purchases of merchandise are first recorded in the income statement* (see Chapter 2). You are informed that ending inventory was valued at cost, i.e., 2,000 CU.

2. Post the entries to the ledger, entering your postings by transaction number.

3. Prepare a trial balance, as of 31 January X1.

4. Prepare a balance sheet as of 31 January X1, and an income statement for the month of January.

Assignments

Assignment 3.1
Multiple-choice questions

Select the right answer (only one possible answer unless otherwise stated).

1. The balance sheet emphasizes the dynamics of the cash flowing in and out of the business

   (a) True
   (b) False

2. The balance sheet offers a dynamic vision of the financial position

   (a) True
   (b) False

3. The choice made of the _____ approach for the recognition of revenues and expenses creates a need for the statement of cash flows

   (a) Cash
   (b) Prudence
   (c) Valuation
   (d) Accrual
   (e) None of these

4. The statement of cash flows consists of the following sections

   (a) Operating and non-operating
   (b) Current and non-current
   (c) Operating, investing and financing
   (d) Trading and financial
   (e) Operating, financing and investing
   (f) None of these

5. What does the cash balance in the opening balance sheet represent in the statement of cash flows?

   (a) It is not used in the statement of cash flows
   (b) The opening cash balance
   (c) The closing cash balance
   (e) None of these

6. By convention, the right-hand side of a T-account is called

   (a) Debt side
   (b) Cash side
   (c) Debit side
   (d) Credit side
   (e) None of these

7. In terms of debit and credit, expenses accounts function in a similar way to

   (a) Liabilities accounts
   (b) Assets accounts
   (c) Shareholders' equity accounts
   (d) Revenues accounts

8. Banks use the terms 'debit' and 'credit' to mean the opposite of what a business records

   (a) True
   (b) False

9. Which of the following statements is true?

   (a) If you increase an asset account, you could increase a liability account
   (b) If you increase a liability account, you could decrease a shareholders' equity account
   (c) If you increase an asset account, you could decrease another asset account
   (d) All of these

10. A supporting document serves as the basis for an entry in a

   (a) Trial balance
   (b) Journal
   (c) Financial statement
   (d) Ledger
   (e) None of these

Assignment 3.2

Industry identification[3]

Common-size statements (see more on this concept in Chapters 2, 15 and 16) and selected ratio values, related to the same financial year, are provided in Exhibit 1 for six well-known French companies. The name and some characteristics of these companies are given in Exhibit 2.

Required

Use your knowledge of general business practices to match the industries to the company data.

Exhibit 1: Common-size consolidated balance sheets						
Company	A %	B %	C %	D %	E %	F %
Balance sheet						
Assets						
Intangible fixed assets	10.4	10.6	25.4	4.6	69.1	2.6
Tangible fixed assets (net)	20.9	40.9	33.1	19.0	7.7	35.7
Financial fixed assets	2.3	10.6	6.0	0.7	4.4	3.6
Inventories	47.7	2.4	16.0	30.7	4.0	17.7
Accounts receivable	1.4	14.5	7.8	27.1	5.9	18.1
Other receivables	14.1	7.4	4.2	6.4	5.7	12.1
Cash	3.2	13.6	7.5	11.5	3.2	10.2
Total assets	100.0	100.0	100.0	100.0	100.0	100.0
Equity and liabilities						
Capital and reserves	31.5	17.3	17.8	24.7	51.5	25.7
Net income	−2.7	2.9	3.6	2.0	−4.7	3.2
Provisions for risks	1.3	23.3	4.5	3.2	7.5	18.5
Financial liabilities	24.8	31.9	24.9	43.9	20.9	30.2
Accounts payable	33.9	20.2	36.8	13.9	3.6	9.9
Other debts	11.2	4.4	12.4	12.3	21.2	12.5
Total equity and liabilities	100.0	100.0	100.0	100.0	100.0	100.0
Financial ratios						
Net income/sales (%)	−1.5	4.4	1.9	1.5	−24.0	3.3
Sales/total assets (%)	182.0	65.0	186.0	131.0	20.0	97.0
Salaries and social charges/total assets (%)	27.0	12.0	17.0	22.0	n/a	30.0
Average collection period (days)	2.7	81.6	5.3	75.5	109.2	67.9

Exhibit 2: Name and characteristics of the companies
(Based on WVB Business Summaries and Multex Business Summaries – Source: www.infinancials.com)

Carrefour Group

Carrefour is a French company, incorporated in 1959, primarily engaged in retail distribution. The company manages hypermarkets, supermarkets, hard discounters, convenience stores, and cash-and-carry and food service. Headquartered near Paris, the company is present in 35 countries worldwide. It has enjoyed a dazzling growth with a high level of profitability before plateauing in 2009.

Go Sport Group

Go Sport retails sports shoes, sportsgear and related accessories. It operates 160 *Go Sport* stores and 240 *Courir* shops mostly located in shopping malls in Europe and the Middle East. Products sold include all leading sports brands, such as Nike, adidas, Timberland and Ellesse.

Michelin Group

The main activity of this global company is the production and sale of tires. The company distributes its products in 177 countries under several brand names, including Michelin, Kleber, BF Goodrich, Uniroyal, Riken, Taurus and Warrior. It manages important capital investments in 19 countries. Despite the recession, it has maintained a higher level of profitability than most of its competitors.

Sanofi-Aventis

Sanofi-Aventis, formerly known as Sanofi-Synthélabo, is a pharmaceutical group engaged in the research, development, manufacture and marketing of healthcare products. The company's business includes two activities: pharmaceutical (prescription drugs) and human vaccines; the latter is conducted through its wholly-owned subsidiary, Sanofi Pasteur (formerly Aventis Pasteur). On 20 August 2004, Sanofi-Synthélabo acquired control of Aventis. On 31 December 2004, Aventis merged with and into the company. The group manages a large portfolio of patents.

Skis Rossignol

Well-known by skiers, Skis Rossignol SA, together with its subsidiaries, operates in the sporting goods sector, with its focus on the winter sports business. The company manufactures winter sporting goods, and offers a full range of products for all disciplines (alpine, Nordic and snowboard) and all product families (boards, bindings, boots and poles). Its product range also includes textile goods and accessories. Its growth is supported by important capital investment.

GDF Suez

One of the leading energy providers in the world, GDF Suez is active, worldwide, across the entire energy value chain, in electricity and natural gas, upstream to downstream. It develops its businesses (energy, energy services and environment) around a responsible-growth model to take up the great challenges: responding to energy needs, ensuring the security of supply, fighting against climate change and optimizing the use of resources.

Assignment 3.3

Schumann Company (1)

Topic: Link between balance sheet, income statement, and statement of cash flows (Income statement by nature)
The Schumann Company is a small-sized business that makes and sells computers on a limited national market. The balance sheet at 31 December X1 is presented below.

Balance sheet at 31 December X1 (in 000 CU)			
Assets			Shareholders' equity and liabilities
Fixed assets		*Shareholders' equity*	
Equipment (net value)	600	Capital	500
		Accumulated retained earnings	200
Current assets		Net income for X1[a]	168
Inventories			
■ Raw materials	80	*Liabilities*	
■ Finished products	120	Financial debt	100
Accounts receivable[b]	140	Accounts payable[c]	110
Cash at bank	250	Income tax payable[c]	112
Total	1,190	Total	1,190

[a] To be appropriated in X2: one half will be distributed.

[b] To be received in X2.

[c] To be paid in X2.

The following budgeted (anticipated) activities are considered for period X2 (000 CU):

1. Sales budget: 1,300 (1,140 in cash will be received from customers during the year).

2. Purchases budget (raw materials): 520 (380 will be paid cash to suppliers during the year).

3. Rental expenses budget: 220 (entirely paid before the end of year).

4. Estimated property taxes: 100 (entirely paid before the end of year).

5. Remunerations and social charges budget: 400 (entirely paid before the end of year).

6. Financing budget: repayment of financial debt for 60. Interest expense: 10 (entirely paid before the end of year).

7. Investment budget: acquisition of fixed assets for 200 (entirely paid before the end of year).

8. Budgeted depreciation expense: 20.

9. New shares will be floated on 1 January X2. The net proceeds, all in cash amount to 100, received from old and new shareholders.

10. Budgeted inventory level:
    - Finished products ending inventory: 140
    - Raw materials ending inventory: 120.

The income tax rate is 40% (taxes are paid in the year following that for which the income is calculated).

Required

Prepare the following forecasted or *pro forma* documents: balance sheet, income statement (or P&L) and cash flow budget (forecasted statement of cash flows) for the year X2.

Assignment 3.4
Schumann Company (2)

Topic: Link between balance sheet, income statement, and statement of cash flows (Income statement by function)

Required

Referring to Assignment 3.3 Schumann Company (1), prepare the three documents: balance sheet, income statement and cash flow budget (forecasted statement of cash flows) for the year X2 integrating the following additional information: the rental expense is related to the factory site and the item 'remunerations and social expenses' budget (400, paid during the year) can be separated between production activities for 300 and sales and administration activities for 100.

The income statement will be presented by function. For the sake of simplicity, because we are dealing with a multi-period situation, we choose, rather than entering into cost accounting discussions, to consider, in this exercise, that all depreciation is charged to the income statement as a single item after all other operating expenses.

Assignment 3.5
Bach Company

Topic: Link between balance sheet, income statement, and statement of cash flows – notion of management

1 – Introduction

Bach Company is used in a simulation exercise, carried out in teams. It is intended to give realistic training in the use of accounting and financial statement for decision-making, use of concepts, language and the preparation of financial documents. To this end, the participants in the simulation are expected to prepare balance sheets, income statements and cash flow budgets/statement of cash flows deriving from their decisions. All decisions, notably production and sourcing volumes, are made on a yearly basis and, once decided on, are not modifiable. Although each team decides on its intended sales volume (and all corollary decisions to make this estimation materialize) the *actual* volume of sales is not selected by the team and is determined externally, for each team, by the instructor.

2 – Your company and its market (each firm operates under these conditions)

On 1 January X7, each team takes responsibility for the management of a firm called Bach-n, where n is the identifier of the team. On day 1 of period X7, all Bach Co. firms in the simulation are identical to all the other ones. Each firm is a rather small-sized business. It designs, assembles and sells hairdryers on a limited domestic market. At the beginning of the simulation, the market is shared equally, between five companies, all of similar size.[4]

The overall market for the year X7 is estimated to be about 500,000 units (see endnote 4). It is reasonable to anticipate that the total market size will increase or decrease, beyond X7 at a trend average rate of about $x\%$ per year (where x is decided by the instructor), but this will depend on the decisions taken by each firm in such matters as the selling price and its evolution for the firm, advertising and marketing expenses and so on. The market is extremely sensitive to prices and to marketing expenses (in a down-market, for example, the firm with the highest marketing and sales expenses might see its market share grow, and, maybe, even its sales volume grow, even if the overall market is shrinking).

3 – Manufacturing equipment (same initial conditions apply to each firm)

On the opening date (1 January X7), the production capacity of each firm consists of nine assembly lines. Each one can assemble a maximum of 10,000 dryers per year. An additional assembly line would represent

an investment of 50,000 CU. It would be depreciated over five years using the straight-line method, which implies a yearly depreciation expense of 10,000 CU for each new line acquired. Old lines, in this fictitious world with no inflation, were acquired, at different times, at the same price of 50,000 CU per line. They have been depreciated using the straight-line method on the basis of a useful life of five years.

The existing equipment (nine assembly lines) is broken down, for each company, as follows (values are in thousands of CU):

# of lines		Years operated		Gross value		Accumulated depreciation		Net book value
2	Lines	4 years	Their accounting	(2 × 50)	−	(2 × 40)	=	(2 × 10)
3	which have	3 years	book value is	(3 × 50)	−	(3 × 30)	=	(3 × 20)
3	already	2 years	therefore	(3 × 50)	−	(3 × 20)	=	(3 × 30)
1	operated for	1 year		50	−	10	=	40

Each company may invest (on January 1) in as many new assembly lines as it feels is necessary to achieve its business plan. Each new assembly line is operational immediately in the period of purchase. All purchases are assumed to take place at the beginning of the period and therefore a new line increases the capacity of production by 10,000 units. Once an assembly line is fully depreciated, it is scrapped and has neither residual value nor production capabilities.

4 – Inventories (same conditions apply to each firm)

The firms acquire from outside suppliers the motors and parts, which enter into the assembly of the hair

dryers. There is no risk of shortage of motors or parts and there is no competition to access the parts and motors markets. The motors are purchased for a cost of 8 CU per unit in X7 (each dryer requires one motor). The various other parts are acquired at a cost of 10 CU in X7 for a set of parts allowing the assembly of one dryer. The total material cost is therefore 18 CU for each hairdryer.

On 1 January X7, each company holds an inventory on hand of motors and parts which allows the production of 10,000 hairdryers without any additional purchases. In addition, the company has 5,000 finished dryers in inventory, ready for delivery, whose unit direct cost (materials and labor) amounts to 27 CU, calculated as follows:

Motor, per unit		8
Parts, per unit		10
Direct labor		
Annual salary cost of one worker	18,000 CU	
Number of dryers made in a year (per worker)	2,000	
Labor cost of one dryer		9
Total cost		**27**

5 – Personnel (same conditions apply to each firm)

As of 1 January X7, 50 employees are working on the production lines in each firm. Each worker can normally assemble up to 2,000 hairdryers in a year. As far as production is concerned, each company can hire additional personnel or dismiss redundant workers. Every dismissal must first be notified to an Inspector from the Ministry of Labor who may refuse the lay-off,

and will be subject to the payment, to the worker, of a cash indemnity equivalent to four months of salary. No social charges will be applied to this indemnity. Dismissals are presumed to take place at the beginning of the period in which they take place. (The indemnity is consequently based on the salary before any increase.)

In X7 the minimum annual salary is 12,000 CU per assembly worker. In addition to the salary, the employer must pay social charges (healthcare, retirement, unemployment, vacations, etc.) amounting to 50% of the employee's remuneration. Thus the total labor cost incurred by the firm is 18,000 CU per year for each employee. In each successive period, the management of each company is free to raise the base pay by whichever amount it feels is necessary.

Management, selling and administrative personnel as a whole receive a total remuneration amounting to 200,000 CU per year in X7. Once social charges are added at the rate of 50%, the payroll cost to the employer for management, selling and administrative personnel is 300,000 CU. This category of personnel will benefit from any percentage increase granted to production workers. Thus, the per person payroll cost for both assembly production personnel and management, selling and administrative personnel would increase, in a firm, by the exact same proportion if a raise were decided by management. The management, selling and administrative personnel fulfills essential functions in the company and cannot be dismissed, regardless of the level of activity. Unlike the manual labor used in assembly work, this category of personnel uses a lot of computerized and automated routines and could handle a significant increase in the workload without requiring any new hiring.

6 – Financing (same conditions apply to all firms)

The opening balance sheet shown below indicates that the shareholders have paid-in 250,000 CU of share capital and that the company has realized profits in the past since the accumulated retained earnings amount to 110,000 CU.

A debt of 200,000 CU was contracted in the first days of X4 with interest payable at the annual rate of 8%. It is repayable on 31 December X8. The interest is due every 12 months on the last day of the accounting period. The amount of any new (medium or long-term) debt financing a firm may require for its planned activities would have to be negotiated in light of justified needs.

The banker(s) or the shareholders must pre-approve any request for additional debt financing or issuance of new capital. Their final decision can only be taken after they have been provided with the firm *pro forma* financial statements and they have been able to review the financial situation of your company.

'Temporary' financial needs can be covered by short-term overdrafts granted by the bank. Interest is charged at the rate of 10% on the amount of overdraft calculated on the last day of the accounting period and is payable immediately.

Balance sheet at 31 December X6 (000 CU)			
Assets		Shareholders' equity and liabilities	
Fixed assets		*Shareholders' equity*	
Manufacturing equipment (net)	210	Capital	250
Gross value: 450		Accumulated retained earnings	110
Accumulated depreciation: 240		Net income X6 (to be appropriated in X7)	100
Current assets			
Inventories		*Liabilities*	
Raw materials (18 × 10,000)	180	Debt 8% X4 (due 31/12/X8)	200
Finished products (27 × 5,000)	135	Accounts payable	235
Accounts receivable	350	Income tax payable	50
Cash at bank	70		
Total	945	**Total**	945

7 – Other purchases and external expenses (yearly amounts, applicable to each firm)

- Each firm rents its factory buildings for 300,000 CU per year. (The offices of the administration and sales team are generously provided for free by one of the firm's major shareholders.)

- Property taxes (non-income related) amount to 40,000 CU.

The amount of other expenses, such as advertising, marketing and promotion expenses, will result from the team's decisions. For the sake of simplicity in the simulation, expenses of this nature are expressed, here, as a percentage of total costs (excluding advertising expenses); for instance: commercial costs, excluding remuneration of the sales force, can be decided by the team as being any figure between at least 2% and 5% (or more). Future sales are sensitive to the level of spending for market development and maintenance.

8 – Credit conditions (same conditions apply to all firms)

Investments in manufacturing equipment, all personnel expenditure, other purchases and external expenses are paid cash during the accounting period concerned.

90% of the value of the purchases of motors and parts are paid cash in the period concerned and the remaining 10% (debt to suppliers) are paid in the immediately following period.

Customers pay the company 85% of the invoiced value of the sale in the period during which delivery takes place. The credit sales amount is therefore 15% of sales revenue. Credit sales are included in accounts receivable and will be settled in the following accounting period.

9 – Income tax and dividends (same conditions apply to all firms)

If the income statement shows a profit, it is assessed for income tax purposes at a rate of 40%. Income tax is due to the State at the end of the year and paid the following year. No fixed minimum income tax is due when the company incurs a loss. Unlike in the real world, losses in previous years cannot be used to offset current taxable income.

The net after tax income may be distributed wholly or partially as a dividend to shareholders. The amount of the dividend (if any) distributed during any year cannot exceed the income of the preceding year, i.e., it has been agreed by shareholders that, once earnings have been retained, they should not be distributed.

10 – Decisions to be taken by the Board

See Appendix 1.

11 – Procedure for a one-year simulation

(a) Prepare the batch of budgeted documents (balance sheet, income statement, and cash flow forecast) to test the validity of your decisions (see Appendix 2).

(b) Hand in your decision sheet to the instructor.

(c) The instructor will advise each firm of the volume of its actual sales for the period. This amount is a maximum figure. If a business has not planned to produce enough to meet the revealed demand, that firm's sales will be limited to the quantities available for shipment (production of the period plus available beginning inventory). The calculation of the potential maximum sales available to any firm reflects the decisions taken by both the firm itself and its competitors.

(d) Once each firm knows its actual demand, each management team will prepare the resulting definitive accounting documents (balance sheet, income statement [or P&L], statement of cash flows), which will be presented to the shareholders. These documents have to be certified by the statutory auditor (see Appendix 2).

The instructor can ask the student teams to present the income statement or P&L either by nature (Appendix 2a) or by function (Appendix 2b). All the necessary information is included in the text of the case and the ready-lined Appendices 2a and 2b can help the students. For the sake of simplicity, because we are dealing with a multi-period situation, we choose, rather than entering into cost accounting discussions, to consider, in this exercise, that all depreciation is charged to the income statement as a single item after all other operating expenses and that unit manufacturing cost is, thus, essentially comprised of only materials and labor.

| NAME OF THE FIRM BACH _____ | | YEAR | |

Appendix 1: Decision sheet

1   ***Sales***

1.1   Unit sales price (in CU)

1.2   Quantities you intend to sell

2   ***Production*** *(these decisions are not modifiable once handed in)*

2.1   Investment (number of acquired new assembly lines)

2.2   Number of operational assembly lines: existing lines at the end of the previous period minus fully depreciated lines at the end of the previous period plus newly acquired lines = number of productive lines available this period

2.3   Production you will launch (quantity of hairdryers)

2.4   Outside purchases of motors and parts (quantity)

2.5   Consumption of motors and parts (quantity) (hopefully equal to quantity in 2.3)

3   ***Personnel*** *(these decisions are not modifiable once handed in)*

3.1   New hires (number of persons)

3.2   Personnel dismissed (number of persons)

3.3   Annual total remuneration (excluding employers' social security charges) – in CU per employee [Do not forget any salary increase, if applicable]

4   ***External expenses (in 000 CU)*** *(these decisions are not modifiable once handed in)*

4.1   Budget for advertising, marketing and promotion

4.2   Auditing fees (of the past year)

5   ***Dividends and others (in 000 CU)*** *(these decisions are not modifiable once handed in)*

5.1   Dividends distributed

5.2   Profit not distributed (and transferred to retained earnings)

5.3   Increase of capital in cash (on the basis of approval by shareholders)

5.4   Increase of capital by incorporation of retained earnings (on the basis of approval by shareholders)

5.5   New debt received (according to agreements made)

5.6   Interest expense on bank overdraft (of the past year)

Appendix 2a: Summary Financial Statements (income statement by nature)

FIRM: BACH _____   YEAR

CASH FLOW BUDGET/STATEMENT (in 000 CU)

Opening balance (1) . . . .
Cash flows from operating activities
Cash from sales: 85% of sales revenue . . . .
Cash from receivables (see preceding balance sheet) . . . .
Cash purchases: 90% of annual purchases . . . .
Accounts payable: 90% of preceding balance sheet) . . . .
Income tax payable . . . .
Other taxes . . . .
Personnel expenses . . . .
Rent expense . . . .
Advertising and commercial expenses . . . .
Auditing fees . . . .
Financial expenses . . . .

Net cash flows from operating activities (2) . . . .

Cash flows from investing activities
Investments (assembly lines) . . . .

Net cash flows used in investing activities (3) . . . .

Cash flows from financing activities
Increase in capital . . . .
New debt . . . .
Repayment of debt . . . .
Dividends paid . . . .

Net cash flows used in financing activities (4) . . . .

Net increase (decrease) in cash (5) = (2) + (3) + (4)

Ending balance (6) = (1) + (5)

INCOME STATEMENT (in 000 of CU)

Operating expenses		**Operating revenues**	
Purchases of motors and parts	. . .	Sales	. . .
Change in inventory of raw materials (B-E)	. . .	Change in inventories of finished products (E-B)	. . .
External expenses	. . .	(Where E = ending and B = beginning)	
Property taxes	. . .		
Personnel expenses	. . .		
Depreciation allowance for the period	. . .		
Financial expenses	. . .	**Financial income**	. . .
Exceptional expenses	. . .	**Exceptional income**	. . .
Subtotal	. . .	Subtotal	. . .
Income tax	. . .		
Net income	. . .	Net loss	
Total		Total	

BALANCE SHEET (in 000 of CU)

	Beg	+	–	End		Beg	–	+	End
Fixed assets					*Shareholders' equity*				
Manufacturing equip. (net)	. . .	. . .	. . .	. . .	Capital	. . .	. . .	. . .	. . .
Current assets					Retained earnings	. . .	. . .	. . .	. . .
Inventories					Net income/loss	. . .	. . .	. . .	. . .
Motors and parts	. . .	. . .	. . .	. . .	Subtotal	. . .	. . .	. . .	. . .
Finished products	. . .	. . .	. . .	. . .	*Liabilities*				
Accounts receivable (15% of sales revenue)	. . .	. . .	. . .	. . .	Debt 8% X4 (due end of X8)	. . .	. . .	. . .	. . .
					Bank overdraft	. . .	. . .	. . .	. . .
Cash at bank	. . .	. . .	. . .	. . .	Accounts payable (10% of purchases)	. . .	. . .	. . .	. . .
					Income tax payable	. . .	. . .	. . .	. . .
Total					Total				

Appendix 2b: Summary Financial Statements (income statement by function)

FIRM: BACH _____   YEAR [ ]

CASH FLOW BUDGET/STATEMENT (in 000 CU)

Opening balance (1) [ ]

Cash flows from operating activities
Cash from sales: 85% of sales revenue ....
Cash from receivables (see preceding balance sheet) ....
Cash purchases: 90% of annual purchases ....
Accounts payable (see preceding balance sheet) ....
Income tax payable ....
Property taxes ....
Personnel expenses ....
Rental expense ....
Advertising expenses ....
Auditing fees ....
Financial expenses ....
Net cash flows from operating activities (2) [ ]

Cash flows from investing activities
Investments (assembly lines) ....
Net cash flows used in investing activities (3) [ ]

Cash flows from financing activities
Increase in capital ....
New debts ....
Repayment of debts ....
Dividends paid ....
Net cash flows used in financing activities (4) [ ]

Net increase (decrease) in cash (5) = (2) + (3) + (4) [ ]

Ending balance (6) = (1) + (5)

INCOME STATEMENT (in 000 of CU)

Sales [ ]
Cost of goods sold (COGS) =
Purchases of motors and parts ....
Change in inventories of raw materials (B-E) ....
Change in inventories of finished products (B-E) ....
Rental expense
Production personnel expenses
Sub-total (COGS) [ ]
Sales and marketing expenses
Administration expenses
Property taxes ....
Non production personnel expenses
Auditing fees
Sub-total admin expenses
Depreciation allowance for the period
Financial expenses
Total expenses [ ][ ][ ][ ]
Income before income tax
Income tax
Net income [ ]

BALANCE SHEET (in 000 of CU)

	Beg	+	–	End
Fixed assets				
Manufacturing equip. (net)	....	....	....	....
Current assets				
Inventories				
Motors and parts	....	....	....	....
Finished products				
Accounts receivable (15% of sales revenue)	....	....	....	....
Cash at bank	....			....
Total				

	Beg	–	+	End
Shareholders' equity				
Capital	....	....	....	....
Retained earnings	....	....	....	....
Net income/loss				
Subtotal				
Liabilities				
Debt 8% X4	....	....	....	....
Bank overdraft				
Accounts payable (10% of purchases)	....	....	....	....
Income tax payable				
Total				

Assignment 3.6

Sibelius Company

Topic: The beginning of the accounting process: the journal.

The Sibelius Company was incorporated on 1 March X1. It carries a commercial activity. The following transactions were undertaken during the first month of operation of Sibelius Co.

1	March 1	Sibelius company was incorporated with a share capital of 600 CU. A bank account was opened with Commercial Credit Bank.
2	March 6	Purchased merchandise on credit: 350 CU.
3	March 12	Paid telephone expense for the month of March: 50 CU.
4	March 20	Sold merchandise for 500 CU (260 CU cash and 240 CU on credit). (The purchase price of the merchandise sold was 300 CU).
5	March 29	Paid the supplier of merchandise (see transaction 2).
6	March 30	Organized a physical inventory and computed an ending inventory of 50 CU.

Required

Prepare the journal entries for the month of March X1. Note that:

■ The company wants to compute the income that reflects the economic situation at 31 March. Consequently, the ending inventory must appear in the records of the company.

■ In order to record purchases, sales and inventory, you can choose to record the purchases of merchandise either in the inventory (balance sheet) or as a purchase (income statement). You must indicate your choice clearly at the top of your journal (see appendix below).

■ A partial excerpt from the chart of accounts of Sibelius Company is given below (note that the authorized accounts are provided in alphabetical order without reference to their expected ending balance):

Accounts payable
Accounts receivable
Capital
Cash in bank
Change in inventories (if purchases recorded in the income statement)
Cost of goods sold (if purchases recorded in the balance sheet)
Inventories
Purchases of merchandise (if purchases recorded in the income statement)
Sales of merchandise
Telephone expenses

Appendix

Recording of purchases, sales and inventory.
  Indicate the system chosen:

Model journal					
Transaction number	Date	Accounts		Amounts	
		Debit	Credit	D	C

Assignment 3.7

Internet-based exercise

- Search the Internet for job offers concerning vacancies for accounting and related personnel (auditor, financial director, management controller, treasurer, etc.).
- Using the offers located, draw up a list of the characteristics of each position.
- Compare and contrast the positions in accounting and related professions.

Assignment 3.8

Accounting history

- Prepare and give a 15-minute presentation on the history of charts of accounts, with particular reference to the French chart of accounts (dating from 1942).
- Prepare and give a 15-minute presentation of how accounts have been kept and presented in the past, to the present day.

Assignment 3.9

Lavender Soap Company case[5]

Topic: Financial statements and decision-making

Salamah Hijazi, an Egyptian immigrant, founded The Lavender Soap Company (LSC) in Seattle at the end of X1 with a capital at par of $60,000. The business mission of Lavender Soap was to distribute organic soaps, cleansing and beauty products both in retail stores located in shopping malls, and wholesale to corporate clients such as hotels and cruise ship operators (Seattle is home port for 11 large cruise ships per week during the six-month season). The business started operations on 1 January X2.

Sales in X2 were both to retail customers (40% of net sales revenue, but providing 50% of the total gross margin) and to 'wholesale' clients (60% of net sales revenue and providing 50% of total gross margin). LSC does not operate a web-based marketplace at this time but is considering creating one soon.

So far, LSC operates only one store, located in South Center Mall, a middle-class mall in suburban Seattle. The owner-manager is intent on growing the business and is looking for additional locations to open new stores. A possible store front will become available in mid-March X3 at the upscale brand-new Bravern Shopping Center in Bellevue, a very wealthy eastern suburb of Seattle, some 10 miles to the north of South Center Mall. Salamah Hijazi has obtained the right of first refusal. A prompt decision on this opportunity is thus required on his part, or another retailer will snap up the storefront and no new desirable opportunities appear to be in the making, despite the economic slowdown in the region.

Opening this new store would require acquiring the leasehold for $45,000 cash, acquiring furniture and fixtures for another $55,000, which would probably have to be paid in cash, and the decoration of the store would require an additional $25,000 cash payment. The minimum starting inventory for the store would be worth about $58,000. The new store would open toward the very beginning of the second quarter of X3.

The results for the operations of the fourth quarter X2 were as follows (Q4 X2 is considered a 'normal' quarter, after three losing quarters – accumulated losses as of the end of Q3 X2 were $28,300):

Sales revenue	208,000
Cost of merchandise sold	105,000
Gross margin	103,000
Cost of selling (rent, procurement, sales force, etc.)	35,000
Cost of administration (manager, accountant, etc.)	5,000
Financial expenses (on a 3-year loan of $133,000 at 6%)	2,000
Income before tax	**61,000**
Minus income taxes (net rate of 30%)	18,300
Net income after taxes	**18,300**

Additional information:
1. Salamah Hijazi expects sales at the South Center Mall store (which, he feels, has not yet reached its full potential) to increase by 10% in each of the next two quarters (early X3). Wholesale business is expected to grow, hopefully, by 5% per quarter for at least 2 quarters.
2. Retail sales are paid cash or by credit or debit cards (essentially equivalent to cash for the purpose of this mini-case). Wholesale sales are collected two months after delivery and invoicing. The balance in accounts receivable at the end of X2 is thus expected to be about $84,000.
3. Purchases of merchandise-for-sale in the fourth quarter X2 are expected to approximate $96,000.
4. Purchases are paid to suppliers within a month after receiving the goods. Accounts payables at the end of the fourth quarter X2 are expected to stand at $32,000.

5. The ending inventory (of sellable merchandise) at the end of X2 is expected to be $82,500. The policy of LSC is to aim for inventory on hand at any time to be approximately equal to three quarters of the cost of merchandise expected to be sold in the subsequent three months.

6. An advertising campaign is planned for early X3 to promote the South Center Mall store after the holyday period, and thus avoid any seasonal effect on sales revenue. This advertising campaign will cost about $8,000. All other selling and administrative expenses are expected to be about the same per quarter, for at least the next two quarters (excluding any additional expenses due to the new store). All expenses, including interest expenses, other than purchases of merchandise for sale are paid cash in the quarter incurred.

7. Selling expenses include a depreciation expense of $5,000 for the depreciation of the store's furniture and fixtures, computerized cash register, and phone and credit card electronics (which have a gross historical cost of $60,000 and will have a net book value of $40,000 at the end of X2).

8. Administrative expenses include a depreciation expense of $1,700 for office furniture, computer and information technology equipment. These assets have a gross historical cost of $34,000 and will have a net book value of $27,200 at the end of X2.

9. The income tax rate, starting in X3, is expected to remain at 30% of taxable income and remain at that level in the foreseeable future. Taxes are paid in the quarter following (i.e. taxes on income of Q4 X2 would be paid in Q1 of X3).

10. The cash balance at the end of X2 is expected to be $24,000.

Required

Assuming LSC wishes to have at least $25,000 in cash (or cash equivalents) on hand at the end of the first quarter of X3, can the new store be opened without obtaining external funds? What questions would you raise to know whether or not the new store in the Bravern Shopping Center should be opened?

To answer the first part of the question, you need to prepare both a *pro forma* or budgeted statement of cash flows and a *pro forma* or budgeted income statement for the first quarter of X3. Should you need external funding, the financial institution would also require LSC to provide a *pro forma* or budgeted balance sheet as of the end of Q1 X3.

References

Colasse, B. (1993) *Gestion financière*, 3rd edn, Paris: PUF.

IASB (1989) Framework for the Preparation and Presentation of Financial Statements, London.

IASB (1992) International Accounting Standard No. 7, Statement of Cash Flows, London.

IASB (2007) International Accounting Standard No. 1, Presentation of Financial Statements, London.

Vlaemminck, J.H. (1979) *Histoire et doctrines de la comptabilité*, Pragnos, quoted by Colasse, B. and Lesage, C. (2007) *Comptabilité générale*, 10th edn, p. 177, Paris: Economica.

Further reading

Bechtel, W. (1995) 'Charts of accounts in Germany', *European Accounting Review* 4(2): 283–304.

Chauveau, B. (1995) 'The Spanish Plan General de Contabilidad: Agent of development and innovation?', *European Accounting Review* 4(1): 125–38.

Inchausti, B.G. (1993) 'The Spanish accounting framework: some comments', *European Accounting Review* 2(2): 379–86.

Jaruga, A. A., and A. Szychta (1997) 'The origin and evolution of charts of accounts in Poland', *European Accounting Review* 6(3): 509–26.

Parker, R.H. (1996) 'Harmonizing the notes in the UK and France: a case study in *de jure* harmonization', *European Accounting Review* 5(2): 317–37.

Plan comptable général (General accounting plan), France, http://www.minefi.gouv.fr/directions_services/CNCompta/ (English version available).

Plano Oficial de Contabilidade (General accounting plan), Portugal, http://www.cnc.min-financas.pt/POC/POContabilidade.pdf (in Portuguese)

Richard, J. (1995) 'The evolution of accounting chart models in Europe from 1900 to 1945: some historical elements', *European Accounting Review* 4(1): 87–124.

Richard, J. (1995) 'The evolution of the Romanian and Russian accounting charts after the collapse of the communist system', *European Accounting Review* 4(2): 305–22.

Roberts, A. (1997) 'Charts of accounts in Europe: An overview', *Management Accounting* 75(6): 39–40.

Additional material on the website

Go to http://www.cengage.co.uk/stolowy3 for further information, journal entries and extra assignments for each chapter.

The following appendices to this chapter are available on the dedicated website:

Appendix 3.1 Concepts of use and source

Appendix 3.2 Trial balance errors

Appendix 3.3 Organization of the accounting system.

Notes

1. Which will be the beginning balance for the subsequent period. Also called 'balance carried forward'.

2. Before computerization, the 'general ledger' was a large, bound volume with pre-numbered pages (to avoid modification of the figures or accounts after the initial recording). The general ledger was a voluminous tome because a certain number of pages were reserved, by anticipation, for each account. The number of pages assigned to each account needed to be large enough to allow for the recording of all transactions of the upcoming year. It was prudent to reserve more pages than needed as a security precaution, thus the general ledger was quite voluminous, as described, often darkly, by authors such as Charles Dickens or Honoré de Balzac or illustrated, sometimes humorously, by artists such as Honoré Daumier. Since the generalization of the use of computers, the general ledger is merely a database, which has, nonetheless, kept the name 'general ledger'.

3. Based on an idea developed by Colasse (1993). The figures have been updated and several companies are different.

4. The number of teams in the simulation will, in fact, vary according to the number of participants. The average quantity of units potentially sold by any firm is always 100,000 in the first period. Thus the market potential in period X7 is equal to the number of teams times 100,000 units.

5. This case is an adaptation, with permission, by Professor Michel J. Lebas of a case written by Professor James Jiambalvo, Foster School of Business, University of Washington.

C4

Chapter 4
Accounting Principles and End-of-Period Adjustments

Learning objectives

After studying this chapter, you will understand:

- How accounting principles (conventions, broad guidelines, rules, and detailed procedures) structure and organize accounting and reporting.
- That the accounting principles can be classified around four objectives or requirements: objectivity, quality of information, prudence and periodicity.
- That, in coherence with the matching principle, end-of-period adjustments (entries) are needed to give a 'true and fair view' of both the financial position at the end of an accounting period, and the income statement for the accounting period.
- That adjusting entries originate in the passage of time, not from specific support documents.
- That end-of-period entries are adjusting entries that reflect:
  - uncompleted transactions (such as revenues earned but not recorded, revenues recorded but unearned, expenses consumed but not recorded and expenses recorded but not consumed);
  - changes in value of fixed assets;
  - changes in value of current assets;
- That end-of-period entries also include some corrections of errors and recording of ending inventories.
- That these entries will be carried out any time one 'closes' the books (yearly, half-yearly, quarterly, monthly, etc.).
- That end-of-period entries are often mentioned and explained in the notes to financial statements.

Chapter 3 described how transactions are recorded during the year in the accounting process. We explained how data enter the accounting process and how they are recorded in the journal and ledgers. The overall objectives of the accounting procedures during the phase of recording are to ensure that:

- All data recorded are relevant to the description of the financial performance of the entity.
- The descriptors of every transaction can be verified from source documents.
- The structure of the data in the ledgers is relevant to the business model held by the management and to their decision-making needs.
- Accurate and significant data can be extracted rapidly from the ledgers on a periodical basis.

In order for the techniques introduced in Chapters 2 and 3 to deliver data that meet these objectives, transactions recording follows a certain number of guidelines or principles, which are accepted by accountants around the world.

This chapter will present these key principles (a broad term that encompasses conventions, broad guidelines, rules, and detailed procedures), around which accounting is organized. These principles apply to all accounting entries and provide a common foundation for greater understandability and comparability of financial statements.

The **matching principle,** introduced in Chapter 2, is one of these principles. It is connected to the concept and definition of the **accounting period**. The matching principle specifies that costs or expenses should be recorded at the same time as the revenues to which they correspond, i.e., costs and revenues that are linked during an accounting period should be reported in the same period. What we have recorded in Chapters 2 and 3 are the current operations of a business. However, the cut-off between periods (specifying to which of two sequential periods a revenue or an expense 'belongs', i.e., should be attached) will require carrying out end-of-period adjustments. These allow one to close the books of one period and open those of the next. This chapter will, therefore, also introduce these entries that are essential to the completion of the periodic **accounting cycle**.

At year-end, adjusting entries, correction of errors, entries relating to ending inventories and closing entries will be recorded.

1 Accounting principles

As indicated in Chapter 1, accounting produces a social good: information. The output of accounting is aimed at a variety of users who use it in their decision-making. It is therefore crucial that a large number of users be able to understand the meaning of the accounting reports, and that these describe fairly the situation of the economic entity. Consequently, it is necessary that 'rules of the game' be established and followed by everyone. These rules, as mentioned previously, are the **accounting principles**. They form a coherent set (see Figure 4.1) of behavioral rules and guidelines that range from pure concepts to very operational guidelines about practice.

Words used to refer to these principles vary between authors, between practitioners, and between countries. What we call principles is called elsewhere 'concepts', 'conventions', or 'assumptions'. In countries of Roman Law tradition, these principles are generally integrated in the body of business or company law and/or in legal accounting rules. It is notably the case in Belgium, France and Switzerland where these principles have been adopted by the appropriate legislative bodies. In countries where the legal system is one of Common Law, such as in the 'Anglo-Saxon' world, the power of these principles is most of the time derived from the consensus within the accounting profession and between it and the business world.

In a given country, the set of principles is referred to, in short, as the local GAAP (for Generally Accepted Accounting Principles, a concept defined in Chapter 1). We will therefore specify which country's set of GAAP to refer to when it will be useful in understanding a specific real-world example. We will thus speak of US GAAP, or Dutch GAAP, or German GAAP. The trend is, however, to evolve towards a single set of GAAP (which would, in all likelihood, lead to increased international comparability between – and greater ease of consolidation of – financial statements). There are however, to date, still two different main sets of GAAP: the US GAAP, largely influenced by the US financial market regulators, and the IFRS/IAS GAAP which reflects the views of a broad international community of users. There appears to be, especially after the market crash of October 2008 and its ensuing recession, serious effort toward unifying the two sets of GAAP. However, choices are quite political in nature (power play between financial markets among other issues). Which one of the leading two contenders will dominate in the end or whether some compromise will be found between the two sets is, however, still pure speculation at the time of writing (see more on this in Chapter 5).

It is useful to understand why these principles have been retained over time, as they help producers, and users as well, understand the value and the limits of accounting information. It also provides an opportunity to explore how the usefulness and quality of accounting information can be improved (the qualitative characteristics of useful information have been presented in Chapter 1 – see Figure 1.5).

Figure 4.1 aims at classifying the accounting principles in four broad categories based on four critical requirements or constraints information users place on accounting.

Figure 4.1 Accounting principles

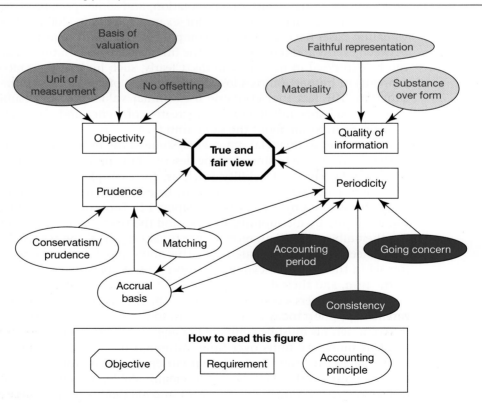

1.1 Main objective of accounting principles: Give a true and fair view

The purpose of the financial statements is to give a **true and fair view** of a business' financial performance and situation. The term 'true and fair view' does not really represent a principle *per se* but defines the intent of the adoption of the principles we list below, as shown in Figure 4.1:

> **True** means that the financial statements do not falsify or dissimulate the financial situation of the company at period-end or its profits (or losses) for the period then ended.
>
> **Fair** means that accounts give all users the same complete, unbiased and relevant information for decision-making.

There is, as a matter of fact, no officially recognized and generally accepted definition of 'true and fair' as it applies to financial statements. The term is used but never precisely defined. IAS 1 (IASB 2007: § 15) requires that financial statements 'present fairly the financial position, financial performance and cash flows of an entity', without explaining explicitly the concept of 'fair' presentation. We choose to say that 'true and fair' is the result of the application of the principles we are now going to explore in further detail.

1.2 Objectivity

1.2.1 Unit of measurement

Financial accounting only records transactions expressed in financial units (euro, pound sterling, US dollar, renmimbi, ruble, dinar, etc.). No principle prevents accounting from keeping accounts of value creation and value consumption in terms other than financial.[1] For example, it is conceivable to account for the environmental effect of a firm's behavior or its impact on the health of a population, and some specialized accounting approaches exist to handle such issues (see, for example, Epstein 2008). However, all alternative valuation bases have a subjective component. The most objective common denominator between events and transactions is the financial measure of their economic impact, which can be expressed in monetary terms. Clearly, such limitation to recording only financial elements in transactions is a loss of the richness of description of the reality of a business situation. The fact that everyone uses similar valuation bases (subject to market-based currency exchange rate fluctuations) creates coherence and allows all users to understand each figure to mean about the same thing.

In the notes to financial statements, some of the reality of the 'non-financial' elements of the situation of a business can be described in approximate monetary terms. For example, an environmental liability (such as, for example, all issues and possible liabilities relating to past uses of asbestos) might be estimated as a range of possible damages that might be assessed by a court (see Chapter 12). Footnoting is an effective way to achieve full disclosure by mentioning an issue and the risks inherent in its existence, while keeping the ambiguity of any monetary estimation out of the reported numbers on the balance sheet and income statement. The notes allow each user to interpret the possible impact of the non-financial information on their personal view of the financial position of the firm, and their decisions.

To give the users a complete vision of the history of events that have shaped the firm's financial position today and allow them to estimate its evolution in the future, figures of different periods must be compared or aggregated. Accounting must therefore use homogeneous monetary units over time. Although the purchasing power of monetary units may change over time and between currencies, accounting implicitly assumes the purchasing power of the monetary unit remains stable. Accounts, for example, consider that a euro in 2010 is comparable to a euro in 2008 (and conversely). This assumption clearly facilitates the work of the accountant, but at the expense of a likely loss of relevance. As long as inflation remains within 'normally accepted limits' (for example a rate of less than 3% a year and is, more or less, applicable to both revenues and expenses, and assets and liabilities) the loss of relevance is not perceived as 'dramatic'. All users can recast the figures to reflect their understanding of the 'real' situation of the firm. But since it is impossible to account for the way all people experience inflation, the accountant *de facto* ignores inflation. In cases where the hypothesis of modest inflation rate is not satisfied, specific methods will be required to keep the purchasing power of the monetary unit in line with reality, while attempting to separate the inflationary effects on profit and cash flows from the fruit of managerial decisions.

1.2.2 Basis of valuation and measurement

'Measurement is the process of determining the monetary amounts at which the elements of the financial statements are to be recognized and carried in the balance sheet and income statement' (Conceptual framework, IASB 1989: § 99). Defining the numbers that describe the effects of a transaction involves the selection of a particular basis of measurement. A number of different measurement bases can be employed and even mixed to different degrees in financial statements. They include the following (IASB 1989: § 100):

- *'Historical cost*: Assets are recorded at the amount of cash or cash equivalents paid or the fair value of the consideration given to acquire them at the time of their acquisition. Liabilities are recorded at the amount or proceeds received in exchange for the obligation, or in some circumstances (for example, income taxes), at the amounts of cash or cash equivalents expected to be paid to satisfy the liability in the normal course of business.

- *Current* [or replacement] *cost*: Assets are carried at the amount of cash or cash equivalents that would have to be paid if the same or an equivalent asset were acquired currently. Liabilities are carried at the undiscounted amount of cash or cash equivalents that would be required to settle the obligation right now.

- *Realizable (settlement* [or liquidation]) *value*: Assets are carried at the amount of cash or cash equivalents that could currently be obtained by selling the asset in an orderly disposal. Liabilities are carried at their settlement values; that is, the undiscounted amounts of cash or cash equivalents expected to be paid to satisfy the liabilities in the normal course of business.

- *Present value*: Assets are carried at the net present value of the future net cash inflows that the item is expected to generate in the normal course of business. Liabilities are carried at the net present value of the future net cash outflows that are expected to be required to settle the liabilities in the normal course of business'.

Historical cost is the **measurement** basis most commonly adopted by economic enterprises in preparing their financial statements, since it is the one that requires the fewest hypotheses. This choice is coherent with the philosophy of 'better approximate, unchallengeable and understandable than more descriptive but debatable and difficult to interpret'. Historical costing is usually combined with other measurement bases. For example, inventories are usually carried at the lower of (historical) cost and net realizable value (often referred to as 'lowest of cost or market' valuation). Such a choice makes sense, especially in high-tech fields such as in electronic products where the cost of components (i.e., their price on the market) may fall very rapidly with volume growth and technology evolution. It would not be fair to shareholders to describe an asset at its purchase price if the replacement value (or the resale value) is lower than the historical cost. We have to keep in mind that the objective of financial statements is to report to shareholders the financial situation of their investment. Overvaluation of inventories, even more so than their undervaluation, misrepresents the actual situation, i.e., the potential future cash flows. However, as we will see below, accountants will always shy away from the possibility of overestimation, seen as resulting from subjective and unproven assumptions, and prefer living with the risk of undervaluation, which accounting information users can correct on the basis of their own awareness of the markets (see: Prudence principle, § 1.4).

1.2.3 No offsetting

Offsetting of opposite net effects of different transactions could hide some of the richness of the situation accounting is supposed to report on. Such practice would obscure the reality of the risks faced by the firm in each transaction. Two transactions may have the same absolute value effect with opposite algebraic signs. The net balance of these two transactions would, arithmetically, be zero. Such a presentation would not reflect the complete 'truth' or 'reality'. For example, an overdrawn account at one bank and a positive bank balance with another bank may have equivalent amounts, but the risks they carry, and the signals they communicate, are not equivalent.

Accountants have established the principle that 'an entity shall not offset assets and liabilities or income and expenses, unless [explicitly] required or permitted by an IFRS' (IAS 1, IASB 2007: § 32).

For this reason all ledgers and specialized ledgers provide the richness of records where all details of all transactions remain un-offset against one another. Accounting is not only the way to report on the financial position of the firm, it is also the way to create and maintain a full archive of how such a position was achieved. Such an archive is essential for better understanding what went right and what went wrong, so that more performance can be created in the future.

Example 1

If a business has two bank accounts, one in Acme Bank with a positive balance of 1,000 CU and a second one in Everyone Thrift Bank with a negative balance of 400 CU, offsetting would be to report a net balance of positive cash-at-bank of 600 CU. However, the no offsetting principle requires that the positive balance be reported on the assets side and the negative balance be reported on the liabilities side of the balance sheet.

Example 2

If a business owes a supplier 5,000 CU and simultaneously has a claim on that very supplier for the same amount (for example, as the result of a down-payment on another order) it would not make sense to offset the two events as they reflect different parts of the business. The debt will be on the liabilities side and the claim on the supplier will be an asset.

Example 3

As a rule, fixed assets are reported on two lines that, theoretically, should not be offset against each other (even if, in addition to the detailed information, the arithmetic sum of the two lines can also be reported as *net* asset): one line reports the gross or historical value of acquisition of the asset and the second line reports the accumulated depreciation on the asset (i.e., its reduction in 'value' through consumption). Even if an asset is fully depreciated (i.e., its net book value is zero), it should be reported as two lines as long as the firm has not physically disposed of it. In this case, the application of the no offsetting principle, for example, allows the financial statements users to evaluate the approximate expected average life of the fixed assets by calculating the ratio between the gross value and the depreciation expense, thus enriching his or her view of the condition of the firm (more on this in Chapter 7).

1.3 Quality of information

The usefulness of financial statements to decision-makers rests on the reports being detailed enough, but not too detailed to the point of being overwhelming (**materiality**

and aggregation principle), providing a faithful description of the economic situation of the business, and being meaningful in the sense that they result from a choice of **substance over form**.

1.3.1 Materiality and aggregation

'Omissions or misstatements of items are material if they could, individually or collectively, influence the economic decisions of users taken on the basis of the financial statements' (IAS 1, IASB 2007: § 7). 'An entity shall present separately each material class of similar items. An entity shall present separately items of a dissimilar nature or function unless they are immaterial' (IAS 1, IASB 2007: § 29).

1.3.2 Faithful presentation

'To be reliable, information must represent faithfully the transactions and other events it either purports to represent or could reasonably be expected to represent. Thus, for example, a balance sheet should represent faithfully the transactions and other events that result in assets, liabilities and equity of the entity at the reporting date (…). Most financial information is subject to some risk of being less than a faithful representation of that which it purports to portray. This is not due to bias, but rather to inherent difficulties either in identifying the transactions and other events to be measured, or in devising and applying measurement and presentation techniques that can convey messages that communicate the full complexity of those transactions and events' (Conceptual framework, IASB 1989: §§ 33–34).

1.3.3 Substance over form

'If information is to represent faithfully the transactions and other events that it purports to represent, it is necessary that they are accounted for and presented in accordance with their substance and economic reality and not merely their legal form. The substance of transactions or other events is not always consistent with that which is apparent from their legal or contrived form. For example, an entity may dispose of an asset to another party in such a way that the documentation purports to pass legal ownership to that party; nevertheless, agreements to pay exist that ensure that the entity continues to enjoy the future economic benefits embodied in the asset. In such circumstances, the reporting of a sale would not represent faithfully the transaction entered into (if indeed there was a transaction)' (Conceptual framework, IASB 1989: § 35). In short, several transactions exist in which the legal 'property' of an asset or of a liability changes hands, but the benefits to be derived from the assets or the obligations contained in the liability remain in the same hands as previously.

One such operation is, for example, the one called leaseback (see Chapter 12). It is commonly used by businesses both to raise cash without having to go through the process of obtaining a loan from financial institution and, often, to rebuild a depleted shareholders' equity. For example, a business may sell the building in which their headquarters is housed, and lease it back immediately from the buyer. A profit or a loss may be recorded on the sale, which would, of course, affect the shareholders' equity. The proper way of recording such an operation should be to recognize, on the one hand, the sale and the cash it generated, as well as the gain or loss on the sale, and, on the other hand, recognize the fact the business now has a commitment to pay rent, which can be measured through the net present value of the rental payments (a liability) and an asset of equivalent amount (to the liability) that recognizes the building is actually at the disposal (under the control) of the firm and will therefore permit future economic benefits. The second 'operation' (recognizing both the liability and the asset) would not affect retained earnings, since we would have the same amount on both sides of the balance sheet. After both transactions have been recorded, the balance sheet would fully reflect the reality of the situation.

The substance over form principle, although logical and useful, is not universally accepted, especially as it affects the recording of leases. To make an oversimplification, the substance over form principle is accepted and used mainly in the North American zone of influence. Many countries have adopted specific rules or principles for the recording of leases, which represent a major issue in this area (see Chapter 12). Other areas where substance over form can be a significant issue involve all trades related to intellectual property such as licensing or sale of patents.

1.4 Prudence

An accountant is prudent by nature. He or she does not wish to recognize profit (or loss) before it has been 'earned' with a high degree of certainty. Three principles serve to achieve this requirement: conservatism, accrual, and matching.

1.4.1 Conservatism

Preparers of financial statements 'have to contend with the uncertainties that inevitably surround many events and circumstances, such as the collectability of doubtful receivables, the probable useful life of plant and equipment, and the number of warranty claims that may occur. Such uncertainties are recognized by the disclosure of their nature and extent and by the exercise of prudence [or **conservatism**] in the preparation of the financial statements. Prudence [conservatism] is the inclusion of a degree of caution in the exercise of the judgments needed in making the estimates required under conditions of uncertainty, such that assets or income are not overstated and liabilities or expenses are not understated' (Conceptual framework, IASB 1989: § 37).

The exercise of prudence does not allow, for example, excessive provisions, i.e., the deliberate (1) understatement of assets or income, or (2) overstatement of liabilities or expenses, because the financial statements would not be neutral, and, therefore, not have the quality of reliability.

Practically, this principle means that profits should not be anticipated. They should only be taken into the accounts when they are earned or realized. For example, revenue attached to sales should be recorded only when the goods have been shipped and invoiced, and not when the order was received.

As far as losses are concerned, however, they should be recognized as soon as the events giving rise to them take place. For example, when the resale value of an item in inventory decreases below its acquisition or manufacturing cost, the loss in value should be recognized immediately, even if the item is not sold. One example of a practice coherent with conservatism is that of always valuing inventories at the '**lower of cost or market**'. Provisions or valuation allowances used to recognize these losses will be further explored later in this chapter.

Conservatism is, like the historical basis in the measurement unit, generally accepted but still controversial at times, as there are many situations in which its usefulness is debatable, as is the case in the valuation of marketable securities in a volatile market. The practice of '**mark to market**' for **financial instruments**, followed by many financial institutions, requires that a security (even if it is not 'for sale') be reported at its current market value (on the date the books are closed) and not at its cost of acquisition. This rule is, understandably, highly debated after the crisis of 2008 as it is in blatant contradiction with the prudence principle, but allowed firms using this practice to show outstanding results as long as the financial market was 'going up and up and up'.

1.4.2 Accrual basis

As we stated in Chapter 2, the accrual principle consists in recognizing or recording an event when it occurs and not when the cash transaction it induces has been completed.

IAS 1 (IASB 2007: § 27) stipulates that 'an entity shall prepare its financial statements, except for cash flow information, under the accrual basis of accounting'. Financial statements must only reflect revenues, expenses, and income that relate to a given accounting period. The resulting difference between cash transactions and amounts recognized under the accrual basis must be shown as either an **accrued expense** (an expense recognized but not yet paid, i.e., a liability), a prepaid expense (an expense already paid but not yet consumed, i.e., an asset), **accrued revenue** (revenue earned but not yet received in cash, i.e., an asset), or prepaid revenue (revenue recognized as cash but for which the services have not yet been rendered, i.e., a liability) (see section 2 in this chapter).

1.4.3 Matching

This principle, also introduced earlier, is a corollary of the accrual basis. Expenses are recognized in the income statement of a period on the basis of their direct association with the revenues also recognized in that period. **Matching** of costs with revenues is defined in the IASB Framework (IASB 1989: § 95) as the simultaneous or combined recognition of revenues and expenses that result directly and jointly from the same transactions or other events.

1.5 Periodicity

This requirement consists of three principles: accounting period, **going concern**, and **consistency of presentation**. It is also connected to the accrual and matching concepts introduced earlier.

1.5.1 Accounting period

As stated in Chapter 1, reporting to shareholders occurs at regular intervals, these defining the accounting period. The yearly accounting period is generally some arbitrary segmentation of the lifecycle of any business.

The outcome of the managers' decisions and actions (income) must be known at least once a year mainly for the following economical and legal reasons:

1. Need to (a) know changes in the overall performance potential of the firm and (b) evaluate the quality of the management and of their decisions as agents of the shareholders.

2. Need to know the amount of income (or wealth created) that is to be shared between shareholders and other stakeholders or partners.

3. Need to provide a basis for the state to levy taxes based on income.

The only definitive measure of the income or value created by a business is the one that would be established through an income statement that would span the entire life of the firm. However, no shareholder or regulatory agency wants to have to wait that long to know (a) how much wealth has been created, and (b) whether the managers, who are the shareholders' agents or representatives, are making the 'right' decisions or, at least, decisions that the shareholders approve. Businesses are controlled by checking the outcome of decisions against the firm's plans and strategic intent. If there is an unacceptable gap between intent and result, corrective actions are decided (both by investors and by managers) to bring the firm's financial position ever closer to fulfilling its strategic intent or by shareholders selling their holdings. A year-long accounting period is the longest periodicity that appears acceptable to all parties. However, many require more frequent information. In fact, most financial markets require reporting the financial position of listed firms on a quarterly basis.

The measurement of income is carried in sequential, yet clearly separated time slices. The accrual principle and the **end-of-period entries** (see later in this chapter) permit this pairing of time and income in coherent sets, useful for forecasting and decision-making.

1.5.2 Going concern

The ability to accrue revenues and expenses, and therefore income, in the appropriate time periods rests on the assumption that a business entity has a life expectancy that exceeds the accounting reporting period. This assumption of continuity is called the 'going concern principle'. Unless the accountant has specific knowledge to the contrary, he or she will assume continuity when establishing the financial statements. It is management's responsibility to take decisions so the business goes on as long as possible for the benefit of the shareholders. Failure in exercising this responsibility leads to bankruptcy, or to the business entity being bought-out or liquidated.

The going concern principle is a key reason for valuing assets and resources or liabilities at their historical cost rather than at their liquidation value. During future periods, the firm will be able to gain economic benefits from the existence of these assets. The least debatable proxy for the net present value of these future benefits remains the purchase price of the asset, eventually adjusted over time through **depreciation** to recognize reduction of the potential since acquisition.

IAS 1 (IASB 2007: § 25) stipulates: 'When preparing financial statements, management shall make an assessment of an entity's ability to continue as a going concern. An entity shall prepare financial statements on a going concern basis unless management either intends to liquidate the entity or to cease trading, or has no realistic alternative but to do so. When management is aware, in making its assessment, of material uncertainties related to events or conditions that may cast significant doubt upon the entity's ability to continue as a going concern, the entity shall disclose those uncertainties. When an entity does not prepare financial statements on a going concern basis, it shall disclose that fact, together with the basis on which it prepared the financial statements and the reason why the entity is not regarded as a going concern'.

In other words, this principle means that there is no reason to suppose that the company will not be carrying on its business throughout the following financial year and following years.

1.5.3 Consistency of presentation

Financial statements must be useful to decision-makers. They must provide not only comparability from period to period, so the user is able to detect trends and evolutions but also comparability with other firms involved in the same line of business (same types of risk factors). It is therefore critical that the financial statements be presented in consistent fashion over time and using consistent parameters. If principles of presentation or parameters change, following alterations of strategy or necessity, it is essential, in order to give a true and fair view of the firm's situation, to recast the old data so that a minimum number of years (generally three) are presented in homogeneous fashion for comparison purposes. This principle allows changes and regulates how these can be implemented (see Chapter 6 for more details).

IAS 1 (IASB 2007: § 45) indicates that 'an entity shall retain the presentation and classification of items in the financial statements from one period to the next unless:

(a) It is apparent, following a significant change in the nature of the entity's operations or a review of its financial statements, that another presentation or classification would be more appropriate having regard to the criteria for the selection and application of accounting policies in IAS 8 [Accounting policies, changes in accounting estimates and errors]; or

(b) An IFRS requires a change in presentation'.

In practice, the valuation methods used at the end of a financial year must be the same as those applied at the end of the preceding year. As a consequence, comparative figures for the preceding year appearing in a statement of financial position (which are required by IAS 1, and by many other national standards) are fully comparable with the figures for the current year. The importance of this principle will become apparent when we look later at the different methods of valuation used for various assets (concepts of depreciation, provision, or valuation allowance).

1.6 The entity concept

Although not quite a real 'principle' for many authors, the **entity concept**, illustrated in the Costas example (see Chapter 1, section 5), is a key foundation of accounting and of financial reports. It specifies that regardless of the legal form of the economic entity (sole proprietorship, partnership, limited company, etc. – see Chapter 11), economic transactions carried by the entity must be recorded separately from that of the personal transactions of actors involved in or with the entity.

2 End-of-period entries

Accounting principles, and especially the matching, accrual and periodicity principles, create the need to know exactly what transactions pertain to a period (and provide the techniques to handle that requirement). Some events that took place during the period are linked only to the passage of time or to other causes, such that they are not effectively documented through a transaction with a physical or electronic support. Other events straddle two periods and need to be partitioned between the two. Inventories and some asset values have to be adjusted if their market value has decreased below their cost, the consumption of assets must be acknowledged through depreciation, etc.

End-of-period entries refer to any such entries that are necessary to give a true and fair view of both the financial position at the end of an accounting period and the income statement for the accounting period. These entries will be carried out every time one closes the books (yearly, half-yearly, quarterly, monthly, etc.).

Figure 4.2 outlines the main categories of end-of-period entries and identifies the principles that are at the source of the issue.

The accounting principles studied earlier in this chapter become particularly important when the year-end entries are recorded. In order to apply these principles, management has to exercise considerable judgment. This confirms that accounting cannot be considered as an exact mathematical science.

2.1 Adjusting entries

The fundamental difficulty encountered with year-end financial statements is that the accounting period (generally the year, and even more so in the case of quarterly reporting), does not correspond to the duration of a normal operating cycle, whatever the entity's activities. In manufacturing, distribution, services, utilities, etc., the economic cycle may be either longer or shorter than the reporting period.

However, in order to provide regular periodic information to shareholders, employees, financial institutions and markets, and, incidentally, to tax authorities, annual financial statements have to be prepared despite the economic entity continuing to carry on its operational activities on an ongoing basis. This means that a **cut-off date** has to be selected by management, in agreement with the shareholders. This date will be used as a watershed, separating transactions pertaining to the closing period and those pertaining to the next one. As a result, many year-end adjustments are related to the influence of time: for example, an insurance premium invoice is probably not going to be received on the first day of a 12-month accounting period, and since it generally corresponds to an

Figure 4.2 Main categories of end-of-period entries

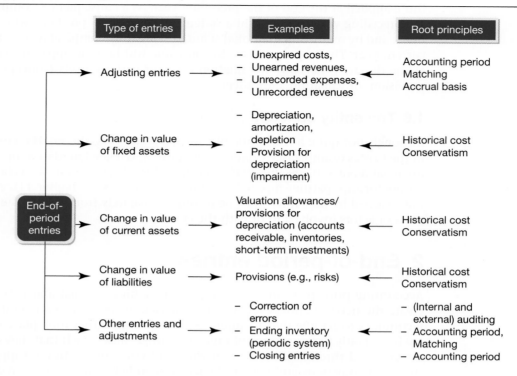

insurance coverage for a year, the amount of the premium must be partitioned between at least two accounting periods.

The most common **adjusting entries** may be classified in four categories as shown in Figure 4.3.

2.1.1 Revenues

The principles of revenue recognition, which will be developed in Chapter 6, prescribe that revenues affect net income in the period during which they are earned, and not the period in which their cash equivalent are collected. In other words, net income must include all and only the revenues which have been earned during the accounting period. This principle has two major consequences:

1. Revenues which have been earned but not yet recorded, mainly because the triggering event has not occurred yet, must be recorded and 'attached' to the current period in calculating its income. Examples of such a situation would be (a) the case of interests earned by the firm on a loan (extended to a customer or a supplier) which are not due until a date posterior to the closing date, or (b) sales delivered but not invoiced, etc.

2. Conversely, revenues which have been recorded in advance and which cover a service to be rendered at a later date must be adjusted to 'leave in the period' only the relevant part. Examples of such situations where the revenue must be apportioned are rent received in advance, subscription received from a customer for a newspaper service, etc.

Revenues earned but not recorded It is necessary, at year-end, to recognize revenues that have been earned but have not yet been recorded. No entry has been recorded, mainly due to the fact that the event, which would trigger the recognition of revenue, will only

Figure 4.3 Main adjusting entries

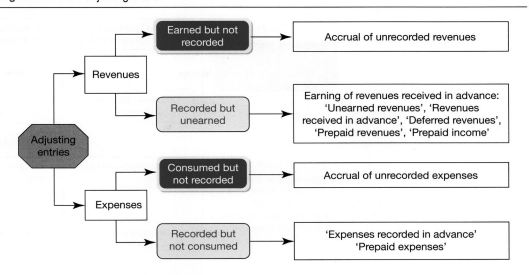

happen in the future. For example, let us assume that annual interest revenue on a loan (for example, granted to a customer at the beginning of March X1) becomes due only on the anniversary of the loan. When the financial statements are drawn on the closing date of 31 December X1, the triggering event has not happened yet. However, during the period ending on that date, the firm has earned 10/12th of the annual interest on the loan. However, the interest revenue is not due from the customer. No source document will be issued saying the customer owes the firm 10/12th of the annual interest. Because of the matching principle, it is essential to recognize, since interest is due to the passage of time, part of the annual interest revenue in this period even though it will be claimed and collected only during the next period. This unrecorded revenue will be accrued and recognized as revenue in period X1 for 10/12th of the interest and, since the interest has not yet been received, capitalized as an asset in the balance sheet at the end of X1 for the same amount. The remaining 2/12th of interest (that will earned in X2) are not mentioned in the balance sheet (see details in section 3 below).

Revenues recorded but unearned   When revenues are received in advance (for example, rent received in advance for several months, retainer fee received, etc.), two alternative solutions can be used to record this event and to recognize the revenues in the appropriate accounting period. They are listed in Figure 4.4 and will be detailed in section 3. In each country, one of the alternatives is generally preferred, but the other one is often tolerated.

2.1.2 Expenses

Expenses should affect net income in the period during which the resources they represent are consumed, and not the period in which their acquisition transaction is settled in cash or cash equivalent. In other words, net income must include all and only those expenses which have been consumed during the accounting period. This principle has two major consequences:

1. Expenses which have been consumed but not recorded, in particular because the triggering event has not occurred (such as interest to be paid after closing date, purchases received but invoice not received from supplier, etc.) must be recorded and 'attached' to the current net income calculation.

2. Conversely, expenses which have been recorded in advance (for example, rent paid in advance, retainer fee paid to a lawyer) must be adjusted so as to recognize, in the income statement, only that part which is relevant for the accounting period.

Figure 4.4 Revenues recorded but unearned

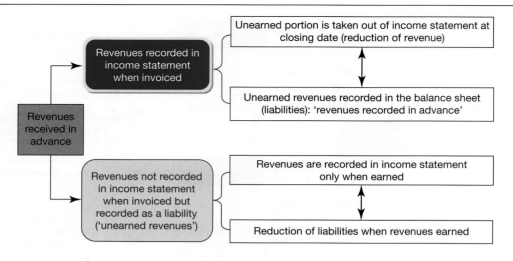

Expenses consumed but not recorded   It is necessary to recognize expenses that have been consumed but not yet recorded because the triggering event that will create the source document which will initiate the recording has not yet occurred. This would, for example, be the case of an interest expense on debt, which would be due by the business to its lender on 30 June X2 while the closing date is 31 December X1. Interest from 1 July X1 to 31 December X1 has actually builtup and represents a relevant expense of the closing period (the use of the funds during the period contributed to the creation of the income of X1). However, interest is not due until 30 June X2. This accrued but unrecorded expense must be recognized as both an expense in the income statement (for the relevant part) and a liability as accrued interest payable in the balance sheet for the same amount. (See example in section 3.3).

Expenses recorded but not consumed   When an expense is paid in advance it often straddles two accounting periods. For example, the subscription fee to a software helpline is generally paid in advance for the coming year but these 12 months rarely correspond to the accounting period.

Two solutions can be used to record such an event and to divide or apportion the expense between the proper periods. Figure 4.5 illustrates the choice. Although each country's accounting regulators generally indicate a preferred approach, it is not unusual to see both approaches coexist.

An illustrated comparison of the two methods is presented in section 3.

2.2 Value adjustments to fixed asset accounts

2.2.1 Principles

Tangible assets are defined in IAS 16 (IASB 2003: § 6) under the term of 'property, plant and equipment'. They 'are tangible items that:

(a) Are held for use in the production or supply of goods or services, for rental to others, or for administrative purposes; and

(b) Are expected to be used during more than one period'.

The value of fixed assets in the balance sheet is initially carried at their purchase price or acquisition cost (i.e., purchase price plus all costs incurred to make the asset useable in the context of the business strategy). This book value of the asset needs to be adjusted

Figure 4.5 Expenses paid in advance

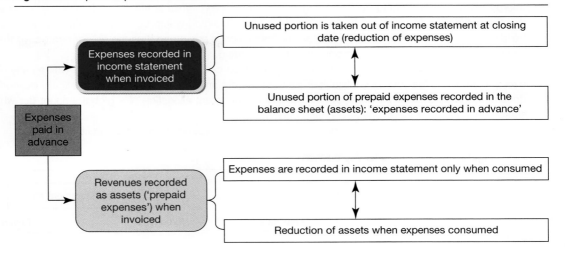

periodically to recognize that (a) it has been used and has, thus, contributed to the creation of revenue (wear and tear on the equipment due to its use has reduced its potential to create a stream of future economic benefits); and (b) its technological obsolescence. This adjustment should only be applied to assets with a limited economic life. For example, land is not considered subject to these downward value adjustments (although it satisfies all the criteria of definition of an asset) because the stream of future economic benefits is not, normally, affected by use. Incidentally, any increase in value of land is also going to remain unrecorded in accounting because of the prudence principle.

Depreciation[2] is the process of allocating the cost of a tangible asset (or some intangible assets, as we will see in Chapter 8, where it is referred to as *amortization*) over the period during which economic benefits are likely to be received by the firm. The justification for this process is found in the matching principle because each period benefits from the existence of the asset and is therefore deemed to consume a share of the original cost. Depreciation has already been mentioned in Chapter 2. Chapter 7 will give us the opportunity to explore further the depreciation mechanisms and their implication in the management of the business.

Example Ravel Company

The local tax authorities have informed the accountant that the normal useful life for Ravel Co.'s buildings was 50 years. The acquisition cost of the building was 5,000 CU. This cost should be distributed over that period of time. The managers agree with the accountant that a fixed annual depreciation charge of 100 CU (i.e., 5,000 CU/50 years) should be attached to each accounting period.

Tax authorities and most accounting regulatory bodies endorse the no offsetting principle, whose application forbids netting the cost of acquisition, and the accumulated depreciation of any asset. As long as an asset is the property of the economic entity, it should be shown in its financial statements. The acquisition cost of a fixed asset will be shown separately from the accumulated depreciation. This separate depreciation account is called a 'contra asset' account because it will be listed in the balance sheet on the assets side but with a negative (credit) balance. The financial information users are also interested in the no offsetting of book value and accumulated depreciation; for example, whether Ravel's building is reported as '4,000 CU net' or is reported as 5,000 CU minus 1,000 CU of accumulated depreciation does not give the same information on the business. In the first case it might, with equal probability, be a small, brand new building (which could be highly productive with built-in IT technology and high energy efficiency) or it could be a very old, inefficient building, while in the second case, it is clear to any reader that the building is 10 years old (the expected life of the building would be mentioned in the Notes, and since the building's accumulated depreciation is 20%, the deduction is easy) and thus the reader can derive the appropriate inferences about the value creation potential of that building.

As far as the calculation of income is concerned, depreciation is treated in the same way as any expense item, even though it is a 'calculated charge', i.e., an expense the amount of which is not specifically defined by a source document, but is defined by a somewhat arbitrary but coherent allocation of a global amount (for which there are source documents) over several accounting periods.

Figure 4.6 illustrates the entries required to account for depreciation related to the first year.

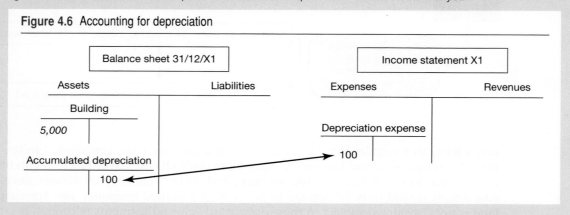

Figure 4.6 Accounting for depreciation

2.3 Value adjustments to current asset accounts

The application of the prudence or conservatism principle, so that information given in the annual accounts satisfies the true and fair view objective, implies that the accounting values recorded during the year for current assets must be validated against economic realities at year-end.

This implies checking that:

■ assets really do physically exist, and

■ their value is not overstated in relation to the future benefits that they represent.

The first point, an asset protection issue (internal control issue), is addressed through carrying a physical inventory of the existing current and fixed assets on a regular basis. The second point refers to the lower of cost or market rule: if the price that a willing purchaser is prepared to pay for an asset (i.e., its market value) is below its original cost, its accounting value should be reduced to this lower value.

To ensure that the 'market value' of the current assets is equal to or greater than the value in the ledger accounts, the Ravel Company accountant would have to study the underlying supporting documents and other data. As far as cash and bank balances are concerned there is usually no problem since both accounts are held in one given currency unit.

For inventories of *finished products*, the accountant confirmed with management that the current sales prices and the future sales forecasts gave every assurance that customers would pay an amount at least equal to the recorded cost of the products held in the inventories.

For inventories of *raw materials*, the accountant verified that the production program indicated clearly that all items held in inventory will be used (i.e., there are no obsolete materials, components or parts) and the cost of acquisition is not higher than the current replacement cost (i.e., their market price plus procurement costs).

Therefore, in our illustration, no value adjustment is necessary for these categories of current assets. The accountant also needs to evaluate the probability that Ravel Company

Figure 4.7 Recording of a provision expense

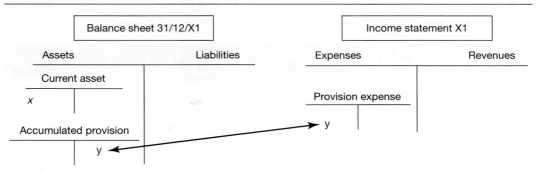

will recover the full value of claims held by Ravel over its customers (accounts receivable). To do this, he or she studies the situation of each individual customer, looking, for example, at the following aspects:

- Has the customer challenged the validity of the receivable?
- Has the customer returned goods and/or complained about Ravel Co.'s service?
- Is the customer up to date with payments in accordance with the agreed contractual terms governing the sales?
- Is there any correspondence (or other data) indicating that the customer has or had financial difficulties?
- Have any letters from Ravel Company been returned as undeliverable from the customer's address?

Although value adjustment to current assets will be developed more fully in Chapter 10, suffice it to say at this stage that a loss of value of a current asset will be recorded through contra asset accounts such as provisions, allowances or impairment losses for which the mechanism is very similar to that of depreciation (with the main difference that depreciation is established in a systematic way and provisions, allowances or impairment losses for adjustments are established on an *ad hoc* basis only). Such a process is illustrated in Figure 4.7. Provision or allowance entries conform to the **no offsetting** principle as well as the lower of cost or market value seen under the units of measurement principle (section 1.2.1).

2.4 Reporting for adjusting entries

Some illustrations of actual notes to financial statements follow that provide details, in conformance with the no offsetting principle, of the elements affected by adjusting entries and which create the balances reported.

KPN, LVMH, Telefonica

Notes to the financial statements

- 'Accrued income' and prepayments mainly consist of prepaid rent recognized at net present value. (KPN – Netherland s – IFRS – Annual report 2008 – Fixed line telecommunications)

- 'Prepaid expenses' include samples and advertising materials, particularly for Perfumes and Cosmetics. (LVMH – France – IFRS - Annual report 2008 – Clothing and Accessories)

- 'Deferred income' principally includes the amount of connection fees not yet recognized in the income statement. These will be recognized as revenue over the estimated customer relationship period (Telefónica –Spain – IFRS – Annual report 2008 – Fixed line telecommunications)

Philips (Netherlands – IFRS – Source: Annual report 2008 – Consumer electronic products) offers, in its annual statements notes, an example of a very detailed list of components of accrued liabilities:

Note 18. Accrued liabilities

Accrued liabilities are summarized as follows:	2007	2008
Personnel-related costs:		
Salaries and wages	433	438
Accrued holiday entitlements	178	192
Other personnel-related costs	169	161
Fixed-asset-related costs:		
Gas, water, electricity, rent and other	62	69
Taxes:		
Income tax payable	154	132
Other taxes payable	12	16
Communication & IT costs	31	23
Distribution costs	109	92
Sales-related costs:		
Commissions payable	43	53
Advertising and marketing-related costs	66	87
Other sales-related costs	206	249
Material-related accruals	134	170
Interest-related accruals	110	79
Deferred income	564	671
Derivative instruments – liabilities	144	505
Restructuring-related liabilities	20	163
Other accrued liabilities	549	536
Total	**2,984**	**3,636**

Meritage Hospitality Group (USA – US GAAP – Source: Annual report 2008 – Quick-service and casual dining restaurant industries) provides a different level of details in its Note 8 (accrued liabilities are very business specific and thus, as a rule, only an aggregate balance is reported in the balance sheet, and business-specific details are provided in the notes, when appropriate):

Excerpts from the Balance sheet at year end

Year ended (amounts in dollars)	30 November 2008	2 December 2007
LIABILITIES AND STOCKHOLDERS' EQUITY		
(…)		
Accrued liabilities	1,919,823	2,013,917
(…)		

Notes to financial statements

8. Accrued liabilities

The following is a detail of accrued liabilities:

$	2008	2007
Payroll and related payroll taxes	1,276,779	1,329,068
Property taxes	412,220	376,074
Interest expense	65,409	95,951
Sales tax	30,567	51,965
Michigan business tax	106,000	33,461
Other expenses	28,848	127,398
Total accrued liabilities	1,919,823	2,013,917

Comment: This example illustrates how to reconcile the amount reported in the balance sheet (1,919,823 $ at the end of 2008) and the detail provided in the notes.

adidas Group (Germany – IFRS – Source: Annual report 2008 – Footwear), like Philips or Meritage, reports details of its accrued liabilities in one of its notes, and, as the illustration below shows, the composition of – and information on – the account balance is specific to adidas' business model

Note 16. Accrued liabilities and provisions		
€ in millions	31 Dec 2008	thereof non-current
Marketing	54	–
Employee benefits	42	13
Returns, allowances, warranty	114	1
Taxes, other than income taxes	13	–
Other provisions	123	14
Total provisions	**346**	**28**
Goods and services not yet invoiced	327	–
Marketing	155	4
Payroll and commissions	157	23
Other accruals	88	10
Total accrued liabilities	**727**	**37**
Total accrued liabilities and provisions	**1,073**	**65**

Accrued liabilities for payroll and commissions mainly consist of accruals for outstanding salary payments, such as bonuses and overtime, as well as outstanding vacation. Other accrued liabilities mainly include items not otherwise allocated and also accruals for interest.

3 Recording of adjusting entries in practice

After the introduction of the main types of adjusting entries, we will now explore the details of how each is being recorded in accounting.

3.1 Revenues earned but not recorded

Let us use the example of royalty revenue not invoiced because the department in charge has been overworked and lags behind in invoicing. At the end of the year, the accountant records an amount of 20 CU, as an *estimate* of the royalty to be recovered.

Figure 4.8 Accrual of revenues at year-end – Year X1

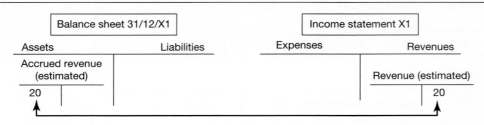

During the next accounting period, when the royalty department has time to calculate the definitive amount to claim, an invoice is issued for 25 CU. Figures 4.8 and 4.9 describe the way to handle the situation. First the estimate is recorded when the X1 accounts are closed (Figure 4.8) and then the correcting or completing entry will be made in X2 (Figure 4.9)

Two possible solutions for handling the completion of the transaction in the second period are illustrated in Figure 4.9.

Appendix 4.1 analyzes these two alternative solutions in more detail.

3.2 Revenues recorded but unearned

The general principles for handling such an entry have been introduced above. Two possible methods have been mentioned:

- **Method 1**: Revenues received in advance (i.e., consideration or cash received) are recorded, in their entirety, as a liability. The end of period adjusting entry calculates how much of that liability, created when the early payment was received, should be recognized as earned in the X1 income statement, thus reducing it by that amount.

Figure 4.9 Accrual of revenues – Year X2

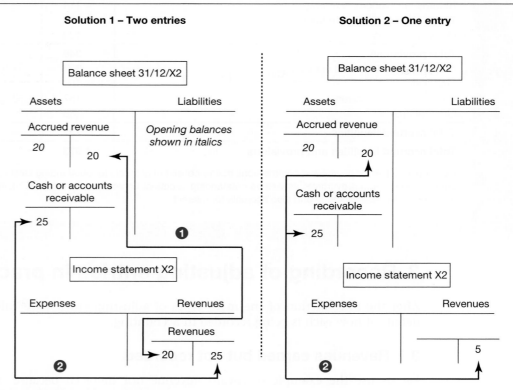

❶ Opening date (of accounting period X2)
❷ On the date the source document is received (date of the event).

■ **Method 2**: Revenues are recorded as fully earned when received in advance for their full amount and adjusted (reduced) later by a second entry at book-closing time.

The example below allows us to compare, side by side, the two methods.

Example

A property owner received, on 15 December X1, 200 CU for the rental of a property. The lease agreement specifies the rent is to be paid upfront for two months. Thus the payment grants the right of occupancy of the property to the tenant for the period extending from 15 December X1 until 14 February X2. The landlord's business books close on 31 December X1. The rent received upfront must therefore be apportioned between period X1 (for half a month or ¼ of the amount) and period X2 (for a month and a half or ¾ of the amount received). Figure 4.10 illustrates the two ways accounting can record the situation in the books of the landlord:
-   Method 1: only the 50 CU earned are recorded as revenue.
-   Method 2: the entire 200 CU are recorded as revenue upon receipt and will be adjusted (reduced) at the end of the accounting period for the unearned part (150 CU).

Figure 4.10 Revenues recorded in advance – Year X1

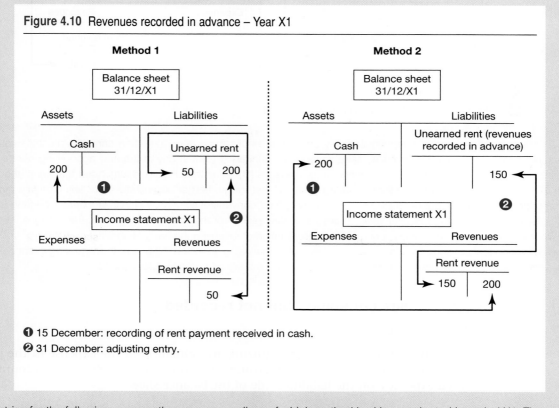

❶ 15 December: recording of rent payment received in cash.
❷ 31 December: adjusting entry.

Entries for the following year are the same, regardless of which method had been adopted in period X1. They are presented in Figure 4.11.

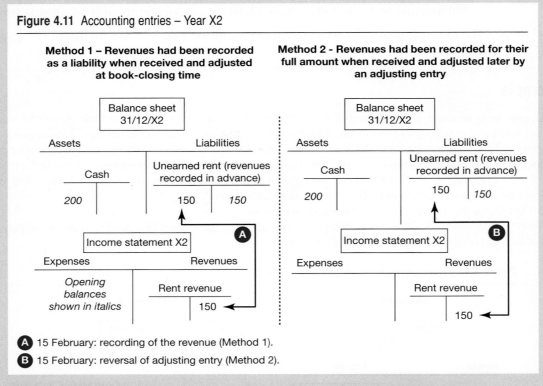

Figure 4.11 Accounting entries – Year X2

Method 1 – Revenues had been recorded as a liability when received and adjusted at book-closing time

Method 2 - Revenues had been recorded for their full amount when received and adjusted later by an adjusting entry

Ⓐ 15 February: recording of the revenue (Method 1).

Ⓑ 15 February: reversal of adjusting entry (Method 2).

In the case of method 2, firms which rarely close their books more frequently than annually (mostly small and medium firms), often, and for simplicity sake, reverse, on January 1 (or first day of the new accounting period), the adjusting entries of the same type as the one shown here as **(B)** so as to not have to remember to reverse the entry on the date the revenue will actually be earned (here: 15 February). Larger organizations, or any firm with modern accounting software, do not need to use this simplifying and convenient solution, which is incoherent with the principles. Since the reversing of the entry will, in any case, take place, for the immense majority of transactions, at some point during the annual accounting period, the approximation of reversing the entry on the first day of the accounting period is of no real consequence, as long as no intermediate closing is carried out before the triggering event causing the actual reversal of the entry. Comments on the two solutions are provided in Appendix 4.2.

3.3 Expenses consumed but not recorded

3.3.1 Principle

The adjusting entry consists in recognizing an estimation of the expense in the income statement of the current period and creating a corresponding 'debt' in an account called 'accrued expenses' on the liabilities side of the balance sheet.

Example

An electricity utility company invoices its customers on a bimonthly basis after the customers' meters have been read. Customer Michael received, on 15 December X1, the invoice for its consumption of electricity in October and November of X1. Michael's accountant must, therefore, at year-end, calculate or estimate the cost of electricity consumed in December. Michael's own electrical engineer, using the installed base and past consumption of previous years, provides the accountant with an *estimate* of the number of kWh (kilowatt hours) consumed in December. Thus, using the rate known from previous invoices, the accountant calculates that the estimated electricity expense for December X1 amounts will be around 175 CU (see Figure 4.12). Michael's accountant thus recognizes both an expense of 175 CU in the income statement of X1 and an 'accrued electricity payable' for the same amount, indicating that the estimated expense will, in fact, be paid in February of X2 or later, after the relevant invoice is received (and the actual consumption known).

Figure 4.12 Accrual of electricity expense – Year X1

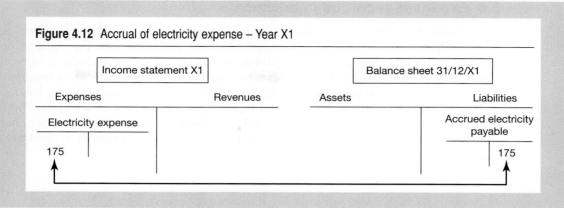

This illustration shows the recording process of the expense consumed but not recorded is the same, whether the income statement is presented 'by nature of expense' or 'by function' (see these concepts in Chapters 2 and 5). This example has also illustrated the way to close the books at the end of the year for events that straddle the closing date.

The next issue is to see how to handle the second part of this transaction in the following year. Two solutions are possible: either we use two entries or we use a single entry. We continue the procedure with the last transaction. Let us assume further that an analysis of the detailed invoice received in mid-February shows the real cost of electricity for December of X1 was 180 CU (instead of the 175 estimated). Figure 4.13 illustrates how accounting will handle the situation. Regardless of the method selected the underestimation of the electricity cost will be charged to the income statement of X2.

Appendix 4.3 presents some comments on this type of entry.

Figure 4.13 Recording – Year X2

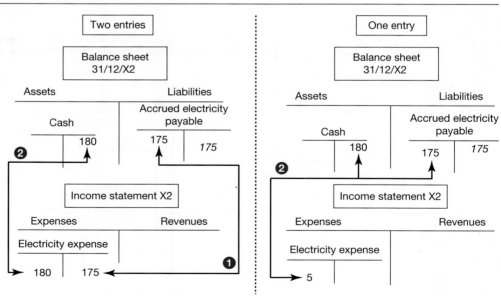

Opening balances shown in italics

1 Opening date (beginning of X2).

2 Source document is received in X2 (i.e., date of the confirming event).

3.4 Expenses recorded in advance

This situation is often encountered when a business acquires any kind of prepaid service such as insurance coverage (the premium is always paid upfront), the right to occupy space in a building (rent is generally paid at the beginning of the period), or subscription to a variety of services such as phone, Internet provider, utilities, preventive maintenance, etc. (as opposed to the cost of consumption, which can only be known after the fact).

Here again two methods can be used to record expenses paid in advance. They have been mentioned earlier in the chapter and are similar, in principle, to the two methods used for revenue above (section 3.2). Let us now look at some examples to illustrate these methods.

Michael's business pays its 120 CU Property and Liability Insurance premium on 1 September for coverage to be received during the next 12 months. The closing date for the accounts is 31 December (see Figure 4.14).

Year X2 entries are described in Figure 4.15. Regardless of the method used upon payment (period X1), the entries for period X2 are the same. The adjustment takes place at any time during the period of coverage of the insurance premium whenever books are closed (if the date is earlier than the expiration of coverage), or, more likely if books are closed yearly, whenever the benefits received (insurance coverage) expire.

Appendix 4.4 compares the two methods and comments on their implementation.

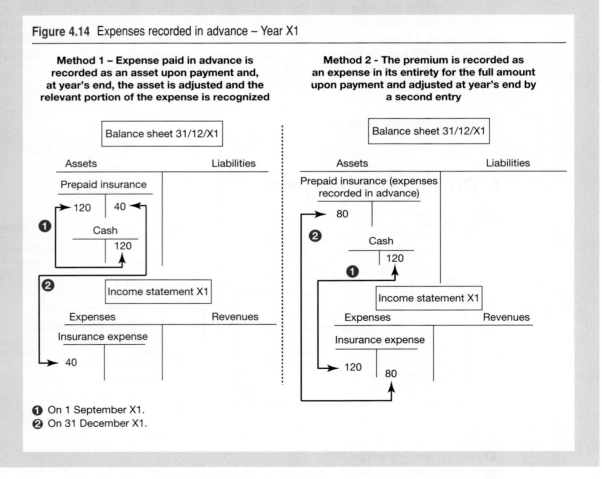

Figure 4.14 Expenses recorded in advance – Year X1

Method 1 – Expense paid in advance is recorded as an asset upon payment and, at year's end, the asset is adjusted and the relevant portion of the expense is recognized

Method 2 - The premium is recorded as an expense in its entirety for the full amount upon payment and adjusted at year's end by a second entry

❶ On 1 September X1.
❷ On 31 December X1.

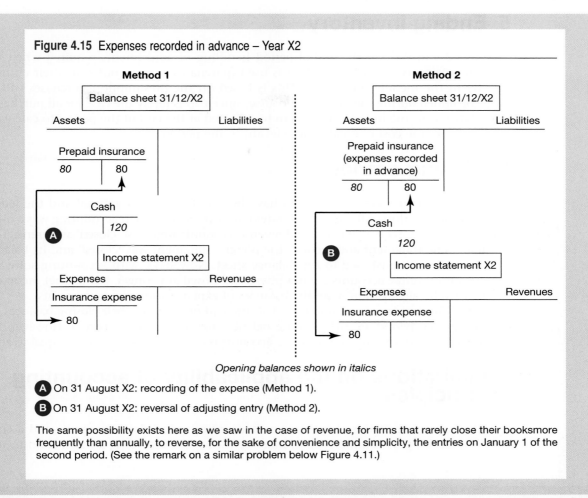

Figure 4.15 Expenses recorded in advance – Year X2

Opening balances shown in italics

A On 31 August X2: recording of the expense (Method 1).

B On 31 August X2: reversal of adjusting entry (Method 2).

The same possibility exists here as we saw in the case of revenue, for firms that rarely close their booksmore frequently than annually, to reverse, for the sake of convenience and simplicity, the entries on January 1 of the second period. (See the remark on a similar problem below Figure 4.11.)

4 Correction of errors

Accounting records may contain errors. We saw in Chapter 3 that computerization of accounting could guarantee a quasi-perfect reliability of transfers between accounts, but errors in the original recording, generally involving a human intervention, may have been introduced without being immediately detected. It is part of normal procedures for all firms establishing financial statements to carry out an internal audit of their procedures and practices to create assurance that the figures are true and fair and devoid of mistakes. When carried out with rigor, this internal audit can detect the majority of errors and allow for their immediate correction. In addition, because financial statements are so important for a variety of users, especially the shareholders, the latter mandate (during the annual General Assembly) an external accountant (external auditor) to carry out an independent audit so as to make doubly sure that all figures are true and fair.

When an error is uncovered, the most common solution is the cancellation of the erroneous entry through a 'reversing entry' and the re-entry of the correct data for the same event. Some accounting software packages allow a pure and simple cancellation or modification of an entry until it has been validated and rendered 'definitive'. Such a possibility is convenient, but can be dangerous because it does not leave any trace of the original (erroneous) entry, the identification of which, in many cases, can be a source of improvement and learning.

Errors and omissions that are uncovered after the books are definitely closed and the financial statements drawn require a special procedure, which will be dealt with in Chapter 6.

5 Ending inventory

Chapters 2 and 9 cover the end-of-period handling of adjustments required when the periodic inventory valuation method is used (purchases were recorded in their entirety directly in the income statement). This is based on the presumption purchases will be fully consumed during the period. Of course, since this is rarely the case for all purchases, as we have seen, the initial entry has to be adjusted at the end of the period to calculate, by deduction, the cost of goods sold relevant to the period.

6 Closing entries

Once the year-end accounting entries have been entered in the journal and the ledger accounts, preparation of the financial statements can begin. When accounting was a manual process, all individual expense and revenue accounts were first 'closed' and transferred to the income statement and second, the income statement was 'closed' and its balance (the net income) transferred to the balance sheet. Nowadays, with accounting software, expense and revenue accounts are not physically closed any longer, but the net income is still defined by aggregation of all the balances of expense and revenue accounts.

Balance sheet accounts are not 'closed' at the end of the year: their closing balances for one accounting period are the opening balances for the following period. However, the opening balance of expense and revenue accounts is always, by construction, equal to zero.

7 Limitations on the applicability of accounting principles

As indicated earlier in this chapter, some accounting principles have limits and a cost/benefit analysis, plus common sense, must be used when recording a transaction to stay

Key points

- Accounting for transactions follows a certain number of guidelines or principles, which are accepted by all accountants around the world.

- These principles apply to all accounting entries and provide a common foundation for improved understandability and comparability of financial statements.

- In order to reach its final objective of providing a 'true and fair view', accounting information must respect four major requirements: (1) objectivity (unit of measurement, basis of valuation and no offsetting); (2) quality of information (materiality, faithful representation and substance over form); (3) prudence (conservatism, accrual basis and matching); and (4) periodicity (accounting period, consistency and going concern).

- The term 'end-of-period entry' refers to any entry that is necessary to give a true and fair view of both the financial position and the income statement. These entries will be carried out every time one closes the books (yearly, half-yearly, quarterly, monthly, etc.).

- The main categories of end-of-period entries are: adjusting entries, entries relating to changes in value of fixed assets (depreciation and amortization), entries concerning changes in value of current assets (provision or valuation allowance), corrections of errors, entries relating to ending inventory (if necessary) and closing entries.

- One fundamental difficulty encountered with year-end financial statements is that the accounting period (generally the year, and, for companies quoted on a stock exchange, more and more the quarter), does not correspond to the duration of a normal operating cycle. Consequently, a cut-off date has to be selected to allow proper matching and year-end adjustments must be recorded.

- The four main categories of adjusting entries are: 'revenues earned but not recorded', 'revenues recorded but unearned', 'expenses consumed but not recorded' and 'expenses recorded but not consumed'.

Review (solutions are at the back of the book)

in line with the intent of the whole process, which remains to create as true and fair a view as possible of the financial situation of the business (see one example in Appendix 4.5).

Review 4.1 Adam

Topic: Accounting principles and end-of-period entries

Eve Adam, a recent hire at the accounting firm Dewey, Billem and How, is puzzled by the preliminary balance sheet of four of the clients she is in charge of.

Company 1 – Balance sheet on 31 December (000 CU)			
Assets		Shareholders' equity and liabilities	
Fixed assets (gross)	300,000	**Shareholders' equity**	
Less accumulated depreciation	–160,000	Share capital and retained earnings	330,000
Fixed assets (net)	140,000	Net income of the period	20,000
Current assets		**Liabilities**	40,000
Inventories	120,000		
Accounts receivable	130,000		
Total assets	390,000	**Total shareholders' equity and liabilities**	390,000

Eve Adam has learned that a freeway is going to be built in the next year adjacent to one large property the company had set aside to build housing for its employees. This piece of land is carried in the books at its historical acquisition cost of 100,000 CU. The market value of land in the area has fallen by 40% as soon as the news of the construction of the freeway became public.

Company 2 – Balance sheet on 31 December (000 CU)			
Assets		Shareholders' equity and liabilities	
Fixed assets (gross)	250,000	**Shareholders' equity**	
Less accumulated depreciation	–130,000	Share capital and retained earnings	300,000
Fixed assets (net)	120,000	Net income of the period	50,000
Current assets		**Liabilities**	20,000
Inventories	100,000		
Accounts receivable	150,000		
Total assets	370,000	**Total shareholders' equity and liabilities**	370,000

When analyzing the accounts receivable, Eve Adam finds out that the Lakme Corp. accounts receivable, has been in arrears for the past three years over an invoice of 60,000 CU. Company 2 has never handled the situation in accounting terms. Exploring a little further, Eve Adam discovers that Lakme Corp. has actually filed for bankruptcy two years ago and that the probability of collecting on the receivable is probably nil.

Company 3 – Balance sheet on 31 December (000 CU)			
Assets		Shareholders' equity and liabilities	
Fixed assets (gross)	500,000	**Shareholders' equity**	
Less accumulated depreciation	–240,000	Share capital and retained earnings	520,000
Fixed assets (net)	260,000	Net income of the period	20,000
Current assets		**Liabilities**	200,000
Inventories	330,000		
Accounts receivable	150,000		
Total assets	740,000	**Total shareholders' equity and liabilities**	740,000

Eve Adam is rather surprised by the valuation of the inventory of 300,000 pieces of gold jewelry. On average, the jewelry pieces were acquired at a cost of 1,000 CU each. On 31 December, the wholesale market price of the jewelry pieces is 1,100 CU each. The head accountant of Company 3 seems to have valued the inventory at its replacement cost.

Company 4 – Balance sheet on 31 December (000 CU)			
Assets		Shareholders' equity and liabilities	
Fixed assets (gross)	210,000	**Shareholders' equity**	
Less accumulated depreciation	–90,000	Share capital and retained earnings	150,000
Fixed assets (net)	120,000	Net income of the period	10,000
Current assets		**Liabilities**	120,000
Inventories	40,000		
Accounts receivable	120,000		
Total assets	280,000	**Total shareholders' equity and liabilities**	280,000

Eve Adam observes that the income statement includes in the sales revenue one 100,000 CU sale to Godounov, Inc. Despite being in an advanced stage of negotiation, the sale has, however, not yet been concluded and the purchase order signed; however the chief salesperson feels very strongly the sale will actually be signed in the first days of January. The goods that would be sold to Godounov Inc. have been acquired for 70,000 CU and would be sold with a margin on sales of 30%.

Required

Establish the definitive balance sheet for each of the four companies by incorporating the information provided. For each case, specify both the accounting principle concerned and the entry that should be recorded to correct the preliminary balance sheet. The impact of taxation will be omitted.

Review 4.2 Offenbach Company

Topic: Accounting for **adjusting entries**

The Offenbach Company prepares its financial statements for the year ending on 31 December X1.

Required

The table below lists events or transactions that took place during the year X1. Indicate by a checkmark to which category of adjusting entries each event is related.

Closing date is 31 December X1 Event	Revenues recorded but unearned	Revenues earned but not recorded	Expenses recorded and not entirely consumed	Expenses consumed but not recorded
Offenbach Company granted a four-month loan to a related company. Interest on this loan has accrued for one month and is expected to be collected when the loan is due at the end of March X2.				
Offenbach Company owns office space that it rents out to other businesses. On 1 April X1, Offenbach rented out an office and received rent upfront for one full year. At that time, the entire amount was recorded to increase rent revenue of the year.				

Closing date is 31 December X1 Event	Revenues recorded but unearned	Revenues earned but not recorded	Expenses recorded and not entirely consumed	Expenses consumed but not recorded
On 1 October X1, Offenbach Company received from its bank a loan to be repaid at the end of September X2. The applicable annual interest rate is 10% and payable in full at the time the loan will be repaid.				
On 1 September X1, Offenbach Company paid an insurance premium for coverage over the next six months. At the time of payment, insurance expense was increased by the full amount of the premium paid.				
The minutes of the last board meeting in Year X1 recorded the board of directors' decision to give managers and employees year-end bonuses on the basis of X1's income. This amount has not been paid out before the end of the year.				
Offenbach Company placed an advertisement in the local paper in the last week of December X1. The newspaper has published the advertisement but has not yet sent the invoice.				

Assignments

Assignment 4.1
Multiple-choice questions

Select the right answer (only one possible answer unless otherwise stated).

1. Which of the following measurement bases does not exist?

    (a) Historical cost
    (b) Decreasing cost
    (c) Realizable value
    (d) Present value

2. A business has two bank accounts: one has a positive balance of 100 CU and the second has a negative balance of 40 CU. What should be reported in the balance sheet?

    (a) A net positive balance of 60 CU on the assets side
    (b) A net positive balance of 60 CU on the liabilities side
    (c) A balance of 100 CU on the assets side and a balance of 40 CU on the liabilities side
    (d) A balance of 40 CU on the asset side and a balance of 100 CU on the liabilities side

3. Information which, if not disclosed on the financial statements, could influence the economic decisions of users, is known as:

    (a) Material
    (b) Substantial
    (c) Interesting
    (d) Important
    (e) None of these

4. Which principle(s) serve(s) to achieve the objective of prudence?

    (a) Conservatism
    (b) Matching
    (c) Accrual
    (d) All of these
    (e) None of these

5. Sales should be recorded only when:

    (a) The order is received
    (b) The sales manager has negotiated the price with the customer
    (c) The customer is satisfied
    (d) The goods have been shipped and invoiced

6. Which of the following fixed assets are generally *not* subject to depreciation?

   (a) Building
   (b) Equipment
   (c) Land
   (d) Office furniture

7. On 1 June, The Dukas Company paid three months rent in advance, for a total cost of 900 CU. At the time of payment, prepaid rent was increased by this amount. What adjusting entry is necessary as part of the 30 June closing?

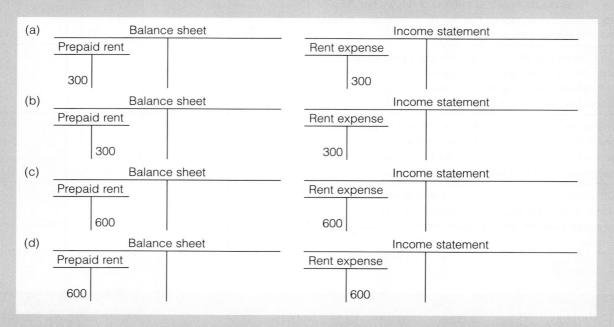

8. The Dukas Company signed a 3,000 CU debit note to Bankix, their local bank on 1 September X3. At that time, the accountant of the company made the appropriate entry. However, no other entry relating to the note has been made. Given that the bank is charging interest at a yearly rate of 10%, what adjusting entry, if any, is necessary on Dukas Company's year-end date of 31 December X3?

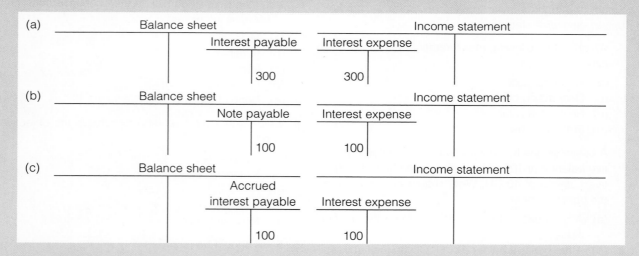

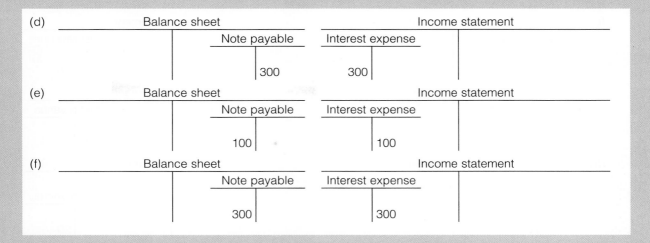

(d) Balance sheet — Note payable 300; Income statement — Interest expense 300

(e) Balance sheet — Note payable 100; Income statement — Interest expense 100

(f) Balance sheet — Note payable 300; Income statement — Interest expense 300

9. The Dukas Company owns offices, which are rented to other businesses. On 1 February, Dukas rented some office space and received six months rent in advance, totaling 6,000 CU. At that time, the entire amount was recorded to increase unearned rent. What adjusting entry is necessary on 28 February, if the company decides to prepare financial statements on that date?

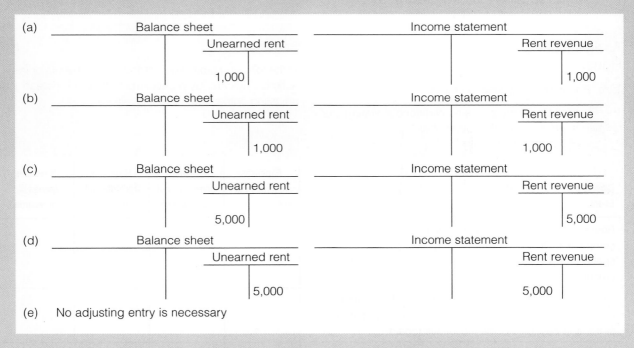

(a) Balance sheet — Unearned rent 1,000; Income statement — Rent revenue 1,000

(b) Balance sheet — Unearned rent 1,000; Income statement — Rent revenue 1,000

(c) Balance sheet — Unearned rent 5,000; Income statement — Rent revenue 5,000

(d) Balance sheet — Unearned rent 5,000; Income statement — Rent revenue 5,000

(e) No adjusting entry is necessary

10. The Dukas Company owns an interest-bearing note receivable with a nominal value of 1,000 CU. Interest at 8% per annum on the note receivable has accrued for three months and is expected to be collected when the note is due in July. What adjusting entry is necessary on 31 March, if the company decides to prepare financial statements at that date?

(a) Balance sheet — Accrued interest receivable 20; Income statement — Interest revenue 20

(b)

Balance sheet		Income statement	
Notes receivable			Interest revenue
80			80

(c)

Balance sheet		Income statement	
Notes receivable			Interest revenue
	80		80

(d)

Balance sheet		Income statement	
Accrued interest receivable			Interest revenue
20			20

(e)

Balance sheet		Income statement	
Notes receivable			Interest revenue
20			20

(f)   No adjusting entry is necessary

Assignment 4.2
Roussel

Topic: Recording of adjusting entries

The Roussel Company prepares its financial statements for the period ending on 31 December X1.

Required

In the following table, you will find a list of events or transactions. Indicate, by a checkmark, to which category of adjusting entries each event is related.

Closing date is 31 December Event	Expenses recorded but not consumed	Expenses consumed but not recorded	Revenues recorded but unearned	Revenues earned but not recorded
Roussel Company owns offices which are rented to other companies. On 1 September X1, Roussel rented some office space and was paid for six months. At that time, the entire amount was recorded to increase rent revenue.				
On 1 April X1, Roussel Company received from its bank a loan to be repaid in March X2. Interest is charged at the rate of 8% and payable at time the loan is repaid.				
On 1 December X1, Roussel Company paid, up-front, a one year subscription fee to a software help-line up front. At the time of payment, maintenance expense was increased by the total amount of the expense.				
The minutes of the last board meeting in X1 recorded the board of directors' decision to give managers and employees year-end bonuses. This amount has not been paid out before the end of the year.				

Closing date is 31 December	Expenses recorded but not consumed	Expenses consumed but not recorded	Revenues recorded but unearned	Revenues earned but not recorded
Roussel Company has delivered some merchandise to a customer but the sales department did not have time to issue the invoice before the end of X1. The invoice is printed and sent to the customer on 15 January X2.				
Roussel Company received some advice from its lawyer during the month of December X1. The lawyer will send her invoice in February X2.				

Assignment 4.3
Gounod Company

Topic: Accounting principles

Guillemette Gounod is CEO of the Gounod Corporation, a manufacturer of smartcards and electronic personal identification devices. As chair of the annual meeting of shareholders she is reporting on the performance of the previous period and commenting on some of the key points revealed by the financial statements. Her remarks follow.

1. Despite the figures you can observe in the comparative income statements, sales activity of X1 is significantly greater than that of period X0. Several major customers, essentially government and semi-government agencies with unused budget allowances in X0 had paid in advance in X0 for deliveries that did not take place until X1. This shifted sales that really took place in X1 towards X0, thus creating the erroneous perception that X1 sales were only 10% greater than those of X0. In reality the sales of your company have increased brilliantly by 40% in X1 over X0. This is quite an achievement in this down economy.

2. Further to this understatement of the X1 sales, our X1 purchases have been inflated because we accepted early delivery of about three months' worth of card readers we purchase from MG-Electronics. MG-Electronics is a subsidiary of Silver Electric International and the CEO of MG-E asked us, and we accepted, to help him meet his X1 sales growth target by accepting early delivery and invoicing. His unit was particularly hit by the downturn in the economy and we were happy to help a key supplier. In addition, as a counterpart to this early delivery and invoicing, credit terms were extended to six-months from the actual delivery, thus this agreement will have no impact on our cash situation, especially since we have plenty of available storage space.

These two events together, deflated sales and inflated purchases, affect negatively the reported income of X1, as you can well understand.

3. You will observe that the balance sheet shows an asset called capitalized R&D. The net addition, this year, to that asset has been lower than last year. The R&D team is involved in a long-term project, a new-generation smartcard, which we do not expect to see hitting the market for another year at least. The headcount of our R&D team has been reduced this year by one person, due to our seconding Dr. Thaddeusz Czapik to PT-Microelectronics to work on the development of the new generation of microchips we will use in our new smartcard.

4. As you know we capitalize the work (engineering and legal) that leads to our taking patents to protect our intellectual capital. In X1 we are valuing the new patents registered in our name at 160,000 CU, down from 340,000 CU in X0. I have been worried by this downward trend and have investigated. I found our patents department has been understaffed due to long sick-leaves of two of its members (and no suitable replacement was procured) and is way behind in filing applications for new patents.

5. Our company's reputation and market share have been increasing significantly. I have been asking, repeatedly, our external auditor to allow us to recognize, as an asset, this increase in value of the firm due to both our name and the quality of our products and labor force in the larger sense. The auditor refused once again to recognize this value creation, fruit of the labor of my team and I will later propose a motion to change auditors.

6. Our tangible assets are essentially numerically-controlled machines, which still work magnificently well in the manufacturing of our products. These machines have not lost any of the potential they had when we bought them. However, I have had

to reluctantly accept the demand by the CFO to depreciate them on the balance sheet. Fortunately the machines were purchased before a price increase. Therefore, despite that added cost of depreciation, we are still comparatively the most competitive producer in the market, despite our older equipment.

7. The chief accountant has told me that each year he chooses the best methods for depreciating the building and fixtures in order to minimize taxable income. This year I understand we used the straight-line method but last year we had used a form of accelerated depreciation (the declining balance method).

8. My last remark also leads me to be critical of our auditor. I still do not understand why we are not allowed to build a provision for the cost of laying-off all or most of our personnel. Such a provision would, of course, reduce taxes if it were allowed by the tax authorities but, mainly, it would give us a true and fair view (accountants have been using this buzzword around me too much!) of the situation of our company in case of a continuation of the downturn in the economy.

Required

Ms. Guillemette Gounod seems to have an incomplete understanding of some key accounting principles. For each of the points of her speech to the shareholders, identify the relevant accounting principle(s) that may have been ignored, or applied properly or improperly and explain to her, each time it is required, the correct position she should accept.

Assignment 4.4
Lalo Company

Topic: End-of period entries

The company

Lalo Company, headquartered in Vaduz, is a company listed in Amsterdam, Paris and Zurich. It is the third largest small home appliance manufacturer in Europe. The company was founded in 1955 by Patrick O'Share, a self-made millionaire, whose family emigrated from Ireland during the 1930s. Despite Lalo being a public company, the O'Share family still holds a significant interest in the company through the ownership of 20% of the outstanding voting shares. The remainder of the shares is actively traded and the stock ownership is diversified. Patrick O'Share, now 70 years old, serves in the largely

honorary position of Chairman of the Board. His eldest daughter, Minnie Mize (her married name), 45, is the current President and Chief Executive Officer.

The company has a 31 December fiscal year-end. Today is 10 January X2 and the books for year X1 are about to be physically closed (as of 31 December X1). All normal and recurring transactions have been recorded in the accounts and a preliminary balance sheet and income statement have been prepared (see Exhibits 1 and 2).

Eric Faithful, Vice President of Finance, has organized a meeting to discuss several issues concerning seven year-end adjustments and closing entries. All parties interested in the year-end adjusting entries have been invited to attend. The meeting will include, among others, Eric Faithful, Minnie Mize (CEO), Max E. Mumm (Vice President for Investor Relations), Celia Vee (Vice President for Sales) and Gunther Somday (Vice President for Production).

Key players

After graduating from a French Graduate School of Business, Eric Faithful qualified as a Certified Public Accountant. He worked as an Audit Supervisor for a 'Big Four' accounting firm in Frankfurt before joining Lalo two years ago. In his opinion, compliance with the letter and spirit of generally accepted accounting principles is essential. He is opposed to any form of manipulation of the accounts. He often declares: 'Our mission is to give a clear and truthful view of the financial position and results of operations of the company'.

Minnie Mize, being both the daughter of the founder of the Company and having progressed through the ranks from being a salesperson to her current position as President and CEO, is a firm believer, especially in the difficult economy that affects the globe at this time, in reinvesting profits and generating enough operating cash flows to support growth without having to depend too much on external financing. Her philosophy is that the accounting experts should 'use conservative accounting methods and take advantage of all legal loopholes to minimize reported and taxable income and avoid unnecessary drains on the cash flow of the company. A better future for all comes from our ability to generate and reinvest as large a cash flow as possible'.

After five years in the Investor Relations Department of a large North American conglomerate, Max E. Mumm assumed the position of Vice President for Investor Relations at Lalo approximately 12 months ago. He has been critical of what he sometimes refers to as the 'lack of vision of the family'. He believes that presenting the company in the most favorable light, and maintaining effective communications with financial analysts and the investment community, are key to the company's success. 'If we are to continue expanding in the face of increased international competition and the consolidation trend in the industry in this depressed economic environment, we are going to need to obtain additional equity capital. We must keep the loyalty of our shareholders and attract new ones. It is essential for a growing business like ours to earn a high return on equity in order to lower our cost of capital'.

Minutes of the meeting

Item on the agenda: Seven adjusting entries still need to be finalized and this is the major objective of the meeting.

1. Depreciation

Eric Faithful: 'Last 1 July, we purchased a new sheet metal press for 1 million CU. The cost of the press was added to property, plant and equipment, but no decision has been made yet about its useful life or depreciation. Gunther, what do you think of the useful life of this press?'

Gunther Somday (VP-Production): 'Technically the useful life of the press should be between five and ten years. Although I do not want to interfere with your accounting discussion, I know we have to choose between a straight-line and an accelerated method of depreciation'.

Minnie Mize: 'This is a no-brainer, let's choose the accelerated method and let's do it over the shortest acceptable life, i.e., five years here. The machine will become obsolete in a few years and I'd rather depreciate it to the maximum before we have to scrap it, or at least, as soon as we have benefited from all the production that we're going to get from the machine. Eric, I believe we should multiply the straight-line amount by two to get the accelerated amount, is that right?'

Eric Faithful: 'Yes, it would be two, if we use double-declining balance depreciation. That would give a depreciation rate equal to twice as much as straight-line. This rate would be applied to the remaining balance, until you have to switch back to straight-line when the amount of depreciation expense is lower than the straight-line amount calculated over the remaining years. Of course, whatever method of depreciation we choose, we must start depreciating as of 1 July X1'.

Max E. Mumm: 'I don't agree with that approach. This machine will have a remaining life expectancy of at least ten years. With our projected sales demand we can use the machine's capacity for at least ten years to come. And, on top of that, I hear it's a good machine with a technology that will not become obsolete that soon. Based on these facts, I feel the straight-line method is the one that is most appropriate. In addition, analysts tell me that straight-line depreciation is the method that is most commonly used by our competitors. Furthermore, if we choose to depreciate the machine over ten years, we will show a better bottom line. If the machine were to become obsolete, we could just expense the remaining un-depreciated book value at that point in time. Why penalize ourselves in the eyes of shareholders?'

Eric Faithful: 'I don't necessarily agree with either of you. Our accounting methods should reflect as accurately as possible the actual position of the company. Gunther says that given the new products in the pipeline, he expects to use the machine at least for the next eight years, but beyond that he is not sure we'll still use this technology. I would therefore suggest we take the eight-year time frame into consideration in our decision about depreciation. As for the method of depreciation, the accelerated method seems to me to be the most appropriate because the market indicates that the resale value of the machine falls off dramatically after the first year of operation. I second Minnie's motion in favor of the double-declining balance method'.

2. Allowance for doubtful accounts

Eric Faithful: 'A 200,000 CU invoice for a sale of microwaves that we made last 15 May to Worldapart is still outstanding and the receivable is still unpaid. The sales people estimate that, in all probability, we will not collect more than 10% to 40%. Their best educated guess is that we will collect about 30%'.

Minnie Mize: 'How about creating a provision for 90% of that receivable? It is conservative since, at worst, we'll collect only 10%, and it is easy to defend if we are criticized'.

Max E. Mumm: 'Why not provide a 60% allowance? The financial analysts will not be happy if we signal that we might have collection problems that could lead to lower earnings numbers. It would raise our cost of capital at the worst time. Let's work hard on making sure we collect the 40% of that receivable instead of giving up so easily'.

3. Contingent liabilities

Eric Faithful: 'We are also involved in a lawsuit brought against us by Fairprice for patent infringement. They are asking for damages of 200,000 CU. I really see no merit in the suit and we will definitely not settle out of court. I don't know which way the judge will go. I estimate we have a fifty-fifty chance of losing the case. I would suggest recording a liability for half the amount they are seeking'.

Minnie Mize: 'Absolutely not. Let's plan for the worst. What happens if our lawyers blow it? We should provide for the worst case: the full amount. We can reverse the accrual later if our lawyers get us off the hook'.

Max E. Mumm: 'I think that this is another unneeded accrual. The more you accrue, the less earnings you report. Let's face it, this is an era of global capital markets. You may not like it, but the view that the analysts have about the company can make or break it. In any case the amount of damages Fairprice is seeking is ridiculously high. In a lawsuit you know that you always ask for five if you want to get one. If we make the accrual, we would be admitting that we would be willing to pay that amount. So, I don't see any need to make an accrual here at this time'.

4. Revenue recognition

Celia Vee (VP-Sales): 'We may have a problem with determining the exact X1 sales revenue. We shipped a truckload of mini-ovens to Pricelead's warehouse on 28 December. I understand the bookkeeper did not have time to record the invoice until 2 January X2, and I am not sure whether the truck got to their warehouse before that date. We are talking here about an invoice for 500,000 CU; so it is no small change. The question is whether to record the sale in X1 or postpone its recognition into X2'.

Max E. Mumm: 'Since we shipped the goods in December X1, it seems logical to consider it as an X1 sale'.

Minnie Mize: 'But, wait a minute, the invoice was recorded and mailed in X2 and the goods may have been delivered in X2. The preliminary income figures I received show that the operating income for X1 will be great. Wouldn't it be better to shift the revenue into X2? Why make X1 even better? In addition, it would be good for the sales force to know they are starting the year X2 with a little plus, don't you think, Celia? Competition is getting harder every day and we all know they have an uphill battle in front of them. Let's give them a push and record that sale in X2'.

Eric Faithful: 'Sorry to rain on your parade, but I think Celia forgot to tell you that our shipments are always made FOB Shipping Point, from our warehouse'.

5. Accrued warranty expense

Eric Faithful: 'Because of our quality control systems, we have relatively low warranty claims. However, we still need to record a liability for our potential warranty claims. Ramon Psikotic, in the sales department, has estimated the warranty expense for X1 at about 100,000 CU'.

Minnie Mize: 'Yes but the repair department thinks that the cost of warranties is going to increase. The total amount should be 120,000 CU. We can always adjust

the figure downwards later if the real figure ends up being less than anticipated'.

Max E. Mumm: 'Personally, I've reviewed Ramon's calculations and I think that the accrual should only be 80,000 CU. That's the number I would go with'.

6. Deferred revenue

Eric Faithful: 'On 1 November, we received a 300,000 CU cash payment for the rent on the warehouse that we leased to Ready-Sol, our European distributor. This represents the rent for three months, i.e., through the end of January X2. We recorded the full payment as rent revenue in the year X1'.

Max E. Mumm: 'I agree. Since the cash is in, it ought to be recorded as revenue in X1'.

Minnie Mize: 'Sorry, Max, I don't agree! One month of that rent relates to January and therefore only two-thirds of the rent payment should be recognized as revenue for X1'.

7. Deferred expenses

Eric Faithful: 'On 1 September, we paid 90,000 CU for our annual liability insurance premium. We recorded the payment as insurance expense (external expense). The period of coverage extends from 1 September X1, to 31 August X2'.

Minnie Mize: 'What matters is when the payment took place. Keep it fully in X1 expenses'.

Max E. Mumm: 'Wait a minute, here! Since we had no liability claim in X1, the period during which we will receive the benefits from that premium can only be for X2. It would seem more logical to recognize the expense as belonging to X2'.

Required

1. What are the bases for the arguments of each of the three protagonists? What relevant principle(s) support or undermine their position?

2. Prepare the three sets of financial statements (balance sheet as of 31 December X1, plus income statement for year X1) strictly reflecting the points of view of each of the three protagonists on the seven points evoked during the meeting (assume for this question that each protagonist is legitimate in his or her position).

3. Prepare the set of financial statements as of 31 December X1 (balance sheet and income statement) that reflect the correct application of the accounting principles described in the chapter. Arguments advanced, and positions taken, should be backed-up with references to the relevant accounting principles whenever possible.

Exhibits 1 and 2 present the preliminary balance sheet and income statement established by the accountant *before any year-end adjusting entry*. Exhibits 3 and 4 present the financial statements using a different format (see this concept in Chapters 2 and 5): vertical, decreasing for the balance sheet and by function for the income statement. Use either Exhibits 1 and 2 or Exhibits 3 and 4 in your answers to the questions above.

- Calculations should ignore the impact of both income tax and value added tax.
- The only adjustments that need to be made to the balance sheet and income statement are those relating to the seven issues that were discussed above. (Students should not attempt to record the entries that produced the preliminary balance sheet and income statement shown in the exhibits).

Exhibit 1: Preliminary balance sheet before year end adjustments (horizontal, increasing format) 31 December X1 (000 CU)			
Assets			Shareholders' equity and liabilities
Fixed assets (gross)	17,300	Capital	5,000
– Accumulated depreciation	–8,300	Retained earnings	3,000
Fixed assets (net)	9,000	Net income of the period	200
Inventory	4,800		
Accounts receivable (gross)	2,400	Liabilities	8,705
– Accumulated provisions	–95		
Accounts receivable (net)	2,305		
Cash	800		
Total	16,905	Total	16,905

Exhibit 2: Preliminary income statement for X1 before year-end adjustments (format by nature) (000 CU)	
Sales	29,000
Rent revenue	300
Purchases	–20,000
External expenses	–230
Personnel expenses	–6,825
Depreciation expense	–1,100
Provision allowance expense	–95
Operating income	1,050
Financial revenues	220
Financial expenses	–1,070
Financial income	–850
Income before income tax	200

Exhibit 3: Preliminary balance sheet before year-end adjustments (vertical, decreasing format) 31 December X1 (000 CU)	
Assets	
Cash	800
Accounts receivable (gross)	2,400
– Accumulated allowance	–95
Accounts receivable (net)	2,305
Inventory	4,800
Fixed assets (gross)	17,300
– Accumulated depreciation	–8,300
Fixed assets (net)	9,000
Total	16,905
Liabilities and shareholders' equity	
Current liabilities	8,705
Common stock	5,000
Retained earnings and income of the period	3,200
Total	16,905

Exhibit 4: Preliminary income statement for X1 before year-end adjustments (format by function) (000 CU)

Sales	29,000
Cost of goods sold	−20,000
Gross margin	9,000
S, G & A expenses	−8,250
Operating income	750
Rent revenue	300
Interest revenue	220
Interest expense	− 1,070
Net interest expense	−850
Income before income tax	200

Assignment 4.5
Electrolux*

Topic: Reporting for adjusting entries

The Electrolux Group (hereafter 'Electrolux') is a producer of home appliances and appliances for professional use, selling more than 40 million products to customers in 150 countries. The company's operations are divided into consumer durables and professional products. Products for consumers comprise major appliances, such as refrigerators, freezers, cooking ranges, tops and stoves, clothes dryers, washing machines, dishwashers, room air-conditioners and microwave ovens, as well as floor-care products. The financial statements are prepared in accordance with the International Financial Reporting Standards (IFRS). From the consolidated balance sheet (annual report 2008), we extracted the following data (amounts in millions of Swedish Krona, SEK):

Equity and Liabilities

	31 December 2008	31 December 2007
(...)		
Current liabilities		
Accounts payable	15,681	14,788
Tax liabilities	2,329	2,027
Other liabilities	10,644	10,049
Short-term borrowings	3,168	5,701
Derivatives	784	280
Other provisions	2,490	1,303
	35,096	**34,148**

Notes payable (balance sheet)	20,000	Prepaid insurance (balance sheet)	3,600
Unearned fees (balance sheet)	1,200	Fees earned (income statement)	1,800

The notes to financial statements provide, *inter alia*, the following information on 'Other liabilities'.

Note 24 Other liabilities (in SEKm)

	31 December 2008	31 December 2007
Accrued holiday pay	840	863
Other accrued payroll costs	1,453	1,421
Accrued interest expenses	116	295
Prepaid income	309	145
Other accrued expenses	5,714	4,712
Other operating liabilities	2,212	2,613
	10,644	**10,049**

Other accrued expenses include accruals for fees, advertising and sales promotion, bonuses, extended warranty, and other items. Other operating liabilities include VAT and other items.

Required

1. Verify that what is detailed in the notes is coherent with the balance sheet, i.e., crosscheck or 'reconcile'.

2. Explain the principle behind the first three items of 'accrued liabilities' and illustrate your explanation showing the impact on the financial statements of the adjusting entries that have probably been recorded for each of these three items at the end of 2008.

3. What is the conceptual difference between these three items and the line 'prepaid income'?

Assignment 4.6
Poulenc Company

Topic: Adjusting entries

Poulenc & Associates, a consulting firm, was incorporated on 1 June X1. On 30 June, the trial balance shows the following balances for selected accounts:

Analysis reveals the following additional data relating to these accounts (no adjusting entry has been recorded):

1. A customer paid 1,200 CU towards a yearly subscription to a service which Poulenc started providing in June.

2. Prepaid insurance is the cost of a nine-month insurance policy, effective as of 1 June.

3. The note payable is dated 1 June. It is a twelve-month, 10% note.

4. Services rendered to customers but not billed at 30 June totaled 1,500 CU.

Required

Show the impact on the balance sheet and the income statement for Poulenc Company as of 30 June, for each of the above transactions.

Assignment 4.7
Debussy Company

Topic: End-of-period entries and preparation of financial statements

Debussy Company has prepared a set of financial statements in accordance with US GAAP: balance sheet, income statement, and statement of retained earnings (see Exhibit 1). The accounting period X1 ends on 30 September X1. Due to the illness of the company's accountant, none of the end-of-period entries have been recorded.

Required

1. Show the impact on the financial statements of the end-of-period transactions or events which are described in Exhibit 2.

2. Update the financial statements taking into account these transactions and events.

Exhibit 1: Preliminary financial statements (000 CU)

Income statement
For the year ended 30 September X1

Sales	10,000
Cost of goods sold	–6,200
Gross profit	3,800
Operating expenses	
Salaries	–1,300
Advertising	–800
Insurance	–30
Telephone	–40
Maintenance	–20
Rent	–25
Miscellaneous expense	–21
Total operating expenses	– 2,236
Operating income	1,564
Deduct interest expense	–26
Income before income taxes	1,538

Balance sheet – 30 September X1

Assets		Liabilities and shareholders' equity	
Current assets		*Current liabilities*	
Cash	1,000	Accounts payable	600
Accounts receivable	1,178	Notes payable	300
Note receivable	400	Unearned rent revenue	60
Merchandise inventory	2,000	Total current liabilities	960
Unexpired insurance	20		
Total current assets	4,598		
Long-term assets		*Shareholders' equity*	
Land	1,700	Paid-in capital	5,000
Building	3,000	Retained income	3,038
Accumulated depreciation	–300		
Total assets	8,998	Total liabilities and shareholders' equity.	8,998

Statement of retained earnings

Retained income, 1 October X0	1,500
Net income for X1	1,538
Total	3,038
Cash dividends declared	0
Retained income, 30 September X1	3,038

Exhibit 2: End-of-period entries (all amounts in 000 CU)

1. Depreciation expense on the building is 80 CU for X1.
2. Part of the building owned by the company has been rented to other companies with occupancy starting on 1 September X1. The amount invoiced to the tenants (60 CU in total) was paid in advance for three months and collected in cash. It has been recorded in the item 'Unearned rent revenue'.
3. Salaries are paid on a weekly basis. The amount corresponding to the last week of September (100 CU) will be paid at the beginning of October.
4. Interest on the note receivable has accrued for one month. It will be collected when the note is due at the end of December. The rate is 6% per annum.
5. Income tax at the rate of 30% applies to X1. The tax owed will be paid in the following accounting period.
6. Cash dividends of 800 CU were declared in September X1. They will be paid-out in October X1. Such an announcement is common in the United States, where quarterly dividend payments are generally decided by the board, announced by the CEO and, sometimes, later ratified or adjusted *ex post* by shareholders. In many other countries, dividends are commonly decided and paid out on a yearly basis. Their amount can only be decided by the General Assembly and cannot be known before a vote is held.

References

Epstein, M.J. (2008) *Best Practices in Managing and Measuring Corporate Social, Environmental and Economic Impacts*, San Francisco: Berrett-Koehler Publishers.

IASB (1989) Framework for the Preparation and Presentation of Financial Statements, London.

IASB (2003) International Accounting Standard No. 16: Property, Plant and Equipment, London.

IASB (2007) International Accounting Standard No. 1: Presentation of Financial Statements, London.

Further reading

Alexander, D. and Archer, S. (2000) 'On the myth of "Anglo-Saxon" financial accounting', *The International Journal of Accounting* 35(4): 539–57.

Brorstom B. (1998) 'Accrual accounting, politics and politicians', *Financial Accountability & Management* 14(4): November, 319-33.

Colasse, B. (1997) 'The French notion of the *image fidèle*: the power of words', *European Accounting Review* 6(4): 681–91.

Dunk, A.S. and Kilgore, A. (2000) 'The reintroduction of the true and fair override and harmonization with IASC standards in Australia: Lessons from the EU and implications for financial reporting and international trade', *The International Journal of Accounting* 35(2): 213–26.

Evans, L. and Nobes, C. (1996) 'Some mysteries relating to the prudence principle in the Fourth Directive and in German and British Law', *European Accounting Review* 5(2): 361–73.

Evans, L. (2003) 'The true and fair view and the "fair presentation" override of IAS 1', *Accounting and Business Research* 33(4): 311–25.

Gangolly, J.S. and Hussein, M.E.A. (1996) 'Generally accepted accounting principles: Perspectives from philosophy of law', *Critical Perspectives on Accounting* 7(4): 383–407.

Jun Lin, Z. and Chen, F. (1999) 'Applicability of the conservatism accounting convention in China: Empirical evidence', *International Journal of Accounting* 34(4): 517–37.

Livne, G. and McNichols, M.F. (2009) 'An empirical investigation of the true and fair override in the United Kingdom', *Journal of Business Finance & Accounting* 36(1–2): 1–30.

Ordelheide, D. (1993) 'True and fair view: A European and a German perspective', *European Accounting Review* 2(1): 81–90.

Van Hulle, K. (1997) 'The true and fair view override in the European accounting directives', *European Accounting Review* 6(4): 711–20.

Zeff, S.A., Buijink, W. and Camfferman, K. (1999) '"True and fair" in the Netherlands: *inzicht* or *getrouw beeld?*', *European Accounting Review* 8(3): 523–48.

Additional material on the website

Go to http://www.cengage.co.uk/stolowy3 for further information, journal entries and extra assignments for each chapter.

The following appendices to this chapter are available on the dedicated website:

Appendix 4.1: Revenues earned but not recorded
Appendix 4.2: Revenues recorded but unearned
Appendix 4.3: Expenses consumed but not recorded
Appendix 4.4: Expenses recorded in advance
Appendix 4.5: Limitations on the applicability of accounting principles.

Notes

1. It can be noted that the Hammurabi Code (circa 1750 BCE, see http://www.wsu.edu/~dee/MESO/CODE.HTM) specified that payment in a drinking establishment could be paid either in currency or in 'corn', as long as the market price of the quantity of corn demanded by the owner of the establishment, was equivalent to the amount of currency required to obtain the same level of service. Since market prices create equivalencies between goods and currency, it can be said that, even in barter economies, accounting only uses monetary units.
2. There is of course the exception of land, or of inalienable rights for perpetuity which cannot be depreciated but can in some cases be *impaired*.

P2

Part 2

Major Accounting Topics

C5

Chapter 5
Regulation of Accounting and Financial Reporting

Learning objectives

After studying this chapter, you will understand:

- That financial accounting is based on a set of rules and accounting standards, also called financial reporting standards.
- The role of the International Accounting Standards Board (IASB) in harmonizing accounting rules and standards between countries to make financial statements more comparable.
- That the balance sheet and income statement can be presented in different ways but that the logic of their construction remains the same and the informational content is generally not affected by differences in presentation.
- That the balance sheet can be presented vertically or horizontally, using a single-step or a multiple-step approach, and using a classification of assets and liabilities either by nature or by term.
- That the income statement can be presented vertically or horizontally, using a single-step or a multiple-step approach, and using a classification of expenses by nature or by function.
- That no presentation is intrinsically 'better' (i.e., leads to better decisions), as long as it is exhaustive, and the users understand the choices made by the statements' producer.
- The main purpose and contents of the notes to financial statements.
- That the content of the full annual report is more than a mere packaging of the three financial statements plus the relevant notes.
- That accounting terminology in English may differ between countries using English as their business language, and mainly between US English and UK English.

Financial accounting is a producer of a common good: information. The quality of the production system relies on the principles we explored in Chapter 4. However, as we have seen, principles leave leeway and do not resolve all issues. Thus, each country has developed its own series of **'rules and standards'** aimed at creating comparable reporting within like entities in a country. Originally, standards were established country-by-country (we called them the local GAAP) to reflect its specific tax and commercial laws. With the development of international trade, multinational companies and globalization of financial markets, the need for standards common to many countries and markets became imperative as a way to reduce on one hand the cost of financial data production and on the other the cost of data analysis and information production.

The movement towards common standards is called **'harmonization'**. It is a complex political bargaining process, as each participant to a coherent set of standards renounces all or part of its own local standards in favor of the common ones. We will offer our viewpoint on the future of the process of international harmonization.

Each country, because of history and, as we mentioned earlier, because of different cultural sensitivities, has, over time, adopted a preferred specific **format of reporting** for the financial statements of its businesses. There currently coexists, around the world, a variety of reporting formats for each statement.

Although common standards often indicate a preference for some format of presentation, they generally do not impose one. As we will see, regardless of the format followed (affecting mainly the order of presentation of the reported items and the level or nature of detail offered), financial statements contain essentially the same data and have the same informational power for any educated analyst. These different financial statements presentations will be reviewed and compared.

The **annual report** to shareholders exceeds the simple presentation of the three statements we have discussed so far plus their relevant notes. It also includes additional optional statements and details and, most importantly, managerial commentary on the figures provided, with regards to both understanding past achievements and formulating expectations for the future. We will discuss the kinds of additional data, commentary and information that can be found in the annual report.

1 Financial reporting standards

1.1 Necessity of financial reporting standards

The various (and numerous) users of financial statements mentioned in Chapter 1 need to understand that financial information is the result of a unique coding of events. For that reason, within each country, local regulations issue generally accepted accounting principles (GAAP)[1] that are called **accounting standards** or **financial reporting standards**.

Accounting standards are authoritative statements of how particular types of transactions and other events should be reflected in financial statements. These standards include specific principles, bases, conventions, rules, and practices necessary to prepare the financial statements.

In each country, regulatory bodies (such as the Accounting Standards Board in the UK, or the *Deutsches Rechnungslegungs Standards Committee* in Germany) and/or the professional accountancy bodies promulgate financial reporting standards. Each national official source of regulation issues pronouncements that may take the form of standards, laws, doctrines, etc.

Because of differences in, *inter alia*, (a) culture and traditions, (b) taxation policies, (c) preferred financing policies, (d) the importance and recognition of the accounting profession, (e) nature of accounting regulation, etc., there are differences of form and contents between the published financial reporting standards of most countries. However, comparability of financial information is a key issue in an international environment. The various users act more and more globally and should be able to understand, and also trust, the financial statements issued in any country of the world. Further, lack of commonly accepted standards can increase the preparation costs of financial reports: for instance a multinational group having to prepare financial statements in the many countries where it operates must follow the possibly different accounting standards in each. Doing so would cause a much higher cost of preparation (and a possible loss of quality of the aggregate description of the whole business) than would be incurred had there been one single set of firm-wide standards across the world. The relationship between internal and external reporting would also militate in favor of accounting harmonization, both within a firm and between countries and firms. More precisely, an international business group, having generally harmonized its internal measure of performance, is also likely to want to harmonize its rules of preparation of its external reporting.

1.2 The International Accounting Standards Board

In this context, the International Accounting Standards Board (IASB) was established in 2001 as an independent, private sector regulatory body. It is recognized by those national regulatory agencies that choose to adopt its statements and mandate businesses in that country to follow these rules and pronouncements. It is the successor to the International Accounting Standards Committee (IASC), which had been established in 1973 with essentially the same mission, but with a different structure of the sources of funding, membership and governance rules. Its main objective is to promote convergence of accounting principles and practices that are used by businesses and other organizations for financial reporting around the world.

1.2.1 Objectives of the IASB

The IASB is the standard-setting body of the IASC Foundation. The objectives of the IASC Foundation, as stated in its constitution (IASB 2009: § 2), are:

(a) 'to develop, in the public interest, a single set of high quality, understandable and enforceable global accounting standards that require high quality, transparent and comparable information in financial statements and other financial reporting to help participants in the world's capital markets and other users make economic decisions;

(b) to promote the use and rigorous application of those standards;

(c) in fulfilling the objectives associated with (a) and (b), to take account of, as appropriate, the special needs of small and medium-sized entities and emerging economies; and

(d) to bring about convergence of national accounting standards and International Accounting Standards and International Financial Reporting Standards to high quality solutions.'

1.2.2 History of the IASB

The confidence crisis which began in 1998 in certain Asian countries and spread to other regions of the world showed the need for more reliable and transparent accounting to support sound decision-making by investors, lenders and regulatory authorities. This led to a restructuring of the standard setting processes that culminated on 1 April 2001, when the IASB assumed accounting standard setting responsibilities from its predecessor body, the IASC.

1.2.3 Structure

In March 2001, the IASC Foundation, a not-for-profit corporation incorporated in the State of Delaware, USA, was formed and is the parent entity of the IASB, which is based in London, UK. The new structure has the following main features: the IASC Foundation is an independent organization having two main bodies, the Trustees, coming from the accounting and financial community, and the IASB, as well as a Standards Advisory Council and the International Financial Reporting Interpretations Committee. The IASC Foundation Trustees appoint the IASB Members, exercise oversight and raise the funds needed, whereas IASB, which consists of 14 individuals (12 full-time members and two part-time members), has sole responsibility for setting accounting standards. The Standards Advisory Council provides a formal vehicle for groups and individuals having diverse geographic and functional backgrounds to give advice to the IASB and, at times, to advise the trustees. The International Financial Reporting Interpretations Committee (IFRIC) assists the IASB in establishing and improving standards. Its role is to provide timely guidance on newly identified financial reporting issues not specifically addressed in the IASB's standards or issues where unsatisfactory or conflicting interpretations have developed, or seem likely to develop.

Figure 5.1 below summarizes this structure.

1.2.4 Past international accounting standards

On April 2001, the IASB approved that 'all standards and interpretations issued under previous constitutions continue to be applicable unless and until they are amended or withdrawn'. These standards adopted by the IASC are named 'International Accounting Standards' (IAS for one standard – when referring to several standards, some authors use the plural form IASs). But, for the sake of simplification, we will use IAS to refer to one or several standards.

1.2.5 New terminology

The IASB also announced in April 2001 that the IASC Foundation trustees have agreed that accounting standards issued by IASB shall be designated 'International Financial Reporting Standards' (IFRS for one standard – or IFRSs in the plural form). For the same reason as mentioned above, we will only use the term IFRS. In the introduction to the

Figure 5.1 The IASB structure

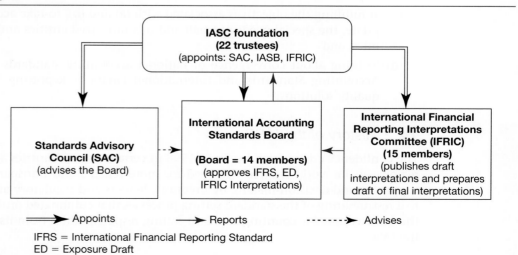

→ Appoints → Reports ------▸ Advises

IFRS = International Financial Reporting Standard
ED = Exposure Draft

Source: Adapted from the IASB website, www.iasb.org

bound volume of its accounting standards (IASB 2009: 12), the IASB states that 'the term "International Financial Reporting Standards" [in a broad sense, should we add], includes IFRSs, IASs and Interpretations developed by the IFRIC (International Financial Reporting Interpretations Committee) or its predecessor, the former Standing Interpretations Committee (SIC).'

It should be noted that the terminology adopted by the European Union texts (see below) is not consistent with that of the IASB. European regulation 1606/2002 refers to 'International accounting standards' or IAS that include both IAS (created by the IASC, predecessor of the IASB) and IFRS (created by the IASB).

Consequently, in order to reduce a possible confusion for the reader, arising from this unfortunate dual meaning of the acronym IAS, we adopt in this book the following policy: when we mention, in a row, 'IFRS and IAS', we make a distinction between IFRS in the strict sense (i.e., standards adopted by the IASB after 2001) and IAS (i.e., standards adopted by the IASC before 2001, some of them having, since, been revised, amended, or otherwise reformatted by the IASB). When we need to mention the set of *all* accounting standards, we use the term 'IFRS/IAS'.

1.2.6 List of standards

Table 5.1 provides a list of the International Financial Reporting Standards and the International Accounting Standards issued as of 31 August 2009. This table is based on the original pronouncements and the website maintained by the accounting firm Deloitte (http://www.iasplus.com/standard/standard.htm). Some terminology must be explained. After its first adoption, a standard can be:

■ revised: the content is significantly modified (but not to such an extent that a new standard would be necessary);

■ amended: some parts are modified, especially because of the application of other standards;

■ reformatted/restructured: the structure of the standard is modified.

1.2.7 Implementation of International Financial Reporting (Accounting) Standards (IFRS or IAS)

The IASB has no authority to require compliance with its accounting standards. However, many countries already endorsed, required or recommended IFRS and IAS as their own reporting standards either without amendment, or with minor additions or deletions (as was the case, for example, for Armenia, Bahrain, Barbados, Botswana, Cyprus, Egypt, Georgia, Hungary, Kenya, Lesotho, Malta, Nepal, the Philippines, Tajikistan, Trinidad and Tobago, Ukraine).

Furthermore, important developments towards harmonization continue to take place around the world: a European regulation (EC No. 1606/2002) adopted on 19 July 2002 by the European Parliament and published on 11 September 2002, required the application of 'international accounting standards' (i.e., IFRS and IAS) in consolidated financial statements of approximately 7,000 listed companies for each financial year starting on or after 1 January 2005. Australia and Russia have adopted a similar requirement also enforceable since 2005. Canada has decided to adopt IFRS in full as Canadian Financial Reporting Standards effective 2011. Companies were allowed to begin using IFRS as early as 2008 on approval of their provincial securities regulator.[2] Some countries have not adopted IFRS/IAS but are converging towards these standards. For example, in August 2007, the Accounting Standards Board of Japan (ASBJ) and the IASB agreed on a process of convergence of Japanese GAAP and IFRS. 'Major differences' between Japanese GAAP and IFRS should be eliminated by 30 June 2011. The target date of 2011 does not apply to any major new IFRS now being developed that would become effective after 2011.[3]

Table 5.1 List of IFRS and IAS

Number	Name	Date of approval or modification
IFRS 1	First-time adoption of IFRS	2003, amended 2005, 2008, restructured 2008
IFRS 2	Share-based payment	2004, amended 2008, 2009
IFRS 3	Business combinations	2004, revised 2008
IFRS 4	Insurance contracts	2004, amended 2005
IFRS 5	Non-current assets held for sale and discontinued operations	2004, amended 2008, 2009
IFRS 6	Exploration for and evaluation of mineral resources	2004, amended 2005
IFRS 7	Financial instruments: Disclosures	2005, amended 2008, 2009
IFRS 8	Operating segments	2006, amended 2009
IAS 1	Presentation of financial statements	1975, 1997, revised 2003, amended 2005, revised 2007, amended 2008, 2009
IAS 2	Inventories	1975, revised 2003
IAS 3	Consolidated financial statements (superseded by IAS 27 and 28)	—
IAS 4	Depreciation accounting (superseded by IAS 16, 22 and 38)	—
IAS 5	Information to be disclosed in financial statements (superseded by IAS 1)	—
IAS 6	Accounting responses to changing prices (superseded by IAS 15)	—
IAS 7	Statement of cash flows	1977, revised 1992, amended 2009
IAS 8	Accounting policies, changes in accounting estimates and errors	1978, revised 1993, 2003
IAS 9	Accounting for research and development activities (superseded by IAS 38)	—
IAS 10	Events after the reporting period	1978, revised 1999, 2003
IAS 11	Construction contracts	1979, revised 1993
IAS 12	Income taxes	1979, revised 1996, 2000
IAS 13	Presentation of current assets and current liabilities (superseded by IAS 1)	—
IAS 14	Segment reporting (superseded by IFRS 8)	—
IAS 15	Information reflecting the effects of changing prices (superseded by IAS 29)	—
IAS 16	Property, plant and equipment	1982, revised 1993, 1998, 2003, amended 2008
IAS 17	Leases	1982, revised 1997, 2003, amended 2009
IAS 18	Revenue	1982, revised 1993, amended 2008, 2009
IAS 19	Employee benefits	1983, revised 1993, 1998, amended 2002, 2004, 2008
IAS 20	Accounting for government grants and disclosure of government assistance	1983, reformatted 1994, amended 2008
IAS 21	The effects of changes in foreign exchange rates	1983, revised 1993, 2003, amended 2005
IAS 22	Business combinations (superseded by IFRS 3)	—
IAS 23	Borrowing costs	1984, revised 1993, amended 2007
IAS 24	Related party disclosures	1984, reformatted 1994, revised 2003
IAS 25	Accounting for investments (superseded by IAS 39 and 40)	—
IAS 26	Accounting and reporting by retirement benefit plans	1987, reformatted 1994

(continued)

Table 5.1 (*continued*)

Number	Name	Date of approval or modification
IAS 27	Consolidated and separate financial statements	1989, reformatted 1994, amended 1998, revised 2003, 2008
IAS 28	Investments in associates	1989, reformatted 1994, amended 1998, revised 2003, 2008
IAS 29	Financial reporting in hyperinflationary economies	1989, reformatted 1994, amended 2008
IAS 30	*Disclosures in the financial statements of banks and similar financial institutions (superseded by IFRS 7)*	—
IAS 31	Interests in joint ventures	1990, reformatted 1994, revised 1998, 2003, 2008
IAS 32	Financial instruments: Presentation (partly superseded by IFRS 7 – former title: Financial instruments: Disclosure and presentation)	1995, revised 1998, 2003, 2005, amended 2008
IAS 33	Earnings per share	1997, revised 2003
IAS 34	Interim financial reporting	1998
IAS 35	*Discontinuing operations (superseded by IFRS 5)*	—
IAS 36	Impairment of assets	1998, revised 2004, amended 2008, 2009
IAS 37	Provisions, contingent liabilities and contingent assets	1998
IAS 38	Intangible assets	1978 (IAS 9), 1998 revised 2004, amended 2008, 2009
IAS 39	Financial instruments: recognition and measurement	1986 (IAS 25), 1998, Revised 2000, 2003, 2004, amended 2005, 2008, 2009
IAS 40	Investment property	1986 (IAS 25), 2000, revised 2003, amended 2008
IAS 41	Agriculture	2000, amended 2008

Note: Standards superseded are shown in *italics*

The European Union requires the application of IFRS/IAS, but only once these have been endorsed by the European Parliament after a positive recommendation by the European Accounting Regulatory Committee (ARC). So far, the procedure of endorsement has been straightforward, with the major exception of the standard referring to financial instruments, about which the European Union strongly disagrees with the approach taken by the IASB. In 2004, there were two carve-outs in IAS 39 concerning: the fair value option, and hedge accounting (see more on this subject in Chapter 10). Subsequently, the fair value option carve-out was resolved through Commission Regulation (EC) No. 1864/2005 of 15 November 2005. The accounting services of the EU are working with IASB to resolve the remaining hedge accounting carve-out.[4]

1.2.8 The relationship IASB-SEC

The success of IASB partly depends on the attitude of the stock markets regulators, and, in particular, of the United States' Securities and Exchange Commission (SEC), towards the IFRS/IAS. The major issue at stake (and one of the main targets of the IASB) is the recognition *without the need of reconciliation* of financial statements prepared in accordance with IFRS/IAS for cross-listing in the USA.

The SEC has been working with the IASB, through the International Organization of Securities Commissions (IOSCO), which is the representative body of the world's securities markets regulators.[5] The SEC has already accepted the use of IFRS/IAS by foreign companies quoted on a US stock exchange, but *with* reconciliation to US GAAP. A major step towards harmonization was taken when, on 15 November 2007, the SEC approved rule amendments under which financial statements from foreign private issuers in the US will be accepted *without* reconciliation to US GAAP only if they are prepared using IFRS/IAS as issued by the IASB. On 21 December 2007, the SEC issued its final rule on Acceptance from foreign private issuers of financial statements prepared in accordance with IFRS without reconciliation to US GAAP.

1.2.9 IFRS/IAS in the US?

In parallel to this evolution, the IASB and the FASB (Financial Accounting Standards Board, the US standard-setting body), have developed closer relationships. A common program of joint revision of several standards has been initiated, leading to a likely convergence of the two sets of standards.

On 27 August 2008, the US SEC voted to publish for public comment a proposed 'roadmap' that could lead to the use of IFRS by US issuers beginning in 2014. Currently, US issuers must use US GAAP, though foreign registrants (of which there are around 1,100 from 52 jurisdictions) may elect to use IFRS.[6] The proposal suggests mandatory adoption of IFRS by US registrants could be phased in from 2014 to 2016 depending on company size:

- large accelerated filers in 2014
- accelerated filers in 2015
- non-accelerated filers in 2016.[7]

The proposal also permitted voluntary early adoption for a limited group of large US registrants (based on industry and size) for periods ending after 15 December 2009 (i.e., firm filing in 2010). However, mandatory IFRS adoption starting in 2014 would not be automatic. In 2011, according to the roadmap, the SEC would evaluate the progress of IFRS against certain defined milestones and make a decision on whether to go ahead with adoption starting in 2014, later, or not at all.

However, at the beginning of 2009, with the appointment of Mary L. Schapiro as new SEC Chairman, and in the context of a world economic and financial crisis, several public statements by a variety of public figures or appointed officials have been made in the USA showing a clear will to slow down the move towards IFRS/IAS. The new SEC chairman even declared in January 2009 during her confirmation hearing before the US Senate Committee on Banking, Housing, and Urban Affairs: 'I have some concerns with the roadmap that has been published by the SEC and is out for comment now. I have some concerns about the IFRS standards generally. They are not as detailed as the US standards. There's a lot left to interpretation. Even if adopted, there will still be a lack of consistency, I believe, around the world in how they are implemented and how they are enforced. The cost to switch from US GAAP to IFRS is going to be extraordinary.' At the time of writing this text[8], the future of IFRS/IAS in the US for US listed companies is still uncertain.

2 The content of the annual report

The annual report is a document published annually by listed companies (as well as some non-listed but large companies). Table 5.2 provides some examples of items commonly found in annual reports. This list is in no way exhaustive, nor does it represent any kind of average or recommended practice. The content, the order and the terminology may vary across countries and companies, as this document is not standardized.

In the remaining part of this chapter, we will focus on the financial statements, more specifically their presentation, and the accompanying notes.

Table 5.2 Illustrative components of an annual report

First part: Business reporting

■ Key financial information (or financial highlights – the year in brief)

■ Letters from the President and/or from the CEO (also called Review by the President)

■ Management report (or Review of operations): Overview of the group and divisional reviews, personnel, research and development

■ Report of the Board of Directors (or financial review – management discussion and analysis): markets evolution, changes in group composition, earnings, production, personnel, capital expenditure, research and development, financing, shares, outlook for the following year, dividend.

Second part: Financial reporting

■ Consolidated financial statements: balance sheet, income statement, statement of cash flows, statement of changes in equity

■ Notes to the consolidated financial statements

■ Report of the auditors (on the consolidated financial statements)

■ Parent company financial statements: balance sheet, income statement, statement of cash flows

■ Notes to the parent company financial statements

■ Report of the auditors (on the parent company financial statements)

■ Information on shares (shareholder information)

■ Composition of the executive board (directors and corporate officers)

Comments:
■ The management report and the report of the Board of Directors are sometimes merged.
■ The parent company financial statements as such are not always included in the annual report when consolidated statements are published (see Chapter 13). For instance, in North America, they are almost never published.
■ The notes to the consolidated and parent company financial statements are often mixed. (See for instance Irish, Nordic countries or UK companies annual reports).
■ The statement of movements of fixed assets (see Chapters 7 and 8) is often reported as a separate document after the balance sheet and income statement in Austria and Germany.
■ Similarly, segment reports (see Chapter 18) are sometimes presented as a separate document in Austria.

3 Financial statements presentation

As mentioned in the IASB Conceptual Framework (IASB 1989: § 47), 'financial statements portray the financial effects of transactions and other events by grouping them into broad classes according to their economic characteristics. These broad classes are termed the elements of financial statements.'

As mentioned earlier, the issue of comparability of the financial situation of firms is essential for accounting information users. However, this objective of ease of comparability is far from being achieved today, despite the ever-growing adoption of either the IFRS or the US GAAP standards for the recording of transactions.

Many countries still encourage, or require, or accept a diversity of **formats of presentation** of the key documents. Each presentation emanates from a certain vision of the business model financial statements are supposed to describe. Chapter 2 has mentioned that the order in which assets and liabilities are listed in a balance sheet depends on the choice of the image the firm wants to give to information users (or the regulatory authorities want businesses to provide). For example, a firm may be deemed to be 'secure' or 'solid' either because (a) it has a strong productive capacity (it wants to highlight its physical and intellectual assets first to a reader from a western culture who reads from the top to the bottom and left to right); or (b) because it is potentially very liquid (it wants to emphasize its ability to pay its debt by presenting liquid assets first in the list). Neither position is intrinsically better. Each is coherent with a certain philosophy of business or communication approach.

A good understanding of the different formats of financial statements is, however, necessary to be able to compare financial statements of different firms, even if they do not appear to be following the same format. The knowledge of the different formats will allow the user to analyze almost any type of financial statements published by any company from any country in the world. Each format of presentation will be, as we will see in Chapters 15 and 16, more, or less, supportive of certain financial statement analysis tools, or will require additional reformatting of the data to be able to derive certain ratios perceived as important by analysts.

The section below will be an opportunity to explore the different presentations of a content that is essentially the same. We will focus on the format of the statements and not on specific accounts, which will only be introduced in later chapters.

3.1 Possible presentations of the balance sheet

The **balance sheet** shows the financial position of a business on a given date. The IASB specifies that 'the elements directly related to the measurement of financial position are assets, liabilities and equity' (IASB 1989: § 49). In terms of presentation, the key choices are essentially pertaining to format of the list (**horizontal** or **vertical**), to the degree of fineness (**single-step** or **multiple-step**) and to the type of classification of assets and liabilities (**by term** or **by nature**, see Figure 5.2).

3.1.1 Formats

The balance sheet is a list of account balances. The list can be continuous (vertical format, see Figure 5.3), or presented as two lists side by side (horizontal format, see Figure 5.4)

The 'horizontal' format is often represented as two blocks as in Figure 5.5.

Degree of fineness in the vertical format   The 'single-step' format provides a simple list of accounts with very little detail or value added by the presentation, while the 'multiple-step' format creates a list of subsets of the main categories of both assets and liabilities, and identifies managerially useful subtotals by subtracting relevant other subcategories of assets or liabilities.

The single-step and the multiple-step approaches reflect different readings of the basic business equation and different perspectives on the firm's position:

Single-step	→	Assets = Liabilities + Shareholders' equity
Multiple-step	→	Assets − Liabilities = Shareholders' equity

The two examples of multiple-step format provided in Table 5.3 illustrate the fact that any balance sheet presentation is essentially a specific expansion of the business equation.

In the Example 1 presentation, shareholders' equity is the end result. It is a format widely used in the UK and Ireland. The format illustrated by Example 2 is less common. It focuses attention on **long-term funding** of the firm. It is found in some Indian annual reports.

Neither of the two illustrated formats provides an intrinsically superior presentation to the others. Each is coherent with a certain vision of the firm and the perceived informational needs of shareholders.

Figure 5.2 Presentation of the balance sheet

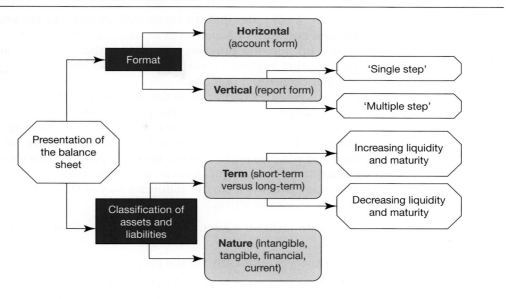

Figure 5.3 Vertical format

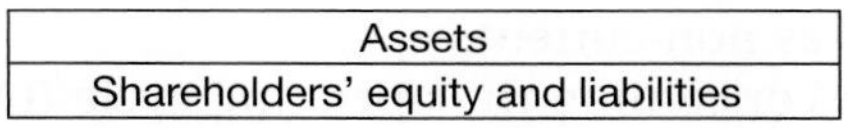

Assets
Shareholders' equity and liabilities

Figure 5.4 Horizontal format

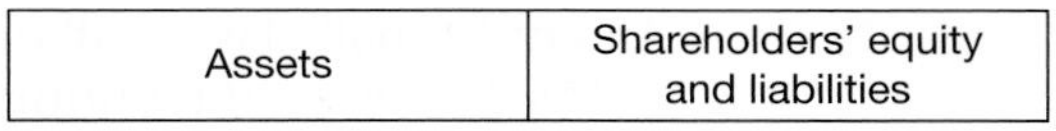

Assets	Shareholders' equity and liabilities

Figure 5.5 Balance sheet horizontal format

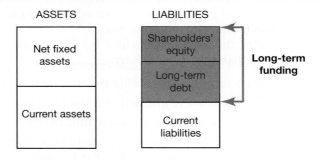

Table 5.3 Balance sheet examples using the 'multiple-step' vertical format

Example 1	Example 2
Assets	Assets
– Current liabilities	– Current liabilities
= Assets minus current liabilities	= Assets minus current liabilities
– Non-current liabilities	Shareholders' equity
= Total net assets	+ Long-term liabilities
= Shareholders' equity	= Long-term funding
Control: Net assets = Shareholders' equity	*Control: Assets minus current liabilities = Long-term funding*

3.1.2 Classifications of assets and liabilities

IAS 1 (IASB 2007: § 60) states that 'an entity shall present current and non-current assets, and current and non-current liabilities as separate classifications (...) except when a presentation based on liquidity provides information that is reliable and is more relevant. When that exception applies, all assets and liabilities shall be presented broadly in order of [increasing or decreasing] liquidity.'

IAS 1 does not provide a definition of the presentation 'by liquidity' described as exception in § 60. It simply mentions that this presentation could be used 'for some entities, such as financial institutions (...) because the entity does not supply goods or services within clearly identifiable operating cycle' (§ 63). Consequently, we will not discuss this classification and will concentrate on the most frequent practice for commercial or manufacturing enterprises, the 'current/non-current' distinction.

A current asset is defined in the following way (IASB 2007: § 66): 'An entity shall classify an asset as current when:

(a) it expects to realize the asset, or intends to sell or consume it, in its normal operating cycle;

(b) it holds the asset primarily for the purpose of trading;

(c) it expects to realize the asset within twelve months after the reporting period; or

(d) the asset is cash or a cash equivalent (as defined in IAS 7) unless the asset is restricted from being exchanged or used to settle a liability for at least twelve months after the reporting period.

An entity shall classify all other assets as non-current.'

IAS 1 adds an interesting precision concerning the operating cycle (IASB 2007: § 68): 'The operating cycle of an entity is the time between the acquisition of assets for processing and their realization in cash or cash equivalents. When the entity's normal operating cycle is not clearly identifiable, it is assumed to be twelve months. Current assets include assets (such as inventories and trade receivables) that are sold, consumed or realized as part of the normal operating cycle even when they are not expected to be realized within twelve months after the reporting period.'

A symmetric definition is provided for current liabilities (IASB 2007: § 69): 'An entity shall classify a liability as current when:

(a) it expects to settle the liability in its normal operating cycle;

(b) it holds the liability primarily for the purpose of trading;

(c) the liability is due to be settled within twelve months after the reporting period; or

(d) the entity does not have an unconditional right to defer settlement of the liability for at least twelve months after the reporting period.

An entity shall classify all other liabilities as non-current.'

In the definitions provided in §§ 66 and 69 of IAS 1, the list of the criteria can be summarized as two main alternative criteria emerge: (a) the realization/settlement in the operating cycle or (b) the realization/settlement within twelve months after the balance sheet date.

In practice, when looking at the financial reporting of companies around the world, it appears that companies are consistent in their choice of classification of assets and liabilities: the same classification is adopted, as is logical, on both sides of the balance sheet.

In summary, two types of references, coherent with IAS 1, can be used to classify assets and liabilities that are:

■ Reference to the duration of the operating cycle: we call this classification 'by nature' (i.e., financial versus operating).

■ Reference to the twelve months after the balance sheet date realization/settlement time horizon: we call this second classification 'by term' (i.e., short-term versus long-term).

Even if IAS 1 appears to rank the operating cycle in the first place (see § 61), a cursory observation of financial reporting practices leads to the conclusion that the presentation 'by term' is nonetheless the one most frequently used in practice. We will therefore start our presentation with this classification.

Classification of assets and liabilities 'by term' (short-term versus long-term)   Assets and liabilities are split respectively between items that should be recovered/settled in more than twelve months after the balance sheet date (which we call 'long-term') and other items that will be recovered/settled within twelve months (called 'short-term'). For example, liabilities can be classified in the following subsets:

> Long-term (non-current) liabilities (amounts falling due more than twelve months after the balance sheet date):
> ■ financial debts (long-term portion)
> ■ accounts payable, for those (rare) payables due in more than twelve months.
> Short-term (current) liabilities (amounts falling due within twelve months after the balance sheet date):
> ■ financial debts (short-term portion)
> ■ bank overdrafts
> ■ accounts payable, for which the due date is (typically) less than twelve months from the balance sheet date.

A parallel classification must also be applied to assets: long-term assets will be recognized as fixed assets (the stream of economic benefits they create for the firm extends beyond one year) and will be distinguished from short-term or current assets which are expected to be consumed within twelve months after the balance sheet date.

When the balance sheet is presented according to the 'term' (short-term vs long-term), two approaches exist: increasing (Table 5.4) or decreasing (Table 5.5) order of liquidity and maturity.[9] Each approach once again emphasizes a different point: long-term strength or short-term liquidity. Neither one is, however, intrinsically superior to the other.

The decreasing liquidity approach is most commonly used in North America and in countries that follow the 'American model'. The increasing liquidity approach is most commonly used in continental Europe.

Classification of assets and liabilities 'by nature' (tangible versus intangible, financial versus operating/ trading)   This classification emphasizes the nature of the assets and liabilities and their role in the operating cycle or operations of the business that were illustrated in Chapter 3, Figure 3.1.

Table 5.4 Increasing liquidity and maturity

Assets	Shareholders' equity and liabilities
Fixed assets	Shareholders' equity
	Liabilities
Current assets	– Long-term
– Inventory	(non-current)
– Accounts receivable	– Short-term (current)
– Cash	

Table 5.5 Decreasing liquidity and maturity

Assets	Liabilities and shareholders' equity
Current assets	Liabilities
– Cash	– Short-term (current)
– Accounts receivable	– Long-term (non-current)
– Inventory	
Fixed assets	Shareholders' equity

Liabilities can be, in the by-nature approach, structured as:

Financial liabilities (regardless of their due date):
- debts to financial institutions (long-term and short-term portions of loans obtained)
- bank overdrafts.

Trading (or operating) liabilities (debts linked to trading and relations with other partners):
- advance payments received from customers on contracts to be delivered in the future
- accounts payable (debts contracted from suppliers in the course of running the business)
- debts to tax authorities.

On the assets side, a parallel distinction will apply. Financial assets generally are financial investments or loans to business associates (such as key suppliers), while operating or trading assets are connected to the cycle of operations. Inventories and accounts receivable are considered to be operating or trading assets (see Table 5.6).

Operating and trading liabilities and operating and trading assets are generally referred to as 'current liabilities' or 'current assets'. In this context, the term 'current' means 'related to the operating cycle of the business'.

In summary, there is an ambiguity, relating to the use of the terminology 'current/non-current' which has, across firms, a dual meaning: based on the context, it either refers to the distinction short-term/long-term or to the distinction operating/financial. This ambiguity arises from the flexibility given by IAS 1 in its definitions of current assets and liabilities (see above).

IAS 1 (IASB 2007: § 61) also specifies that, 'whichever method of presentation is adopted, an entity shall disclose the amount expected to be recovered or settled after more than twelve months for each asset and liability line item that combines amounts expected to be recovered or settled: (a) no more than twelve months after the reporting period, and (b) more than twelve months after the reporting period.'

3.1.3 Examples of presentations

This paragraph provides illustrations of the various presentations of the balance sheet we introduced above.

Table 5.6 Classification of assets and liabilities 'by nature'

Assets	Shareholders' equity and liabilities
Fixed assets - Intangible assets - Tangible assets - Financial fixed assets	Shareholders' equity
Current assets - Inventory - Accounts receivable - Cash	Liabilities - Financial (including the current portion) - Operating (due within the time horizon of the operating cycle)

International model IAS 1 (2007: § IG6) includes an *illustrative* balance sheet showing one way in which a balance sheet may be presented, distinguishing between short-term and long-term items. This example corresponds to the format 'by term' (see Table 5.7).

UK model In the United Kingdom, for example, limited companies must use one of the two formats prescribed in the Companies Act. Of these two formats, the one illustrated in Table 5.8 represents the most commonly used. It is a variation on the multiple-step 'vertical balance sheet'.

Balance sheet 'by nature' Table 5.9 illustrates the traditional format by nature.

US model As opposed to a continental European balance sheet that reflects a patrimonial approach and thus lists fixed assets at the top, a North American approach tends to emphasize the short-term liquidity of the firm and thus lists assets in the order of decreasing liquidity with fixed assets at the bottom of the list. Table 5.10 illustrates a 'typical' North American balance sheet structure.

3.2 Possible presentations of the income statement

The **income statement** reports the revenues and expenses incurred during a period and serves to establish the net income. Net income is the remainder after all expenses have been deducted from revenues. It is a measure of the wealth created by an economic entity (increased shareholders' equity) during an accounting period. The income statement reports how the company's financial performance was achieved. As was the case for the balance sheet, there are several ways of presenting an income statement (horizontal or vertical format) and a choice of degree of fineness as well as of types of account classifications (see Figure 5.6).

3.2.1 Formats

An income statement is a list of account balances. The list can be presented (see Figure 5.7) as a continuous list (vertical format) or as two lists side by side (horizontal format).

Although not commonly used in business reporting, the **horizontal format** is very practical in a pedagogical context as it essentially presents the income statement in the form of a T-account.

3.2.2 Degree of fineness

Expenses are first grouped in homogeneous meaningful categories and then deducted step-by-step from revenues. The choice is between **single-step** and **multiple-step**.

Single-step It is the most simplified version of the income statement. Expenses and revenues are each considered as one category (see for example the left panel of Figure 5.7).

Multiple-step Revenue and expense categories are paired so as to highlight the components of total net income (see Table 5.11). For example, trading (or operating) revenues and trading (or operating) expenses will be grouped to create the trading (or operating) income. Financial revenues and expenses will be offset against one another to inform the users about the role of the financial activity in total net income. This format is also used in reporting income by segments such as types of business, products, markets, regions, etc. (see Chapter 18).

This rich format of reporting income is the most commonly used in business reports because it is more informative than the single-step approach. Its usefulness rests on the ability for the firm to separate revenues and expenses on sound and meaningful bases,

Table 5.7 IASB format

XYZ Group – Statement of financial position as at 31 December X7 (in thousands of currency units)

ASSETS	31 Dec X7	31 Dec X6
Non-current assets		
Property, plant and equipment	350,700	360,020
Goodwill	80,800	91,200
Other intangible assets	227,470	227,470
Investments in associates	100,150	110,770
Available-for-sale financial assets	142,500	156,000
	901,620	945,460
Current assets		
Inventories	135,230	132,500
Trade receivables	91,600	110,800
Other current assets	25,650	12,540
Cash and cash equivalents	312,400	322,900
	564,880	578,740
Total assets	1,466,500	1,524,200
EQUITY AND LIABILITIES	31 Dec X7	31 Dec X6
Equity attributable to owners of the parent		
Share capital	650,000	600,000
Retained earnings	243,500	161,700
Other components of equity	10,200	21,200
	903,700	782,900
Non-controlling interest	70,050	48,600
Total equity	973,750	831,500
Non-current liabilities		
Long-term borrowings	120,000	160,000
Deferred tax	28,800	26,040
Long-term provisions	28,850	52,240
Total non-current liabilities	177,650	238,280
Current liabilities		
Trade and other payables	115,100	187,620
Short-term borrowings	150,000	200,000
Current portion of long-term borrowings	10,000	20,000
Current tax payable	35,000	42,000
Short-term provisions	5,000	4,800
Total current liabilities	315,100	454,420
Total liabilities	492,750	692,700
Total equity and liabilities	1,466,500	1,524,200

Table 5.8 UK Format – Multiple-step vertical balance sheet

Fixed assets	(1)	100
Current assets	(2)	70
Creditors (amounts falling due within one year)	(3)	–60
Net current assets/(liabilities)	(4) = (2 + 3)	10
Total assets less current liabilities	(5) = (1 + 4)	110
Creditors (amounts falling due after more than one year)	(6)	–20
Provisions for liabilities and charges	(7)	–10
Total net assets	(8) = (5 + 6 + 7)	80
Capital and retained earnings	(9)	80
Total equity	(10) = (9)	80

The balance sheet balances with (10) = (8)

Table 5.9 Single-step vertical balance sheet by nature

Fixed assets	(1)	100
Current assets	(2)	70
Total assets	(3) = (1 + 2)	170
Capital and retained earnings (reserves)	(4)	80
Provisions for liabilities and charges	(5)	10
Financial liabilities	(6)	50
Operating liabilities	(7)	30
Total equity and liabilities	(8) = (4 + 5 + 6 + 7)	170

The balance sheet balances with (8) = (3)

without using rules of allocation that would create doubt about the usefulness for decision-making of the sub-categories of the net income.

3.2.3 Classification of expenses

IASB (2007: § 99) states that 'an entity shall present an analysis of expenses recognized in profit or loss using a classification based on either their nature or their function within the entity, whichever provides information that is reliable and more relevant.' This standard adds (§ 101) that 'expenses are sub-classified to highlight components of financial performance that may differ in terms of frequency, potential for gain or loss and predictability.' This information is provided either **by nature** or **by function**. Classification issues are especially important for operating expenses. Thus, in the development below we do not explore classification schemes beyond those of operating income, as most other sources of income are self-explanatory.

Table 5.10 A typical US balance sheet	
ASSETS	
Current assets	
Cash and cash equivalents	
Accounts receivable	
Inventories	
Prepaid expenses and other current assets	
Total current assets	*(1)*
Fixed assets	
Investments	
Property, plant and equipment	
Intangible assets	
Total fixed assets	*(2)*
Total assets	**(3) = (1) + (2)**
LIABILITIES AND SHAREHOLDERS' EQUITY	
Current liabilities	
Accounts payable	
Income taxes payable	
Accrued expenses	
Dividends payable	
Current portion of long-term debt	
Total current liabilities	*(4)*
Long-term debt	
Borrowings	
Other long-term liabilities	
Total long-term debt	*(5)*
Stockholders' equity	
Capital stock	
Capital in excess of par value of stock	
Retained earnings	
Total stockholders' equity	*(6)*
Total liabilities and shareholders' equity	**(7) = (4) + (5) + (6)**
Balance	**(3) = (7)**

Classification by nature (or 'nature of expense method') In this approach, expenses are aggregated in the income statement directly according to their nature. Examples of nature of expenses are: purchases of materials, transportation costs, taxes other than income tax, salaries, social contribution expenses, fringe benefits (the latter three can be aggregated to form the category 'remuneration expenses' or 'labor and personnel expenses'), depreciation, etc. (see Table 5.12). This method is simple to apply, even in small enterprises, because no allocation or partition of expenses or costs is required (see IASB 2007: § 102). The structure follows the nature of source documents such as invoices or payment vouchers.

Figure 5.6 Choices in the presentation of income statement

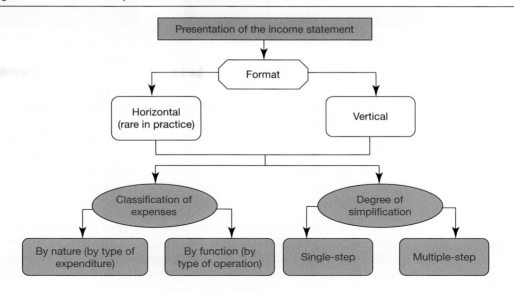

Figure 5.7 Vertical versus horizontal presentations

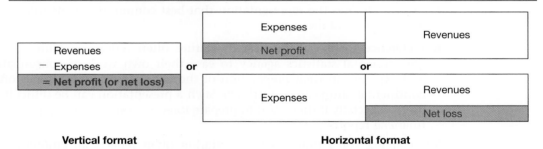

Vertical format   **Horizontal format**

Classification by function (or 'cost of sales method') The second form of analysis is the 'function of the expense' or 'cost of sales' method. It classifies expenses according to their 'function' i.e., they are either part of cost of sales (also known as cost of goods sold) or not. If they are not part of the cost of sales, they can be classified, for example, as marketing and commercial costs, costs of physical distribution, cost of after-sale service, or cost of administrative and coordination activities. At a minimum, an entity discloses, under this method, its cost of sales separately from other expenses (IASB 2007: § 103), see Table 5.13.

Table 5.11 Example of multiple-step income statement (vertical)		
		Operating revenues
	−	Operating expenses
	=	Operating income (or margin) (1)
		Financial revenues
	−	Financial expenses
	=	Financial income (or margin) (2)
	=	Net income (1) + (2)

Table 5.12 Income statement by nature (vertical presentation)	
	Net sales
+	Other operating revenues
−	Purchases of merchandise
−	Change in inventories of merchandise
−	Labor and personnel expense
−	Other operating expenses
−	Depreciation expense
=	Operating income

Table 5.13 Income statement by function (vertical presentation)	
	Net sales
−	Cost of goods sold (cost of sales)
=	Gross margin
−	Commercial and distribution expenses
−	Administrative expenses
−	Other operating expenses
=	Operating income

Choice of a classification approach The criteria 'degree of fineness' and 'classification of expenses' are not exclusionary and can form a 2×2 matrix, as shown in Table 5.14. For example an income statement by nature can be presented according to the single or the multiple-step method. An income statement prepared according to the functional approach can be either single or multiple-step. The 'horizontal × functional' approach is however rather rare and thus is ignored here.

No single format of the multiple-step approach appears to be dominating in practice. Each firm chooses the representation that best communicates its intended emphasis on specific points and messages.

■ Preference for a classification by nature often reflects pressure exercised by some governmental statistics agency to ease their own work of consolidation of income and expenses in their preparation of the national accounts (this is often the case in continental European countries[10]). Such a presentation can be difficult to decipher by users, especially if they want to prepare forecasts, one of the key purposes of the use of financial reports.

■ Preference for a functional presentation often reflects an emphasis on the income creation process. It is the preferred method in North America and is also used by most firms quoted on the New York Stock Exchange. The informational content of such annual statements is easily understandable and usable by ordinary investors.

The IASB chooses sides by stating that the presentation by function can 'provide more relevant information to users than the classification of expenses by nature' (IASB 2007: § 103). However, it draws the attention of the report preparer, in the very same paragraph, to the fact that 'allocating costs to functions may require arbitrary allocations and involve considerable judgment'. In conclusion, paragraph 105 recognizes that 'the choice between the function of expense method and the nature of expense method depends on historical and industry factors and the nature of the entity. Both methods provide an indication of those costs that might vary, directly or indirectly, with the level of sales or production of the entity.'

Proponents of the classification by nature highlight the fact that this method may allow for a user-specific analysis of the performance of the firm. They point out that, in theory,

Table 5.14 Nature/function and single/multiple step		
	Single-step	Multiple-step
Nature	Rare in practice	Frequent
Function	Almost impossible	Frequent

the cost of goods sold (or the cost of sales) can be reconstructed to suit the analysis of the user. However, most reports presented by nature fail to offer any partition of key natures of expenses between manufacturing, selling and administration. Proponents of the classification by function highlight the fact that **gross profit** (revenues minus manufacturing cost of goods sold) and the commercial and distribution expenses are two key figures in monitoring the performance of a business and are easily understandable by any user.

In conclusion we will not choose sides and will agree with IASB that 'each method of presentation has merit for different types of entities' (IASB 2007: § 105). We will go further and acknowledge the fact that the choice between classifications must be in favor of that which most fairly presents the elements of the entity's performance.

However, 'because information on the nature of expenses is useful in predicting future cash flows, additional disclosure is provided when the function of expense classification is used' (IAS 1: § 105). Depreciation and amortization (concept equivalent to depreciation and applied to intangible assets – see Chapter 8) must critically be disclosed in a footnote or in the statement of cash flows (in the 'indirect method', see this concept in Chapter 14). It can prove useful for forecasting purposes, especially in internal reporting, to break up the cost of goods sold through a local application of the by-nature approach, distinguishing consumption of consumables, raw materials, manufacturing labor and services purchased from third parties. Employee benefits expense should also be disclosed.

3.2.4 Examples of presentations

International models IAS 1 (2007: § IG6) provides two income statements to illustrate the alternative classification of revenues and expenses, by nature and by function (see Tables 5.15 and 5.16).

US model Table 5.17 illustrates a commonly found multiple-step income statement.

3.2.5 Comparison nature vs function

Expenses in the income statement by function are divided in three or four main categories:

- cost of sales (or **cost of goods sold**) (this concept is further developed in Appendix 5.1)
- commercial, selling and distribution expenses
- administrative expenses
- some firms add research & development (R&D) expenses to this list.

In order to compare presentations of an income statement by nature and by function, let us look at a quantified example.

Brahms Company is a retailer. Its beginning inventory of merchandise is valued at 2,000 (all figures are in thousands of CU). During the period we are considering, Brahms Co. incurred total purchases of 8,000 and recorded invoicing customers for 17,000. The cost of goods sold pertaining to these sales was 9,000 (the 2,000 CU worth of beginning inventory plus 7,000 CU of the newly purchased merchandise – we assume here that oldest merchandise is sold first so as to avoid holding obsolete products on the shelves). Thus the ending inventory of merchandise is 1,000 (i.e., 2,000 + 8,000 = goods available for sale, minus 9,000 withdrawn to meet demand, i.e., the cost of sales). Labor and personnel expenses include the compensation of the sales force (4,000) and of the accounting and administration staff (2,000). The depreciation of administrative equipment for the period was estimated at 1,000.

Table 5.18 shows side-by-side the calculation of the operating income by nature and by function. The net operating income we find under either approach will, mechanically, be exactly the same. The potential for interpretation and uses of the information contained in the income statement may however be different.

Table 5.15 IASB format by nature

XYZ Group – Income statement for the year ended 31 December X7
Classification of expenses within profit by nature (in thousands of currency units)

	X7	X6
Revenue	390,000	355,000
Other income	20,667	11,300
Changes in inventories of finished goods and work in progress	–115,100	–107,900
Work performed by the entity and capitalized	16,000	15,000
Raw material and consumables used	–96,000	–92,000
Employee benefits expense	–45,000	–43,000
Depreciation and amortization expense	–19,000	–17,000
Impairment of property, plant and equipment	–4,000	–
Other expenses	–6,000	–5,500
Finance costs	–15,000	–18,000
Share of profit of associates	35,100	30,100
Profit before tax	161,667	128,000
Income tax expense	–40,417	–32,000
Profit for the year from continuing operations	121,250	96,000
Loss for the year from discontinued operations	–	–30,500
PROFIT FOR THE YEAR	121,250	65,500
Profit attributable to:		
Owners of the parent	97,000	52,400
Non-controlling interests	24,250	13,100
	121,250	65,500

4 Notes to financial statements

The accounting system must provide relevant information with as much precision and reliability as possible so that users of the financial statements trust their informational content. Such understandability requires that no ambiguity remains about how they were developed. The rules, procedures and principles that were followed in the establishment of the financial statements must be made clear so that the users can interpret their implications and, if needed, recode the information to suit their specific needs. In some countries, accounting rules and regulations governing the establishment of financial statements are very precisely defined. Other countries prefer principles to rules. Principles leave more room for adaptation (and interpretation) of the descriptors of the financial position of the firm.

Since the purpose of the financial statements is to give a true and fair view of a business' financial performance, the **notes** (often called 'notes to the financial statements' or 'footnotes') are essential. They provide any additional information the format of presentation selected failed to communicate since no format of presentation is actually perfect or serves the interests of all parties.

Notes to financial statements constitute a clarification and a supplement to the balance sheet and the income statement. They list such 'off balance sheet' information as litigation in which the firm is involved, or hypotheses used in valuing specific assets such as the rate of recovery of accounts receivable. Notes are required by the IASB (IAS 1, IASB 2007: § 10): 'A complete set of financial statements

Table 5.16 IASB format by function

XYZ Group – Income statement for the year ended 31 December X7
Classification of expenses within profit by function (in thousands of currency units)

	X7	X6
Revenue	390,000	355,000
Cost of sales	–245,000	–230,000
Gross profit	145,000	125,000
Other income	20,667	11,300
Distribution costs	–9,000	–8,700
Administrative expenses	–20,000	–21,000
Other expenses	–2,100	–1,200
Finance cost	–8,000	–7,500
Share of profit of associates	35,100	30,100
Profit before tax	161,667	128,000
Income tax expense	–40,417	–32,000
Profit for the year from continuing operations	121,250	96,000
Loss for the year from discontinued operations	–	–30,500
PROFIT FOR THE YEAR	121,250	65,500
Profit attributable to:		
Owners of the parent	97,000	52,400
Non-controlling interests	24,250	13,100
	121,250	65,500

comprises: (…) (e) notes, comprising a summary of significant accounting policies and other explanatory information.'

The IASB (IAS 1: § 7) also states that 'Notes contain information in addition to that presented in the statement of financial position, statement of comprehensive income, separate income statement (if presented), statement of changes in equity and statement of cash flows. Notes provide narrative descriptions or disaggregation of items presented in those statements and information about items that do not qualify for recognition in those statements.'

IAS 1 (IASB 2007: § 112) states that the notes shall:

(a) 'present information about the basis of preparation of the financial statements and the specific accounting policies used in accordance with paragraphs 117–124 [which deal with 'Disclosure of Accounting Policies'];

(b) disclose the information required by IFRSs that is not presented elsewhere in the financial statements; and

(c) provide information that is not presented elsewhere in the financial statements, but is relevant to an understanding of any of them.'

Notes to the statements are a set of qualitative and quantitative comments or specification of hypotheses required to provide a really 'true and fair view' of both the financial position of the firm and of its financial performance over the previous period and periods. They state the valuation hypotheses used and principles followed by management in establishing the figures that are in the financial statements.

Table 5.17 US multiple-step income statement

Net sales	(1)
Cost of goods sold	(2)
Gross profit	**(3) = (1) − (2)**
Commercial, selling and distribution expenses	(4)
Administrative expenses	(5)
Operating income	**(6) = (3) − (4) − (5)**
Interest revenue and expenses	(7)
Gain or loss on sale of equipment	(8)
Pretax income from continuing operations	**(9) = (6) − (7) ± (8)**
Income tax expense	(10)
Income from continuing operations	**(11) = (9) − (10)**
Discontinued operations (gain or loss on disposal)	(12)
Extraordinary items	(13)
Cumulative effect of change in accounting principle	(14)
Net income	**(15) = (11) + (12) ± 13) ± (14)**

Table 5.18 Comparison between income statement by nature and by function

Income statement by nature		Income statement by function	
Sales of merchandise	17,000	Sales of merchandise	17,000
− Purchases of merchandise	−8,000	− Cost of goods sold	−9,000
− Inventory change of merchandise[a]	−1,000	= Gross margin	8,000
− Personnel expense[b]	−6,000	− Commercial and selling expenses[c]	−4,000
− Depreciation expense	−1,000	− Administrative expenses[d]	−3,000
= Operating income	1,000	= Operating income	1,000

[a] Beginning minus ending
[b] Sales personnel (4,000) plus administrative personnel (2,000)
[c] Sales personnel remunerations
[d] Administrative labor (2,000) + Depreciation (1,000)

Notes should not, however, become so cumbersome to use that they defeat their purpose of clarification. They should be reserved for remarks that are significant and may have a material effect on the meaning of figures.

Table 5.19 offers a list of some commonly found remarks in notes to financial statements.

Table 5.19 Example of information found in the notes

Qualitative information	Quantitative information
Accounting policies:	Fixed assets – movements for the year
■ Accounting principles	Depreciation – movements for the year
■ Basis of consolidation	Amortization and provision – movements for the year
Measurement bases	Analysis of debt by maturity
Specific accounting policy	

Real-life example

The structure of the notes to the 2008 financial statements of Sandvik, a Swedish engineering company is presented below (source: annual report 2008). The example contains two sections, a first one called 'Accounting principles' [and policies followed] and a second one, more technical, called 'Notes to the consolidated financial statements'.

Accounting principles

- Statement of compliance
- Basis of measurement in preparation of the financial reports
- Changes in accounting policies
- New or revised IFRS and interpretations coming into effect in future accounting periods
- Classification
- Segment reporting
- Basis of consolidation subsidiaries
  - Associated companies
  - Transactions eliminated on consolidation
- Foreign currency
  - Foreign currency transactions
  - Financial statements of foreign operations
- Revenue
  - Revenue from sales and service
  - Construction contracts
  - Other revenue
  - Government grants
- Operating and financial income and expenses
  - Operating lease agreements
  - Finance lease agreements
- Financial income and expenses
- Income tax
- Financial instruments
  - Recognition and derecognition
  - Classification and measurement
- Derivatives and hedge accounting
  - Receivables and liabilities denominated in foreign currencies
  - Cash-flow hedges
  - Fair value hedges
  - Hedging of net investment
- Intangible assets
  - Goodwill
  - Research and development

- Other intangible assets
- Subsequent expenditure
- Amortization of intangible assets
- Tangible fixed assets
  - Property, plant and equipment owned assets
  - Leased assets
  - Subsequent expenditure
  - Depreciation
- Impairment and reversal of impairment
- Inventories
- Equity
- Earnings per share
- Employee benefits
  - The group's pension plans
  - Defined-contribution plans
  - Defined-benefit plans
  - Termination benefits
  - Share-based payments
- Provisions
  - Warranties
  - Restructuring
  - Site restoration
  - Onerous contracts
- Contingent liabilities
- Cash-flow statement
- Parent company's accounting policies
  - Classification of reporting formats
  - Shares in group companies and associated companies
  - Property, plant and equipment
  - Leased assets
  - Intangible assets
  - Employee benefits
  - Income tax
  - Group contributions

- Anticipated dividends
- Financial instruments
- Financial guaranties
- Critical accounting estimates and judgments
  - Key sources of estimation uncertainty
  - Impairment tests of goodwill
  - Impairment tests of other fixed assets

- Pension assumptions
- Income tax
- Disputes
- Key assessments in applying the group's accounting policies
- Inventory accounting
- Accounting for actuarial gains and losses

Notes to the consolidated financial statements

Segment information
Categories of revenue
Personnel information and remuneration to
    management and auditors
Research, development and quality assurance
Other operating income
Other operating expenses

Information on the nature of operating expenses
Fees for finance and operating leases
Net financing cost
Appropriations
Income tax
Earnings per share
Intangible assets, property, plant and equipment – group
Intangible assets, property, plant and equipment –
    parent Company
Shares in group companies
Investments in associated companies
Other financial assets

Non-current receivables and other current receivables
Inventories
Capital and reserves [including retained earnings]

Parent company's accelerated depreciation
Parent company's other untaxed reserves
Provisions for pensions and other non-current
    post-employment benefits
Other provisions
Non-current interest-bearing liabilities
Other interest-bearing liabilities
Other non-interest-bearing liabilities
Accrued expenses and deferred income
Contingent liabilities and pledged assets
Related parties
Supplementary information to the cash-flow statements

Business acquisitions
Parent company particulars
Information on shares, owners and rights

5 Terminology variations

As early as Chapter 2 we made it clear that differences existed between US and UK terminology. For example, we pointed out that the income statement (in US terminology) is generally called 'Profit and Loss Account' (or P&L) by UK or other European firms However, since the vocabulary is not standardized within most countries, there exist plenty of variations on a same theme as is the case, particularly in the United States where P&L and income statement coexist with no problem. To make things somewhat more complex, the IASB tends to use its own terminology, which mixes both US and UK terminologies and leaves a lot of room for individual choices. However, comparability implies that any terminology cover definitions that are essentially coherent and we will therefore try to stay with one set of terms.

Table 5.20 recapitulates the differences and defines the terminology we will use in this text. Our choice has been to stay as close as possible to the IASB terminology but to make a clear choice when the official terminology leaves some leeway. We opted for simple options that reflect practice as observed in the hundreds of annual reports we have consulted.

Table 5.20 Accounting terminology differences

USA	UK	IASB	Terminology used in this book
Financial statements	**Accounts**	**Financial statements**	**Financial statements**
Balance sheet			
Balance sheet (or statement of financial position)	Balance sheet	Statement of financial position (or balance sheet)	Balance sheet
Long-term (or fixed) assets	Fixed assets	Non-current assets	Fixed assets
Real estate	Land and buildings	Land and buildings	Land and buildings
Property, plant and equipment	Tangible fixed assets	Property, plant and equipment	Tangible assets
Inventories	Stocks	Inventories	Inventories
Work in process (WIP) in manufacturing industries	Work in process (WIP) in manufacturing industries	Work in progress (WIP) in manufacturing industries	Work in process (WIP) in manufacturing industries
Work in progress (WIP) in services, construction or engineering services	Work in progress (WIP) in services, construction or engineering services	Work in progress (WIP) in services, construction or engineering services	Work in progress (WIP) in services, construction or engineering services
Receivables	Debtors	Receivables	Receivables
Accounts receivable	Trade debtors	Accounts receivable	Accounts receivable
Doubtful accounts	Bad debts, doubtful debts	Bad debts	Doubtful accounts
Allowance for doubtful accounts	Provision for doubtful debts	Allowance for bad debts	Provision for doubtful accounts
Treasury stock	Own shares	Treasury shares	Treasury shares
Stockholders' equity	Shareholders' equity, Shareholders' funds (or capital and reserves)	Shareholders' equity	Shareholders' equity
Common stock	Ordinary shares	Share capital	Share capital
Preferred stock	Preference shares	–	Preference shares
Additional paid-in capital	Share premium	–	Share premium
Retained earnings, retained income	Reserves, retained profit, profit and loss account	Retained earnings, reserves, accumulated profits (losses)	Retained earnings, retained income
Loans	Debts	Loans	Borrowings
Bonds, notes payable	Debenture loan	–	Bonds, notes payable.
Long-term liabilities	Creditors: amounts falling due after more than one year	Non-current liabilities	Long-term liabilities
Payables	Creditors	Payables	Payables
Current liabilities	Creditors: amounts falling due within one year	Current liabilities	Current liabilities
Accounts payable	Trade creditors	Accounts payable	Accounts payable
Income statement			
Income statement, statement of operations, statement of income	Profit and loss account	Statement of comprehensive income (income statement, if presented separately)	Income statement
Sales	Turnover	Revenue	Sales or sales revenue
Expense	Charge	Expense	Expense
Interest expense	Interest payable	Finance cost	Interest expense
Interest income	Interest received	–	Interest income
Income	Profit	Profit	Income

(continued)

Table 5.20 *(continued)*

USA	UK	IASB	Terminology used in this book
Others			
Statement of cash flows	Cash flow statement	Statement of cash flows	Statement of cash flows
Leverage	Gearing	–	Leverage
Stock	Share	Share	Share
Residual value, salvage value, terminal value	Scrap value	Residual value	Residual value
Declining balance method	Reducing balance method	–	Declining balance method
Pay check	Pay slip	–	Pay slip
Corporation	Company	–	Company
Conservatism	Prudence	Prudence	Prudence

Key points

- The various (and numerous) users of financial statements need to understand the financial information in the same way. For that reason, within each country, local regulations issue generally accepted accounting principles (GAAP) that are called accounting standards or financial reporting standards which include specific principles, bases, conventions, rules and practices necessary to prepare the financial statements.
- The International Accounting Standards Board's main objective is to promote convergence of accounting principles that are used by businesses and other organizations for financial reporting around the world.
- An annual report includes financial data describing the activity of a company, notes on policies followed plus a managerial commentary and additional relevant financial information.

- Financial statements include, as a minimum, a balance sheet, an income statement and notes to these statements. Additionally, they tend to also comprise a statement of cash flows and a statement of changes in shareholders' equity.
- The several possibilities of presentation that exist for the balance sheet do not affect its generic content.
- There are several ways of presenting an income statement. They all provide the same bottom line.
- For the income statement, the choice between a presentation by nature or by function is always debatable.
- The notes to the financial statements (often called 'footnotes') are an essential component of the information provided through financial statements.
- Notes to financial statements constitute a clarification of – and a supplement to – the balance sheet, income statement and statement of cash flows (when reported).

Review (solutions are at the back of the book)

Review 5.1 Orkla*

Topic: Constructing a balance sheet

Orkla is a Norway-based group operating in the branded consumer goods, aluminum solutions, materials, renewable energy and financial investment sectors. Listed below are *in alphabetical order* items and amounts taken from the group's consolidated balance sheet for the accounting year ended on 31 December 2008. All numbers are in millions of Norwegian Krone (NOK) (source: annual report 2008). The consolidated financial statements for 2008 have been prepared and presented in compliance with the International Financial Reporting Standards (IFRS), as adopted by the EU.

Assets in discontinued operations	3,148	Minority interests	2,686
Cash and cash equivalents	4,438	Non-current assets	62,000
Current assets	42,926	Non-current interest-bearing liabilities	29,598
Current interest-bearing liabilities	3,654	Non-current liabilities	34,831
Current liabilities	20,026	Other current liabilities	14,702
Deferred tax	2,872	Other non-current financial assets	1,219
Deferred tax assets	984	Paid-in equity	1,993
Equity	50,069	Property, plant and equipment	26,368
Equity and liabilities	104,926	Provisions and liabilities	2,361
Income tax payable	1,005	Receivables	14,331
Intangible assets	16,317	Retained earnings	45,390
Inventories	9,564	Share portfolio etc.	11,445
Investments in associates	17,112	Total assets	104,926
Liabilities in discontinued operations	665		

N.B.
- Minority interests represent the part of the net assets of a subsidiary attributable to interests, which are not owned, directly or indirectly through subsidiaries, by the parent company (minority shareholders). This item will be presented in a more detailed manner in Chapter 13.
- 'Provisions' are, here, assimilated to long-term liabilities.

Required

1. Reconstruct the balance sheet in a vertical, single-step and increasing format (check figure: total balance sheet = 104,926).

2. Given the terminology used, was the original balance sheet organized by nature or by term?

Review 5.2 Holcim*

Topic: Constructing an income statement

Holcim is a Switzerland-based group producing and selling cement and clinker, as well as aggregates. It is closely linked to the building industry. Listed below are *in alphabetical order* items and amounts taken from the group's consolidated statement of income for the accounting year ended on 31 December 2008. All numbers are in millions of Swiss Francs (source: annual report 2008). The consolidated financial statements have been prepared in accordance with International Financial Reporting Standards (IFRS).

Administration expenses	(1,760)	Net income	2,226
Distribution and selling expenses	(5,921)	Net income before taxes	2,889
Equity holders of Holcim Ltd	1,782	Net sales	25,157
Financial expenses	(990)	Operating profit	3,360
Financial income	271	Other income	19
Gross profit	11,041	Production cost of goods sold	(14,116)
Income taxes	(663)	Share of profit of associates	229
Minority interest	444		

N.B. Minority interests, see note to Review problem 5.1.

Required

1. Prepare the income statement in a multiple-step format (check figure: bottom line = 2,226).

2. Given the terminology used, was the original income statement organized by nature or by function?

Assignments

Assignment 5.1
Multiple-choice questions

Select the right answer (only one possible answer unless otherwise stated).

1. Which of the following does IASB stand for?
   (a) Internationally Accepted Standards Board
   (b) International Accounting Standards Board
   (c) International Accounting Standards Building
   (d) Internationally Accepted Standards Building

2. The main objective of the IASB is:
   (a) To control local accounting regulators
   (b) To help firms to apply local accounting standards correctly
   (c) To protect European investors
   (d) To promote convergence of accounting principles used by businesses and other organizations for financial reporting around the world
   (e) All of these
   (f) None of these

3. None of the standards and interpretations issued before the creation of IASB in 2001 are now applicable
   (a) True
   (b) False

4. The IASB has authority to require compliance with its accounting standards
   (a) True
   (b) False

5. The key choice(s) concerning the presentation of the balance sheet is (are):
   (a) The format of the list (vertical or horizontal)
   (b) The type of classification (by term or by nature)
   (c) The degree of fineness (single- or multiple-step)
   (d) All of these

6. Which categories are used to classify assets?
   (a) Short-term versus long-term
   (b) Financial versus operating/trading
   (c) Tangible versus intangible
   (d) All of these

7. The IASB imposes the use of the classification by function
   (a) True
   (b) False

8. According to IAS 1, the purpose(s) of the notes to financial statements is (are):
   (a) To present information about the basis of preparation of the financial statements
   (b) To provide additional information that is not presented on the face of the financial statements but that is relevant to an understanding of any of them
   (c) To disclose information required by IFRS that is not presented elsewhere in the financial statements
   (d) All of these

9. An annual report includes:
   (a) Only information on the activity of a company
   (b) Only commercial information
   (c) Only financial information
   (d) Information on the activity of a company

10. The income statement in North America is generally called the _____ in the UK
    (a) Revenue and expense account
    (b) Result account
    (c) Profit and loss account
    (d) Statement of comprehensive income
    (e) Statement of operations
    (f) Statement of income
    (g) None of these

Assignment 5.2
adidas Group*

Topic: Constructing a balance sheet

The company was founded on 18 August 1949. It offers its products through three main brands: adidas, Reebok and TaylorMade-adidas Golf. adidas products include footwear, apparel and hardware, such as bags and balls. The company's shares were first listed on Frankfurt Stock Exchange and Paris Stock Exchange in 1995. In December 1997, the company acquired the Salomon Group with the brands Salomon, TaylorMade, Mavic and Bonfire. The new company was named adidas-Salomon AG. The Salomon Group (including Salomon, Mavic, Bonfire, Cliché and Arc'Teryx) was sold to Amer Sports in October 2005. The new adidas Group focused itself on its core strength in the athletic footwear and apparel market as well as the growing golf sector. The legal name of the company was changed to 'adidas AG' in May/June 2006. The company acquired Reebok in 2006.

Effective 3 January 2008, adidas Canada acquired Saxon Athletic Manufacturing Inc. Effective 11 February 2008, TaylorMade-adidas Golf divested the Maxfli brand. The company is headquartered in Herzogenaurach, Germany.

Listed below are *in alphabetical order* items and amounts taken from the consolidated balance sheet as of 31 December 2008. All numbers are in millions of euros. Some items have been grouped, in order to simplify the balance sheet.

Accounts payable	1,218	Other non-current liabilities	515
Accounts receivable	1,624	Pensions and similar obligations	132
Assets classified as held for sale	31	Property, plant and equipment	886
Cash and cash equivalents	244	Reserves	−10
Current accrued liabilities and provisions	1,008	Retained earnings	3,202
Goodwill	1,499	Share capital	194
Income taxes	321	Shareholders' equity	3,386
Inventories	1,995	Short-term borrowings	797
Liabilities classified as held for sale	6	Short-term financial assets	141
Long-term borrowings	1,776	Total assets	9,533
Long-term financial assets	96	Total current assets	4,934
Minority interests	14	Total current liabilities	3,645
Non-current accrued liabilities and provisions	65	Total equity	3,400
Other current assets	899	Total liabilities and equity	9,533
Other current liabilities	295	Total non-current assets	4,599
Other intangible assets	1,594	Total non-current liabilities	2,488
Other non-current assets	524		

N.B.
- Minority interests, see note to Review problem 5.1.
- Goodwill represents any excess of the cost of the acquisition over the acquirer's interest in the fair value of the identifiable assets and liabilities acquired as at the date of the exchange transaction. This item will be presented in a more detailed manner in Chapters 8 and 13.

Required

Prepare a vertical balance sheet, knowing that this German group prepares its financial statements in accordance with the International Financial Reporting Standards (IFRS) (check figure: total assets = 9,533).

Assignment 5.3
Ona Group*

Topic: Constructing an income statement

Ona Group is an industrial and financial private Moroccan group. Operating in Morocco, France and sub-Saharan Africa, the Ona Group is organized into five strategic areas: mines and construction materials, agribusiness and beverages, tourism, distribution and development and financial activities. Listed below are *in alphabetical order* items and amounts taken from the consolidated income statement for the accounting year ending on 31 December 2008 (source: company's website: www.ona.ma). All numbers are in millions of Moroccan Dirhams (MDH).

Consolidated net income	792	Net income of consolidated companies	(189)
Deferred tax	192	Operating income	1,351
Depreciation, amortization and provisions	(1,865)	Other external expenses	(3,545)
Income before taxes of consolidated companies	775	Other financial revenues and expenses	(27)
Income from financial instruments	(151)	Other non-recurring operating revenues and expenses	(98)
Income from ordinary activities	1,571	Other operating revenues	421
Income from the disposal of assets	27	Other operating revenues and expenses, net	3,061

(*continued*)

Income from the disposal of subsidiaries and investments	3	Purchases	(29,713)
Income tax	(1,156)	Recurring operating expenses	(35,485)
Interest expense	(692)	Revenues from ordinary activities	37,056
Interest income	144	Sales	36,635
Net financial income	(576)	Share of income of companies accounted for under the equity method	981
Net income from continuing activities	792	Staff costs	(3,195)
Net income from discontinued activities	0	Taxes other than on income	(227)

N.B. Portion of the results of companies valued at equity represent the share in companies where the group only exerts a significant influence (ownership between 20% and 50% of share capital). This item is covered in more detail in Chapter 13.

Required

1. Prepare the income statement in a multiple-step format (check figure: bottom line = 792).
2. Given the terminology used, was the original income statement organized by nature or by function?

Assignment 5.4
Nokia* and others

Topic: Determination of financial statements format

You will find below in Exhibits 1 and 2 the balance sheets and income statements from eight different companies.

- **Nokia** (Finland) is a leader in the communication industry, with emphasis on cellular phones and other wireless solutions. The consolidated financial statements of Nokia are prepared in accordance with International Financial Reporting Standards as issued by the IASB and in conformity with IFRS as adopted by the European Union.
- **Aracruz Celulose** (Brazil) is the world's leading producer of bleached eucalyptus pulp. The consolidated financial statements have been prepared in conformity with accounting principles generally accepted in the United States of America (US GAAP).
- **Metro** (Germany) is one of the most important international trading and retailing companies. Metro AG's consolidated financial statements as of 31 December 2008 were prepared in accordance with the IFRS of the International Accounting Standards Board (IASB), London.
- **Trigano** (France) is a European manufacturer of leisure equipment and leisure vehicles. Pursuant to European regulation 1606/2002 of 19 July 2002 on international accounting standards, the consolidated financial statements of Trigano as at 31 August 2008 have been prepared in accordance

with the standards and interpretations published by the IASB and adopted by the European Union as at 31 August 2008. These accounting standards include the international accounting standards (IAS and IFRS) and interpretations of the Standing Interpretations Committee (SIC) and the International Financial Reporting Interpretations Committee (IFRIC).
- **easyJet** (UK) is a low-cost airline carrier. easyJet's financial statements are prepared in accordance with IFRS as adopted by the European Union, taking into account International Financial Reporting Interpretations Committee (IFRIC) interpretations and those parts of the Companies Acts 1985 and 2006 applicable to companies reporting under IFRS.
- **Continental Airlines** (USA) provides scheduled air transportation for passengers and cargo throughout the US and around the world. With the company's domestic and international partners, its route network covers 241 cities. The consolidated financial statements have been prepared in conformity with accounting principles generally accepted in the United States of America (US GAAP).
- **Bayer CropScience** (India) is engaged in the area of crop protection (Crop Protection), non agricultural pest-control (Environmental Science), seeds and plant biotechnology (BioScience). The Company's Crop Protection activities are focused on four fields: Herbicides, Insecticides, Fungicides and Seed Treatment. The financial statements have been prepared in conformity with accounting principles generally accepted in India and comply with the accounting standards notified under Section 211(3C) of the Companies Act, 1956 and the relevant provisions of this act.
- **China Communications Construction** (China) is based in the People's Republic of China and

principally engaged in infrastructure construction, infrastructure design, dredging and manufacturing of port machinery and other businesses. The consolidated financial statements of the group have been prepared in accordance with IFRS.

Required

Analyze the financial statements and classify each balance sheet and income statement as described in the following table.

Company	Balance sheet			
	Format	**Classification**		**Presentation**
	Vertical (V) Horizontal (H)	Single-step (S) Multiple-step (M)	Nature (N) Term (T)	Increasing (I) Decreasing (D)
Nokia (Finland)				
Aracruz (Brazil)				
Metro (Germany)				
Trigano (France)				
easyJet (UK)				
Continental Airlines (US)				
Bayer CropScience (India)				
China Communications Construction (China)				

Company	Income statement		
	Format	**Degree of simplification**	**Classification of expenses**
	Vertical (V) Horizontal (H)	Single-step (S) Multiple-step (M)	Nature (N) Function (F)
Nokia (Finland)			
Aracruz (Brazil)			
Metro (Germany)			
Trigano (France)			
easyJet (UK)			
Continental Airlines (US)			
Bayer CropScience (India)			
China Communications Construction (China)			

Exhibit 1: Balance sheets (source: annual reports)

The balance sheets listed hereafter are excerpted from the actual annual reports of the companies. Some of the data has been simplified for pedagogical reasons.

Nokia – Consolidated balance sheets (IFRS) Financial year ended 31 December 2008 (in € millions)

	2008	2007
ASSETS		
Non-current assets		
Capitalized development costs	244	378
Goodwill	6,257	1,384
Other intangible assets	3,913	2,358
Property, plant and equipment	2,090	1,912
Investments in associated companies	96	325
Available-for-sale investments	512	341
Deferred tax assets	1,963	1,553
Long-term loans receivable	27	10
Other non-current assets	10	44
	15,112	8,305
Current assets		
Inventories	2,533	2,876
Accounts receivable, net of allowances for doubtful accounts	9,444	11,200
Prepaid expenses and accrued income	4,538	3,070
Current portion of long-term loans receivable	101	156
Other financial assets	1,034	239
Available-for-sale investments, liquid assets	1,272	4,903
Available-for-sale investments, cash equivalents	3,842	4,725
Bank and cash	1,706	2,125
	24,470	29,294
Total assets	39,582	37,599
SHAREHOLDERS' EQUITY AND LIABILITIES		
Capital and reserves attributable to equity holders of the parent		
Share capital	246	246
Share issue premium	442	644
Treasury shares, at cost	−1,881	−3,146
Translation differences	341	−163
Fair value and other reserves	62	23
Reserve for invested non-restricted equity	3,306	3,299
Retained earnings	11,692	13,870
	14,208	14,773
Minority interests	2,302	2,565
Total equity	16,510	17,338
Non-current liabilities		
Long-term interest-bearing liabilities	861	203
Deferred tax liabilities	1,787	963
Other long-term liabilities	69	119
	2,717	1,285
Current liabilities		
Current portion of long-term loans	13	173
Short-term borrowings	3,578	714
Other financial liabilities	924	184
Accounts payable	5,225	7,074
Accrued expenses	7,023	7,114
Provisions	3,592	3,717
	20,355	18,976
Total shareholders' equity and liabilities	39,582	37,599

Source: Nokia, annual report 2008

Aracruz – Consolidated balance sheets on 31 December (in US$ 000)

ASSETS	31 December 2007	2008	LIABILITIES AND STOCKHOLDERS' EQUITY	31 December 2007	2008
Current assets			Current liabilities		
Cash and cash equivalents	53,321	60,033	Suppliers	119,950	149,679
Short-term investments	439,940	368,862	Payroll and related charges	33,310	20,640
Derivative instruments	3,417		Income and other taxes	31,237	47,647
Accounts receivable, net	361,603	288,611	Short-term borrowings	5,646	115,579
Inventories	225,023	310,383	Current portion of long-term debt		
Deferred income tax	12,280	16,425	Related party	76,082	39,405
Recoverable taxes	140,390	134,268	Other	5,897	153,230
Prepaid expenses and other current assets	18,843	15,070	Accrued finance charges	12,560	38,138
			Derivative instruments		37,515
Total current assets	1,254,817	1,193,652	Accrued dividends - interest payable on stockholders' equity	45,495	950
			Other accruals	959	1,221
Property, plant and equipment, net	2,518,700	3,009,367	Total current liabilities	331,136	604,004
			Long-term liabilities		
			Long-term debt		
Investment in affiliated company	415,394	556,410	Related party	350,274	267,361
Goodwill	192,035	192,035	Other	962,077	3,299,334
			Derivative instruments		23,467
Derivative instruments	29,699		Litigation contingencies	130,999	105,357
Advances to suppliers	100,922	119,158	Liabilities associated with unrecognized tax benefits	92,449	60,135
Accounts receivable	24,671	15,973			
Deposits for tax assessments	22,520	18,866	Interest and penalties on liabilities associated with unrecognized tax benefits	69,046	
Deferred income tax, net		270,970			
Recoverable taxes	64,899	19,117			
Other	4,623	3,867	Deferred income tax, net	248,879	41,607
Total other assets	247,334	447,951	Other	44,905	48,851
			Total long-term liabilities	1,898,629	3,846,112
			Commitments and contingencies (Note 13)		
			Minority interest	11,397	11,662
			Stockholders' equity		
			Share capital - no-par-value shares authorized issued and outstanding		
			Preferred stock		
			Class A	41,305	41,303
			Class B	853,439	853,441
			Common stock	518,385	518,385
			Treasury stock	(2,639)	(2,639)
			Total share capital	1,410,490	1,410,490
			Appropriated retained earnings	1,434,228	
			Unappropriated retained deficit	(457,600)	(472,853)
			Total stockholders' equity	2,387,118	937,637
Total assets	4,628,280	5,399,415	Total liabilities and stockholders´ equity	4,628,280	5,399,415

Source: Aracruz, annual report 2008

Metro – Balance sheet on 31 December (in € millions)

ASSETS

	As of 31 Dec 2008	As of 31 Dec 2007
Non-current assets	**18,808**	**18,882**
Goodwill	3,960	4,328
Other intangible assets	552	515
Tangible assets	12,524	12,332
Investment properties	133	116
Financial assets	144	152
Other receivables and assets	450	490
Deferred tax assets	1,045	949
Current assets	**15,017**	**14,990**
Inventories	7,001	7,328
Trade receivables	446	508
Financial assets	8	28
Other receivables and assets	3,132	3,076
Entitlements to income tax refunds	326	275
Cash and cash equivalents	3,874	3,433
Assets held for sale	230	342
	33,825	**33,872**

LIABILITIES

	As of 31 Dec 2008	As of 31 Dec 2007
Equity	**6,074**	**6,509**
Share capital	835	835
Capital reserve	2,544	2,544
Reserves retained from earnings	2,441	2,876
Minority interests	254	254
Non-current liabilities	**7,369**	**7,357**
Provisions for pensions and similar commitments	964	973
Other provisions	533	524
Financial liabilities	5,031	5,030
Other liabilities	620	647
Deferred tax liabilities	221	183
Current liabilities	**20,382**	**20,006**
Trade liabilities	13,839	14,088
Provisions	522	576
Financial liabilities	3,448	2,708
Other liabilities	2,161	2,267
Income tax liabilities	266	337
Liabilities related to assets held for sale	146	30
	33,825	**33,872**

Source: Metro, annual report 2008

Trigano – Consolidated balance sheets as of 31 August (in € 000)

ASSETS	31/08/2008	31/08/2007
Intangible fixed assets	5,132	4,138
Goodwill	39,504	45,127
Tangible fixed assets	117,447	120,932
Investments in associated companies	9,549	9,392
Other financial assets	1,661	1,580
Deferred tax assets	10,469	12,705
Other long-term assets	43	470
Total non-current assets	**183,805**	**194,344**
Stocks [inventories] and work in progress	334,925	250,726
Trade and other debtors	142,035	149,268
Tax receivables	18,936	7,203
Other current assets	35,317	41,955
Cash and cash equivalents	36,227	60,145
Total current assets	**567,440**	**509,297**
Total assets	**751,245**	**703,641**

EQUITY AND LIABILITIES	31/08/2008	31/08/2007
Share capital and share premium	94,341	94,239
Reserves, retained earnings and consolidated profit	213,199	215,746
Total equity attributable to the Group	**307,540**	**309,985**
Minority interests	369	757
Equity of the consolidated group	**307,909**	**310,742**
Non-current financial liabilities	11,059	19,796
Long-term provisions	14,735	12,759
Deferred tax liabilities	6,285	6,067
Other non-current liabilities	1,022	1,030
Total non-current liabilities	**33,101**	**39,652**
Current financial liabilities	195,813	116,565
Current provisions	7,655	6,713
Trade and other creditors	162,881	170,733
Taxes payable	2,576	13,120
Other current liabilities	41,310	46,117
Total current liabilities	**410,235**	**353,248**
Total liabilities	**751,245**	**703,641**

Source: Trigano, annual report 2008

easyJet – Consolidated balance sheet as of 30 September (in £ millions)

	30 September 2008	30 September 2007
Non-current assets		
Goodwill	359.8	309.6
Other intangible assets	80.6	1.8
Property, plant and equipment	1,102.6	935.8
Derivative financial instruments	21.3	—
Loan notes – The Airline Group Limited	12.0	11.1
Restricted cash	42.9	32.9
Other non-current assets	61.1	58.1
Investments in associates	—	0.3
Deferred tax assets	0.5	0.4
	1,680.8	**1,350.0**
Current assets		
Assets held for sale	195.8	—
Trade and other receivables	236.9	223.6
Derivative financial instruments	96.5	14.4
Restricted cash	23.3	15.9
Money market deposits	230.3	193.4
Cash and cash equivalents	632.2	719.1
	1,415.0	**1,166.4**
Current liabilities		
Trade and other payables	(653.0)	(461.7)
Borrowings	(56.7)	(40.5)
Derivative financial instruments	(76.0)	(26.6)
Current tax liabilities	(75.1)	(89.7)
Maintenance provisions	(49.0)	(2.8)
	(909.8)	**(621.3)**
Net current assets	**505.2**	**545.1**
Non-current liabilities		
Borrowings	(570.2)	(478.6)
Derivative financial instruments	(0.3)	(6.3)
Other non-current liabilities	(68.8)	(86.8)
Maintenance provisions	(160.4)	(136.0)
Deferred tax liabilities	(108.1)	(35.0)
	(907.8)	**(742.7)**
Net assets	**1,278.2**	**1,152.4**
Shareholders' funds		
Share capital	105.7	104.8
Share premium	640.2	633.9
Hedging reserve	27.6	(13.7)
Translation reserve	0.1	—
Retained earnings	504.6	427.4
	1,278.2	**1,152.4**

Source: easyJet, annual report 2008

Continental Airlines – Consolidated balance sheets as of 31 December (in US $ millions)

ASSETS	31 December 2008	31 December 2007	LIABILITIES AND STOCKHOLDERS' EQUITY	31 December 2008	31 December 2007
Current assets:			Current liabilities:		
Cash and cash equivalents	2,165	2,128	Current maturities of long-term debt and capital leases	519	652
Short-term investments	478	675	Accounts payable	1,021	1,013
Total unrestricted cash, cash equivalents and short-term investments	2,643	2,803	Air traffic and frequent flyer liability	1,881	1,967
Restricted cash, cash equivalents and short-term investments	190	179	Accrued payroll	345	545
Accounts receivable, net of allowance for doubtful receivables	453	606	Accrued other liabilities	708	272
Spare parts and supplies, net of allowance for obsolescence	235	271	Total current liabilities	4,474	4,449
Deferred income taxes	216	259			
Prepayments and other	610	443	Long-term debt and capital leases	5,353	4,337
Total current assets	4,347	4,561	Deferred income taxes	216	369
Property and equipment:			Accrued pension liability	1,417	534
Owned property and equipment:			Accrued retiree medical benefits	234	235
Flight equipment	8,446	7,182	Other	869	612
Other	1,694	1,548	Commitments and contingencies		
	10,140	8,730	Stockholders' equity:		
Less: accumulated depreciation...	3,229	2,790	Preferred stock	—	—
	6,911	5,940	Class B common stock	1	1
Purchase deposits for flight equipment	275	414	Additional paid-in capital	2,038	1,647
Capital leases	194	297	Retained earnings (accumulated deficit)	(160)	426
Less: accumulated amortization	53	93	Accumulated other comprehensive loss	(1,756)	(505)
	141	204	Total stockholders' equity	123	1,569
Total property and equipment, net	7,327	6,558			
Routes and airport operating rights, net of accumulated amortization	804	706			
Investment in other companies	0	63			
Other assets, net	208	217	Total liabilities and		
Total assets	12,686	12,105	stockholders' equity	12,686	12,105

Source: Continental Airlines, annual report 2008

Bayer CropScience Limited – Balance sheet as of 31 March (in rupees 000)

	As at 31.03.2008		As at 31.12.2006	
SOURCES OF FUNDS				
SHAREHOLDERS' FUNDS				
Share capital	394,987			394,987
Reserves and surplus (retained earnings)	3,299,436			2,919,319
		3,694,423		3,314,306
LOAN FUNDS				
Secured loans	133,022			203,459
Unsecured loans	559,082			877,960
		692,104		1,081,419
		4,386,527		**4,395,725**
APPLICATION OF FUNDS				
FIXED ASSETS				
Gross block	4,161,840			3,397,464
Less: Depreciation/ amortization/ impairment loss	1,794,955			1,880,672
Net block	2,366,885			1,516,792
Capital work-in-progress	112,040			37,519
		2,478,925		1,554,311
INVESTMENTS		603,324		40,043
DEFERRED TAX ASSET (NET)		165,089		25,698
CURRENT ASSETS, LOANS AND ADVANCES				
Inventories	2,018,151			1,887,201
Sundry debtors	1,808,703			2,144,059
Cash and bank balances	275,767			265,892
Other current assets	—			39,499
Loans and advances	1,052,878			476,648
	5,155,499			4,813,299
Less: CURRENT LIABILITIES AND PROVISIONS				
Current liabilities	3,712,130			1,803,496
Provisions	304,180			234,130
	4,016,310			2,037,626
NET CURRENT ASSETS		1,139,189		2,775,673
		4,386,527		**4,395,725**

Source: Bayer CropScience, annual report 2008

China Communications Construction – Balance sheets as of 31 December (in RMB millions)

	2008	2007
ASSETS		
Non-current assets		
Property, plant and equipment	37,205	26,129
Lease prepayments	3,406	2,979
Investment properties	320	374
Intangible assets	6,218	4,873
Investments in subsidiaries	—	—
Investments in jointly controlled entities	651	370
Investments in associates	3,146	3,222
Available-for-sale financial assets	6,733	16,621
Held-to-maturity financial assets	2	2
Deferred income tax assets	1,900	2,251
Trade and other receivables	11,229	7,744
Other non-current assets	98	83
	70,908	64,648
Current assets		
Inventories	16,360	5,863
Trade and other receivables	63,777	44,782
Loans to subsidiaries	—	—
Amounts due from subsidiaries	—	—
Amounts due from customers for contract work	38,682	28,488
Derivative financial instruments	1,382	508
Other financial assets at fair value through profit or loss	49	160
Restricted cash	662	475
Cash and cash equivalents	26,278	22,473
	147,190	102,749
Total assets	218,098	167,397
EQUITY		
Capital and reserves attributable to equity holders of the company		
Share capital	14,825	14,825
Share premium	13,853	13,853
Other reserves (retained earnings)	11,040	15,162
Proposed final dividend	1,453	1,305
	41,171	45,145
Minority interests	10,998	8,817
Total equity	52,169	53,962
LIABILITIES		
Non-current liabilities		
Borrowings	19,996	12,633
Deferred income	313	246
Deferred income tax liabilities	972	3,817
Early retirement and supplemental benefit obligations	2,856	3,153
	24,137	19,849
Current liabilities		
Trade and other payables	88,031	62,099
Amounts due to subsidiaries	—	—
Amounts due to customers for contract work	13,224	7,627
Current income tax liabilities	1,647	1,562
Borrowings	37,878	21,828
Derivative financial instruments	725	158
Early retirement and supplemental benefit obligations	197	202
Provisions	90	89
Other current liabilities	—	21
	141,792	93,586
Total liabilities	165,929	113,435
Total equity and liabilities	218,098	167,397
Net current assets	5,398	9,163
Total assets less current liabilities	76,306	73,811

Exhibit 2: Income statements (source: annual reports)

The income statements listed hereafter are excerpted from the actual annual reports of the companies. Some of the data has been simplified for pedagogical reasons.

Nokia – Consolidated profit and loss accounts (IFRS) for the year ended 31 December (in € million)

Financial year ended 31 December	2008	2007
Net sales	50,710	51,058
Cost of sales	–33,337	–33,781
Research and development expenses	–5,968	–5,636
Selling and marketing expenses	–4,380	–4,379
Administrative and general expenses	–1,284	–1,165
Other income	420	2,312
Other expenses	–1,195	–424
Operating profit	4,966	7,985
Share of results of associated companies	6	44
Financial income and expenses	–2	239
Profit before tax	4,970	8,268
Tax	–1,081	–1,522
Profit before minority interests	3,889	6,746
Minority interests	99	459
Profit attributable to equity holders of the parent	3,988	7,205

Source: Nokia, annual report 2008

Aracruz – Consolidated statements of income for the year ended 31 December (in $ 000)

	Year ended 31 December		
	2006	2007	2008
Domestic	77,431	137,086	152,285
Export	1,845,026	2,007,017	1,999,605
Gross operating revenues	1,922,457	2,144,103	2,151,890
Sales taxes and other deductions	(241,624)	(260,328)	(240,587)
Net operating revenues	1,680,833	1,883,775	1,911,303
Operating costs and expenses			
Cost of sales	1,037,896	1,190,957	1,337,797
Selling	74,005	78,832	88,329
Administrative	57,020	58,708	64,738
Other, net	12,514	(38,624)	77,973
Total operating costs and expenses	1,181,435	1,289,873	1,568,837
Operating income	499,398	593,902	342,466
Non-operating (income) expenses, net			
Financial income	(92,867)	(72,400)	(65,380)
Financial expenses	149,719	100,864	112,690
Results of derivative transactions, net	(88,866)	(95,637)	2,159,255
Gain on currency remeasurement, net	(7,641)	(908)	(71,146)
Other, net	(7)	(61)	
Total non-operating (income) expenses, net	(39,662)	(68,142)	2,135,419
Income before income taxes, minority interest and equity in results of affiliated companies	539,060	662,044	(1,792,953)
Income tax expense			
Current	30,754	41,343	34,305
Deferred	38,740	155,969	(524,063)
Total income tax expense (credit)	69,494	197,312	(489,758)
Minority interest	(544)	(10,522)	735
Equity in results of affiliated companies	(13,705)	(32,141)	63,766
Net income (loss)	455,317	422,069	(1,238,694)

Source: Aracruz, annual report 2008

Metro – Income statement for the financial year from 1 January to 31 December (in € millions)

	2008	2007
Net sales	**67,956**	**64,210**
Cost of sales	(53,636)	(50,810)
Gross profit on sales	**14,320**	**13,400**
Other operating income	1,518	1,554
Selling expenses	(12,332)	(11,443)
General administrative expenses	(1,426)	(1,352)
Other operating expenses	(92)	(81)
Earnings before interest and taxes (EBIT)	**1,988**	**2,078**
Result from associated companies	0	0
Other investment result	14	11
Interest income	196	185
Interest expenses	(682)	(676)
Other financial result	(101)	(37)
Net financial result	**(573)**	**(517)**
Earnings before taxes (EBT)	**1,415**	**1,561**
Income taxes	(426)	(560)
Income from discontinued operations	(429)	(18)
Net profit for the period	**560**	**983**
Profit attributable to minority interests	157	158
Profit attributable to shareholders of METRO AG	403	825

Source: Metro, annual report 2008

Trigano – Consolidated income statement for years ended 31 August (in € 000)

	2008	2007
Sales	**875,503**	**934,630**
Other income from business activities	5,276	6,322
Purchases consumed	(659,439)	(655,604)
Personnel costs	(139,273)	(137,645)
External expenses	(97,035)	(96,865)
Taxes and duties	(6,772)	(6,960)
Depreciation, amortization and impairment	(19,987)	(15,106)
Change in stocks of finished products and work in progress	79,856	27,763
Current operating income	**38,129**	**56,535**
Other operating income and expenses	(3,675)	238
Operating income	**34,454**	**56,773**
Financial result	(12,597)	(5,899)
Tax charge	(7,084)	(22,079)
Share in net income of associated companies	1,278	1,204
Net income	**16,051**	**29,999**

Source: Trigano, annual report 2008

easyJet – Consolidated profit and loss account for the year ended 30 September (in £ million)

	Year ended 30 September 2008	Year ended 30 September 2007
Passenger revenue	1,996	1,626
Ancillary revenue	367	171
Total revenue	**2,363**	**1,797**
Ground handling charges	(212)	(156)
Airport charges	(397)	(306)
Fuel	(709)	(426)
Navigation charges	(196)	(142)
Crew costs	(263)	(204)
Maintenance	(148)	(98)
Advertising	(47)	(38)
Merchant fees and commissions	(34)	(21)
Aircraft and passenger insurance	(9)	(12)
Other costs	(88)	(97)
GB Airways integration costs	(13)	—
EBITDAR[a]	**249**	**298**
Depreciation	(44)	(33)
Amortization of other intangible assets	(3)	(1)
Aircraft dry lease[b] costs	(111)	(91)
Aircraft long-term wet lease[c] costs	—	(1)
Operating profit	**91**	**172**
Interest receivable and other financing income	53	55
Reversal of prior year impairment losses on financial assets	—	11
Interest payable and other financing charges	(34)	(35)
Net finance income	**19**	**30**
Share of profit of associate	—	0
Profit before tax	**110**	**202**
Tax	(27)	(50)
Profit for the year	**83**	**152**

Notes

[a] EBITDAR = Earnings Before Interest, Taxes, Depreciation, Amortization and Rent

[b] Dry lease = leasing arrangement whereby an aircraft financing entity, such as GECAS and ILFC (lessor), provides an aircraft without insurance, crew, ground staff, supporting equipment, maintenance, etc.

[c] Wet lease = a short-term leasing arrangement whereby one airline (lessor) provides an *aircraft, complete crew, maintenance, and insurance (ACMI)* to another airline (lessee), which pays by hours operated. The lessee provides fuel, covers airport fees and any other duties, taxes, etc.

Source: easyJet, annual report 2008

Continental Airlines – Consolidated statements of operations for the year ended 31 December (in $ millions)	2008	2007	2006
Operating revenue:			
Passenger	13,737	12,995	12,003
Cargo	497	453	457
Other	1,007	784	668
	15,241	14,232	13,128
Operating expenses:			
Aircraft fuel and related taxes	5,919	4,034	3,697
Wages, salaries and related costs	2,957	3,127	2,875
Regional capacity purchase, net	1,059	1,113	1,128
Aircraft rentals	976	994	990
Landing fees and other rentals	853	790	764
Distribution costs	717	682	650
Maintenance, materials and repairs	612	621	547
Depreciation and amortization	438	413	391
Passenger services	406	389	356
Special charges	181	13	27
Other	1,437	1,369	1,235
	15,555	13,545	12,660
Operating income (loss)	(314)	687	468
Non-operating income (expense):			
Interest expense	(376)	(393)	(409)
Interest capitalized	33	27	18
Interest income	65	160	131
Gains on sale of investments	78	37	92
Other, net	(181)	38	61
	(381)	(131)	(107)
Income (loss) before income taxes and cumulative effect of change in accounting principle	(695)	556	361
Income tax benefit (expense)	109	(117)	—
Income (loss) before cumulative effect of change in accounting principle	(586)	439	361
Cumulative effect of change in accounting principle	—	—	(26)
Net income (loss)	(586)	439	335

Source: Continental Airlines, annual report 2008

Bayer CropScience Limited – Profit and loss account for the period from 1 January 2007 to 31 March (in rupees 000)

	01.01.2007 to 31.03.2008		01.01.2006 to 31.12.2006
INCOME			
Sales	12,456,334		8,008,921
Less: excise duty	822,817		730,470
		11,633,517	7,278,451
Operating income		749,683	468,047
Other income		230,407	337,557
		12,613,607	8,084,055
EXPENDITURE			
Materials consumed		3,178,058	3,111,927
Cost of traded goods sold		4,484,409	1,415,306
Employee cost		1,221,699	671,229
Other expenses		2,539,728	1,640,409
Finance charges		75,507	85,335
Depreciation/ amortization		261,223	218,637
Impairment loss on fixed assets (net)		1,614	68,278
Decrease/ (increase) in stock		60,840	(21,789)
		11,823,078	7,189,332
PROFIT BEFORE EXCEPTIONAL ITEM AND TAXATION		790,529	894,723
Exceptional items			
—Profit on sale of long term investments	194,021		—
—Voluntary retirement expenditure	(304,987)		(4,192)
		(110,966)	(4,192)
PROFIT FOR THE PERIOD BEFORE TAXATION		**679,563**	**890,531**
Taxation			
— Current tax	284,069		312,000
— Deferred tax	(139,391)		(10,657)
— Fringe benefit tax	43,860		20,610
		188,538	321,953
PROFIT AFTER TAXATION		491,025	568,578
Add: Balance brought forward from previous year		2,019,232	1,618,420
AMOUNT AVAILABLE FOR APPROPRIATION		**2,510,257**	**2,186,998**

Source: Bayer CropScience, annual report 2008

China Communications Construction – Consolidated income statement for the year ended 31 December (in RMB millions)		
	2008	2007
Revenue	178,889	150,601
Cost of sales	(161,031)	(135,033)
Gross profit	17,858	15,568
Other income	2,212	2,226
Other gains — net	1,171	243
Selling and marketing expenses	(490)	(409)
Administrative expenses	(7,447)	(6,059)
Other expenses	(1,417)	(983)
Operating profit	11,887	10,586
Interest income	657	491
Finance costs, net	(2,636)	(1,545)
Share of loss of jointly controlled entities	(88)	(41)
Share of profit of associates	11	132
Profit before income tax	9,831	9,623
Income tax expense	(1,955)	(2,049)
Profit for the year	7,876	7,574

Source: China Communications Construction, annual report 2008

References

IASB (1989) Framework for the Preparation and Presentation of Financial Statement, London.

IASB (2003) International Accounting Standard No.8: Accounting policies, changes in accounting estimates and errors, London.

IASB (2007) International Accounting Standard No. 1: Presentation of Financial Statements, London.

IASB (2009a) Constitution in *International Financial Reporting Standards*, bound volume, London.

IASB (2009b) Introduction in *International Financial Reporting Standards*, bound volume, London.

Further reading

Ball, R. (2006) 'International financial reporting standards (IFRS): Pros and cons for investors', *Accounting & Business Research* 36(Special issue): 5–27.

Carmona, S. and Trombetta, M. (2008) 'On the global acceptance of IAS/IFRS accounting standards: The logic and implications of the principles-based system', *Journal of Accounting and Public Policy* 27(6): 455–61.

Chua, W. F. and Taylor, S. L. (2008) 'The rise and rise of IFRS: An examination of IFRS diffusion', *Journal of Accounting and Public Policy* 27(6): 462–73.

Ding, Y. and Su, X. (2008) 'Implementation of IFRS in a regulated market', *Journal of Accounting and Public Policy* 27(6): 474–79.

Haller, A. (2002). 'Financial accounting developments in the European Union: Past events and future prospects', *European Accounting Review* 11(1) (May): 153–90.

Murphy, A.B. (2000) 'Firm characteristics of Swiss companies that utilize international accounting standards', *International Journal of Accounting* 34(1): 121–31.

Nobes, C., and Parker, R. (2008) *Comparative international accounting*, 10th edn, Harlow: Pearson/Prentice-Hall.

Nobes, C. (2006) 'The survival of international differences under IFRS: Towards a research agenda', *Accounting & Business Research* 36(3): 233–45.

Street, D.L., Gray, S.J. and Bryant, S.M. (1999) 'Acceptance and observance of international accounting standards: An empirical study of companies claiming to comply with IASs', *International Journal of Accounting* 34(1): 11–48.

Street, D. L. and Linthicum, C. L. (2007) 'IFRS in the US: It may come sooner than you think: A commentary', *Journal of International Accounting Research* 6(1): xi–xvii.

Tarca, A. (2004) 'International convergence of accounting practices: Choosing between IAS and US GAAP', *Journal of International Financial Management and Accounting* 15(1): 60–91.

Thomas, J. (2009) 'Convergence: Businesses and business schools prepare for IFRS', *Issues in Accounting Education* 24(3): 369–76.

Additional material on the website

Go to http://www.cengage.co.uk/stolowy3 for further information, journal entries and extra assignments for each chapter.

The following appendix to this chapter is available on the dedicated website:

Appendix 5.1: Cost of goods sold.

Notes

1. The AICPA (American Institute of Certified Public Accountants) in its APB Statement No. 4 'Basic Concepts and Accounting Principles Underlying Financial Statements of Business Enterprises' (New York, 1970) defines a GAAP as encompassing 'conventions, rules and procedures necessary to define accepted accounting practice at a particular time. It includes not only broad guidelines of general application but also detailed practices and procedures. Those conventions, rules and procedures provide a standard by which to measure financial presentations'. Every country, every culture or society creates its own GAAP, adapted to its tradition, principles, values and practices.

2. *Source:* www.iasplus.com.

3. *Source:* www.iasplus.com.

4. See http://ec.europa.eu/internal_market/accounting/ias/index_en.htm and more specifically http://ec.europa.eu/internal_market/accounting/ias/ias_39_carve-out_en.htm.

5. Members include, among others, the Australian Securities and Investments Commission, the members of the Canadian Securities Administrators (CSA), the French Autorité des Marchés Financiers (AMF), the Italian Commissione Nazionale per le Società e la Borsa (CONSOB), the UK's Financial Services Authority (FSA), and the United States Securities and Exchange Commission (SEC).

6. These developments are based on the website www.iasplus.com.

7. The concept of 'accelerated filers' is, in summary, based on the size of the company. It means that for large companies, the deadlines for filing are shorter (i.e., the filing procedure is 'accelerated').

8. 6 September 2009.

9. A debt is 'mature' when it should be paid. For example, United Airlines, in its statement of consolidated financial position (annual report 2008), refers to 'long-term debt maturing within one year', i.e., debts falling due within one year.

10. This presentation allows the calculation of the so-called 'value added' of the firm. This concept emanates essentially from a tax preoccupation (value added tax) and a national statistics viewpoint. It will be further explored in Chapters 10 and 16. Simply stated, this value added concept (not to be confused with that of 'economic value added', developed in Chapter 18 – used in the rank ordering of firm performance – essentially operating profit minus cost of capital employed) measures the amount of value created by the firm beyond 'what it acquired from outside the economic entity'. The definition of the business perimeter, although provided by tax authorities, rarely reflects a decision-makers' preoccupation.

C6

Chapter 6
Revenue Recognition Issues

Learning objectives

After studying this chapter, you will understand:

- What the concept of revenue recognition represents.
- When to recognize revenue.
- What accounting consequences result from divergences between tax regulation and financial reporting standards and guidelines.
- How deferred taxation is recorded and reported.
- How losses can be carried forward or carried back to reduce taxes (future tax reduction or tax refund).
- Which methods can be applied to revenue recognition for long-term contracts.
- How to distinguish between ordinary, extraordinary and exceptional items in the income statement.
- What the different types of accounting changes are and how to deal with them: changes in accounting policies, changes in estimates and correction of errors.
- What is meant by comprehensive income and why it was introduced.
- What accounting issues relate to recording and reporting government assistance.

Before exploring in detail the various accounts composing the balance sheet (Chapters 7–12), it is essential to gain a better understanding of the income statement, the most common source of evolution of shareholders' equity. As we saw in Chapter 2, the income statement is conceptually a subset of the balance sheet, summarizing those entries related to operations that affect shareholders' equity.

Besides the handling of costs and expenses which was covered in Chapters 3 and 4, several issues remain that need clarification:

1. Revenue recognition: when and how much revenue to recognize?

2. Issues arising from (a) the existence of different purposes in tax and shareholder reporting, and (b) the impact of the use of different rules used for financial reporting and for tax assessment purposes.

3. Separation of ordinary (recurrent) and extraordinary events (i.e., events not occurring in the normal course of business) so as to create a truly useful and comprehensive description of how the firm created wealth during a given period, so that investors and financial information users can anticipate what future performance might look like.

4. Handling and reporting of a variety of odd issues including accounting rule changes and government subsidies.

1 Revenue recognition

Revenue, **revenues** or **sales revenue**[1] are three totally interchangeable terms. In this book, we use the three terms as completely substitutable. Revenue is the inflow of funds that a *business* receives from customers in the course of its normal business activities, usually from the sale of *goods and services*. Revenue can also be received in the form of *interest*, *dividends*, or *royalties* paid to the firm by third parties.

According to the IASB (IAS 18, IASB 1993b: § 7), revenue is 'the gross inflow of economic benefits during the period arising in the course of the ordinary activities of an entity when those inflows result in increases in equity, other than increases relating to contributions from equity participants'.

To recognize revenue is to record the impact of a transaction on the revenue component of the income statement. One major accounting issue, derived from the matching and periodicity principles (see section 1 in Chapter 4) is to determine **when** to recognize revenue. IAS 18 (IASB 1993b: §§ 1–5) provides guidance for **revenue recognition** for the following three categories of transactions and events:

1. The sale of goods (goods purchased for resale, or goods manufactured by the selling firm, or land and other property held for resale).

2. The rendering of services (performance by the entity of a contractually-agreed task benefiting a customer over an agreed period of time).

3. The use by others of entity assets yielding:

    - interest (charges for the use of cash or cash equivalents or amounts due to the entity);

    - royalties (charges for the use of long-term assets of the entity, for example, patents, trademarks, copyrights and computer software);

    - dividends (distributions of profits to holders of equity investments in proportion to their holdings of a particular class of capital).

Criteria for recognition vary according to each type of **transaction**. Although some implementation differences may exist between countries, IAS 18 offers a set of generally accepted practices for revenue recognition. We will essentially adopt, in this chapter, the position presented in that standard.

1.1 Sale of goods

1.1.1 Principles

Revenue from the sale of goods should be recognized (IAS 18, § 14) when *all* of the following conditions 'have been satisfied:

(a) the entity has transferred to the buyer the significant risks and rewards of ownership of the goods;

(b) the entity retains neither continuing managerial involvement to the degree usually associated with ownership nor effective control over the goods sold;

(c) the amount of revenue can be measured reliably;

(d) it is probable that the economic benefits associated with the transaction will flow to the enterprise;

(e) the costs incurred or to be incurred in respect of the transaction can be measured reliably.'

These five criteria call for several comments. The assessment of when an entity has transferred the significant risks and rewards of ownership to the buyer requires an examination of the circumstances of the transaction. In most cases, this transfer coincides with the transfer of the legal title or of possession to the buyer. This is the case for most retail sales. However, the seller, especially in bundled or business-to-business transactions, may retain a significant risk of ownership in a number of ways, such as:

■ When the seller retains an obligation of service to the buyer such as in the sale of a bundled electronic product including a promise of future upgrades of the software or in the case of a sale conditional on a specific performance-level clause not covered by normal warranty provisions.

■ When the receipt of the revenue from a particular sale is contingent on the derivation of revenue by the buyer from its sale of the goods (for example, consignment sales).

■ When the goods are shipped subject to installation, and that installation is a significant part of the contract, which has not yet been completed by the selling enterprise or on its behalf.

■ When the buyer has the right to rescind the purchase for a reason specified in the sales contract and the entity is uncertain about the probability of return (for example, a sale on approval).

If an entity retains an 'insignificant' risk of ownership, the transaction can be considered to be a finalized sale, and revenue should be recognized. An example would be a retail sale for which a refund is offered if the customer is not satisfied. Revenue in such a case would be recognized at the time of the sale, provided the seller can reliably estimate the risk of future returns, and recognizes a liability for probable returns (a provision), calculated on the basis of previous experience and other relevant factors.

The term 'insignificant' is critical here as it is a fairly subjective concept. For example, the issue of the revenue from sale of bundled electronic products and software is complex in that the sale includes several products and implied services. PricewaterhouseCoopers's Dean Petracca in an interview with *CFO Magazine* (Leone, 2009) stated: 'The requirements are that when you sell more than one product or service at one time, you have to break down the total sale value into individual pieces. Establishing the individual values [...] is solely a function of how the company prices those products and services over time.'

Contracts typically include such multiple 'deliverables' as hardware, software, professional services, maintenance, and support — all of which are valued and accounted for differently by different firms.

The rules that govern revenue recognition are all practical applications of the matching principle. They are conceived to facilitate the co-temporal recognition of revenues and expenses that are related to the same transaction or other event.

1.1.2 Costs associated to the sale

Some expenses or costs, including, for example, software maintenance and upgrades, warranty work, or end-of-life-of-product recycling costs, are incurred after the shipment of the goods takes place and ownership changes hands. That is why co-temporality is an issue if we want to strictly respect the matching principle. These expenses or costs can generally be estimated with some statistical reliability and therefore appropriately provisioned so as to be matched with the corresponding revenue.

A provision is an estimation of the future probable cost created by an uncertain or risky situation (see Chapter 12). A provision allows the recognition of an expense at the time of the triggering event, therefore matching it to revenue. A provision is a cost or reduction in shareholders' equity. In order to keep the balance sheet balanced, the provision expense will lead to the creation of a liability for the very same amount. The provisioned liability will be used to 'compensate' or offset the actual expense when it is actually incurred (in the future). This way the expense, when incurred, will not affect profit, at least up to the provisioned amount. If it becomes established the actual expense will be less than what was provisioned or will not happen at all, the amount of the provision must be, at the time this 'knowledge' becomes available, reintegrated in the current profit (the provision is said to be 'reversed' or 'released').

Example

Assume a sale generates a gross margin (revenue minus cost of goods sold) of 150 CU. This sale carries a 100% chance that the seller will need to provide additional services at a cost of 40 CU two years from the date of the sale. The gross profit from the sale is recognized as 150 CU and a provision is constituted for 40 CU. In keeping with the no offsetting principle, the net effect of that sale in the income statement is 110 CU and, simultaneously, a liability is created for 40 CU, which acknowledges the anticipated recording of a future expense. When the actual cost of 40 CU is incurred, it might appear to have all the characteristics of an expense but this cannot be the case since that amount has already been deducted from revenue as an anticipated expense. Therefore, that cost will be compensated by the cancellation of the provision taken as a liability two years before. With this procedure the matching principle has been fully respected, and the shareholders' equity has only been affected at the time of the triggering event, not when the actual cost is incurred.

If, however, it were difficult or impossible to estimate these post-sale expenses, the revenue should not be recognized at all at the time of shipment (and postponed until the uncertainties about these future costs are sufficiently reduced). Any cash or consideration received for the sale of the goods or service should, in this case, be recognized as a debt towards the customer. If we increase cash and create a liability of the same amount, there is no impact on shareholders' equity.

1.2 Rendering of services

Services rendered contracts such as long-term construction or consulting contracts, legal cases or research contracts tend to span several accounting periods. This creates specific problems of measurement of both periodic revenue recognition and measurement of the degree of 'completion' of the contract. We will cover these in section 3 of this chapter.

IAS 18 (§ 20) states that, 'when the outcome of a transaction involving the rendering of services [such as in **long-term contracts**] can be estimated reliably, revenue associated with the transaction shall be recognized by reference to the stage [or percentage] of completion of the transaction at the end of the reporting period. The outcome of a transaction can be estimated reliably when all the following conditions are satisfied:

(a) the amount of revenue [that will be obtained upon completion] can be measured reliably [i.e., the terms of the sales contract are clear, including how both parties can agree the contract has been completed];

(b) it is probable that the economic benefits associated with the transaction will flow to the entity;

(c) the stage [or percentage] of completion of the transaction at the end of the reporting period can be measured reliably; and

(d) the costs incurred for the transaction and the costs to complete the transaction can be measured reliably.'

The recognition of revenue by reference to the degree of completion of a transaction is often referred to as the 'percentage of completion' method. Under this method, a portion of the final revenue is recognized in each of the accounting periods in which the services are rendered, in proportion to the increase in the degree of completion that took place during each period (i.e., the increase over the previous period of the percentage achieved of total fulfillment of the contract obligation).

The percentage of completion of a transaction may be determined by a variety of methods. Each entity uses the method that, in their view, best measures reliably the services performed and gives what they feel is the fairest representation of the actual financial situation of the firm. Some methods are more suited for certain type of transactions. Methods include:

(a) Actual measurement of work performed (a feasible option when only one activity is performed and the resources or work required to completion are known without ambiguity).

(b) Quantity of services performed to date as a percentage of total services to be performed (a feasible option when the completed, possibly complex service can be decomposed in small discrete and measurable sections or segments separated by clearly defined milestones).

(c) The proportion that costs incurred to date represent as a percentage of the re-estimated total costs of the transaction at completion, i.e., actual costs plus committed costs plus re-estimated costs remaining to be incurred until completion. This is the preferred option when the service rendered is complex and requires the cooperation of several different types of expertise.

Progress payments and advances received from customers often do not reflect the services performed. Even though agreed milestones of completion generally trigger invoicing for a predefined portion of the contractual revenue, it would be a rare case to find that the cumulated costs to date represent the same proportion of the total cost as the cumulated billing or invoicing (cumulated revenue to date) does. Given possible interpretations of the matching principle, three situations can occur at any point during the life of a long-term contract:

1. Cumulated actual costs exceed cumulated revenue: the seller finances the difference and incurs a cost of financing. It is equivalent to the seller giving a hidden discount on the selling price. Defining the relevant revenue figure becomes a matter of discussion and of availability of proper traceability systems: the relevant revenue should be equal to [sales price] multiplied by [increase in the degree of completion] minus [financing cost incurred during the period due to the contract negative cash balance in the seller's books]. However, all too often the inability (or unwillingness[2]) to match cash inflows and outflows relevant to a given contract leads to misreporting of the revenue (and, consequently, of the profit or loss) on a given contract. The lack of tracing financial costs attached to a contract leads to overestimating a given contract's revenue during that accounting period.

2. Cumulated revenue exceeds cumulated actual costs: the customer finances the difference. It is equivalent to a hidden premium on the agreed upon sales price paid by the buyer. The issue of defining the relevant revenue stream is the converse of that mentioned in point 1 above. Simply, this time, revenue is underestimated: the percentage of the selling price earned in the period should be increased by the financial revenue earned on the positive cash balance, during the period, on the contract's positive cash position.

3. The two streams are pretty well balanced. The agreed sales price includes neither discount nor premium. Revenue recognition of the contract is straightforward and will be the result of the application of any of the percentage of completion methods evoked earlier.

Clearly, the recognition of revenue leaves some room to choice. That is why long-term contracts are such an important subject in today's economy. The rule of prudence, in the uncertain environment in which most long-term contracts take place today, has led the IASB to recommend that 'when the outcome of the transaction involving the rendering of services cannot be estimated reliably, revenue shall be recognized only up to the extent of the expenses recognized that are recoverable' (IAS 18: § 26), i.e., no profit should be recognized before the end of the contract. The same prudence principle leads to the practice that, once it has been established without ambiguity that billable revenue will not allow a recovery of the incurred costs, the loss should be recognized as fully as the situation warrants.

1.3 Interest, royalties, and dividends

When (a) it is probable that the economic benefits associated with the transaction will flow to the entity, and (b) the amount of the revenue can be measured reliably, revenue arising from the use by others of entity assets yielding interest, royalties and dividends should be recognized on the following bases (see IAS 18: §§ 29–30):

■ **Interest**: Proportionately to the length of the period during which the asset was actually made available and on the basis of the agreed interest rate.

■ **Royalties**: On an accrual basis in accordance with the substance of the relevant agreement.

■ **Dividends**: When the shareholders' right to receive payment is established (decision of the shareholders' general meeting).

1.4 Revenue recognition and reporting

1.4.1 Principles

The revenue recognition policy of a firm may have a significant impact on its income and on the image it will communicate of its future economic potential (going concern principle) to the variety of users of accounting information and especially to the financial markets. The rules can be applied with more or less flexibility. Managers and accountants alike can use this flexibility to anticipate or delay recognition of profit or losses. Such a deliberate action on the timing of recognition of revenues (and of expenses) may create a lack of comparability between firms[3] and open the possibility for management to engage in 'income smoothing' (i.e., attempts to avoid reporting peaks and troughs in revenue and/or income which the manager or accountant thinks might give an alarming message to financial markets – see Chapter 17).

Although financial markets can generally 'see' through most income smoothing practices and are not fooled by them, these may have a significant impact in terms of taxation, and, therefore, on cash outflows. The consistency accounting principle (see Chapter 4) is theoretically designed to prevent such abuses of flexibility but the recognition criteria have such a large built-in subjectivity component that flexibility always legitimately exists.

This is probably a reason why shareholders require (in keeping with full disclosure) that the notes to the financial statements reveal the methods of recognition retained and highlight any deviation from these. IAS 18 (§ 35) defines the minimum that 'an entity shall disclose:

(a) the accounting policies adopted for the recognition of revenue, including the methods adopted to determine the stage [or percentage] of completion of transactions involving the rendering of services;

(b) the amount of each significant category of revenue recognized during the period, including revenue arising from: (i) the sale of goods, (ii) the rendering of services, (iii) interest, (iv) royalties, (v) dividends; and

(c) the amount of revenue arising from exchanges of goods or services [bartering] included in each significant category of revenue.'

1.4.2 Real-life examples of revenue-recognition-relevant notes to financial statements

Some illustrative notes excerpted from the financial statements of some large international corporations follow.

Real-life example Bull

(France – IFRS – Source: Annual report 2008 – International IT group)

The Bull Group's revenue consists of the sale and rental of hardware and software as well as services related to the processing of data under various contractual terms and conditions.

A sale is deemed to have taken place when the services of the Bull Group have been performed in accordance with contractual clauses, which usually refer to the delivery or availability of hardware. Usually, sales contracts contain a retention-of-title clause in all countries where such a clause is allowed by legislation.

Revenue from software licenses that is invoiced once is recognized when the software is made available and depending on the completion of the services contractually owed. Monthly licensing fees are recognized as revenue on the due date in each period.

Revenue from leases is recognized at each due date during the term of the contract. Depreciation and amortization is the main cost related to these contracts. Non-terminable medium-term rental contracts that usually span three to five years are recognized as revenue at the discounted value of the minimum rental payments receivable. The costs of products and services sold include the cost of the hardware rented under such contracts and provisions for the estimated costs and expenses to be incurred during the term of the contract.

Real-life example Ericsson

(Sweden – IFRS – Source: Annual report 2008 – Communications solutions)

Sales are recorded net of value added taxes, goods returned, trade discounts and rebates. Revenue is recognized with reference to all significant contractual terms when the product or service has been delivered, when the revenue amount is fixed or determinable and when collection is reasonably assured. Specific contractual performance may impact the timing and amounts of revenue recognized.

Real-life example China Unicom

(China – Hong Kong GAAP and IFRS – Source: Annual report 2008 – Cellular phone business)

Revenue comprises the fair value of the consideration received or receivable for the services and sales of goods or telecommunications products in the ordinary course of the Group's activities. Revenue is shown net of business tax, government surcharges, returns and discounts and after eliminating sales within the Group.

The Group recognizes revenue when the amount of revenue can be reliably measured, it is probable that future economic benefits will flow to the entity and specific criteria have been met for each of the Group's activities as described below. The amount of revenue is not considered to be reliably measurable until all contingencies relating to the sale have been resolved. The Group bases its estimates on historical results, taking into consideration of the type of customer, the type of transaction and the specifics of each arrangement.

(a) Sales of services and goods
- Usage fees are recognized when the service is rendered.
- Revenues from the provision of broadband and other Internet-related services and managed data services are recognized when the services are provided to customers.

- Revenue from telephone cards, which represents service fees received from customers for telephone services, is recognized when the related service is rendered upon actual usage of the telephone cards by customers.

- Lease income from leasing of lines and customer-end equipment are treated as operating leases with rental income recognized on a straight-line basis over the lease term.

- Value-added services revenue, which mainly represents revenue from the provision of services such as short message, cool ringtone, personalized ring, CDMA 1X wireless data services, caller number display and secretarial services to subscribers, is recognized when service is rendered.

- Standalone sales of telecommunications products, which mainly represent handsets and accessories, are recognized when title has been passed to the buyers.

- (…)

- Revenue from information communications technology services are recognized when goods are delivered to the customers (which generally coincides with the time when the customers have accepted the goods and the related risks and rewards of ownership have been transferred to the customers) or when services are rendered to the customers using the percentage of completion method when the outcome of the services provided can be estimated reliably. If the outcome of the services provided cannot be estimated reliably, the treatment should be as follows: (i) if it is probable that the costs incurred for the services provided is recoverable, services revenue should be recognized only to the extent of recoverable costs incurred, and costs should be recognized as current expenses in the period in which they are incurred; (ii) if it is probable that costs incurred will not be recoverable, costs should be recognized as current expenses immediately and services revenue should not be recognized.

(b) Interest income

Interest income from deposits in banks or other financial institutions is recognized on a time proportion basis, using the effective interest method.

(c) Dividend income

Dividend income is recognized when the right to receive payment is established.

Real-life example Apple, Inc.

(USA – US GAAP – Source: Form 10-K 2008 – Electronics, software and support services)
The Company recognizes revenue when persuasive evidence of an arrangement exists, delivery has occurred, the sales price is fixed or determinable, and collection is probable. (…)

For both Apple TV and iPhone, the Company has indicated that from time-to-time it may provide future unspecified features and additional software products free of charge to customers. Therefore, sales of Apple TV and iPhone handsets are recognized under subscription accounting in accordance with SOP No. 97-2. The Company recognizes the associated revenue and cost of goods sold on a straight-line basis over the currently estimated 24-month economic lives of these products, with any loss recognized at the time of sale. Costs incurred by the Company for engineering, sales, marketing and warranty are expensed as incurred.

Real-life example Nokia

(Finland – IFRS – Source: Annual report 2008 – Cell-phones and telecommunication systems)
Sales from the majority of the Group are recognized when the significant risks and rewards of ownership have transferred to the buyer, continuing managerial involvement usually associated with ownership and effective control have ceased, the amount of revenue can be measured reliably, it is probable that economic benefits associated with the transaction will flow to the Group and the costs incurred or to be incurred in respect of the transaction can be measured reliably. An immaterial part of the revenue from products sold through distribution channels is recognized when the reseller or distributor sells the products to the end users.

2 Accounting for differences in net income calculations originating from diverging financial reporting and tax regulations

In most countries, an income tax is levied on **taxable income**, which is generally defined as the difference between taxable revenues and deductible (or tax-deductible) expenses or costs. In principle, all sources of revenue are taxable and all ordinary and necessary expenses of doing business are deductible. But there are notable, large exceptions to this generalization.

In addition, the rules used for reporting to shareholders and for accounting for taxation do not have similar or coherent intents:

- Accounting rules and policies are designed to support a true and fair reporting of the financial situation of a firm (i.e., measuring and reporting fairly and usefully the wealth created in a period of time) to the shareholders and to other users.

- Tax policies regarding calculation of the income tax base (i.e., taxable income) are a practical compromise between stimulating the economy by encouraging certain behavior in a context of industrial policies, income redistribution, and the need for any state administration to obtain sufficient resources for its own policies. It is not within the scope of this book to explore exhaustively the tax regulations about costs deductibility and revenue taxability. Each country has its own rules, recorded, for example, in the Internal Revenue Code in the USA, the *Code général des impôts* in France, or different sections of tax law in the UK (Income and Corporation Taxes Act, Value Added Tax Act, etc.).[4]

This section deals with accounting for generic differences between reporting and taxation in unconsolidated financial statements. Accounting for income tax effects in consolidated financial statements will be covered in Chapter 13.

2.1 Pre-tax income and taxable income

Pre-tax income and taxable income do not derive from the same purposes and set of principles. Examples of differences in policies and practices include:

- **Depreciation** is generally computed on a straight-line basis for financial reporting purposes, while an accelerated method is often used for tax purposes (see more on this in Chapter 7). This tax-accepted acceleration of depreciation actually postpones the taxation of profits. A common argument supporting **accelerated depreciation** methods is that it provides larger deductions from taxable revenue in the early life of the asset. This creates a larger cash flow from operations available early for reinvestment[5] and hopefully growth, thus encouraging the acquisition of assets and boosting the econ-omy, which is generally in the interest of the government.

- **Warranty costs** are most often recognized for financial reporting purposes in the period in which the sale took place (matched with the sales revenue through the use of provisions for future warranty costs), while they are often deductible for tax purposes only when actually incurred. Here tax authorities do not want to leave open the door to possible easy abuses of provision expenses used to postpone paying taxes.

- **Expenses benefiting several years** can sometimes be immediately deductible for tax purposes but can be amortized (distributed) over several years for reporting purposes.

Differences between income tax rules and accounting rules lead to different figures for income. Since only one uniquely defined figure can serve as the actual tax basis (and thus affect the cash flow through the payment of income taxes), it is important to reconcile the two income figures for the same period so as to give a true and fair view of the financial position.

Revenue and expense recognition rules for tax purposes can differ from accounting rules in two ways:

■ whether or not an item is recognized (taxable or deductible);

■ the date on which an item is recognized (the current period, when the triggering event takes place, or one or several subsequent periods).

These differences in rules create two types of differences between tax-basis income and pre-tax accounting income:

■ permanent differences (linked to recognition or non-recognition);

■ temporary differences (linked to the timing of recognition).

Figure 6.1 illustrates how these differences arise.

Tables 6.1 and 6.2 illustrate the two methods for the calculation of taxable income: either a 'direct dedicated' approach, or one based on a 'reconciliation' starting from the accounting income.

2.1.1 'Direct dedicated' approach

This approach is used in some countries where tax and financial accounting rules are largely or totally similar (generally at the cost of a loss of relevance to the other users of financial information). It is also frequently used in unlisted small and medium enterprises. They do not wish to go through the reconciliation and keep only the set of required tax books, applying tax rules for all recognition issues. Since the users are generally limited to the banker(s), the owners, or a limited group of close-knit shareholders, they often have an intimate knowledge of the reality of the situation of the firm and do not rely greatly on financial statements for interim information. Thus, the loss of information created by the integration of tax- and reporting-accounting is not significant. However, larger businesses, and especially listed companies, must use the reporting format required by financial markets and thus may deviate from tax rules in their reporting.

2.1.2 'Reconciliation and detailed description of steps' approach

In this second approach, the steps describing the differences of rules and practices are detailed so that one can go, step-by-step, from the pre-tax income of the period to the taxable income. The interest of this method, when it is disclosed, is that it allows the reader

Figure 6.1 Differences between taxable and pre-tax income

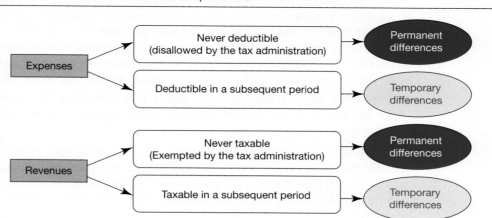

Table 6.1 Method 1 – Direct computation
Taxable revenues
– Deductible expenses
= Taxable income = reported income

of financial statements to better understand the choices made by the firm and to therefore better anticipate the future cash flows from operations.

2.2 Impact of permanent differences

<u>**Permanent differences**</u> are created by revenue and expense items that are recognized for accounting purposes, but not for tax purposes, or the converse, such as:

- interest revenue on state and municipal bonds are, in some countries, not taxable;
- life insurance premiums (taken on the head of executives), paid by a firm that is the designated beneficiary of the life insurance in case of death, are not always tax deductible;
- penalties and fines for violation of laws or regulations are rarely tax deductible;
- depreciation on certain assets may not be tax deductible (for instance, on cars of a value in excess of certain tax-specified purchase price);
- interest expense on shareholders' current accounts in excess of certain tax-specified limitation can be non-tax deductible in some countries;
- provisions for doubtful accounts receivable are not always tax deductible;
- non-deductibility of charitable contributions in excess of a tax-specified ceiling.

We will see how these permanent differences are affecting accounts through the example of non-tax deductible parking violation fines for a firm whose main activity is the on-site maintenance of photocopying equipment in a small medieval town without much public parking. From an accounting point of view, these fines are legitimate expenses because repair persons have no choice but to often park illegally while visiting their customers. The tax authorities cannot condone the violation of the law and thus legitimately

Table 6.2 Method 2 – Reconciliation in year X1
Pre-tax income for the year X1 (i.e., using accounting rules for reporting to shareholders)
Positive tax adjustments
+ Expenses in X1 never deductible
+ Expenses in X1 deductible in X2 or later
+ Revenues in X0 not taxable in X0 but taxable in X1
Negative tax adjustments
– Revenues in X1 never taxable
– Revenues in X1 taxable in X2 or later
– Expenses in X0 not deductible in X0 but deductible in X1
= **Taxable income in X1**

deny the deductibility of these parking violation fines. There is therefore a divergence between the two sets of rules. Let us assume the pre-tax income before deducting the non-deductible fines is 110 CU. The amount of parking fines is 20 CU and represents the only expense that is treated differently between accounting for reporting and accounting for tax purposes. The tax rate is 40%.

Table 6.3 illustrates the detailed steps followed to calculate the income tax applicable to both the tax basis and the reporting basis income.

Any other permanent difference would be handled in a similar way. Thus, we can state that 'permanent differences' do not impair reporting (as long as the non-deductible penalty is fully reported, as was the case here in the financial statements side of Table 6.3):

- permanent differences do not reverse themselves over time;
- they have no future tax consequences.

2.3 Impact of temporary differences

As we mentioned earlier in the case of warranty costs, the impact of the divergence between tax and accounting rules is on the timing of the recognition, not on the amount recognized as was the case for permanent differences.

Temporary differences arise when some expenses are recognized immediately for reporting to shareholders and at a later date for tax purposes, or the reverse. If the tax rules lead to a later recognition of the tax burden than under financial accounting rules, a tax liability is created which is called deferred tax liability, often shortened to 'deferred taxes'. It is the most common case. If, on the contrary, the tax rules lead to recognizing taxes earlier than what would have been found according to financial accounting rules, a prepaid tax asset is created which is called 'deferred tax asset'. Temporary differences also arise with regard to revenues (see below).

Figure 6.2 summarizes the process of creation of these deferred tax assets and liabilities (numbers refer to the case examples that follow).

The basic principle of (temporary) deferred taxation is that the difference is expected to be reversed in future periods. These differences are said to originate in one period and be 'capable of reversal' in one or more subsequent periods.

Temporary differences arise not only from different rules of recognition of revenues and expenses in the income statement, but also from differences in tax and accounting bases of valuation of either assets or liabilities.

IAS 12 (IASB 2000, § 5) states that 'temporary differences are differences between the carrying amount of an asset or liability in the statement of financial position and its tax base'. They 'may be either:

Table 6.3 Permanent differences

Financial statements			Income tax return	
Pre-tax income before non deductible penalty	110			
– Non deductible penalty	–20			
= Pre-tax income	90	→	Pre-tax income	90
			+ Permanent difference (expense added back)	20
			= Taxable income	110
– Income tax expense	44	←	Income tax expense (taxable income × rate: 110 × 40%)	44
= Net income (after tax) (pre-tax income – income tax = 90 – 44)	46			

Figure 6.2 Temporary differences and income

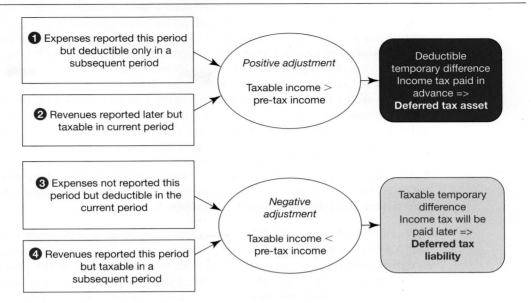

(a) *Taxable temporary differences*, which are temporary differences that will result in taxable amounts in determining taxable profit (tax loss) of future periods when the carrying amount of the asset or liability is recovered or settled; or

(b) *Deductible temporary differences*, which are temporary differences that will result in amounts that are deductible in determining taxable profit (tax loss) of future periods when the carrying amount of the asset or liability is recovered or settled.'

The tax base of an asset or liability is the value attributed to that asset or liability for tax purposes. For instance, if a provision for doubtful accounts receivables (see Chapter 10) is considered by tax authorities to have been overstated, the tax administration might disallow part of it. As a consequence, the tax value of the asset (accounts receivable net of accumulated provision) is greater than the carrying amount (net book value). This situation leads to the recording of a deferred tax asset, as the 'excess' provision expense will be reversed when the actual bad debt will be recognized (assuming the provision for doubtful receivables was based on realistic estimates, and that the tax authorities had simply placed some arbitrary ceiling on this type of provision), but the excess actual cost over the tax-allowed provision will not affect the taxable income at the time of reversal.

> For pedagogical purposes, we prefer to focus our analysis of deferred taxation by reference to only revenues and expenses, as we believe that the approach based on assets and liabilities is less common and might lead to confusion, especially for beginners.

Temporary differences are essentially 'timing differences'. In practice many accountants use the terms 'temporary' and 'timing' interchangeably when discussing differences between tax accounting and accounting for reporting to shareholders.

Let us now illustrate some of the sources of temporary differences (numbered cases refer to Figure 6.2).

Case ❶ – Expenses that are tax deductible in a later period than they are recorded under financial accounting rules   Table 6.4 provides examples of situations of this type that abound in the life of any business.

A quantified warranty provision example will provide an illustration. Lorentz Co. sells products with a short life cycle. Every year a new product replaces the previous year's product. In year X1, product A is still pretty experimental and Lorentz Co. feels it is appropriate to create a provision of 10 CU for future warranty costs on product A. Product B is introduced in year X2, completely replacing product A, which is no longer sold. B is a second-generation product and is considered to be extremely robust and, thus, in year X2, Lorentz Co. sees no need to create a provision for future warranty costs. In year X2 however, all the fears about the warranty service to be provided on product A materialize and the actual warranty service cost is 10 CU. The tax rate in this illustration is assumed to be 40%. We assume the company has a pre-tax income before warranty expense and provision of 100 CU each year. The provision is tax deductible only in the year of the actual expense (year X2 in our example).

Two alternative accounting solutions exist: either the firm does report taxes as they are owed (no use of the deferred tax mechanism) as shown in Table 6.5, or they use the deferred tax mechanism as shown in Table 6.6.

First solution: the local GAAP do not allow (or require) the deferred tax mechanism   In year X2 the actual expense of 10 CU is compensated by the pre-existing provision. The recognition of the expense goes along with the cancellation of the provision, thus creating no impact on the income statement of year X2 as can be seen in Table 6.5.

Since no deferred taxes mechanism is used, the left panel of Table 6.5 shows what is recorded according to the local GAAP. The tax accrued in each year is the same in the fiscal calculation (right panel), and in the GAAP statements.

Second solution: the local GAAP accept or require the use of deferred tax accounting   Table 6.6 shows, in the left panel, that the tax recorded in the financial accounting books is calculated on the basis of the GAAP-based pre-tax income. It is, in a way, a 'theoretical' amount since the taxes that will really be owed to the tax authority are calculated as a function of the taxable income in the right panel of the table. There is a timing difference

Table 6.4 Examples of expenses that are tax deductible in a period later than they are recorded under financial accounting rules

Examples	Accounting timing	Tax timing
Tax on net sales revenue	At time of original sale (possibly subject to the establishment of a provision for returns)	After returns and claims are known
Product warranty-costs provision	At time of sale	When costs are actually incurred
Bad debt expense (or doubtful accounts) provision	When claim is created	When risk materializes
Interest or royalties payable	Accrued with passage of time	When actually paid
Provisions for repairs and maintenance	When established	When actual costs incurred
Retirement benefit costs	As employee accrues benefits	When retirement contribution to pension fund (or benefit) is paid out
Research costs (incorporation or other start up costs)	Year incurred	May be amortized over a few years (actual duration is specified by tax code)

Table 6.5 Effect of a provision when local GAAP do not allow deferred tax accounts

GAAP Financial statements	Year X1	Year X2	Income tax return	Year X1	Year X2
Pre-tax income before actual warranty expense	100	100			
Actual warranty expense	0	−10			
Pre-tax income before accounting for product warranty provision	100	90	Pre-tax income	90	100
Product warranty provision expense	−10	0	Provision added back	+10	
Reversal of provision	0	+10	Reversal of provision		−10
Pre-tax income	90	100	Taxable income	100	90
Income tax expense	−40	−36	Income tax expense	40	36
Net reported income after tax	50	64			

between the recorded tax expense, calculated on the basis of pre-tax income (36 for year X1), and the tax due (40 for year X1). The actual tax liability for year X1 is greater than the tax recorded in the books.

Note that, if cumulated over the two years of the illustration, both the after tax income and the taxes due are the same (in nominal CU) regardless of whether one takes the GAAP or the tax basis. The difference between the two approaches is only one of timing.

The accounting tax expense is, like any expense, a reduction of the shareholders' equity. Thus, in order to keep the financial accounting balance sheet balanced (the cash outflow for taxes in year X1 was indeed 40 CU, while the 'books' only show it theoretically should have been 36 CU), the firm must recognize the creation of a 'deferred tax asset', which is equivalent to saying it has 'prepaid taxes' in the amount of 4 CU (i.e., 40 − 36 = 4) (see Figure 6.3).

Table 6.6 Accounting for deferred income taxes

Tax expense based on financial reporting	Year X1	Year X2	Reminder: Tax expense based on tax return	Year X1	Year X2
Pre-tax income (from Table 6.5)	90	100			
(Theoretical) income tax expense (40 % of pre-tax income)	36	40	(Actual) income tax expense (40% of taxable income from Table 6.5)	40	36
Net income	54	60			
	Year X1	Year X2			
Deferred tax	+4	−4			

Figure 6.3 Recording a deferred tax asset in the financial accounting (GAAP-based) books

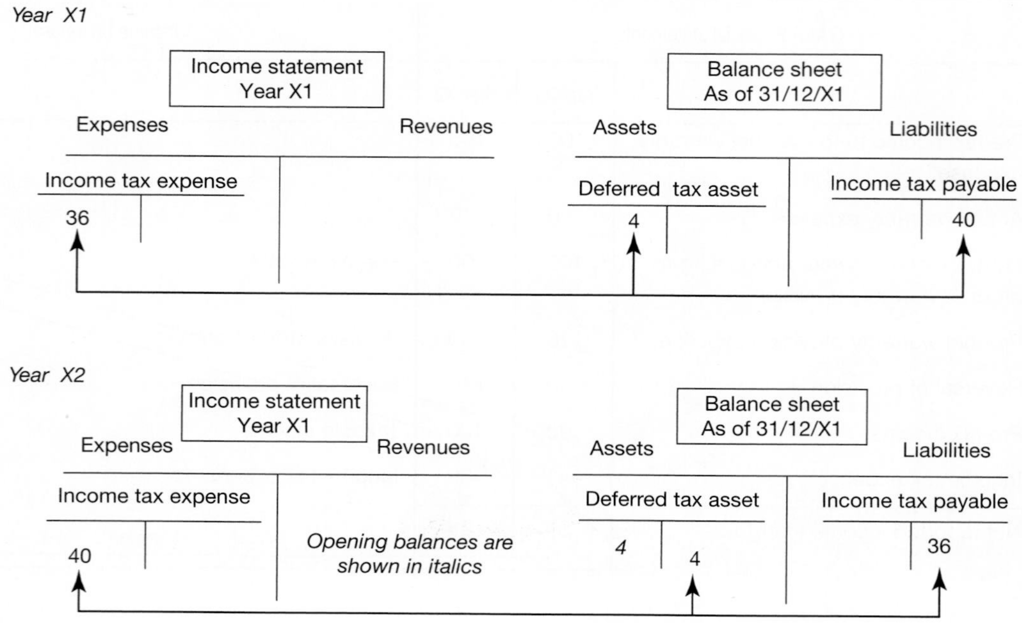

Year X1

Income statement Year X1		Balance sheet As of 31/12/X1	
Expenses	Revenues	Assets	Liabilities

Income tax expense		Deferred tax asset	Income tax payable
36		4	40

Year X2

Income statement Year X1		Balance sheet As of 31/12/X1	
Expenses	Revenues	Assets	Liabilities

Income tax expense		Deferred tax asset	Income tax payable
40	*Opening balances are shown in italics*	4 4	36

The deferred tax asset records the temporary differences due to using differing rules and regulations between accounting for taxes and accounting for reporting. This example shows that the deferred tax assets do indeed reverse in the second period. The deferred taxation mechanism's impact is only to modify the timing of the recognition of taxes on income.

Not all countries allow the deferred taxation mechanism. Some countries require that the tax calculated according to tax rules be the one reported in financial accounting statements. In this case, the reported tax liability would be 40 for year 1 and 36 for year 2 in our example.

Case ❷ – Revenues or gains that are taxable in an earlier period than they are recognizable under financial accounting rules   Several such situations may occur in the normal course of business:

- A latent gain on marketable securities (see Chapter 10) is, in fact, taxable in some countries in the period incurred, but is reported under GAAP only at the time of the sale of these marketable securities. (Remember, the logic of taxation is sometimes just an expedient to get the cash into the coffers of the government sooner).

- Cash received in advance for rent is sometimes taxable in the year received while it generally must be accrued under the local GAAP. Only that part of the cash payment relevant to the period is recognized as revenue under financial reporting rules and the remainder is recognized as 'prepaid rent received', i.e., a liability.

These temporary differences will generate a deferred tax asset because, as was the situation in the previous example, there is a timing difference between the GAAP and the tax calculation.

Case ❸ – Expenses (or losses) that are deductible in earlier periods for tax purposes than they are recorded under financial accounting rules   This is, for example, the case for:

- Expenses spread over several years according to the local GAAP (in application of the matching principle) but that are tax deductible for the full amount in the year initially incurred. This is, for example, the case for product development costs that can be, in some countries, capitalized for reporting purposes and, thus, will be amortized in the income statement over several periods covering the life expectancy of the product. Meanwhile, the full amount of such an expense may be tax deductible in the period in which the development costs were incurred.

■ Greater depreciation for tax purposes than for financial reporting purposes in the early periods of an asset's life, as is the case when accelerated depreciation is used for tax reporting while straight-line is used for reporting to shareholders or when the depreciation period used for tax purposes is shorter than the useful economic life of the asset.

Such situations create a tax liability as is shown in the following very simple example of Gade Company. The firm's business requires the acquisition of an asset worth 20 CU. The pre-tax income before any depreciation expense is 180 CU in both years X1 and X2. Let us further assume that, for tax purposes, the asset can be fully depreciated in the year of acquisition (i.e., the tax deductible depreciation expense will be fully incurred in year X1) while, under local GAAP, the asset depreciation is recognized for reporting purposes over two years.

The data can be summarized as follows:

Income before depreciation and taxes	180
Asset purchased	20
Depreciation for tax purposes (asset is depreciated in one year)	20
Depreciation for reporting purposes (asset is depreciated over two years)	10
Income tax rate	40%

The impact of the different accounting and tax rules regarding depreciation expense is described in Tables 6.7 and 6.8. Two alternative treatments exist:

(a) The financial accounting report to shareholders shows the actual tax expense (with an income before tax figure calculated according to tax rules), or

(b) the financial statements report to shareholders the tax that would have been owed if tax rules regarding income determination had been identical to GAAP rules (i.e., a theoretical amount different from the actual income tax paid) and, thus, requires a deferred tax liability account to reconcile the two ways of calculating the net income after tax.

First alternative: GAAP indicate that financial statements show (or are allowed to show) the real tax owed (calculated according to tax rules) as the tax expense　The left-hand panel of Table 6.7 shows the reported statement while the right-hand panel of Table 6.7 shows the calculation mechanism for the taxes on income that will actually be paid to the local fiscal administration.

Second alternative: local GAAP allows or states that reported tax expense should be calculated according to GAAP rules, and not according to tax rules (thus creating a deferred taxation issue)　Table 6.8 shows the calculations required for the establishment of the financial statements.

There will exist a timing difference between the two flows: in year X1, for example, the tax expense actually owed to the fiscal administration is only 64 CU, while under GAAP it will appear as 68 CU. In the first year, Gade Company actually pays 4 CU less in taxes than it reports to shareholders. The situation is the reverse in year X2. Over the two years taken together, the taxes owed are, of course, the same (136) in nominal CU. Therefore it is essential for the financial statements to inform the shareholders that a debt to the tax

Table 6.7 Case of an expense which is deductible, under tax rules, earlier than under GAAP

Financial statements as reported			Income tax return		
	Year X1	Year X2		Year X1	Year X2
Pre-tax income before accounting for depreciation expense	180	180	Pre-tax income	►170	►170
Depreciation expense (GAAP based)	–10	–10	Reported depreciation expense added back	+10	+10
Pre-tax income	170	170	Deductible expense (full depreciation in year X1)	–20	
			Taxable income (under tax rules)	160	180
Income tax expense	–64	–72	Income tax expense	64	72
Net income reported	106	98			

authorities has been created by the use of GAAP rules to calculate the reported income tax owed in year X1. The accountant does so by recognizing a deferred tax liability of 4 CU at the end of year X1 (see Figure 6.4).

In this illustration, the deferred tax liability is indeed the result of a temporary difference since it clearly was reversed in the second year. Once again this illustrates the fact that the deferred tax mechanism only impacts the timing of recognition of the tax expense. The deferred tax liability may be classified, as a function of the expected timing of the reversal, as either long-term or current liability (when the balance sheet distinguishes the time horizon of liabilities – see Chapter 5).

Case ❹ – Revenues (or gains) that are taxable in later periods than they are recognized under GAAP
This is the case for example in the following situations:

■ In some countries, the revenue from credit sales (that give rise to an account receivable) may be fully recognized under GAAP when the sale takes place, but only be taxable for tax purposes on a cash basis, i.e., only when the customer settles his/her debt.

■ Interest revenue is generally received in arrears and is included in GAAP accounting profit on a time-apportioned accrual basis (in application of the matching principle) but is included in taxable profit only on a cash basis.

Table 6.8 Accounting for deferred income taxes

Tax expense as reported in the Financial statements			Reminder: Tax expense based on tax return		
	Year X1	Year X2		Year X1	Year X2
Pre-tax income based on local GAAP (see Table 6.7)	170	170			
Income tax expense (40% of pre-tax reported income)	68	68	Income tax expense (40% of taxable income) (Table 6.7)	64	72
Net income reported	102	102			
	Year X1	Year X2			
Deferred tax	–4	+4			

Figure 6.4 Recording a deferred tax liability

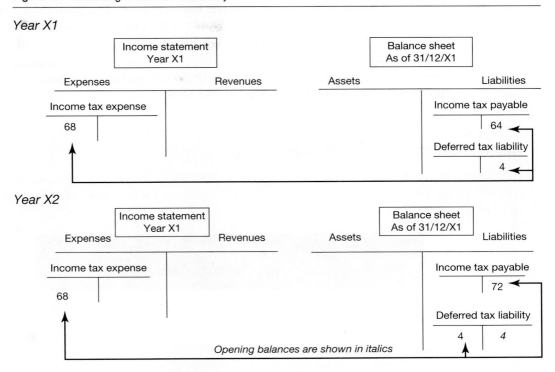

These differences are only temporary as their effect will reverse over time. They generate a deferred tax liability.

2.4 Accounting for and reporting income taxes

The choice of reporting method for income taxes should answer the fundamental question: Should the expected tax consequences of the existing temporary differences be recognized in financial statements? In other words, should deferred taxation be reported?

Two basic alternatives can be identified:

1. **Taxes payable accounting** (or **flow-through method** or **integrated model**): This approach consists in ignoring temporary differences, recognizing income tax expense (in the financial statements for shareholders) as identical to the actual income tax payable. This view is defended by experts and countries who hold the position that taxation is, in fact, a sharing mechanism in which the tax is the share of income that should go to the state, government or fiscal administration (in return for granting the business the right to exist and providing the conditions for its existence, such as the enforcement of the rule of law and open markets for resources and output) rather than a cost of doing business that needs to be recorded on an accrual basis in the income statement. This view is in opposition to the matching principle since, in the reported net income to shareholders, the link between the tax recognized and the triggering event is weak or non-existent.

2. **Deferred taxation accounting** (or **full provision method** or **deferred tax model**): This approach consists in recognizing the tax consequences of the temporary differences by including their tax effect as income tax expense on

the income statement and as an asset or a liability (called a deferred tax asset or a deferred tax liability) in the balance sheet. This method actually reports an economic tax expense based on the (financial accounting) pre-tax income. This method is in full compliance with the matching principle.

While reporting deferred taxation in the consolidated financial statements is an almost universal practice, many countries' GAAP do not include or require the use of deferred taxes in the unconsolidated financial statements.

Real-life example Procter & Gamble

The Procter & Gamble Company engages in the manufacture and sale of consumer goods worldwide. The company operates in three global business units: beauty, health and well-being and household care. Its annual report 2008 reports the following figures relating to income taxes:

Procter and Gamble Consolidated statement of earnings (in US$ millions) for the years ended 30 June 2006–2008 (source: Annual report 2008)			
	2008	2007	2006
Income taxes	4,003	4,370	3,729

In note 10 to the financial statements, the following information appears:

	2008	2007	2006
Current tax expense			
US federal	1,016	2,667	1,961
International	1,546	1,325	1,702
US state and local	227	125	178
	2,789	4,117	3,841
Deferred tax expense			
US federal	1,267	231	226
International	(53)	22	(338)
	1,214	253	(112)
Income taxes	4,003	4,370	3,729

2.5 Recognition of a net deferred tax asset

The recognition of a net deferred tax asset (excess of deferred tax assets over deferred tax liabilities) raises an issue of both value and reality and is developed in Appendix 6.1.

2.6 Accounting for net operating losses

Some tax regulations allow the carry-back and/or **carry-forward** of net operating losses. It means that the losses of one period can be carried-back, i.e., used to offset profits made in previous periods (thus calling for a tax refund), or carried-forward to be offset against future profits, so as to avoid paying taxes in the future. The carry-back/carry-forward issue can affect greatly the cash flow of any business and is a major way of supporting start-up companies (the accumulated tax losses can be offset against future profits thus maintaining cash inside the firm when it needs it the most), and a significant element of financing in mergers and acquisitions (a profitable firm buys a business with large accumulated losses to shield its current and possibly future profits against taxation, thus reducing the net cash cost of the acquisition).

Table 6.9 indicates whether such practice is allowed in a given country (the list is not exhaustive and does not identify special cases).

Appendix 6.2 illustrates the mechanism of carry-back and carry-forward. A loss carry-back allows the business to carry the net operating loss back a certain number of years (generally between 1 and 3 years – see Table 6.9) and receive refunds for income taxes already paid in those years.

A **loss carry-back** is not a complex accounting issue as the claim on the tax authority is definite and real. Thus, the following entry is perfectly legitimate: increase in assets (income tax refund receivable or cash received for the refund) and increase in revenues (benefit due to loss carry-back) [or, in some countries, decrease in expenses (income tax expense)].

For example, in September 2004 Lucent Technologies, the US telecom-equipment maker (later acquired by Alcatel to form Alcatel-Lucent) declared the US Internal Revenue Service had tentatively agreed, subject to an audit of its 2001 tax return and a review by the congressional Joint Committee on Taxation, to a net operating loss carry-back yielding the record-breaking tax refund (at the time) of $816 million. (Lucent Technologies claimed the refund by carrying its $16.2 billion net operating loss in 2001 back to 1996[7]).

Table 6.9 Net operating losses[6]

Country	Loss carry-forward	Loss carry-back
Australia	Unlimited	No
Austria	Unlimited	No
Belgium	Unlimited	No
Canada	20 years	3 years
Denmark	Unlimited	No
Finland	10 years	No
France	Unlimited	3 years
Germany	Unlimited	1 year
Greece	5 years	No
Ireland	Unlimited	3 years
Italy	5 years	No
Japan	7 years	1 year (suspended)
Luxembourg	Unlimited	No
Netherlands	9 years	1 year
Norway	Unlimited	2 years (if ceased activity)
Portugal	6 years	No
Spain	15 years	No
Sweden	Unlimited	No
Switzerland	7 years	No
United Kingdom	Unlimited	3 years
United States	20 years	2 years

A **loss carry-forward** allows the enterprise to offset future taxable income against the accumulated losses for up to a certain number of years (20 in the USA) or during an unlimited period (Australia or France, for example). The tax effect of a loss carry-forward represents future tax savings. To the contrary of a carry-back, the carry-forward encompasses a certain degree of uncertainty because the claim against future taxes can only be used if taxes payable result from future profits. In this context, the key accounting issue is whether the requirements for recognition of a deferred asset for operating loss carry-forwards should be different from those for recognition of a deferred tax asset for deductible temporary differences.

According to IAS 12 (IASB 2000: § 35), 'the criteria for recognizing deferred tax assets arising from the carry-forward of unused tax losses and tax credits are the same as the criteria for recognizing deferred tax assets arising from deductible temporary differences. However, the existence of unused tax losses is strong evidence that future taxable profits may not be available. Therefore, when an entity has a history of recent losses, the entity recognizes a deferred tax asset arising from unused tax losses or tax credits only to the extent that the entity has sufficient taxable temporary differences or there is convincing other evidence that sufficient taxable profit will be available against which the unused tax losses or unused tax credits can be utilized by the entity.'

The US answer is that there should not be different requirements. Different solutions have, however, been adopted in other countries. When local GAAP and regulation authorize the recognition of a deferred tax asset in the case of loss carry-forward, an entry similar to the one mentioned above for carry-back is recorded, with one difference: 'income tax refund receivable' is replaced by 'deferred tax asset'.

2.7 Changes in tax rates

Appendix 6.3 develops the impact of changes in tax rates on deferred taxation.

3 Long-term contracts

Earlier sections of this chapter dealt with the general principles of revenue recognition. We will now examine the specific revenue recognition issues raised by some business practices. As shown earlier in this chapter, long-term contracts represent a very common situation in which the revenue and cost recognition principles find all their usefulness.

Long-term contracts are referred to by IASB as 'construction contracts' (IAS 11, IASB 1993a). We will however keep using the expression 'long-term contracts' since contracts that span several accounting periods include many other categories of contracts than construction contracts. For example, research contracts, contracts for the delivery of a series of locomotives or aircraft, facilities management contracts, computer service contracts, law suits, consulting contracts, etc., are all long-term contracts which span several accounting periods.

This section is largely inspired by IAS 11, which states the problems arising with the accounting for long-term contracts in a very clear way. The primary issue with long-term contracts is the allocation of contract revenues and contract costs to the accounting periods in which work is performed. The general rules of revenue recognition introduced in section 1 above apply.

IAS 11 (§ 3) distinguishes two types of long-term contracts based on the revenue determination formula:

■ A *fixed price contract* is one 'in which the contractor agrees to a fixed contract price, or a fixed rate per unit of output, which in some cases is subject to cost escalation clauses' to reflect inflation on the cost of resources consumed.

■ A *cost plus contract* is one 'in which the contractor is reimbursed for allowable or otherwise defined costs, plus a ['margin' represented by a] percentage of these costs, or a fixed fee'.

'When the outcome of a construction [long-term] contract can be estimated reliably, contract revenue and contract costs associated with [this] contract shall be recognized as revenue and expenses respectively by reference to the stage of completion of the contract activity at the end of reporting date' (IAS 11: § 22). The IASB, and a majority of countries prefer the 'percentage of completion method' over any other. It consists in recording costs and revenues associated with the contract in increments linked (generally proportionally) to the degree of completion of the contract during the period.

The IASB endorses this method if several stated conditions are met. In the case, for example, of a fixed price contract (see IAS 11 [Construction contracts]: § 23 – totally coherent, somewhat redundant, with IAS 18 [Revenue recognition]: § 20 we mentioned earlier in section 1), 'the outcome of a construction contract can be estimated reliably when all the following conditions are satisfied:

(a) total contract revenue can be measured reliably;

(b) it is probable that the economic benefits associated with the contract will flow to the entity;

(c) both the contract costs to complete the contract and the stage of contract completion at the end of the reporting period can be measured reliably; and

(d) the contract costs attributable to the contract can be clearly identified and measured reliably so that actual contract costs incurred can be compared with prior estimates'.

If any one of these conditions cannot be met, IAS 11 recommends a prudent approach for the recognition of revenue, which is a variation on the percentage of completion method (IAS 11: § 32):

(a) 'revenue shall be recognized only to the extent of contract costs incurred that it is probable will be recoverable; and

(b) contract costs shall be recognized as an expense in the period in which they are incurred.'

An alternative method exists that is not endorsed under IAS 11 but which is still used by many entities in countries that accept its use: the 'completed contract method'. Its mechanism consists in waiting until the contract is fully completed to recognize all its revenues and costs. Under this method the costs pertaining to the contract are capitalized as an asset and revenues received from interim billing are recorded as a liability and thus they do not impact the income statement of the firm until completion (although they impact changes in shareholders' equity, if the two amounts capitalized are different). This method is extremely simple to apply. It is built on the premise that the final outcome of a long-term contract cannot be known until the contract is fully completed, because too many uncertainties taint any attempt at estimating the end result. While the 'percentage of completion method' is a direct application of the matching principle, the 'completed contract method' is a direct application of the prudence principle. The completed contract method was used extensively in the past, when it was allowed, and is still used where it is still acceptable, as a powerful income-smoothing instrument. Such blatant abuse of the intent of the prudence principle is likely to be reason enough for most countries to have banned its use and for the IASB to have not endorsed it.

Regardless of the method used for the recognition of income pertaining to a long-term contract, both require immediate recognition of potential losses on a contract as soon as they can be legitimately established. Appendix 6.4 provides a detailed illustration of both methods of recording long-term contracts.

Real life example Ericsson

(Sweden – IFRS - Source: Annual report 2008 - Communications solutions)

Construction-type contracts. In general, a construction-type contract is a contract where the company supplies to a customer, a complete network, which to a large extent is based upon new technology or includes major components which are specifically designed for the customer. Revenues from construction-type contracts are recognized according to stage of completion, generally using the milestone output method.

Inventories (in millions of Swedish Krona)	2008	2007
(…)		
Contract work in process	12,807	10,338
Less advances from customers	–	–677
(…)		

For construction-type contracts in progress (in millions of Swedish Krona)	2008	2007
Aggregate amounts of costs incurred	2,156	9,599
Aggregate amount of recognized profits (less recognized losses)	971	2
Gross amount due from customers*	204	733
Gross amount due to customers**	406	2

Notes:
* For all contracts in progress for which costs incurred plus recognized profits (less recognized losses) exceeds progress billings.
** For all contracts in progress for which progress billings exceed costs incurred plus recognized profits (less recognized losses). The aggregate amounts of costs incurred relate to all construction-type contracts that were not finalized as per 31 December 2008, and include all costs incurred since the start of these projects, including any costs incurred prior to 1 January 2008. Net sales for construction-type contracts for 2008 amount to SEK 2,488 (7,121) million, see note c4, 'Net sales'.

Real life example Atos Origin

(France – IFRS – Source: Annual report 2008 – IT business processes)

Where the outcome of fixed price contracts such as consulting and systems integration contracts can be estimated reliably, revenue is recognized using the percentage-of-completion (POC) method. Under the POC method, revenue is recognized based on the costs incurred to date as a percentage of the total estimated costs to fulfil the contract. Revenue relating to these contracts is recorded in the consolidated balance sheet under 'trade accounts and notes receivable' for services rendered in excess of billing, while billing exceeding services rendered is recorded as deferred income under 'other current liabilities'. Where the output of a fixed price contract cannot be estimated reliably, contract revenue is recognized to the extent of contracts costs incurred that are likely to be recoverable.

Revenue for long-term fixed price managed operations services is recognized when services are rendered.

4 Installment sales

Installment sales are developed in Appendix 6.5.

5 Extraordinary and exceptional items

Most country-specific GAAP include explicitly or implicitly the principle that it is essential for an income statement to be useful for decision-makers. Its measurement of past performance must be unambiguous so it can be used to prepare extrapolations and expectations regarding future performance. Consequently, an income statement must present, separately and distinctly, what pertained to 'normal' and recurrent business activities, and what pertained to actions, decisions, and events that were occasional and unusual.

There are, however, some divergent views about what are 'normal' (in the course of carrying out the business activity) and what are 'abnormal' or 'unusual' activities (reflected in the choice of terms used to refer to this dichotomy).

The IASC, actually followed in its choice by many countries, did originally distinguish 'extraordinary' items from 'ordinary' items. The IASB, however deviated from its predecessor's initial position and prescribed that 'an entity shall not present any items of income and expense as extraordinary items, in the statement of **comprehensive income** or the separate income statement (if presented), or in the notes' (IAS 1, IASB 2007: § 87).

The difficulty of defining the words 'ordinary' and 'extraordinary' in generic terms for any and all businesses is undoubtedly daunting. One can nonetheless wonder whether the best remedy to this debatable categorization of events is the pure and simple suppression of any information about the subject. To make things worse and add to the confusion, the IASB, since its revision of IAS 1 in 2003, failed to define what is to be understood as 'ordinary or extraordinary' activities. At best, one can still refer to a definition in IAS 8 superseded in 2002: [extraordinary] 'income or expenses [are those] that arise from events or transactions that are clearly distinct from the ordinary activities of the enterprise and therefore are not expected to recur frequently or regularly'. One can also refer for guidance to the IASC's original Conceptual Framework (1989: § 72) which has not been invalidated, and in which one can read that 'when distinguishing between [ordinary and extraordinary] items (...) consideration needs to be given to the nature of the entity and its operations. Items that arise from the ordinary activities of one entity may be unusual in respect of another'. For example, selling productive assets such as machinery may unambiguously be recognized as an 'ordinary' activity for a business whose strategy implies they always have in their production process the machinery with the latest technology, while the sale of a similar machine, if sold by a company that has a strategy of using all machinery to the full extent of their useful life, would clearly be an extraordinary event. The distinction between the two terms is not easy.

For lack of a better rule, we will consider that events or transactions that give rise to truly extraordinary items for most entities, and thus must be distinguished from normal operating transactions, are transactions that are not recurrent or coherent with the long-term strategy of the firm, or events over which the management of the firm has no control, such as an expropriation of assets, or an act of God such as an earthquake, a flood or other natural disaster. Some countries introduce a slightly different meaning to the word extraordinary by choosing other words: for example by distinguishing extraordinary from exceptional items and from current items (the latter term referring to both operating and financial data).

Appendix 6.6 provides further developments on the concepts of extraordinary and exceptional items.

6 Reporting accounting changes

6.1 Changes in accounting policies

The consistency principle evoked in Chapter 4 states that identical accounting policies ought normally to be followed in each successive period in order to allow users to compare the financial statements of an entity over a period of time and to identify trends in its financial position, wealth creation, and cash flows. Therefore, in this context, 'an entity shall change an accounting policy only if the change:

(a) is required by an IFRS; or

(b) results in the financial statements providing reliable and more relevant information about the effects of transactions, other events or conditions on the entity's financial position, financial performance or cash flow' (IAS 8, IASB 2003: § 14).

IAS 8 prescribes the retrospective method as benchmark treatment: 'when (…) an entity changes an accounting policy voluntarily, it shall apply the change retrospectively' (§ 19b), i.e., 'as if the new accounting policy had always been applied' (§ 22). The entity 'shall adjust the opening balance of each affected component of equity for the earliest prior period presented and the other comparative amounts disclosed for each period presented' (§ 22).

However, two exceptions are possible:

■ 'When it is impracticable to determine the period-specific effects of changing an accounting policy on comparative information for one or more prior periods presented, the entity shall apply the new accounting policy to the carrying amounts of assets and liabilities as at the beginning of the earliest period for which retrospective application is practicable, which may be the current period, and shall make a corresponding adjustment to the opening balance of each affected component of equity for that period' (IAS 8: § 24).

■ 'When it is impracticable to determine the cumulative effect [of the change], at the beginning of the current period, of applying a new accounting policy to all prior periods, the entity shall adjust the comparative information to apply the new accounting policy prospectively from the earliest date practicable' (IAS 8: § 25), which means 'applying the new accounting policy to transactions, other events and conditions occurring after the date as at which the policy is changed' (IAS 8: § 5).

In the case of a voluntary change, IAS 8 (§ 29) prescribes disclosure of:

(a) 'the nature of the change in accounting policy;

(b) the reasons why applying the new accounting policy provides reliable and more relevant information;

(c) for the current period and for each period presented, to the extent practicable, the amount of the adjustment (…) for each financial statement line item affected (…);

(d) the amount of the adjustment relating to periods before those presented, to the extent practicable; and

(e) if retrospective application is impracticable for a particular prior period, or for periods before those presented, the circumstances that led to the existence of that condition and a description of how and from when the change in accounting policy has been applied'.

6.2 Changes in accounting estimates

'As a result of the uncertainties inherent in business activities, many items in financial statements cannot be measured with precision but can only be estimated. Estimation involves judgments based on the latest available, reliable information. For example, estimates may be required of: (a) [future] bad debts; (b) inventory obsolescence [rate]; (c) the fair value of financial assets or financial liabilities [see more on this in Chapter 10]; (d) the useful lives of, or expected pattern of consumption of the future economic benefits embodied in, depreciable assets; and (e) warranty obligations. The use of reasonable estimates is an essential part of the preparation of financial statements and does not undermine their reliability' (IAS 8: §§ 32–33).

'An estimate may need revision if changes occur in the circumstances on which the estimate was based or as a result of new information, or more experience. By its nature, the revision of an estimate does not relate to prior periods and is not the correction of an error' (IAS 8: § 34).

IAS 8 (§ 36) prescribes that the 'effect of a change in an accounting estimate (...) shall be recognized prospectively'. According to this Standard (§ 38), 'a change in an accounting estimate may affect only the current period's profit or loss, or the profit or loss of both the current period and future periods. For example, a change in the estimate of the amount of bad debts affects only the current period's profit or loss and therefore is recognized in the current period. However, a change in the estimated useful life of, or the expected pattern of consumption of the future economic benefits embodied in, a depreciable asset affects depreciation expense for the current period and for each future period during the asset's remaining useful life. In both cases, the effect of the change relating to the current period is recognized as income or expense in the current period. The effect, if any, on future periods is recognized as income or expense in those future periods.'

'An entity shall disclose the nature and amount of a change in an accounting estimate that has an effect in the current period or is expected to have an effect in future periods, except for the disclosure of the effect on future periods when it is impracticable to estimate that effect' (IAS 8: § 39).

6.3 Prior period errors

'Errors can arise in respect of the recognition, measurement, presentation or disclosure of elements of financial statements' (IAS 8, IASB 2003: § 41).

'A prior period error shall be corrected by retrospective restatement except to the extent that it is impracticable to determine either the period-specific effects or the cumulative effect of the error' (IAS 8: § 43). 'When it is impracticable to determine the cumulative effect, at the beginning of the current period, of an error on all prior periods, the entity shall restate the comparative information to correct the error prospectively from the earliest date practicable' (IAS 8: § 45).

IAS 8 adds that (§ 49) 'an entity shall disclose:

(a) the nature of the prior error;

(b) for each prior period presented, to the extent practicable, the amount of the correction: (...) for each financial statement line item affected (...);

(c) the amount of the correction at the beginning of the earliest prior period presented; and

(d) if retrospective restatement is impracticable for a particular prior period, the circumstances that led to the existence of that condition and a description of how and from when the error has been corrected.'

7 Reporting discontinued operations

Any business entity may, in the normal course of its activity, discontinue, spin-off or cede some segments of its activity so as to, for example, reallocate its resources towards potentially more profitable markets. Entire sections of a business can therefore, at times, be either sold or discontinued. Since users need to be able to interpret the current performance of the firm by comparing it against previous periods' performance, it is critical to be able to reconstitute an equivalent economic perimeter so that the basis of comparability can be re-established. The handling of **discontinued operations** is therefore a very important element of quality reporting.

As defined in IFRS 5 (IASB 2004: § 32), which replaces IAS 35, 'a discontinued operation is a component of an entity that either has been disposed of, or is classified as held for sale, and:

(a) represents a separate major line of business or geographical area of operations;

(b) is part of a single coordinated plan to dispose of a separate major line of business or geographical area of operations; or

(c) is a subsidiary acquired exclusively with a view to resale.'

The standard establishes principles for reporting information about discontinued operations, thereby enhancing the ability of users of financial statements to make projections of an entity's cash flows, earnings-generating capacity, and financial position by segregating information about discontinued operations from information about continuing operations.

According to IFRS 5 (IASB 2004: § 33), 'an entity shall disclose:

(a) A single amount on the face of the income statement comprising the total of: (i) the post-tax profit or loss of discontinued operations; and (ii) the post-tax gain or loss recognized on the measurement to fair value less costs to sell or on the disposal of the assets or disposal group(s) constituting the discontinued operation.

(b) An analysis of the single amount in (a) [above] into: (i) the revenue, expenses and pre-tax profit or loss of discontinued operations; (ii) the related income tax expense as required by paragraph 81(h) of IAS 12; (iii) the gain or loss recognized on the measurement to fair value less costs to sell or on the disposal of the assets or disposal group(s) constituting the discontinued operation; and (iv) the related income tax expense as required by paragraph 81(h) of IAS 12.

The analysis may be presented in the notes or in the statement of comprehensive income. If it is presented in the statement of comprehensive income it shall be presented in a section identified as relating to discontinued operations, i.e., separately from continuing operations. (…)

(c) The net cash flows attributable to the operating, investing and financing activities of discontinued operations. These disclosures may be presented either in the notes or on the face of the financial statements (…).'

Real-life example Siemens

(Germany - IFRS - Source: Annual report 2008 - Diversified industries)

Siemens AG (Siemens) is engaged in electronics and electrical engineering. During the fiscal year ended 30 September 2008, the company reorganized its operations. It operates in six segments: industry, energy, healthcare, Siemens IT Solutions, Services and Siemens Financial Services (SFS) and equity investments.

Excerpts from the notes to the consolidated financial statements and the management report

Discontinued operations are reported when a component of an entity comprising operations and cash flows that can be clearly distinguished, operationally and for financial reporting purposes, from the rest of the entity is classified as held for sale or has been disposed of, if the component either (a) represents a separate major line of business or geographical area of operations or (b) is part of a single coordinated plan to dispose of a separate major line of business or geographical area of operations or (c) is a subsidiary acquired exclusively with a view to resale.

Siemens VDO Automotive (SV) – discontinued operation

At the beginning of December 2007, Siemens sold its SV activities to Continental AG, Hanover, Germany for a sale price of approximately €11.4 billion. The transaction resulted in a preliminary gain, net of related costs of €m5,522, which is included in discontinued operations. The historical results of SV are reported as discontinued operations in the consolidated statements of income for all periods presented.

The net results of SV reported in the consolidated statements of income consist of the following components (in €m):

	30 September	
	2008	2007
Revenue	1,842	10,324
Costs and expenses, including gain on disposal	3,553	(9,744)
Income from discontinued operations before income taxes	**5,395**	**580**
Income taxes	65	(1,130)
Income from discontinued operations, net of income taxes	**5,460**	**(550)**

As a result of taxable reorganizations in fiscal 2007, prior to the completion of the sale, no disposal gain related income taxes arose on the disposal of SV in December 2007.

8 Comprehensive income

The Glossary of Terms published by the IASB does not include a definition of the concept of 'comprehensive income' *per se*. However, it defines:

■ The 'total comprehensive income' as 'the change in equity during a period resulting from transactions and other events, other than those changes resulting from transactions with owners in their capacity as owners' and

■ The 'other comprehensive income' as 'items of income and expense (including reclassification adjustments) that are not recognized in profit or loss as required or permitted by other IFRSs)' (see also IAS 1, 2007: § 7).

IAS 1 (2007) constantly refers to 'comprehensive income (i.e., non-owner changes in equity)' throughout the standard. Comprehensive income is defined in US GAAP as the sum of all 'change[s] in equity of a business enterprise during a period [arising] from transactions and other events and circumstances from non-owner sources. It includes all changes in equity during a period except those resulting from investments by owners and distributions to owners' (FASB 1997: § 8).

Certain changes in assets and liabilities, which, according to accounting principles, are not considered as part of the business activity (i.e., neither ordinary nor exceptional nor extraordinary) and thus are not part of the business net income, are sometimes not reported in the income statement for the period in which they are recognized but, instead, are included directly in a separate component of equity in the balance sheet. For example, the potential gain resulting from a rise in the market value of 'available-for-sale' marketable securities (see Chapter 10) would not be recorded in the income statement but directly in the shareholders' equity.

Figure 6.5 Components of the total comprehensive income

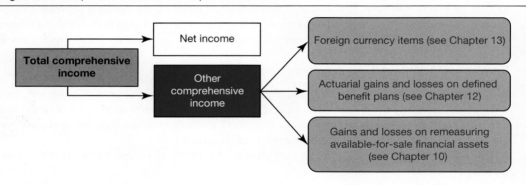

Some users of financial statement information have expressed concerns about the increasing number of items that bypass – or are not reported in – the income statement. In this context, the FASB issued in June 1997 the Statement of Financial Accounting Standard (SFAS) No. 130 – Reporting Comprehensive Income – that discusses how to report and display these items to arrive at a 'total comprehensive income'. The IASB, which has been discussing the idea of reporting a comprehensive income for several years, has adopted this idea in the revised version of IAS 1 (2007).

Those items 'bypassing' the income statement are referred to as 'other [elements of] comprehensive income'. Figure 6.5 presents the components of the total comprehensive income. Some examples of other comprehensive income are provided below.

In summary, 'IAS 1 requires an entity to present, in a statement of changes in equity, all owner changes in equity. All non-owner changes in equity (i.e., comprehensive income) are required to be presented in one statement of comprehensive income or in two statements (a separate income statement and a statement of comprehensive income). Components of comprehensive income are not permitted to be presented in the statement of changes in equity' (IAS 1: § IN6).

More precisely, 'An entity shall present all items of income and expense recognized in a period:

(a) in a single statement of comprehensive income; or

(b) in two statements: a statement displaying components of profit or loss (separate income statement) and a second statement beginning with profit or loss and displaying components of other comprehensive income (statement of comprehensive income)' (IAS 1: § 81).

Example IAS 1

IAS 1 includes in its appendix an example of statement of comprehensive income with the two allowed formats: one-statement approach or two-statements approach.

Table 6.10 lists the elements that are added to the net income to obtain the comprehensive income.

In the one-statement approach, the income statement (see Tables 5.15 and 5.16 in Chapter 5) is listed first, followed by the comprehensive income statement (Table 6.10). They, together, form a single statement.

Table 6.10 Comprehensive income in IAS 1

	20X7	20X6
Profit for the year	121,250	65,500
Other comprehensive income:		
Exchange differences on translating foreign operations	5,334	10,667
Available-for-sale financial assets	(24,000)	26,667
Cash flow hedges	(667)	(4,000)
Gains on property revaluation	933	3,367
Actuarial gains (losses) on defined benefit pension plans	(667)	1,333
Share of other comprehensive income of associates	400	(700)
Income tax relating to components of other comprehensive income	4,667	(9,334)
Other comprehensive income for the year, net of tax	(14,000)	28,000
TOTAL COMPREHENSIVE INCOME FOR THE YEAR	107,250	93,500
Total comprehensive income attributable to:		
Owners of the parent	85,800	74,800
Non-controlling interests	21,450	18,700
	107,250	93,500

In the two-statements approach, the data shown in Table 6.10 are listed separately, but reported after the income statement (see Tables 5.15 and 5.16 in Chapter 5). The reader will have noticed that the two approaches are, in fact, largely similar.

We will not delve into the details of the different items of the other comprehensive income. The interested reader is encouraged to consult IAS 1. In Chapter 11, we will develop the Statement of Changes in Equity and will explain how total comprehensive income is integrated in this statement.

Real-life example Hellenic Petroleum SA

(Greece – IFRS – Source: Interim report June 2009 – Energy)

This example illustrates the reporting for comprehensive income using the single statement approach.

Interim statement of comprehensive income (in € 000)		
For the six-month period ended	30 June 2009	30 June 2008
Sales	2,908,242	4,880,897
Cost of sales	(2,634,761)	(4,517,962)
Gross profit	273,481	362,935
Selling, distribution and administrative expenses	(88,047)	(93,218)
Exploration and development expenses	(2,931)	(13,826)
Other operating income/(expenses) - net	(16,362)	(49,979)
Dividend income	17,110	13,462
Operating profit	183,251	219,374
Finance (expenses)/income -net	(5,132)	(8,023)
Currency exchange (losses)/gains	4,435	17,414
Profit before income tax	182,554	228,765
Income tax expense	(43,133)	(64,786)
Profit for the period	139,421	163,979
Other comprehensive income:		
Unrealized gains (losses) on revaluation of hedges	(36,658)	(165,527)
Other comprehensive income for the period, net of tax	(36,658)	(165,527)
Total comprehensive income/(loss) for the period	102,763	(1,548)

This example is based on interim financial statements for the first half year of 2009 because the revised IAS 1 became effective only on 1 January 2009 and, at the time of the writing of this text, only interim financial statements applying the revised version of IAS 1 were available.

9 Government assistance: Grants and subsidies

Government direct financial support to businesses for special purposes (grants or subsidies) is a relatively common practice in many countries. IAS 20 (IASB: 1994) uses the term 'government assistance' to show that the aid provided takes many forms varying both in the nature of the assistance given and in the conditions which are usually attached to it. Such assistance creates a serious revenue recognition question, the answer to which can affect the interpretation of financial statements by users. Is government assistance revenue, or a compensation of costs (which is, technically, equivalent to a revenue), or a source of financing?

There are several categories of government assistance, and each category may require a different answer to the question we raised. They are:

- grants related to assets;
- grants related to income;
- forgivable loans (i.e., loans that will not need to be reimbursed if certain conditions are met).

Let us analyze in turn the specificity of each type of assistance.

9.1 Grants related to assets

<u>Grants related to assets</u> are government grants whose purpose is to specifically encourage qualified entities to 'purchase, construct or otherwise acquire long-term assets' (IAS 20: § 3). These grants are mostly a targeted aid to investment in economic sectors or geographical areas selected for development. Often called 'investment grants', they can be used to finance green-field operations as well as part of the cost of additions or modifications to existing fixed assets.

Figure 6.6 illustrates the several possible ways to account for such government assistance.

Figure 6.6 shows that the IAS 20 preferred solution consists in recognizing the grant as revenue in systematic and rational sections that allow matching, over the relevant periods, of the government assistance with the related costs (in practice the depreciation expenses). The full recognition of the whole investment grant in the first year would only be acceptable if no basis existed for allocating it to periods other than the one in which it was received.

Alternative solutions, however, exist without violating the intent of IAS 20. For example, under French GAAP, an investment grant is reported not in the income statement but in the balance sheet as a separate item within shareholders' equity (in the unconsolidated financial statements), or as a non-current liability (in the consolidated financial statements). The amount so recorded is 'amortized' following the method prescribed by IASB, i.e., a systematic and rational matching to revenue. The separate item is then equivalent to the 'deferred income' account prescribed by IASB as shown in Figure 6.6.

Theoretical example

Kunzen SA acquires on 1 January X1 an asset in exchange for a cash payment of 200 CU. This asset will be depreciated over five years on a straight-line basis. Because Kunzen is located in a special economic zone, it qualifies for government assistance related to this asset for an amount of 150 CU. Figure 6.7 illustrates the accounting for the grant in year X1.

Figure 6.6 Accounting and reporting for investment grant in IAS 20

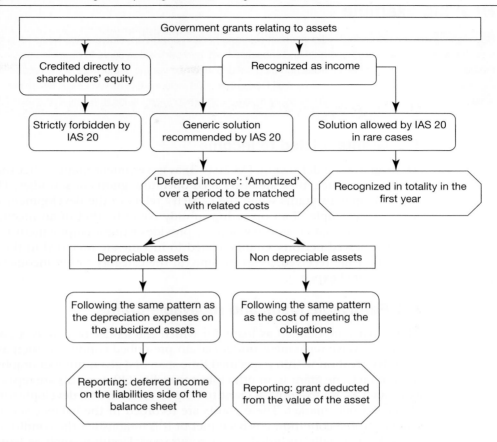

Figure 6.7 Accounting for an investment grant

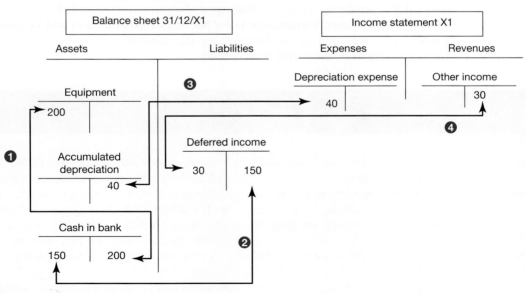

❶ Purchase of the equipment on cash.

❷ Receipt of the investment grant, which is recorded as a deferred income on the liabilities side of the balance sheet.

❸ Depreciation of the equipment over five years (annual depreciation allowance is 200 CU/5 = 40 CU per year).

❹ Every year, during five years, the deferred income is transferred to the income statement, following the pattern of the depreciation of the fixed asset (150/5 = 30).

Real-life example

Bayer, the Germany-based international chemicals and health care group, states in the notes to its annual report 2008 that, in accordance with IAS 20, grants and subsidies from third parties that serve to promote investment are reflected in the balance sheet under other liabilities and amortized to income over the useful lives of the respective assets. Accrued expenses (reflected in other liabilities) as of 31 December 2008 includes €49 million (2007: €44 million) in grants and subsidies received from government. The amount reversed and recognized in income was €18 million (2007: €7 million).

9.2 Grants related to income

These grants are defined by IAS 20 (§ 3) as government grants other than those related to assets. In practice, they are also called operating grants or subsidies. They include capacity development grants when the capacity refers to the development of competences or skills. An example of an operating subsidy could be that of an incentive grant awarded to a business that creates new jobs or provides gainful employment to certain categories of unemployed persons. Grants related to income are included in the income statement when they are received, as an income (in the category 'other income') or as a deduction of the related expense.

9.3 Forgivable loans and repayable grants

These loans are defined as loans for which the lender (generally a government agency) agrees to waive repayment under certain prescribed conditions such as, for example, the effective creation within a specified time span of a given number of jobs. If the conditions are not met, the grant is, in principle, repayable. Other grants are repayable in case of success, such as, for example, a grant to help in research and development or a grant to help develop a new market. These grants are recorded in the balance sheet (on the liabilities side) until the condition has been met or it is established the conditions will not be met. They are generally recorded under some special caption such as 'conditional advances received from the state'. These grants should, logically, be listed immediately next to shareholders' equity to recognize their special nature. If the conditions are not met at the end of the life of such a grant, the latter becomes repayable and will be handled exactly as would a normal loan. If, on the contrary, the conditions are met, an operating revenue or an exceptional revenue will be recorded.

Key points

- The issue of revenue recognition deals with when and how much revenue to recognize.
- Criteria for recognition vary according to the type of transaction: sales of goods, rendering of services or use of entity assets yielding interest, royalties, or dividends.
- Revenue from the sale of goods should be recognized when several conditions have been satisfied, and mainly when the entity has transferred to the buyer the significant risks and rewards of ownership of the goods.
- Some transactions involve the rendering of services spanning several accounting periods (such as in long-term contracts). When the outcome of such transactions can be estimated reliably, revenues and costs associated with it should be recognized on the balance sheet date, as a function of the stage or percentage of completion of the transaction.
- The 'percentage of completion method', which consists in recording costs and revenues associated with the contracts as the work proceeds, is the preferred method for the recognition of profit in long-term contracts.
- There may be some divergences between tax regulation and accounting rules. When these differences relate to the timing of the recognition, they are called 'temporary differences'.
- Deferred tax assets or liabilities are created when the income tax expense is based on the pre-tax reported

income (defined according to accounting rules) and not on the taxable income (based on the tax rules).

■ Accounting standards stipulate that for an income statement to be useful in terms of evaluation of performance and supporting extrapolations, it must present, separately and distinctly, what pertains to 'normal' and recurrent business activities, and what pertains to actions, decisions and events that are occasional and unusual.

■ The comprehensive income includes revenues and expenses that are usually excluded from net income (e.g., unrealized gains and losses on short-term investments). This concept aims at showing the global performance of the company.

■ Government assistance (grants, subsidies, subventions or premiums) must be recognized separately as they are, by nature, not recurrent, and thus raise revenue recognition issues.

Review (solutions are at the back of the book)

Review 6.1 Schultz Accountancy Firm (1)

Topic: Revenue recognition

Mr. Schultz, the senior partner of an accounting firm, is concerned by the revenue recognition rules some of the firm's clients have adopted. He provides the following list of some of the revenue recognition rules he found in the notes to the firm's customers' financial statements:

(a) An advertising agency records as revenue the full commission as soon as the advertisement campaign has been fully prepared.

(b) Atrium Auditorium Inc. (AA Inc.) sells subscription packages to several series of concerts to be held between October X1 and September X2. Most concerts will take place in the fall and the spring and a sprinkling of events will take place during the summer. Customers are expected to pay cash for their subscription. AA Inc.'s reporting year ends on 31 December. In its income statement for period X1, AA Inc. records as revenue 3/12 (3 months) of the amounts received as subscription from paying-customers. The remaining 9/12 of the cash intake will be recognized in X2.

(c) Boticcelli Markets is specialized in home delivery of groceries, fruit and produce. It expects cash on delivery. It recognizes revenue at the time of payment.

(d) The Olympic Sports Club is a membership-only club. The yearly admission fee allows the members to enter the premises. Members have the possibility of paying the membership fee in installments for a small surcharge. All services within the club are billed to the members at about 20% below the open enrolment market prices of competing clubs. Membership fees are recognized in the income statement in equal installments over the duration of the membership (generally one year, although discounts are granted to members who pay upfront for longer periods). Membership fees already paid cannot be reimbursed.

Required

Evaluate whether the accounting policies adopted by the different companies are acceptable or not. If you feel they are not, which policy should have been adopted?

Review 6.2 Schall Company

Topic: Deferred taxation

Schall Company realized in the year X1 a fiscal pre-tax income of 100 CU. This income includes taking into account a one-off royalty fee expense for 10 CU (which was paid upfront in X1). The royalty fee is for the use by Schall Co. of a new technology for two years. Accordingly, Schall Co.'s accountant chose to recognize as an expense, for reporting purposes, half the fee in year X1, and the second half in year X2. However, tax regulations require an immediate deduction in tax accounts. The income tax rate is 40%.

The following table summarizes the data:

Pre-tax income before recording the royalty fee	110
Royalty fee expense paid	10
Royalty fee expense recorded for tax purposes	10
Pre-tax income after recording the fee	100
Yearly amortization of the fee expense (over 2 years)	5
Income tax rate	40%

Required

1. Compute the deferred taxation, assuming that the pre-tax income before recording the royalty fee expense is the same in X2 as it was in X1.

2. Record the deferred taxation at the end of X1 and at the end of X2.

Assignments

Assignment 6.1
Multiple-choice questions

Select the right answer (only one possible answer unless otherwise stated).

1. Which category(ies) of transactions and events is (are) specified in IAS 18 rules guiding the revenue recognition process?

   (a) The sale of goods
   (b) The use by others of entity assets
   (c) The rendering of service
   (d) All of these

2. In which of the following situations can one consider that the seller does not retain a significant risk of ownership?

   (a) For a retail sale, refund is offered if the customer is not satisfied. The seller can reliably estimate future returns and recognizes a liability for returns
   (b) The entity retains an obligation in case of unsatisfactory performance not covered by normal warranty provisions
   (c) The receipt of the revenue from a particular sale is contingent on the derivation of revenue by the buyer from its sale of the goods
   (d) The goods are shipped subject to installation, and that installation is a significant part of the contract which has not yet been completed by the selling entity or on its behalf

3. The recognition of revenue by reference to the degree of completion of a transaction is often referred to as the percentage of completion method.

   (a) True
   (b) False

4. Progress payments and advances received from customers often reflect the services performed and can so be used to reliably determine the percentage of completion.

   (a) True
   (b) False

5. When the outcome of a transaction involving the rendering of services cannot be estimated reliably, which of the following statements is correct?

   (a) Revenue should not be recognized
   (b) Revenue should be recognized for the total amount specified in the contract
   (c) Revenue should be recognized only up to the amount of the recoverable recognized expenses
   (d) None of these

6. When should revenue which arises from others' use of entity assets (interest, royalties and dividends) be recognized? (More than one possible answer)

   (a) When it is probable that the economic benefits associated with the transaction will flow to the enterprise
   (b) When the amount of the revenue can be measured reliably
   (c) When the contract is signed
   (d) When the payment is received

7. When it is decided to deliberately anticipate or delay recognition of profit or losses to avoid reporting peaks and troughs in income, this is known as _____

   (a) Income hiding
   (b) Income smoothing
   (c) Income covering
   (d) Income cheating

8. What is created when the tax rules lead to a later recognition of the tax burden than under financial accounting?

   (a) Deferred tax liability
   (b) Deferred tax revenue
   (c) Deferred tax asset
   (d) Deferred tax expense

9. A change in accounting policy should be made only: (more than one possible answer)

   (a) If required by an Interpretation
   (b) If required by a Standard
   (c) If the change will result in a more appropriate presentation of events or transactions in the financial statements of the enterprise
   (d) If suggested by the CEO

10. What is (are) the main source(s) of 'other comprehensive income' (i.e., items not recorded in the income statement but directly in the shareholders' equity)? (More than one possible answer.)

    (a) Foreign currency items
    (b) Unrealized gains and losses on certain investments in debt and equity securities
    (c) Minimum pension liability adjustments
    (d) Restructuring costs

Assignment 6.2
Schultz Accountancy Firm (2)

Topic: Revenue recognition

Mr. Schultz, the managing partner of an accounting firm, is concerned by some specific rules of revenue recognition adopted by some of his clients. The following list contains some of the rules he found in their notes to financial statements:

(a) DPS Business School Inc. (DPSBS Inc.) invoices its students at the beginning of each quarter for the quarterly tuition fees. DPSBS Inc. recognizes revenue only when tuition is actually paid by the students (or whomever, on their behalf). The first quarter X2 tuition invoices were mailed on 1 December X1 and all the tuition fee payments have been received in full by 15 December X1. No adjusting entry has been recorded.

(b) The *Commercial Times* is a newspaper, which receives payment for subscriptions. *Commercial Times* has a circulation of 750,000 copies and sells over three-quarters of these through annual subscription. Readers subscribe at any time during the year and there seems to be no clear seasonality in new subscriptions or cancellations. The *Commercial Times'* accountant is in the habit of recognizing as revenue for any year half of the cash received for annual subscriptions in that year plus half the subscriptions payments received in the previous year.

(c) A bridge club invoices a membership fee to its members who receive in return the magazine *Bridge Forever* and are entitled to special prices on other magazines. The club, in order to simplify its recording of fees, spreads the fee revenue on a straight-line basis over the period of membership.

(d) A seller (shipper) transfers goods to a buyer (recipient) who undertakes to sell the goods on behalf of the seller (consignment sales). The shipper recognizes the revenue at the time of delivery to the buyer.

Required

Evaluate whether the policies adopted by the different firms are acceptable or not. In the latter case, which policy should have been adopted?

Assignment 6.3
Nielsen Company

Topic: Deferred taxation

During year X1, the Nielsen Company reported sales for 2,400 CU and total expenses for 1,800 CU. It has no pre-existing deferred tax liability or tax asset. The following information is provided in relation to year X1:

1. Marketable securities held by Nielsen Co. have a market value at the end of the year which exceeds their book value by an amount of 8 CU. This potential gain is taxable as pertaining to year X1, but will be reported to shareholders only at the time of the sale.

2. The company accrued interest due on a bank loan for 16 CU. This interest (included in the expenses mentioned) will be tax deductible only when paid (which will be the case in year X2).

3. For some assets, Nielsen Co. uses different methods of depreciation for tax and for reporting purposes. The depreciation allowance for year X1 for tax purposes exceeds that reported to shareholders (included in the total expenses mentioned above) by 250 CU.

4. During year X1 a fine for an accidental pollution occurrence (included in the total expenses mentioned above) was paid for a total amount of 10 CU.

5. Part of the liquidity of Nielsen Co. is invested in tax-free municipal bonds. During year X1 these yielded a return of 40 CU (not included in the sales revenue mentioned above).

6. Warranty costs are provisioned at the level of 1.5% of sales. The corresponding amount has been included in the total expenses mentioned above. Actual expenses incurred during year X1 for services and repairs included in the warranty contract amounted to 15 CU.

Assume the tax rate is 40%.

Required

1. Compute the income before income tax for shareholder reporting.

2. Analyze each event with regard to taxation in terms of permanent and timing differences.

3. Compute the income tax payable to the tax authorities and income tax expense for shareholder reporting. (Local GAAP allow that reported tax expense be calculated according to GAAP rules).

4. Record the income tax expense for year X1.

Assignment 6.4
UBS AG* and Konica Minolta*

Topic: Extraordinary/exceptional items

UBS AG is a global provider of financial services to private, corporate and institutional clients. The company's financial businesses are organized on a worldwide basis into three business divisions and the Corporate Center. Global Wealth Management & Business Banking consists of three segments: Wealth Management International & Switzerland, Wealth Management US, and Business Banking Switzerland.

Konica Minolta is a Japan-based holding company. The company operates five business segments through its subsidiaries and associated companies. The information equipment segment manufactures and sells multi-function printers (MFPs), printers and related materials.

UBS and Konica Minolta publish the following information (source: annual reports 2008 and 2008/2009). The detail of the extraordinary income and expenses included in the accompanying financial statements are as follows:

UBS (Parent Bank)

Income statement (excerpts) (in CHFm)	31/12/2008	31/12/2007
Profit before extraordinary items and taxes	**(36,852)**	(8,797)
Extraordinary income	**1,002**	4,665
Extraordinary expenses	**482**	4
Tax expense	**157**	115
Profit (loss) for the period	**(36,489)**	(4,251)

In the notes one can find additional information regarding the composition of extraordinary income and expenses:

Extraordinary income includes a gain from the sale of the Bank of China investment of approximately CHF 360 million in 2008, whereas 2007 included a gain on the sale of UBS's 20.7% stake in Julius Baer of CHF 3,180 million. Further, 2008 includes a release of provisions of CHF 72 million, a release on reserves on investments in subsidiaries of CHF 490 million and a write-up of investments in associated companies of CHF 30 million (2007: CHF 409 million). Amounts in 2007 include a release on reserves on own properties of CHF 824 million and for lapsed employee options of CHF 165 million.

In 2008, extraordinary expenses include CHF 478 million related to an overstatement of trading income in 2007. Extraordinary expenses in 2007 were immaterial.

Konica Minolta

Income statement (excerpts) (in ¥ millions)	31 March	
	2008	2009
Extraordinary income		
Gain on sales of noncurrent assets	1,308	249
Gain on sales of investment securities	20	6
Gain on sales of subsidiaries and affiliates' stocks	47	2,803
License related income	8,080	560
Gain on transfer of business	—	3,063
Reversal of provision for loss on business liquidation	590	932
Other	—	458
Total extraordinary income	**10,045**	**8,071**
Extraordinary loss		
Loss on sales and retirement of non-current assets	4,533	3,115
Loss on sales of investment securities	0	0
Loss on valuation of stocks of subsidiaries and affiliates	54	—
Loss on valuation of investment securities	313	3,826
Impairment loss	5,702	1,168
Loss on litigation	625	—
Environmental expenses	1,856	—
Special extra retirement payments	460	—
Extraordinary loss in foreign subsidiaries	1,731	—
Business structure improvement expenses	—	10,094
Loss on revision of retirement benefit plan	—	2,046
Total extraordinary losses	**15,274**	**20,249**

Required

1. For each firm, how well do expenses and income reported correspond to the definitions of extraordinary items indicated in section 5 of this chapter?

2. What do you think of the terminology used by UBS and Konica Minolta? How helpful are the categories provided by each firm for an investor to understand the implication of these items on future performance?

3. For Konika Minolta, what do you think might be the reaction of a long-term investor discovering the rubric 'Gain (or loss) on sales of subsidiaries' and affiliates, stocks [i.e. shares]'?

References

FASB (1997) Statement of Financial Accounting Standards, No. 130: Reporting Comprehensive Income, Norwalk, CT.

IASC/IASB (1989) Framework for the Preparation and Presentation of Financial Statements, London.

IASB (1993a) International Accounting Standard, No. 11: Construction Contracts, London.

IASB (1993b) International Accounting Standard, No. 18: Revenue, London.

IASB (reformatted 1994) International Accounting Standard, No. 20: Accounting for Government Grants and Disclosure of Government Assistance, London.

IASB (2000) International Accounting Standard, No. 12: Income Taxes, London.

IASB (2003) International Accounting Standard, No. 8: Net Profit or Loss for the Period, Fundamental Errors and Changes in Accounting Policies, London.

IASB (2004) International Financial Reporting Standard, No. 5: Non-current Assets Held for Sale and Discontinued Operations, London.

IASB (2007) International Accounting Standard, No. 1: Presentation of Financial Statements, London.

Leone, M. (2009) New Revenue-Recognition Rules: The Apple of Apple's Eye? CFO Magazine.com September 16, 2009.

Further reading

Artsbert, K. (1996) 'The link between commercial accounting and tax accounting in Sweden', *European Accounting Review* 5(Supplement): 795–814.

Ballas, A.A. (1999) 'Valuation implications of exceptional and extraordinary items', *British Accounting Review* 31(3): 281–95.

Bauman, C.C., Bauman, M.P. and Halsey, R.F. (2001) 'Do firms use the deferred tax asset valuation allowance to manage earnings?', *Journal of the American Taxation Association* 23(Supplement): 27–48.

Christiansen, M. (1996) 'The relationship between accounting and taxation in Denmark', *European Accounting Review* 5(Supplement): 815–33.

Eberhartinger, E.L.E. (1999) 'The impact of tax rules on financial reporting in Germany, France, and the UK', *International Journal of Accounting* 34(1): 93–119.

Eilifsen, A. (1996) 'The relationship between accounting and taxation in Norway', *European Accounting Review* 5(Supplement): 835–44.

Frydlender, A. and Pham, D. (1996) 'Relationships between accounting and taxation in France', *European Accounting Review* 5(Supplement): 845–57.

Holeckova, J. (1996) 'Relationship between accounting and taxation in the Czech Republic', *European Accounting Review* 5(Supplement): 859–69.

Holland, K. and Jackson, R.H.G. (2004) 'Earnings management and deferred tax', *Accounting and Business Research* 34(2): 101–23.

Hoogendoorn, M.N. (1996) 'Accounting and taxation in Europe – A comparative overview', *European Accounting Review* 5(Supplement): 783–94.

Hoogendoorn, M.N. (1996) 'Accounting and taxation in the Netherlands', *European Accounting Review* 5(Supplement): 871–82.

Jaruga, A., Walinska, E. and Baniewicz, A. (1996) 'The relationship between accounting and taxation in Poland', *European Accounting Review* 5(Supplement): 883–97.

Järvenpää, M. (1996) 'The relationship between taxation and financial accounting in Finland', *European Accounting Review* 5(Supplement): 899–914.

Jorissen, A. and Maes, L. (1996) 'The principle of fiscal neutrality: The cornerstone of the relationship between financial reporting and taxation in Belgium', *European Accounting Review* 5(Supplement): 915–31.

Lamb, M. (1996) 'The relationship between accounting and taxation: The United Kingdom', *European Accounting Review* 5(Supplement): 933–49.

Pierce, A. (1996) 'The relationship between accounting and taxation in the Republic of Ireland', *European Accounting Review* 5(Supplement): 951–62.

Pfaff, D. and Schröer, T. (1996) 'The relationship between financial and tax accounting in Germany – the authoritativeness and reverse authoritativeness principle', *European Accounting Review* 5(Supplement): 963–79.

Rocchi, F. (1996) 'Accounting and taxation in Italy', *European Accounting Review* 5(Supplement): 981–89.

Stice, J., Stice, E.K. and Skousen, F. (2009) *Intermediate Accounting*, 17th edn, South-Western Cengage Learning, Mason, OH.

Additional material on the website

Go to http://www.cengage.co.uk/stolowy3 for further information, journal entries and extra assignments for each chapter.

The following appendices to this chapter are available on the dedicated website:

Appendix 6.1 Recognition of a net deferred tax asset

Appendix 6.2 Illustration of the principle of carry-back and carry-forward

Appendix 6.3 Deferred taxation and changes in tax rates

Appendix 6.4 Illustration of the two methods for reporting of long-term contracts

Appendix 6.5 Installment sales

Appendix 6.6 Extraordinary and exceptional items.

Notes

1. In many countries, including the UK, what we call revenue is referred to as 'turnover' or 'sales turnover'. We will refrain from using these terms as we reserve the term turnover for the metric indicating the speed with which an account renews itself (as in 'inventory turnover', a metric describing how fast the normal business cycle consumes the existing inventory of a firm.)

2. When a business simultaneously manages several contracts, some generating a positive cash balance and some generating a negative one, the management may choose, deliberately but erroneously, to blur the results of each contract and consolidate the cash flows. This bad practice is depriving both management and shareholders of relevant information about the risks and profitability of the types of contracts the firms manages, deliberately but erroneously, to blur the results of each contract and consolidate the cash flows. This bad practice is depriving both management and shareholders of relevant information about the risks and profitability of the types of contracts the firms manages.

3. For example, Apple's iPhone versus Nokia's N97: both products are fairly equivalent 'smart phones', but Apple uses revenue deferral to acknowledge its commitment to offer future upgrades to the phone's software, while Nokia considers upgrades represent a normal business cost and does not in any way attach that future cost to part of the sale revenue in calculating its income. Thus the financial statements of Apple and Nokia are not truly comparable. (See Leone 2009, and Apple's Form 10-K and Nokia's annual report).

4. For more detail, see 'corporate taxes, worldwide tax summaries', PricewaterhouseCoopers, available online: http://www.pwc.com/gx/en/worldwide-tax-summaries/index.jhtml.

5. The link between depreciation and cash flow is developed in Chapter 7.

6. From Corporate Taxes, Worldwide Tax Summaries, PricewaterhouseCoopers, available online: http://www.pwc.com/gx/en/worldwide-tax-summaries/index.jhtml.

7. Mochari, I. (2004), 'Back to the Present: How some companies are taking advantage of extensions to net operating loss carry-backs', *CFO Magazine* November, 2004.

C7

Chapter 7
Tangible Assets

Learning objectives

After studying this chapter, you will understand:

■ That tangible assets are physically observable items that are held for use in the production, sale or supply of goods or services, for rental to others, or for administrative purposes; and are expected to be used during more than one period.
■ That tangible assets are different from inventories.
■ That tangible assets represent a significant portion of both total and fixed assets. This proportion is heavily industry-related. The depreciation expense on tangible assets often represents a large expense item in the income statement.
■ How to distinguish capital expenditures (which are capitalized as assets) and revenue expenditures (which are included in expenses).
■ More in depth what the concept of depreciation represents.
■ What the main methods of depreciation are.
■ The main concepts needed for the preparation of a depreciation schedule (residual value, depreciable amount, useful life).
■ How to record internally constructed tangible assets.
■ How to handle financing or borrowing (interest) costs.
■ How to integrate tangible assets and depreciation in financial statement analysis.

The **assets** side of the balance sheet comprises both 'current' and 'fixed' – also called 'long-term' – assets. As we saw as early as Chapter 1, current assets are those that are created by or used in the operating cycle of the firm. They turn over rather rapidly (the speed of rotation is, of course, specific to each industrial or commercial sector), and, in the case of most well-managed firms, their turnover cycle is generally much shorter than the accounting period. Fixed assets are those that reflect the facilities and the 'capability' and 'capacity' provided by the firm that allow the operating cycle to take place. These assets create economic benefits over several periods, and represent significant investments that must be put in place before any activity can take place.

Among fixed assets, **tangible assets** represent a significant portion of total assets. Their use, which leads, as we have seen, to recognizing a depreciation expense, can be a large expense item in the income statement. A policy of depreciation choices is, thus, likely to greatly impact the calculated income. Table 7.1 illustrates the diversity of the proportion tangible assets represent in balance sheets of an illustrative, but non-statistically representative, sample of industries and countries. The importance of tangible assets in

Table 7.1 Weight of tangible assets

Company (country – activity)	Currency	Tangible assets (net amount) (1)	Total assets (net amount) (2)	Tangible assets as % of total assets (1)/(2)	Depreciation expense (3)	Sales revenue (4)	Depreciation expense as % of sales (3)/(4)
Irish Continental (Ireland – Shipping, transport)	€m	236	311	75.9	23	343	6.7
Club Méditerranée (France – Leisure)	€m	919	1,527	60.2	65	1,502	4.3
China Petroleum & Chemical Corporation (China – Oil and chemistry)	RMBm	403,265	767,827	52.5	45,823	1,452,101	3.2
Repsol (Spain – Oil and gas)	€m	25,732	49,429	52.1	2,974	57,740	5.2
Stora Enso (Finland – Paper production)	€m	5,413	12,241	44.2	666	11,029	6.0
Heineken (Netherlands – Brewery group)	€m	6,314	20,563	30.7	825	14,319	5.8
Temple-Inland (USA – Paper packaging products)	$m	1,664	5,869	28.4	206	3,884	5.3
Orkla (Norway – Metals and materials [production])	NOKm	26,368	104,926	25.1	2,003	63,937	3.1
Pirelli (Italy – Tires, cables and systems)	€000	1,598,046	6,933,218	23.0	198,742	4,660,175	4.3
Anheuser Busch InBev (Belgium – Brewery group)	€m	14,137	81,313	17.4	1,198	16,102	7.4
Mitsubishi Electric (Japan – Electrical equipment)	¥m	554,424	3,334,123	16.6	148,018	3,665,119	4.0
Philips (Netherlands – Consumer products)	€m	3,484	33,041	10.5	725	26,385	2.7
Securitas (Sweden – Security systems and services)	SEKm	2,460	35,719	6.9	772	56,572	1.4
ISS (Denmark – Support services)	DKKm	2,276	53,605	4.2	1,348	68,829	2.0
WPP (UK – Market information)	£m	691	24,463	2.8	145	36,920	0.4

financial statements is generally defined through two ratios: net tangible assets/total net assets, and depreciation expense/net sales. All data are excerpted from 2008 annual reports. The currencies used are the ones used in the annual report.

Table 7.1 lists firms in decreasing order of their percentage of net tangible assets over net total assets. The table shows that this ratio is heavily influenced by the sector of activity, services companies appearing at the bottom. The ratio varies from 75.9 to 2.8%.

After a short presentation of the various categories of fixed assets, this chapter will mainly deal with reporting and accounting issues (valuation and income effects) regarding tangible assets.

The qualifier 'tangible' distinguishes assets from those that are called 'intangible' (see Chapter 8) or 'financial' (see Chapter 10). A tangible asset is one that has a physical reality or substance, such as a building or a piece of equipment, while an intangible asset does not have a physical substance but represents an idea or knowledge (for example, the capitalized costs incurred in developing a patented product, technique or technology) or a right (for example, the price paid for a license to use a technology developed by someone else, or for a leasehold). The most common financial assets (i.e., neither tangible nor intangible) are generally either participations of the entity in the capital of some other business or enterprise (valued at historical cost), or long-term loans to a subsidiary, a customer or a supplier (valued at face value).

Fixed assets are, by nature, the most illiquid assets on the balance sheet. In countries where the accounting tradition is more 'patrimonial' they will be shown at the top of the list of assets, while in countries where the accounting culture emphasizes operations or liquidity, the tangible assets will be listed at the bottom of the list.

1 General principles

1.1 Categories of fixed assets

As mentioned in the introduction, fixed assets are divided into three categories: tangible, intangible and financial.

The first two categories are sometimes confused because their difference is not one of purpose or life cycle, but only one of physical substance. Table 7.2 presents the common and distinguishing characteristics of the three categories of fixed assets.

Since all three categories of fixed assets are long lived, a distinguishing feature is also the way their historical cost of acquisition is allocated (distributed) over time to reflect its use in the carrying out of normal business operations. The distribution over time of the cost of an asset is called depreciation (mainly for tangible assets), amortization (mainly for intangible assets – the same term is also used for reducing liabilities, as we will see in Chapter 12), or is described by other terms (such as depletion or impairment) for special cases, as we will see later. For the time being, we will discuss the concept of distribution over time of the **acquisition cost** of an asset under the generic term depreciation.

Table 7.2 Tangible, intangible and financial assets compared

Tangible assets	Intangible assets	Financial assets
Used in the course of the operations of the business (production, sale or distribution of goods and services) and not acquired for the purpose of resale		
Long-term (long-lived) in nature and usually subject to 'consumption' reflected by depreciation, amortization, depletion or impairment		Long-term (long-lived) in nature and are generally not susceptible to depreciation
Possess physical substance	Lack physical substance	

The matching principle calls for the depreciation pattern over time to, more or less, reflect the consumption of the 'productive[1] capacity' or 'productive potential' of the asset (at least in principle; as we will see below, there are exceptions to this rule). Table 7.3 highlights how each category's and sub-category's cost of consumption of the productive capacity provided by the asset (i.e., depreciation expense) is recorded for reporting income to shareholders.

When the allocation of the acquisition cost of an asset (i.e., depreciation, amortization or depletion[2]) reflects an ongoing process of consumption of the potential offered by that asset (in the course of business and in a way reflecting, as much as possible, the pace of activity), it is called a **systematic** allocation.

However, when the allocation (in this case called impairment) reflects the recognition of some form of random, unpredictable, or catastrophic event (often from external causes) that modifies the value (potential of generating future economic benefits) of the asset, rather than reflecting the consumption of economic-benefit generation potential of the fixed asset, it is called an **unsystematic** allocation.

1.2 Accounting issues relating to tangible assets

Figure 7.1 summarizes the various accounting issues that arise when reporting truly and fairly on tangible assets in the three phases in the life of an asset: birth, usage, death. The diagram also indicates in which part of this chapter each issue will be dealt with.

The valuation at acquisition of a tangible asset will be assumed to be unambiguous because it is market-based. An asset can be acquired through other processes than a straightforward purchase. The financing of the acquisition (by loan, by deferred payments, by exchange of another asset other than cash [barter][3], by the issuance of specific new financial instruments such as shares or bonds, by gifting or donation, etc.) has no impact on the depreciation mechanism *per se*. It only raises issues of valuation of the asset. Such issues are beyond the scope of this book.

1.3 Definition of tangible assets

1.3.1 General definition

The vocabulary used in businesses to refer to tangible assets tends to be diverse and even sometimes misleading: terms like 'property, plant and equipment'[4] (PPE), and the

Table 7.3 Fixed assets and cost allocation

Asset classification	Examples	Systematic cost allocation	Unsystematic cost allocation
Tangible assets	Buildings, machinery, equipment, furniture and fixtures	Depreciation	Impairment (rare)
	Land	No systematic cost allocation	Impairment (rare)
	Natural resources (oil and gas reserves, mineral deposits – e.g., mines and quarries)	Depletion	Impairment (rare)
Intangible assets	With a finite useful life: patents, copyrights, franchises, leaseholds, software	Amortization	Impairment (possible and no longer rare in this era)
	With an indefinite useful life: brands, trademarks, goodwill	No systematic cost allocation	Impairment (common when appropriate)
Financial assets	Investments	No systematic cost allocation	Impairment (common when appropriate)

Figure 7.1 Accounting issues in reporting tangible assets

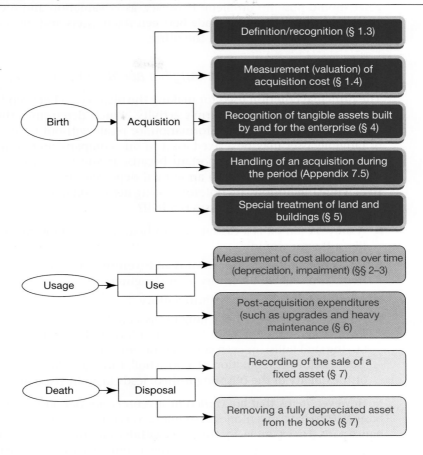

sometimes less appropriate 'plant assets', 'operational assets', or 'fixed assets', are often used interchangeably with the proper term of 'tangible assets'.

IAS 16 (IASB 2003) (§ 6) defines as 'property, plant and equipment' the 'tangible items that:

(a) are held for use in the production or supply of goods or services, for rental to others, or for administrative purposes; and

(b) are expected to be used during more than one period.'

In the remainder of this chapter, we will use the term 'tangible assets' as synonymous with 'property, plant and equipment' and all the other equivalent terms. Tangible assets include:

- land, freeholds and leaseholds;
- building structures (stores, factories, warehouses, offices);
- equipment (machinery, tools, fixtures);
- vehicles;
- furniture and fittings;
- payments on account (payments made by a business towards the acquisition of as yet undelivered tangible assets);
- tangible assets during their construction (cost of purchasing, constructing and installing tangible assets ahead of their productive use).

From the preceding definition, it would appear that the identification of a tangible asset should pose no problem. However, asset valuation and revenue recognition require that a clear distinction be made between fixed assets and inventories, on one hand, and fixed assets and expenses, on the other.

1.3.2 Difference between tangible assets and inventories

The principal criterion used for making the distinction between tangible assets and inventories is the nature of the firm's activity, which determines the purpose for which the asset is held – own use, transformation, or resale without transformation. Thus, any type of tangible asset may be a fixed asset in one company and an inventory in another. The distinction is, of course, important because it affects the timing of income recognition. Tangible assets are subject to an annual depreciation expense over their normal **useful life**, while inventories are not. Interesting definitional issues can arise in many situations. For example, what kind of asset is a bull?

- A dray ox (an ox is a castrated bull) held for providing traction is a tangible asset (just like a tractor would).

- An ox or a bull reared for meat is an inventory (work-in-process inventory while on the hoof, and sellable inventory after slaughter).

- A bull held for trading is an inventory.

- A stud bull may be either a tangible asset (if the owner mainly uses the bull for breeding for a fee and does not trade it), an inventory (if the owner is in the business of selling and buying stud bulls), or even could, at the same time, contain some components of an intangible asset if the reputation of a prize bull, through acknowledgement by respected judges or the quality of the offspring it sired, leads to an increase in the value of its services!

However, items that are carried in inventory are not all for direct resale. It is normal for businesses to have inventories of supplies, consumables, components and consumable maintenance parts. For example, for the latter, withdrawals from inventory will normally be expensed (consumed and recognized as such in the income statement) as repair and maintenance costs. However, when the unit cost of a spare part is intrinsically large and is an integral part of the business process' ability to remain operational, it may be accounted for as a fixed asset. For example, an airplane jet engine in working order kept in inventory to be used, as a temporary or permanent replacement, during maintenance or repair operations (off line) on the original engine, would be treated as a tangible asset (no scheduled airline can operate effectively unless it has access to available replacement engines), and, as such, the spare engine should be subject to an annual depreciation expense, even before being brought into operational use.

1.3.3 Difference between tangible assets and expenses (expenditures)

The IASB defines 'an asset [as] a resource (a) controlled by an entity as a result of past events and (b) from which future economic benefits are expected to flow to the entity' (IASB 1989: § 49 and IASB 2004b: § 8).

Revenue and capital expenditure   A 'revenue expenditure' is a consumption of resources for the purpose of generating revenue. They include the costs of production and transformation, costs of marketing, selling and distributing the product or services and the costs of administering and coordinating the entity. Following the matching principle, all expenses incurred in creating, sustaining and satisfying demand are called **revenue expenditures** and, as such, recognized (expensed) in the income statement when incurred. The general case is that no marketing expense (creating and sustaining demand) ought to be capitalized (turned into a depreciable asset) because of the uncertainty affecting the correlation between the expenditure and the future economic benefits it may create for the firm.

Some expenses or expenditures are incurred in (1) the course of bringing an asset 'online', or (2) in upgrading it, or (3) in carrying out a major maintenance operation required to ensure or extend the economic life of the asset. Any of these expenses change (modify and, hopefully, extend) the potential for future economic benefits offered by the asset.

In the first case, the expenditure should, normally, be considered as an increase in the value of the original cost of acquisition (historical **book value**) of the asset. The asset cannot be brought in operations without these upfront preparation costs. However some businesses, in application of their understanding of the materiality concept (and the specifics of the situation) consider such an expense as a normal consumption of resources in the course of doing business, and, as such, recognize it as an expense of the period.

The latter two cases [(2) and (3)] call unambiguously for a capitalization of the expense. The historical book value to date (gross historical cost of acquisition) of the asset is incremented by the amount of the expense (and probably leading to a recalculation of the depreciation schedule from that moment onwards).

The ambiguity of the materiality of an upgrade or maintenance expense (proportion of the expenditure to the value of a new asset) leads sometimes to debate as to the proper handling of that expense. Some businesses argue they serve their shareholders best in expensing (in the period incurred) these upgrading or maintenance expenses, while others prefer to capitalize them and depreciate them over the periods during which benefits will be derived. Table 7.4 summarizes the distinction between '**capital expenditure**', which are recorded as assets (i.e., capitalized), and 'revenue (generating) expenditure' which will be recognized in the period in which they are incurred.

Focus on capital expenditure   Capital expenditure should meet at least one of the following three criteria:

1. The quantity of (economic benefit generating) services received from using the asset will be increased through a longer useful life.
2. The quantity of economic benefits received from using the asset will be increased with more units of output.
3. The quality of the services received from using the asset will be increased (presumably leading to a possible increase of the price, or to the prevention of a price decrease in order for the firm or the product to remain competitive).

An expense or expenditure that meets at least one of these three conditions is considered a capital expenditure.

'Small' equipment   The decision of whether a specific expenditure should be handled as either the creation of a tangible asset or an expense is often made solely on grounds of materiality. Many countries' GAAP and tax regulations have established minimum

Table 7.4 Capital and revenue expenditure

Type of expenditure	Definition	Accounting	Depreciation
Capital expenditure	Expenses incurred for the purpose of generating future economic benefits	Recorded as assets	Yes
Revenue expenditure	Expenses caused by the short-term usage – or normal maintenance – of the revenues generating potential of an asset (examples: minor spare parts, lubricants and cooling fluids, maintenance labor expenses, minor repairs expenses)	Charged as expense as incurred	No

threshold amounts (arbitrary, thus not necessarily coherent between the two sources of regulation) to facilitate the distinction between expense (expensing) and asset (capitalizing). Thus, acquired resources of small unitary value that may benefit future periods (such as off-the-shelf software packages, small tools, furniture, and office equipment) may be fully expensed in the year of acquisition and not ever be listed as a fixed asset. For example, French tax law states that any industrial or office equipment with an invoiced price below €500 can be expensed, but must be dealt with as an asset if its amount is above that threshold. Thresholds are often relative to the size of the firm (however defined). For example, in the USA, a quick, non-exhaustive and not statistically significant survey of a variety of firms in Western Washington State, showed the following approximate average internal thresholds: $1,000 (for 'small or medium' businesses) and $10,000 (for 'large' firms).

As regulatory texts or practice allow companies to expense capital expenditures and revenue expenditures of an amount below a certain limit, most entities have generally opted for immediately expensing all those expenses below that threshold. Doing so has two advantages:

1. It will reduce taxable profit in the year of acquisition by an amount much greater than an allowance for depreciation expense. Lower taxable profit early means a higher immediate cash flow, all things being equal, and larger cash flows are generally considered to be good for the business. Of course if the expense is recognized this year, the taxable profit next year will be higher (than it would have been had a depreciation procedure been engaged in), but 'sooner is always better than later' when it comes to cash flow … This leads, at times, to some businesses requesting their suppliers to break up large purchases of maintenance contracts with a value above the threshold into several smaller invoices, so as to be able to expense each individual invoice immediately, and thus reduce their immediate tax burden. Such a practice is, of course, misleading to the shareholders and other financial information users and should not be condoned.

2. There will be no fiscal obligation to maintain, for these items, the detailed records of acquisition cost and accumulated depreciation that are usually mandated by tax regulations.

1.4 Cost of acquisition

1.4.1 Definition

Acquisition 'cost is the amount of cash or cash equivalents paid or the fair value of the other consideration given, to acquire an asset at the time of its acquisition or construction (…)' (IAS 16: § 6). In general, the cost of acquisition is the cash or cash equivalents paid to obtain the asset and to bring it to the location and condition necessary for its intended use.

More precisely, IAS 16 (§ 16) states: 'The cost of an item of property, plant and equipment comprises (a) its purchase price, including import duties and non-refundable purchase taxes, after deducting trade discounts and rebates; (b) any costs directly attributable to bringing the asset to the location and condition necessary for it to be capable of operating in the manner intended by management; (c) the initial estimate of the costs of dismantling and removing the item and restoring the site on which it is located, the obligation for which an entity incurs either when the item is acquired or as a consequence of having used the item during a particular period for purposes other than to produce inventories during that period.'

1.4.2 Recording of the acquisition of an asset

Let us take the example of a piece of equipment with a cost of acquisition, which can be broken down as follows (in CU):

Purchase price	40
Import duties	3
Transportation	5
Professional fees	2
Total	50

The acquisition cost is therefore 50 CU. Figure 7.2 describes the recording procedure when the asset is acquired.

1.4.3 Examples of components of the acquisition cost

IASB (IAS 16: § 17) provides six examples of directly attributable costs that 'should be included in the cost of acquisition:

(a) costs of employee benefits (…) arising directly from the construction or acquisition of the item of property, plant and equipment;

(b) costs of site preparation;

(c) initial delivery and handling costs;

(d) installation and assembly costs;

(e) costs of testing whether the asset is functioning properly, after deducting the net proceeds from selling any items produced while bringing the asset to that location and condition (such as samples produced when testing equipment); and

(f) professional fees' such as those paid to architects or external engineers.

However, according to IAS 16 (§ 19), 'examples of costs that are not costs of an item of property, plant and equipment are:

(a) costs of opening a new facility;

(b) costs of introducing a new product or service (including costs of advertising and promotional activities);

(c) costs of conducting business in a new location or with a new class of customer (including costs of staff training); and

(d) administration and other general overhead costs.'

Appendix 7.1 lists some examples of components of the acquisition cost of tangible assets as reported in notes to financial statements.

Figure 7.2 Recording of the acquisition

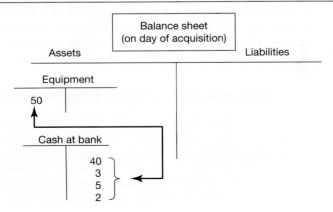

2 Depreciation

IAS 16 (§ 6) defines depreciation as 'the systematic allocation of the **depreciable amount** of an asset over its useful life'. In other words, depreciation is the process of allocating the cost of a long-term asset in a **rational and systematic manner** over its useful life in order to achieve a matching of expenses and revenues. The yearly depreciation allowance ('depreciation expense') is therefore a normal component of the expense side of the income statement.

With the notable exception of land, the net book value (acquisition cost minus accumulated depreciation) of each and all tangible assets will diminish irreversibly due to use, the effect of the passage of time, technological evolution and any other reason, reflecting the diminution of the productive potential of the assets. When the obsolescence of the potential for future benefits is unpredictable (unsystematic reduction in value due to unexpected or catastrophic events), the loss of value of an asset is not recognized through depreciation but will lead to a write-down (see the concept of 'impairment' later in section 4).

In the definition of depreciation, two concepts are important:

- *Rational manner*: The depreciation expense should be related to the flow of benefits expected to arise from the asset.

- *Systematic manner*: The computation of the depreciation expense is based on a formula, which was decided at the time of acquisition or before, and cannot be modified during the life of the asset. This characteristic is designed to prevent any possibility of 'earnings management' that might have happened if the amount of the depreciation allowance had been left to the whim of the management or of the accountant.

In order to establish the systematic and rational schedule of depreciation of a tangible asset, several parameters need to be documented:

- existence of different 'components' ('parts') of the asset (see 2.1 below);
- residual value of the asset;
- depreciable base amount;
- useful life duration;
- choice of a depreciation method.

They will lead to:

- A depreciation schedule (or several, in case of the existence of different 'components' of the asset, each having, for example, a specific life duration)
- A net book value, which is periodically updated.

Each of these points will be covered in succession. '**Depletion**' (depreciation recorded for natural resources or mineral deposits) is a specific topic especially relevant for countries with important exhaustible natural resources. It is not, however, covered in detail in this book[5] since its logic is the same as depreciation and the key impact of the recording of depletion is that the reporting rules and the tax rules are generally quite different (but here again, the principle is similar to that of depreciation, simply more acute).

2.1 Components of a complex tangible asset

'Each part of an item of property, plant and equipment with a cost that is significant in relation to the total cost of the item shall be depreciated separately' (IAS 16: § 43). 'An entity allocates the amount initially recognized in respect of an item of property, plant and equipment to its significant parts and depreciates separately each such part. For example, it may be appropriate to depreciate separately the airframe and engines of an aircraft' (IAS 16: § 44). What the IASB calls 'part' of an asset is often referred to by practitioners as '**component**' of that asset. The method required by the IASB is thus called 'depreciation by component' or 'component accounting'.

An asset can, if appropriate, be separated between its 'structure' and its 'components' (these, in turn, can be separated between hardware and software, etc.), each part having its own depreciation schedule. For example, a long-haul truck is generally separated in at least three parts: the structure (the truck itself, with a life expectancy of about five years) and two components, the engine plus transmission and the tires. The structure can be depreciated, for example, over 1,000,000 kilometers (621,371 miles), while the motor and transmission can be depreciated over 500,000 kilometers (310,686 miles) and the tires are depreciated, for example, over 80,000 kilometers (49,710 miles).

Depreciation by components does not modify the total depreciable cost of the asset. If a tangible asset is acquired and it appears depreciation by component would be appropriate, the depreciable cost of the structure is often found by deduction. If a 40-ton truck is acquired for 100 CU and the cost of a replacement engine plus transmission is 25 CU and the cost of a set of tires is 15 CU, by deduction the depreciable cost of the structure would be 60 CU. The full 100 CU cost of the whole truck would, in this case, be depreciated through three different historical costs of acquisition and depreciation schedules.

2.2 Residual value

IAS 16 (§ 6) defines 'residual value' as 'the estimated amount that an entity would currently obtain from disposal of the asset, after deducting the estimated costs of disposal if the asset were already of the age and in the condition expected at the end of its useful life'. In order to avoid double counting, IAS 16 (§ 16) adds that if the estimated costs of disposal, including costs relating to dismantling the equipment cleanly, removing the asset and restoring the site, etc. were already included in the depreciable cost of acquisition, they should not be deducted from the **residual value** (which in this case is only the naked revenue, net of transaction costs, expected to be obtained from the resale of the obsolete asset).

The actual depreciable cost of an asset can only be the actual cost incurred to create the economic benefits over its life expectancy. The residual value is not depreciated because the company will, eventually, recover it. If an asset, at the end of its useful economic life, still has a residual value (through for example scrap, resale or reuse), the depreciable asset value should, conceptually, be the cost of acquisition *minus* the residual value.

The residual value (also called salvage value, terminal value, end-of-life salvage value or scrap value) is often difficult to estimate. As a consequence, it is often neglected in the computation of the depreciation expense, i.e., assumed to be zero. IAS 16 explicitly allows this possibility: 'In practice, the residual value of an asset is often insignificant and therefore immaterial in the calculation of the depreciable amount' (§ 53). Another possibility, often found in practice, is to adopt a discretionary standard percentage of the acquisition cost to determine the residual value, or to assume, by convention, the residual value is one currency unit.[6]

2.3 Depreciable amount

IAS 16 (§ 6) defines the 'depreciable amount' as the 'cost of an asset, or other amount substituted for cost in the financial statements, less its residual value':

Depreciable amount = Acquisition cost – Estimated residual value

It is in the interest of the firm to select as high a depreciable amount as possible as the depreciation expense generally reduces taxable profit and thus creates a higher cash flow[7] potentially retained in the firm.

2.4 Useful life (or service life) for accounting purposes

IAS 16 (§ 6) defines the 'useful life' as 'either:

(a) the period of time over which an asset is expected to be available for use by an entity; or

(b) the number of production [output] or similar units expected to be obtained from the asset by an entity.'

> Useful life = Time period over which an asset is available for use
>
> **or**
>
> Maximum expected number of units of output before the asset is declared unproductive

'The useful life of an asset is defined in terms of the asset's expected utility to the entity. The asset management policy of the entity may involve the disposal of assets after a specified time or after consumption of a specified proportion of the future economic benefits embodied in the asset. Therefore, the [accounting] useful life of an asset may be shorter than its [true] economic life. The estimation of the [accounting] useful life of the asset is a matter of judgment based on the experience of the entity with similar assets' (IAS 16: § 57). The estimation of the duration of the useful life of a type of asset can vary from country to country but this is frequently due to businesses adopting depreciation rates consistent with that allowed for taxation purposes and these allowances vary between countries. Table 7.5 presents the most commonly accepted ranges of useful lives for a selection of classes of tangible assets.

Long-haul truck tires are generally not depreciated *prorata temporis* (i.e., on the basis of time elapsed) but on the basis of mileage covered. For a tractor-trailer, the expected mileage for a set of tires varies from country to country, but is generally in the range of 60,000 to 80,000 kilometers (37,282 to 49,710 miles).

In practice, as it is often difficult to forecast the real useful life of a fixed asset, the selected useful life may prove, *ex post* (i.e., after complete use of the asset), to be shorter than the real life of the asset. The principle of prudence (combined with the desire to create as much cash flow as early as possible) may explain the fact that many businesses

Table 7.5 Common useful lives

Tangible assets	Useful life (in years)	Corresponding straight-line annual rate (in %)
Commercial buildings	20 to 50	5 to 2
Industrial buildings	20	5
Equipment	8 to 10	12.5 to 10
Industrial equipment (tooling)	5 to 10	20 to 10
Transportation (trucks, vans, cars)	4 to 5	25 to 20
Furniture	10	10
Computers	3	33.33
Office equipment	5 to 10	20 to 10
Fixtures and fittings	10 to 20	10 to 5

deliberately choose shorter useful lives than they really expect to experience. The choice of a useful life may have a great impact on the timing of future net income and cash flows. Sometimes, however, the reverse may be true and the entity may choose to lengthen its original estimate of the useful life as shown in the example below.

Example EDF Group

At 1 January 2003, EDF Group, the French national electrical utility (production and distribution of electricity), decided to increase the depreciation period of its nuclear installations in France from 30 years to 40. The annual report specified that this change was 'prompted by operating experience, technical surveys, the renewal in the United States of operating licenses for nuclear installations using the same technology and the application filed by the Group with the Nuclear Safety Authority to define the operating conditions of installations after a 30-year term. This change is recognized prospectively and therefore has no impact on equity at 31 December 2002. The extension of the period of useful life of nuclear power stations affected the amortization of nuclear power stations by €853 million. In addition the change in amortization method affected the depreciation of these assets by €(224) million. The extended useful life of nuclear power stations introduced with effect from 1 January 2003 has deferred decommissioning and last core disbursements by ten years'.

(*Source:* Annual report 2003)

2.5 Choice of a depreciation method

Several methods have been developed. According to IAS 16 (§ 60), 'the depreciation method used shall reflect the pattern in which the asset's future economic benefits are expected to be consumed by the entity'. The choice of the appropriate method should therefore be specific to each class of tangible asset and to the understanding, by the management team, of the pattern of consumption.

2.5.1 Classification of methods

Table 7.6 presents a classification of the main depreciation methods in two families: time-based and activity level-based methods.

The methods most commonly used are **the straight-line method** and the **declining balance method**. All methods are first described, and then illustrated through the same example, with data pertaining to a piece of equipment purchased by the Purcell Company on 1 January X1. Purcell Co. closes its books on 31 December each year. The data we will use are described in Table 7.7.

Table 7.6 Main depreciation methods

Time-based depreciation methods	Depreciation methods based on activity level produced or consumed (or service level or level of use)
1. Straight-line	3. Productive output
2. Accelerated (reducing charge) 2.1 Declining (reducing) balance 2.2 Sum-of-the-years'-digits (sum of digits)	4. Service quantity
Depreciation expense will be determined regardless of the level of activity during the period.	*The depreciation expense is the result of the multiplication of a constant depreciation (expense) rate per unit of activity times the number of units of activity consumed or produced during the period.*

Table 7.7 Basic data

Basic data	
Acquisition cost (in 000 CU)	6,000
Estimated residual value (in 000 CU)	1,000
Depreciable amount (in 000 CU)	5,000
Estimated useful life (in years)	5

Expected units of output over the life of the asset	25,000 units	Expected number of machine hours over the life of the asset	50,000 hours
Year 1	8,000	Year 1	12,000
Year 2	7,000	Year 2	12,000
Year 3	6,000	Year 3	12,000
Year 4	3,000	Year 4	8,000
Year 5	1,000	Year 5	6,000

2.5.2 Straight-line method

This method is appropriately used if the decline in service potential relates primarily to the passage of time rather than to the level of activity, or if it can be assumed the asset will be equally productive each year.

Principles The asset is depreciated evenly over its useful life. In other words, the company allocates an equal amount of depreciation expense to each year of the asset's estimated useful life. Periodic depreciation expense is computed as follows:

Annual depreciation expense = (Acquisition cost − Residual value)/Number of years of useful life
= Depreciable amount/Estimated useful life in years
= Depreciable amount × Depreciation rate
(with Depreciation rate = 1/Number of years of useful life of the asset)

The straight-line method is the most frequently used method because of its simplicity of application (and interpretation by financial information users) and because it often reflects accurately the schedule of consumption of the productive potential.

Illustration: Purcell Company Table 7.8 shows an example of depreciation using the straight-line method. The annual depreciation rate = 1/5 years = 20%.

2.5.3 Declining balance method

The objective of any **accelerated** (or **reducing charge**) method is to recognize greater amounts of depreciation in the early years of an asset's life and smaller amounts in the later years. The logic behind using an accelerated method of depreciation is twofold. First, it is a way of recognizing that a large loss of resale value is incurred in the first period of use. For example, the market resale value of a car is, according to published sales records

Table 7.8 Depreciation schedule – Straight-line method

End of year	Depreciable amount	Depreciation rate (%)	Depreciation of the year	Balance: accumulated depreciation	Year-end book value
Date of acquisition					6,000
Year 1	5,000	20	1,000	1,000	5,000
Year 2	5,000	20	1,000	2,000	4,000
Year 3	5,000	20	1,000	3,000	3,000
Year 4	5,000	20	1,000	4,000	2,000
Year 5	5,000	20	1,000	5,000	1,000

Depreciable amount = 6,000 (acquisition cost) – 1,000 (residual value) = 5,000.
Yearly depreciation expense = 5,000 (depreciable amount) × 20% (depreciation rate) = 1,000.
Year-end book value (year 1) = 6,000 (year-end book value of the preceding year) – 1,000 (depreciation of the year).

in many countries, reduced by up to 15 to 20% in the first few months after acquisition – i.e., the market offers a premium for a pristine car. Second, it is also a way of shielding more income from immediate taxation, thus leaving more cash in the firm in the early years to be used, hopefully, for the development of the firm.

However, in keeping with the matching principle, depreciation methods are supposed to be, first and foremost, ways to allocate the cost of the asset to the periods during which the economic benefits are derived from the use of the asset. Accelerated depreciation can be seen as diverging from the strict application of the matching principle.

Accelerated depreciation is conceptually sound if the declining pattern of expense recognition is consistent with the actual contribution the asset makes to the revenue-generating process. Accelerated depreciation methods are logical when an asset is believed to provide superior performance in the early years of its life (i.e., operate with greater efficiency or provide more or higher quality benefits), or if repairs and maintenance costs will burden the last years of the useful life more than the earlier years.

Of the several variations of accelerated depreciation, the most widely used is the declining balance method: it consists in applying a constant rate to a declining base. A second method, known as 'the sum-of-the years'-digits method', consists in applying a declining rate to a constant base. It is, despite its simplicity, rarely applied outside North America. In this method, for example, in the case of an asset with a life expectancy of five years, the sum of the years' digits is 1 + 2 + 3 + 4 + 5 = 15; the first year 5/15 of the depreciable amount would be expensed (depreciated), 4/15 of the depreciable amount the second year, etc. until it would be 1/15 for the fifth year.

Determination of a multiple in the declining balance method   The percentage applied to the base is defined as some multiple of the straight-line rate. The selection of the multiple is highly variable from country to country. In some countries the choice of a multiple is totally open, subject to some unspecified criterion of reasonableness. In the USA, where the choice is essentially open, the most common application of this method is the 'double-declining balance', in which the accelerated percentage is twice the straight-line rate. By way of contrast, in some countries, such as France, the tax authorities have defined, for each class of assets, a standardized multiple.

Most accelerated methods (with the notable exception of the sum-of-the-years'-digits method) have to switch, at some point in time, to a straight-line method, so as to arrive at a book value equal to the residual value at the end of the useful life. In order to avoid

Table 7.9 Examples of multiples used for accelerated depreciation

Country	Determination of the multiple M (or rate of depreciation) Where N = asset's useful life, expressed in years
France	M = 1.25, if N = 3 or 4 years M = 1.75, if N = 5 or 6 years M = 2.25, if N > 6 years.
Germany	Limitation of application of the accelerated rate to 30% of the depreciable amount.
UK	Depreciation rate = $1 - (Residual\ value/Cost\ of\ acquisition)^{1/N}$ If the residual value is 0, assume a residual value of 1.[8]
USA	M = 2 (common practice). However, 1.5 is also used on occasion.

this switching, a method, mainly used in the UK, called 'fixed percentage of book value method' or 'fixed percentage of declining balance method' has been devised that selects a rate that depreciates the asset exactly down to the residual value. The formula for this method is shown in Table 7.9 along with some illustrations of practice in other countries.

Application to the declining book value   This fixed percentage is applied to the book value of the asset, giving a depreciation figure that declines throughout the life of the asset.

> Declining balance (DB) depreciation expense for a period = (DB rate) × (net book value at beginning of period)
> **or**
> DB depreciation expense = (DB rate) × (Depreciable cost minus accumulated depreciation)

Table 7.10 provides an illustration of the method.

How to end the depreciation process   If applied consistently, the mathematics of the declining balance method are such that the book value would never be equal to the residual value. If the method was applied without adjustments, not only would the asset never be fully depreciated but also its net book value would eventually end up below the residual value. It is, therefore, important to decide beforehand how to terminate the depreciation to end up exactly at the level of the residual value.

In this context, several possibilities exist. They consist in either:

- Method 1: switching to a straight-line method (over the remaining useful life) at the point where the straight-line rate (calculated over the remaining useful life) exceeds or equals the declining balance rate selected (illustrated in Table 7.10).
- Method 2: switching to straight-line (over the remaining useful life) at the midpoint of the life of the asset (illustrated in Table 7.11).
- Method 3: defining the depreciation expense as the difference between the preceding book value and the residual value in the year in which the accelerated depreciation expense would bring the book value to be lower than the residual value (illustrated in Table 7.12).

Table 7.10 Method 1: Double-declining balance (DDB) with reversal to straight-line when rate of straight-line (SL) over remaining life exceeds or equals that of DDB

End of year	Depreciable basis	Depreciation expense of the year	Balance: accumulated depreciation	Year-end book value
Date of acquisition				6,000
Year 1	6,000	2,400	2,400	3,600
Year 2	3,600	1,440	3,840	2,160
Year 3	2,160	864	4,704	1,296
Year 4	1,296	148	4,852	1,148
Year 5	1,296	148	5,000	1,000

Depreciable amount = 6,000 (initial book value). Depreciation expense of year 1 = 6,000 (depreciable amount) × 40% (DDB rate) = 2,400. Depreciation expense of year 2 = 3,600 (ending book value of the preceding year) × DDB rate = 1,440. In year 4, the DDB approach would lead to a lower residual value than agreed upon [1,296 − (1,296 × 40%)] = [1,296 − 518] = 778. Since this is less than 1,000, there is a reversal to straight-line over the remaining useful life (two years at 50%). Note that we could also have said the switch to SL was due to the straight-line rate over the remaining useful life, i.e., 50% exceeding the DDB rate i.e., 40%. Thus, since we switch to straight-line for the remaining two years, the annual depreciation expense for each of these years is 148 = [1,296 (the depreciable basis) − 1,000 (residual value)]/2.

The 'fixed percentage of book value method' used mainly in the UK for computing the depreciation rate (see Table 7.9) avoids the entire problem of how to reach the residual value.

In choosing a method, the most important thing is to be rational and systematic. These conditions are met if the method for handling the end of depreciation is selected at the time of acquisition and applied to all assets of one homogeneous category.

Tables 7.10, 7.11 and 7.12 illustrate the three possible methods as applied to the Purcell Company example. If we choose a multiple equal to 2, we have: double-declining balance (DDB) rate = straight-line (SL) rate × 2 = 20% × 2 = 40%.

Method 2, although simple, does not give the entity the full benefit of the cash flow impact of the accelerated depreciation and is thus less frequently used than method 1.

Method 3, is not recommended because it leads to the violation of the agreed upon expected depreciable (useful) life of five years.

Table 7.11 Method 2: Declining balance with switch to straight-line in mid-life

End of year	Depreciable basis	Depreciation expense of the year	Balance: accumulated depreciation	Year-end book value
Date of acquisition				6,000
Year 1	6,000	2,400	2,400	3,600
Year 2	3,600	1,440	3,840	2,160
Year 3	1,160	387	4,227	1,773
Year 4	1,160	387	4,614	1,386
Year 5	1,160	386	5,000	1,000

Switch to straight-line at the midpoint of the life of the asset (2.5 years is conventionally translated as third year). Depreciable basis at the time of the switch to straight-line = 2,160 (book value at the end of year 2) − 1,000 (residual value) = 1,160. Depreciation expense for years 3, 4 and 5 = 1,160 (the depreciable basis)/3 = 387 (or 386, due to rounding).

Table 7.12 Method 3: Double-declining balance with switch to SL as soon as DDB would lead to a book value lower than the residual value

End of year	Depreciable basis	Depreciation expense of the year	Balance: accumulated depreciation	Year-end book value
Date of acquisition				6,000
Year 1	6,000	2,400	2,400	3,600
Year 2	3,600	1,440	3,840	2,160
Year 3	2,160	864	4,704	1,296
Year 4	1,296	296	5,000	1,000
Year 5	0	0	5,000	1,000

In year 4, the depreciation expense would bring the book value to be lower than the residual value [(1,296 – (1,296 × 40%)] = [1,296 – 518] = 778 which is lower than 1,000. Therefore the depreciation expense is, at this point, set as the difference between the preceding book value and the residual value, i.e., 1,296 – 1,000 = 296. The result is that there is no depreciation in year 5, in violation of the hypothesis of a 5 year useful life.

2.5.4 Sum-of-the-years'-digits method (sum of the digits method)

This method belongs to the category of accelerated (reducing charge) methods of depreciation. Tax authorities rarely allow it and its use in reporting to shareholders is declining. It is presented in Appendix 7.2.

2.5.5 Productive-output method (units-of-output method)

The use of this method, matching the depreciation schedule with the 'consumption' of the potential of economic benefits the asset can provide, is appropriate only if the asset's output is discretely and distinctly measurable and if the useful life of the asset is better expressed in terms of maximum number of units of output than in terms of time periods.

Principle   The depreciation schedule matches the timing of the output of the asset expressed in units of products or services such as miles or kilometers driven, units shipped, or tons produced. A depreciation cost per unit of output is calculated by dividing the depreciable amount by the total potential number of units of output expected of that asset over its useful life. This depreciation rate per unit is then applied to the actual output for the period to determine the depreciation expense of the period.

The amount of depreciation expense cannot be determined in advance for any given period, because it is dependent on the level of output during the period.

$$\text{Depreciation expense} = \frac{\text{Depreciable amount}}{\text{Life expressed in units of output}} \times \text{Units of output for the period}$$
$$= \text{Depreciation rate per unit} \times \text{Units of output for the period}$$

This method is easy to apply when the required information is readily available as, for example, for a bottling machine whose quantity of output (number of bottles filled and capped) would automatically be recorded.

One of the advantages of this method is that it allows the enterprise to record the depreciation expense in proportion to the intensity of use of the asset. It is clear that a machine that produces 48,000 containers of yogurt per hour during one 8-hour shift for 5 days a week will not wear out as quickly as it would if it were used 20 hours a day for 6½ days a week (5 shifts).

However, the determination of the rated lifetime output is not completely objective: the difficulty of choosing the useful economic life is compounded with that of defining the maximum output over the lifetime of the machine and for each period (generally estimated by the manufacturer or production engineers). For example, the yogurt-packaging machine just mentioned was rated by its manufacturer at 36,000 containers per hour; but the dairy's maintenance and production engineers were able to increase the rated output to 48,000 containers per hour after only three months of operation without any noticeable increased wear and tear on the machine. Which is the appropriate figure in determining the key element of the denominator number (the lifetime output): 36,000 or 48,000?

Another major source of ambiguity concerning the number of units constituting the total life potential of the machine comes from the fact that there is no guarantee the market will absorb the whole output potential over the expected useful life of the machine. If the cumulated market demand does not materialize and does not match the expected output, the asset may be completely obsolete much before it is fully depreciated. This method thus requires that the accountant use, as the denominator, only the total cumulated output that will *reasonably* be absorbed by the market.

The productivity of many plant assets, such as buildings and fixtures, however, cannot be measured in terms of a unit of output. For such classes of assets, this method of depreciation is inappropriate.

Illustration: Purcell Company   Table 7.13 offers an illustration of this method for the Purcell Company.

2.5.6 Service-quantity method

Principle   While the mechanics of applying the service quantity (or unit depreciation) method are similar to those of the productive-output method, the concepts underlying the methods are somewhat different. Under the service-quantity method, the contribution to operations is stated in terms of productive-output factors rather than physical sellable output of the production process. This method is commonly employed in air or ground transportation businesses. Aircraft are depreciated on the basis of flying hours (but the landing gear should logically be depreciated on the basis of the number of landings), locomotives or trucks are depreciated on the basis of kilometers (or miles) driven.

Table 7.13 Depreciation schedule – productive-output method

End of year	Annual output in units	Depreciation rate per unit	Annual depreciation expense	Balance: accumulated depreciation	Year-end book value
Date of acquisition					6,000
Year 1	8,000	0.20	1,600	1,600	4,400
Year 2	7,000	0.20	1,400	3,000	3,000
Year 3	6,000	0.20	1,200	4,200	1,800
Year 4	3,000	0.20	600	4,800	1,200
Year 5	1,000	0.20	200	5,000	1,000

Depreciable amount: 5,000 CU (cost of acquisition of 6,000 minus the residual value of 1,000). The expected normal number of units of output the asset can create, and which are expected to be sold, has been estimated at 25,000 units. The estimated depreciation rate per unit of output is therefore 0.20 CU (5,000/25,000 = 0.20). Depreciation of year 1 = 8,000 (units produced and sold) × 0.20 (depreciation rate per unit) = 1,600 CU.

The same issue arises as was found in the case of the productive-output method, namely the definition of the accumulated number of units of service the equipment can handle. A truck may be rated for a million miles for use over 'normal roads under normal driving conditions' but the actual mileage that will be obtained from the same truck may vary greatly with the load factor and the road conditions as well as with the driving style and intensity of use. For example, the mileage wear and tear cannot be equivalent between a truck driven over dirt roads in the Sahel and one driven over modern freeways in the Netherlands or over alpine roads in Switzerland or Austria. The actual number of useful productive units is a strategic choice: the same aircraft can produce a different number of flight hours depending on whether it is used by a low-cost carrier or used on a feeder line by a legacy airline using the hub and spoke system in a long-haul route system.

The depreciation rate per unit of productive service is determined as follows:

$$\text{Depreciation expense} = \frac{\text{Depreciable amount}}{\text{Total quantity of productive service}} \times \text{Productive service for the period}$$

$$= \text{Depreciation cost per unit of service} \times \text{Units of output for the period}$$

Illustration: Purcell Company Table 7.14 provides an illustration using the Purcell Co. data.

2.5.7 Limitations of the methods based on activity level

The unit depreciation methods are not widely used outside of small niches, probably for two major reasons:

■ These methods produce schedules of depreciation for the first years of the asset that are often not very different from those that would be obtained through the use of either the straight-line or accelerated depreciation methods.

■ As mentioned in the text, the ambiguity linked to the definition of the reference figures can be rather large and the data-collection costs might prove to be high.

2.6 Depreciation schedule

The depreciation schedule is the pre-established list of depreciation amounts for each year of an asset's useful life. Such a schedule cannot, as mentioned above, be prepared for

Table 7.14 Depreciation schedule – service-quantity method

End of year	Life-time number of units of service	Depreciation rate per unit of service	Annual depreciation expense	Balance: accumulated depreciation	Year-end book value
Date of acquisition					6,000
Year 1	12,000	0.10	1,200	1,200	4,800
Year 2	12,000	0.10	1,200	2,400	3,600
Year 3	12,000	0.10	1,200	3,600	2,400
Year 4	8,000	0.10	800	4,400	1,600
Year 5	6,000	0.10	600	5,000	1,000

Depreciable amount: 5,000 CU (cost of acquisition of 6,000 minus the residual value of 1,000). Estimated life-time number of units of service: 50,000 units of service. Estimated cost per unit of service = 0.10 (5,000/50,000). Depreciation expense for year 1 = 12,000 (number of units of service) × 0.10 (depreciation cost per unit of service) = 1,200.

either of the depreciation methods based on activity level. The elaboration of a depreciation schedule is based on the choice of depreciation method as illustrated in Tables 7.8, 7.10, 7.11, 7.12, 7.13 and 7.14.

2.7 Book value (also called 'net book value' or 'carrying amount')

The book value is the difference between the asset's cost (cost of acquisition) and the balance of its accumulated depreciation. After the book value has reached the residual value (which can be equal to zero), the asset might not be taken out of service if it is still reliable and usefully productive. It will be reported (carried) in the balance sheet at the residual value or for a book value of zero, so that the asset remains identified as belonging to the productive potential of the firm.

2.8 Recording the depreciation expense

2.8.1 Principle

In countries where the income statement is organized by nature of expenses (see this concept in Chapters 2 and 5), depreciation is recorded as shown in Figure 7.3 below.

The 'accumulated depreciation' is a reduction of assets and is called a 'contra-asset' account, i.e., is displayed on the assets side of the balance sheet, with a negative sign or by placing the amount in parentheses.

In countries where the income statement is presented by function (see this concept in Chapters 2 and 5), the depreciation expense on manufacturing assets is included in the cost of the goods manufactured[9] at the stage of the manufacturing process when that asset is used. The depreciation expense is recorded as an increase of the 'work in progress' account of that stage. The depreciation expense will flow to the cost of goods sold account (and thus be matched in due course against revenue) after having transited through the various levels of inventories. The depreciation expense ends up, therefore, being potentially distributed over the cost of goods sold and the various inventories (if there has been an increase of the inventory levels). For non-manufacturing equipment (such as a computer used in the accounting department), the depreciation expense is a 'period cost' that does not flow through inventory accounts, and the accounting entries are similar to the ones described for countries using a by-nature income statement structure.

2.8.2 Illustration: Purcell Company

Figure 7.3 illustrates the accounting entries for the recording of depreciation (year 1 only), using the straight-line method.

Figure 7.3 Recording the depreciation expense

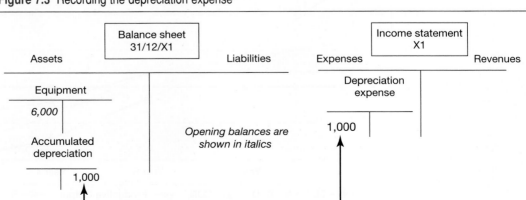

Table 7.15 Summary of the different methods

Year	Straight-line (see Table 7.8)		Sum-of-years' digits (see Appendix 7.2)		Double-declining balance (see Table 7.10)		Productive-output (see Table 7.13)		Service-quantity (see Table 7.14)	
	Depr. expense	Net book value	Depr. expense	Net book value	Depr. expense	Net book value	Depr. expense	Net book value	Depr. expense	Net book value
At acquisition		6,000		6,000		6,000		6,000		6,000
Year 1	1,000	5,000	1,667	4,333	2,400	3,600	1,600	4,400	1,200	4,800
Year 2	1,000	4,000	1,333	3,000	1,440	2,160	1,400	3,000	1,200	3,600
Year 3	1,000	3,000	1,000	2,000	864	1,296	1,200	1,800	1,200	2,400
Year 4	1,000	2,000	667	1,333	148	1,148	600	1,200	800	1,600
Year 5	1,000	1,000	333	1,000	148	1,000	200	1,000	600	1,000

2.9 Summary of the income statement impact of the different methods

Table 7.15 summarizes, in the illustrative case of the Purcell Company, the depreciation expense and the closing book value of the same asset under the five main depreciation methods described above (including Appendix 7.2).

Figure 7.4 graphically illustrates evolution of the annual depreciation expense over time under each of the alternative depreciation methods and Figure 7.5 graphically illustrates the resulting net book value at each year-end.

In practice, tangible assets are rarely purchased or sold on the first day of the accounting period. The issues which arise for a purchase or sale during the year are dealt with in Appendix 7.3.

Figure 7.4 Annual depreciation expense

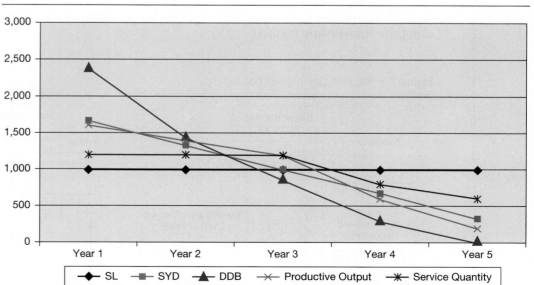

Figure 7.5 Closing net book value

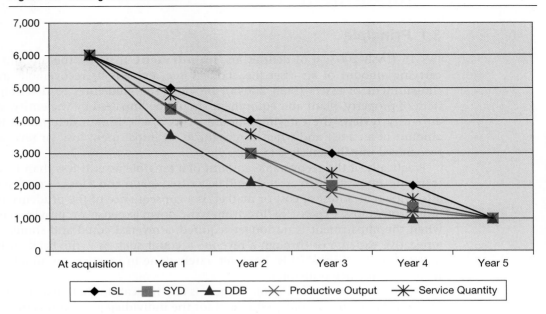

2.10 Reporting depreciation policies

Real-life example Weyerhaeuser

(USA – US GAAP – Source: Annual report 2008 – International forest products company)

Excerpts from the notes.

Property and Equipment. The company's property accounts are maintained on an individual asset basis. Improvements to and replacements of major units of property are capitalized. Maintenance, repairs and minor replacements are expensed. Depreciation is calculated using a straight-line method at rates based on estimated service lives. Logging railroads and truck roads are generally amortized – as timber is harvested – at rates based on the volume of timber estimated to be removed. Cost and accumulated depreciation of property sold or retired are removed from the accounts and the gain or loss is included in earnings.

Timber and Timberlands. Timber and timberlands are carried at cost less depletion charged to disposals. Depletion refers to the carrying value of timber that is harvested, lost as a result of casualty, or sold. Key activities affecting how timber and timberlands are accounted for include reforestation, depletion and forest management in Canada.

Reforestation. Generally, all initial site preparation and planting costs are capitalized as reforestation. Reforestation is transferred to a merchantable timber classification when the timber is considered harvestable. That generally occurs after 15 years in the South and 30 years in the West. Generally, costs are expensed after the first planting as they are incurred over the period of expected benefit. These costs are considered to be maintenance of the forest and include fertilization, vegetation and insect control, pruning and precommercial trimming, property taxes and interest. Accounting practices for these costs do not change when timber becomes merchantable and harvesting starts.

Depletion. To determine depletion rates, the net carrying value of timber is divided by the related volume of timber estimated to be available over the growth cycle. To determine the growth cycle volume of timber, regulatory and environmental constraints, management strategies, inventory data improvements, growth rate revisions and recalibrations and known dispositions and inoperable acres are considered. The cost of timber harvested is included in the carrying values of raw materials and product inventories. As these inventories are sold to third parties, they are included in the cost of products sold.

3 Impairment

3.1 Principle

IAS 16 (IASB 2003: § 6) defines an '**impairment loss**' as 'the amount by which the carrying amount of an asset [i.e., book value] exceeds its recoverable amount'. IAS 36 (Impairment of assets [IASB 2004a]) provides the guidelines to determine whether an item of property, plant and equipment should be impaired by the entity. It explains how an entity reviews the carrying amount of its assets, how it determines the recoverable amount of an asset and when it recognizes an impairment loss, or reverses a previously recognized impairment loss (§ 63).

Practically, if the recoverable amount of a tangible asset is less than its net book value (carrying amount), such asset should be written down and a loss recognized (this practice, also known as 'lower of cost or market' is a consequence of the prudence principle) as an 'impairment loss' expense or 'loss from write-down expense' or 'provision expense'. If and when the impairment is no longer required, a reversal could and should be recorded as a negative expense or through a revenue account such as 'write-back on impairment' or 'reversal of provisions' (it is, however, rarely done in practice, essentially to keep in line with the prudence principle).

As indicated by IAS 36 (§ 66), 'if there is any indication that an asset may be impaired, recoverable amount shall be estimated for the individual asset. If it is not possible to estimate the recoverable amount of the individual asset, an entity shall determine the recoverable amount of the cash-generating unit to which the asset belongs'. A cash-generating unit is defined by the same standard (§ 6) as 'the smallest identifiable group of assets that generates cash inflows that are largely independent of the cash inflows from other assets or groups of assets'.

Practice and regulation regarding impairment have varied over time and between countries in the world. Apart from IAS 36 (IASB 2004a), rules for impairment exist in many countries, such as the USA (SFAS 144, Accounting for the Impairment or Disposal of Long-Lived Assets) and the UK (FRS 11, Impairment of Fixed Assets and Goodwill).

The topic of impairment may become increasingly relevant, with the change of rules relating to impairment of intangibles (see Chapters 8 and 13). In practice, tests for impairment are very difficult to design and implement reliably.

Real-life example France Telecom

(France – IFRS – Source: Annual report 2008 – Telecommunications)

Impairment of non-current assets other than goodwill and trademarks (note 2.13): In the case of a decline in the recoverable amount of an item of property, plant and equipment (…) to below its net book value, due to events or circumstances occurring during the period (such as obsolescence, physical damage, significant changes to the manner in which the asset is used, worse than expected economic performance, a drop in revenues or other external indicators) an impairment loss is recognized. The recoverable amount of an asset is the higher of its fair value less costs to sell and its value in use, assessed by the discounted cash flows method, based on management's best estimate of the set of economic conditions. The impairment loss recognized is equal to the difference between the net book value and the recoverable amount. Given the nature of its assets and activities, most of France Telecom's individual assets do not generate independent cash flows that are independent of those from cash-generating units (CGU). The recoverable amount is then determined at the level of the CGU to which the asset belongs, except where the fair value less costs to sell of the individual asset is higher than its book value; or the value in use of the asset can be estimated as being close to its fair value less costs to sell, where fair value can be reliably determined.

Excerpts from the consolidated income statement		
Amounts in € millions	Period ended 31 December 2008	Period ended 31 December 2007
Revenues	**53,488**	**52,959**
(...)		
Depreciation and amortization	(7,776)	(8,111)
Impairment of goodwill	(271)	(26)
Impairment of non-current assets	(9)	(107)
(...)		
Operating income	**10,272**	**10,799**

4 Assets constructed by and for the enterprise (internally generated assets)

Businesses often use their own resources to build an asset for their own use. These can be machinery, buildings, or fixtures. The issue of valuation of such assets is especially problematic since the 'at arm's length' or market relation that exists in an acquisition from a third party does not exist and therefore cannot remove any and all ambiguity and arbitrariness in the valuation of the asset. We will approach this valuation issue in three steps:

1. Definition of the term 'asset constructed by and for the enterprise'
2. Valuation of such asset (cost measurement)
3. Recording of such asset in the accounting system.

4.1 Definition – Principle

In certain circumstances, companies construct or build their own tangible assets instead of acquiring them from other businesses. This practice happens frequently in certain industrial sectors such as construction, automotive, railroad, utilities (building a power plant or a water treatment facility or laying the network of pipes for gas distribution), etc. For instance, when Bouygues Company, a French-based global construction, civil engineering and telecommunication firm, built their showcase headquarters near Paris, they did it with their own human and physical resources. It would not have made sense to ask a competitor to develop such a building that was meant to showcase all the best facets of Bouygues' *savoir-faire*. Similarly, a machine tool manufacturer might develop its own machines to make the machine tools it sells, or an automotive manufacturer might make the dies for its body shop or an airplane manufacturer might create a dedicated lift to hoist the tail reactor (for power and air conditioning) in place on a commercial jet. Assets built by and for the firm are extremely common occurrences in many businesses.

4.2 Valuation

Tangible assets, which are created or developed internally, must be valued at their production cost. The production cost of an object is generally broken down into several components, which can be traced to the object with varying degrees of accuracy:

- Cost of raw materials and components.
- Cost of the labor that was directly involved in the creation of the object (whether it is in the research and development phase or the manufacturing and testing phase).

- Overhead (or indirect) costs that include supplies, energy and fluids, supervisory labor, and all the costs of the facilities and support functions that permitted the creation of the object.
- Financial costs, which can be very significant when the asset is extremely costly and the construction process spans a long period, as is the case, for example, in the building of a power plant or the construction of a large office building.

4.2.1 Overhead

While there are generally few problems arising from the tracing of direct materials and components or direct labor cost to the object, allocation of overhead costs (support costs) is a difficult issue (see Appendix 7.4) and is a key subject of Managerial Accounting textbooks.

4.2.2 Financing costs: Interest costs (or borrowing costs)

While the asset is being constructed, resources are consumed but no revenue is generated. The revenue will be generated when the asset will be operational and for the duration of its useful life. The firm must, therefore, finance the cost of the resources consumed, either out of its own funds (possibly losing an opportunity to earn revenue) or by borrowing funds to cover the need. There is, therefore, little doubt that there is a causal link between the construction and the financing costs, but it is not so clear how much of it should be attached to the cost of the asset.

IAS 23 (IASB 1993, amended 2007: § 5) defines '**borrowing costs**' as 'interest and other costs that an entity incurs in connection with the borrowing of funds'. The standard states (§ 1) that 'borrowing costs that are directly attributable to the acquisition, construction or production of a qualifying asset form part of the cost of that asset. Other borrowing costs are recognized as an expense'. Before the modification of IAS 23 in 2007, the inclusion of borrowing costs in the cost of an asset, referred to as the '**capitalization**' of borrowing/ interest costs' was only an option. A qualifying asset is 'an asset that necessarily takes a substantial period of time to get ready for its intended use or sale' (IAS 23: § 5).

An example of computation of capitalized interest costs is provided in Appendix 7.5. Capitalized interest may represent a very large share of the asset cost and, thus, a big stake in the determination of income.

Real-life example Bayer

(Germany – IFRS Source: Annual report 2008 – Biotechnology)

If the construction phase of property, plant or equipment extends over a long period, the interest incurred on borrowed capital up to the date of completion is capitalized as part of the cost of acquisition or construction in accordance with IAS 23 (Borrowing costs). (...) In 2008, borrowing costs of €29 million (2007: €9 million) were capitalized as components of the cost of acquisition and construction of qualifying assets, applying an average financing cost factor of 6.2% (2007: 5%).

4.3 Recording of the transactions

This section uses the data from the example of a piece of machinery constructed by the Purcell Company for its own use. The production cost includes the following cost items (all are assumed to be paid cash, for simplicity sake):

- materials and components (already in inventory): 30 CU;
- labor (personnel expense): 55 CU;

■ overhead (various expenses, including depreciation of productive equipment used): 15 CU.

The new machine will be depreciated over five years.

One way of recording the capitalization of the costs incurred in the construction is presented in Figure 7.6.

Figure 7.6 Accounting for tangible assets constructed by and for Purcell Company

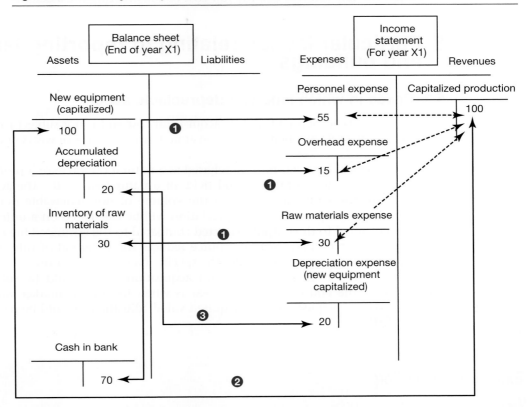

Across countries, several alternative solutions are possible at the time of capitalization. The three most common approaches are described below:

1. To record, in the income statement, an increase in the costs or expenses incurred for the capitalized asset (step ❶), and, to neutralize the income effect of such an entry, increase a revenue account (production capitalized), with a counterpart for that same amount to the balance sheet, thus creating the capitalized asset (step ❷). This is the solution illustrated in Figure 7.6.

2. To record, in the income statement, an increase in the costs or expenses incurred for the capitalized asset (step ❶) and decrease the same accounts, thus creating the capitalized asset (second step). This solution is not illustrated in Figure 7.6.

3. To open a 'project account' (directly in the balance sheet) in which all expenses pertaining to the new asset being developed are transferred, thus creating directly, by accretion, the value of the asset without having to go through the income statement. This solution is very simple, but does not give the same visibility for shareholders to see (through the income statement) what their business is really doing with its resources. (This solution is not illustrated here).

In all three cases, regardless of the capitalization process adopted, depreciation will have to be recognized for the year. Here, assuming a depreciation of the new equipment over five years (100/5 = 20 if we choose straight-line) the annual depreciation expense of the asset is recognized through step ❸.

After capitalization, the impact of the new machine on income for the first year is limited to the depreciation expense, i.e., 100/5= 20. If the machine built in-house had not been capitalized and considered to be an asset, the impact on the first year income would have been the full 100 CU, i.e., the full cost of constructing the asset.

5 Particular issues relating to reporting land and buildings

5.1 Cases in which land is a depreciable asset

Normally, land is accounted for at its acquisition cost and is not subject to any depreciation, since it theoretically neither gets consumed through use, nor wears out, nor becomes obsolete.

However, where land has been purchased as a natural resource for a productive potential – such as a quarry, a mine, an oil field, or a natural gas well – the acquisition cost relates not to the land surface but to the volume of non-renewable riches which are hidden beneath it. In such cases, depreciation will be calculated on a unit consumption basis (proportional to the output extracted compared to the estimated life capacity of the deposit) since exploitation of the resource reduces the potential of future exploitation. This depreciation is recognized under the specific name of 'depletion'.

Another situation in which the land acquisition costs would be subject to value adjustment at the end of a financial year is when its current market value has fallen below the cost of acquisition. The required value adjustment would be recognized as an 'impairment'.

Example Britten Corp.

Britten Corp. purchased, unconditionally, a well-located piece of suburban farmland for 850,000 CU (much higher than the price of land for farming but much lower than the price of constructible land) in the anticipation that it could be re-zoned and developed as a shopping center. However, three years later the company formally learns from its lawyer that, despite her efforts to get the zoning regulations changed, there will be no possibility of obtaining a building permit. As a consequence the market value of the land is not more than 305,000 CU (farmland price). In this case the company should take an impairment loss expense of 545,000 CU in the income statement of the year.

5.2 Land and building

Because they cannot be depreciated, land assets must always be reported separately from buildings which are constructed on them. Even if a purchase contract provides only one global acquisition cost for a property comprising land and buildings, the firm acquiring the property has to obtain the necessary information to split that amount between two separate accounts. Such a correction is necessary not only to provide correct information on the assets (the market value of land and of constructed buildings do not evolve in parallel), but also because buildings and constructions are, unlike land, depreciable assets.

Buildings shown in the tangible asset category on the balance sheet include only those that are held as long-term investments, thus excluding short-term or speculative holdings.

This means that, in principle, all industrial, commercial and administrative buildings should give rise to the recognition of an annual depreciation expense throughout their expected useful life.

During a very inflationary period, depreciation of buildings might not be coherent with truthful reporting because the residual value of the asset might increase to the point of exceeding the acquisition cost or the book value. Since the depreciable base is the difference between the cost of acquisition and the residual value, there might not be anything to depreciate in such a context. Such a situation is very rare in developed economies but was not uncommon in the 1980s in countries with high inflation rates such as Brazil or Argentina, and would require, in any case, full disclosure in a note to the financial statements.

6 Costs subsequent to acquisition

The way to handle costs subsequent to acquisition is based on the rule, mentioned earlier, about the distinction between capital and revenue expenditure (see section 1), that 'the cost of an item of property, plant and equipment shall be recognized as an asset if, and only if: (a) it is probable that future economic benefits associated with the item will flow to the entity; and (b) the cost of the item can be measured reliably' (IAS 16: § 7). The text of IAS 16 refers constantly to this rule to distinguish, among costs incurred after acquisition, between those that must be capitalized and those that should be expensed (IAS 16: §§ 12-14).

Therefore, costs incurred after the acquisition of an asset, such as additions, improvements, or replacements, are added to the asset's depreciable cost base if they provide future service potential, extend the useful life of the asset, or increase either the quantity or quality of service rendered by the asset. Otherwise, they are expensed immediately.

Examples of improvements that result in increased future economic benefits are the following:

■ Modification of an asset to extend its useful life, or increase its productive capacity.

■ Upgrading machine parts to achieve a substantial improvement in the quality of output.

■ Adoption of new production processes enabling a substantial reduction in previously assessed operating costs.

■ Relining of a blast furnace required after a specified number of hours of use, or replacement of aircraft interiors such as seats and galleys (example given in IAS 16: § 13).

However, 'an entity does not recognize in the carrying amount of an item of property, plant and equipment the costs of the day-to-day servicing of the item' (IAS 16: § 12). An expenditure on repairs or maintenance of a tangible asset is made only to maintain or restore the stream of future economic benefits. As such, it is usually recognized as an expense when incurred. For example, the cost of servicing or repairing plant and equipment is usually an expense since it maintains, rather than increases, the originally assessed standard of performance.

The developments (in section 1) relating to the difference between an asset and an expense can be applied to the concept of 'subsequent expenditure', especially in the case of small expenditures.

7 Disposal of long-term assets

Tangible assets can be (and often are) disposed of at any time during their useful life and for many different reasons and in a variety of ways. Examples of disposal include outright sale, abandonment and loss (flood, fire, natural disaster, etc.).

We will mainly focus on the outright sale of tangible assets. The other two categories of disposal will be dealt with later.

7.1 Recording of the sale of an asset

When long-term assets are sold before their useful lives are completed, the difference between the book value and the disposition proceeds (sales proceeds or selling price) is treated as a gain or a loss.

Some countries (e.g., the USA) record the net impact from the sale in a single line (gain or loss on sale of asset, depending on the nature of this difference) directly in the income statement. Other countries record separately in the income statement the selling price as revenue and the cancellation of the net book value as an expense (e.g., France), or open an asset disposal account (reported in the notes), the balance of which is transferred to the income statement account (e.g., the UK). Of course, the reported impact on net income is the same, whichever method is chosen. Depreciation must be recorded for the period of time between the date of the last depreciation entry and the date of sale. A detailed illustration of the recording of a sale of a fixed asset is given in Appendix 7.6 and the treatment of the removal of a fully depreciated tangible asset from the book is provided in Appendix 7.7.

We provide below an example which assumes that the equipment of the Purcell Company is sold on 31 December X4 for a sale price of 2,500. This asset was depreciated following the straight-line method. As the sale takes place on 31 December, we assume that the depreciation expense of year four has already been recorded. Had the sale taken place at another date not corresponding to the end of the fiscal period, a partial year depreciation would have had to be recorded first. Figure 7.7 describes the recording of a sale of a fixed asset using one entry.

7.2 Classification in the income statement

Gains and losses from the sale of long-term assets need to be reported to shareholders. The choice of where in the income statement to report these items (exceptional, extraordinary, or ordinary income) differs from country to country. In the USA, gains and losses from

Figure 7.7 Accounting for the sale of fixed assets (one entry – gain or loss recorded in one account) (country example: USA)

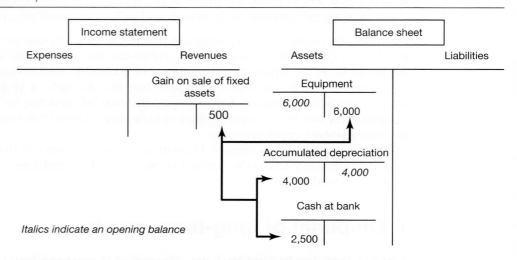

- Accumulated depreciation: see depreciation schedule (straight-line method at end of year 4).
- Book value = 6,000 (acquisition cost) – 4,000 (accumulated depreciation) = 2,000
- Gain on sale = 2,500 (selling price) – 2,000 (book value) = 500

asset sales do not satisfy the criteria for the 'extraordinary item' treatment (see Chapter 6). They are included in the income statement 'above the line', i.e., they are considered to be part of the normal business of the firm. In continental Europe, the book value of fixed assets sold and the sales price are often classified as 'exceptional items'. In the UK, profits and losses on disposals (sales) of fixed assets must be disclosed after the operating profit as an 'exceptional item'.

8 Financial aspects of tangible assets

8.1 Depreciation and cash flow

Depreciation expenses (and impairment losses) are non-cash expenses. This means that they have no direct impact on the cash balance, but an indirect one arising from the income tax effect of expenses. This will be illustrated through the example of the Lloyd Webber Company.

Assume that the company realized sales (all for cash) for 200 CU and the corresponding cash operating expenses (materials, labor and overhead excluding depreciation) amounted to 120 CU. In addition, since Lloyd Webber Co. used its tangible assets (which amounted to 100 CU and had a useful economic life of five years), depreciation expense (a component of the class of costs called 'overhead') is another expense to be matched with the revenue. If Lloyd Webber Co. uses the straight-line method, the depreciation expense for the first year amounts to 20 CU, while if it uses the double-declining balance depreciation method, the first year depreciation expense amounts to 40 CU. In both cases we assume the income tax rate to be 40%. Table 7.16 presents the income statement and the operating cash flow (extracted from the statement of cash flows – see Chapters 3 and 14).

Table 7.16 illustrates some important points:

■ The choice of method of depreciation impacts both income before tax and income after tax.

■ Cash flow (either before or after tax) from operating activities is not influenced by depreciation expense because its calculation does not include the depreciation expense, which is a non-cash expense since the cash impact (immediate or delayed through financing) took place when the asset was first acquired.

■ The higher the depreciation expense in one year, other things being equal otherwise, the larger the net after-tax cash flow. This is due to the different income tax shield provided by each method. In reality, this is, of course, the case only where tax regulation allows the use of accelerated depreciation methods.

8.2 Reporting movements in tangible assets

In most countries, the notes to financial statements must include two separate statements, one reporting the **movements** in the gross value of tangible assets and the other with the changes in accumulated depreciation (with the exception of the USA and Canada where both are merged). One example of such a statement is provided in Table 7.17.

According to IAS 16 (§ 73), 'the financial statements shall disclose, for each class of property, plant and equipment:

  (a) the measurement bases used for determining the gross carrying amount;

  (b) the depreciation methods used;

  (c) the useful lives or the depreciation rates used;

  (d) the gross carrying amount and the accumulated depreciation (aggregated with accumulated impairment losses) at the beginning and end of the period; and

Table 7.16 Lloyd Webber Co. Depreciation and cash flow

	Straight-line depreciation	Double-declining balance depreciation
Income statement		
Sales	200	200
Cash operating expenses	(120)	(120)
Earnings before interest, taxes, depreciation and amortization (EBITDA)	80	80
Depreciation expense	(20)	(40)
Income before interest and income tax (EBIT)	60	40
Income tax expense (40%)	(24)	(16)
Net income after tax	36	24
Statement of cash flows		
Cash received from customers	200	200
Cash paid for operating expenses	(120)	(120)
Cash flow before tax from operating activities	**80**	**80**
Cash paid for income tax	(24)	(16)
Cash flow after tax provided from operating activities	56	64
Alternative presentation of the statement of cash flows		
	Net income after tax	36	24
Add back	Depreciation expense (a non-cash expense already deducted)	20	40
Equals	Cash flow (after tax) from operating activities	56	64
Add back	Cash paid for income tax (already paid)	24	16
Equals	Cash flow (before tax) from operating activities	**80**	**80**

(e) a reconciliation of the carrying amount at the beginning and end of the period showing:

(i) additions;

(ii) assets classified as held for sale or included in a disposal group classified as held for sale in accordance with IFRS 5 and other disposals;

(iii) acquisitions through business combinations;

(iv) increases or decreases resulting from revaluations under paragraphs 31, 39 and 40 and from impairment losses recognized or reversed directly in equity in accordance with IAS 36;

(v) impairment losses recognized in profit or loss in accordance with IAS 36;

(vi) impairment losses reversed in profit or loss in accordance with IAS 36;

(vii) depreciation;

(viii) the net exchange differences arising on the translation of the financial statements from the functional currency into a different presentation currency, including the translation of a foreign operation into the presentation currency of the reporting entity; and

(ix) other changes.'

Table 7.17 Movements in tangible assets

Beginning value	+	Increases	–	Decreases	=	Ending value
Gross value	+	Acquisitions	–	Disposals	=	Gross value
Beginning accumulated depreciation	+	Depreciation expense	–	Cancellation of depreciation of fixed assets sold or disposed of	=	Ending accumulated depreciation

Real-life example Atos Origin

(France – IFRS – Source: Annual report 2008 – IT business processes)

(in € millions)	Land and buildings	IT equipments	Other assets	Total
GROSS VALUE				
At 1 January 2008	**266.5**	**800.5**	**77.0**	**1,144.0**
Additions	23.7	178.5	32.7	234.9
Disposals	(24.0)	(57.0)	(9.7)	(90.7)
Impact of business combinations	0.1	0.1	0.1	0.3
Disposal of subsidiaries	(0.9)	(8.4)	(1.3)	(10.6)
Exchange differences	(16.5)	(21.0)	(1.4)	(38.9)
Reclassified as held for sale	–	–	–	–
Others	7.7	14.7	(18.8)	3.6
AT 31 DECEMBER 2008	**256.6**	**907.4**	**78.6**	**1,242.6**
ACCUMULATED DEPRECIATION				
At 1 January 2008	**(129.0)**	**(540.7)**	**(37.2)**	**(706.9)**
Depreciation charge for the year	(27.2)	(152.8)	(6.2)	(186.2)
Eliminated on disposal	14.5	55.6	7.2	77.3
On assets reclassified as held for sale	–	–	–	–
Exchange differences	8.6	13.5	0.9	23.0
Disposal of subsidiaries	1.0	4.7	0.2	5.9
Impairment	–	–	–	–
Others	–	(2.9)	1.6	(1.3)
AT 31 DECEMBER 2008	**(132.1)**	**(622.6)**	**(33.5)**	**(788.2)**
NET VALUE				
At 1 January 2008	137.5	259.8	39.8	437.1
AT 31 DECEMBER 2008	**124.5**	**284.8**	**45.1**	**454.4**

- It should be noted that the movements are presented in line and the assets in columns.
- The book value is computed as the difference between the gross value and the accumulated depreciation at year-end.
- The lines 'impact of business acquisitions' and 'disposal of subsidiaries' represent the impact of acquisitions and sales of group companies on the movements in tangible assets.

8.3 Financial statement analysis

Several ratios may be computed to help the user of financial information gain a better understanding of the financial position of the business regarding its ability to use its tangible assets.

8.3.1 Capital intensity ratios

There are two key ratios:

> Rate of return on tangible assets = Net income/Net tangible assets
> Tangible asset turnover = Net sales/Average net tangible assets (net book value)

They answer the questions 'how much profit does the business create per currency unit invested in tangible assets' or 'how much sales revenue is generated per currency unit originally invested in tangible assets'. These ratios are essential for extrapolating the consequences of an investment strategy. Their value is clearly influenced by the depreciation method chosen.

Although commonly used, these ratios are somewhat misleading in that when the net *book value* is used as the denominator, the ratio increases with the passage of time, even if the firm does nothing (the ratio may even improve when things go bad if the speed of depreciation of the denominator exceeds the rate of decline of income!). More relevant denominator values that are sometimes used, especially in business communication with the financial community, are (most commonly) the historical book value (i.e., the cost of acquisition before accumulated depreciation) or (still unusual) the replacement value of the tangible assets.

8.3.2 Average age and life of tangible assets

Shareholders (potential or actual) and financial analysts need to evaluate the risk of obsolescence of the assets of the firm. When an exact, engineering-based knowledge of the average age or life of the assets is not available, a quick estimate can be found by exploiting the fact that financial statements report both the gross value of the assets and their accumulated depreciation.

> Average age = Accumulated depreciation at year-end/Depreciation expense for the year
> Average useful life = Gross value of depreciable assets at year-end/Depreciation expense for the year

These two ratios suffer several limits since the depreciation allowance (and thus the timing of the accumulated depreciation) varies with the method of depreciation selected (straight-line versus accelerated):

- they provide reasonably good information only in the case of use of the straight-line depreciation method;
- they assume the cost of acquisition of equivalent assets over time is stable;
- they are influenced by acquisitions and disposals during the year.

A further problem with the meaningfulness of these ratios derives from the fact managers could manipulate tangible assets valuation and depreciation expense in order to increase (or decrease) net income. The three major sources of manipulation are:

- increase (or decrease) an asset's useful life;
- change depreciation method (from straight-line to declining balance or the opposite, for example), with the limitation of the need to respect the consistency accounting principle;
- decide to capitalize (or not) elements of the acquisition cost (such as financial expenses) or upgrade of the asset (by decomposing the upgrade in slices that all meet the capitalization threshold).

The notes to financial statements, particularly the section devoted to accounting policies, are very helpful for the user of financial statements. Managers must use them to reveal the accounting choices they have made during the year and thus allow the analyst or any reader to recast the figures in the light that suits them.

The impact of the choice of a depreciation method on the financial statements is dealt with in Appendix 7.8.

Key points

- Tangible assets ('property, plant and equipment' [PPE], 'plant assets', 'operational assets' or 'fixed assets') create economic benefits over several periods and represent significant investments that must be put in place before any economic activity can take place.
- Fixed assets are, by nature, the most illiquid assets on the balance sheet. In countries where the accounting tradition is more 'patrimonial' they will appear at the top of the list of assets, while in countries where the accounting culture favors liquidity, the tangible assets will be listed at the bottom of the list.
- Fixed assets can be divided into three categories: (1) tangible assets; (2) intangible assets (see Chapter 8); and (3) financial assets (see Chapter 10).
- The various accounting issues that arise when dealing with tangible assets are related to their acquisition (definition, recognition, measurement), use (depreciation) and disposal (sale or removal).
- Depreciation is 'the systematic allocation of the depreciable cost of an asset over its useful life'.

- Several depreciation methods have been developed. The choice of the most appropriate method for reporting to shareholders should theoretically be made so as to best reflect the pattern of decline in the asset's service potential and should therefore be specific to each class of tangible assets.
- Two categories of methods are available: (1) time-based depreciation methods (straight-line, declining balance and sum-of-the-years' digits); and (2) methods based on activity level (productive-output and service-quantity).
- In any given year, depreciation expenses are 'non-cash expenses' (the tangible assets have already been paid for, and depreciation expenses are only a time-based allocation of that original cost, as mentioned above). This means that the depreciation expenses have *no direct impact* on the cash balance (the *impact is only indirect*, through the tax deductibility of the depreciation expenses). The indirect impact on after-tax cash is even greater when an accelerated depreciation method is allowed for tax purposes.

Review (solutions are at the back of the book)

Review 7.1 Gibbons

Topic: Determining the cost of acquisition

Gibbons Co., a coffee shop, purchases a new coffee machine. The list price for the machine is 1,500 CU. However, the manufacturer is running a special offer, and Gibbons Co. obtains the machine for a price which is 20% lower than the list price. Freight expenses for the delivery of the machine are 150 CU, and installation and testing expenses amount to 100 CU. During installation, uninsured damages are incurred resulting in repair expenses of 200 CU.

Required

1. Compute the acquisition cost of the machine.
2. Record the acquisition in the format of your choice ('ledger-financial statements', ledger, journal, financial statements).

Assignments

Assignment 7.1
Multiple-choice questions

Select the right answer (only one possible answer unless otherwise stated).

1. The most appropriate method of depreciation of land is
   (a) The straight-line method
   (b) The declining balance method
   (c) Either method
   (d) None of these

2. Depreciation will directly generate
   (a) An increase in cash
   (b) An increase in liabilities
   (c) A decrease in liabilities
   (d) A decrease in assets
   (e) A decrease in cash

3. At the end of the useful life of a tangible asset originally purchased for 100 CU and fully depreciated over five years, the gross value is
   (a) 0
   (b) 100
   (c) 20
   (d) None of these

4. Which of the following items would not be considered a tangible asset?
   1. Land
   2. Trademark
   3. Building
   4. Oil well
   5. Software

   (a) 1, 3 and 4
   (b) 2 and 4
   (c) 2 and 5
   (d) 2, 3, 4 and 5
   (e) 3 and 5

5. Examples of tangible assets include land, buildings and equipment
   (a) True
   (b) False

6. All tangible assets are charged to expense over a period of years in some systematic and rational manner
   (a) True
   (b) False

7. Companies can only use one method of depreciation for all of its depreciable assets
   (a) True
   (b) False

8. When using the double-declining balance method, in calculating the annual depreciation expense, the depreciation rate is multiplied by the
   (a) Purchase cost of the asset
   (b) Fair value of the asset at beginning of the period
   (c) Depreciable amount
   (d) Book value at beginning of that year
   (e) None of these

9. The share of a natural resource deposit's cost of acquisition that is expensed each year is called
   (a) Depreciation
   (b) Amortization
   (c) Depletion
   (d) Exhaustion
   (e) None of these

10. Which ratio(s) is (are) used to define the importance of tangible assets in financial statements?
    (a) Net tangible assets/total net assets
    (b) Rate of return of tangible assets
    (c) Tangible assets turnover
    (d) Depreciation expense/net sales
    (e) Average life of tangible assets

Assignment 7.2
Discussion questions

1. Give some arguments in favor of at least four different methods of depreciation.

2. Does depreciation provide or consume cash?

3. Give some arguments in favor of each method of reporting the sale of tangible assets.

4. Does the acquisition of a tangible asset influence net income?

Assignment 7.3
Reporting in different sectors of activity

On the Internet, or in the library, find the annual reports of four companies from different sectors of activity in a given country.

Required

1. How are tangible assets presented in their balance sheets? What decisions on the basis of this information can investors or shareholders take? What decisions would be difficult to take on the basis of just this information?

2. Are there any notes relating to tangible assets? How do they enlarge the decision analysis possibilities offered to shareholders and investors?

3. What are the accounting treatments applied to these assets?

4. What appears to be the estimated useful lives of the major categories of tangible assets in each firm?

5. What is the weight of tangible assets as a percentage of total assets for each firm? What strategic implications would an investor derive from this ratio?

6. What is the weight of depreciation expense as a percentage of sales? What strategic implications would an investor derive from this ratio?

Assignment 7.4
Reporting in the same sector of activity

On the Internet, or in the library, find the annual reports of three companies essentially in roughly identical or similar industries in a given country or in different countries.

Required

Use questions from Assignment 7.3.

Assignment 7.5
Choice of depreciation methods

Choose a country you know well, either because you come from this country or have worked there.

Required

Identify the depreciation methods which are the most commonly used in practice. You can base your presentation on official statistics (if they exist) or on a sample of annual reports you will survey.

Assignment 7.6
Tippett

Topic: Popular depreciation methods

Tippett Company acquired new machine tools for 10 million CU. Their aggregate predicted useful lives is four years and their predicted residual value is 1 million CU.

Depreciation expense of this class of asset can be computed through one of five methods:

■ straight-line;
■ double-declining balance (switching to a straight-line method [over the remaining useful life] at the point where the straight-line rate [calculated over the remaining useful life] exceeds or equals the declining balance rate selected);
■ sum of the years' digits;
■ units of output basis;
■ service hours basis.

Units of output and service hours for each year and in total are listed in the following table.

	Annual	Total
Units of output		15,000
Year 1	7,000	
Year 2	4,000	
Year 3	2,000	
Year 4	2,000	
Service hours		36,000
Year 1	12,000	
Year 2	9,000	
Year 3	8,000	
Year 4	7,000	

Required

■ Variation 1: Prepare a depreciation schedule comparing the first two depreciation methods, assuming that the acquisition date was 1 January X1.
■ Variation 2: Prepare a depreciation schedule comparing the five depreciation methods, assuming that the acquisition date was 1 January X1.

Assignment 7.7
Britten Inc.

Topic: Determining the cost of acquisition – recording the acquisition and the depreciation

Britten Inc. is a large European civil engineering and construction enterprise. They have just finished building, for their own use, a large hangar, which will serve as both a warehouse for their inventory of raw construction materials and as a garage for idle equipment between assignments. Construction began on 14 July X1 and was completed on 1 October of the same year. Resources consumed by the construction project were:

■ Raw materials which were already in inventory for an amount of 10,000 CU
■ Labor costs amounting to 20,000 CU.

This type of light construction is generally depreciated over 10 years and Britten Inc. chose to use the double-declining balance method. The residual value of the building will essentially be zero. The hangar will be fully depreciated by:

- Either switching to the straight-line method when the double-declining rate on the balance becomes smaller than the straight-line rate over the remaining years.
- Or switching to straight-line method at the mid-point of useful life of the hangar.

The closing date is 31 December.

Required

1. Record the acquisition cost of the hangar (depreciable amount).
2. Prepare the depreciation schedule under both possibilities for switching to straight-line, assuming that the hangar will be fully depreciated at the end of year X10.
3. Record the depreciation expense pertaining to the hangar in the income statement of Britten Inc. for the year ended 31 December X1.

Assignment 7.8
Merck*

Topic: Reporting for movements of tangible assets

Merck KGaA is a German-based company, operating in the pharmaceutical and chemical business sectors.

We provide below an excerpt from the consolidated balance sheet.

Consolidated balance sheet (excerpt)			
(€ million)	Note	2008	2007
Non-current assets			
(…)			
Property, plant and equipment	(#24)	2,440.1	2,274.5

Note 24 in the 2008 consolidated annual report – prepared under IFRS – pertains to property, plant and equipment. It states the following:

(€ million)	Land, land rights and buildings, including buildings on third-party land	Plant and machinery	Other facilities, operating and office equipment	Construction in progress and advance payments to vendors and contractors	Total
Net carrying amount as of 31 December 2007	**1,108.4**	**780.9**	**211.6**	**173.6**	**2,274.5**
Acquisition cost 1 January 2008	**1,754.9**	**2,325.3**	**760.2**	**187.4**	**5,027.8**
Currency translation	72.5	37.5	4.7	4.8	119.5
Changes in companies consolidated	–	−2.4	1.4	0.2	−0.8
Additions	25.2	44.6	46.4	278.5	394.7
Disposals	−16.4	−80.8	−71.1	−4.1	−172.4
Transfers	48.3	65.6	32.5	−151.2	−4.8
Reclassification of assets held for sale	1.3	1.8	0.6	0.1	3.8
31 December 2008	**1,885.8**	**2,391.6**	**774.7**	**315.7**	**5,367.8**
Accumulated depreciation and impairment losses 1 January 2008	**−646.5**	**−1,544.4**	**−548.6**	**−13.8**	**−2,753.3**
Currency translation	−19.2	−32.3	−4.4	−0.4	−56.3
Changes in companies consolidated	−0.5	1.7	−1.6	−0.1	−0.5
Depreciation and impairment losses	−68.4	−146.0	−62.5	−1.1	−278.0
Disposals	13.9	76.7	67.9	0.1	158.6
Transfers	0.4	0.4	2.1	–	2.9
Write-ups	0.4	0.5	0.1	–	1.0
Reclassification of assets held for sale	−0.5	−1.2	−0.4	–	−2.1
31 December 2008	**−720.4**	**−1,644.6**	**−547.4**	**−15.3**	**−2,927.7**
Net carrying amount as of 31 December 2008	**1,165.4**	**747.0**	**227.3**	**300.4**	**2,440.1**

Required

1. Reconcile the balance sheet figures and the statement of Note 24.

2. Double-check (reconcile) the amount of 'Net carrying amount as of 31 December 2008' between the various tables.

3. Double-check (reconcile) the amount of 'Net carrying amount as of 31 December 2007' between the various tables.

4. In the line 'Changes in companies consolidated', why are the figures not always positive?

5. Explain what the figures represent under the heading 'Reclassification of assets held for sale'. (The full annual report might help to answer this question).

6. Explain why is there no line 'Additions' in the section 'Accumulated depreciation and impairment losses'.

7. Explain and provide an illustration of what happens in the line 'Transfers' (at acquisition cost).

8. Explain why, in the lines 'Disposals' and 'Transfers' (depreciation), the signs are positive.

NB. Although the topic of business combinations (see Chapter 13) has not yet been developed, we can deduce that the line 'Changes in companies consolidated' represents the impact of acquisitions and sales of companies. The column 'Currency translation' is related to the translation of financial statements of the various subsidiaries originally established in their local currencies.

Assignment 7.9
Honda Motor Co.*

Topic: Analysis of tangible assets

Honda Motor Co. and its subsidiaries (collectively 'Honda') develop, manufacture, distribute and provide financing for the sale of its motorcycles, automobiles and power products. The consolidated financial statements have been prepared in a manner and reflect the adjustments that are necessary to be in conformity with accounting principles generally accepted in the United States of America.

You will find below the consolidated balance sheets as at 31 March 2004 to 2009, as well as some additional information (Source: Annual reports 2004 to 2009).

	31 March					
Additional information (in Yen millions)	2004	2005	2006	2007	2008	2009
Sales	8,162,600	8,650,105	9,907,996	11,087,140	12,002,834	10,011,241
Net income	464,338	486,197	597,033	592,322	600,039	137,005
Depreciation expense including property on operating leases	213,445	225,752	262,225	371,488	518,425	637,644
Depreciation of property on operating leases	0	0	0	9,741	101,032	195,776
Depreciation expense excluding property on operating leases	213,445	225,752	262,225	361,747	417,393	441,868

Required

1. Compute for the years 2004 to 2009 the following ratios:

    ■ weight of tangible assets (net tangible assets/total assets);

    ■ rate of return on tangible assets (net income/net tangible assets);

    ■ tangible assets turnover (net sales/average tangible assets – at book value);

    ■ average age of tangible assets (accumulated depreciation at year-end/depreciation expense for the year);

    ■ average useful life of tangible assets (gross value of depreciable assets at year-end/depreciation expense for the year).

    Explain in detail your computation and the assumption(s) you must make.

2. Comment on your results.

Honda Motor Co. – Consolidated balance sheets – 31 March 2004 to 31 March 2009
(in Yen millions)

Assets	March 31					
	2004	2005	2006	2007	2008	2009
Current assets:						
Cash and cash equivalents	724,421	773,538	716,788	945,546	1,050,902	690,369
Trade accounts and notes receivable, net of allowance for doubtful accounts	688,303	791,195	963,320	1,055,470	1,021,743	854,214
Finance subsidiaries-receivables, net	949,733	1,021,116	1,230,912	1,426,224	1,340,728	1,172,030
Inventories	765,433	862,370	1,036,304	1,183,116	1,199,260	1,243,961
Deferred income taxes	222,179	214,059	221,294	215,172	158,825	198,158
Other current assets	303,185	346,464	406,985	426,863	460,110	462,446
Total current assets	**3,653,254**	**4,008,742**	**4,575,603**	**5,252,391**	**5,231,568**	**4,621,178**
Finance subsidiaries – receivables, net:	**2,265,874**	**2,623,909**	**2,982,425**	**3,039,826**	**2,707,820**	**2,400,282**
Investments and advances:						
Investments in and advances to affiliates	298,242	349,664	408,993	487,538	549,812	505,835
Other, including marketable equity securities	242,824	264,926	298,460	254,610	222,110	133,234
Total investments and advances	**541,066**	**614,590**	**707,453**	**742,148**	**771,922**	**639,069**
Property on operating leases:						
Vehicles	—	—	—	345,909	1,014,412	1,557,060
Less accumulated depreciation	—	—	—	9,700	95,440	269,261
Net property on operating leases	**—**	**—**	**—**	**336,209**	**918,972**	**1,287,799**
Property, plant and equipment, at cost:						
Land	354,762	365,217	384,447	429,373	457,352	469,279
Buildings	968,159	1,030,998	1,149,517	1,322,394	1,396,934	1,446,090
Machinery and equipment	2,072,347	2,260,826	2,562,507	2,988,064	3,135,513	3,133,439
Construction in progress	49,208	96,047	115,818	204,318	227,479	159,567
	3,444,476	3,753,088	4,212,289	4,944,149	5,217,278	5,208,375
Less accumulated depreciation and amortization	2,008,945	2,168,836	2,397,022	2,865,421	3,015,979	3,060,654
Net property, plant and equipment	**1,435,531**	**1,584,252**	**1,815,267**	**2,078,728**	**2,201,299**	**2,147,721**
Other assets	**433,043**	**485,477**	**550,652**	**587,198**	**783,962**	**722,868**
Total assets	**8,328,768**	**9,316,970**	**10,631,400**	**12,036,500**	**12,615,543**	**11,818,917**

Liabilities, minority interests and stockholders' equity	2004	2005	2006	2007	2008	2009
Current liabilities:						
Short-term debt	734,271	769,314	693,557	1,265,868	1,687,115	1,706,819
Current portion of long-term debt	487,125	535,105	657,645	775,409	871,050	977,523
Trade payables: Notes	29,096	26,727	31,698	33,276	39,006	31,834
Trade payables: Accounts	882,141	987,045	1,015,409	1,133,280	1,015,130	674,498
Accrued expenses	813,733	913,721	786,972	807,341	730,615	562,673
Income taxes payable	31,194	65,029	110,160	76,031	71,354	32,614
Other current liabilities	357,259	451,623	198,226	196,322	258,066	251,407
Total current liabilities	**3,334,819**	**3,748,564**	**3,493,667**	**4,287,527**	**4,672,336**	**4,237,368**
Long-term debt, excluding current portion:	**1,394,612**	**1,559,500**	**1,879,000**	**1,905,743**	**1,836,652**	**1,932,637**
Other liabilities:	**724,937**	**719,612**	**1,045,523**	**1,237,712**	**1,414,270**	**1,518,568**
Total liabilities	**5,454,368**	**6,027,676**	**6,418,190**	**7,430,982**	**7,923,258**	**7,688,573**
Minority interests in consolidated subsidiaries:	—	—	**87,460**	**122,907**	**141,806**	**123,056**
Stockholders' equity:						
Common stock	86,067	86,067	86,067	86,067	86,067	86,067
Capital surplus	172,719	172,531	172,529	172,529	172,529	172,529
Legal reserves	32,418	34,688	35,811	37,730	39,811	43,965
Retained earnings	3,589,434	3,809,383	4,267,886	4,654,890	5,106,197	5,099,267
Accumulated other comprehensive income (loss), net	(854,573)	(793,934)	(407,187)	(427,166)	(782,198)	(1,322,828)
Treasury stock, at cost	(151,665)	(19,441)	(29,356)	(41,439)	(71,927)	(71,712)
Total stockholders' equity	**2,874,400**	**3,289,294**	**4,125,750**	**4,482,611**	**4,550,479**	**4,007,288**
Total liabilities, minority interests and stockholders' equity	**8,328,768**	**9,316,970**	**10,631,400**	**12,036,500**	**12,615,543**	**11,818,917**

References

IASB (1989) Framework for the Preparation and Presentation of Financial Statements, London.

IASB (2003) International Accounting Standard No. 16: Property, Plant and Equipment, London.

IASB (2004a) International Accounting Standard No. 36: Impairment of Assets, London.

IASB (2004b) International Accounting Standard No. 38: Intangible Assets, London.

IASB (amended 2007) International Accounting Standard No. 23: Borrowing Costs, London.

Stice J., Stice E.K. and Skousen F. (2009) *Intermediate Accounting*, 17th edition, South-Western Cengage Learning, Mason, OH.

Further reading

Burlaud, A. Messina, M. and Walton, P. (1996) 'Depreciation: Concepts and practices in France and the UK', *European Accounting Review* 5(2): 299–316.

Chambers, D., Jennings, R. and Thompson, R. (1999) 'Evidence on the usefulness of capital expenditures as an alternative measure of depreciation', *Review of Accounting Studies* 2(3–4): 169–95.

Collins, L. (1994) 'Revaluation of assets in France: The interaction between professional practice, theory and political necessity', *European Accounting Review* 3(1): 122–31.

Mohrman, M.B. (2009) 'Depreciation of airplanes and garbage trucks: Information value and fraud prevention in financial reporting', *Issues in Accounting Education* 24(1): 105–07.

Paterson, R. (2002) 'Impairment', *Accountancy* 130(1312): 105.

Additional material on the website

Go to http://www.cengage.co.uk/stolowy3 for further information, journal entries and extra assignments for each chapter.

The following appendices to this chapter are available on the dedicated website:

Appendix 7.1: Examples of components of the acquisition cost

Appendix 7.2: Sum-of-the-years' digits method

Appendix 7.3: Depreciation for partial years (fractional year problems)

Appendix 7.4: Overhead

Appendix 7.5: Calculation of capitalized interest costs

Appendix 7.6: Accounting for a sale of a fixed asset: Illustration: Purcell Company

Appendix 7.7: Removing a fully depreciated tangible asset from the book

Appendix 7.8: Impact of the choice of a depreciation method on the financial statements.

Notes

1. Productive, here, refers to the potential of economic benefit generation provided by the fixed asset.
2. Depletion is the term used to refer to depreciation of natural resources assets (generally non-renewable) and is used most often in mining, timber, oil production, or other extractive industries.
3. The reader can read Stice, Stice and Skousen (2009) to find an explanation referring to US GAAP.
4. The term 'equipment' refers to the variety of machinery, vehicles, computers, etc. that are used by a business.
5. The interested reader can consult the following US textbook: Stice, Stice and Skousen (2009).
6. This is the practice, for example, in Argentina, Austria, Germany, and Switzerland.
7. The concept of non-cash item and the mechanism linking the depreciation expense to the cash flow are developed in Chapter 14.
8. Let us illustrate this computation: a machine having a useful economic life of five years has been purchased for 1,000 CU and is expected to have a residual value of 50 CU. The depreciation rate will be: $1 - (50/1,000)^{1/5} = 1 - 0.549 = 0.451 = 45.1\%$. A depreciation schedule with this rate will generate a residual value of 50. If the residual value had been 1 CU the depreciation rate would amount to 74.9%.
9. Without wanting to get into too many details – that would be the purpose of a Cost Accounting book – let us say that the cost of an object, at any point in the manufacturing to distribution cycle of the object, is the sum of all materials and components costs, labor costs and the cost of various and assorted services (including support costs or overhead) that the object has received at that point. These aggregated costs 'travel' with the object as it physically moves from workshop to warehouse, to another workshop, to storage, to the delivery truck, etc. These costs are matched against revenue when the object is sold. The depreciation cost is one the services received by the object since it represents the consumption, by the object, of the productive capacity of the tangible asset.

C8

Chapter 8
Intangible Assets

Learning objectives

After studying this chapter, you will understand:

- That intangible assets are usually divided into three categories: research and development (R&D), goodwill and other intangible assets.
- That intangible assets may represent a significant proportion of total assets.
- That intangible assets raise issues of definition, recognition and recording of their change in value.
- How the concept of goodwill is defined and what it represents.
- That some accounting principles favor recognition of intangible assets while others oppose it.
- What the criteria are for recognition of an intangible asset.
- How accounting handles changes in value of intangible assets after their initial recognition.
- What the conditions are for appropriate R&D capitalization.
- What the arguments are in favor and against R&D capitalization.
- What accounting rules apply to reporting development of computer software.

As defined in Chapter 7, **intangible assets** are long-lived (long-term) assets that lack physical substance and whose acquisition and continued possession represent rights to future economic benefits. Intangible assets comprise **goodwill** (essentially the premium paid over the fair value of acquired assets, reflecting the expected stream of future economic benefits – see section 1.2.2 for a more precise definition), **patents**, **franchises**, licenses, **trademarks**, brands, **copyrights**, etc., and, if certain conditions are met, capitalized R&D.

The valuation and reporting of intangibles has been controversial and a source of debate for many years, mainly because it is often very difficult to define objectively and value future economic benefits derived from such assets. How can one establish an 'objective' value for a brand, especially if the brand was developed by the firm itself and not purchased from someone else in an 'at arm's length' transaction? Unlike physical assets where the historical value results from clear market-based transactions or from a measurable consumption of resources and where the future economic benefits are generally unambiguously measurable (the market uncertainty regarding the existence of demand is generally ignored), it is the 'quality' of the usage made of intangible assets by a management team that creates both the 'value' of the asset and the stream of future economic benefits.

For example, when a European pharmaceutical laboratory with a cosmetics division acquired a firm owning a well-known perfume brand, their intention was to use the well-known brand as a locomotive for the rest of their cosmetics division and develop the stream of future economic benefits of both the newly acquired firm but also, by ricochet and osmosis, of the other pre-existing products and brands in the portfolio of that division. Immediately after the completion of the acquisition, the book value of the 'brand' was clearly the (market) price paid for it. However, the culture of that pharmaceutical laboratory was so different from that of a cosmetics and perfume business that it drowned the image of the acquired brand and management was unable to capitalize on its acquisition. It ended up choosing to sell the whole cosmetics division a couple of years later at a loss (i.e., at a selling price below the book-value of the division, including valuing the acquired brand below its original purchase price). The buyer, in turn, having a culture that proved to be more coherent with the potential of the brand was able to reap significant profit from the acquisition. Although it listed the brand only at its (now deflated) purchase price, the reality of the future economic benefits would have called for a higher valuation, had the firm sought a new (strategically coherent) buyer for that brand. Of course, the prudence principle did not allow the new owner of the brand to revaluate upwards that intangible asset in its books. 'Same intangible asset, different values', depending on in whose hands it is held.

Accountants and financial analysts have long been quite cautious about intangible assets. Accountants tended to expense the cost of any intangibles acquisition (or development costs) in the period incurred. Financial analysts, when faced with financial statements in which these costs had been recorded as assets, tended to consider them as 'virtual' assets and excluded them from their analyses.

However, today's information- and knowledge-based economy relies quite heavily on intangibles (see Table 8.1). These assets have to be reported accurately if the financial statements are to give the shareholders a true and fair view of the business. Both the accountants and financial analysts communities are therefore reconsidering their positions. The development of brands or the sale of rights to patents may, in some cases, represent the major source of value creation by a business (for example, in retail, cosmetics or luxury products, biotechnology, or software development).

The reporting of intangible assets raises the three major issues listed in Figure 8.1. Each will be dealt with in turn in sections 1, 2 and 3 of this chapter.

Among the various intangible assets, capitalized research and development costs and computer software deserve special attention and will be covered in sections 4 and 5.

Most businesses report at least some intangible assets in their year-end 2008 balance sheet, as exemplified by the sample of firms listed in Table 8.1.

Figure 8.1 Intangible assets issues

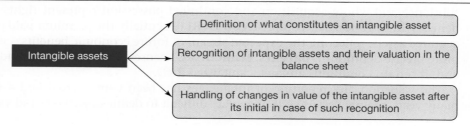

Table 8.1 Weight of intangible assets in balance sheets

Company (country – activity)	Currency	Types of intangibles	Intangible assets (net amount)	Total assets (net amount)	Intangibles as % of total assets
RC2 (USA – Racing replicas)	$000	Goodwill	0		0.00
		Intangible assets, net	82,504		24.51
		Total intangible assets	82,504	336,650	24.51
ISS (Denmark – Support services)	DKKm	Goodwill	27,259		50.85
		Customer contracts	6,918		12.91
		Brands	1,526		2.85
		Software and others	298		0.56
		Total intangible assets	36,001	53,605	67.16
Anheuser-Busch InBev (Belgium – Brewery group)	€m	Intangible assets	17,010		20.92
		Goodwill	35,608		43.79
		Total intangible assets	52,618	81,313	64.71
Securitas (Sweden – Security services and alarm systems)	SEKm	Goodwill	14,104		39.49
		Other intangible fixed assets	1,007		2.82
		Total intangible assets	15,111	35,719	42.30
EMI (UK – Music)	£m	Music copyrights	3,553		55.26
		Goodwill	1,507		23.44
		Total intangible assets	5,060	6,430	78.69
Saint-Gobain (France – Glass, building materials and high performance industrial materials)	€m	Goodwill	10,671		24.59
		Other intangible assets	2,868		6.61
		Total intangible assets	13,539	43,395	31.20
Roche (Switzerland – Pharmaceuticals and chemicals)	CHFm	Goodwill	8,353		10.98
		Patents, licenses, trademarks and other	7,121		9.36
		Total intangible assets	15,474	76,089	20.34
Club Méditerranée (France – Leisure)	€m	Goodwill	32		2.10
		Intangible assets	53		3.47
		Total intangible assets	85	1,527	5.57
Repsol (Spain – Oil and gas)	€m	Intangible assets	1,228		2.48
		Goodwill	2,851		5.77
		Total intangible assets	4,079	49,429	8.25
Philips (Netherlands – Consumer and professional electronics)	€m	Intangible assets	4,477		14.08
		Goodwill	7,280		22.90
		Total intangible assets	11,757	31,790	36.98
Pirelli (Italy – Tires and cables for energy distribution and telecommunication)	€000	Patents and intellectual property rights	424		0.01
		Concessions, licenses and trademarks	25,070		0.36
		Software	12,129		0.17
		Goodwill	1,007,685		14.53
		Other intangible assets	800		0.01
		Total intangible assets	1,046,108	6,933,218	15.09

Table 8.1 *(continued)*					
Company (country – activity)	Currency	Types of intangibles	Intangible assets (net amount)	Total assets (net amount)	Intangibles as % of total assets
EVN (Austria – Electricity and gas production and retail and wholesale distribution, heating services)	€000	Goodwill Other intangible assets	215,489 142,061		3.25 2.14
		Total intangible assets	357,550	6,636,275	5.39
Aluminum Corporation of China (China – Aluminum production – Annual report 2007)	RMB000	Goodwill Mining rights Other intangible assets	2,330,949 308,071 37,708		2.47 0.33 0.04
		Total intangible assets	2,676,728	94,338,362	2.84

1 Definition of intangibles

The definition of intangibles has evolved over the last few years trying to provide a better understanding of the concept, allow reliable measurement of intangible investments and promote understanding and communication between researchers, managers, users of financial information and policy makers. Intangible assets are usually considered to have no physical substance and to be linked to legal rights (trademarks, patents, copyrights). Generally, the definition of intangibles is based on the existence of the following four criteria:

1. Identifiability;
2. Lack of physical substance;
3. The entity claiming it as an asset must have control over the asset; and
4. Existence of defined future economic benefits deriving from the asset.

1.1 Principles

The IASB defines an intangible asset as 'an identifiable non-monetary asset without physical substance' (IASB 2004b, IAS 38: § 8). Remember that an asset is 'a resource: (a) controlled by an entity as a result of past events; and (b) from which future economic benefits are expected to flow to the enterprise', while '**monetary assets** are money held and assets to be received in fixed or determinable amounts of money' (IAS 38: § 8).

All countries' GAAP acknowledge the existence and the importance of intangible assets. However, each may have its own specific definition of the concept with more or fewer details than contained in the IASB definition. For example, in the United States, intangible assets are 'assets (not including financial assets) that lack physical substance' (FASB 2001, SFAS 142, Appendix F). In the UK, intangible assets are 'non-financial fixed assets that do not have physical substance but are identifiable and are controlled by the entity through custody or legal rights' (ASB 1997: § 2).

1.2 Main categories of intangibles

Intangible assets are usually divided into three categories: research and development (R&D), goodwill and other intangible assets.

1.2.1 Research and Development

In certain circumstances, R&D expenses may be capitalized, i.e., recorded as an asset. This topic is developed in section 4.

1.2.2 Goodwill

The term *goodwill* has been adopted around the world to refer to the difference between the purchase price of an acquired business and the 'value' of its identifiable assets (minus identifiable liabilities). The term goodwill has two somewhat different meanings depending on whether it is reported in consolidated financial statements (corresponding to the group – see Chapter 13) or in unconsolidated (individual company) financial statements.

'Goodwill recognized in a business combination [i.e., which will be recorded in consolidated financial statements] is an asset representing the future economic benefits arising from other assets acquired in a business combination that are not individually identified and separately recognized' (IAS 38: § 11). Goodwill represents any excess of the cost of the acquisition over the acquirer's interest in the fair value of the identifiable assets and liabilities acquired as of the date of the exchange transaction (IASB, 2008: based on § 32). The calculation of goodwill is presented in Chapter 13.

Figure 8.2 below explains the difference between the purchase price and the book value of assets and liabilities acquired.

The difference between the fair value of each identifiable asset or liability and their book value is called a 'valuation difference' (see Figure 8.2). Unlike goodwill, valuation differences are not explicitly reported in the balance sheet. Since each asset or liability is recorded in the acquirer's books at their fair value, the valuation differences are not reported as such. They are included in the new book value of the item in the acquirer's accounts (fair value in the acquirer's books equals book value in the seller's books plus valuation difference). We consider it is important conceptually to identify valuation differences, because we feel it is crucial to avoid overestimating the goodwill. We agree with the IASB's position that goodwill should only represent the premium paid for – or value of – the unidentified intangible assets acquired (see below).

In consolidated financial statements, goodwill is often referred to in the balance sheet as 'consolidation goodwill'. In the unconsolidated financial statements, some countries' GAAP recognize goodwill and call it 'purchased goodwill'.

Goodwill, whether in consolidated or unconsolidated financial statements, often represents the value of intangible elements of the value of the firm such as the loyal customer base of the enterprise, the brand name or the reputation of the firm, the 'pipeline' of R&D projects or new products, the expertise and loyalty of key personnel, etc.

1.2.3 Other intangible assets

Patent   A patent is a document granted by a government or an official authority bestowing on the inventor of a product or manufacturing process the exclusive right to use or sell the

Figure 8.2 Goodwill and valuation differences

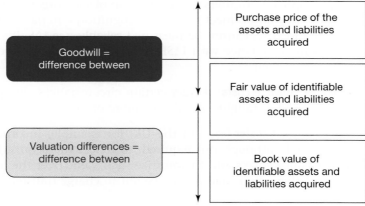

invention or rights to it. The duration of the protection offered by a patent varies between countries (17 years in the USA, 20 in France, etc.). A patent cannot be renewed, but obtaining a new patent on the basis of modifications and improvements to the original invention may extend its effective life.

Trademark   A trademark (or trade name, brand or brand name) is a distinctive identification (symbol, logo, design, word, slogan, emblem, etc.) of a family of manufactured products and/or services that distinguishes it from similar families of products or services provided by other parties. Legal protection for trademarks is usually granted by registration with a specialized (government-regulated or supervised) office or agency. This registration is effective for an initial duration which varies from country to country (for example 20 years in the USA or 10 years in France) and which can be renewed periodically for the same period under specified conditions (mainly that the trademark be effectively used by the entity in carrying out its business).

Copyright   A copyright provides the holder with exclusive rights to the publication, production and sale of the rights for an intellectual creation, be it a musical, artistic, literary, or dramatic work (and often, by extension, software). Usually, the protection is granted for the remaining life of the author plus 50 years.

Franchises   A franchise is a contractual agreement that grants, for a fee, and within a limited geographical territory, the holder (franchisee), with or without direct support from the franchisor, the right to produce and/or sell certain products or services, to use certain trademarks, or to do other specific things identified in the franchise agreement without loss of ownership over these by the franchisor. The duration and terms of the franchise agreement are specified in each contract. When one party feels the other one is not upholding its end of the intent or the letter of the franchise contract, the latter can be broken, with or without litigation proceedings in front of the proper judicial authority.

Licensing agreements   A licensing agreement allows a company to use properties or rights owned by other entities for a fee and for an agreed-upon duration. It applies specifically to patents and trademarks.

Organization (or set-up) costs   **Organization costs (incorporation or set-up costs)** are the costs incurred during the process of establishing or incorporating a business. They include incorporation fees, legal fees (such as those incurred for the writing of by-laws or articles of incorporation), underwriting fees, accounting fees and promotional fees. Some countries allow these costs to be recorded as intangible assets. If these costs have been capitalized, they must be amortized over a fairly short period (up to five years), generally using a straight-line approach.

For example, Albeniz NA was created on 1 January X1. The costs incurred during the incorporation process amount to a total of 200 CU. The manager decides to capitalize these costs and amortize them over four years. Figure 8.3 describes the ensuing accounting entries.

IASB (IAS 38) prohibits the recognition of such organization costs as an intangible asset because they do no meet the asset recognition criteria (future economic benefits are not certain and costs cannot be measured reliably, see IAS 38: §§21-23). If a business entity reports in accordance with IASB standards, the organization or incorporation costs are expensed as incurred.

Computer software costs   Under certain circumstances, computer software can be considered to be an 'intangible asset'. (See more on this point in section 5.)

Soccer player transfer fees   In the UK, for example, incorporated soccer (football) clubs are allowed, although not required, to reflect the acquisition value of their players on their balance sheets and to amortize such value over the length of their contract. Until recently, these clubs had no choice but to charge transfer fees against profits in the year

Figure 8.3 Albeniz NA Accounting for organization costs

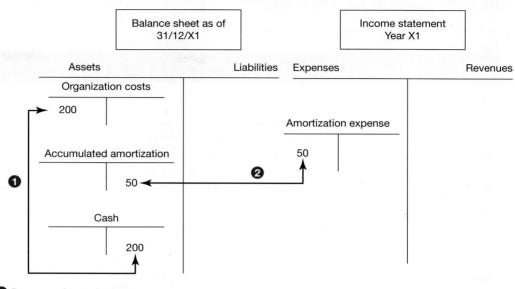

1 Payment of organization costs.

2 Amortization: 200/4 years = 50 CU per year.

they occurred, thus leading to wild fluctuations in yearly reported income without fairly representing the situation of the business.

Similar dispositions exist in other countries. For example, in France (CRC ruling 2004–07), amounts paid by a sports team to another in order to obtain the transfer of a player are grounds for the creation of an intangible asset because the new team controls the employment of the player and expects to derive future economic benefits from the player being a member of the team. Such an asset can be amortized over the life of the contract or over five years, whichever is the shortest.

Deferred charges (deferred assets)   Deferred charges are sometimes considered to be intangible assets. They are conceptually identical to prepaid or deferred expenses but they have longer-term economic benefits and must therefore be recognized over several periods to be coherent with the matching principle. Examples of such deferred charges are debt issuance costs (e.g., fees paid to banks or brokerage firms for a new flotation of stock or bonds) or fixed assets acquisition costs (when they are not included in the cost of the asset). Accountants often use this category as a catch all for items hard to classify anywhere else. Deferred charges, therefore, deserve significant attention on the part of any user of financial information to understand what is actually covered in this category. However, as IASB (IAS 38) prohibits their recognition because they do not meet the asset recognition criteria, the use of deferred charges should decrease in world practice.

Real-life example EVN AG

(Austria – IFRS – Source: Annual report 2007/08 – Energy, gas, heating services)

Notes to financial statements

Other intangible assets include electricity procurement rights, transportation rights for natural gas pipelines and other rights, in particular software licenses and the customer base of the Bulgarian and Macedonian electricity supply companies.

Real-life example Club Méditerranée

(France – IFRS – Source: Annual report 2008 – Leisure)

This company provides an interesting detailed list of its intangible assets.

Note 7 to the consolidated financial statements

Intangible assets

(in € millions)	Brands and licenses	Software	Lease premiums	Other intangible assets	Assets under construction	Total
Cost at 31 October 2007	**28**	**119**	**18**	**6**	**4**	**175**
Accumulated amortization	(3)	(83)	(3)	(3)		(92)
Net at 31 October 2007	**25**	**36**	**15**	**3**	**4**	**83**
Acquisitions		2			4	6
Amortization for the period		(7)		(1)		(8)
Sale of Jet tours operations	(23)	(2)			(1)	(26)
Sale of Club Med Gym operations	(1)		(1)			(2)
Reclassifications and other		3			(3)	0
Cost at 31 October 2008	**4**	**117**	**17**	**6**	**4**	**148**
Accumulated amortization	(3)	(85)	(3)	(4)	0	(95)
Net at 31 October 2008	**1**	**32**	**14**	**2**	**4**	**53**

Real-life example Saint-Gobain

(France – IFRS – Source: Annual report 2008 – Production, processing and distribution of glass, high-performance materials, and construction supplies)

Note 1 to the consolidated financial statements

Other intangible assets (see Note 4) primarily include patents, brands, software and development costs. They are measured at historical cost less accumulated amortization and impairment

Note 4 – Other intangible assets

(in € millions)	Patents	Non-amortizable brands	Software	Development costs	Other	Total
At 31 December 2007						
Gross value	106	2,763	631	47	279	3,826
Accumulated amortization and impairment	(90)		(441)	(22)	(148)	(701)
Net	16	2,763	190	25	131	3,125
Movements during the year						
Changes in group structure	1		46	1	(26)	22
Acquisitions			43	8	28	79
Disposals			(3)		1	(2)
Translation adjustments		(250)	(8)		(2)	(260)
Amortization and impairment	(2)		(76)	(7)	(11)	(96)
Total	(1)	(250)	2	2	(10)	(257)
At 31 December 2008						
Gross value	113	2,513	684	54	276	3,640
Accumulated amortization and impairment	(98)		(492)	(27)	(155)	(772)
Net	15	2,513	192	27	121	2,868

Real-life example Volvo Group

(Sweden – IFRS – Source: Annual report 2008 – Automotive industry)

Intangible assets, acquisition costs (in SEK millions)	Goodwill	Entrance fees, industrial programs	Product and soft- ware development	Other intangible assets	Total intangible assets
Value in balance sheet 2007	19,969	3,168	19,123	5,387	**47,647**
Capital expenditures	0	399	2,150	326	**2,875**
Sales/scrapping	0	0	(549)	(14)	**(563)**
Acquired and divested operations	1,028	0	185	381	**1,594**
Translation differences	3,634	2	2,386	1,287	**7,309**
Reclassifications and other	182	0	(5)	(380)	**(203)**
Value in balance sheet 2008	**24,813**	**3,569**	**23,290**	**6,987**	**58,659**

Accumulated depreciation and amortization (in SEKmillions)	Goodwill	Entrance fees, industrial programs	Product and soft- ware development	Other intangible assets	Total intangible assets
Value in balance sheet 2007	–	1,639	7,954	1,546	11,139
Depreciation and amortization	–	60	2,864	362	3,286
Write-downs	–	–	–	–	0
Sales/scrapping	–	0	(547)	(12)	(559)
Acquired and divested operations	–	0	(16)	0	(16)
Translation differences	–	0	633	209	842
Reclassifications and other	–	0	21	(12)	9
Value in balance sheet 2008	**0**	**1,699**	**10,909**	**2,093**	**14,701**
Net carrying value in balance sheet 2008	**24,813**	**1,870**	**12,381**	**4,894**	**43,958**

Note: The second column in the list of intangible assets (entrance fees, industrial programs) is less and less rare and is directly derived from the industrial strategy of Volvo Group not to develop its own products alone but in a consortium with partners and, sometimes, competitors. It reflects the fact that, (a) when joining an international, multi-company R&D program such as the ones referred to here, each partner must provide some seed capital and (b) when new partners join an already existing such program they must 'buy into' the program, i.e., compensate the pre-existing partners for the investment they have already incurred and which they are willing to share, thus seeing a dilution of their future returns.

2 Recognition of intangible assets

Different accounting principles favor or oppose **recognition of intangible assets**.

Matching principle: Intangible assets should first be recognized, and then, amortized over the period during which economic benefits are derived.

Prudence principle: Since economic benefits derived from intangible assets are uncertain, the cost that could be considered for capitalization as an intangible asset should, instead, be expensed in the period when incurred.

The recognition of intangible assets is the result of an informativeness trade-off between relevance and reliability or conservatism and prudence (see Høegh-Krohn and Knivsflå, 2000). Accounting standards in local GAAP generally provide recognition criteria for each of the three categories of intangible assets: research and development costs (R&D), goodwill (G) and other intangible assets (O).

Figure 8.4 illustrates the possibilities of recognizing (R) or not recognizing (NR) intangible assets.

As mentioned earlier, IASB (2004b: IAS 38) states: 'the recognition of an item as an intangible asset requires an entity to demonstrate that the item meets: (a) the definition of an intangible asset (...); and (b) the recognition criteria (...)' (§ 18). More precisely, 'an intangible asset shall be recognized if, and only if:

(a) it is probable that the expected future economic benefits that are attributable to the asset will flow to the entity; and

(b) the cost of the asset can be measured reliably' (§ 21).

In case of an acquisition of a discrete asset, the issue is simple; the probability of attributable future economic benefits, mentioned in the recognition criterion (...) 'is always considered to be satisfied for separately acquired intangible assets' (IAS 38: § 25).

In the case of an acquisition as part of a business combination, the situation is more complex. IAS 38 states that, 'in accordance with this Standard and IFRS 3 (as revised in 2008), an acquirer recognizes at the acquisition date, separately from goodwill, an intangible asset of the acquiree, irrespective of whether the asset had been recognized by the acquiree before the business combination'(§ 34). One example of such a situation could be the valuation of the air-rights over a piece of real estate in a dense urban environment. The use of a real estate property represented by, say, a railroad station can hardly be modified, but the right to build over the building or the railroad right of way, can prove to be very valuable when urban constructible land is scarce. The railroad company owning the land probably never valued the air-rights in its books (it did not explicitly acquire that right, and, therefore, cannot put a value on it). For example the new owner of the Pennsylvania Railroad real estate, after the railroad's bankruptcy, was entitled to value – and sell or develop – the air-rights over both Penn station and Grand Central Station in central Manhattan in New York.

The writing-off of goodwill against reserves or retained earnings in business combinations, even if it was used only exceptionally, is no longer supported by the IASB (see IFRS 3, 2008), and is therefore more rarely recommended in national GAAP. The United Kingdom, a proponent for many years of goodwill write-off, has reversed its position and standard FRS 10 (adopted in 1997 by the ASB) disallows this possibility.

Figure 8.4 Recognition of intangible assets

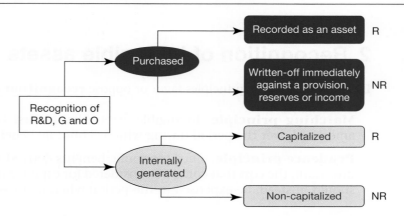

IAS 38 also states clearly: 'internally generated goodwill shall not be recognized as an asset' (§ 48). Finally, IAS 38 (§ 51) acknowledges that 'it is sometimes difficult to assess whether an internally generated intangible asset qualifies for recognition'. An entity should assess if the asset meets the criteria for recognition. The Standard provides some specific developments concerning research and development (see section 4 below).

3 Reporting of changes in intangible assets value

As seen in Chapter 7, the process of allocation of the cost of an intangible asset over its useful life is called amortization instead of depreciation.

3.1 Different possibilities exist of changes in intangible assets value

In principle, three possibilities for reporting changes in value of intangible assets exist and are summarized in Figure 8.5. Either the asset cost is amortized (over different periods: e.g., 5 years, 20 years, or the useful life), or a decrease in value is recognized through impairment, if necessary. A revaluation based on the fair value of the intangible asset is allowed by some countries' GAAP and represents the third possibility of recording a change in value of intangible assets.

Duration and practices of amortization, when the method is allowed, vary between countries, often rendering international comparisons difficult without considerable rework. Some local GAAP simply indicate that amortization must be recorded over the useful life of the asset without any further specification; others require amortization over the useful life up to an upper limit (5, 20 years, or even 40 years as was the case in the USA before the reform of 2001 – see below).

In the USA, the Statement of Financial Accounting Standard No. 142, Goodwill and Other Intangible Assets, adopted in June 2001, abolished amortization over 40 years and replaced it by an impairment test. The same modification has been adopted in Canada. The new regulation has been implemented in the majority of cases in 2002. Following this move, the IASB has revised IAS 38 (IASB 2004b) on intangible assets and issued IFRS 3 (IASB: 2008) on business combinations barring amortization of goodwill.

Figure 8.5 Processes of changes in value of intangible assets (different theoretical possibilities)

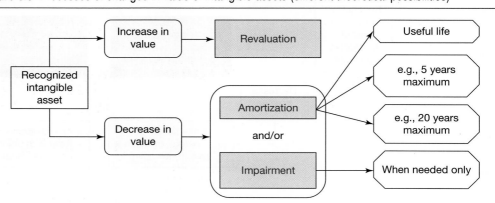

In IAS 38, the treatment of changes in value after recognition concerning intangible assets (excluding goodwill) is now based on the distinction between intangible assets with finite or indefinite useful lives.

- Finite useful life: 'The depreciable amount of an intangible asset with a finite useful life shall be allocated on a systematic basis over its useful life' (IAS 38: § 97).

- Indefinite useful life: 'An intangible asset with an indefinite useful life shall not be amortized' (IAS 38: § 107). 'In accordance with IAS 36 [Impairment of assets], an entity is required to test an intangible asset with an indefinite useful life for impairment by comparing its recoverable amount with its carrying amount' (IAS 38: § 108).

Figure 8.6 summarizes the treatment of changes in intangible assets value after recognition, according to the IASB.

The handling of changes in value of goodwill is somewhat different from that applied to all other intangible assets, and dealt with in IFRS 3. It is based on the following rules:

- no amortization;

- annual impairment test (in accordance with IAS 36: 2004a);

- no reversal of any impairment loss.

This latest element should be highlighted: the reversal of the impairment loss is not possible for goodwill, whereas it is still an open possibility for other intangible assets.

In the case of intangible assets with a finite useful life, amortization and impairment are not exclusive of each other. The impairment amount can be added to the predefined amortization expense if the accountant feels the environment has changed and the pattern of depreciation does not offer a fair net value of the asset (the principle of the 'lower of cost or market' applies here). Many countries, including the Netherlands, Canada, Ireland, the United Kingdom and France, have adopted this position. In addition, the IASB allows the possibility of revaluation for intangible assets (IAS 38: § 75).

Figure 8.6 Processes of changes in value of intangible assets (IASB)

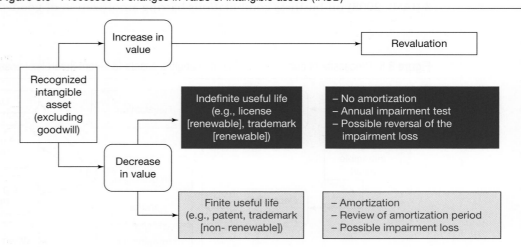

3.2 Comparison of the approaches of the IASB and the FASB (USA)

Figure 8.7 summarizes the evolution of accounting standards at the international level (IASB) and in the USA (FASB) over the past last 40 years.

As shown in Figure 8.7, the treatment of goodwill is now similar at the international level (IFRS/IAS) and in the US GAAP.[1] The treatment of other intangible assets is also similar (no amortization but impairment test required for assets with indefinite useful life). However, there is still a difference between the two sets of standards. It concerns the treatment of the reversal of an impairment loss: this reversal is prohibited under US GAAP while it is allowed under IFRS/IAS (for intangible assets other than goodwill).

We quote below the relevant accounting standards:

- SFAS 142, § 17: 'Subsequent reversal of a previously recognized impairment loss is prohibited.'

- IAS 38, § 111: 'To determine whether an intangible asset is impaired, an entity applies IAS 36. That Standard explains when and how an entity reviews the carrying amount of its assets, how it determines the recoverable amount of an asset and when it recognizes or reverses an impairment loss.'

- IAS 36, § 114. 'An impairment loss recognized in prior periods for an asset other than goodwill shall be reversed if, and only if, there has been a change in the estimates used to determine the asset's recoverable amount since the last impairment loss was recognized. If this is the case, the carrying amount of the asset shall (…) be increased to its recoverable amount. That increase is a reversal of an impairment loss.'

Figure 8.7 Comparison of treatment of goodwill between IFRS and US GAAP

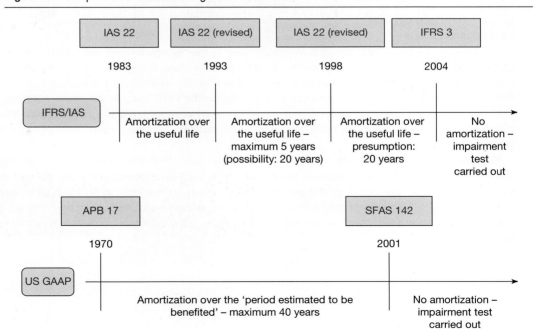

Real-life example Club Méditerranée

(France – IFRS - Source: Annual report 2008 – Leisure)

Note 2.4.3 to the consolidated financial statements: Intangible assets

Intangible assets consist mainly of the Jet tours brand, sold in 2008, lease premiums and software. Purchased intangible assets are carried at cost less accumulated amortization and any accumulated impairment losses. Intangible assets are analyzed to determine whether they have a finite or indefinite life. Based on this analysis, the Jet tours brand and lease premiums in France have been qualified as having an indefinite life. Consequently, they are not amortized but are tested for impairment at least once a year and whenever events or circumstances indicate that their recoverable amount may be less than their carrying amount, in accordance with the policy described in Note 2.7 'Impairment of assets'. All other intangible assets (software and licenses) are qualified as having a finite life and are amortized over their estimated useful life. The main useful lives are as follows:

- Financial information system: 3 to 15 years
- Marketing system: 3 to 24 years
- Other software: 3 to 8 years
- Other intangible assets: 3 to 10 years

These useful lives are reviewed at each year-end and adjusted if necessary. The adjustments are treated as a change in accounting estimates and are made prospectively. Intangible assets with a finite life are tested for impairment whenever there is an indication that their recoverable amount may be less than their carrying amount (see Note 2.7 'Impairment of assets').

Note 2.7.2 Impairment of goodwill and intangible assets with indefinite useful lives

In accordance with IAS 36 – Impairment of assets, goodwill and intangible assets with an indefinite life are tested for impairment annually and whenever there is an indication that their recoverable amount may be less than their carrying amount.

For impairment testing purposes, goodwill is allocated to the cash-generating unit (CGU) to which it relates. The CGUs used by the Group are based on the groups of assets used to organize its businesses and analyze their results. (...) Impairment tests are based on recoverable amounts estimated by reference to market multiples (to determine estimated fair value less costs to sell) and discounted cash flows (to determine estimated value in use). Cash flow projections for subsequent periods are estimated by extrapolating the projections over a five- year period based on a three-year operational plan, a growth rate to perpetuity and the present value of the assets concerned at the end of their useful lives.

When the CGU's recoverable amount determined by the above methods is less than the carrying amount of its assets, an impairment loss is recognized to write down the CGU to recoverable amount, defined as the higher of value in use and fair value less costs to sell. Impairment losses are recorded in priority against any goodwill allocated to the CGU. Estimates of recoverable amounts are based on assumptions concerning village occupancy rates, normative investment rates, growth rates for the region or the business, perpetual growth rates and discount rates.

Real-life example Saint-Gobain

(France – IFRS – Source: Annual report 2008 – Production, processing and distribution of glass, high-performance materials, and construction supplies)

Note 1 to the consolidated financial statements

Acquired retail brands and certain manufacturing brands are treated as intangible assets with indefinite useful lives as they have a strong national and/or international reputation. These brands are not amortized but are tested for impairment on an annual basis. Other brands are amortized over their useful lives, not to exceed 40 years.

Costs incurred to develop software in-house – primarily configuration, programming and testing costs – are recognized as intangible assets. Patents and purchased computer software are amortized over their estimated useful lives, not exceeding 20 years for patents and 3 to 5 years for software.

Research costs are expensed as incurred. Development costs meeting the recognition criteria under IAS 38 are included in intangible assets and amortized over their estimated useful lives (not to exceed five years) from the date when the products to which they relate are first marketed.

Real-life example Repsol YPF

(Spain – IFRS – Source: Annual report 2008 – Oil and gas)
According to notes 4.5 and 4.9 to the consolidated financial statements, the following periods are adopted:

Goodwill	Not amortized but, in accordance with IFRS 3, subsequently measured at cost less any accumulated impairment losses
Leasehold assignment	Related contract terms (from 9 to 50 years)
Reflagging rights	Straight-line basis over the related contract term
Exclusive supply contracts	Straight-line basis over the related contract term (currently five years on average)
Emission allowances	Not amortized but subject to an annual analysis on impairment
Other intangible assets	Straight-line basis over the useful lives of the assets (period ranging between 3 and 20 years)

Real-life example EVN AG (Austria – IFRS – Source: Annual report 2007/08 – Energy, gas, heating services)

(Austria – IFRS – Source: Annual report 2007/08 – Energy, gas, heating services)

Note 24 Intangible assets

(...)

The impairment test for intangible assets in the previous year led to a reversal of impairment losses amounting to TEUR 3,206.2 that were previously recorded to electricity purchasing rights.

(...)

4 Accounting for research and development

4.1 Definition

IAS 38 (IASB 2004b: § 8) states that:

(a) **Research** is 'original and planned investigation undertaken with the prospect of gaining new scientific or technical knowledge and understanding'. 'Examples of research activities are:

   – activities aimed at obtaining new knowledge;

   – the search for, evaluation and final selection of, applications of research findings or other knowledge;

   – the search for alternatives for materials, devices, products, processes, systems, or services; and

   – the formulation, design, evaluation, and final selection of possible alternatives for new or improved materials, devices, products, processes, systems, or services' (IAS 38: § 56).

(b) **Development** is 'the application of research findings or other knowledge to a plan or design for the production of new or substantially improved materials, devices, products, processes, systems or services before the start of commercial production or use' (IAS 38: § 8). 'Examples of development activities include:

   – the design, construction, and testing of pre-production or pre-use prototypes and models;

   – the design of tools, jigs, molds and dies involving new technology;

   – the design, construction, and operation of a pilot plant that is not of a scale economically feasible for commercial production; and

   – the design, construction, and testing of a chosen alternative for new or improved materials, devices, products, processes, systems, or services' (IAS 38: § 59).

Some countries distinguish between **fundamental** and **applied** research within the category of research and development and recommend differentiated reporting:

■ Pure research is experimental or theoretical work undertaken primarily to acquire new scientific or technical knowledge for its own sake, rather than directed towards any specific aim or application.

■ Applied research is original or critical investigation undertaken in order to gain new scientific or technical knowledge and directed towards a specific practical aim or objective.

4.2 Accounting for R&D expenses or costs

The default position, in coherence with the prudence principle, is to expense research and development costs when incurred. This principle applies, with no exception, to research costs: 'No intangible asset arising from research (or from the research phase of an internal project) shall be recognized. Expenditure on research (or on the research phase of an internal project) shall be recognized as an expense when it is incurred' (IAS 38: § 54). However, under certain circumstances and if specified criteria are met, some development (and applied research – when the distinction is made) costs may be capitalized and recorded as an intangible asset.

4.2.1 Conditions for capitalization

According to IAS 38 (IASB: 2004b: § 57), 'an intangible asset arising from development (or from the development phase of an internal project) shall be recognized if, and only if, an entity can demonstrate *all* [our emphasis] of the following criteria are met:

(a) The technical feasibility of completing the intangible asset so that it will be available for use or sale.

(b) Its intention to complete the intangible asset and use or sell it.

(c) Its ability to use or sell the intangible asset.

(d) How the intangible asset will generate probable future economic benefits. Among other things, the entity can demonstrate the existence of a market for the output of the intangible asset or the intangible asset itself or, if it is to be used internally, the usefulness of the intangible asset.

(e) The availability of adequate technical, financial and other resources to complete the development and to use or sell the intangible asset.

(f) Its ability to measure reliably the expenditure attributable to the intangible asset during its development'.

The wording 'shall' is important here as it might lead the reader to think that capitalization of R&D is required if the six above-mentioned criteria are met. In practice, we believe that there is still maneuvering room for businesses. Given that some of these criteria are extremely subjective in their application, it is fairly easy to claim that, even using the same identical facts, a condition has not been met or has been met.

Table 8.2 summarizes the seven necessary criteria stated (explicitly or implicitly) in IAS 38 that must be met for capitalization and provides examples of excerpts from accounting standards around the world, corresponding to these criteria.

Table 8.2 Criteria for R&D capitalization

	Criterion	Illustrative language used in various country GAAP that are in coherence with IAS 38
(1)	Identifiability	■ 'The projects concerned are clearly identifiable'; ■ 'A detailed description has been made of the product and process'; ■ 'The R&D work and the expenditures accrued on the work shall be well defined and the R&D work should have a fixed application'.
(2)	Evaluation	■ 'Their respective costs are distinctly evaluated in order to be allocated over time'; ■ 'Costs to be allocated are determinable'; ■ 'Ability to measure the expenditure attributable to the intangible asset during its development'.
(3)	Technical feasibility	■ 'Proof exists of technical feasibility of the product or process'; ■ 'The technical feasibility of the product or process has been established'; ■ 'The technical feasibility of completing the intangible asset so that it will be available for use or sale'.
(4)	Commercial success	■ 'Each project has a serious chance of commercial success at the date of closing of financial statements'; ■ 'The new product or process will be introduced in the market'; ■ 'There is a clear market potential or other beneficial use'; ■ 'The enterprise should demonstrate the existence of a market for the output of the intangible asset'; ■ 'Ability to use or sell the intangible asset'.
(5)	Future economic benefits	■ 'It will generate future economic benefits over several years'.
(6)	Financial feasibility	■ 'The development process can be completed (i.e., is financially feasible)'; ■ 'There must be resources both for the completion of the R&D work and for the marketing of the product or process if it is intended for sale'; ■ 'Adequate resources exist, or are expected to be available, to complete the project'.
(7)	Intention to complete	■ 'Intention to complete the intangible asset and use or sell it'.

4.2.2 Elements of the debate over capitalization of R&D

Many users of financial statements (financial analysts and banks being among the most vocal[2]) see capitalization of R&D as a grave violation of the prudence principle (see Chapter 4). Any position on the subject is therefore controversial. Arguments for and against are traded by both sides, arguing matching versus prudence.

Arguments in favor R&D expenses, in case of a favorable outcome, should be related to future periods when the benefits will accrue (matching principle). Therefore, R&D expenses should be accrued (capitalized) and not expensed immediately.

Arguments against Future economic benefits potentially derived from R&D are not sufficiently objectively defined or certain to flow to the enterprise at the time the expense is incurred to justify capitalization. The principle of prudence militates therefore in favor of expensing R&D costs as incurred.

Impact of capitalization Let us take an example. Albeniz NA has incurred a development cost for a total amount of 150 CU (80 for labor expenses and 70 of depreciation expense for equipment and facilities used in carrying the development project). The manager of Albeniz NA has decided to capitalize the expenditure and to amortize it over the next five years as she feels the economic benefits will be derived for that period. Figure 8.8 illustrates the accounting entries required to record the first year of the project.

Figure 8.8 Accounting for R&D

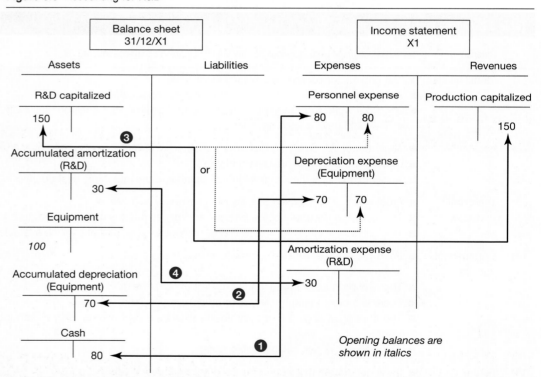

Entries ❶ and ❷ record the cost of the development project. If the conditions for capitalization are met, the total cost of the project is transferred to the assets side of the balance sheet (❸).
Two solutions are available in order to carry out this transfer (❸):

– Cancel (through a reduction of expenses) the original expense accounts (labor expense and depreciation expense) [dotted lines]; or

– Create (through an increase in revenue) a revenue account (production capitalized) [solid lines].

Each country GAAP recommend either one, and on a large sample of countries neither approach seems to show dominance.

❹ Amortization is calculated on the basis of a useful life of five years (150/5 = 30).

The impact of capitalization on the bottom line can be broken down as shown in Table 8.3.

The impact on net income of the choice of method for handling R&D over the amortization period is shown in Table 8.4.

In practice, the impact of R&D capitalization on the timing of income recognition is more complex than shown in this simple illustration because R&D is rarely limited to a one-time project. It is likely that additional R&D costs will be incurred in year 2 and following and capitalized (to be coherent – principle of consistency of accounting methods – see Chapter 4) and thus amortized, and so on. A business whose bottom line is not exactly looking prosperous may be tempted to improve its situation by capitalizing R&D expenses for the sole objective of improving the reported income. In this case it might find itself in a vicious circle: the annual amount of cumulated R&D amortization expense (on past projects) might become so large that the capitalization of the year's R&D expense might become needed for the sole purpose of offsetting the amortization of the previous year's R&D costs. In such a situation, the only rational behavior is to stop capitalizing, even if it leads to reporting significant losses in the first year after the decision (see an illustration in Assignment 8.7 Granados Company).

4.3 Reporting R&D activity

R&D costs are an essential investment in the firm's growth, profitability and ability to remain a going concern. It should therefore be essential to report their amount as accurately and truthfully as possible, in all parts, financial and non-financial, of the annual statements.

4.3.1 Income statement by function

The income statement presentation by function (Chapter 5) is the only one in which R&D expenses can be reported as such. The following three examples illustrate the diversity with which business entities report their R& D expenses:

Table 8.3 Impact on net income of expensing versus capitalization

		R&D is expensed	R&D is capitalized
Net income before R&D		500	500
R&D expenses	Personnel expense	−80	−80
	Depreciation expense	−70	−70
Net income after R&D expenses		350	350
Capitalization of R&D		0	150
Net income after R&D recording		350	500
Amortization of R&D if capitalized		0	−30
Income before income tax		350	470
Differential net income before tax in year 1, due to treatment of R&D		+ 120	

Table 8.4 Impact on net income over the life of the project

	Year 1	Year 2	Year 3	Year 4	Year 5	Total
(1) R&D is expensed first	−150					−150
(2) If R&D is capitalized, expense is reversed	+150					+150
(3) Capitalized R&D is expensed through amortization over 5 years	−30	−30	−30	−30	−30	−150
Yearly impact on net income of capitalization of R&D versus expensing it (2) + (3)	+120	−30	−30	−30	−30	0

■ Bayer estimates that, because of the uncertainties regarding future economic benefits, all its R&D expenses are expensed.

■ Sandvik reports its R&D expenses as a separate function, item or line and then breaks it down between the part expensed and, by deduction, the part capitalized.

■ Saint-Gobain does capitalize the development part of R&D when appropriate and reports expensing the research costs as part of operating expenses (other firms have been known to report their expensing research costs as part of the broader functional category 'selling, general and administrative expenses').

Real-life example Bayer

(Germany – IFRS – Source: Annual report 2008 – Pharmaceuticals, chemicals)

Basic principles of the consolidated financial statements

Research and development expenses. According to IAS 38 (Intangible assets), research costs cannot be capitalized; development costs must be capitalized if, and only if, specific narrowly defined conditions are fulfilled. Development costs must be capitalized if it is sufficiently certain that the future economic benefits to the company will also cover the respective development costs. Since development projects are often subject to regulatory approval procedures and other uncertainties, the conditions for the capitalization of costs incurred before receipt of approvals are not normally satisfied.

Real-life example Sandvik

(Sweden – IFRS – Source: Annual report 2008 – Engineering group in tooling and materials technology)

Note 4 Research, development and quality assurance

(in SEK millions)	2008	2007
Expenditure for		
Research and development	2,347	2,195
Quality assurance	464	544
Total	**2,811**	**2,739**
of which expensed	2,478	2,362
of which expensed relating to research and development	2,014	1,818

Research and quality assurance expenditures are expensed as incurred. Expenditure for development is reported as an intangible asset if it meets the criteria for recognition as an asset in the balance sheet.

Real-life example Saint-Gobain

(France – IFRS – Source: Annual report 2008 – Production, processing and distribution of glass, high performance materials, and construction supplies)

NOTE 1 – ACCOUNTING PRINCIPLES AND POLICIES

Research costs are expensed as incurred. Development costs meeting the recognition criteria under IAS 38 are included in intangible assets and amortized over their estimated useful lives (not to exceed five years) from the date when the products to which they relate are first marketed.

5 Accounting for computer software

5.1 Accounting rules

Reporting computer software costs has long been a debated issue but today's practice is stabilized along the lines described in Figure 8.9.

As can be expected, the most delicate issue is deciding on the accounting treatment of internally developed software for use by the developing firm itself. The costs that can be capitalized in this case vary between countries (see an illustration in Appendix 8.1).

5.2 Reporting computer software costs

5.2.1 Expensing versus capitalizing

Table 8.5 provides some examples of notes relating to computer software issues (excerpted from year 2008 annual reports).

5.2.2 Duration of the amortization period

The term 'useful life' used in the preceding examples remains quite subjective. The possible change of such period of amortization may have a significant impact on the perceived timing of income.

The example below illustrates how the government of the Commonwealth of Australia modified the useful life of its software and thus modified its calculated income.

Figure 8.9 Accounting for computer software

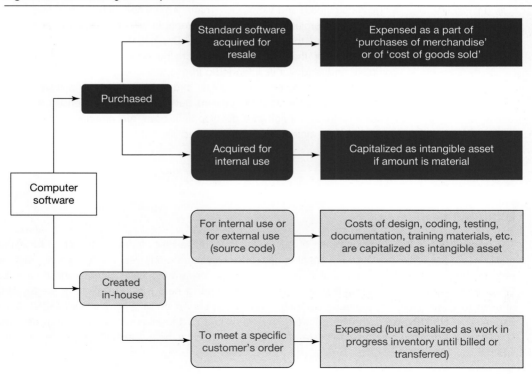

Table 8.5 Examples of reporting for computer software

Company	Type of software and comments	Period of amortization
Bayer (Germany – IFRS)	Costs of €20 million for internally generated software incurred during the application development phase were capitalized in 2008. The carrying amount of internally generated software is €31 million (2007: €27 million) and is recognized in other rights and advance payments.	Useful life
Bull (France – IFRS)	Software development expenses are accounted for in accordance with SFAS 86 principles (US GAAP applied by the Bull Group since 1987) and the French Chart of Accounts, which are consistent with IFRS. However, IFRS extends the principles followed for software development expenses to hardware. Development expenses are accounted for as assets for clearly identified projects whose technical and sales risks are reasonably controlled and on which a return is certain. Only projects with a total development cost exceeding €1 million are recognized. Development expenses cease being accounted for as assets when the product is rolled out as part of its overall marketing stage. Maintenance and continuation expenses are expensed as soon as they are incurred. Lastly, the amounts accounted for assets are amortized using the straight-line method over a maximum of three years and they are tested for impairment each year. Amortization for the period is recognized in the income statement as an expense by type.	Useful life Maximum three years
VimpelCom (Vimpel-Communications) (Russia – Russian/US GAAP)	Software Costs: Under the provision of Statement of Position No. 98-1, 'Accounting for the Costs of Computer Software Developed or Obtained for Internal Use', VimpelCom capitalizes costs associated with software developed or obtained for internal use when both the preliminary project stage is completed and VimpelCom management has authorized further funding of the project which it deems probable will be completed and used to perform the function intended. Capitalization of such costs ceases no later than the point at which the project is substantially complete and ready for its intended purpose. Research and development costs and other computer software maintenance costs related to software development are expensed as incurred. Capitalized software development costs are amortized using the straight-line method over the expected life of the product.	Estimated useful lives

Example

The government of the Commonwealth of Australia has increased the depreciation period for expenditure on 'in-house computer software' which is capital in nature from two-and-a-half years to four years. This measure has an ongoing gain to revenue estimated at $1.3 billion over the forward estimates period, and demonstrates the Rudd Government's commitment to finding savings in the budget to help tackle inflationary pressures. This measure applied to expenditure on 'in-house computer software' incurred on or after 7.30 pm (AEST) on 13 May 2008. Expenditure on 'in-house computer software' is expenditure by the taxpayer on acquiring, developing or having someone else develop computer software which is mainly used by the taxpayer. Expenditure on 'in-house computer software' will continue to be depreciated on a straight-line basis. A four-year depreciation period for expenditure on 'in-house computer software' is the same period as the Commissioner for Taxation's 'safe harbour' effective life for computer hardware. Australian taxpayers are entitled to a tax system that is as fair and efficient as possible and this measure will help achieve that goal.[3]

6 Financial statement analysis

Many financial analysts feel too many would-be-intangible assets are often omitted from the balance sheet due to 'excessive' prudence on the part of accountants. As the economy is moving gradually into a knowledge-based, technology-intensive world, intangibles become ever more important in the competitive strategy of a firm. Investments in information technology, research and development, human resources and advertising have become essential in order to strengthen the firm's competitive position and ensure its future viability (see Cañibano *et al.* 2000, Zambon and Marzo 2007). Because some intangibles are not reflected in the balance sheet, a loss of relevance of accounting information has been highlighted by many studies and one evidence of this phenomenon is the gap existing between the book value and the market value of companies (Hope and Hope 1998; Lev and Zarowin 1999).

Among intangibles, R&D has received special attention on the part of financial analysts as it helps describe the effort of the firm to be innovative and build its future competence. Numerous academic studies (Lev and Sougiannis 1996, for example) have documented the positive relationship between a company's R&D investment and its market value both in the USA and in the UK.

Several ratios are often used in such evaluation, which we will explore further in turn. They are:

- R&D expenses/sales (or R&D expenses/operating expenses), often called '**R&D intensity**'.
- R&D expenses/number of employees: **R&D per employee**, one measure of knowledge intensity.
- Annual growth rate of R&D expenses = {([[(R&D expenses year 2 – R&D expenses year 1)/R&D expenses year 1] – 1)* 100}.

6.1 R&D intensity

Table 8.6 provides some examples of R&D intensity based on 2008 annual reports.

Table 8.6 confirms that the R&D intensity is clearly a function of the line of business of the firm. In industries operating in rapidly evolving technological environments or with short product-life cycles (such as Microsoft), or requiring gigantic investments in innovation (such as Roche, Nokia or Bayer), the need to invest in R&D is much greater than it is in industries where products and processes have a long life cycle and innovation is incremental (Sandvik or Saint-Gobain, for example). The average R&D intensity for a sample of 1,000 EU firms and 1,000 international firms (R&D Scoreboard) reported by the 2008 EU Industrial R&D Investment Scoreboard of the European Commission[4] is 2.3% and 3.8% respectively for 2008 with significant positive skewness and very large standard deviations both between and within countries.

6.2 Link between R&D and growth

Several surveys showed that R&D intensity is linked to subsequent sales growth. For instance, Morbey (1988) demonstrated that companies sustaining R&D investment

Table 8.6 R&D intensity				
Companies	Currency	R&D expenses	Sales	R&D/ sales %
Roche (Switzerland – pharmaceuticals, chemicals)	CHFm	8,845	45,617	19.39
Microsoft (USA – computer industry)	$m	8,164	60,420	13.51
Nokia (Finland – telecommunication)	€m	5,968	50,710	11.77
Bayer (Germany – chemicals, health care)	€m	2,653	32,918	8.06
Procter & Gamble (USA – consumer products)	$m	2,226	83,503	2.67
Sandvik (Sweden – tools and engineering)	SEKm	2,014	92,654	2.17
Bull (France – IT group)	€m	23	1,132	2.03
Saint-Gobain (France – glass and building materials)	€m	377	43,800	0.86

over 4% of sales were particularly likely to achieve higher long-term growth. The R&D Scoreboard reaches a similar conclusion. However Hunter *et al.* (2009) emphasize that corporate spending decisions on intangibles and R&D are likely to be based more on rules-of-thumb than objective evidence. R&D budgets and spending on intangibles remain a discretionary variable and are no guarantee of success. Although it is commonly admitted that the development of a successful new molecule in pharmaceuticals requires an average R&D spending of roughly one billion dollars, spending that much may not always yield the results intended. New blockbuster drugs are somewhat rare, even with the high talent involved in R&D.

6.3 Link between R&D and market value

The success of the NASDAQ as an effective stock exchange has drawn attention to the market value of technology-based companies. Numerous academic studies (e.g., Lev and Sougiannis 1996) have showed the relationship between a company's R&D investment and its market value both in the USA and in the UK. It is therefore quite important, in a spirit of true and fair view, for management to inform its shareholders of the R&D expenditures of their company.

Key points

- Intangible assets are long-lived (long-term) assets that lack physical substance and whose acquisition and continued possession represent rights to future economic benefits.
- Intangible assets comprise patents, franchises, licenses, trademarks, brands, copyrights, etc., and may include R&D costs if these are capitalized.
- It is very difficult to be objective in the valuation of intangible assets as their value may be a function of the firm's ability to use them.

- Intangible assets raise three major questions: (1) What is an intangible asset? (2) How to recognize its value in the books? and (3) How to treat a change in its value over time?
- When purchased, intangibles are valued without any ambiguity; the valuation of internally generated intangibles is a highly debated issue among accountants and analysts, as well as between them.
- The choice of capitalization versus expensing is the result of a trade-off between the matching and the prudence principles.

- Intangible assets may be amortized and/or impaired over an appropriate horizon regulated by local GAAP.
- Research and development costs are usually expensed when incurred. However, under certain circumstances, some development expenses may be capitalized and recorded as an intangible asset if a set of specified 'capitalization criteria' are met.
- R&D intensity, R&D per employee and R&D growth rate are ratios that help analysts and investors monitor the policies of a management team regarding its investment in the future.

Review (solutions are at the back of the book)

Review 8.1 Turina

Topic: Various intangibles

The head accountant of the Turina Company provides you with the following information on three transactions or events in the life of the firm.

1. The Turina Company acquired a franchise on 1 July X3 by paying an initial franchise fee of 160,000 CU. The franchise term is eight years.
2. The Turina Company incurred advertising expenses amounting to 300,000 CU related to various products. According to the marketing department, these expenses could generate revenue for approximately four years.
3. During X3, Turina incurred legal fees of 40,000 CU in connection with the unsuccessful defense of a patent. The patent had been acquired at the beginning of X2 for 150,000 CU and was being amortized over a five-year period. As a result of the unsuccessful litigation, the patent was considered to be worthless at the end of year X3.

Required

Analyze each piece of information and show how you would record each event. Calculate its impact on the financial statements.

Review 8.2 De Falla

Topic: Accounting for R&D

During X1, the De Falla Company incurred the following costs in relation to its R&D activities (all figures in 000 of CU):

- Wages and salaries of researchers, technicians and R&D managers: 100.
- Supplies used in R&D activities (all drawn from existing inventory): 20.
- Depreciation of the building where R&D activities take place: 30.
- Depreciation of machinery and equipment specifically devoted to R&D: 50.
- Allocation of general and administrative expenses: 60.

Required

Assuming that the income statement is presented by function, show the impact of R&D on the financial statements.

Assignments

Assignment 8.1
Multiple-choice questions

Select the right answer (only one possible answer unless otherwise stated).

1. An example of an item that is not an intangible asset is
   - (a) Patent
   - (b) Goodwill
   - (c) Computer
   - (d) Computer software
   - (e) Trademark

2. An example of a trademark which should unambiguously be capitalized is
   - (a) The logo of a business school designed and created by the school
   - (b) The trademark 'Chivas' acquired by Pernod Ricard within the purchase of the whole Seagram company
   - (c) The name 'Oneworld', referring to a group of airlines including, among others, American Airlines, British Airways and Cathay Pacific
   - (d) None of these
   - (e) All of these

3. All recorded intangible assets should be amortized to match their cost with the revenue they contribute to generate.
   - (a) True
   - (b) False

4. Albeniz company spent 500 CU throughout X1 in promoting a not well-known trademark it created internally during that same year. This trademark is supposed to have an indefinite life. The company applies IFRS/IAS GAAP in its financial statements. The 500 CU should be
   - (a) Capitalized and amortized over 40 years
   - (b) Capitalized and not amortized but tested for impairment
   - (c) Not capitalized but expensed in X1
   - (d) Capitalized and amortized over 20 years
   - (e) None of these

5. Same question as (4) but Albeniz applies US GAAP
   - (a) Capitalized and amortized over 40 years
   - (b) Capitalized and not amortized but tested for impairment
   - (c) Not capitalized but expensed in X1

   - (d) Capitalized and amortized over 20 years
   - (e) None of these

6. Same question as (4) but Albeniz purchased the trademark (instead of having developed it internally a long time ago) and applies IFRS/IAS
   - (a) Capitalized and amortized over 40 years
   - (b) Capitalized and not amortized but tested for impairment
   - (c) Not capitalized but expensed in X1
   - (d) Capitalized and amortized over 20 years
   - (e) None of these

7. Same question as (4) but Albeniz purchased the trademark (instead of having developed it internally a long time ago) and applies US GAAP
   - (a) Capitalized and amortized over 40 years
   - (b) Capitalized and not amortized but tested for impairment
   - (c) Not capitalized but expensed in X1
   - (d) Capitalized and amortized over 20 years
   - (e) None of these

8. Training costs of personnel should be
   - (a) Capitalized and amortized over 40 years
   - (b) Capitalized and not amortized but tested for impairment
   - (c) Not capitalized but expensed
   - (d) Capitalized and amortized over 20 years
   - (e) None of these

9. Since economic benefits derived from intangible assets are uncertain, the cost should be expensed in the period when it incurs. Which principle is put into practice in this statement?
   - (a) Going concern principle
   - (b) Matching principle
   - (c) Prudence principle
   - (d) Accrual principle

10. Among intangible assets, R&D has received special attention on the part of financial analysts as it helps describe the effort of the firm to be innovative and build its future competence. Which ratio(s) is (are) often used in such evaluation?
    - (a) R&D intensity = Sales/R&D expenses
    - (b) R&D per employee = R&D expense/number of employees
    - (c) Annual growth rate of R&D = [(R&D expenses year 2 − R&D expenses year 1)/R&D expenses year 1] − 1
    - (d) All of these

Assignment 8.2
Discussion questions

Topic: Types of intangibles

Required

1. Accounting for intangible assets. Discuss relevance versus reliability as they apply to reporting on the intangible assets of the firm.
2. Goodwill. Discuss the pros and cons of the choice between the different possible methods of handling goodwill over time in the financial statements (no amortization, amortization, impairment, immediate write-off).
3. Research and development costs. Discuss the choice between capitalization versus expensing or R&D costs.

Assignment 8.3
Reporting for intangibles

Topic: Usefulness of reported intangibles

On the Internet or in the library find and compare the recent annual reports of four companies from one or different countries in approximately the same economic sector.

Required

1. How are intangible assets presented in their balance sheet? What decisions on the basis of this information can investors or shareholders take? What decisions would be difficult to take on the basis of just the information reported in their balance sheet?
2. Are there any notes relating to intangible assets? In what way does their content enlarge the decision analysis possibilities offered to shareholders and investors?
3. How are the intangible assets being reported? What method and level of detail is used in reporting? Which ones of the four firms in your sample seem, according to you, to provide the most useful information on intangibles to their investors?

Assignment 8.4
Searching for specific intangibles

Topic: Usefulness of reported intangibles

Required

On the Internet or in the library find and analyze recent illustrations or examples of industry-specific intangible assets in the annual reports of four companies from different sectors of activity in a single country or in different countries. Why do you think each industry seems to handle the issue of intangibles in different ways (beyond the differences in communication style)?

Assignment 8.5
R&D intensity

Topic: Comparison of R&D intensity

On the Internet or in the library find the recent annual reports of four companies from different sectors of activity in a given country or in different countries for which you anticipate that R&D expenses may be quite important.

Required

Compare and contrast the firms in your sample.
1. Look for the data relating to R&D expenses and sales.
2. Compute the ratio R&D expenses/sales revenue.
3. Look for the data relating to the workforce.
4. Compute the ratio R&D expenses/number of employees.

Assignment 8.6
CeWe Color*

Topic: Accounting for changes in intangibles

CeWe Color Holding AG is a Germany-based photofinishing holding company. It provides retail customers with color prints and offers digital and Internet services. It divides its business activities into the geographical segments Central Europe, Benelux, Western Europe and Central Eastern Europe. From the notes to the consolidated financial statements (annual report 2008), the following information (in thousands of €) is provided below:

	Industrial property rights and similar rights	Goodwill
Additions	6,082	0
Additions (depreciation)	7,941	0
Amount carried forward on 01.01.2008	52,113	40,391
Amount carried forward on 01.01.2008 (depreciation)	30,998	35,106
Balance on 31.12.2008	62,277	45,610
Balance on 31.12.2008 (depreciation)	40,303	35,285
Book value 31.12.2007	21,115	5,285
Book value 31.12.2008	21,974	10,325
Change in consolidated companies	2,181	5,155
Change in consolidated companies (depreciation)	0	0
Disposals	566	93
Disposals (depreciation)	553	21
Price adjustments	1,748	157
Price adjustments (depreciation)	1,902	200
Reposting/reclassifications	719	0
Reposting/reclassifications (depreciation)	−8	0
Unscheduled depreciation	23	

Required

1. From the information given, which is presented in alphabetical order, prepare a statement showing the movements in intangible assets, using the format presented in Chapter 7 for tangible assets.

2. Show which figures could be used as 'check figures' or 'control figures' in this exercise.

3. Explain briefly the meaning of each line.

Assignment 8.7
Granados Company

Topic: Accounting for Research and Development

Granados Company's current accounting policies call for the expensing of R&D expenditures in the year incurred. The following table presents the amount of expenditures from Year 1 to Year 5.

Year 1	Year 2	Year 3	Year 4	Year 5
200	150	150	100	50

The managers of the company feel the R&D expenditures now probably meet the criteria for capitalization. They are considering modifying their accounting policies and capitalize R&D with an amortization over five years. Before changing over, they ask you to evaluate the pros and cons of such a switch.

Required

1. Compute the impact capitalization versus expensing would have on net income for each year of the period.

2. In which year, if any, will the total annual amount of amortization of past R&D be at least equal to the R&D expense incurred during that year.

3. What would you suggest to the managers of the company, with regard to possible modifications in their accounting policies?

Assignment 8.8
Sanofi-Aventis*

Topic: R&D intensity

Sanofi-Synthelabo and Aventis are two French-based groups, heavily involved in the pharmaceutical business. On 20 August 2004, Sanofi-Synthelabo acquired control of Aventis and the two groups merged on 31 December 2004 under the name of Sanofi-Aventis.

We present below the following income statements:

■ Before merger:
  – Sanofi-Synthelabo (years 2001, 2002 and 2003)
  – Aventis (years 2001, 2002 and 2003)
■ After merger: Sanofi-Aventis (years 2004 to 2008).

The consolidated financial statements of the three structures have been prepared in accordance with French law, and more specifically with Rule 99-02 of the Accounting Regulatory Committee (*Comité de la Réglementation Comptable*, 'CRC') issued 29 April 1999 which, for the purpose of the assignment, can be considered to be equivalent to the IFRS GAAP.

Sanofi-Synthelabo – Consolidated statements of income

(in € millions)	Year ended 31 Dec 2001	Year ended 31 Dec 2002	Year ended 31 Dec 2003
Net sales	6,488	7,448	8,048
Cost of goods sold	(1,253)	(1,378)	(1,428)
Gross profit	5,235	6,070	6,620
Research and development expenses	(1,031)	(1,218)	(1,316)
Selling and general expenses	(2,306)	(2,428)	(2,477)
Other operating income/(expense), net	208	190	248
Operating profit	2,106	2,614	3,075
Intangibles – amortization and impairment	(68)	(129)	(129)
Financial income/(expense), net	102	85	155
Income before tax and exceptional items	2,140	2,570	3,101
Exceptional items	281	10	24
Income taxes	(842)	(746)	(1,058)
Net income before income from equity investees, goodwill amortization and minority interests	1,579	1,834	2,067
Income from equity investees, net	14	20	20
Goodwill amortization	(7)	(8)	(8)
Net income before minority interests	1,586	1,846	2,079
Minority interests	(1)	(87)	(3)
Net income	1,585	1,759	2,076

Aventis – Statements of operations

(in € millions)	2001	2002	2003
Net sales	22,941	20,622	17,815
Co-promotion income		161	252
Production costs and expenses	(7,943)	(6,578)	(5,377)
Selling, general and administrative costs and other operating income (expenses)	(7,178)	(6,866)	(5,365)
Research and development	(3,481)	(3,420)	(2,924)
Restructuring expenses	(50)	(68)	(251)
Goodwill amortization	(650)	(1,021)	(480)
Operating income	3,639	2,830	3,670
Equity in earnings of affiliated companies	85	51	(107)
Interest (expense) income – net	(704)	(309)	(151)
Miscellaneous non-operating income and expenses – net	(134)	1,120	(501)
Income before taxes and minority interests	2,886	3,692	2,911
Provision for income taxes	(1,111)	(1,430)	(929)
Minority interests	(142)	(86)	(29)
Preferred remuneration	(128)	(85)	(52)
Net income	1,505	2,091	1,901

Sanofi-Aventis – Statements of income

(in € millions)	2004 (as reported in 2004)	2004 (as restated in 2005)	2005	2006	2007	2008
Net sales	**15,043**	**14,871**	**27,311**	**28,373**	**28,052**	**27,568**
Other revenues		862	1,202	1,116	1,155	1,249
Cost of goods sold	(3,753)	(4,439)	(7,566)	(7,587)	(7,571)	(7,337)
Gross profit	11,290	11,294	20,947	21,902	21,636	21,480
Research and development expenses	(7,455)	(2,389)	(4,044)	(4,430)	(4,537)	(4,575)
Selling and general expenses	(4,500)	(4,600)	(8,250)	(8,020)	(7,554)	(7,168)
Other operating income/(expense), net	360	214	261	391	522	556
Other operating expenses		(38)	(124)	(116)	(307)	(353)
Operating profit	**(305)**					
Amortization and impairment of intangibles	(1,563)					
Amortization of intangibles		(1,581)	(4,037)	(3,998)	(3,654)	(3,483)
Operating income before restructuring, impairment of property, plant and equipment and intangibles, gains and losses on disposals, and litigation		**2,900**	**4,753**	**5,729**	**6,106**	**6,457**
Restructuring costs		(679)	(972)	(274)	(137)	(585)
Impairment of property, plant and equipment and intangibles			(972)	(1,163)	(58)	(1,554)
Gains and losses on disposals, and litigation		205	79	536	–	76
Operating income		**2,426**	**2,888**	**4,828**	**5,911**	**4,394**
Financial expenses		(239)	(532)	(455)	(329)	(335)
Financial income		124	287	375	190	103
Financial income/(expense), net	25					
Income before tax and exceptional items	**(1,843)**					
Income before tax and associates		**2,311**	**2,643**	**4,748**	**5,772**	**4,162**
Exceptional items	(402)					
Income taxes	(819)	(479)	(477)	(800)	(687)	(682)
Share of profit/loss of associates		409	427	451	597	812
Net income before income from equity investees, goodwill amortization and minority interests	**(3,064)**					
Income from equity investees, net	(261)					
Goodwill amortization	(292)					
Net income before minority interests	(3,617)					
Minority interests	7					
Net income	**(3,610)**	**2,241**	**2,593**	**4,399**	**5,682**	**4,292**
Net income attributable to minority interests		255	335	393	419	441
Net income attributable to equity holders of the company		**1,986**	**2,258**	**4,006**	**5,263**	**3,851**

In the notes to the financial statements of the three groups (Sanofi-Synthelabo, Aventis and Sanofi-Aventis), we can read that Research and Development expenses are charged to the income statement as incurred.

Required

1. Compute the R&D intensity over the period for each company.

2. Comment on the evolution over time of the figures you have calculated.

References

ASB (1997) Financial Reporting Standard No. 10: Goodwill and Intangible Assets, London.

Cañibano, L., García-Ayuso, M. and Sánchez, M.P. (2000) 'Accounting for intangibles: A literature review', *Journal of Accounting Literature* 19: 102–30.

Ding, Y., Richard, J. and Stolowy, H. (2008) 'Towards an understanding of the phases of goodwill accounting in four western capitalist countries: From stakeholder model to shareholder model', *Accounting, Organizations and Society* 33(7–8): 718–55.

FASB (2001) Statement of Financial Accounting Standards No. 142: Goodwill and Other Intangible Assets, Norwalk, CT

Høegh-Krohn, N.E.J. and Knivsflå, K.H. (2000) 'Accounting for intangible assets in Scandinavia, the UK, the US, and by the IASC: Challenges and a Solution', *The International Journal of Accounting* 35(2): 243–65.

Hope, T. and Hope, J. (1998) *Managing in the Third Wave*, Cambridge, MA: Harvard Business Press.

Hunter, L.C., Webster E. and Wyatt A. (2009) 'Identifying Corporate Expenditures on Intangibles Using GAAP', *Melbourne Institute Working Paper Series Working Paper No. 12/09*, Melbourne: University of Melbourne.

IASB (2004a) International Accounting Standard No. 36: Impairment of Assets, London.

IASB (2004b) International Accounting Standard No. 38: Intangible Assets, London.

IASB (2008) International Financial Reporting Standard No. 3: Business Combinations, London.

Lev, B. and Sougiannis, T. (1996) 'The capitalization, amortization and value relevance of R&D', *Journal of Accounting and Economics* 21: 107–38.

Lev, B.,and Zarowin, P. (1999) 'The boundaries of financial reporting and how to extend them', *Journal of Accounting Research* 37(2): 353–85.

Morbey, G.K. (1988) 'R&D: Its relationship to company performance', *The Journal of Product Innovation Management* 5(3): 191–201.

Zambon, S. and Marzo, G. (eds.) (2007). *Visualising intangibles: Measuring and reporting in the knowledge economy*, Aldershot, UK: Ashgate.

Further reading

Cazavan-Jeny, A. and Jeanjean, T. (2006) 'The negative impact of R&D capitalization: A value relevance approach, *European Accounting Review* 15(1): 37–61.

Kohlbeck, M.J., Cohen, J.R. and Holder-Webb, L.L. (2009) 'Auditing intangible assets and evaluating fair market value: The case of reacquired franchise rights', *Issues in Accounting Education* 24(1): 45–61.

Nixon, B. (1997) 'The accounting treatment of research and development expenditure: Views of UK company accountants', *European Accounting Review* 6(2): 265–77.

Power, M. (1992) 'The politics of brand accounting in the United Kingdom, *European Accounting Review* 1(1): 39–68.

Stolowy, H., Haller, A. and Klockhaus, V. (2001) 'Accounting for brands in France and Germany compared with IAS 38 (intangible assets) – An illustration of the difficulty of international harmonization', *The International Journal of Accounting* 36(2): 147–67.

Stolowy, H. and Jeny-Cazavan, A. (2001) 'International accounting disharmony: The case of intangibles', *Accounting, Auditing and Accountability Journal* 14(4): 477–96.

Additional material on the website

Go to http://www.cengage.co.uk/stolowy3 for further information, journal entries and extra assignments for each chapter.

The following appendices to this chapter are available on the dedicated website:

Appendix 8.1: Accounting for computer software

Notes

1. See more on this in Ding, Richard and Stolowy (2008).
2. However, the capitalization of R&D expenses is one of the major adjustments to income suggested by Stern Stewart & Co., the firm that invented EVA (economic value added – a variation return on capital employed) and promotes its use for the evaluation of the return on capital invested by shareholders (more on this in Chapter 18).
3. Source: Treasury of the Commonwealth of Australia, Media Release No 049, 13 May 2008.
4. http://iri.jrc.ec.europa.eu/research/scoreboard_2008.htm.

C9

Chapter 9
Inventories

Learning objectives

After studying this chapter, you will understand:

- That inventories play an important role in the operating cycle of a business entity.
- That inventories may represent a significant part of an entity's assets and, consequently, that an important quantity of funds may be required to finance them.
- That there are different categories of inventories (such as finished goods, semi-finished goods, components and materials).
- That there are different methods for valuing the cost of goods withdrawn from inventory.
- How to record movements in inventory.
- How profit is affected by the choice of how to attach costs to objects that transit through an inventory before their sale.
- How inventory valuation methods affect cash flow.
- What the accounting consequences are of a decline in the value of an inventory.
- Why knowledge of detailed information about inventories is important to restate an income statement by nature into an income statement by function (and vice-versa).
- How inventory valuation policies are disclosed.
- How to analyze inventory turnover.

Inventories play a critical role in the operating cycle of all manufacturing entities and can play a significant role even in service industries as **work in progress** and work in process. They play the role of buffers of differences in timing between demand and production (supply). In accounting, an inventory helps in the application of the matching principle.

An inventory is akin to a storage tank that can release its content (the costs attached to the objects held in inventory) when certain triggering events take place. For example, as long as a product (or service in the case of a long-term contract) has not been sold, all costs attached to it should be withheld from the income statement. They are temporarily 'stored' in an inventory account, which is an asset, i.e., a potential source of future economic benefits.

Even if, in a world of just in time, the role of **inventories** is decreasing as a management tool for adjusting the needs of cost minimization (long series, for example) and production smoothing (avoidance of set up costs, for example) to the randomness or seasonality of demand, inventories still create significant issues in reporting to shareholders: (a) inventories represent an immobilization of funds (required to finance them), and (b) the choice of how to attach costs to objects that transit through an inventory before their sale affects profit. It is therefore important to examine how inventories are recorded and reported.[1]

The three major issues relating to accounting for inventories valuation are shown in Figure 9.1. They are: **periodicity of recording** (perpetual or periodic), **costing of inflows and outflows** (specific identification, versus FIFO, LIFO or weighted average cost), and **valuation adjustments** (cost based or market based).

1 Classification of inventories

1.1 Definition

According to IAS 2 (IASB 2003: § 6), 'inventories are assets:

(a) held for sale in the ordinary course of business;

(b) in the process of production for such sale; or

(c) in the form of materials or supplies to be consumed in the production process or in the rendering of services.'

1.2 Different types of inventories

Figure 9.2 illustrates the six basic types of inventories found on a balance sheet, each reflecting a different degree of saleability of the items each contains.

The six inventory types displayed in Figure 9.2 are shown in three colors of background: from dark blue for inventories of goods closest to the customer (they represent potential sales and it is only a question of time until these inventories can be turned into receivables or cash) to light blue for inventories in the process of transformation that will eventually, but certainly, turn into sellable products, to grey to reflect the fact these last two categories of inventories are not potentially sellable in the condition in which they

Figure 9.1 Inventories major issues

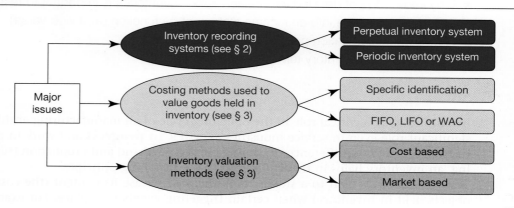

Figure 9.2 Classification of inventories

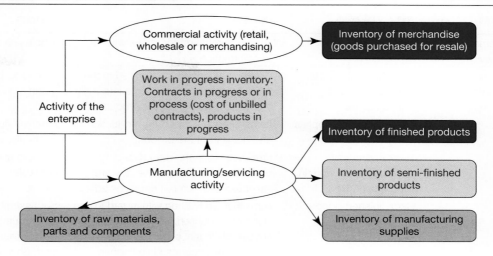

are held (for example, a contract, even completed at a 99% level, is not complete until the customer has formally accepted its delivery). The items referred to in the 'grey' boxes are resources that will require before being attached to the cost of good sold, that they be transformed or integrated in the products themselves (**raw materials** and supplies) or being used in supporting the production process or the machinery and devices that contribute to production (supplies).

Many businesses, as mentioned in Chapter 6, report in a single line their work in process and their contracts in progress even though the two items are not of the same nature.

Work in process measures the value of the resources attached to items that are still left in the process of production on the closing date. Normally, work in process should be a pretty small investment, equal to, at the worst, less than the sum of the resources required to manufacture the quantity produced in half a product production cycle.

Contract(s) in progress (see Chapter 6) can legitimately represent large amounts of investment since that item on the balance sheet measures the amount of resources consumed in realizing all or part of a (long-term) contract but for which no invoicing has been issued to the customer. If invoicing takes place, for example, only every four months, the cost of up to four months of production may be listed under contracts in progress. As soon as an invoice is issued, all corresponding resources (in application of the matching principle and subject to long-term contract rules) are carried, as cost of goods sold, to the income statement. On average, in the example of billing every four months, the contracts in progress account will represent about two months worth of activity or 16% of the annual cost of goods sold in a steady stream of business, i.e., a significant amount invested.

The terms 'in progress' and 'in process' are often seen as clearly interchangeable, despite their representing, as already mentioned, fundamentally different concepts. However, in coherence with IASB terminology, we will use the term 'work in progress', and specify, when needed, the specifics of what is meant. The reader will take solace in the fact that most of the time the initials, i.e. WIP, are used to refer to either of these items.

Table 9.1 presents and illustrates the various categories of inventories.

The reader will take solace in the fact that most of the time the initials, i.e., WIP, are used to refer to either of these items

Table 9.1 Main categories of inventories[2]

Activity	Name of the goods	Definition	Examples
Commercial activity	Merchandise	Goods purchased for resale without transformation	Wholesale and retail activities
Manufacturing activity	Raw materials, parts, components and consumables	Goods that, once incorporated in the production process, become integrally and physically part of the product	Electronic parts in a computer manufacturing business
	Manufacturing supplies	Items used in supporting production and not part of the product	Machine fluids, cleaning materials, spare parts
	Work in process called by IASB work in progress (WIP)	Products still in the manufacturing process at the close of the day and services rendered but not invoiced	Chassis and parts of a computer still on the assembly line at the end of the day
	Semi-finished goods	Items that are finished with regard to one stage of production but are nonetheless not sellable in that condition. They will generally be integrated in a finished product at a later date	Subassembly of the chassis of a computer waiting to receive the microprocessor and the skirt, once the customer order is known
	Finished goods	Completed products ready for sale	Computers ready to be shipped
Service activity	Work in progress	Accumulated costs incurred in fulfilling a contract and not yet billed	Consultancy projects, law suit, engineering projects

Real-life example Siemens

(Germany – IFRS – Source: Annual report 2008 – Energy, industry components, automotive systems, information and communication products)

Excerpts from the notes to the consolidated balance sheet		
Inventories		30 September
(in € million)	2008	2007
Raw materials and supplies	2,593	2,201
Work in process	3,588	3,196
Costs and earnings in excess of billings on uncompleted contracts	7,537	7,099
Finished goods and products held for resale	2,835	2,558
Advances to suppliers	794	751
	17,347	15,805
Advance payments received	(2,838)	(2,875)
	14,509	12,930

Comments

■ The amounts in the notes are net of allowances for provisions (see Chapter 4 and section 5 of this chapter).

■ Finished products and merchandise are reported as a single item, thus not allowing the information users to understand the breakdown between inventories of finished products (manufactured in house) and inventories of merchandise (acquired from third-party suppliers, for resale without transformation).

■ The large amount listed under 'work in process' possibly reflects a choice made by Siemens to pool together work in process and semi-finished products. That choice is not unreasonable since a large part of Siemens' activity is in heavy equipment and long-term contracts and therefore much of the semi-finished products are probably part of a product that will take more than the interim reporting period to complete.

Real-life example Sony Corporation

(Japan – Japanese/US GAAP – Source: Annual report 2009 – Electronics [such as AV/IT products and components], games [such as PlayStation], entertainment [such as motion pictures and music], and financial services)

Excerpts from the notes to the consolidated balance sheet

Note 3 Inventories (in Yen million)

	31 March	
	2008	2009
Finished products	687,095	573,952
Work in process	119,656	79,848
Raw materials, purchased components and supplies	214,844	159,268
	1,021,595	813,068

Note 4 Film costs (in Yen million)

	31 March	
	2008	2009
Theatrical:		
Released (including acquired film libraries)	130,280	112,425
Completed not released	5,369	23,778
In production and development	133,829	120,374
Television licensing:		
Released (including acquired film libraries)	25,801	37,935
In production and development	1,652	4,180
Broadcasting rights	16,808	18,632
Less: current portion of broadcasting rights included in inventories	(9,496)	(10,447)
Total film costs	304,243	306,877

Comments

Sony is a very complex organization dealing both in manufacturing and selling diversified electronic equipment and in creating and selling cultural material (music and films). In the past, it used to distinguish current from non-current inventories (a rather unusual situation but quite legitimate in the entertainment field). The first ones are used in the course of the operating cycle (i.e., within less than 12 months after acquisition or creation). This includes both manufactured goods and entertainment products whose release is expected within the next 12 months. The non-current inventories represent film rights, which are held for use over a period of time extending beyond one year. Technically one might have been tempted to consider non-current inventories as long-lived (fixed) assets since they represent a right to future stream of economic benefits. However, such assets (films already released for which Sony holds future TV and DVD rights as well as films under development whose release date is not within 12 months, i.e., work in progress) do not qualify as tangible assets since they have been acquired (or created) for the sole purpose of being sold as such. Sony changed its reporting method in 2005 and now discloses 'inventories' (note 3, formerly 'current' inventories), separately from 'film costs' (note 4, formerly 'non-current' inventories) which is reported on a specific line between current assets and financial assets.

Real-life example Alstom

(France – IFRS – Source: Annual report 2008 – Engineering and manufacturing in power generation, transportation systems and maintenance)

The following two notes to the financial statements indicate the situation of inventories, in the larger sense, of Alstom. The notes distinguish between 'true' inventories and 'construction [i.e., long-term] contracts in progress', another form of inventory created by the difference of timing between incurrence of costs and recognition of these costs when sales are invoiced. The reporting of construction contracts is more akin to an inventory than to a receivable.

NOTE 16. INVENTORIES			
At 31 March (in € million)	**2009**	**2008**	**2007**
Raw materials and supplies	1,019	750	663
Work in progress	1,995	1,742	1,291
Finished products	147	123	116
Inventories, gross	3,161	2,615	2,070
Write-down	(285)	(299)	(300)
Inventories	2,876	2,316	1,770
NOTE 17. CONSTRUCTION CONTRACTS IN PROGRESS			
At 31 March (in € million)	**2009**	**2008**	**2007**
Construction contracts in progress, assets	3,139	2,807	2,858
Construction contracts in progress, liabilities	(10,581)	(8,931)	(7,239)
Construction contracts in progress	(7,442)	(6,124)	(4,381)
At 31 March (in € million)	**2009**	**2008**	**2007**
Contract costs incurred plus recognized profits minus recognized losses to date	46,180	39,681	35,197
Less progress billings	(49,258)	(42,504)	(37,084)
Construction contracts in progress excluding down payments received from customers	(3,078)	(2,823)	(1,887)
Down payments received from customers	(4,364)	(3,301)	(2,494)
Construction contracts in progress	(7,442)	(6,124)	(4,381)

Comments

■ Note that since Alstom does most of its business in long-term contracts, they report their inventories of work in progress pertaining to these contracts separately from the inventories more linked to the manufacturing side.

■ While the inventories (strictly speaking) are using funds, the contracts in progress are, in Alstom's case, a net source of funds because customers provide down payments and billing is generally negotiated in such a way the customer finances the project (in exchange for a lower price).

1.3 Weight of inventories in the balance sheet

Inventories sometimes represent a large portion of assets and therefore their correct valuation is essential for reporting shareholders' equity. The larger the proportion of total assets is represented by inventories, the more important it is to correctly estimate the physical inventories and their value.

For example, when Charbonnages de France (the now defunct French coal monopoly) was holding inventories of about one year's supply of coal in the early 1960s (when coal was still a major source of fuel in France), it was rumored that an error of estimation of less than 1% of the physical inventory of coal could either entirely erase the losses of the firm or double them. When one knows how difficult it is to estimate the physical quantity of coal in a coal storage bin (and even harder when we are talking about tens of millions of tons), one realizes that errors of more than 1% either way were very likely.

Table 9.2 Weight of inventories

Company	Currency (millions)	Inventory	Total assets	Inventories/ total assets (%)
Siemens (Germany – Energy, industry components, automotive systems, communication products)	€	14,509	94,463	15.4
Volvo (Sweden – Cars, trucks, buses, construction equipment, aero, marine and industrial engines)	SEK	55,045	372,419	14.8
Bosch (Germany – Automotive equipment, consumer goods, communication technology, capital goods)	€	6,826	46,761	14.6
Pirelli (Italy – Tires, cables and broadband systems)	€	921	6,933	13.3
Norsk Hydro (Norway – Aluminum and energy)	NOK	12,227	92,046	13.3
Kerry (Ireland – Consumer foods, agribusiness)	€	513	3,877	13.2
Aluminum Corporation of China (China – Aluminum production)	RMB	9,655	76,383	12.6
Unilever (Netherlands/Great Britain – Food business, detergents, home and personal care)	€	3,889	36,142	10.8
Philips (Netherlands – Technological consumer products, components, semiconductors)	€	3,371	31,790	10.6
L'Oréal (France – Beauty and cosmetic products, toiletries and pharmaceuticals)	€	1,636	22,957	7.1
Hewlett–Packard (USA – Computers and printers)	US$	7,879	113,331	7.0
Sony (Japan – Electronics, games, music, pictures)	¥	813,068	12,013,511	6.8
SEB (France – Small domestic appliances)	€	84	2,035	4.1
Telefónica (Spain – Telecommunications, media)	€	1,188	99,896	1.2

Each industry (and probably to some extent each firm's strategy) has its own appropriate level of inventory and there is a lot of diversity between industries (as can be seen in Table 9.2) but the interesting exercise is to compare firms in the same industry. However, the lower level of inventory is not always (but it most often is) synonymous with better management unless the services offered by the firm are completely comparable (a rare occurrence). In Table 9.2 Sony and Philips are not directly comparable because of the weight of the entertainment products in Sony's inventories, products which Philips no longer has. However, from the note on Sony's balance sheet (seen earlier) we know that the manufacturing inventories of Sony can be estimated at 813,068 million yen thus giving an industrial inventory as a percentage of total assets of 6.8% which compares favorably to Philips' 10.6%. This is, of course, a first pass at an analysis but it is the way financial reporting becomes useful.

Not surprisingly a service industry like the telephone industry, in which Telefónica operates, shows little inventory compared to other assets (probably parts for repair of telephone exchanges and network infrastructure).

2 Inventory recording systems

Chapter 2 introduced the two methods most commonly used to report inventory movements (whether they pertain to purchases of goods or raw materials or to addition of goods manufactured in-house): purchases recorded in the balance sheet and transferred to the income statement or, conversely, purchases recorded in the income statement and transferred to the balance sheet. In practice, there are two methods for recording inventory movements: **perpetual** and **periodic inventory systems**. We will now study these two practices in details as they impact differently on the profit and on the ending balance sheet structure. We will also examine the possibility that items carried in inventory are either so large, so valuable and/or so specific that they cannot be considered fungible (a basic assumption of both perpetual and periodic inventories) and are therefore kept in inventory under the so-called '**specific identification method**'.

2.1 Perpetual (or permanent) inventory system

Under a perpetual inventory system, a continuous record of changes in inventory quantities and values (entries as well as withdrawals) is maintained in the inventory account. Practically, all movements flow through an inventory account (in the general ledger). Purchases are recorded as increases of the inventory assets in the balance sheet and all withdrawals and consumption are reduction of the inventory assets.

The inventory account is presented in the following way:

Perpetual inventory account

Asset increase	Asset decrease
■ Beginning inventory ■ Purchases (cost of goods purchased) or additions to the inventory (cost of goods manufactured)	■ Withdrawals from inventory (cost of goods sold or cost of goods consumed in the next segment of the 'manufacturing' process)

Balance: Ending inventory (by deduction)

This system provides a continuous record of the balances in both the 'inventory account' and the 'cost of goods sold account'.

Let us illustrate the mechanism with an example. The relevant complete data for the Borodine Company are:

Inventory of goods for resale (merchandise) at beginning of year	200
Purchases of goods for resale (merchandise) during the year	900
Sales revenue from the sale of goods for resale (merchandise)	1,200
Cost of goods sold (valued at their purchase price)	800
Inventory of goods for resale (merchandise) at end of year	300

In a perpetual inventory system, the fundamental inventory equation is used to calculate the ending inventory as follows:

Beginning inventory	+	Purchases or additions	−	Withdrawals	=	Ending inventory (the unknown)
200	+	900	−	800	=	X

$$X = 200 + 900 - 800 = 300$$

This system has two main characteristics:

1. All additions to inventory through manufacturing or purchase are recorded as an increase of the inventory account (asset increase).

2. All withdrawals for sale or further manufacturing are recorded as a decrease of the inventory account (asset decrease) and are eventually charged to the income statement as cost of goods sold.

Dedicated accounting software will help any company record purchases, additions, and withdrawals nearly instantaneously at an acceptable cost if a proper system of control and measurement is introduced. However, creating a closed storeroom with rigorous controls counting all movements (in and out) can be a complex and expensive procedure, even if barcoding has often simplified recording (and the reduction in the cost of Radio Frequency Identification - RFID - will soon make manual or optical tracking obsolete for most businesses). Many small companies do not have the administrative and technical capacity and resources to record all movements in and out of inventory. These companies, in particular, take advantage of the simplification allowed under the periodic inventory system.

2.2 Periodic inventory system

This method is minimalist. It simply follows the general requirement that at least once every period (commonly the year) a business physically counts – and attests to – what is really in inventory and what assets and liabilities really exist (opportunity to record impairment or provisions when needed). The periodic inventory system relies on the required periodic (annual) physical counting to establish the quantities in the ending inventory so that they can be valued.

This system has two main characteristics:

1. All beginning inventories and additions to inventory (through manufacturing or purchase) are, in a first step, presumed consumed and recorded directly as an expense in the income statement.

2. In a second step, the presumed consumption cost is adjusted at the end of the period (adjusting entry) by deducting the independently measured ending inventory(ies).

The cornerstone of the periodic inventory method is therefore the physical inventory figures (always assumed to be measured on the balance sheet date).[3] Appendix 9.1 deals with differences between physical and accounting inventory count. The balance shown on an inventory account in the ledger is only changed when a new physical inventory is taken.

The inventory account is presented in the following way (it must be noted that purchases or acquisitions are not presumed to transit through the inventory account, thus the account is somewhat of a tautology):

Periodic inventory account

Asset increase	Asset decrease
■ Beginning inventory (opening balance)	■ Beginning inventory (assumed consumed)
■ Ending inventory (measured at year end)	

Balance: Ending inventory (measured at year end)

The fundamental inventory equation is expressed as follows (continuing the Borodine Company example):

Beginning inventory	+	Purchases or additions	−	Ending inventory (independently measured)	=	Cost of goods sold or cost of goods transferred (deducted or consumed)
200	+	900	−	300	=	X
			$X = 200 + 900 - 300 = 800$			

2.3 Comparison of recording

As the example shows, cost of goods sold, profit and inventory values are the same under either method, as long as the basic data do not show any inflation or deflation. The preference of most businesses for the perpetual inventory (subject to cost-benefit criteria applied to the information the system generates) comes from the superior managerial information and internal control it provides. A more detailed comparison of advantages and limits of both methods is presented in Appendix 9.2.

Figure 9.3 illustrates side by side the impact of the perpetual and periodic inventory methods on the financial statements of the Borodine Company.

■ The ending inventory value, 300 CU, is the same under either method. It is calculated as follows:

● Perpetual inventory: Beginning inventory (i.e., 200) + Purchases or additions (i.e., 900) − Withdrawals (cost of goods sold or consumption) (i.e., 800) = 300.

● Periodic inventory: The ending inventory is declared to be 300 after an end-of-period physical inventory count.

■ Both methods provide the same cost of goods sold (or cost of goods consumed) which is calculated as follows:

● Perpetual inventory: directly by summing the withdrawal or requisition slips that recorded the movements.

● Periodic inventory (by deduction): Purchases (i.e., 900) + Change in inventory (i.e., 200 − 300).

2.4 Presentation of inventories in the income statement by nature

Figure 9.4 illustrates how inventories are reported in an income statement presented by nature, in companies from countries such as Belgium, France, Italy and Spain.

3 Inventory valuation and reported income

3.1 The basic issue

The value of the cost of goods sold (which by definition is linked to the value of the ending inventory in the balance sheet) directly impacts the gross margin, and, consequently, net income. As a consequence, inventory valuation and costing methods have a great impact on net income.

IAS 2 (IASB 2003: § 10) states: 'the **cost of inventories** shall comprise all costs of purchase, costs of conversion and other costs incurred in bringing the inventories to their present condition and location' (i.e., historical cost of acquisition). IAS 2, like most accounting standards, defines the *value of the inventory* as the critical element (i.e., taking a balance

Figure 9.3 Recording of inventory – impact on the financial statements

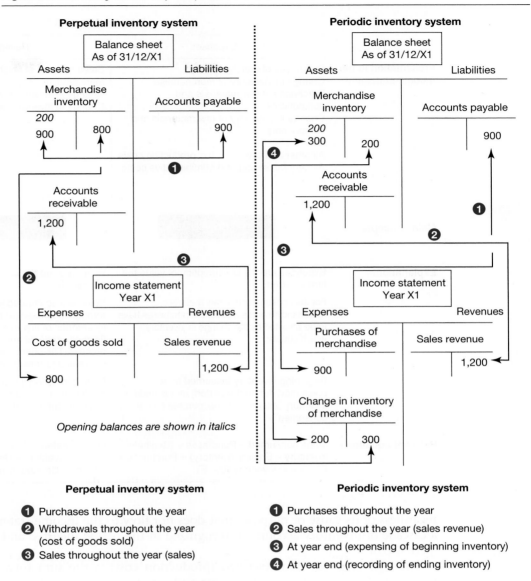

Perpetual inventory system

❶ Purchases throughout the year

❷ Withdrawals throughout the year
(cost of goods sold)

❸ Sales throughout the year (sales)

Periodic inventory system

❶ Purchases throughout the year

❷ Sales throughout the year (sales revenue)

❸ At year end (expensing of beginning inventory)

❹ At year end (recording of ending inventory)

sheet view of the firm). On the other hand, a manager would probably take an income statement view of the firm. Her or his responsibility is to allocate resources in order to manage products and customers portfolios and increase wealth. The *cost of goods sold* is the metric that is the most important element to the manager (and, for her or him, inventory valuation is often only residual data).

Any cost that flows to the income statement by being attached to a 'product' (following the physical flow of goods in their production, transformation and conversion process) is called a 'product cost' or 'inventoriable cost'. Resources entering the inventory are valued at their acquisition cost which is comprised of the purchase price plus supplier qualification costs, sourcing costs, purchasing costs, ordering costs, receiving costs, in-bound transportation costs, warehousing costs, etc. Some components of the acquisition cost beyond the purchase price may prove to be difficult to trace in businesses with weak or non-extant cost-accounting systems. If these items are not included in the acquisition cost they will flow directly to the income statement of the period when incurred. Any cost,

Figure 9.4 Inventories in the income statement by nature

	Income statement	
	Expenses	Revenues
Presentation in the income statement	Purchases of merchandise Change in inventory of merchandise Purchases of raw materials and components Change in inventory of raw materials and components All other non 'inventoriable' production costs All general, selling and administrative costs	Sales revenue of finished products and merchandise Change in inventory of finished products Change in inventory of work in progress
Main concepts	VALUE CONSUMED	VALUE CREATED
Explanations	Expenses are the consumption of value the firm incurred. For the consumption of raw materials, merchandise and supplies, the purchases have to be adjusted by the change in inventory which equals: Beginning inventory [assumed to be consumed during the period] minus ending inventory [assumed to be 'purchases not consumed']	Revenues are the creation of value during the period. Value is also created [or destroyed] through increases [or decreases] in inventories of finished products, semi-finished products and work in progress/in process. The change in inventory is calculated to reflect this value creation: Ending inventory [assumed to have been produced this period] minus beginning inventory [produced in prior periods]
Relevant equation	Value consumed = Purchases + (Beginning inventory − Ending inventory) = Purchases + Change in inventory (B − E)	Value created = Sales + (Ending inventory − Beginning inventory) = Sales + Change in inventory (E − B)

regardless of its cause or purpose, that does not flow to the income statement by way of a cascade of inventory accounts is recognized in the period incurred and is thus called a 'period cost'.

The cost of goods manufactured (production cost) is the sum total of the acquisition cost of raw materials, components and supplies consumed, direct production costs (mainly labor and conversion costs) and a reasonable proportion of production support and infrastructure costs (called 'overheads'). The tracing of overheads to products is a key topic in cost accounting[4] and is not guided by one unambiguous dominant solution.

The cost of acquisition or of manufacturing of an item is not stable over time, even in the course of a year, as the market price of any and all resources change in response to the evolution of their supply and demand.

3.2 Methods for the valuation of inventory outflows (costing formulae for withdrawals)

Four procedures exist for the valuation of withdrawals but only three are outlined and allowed in IAS 2 (IASB 2003: §§ 23–27). The issue is about the relative fungibility of items in inventory. Either they are not fungible and we must use the method of specific identification or they are at least partially fungible (within a batch received or produced) and the issue is that of time-ordering of entries and withdrawals (**first-in, first-out [FIFO]** versus last-in, first-out [LIFO]); it should be noted that the latter method is no longer allowed by the IASB – see below), or they are completely fungible and an average cost can be used.

3.2.1 Specific identification method

Items that are not ordinarily interchangeable or fungible (such as jewels, diamonds, paintings, custom orders, etc.) and goods that were produced for a specifically identified project or customer, will keep their specific cost when carried in inventory. This means that their cost upon withdrawal i s absolutely identical to the one they had when entering in inventory (cost of acquisition or cost of goods manufactured). This method is known as the 'specific identification method'. When this method is used, the distinction between periodic or perpetual inventory system is not needed since the item will be entered or withdrawn only once during the accounting period. This method is simple but extremely costly to implement when the individual value of the items involved is moderate or small. It is also a method that could be used deliberately to affect (manipulate) the bottom line by carefully selecting those items that are sold and those that remain in inventories. Usually, this method is reserved for high-priced items or items that must not be considered to be fungible for legal reasons, such as cars at a dealer's showroom (cars from the accounting point of view of the car manufacturer are generally considered to be fungible within their production series), heavy equipment, farm equipment, works of art, furs, jewelry.

3.2.2 Methods used for fungible and semi-fungible items

When items are fungible to some degree, it is not simple (in fact it is quasi-impossible!) to trace the cost of acquisition of a given item. The specific identification method is unworkable if large quantities of items flow through an inventory account, as it would be impractical to maintain individualized inventory records for each item. Specific identification would be impossible and unnecessary for generic microprocessors, nails or cans of beer, difficult for a hand-finished motor vehicle, necessary for a classic antique piece of furniture, essential for an item produced to contractually defined customer specifications. In other words, it is rarely feasible to trace the cost of a specific item in inventory.

As a consequence, businesses recognize the partial or total fungibility of products and make assumptions about the timing sequence according to which inventory items enter and leave an inventory account to either become part of goods consumed in a further step of transformation (manufacturing) or become part of the cost of goods sold. There are two sets of hypotheses.

Either products are totally fungible, or they are fungible only within a batch defined by a date of acquisition or a period of manufacturing.

When products are considered partially or totally fungible, three possibilities for time ordering withdrawals exist,[5] each reflecting a specific assumed pattern of goods flow:

1. Goods withdrawn are valued batch by batch in the order they entered inventory (first-in, first-out, or FIFO).

2. Goods withdrawn are valued batch by batch in the reverse order from the one they followed when entering inventory (last-in, first-out, or LIFO).

3. Goods withdrawn (considered totally fungible) are valued at the average cost of available goods (**weighted average cost method**, or WAC).

Both the FIFO and LIFO approaches require that a record of each acquisition be kept by date and that the withdrawals be valued by adding complete (or parts of) batches. The WAC is simpler and potentially less costly to operate. It consists in using a continuously updated weighted average for the unit cost of any item in inventory.

In periods of inflation the price (and thus the cost of acquisition) of resources does go up. FIFO or WAC methods do not give a true view of the financial condition of the business. Especially, they may lead to an overestimation of the real value created. If goods purchased three months ago for 100 CU are sold for 150 the apparent profit margin is 50. But if the replacement of these units (a must if the business is to remain a going concern) requires that 120 CU be spent, the 'real' (sustainable) profit is only 30 CU. The LIFO method is more reactive to the evolution (up or down) of the market price of resources and is often preferred to FIFO or WAC in the context of managerial decisions. However, the historical costing and prudence principles would tend to favor FIFO or WAC for reporting purposes. Some other LIFO considerations are shown in Appendix 9.3.

LIFO is permitted as a valid basis for the valuation of withdrawal flows by the European Union but is not allowed any longer by the IASB for consolidated accounts (reporting purpose) in the latest revision of the accounting standard IAS 2 (2003): 'The cost of inventories, other than those dealt with in paragraph 23 [subject to specific identification], shall be assigned by using the first-in, first-out (FIFO) or weighted average cost formula' (§ 25).

The three main reasons for not using LIFO are:

- **Reporting**: Inflation is very limited today in developed economies and there is often simultaneously inflation and deflation on different products or resources, thus the reporting benefit might not be significant.

- **Taxation**: With even a small inflation, the LIFO-based taxable income would be less than it would be under FIFO or WAC and, if there is a reversal of inflation, LIFO might create larger swings in taxable income levels than would WAC or FIFO. In fact, the use of LIFO is forbidden for tax purposes in many countries.

- **Accounting**: LIFO in periods of heavy inflation may lead to a valuation of an inventory that is physically and concretely real but is valued at meaningless costs, thus giving less credibility to the balance sheet.

Figure 9.5 summarizes the different costing methods.

The Glinka Company example summarized in Tables 9.3 and 9.4 illustrates the effect on income and the balance sheet of using FIFO, LIFO or WAC. In this illustration, we assume, without loss of generality, no beginning inventory. Glinka's relevant data for the period under scrutiny were the following:

- 1st purchase: 10 units are purchased and are recorded for an acquisition cost of 10 CU per unit.

- 2nd purchase: 10 units are purchased and are recorded for an acquisition cost of 12 CU per unit.

- 15 units are sold at the end of the period for a unit selling price of 18 CU per unit.

Figure 9.5 Costing inventories

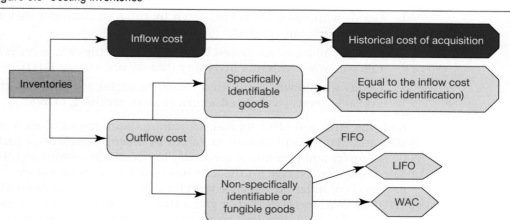

Table 9.3 Cost of consumption and value of remaining inventory

		Transactions (in and out)			Ending inventory		
		Quantity	Cost per unit	Total cost	Quantity	Cost per unit	Total cost
FIFO	Purchase 1	10	10	100	10	10	100
	Purchase 2	10	12	120	20	10 units at 10	100
						10 units at 12	120
	COGS	−10	10	−100			
		−5	12	−60	5	12	60
		Quantity	Cost per unit	Total cost	Quantity	Cost per unit	Total cost
LIFO	Purchase 1	10	10	100	10	10	100
	Purchase 2	10	12	120	20	10 units at 12	120
						10 units at 10	100
	COGS	−10	12	−120			
		−5	10	−50	5	10	50
		Quantity	Cost per unit	Total cost	Quantity	Cost per unit	Total cost
WAC	Purchase 1	10	10	100	10	10	100
	Purchase 2	10	12	120	20	20 units at 11	220
	COGS	−15	11	−165	5	11	55

Table 9.4 Impact on income statement

	FIFO	LIFO	WAC
Sales	270	270	270
Cost of goods sold (direct computation)	160	170	165
Alternatively the COGS can be obtained by applying the full equation			
Purchases	*220*	*220*	*220*
Plus beginning inventory	*0*	*0*	*0*
Equals cost of goods available for sale	*220*	*220*	*220*
Minus ending inventory	*−60*	*−50*	*−55*
Equals cost of goods sold	*160*	*170*	*165*
Gross margin (before tax)	110	100	105
− Income tax (assuming a 40% rate)	−44	−40	−42
Gross margin (after tax)	66	60	63
Control:	220	220	220
Cost of goods sold + Ending inventory	220	220	220
Purchases + Beginning inventory			

In the example presented in table 9.4, the sum of 'cost of goods sold plus ending inventory' is equal to the sum of 'purchases plus beginning inventory' as a consequence of the fundamental inventory equation which can be reformulated:

Beginning inventory + Purchases – Cost of goods sold = Ending inventory
Beginning inventory + Purchases = Cost of goods sold + Ending inventory

The example confirms that, in an inflationary world, LIFO gives the highest cost of goods sold of the three methods and thus the lowest value for ending inventory and the lowest reported income. The situation would be the exact opposite if Glinka had operated in a deflationary world. The effect of LIFO is that, after a period of years in an inflationary world, the balance sheet might no longer present a true and fair view of the company's real assets. However, over the same years the LIFO method has provided management with a true and fair measure of the COGS and thus allowed them to manage both products and customers appropriately to create more value for the shareholders. The debate between the various methods is thus a question of whether one prefers to have a 'correct' income statement or a 'correct' balance sheet.

Table 9.5 summarizes the impact on income and ending inventory of the three methods in the context of rising or falling costs of acquisition.

Inventory misstatements may have an impact on net income (see Appendix 9.4).

4 Inventories and cash flow

The choice of inventory valuation methods has no impact on the cash flow before tax. However, it has an impact on the tax expense that will accrue (because of the differences in gross margins). It will thus change the cash flow after tax. The effect of the choice of a method of cost flow (i.e., inventory valuation) on cash flows is illustrated in Table 9.6 using the data from the Glinka Company example (see above) assuming that sales and purchases are both paid in cash.

Table 9.6 illustrates that, in an inflationary resources market with stable market prices for units sold, it is the use of LIFO that generates the highest cash flow after tax because it provides the lowest gross margin before income tax (Table 9.4). It is therefore easily understood why LIFO might not be authorized for tax reporting in most countries.

Table 9.5 Impact on net income and ending inventory

Context	Impact on net income	Impact on ending inventory
Rising costs	FIFO ⟶ higher income reported WAC ⟶ medium income reported LIFO ⟶ lower income reported	FIFO ⟶ higher ending inventory reported WAC ⟶ medium ending inventory reported LIFO ⟶ lower ending inventory reported
Falling costs	FIFO ⟶ lower income reported WAC ⟶ medium income reported LIFO ⟶ higher income reported	FIFO ⟶ lower ending inventory reported WAC ⟶ medium ending inventory reported LIFO ⟶ higher ending inventory reported

Table 9.6 Impact on cash flow	FIFO	LIFO	WAC
Cash inflow from sales	270	270	270
Minus Cash outflows for purchases	–220	–220	–220
Equals Cash flow before tax	50	50	50
Minus Income tax (40% rate) (see Table 9.4)	–44	–40	–42
Equals Cash flow after tax	6	10	8

5 Decline in value of inventories (end of year adjustments)

Decline in replacement prices, physical deterioration or obsolescence are some of the reasons why the inventory at the end of the year may be worth less than its value shown in the books (assuming all physical discrepancies have been accounted for already). The rule of 'lower of cost or market' is outlined in IAS 2 (§ 9), 'Inventories shall be measured at the lower of cost and net realizable value'. Net realizable value is defined as the 'estimated selling price in the ordinary course of business less the estimated costs of completion and the estimated costs necessary to make the sale' (IAS 2: § 6). This rule requires that a business 'realigns' the books when it finds itself in a situation in which the book value of inventories is greater than their market value (expressed either in terms of disposal or liquidation cost or in terms of sale price that the business hopes to obtain from customers for the goods in inventory). If the 'market value' is lower than the recorded cost, the inventory is written-down to current market value. The corresponding unrealized loss must be recognized in the income statement.

Let us illustrate this point with an example. Glazunov GmbH purchased 1,000 stuffed wombats at a unit cost of acquisition of 20 CU. An Indonesian producer of stuffed wombats has provided all retailers competing with Glazunov GmbH with fairly similar products at 15 CU each. Thus the wholesale market unit price of stuffed wombats has effectively dropped to 15 CU for a product that Glazunov had been purchasing at 20 CU per unit. Glazunov GmbH still holds 100 units in inventory at the end of the accounting period. A provision for loss of value of inventory must be recorded. It amounts to (20 – 15) × 100 = 500 CU. Figure 9.6 illustrates the year-end adjusting entries.

The 'inventory' account is reduced in the form of a contra-asset account ('Provision for depreciation of inventories') so as to not lose information. If the market value recovers by year-end, the write-down (provision) should be reversed either by reversing the expense itself or creating an income or a revenue.

6 Income statement by nature and income statement by function

Expenses in the income statement can be classified either by nature or by function. In Chapter 5 we illustrated how to go from one presentation to the other for Brahms Company, a retailer. We can now illustrate the passage from one presentation to the other for a manufacturing company. Our illustration will be about the Moussorgski Company. The relevant data are provided in Table 9.7 (in thousands of CU).

Figure 9.6 End-of-year adjustments

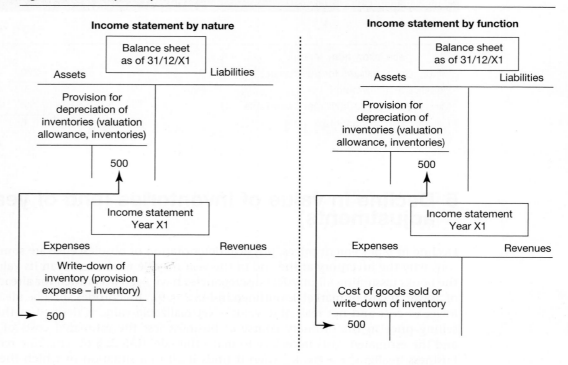

Table 9.8 shows side by side the calculation of the operating income by nature and by function (we assume, for the sake of simplicity, that no general and administrative overhead is allocated to the production costs). The operating income is mechanically exactly the same under both approaches. The difference in presentation offers different possible learning from – and uses of – the information contained in the income statement.

Table 9.7 Data			
Beginning inventory of raw materials	20	Depreciation expenses	
Purchases of raw materials	40	■ Production equipment	19
Sales revenue (finished products sold)	100	■ Sales equipment	5
Raw materials consumed in manufacturing	50	■ Administrative equipment	3
Ending inventory of raw materials	10		
Personnel expenses		Rent expenses	
■ Direct labor	20	■ Production	3
■ Supervisory labor	6	■ Administration	1
■ Sales personnel	4	Beginning inventory of work in process	2
■ Accounting and administration personnel	3	Cost of units transferred into finished goods inventory during the period	88
Total cost of units sold during the period	80	Ending inventory of work in process	12
		Beginning inventory of finished products	3
		Ending inventory of finished products	11

Table 9.8 Income statement by nature and by function

Income statement by nature			Income statement by function		
	Sales revenue from finished products	100		Sales revenue from finished products	100
+	Change in inventory of finished products (a)	8	−	Cost of goods sold (f)	−80
+	Change in inventory of work in process (a)	10	=	Gross margin	20
−	Purchases of raw materials	−40	−	Selling expenses (g)	−9
−	Change in inventory of raw materials (b)	−10	−	Administrative expenses (h)	−7
−	Rent expenses (c)	−4	=	Operating income	4
−	Personnel expenses (d)	−33	(f)	Cost of goods sold	
=	Depreciation expense (e)	−27	+	Raw materials consumed	50
	Operating income	4	+	Direct labor	20
			+	Supervisory labor	6
(a)	Ending minus beginning		+	Depreciation (production equipment)	19
(b)	Beginning minus ending (subtraction of the change)		+	Rent expense (production overhead)	3
(c)	3 + 1		=	Production costs incurred this period	98
(d)	20 + 6 + 4 + 3		−	Change in inventory of finished products (a)	−8
(e)	19 + 5 + 3		−	Change in inventory of work in process (a)	−10
			=	Cost of goods sold (f)	80
			(g)	Selling expenses	
			+	Personnel expenses (sales person)	4
			+	Depreciation (sales equipment)	5
			=	Selling expenses (g)	9
			(h)	Administrative expenses	
			+	Personnel expenses (administration)	3
			+	Depreciation (administration)	3
			+	Rent expense (administration)	1
			=	Administrative expenses (h)	7

7 Disclosure of inventory valuation policies

Although disclosure practices in the notes to financial statements may vary between countries, the following minimum information should be given according to IAS 2 (§ 36):

- Accounting policies adopted in measuring inventories, including the cost formula used.
- Total carrying amount of inventories and carrying amount in classifications appropriate to the entity.
- Carrying amount of inventories carried at fair value less costs to sell (mainly applicable to retail or wholesale trading).
- Amount of any write-down of inventories recognized as an expense in the period (…).
- Amount of any reversal of any write-down of inventories that is recognized as a reduction in the amount of inventories recognized as expense in the period (…).
- Circumstances or events that led to the reversal of a write-down of inventories (…).
- Carrying amount of inventories pledged as security for liabilities.

Real-life example Saurer

(Switzerland – IFRS – Source: Annual report 2006 – Full service solutions in textile machinery and mechanical power transmission systems)

Income statement (excerpts)				
(€ 000)	2006	%	2005	%
Sales	1,894,289	100.0	1,569,786	100.0
Cost of goods sold	−1,526,628	80.6	−1,254,557	79.9
Gross profit	367,661	19.4	315,229	20.1

Note 8 Inventories	31.12.2006	31.12.2005
Raw materials	155,695	128,178
Work in process	190,130	136,472
Finished goods	113,776	99,437
Provision for slow-moving and obsolescent inventories	−50,830	−47,002
Total inventories before customer payments on account	408,771	317,085
Customer payments on account	−76,421	−84,415
Total inventories (net)	332,350	232,670
Write-down of inventories recognized as expense in the period	5,980	6,310

Inventories. Raw materials are valued at the lower of cost and market, using the weighted average cost method. Finished goods and work in process are valued at production cost, reduced to net realizable value should this be lower than cost. Provisions are made for items of reduced salability and excess stocks. Customer payments on account are deducted from inventories.

Several comments can be made on this note.

■ Advances received on orders are subtracted here from inventories. Usually, this item is reported as a liability. We could say the presentation adopted by Saurer, if the offset were not mentioned explicitly in note 8, might be considered in violation of the 'non-offsetting principle'.

■ The notes allow the calculation of the change in inventories of raw materials and supplies, which could not be obtained from the income statement because Saurer reports the cost of goods sold and therefore these variations are hidden in the COGS figures.

■ The fact we have two years of financial statements allows the calculation of the net variation of the provision for slow-moving and obsolescent inventories.

Real-life example Sauer-Danfoss

(USA – US GAAP – Source: Annual report 2008 – Mobile hydraulics industry)

Sauer-Danfoss, one of the largest worldwide companies in the mobile hydraulics industry, designs, manufactures and sells a complete range of engineered hydraulic, electric and electronic systems as well as components. Sauer-Danfoss grew largely by mergers and acquisitions. Since 2008 the company has been a subsidiary of Danfoss A/S of Denmark, which holds a more than 50% interest.

In the notes to consolidated financial statements for the year 2008, we find the following information:

'Inventories are valued at the lower of cost or market, using various cost methods, and include the cost of material, labor and factory overhead. The last-in, first-out (LIFO) method was adopted in 1987 and is used to value inventories at the US locations which existed at that time. Inventories at all of the non-US locations and the US locations obtained through acquisition after 1987, which produce products different from those produced at US locations existing at 1987, are valued under the inventory valuation method in place prior to acquisition, either weighted average or first-in, first-out (FIFO) inventory valuation method. The percentage of year-end inventory using LIFO and FIFO cost methods was 11% and 89%, respectively, for 2008 and 14% and 86%, respectively, for 2007.'

The fact the note gives the opportunity to the reader of the financial statements to recast the income statement according to any of the three basic inventory valuation methods is rather unusual. It helps identify better the earnings potential of the firm in allowing one to understand what comes from past events (FIFO) and what comes from current competitive edge (LIFO), which is a good indicator of future earnings potential. It would appear that the choice of inventory valuation methods favors avoiding the tax effect of switching old LIFO inventories to a FIFO or WAC basis over a coherent presentation of inventories throughout the group. Thus, only the more recently acquired businesses are using the FIFO or WAC methods. This reflects the fact, as mentioned above, that under LIFO, the value of the inventories in the balance sheet might end up being completely disconnected from the reality of the value of the goods held on hand. If Sauer-Danfoss were to convert these 'old' inventories to a FIFO basis, it would have to acknowledge an unrealized gain on the inventory, which would be taxable in the year of conversion.

8 Financial statement analysis pertaining to inventories

The financial analysts' main concern is with the coherence between the actual level of inventory and the one they feel would be desirable, given the operating cycle, the firm's strategy and its competitive business environment. Two metrics are commonly used in this respect:

- *Inventory turnover*: This metric, introduced in Chapter 2, is defined as the number of times the inventory 'turns' during the accounting period. The shorter the operating cycle, the higher the turnover. This ratio is obtained by dividing the cost of goods sold by the average value of the relevant inventory (beginning inventory plus ending inventory divided by 2). For a given industry, the higher the turnover ratio, the more likely the management of the physical flows is efficient. With the development of just-in-time relations between suppliers and customers, ratios of 26 (equivalent to an inventory sufficient to meet the needs of 2 weeks of average demand or consumption) or even 52 (one week) are no longer unusual in the automotive industry or the assembly of washing machines.

- *Average days of inventory available*: This metric is essentially the inverse of the turnover ratio. It expresses the inventory in terms of number of days of activity that can be 'supplied' without having to purchase (or produce) any new products or materials. It is obtained as the 'number of activity days in the year divided by the turnover ratio'. Given the actual number of activity days is different with each country, it is common practice to use 365 days as the numerator in the calculation of the average days of inventory.

The choice of presentation of the income statement (by nature or by function) facilitates or hinders the calculation of these ratios. In an income statement by nature, extensive information is available describing the inventories for each type of object (**finished goods**, intermediate products, raw materials, WIP, components or **merchandise**) but the cost of goods sold is difficult to measure. An income statement by nature is best used in retail businesses since such businesses do not carry any transformation activity. The

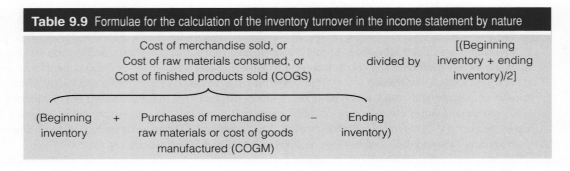

Table 9.9 Formulae for the calculation of the inventory turnover in the income statement by nature

Cost of merchandise sold, or Cost of raw materials consumed, or Cost of finished products sold (COGS)	divided by	[(Beginning inventory + ending inventory)/2]

(Beginning inventory + Purchases of merchandise or raw materials or cost of goods manufactured (COGM) − Ending inventory)

calculation illustrated in Table 9.9 assumes that the cost of goods manufactured (COGM) is known. However, the COGM is a cost best known by using the income statement by-function approach. Creating such a piece of data from an income statement by-nature would require a complex job of reclassification and allocation, carried out more efficiently in Management or Cost Accounting which are, by definition, 'by-function' approaches.

The proponents of the by-nature approach in reporting inventories favor providing the value of inventories (beginning and closing) in both the income statement and the balance sheet and must accept that the COGM be provided externally. In a 'by-function' approach, the inventory values are only found in the balance sheet and two balance sheets are required to have the beginning and closing balances of inventories. It should be noted, however, that this is not a real problem as companies always report, as a minimum, the current balance sheet and the preceding one.

In an income statement presented by function, the cost of goods sold is not separated between merchandise, raw materials and finished products. A general inventory turnover is then calculated by dividing the cost of goods sold (obtained from the income statement) by the average inventory (obtained from the balance sheet).

Real-life example Toray Industries

(Japan – Japanese GAAP – Source: Annual report 2008/09 – Manufacturer of synthetic fibers and textiles)

(in Yen million) Note 3 to financial statements		2009	2008
Balance sheet			
Merchandise and finished goods		175,572	174,801
Work in process		86,524	86,455
Raw materials and supplies		57,866	67,191
		(A) 319,962	(B) 328,447
Income statement			
Cost of goods sold	(1)	1,208,056	
Computation			
Average inventory	(2) = [(A) + (B)]/2	324,205	
Inventory turnover	(3) = (1)/(2)	3.73 times	
Average days of inventory available	(4) = 1/(3)*365	98 days	

Key points

- Inventories are essential assets (potential source of future economic benefits): (1) held for sale in the ordinary course of business; (2) in the process of production for such sale; or (3) in the form of materials or supplies to be consumed in the production process or in the rendering of services.
- As long as a product has not been sold, all costs attached to it are withheld from the income statement and essentially stored in an inventory account.
- The three major issues relating to accounting for inventories are: (1) inventory recording systems, (2) inventory costing methods and (3) inventory valuation methods.
- The main categories of inventories are: (1) merchandise (commercial activity), and (2) raw materials, manufacturing supplies, work in progress and process, semi-finished goods and finished goods (manufacturing activity).
- Inventories may represent a large portion of total assets and therefore their correct valuation is essential for reporting accurately and fairly the value of the shareholders' equity.
- The fundamental inventory equation is: [withdrawals = purchases (additions) + beginning inventory – ending inventory].

- A perpetual inventory system is a continuous record of changes in inventory (additions as well as withdrawals).
- The periodic inventory system relies on the required periodic (annual) physical counting to establish and value the quantities in the ending inventory.
- Inventory valuation and costing methods have a great impact on net income.
- There are four methods for costing items withdrawn from inventory: 'specific identification method', FIFO (first-in, first-out), LIFO (last-in, first-out) and WAC (weighted average cost).
- The IASB no longer allows the use of LIFO for external reporting of a business financial position.
- Financial analysts are mainly concerned with the coherence between the current or actual level of inventory of a business with that which would appear to be appropriate given the firm's business's environment and strategy. Their measures to evaluate this coherence are: (1) inventory turnover (number of times the inventory 'turns' during the accounting period), and/or (2) average days of inventory available (365 times the inverse of the turnover ratio).

Review (solutions are at the back of the book)

Review 9.1 Ericsson*

Topic: Reporting for inventory

Based in Sweden, Ericsson is a leading provider in the telecom world, with communication solutions that combine telecom and datacom technologies with freedom of mobility for the user.

The 2008 annual report shows inventories to be as follows:

31 December, SEK million	Note	2008	2007
Assets			
(...)			
Inventories	C13	27,836	22,475

The notes to the consolidated financial statements contain the following information:

Note 13: INVENTORIES	2008	2007
Raw materials, components, consumables and manufacturing work in progress	7,413	7,476
Finished products and goods for resale	7,616	5,338
Contract work in progress	12,807	10,338
Less advances from customers	—	-677
Inventories – net	**27,836**	**22,475**

Contract work in progress includes amounts related to delivery-type contracts, service contracts and construction-type contracts with ongoing work in progress. Reported amounts are net of obsolescence allowances of SEK 3,493 (2,752 million, 2007).

Movements in obsolescence allowances	2008	2007	2006
Opening balance	2,752	2,578	2,519
Additions, net	1,553	1,276	857
Utilization	-1,039	-1,114	-693
Translation difference	250	17	-81
Balances regarding acquired /divested businesses	-23	-5	-24
Closing balance	**3,493**	**2,752**	**2,578**

The amount of inventories recognized as an expense and included in cost of sales was SEK 58,155 (52,864 million, 2007).

Required

1. What are 'obsolescence allowances' usually called?
2. What do the 'Additions' in these allowances represent?
3. What does the item 'Utilization' in these allowances refer to?
4. What restatement is necessary to obtain the gross amount of inventories?

Assignments

Assignment 9.1
Multiple-choice questions

Select the right answer (only one possible answer unless otherwise stated).

1 Raw materials and merchandise are included in

(a) Expenses
(b) Fixed assets
(c) Cash
(d) Current assets
(e) None of these

2 According to IAS 2, inventories are assets: (several possible answers)

(a) Held for sale in the ordinary course of business.

(b) In the process of production for sale in the ordinary course of business.
(c) In the form of materials or supplies to be consumed in the production process or in the rendering of services.
(d) Providing necessary supports to the production process

3 In an income statement by nature, change in inventory of finished products is reported

(a) On the revenues side, under the sales of finished products
(b) On the expenses side, under the purchases of raw materials

(c) Both solutions are possible

(d) None of these

4 In an income statement by nature, change in inventory of merchandise is reported

(a) On the revenues side, under the sales of merchandise

(b) On the expenses side, under the purchases of merchandise

(c) Both solutions are possible

(d) None of these

5 In the balance sheet, the item 'inventories' may be subject to

(a) Depreciation

(b) Amortization

(c) Depletion

(d) Provision

(e) None of these

6 The following inventory costing method provides a value for *ending inventory* which approximates most closely its current cost

(a) FIFO

(b) LIFO

(c) None of these

7 Which of the following statements are true? (several answers possible)

(a) The increase of a business' size generally induces more inventories.

(b) The ending inventory is always a good proxy for the firm's average inventory level.

(c) The weight of inventory as a % of total assets is a function of the firm's business sector.

(d) Firms should accumulate more inventories for paying the liabilities.

8 An audit shows that the beginning inventory at 1 January X1 had been overstated by 1,000 CU and the ending inventory (31/12/X1) was overstated by 400 CU. As a consequence, the cost of goods sold for X1 was

(a) Overstated by 1,000

(b) Understated by 1,000

(c) Overstated by 400

(d) Understated by 400

(e) Overstated by 1,400

(f) Understated by 1,400

(g) Overstated by 600

(h) Understated by 600

(i) None of these

9 In periods of steadily decreasing prices, the following method will give the highest ending inventory value (assuming quantities purchased exceed quantities withdrawn)

(a) FIFO

(b) LIFO

(c) Weighted average cost (WAC)

10 The average day's inventory available is defined as: (Cost of goods sold/Average inventory) × 365

(a) True

(b) False

Assignment 9.2
Discussion questions

Topic: Inventory valuation methods

1. Give at least three arguments in favor of each of the three basic methods of inventory valuation (FIFO, LIFO and WAC).

2. Provide at least three arguments in favor of perpetual and three for periodic inventory accounting methods.

Assignment 9.3

Taylor Nelson Sofres* and Irish Continental*

Topic: Nature of inventory

Taylor Nelson Sofres is a UK group specializing in market information, providing continuous and custom research and analysis. It is active in managing consumer panels and measuring television audiences. Irish Continental Group is a shipping, transport and leisure group (Irish Ferries) principally engaged in the transport of passengers and cars, freight and containers.

Both companies have in common the fact that their inventories are very low, particularly in relation to total assets, as shown in the following table where figures have been extracted from the 2008 annual reports of each company.

Taylor Nelson Sofres		
(in £m)	2008	2007
Inventory and work in progress	343.9	343.9
Total assets	24,463.3	17,252.0
Inventories /total assets	1.41%	1.99%

Irish Continental Group		
(in €m)	2008	2007
Inventory and work in progress	0.8	1.3
Total assets	311.3	386.6
Inventories /total assets	0.26%	0.34%

Required

Provide a list of possible items that could be included under the item 'inventories' for each of these companies.

Assignment 9.4
Stravinsky

Topic: Application of the FIFO, LIFO and WAC methods.

Stravinsky Company, a retailer selling a single product, opened shop on 2 April. The first months' transactions were as follows:

April 02: Takes delivery and is invoiced for 220 units @ 22 CU each

April 08: Takes delivery and is invoiced for 180 units @ 18 CU each
April 17: Sale of 240 units @ 25 CU each.

Required

Using successively each of the three costing methods (FIFO, LIFO and WAC), prepare a table allowing you to compare the impact of the three methods on:

1. the ending inventory;
2. the net income, assuming a 40% income tax rate;
3. the cash flow.

Assignment 9.5
Repsol*

Topic: Reporting inventories

Repsol is a Spanish group involved in the oil and gas sector. From the financial statements (annual report 2008), which are prepared in accordance with IFRS, we extracted the following information relating to inventory.

Excerpts from the consolidated income statement		
(in € million)	2008	2007
Expenses		
Materials used	40,861	36,294
(...)		
Revenues		
Net sales	57,740	52,098
Services rendered and other income	1,892	1,767
Changes in inventories of finished goods and work in progress inventories	(274)	387
Income from reversal of impairment losses and gains on disposal of non-current assets	183	844
Allocation of subsidies on non-financial assets and other subsidies	18	13
Other operating income	1,416	814
	60,975	55,923

Excerpts from the consolidated balance sheet		
	31 December	
(in € million)	2008	2007
Assets		
Inventories (Note 16)	3,584	4,675

Excerpts from the notes

(in € million)	Cost	Allowance for decline in value	Net
2008			
Crude oil and natural gas	982	–	982
Finished and semi-finished products	2,429	(253)	2,176
Supplies and other inventories	449	(23)	426
	3,860	**(276)**	**3,584**
2007			
Crude oil and natural gas	1,543	–	1,543
Finished and semi-finished products	2,302	(2)	2,300
Supplies and other inventories	863	(31)	832
	4,708	**(33)**	**4,675**

Required

1. Identify the links between the figures of the balance sheet and the figures in the notes.

2. Explain why some figures of the income statement cannot be double-checked.

Assignment 9.6
Tchaïkovsky

Topic: Income statement by nature and by function

Tchaïkovsky Company manufactures and sells various and assorted products. Information relating to year X1 is given below (in 000 of CU).

Required

Prepare an income statement by nature and an income statement by function. (Check figure [operating income] is 21.)

Beginning inventory of raw materials	18	Rent expenses	
Purchases of raw materials	60	■ Production	4
Sales of finished products	150	■ Administration	5
Raw materials consumed	55	Beginning inventory of work in process	10
Ending inventory of raw materials	23	Units completed during the period	105
Personnel expenses		Ending inventory of work in process	5
■ Direct labor	16	Beginning inventory of finished products	3
■ Supervisory labor	5	Cost of units sold during the period	107
■ Sales personnel	3	Ending inventory of finished products	1
■ Accounting and administration	4		
Depreciation expenses			
■ Production equipment	20		
■ Sales equipment	6		
■ Administrative equipment	4		

Assignment 9.7
McDonald's* and others

Topic: Comparative inventory turnover

The following information concerns seven US companies operating solely or mainly restaurants.

McDonald's Corporation

McDonald's Corporation franchises and operates McDonald's restaurants in the food service industry.

These restaurants serve a limited, value-priced menu in more than 100 countries globally. The restaurants are operated either by the company or by franchisees, including franchisees under franchise arrangements, and foreign-affiliated markets and developmental licensees under license agreements. Extracted from the consolidated balance sheet and income statement (annual report 2008) the following data are provided.

(in US$ million)	31 December 2008	31 December 2007
Inventory, at cost, not in excess of market (balance sheet)	111.5	125.3
Company-operated restaurant expenses – Food and paper (income statement)	5,586.10	5487.4

There is no note to the financial statements indicating the detail of inventory.

Benihana

Benihana operates teppanyaki-style Japanese restaurants in the United States. The company also operates other Asian restaurant concepts, which include RA Sushi and Haru. Its Benihana restaurants offer fresh steak, chicken and seafood; RA Sushi's concept is to provide sushi and Pacific-Rim dishes; and Haru's concept features Japanese and Japanese fusion dishes. From the consolidated balance sheet and income statement (annual report 2009), the following data were extracted.

(in US$ 000)	29 March 2009	30 March 2008
Inventories (balance sheet)	6,529	6,477
Cost of food and beverage sales (income statement)	72,646	69,727

A note to the financial statements indicates that inventory consists principally of restaurant operating supplies (000$ 3,744) and food and beverage (000$ 2,785). The company has a 52/53-week fiscal year. The company's first fiscal quarter consists of 16 weeks and the remaining three quarters are 12 weeks each, except in the event of a fifty-three week year with the final quarter composed of 13 weeks. Because of the differences in length of these accounting periods, results of operations between the first quarter and the later quarters of a fiscal year are not comparable.

Darden Restaurant Inc

Darden Restaurants, Inc. (Darden) operates a full-service restaurant company and served approximately 404 million meals during the fiscal year ended 31 May 2009 (fiscal 2009). As of 31 May 2009, the company operated through subsidiaries 1,773 restaurants in the United States and Canada. In the United States, the company operated 1,738 restaurants in 49 states (the exception being Alaska), including 661 Red Lobster, 685 Olive Garden, 321 LongHorn Steakhouse, 37 The Capital Grille, 24 Bahama Breeze, eight Seasons 52 and two specialty restaurants: Hemenway's Seafood Grille & Oyster Bar and The Old Grist Mill Tavern. In Canada, it operated 35 restaurants, including 29 Red Lobster and six Olive Garden restaurants. From the consolidated balance sheet and income statement (annual report 2009), the following data were extracted.

(in US$ million)	31 May 2009	25 May 2008
Inventories (balance sheet)	247.0	216.7
Food and beverage costs (income statement)	2,200.3	1,996.2

A note to the financial statements indicates that inventory consists principally of food and beverages. The company's fiscal year is a 52- or 53-week year ending on the last Sunday in May each year.

Diedrich Coffee

Diedrich Coffee is a specialty coffee roaster, wholesaler and retailer. The company's brands include Diedrich Coffee, Gloria Jean's and Coffee People. The majority of its revenue is generated from wholesale customers located across the United States. In addition, the company operates a coffee roasting facility in central California that supplies freshly roasted coffee beans to its retail locations and to its wholesale customers. From the consolidated balance sheet and income statement (annual report 2008), the following data were extracted.

(in US$)	25 June 2008	27 June 2007
Inventories (balance sheet)	4,652,000	4,323,000
Cost of sales and related occupancy costs (exclusive of depreciation shown separately) (income statement)	35,886,000	24,244,000

Note to financial statements indicates that inventory consists principally of raw materials (green bean coffee), and finished goods, which include roasted coffee, tea, accessory products, and packaged foods. The company's fiscal year ends on the Wednesday closest to 30 June.

Frisch's Restaurants

Frisch's Restaurants, Inc. operates full-service, family-style restaurants under the name Frisch's Big Boy. The company also operates grill buffet-style restaurants under the name Golden Corral pursuant to certain licensing agreements. As of 2 June 2009, the company's operations consisted of 88 family-style restaurants using the Big Boy trade name and 35 Golden Corral grill buffet-style family restaurants. Additionally, 26 Big Boy restaurants were in operation under licensing rights granted by the company to other operators. The restaurants licensed to other operators are located in various markets of Ohio, Kentucky and Indiana. From the consolidated balance sheet and income statement (annual report 2009), the following data were extracted.

(in US$)	2 June 2009	3 June 2008
Inventories (balance sheet)	6,531,127	5,647,629
Cost of sales – food and paper (income statement)	105,859,982	106,895,380

A note to the financial statements indicates that inventory consists principally of food items. The closing date is the Tuesday nearest to the last day of May. The first quarter of each fiscal year contains 16 weeks, while the last three quarters each normally contain 12 weeks. Every fifth or sixth year, an additional week is added to the fourth quarter, which results in a 53-week fiscal year.

Meritage Hospitality Group

Meritage Hospitality Group Inc. (Meritage) operates 49 Wendy's Old Fashioned Hamburgers quick-service restaurants in Western and Southern Michigan. Meritage, a Wendy's franchisee, serves approximately nine million customers annually. The Wendy's menu features hamburgers and chicken sandwiches, all of which are prepared to order with the customer's choice of condiments, and also includes items such as chili, baked and French fried potatoes, chicken nuggets, salads, soft drinks, Frosty desserts and children's meals. The company is also an O'Charley's franchisee, operating four O'Charley's casual dining restaurants in Michigan. From the consolidated balance sheet and income statement (annual report 2008), the following data were extracted.

(in US$)	30 November 2008	2 December 2007
Inventories (balance sheet)	375,345	324,115
Cost of food and beverages (income statement)	16,258,615	15,725,434

A note to the financial statements indicates that inventory consists principally of restaurant food items, beverages and serving supplies. The company has elected a 52/53-week fiscal period for tax and financial reporting purposes. The fiscal period ends on the Sunday closest to 30 November.

Morton's restaurant group

Morton's Restaurant Group, Inc. (MRG) is engaged in the business of owning and operating restaurants under the names Morton's The Steakhouse ('Morton's'), Trevi ('Trevi') and Bertolini's Authentic Trattorias ('Bertolini's'). As of 4 January 2009, the company owned and operated 83 restaurants (80 Morton's and three Italian restaurants: one Trevi and two Bertolini's). Morton's are upscale steakhouse restaurants. Morton's and the company's Italian restaurants appeal to a broad spectrum of consumer tastes and target separate price points and dining experiences. From the consolidated balance sheet and income statement (annual report 2009), the following data were extracted.

(in US$ 000)	4 January 2009	30 December 2007
Inventories (balance sheet)	12,545	13,394
Food and beverage costs (income statement)	115,430	117,010

A note to the financial statements indicates that inventory consists principally of food, beverages and supplies. The company uses a 52/53-week fiscal year which ends on the Sunday closest to 1 January. Approximately every sixth or seventh year, a 53rd week will be added.

Required

1. Compute the inventory turnover for each company.
2. Compute the average days' inventory available for each company.
3. Compare and contrast the figures obtained.

Assignment 9.8
Toyota*

Topic: Inventory ratios

Toyota Motor Corporation (Toyota) primarily conducts business in the automotive industry. Toyota also conducts business in the finance and other industries. It is organized in three segments: automotive operations, financial services operations and all other operations. Toyota's automotive operations include the design, manufacture, assembly and sale of passenger cars, minivans and commercial vehicles, such as trucks, and related parts and accessories. Toyota's financial services business consists primarily of providing financing to dealers and their customers for the purchase or lease of Toyota vehicles.

Toyota's financial services also provide retail leasing through the purchase of lease contracts originated by Toyota dealers. Related to Toyota's automotive operations is its development of intelligent transport systems (ITS). Toyota's all other operations business segment includes the design and manufacture of prefabricated housing and information technology-related businesses.

The parent company and its subsidiaries in Japan maintain their records and prepare their financial statements in accordance with US generally accepted accounting principles, and its foreign subsidiaries in conformity with those of their countries of domicile.

From the consolidated balance sheet and income statement (annual reports 2004 to 2009), we extracted the following information:

(in Yen million)	31 March					
	2004	2005	2006	2007	2008	2009
Inventories	1,083,326	1,306,709	1,620,975	1,803,956	1,825,716	1,459,394
Cost of products sold	13,506,337	14,500,282	16,335,340	18,356,255	20,452,338	17,468,416

Required

1. Compute the inventory turnover and analyze its evolution over the years.

2. Compute the average days' inventory available and analyze its evolution over the years.

3. Comment on the results of your computations.

References

Drury, C. (2007) *Management and Cost Accounting*, 7th edn, London: Thomson Learning.

IASB (2003) International Accounting Standard No. 2: Inventories, London.

Further reading

Ahmed, M.N. and Scapens, R.W. (2000) 'Cost allocation in Britain: Towards an institutional analysis', *European Accounting Review* 9(2): 159–204.

Chung, J.O.Y., Cohen, J.R. and Monroe, G.S. (2008) 'The effect of moods on auditors' inventory valuation decisions', *Auditing: A Journal of Practice & Theory* 27(2): 137–59.

Jennings, R., Simko, P.J. and Thompson II, R.B. (1996) 'Does LIFO inventory accounting improve the income statement at the expense of the balance sheet?', *Journal of Accounting Research* 34(1): 85–119.

Knapp, M.C. and Knapp, C.A. (2000) 'Perry Drug Stores, Inc.: Accounting and control issues for inventory in a retail environment', *Issues in Accounting Education* 15(2): 237–55.

Pfaff, D. (1994) 'On the allocation of overhead costs', *European Accounting Review* 3(1): 49–70.

Additional material on the website

Go to http://www.cengage.co.uk/stolowy3 for further information, journal entries and extra assignments for each chapter.

The following appendices to this chapter are available on the dedicated website:

Appendix 9.1: Differences between physical and accounting inventory count

Appendix 9.2: Comparison of advantages and limits of perpetual and periodic inventory systems

Appendix 9.3: Other LIFO considerations

Appendix 9.4: Effect of an inventory misstatement

Notes

1. The reader wishing to explore the topics of inventory management or 'costing' of inventory inflows is encouraged to consult books respectively on production management and managerial accounting. See for example Drury (2007).

2. Inventories related to long-term contracts have been developed in Chapter 6, Appendix 6.1.

3. Even if the physical inventory is not taken on the very date of closure of the books, the modification of said inventory between the two dates only requires minor adjustments, which can be handled by keeping track, exceptionally, of each movement between inventory and closing dates.

4. See Drury (2007) for an example.

5. In a physical inventory management system the first-in, first-out approach is the only one to make sense so as to avoid the build-up of obsolete inventories.

C10

Chapter 10

Financial Instruments in the Balance Sheet and Fair Value Accounting

Learning objectives

After studying this chapter, you will understand:

- That there are several and different types of financial instruments.
- How financial assets and financial liabilities are valued.
- What cash and cash equivalents represent and how they are reported.
- What financial assets and liabilities 'at fair value through profit or loss' mean.
- What 'held-to-maturity' financial assets represent and how they are reported.
- What accounts receivable, also known as receivables, represent and how they are reported.
- What 'available-for-sale' financial assets represent and how they are reported.
- How to analyze financial instruments in the balance sheet for decision making.

Financial instruments are found in many parts of any balance sheet, on the left side (assets such as receivables or marketable securities) as well as on the right side (liabilities such as debt instruments or payables), in the current part of the balance sheet as well as in its long-term portions. While the term financial instruments is more spontaneously associated with the core business of financial institutions, industrial and commercial firms also do use such elements for many reasons, such as:

- Operational decisions, such as sales on credit (the financial instrument is accounts receivable on the assets side) or purchases on credit (the financial instrument is accounts payable on the liabilities side – see more on this in Chapter 12).

- Risk management (hedging elements in assets or liabilities). The purpose of a business is to manufacture, sell or trade goods or services, not to speculate or be the victim of fluctuations beyond its control, or to manage risks directly. Hedging allows a separation of results between management results and the cost of protection against risks (more on this in Appendix 10.1).

- Financing or funding arrangements to supplement long-term funds provided by shareholders or short-term financing provided by suppliers (other than payables) or other creditors (debt or financial liabilities).

- Investing funds for short-term or long-term financial gain or to protect the purchasing power of their liquidities (securities held for trading, securities held to maturity, or securities available for sale).

- Investing for strategic partnership or control in another business entity (long-term investments in associated companies or subsidiaries).

In this chapter, we will study these financial instruments, except those concerning investments for strategic partnership or control, which are covered in Chapter 13 relating to business combinations.

1 Definition of financial assets and liabilities

The IASB defines 'financial instruments' (IAS 32, IASB 2008a: § 11) as 'any contract that gives rise to a financial asset of one entity and a financial liability or equity instrument of another entity.

A **financial asset** is any asset that is:

(a) cash;

(b) an equity instrument of another entity;

(c) a contractual right:

    (i) to receive cash or another financial asset from another entity; or

    (ii) to exchange financial assets or financial liabilities with another entity under conditions that are potentially favorable to the entity; or

(d) a contract that will or may be settled in the entity's own equity instruments and is:

    (i) a non-derivative[1] for which the entity is or may be obliged to receive a variable number of the entity's own equity instruments; or

    (ii) a **derivative** that will or may be settled other than by the exchange of a fixed amount of cash or another financial asset for a fixed number of the entity's own equity instruments. For this purpose the entity's own equity instruments do not include instruments that are themselves contracts for the future receipt or delivery of the entity's own equity instruments.

A **financial liability** is any liability that is:

(a) a contractual obligation:

    (i) to deliver cash or another financial asset to another entity; or

    (ii) to exchange financial assets or financial liabilities with another entity under conditions that are potentially unfavorable to the entity; or

(b) a contract that will or may be settled in the entity's own equity instruments and is:

    (i) a non-derivative for which the entity is or may be obliged to deliver a variable number of the entity's own equity instruments; or

    (ii) a derivative that will or may be settled other than by the exchange of a fixed amount of cash or another financial asset for a fixed number of the entity's own equity instruments. For this purpose the entity's own equity instruments do not include instruments that are themselves contracts for the future receipt or delivery of the entity's own equity instruments'.

IAS 39 (IASB 2008b: § 9) defines four categories of financial instruments in assets:

- financial assets held 'at fair value through profit or loss' [i.e., held for trading or sale, and for which latent (potential or unrealized) gains or losses are transferred to the income statement on the basis of the fair value on the closing date];
- held-to-maturity investments;
- loans and receivables;
- available-for-sale financial assets.

IAS 39 (§ 9) also defines financial liabilities 'at fair value through profit or loss', and by default creates a category of all other financial liabilities which are not carried 'at fair value through profit or loss'. This second category that includes bonds is covered in Chapter 12.

IAS 39 does not apply directly to investments in subsidiaries, associates and joint ventures, which constitute, in our view, a fifth category, and is covered in Chapter 13.

In the balance sheet, financial assets and liabilities 'held for trading' are reported as part of current assets and current liabilities respectively, while 'held-to-maturity' investments and 'available-for-sale' financial assets are normally reported as part of long-term (non-current) assets. Loans and receivables can be reported either in the current or long-term sections, depending on their maturity terms.

IAS 39 (§ 43) states that 'when a financial asset or financial liability is recognized initially, an entity shall measure it at its fair value plus, in the case of a financial asset or financial liability not at fair value through profit or loss, transaction costs that are directly attributable to the acquisition or issue of the financial asset or financial liability'.

The measurement of a financial asset after its initial recognition will depend on how it will have been classified between the four above-mentioned categories. Table 10.1 summarizes the rules of subsequent valuation of financial instruments.

Sections 2 to 6 of this chapter explore the different types of financial assets one by one: **Cash** and **cash equivalents**, held-for-trading investments, **held-to-maturity investments**, **loans and receivables** and **available-for-sale financial assets**. The last section focuses on how a financial information user can interpret the financial instrument data reported in the financial statements.

Table 10.1 Subsequent measurement of financial assets

Category	IASB (IAS 39)	
	Valuation or measurement of the current investment in the balance sheet	Treatment of potential (unrealized) gains and losses measured by comparing cost to fair market value
Financial assets at fair value through profit or loss	At 'fair value' (unless the asset has no quoted market price in an active market or the fair value cannot be reliably measured)	Included in net profit or loss of the period in which it arises
Held-to-maturity investments	At cost	–
Loans and receivables	At cost	–
Available-for-sale financial assets	At 'fair value' (unless the asset has no quoted market price in an active market or the fair value cannot be reliably measured)	Recognized (recorded) directly in equity

2 Cash and cash equivalents

IAS 7 (IASB 1992) states that 'cash comprises cash on hand' (coins, banknotes and currency available) and 'demand deposits' (deposits in bank accounts that are available on demand). 'Cash equivalents are short-term, highly liquid investments that are readily convertible to known amounts of cash and which are subject to an insignificant risk of changes in value' (§ 6). 'Cash equivalents' are financial instruments (such as money market securities) held for the purpose of meeting short-term cash commitments rather than for investment or other purposes. An investment normally qualifies as a cash equivalent only when it has a short maturity of, say, three months or less from the date of acquisition.

The concept of '**net cash**' represents the difference between 'cash and cash equivalents' (defined above) and liabilities accounts corresponding to negative cash (essentially bank overdrafts).

The weight of cash and cash equivalents in a balance sheet can vary greatly between firms (see Table 10.2, which is based on 2008 annual reports). Unlike what was stated in previous chapters about other balance sheet items, there appears to be no link between the nature of the industrial sector the firm is involved in and its level of cash and cash equivalents. The level of cash and cash equivalents plus **current investments** is, in fact, considered to be the cash reserve a firm chooses to build in order to (a) be able to operate the cash pump smoothly (see Chapter 1) and (b) be able to act rapidly in case opportunities appear. For example, Microsoft's 'cash and cash equivalent plus short-term investments' as at 30 June 2009 was equal to $31,447 million. It is, for Microsoft, a

Table 10.2 Weight of cash and cash equivalents

Company (country - activity)	Currency (millions)	Cash and cash equivalents	Total assets	Cash and cash equivalents/ Total assets (%)
Bull (France – IT group)	€	288.9	727.0	39.7
Weyerhaeuser (USA – Building materials and fixtures)	$US	2,288	16,735	13.7
Sulzer (Switzerland – Advanced materials technologies and fluid dynamics applications)	CHF	447.2	3,430.2	13.0
Philips (Netherlands – Consumer and professional electronics)	€	3,620	31,790	11.4
Iberia (Spain – Airline)	€	600	5,634	10.6
RC2 corporation (USA – Racing cars replicas)	US$ (000)	32,095	336,650	9.5
Sony (Japan – Music, entertainment, games, and professional and consumer electronics)	¥	1,086,431	12,552,739	8.7
Fiat (Italy – Car manufacturer)	€	3,683	61,772	6.0
ISS (Denmark – Support services)	DKK	2,961	53,605	5.5
Orkla (Norway – Food)	NOK	4,438	104,926	4.2
Stora-Enso (Finland – Paper production)	€	415.8	12,240.8	3.4
Heineken (Netherlands – Brewery)	€	698	20,563	3.4
Pernod Ricard (France – Beverages)	€	421	18,431	2.3
China Petroleum & Chemical Corporation (China – Oil and chemistry)	RMB	6,948	767,827	0.9

strategic reservoir of resources coherent with its strategy of searching for acquisitions, either representing major enlargement of the scope of the firm (major acquisitions such as the partially ill-fated courting of Yahoo! by Microsoft in 2008) or on the frontier of their scope (such as the acquisition in May 2009 of BigPark Inc., based in Vancouver BC, to expand the video gaming talent for the Xbox 360 group) in a very turbulent world in which an exchange of shares may no longer be considered as attractive as it may have been in previous years.

Real-life example Darden

(USA – US GAAP – Source: Annual report 2009 – Restaurants)

Excerpts from the consolidated balance sheet (USD million)		
	31 May 2009	25 May 2008
(...)		
Current assets		
Cash and cash equivalents	62.9	43.2
(...)		
Note to the financial statements		
CASH EQUIVALENTS		

Cash equivalents include highly liquid investments such as US treasury bills, taxable municipal bonds and money market funds that have an original maturity of three months or less. Amounts receivable from credit card companies are also considered cash equivalents because they are both short-term and highly liquid in nature and are typically converted to cash within three days of the sales transaction.

The topic of cash and cash equivalents is developed in greater detail in Chapter 14.

3 Financial asset and liability at fair value through profit or loss

3.1 Definitions

This category corresponds to financial assets and liabilities that meet any of several conditions defined in IAS 39 (IASB 2008b: § 9):[2] 'A financial asset or financial liability at fair value through profit or loss is a financial asset or financial liability that meets either of the following conditions.

(a) It is classified as held for trading. A financial asset or financial liability is classified as held for trading if:

  (i) it is acquired or incurred principally for the purpose of selling or repurchasing it in the near term;

  (ii) on initial recognition it is part of a portfolio of identified financial instruments that are managed together and for which there is evidence of a recent actual pattern of short-term profit-taking; or

(iii) it is a derivative (except for a derivative that is a financial guarantee contract or a designated and effective hedging instrument).

(b) Upon initial recognition it is designated by the entity as at fair value through profit or loss (…)' (see § 3.4 below).

The sub-category of 'held for trading' assets often refers to 'current investment', 'marketable securities' or 'short-term investments'. These assets can be sold readily and are held by the firm as a cash substitute with the intention of protecting the purchasing power of a liquid asset and, when possible, earning a return on the sums invested.

The liabilities in this category result mainly from hedging instruments that the firm uses to protect its financial assets value from the fluctuations of interest rates, currency exchange rates, market price variations, etc.

The valuation of these instruments is critical as their fair value (market value) is constantly changing, thus creating latent or potential (i.e., unrealized) gains or losses. The way these losses or gains are recognized, if at all, and reported may affect both the perceived inherent risk level of the firm and the measurement of the value created by the business.

IAS 39 (§ 9) states that financial assets or liabilities classified as held for trading should be valued at **fair value** through profit or loss. 'Fair value is the amount for which an asset could be exchanged, or a liability settled, between knowledgeable, willing parties in an [at] arm's length transaction' (IAS 39: § 9). 'The existence of published price quotations in an active market is the best evidence of fair value' (IAS 39: § AG71). The standard, however, acknowledges that, for many financial assets (such as shares of unlisted companies or untraded commercial paper), the ability to evaluate the market or fair value of these assets is a highly debatable topic. Thus, in practice, unless a credible valuation model can be approved by both the Audit Committee and the Board of Directors, the assets (or liabilities) should be carried at cost, with duly informed comment in the notes.

3.2 Accounting for financial assets at fair value through profit or loss

IASB, through IFRS 7 (IASB 2008c) and IAS 39 (IASB 2008b), mandates that unrealized gains or losses on current financial investments or liabilities held for trading be recognized in the income statement of the period for which the gain or loss was calculated.

Let us illustrate. Mozart Company holds securities of two other businesses (Alpha Company and Beta Company) as current investments. Let us examine the key operations that can affect this current investment using the data displayed in Table 10.3.

Although the no-offsetting principle would normally call for the recording of unrealized gains and losses for each separate security (individual basis), IAS 39 has endorsed the portfolio basis approach in which only the unrealized gains or losses of the aggregate portfolio of current investments are reported. One can surmise that the choice made results from the observation that since the financial instruments involved in this category are

Table 10.3 Data of Mozart Company's current investment example

Date of purchase	Security	Quantity	Unit cost	Total cost	Market value at year-end	Total market value	Period-end adjustment (individual basis)	Period-end adjustment (aggregate portfolio basis)
25/10/X1	Bonds Alpha Company	10	150	1,500	160	1,600	100	
23/11/X1	Shares Beta Company	20	100	2,000	90	1,800	−200	
Total	Portfolio	10B + 20S		3,500		3,400	−100	−100

meant to be traded in the very short-term after closing, the specific nature of each item is not relevant to the analyst.

Let us pursue the example using the aggregate portfolio basis method required by IAS 39. Potential losses on the shares of Beta Company are offset against potential gains on the bonds of Alpha Company. The difference is a net loss and recorded as such (see Figure 10.1). In this example, we record the change in fair value as a provision expense. In keeping with IFRS/IAS usual policy of not mentioning which accounts should be used, IAS 39 states only that the change in fair value should be recognized 'in profit or loss'. The provision mechanism thus appears to be perfectly appropriate for handling this situation. In the case of a potential gain (not dealt with in our example), a revenue account should be created for this purpose.

On 20 February X2, 8 shares of Beta Company are sold at a unit price of 85. Since they had been purchased for 100 each, there is a total loss of 120 on that sale ([85 – 100] × 8 = −120). For simplicity's sake, we assume that the value of the bonds of Alpha Company has not changed between the close of X1 and the close of the first quarter Q1 of X2. We also assume that the end-of-quarter market value of one share of Beta Company is 85. The appropriate entries are illustrated in Figure 10.2.

Some countries (but most do not) merge the two entries by recording in the income statement the difference between the reversal of the provision and the loss on the sale. In our example, an entry or a loss of 20 would have been recorded directly in the income statement, but the additional provision for the recognition of the additional unrealized loss on the remaining 12 shares of Beta Company would have been recorded separately.

3.3 Reporting financial asset at fair value through profit or loss

The IASB encourages transparency as a way of delivering a true and fair view. It does not specify one favored method of reporting as long as the notes to the financial statements contain any relevant facts that allow the reader to understand the whole situation. An analysis of annual reports shows that current investments are reported in four different

Figure 10.1 Accounting for current investments – Year X1

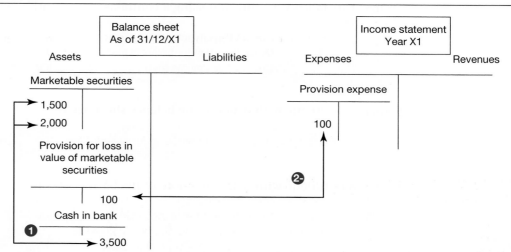

❶ Purchase of marketable securities. The entries on 25 October X1 and 23 November X1 are merged into one here. There would be two distinct entries if we were describing a real accounting system. Since our concern is the valuation of the financial assets at year-end, the separation of the transactions into two entries is unnecessary.

❷ At year-end, entry to account of the potential loss (computed on an aggregate basis using the market value of the securities on the last day of trading before closing or the closing date). The loss remains latent, unrealized, or potential as long as the securities have not been sold. The terminology for unrealized losses or potential losses is not settled and several alternative terms can be found in published financial statements.

Figure 10.2 Accounting for current investments – Quarter 1 of X2

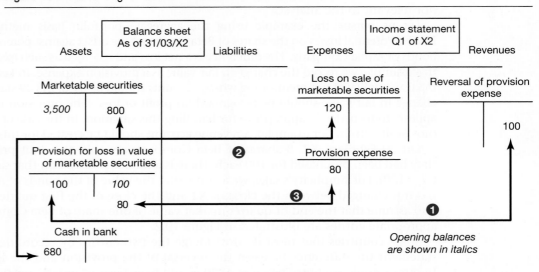

❶ The provision (allowance) is cancelled (reversed) at the beginning of the first quarter of X2.

❷ The sale is recorded without taking the provision into account. The loss is: (8 × [85 − 100]) = 8 × [−15] = −120.

❸ The provision (allowance) is recalculated on the basis of acquisition costs compared to current market prices for the portfolio constituted of 10 bonds of Alpha and 12 shares of Beta. The bonds still have a potential gain of 100 and the shares of Beta have a potential loss of 180 (12 × [85 − 100]). Thus the portfolio requires a new net provision of 80.

ways; when the reporting format deviates from the full reporting (Format 1), the appropriate additional information is provided, if needed, in the notes.

If we use Mozart company data for year X1, the current investments can be reported in one of the four following formats

Format 1 (detailed vertically and using a contra-asset account)

Current investments (gross – at cost)	3,500
Minus provision for potential loss	− 100
Current investments (net)	3,400

Format 2 (synthetic with detail in the balance sheet itself)

Current investments (net of provision for potential loss: 100)	3,400

Format 3 (synthetic with detail in a note to the balance sheet)

Current investments (net) (see note X)   3,400

Notes to the financial statements:

Note X – Current investments:

The accumulated amount of provision for potential losses is equal to 100.

Format 4 (detailed horizontally)

	Gross value	Accumulated provisions	Net value
Current investments	3,500	100	3,400

Real-life example Bosch

(Germany – IFRS – Source: Annual report 2008 – Electrical systems)

Excerpts from the consolidated balance sheet (€ million)		
	31/12/2008	31/12/2007
(...)		
Marketable securities	396	551
(...)		

Note 11 The securities classified as current are listed securities with a residual term of less than one year as well as securities which are intended for sale within a year.

Real-life example Toray Industries

(Japan – Japanese GAAP – Source: Annual report 2008 – Manufacturer of synthetic fibers and textiles)

Consolidated balance sheet – 31 March 2009 and 2008 (Yen million)		
	2009	2008
(...)		
Prepaid expenses and other current assets (Note 5)	36,341	39,111
(...)		
Investment securities (Notes 4 and 5)	89,305	127,799
(...)		

Notes to the financial statements

1. Significant accounting policies

Securities

Other securities [than held-to-maturity debt securities] for which market quotations are available are stated at fair value. Net unrealized gains or losses on these securities are reported as a separate item in net assets at a net-of-tax amount. Other securities for which market quotations are unavailable are stated at cost, except as stated in the paragraph below. In cases where the fair value of (...) other securities has declined significantly and such impairment of the value is not deemed temporary, those securities are written down to fair value and the resulting losses are included in net income or loss for the period.

5. Securities

At 31 March 2009 (...), the acquisition cost and aggregate fair value of the securities classified as held-to-maturity debt securities and other securities for which market quotations were available were as follows:

(Yen million)	2009			
	Acquisition cost	Unrealized gains	Unrealized losses	Fair value
Held-to-maturity debt securities	74	–	–	74
Other securities	66,217	27,870	11,377	82,710

At 31 March 2009, the carrying amount of the securities classified as held-to-maturity debt securities and other securities for which market quotations were unavailable were as follows:

(Yen million)	2009	2008
Held-to-maturity debt securities	134	151
Other securities	6,647	7,567

Comment: We can observe that the notes of Toray Industries do not make a distinction between securities included in current assets and those included in financial fixed assets. This makes a reconciliation between balance sheet and figures in the notes essentially impossible.

3.4 Evolution and debate over regulation and practice

This category '<u>**financial asset at fair value through profit or loss**</u>' includes two sub-categories: financial assets designated as such on initial recognition and financial assets 'held for trading'.

IAS 39 (§ 9) stipulates that a 'financial asset at fair value through profit or loss' could be 'upon initial recognition (...) designated by the entity as at fair value through profit or loss. An entity may use this designation only when permitted by paragraph 11A [which concerns 'embedded derivatives'], or when doing so results in more relevant information[3] (...)'. This version represents an amendment to what has been called the 'fair value option'. It is a much more restrictive version, compared to the original standard, which had not been accepted by the European Union. However, the EU Commission, following the Accounting Regulatory Committee (ARC), the EU advisory body on the endorsement of individual IFRS for use in the European Union, has accepted on 15 November 2005 an amended version of IAS 39 relating to the fair value option (FVO).

Current asset financial instruments are meant to be disposed of, one way or another, in the near future. A financial fixed asset is, by nature, not a current asset since it is held for the long-term (a value-adding network exists only if the financial relationships between its members are for the long-term). Thus, it takes a deliberate decision by the management of the entity at the time of acquisition to classify a financial instrument as a long-term financial asset.

The introduction of 'financial asset at fair value through profit or loss' has made a revolutionary change in financial accounting. In fact, before this adoption, the principle of prudence (conservatism) had required accountants to deliberately undervalue the book value (accounting value) of the firm by only recognizing potential losses in the income statement through provision, while ignoring totally potential gains. The issue linked to this original conservatism and the switch to fair valuation (mark to market) has raised, especially since the 2008 crisis, some intense debates well beyond the accounting sphere.

The proponents of fair value applaud the improvement of timeliness and relevance of accounting information, believing that the adoption of fair value brings the accounting value closer to the market value. They argue that, especially for firms with large proportions of financial assets eligible for the fair value treatment, the traditional method of historical cost plus depreciation/amortization/provision did not provide relevant information and that the undervalued book value provided a hidden cookie jar for managers for discretionary improvement of earnings by selling some of these assets.

The opponents of fair value accounting criticize the new approach because of its pro-cyclicality: When the market price goes up, the unrealized gains will be reported and improve the accounting earnings. And then, the disclosure of 'better' accounting performance might tend to comfort the market positively and bring the value of the share to an even higher level. The fair value can also play such an accelerator effect in a downturn market, but, of course, in the opposite way.

4 Held-to-maturity financial assets

Held-to-maturity investments are 'non-derivative financial assets with fixed or determinable payments and fixed maturity that an entity has the positive intention and ability to hold to maturity (...)' (IAS 39: § 9). These are not speculative investments, unlike the ones examined in the previous section. It is however clear that the distinction is merely one of intent.

As mentioned earlier, 'when a financial asset or financial liability is recognized initially, an entity shall measure it at its fair value plus, in the case of a financial asset or financial liability not at fair value through profit or loss, transaction costs that are directly attributable to the acquisition or issue of the financial asset or financial liability' (IAS 39: § 43).

After initial recognition, held-to-maturity investments 'shall be measured at amortized cost using the effective interest method' (IAS 39: § 46). 'The **amortized cost** of a financial asset or financial liability is the amount at which the financial asset or financial liability is measured at initial recognition minus principal repayments, plus or minus the cumulative amortization using the effective interest method of any difference between that initial amount and the maturity amount, and minus any reduction (directly or through the use of an allowance account) for impairment or uncollectibility. The **effective interest method** is a method of calculating the amortized cost of a financial asset or a financial liability (…) and of allocating the interest income or interest expense over the relevant period. The effective interest rate is the rate that exactly discounts estimated future cash payments or receipts through the expected life of the financial instrument or, when appropriate, a shorter period to the net carrying amount of the financial asset or financial liability'. (IAS 39: § 9)

In practice, this category of assets is quite similar to the one on receivables that we present in the following section.

5 Receivables

Accounts receivables are created when the customer is granted a delay in paying for the goods or services delivered. Businesses may be led to lend money to their suppliers or their customers to allow them to weather the float between their own payments and receivables. Loans and receivables are 'non-derivative financial assets with fixed or determinable payments that are not quoted in an active market' (IAS 39: § 9). Through securitization,[4] receivables or loans can be transformed into 'available for sale' financial assets.

5.1 Accounts receivable or 'receivables'

Accounts receivable, which may be abbreviated as A/R, often represent a sizeable component of the assets side of a balance sheet, as shown in Table 10.4, which lists companies in decreasing percentage of accounts receivable (or, more broadly, receivables) over total assets in their 2008 annual financial statements. The percentage represented by receivables appears, of course, much higher for firms involved in service activities (such businesses require few fixed assets) or for firms relying heavily on outsourcing their production, than in a business involved in some 'heavy' industry (which may require large fixed assets).

This table, like equivalent tables in previous chapters, is provided for the sole purpose of illustrating the diversity of situations. It is interesting to note the variety of terms used in annual accounts to describe a similar reality.

Several accounting issues affect the reporting of receivables:

- application of the no-offsetting principle;
- links between subsidiary ledgers (mainly per transaction type or per customer) and accounts receivable;
- handling of the probability the claim reflected in the receivable will effectively be collected (collectibility), leading, if such probability is not 100%, to 'bad debt' expenses and 'doubtful accounts' expenses;
- reporting the receivables;
- handling of value added tax (VAT) or sales taxes (covered in Appendix 10.2).

Table 10.4 Weight of accounts receivable

Company (country – activity)	Currency (millions)	Account name	Receivables (rounded)	Total assets	A/R/ Total assets (%)
RC2 corporation (USA – Production and sales of collectibles)	US$ (000)	Accounts receivable, net of allowances for doubtful accounts	91,647	336,650	27.2
Sulzer (Switzerland – High-tech material technologies and fluid dynamics applications)	CHF	Trade accounts receivable	859	3,430	25.1
Bull (France – IT group)	€	Trade receivables (less allowances for doubtful accounts)	157	727	21.6
Orkla (Norway – Food products)	NOK	Receivables	14,331	104,926	13.7
Stora-Enso (Finland – Paper production)	€	Short-term operative receivables	1,583	12,241	12.9
Philips (Netherlands – Consumer and professional electronic products)	€	Accounts receivable (net)	3,813	33,041	11.5
Iberia (Spain – Airline)	€	Accounts receivable	586	5,634	10.4
EDF (France – Electricity)	€	Trade receivables	19,144	200,288	9.6
Sony (Japan – Music, movies, games, consumer and professional electronics)	¥	Notes and accounts receivable, trade	963,837	12,013,511	8.0
easyJet (UK – Airlines)	£	Trade and other receivables	237	3,096	7.7
Fiat (Italy – Car manufacturer)	€	Trade receivables	4,390	61,772	7.1
Linde (Germany – Commodity chemicals)	€	Trade receivables	1,641	23,824	6.9
Pernod Ricard (France – Beverages)	€	Accounts receivable, net value	1,146	18,431	6.2
Alcoa (USA – Aluminum)	US$	Receivables from customers, less allowances	1,883	37,822	5.0
China Petroleum & Chemical Corporation (China – Oil and chemistry)	RMB	Trade accounts receivable, net	12,989	767,827	1.7

5.1.1 Application of the no-offsetting principle to accounts receivable

Accounts receivable are the result of credit sales. Accounts receivable are generally found on the left-hand side of the balance sheet, since an account receivable represents an increase of assets when the sale (increase of revenues in the income statement) is recorded. However, a customer may provide a down-payment, thus creating a liability acknowledging the fact the firm is now obligated to deliver some service or goods to the customer. Accounts receivable on the assets side cannot be offset against the down-payment on the liabilities side for the same customer (or for any customer). Similarly, several transactions with a single customer cannot be offset against each other.

Assume customer C buys goods or services for 100 CU in month 1 and 200 CU in month 2. The sales were granted with two months of credit. In month 3 the customer sends a payment of 150. That payment must be specifically applied to the account the customer intended to settle. It is not the same thing to say one of these two possible ways:

- The payment should be applied to transaction 1 for a full on-time payment of 100 and there is an early payment of 50 on transaction 2;

- Both transactions are considered settled for 50% (one on time for 50% and the other early for 50%).

Obviously, the first case is the more logical one, but would it be so obvious if the payment came in month 4? The fact is, in an account receivable, transactions cannot be merged (see subsidiary ledgers below).

Similarly, when a firm is both a customer and a supplier of a business, it cannot offset the receivables and the payables from and to that partner. When customers settle their accounts by transferring some of their resources (generally cash) to their creditor, the receivable balance is reduced by the appropriate amount and the cash account recognizes the payment.

However, accounts receivable that are liabilities (lay-away plans or down-payments) operate in reverse and their balance is reduced as the goods or services are delivered or the excess payment is refunded.

5.1.2 Subsidiary ledgers

In previous chapters we have recorded credit sales by increasing the assets with a generic 'accounts receivable'. For accounting to be useful to managers, such a generic account is not a sound basis for monitoring transactions with customers. Although reports to outside users of accounting information need only contain one (or very few) line(s) for accounts receivable, internally the firm will generally use one sub-division of accounts receivable per customer (called subsidiary ledger) so it can keep track of payments and of possible lateness in payment.

Most accounting software programs code accounts on an alphanumeric basis (see Chapter 3). At the end of the accounting period, individual subsidiary ledger accounts are centralized (accumulated) and transferred to the controlling 'accounts receivable' in the general ledger.

Subsidiary ledgers are generally organized both by customer and by due date so the specialized accountants can keep track of payments. Aging the receivables consists in creating a table that lists all customers (and each transaction for a given customer) by due date or by category of delay past due if applicable.

5.1.3 Collectibility of receivables

The development of credit sales or sales on account is a legitimate way for reaching new retail customers and growing sales and a requirement in most business to business transactions. The existence of receivables leads to the necessity of evaluating, at the end of each accounting period, the probability that the account will effectively be collected. This evaluation is based on both commercial information (customer satisfaction, returns, complaints, etc.) and external information pertaining to the economic or financial situation of the debtor. Figure 10.3 highlights the four categories of accounts receivable such an analysis will lead to.

The write-down or write-off procedures are highlighted in Figure 10.4 and described subsequently.

❶ **Identification of doubtful or disputed accounts** As mentioned earlier, the balances of each individual customer account receivable are individually reviewed and structured by due

Figure 10.3 Different categories of claims

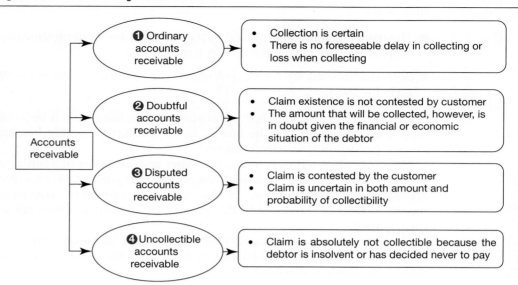

Doubtful (❷) or disputed (❸) accounts, which are partly or totally uncollectible, are referred to as 'bad' or 'doubtful' debt(s).[5] The value of these accounts will have to be written-down by taking a provision expense – or valuation allowance – in the income statement. Uncollectible accounts (❹) must be written-off through a bad debt expense in the income statement. Sometimes, both written-down and written-off amounts are, collectively, called 'bad debt expense'.

Figure 10.4 Doubtful accounts receivable

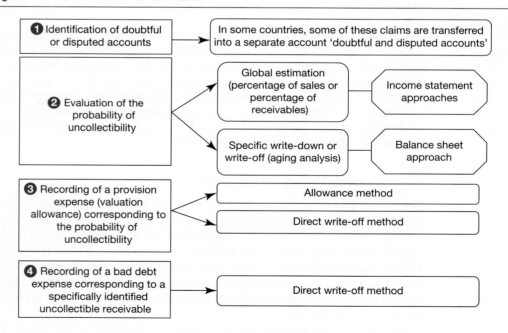

date in an **aged balance**.[6] Any transaction whose age is considered to fall outside the customary credit terms for this type of clientele is potentially a **doubtful** or a disputed account. Specific research about the cause of the lateness of the payment to an account can establish whether it should be considered doubtful or disputed.

Real-life example Bayer

Bayer, the German chemical group, published an aged table of overdue receivables in its 2008 annual report:

[Note 22] Trade accounts receivable

Trade accounts receivable less write-downs amounted to €5,953 million on the reporting date (2007: €5,830 million), including €5,936 million (2007: €5,775 million) maturing within one year and €17 million (2007: €55 million) maturing after one year. Write-downs in 2008 amounted to €256 million (2007: €295 million).

	Carrying amount	Of which neither impaired nor overdue at the balance sheet date	Of which not impaired but overdue at the balance sheet date			
			up to 3 months	3 to 6 months	6 to 12 months	12 months
31 December 2008	5,953	4,699	739	156	142	100
31 December 2007	5,830	4,493	638	119	84	103

Trade accounts receivable not yet due as of the reporting date are deemed to be collectible on the basis of established credit management processes such as regular analyses of the creditworthiness of our customers and selective use of credit insurance.

Credit terms are strategic elements that are firm-specific, but there are ranges that are common acceptable practice within both countries and industries or business size. Tables 10.5 and 10.6 illustrate the range of average credit terms observed in several European countries and in the USA respectively.

The more a receivable is past due (i.e., exceeds its 'normal' credit terms), the higher the likelihood of its uncollectibility.

❷ Evaluation of the probability of uncollectibility

Global estimation (percentage of sales or percentage of receivables)   The uncollectibility probability can be estimated globally using historical statistical elements as long as these are specific to the firm. The most commonly-used methods consist in applying a historically based selected percentage to either total sales or total receivables. This method is however

Table 10.5 Average payment delay and contractual payment terms in some European countries in 2007[7]

Country	Payment delay over contractual terms (days)	Range of payment contractual terms (days)
Germany	9.4	14–60
Netherlands	11.7	30–90
France	12.2	30–90
Italy	12.6	30–120
Great Britain	13.6	30–60
Spain	14.8	30–120
Belgium	16.2	30–90
Irland	19.6	30–60
Portugal	24.1	30–120

Table 10.6 Average US credit terms based on company size[8]

	2008	2009
Bill collection (days)		
Companies with annual sales over $5 billion	41.9	41.0
Companies with annual sales less than $500 million	54.4	58.9
Bill payment (days)		
Companies with annual sales over $5 billion	53.2	55.8
Companies with annual sales less than $500 million	42.9	40.1

less and less used in practice since the generalization of efficient accounting software supports the specific write-down (through provision expense) or write-off (through **bad debt expense**) of individualized transactions.

Specific write down or write-off (aging analysis)   The aging analysis permits a transaction-by-transaction decision. The situation of each individual customer (or transaction) determined to be problematic is further documented through questions such as:

- Has the customer challenged the validity of the receivable or expressed dissatisfaction with the product or service?
- Has the customer been, so far, up-to-date in its payments according to the specifically agreed schedule pertaining to this and other transactions?
- Has there been any correspondence or other piece of information indicating that the customer has been experiencing financial difficulties?
- Have any letters from the company to the customer's address been returned undelivered?

An overdue claim might often prove to be collectible if the conditions for its lateness are detected and handled appropriately (partial refund or credit, replacement, free products supplied, etc.). It is also critical to use the information about the uncollectibility of a claim to help prevent the occurrence of future uncollectible receivables.

❸ Recording of a provision expense corresponding to the probability of uncollectibility   'When an uncertainty arises about the collectibility of an amount already included in revenue, the uncollectible amount, or the amount in respect of which recovery has ceased to be probable, is recognized as an expense, rather than as an adjustment of the amount of revenue originally recognized' (IAS 18, IASB 1993: § 22).

When the total or partial uncollectibility of the claim is established, an 'allowance for uncollectibles' is recorded as a provision (the term 'allowance for impairment' [of receivables] is also used and that choice of wording underscores the fact the assumed level of uncollectibility is still somewhat of a judgment call). This method is therefore known as the 'allowance method'. To be in total conformity with the matching principle, the allowance should be expensed and matched with the revenue which has generated the accounts receivable. The time required to establish the probability of collectibility means that the provision/allowance can only be calculated in the few weeks after the closing date. Its recording is part of the entries that take place in what is often called the 13th month of entries.

To illustrate: Brückner GmbH holds, at the close of the year, a 100 CU claim over customer Anton Corp. In the latter part of X1, Anton Corp. has been experiencing financial difficulties. The potential loss is estimated to reduce the collectible claim to 60 CU (a loss of 40% of the receivable). At the end of period X2, the estimation of the non-collectible part of the claim has grown to 70. During X3, Anton Corp. is liquidated and the receiver settles the claim in full with a payment of 10. This succession of events is illustrated in Figures 10.5–10.7.

Brückner records an expense of 40 corresponding to its estimation of the likely loss. At this stage, the 'accounts receivable' is not decreased (no reduction of assets). A contra-asset

Figure 10.5 Doubtful accounts – Year X1

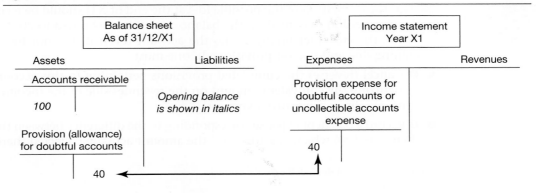

Figure 10.6 Doubtful accounts – Year X2

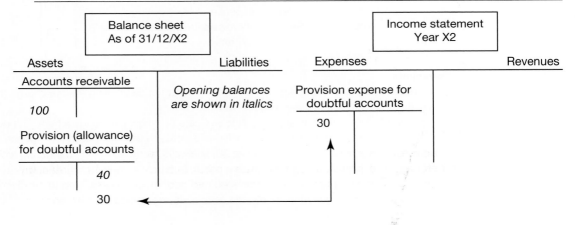

Figure 10.7 Doubtful accounts – Year X3

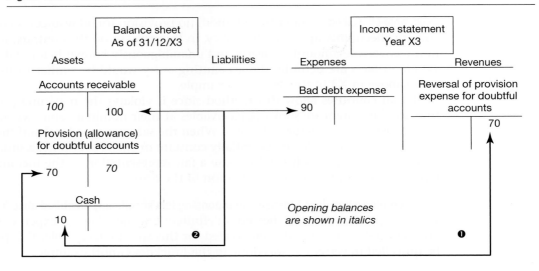

account is used: 'provision' (or 'allowance') for 'bad debts' (or 'for doubtful accounts'). One should absolutely not reduce directly the individual customer account receivable as it would give the impression that the receivable has decreased (i.e., been partially settled). As a matter of fact, the claim Brückner holds over Anton remains integral as long as Anton Corp. has not been liquidated. What is at stake here is the probability of collection, not the claim itself.

In X2, the possible loss is now estimated to be 70. The allowance must be raised to recognize the further devaluation of the claim. An additional allowance amounting to 70 − 40 = 30 (40 was the estimation of the possible loss at the end of X1) should be recorded. The accumulated provision (recorded on the balance sheet) is now raised to 70.

When the customer finally settles the account (even if it is not for the full amount remaining due and not yet provisioned), one must:

- ❶ Cancel (reverse) the cumulated provisions pertaining to this account receivable by recognizing the equivalent amount on the revenues side of the income statement (i.e., conceptually as a negative expense).
- ❷ Record a bad debt expense corresponding to the difference between the original claim (here it is 100) which is settled and the amount actually collected (here it is 10).

Impact on income of each of the years' entries

Year X1	Provision expense	−40	
Year X2	Provision expense	−30	−90
Year X3	Reversal of provision expense	+70	−20
	Bad debt expense	−90	

Comments
- The mechanism of allowance (provision) has the effect of distributing the net charge (here 90) over the years it takes to clear the receivable.
- The possible loss was originally difficult to evaluate (as shown in the case here, first evaluated at 40 and later revised at 70). The net difference between the total bad debt expense and the cumulated provisions (here it amounts to 20) is always recorded in the year during which the bad debt expense is finally recognized (here it is X3). In practice, there is almost always a difference (one way or another) between the estimated bad debt expense (which led to provisioning) and the actual amount of accounts receivable written-off (actual bad debt expense).

Direct write-off method   Under this method, no provision (or allowance) is created when the risk uncollectibility appears. The policy, in this case, is, on the contrary, to wait until the non-recoverable amount is clearly and unambiguously known before taking any action. When all facts are definite, the accounting entry would be similar to the second entry taken above in X3 in the Brückner example.

Not all countries allow this method since it violates the matching principle and the true and fair intent by showing receivables at their nominal value, when, in fact, a risk of uncollectibility is actually known. When the sales revenue level and the percentage of uncollectible receivables are essentially constant or stable over time, a situation obviously quite rare, this approach would create a fair representation of the income but an unfair representation of the financial situation of the firm.

❹ **Recording a bad debt expense corresponding to a specifically identified uncollectible receivable** When a specific receivable becomes definitely uncollectible, an expense is recorded. If a provision (allowance) had been created for this specific receivable, this provision has to be cancelled (reversed) as was done in the Brückner GmbH example.

As the reader will have gathered while reading this section, there is some maneuvering room, despite the existence of guidelines, in the valuation of the uncollectibility provision. Such a mechanism constitutes one of the tools managers often use to 'manage their earnings' (see 'accounts manipulation' in Chapter 17).

5.1.4 Reporting accounts receivable

In the balance sheet   Businesses follow one of four methods for reporting accounts receivable as illustrated below using the data from year X2 of the Brückner GmbH example:

Method 1 (detailed vertically and using a contra-asset account)

Accounts receivable (gross)	100
Less provision for doubtful accounts	−70
Accounts receivable (net)	30

Method 2 (synthetic with detail in the balance sheet)

Accounts receivable (net of provision for doubtful accounts: 70)   30

Method 3 (synthetic with detail in a note to the balance sheet)

Accounts receivable (net) (see note X)   30

Notes to the financial statements:
Note X – Accounts receivable
The accumulated amount of provision for doubtful accounts is equal to 70.

Method 4 (detailed horizontally)

	Gross value	Accumulated provisions	Net value
Accounts receivable	100	70	30

Whichever method is used, it is most important for the user of financial information to get access to the gross amount of receivables, which is used to compute ratios (see developments on financial statement analysis in section 7 of this chapter).

Real-life example Ericsson

(Sweden – IFRS – Source: Annual report 2008 – Telecommunications and network solutions)

Balance sheet (excerpts)

31 December, SEK million	2008	2007
Current assets		
Receivables		
Trade receivables - trade (note 14)	75,891	60,492
Customer finance (note 14)	1,975	2,362
(...)		

Note 11 - Trade receivables and customer finance		
31 December, SEK million	2008	2007
Trade receivables excluding associated companies and joint ventures	76,827	60,669
Allowances for impairment [of receivables]	−1,471	−1,351
Trade receivables, net	75,356	59,318
Trade receivables related to associated companies and joint ventures	535	1,174
Trade receivables, total	**75,891**	**60,492**
Customer finance [essentially loans to the customers]	3,147	3,649
Allowances for impairment	−326	−275
Customer finance, net	**2,821**	**3,374**
of which short term	1,975	2,362

Reporting movements in provision for doubtful accounts   Chapter 7 evoked the changes in valuation of fixed assets regarding the evolution of the gross value of fixed assets and of the accumulated depreciation. It is possible to create a similar table to report the changes in the receivables provision accounts.

Real-life example Ericsson

Ericsson, the Swedish telecommunication company (see real-life example above) publishes in its annual report 2008, a table with a detailed analysis of movements in allowances for impairment of its trade receivables and its customer finance:

Note 11 −Movements in allowances for impairment						
	Trade receivables			Customer finance		
	2008	2007	2006	2008	2007	2006
Opening balance	1,351	1,372	1,382	275	418	1,755
Additions	651	564	686	90	49	79
Utilization	−492	−554	−139	−3	−43	−284
Reversal of excess amounts	−81	−137	−527	−74	−141	−1,082
Reclassification	−69	56	56	−	−	−5
Translation difference	115	50	−86	38	−8	−45
Balances regarding acquired/ divested business	−4	−	−	−	−	−
Closing balance	1,471	1,351	1,372	326	275	418

- Additions: these are provision expenses for the year (i.e., provisions on new receivables plus additional provisions on receivables for which the probability of uncollectibility is considered to have increased).
- Ericsson does not explain the difference between 'utilization' and 'reversal of excess amounts' of allowances for impairment. Our interpretation is that deductions due to utilization represent cancellation of provisions because the receivable has been settled. This cancellation can be recorded as either a reduction in expenses or an increase in revenues (reversal of provision). Reversal of excess amounts is a modification of the level of risk attached to existing claims because the probable loss is perceived to have decreased on some of the receivables.
- Other movements: these are movements linked to the consolidation of subsidiaries (see Chapter 13), such as:
  - exchange differences on the conversion of financial statements of subsidiaries labeled in a currency other than the one of the parent company;
  - changes in the scope of consolidation resulting from acquisition or sale of subsidiaries.

5.2 Notes receivable

5.2.1 Principle

Credit sales are sometimes settled through specific monetary instruments called 'notes' or 'commercial paper'. These instruments are either a 'draft' or 'bill of exchange' when issued by the seller or a 'promissory note' when issued by the purchaser. Such instruments are used extensively, mainly in Southern Europe in countries such as Spain, Italy, France, and Greece, but also in the USA, Japan, Finland and the UK. Commercial paper or notes are defined as follows:

- A draft (or bill of exchange) is a written order by a first party (the drawer, i.e., the seller) instructing a second party (the drawee, i.e., the buyer) to pay a third party (the payee or beneficiary, who may be the drawer himself) a specified amount at a specified date (maturity) without conditions. It is common practice to have the draft prepared by the seller and sent to the buyer along with the invoice as a suggested preferred method of payment. The buyer then returns the signed ('accepted') draft to the seller, thus creating the contract by their signature.

- A promissory note is a written document in which a person or business (generally known as the 'maker') promises to pay a given amount to a third party (individual or business), referred to as the 'beneficiary', on a specified date (maturity date). The maker is the customer and the beneficiary is generally the supplier.

Since the accounting handling is the same for a draft, a bill of exchange or a promissory note, we will refer to this class of financial instruments by using the generic term of '**notes receivable**' on the supplier side and 'notes payable' on the buyer side (the latter is covered in Chapter 12).

Notes receivable offer three advantages to the seller over the traditional credit sale in which an invoice leads to the recording of a receivable:

- A note is a contract since it has been 'accepted' by the buyer. It offers a higher level of guarantee of payment to the seller than a simple combination 'order, delivery, acknowledgement of receipt plus invoice'.

- A note is a regular financial instrument. A note can be endorsed over to a third party (not limited to financial institutions) and thus can be traded at the expense of a **discounting fee**, charged by the buyer, and which reflects the specific risk level the firm is exposed to, generally and for the receivable traded.

- A note is a negotiable credit instrument. The seller can sell a note (commercial paper) to a financial institution before its maturity date and receive an amount of cash slightly inferior to the face value. The financial institution charges a fee for its services (generally proportional to the face value of the note plus a fixed administrative fee). The act of selling a note to a financial institution is referred to as '**discounting**' it. Some specialized financial institutions (often subsidiaries of banks or insurance companies), called 'factors', offer similar services to that provided by main-street banks. When a note payable is sold to a factor, it is called 'factoring' instead of discounting but the two mechanisms are essentially identical. Factors, often, are very willing to assume the default risk in return for higher fees than a main-street bank would have charged.

The lifecycle process of a draft or bill of exchange is illustrated in Appendix 10.3 for a payment on the maturity date and in Figure 10.8 for a sale (i.e., discounting or factoring) of the note before that date.

5.2.2 Recording of notes receivable

Several accounting methods coexist. If the note is discounted, the corresponding element of 'notes receivable' is cancelled and the cash account is increased, net of discounting fees

Figure 10.8 Notes receivable discounted (sold) before maturity (draft emitted by the seller and accepted by the buyer)

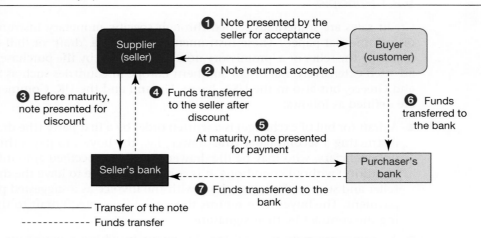

- Any holder of a note (even after an endorsement) can sell it whenever they feel the need to do so.
- In case of a discounting, in phase ❹ the holder of the note does not receive the full face amount of the note. The bank charges a discounting fee which represents (1) the interest for the period separating the date of discounting and the maturity date, (2) an administrative fee, and eventually (3) a risk premium.
- Discounting a note can be done in two ways that involve different risk levels:
  - *without recourse*: the note is sold with complete transfer to the buyer of the note of the default risk of the drawee.
  - *with recourse*: i.e., a conditional sale. If the drawee defaults on the maturity date, the discounting financial institution will demand full reimbursement of the note plus fees from the drawer or seller of the note who discounted it in the first place.

which are recorded as expenses in the income statement. The amount of discounted notes that have been removed from the assets, but which still carry a possibility of **recourse** by the acquirer should be reported in the notes to the financial statements of the seller, in the 'commitments' or the 'accounts receivable' sections. The note allows the reader to understand that the accounts receivable which have been discounted have been removed from the assets but still represent a latent liability.

Another solution is possible: the note receivable, after it has been sold (discounted), remains listed on the assets side and a corresponding liability is recorded (representing the debt towards the financial institution that bought the receivable). IAS 39 (§ 20) favors the second solution when the discounting is with recourse: 'When an entity transfers a financial asset (…) if the entity retains substantially all the risks and rewards of ownership of the financial asset, the entity shall continue to recognize the financial asset.'

The amount of discounted notes is required information to adjust the stated receivables when computing unbiased ratios relating to receivables such as average days of sale on credit (see section 7). The recording of notes receivable is further developed in Appendix 10.4.

Real-life example TCL

(China – IFRS – Source: Annual report 2008 – Consumer electronics)

Note 25 on 'factored trade receivables and bank advances as consideration for factored trade receivables'.

At 31 December 2008, the group's trade receivables of HK$1,835,241,000 (2007: HK$610,306,000) (the 'factored receivables') were factored to certain banks under certain receivables purchase agreements. The group continued to recognize the factored receivables in the balance sheet because, in the opinion of the directors, the group has retained substantially all the risks and rewards of ownership of the factored receivables as at the balance sheet date, including risks in respect of default payments and risks tied to the time value of money.

Accordingly, the advances from the relevant banks of HK$1,665,749,000 (2007: HK$610,306,000) received by the group as consideration for the factored receivables were recognized as liabilities in the consolidated balance sheet.

5.3 Sales returns

When a customer is not satisfied for any reason with the product or service that was delivered (such as non-conformity of delivery with order, defects, lateness, etc.), the product can generally be returned to the seller for partial or full credit or reimbursement. The original sale must therefore be reversed. Two methods exist for recording a **sales return**: cancellation of the sale directly in the sales ledger account, or indirectly through a 'contra-revenue' account which offers a better way than direct cancellation of monitoring the important operating parameter represented by sales returns (see Figures 10.9 and 10.10).

The sales returns account (a rarely reported account, essentially used internally by the firm) creates a measure used by management to monitor the evolution of returns so as to better be able to research and manage their causes. Gross sales (before discounts and other price adjustments) are most of the time reported net of returns in the income statement.

When goods have been returned, they must be entered in inventory before resale or destruction. Accounting entries here depend on whether the firm is using a periodic or perpetual inventory.

If the firm uses a periodic inventory system   (see Chapters 2 and 9), no specific entry is required at the time of the return since the returned goods will automatically be counted in the year-end physical inventory unless they have, by then, already been resold or destroyed.

Figure 10.9 Method 1: Recording of a sales return with direct cancellation

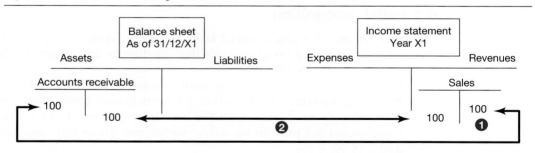

Figure 10.10 Method 2: Recording of a sales return with use of a contra-account

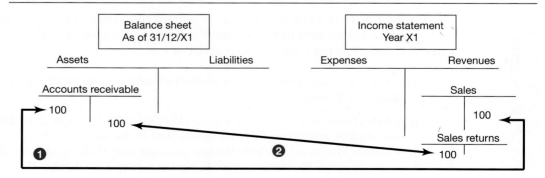

If the firm uses a perpetual inventory system   (see Chapters 2 and 9), and the goods are still in a sellable condition, the goods must be re-entered in the inventory account so as to adjust the cost of goods sold by the appropriate amount, and if they are not sellable, they are simply 'ignored' (in that case only the negative revenue element of the return (i.e., the cost of handling and disposal) is recorded without the offset of an increase in inventory).

Notes receivable and sales returns also impact value added taxes (receivables are generally carried VAT included) and potentially sales tax when applicable (see Appendix 10.2) and bank reconciliations (Appendix 10.5).

6 Available-for-sale financial assets

6.1 Definition

Available-for-sale financial assets 'are those non-derivative financial assets that [either] are [formally] designated as available for sale, or are not classified as (a) loans and receivables, (b) held-to-maturity investments or (c) financial assets at fair value through profit or loss' (IAS 39: § 9).

This class of financial assets is thus partly a residual category defined by opposition to the other three categories. In practice, two main types of investments will be found under this available-for-sale heading:

1. All equity securities except those classified as at fair value through profit or loss. These can represent, for example, long-term equity investments, held for return, without any intention to influence the business whose shares are held as an asset.

2. Investments in non-consolidated companies (because they do not meet the required threshold – see Chapter 13), or (speculative) investments (i.e., not part of an 'industrial strategy') included in the parent company's, or any subsidiary's, stand-alone balance sheet.

6.2 Initial recognition

When an available-for-sale financial asset is recognized initially, an entity shall measure it at its fair value plus transaction costs that are directly attributable to the acquisition of this financial asset (IAS 39: § 43).

After initial recognition, an entity shall measure available-for-sale financial assets, at their fair value, without any deduction for [anticipated] transaction costs it may incur on sale or other disposal, except for the investments in equity instruments that do not have a quoted market price in an active market and whose fair value cannot be reliably measured (IAS 39: § 46).

6.3 Recognition of the evolution of value

However, IAS 39 (§ 55) introduces an important difference in reporting [potential] gains and losses incurred after initial recognition between available-for-sale financial assets and those classified at fair value through profit or loss:

'A gain or loss arising from a change in the fair value of a financial asset (…) shall be recognized, as follows:

(a) A gain or loss on a financial asset (…) classified as 'at fair value through profit or loss' shall be recognized in profit or loss [i.e., in the income statement].

(b) A gain or loss on an available-for-sale financial asset shall be recognized directly in equity, through the statement of changes in equity [see Chapter 11] (…)'.

In practice, value adjustments should be made both when the market value falls below the acquisition cost (potential loss) and when the market value goes beyond the acquisition cost (potential gain). In the first case, the book value of the available-for-sale investment is adjusted (reduced) to its market level on the assets side. As a counterpart, a reduction in equity is also recorded. In the second case, both the book value of the investment and the equity are increased to reflect the positive change of market price.

6.4 Special case of unlisted (untraded) financial assets

Available-for-sale financial assets often include unlisted equity investments (i.e., not readily sold on a financial market). US GAAP and IFRS have adopted similar, but not identical, approaches to handling these investments. The regulations can be analyzed in terms of reporting, measurement and disclosure.

6.4.1 Principle

In the USA, reporting of investments in unlisted equity securities (also called 'investments in closely held companies' or 'investments in privately-held companies') is not regulated by SFAS 115 (FASB 1993), which specifically applies to equity securities with 'readily determinable fair values'. Reporting for this category of investments follows Regulation S-X of the SEC which requires registered investment companies to value their investments for the purposes of financial statements in conformity with the valuation concepts prescribed in the 1940 act (Investment Company Act of 1940). Investments of companies that are not publicly traded are valued at fair value as determined 'in good faith by the Board of Directors' (1940 Act, section 2, § 41) and approved by the Audit Committee. Consequently, a major concept in the US accounting treatment is the 'readily determinable' fair value.

IAS 39 indicates, in the section devoted to financial assets at fair value through profit or loss, that 'investments in equity instruments that do not have a quoted market price in an active market, and whose fair value cannot be reliably measured (...), shall not be designated as at fair value through profit or loss' (§ 9) but 'shall be measured at cost' (§ 46-c). IAS 39 leaves the door open to fair value reporting of investments in unlisted equity instruments, as long as the company believes that their fair value can be reliably measured.

6.4.2 Estimation techniques of the fair value of unlisted investments

In the USA, companies generally use traditional valuation methods to estimate the enterprise value of 'portfolio companies'[9] issuing the securities. In September 2006, the FASB issued Statement 157, Fair Value Measurements ('SFAS 157'), which provides enhanced guidance on the use of fair value to measure assets and liabilities. SFAS 157 applies whenever other standards require (or allow) assets or liabilities to be measured at fair value, but it does not extend the use of fair value to any new circumstances. SFAS No. 157 is effective for fiscal years beginning after 15 November 2007 and is applied by firms operating in the private equity industry.

Under SFAS 157 (FASB 2006: § 18), any one of three valuation techniques (market approach, income approach, and/or cost approach) must be used to measure fair value. The Statement describes the 'inputs' to valuation techniques (SFAS 157: §§ 21–31), a concept which refers broadly to the assumptions that market participants would use. Inputs may be observable or unobservable. Fair values are determined by reference to three types of inputs used to measure the asset:

- ■ Level 1 and 2 asset values are based on observable market data:
  - – level 1: quoted prices for identical assets;
  - – level 2: other observable data, such as quoted prices for similar assets.

- Level 3: absent observable market data, the firm's management must rely on its own assumptions and judgment (decision by the Board, after approval by the Audit Committee).

IAS 39 states that 'the fair value of investments in equity instruments that do not have a quoted market price in an active market … is reliably measurable if (a) the variability in the range of reasonable fair value estimates is not significant for that instrument or (b) the probabilities of the various estimates within the range can be reasonably assessed and used in estimating fair value' (§ AG80). In other words, an unlisted equity instrument can be reported at 'fair value' if it can be 'reliably measured': 'if the market for a financial instrument is not active, an entity establishes fair value by using a valuation technique. Valuation techniques include using recent [at] arm's length market transactions between knowledgeable, willing parties, if available, reference to the current fair value of another instrument that is substantially the same, discounted cash flow analysis and option pricing models' (IAS 39 § AG74).

6.4.3 Disclosure issues

Given that 'fair value' construction defines gains or losses and thus can significantly affect the value of equity, disclosure of the methodology is essential to a true and fair view. Before the implementation of SFAS 157, few current accounting regulations that require fair value measurement also required disclosure of the measurement technique. To improve transparency in financial reporting, the FASB decided to require expanded disclosure of fair value measurements using significant unobservable inputs and the effects of such measurements on earnings (SFAS 157: § C17).

More precisely, for assets reported at fair value on a recurring basis in periods subsequent to initial recognition, the reporting entity must disclose information that enables users of its financial statements to assess the inputs used to develop those measurements; and for recurring fair value measurements using significant unobservable inputs (level 3), the effect of those measurements on earnings (or changes in net assets) for the period must also be disclosed (SFAS 157: § 32).

However, in its Exposure Draft, the FASB had expressed the view that standardizing such disclosures for all assets measured at fair value (for example, requiring disclosure of the assumptions used in fair value valuation) would not be practical. The Board noted that in some cases, an overwhelming volume of information would need to be disclosed to be meaningful. Because fair value evaluations rely largely on the assumptions made by the firm, the issue of sensitivity of these fair value calculation to variations in the parameters is always a critical issue. The Board decided not to require disclosure of such sensitivity. Instead, the Statement establishes broad disclosure objectives, which the Board expects to consider as a basis for requiring more specific disclosures in individual accounting pronouncements that require fair value measurements on a project-by-project basis (SFAS 157: § C101).

IFRS 7 (§ 27) states that 'An entity shall disclose:

(a) the methods and, when a valuation technique is used, the assumptions applied in determining fair values of each class of financial assets (…)

(b) (…)

(c) for fair values that are recognized in the financial statements, if changing one or more of those assumptions to reasonably possible alternative assumptions would change fair value significantly, the entity shall state this fact and disclose the effect of those changes. For this purpose, significance shall be judged with respect to profit or loss, and total assets or total liabilities, or, when changes in fair value are recognized in equity, total equity.

(d) if (c) applies, the total amount of the change in fair value estimated using such a valuation technique that was recognized in profit or loss during the period.'

IFRS 7 refers explicitly to sensitivity analysis: 'To provide users of financial statements with a sense of the potential variability of fair value estimates, the Board decided that information about the use of valuation techniques should be disclosed, in particular the sensitivities of fair value estimates to the main valuation assumptions' (IFRS 7: § BC38).

In summary, while the FASB preferred not to explicitly require sensitivity disclosures, the IASB in contrast chose to require publication of a sensitivity analysis, but only where necessary (a decision effectively left to the management of the firm).

At the time of writing this book, the IASB has published an exposure draft on 'Fair value measurement' (ED/2009/05) which appears to be consistent with SFAS 157.

7 Financial statement analysis

Managers as well as many users are interested in monitoring the operating and cash cycles of a business. The credit policy of a firm has an impact on sales revenue (credit terms can be a key attribute in the customer's decision to buy), on the level of receivables and length of the cash collection cycle. Two ratios, actually linked, are commonly used to monitor the effects of a credit policy. They are the '**average days of sales**' and the '**receivables turnover**'. They are defined as follows:

> **Average days of sales** (in receivables) (or **Average collection period** or **Days Sales Outstanding [DSO]**) = (Average accounts receivable/Net sales) × 365 days

This ratio provides the average duration of credit terms offered to customer.

> Receivables turnover = Net sales/Average accounts receivable

The second ratio, which is proportional to the inverse of the first one, measures the number of times receivables turned over during the year.

Financial information users must monitor closely the change of these two ratios, because in most situations, the slow-down of receivables turnover will have at least four negative effects:

1. increase the risk of bad debts;

2. create opportunity costs (the amount of funds required to offset the receivables cannot be used for alternative investments or projects, potentially more profitable or more pregnant with future results);

3. create higher handling and administrative expenses (needed to monitor and collect this money);

4. paying financial interests for the funds required to finance the receivables.

Comments:

- The gross value of accounts receivable, rather than their net value, should be considered, as it represents the real credit granted to customers. In other words, the net value – after deduction of valuation allowances for doubtful accounts – artificially minimizes the average days of sales in receivables. However, in practice, many companies do not disclose the gross amount of accounts receivable. Consequently, financial analysts often compute the two above-mentioned ratios using the only available net amount of accounts receivable. This practice is acceptable (if a better solution cannot be found) but it should always be borne in mind that it is a by-default solution and could provide biased and misleading figures if amounts of valuation allowances are significant or vary from period to period. If gross amounts are available, they should, of course, be taken into account.

■ Accounts receivable used in ratio calculations are generally the average of the beginning and end of the year. An even better approach, in an attempt to minimize seasonal variations, is to take the weighted average of the four published quarterly receivables, if they are available. External analysts generally only have, in the worst case, annual and, in the best case, quarterly data to build their averages, thus not freeing themselves completely of seasonal variations within the period. An internal manager probably uses rolling weighted averages over 12 months (or even 52 weeks) based on monthly (or weekly) balances for a better vision of the impact of the interaction of the credit policy and the state of the economy on the behavior of customers.

■ Some analysts suggest that only credit sales be used in the calculation of these ratios in order to not introduce a favorable bias due to cash sales. Although theoretically more accurate than the averaging of total sales versus total receivables, this approach is difficult to implement as the breakdown between cash and credit sales is rarely reported in annual statements.

■ Notes receivable that have been discounted to a bank or other financial institution and have been removed from accounts receivable should be added back to the book receivables in order to get as accurate a picture of the real situation as possible. In fact, the possibility for the seller to sell their notes to a financial institution is an encouragement to feel free to extend credit without having to bear the requisite increase in working capital it would involve, but by bearing, in counterpart, a heavy expense in discounting fees.

■ When sales are eligible for VAT the accounts receivable balance includes VAT (see Appendix 10.2). Therefore, in order to use coherent figures in the calculation of ratios, one must verify that numerator and denominator are expressed coherently either VAT-included or VAT-excluded. However, such coherence is not always easy to achieve as, for example, export sales are generally not submitted to VAT in the country of origin and each country tends to have a specific VAT rate for its domestic sales. Current practice calls for ignoring VAT and accepting that the figures give an approximate value of the ratio. It is not, however, a dramatic error in that the general trend of evolution is still the same as long as no major changes in the mix of sales (cash versus credit, and/or domestic versus export) took place.

Real-life example Ericsson

Ericsson, the Swedish telecommunications network solutions manufacturer, shows an excellent example of the difficulty of evaluating the average days of sales when a large proportion of sales are export sales or sales not realized by the parent's country operations. All figures are drawn from its 2008 annual report.

(SEK million)		
Net sales	2008	208,930
Net sales in Sweden	2008	8,876
Trade receivables	2008	75,891
Trade receivables	2007	60,492
Trade receivables	Average	68,192
Average days' sales (68,192/208,930) × 365		119.1
Receivables turnover (208,930/68,192)		3.06

In this example, we have chosen to not extract the VAT which is included in the receivables because the proportion of total sales originating from domestic operations is very small. The credit term appears to be intrinsically long but, as we will see in Chapter 18, no ratio can ever be interpreted on its face value, but only by analyzing its evolution over time and comparing its value to equivalent ratios pertaining to other comparable firms in the same line of business.

In order to analyze the other financial instruments in the balance sheet, a common-size format is very useful. Before drawing any conclusions, please keep in mind that the balance sheet is a static picture of a firm's financial situation at a precise moment. In order to evaluate the current situation, some comparisons across different years and/or with other companies from the same industry are also quite helpful.

Financial assets held for trading are very liquid assets. However, their market prices are highly volatile. Here, the timeliness of the balance sheet is the main issue. When analyzing these assets, users must check the price changes since the issuance day of the balance sheet.

As presented in section 6, the unrealized gains or losses of available-for-sale assets are reported in the equity. In some case, these changes may impact violently the equity-to-debt ratio of the company and so also the financial risk appreciation (see Assignment 10.6 Youngor).

Key points

- Financial instruments comprise four categories: financial asset or financial liability at fair value through profit or loss [including held for trading]; held-to-maturity investments; loans and receivables and available-for-sale financial assets.
- Cash comprises 'cash in hand' (coins, banknotes and currency available) and 'demand deposits' (deposits in bank accounts that are available on demand).
- Cash equivalents are short-term, highly liquid investments that are readily convertible to known amounts of cash and which are subject to an insignificant risk of changes in value.
- According to IASB, current investments held for trading should be carried in the balance sheet at fair value through profit or loss.
- The fair value valuation causes many debates.

- The percentage of total assets represented by receivables is generally related to the entity-specific business activity: the absolute level of receivables (driven by the credit sales policy and sales volume) and the relative importance of fixed assets.
- The probability that an account receivable will effectively be collected must be evaluated at the end of each accounting period. Doubtful or disputed accounts, which are partly or totally uncollectible, are referred to as 'bad' or 'doubtful' debts, or 'doubtful accounts'. Their value has to be written down by recognizing a provision expense equal to the estimated potential loss.
- Uncollectible accounts must be written-off by recognizing a bad debt expense.
- The two main indicators relevant with regard to accounts receivable are (1) the average days of sales, and (2) the receivables turnover.

Review (solutions are at the back of the book)

Review 10.1 Berg

Topic: Accounting for provision on receivables

At the end of their accounting period, on 31 December X3, Berg Enterprises have reviewed their receivables and found two doubtful accounts.

Customer	A/R Balance	Comments	Probable loss
Alban	200	Filed for protection from creditors	25%
Adam	300	Filed for protection from creditors	40%

As of 31 December X4, these doubtful accounts are as follows:

Customer	A/R Balance	Comments	Probable (or real) loss
Alban	200	Filed for protection from creditors	70%
Adam	300	Paid 50 in total settlement of account	250

Required

1. Prepare the doubtful accounts provisions at the end of X3.
2. Prepare the appropriate entries at the end of X3.
3. Prepare the doubtful accounts provisions at the end of X4.
4. Prepare the appropriate entries at the end of X4.

Assignments

Assignment 10.1
Multiple-choice questions

Select the right answer (only one possible answer, unless otherwise stated).

1. Doubtful debts represent
   (a) Liabilities which are challenged by one of the parties
   (b) Receivables which might not be collected
   (c) All of these
   (d) None of these

2. Accounts receivable is equivalent to (several answers possible)
   (a) Trade creditors
   (b) Trade debtors
   (c) Trade accounts payable
   (d) Trade accounts receivable
   (e) All of these
   (f) None of these

3. A bank overdraft should be
   (a) Included in the financial fixed assets
   (b) Reported as a current asset
   (c) Reported as a current liability
   (d) Netted against positive cash balances at other banks
   (e) None of these

4. The direct write-off method is consistent with the matching accounting principle while the allowance method is not
   (a) True
   (b) False

5. Accounts receivable are generally valued at the
   (a) Amounts invoiced to customers
   (b) Net realizable value
   (c) Present value of future cash flows
   (d) None of these

6. Given the following information, determine the accounts receivable turnover (two possible answers)

Beginning accounts receivable	20
Ending accounts receivable	40
Beginning cash	50
Ending cash	60
Cash sales	40
Credit sales	300
Net income	35

   (a) 15
   (b) 7.5
   (c) 10
   (d) 17
   (e) 8.5
   (f) 11.33
   (g) 1
   (h) 2
   (i) 2.5
   (j) 3
   (k) None of these

7. An accounts receivable with a 100% probability of being collected is a cash equivalent
   (a) True
   (b) False

8. When a note receivable is discounted

(a) The note is removed from the assets

(b) The note is maintained in the assets and a liability is recorded

(c) The note is removed from the assets or maintained in the assets with a liability recorded, depending on the national GAAP

(d) None of these

9. When a provision (allowance) is no longer necessary

(a) An expense account is decreased

(b) A revenue account is increased

(c) Both solutions are possible, it depends on the country

(d) None of these

10. Which of the following statements are not true? (several answers possible)

(a) Unrealized gains of financial assets are never recognized

(b) Financial assets held for trading are usually very liquid

(c) Available-for-sale financial assets are always valued at fair value

(d) Liquid financial assets have low risk

(e) Provisions are sometimes needed for held-to-maturity assets

Assignment 10.2
Mahler

Topic: Estimating provision for doubtful accounts

Mahler Company provides the following information relating to sales, accounts receivable and the provision for doubtful accounts for year X2 (000 CU omitted).

Sales for X2	3,000
Sales returns on credit sales	100
Accounts receivable balance, on 1 January X2	400
Provision for doubtful accounts balance, on 1 January X2	40
Cash collected on accounts receivable during X2	1,000
Accounts written-off as bad debt expenses during X2	30

Required

1. Record the write-off of uncollectible doubtful accounts during X2.

2. Prepare the adjusting entry required on 31 December X2 to record the provision on doubtful accounts for each of the following *independent* assumptions:

(a) The provision for doubtful accounts is based on the ending balance of accounts receivable. Eighty percent of the sales during X2 were credit sales. The accountant of Mahler Company, Mr. Gustav, estimates, from past experience, that 10% of the 31 December X2 accounts receivable will prove to be doubtful.

(b) The provision for doubtful accounts is based on net credit sales. The accountant estimated that 80% of the sales are credit sales, and that 5% of the net credit sales will prove to be doubtful.

(c) The provision for doubtful expense is based on aging of accounts receivable. The following aging schedule has been prepared by the accountant:

Days outstanding	Amount	Probability of collection
0–30 days	900	95%
31–60 days	500	90%
61–90 days	250	80%
More than 90 days	20	70%

Assignment 10.3
Bosch*

Topic: Reporting for receivables

Bosch is a German group producing automotive equipment, power tools and home appliances. The consolidated balance sheet and notes to financial statements 2008 show the following elements relating to receivables (source: Annual report 2008).

(in € million)		
Excerpts of the balance sheet	31/12/2008	31/12/2007
Current assets		
Trade receivables (note 12)	6,971	7,844
Other assets (note 13)	1,672	1,955
Note 12 Trade receivables	**2008**	**2007**
Trade receivables	6,971	7,844
– thereof due in more than one year	9	2
Note 13 Other assets (current)	**2008**	**2007**
Loan receivables	167	233
Receivables from finance leases	28	28
Receivables from board of management, associates	27	25
Receivables from tax authorities (without income tax receivables)	663	652
Other assets and sundry other receivables	787	1,017
Total	1,672	1,955

Required

1. Relate the balance sheet items shown to the information contained in the notes.

2. What plausible conclusion can be drawn about the format of presentation in note 12 from the existence of the line 'thereof due in more than one year'?

3. In your best judgment, are the amounts reported in the notes gross or net? Explain your position and, eventually, its possible implications.

4. What are associated companies and is it normal that receivables pertaining to trade with these companies still appear on a consolidated balance sheet (see Chapter 13)?

Assignment 10.4
Bayer*

Topic: Financial statement analysis of receivables

Bayer is a German chemical group. The consolidated balance sheet and income statement (source: Annual report 2008) include the following data.

(in € million)		
Excerpts from the balance sheet	31 Dec 2007	31 Dec 2008
Current assets		
Trade accounts receivables (note 22)	5,830	5,953
Excerpts from the income statement	**2007**	**2008**
Net sales	32,385	32,918

The notes, as mentioned earlier in this chapter, provide the following table concerning changes in write-downs of trade accounts receivable:

	Carrying amount	Of which neither impaired nor overdue at the balance sheet date	Of which not impaired but overdue at the balance sheet date			
			up to 3 months	3–6 months	6–12 months	12 months
31 Dec 2008	5,953	4,699	739	156	142	100
31 Dec 2007	5,830	4,493	638	119	84	103

Required

1. Compute the average days of sales (also called the number of days sales outstanding) and receivables turnover on the sole basis of the information provided in the balance sheet and income statement.

2. Compute the same ratios incorporating data disclosed in the notes.

3. Explain the difference you find between the two methods of computations.

4. Comment on these ratios.

Assignment 10.5
Holmen*

Topic: Financial statement analysis of receivables

Holmen (formerly MoDo) is a Swedish paper and cardboard manufacturer. In the notes to their 2008 consolidated financial statements (source: Annual report 2008), the Company disclosed the following data with regard to operating receivables (in millions of SEK):

	Group		Parent company	
	2008	2007	2008	2007
Accounts receivable	3,144	3,004	2,343	2,191
– thereof accounts receivables from associated companies	64	n.a.	64	n.a.
– thereof accounts receivables from group companies	—	—	162	n.a.
Receivables from associated companies	5	37	5	37
Prepaid costs and accrued income	166	100	135	49
Derivatives	157	27	138	121
Other receivables	220	296	143	221
	3,692	3,464	2,764	2,619

In the income statement, the net turnover (net sales) amounts to:

	2008	2007
Net turnover	19,334	19,159

Required

1. Explain why the 'receivables from group companies' do not appear in the 'group' financial statements.

2. Compute the average days of sales (in receivables) for 2008 and 2007.

3. Comment on these figures.

Assignment 10.6
Youngor*

Topic: Financial instruments

Youngor Group, founded in 1979, has grown over 30 years into a large-scale multinational group with over 50,000 employees in over 40 subsidiaries and interests in as diverse activities as apparel, real estate development and equity investment. Its largest subsidiary, Youngor Group Co. Ltd. (the leading Chinese enterprise involved in designing, manufacturing, selling and trading clothing products and accessories) has been listed on the Shanghai Stock Exchange since 1998. In 2007, the group sales reached 18.4 billion yuan and yielded $865 million in foreign exchange from exports. Its total profit amounted to about 4 billion yuan, with tax contributions of 2,184 million yuan. It was listed in 'China's Top 100 Leading Enterprises in 2007' for its excellent performance and sustained growth. In 2008, it was ranked No.134 on the list of China's Top 500 Manufacturing Enterprises. In addition, it has made several appearances on 'Forbes Charity List' for its good image as corporate citizen and won 'China's Charity Award for Extraordinary contributions'. It had also been listed for two consecutive years in 'Hurun Chinese Top 50 Socially Responsible Enterprises'.

Apparel

One of the group's principal activities is apparel manufacturing and merchandising. It has developed a vertical textile and clothing industry supply chain through continuous efforts since it first engaged in men's apparel manufacturing in 1979.

Youngor Clothing Co. Ltd., the apparel subsidiary, has more than 100 branches, over 400 fully owned specialty stores, and a total of over 1,500 business outlets nationwide. Its brand 'Youngor' is the reference for men's clothing, which includes shirts, business suits, pants and jackets, ties and T-shirts, among others. Its apparel products carry an image of maturity, self-confidence, modesty and a high-quality life.

Youngor Clothing Co. Ltd has been the domestic market share leader in shirts (its main product) for 12 consecutive years. It became the first Chinese apparel manufacturer exempted from export inspection for shirts. It has held the largest domestic market share in business suits for seven consecutive years.

Youngor has ranked No. 1 in China's clothing industry in terms of both sales revenues and total profits for seven consecutive years. Youngor has expanded its apparel business upstream all the way to cotton plantations. In 2008 it extended its integration upstream and downstream by acquiring Smart Apparel Group Limited, Kellwood Company's core menswear business, with strong capabilities in apparel design and international operation management, and bringing to Youngor a solid distribution network throughout the USA.

Real estate development

Since setting foot in real estate development in 1992, Youngor Group has successively developed Donghu Garden, Donghu Xinyuan, City Forest, Suzhou Future City, Sea View Garden, Qianhu Bihuali and other large-scale buildings in Ningbo, Suzhou and other places. The accumulated land area of residential buildings, villas, and commercial buildings developed by Youngor totals three million square meters, and is growing continuously.

Equity investment

Youngor entered the equity investment sector in 1993 and then expanded into other financial sectors like securities and banking. It had invested in many enterprises including Guangbo Group, Yak Technology, Citic Securities, Bank of Ningbo and Hai Tong Securities. With

Consolidated Balance Sheet Youngor Group Co. Ltd

Assets	31 Dec 2008 yuan	31 Dec 2007 yuan	31 Dec 2006 yuan	2008 %	2007 %	2006 %
Current assets:						
Money capital (cash)	3,983,223,090	2,192,846,691	661,165,719	13	6	4
Transactional monetary capital (cash equivalents)	819,802	2,128,334	873,774	–	–	–
Notes receivable	3,070,274	5,382,000	5,329,152	–	–	–
Accounts receivable	795,883,873	456,274,759	407,584,687	3	1	2
Prepaid accounts	1,646,983,950	3,392,962,551	1,428,684,098	5	10	8
Accrued interest receivable	5,245			–	–	–
Other receivables	639,776,469	179,412,898	92,247,134	2	1	1
Inventories	13,334,950,568	7,369,713,562	5,465,662,278	42	21	32
Total current assets	**20,404,713,271**	**13,598,720,795**	**8,061,546,842**	**65**	**38**	**47**
Non-current assets:						
Financial assets available for sale	4,672,338,450	16,496,690,651	4,368,900,098	15	47	25
Long-term accounts receivable	5,831,896	–	–	–	–	–
Long-term equity investments	1,092,565,639	871,012,466	569,554,108	3	2	3
Investments in real estate	53,255,240	17,874,036	18,967,925	–	–	–
Fixed assets	4,506,866,043	3,686,616,267	3,648,993,863	14	10	21
Construction in process	370,305,292	286,969,303	106,497,010	1	1	1
Engineering material	–	68,760,903	–	–	–	–
Intangible assets	368,735,336	258,716,381	389,964,228	1	1	2
Goodwill	47,814,253	45,196,688	45,196,688	–	–	–
Long-term deferred expense	37,083,818	7,276,175	24,474,192	–	–	–
Deferred income tax assets	72,116,404	6,536,212	15,554,967	–	–	–
Other non-current assets	40,464	–	–	–	–	–
Total non-current assets	**11,226,952,835**	**21,745,649,081**	**9,188,103,080**	**35**	**62**	**53**
Total assets	**31,631,666,106**	**35,344,369,876**	**17,249,649,922**	**100**	**100**	**100**

Liabilities and equity	31 Dec 2008 yuan	31 Dec 2007 yuan	31 Dec 2006 yuan	2008 %	2007 %	2006 %
Current liabilities:						
Short-term borrowing	7,455,568,284	5,905,186,413	2,297,429,328	24	17	13
Transactional monetary liabilities	3,761,921	–	–	–	–	–
Bills payable	347,946,162	165,608,596	122,054,253	1	–	1
Accounts payable	666,811,808	439,741,668	325,791,531	2	1	2
Accounts received in advance	5,534,514,769	5,485,733,063	2,294,390,847	17	16	13
Payroll payable	346,061,881	241,704,446	191,005,340	1	1	1
Taxes payable	−293,769,155	586,190,995	485,798,244	−1	2	3
Accrued interest payable	41,372,601	15,715,804	3,913,644	–	–	–
Dividends payable	49,390,739	2,400,000	2,400,000	–	–	–
Other payables	904,830,836	658,284,990	604,077,753	3	2	4
Non-current liabilities due within one year	887,865,000	235,000,000	980,000,000	3	1	6
Other current liabilities	1,903,280,000	–	–	6	–	–
Total current liabilities	**17,847,634,847**	**13,735,565,975**	**7,306,860,939**	**56**	**39**	**42**
Non current liabilities						
Long-term borrowings	2,335,006,252	1,933,930,604	646,985,121	7	5	4
Special accounts payable	7,453,958	9,326,871	5,900,312	–	–	–
Deferred income tax liabilities	1,534,101,191	3,092,751,712	1,337,992,775	5	9	8
Total non-current liabilities	**3,876,561,402**	**5,036,009,187**	**1,990,878,207**	**12**	**14**	**12**
Total liabilities	**21,724,196,249**	**18,771,575,162**	**9,297,739,146**	**69**	**53**	**54**
Shareholders' equity:						
Paid-in capital	2,226,611,695	2,226,611,695	1,781,289,356	7	6	10
Capital surplus	2,306,050,375	9,381,602,567	3,265,440,210	7	27	19
Earned surplus	677,535,305	592,909,549	380,822,537	2	2	2
Undistributed profits	3,882,983,973	3,537,057,216	1,831,024,870	12	10	11
Converted difference in foreign currency statements	−82,072,533	−3,406,950	−1,705,064	–	–	–
Total owners' equity attributable to parent company	9,011,108,815	15,734,774,078	7,256,871,910	28	45	42
Minority shareholders' equity	896,361,043	838,020,636	695,038,865	3	2	4
Total owners' equity	**9,907,469,858**	**16,572,794,713**	**7,951,910,776**	**31**	**47**	**46**
Total liabilities and owners' equity	**31,631,666,106**	**35,344,369,876**	**17,249,649,922**	**100**	**100**	**100**

the near-completion of the Equity Division Reform in 2006, the net assets of Youngor increased significantly and many of its investments represent large potential unrealized capital gains.

In 2007 Youngor established a professional investment company for equity investment in financial institutions, resource-based enterprises and industry leaders which are already listed or are planning to list on Chinese stock exchanges.

In addition to its three major business segments, namely, apparel, real estate development and equity investment, Youngor has also expanded into other fields such as hotel, tourism and international trade. One of its subsidiaries, China-Base Ningbo Foreign Trade Co. Ltd., is the biggest import and export company in Ningbo.

The following financial statements have been extracted from Youngor Group Co. Ltd. annual report 2007 and 2008.

Some background information:
1. In 2007, the Chinese capital market leading index – Shanghai Stock Index increased by 96.1%, while in 2008, it dropped 65.4%.

2. Youngor has a substantial business in real estate development, which is reflected in the following accounts:

- Prepaid accounts in assets: mainly the deposits paid to the local government after land purchase agreements.
- Inventory in assets: land in stock and ongoing real estate projects.
- Accounts received in advance in liabilities: in China, real estate projects are usually pre-sold to owners before construction. Since the transfer of ownership of the houses is only made after the construction, developers keep, as required by Chinese GAAP and IFRS/IAS, these prepaid revenues as liabilities during the construction period.

Required

1. Explain why the 'Financial assets available for sale' change so violently over the period under consideration.

2. Comment on these figures and analyze their impacts on Youngor's strategy and financial structure.

References

FASB (1993) Statement of Financial Accounting Standard No. 115: Accounting for Certain Investments in Debt and Equity Securities, Stamford, CT.

FASB (2006) Statement of Financial Accounting Standards No. 157: Fair value measurements Norwalk, CT.

IASB (1992) International Accounting Standard No. 7: Statement of cash flows, London.

IASB (1993) International Accounting Standard No. 18: Revenue, London.

IASB (2008a) International Accounting Standard No. 32: Financial Instruments: Presentation, London.

IASB (2008b) International Accounting Standard No. 39: Financial Instruments: Recognition and Measurement, London.

IASB (2008c) International Financial Reporting Standard No. 7: Financial Instruments: Disclosure, London.

Further reading

Stice J., Stice E.K. and Skousen F. (2009) *Intermediate Accounting*, 17th edn, South-Western Cengage Learning, Mason, OH.

Additional material on the website

Go to http://www.cengage.co.uk/stolowy3 for further information, journal entries and extra assignments for each chapter.

The following appendices to this chapter are available on the dedicated website:

Appendix 10.1: Hedging
Appendix 10.2: Value added tax
Appendix 10.3: Notes receivable paid at maturity
Appendix 10.4: Recording of notes receivable
Appendix 10.5: Bank reconciliation

Notes

1. A derivative is any financial instrument derived from securities, commodity markets or market indices. The term has become a generic term that is used to describe all types of new and old financial instruments. The most common types of derivatives are *futures, options, warrants* and *convertible bonds*. Beyond these traditional derivatives instruments, 'the derivatives range is only limited by the imagination of investment banks' (adapted from 'derivatives' in www.numa.com/ref/faq.htm).

2. The notion of 'through profit or loss' refers to the fact that since the fair value may change from period to period, the investing business will recognize the potential gain or loss on its investment in its income statement on an as-you-go basis.

3. For example it would be the case if such designation were to eliminate or significantly reduce, in further reporting, a measurement or recognition inconsistency (sometimes referred to as 'an accounting mismatch') that would otherwise arise from measuring assets [or liabilities] or recognizing the gains and losses on them on different bases.

4. Securitization consists in aggregating similar, generally not individually negotiable financial instruments, such as receivables, loans or mortgages, into a negotiable security, which can be partitioned into 'shares' that can be sold and traded on financial markets. The most commonly securitized receivable (or payable) is called 'commercial paper' which is commonly traded in financial markets, directly or through specialized funds (second degree securitization).

5. The term 'debt' is still often used in practice. A more accurate (but rarely used) term ought to be 'bad-' or 'doubtful receivables'. Some countries use the term 'doubtful accounts' or 'uncollectible accounts'.

6. Aging accounts receivable is the process of classifying individual receivable transactions by the time elapsed since the claim came into existence. Most accounting software programs provide an automatic partitioning of the accounts receivable by age class, i.e., due date or overdue delay (30 days, 31 to 60 days, etc.).

7. Source: MOCI (France) no. 1813, 6 March 2008, p. 6.

8. Source: S. Ng and C. Tuna: 'Big firms are quick to collect, slow to pay', 01 September 2009, *Wall Street Journal*, available at http://online.wsj.com/article/SB125167116756270697.html.

9. Essentially firms or entities whose main business is to buy and sell shares or other financial instruments of other firms. The most common type of such entities is known as 'private equity firms'.

C11

Chapter 11

Shareholders' Equity

Learning objectives

After studying this chapter, you will understand:

- The differences between the legal forms of business organization.
- What share capital is.
- How changes in share capital (increase or reduction) are reported.
- What different categories of shares exist.
- What a share premium is and how it is reported.
- How profit appropriation is recorded.
- What kinds of different categories of reserves are found in the balance sheet.
- How stock options plans are recorded.
- How changes in shareholders' equity are reported.
- How shareholders' equity can be analyzed.

As shown in Figure 1.3 (Chapter 1), in order to create value or wealth for its creators, a business must finance upfront the acquisition of its initial means of 'production' so it can create and deliver its value proposition to its customers and thus activate the cash pump. The two main sources of seed financial resources of a firm are:

1. Capital provided, without time limit, by the entrepreneur or by risk-taking investors (such as shareholders) in exchange for a claim on the future returns (positive or negative) of the business venture; and

2. Borrowed funds, generally provided, for a predefined and limited period of time, by financial institutions in a contract specifying the principal will be returned by an agreed upon date plus a fee (interest) which is not conditional on the success of the venture.

Additional financial resources will be generated, on an ongoing basis, through operations but, if these are not sufficient to support growth, further calls on external sources of financing might be required.

Capital can be provided in the form of cash contributions, contribution of tangible or intangible assets (including intellectual property), or, in some forms of business organizations, even of labor (in lieu of remuneration). Capital, unlike borrowed financial resources, has no specified reimbursement date to the provider(s) and generally no return is guaranteed.

The term used to refer to investors (providers of capital) is a function of the legal form of the business organization. In a corporation they are shareholders (or stockholders). In a **partnership** they are partners or associates. A sole proprietor is the investor in a business she or he owns entirely. Whatever the legal organizational format, the separation of private and business rights and responsibilities is essential.

Capital is an investment at risk that implies the investor's participation in managerial decision-making (even if sometimes such participation remains only theoretical or virtual). Investors are therefore liable for the consequences of the actions of 'their' business. That liability may be limited to their contribution to the capital of the firm, for example in 'limited liability corporations', or it may be unlimited, such as, for example, in the case of an unincorporated, sole proprietorship, enterprise.

Since capital, in limited liability companies, represents the upper limit of the potential liability assumed by investors, its nominal or face value must be communicated to all persons dealing (or potentially dealing) with the business. It cannot be modified without public notice and without conforming to the rules defined in the business' by-laws or their equivalent.

Understanding what capital and shareholders' **equity** are and how they are recorded and reported is crucial in the definition of standardized key investment return metrics (such as earnings per share, cash flow per share, share yield, dilution, share [stock] options, etc.) that are used by financial market investors to inform their investment decisions.

This chapter is devoted to business owners' equity: definitions and processes through which equity and capital can be increased (whether it be through operation of the business [such as in the case of retained earnings] or through additional capital contributions) or modified (for example through the payment of **dividends** or the, hopefully rare, absorption of accumulated losses).

The IASB Framework (1989) defines equity as 'the residual interest [of the investors] in the assets of the entity after deducting all its liabilities' (§ 49). The term equity refers to the concept of '**net worth**' introduced in Chapter 1, i.e., the difference between total assets and liabilities.

Because businesses that are incorporated represent a much larger part of the global gross wealth creation (measured, for example, by gross national product) than do the unincorporated firms, the most important form of equity or 'net worth', from an economic point of view, is that of 'shareholders' equity'. For simplicity's sake, we will use in this text the term shareholders' equity to refer to any investor's residual claim on the worth of the company, regardless of the organizational form retained in the by-laws by the founders of the firm. The alternative forms of organization are evoked briefly first as they are important for understanding the extent of the responsibility assumed by the investors in each case.

In the first part of this chapter (sections 1–3), after presenting the different forms of business organization, we will review the two principal components of shareholders' equity: (share) capital and retained (accumulated) earnings (or reserves). We will subsequently study the mechanism of their modification: decrease or increase of capital as well as payment of dividends are some of the most common events that impact on the shareholders' equity.

The second part of the chapter (sections 4–11) will address special situations that deviate from the general principles presented in the first part. Issues that are covered in the second part are:

- Issuance of (new) shares may be the result of non-cash contributions.
- Share issuance costs need to be recorded and reported appropriately.

- Shareholders' equity is affected by the possibility most corporations have to purchase their own shares and cancel them. This is used when no investment alternatives exist to increase the return on equity for the shareholders (by reducing the denominator, while productive investment opportunities would have increased the numerator).

- The comprehensive income (discussed in Chapter 6) may appear in the shareholders' equity.

- The statement of changes in shareholders' equity is an important document.

1 Forms of business organization

Three generic and alternative **legal forms of organization** specify the roles and responsibilities of the capital providers: (1) sole proprietorship; (2) partnership; and (3) **limited liability company**. Each country's legal system defines precisely the rules applying to each generic form. It would be beyond the scope of this book to explore the more detailed specific elements of any country.

A business represents a legal or economic entity that is separate from the individual or corporate capital provider(s). Any business must report on its economic activity by issuing periodic financial statements, even if only for tax purposes. If incorporated as a legal entity, a business can possess wealth, own property, make decisions, contract debts, pay money in its own right, go to court, or be taken to court, etc.

It is essential that the accounting and the reporting systems completely separate economic transactions that concern the business exclusively, from those that concern its individuals or corporate capital providers. Capital providers are distanced and separated from the firm in which they invested. This separation suffers one exception pertaining to risk sharing (assumption of liability for the firm's actions) as mentioned before: some legal organizational forms limit responsibility while others do not.

1.1 Sole proprietorship

In a sole proprietorship, the single capital provider holds claim to 100% of the future wealth creation of the business and bears all the risks of the venture. This legal form is not well adapted to the needs of large businesses. Creating a sole proprietorship generally is simple. This simplicity and the corollary low organizational costs may explain its common usage in the creation of small enterprises.

1.2 Partnership

A partnership is a business with two or more owners. In many countries, incorporation of a partnership is not required and, in this case, each of the associates or partners is fully responsible for all the consequences of the actions of the business. Some countries do not specifically offer the partnership form as such, but generally offer other forms approximating the partnership format such as the 'unlimited liability company', also called 'incorporated partnership'. Examples of such national variations on the theme are: *Société en nom collectif* (SNC) in Belgium, France and Switzerland, *Interessentskab* (I/S) in Denmark, *Offene Handelsgesellschaft* (OHG or oHG) in Germany, *Omorrythmos Etairia* (OE) in Greece, *Unlimited company* in Ireland and the UK, *Società in nome collettivo* (SNC) in Italy, *Vennootschap Onder Firma* (VOF) in the Netherlands, *Sociedad regular colectiva* (SRC) in Spain, and *Sociedade em nome colectivo* in Portugal.

This form of organization is best suited for a limited number of associates or partners (see exception below). Each country's legislation specifies the minimum number of partners and sometimes an upper limit to that number. Both lower and, occasionally, upper limits vary greatly between countries. This form of legal organization is flexible enough to allow a significant expansion of the business activities. New partners (i.e., additional capital providers) can often be added on with minimal formality. The organizational costs of setting up a partnership are greater than those incurred in setting up a sole proprietorship but the procedures are nonetheless not very complex or burdensome.

A well-known example of a special case of a limited liability partnership is the Compagnie Générale des Etablissements Michelin (CGEM). The company is a 'Limited share partnership'[1] (LSP) incorporated in Clermont-Ferrand (France). Its shares are traded on Euronext.

1.3 Limited liability company

The limited liability company, also called corporation in North America, is the most common form of organization for larger businesses. The liability assumed by the investors does not extend beyond their investment. The capital is partitioned in small homogeneous and tradable increments called shares. Each share represents both a contribution to the capital and a claim on future profits. Investors are called shareholders. Shares can generally be traded independently of the enterprise.

Most countries require a minimum level of capital funds be provided by investors as this type of organization is meant to grow and expand, and their level of responsibility of potential liability with them. Since capital measures the maximum level of liability an incorporated enterprise assumes, its trading partners (suppliers, customers, banks, etc.) generally require that the capital be brought to a level coherent with the size of the business activities.

Limited liability companies generally raise capital in the open market. They have an obligation of reporting to their shareholders. An auditor generally is required to certify that the financial statements have been prepared in accordance with the rules and requirements of the country and also that they represent fairly the financial situation of the business. Corporations are generally highly regulated and the incorporation process is often complex, leading to significant organizational costs.

Many countries distinguish two types of limited liability companies:

- *Private limited companies*: They generally have a fairly low minimum level of capital and at least two distinct share capital providers, although there are exceptions such as in Belgium (SPRLU), France (EURL), Germany (*Einmann* GmbH), and Portugal (EIRL) where a single capital provider (individual or corporate entity) may incorporate her, his or its business as a private limited company. Country-specific business legislation generally mentions a maximum number of capital providers. For example, it is 50 shareholders in India, Ireland [Private limited company], Spain [*Sociedad de responsabilidad limitada* (SL)], and the UK [Private limited company], and 100 shareholders in France [*Société à responsabilité limitée* (SARL)]. There is no requirement for a maximum number of proprietors in Germany [*Gesellschaft mit beschränkter Haftung* (GmbH)]. Because the number of shareholders is often small, the shares are generally not traded on a financial market and their sale may even require approval (as is the case for partnerships) by a majority of the remaining shareholders. These shares are thus not very liquid and often represent a cumbersome investment instrument for the capital provider.

- *Public limited companies*: A minimum number of capital providers is required, but no maximum is ever specified. The minimum number of shareholders varies greatly between countries (two in Argentina, Belgium [*Société anonyme* (SA)], Greece [*Anonymos eteria* (AE)], Italy [*Società per azioni* (Spa or SpA)], the Netherlands [*Naamloze vennootschap* (NV)] and the UK [Public limited company (PLC)], three in Denmark [*Aktieselskab* (AS)], Spain [*Sociedad anonima* (SA)], and Switzerland [*Société anonyme* (SA)], five in Germany [*Aktien Gesellschaft* (AG)], and Portugal [*Sociedad anonima* (SA)], seven in France [*Société anonyme* (SA)], India [Public limited company (PLC)] and Ireland [Public limited company (PLC)], etc.). Each country's legislation also specifies a minimum amount of capital and such minimum is generally higher for the public limited companies than it is for the private limited companies. Most of the time, shares of public limited companies can be traded freely on open financial markets. When such a market exists, these shares are liquid and offer a preferred medium of investment for capital providers who can go in and out of an investment with a low transaction cost. A side benefit of such liquidity is that it generally provides the enterprise with a lower cost of capital than the one incurred by businesses where the capital is not as liquid.

Figure 11.1 summarizes the principal characteristics of the various forms of legal organization.

Although shareholders' equity is defined by the IASB as a residual, its framework states that it 'may be sub-classified in the balance sheet [i.e., for reporting purposes]. For example, in a corporate [i.e., incorporated] entity, funds contributed by shareholders, retained earnings, reserves representing appropriations of retained earnings and reserves representing capital maintenance adjustments may be shown separately. Such classifications can be relevant to the decision-making needs of the users of financial statements when they indicate legal or other restrictions on the ability of the entity to distribute or which apply to its equity. They may also reflect the fact that parties with ownership interests in an entity have differing rights in relation to the receipt of dividends or the repayment of contributed equity' (IASB 1989: § 65). The following sections will explore these sub-categories of shareholder's equity.

Figure 11.1 Forms of business organization

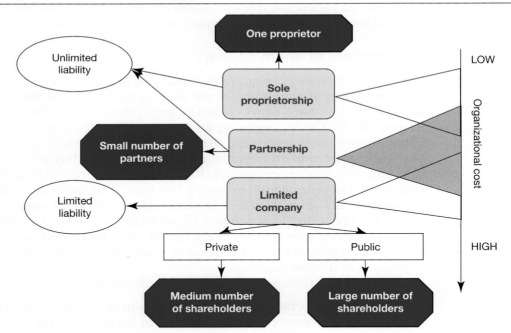

2 Share capital

2.1 Definition

Shares or stock certificates represent the capital. They are evidence of the contribution of the shareholders to the formation of the capital. Shares are attributed to investors proportionately to the value of the resource they provided. A share is a certificate of property.

It can generally be sold, bought or transferred by the shareholder without the consent of the corporation. Each shareholder has the right to:

- influence management decision-making by participating in and voting in general assembly meetings;
- receive dividends and a proportionate share of any eventual liquidations surplus;
- have first pass at acquiring additional shares (proportionately to the current holding) in the case where the business decides to issue new shares.

2.2 Nominal or par value

Generally, at the time of a business' incorporation, its by-laws specify (within the constraints specified by law) the face value of the unitary share, which represents the metric that will determine how many shares constitute the original capital. The face value of a share is called the **nominal or par value**. The capital is therefore equal to the number of shares multiplied by the par value. The market value of the share has generally no relation to its par value. Some countries' regulation, like that of the United States, allows 'no-par' shares. We will ignore this unusual situation here.

The par or nominal value of the capital represents an 'official' measure of the minimum monetary extent of liability assumed by the corporation. The total capital at-par is often mentioned in official documents of the firm addressed to the general public. As a general rule, shares cannot be issued below par. Further increases in capital in the life of the business entity by issuing new shares may bring more resources than the par value (see section 2.5 below). As we will see, this will lead to the payment of a premium that will be part of shareholders' equity but will be reported separately from capital.

2.3 Payment of share capital

Investors are not always required to hand over to the corporation the full amount of their investment as represented by par value of the number of shares they receive. This is due to the fact that a newly created business often does not need to have all the capital available right at the beginning and would not be able to provide the shareholders a return on their (cash) investment that would be competitive. Corporations can therefore offer their shareholders the possibility to subscribe to (or buy on credit) their shares by delivering their funds or resources to the corporation over a period specified by the board of directors but generally not exceeding five years. This subscription process is useful to shareholders as it gives them time to accumulate the funds or resources they will use to pay for the shares they have purchased upon issuance. The 2nd European Directive states that a minimum of one-quarter of the capital needs be handed over to the corporation upon incorporation and initial issuance of shares. Similar constraints on minimum cash payment exist in most countries.

The vocabulary reflects the complexity of this situation:

- **Authorized capital** is the maximum amount of capital (at par) the charter (or by-laws) states the corporation can issue when needed. It is the maximum number of shares authorized multiplied by the par value. Its level can be increased by a decision of the General Assembly of the shareholders.

- **Subscribed** or **issued capital** is that part of the authorized capital that the shareholders have agreed to purchase and pay for when asked (called) to do so. Some countries require that subscribed capital be equal to authorized capital. The fact that there are authorized shares in excess of subscribed shares, however, gives great flexibility to the management of the business in issuing new shares as they see fit without the need to obtain approval of the general assembly of shareholders. It is, for example the case when the compensation package of executives or senior personnel includes stock options or share options. For example BT Group (British Telecom)'s 2009 annual report in the notes to consolidated financial statements (note 23) states that 'Of the authorized but unissued share capital at 31 March 2009, nil ordinary shares (2008 – 21 million) were reserved to meet options granted under employee share option schemes'.

- **Called-up capital** is the fraction of the subscribed capital that the corporation's board decided to collect from the investors (the amount of the par or only a portion of the par).

- **Paid-in capital** or **contributed capital** is the part of the capital that has been effectively contributed by the shareholders and is available to the corporation.

- **Uncalled capital** is the part of the subscribed capital that has not been called up. It will represent a declining balance as the investors actually deliver on their promise to fund the company.

- **Capital receivable** is the part of the subscribed capital that has been called-up and remains unpaid. It will represent a declining balance as the investors actually deliver on their promise to fund the company.

- **Outstanding capital** (outstanding shares times the par value) is subscribed capital (at par) minus the par value of any share that has been bought back by the corporation (treasury shares).

To sum up:

> Outstanding shares ≤ Issued shares ≤ Authorized shares
> and
> Subscribed capital = Paid-in capital + Capital receivable + Uncalled capital

2.4 Different categories of shares

Shares are negotiable instruments that grant certain rights to their owner. However, a corporation may find an interest in giving different rights to different categories of shareholders in order, for example, to make the capital subscription more attractive to certain types of investors or more attractive at certain times such as when the ongoing nature of the business is not fully assured. Shares carrying special rights are called '**preferred shares**' or 'preference shares'. They form a category distinct from 'ordinary shares'.

2.4.1 Preferred versus ordinary shares

The special rights of preferred shares that make them more (or less) attractive to purchase, when issued, than ordinary shares can take many forms, which can be combined. Two of the most common characteristics of preferred shares are:

- Pecuniary advantage such as fully or partially guaranteed dividend, larger dividend than common (ordinary) shares, priority dividend, cumulative dividends,[2] etc.

- Different voting rights in the general assembly (often double but occasionally no voting right at all) than those held by the ordinary shares.

The basic idea behind preferred shares is that they allow raising of capital without necessarily creating a proportional dilution or without creating a shift in stewardship away from the original shareholders (case of no voting shares), or, on the contrary, shifting control towards a certain class of shareholders (case of multiple voting rights).

Preferred shares generally represent a trade-off between return and control: either higher dividends but reduced voting rights, or higher voting rights but lower returns. The common or ordinary shareholders are the residual owners of the corporation after the preferred shareholders have received their dues. Shares carrying the same rights are organized in homogeneous classes.

Real-life example Fresenius

(Germany – IFRS – Source: Annual report 2008 – Pharmaceutical)

Excerpts from note 27 to the consolidated financial statements

(in €)	Ordinary shares	Preference shares	Total
Conditional Capital I Fresenius AG Stock Option Plan 1998	768,306	768,306	1,536,612
Conditional Capital II Fresenius AG Stock Option Plan 2003	2,364,711	2,364,711	4,729,422
Total Conditional Capital as of 1 January 2008	**3,133,017**	**3,133,017**	**6,266,034**
Fresenius AG Stock Option Plan 1998 – options exercised	−85,839	−85,839	−171,678
Fresenius AG Stock Option Plan 2003 – options exercised	−155,586	−155,586	−311,172
Conditional Capital III, approved on 21 May 2008	3,100,000	3,100,000	6,200,000
Total Conditional Capital as of 31 December 2008	**5,991,592**	**5,991,592**	**11,983,184**

Conditional Capital

Corresponding to the stock option plans, the Conditional Capital of Fresenius SE is divided into Conditional Capital I, Conditional Capital II and Conditional Capital III which exist to secure the subscription rights in connection with already issued stock options on bearer ordinary shares and bearer preference shares of the stock option plans of 1998, 2003 and 2008 (see Note 34, Stock options).

Real-life example RWE

(Germany – IFRS – Source: Annual report 2008 – Utility)

Excerpts from note 23 to the consolidated financial statements

	31 Dec 2008		31 Dec 2007		31 Dec 2008	31 Dec 2007
	Number of shares		Number of shares		Carrying amount	
Subscribed Capital	in 000	in %	in 000	in %	€ million	€ million
Common shares	523,405	93.1	523,405	93.1	1,340	1,340
Preferred shares	39,000	6.9	39,000	6.9	100	100
	562,405	**100.0**	**562,405**	**100.0**	**1,440**	**1,440**

Common and preferred shares are no-par-value bearer share certificates. Preferred shares have no voting rights. Under certain conditions, preferred shares are entitled to payment of a preference dividend of €0.13 per preferred share, upon allocation of the company's profits. Pursuant to the resolution passed by the Annual General Meeting on April 17, 2008, the Executive Board was authorized to increase the company's capital stock, subject to the Supervisory Board's approval, of up to €287,951,360.00 until April 16, 2013, through the issuance of new bearer common shares in return for contributions in cash or in kind (authorized capital). In certain cases, the subscription rights of shareholders can be waived, with the approval of the Supervisory Board.

Real-life example Philips

(Netherlands – IFRS – Source: Annual report 2008 – Electronics)

Excerpts from the consolidated balance sheet and note 63		
(in EUR m)	2007	2008
Stockholders' equity:		
Preference shares, par value EUR 0.20 per share:		
– Authorized: 2,000,000,000 shares (2007: 2,500,000,000 shares), issued none		
Common shares, par value EUR 0.20 per share:		
– Authorized: 2,000,000,000 shares (2007: 2,500,000,000 shares)		
– Issued and fully paid: 972,411,769 shares (2007: 1,142,826,763 shares)	228	194

Common shares

In 2008, the company's issued share capital was reduced by 170,414,994 shares, which were acquired pursuant to the EUR 5 billion share repurchase program. As of 31 December 2008, the issued share capital consists of 972,411,769 common shares, each share having a par value of EUR 0.20, which shares have been paid-in in full.

Preference shares

The 'Stichting[3] Preferente Aandelen Philips' has been granted the right to acquire preference shares in the company. Such right has not been exercised. As a means to protect the company and its stakeholders against an unsolicited attempt to acquire (de facto) control of the company, the general meeting of shareholders in 1989 adopted amendments to the company's articles of association that allow the board of management and the supervisory board to issue (rights to acquire) preference shares to a third party. As of 31 December 2008, no preference shares have been issued.

2.4.2 Redeemable or convertible preference shares

When the special rights attached to preferred shares are only temporary, these shares may be redeemable or convertible. In this first case, the preferred shares can be retired or redeemed at the initiative of the corporation at a price and under conditions that were mentioned in the preference share contract. For example, the cash value of the retirement price may be based on the average share price calculated over a contractual period defined in the original contract. In the second case, convertible shares can be converted, within a certain time range and at the initiative of the bearer, into bonds or ordinary shares.

2.4.3 Shares with amended voting rights

The voting power of a common shareholder is, in theory,[4] strictly proportional to the number of common shares she or he holds. Preferred shares may hold voting rights that deviate from the normal 'one share one vote' rule. Preferred shares with special voting rights are often used in new share issuance when the original shareholders are willing to incur a dilution of earnings but not of their power to direct the affairs of the firm. They are also used as defensive or offensive tactics in acquisitions, mergers or takeover bids.

Real-life example Quebecor Inc.

(Canada – Canadian GAAP – Source: Annual report 2008 – Communications, printing and forest products)

This company reports the existence of multiple voting rights shares in the note 22 on capital stock.

a) Authorized capital stock

An unlimited number of Class A Multiple Voting Shares ('A shares') with voting rights of 10 votes per share, convertible at any time into Class B Subordinate Voting Shares on a one-for-one basis.

An unlimited number of Class B Voting Shares ('B shares') convertible into A shares on a one-for-one basis, only if a takeover bid for A shares is made to holders of A shares without being made concurrently and under the same terms to holders of B shares, for the sole purpose of allowing the holders of B shares to accept the offer and subject to certain other stated conditions provided in the articles including the acceptance of the offer by the majority holder.

Holders of B shares are entitled to elect 25% of the Board of Directors of Quebecor Inc.

Holders of A Shares may elect the other members of the Board of Directors.

Real-life example Volvo Group

(Sweden – IFRS – Source: Annual report 2008 – Car and truck manufacturer)

'The share capital of the parent company is divided into two series of shares: A and B. Both series carry the same rights, except that each Series A share carries the right to one vote and each Series B share carries the right to one tenth of a vote' (Note 23 to the 2008 consolidated financial statements).

Real-life example Ericsson

(Sweden – IFRS – Source: Annual report 2008 – Telecommunications network solutions provider)

Capital stock at 31 December 2008 consisted of the following:

Parent company	Number of shares	Capital stock (SEKm)
Class A shares	261,755,983	1,309
Class B shares	2,984,595,752	14,923
Total	**3,246,351,735**	**16,232**

The capital stock of the company is divided into two classes: Class A shares (quota value SEK 5.00) and Class B shares (quota value SEK 5.00). Both classes have the same rights of participation in the net assets and earnings of the company. Class A shares, however, are entitled to one vote per share while Class B shares are entitled to one tenth of one vote per share (Note C16 to the 2008 consolidated financial statements).

2.5 Share premium

The par value of a share is only a way of defining the number of shares in the legal capital and thus the relative power of decision of each shareholder. A share is valued by the market as the net present value of the estimated future cash flows (or dividends plus liquidation value) of the business venture. Most shares are issued at par at the time of incorporation (i.e., the issuance price equals the nominal value) and above their par for subsequent issuances, to reflect the fact the market values the investment already realized.

The **share premium** is the difference between the issue price and the par value. It records a contribution from the 'new' shareholders in excess of the legal share capital. The share premium is also called 'additional paid-in capital' or 'capital in excess of par' or, in the USA, 'capital surplus'. It is reported as a part of the shareholders' equity.

2.6 Accounting for share capital

Accounting for capital issuance follows the same rules whether it is when the capital is first issued or when further capital is raised through a flotation of authorized but unsubscribed shares, i.e., new shares (initial public offering, i.e., IPO, or later) after the business has been in existence for a while. The mechanism is illustrated here through the entries required to record the issuance of capital by Gershwin Corporation.

Gershwin Corporation was incorporated at the beginning of year X0. Its authorized capital is 100,000 ordinary shares with a par of 1 CU. The initial issue was for 10,000 ordinary shares sold at par. This issue was entirely subscribed (paid-in) for a total cash inflow of 10,000 CU. During year X1, 90,000 additional shares were floated at the price of 1.2 CU per share. The terms of the flotation are that the acquirers of the new shares must contribute immediately 50% of the par (the rest to be contributed when called) and 100% of the share premium. This flotation creates a share premium for a total of 18,000 CU [90,000 shares × (1.2 CU – 1 CU at par)]. Of the par value of the 90,000 shares (i.e., 90,000 CU), only 45,000 CU will be contributed while another 45,000 CU will remain uncalled for the time being. The total cash raised immediately is therefore 63,000 CU through the issuance of the new shares.

Figure 11.2 illustrates the accounting mechanism required for recording both transactions (000 CU).

The capital is increased by the par value of the 90,000 shares issued even though one-half has not yet been contributed and remains uncalled. In some countries (e.g., the United States), the uncalled portion of capital ('uncalled capital' or 'subscriptions receivable') is not shown as an asset as done here but as a reduction of share capital, i.e., a contra-liability account. However, the end result is the same and the two different approaches, giving full disclosure, provide a true and fair view of the financial situation of the firm. When the uncalled capital will be called and the shareholders will pay in the rest of their contribution, the only additional entry required will be to balance cash against either the uncalled capital (receivable) or the contra-liability of uncalled capital.

2.7 Reporting share capital

IAS 1 (IASB 2007) stipulates rather detailed rules for the reporting of share capital in financial statements. Paragraph 79 states that 'an entity shall disclose the following, either in the statement of financial position or the statement of changes in equity, or in the notes:

    (a) for each class of share capital:

        (i) the number of shares authorized;

        (ii) the number of shares issued and fully paid, and issued but not fully paid;

Figure 11.2 Accounting for issuance of share capital

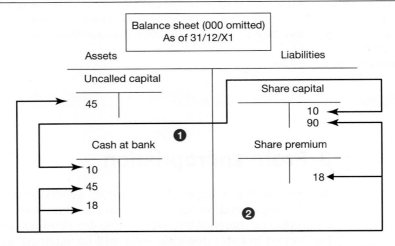

❶ Recording of the capital issued at the time of the incorporation of the company (year X0).
❷ Issuance of additional shares for cash.

(iii) par value per share, or that the shares have no par value;

(iv) a reconciliation of the number of shares outstanding at the beginning and at the end of the period;

(v) the rights, preferences and restrictions attaching to that class including restrictions on the distribution of dividends and the repayment of capital;

(vi) shares in the entity held by the entity or by its subsidiaries or associates; and

(vii) shares reserved for issue under options and contracts for the sale of shares, including terms and amounts; and

(b) a description of the nature and purpose of each reserve within equity'.

IAS 1 (§ 137) adds that 'An entity shall disclose in the notes:

(a) the amount of dividends proposed or declared before the financial statements were authorized for issue but not recognized as a distribution to owners during the period, and the related amount per share; and

(b) the amount of any cumulative preference dividends not recognized'.

'An entity without share capital, such as a partnership or trust, shall disclose information equivalent to that required by paragraph 79(a), showing changes during the period in each category of equity interest, and the rights, preferences and restrictions attaching to each category of equity interest' (IAS 1: § 80).

Real-life example Procter & Gamble

(USA – US GAAP – Source: Annual report 2008 – Beauty and personal care, family health, household care)

Procter & Gamble reports several types of shares.

Consolidated balance sheet (excerpts)		
	30 June	
(Amounts in millions)	2008	2007
Shareholders' equity		
Convertible Class A preferred stock, stated value $1 per share (600 shares authorized)	$1,366	$1,406
Non-Voting Class B preferred stock, stated value $1 per share (200 shares authorized)	–	–
Common stock, stated value $1 per share (10,000 shares authorized; shares issued: 2008 – 4,001.8, 2007 – 3,989.7)	4,002	3,990
Additional paid-in capital	60,307	59,030
(…)		

---

3 Profit appropriation

As mentioned in Chapter 2, all earnings generated by a business are theoretically available for appropriation and distribution to shareholders. However, although the right of ownership by shareholders over all after-tax earnings is not challenged, yearly earnings are partitioned in two categories: some will be 'retained' in the business as retained earnings (i.e., a voluntary reinvestment), also called reserves, and some will effectively be distributed as dividends.

3.1 Dividends

A dividend is a distribution of the earnings of the business to its shareholders. Dividends are allocated proportionately to the rights attached to the shares held by the shareholders on a date of record.[5] The management team of the business generally proposes the dividend payout amount for approval by the general assembly of shareholders, after the financial statements have been approved. Shareholders have the final say (through the general assembly) in what to do with the earnings. Dividends are paid to the shareholders following a schedule which varies with the traditions of each country: monthly or quarterly and mostly by anticipation in the United States or annually and *ex post* in most European countries.

3.2 Reserve accounts

According to the IASB Framework (IASB 1989: § 66): 'The creation of reserves is sometimes required by statute or other law in order to give the entity and its creditors an added measure of protection from the effects of losses. Other reserves may be established if national tax law grants exemptions from, or reductions in, taxation liabilities when transfers to such reserves are made. The existence and size of these legal, statutory and tax reserves is information that can be relevant to the decision-making needs of users. Transfers to such reserves are appropriations of retained earnings rather than expenses'.

All required reserve accounts must be funded before dividends can be paid out. It means that the amount of earnings available to the shareholders for distribution or voluntary reinvestment is equal to:

> Annual earnings minus sum of the allocations to reserve accounts
> = Earnings available for distribution

The 'distributable earnings' are either distributed or transferred to reserves (called optional reserves) or retained (retained earnings) until further decisions are made concerning their possible distribution.[6]

For example, as of 31 December 2008, Ericsson (Swedish telecommunications network provider) described its 'restricted equity' (SEK million 41,954) as the sum of 'amounts to be paid to shareholders' (SEK million 6,005) plus 'Amount to be retained by the parent company' (SEK million 35,948) out of a total 'stockholders' equity' of SEK million 89,678.

In summary, the main categories of **reserves** are the following: legal reserve, statutory reserve, regulated reserve, revaluation reserve, reserve for own shares, optional (or voluntary) reserves and profit/loss brought forward. These different categories are presented in Appendix 11.1.

3.3 Reporting retained earnings and reserves

A balance sheet may be presented 'before' or 'after appropriation'. The term 'appropriation' here refers to the decision taken by the shareholders or directors to distribute dividends and/or to transfer all or part of the income of the period to retained earnings (or to reserves if so required by by-laws or covenants).[7] In the 'after appropriation' method, the earnings of the year are not reported explicitly in the balance sheet; only additions to the retained earnings will be reported. The earnings of the period are added to the retained earnings or to the reserves. The formula defining retained earnings/reserves at any point in time is presented in Table 11.1.

Table 11.1 is a bare bone template for the 'statement of retained earnings' that is required under IFRS rules and in the USA, in Canada, and generally in the annual statements of financial position of any business reporting under the US GAAP (most firms quoted on the New York Stock Exchange) or under a local GAAP which is based on the US GAAP. That statement explains how the retained earnings of the previous year are transformed, in a recurring fashion, into the retained earnings of the current year.

Retained earnings are a part of 'shareholders' equity'. However, an analyst of the financial position of the firm must be aware of the fact that the term 'retained earnings' may cover different realities depending on the country whose laws and practices are followed (see more on this topic in Appendix 11.2).

Table 11.1 Retained earnings and reserves	
	Retained earnings and reserves (up to end of previous period)
+	Net income (after tax) of the year
−	Dividends declared
−	Transfers to specifically identified reserves
=	Retained earnings and reserves (at year-end)

3.4 Reporting and accounting for shareholders' equity

3.4.1 Simple example of reporting of reserves and retained earnings

Continuing with the Gershwin Corporation example, we learn that income and dividend payments for years X1 and X2 are as follows (000 CU):

	Year X1	Year X2
Profit net of taxes	50	70
Dividends	0	30

Table 11.2 illustrates the presentation of shareholders' equity according to each of the two methods commonly used by corporations, i.e., after appropriation or before appropriation. The choice of method has no impact on the actual total shareholders' equity plus liabilities. It is only a matter of presentation.

3.4.2 Accounting for profit appropriation

Figure 11.3 illustrates the process of year X2 profit appropriation on the balance sheet of Gershwin Corporation. This process takes place after the general assembly has approved the appropriation, i.e., in X3. Since the accounting entries for methods 1 and 2 are essentially the same (but the timing is different), we chose to only illustrate method 2, i.e., reporting before appropriation, which appears to be the most frequently used method in Europe.

Table 11.2 Presentation of shareholders' equity in the balance sheet

	Year X1	Year X2
Method 1 (after appropriation)		
Share capital	100	100
Share premium	18	18
Retained earnings (ending balance)	50	90*
Shareholders' equity	168	208
Dividends payable (liabilities)	0	30
Total shareholders' equity and liabilities	168	238
*[50 (beginning balance) + 70 (income of the period) – 30 (dividends payable)]		
Method 2 (before appropriation)		
Share capital	100	100
Share premium	18	18
Retained earnings (beginning balance)	0	50
Net income of the period (to be appropriated)	50	70
Shareholders' equity	168	238

Comments
When method 1 is used, there is a 'dividends payable' only as long as the dividends have not actually been paid out on the reporting date. If the dividends have already been paid out by the date the financial statements are approved, the cash account has already been reduced and there is no need to report 'dividends payable'.

Figure 11.3 Accounting for profit appropriation

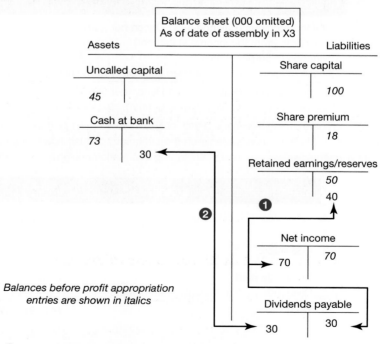

Balances before profit appropriation entries are shown in italics

❶ Cancellation of net income, and transfer to reserves and to dividends payable. Dividends have been declared but not paid.
❷ Payment of dividends.

Real-life examples

Method 1 – Balance sheet after appropriation

ArcelorMittal SA (Luxemburg – IFRS – Source: Annual report 2008 – Steel company)

Consolidated balance sheet (excerpts)		
		31 December
(US$ million)	2007	2008
Shareholders' equity		
Common shares	9,269	9,269
Treasury stock	(1,552)	(5,800)
Additional paid-in capital	20,309	20,575
Retained earnings	23,552	30,403
Reserves	5,107	751
Equity attributable to the equity holders of the parent	**56,685**	**55,198**
Minority interest	4,850	4,032
Total equity	**61,535**	**59,230**

- The topic 'Treasury stock' is further developed in section 7 of this chapter.
- The evolution of retained earnings between 2007 and 2008 is explained in the statement of changes in shareholders' equity, which contains the following information (in US$ millions):

Changes in equity (excerpts US$ million)	
Retained earnings (Balance at 31 December 2007)	23,552
Net income [from the income statement]	9,399
Dividends (1.50 per share)	(2,068)
Dilution of interest in consolidated subsidiary and others	(480)
Retained earnings (Balance at 31 December 2008)	30,403

Dividends have been paid during the year but they only are reported in the statement of cash flows (financing activities). (For refresher and further developments on the statement of cash flows, see Chapters 3, 14 and 17). In the 2008 statement of cash flows, we can find the following information concerning dividends:

Statement of cash flows (excerpts)		
		December 31
(US$ million)	2007	2008
Dividends paid	(1,826)	(2,068)
Dividends paid to minority shareholders	(443)	(508)
Total	**(2,269)**	**(2,576)**

Method 2 – Balance sheet before appropriation

Ericsson (Sweden – IFRS – Source: Annual report 2008 – Telecommunications network solutions)

Parent company balance sheet (excerpts)		
	31 December	
(in SEK million)	2008	2007
Stockholders' equity		
Capital stock	16,232	16,132
Revaluation reserve	20	20
Statuatory reserve	31,472	31,472
Restricted equity	**47,724**	**47,624**
Retained earnings	24,727	22,080
Net income	17,227	13,145
Non-restricted earnings	**41,954**	**35,225**
	89,678	**82,849**

■ Ericsson's annual report indicates clearly restricted and unrestricted equity. This distinction is developed in Appendix 11.3.

■ The 'retained earnings' only represent accumulated earnings in non-restricted reserves.

Repsol YPF (Spain – IFRS – Source: Annual report 2008 – Oil and gas)

Consolidated balance sheet (excerpts)		
	31 December	
(€ million)	2008	2007
Net equity (note 17)		
Share capital	1,221	1,221
Share premium	6,428	6,428
Reserves	247	247
Treasury shares	(241)	4
Retained earnings	11,427	9,459
Results attributable to the shareholders of the parent company [same as in income statement]	2,711	3,188
Dividends	(634)	(610)
Equity	**21,159**	**19,937**

4 Accounting for the issuance of shares granted for non-cash capital contributions

Not all shares are issued against cash. There are three basic situations that may lead to the issuance of shares in return for something other than cash:

1. Shares can be issued in return for a capital contribution in kind.

2. New shares may be issued as the result of a 'capitalization' of reserves or of retained earnings (thus acknowledging that the shareholders renounce their right to have these retained earnings distributable on request).

3. New shares may be the result of the conversion by a creditor of their claim into shares.

4.1 Issuance of shares for capital contributions in kind

Shareholders may contribute assets other than cash. For example, intangible assets such as patents, specific knowledge, provision of access to a market, or tangible assets such as land, buildings or machinery, inventories or receivables (all net of attached liabilities) are often important capital contributions, especially in the early phases of the life of a corporation. Shares issued for capital contributions in kind are also frequent in the case of business combinations such as acquisitions or mergers (see Chapter 13). The contributed value is theoretically the 'fair value' of the net assets; but such a value is often difficult to estimate since their value may be a function of their coherence with the strategy of the buyer.

The mechanism of recording is similar to that of a cash capital contribution, with the only difference being that an asset account different from the cash account is increased (i.e., fixed assets, inventories, accounts receivable ...).

To illustrate the mechanism of recording a contribution in kind, let us go back to the Gershwin Corporation. In year X3, new shareholders contribute a patent valued at 15,000 CU. In exchange for the property transfer of the patent, these new shareholders receive 10,000 ordinary shares with a par of 1 CU. A 5,000 CU share premium therefore needs to be recorded. Figure 11.4 describes the mechanism.

4.2 Issuance of new shares due to capitalization of retained earnings or of some reserves

The action of incorporating retained earnings or some reserves into the share capital is called capitalization. Reserves that are capitalized are essentially discretionary or optional reserves not required to be maintained by law or the articles of incorporation – if legally required reserves

Figure 11.4 Accounting for a share issuance in kind

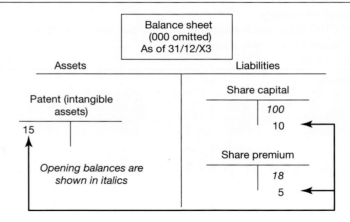

are capitalized, they will need to be rebuilt on the basis of the new capital. When the balance of the accumulated undistributed earnings becomes very large in proportion to the share capital, or when shareholders wish to communicate to the financial markets they are renouncing any claim on future distribution of these earnings, it may be a good idea to incorporate all or part of the retained earnings or reserves into the capital. It is so because (1) it may improve the market liquidity of the shares if additional shares are issued; and (2) it communicates the message (signaling) that the shareholders are willing to increase the level of responsibility they are prepared to accept, thus granting a higher level of protection to creditors.

After the incorporation of retained earnings or reserves in the share capital (restructuring and consolidation of the shareholders' equity), the total book value of the shareholders' equity is unchanged, but the number of shares (or, more rarely, the par value of the shares) has been modified. Such an operation is called by different names: 'stock split'[8] mainly in North America (where an increase of the par value is extremely unusual), and 'bonus issue' or '**capitalization of reserves**' elsewhere (depending on whether or not new shares are issued).

Unless the corporation chooses to reflect this action by increasing the par value of the share, the procedure will lead to the issuance of new shares that will generally be given to the current shareholders. It leads to a 'bonus issue' and the shareholders on record on the date of the issue receive the new shares in proportion to their previous holdings.

Most reserves or retained earnings that are unambiguously the property of the shareholders (essentially all reserves and retained earnings) can be incorporated into share capital. Although each country may have its own specific rules regarding the incorporation of reserves or retained earnings, the eligible reserves (see the definition of each reserve in Appendix 11.1) are generally composed of:

- legal reserve (after a decision of capitalization, this reserve must be reconstituted);
- statutory reserves;
- regulated reserves;
- optional (voluntary) reserves;
- revaluation reserves;
- profit brought forward;
- net income of the year;
- share premium.

While some countries allow both an increase of the par value of the existing shares and the issuance of bonus shares at the initiative of the corporation, others forbid either one or the other.

To illustrate the mechanism of incorporation of reserves in the share capital, let us revisit the Gershwin Corporation example. In year X4, the board of directors decides (and the decision is approved by the general assembly) to incorporate 30,000 CU worth of reserves into the share capital. In order to reduce dilution, some 30,000 new shares of par 1 are therefore created and attributed to the shareholders proportionately to their current holdings (i.e., 3 new shares for 11 old ones – let's keep in mind that Gershwin corporation had 110,000 shares outstanding after the capital contribution in kind in year X3). The appropriate entry is shown in Figure 11.5.

Such an entry involves a mere transfer from retained earnings to capital. The opening balance of the retained earnings account (150) is the sum of the undistributed earnings up to and including those of year X3 (i.e., 90 + the retained earnings of X3).

4.3 Issuance of shares resulting from an increase in capital due to a conversion of liabilities

Creditors of the corporation (suppliers or bankers) may agree to receive shares of capital as a counterpart for canceling their claim. In this case the shares they receive are new shares, thus creating an increase of the share capital.

Figure 11.5 Share issuance by capitalization of reserves

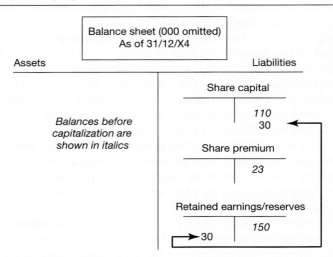

Any combination of the following three reasons may explain the decision of the creditors to surrender a fixed claim in exchange for a conditional claim:

- The debtor corporation is experiencing serious cash difficulties and/or the total interest charge is not compatible with the current operational possibilities of the business. In order to avoid bankruptcy of their debtor, the creditors may find the conversion of loans or payables a less risky operation than the significant definitive loss that the failure of their client might entail. In many cases the creditors use this opportunity to effectively take control of the board of directors to reorient the business activities in a way that provides for what they feel might be a more secure future for the 'investment' their financing represents.

- The corporation had issued convertible debt. The choice of issuing convertible debt is often the result of a bad image of the corporation on the share market. It allows lenders to reduce the risks they are taking: they receive a fixed remuneration if things don't go well, and could receive a dividend remuneration – which may be greater than the original fixed return – if things go well and they decide to convert the loan they provided into capital. This way the lender can take the time to see how the business is evolving before deciding to become a shareholder.

- The lender is, for example, the parent company of the borrower and such an operation is part of the long-term strategy of the parent. It may be an opportunity for the parent to increase its control over the subsidiary, or even to create a possibility for a *de facto* transfer of the debt to an outside party when shares are easier to sell than debt.

The increase in capital is recorded by a simple accounting entry in which debt is eliminated and 'share capital at par' is increased and 'capital surplus' or 'share premium' is incremented for the balance.

5 Accounting for share issuance costs

Incorporating a corporation or increasing its capital are operations that incur significant costs. These costs include legal costs, auditors' fees, bankers' commissions, etc. In theory, these costs can be handled in three different ways at the initiative of the firm. They can be:

- considered to be a period cost and recognized in the corresponding period's income statement;

- capitalized as an intangible asset and amortized (in general over a maximum of five years);
- written off against the total accumulated share premium.

The last possibility, when authorized by the laws and regulations of the country, offers the advantage over both previous methods of not impacting annual income, thus not biasing the time series of earnings.

Logically, then, IASB authorizes only this last solution, although it does not explicitly mention the specific category of equity against which issuance costs should be written-off: 'An entity typically incurs various costs in issuing or acquiring its own equity instruments. Those costs might include registration and other regulatory fees, amounts paid to legal, accounting and other professional advisers, printing costs and stamp duties. The transaction costs of an equity transaction are accounted for as a deduction from equity (net of any related income tax benefit) to the extent they are incremental costs directly attributable to the equity transaction that otherwise would have been avoided. The costs of an equity transaction that is abandoned are recognized as an expense' (IAS 32, 2008: § 37). In practice, the costs are deducted from the share premium.

6 Capital reduction

A corporation may be led to reduce its capital for essentially either of two reasons:

- taking into account the reality created by accumulated losses (see Appendix 11.5);
- cancellation of shares to acknowledge the reduction in the total liability assumed by the population of shareholders because, for example, the business has repurchased its own shares.

The second case is so important that we will devote the following section to the issues such a practice raises. As a reduction of share capital reduces the maximum liability assumed, company laws in most countries strictly regulate reductions of share capital to protect creditors.

7 Treasury shares (or own shares, or treasury stock)

Treasury shares occur when the corporation acquires its own shares.

7.1 Why repurchase one's own shares?

Corporations generally do not acquire or hold their own shares. However, in most countries such a practice is perfectly legal. Corporations are allowed to purchase their own shares (i.e., create 'own shares', 'treasury shares' or 'treasury stock') under certain circumstances. The following situations offer a far from exhaustive list of such conditions:

- A corporation can repurchase its shares in order to reduce its capital by canceling the repurchased shares. This is generally done with the intent of boosting the value of the share (fewer shares hold claim over future earnings), or improve the earnings per share ratio when no better alternative exists to develop the numerator (earnings) of that ratio.[9]
- Shares can be repurchased and given to employees in the context of a profit-sharing plan or in their exercising the stock options they have received. Such a policy would be coherent only if (a) the remaining shareholders do not want to see any dilution take

place due to the distribution, or (b) all the authorized shares have already been issued and it would be difficult to increase the number of authorized shares without asking the general assembly.

- A listed corporation may repurchase its own shares with the intent of smoothing the market value of its shares in a turbulent environment.

- A listed corporation may wish to repurchase its own shares as a preventive measure if it fears a potential takeover. If fewer shares are on the open market, it may be harder for the 'predator' to obtain a majority of the voting rights, even if treasury shares have no voting rights.

- In some countries, the by-laws may require that the sale of a block of shares by a shareholder be made conditional on the approval of the new shareholder by the remaining previous shareholders. In such a situation, the corporation may act as a broker and thus allow the shareholders wanting to sell to do so before an acceptable candidate has been found.

Among these five possible situations, the first one does not, strictly speaking, lead to the creation of 'own shares' or 'treasury stock' since the shares are rapidly cancelled and taken off the books.

7.2 Purchase of treasury shares to reduce the share capital

As we have seen, the main reason for such action, called retirement of shares, is generally a way of boosting the earnings per share or to stabilize the market price of the share. However, it may be used in other circumstances. Retirement of shares may take place, for example, in a small corporation, when one of the shareholders wants to leave the group of shareholders for whatever reason. For example, let us assume that the shareholders of Gershwin Corporation have a falling-out. One of the shareholders, Mr George, owns 20% of the shares and wants out. The remaining shareholders wish neither to buy George's shares nor to welcome an outside buyer of his shares.

The total share capital amounts to 140,000 (at par) (see Figure 11.5). Mr George's claim on the par capital amounts to 28,000 CU but the equity book value of Mr George's shares is 20% of (140 + 23 + 120), i.e., 56.6 thousand CU. The remaining shareholders and Mr George have agreed to value the shares at only 56,000 CU. The simplest solution is to have the corporation repurchase Mr. George's shares and cancel them. As shown in Figure 11.6, this transaction is carried out in two steps. The difference between the market value of the shares in the transaction and their par value will be taken out of the reserves and share premium accounts (the former for 20% of the reserves and the latter only for the balance). In this simplified example, we assume that the share premium and the retained earnings/reserves are unrestricted (see Appendix 11.3).

7.3 Purchase of treasury shares held by the corporation

When own shares are purchased and held for some time for whatever purpose (regulating the market of the share, anti-takeover bid strategy, employees profit-sharing plan, etc.), the accounting transaction recording the purchase is identical to that of phase ❶ in Figure 11.6.

When the shares are eventually sold (or, for example, handed over to employees under a profit-sharing plan), the entry is simply reversed as long as the amounts are the same. However the amounts are rarely identical. When the resale value is different from the purchase value, the difference is recorded, varying between countries, following either:

- Solution 1: in the shareholders' equity, as an increase or decrease of the share premium (this is notably the case under IFRS and in North America).
- Solution 2: in the income statement, as an income or a loss.

If the company reporting follows IFRS/IAS, IAS 32 (§ 33) applies: 'If an entity reacquires its own equity instruments, those instruments ('treasury shares') shall be deducted from equity. No gain or loss shall be recognized in profit or loss on the purchase, sale, issue or

Figure 11.6 Accounting for retirement of shares to reduce share capital

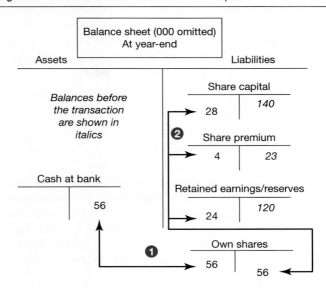

❶ Purchase of the corporation's own shares for the amount accepted by the seller and the remaining shareholders. According to IAS 32 (IASB 2008: §33) and North American practice the own shares are reported as a negative entry in the shareholders' equity. We followed this method in the above figure. Another approach is possible and applied in several European countries: own shares are recognized (positively) on the assets side.

❷ Reduction of the capital by canceling these shares and all the rights pertaining to them.

- Generally, phase 2 (entry ❷) happens simultaneously with phase 1.
- In some countries, both entries are merged into only one and the account 'own shares' is not used.
- In some European countries, the law requires that despite canceling shares, the total amount of the restricted reserves/capital remain unmodified. In such a case a special restricted reserve ('reserve for own shares') must be created for the amount by which the capital was reduced. Here such a reserve would compensate the reduction of capital, i.e., 28,000 CU, as we assume that reserves and the share premium are unrestricted. The following entry would be recorded: decrease of 'reserves' and increase of 'reserves for own shares'.

cancellation of an entity's own equity instruments. Such treasury shares may be acquired and held by the entity or by other members of the consolidated group. Consideration paid or received shall be recognized directly in equity'. In other words, when own shares are finally resold or attributed to employees, the gain or loss on sale is recorded as an increase or decrease of equity. IAS 32 does not mention explicitly which caption to use for the offset. In practice, share premium is often used as the balancing entry. It must then be noted that the IASB only authorizes the above-mentioned solution 1.

7.4 Reporting for treasury shares

There are many ways to report the ownership of one's own shares. Some examples of practice will illustrate the point.

Real-life example Club Méditerranée

(France – IFRS – Source: Annual report 2008 – Leisure)

Transactions on company shares

The authorization given to the board of directors to trade in the company's shares on the stock market, in accordance with articles L.225–209 et seq. of the Commercial Code and European Commission Regulation 2273/2003 was renewed at the shareholders' meeting of 11 March 2008 (seventeenth resolution) for a further period of eighteen months, expiring on 10 September 2009. Under the terms of this authorization, the number of shares purchased may not exceed 10% of the capital. The authorization may be used in the following order of priority:

- To maintain a liquid market in the company's shares under a liquidity agreement that complies with the Code of Ethics of the French Association of Investment Firms (AFEI).
- To purchase shares for allocation on exercise of stock options granted to employees.
- To purchase shares to be exchanged for stock in other companies or to be used as consideration in connection with acquisitions.
- To purchase shares for subsequent cancellation.

The maximum purchase price per share is €70.

The minimum sale price is €30. This minimum sale price applies to the resale of shares acquired under this share buyback program and/or any programs authorized by previous shareholders' meetings and these ceilings are only applicable in case of standardization of rates. On 11 July 2007, Club Méditerranée (ISIN FR0000121568) entered into a liquidity agreement with Natixis Securities that complies with the AFEI Code of Ethics as approved by the French securities regulator (*Autorité des Marchés Financiers*) on 22 March 2005. For its implementation, 2,000,000 euros were initially allocated to this liquidity agreement. The company made an additional contribution of 1,000,000 euros on 2 October 2008.

Between 11 March and 31 October 2008, the company purchased 254,858 shares at an average price of €31.30 and sold 197,500 shares at an average price of 33.08.

At 31 October 2008, a total of 274,837 shares were held in treasury.

Shareholders will be asked to renew the share buyback authorization at the shareholders' meeting on 20 February 2009.

Comments: This note is interesting in that it explains what happened during the period and what were the safeguards placed by the Executive Board on these treasury stock transactions.

Real-life example Toray Industries

(Japan – Japanese GAAP – Source: Annual report 2009 – Manufacturer of synthetic fibers and textiles)

Consolidated balance sheet (excerpts)		
(in Yen million)	2009	2008
Stockholders' equity:		
Common stock:		
*Authorized – 4,000,000,000 shares		
*Issued – 1,401,481,403 shares	96,937	96,937
Capital surplus	85,802	85,821
Retained earnings	353,222	387,070
Treasury stock, at cost	(1,123)	(1,073)
Total stockholders' equity	**534,838**	**568,755**

The own shares (treasury stock) are shown as a reduction of stockholders' equity, as is required by IAS 32 and common in a North American balance sheet.

8 Stock options plan ('Share options plan')

8.1 Definition

A **stock options plan** is a motivational device in which the corporation grants employees the right to acquire a specified personalized number of shares of the corporation at a predetermined invariant price and for a specified time window. These options are generally granted only after a given number of months or years of employment (the vesting period) and if the performance of either or both the employee and the business have met pre-specified levels. The implementation of such a plan is at the discretion of the management of the firm.

Employees exercise their option to buy only when the current market price is sufficiently high for the difference between the exercise price and the current market price to cover the transaction costs (often the employee must borrow funds to exercise her/his options[10]) and leave an appreciable surplus.

The shares sold to the employees can be new shares (authorized previously but unsubscribed or authorized for this special purpose) or shares acquired by the firm on the market to be re-sold to employees. International accounting standards do not make a clear distinction between these two situations and, in both cases, there is an increase in equity.

8.2 Accounting for stock options plan

IFRS 2 (IASB 2004) deals with accounting for stock options plan. The general principle is the following: 'When the goods or services received or acquired in a share-based payment transaction do not qualify for recognition as assets [which is the case with the service provided by employees], they shall be recognized as expenses' (§ 8). The procedure applicable to the attribution of stock options to employees is thus the following:

■ At the date the option is granted to employees, an option pricing model must be applied. The option's value is recorded as an increase in expenses (personnel expense) and an increase of an equity account (share premium). This entry is definitive, whether the option is exercised or not.

■ When the option is exercised, one should record the sale of own shares or the issuance of new shares, for an amount corresponding to the exercise price, which is the price paid by the person benefiting from the option. This concept is illustrated in Figure 11.7.

Figure 11.7 Barber Company – Accounting for stock options

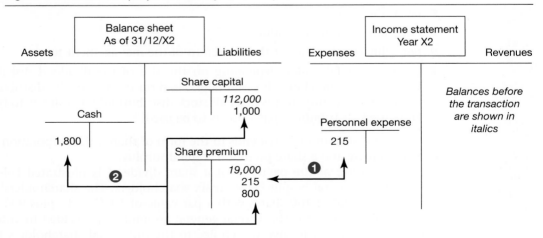

❶ Recording of the fair value of the option at the date of attribution.
❷ When the option is exercised, issuance of 1,000 shares in cash at an issuance price of 1.8 (including 1 of nominal value and 0.8 of share premium).

For example, let us assume that in year X1, the Barber Company board grants its General Manager, Mrs Claire, an option to subscribe 1,000 shares at the exercise price of 1.80 CU per share. This option can be exercised after 1st July X2. On the date of the granting of the option, the market value of a Barber share is 2 CU. A valuation model estimates the value of the option thus granted to be 215 CU. The value of an option is the sum of the intrinsic value plus a speculative value. Here the intrinsic value is equal to the difference between the actual market value of the share and the exercise price: (2 − 1.80) × 1,000 = 200 CU. The speculative value (here 15 CU) reflects the possibility of additional gain, given the exercise date for the option is nine months to a year hence. (The speculative value is based on the estimated volatility of both earnings and the share market value – it is a highly subjective measure although it is generally grounded on past statistics.) When Mrs Claire will exercise her option, the business will create an additional 1,000 shares. The entries required by such a transaction are shown in Figure 11.7.

9 Share dividend and dividend in kind

Normally, dividends are paid-out in cash. However, they could also be paid-out by giving assets to the shareholders (known as 'dividend in kind'). For example, the corporation may distribute third-party securities held in portfolio or may hand over some real property. Such an approach, although perfectly conceivable, encounters significant legal issues about property rights and is, therefore, very rarely used.

More frequently, corporations issue dividends by giving their own shares to their shareholders without requiring any additional contribution on their part (**share dividend** or stock dividend). This method is interesting to an organization because it allows the 'payment' of dividends without placing any strain on the cash situation of the firm. This is an especially attractive approach for often cash-strapped new ventures or fast growing businesses.

By-laws often allow the shareholders to elect, individually or collectively (in the general assembly) whether they prefer their dividend to be paid-out in cash or in the form of additional shares.

In the calculation of the number of shares to be given as dividends, there are several valuation options and the actual choice varies from country to country. The possibilities are:

- par value;
- fair value (i.e., market value);
- par value or fair value, at the discretion of the management team;
- par value or fair value depending on the size of the dividend distribution. (In the United States the choice is essentially based on the size of the distribution relative to shareholder's equity. If it is a 'small stock distribution' fair value is to be used; if it is a large stock distribution, par value is to be used).

When it distributes its dividends in the form of shares, the corporation has to record a capital increase and a share premium (capital surplus).

The recording of the payment of a share dividend is illustrated below. MacDowell Corporation's capital is split between six shareholders. The shareholders' equity is composed of a capital of 100 shares with a par value of 1 CU each, plus 900 CU in retained earnings. For period X1, the annual general assembly has decided to vote a dividend of 100 CU in total and to give the choice to the individual shareholders between a payment in cash or as a share dividend. Five small shareholders holding a total of 10 shares prefer payment in cash while the sixth shareholder, holding a total of 90 shares, prefers to receive a share dividend.

The average market quote over the six weeks prior to the distribution was 15 CU per share. The dividends that the shareholder elected to receive in the form of additional shares, are therefore equivalent to 6 new shares[11] (fair value = 15 CU × 6 shares = 90 CU). Capital at par will increase by 6 CU, while capital surplus will increase by 90 − 6 = 84 CU. Figure 11.8 illustrates the recording of these share dividends.

Figure 11.8 Accounting of the payment of dividends by both cash and share dividends

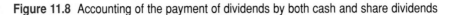

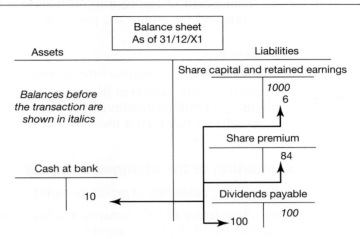

The share dividend mechanism is essentially similar to a share issuance by capitalization of reserves. In North America the practice may differ from that used in our example, which is coherent with IFRS practice (see Appendix 11.6).

10 Comprehensive income

In Chapter 6, comprehensive income was defined. IAS 1 (IASB 2007: § 81) states that: 'An entity shall present all items of income and expense recognized in a period:

(a) in a single statement of comprehensive income; or

(b) in two statements: a statement displaying components of profit or loss (separate income statement) and a second statement beginning with profit or loss and displaying components of other comprehensive income (statement of comprehensive income)'.

An illustration of reporting for comprehensive income is developed in Appendix 11.7.

11 Changes in shareholders' equity

Given the complexity of the shareholders' equity account and the many changes that can affect its composition during the year, IAS 1 (IASB 2007) and the GAAP of many countries require (or suggest) that a table be provided that explains changes in shareholders' equity.

11.1 The prescriptive content of IAS 1

IAS 1 (IASB 2007: § 106) states that: 'an entity shall present a statement of changes in equity showing in the statement:

(a) Total comprehensive income for the period, showing separately the total amounts attributable to owners of the parent and to non-controlling interests;

(b) For each component of equity, the effects of retrospective application or retrospective restatement recognized in accordance with IAS 8; and

(c) [deleted]

(d) For each component of equity, a reconciliation between the carrying amount at the beginning and the end of the period, separately disclosing changes resulting from:

   (i) profit or loss;

  (ii) each item of other comprehensive income; and

 (iii) transactions with owners in their capacity as owners, showing separately contributions by and distributions to owners and changes in ownership interests in subsidiaries that do not result in a loss of control.'

11.2 Presentation of the changes in equity

In practice, there is the possibility of reporting equity changes in two formats:

- a broad one, cumulating all the elements: the 'statement of changes in shareholders' equity' or 'statement of changes in equity';
- a reduced version: the 'statement of recognized income and expense'.

It is important to note that after the amendment of IAS 1 in 2007 (effective since January 2009), the reduced version is no longer allowed under IFRS reporting. We mention it here because not all countries have adopted IFRS reporting and thus may still use this presentation.

11.2.1 Statement of changes in equity

IAS 1 provides in its Appendix 'Guidance on implementing IAS 1' (§ IG6) an illustration of a statement of changes in equity. We consider it to be an illustration of best practice. Table 11.3 is extracted from IAS 1.

11.2.2 Statement of recognized income and expense

Before its revision in 2007, IAS 1 used to provide an example of a statement which presents those changes in equity that represent income and expense (a simplified version of which is shown as Table 11.4).

Table 11.3 XYZ Group – Statement of changes in equity for the year ended 31 December X8 (in thousands of CU)

	Share capital	Retained earnings	Translation of foreign operations	Available-for-sale financial assets	Cash flow hedges	Revaluation surplus	Total	Non-controlling interests	Total equity
Balance at 1 January 20X6	600,000	118,100	(4,000)	1,600	2,000	–	717,700	29,800	747,500
Changes in accounting policy	–	400	–	–	–	–	400	100	500
Restated balance	600,000	118,500	(4,000)	1,600	2,000	–	718,100	29,900	748,000
Changes in equity for 20X6									
Dividends	–	(10,000)	–	–	–	–	(10,000)	–	(10,000)
Total comprehensive income for the year	–	53,200	6,400	16,000	(2,400)	1,600	74,800	18,700	93,500
Balance at 31 December 20X6	600,000	161,700	2,400	17,600	(400)	1,600	782,900	48,600	831,500
Changes in equity for 20X7									
Issue of share capital	50,000	–	–	–	–	–	50,000	–	50,000
Dividends	–	(15,000)	–	–	–	–	(15,000)	–	(15,000)
Total comprehensive income for the year	–	96,600	3,200	(14,400)	(400)	800	85,800	21,450	107,250
Transfer to retained earnings	–	200	–	–	–	(200)	–	–	–
Balance at 31 December 20X7	650,000	243,500	5,600	3,200	(800)	2,200	903,700	70,050	973,750

Table 11.4 XYZ Group – Statement of recognized income and expense for the year ended 31 December X2 (in thousands of CU)

	X2	X1
Gain/(loss) on revaluation of properties	(x)	x
Available-for-sale investments:		
Valuation gains/(losses) taken to equity	(x)	(x)
Transferred to profit or loss on sale	x	(x)
Exchange differences on translation of foreign operations	(x)	(x)
Net income recognized directly in equity	x	x
Profit for the period	x	x
Total recognized income and expense for the period	x	x
Attributable to:		
Equity holders of the parent	x	x
Minority interest	x	x
	x	x
Effect of changes in accounting policy		
Equity holders of the parent		(x)
Minority interest		(x)
		(x)

Real-life example Aluminum Corporation of China (Chalco)

(China – Hong Kong GAAP – Source: Annual report 2007 – Production, sales and research of alumina and primary aluminum)

The detail of the shareholders' equity (consolidated balance sheet) is reproduced below.

Consolidated balance sheet (excerpts)

	31 December	
(in RMB 000)	2007	2006
Share capital and reserves attributable to equity holders of the company		
Share capital	13,524,488	11,649,876
Reserves	20,776,271	15,977,303
Retained earnings	23,643,388	17,168,564
	57,944,147	44,795,743
Minority interest	3,072,622	4,470,819
Total equity	**61,016,769**	**49,266,562**

After the income statement and balance sheet, the group publishes a 'Consolidated statement of changes in equity'.

Consolidated statement of changes in equity (simplified)

(in RMB 000)	Share capital	Capital reserve	Other reserves	Retained earnings	Minority interest	Total
As of 1 January 2007, as previously stated	11,649,876	10,009,225	5,351,968	17,213,665	3,541,192	**47,765,926**
Acquisition of Baotou Aluminum	–	512,255	103,855	(45,101)	929,627	**1,500,636**
As of 1 January 2007, as restated	**11,649,876**	**10,521,480**	**5,455,823**	**17,168,564**	**4,470,819**	49,266,562
Changes in equity for the year ended 31 December 2007						
Fair value gains from available-for-sale investment – gross	–	–	8,879	–	5,608	**14,487**
Fair value gains from available-for-sale investment – tax	–	–	(1,332)	–	(841)	**(2,173)**
Equity pick up from an associate	–	168	0	–	–	**168**
Cumulative translation difference	–	–	10,047	–	–	**10,047**
Net income recognized directly in equity	–	168	17,594	–	4,767	**22,529**
Profit for the year ended 31 December 2007	–	–	–	10,244,545	1,384,379	**11,628,924**
Total recognized income and expense for the year	–	168	17,594	10,244,545	1,389,146	**11,651,453**
Issuance of new shares	1,874,612	7,852,275	–	–	–	**9,726,887**
Share issuance expense	–	(179,000)	–	–	–	**(179,000)**
Acquisition of subsidiaries	–	(3,155,330)	–	–	(2,345,430)	**(5,500,760)**
Capital injection from minority shareholders	–	–	–	–	10,094	**10,094**
Transfers	–	–	1,083,388	(1,083,388)	–	**–**
Dividends	–	–	–	(3,506,460)	(452,007)	**(3,958,467)**
Adjustment to surplus reserves	–	–	(820,127)	820,127	–	–

Consolidated statement of changes in equity (simplified) (Continued)						
(in RMB 000)	Share capital	Capital reserve	Other reserves	Retained earnings	Minority interest	Total
As of 31 December 2007	**13,524,488**	**15,039,593**	**5,736,678**	**23,643,388**	**3,072,622**	**61,016,769**
Retained earnings represented by 2007 final dividend proposed				716,798		
Unappropriated retained earnings				22,926,590		
Retained earnings as of 31 December 2007				**23,643,388**		

One can easily reconcile the beginning (49,266,562) and ending (61,016,769) equity disclosed in the statement of changes in equity with the figures reported in the consolidated balance sheet (see above).

Real-life example Accor

(France – IFRS – Source: Annual report 2008 – Leisure sector, hotels and health clubs)

We disclose below an excerpt of the consolidated balance sheet corresponding to the detail of total equity.

Consolidated balance sheet (excerpts)			
(in € million)	Dec. 2006	Dec. 2007	Dec. 2008
Share capital	635	665	660
Additional paid-in capital	2,321	2,276	2,226
Retained earnings	100	(94)	158
Fair value adjustments on financial instruments reserve	524	66	(6)
Reserve related to employee benefits	32	59	82
Reserve for actuarial gains/losses	(23)	(19)	(23)
Currency translation reserve	8	(145)	(367)
Net profit, group share	501	883	575
SHAREHOLDERS' EQUITY, GROUP SHARE	**4,098**	**3,691**	**3,305**
Minority interests	66	61	258
TOTAL SHAREHOLDERS' EQUITY AND MINORITY INTERESTS	**4,164**	**3,752**	**3,563**

After the primary financial statements (income statement, balance sheet, statement of cash flows), Accor publishes its 'Consolidated statement of changes in equity'.

Consolidated statement of changes in equity (simplified)										
(in € million)	Share capital	Additional paid-in capital	Currency translation reserve	Fair value reserve	Employee benefits reserve	Actuarial reserve	Retained earnings and profits	Share-holders' equity	Minority interests	Consolidated shareholders' equity
31 December 2007	**665**	**2,276**	**(145)**	**66**	**59**	**(19)**	**789**	**3,691**	**61**	**3,752**
Fair value adjustments on financial instruments	–	–	–	(72)	–	–	67	(5)	–	(5)
Currency translation adjustment	–	–	(222)	–	–	–	–	(222)	(45)	(267)
Change in reserve for actuarial gains/losses	–	–	–	–	–	(4)	–	(4)	–	(4)
Profit for the period	–	–	–	–	–	–	575	575	38	613
Recognized income and expense	*–*	*–*	*(222)*	*(72)*	*–*	*(4)*	*642*	*344*	*(7)*	*337*
Exercise of stock options	1	7	–	–	–	–	–	8	–	8
Capital reduction	(6)	(57)	–	–	–	–	–	(63)	–	(63)
Dividends paid	–	–	–	–	–	–	(698)	(698)	(22)	(720)
Change in reserve for employee benefits	–	–	–	–	23	–	–	23	–	23
Effect of scope changes	–	–	–	–	–	–	–	0	226	226
31 December 2008	**660**	**2,226**	**(367)**	**(6)**	**82**	**(23)**	**733**	**3,305**	**258**	**3,563**

The reconciliation table begins with the opening balance of shareholders' funds and ends with the closing balance of shareholders' funds.

12 Financial statement analysis

12.1 Impact on financial structure

Table 11.5 summarizes the different possible key types of capital increase. It also describes their impact on the structure of the balance sheet. In order to facilitate the understanding of the right-most column, the following definitions may prove useful to the reader (the concepts are fully defined in Chapter 15):

■ Working capital = Equity + Long-term liabilities – Fixed assets (or, Working capital = Current assets including cash – Current liabilities).

- Working capital need (simplified definition) = Current assets (excluding cash) – current liabilities (excluding bank overdrafts) = Inventories + receivables – payables.
- Cash = Cash at bank and in hand – bank overdrafts.

12.2 Ratios

The share yield (earnings per share divided by market value of the share – see the definition of earnings per share in Chapter 18) is a key ratio for analysts and investors alike

Table 11.5 Different types of capital increases

Types of increases	Objectives	Procedure	Impact on the balance sheet	Impact on the financial structure
In cash	To obtain additional long-term financial resources without term limits in order to buttress the development potential of the firm	Issuance of new shares either at a price greater than the par value (thus creation of a 'share premium' for the difference) or Increase in the par value of the existing shares	*Increase* of current asset, and *Increase* of the capital account on the liabilities side	Increase in working capital, and Increase in cash
Capitalization of reserves	Reconcile the level of legal capital with the actual value of the assets and/ or strengthen the capital as a gesture of responsibility towards the firm's trading partners	Distribution of shares or Increase of the par value	*Reduction* of the reserves on the liabilities side, and *Increase* of capital on the liabilities side	Financial structure unchanged
In kind	Reinforce the growth potential of the firm by adding new tangible and intangible assets that will enhance the firm's future development	New shares are valued close to their fair market value	*Increase* on the assets side (the contributed asset) and possibly *Increase* on the liabilities side if the contribution is not net of debt, and *Increase* of the capital	If the contribution is a fixed asset, the financial structure is not modified If the contribution is a current asset: ■ Increase in working capital ■ Increase in working capital need If the contribution includes a financial (i.e., long-term) debt, the financial structure is unchanged If the contribution includes operating (i.e., short-term) or non operating debts: ■ Increase in working capital ■ Increase in working capital need

Table 11.5 Different types of capital increases (Continued)				
Types of increases	Objectives	Procedure	Impact on the balance sheet	Impact on the financial structure
Conversion of liabilities	Reimburse debt without impacting on cash: the creditor abandons its claim in exchange for shares	New shares are valued close to their fair market value	*Decrease* in liabilities, and *Increase* of shareholders' equity	If the cancelled debt was long-term debt, the financial structure is unchanged If the cancelled debt was short-term (operating or non operating): ■ Increase in working capital ■ Increase in working capital need If the conversion is one of short-term bank credit such as overdraft: ■ Increase in working capital ■ Increase in cash
Share dividend	Reinforce the capital structure without strapping either the firm or the shareholders for cash	New shares are valued close to their fair market value	*Reduction* of the debt (dividends payables), and *Increase* of the capital	Increase in working capital Increase in working capital need

in deciding whether to move their investment or not. However, many other ratios help analysts evaluate shareholders' equity.

12.2.1 Return on equity

The most common ratio used to evaluate the effectiveness of the management of the investment is undoubtedly the **return on equity** (ROE). The formula is as follows:

$$\text{Net income/Average equity}$$

Managers use this ratio to compare investments opportunities, hopefully from the point of view of the shareholders. If a new investment opportunity does not yield a return on investment (ROI – see Chapter 2) greater than the current ROE, it will, logically, if implemented, lower the *ex post* ROE and is therefore not a desirable opportunity. Incremental investments are rank-ordered by decreasing ROI and all investment opportunities failing to exceed the current ROE are eliminated. Those meeting the expected ROI > ROE will be implemented in decreasing priority based on the availability of funding and their strategic long-term interest.

A variant of ROE, called 'return on common equity' is sometimes used when only the point of view of the common shareholders needs to be taken into account:

$$\text{(Net income minus preferred dividends)/Average common equity}$$

12.2.2 Economic value added

This metric, designed by and proprietary to the financial consulting firm Stern Stewart, and developed in Chapter 18, addresses the concept of return on equity from a slightly different point of view by restating both the income (to reflect the long-term dynamics of the firm) and the equity to show the real investment (beyond the book value of equity) of the shareholders in the firm.

12.2.3 Equity ratio

This ratio measures the contribution of the shareholders in providing the resources required by the firm's operations.

> Shareholders' equity/Total shareholders' equity and liabilities (or total assets)

If the shareholders provide too little of the financing of the assets, either the firm must procure this funding from external costly sources thus reducing the income, or must obtain this funding by an extended suppliers credit, thus creating a dependency on sales growth and on the willingness of the suppliers to maintain these credit terms. It can also be observed that suppliers are not philanthropists and they often include in their price the cost of financing the credit terms granted. Thus, a relevant question is whether, in return for the shareholders financing more of the assets, a lowering of the purchase price of materials or components could not be obtained. A cost-benefit analysis should be carried out regularly as undercapitalization may prove to be very costly in the long run, and overcapitalization often means lost opportunities.

12.2.4 Debt/equity ratio

Debt/equity ratio describes the financial leverage the shareholders have obtained. This ratio has many different definitions as will be shown in the real-life examples below.

> Long-term debts/Shareholders' equity

Let us assume an incremental one-year investment opportunity exists for a firm. The capital required is 100 CU. The expected return is 20 CU. If the firm can finance its own incremental investment, it will obtain an ROI of 20%, but if it funds half of the investment cost through a 6% loan, its own funding will only be 50 and the ROI will be $(20 - 50 \times 0.06)/50 = 34\%$. What is called 'leverage' is the impact of the ability of using someone else's money (for a cost) to finance part of the investment to increase the ROI and, by consequence, the ROE (see Chapter 2). Here again a cost-benefit analysis is needed since an over-leveraged firm may have a great ROI but is also very vulnerable to any change in the market conditions for its products and services. An underleveraged firm may be seen as depriving its shareholders of a possible additional return on equity but also provides more security in a turbulent world. For example, even in the same industry the leverage ratio may differ greatly between firms or over time: as of 31 December 2008, Nokia had roughly six euros of shareholders' equity for one euro of non-current debt, while, at the same date, Ericcson had only 3.6 Swedish krona of shareholders' equity for one krona of debt. As of the third quarter of 2009, Nokia's equity to debt ratio had changed from 6 to 1 to 2.4 to 1, while Ericsson's had changed from 3.6 to 1 to 2.95 to 1. Although these two firms are obviously not completely comparable, they are largely facing similar risks in the broadly defined cell phone industry. It is noteworthy to observe that each firm's strategy leads to different ratios. Comparing ratios between firms is always a difficult task.

12.2.5 Market to book ratio

Shareholders' equity defines the book value of the company. However, the amount at which equity is shown on the balance sheet is dependent on the valuation of assets and liabilities. Since (a) assets and liabilities are recorded in accounting systems at their historical cost (with the exception of some assets and liabilities carried at 'fair value', as seen in Chapter 10); and (b) the market value of a firm (and thus of its shares) is largely a function of its future cash-flow stream and the level of risk or volatility of these cash flows. The market takes into consideration not only the recorded tangible and intangible assets of the firm, it also looks at other elements not explicitly reported and valued in the balance sheet such as: expertise, legitimacy, knowledge base, customer loyalty, employee loyalty, etc. It should be no surprise to find out that the market value of a firm is generally much greater than the book value of its equity. Even the resale value of the assets in the context of liquidation often exceeds their book value by a large amount.

The 'market to book' ratio measures the under-valuation represented by the book value of equity. The higher the ratio, the higher the unreported intangible resources are likely to be, but also the higher the expected growth of cash flow, the lower the risk level perceived by the market regarding the volatility of future cash flows, and the longer the time horizon of visibility shareholders feel they have about future cash flows. The formula is very simple but the interpretation of the ratio remains complex:

> Market price per share/Book value per share

This ratio represents the amount investors appear to be willing to pay for each CU of a firm's net assets. The market value per share varies continuously as analysts and investors continuously trade firms against one another on the basis of their perception of the future of the firm. The **market to book ratio** is only useful if looked at in the long run.

Real-life examples

Table 11.6 compares three ratios as published by three industrial companies in the same country so as to minimize discrepancies that might be due to differing GAAP (all data are from the companies' own 2008 annual reports). Even in the same country, here Sweden, discrepancies exist because technologies (thus assets required), markets, financing and reporting strategies are different. This diversity implies that when ratios are being used to compare companies around the world, great care must be taken to ensure comparability. We should also note that Sandvik calls 'equity ratio' a ratio which is significantly different from the same ratio computed by the two other companies: the denominator is 'total capital' for Sandvik instead of 'total assets' for the others. A direct comparison is thus impossible.

Table 11.6 Examples of ratios based on equity

Company	Name of the ratio	Computation	2008	2007
Holmen (Newsprint and magazine paper)	Return on equity (in %)	Profit for the year, expressed as percentage of the average equity calculated on the basis of quarterly data	3.9	9.2
Rottneros (Production of pulp)	Return on equity (in %)	Net profit as a percentage of average shareholders' equity	Neg.	Neg.
Sandvik (Engineering)	Return on shareholders' equity (in %)	Net profit for the year as a percentage of average shareholders' equity during the year	24.8	34.4

Table 11.6 Examples of ratios based on equity (Continued)

Company	Name of the ratio	Computation	2008	2007
Holmen	Equity ratio (in %)	Equity plus minority interests, if any, expressed as percentage of the balance sheet total	45.2	50.9
Rottneros	Equity/assets ratio (in %)	Shareholders' equity including minority as a percentage of balance sheet total	40	45
Sandvik	Equity ratio (in %)	Shareholder's equity including minority interests in relation to total capital	36	35
Holmen	Debt/equity ratio	Financial net debt divided by the sum of equity and minority interests, if any	0.48	0.35
Rottneros	Debt/equity ratio (multiple)	Interest-bearing liabilities divided by shareholders' equity	1.0	0.6
Sandvik	Net debt/equity ratio (times)	Interest-bearing current and non-current debts (including provision for pensions) less cash and cash equivalents divided by the total of shareholders' equity including minority interests	0.9	1.0

Key points

- The two main providers of seed long-term financial resources of a firm are (1) the entrepreneur or risk-taking investors, and (2) creditors (who 'rent' their funds to the firm and take less risk than the participants in the first category of providers).
- The wealth contributed by the entrepreneur or by investors as capital to a business can be in the form of cash, of tangible or intangible assets, of intellectual property, of inventories, etc.
- Investors bring in capital to the business venture in return for a claim on a portion of the wealth that will be potentially created by the enterprise over the years following the investment.
- Shares, or stock certificates, represent a partition of the capital of incorporated firms. They are granted proportionately to the contribution of the shareholders to the formation of capital.
- The face value of a share is called the nominal or par value. The capital is, therefore, equal to the number of shares multiplied by the par value.
- Equity (or shareholders' equity) is 'the residual interest [of the investors] in the assets of the enterprise after deducting all its liabilities'.
- The two principal components of shareholders' equity are share capital and retained earnings (some of which are reported under the name of reserves).
- 'Ordinary' (or common) shares are distinct from 'preferred' shares. The latter carry rights different from those of common shares.

- The share premium is the difference between the issuance price and the par value.
- The profit of a period can be either distributed to the shareholders in the form of dividends or kept in the organization either as a voluntary re-investment by the shareholders as retained earnings (reserve) or as a legally required reserve for a purpose specified by the law.

- The statement of changes in shareholders' equity is an important document that details how the current year's decisions (beyond operating decisions) have affected shareholder's equity.
- Several important ratios are related to shareholders' equity: return on equity, equity ratio, debt/equity ratio and market to book ratio.

Review (solutions are at the back of the book)

Review 11.1 Copland Company

Topic: Share issuance in cash

Copland has a capital of 300,000 CU, divided into 3,000 shares each with a par of 100 CU. It issues 1,000 new shares (par 100) for a price of 170 each. The legislation of the country in which Copland operates requires that the full share premium (here 70 CU per share) be paid up at the time of the new shares subscription, but only requires that a minimum of 25% of the par value be paid up. The share issuance costs pertaining to this issuance (legal fees, auditors fees, printing costs, financial commissions and sundry fees) are offset against share premium. All providers, whose bills are summed up under issuance costs for an amount of 5,000 CU, have been paid immediately by check.

Required

1. Prepare the accounting entries necessary to record this capital increase.
2. Prepare a comparison of the relevant excerpts of the balance sheet before and after the issuance of new shares.

Review 11.2 Menotti Company

Topic: Profit appropriation

As of 1 January X1, Menotti's capital comprised 4,000 shares of 100 CU par. These shares are divided in two classes: 1,000 class-A shares and 3,000 class-B shares. Class-A shares enjoy a 5% of par preference-dividend over and above the ordinary dividends.
    Before appropriation of the annual earnings, the books show the following year-end data (in CU).

Capital	400,000
Legal reserve	39,000
Regulated reserves	8,000
Losses brought forward	–5,000
Net income after tax (year ending 31/12/X0)	40,000

Tax regulations require that the regulated reserve be incremented by 2,000 CU in X1.
    The by-laws contain the following stipulations:

- Each year the legal reserve must be incremented by an amount of 5% of the net income for the year, net of any loss carry-forward (if the net is positive) as long as the legal reserve is less than 10% of the par capital.
- Class-A shares must receive a preference dividend of 5% of their par value.
- All A and B shares are equally entitled to the payment of ordinary dividends.
    The board of directors proposes that (a) an optional reserve be created for an amount of 10,000 CU, and (b) that an ordinary dividend of 4 CU per share be paid out. The general assembly approves these propositions.
    The balance of income after appropriation will be carried forward.

Required

1. Prepare a table detailing the profit appropriation calculations (including the per share dividend for each class of shares).

2. Prepare the appropriation accounting entries.

3. Prepare a table detailing the shareholders' equity and liabilities before and after appropriation.

Assignments

Assignment 11.1
Multiple-choice questions

Select the right answer (only one possible answer, unless otherwise stated).

1. The sale by a shareholder of shares of a company to another shareholder should be recorded by the company
   (a) True
   (b) False

2. A company received cash subscriptions for 5,000 shares of 20 CU nominal (par) value at 100 CU per share. A down-payment of 50% of the issuance price is required. The remainder of the purchase price is to be paid the following year. At the time that the share is subscribed, share capital should be increased for
   (a) 500,000
   (b) 250,000
   (c) 100,000
   (d) 50,000
   (e) 400,000
   (f) 200,000
   (g) None of these

3. Dividends cannot be distributed if net income is not greater than zero
   (a) True
   (b) False

4. The difference between the price paid for a company's common share and the par value of each share can be called (several possible answers)
   (a) Capital surplus
   (b) Share premium
   (c) Additional paid-in capital
   (d) Paid-in capital
   (e) Additional contributed capital
   (f) Ordinary share capital
   (g) Capital in excess of par value
   (h) Premium fund
   (i) All of these

5. A company has the following shareholders' equity section:

Ordinary shares: par = 2 CU; 250,000 shares authorized; 100,000 shares issued and outstanding	200,000
Share premium	30,000
Reserves	50,000
Net income	20,000
Shareholders' equity	300,000

The market price per share is 15 CU. What is the book value per share?
   (a) 2
   (b) 1.2
   (c) 3
   (d) 0.8
   (e) 15
   (f) 2.3
   (g) 0.92
   (h) None of these

6. In all types of limited liability companies, it is possible to defer the payment of one part of the subscribed capital
   (a) True
   (b) False

7. The number of authorized shares is greater than the amount of issued shares which might be greater that the amount of outstanding shares
   (a) True
   (b) False

8. A share may grant a voting right greater than one but never lower than one
   (a) True
   (b) False

9. The main objective of the legal reserve is to protect the shareholders of the company
   (a) True
   (b) False

10 According to IAS 1, which of the following items should be disclosed either on the balance sheet or in notes?

(a) The number of shares authorized

(b) The number of shares issued and fully paid, and issued but not fully paid

(c) Par value per share, or that the shares have no par value

(d) All of these

Assignment 11.2
Ives Company

Topic: Impact on shareholders' equity

Transactions related to Ives Company's shareholders' equity (far left column) are listed in the following table. For each line you are provided with three choices of impact of the transaction on the total of shareholders' equity: increase, decrease or no impact.

Required

Indicate by a checkmark the impact of each transaction.

	Impact on shareholders' equity		
	Increase	Decrease	No impact
Issuance of ordinary shares in cash at par value			
Issuance of preference shares in cash at par value			
Declaration of the year's cash dividend			
Payment of the above-mentioned cash dividend			
Issuance of ordinary shares in cash at a price greater than par value			
Issuance of preference shares in cash at a price greater that nominal value			
Conversion of preference shares to ordinary shares			
Issuance of share dividends			
Issuance of ordinary shares at par (nominal) value by capitalization of reserves (retained earnings)			
Issuance of ordinary shares by conversion of bonds for a price greater than nominal value			
Issuance of shares in kind for a price greater than nominal value			
Repurchase and retirement of shares by the company			
Purchase of treasury shares (own shares)			

Assignment 11.3
Bernstein Company

Topic: Share issuance in cash

Bernstein Company is a limited liability company. The annual general assembly, held on 6 May X1, voted to issue an additional 2,500 shares (each with a par of 550 CU). The public offering price is set at 700 CU. The capital will be called for the full amount of the legal minimum. Bank X received the subscriptions from 7 to 30 May. On 30 May, the bank issued a certificate stating that the sale was complete and all funds had been collected.

Required

Under both of the following hypotheses:

1. The legal minimum that must be called is half of the issuance price,

2. The legal minimum that must be called is half the par value and the entire share premium,

prepare the appropriate entries.

Assignment 11.4
Gilbert Company

Topic: Profit appropriation

Gilbert Company was created in early X1. Its original capital was 2,500 shares with a par value of 100 CU. The composition of the capital as of 31 December X9, is described in article 7 of the amended by-laws (see exhibit).

At the end of X9 the shareholders' equity account before appropriation stands as shown in the table on the following page.

Share capital	3,780,000
Share premium	7,560,000
Legal reserve	370,000
Retained earnings	2,000,000
Profit/loss brought forward	−100,000
Net income for X9	1,000,000
Total	14,610,000

The board of directors has approved a motion in which, in addition to the appropriation of the earnings from X9, there will be a second dividend, which will be paid to shares of all classes. This second dividend will be the maximum legally possible without, however, exceeding 10 CU per share. The remaining balance, if there is any, will be transferred to the retained earnings account.

The prime rate mentioned in the by-laws and applicable to the year X9 is 6% per annum.

As soon as the amount of the legal reserve represents 10% of the share capital, there is no longer a need to fund this reserve.

Required

1. Prepare a suggested appropriation of the X9 net income.

2. Prepare the appropriate accounting entries that your suggested appropriation requires.

3. Prepare a table describing the shareholders' equity after appropriation.

Exhibit

Article 7 – Share capital

The capital of Gilbert is 3,780,000 (three million seven hundred eighty thousand) CU.

The capital is composed of 37,800 (thirty seven thousand eight hundred) fully subscribed shares, each with a par of 100 (one hundred) CU.

The shares are partitioned into two classes:
- 27,000 A Shares, numbered 1 to 27,000, and
- 10,800 B Shares numbered 27,001 to 37,800.

The B shares are preference shares with a preference dividend for the fiscal years X9 to X15 inclusive. This preference dividend will be calculated as a fixed remuneration on the basis of the prime rate minus 1% for fiscal year X9, prime rate plus 2% for fiscal year X10, and prime rate plus 5% for years X11 to X15.

The fixed remuneration rate will be applied to the full subscription price (including the capital surplus), i.e., 800 CU per share of 100 CU. All holders of B shares will receive this dividend. The dividend will be payable in keeping with the conditions defined by law. (…)

Assignment 11.5
Gerry Weber*

Topic: Reporting for profit appropriation

Gerry Weber International AG is a German group active in the design, manufacture and retail of woman clothing. The following data concerning the parent company were excerpted from the 2008 annual report.

Consolidated balance sheet (excerpts)		
		31 October
(in €)	2008	2007
Equity		
Capital stock	22,508,820.00	22,952,980.00
Capital reserve	33,668,025.21	28,047,398.39
Retained earnings	56,580,017.61	53,880,426.05
AOCI[12] to IAS 39	12,363,091.07	−2,786,859.00
Exchange differences	551,085.25	515,590.38
Accumulated profits	55,407,234.57	42,469,578.13
	181,078,273.71	145,079,113.95

Consolidated income statement (excerpts)		
(in €)	2007/2008	2006/2007
Net income for the year	**39,414,146.44**	**26,964,495.35**
Profit carried forward	30,993,088.13	25,505,082.78
Transfer to retained earnings	−15,000,000.00	−10,000,000.00
Accumulated profits	**55,407,234.57**	**42,469,578.13**

Required

1. Explain the computation of the 'accumulated profits' in the income statement.

2. What does this accumulated profit for the year represent? Is the balance sheet presented before or after profit appropriation?

3. Beginning on 9 September 2008, Gerry Weber International AG acquired 444,160 of its own shares at an average price of €16.04 per share (par value €1/share; total purchase cost €7,123,941.62). In which line item of the balance sheet do you think one can find the 'reserve for own shares'? What influence (in €) did the repurchase of own shares have on this particular line item? How can you use the information given in relation to the 'capital stock' line item?

4. Explain the total change in 'retained earnings'. For that, note the line item 'transfer to retained earnings' disclosed in the income statement and take account of the fact, that €5,620,626.82 have been

taken out of retained earnings because of 'reclassification of redemption of own shares'.

5. From the data excerpted from the balance sheet and income statement provided above, find the amount of the dividends distributed in 2008 with regard to 2007.

6. The annual report indicates that the dividends distributed in 2008 relating to the 2007 profit amounted to €0.50 per share. It also states that the share capital includes 22,952,980 shares (in 2007 and 2008). Double-check the amount of dividends paid in 2008 as found in question 5.

Assignment 11.6
Holmen*

Topic: Statement of changes in equity

Holmen (formerly MoDo), is a Swedish group manufacturing and selling newsprint and magazine paper as well as paperboard. Its financial statements are prepared in accordance with IFRS. The 2008 financial statements contain the following information on 'equity' for the year ended 31 December 2008 (source: Annual report 2008).

Consolidated balance sheet (excerpts)		
	31 December	
(in SEK million)	2008	2007
Equity		
Share capital	4,238	4,238
Other contributed capital	281	281
Reserves	−672	−16
Profits brought forward incl. profit for the year	11,795	12,429
Total equity attributable to the parent company's shareholders	**15,642**	**16,932**

No changes in share capital and other contributed capital took place in 2008. Profit for the year has been 642 MSEK. Total changes stated directly in equity excluding transactions with the company's shareholders in 'profit brought forward' was −121 MSEK. At the same time, dividends taken from 'profit brought forward incl. profit for the year' have been distributed: 1,017 MSEK. Some other transactions (received premiums for call options, buy-back of own shares) affected the profit reserve in an amount of −138 MSEK. The non-restricted reserves ('reserves') changed due to translation differences (55 MSEK) and hedging activities (−712 MSEK) over the last fiscal year.

Required

Prepare the statement of changes in shareholders' equity for the year 2008 using the format recommended in IAS 1 (see Table 11.3 and the example of Aluminum Corporation of China above).

Assignment 11.7
Nokia*

Topic: Ratios based on equity

Nokia (Finland) is among the leaders in the telecommunication industry, with emphasis on cellular phones and other wireless solutions. The consolidated financial statements are prepared in accordance with International Financial Reporting Standards. We disclose below the consolidated balance sheets at 31 December 2004 to 2008 (source: Annual reports 2004–2008) as well as some additional information (2004–2008).

Consolidated balance sheet (assets)

(in € million)	31 December				
	2008	2007	2006	2005	2004
ASSETS					
Non-current assets					
Capitalized development costs	244	378	251	260	278
Goodwill	6,257	1,384	532	90	90
Other intangible assets	3,913	2,358	298	211	209
Property, plant and equipment	2,090	1,912	1,602	1,585	1,534
Investments in associated companies	96	325	224	193	200
Available-for-sale investments	512	341	288	246	169
Deferred tax assets	1,963	1,553	809	846	623
Long-term loans receivable	27	10	19	63	–
Other non-current assets	10	44	8	7	58
	15,112	**8,305**	**4,031**	**3,501**	**3,161**
Current assets					
Inventories	2,533	2,876	1,554	1,668	1,305
Accounts receivable, net of allowances for doubtful accounts (2008: € 415; 2007: € 332, 2006: € 212; 2005: € 281; 2004: € 361 million)	9,444	11,200	5,888	5,346	4,382
Prepaid expenses and accrued income	4,538	3,070	2,496	1,938	1,429
Current portion of long-term loans receivable	101	156	–	–	–
Other financial assets	1,034	239	111	89	595
Available-for-sale investments	–	–	–	–	255
Available-for-sale investments, liquid assets	1,272	4,903	5,012	6,852	9,085
Available-for-sale investments, cash equivalents	3,842	4,725	2,046	1,493	1,367
Bank and cash	1,706	2,125	1,479	1,565	1,090
	24,470	**29,294**	**18,586**	**18,951**	**19,508**
Total assets	**39,582**	**37,599**	**22,617**	**22,452**	**22,669**

Consolidated balance sheet (equity and liabilities)

(in € million)		31 December				
		2008	2007	2006	2005	2004
EQUITY AND LIABILITIES						
Capital and reserves attributable to equity holders of the parent						
Share capital		246	246	246	266	280
Share issue premium		442	644	2,707	2,458	2,272
Treasury shares, at cost		(1,881)	(3,146)	(2,060)	(3,616)	(2,022)
Translation differences		341	(163)	(34)	69	(126)
Fair value and other reserves		62	23	(14)	(176)	69
Reserve for invested non-restricted equity		3,306	3,299	–	–	–
Retained earnings		11,692	13,870	11,123	13,308	13,765
		14,208	**14,773**	**11,968**	**12,309**	**14,238**
Minority interests		**2,302**	**2,565**	**92**	**205**	**168**
Total equity		**16,510**	**17,338**	**12,060**	**12,514**	**14,406**
Non-current liabilities						
Long-term interest-bearing liabilities		861	203	69	21	19
Deferred tax liabilities		1,787	963	205	151	179
Other long-term liabilities		69	119	122	96	96
		2,717	**1,285**	**396**	**268**	**294**
Current liabilities						
Current portion of long-term debt		13	173	–	–	–
Short-term borrowings		3,578	714	247	377	215
Other financial liabilities		924	184	–	–	–
Accounts payable		5,225	7,074	3,732	3,494	2,669
Accrued expenses		7,023	7,114	3,796	3,320	2,606
Provisions		3,592	3,717	2,386	2,479	2,479
		20,355	**18,976**	**10,161**	**9,670**	**7,969**
Total shareholders' equity and liabilities		**39,582**	**37,599**	**22,617**	**22,452**	**22,669**

Additional information

(in € million)	31 December				
	2008	2007	2006	2005	2004
Net profit (income statement)	3,988	7,205	4,306	3,616	3,207
Advance payments from other companies (notes)	182	7	72	121	133

In addition the annual report 2004 mentions that the amount of shareholders' equity on 31 December 2003 was equal to 15,148 millions of euros.

Required

Compute the three following ratios based on equity, as defined by the company in its annual report:

1. Return on shareholders' equity (%): (Profit attributable to the equity holders of the parent) / (average capital and reserves attributable to the company's equity holders during the year).

2. Equity ratio (%): (capital and reserves attributable to the company's equity holders plus minority shareholders' interests) / (Total assets minus advance payments received).

3. Net debt to equity (gearing ratio) (%): (Long-term interest-bearing liabilities [including the current portion thereof] plus short-term borrowings minus cash and other liquid assets)/(capital and reserves attributable to the equity holders of the parent plus minority shareholders' interests).

4. Comment on the evolution of these ratios.

References

IASB (1989) Framework for the Preparation and Presentation of Financial Statements, London.

IASB (2004) International Financial Reporting Standard No. 2: Share-based payment, London.

IASB (2007) International Accounting Standard No. 1: Presentation of Financial Statements, London.

IASB (2008) International Accounting Standard No. 32: Financial instruments: Presentation, London.

Further reading

Dhaliwal, D., Subramanyam, K R. and Trezevant, R. (1999) 'Is comprehensive income superior to net income as a measure of firm performance?' *Journal of Accounting & Economics* 26(1–3): 43–67.

Kanagaretnam, K., Mathieu, R. and Shehata, M. (2009) 'Usefulness of comprehensive income reporting in Canada', *Journal of Accounting and Public Policy* 28(4): 349–65.

Maines, L.A. and McDaniel, L.S. (2000) 'Effects of comprehensive-income characteristics on nonprofessional investors' judgments: The role of financial-statement presentation format', *The Accounting Review* 75(2): 179–207.

Additional material on the website

Go to http://www.cengage.co.uk/stolowy3 for further information, journal entries and extra assignments for each chapter.

The following appendices to this chapter are available on the dedicated website:

Appendix 11.1: Different categories of reserves

Appendix 11.2: Differences in the meaning of retained earnings

Appendix 11.3: Unrestricted and restricted reserves

Appendix 11.4: Share (stock) split

Appendix 11.5: Reduction of the share capital due to accumulated losses

Appendix 11.6: Share dividends in North America

Appendix 11.7: Reporting comprehensive income

Notes

1. 'A limited share partnership (LSP) is a business whose share capital is divided into shares, but with two types of partners: several limited partners with the status of shareholders, whose liability is limited to the amount of their investment in the company; and one or more general partners (they are usually senior managers of the LSP), who are jointly and severally liable, to an unlimited extent, for the debts of the company. A limited share partnership introduces a complete separation between management and financial ownership of the company'. Source: http://www.vernimmen.com/html/glossary/definition_limited_share_partnerships_lsp.html.

2. A *cumulative* dividend means that if there are not enough earnings to pay out the guaranteed dividend during one period, the dividends in arrears (i.e., that were not paid) will be carried over to the next period and paid in priority before any other dividend can be paid out.

3. Stichting = Foundation (in Dutch).

4. Exceptions can be found where, to encourage stability of ownership, shares held for a number of years receive a larger voting right. For example, Michelin's 2008 annual report states that: 'All shares issued are fully paid and registered. Shares held for more than four years have a double voting right'.

5. The date of record is a cut-off: investors who acquired shares beyond this date do not receive dividends emanating from earnings relating to the period(s) during which they were not actually shareholders.

6. All amounts of earnings retained under the heading 'retained earnings' remain distributable at the initiative of shareholders at a later date.

7. This topic has been introduced in Chapter 2.

8. The concept of 'stock split' (or 'share split') is developed in Appendix 11.4.

9. A special case of such a situation may arise when the firm cannot, through its innovation and growth, guarantee to the shareholders a level of return on investment that is coherent with the risk level they are exposed to. Financial markets often see a massive repurchase of shares, for cancellation purposes, as a sign that the firm has run out, at least for the time being, of ideas and opportunities for growing its future earnings and cash flows.

10. Borrowing the funds, exercising the option, reselling all or enough shares to reimburse the loan in full may all be done in a 24 to 48 hour window.

11. Although in reality, the calculations would be more complex because the number of shares each individual shareholder would receive might include partial shares, we ignore such complexity at this stage.

12. Accumulated other comprehensive income.

C12

Chapter 12
Liabilities and Provisions

Learning objectives

After studying this chapter, you will understand:

- How to define a liability.
- How liabilities are usually classified and reported in the balance sheet.
- How to record current and non-current liabilities.
- How to distinguish between liabilities, accrued liabilities, provisions and contingent liabilities.
- How to record bonds issue.
- That the distinction between finance and operating leases is important.
- How to record and report leased assets.
- How to record employee benefits.
- How to analyze liabilities.

Liabilities (in a broad sense) are one of the major components of the balance sheet. IAS 37 (IASB 1998b: § 10) distinguishes:

- liabilities (in a strict sense), i.e., debts with a defined face amount and a specified timing for interest payments and reimbursement of the principal;
- provisions: liabilities of uncertain timing or amount.

In the rest of this chapter we will apply this distinction: liabilities (in a strict sense) and **provisions.**

Liabilities represent, beside shareholders' equity, the other source of funding for any business through either direct contribution of cash (such as in the case of a loan) or postponement of cash outlays (such as in the case of suppliers' credit). A **liability** is the result of a business' past transactions that recognizes an **obligation** to transfer, in the future and for the benefit of 'liability holders' (for example, lenders), some of the business' resources such as assets – and particularly cash – or provide services.

The liability funds providers can be persons or organizations whose main activity is to provide funds, such as bond holders – private or institutional – or financial institutions such as banks or insurance firms. Funds providers can also be business 'partners' such as customers (who prepay for services, as would be the case, for example, of a subscription to a magazine), suppliers (accounts payable), tax or para-fiscal authorities (such as a social security authority, for example), or even salaried employees (who get paid, or receive a bonus, after they have provided the work and thus are owed their salary or bonus until payday, thus providing some cash float to the business). The same issues that applied to assets apply to liabilities, namely issues of:

- definition (what constitutes a liability);
- recognition (when to recognize the obligation);
- valuation (what is the amount of the obligation); and
- classification in reporting.

The principles of liabilities reporting, as well as the handling of provisions and equivalent, will be addressed in sections 1, 3 and 5, while a certain number of special issues including those created by bonds and 'quasi-liabilities', like **leases**, will be dealt with in sections 7 and 8 of this chapter.

A liability reflects an obligation to pay or deliver in the future. However, the definition of what an obligation is, how definitive it is, or its amount, are difficult points the IASB has attempted to clarify. Liabilities or obligations are generally divided between current and non-current. The weight of these obligations in the financing of a business as well as the mix of current and non-current liabilities varies from business to business and between industrial or service sectors.

1 Definitions

IAS 37 (§ 10) defines a liability as [a] 'a present obligation of the entity arising from [b] past events, [c] the settlement of which is expected to result in an outflow from the entity of resources embodying economic benefits'. In this definition, several concepts are important. Each will be reviewed in turn.

1.1 Present obligation

The IASB Framework (IASB 1989: § 60) specifies that an 'essential characteristic of a liability is that the entity has a present obligation'. The concept of obligation is then defined as: 'A duty or responsibility to act or perform in a certain way. Obligations may be legally enforceable as a consequence of a binding contract or statutory requirement. This is normally the case, for example, with amounts payable for goods and services received. Obligations also arise, however, from normal business practice, custom and a desire to maintain good business relations or act in an equitable manner. If, for example, an entity decides as a matter of policy to rectify faults in its products even when these become apparent after the warranty period has expired, the amounts that are expected to be expensed in respect to goods already sold are liabilities.'

1.2 Past events

'Liabilities result from past transactions or other past events. Thus, for example, the acquisition of goods and the use of services give rise to trade payables (unless paid for in advance or on delivery) and the receipt of a bank loan results in an obligation to repay the loan. An entity may also recognize future rebates based on [accumulated] annual purchases by customers (*ex post* quantity discount) as liabilities; in this case, the sale of the goods in the past was the transaction that gave rise to the liability' (IASB 1989: § 63).

1.3 Settlement of the obligation

'The settlement of a present obligation usually involves the entity giving up resources embodying economic benefits in order to satisfy the claim of the other party'. This settlement 'may occur in a number of ways, for example, by: (a) payment of cash; (b) transfer of other assets; (c) provision of services; (d) replacement of that obligation with another obligation; or (e) conversion of the obligation to equity [see Chapter 11]. An obligation may also be extinguished by other means, such as a creditor waiving or forfeiting its rights' (IASB 1989: § 62).

1.4 The current/non-current distinction

As seen in Chapter 5, IAS 1 (IASB 2007: § 60) states: 'an entity shall present (...) current and non-current liabilities (...) except when a presentation based on liquidity provides information that is reliable and is more relevant. When that exception applies, all assets and liabilities shall be presented broadly in order of liquidity'. In practice, businesses are relatively free to choose the format used to report liabilities as separate classifications on the balance sheet. Alternative acceptable classifications to the current/non-current classification include order of maturity [called 'liquidity' in IAS 1] (short-term versus long-term) and distinguishing interest-bearing liabilities from non-interest-bearing ones (and possibly ranking liabilities by order of maturity within each category). Reporting of liabilities is aimed at informing investors, partners and analysts. Any classification is a choice reflecting an emphasis on a given focus. For example, the distinction financial versus operating (❶ in Figure 12.1) emphasizes the operating cycle, while the distinction short-term versus long-term (❷ in Figure 12.1) refers to a preoccupation with solvency.

IAS 1 (IASB 2007) specifies (§ 69) that: 'a **liability** shall be classified as **current** when it satisfies any of the following criteria:

(a) it is expected to be settled in the entity's normal operating cycle;

(b) it is held primarily for the purpose of being traded;

(c) it is due to be settled within twelve months after the reporting period; or

(d) the entity does not have an unconditional right to defer settlement of the liability for at least twelve months after the reporting period.

An entity shall classify all other liabilities as non-current'.

IAS 1 does not provide a definition of the presentation 'by liquidity' described as an exception in § 60. It simply mentions that this presentation could be used 'for some entities, such as financial institutions (...) because the entity does not supply goods or services within a clearly identifiable operating cycle' (§ 63). Consequently, we will not explore the by-liquidity classification and will concentrate on the common rule, the 'current/non-current' distinction.

If we concentrate on the four alternative definitions provided in IAS 1 (§ 69), two main alternative criteria emerge (see Chapter 5):

■ the realization/settlement in the operating cycle: we call this classification 'by nature' (financial liabilities versus operating liabilities) (point (a) in § 69); or

■ the realization/settlement within twelve months after the reporting period: we call this second classification 'by term' (short-term versus long-term) (point (b) in § 69).

Figure 12.1 summarizes the two classifications of liabilities. It shows that the distinction 'current' and 'non-current' is ambiguous as the same terms are used to refer either to the operating versus financial classification or to the short-term versus long-term distinction. This makes the understanding of the liabilities side of the balance sheet more difficult and it is necessary to study the detail of the captions to know which classification is actually used behind the terms 'current' and 'non-current' (this topic was covered in detail in Chapter 5).

The concept of 'operating cycle' was introduced in Chapter 2. 'Some current liabilities, such as trade payables and some accruals for employee and other operating costs, are part of the working capital used in the entity's normal operating cycle. An entity classifies such operating items as current liabilities even if they are due to be settled more than twelve months after the reporting period' (IASB 2007: § 70). This paragraph is rather ambiguous. It should be understood that liabilities such as trade payables can be classified as 'current' (in the sense of IAS 1), i.e., 'operating', even if their term exceeds 12 months. This rule applies if the entity has decided to adopt the 'operating versus financial' classification. Otherwise, a long-term trade payable should remain in long-term liabilities, if the classification 'by term' is used.

Concerning disclosure, IAS 1 (§ 61) adds that 'whichever method of presentation is adopted, an entity shall disclose the amount expected to be recovered or settled after more than twelve months for each asset and liability line item that combines amounts expected to be recovered or settled: (a) not more than twelve months after the reporting period, and (b) more than twelve months after the reporting period'. In practice, this paragraph means that if the operating versus financial distinction is adopted, some liabilities might mix short-term and long-term portions. In that case, the long-term part should be disclosed explicitly in the notes.

Figure 12.1 Classification of liabilities

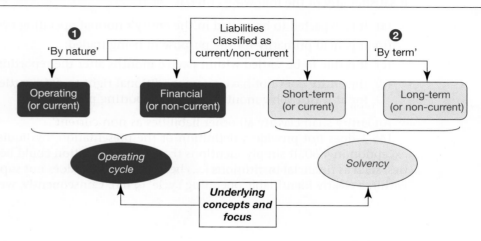

Real-life example Sandvik

(Sweden – IFRS – Source: Annual report 2008 – Engineering in tooling and materials technology)

Consolidated balance sheet (excerpts)		
in Swedish Krona (SEK) million	2008	2007
EQUITY AND LIABILITIES		
Equity		
Share capital	1,424	1,424
Other paid-in capital	1,057	1,057
Reserves	4,651	368
Retained earnings including profit for the year	28,456	25,765
Equity attributable to equity holders of the parent	35,588	28,614
Minority interest	1,137	1,209
TOTAL EQUITY	36,725	29,823
Non-current liabilities		
Interest-bearing liabilities		
Provisions for pensions	2,735	3,100
Loans from financial institutions	4,691	2,682
Other liabilities	17,888	15,695
Total	25,314	21,477
Non-interest-bearing liabilities		
Deferred tax liabilities	1,514	1,786
Provisions for taxes	3,201	2,760
Other provisions	806	701
Other liabilities	398	129
Total	5,919	5,376
Total non-current liabilities	31,233	26,853
Current liabilities		
Interest-bearing liabilities		
Loans from financial institutions	11,324	9,158
Other liabilities	3,225	1,311
Total	14,549	10,469
Non-interest-bearing liabilities		
Advance payments from customers	2,368	1,795
Accounts payable	7,000	6,777
Due to associated companies	80	103
Income tax liabilities	1,301	1,334
Other liabilities	3,312	2,168
Provisions	734	569
Accrued expenses and deferred income	5,925	5,544
Total	20,720	18,290
Total current liabilities	35,269	28,759
TOTAL LIABILITIES	66,502	55,612
TOTAL EQUITY AND LIABILITIES	103,227	85,435

Comment: This excerpt of the Sandvik balance sheet illustrates a presentation of liabilities first according to their non-current versus current nature (i.e., by term) and second, within the first category, according to the interest-bearing and non-interest-bearing distinction.

Real-life example Sony Corporation

(Japan – Japanese/US GAAP – Source: Annual report 2009 – Electronics, games, music, motion pictures)

Consolidated balance sheet (excerpts)		
(in Yen million)	2008	2009
LIABILITIES AND STOCKHOLDERS' EQUITY		
Current liabilities		
Short-term borrowings	63,224	303,615
Current portion of long-term debt	291,879	147,540
Notes and accounts payable, trade	920,920	560,795
Accounts payable, other and accrued expenses	896,598	1,036,830
Accrued income and other taxes	200,803	46,683
Deposits from customers in the banking business	1,144,399	1,326,360
Other	505,544	389,077
Total current liabilities	4,023,367	3,810,900
Long-term liabilities		
Long-term debt	729,059	660,147
Accrued pension and severance costs	231,237	365,706
Deferred income taxes	268,600	188,359
Future insurance policy benefits and other	3,298,506	3,521,060
Other	260,032	250,737
Total long-term liabilities	4,787,434	4,986,009
Total liabilities	**8,810,801**	**8,796,909**

Comment: This excerpt of the balance sheet of this company illustrates the classification presenting liabilities in a decreasing order of maturity (short-term [called here 'current'] vs. long-term).

2 Relative weight of liabilities in the balance sheet

Between businesses, countries, and even between firms in the same economic sector, liabilities (and provisions) represent different weights in the balance sheet. Such diversity is illustrated in Table 12.1 based on 2008 and 2009 annual reports of a not statistically significant sample of companies.

When looking at a single economic sector, it is interesting to notice that not all business entities have similar approaches to trade indebtedness (short-term liabilities), even if they operate essentially in similar markets, and often with the same suppliers. Table 12.2 illustrates the percentage that trade creditors represent out of retail inventory in 11, essentially UK-based, supermarkets or drugstore chains (Plender *et al.*, *Financial Times*, 7 December, 2005, page 13).

From Table 12.2 it is clear that, even if all other aspects were identical, the profitability of the various chains will be very different because they neither use trade credit in the same way, nor manage to have the same inventory turnover (see Chapter 9).

The recourse to liabilities as a source of funding for a business is a very strategic decision. It is therefore essential for the users of financial information to be well informed about what the situation of the firm is.

Table 12.1 Weight of liabilities in the balance sheet

Company (country – activity)	Currency	Types of liabilities	Liabilities	Total equity and liabilities	% of total equity and liabilities
United Internet (Germany – Internet provider)	€000	Current liabilities	399,799		36.28
		Non-current liabilities	556,618		50.51
		Total	956,417	1,101,997	**86.79**
Sony (Japan – Music)	¥m	Current liabilities	3,810,900		31.72
		Long-term liabilities	4,986,009		41.50
		Total	8,796,909	12,013,511	**73.23**
Iberia (Spain – Airline)	€m	Non-current liabilities	1,765		31.33
		Current liabilities	2,305		40.91
		Total	4,070	5,634	**72.24**
Weyerhaeuser (USA – Building materials)	$m	Current liabilities	1,812		10.83
		Long-term debt	5,153		30.79
		Deferred income taxes	1,805		10.79
		Deferred pension and other liabilities	1,538		9.19
		Liabilities held by special purpose entities	764		4.57
		Real estate	849		5.07
		Total	11,921	16,735	**71.23**
Morton's Restaurant (USA – Restaurants)	$000	Current liabilities	59,673		24.30
		Borrowings under senior revolving credit facility	60,800		24.76
		Obligation to financial institutions, less current maturities	3,057		1.24
		Deferred income taxes	–		–
		Joint venture loan payable	2,794		1.14
		Other liabilities	36,138		14.72
		Total	162,462	245,567	**66.16**
ArcelorMittal (Luxembourg – Steel)	$m	Current liabilities	30,760		23.11
		Non-current liabilities	43,098		32.38
		Total	73,858	133,088	**55.50**
Sinopec (China – Oil and chemistry)	RMBm	Current liabilities	274,537		35.76
		Non-current liabilities	143,968		18.75
		Total	418,505	767,827	**54.51**
Fielmann (Germany – Glasses)	€000	Long-term provisions	7,310		
		Long-term financial liabilities	5,086		
		Deferred tax liabilities	7,662		
		Short-term provisions	43,730		
		Short-term financial liabilities	3,412		
		Trade creditors and other liabilities	75,230		
		Tax liabilities	44,013		
		Total	186,443	654,729	**28.48**
Mountain Province Diamonds (Canada – Mining)	$CA	Current liabilities	191,711		0.29
		Non-current liabilities	5,686,567		8.67
		Total	5,878,278	65,559,595	**8.97**

Table 12.2 Relative weight of trade creditors as a percentage of retail inventories

	2000	2001	2002	2003	2004
Wm Morrison	288	301	362	343	264
J Sainsbury	167	194	187	165	255
Tesco	189	201	196	203	216
Tesco UK	200	202	199	219	n/a
Asda (Wal-Mart UK)	163	196	209	262	206
Wal-Mart Group	71	69	69	72.5	74
Alliance Unichem	138	148	149	159	163
John Lewis Partnership	89.5	95.5	88	72.5	88.5
Waitrose	n/a	169	153	128	150
Marks and Spencer	44	61.5	55.5	53	57.5
Boots	56	57	59	58.5	51

3 Non-current (long-term or financial) liabilities

Figure 12.2 illustrates the fact that businesses have both non-current (long-term or financial liabilities, depending on the presentation adopted) and current liabilities (short-term or operating). The operating cycle (the cash pump introduced in Chapter 1) requires that the entity's financial needs be met not only by short-term (or current or operating) liabilities but also by long-term resources. If the current liabilities were to dry-up (for example if the suppliers were to refuse any trade credit, as was the case during the market bust of October 2008), the long-term resources offer a safe financing, giving the business the opportunity to continue operating its cash pump and thus have a chance to 'get back on its feet'.

A business' financing needs come essentially from a combination of three factors:

■ Growth: in order to grow, a business must invest in both long-term fixed assets (tangible or intangible) and in operating assets.

■ The operating cycle: inventories, receivables and payables will generally grow with the expansion of the business activity unless the speed (turnover) of the operating cycle can be increased faster than the rate expansion (which is a highly improbable occurrence). Because the need for operating assets is recurrent, a large part of the growth in these items should be financed through long-term (permanent or semi-permanent) funds.

Figure 12.2 Financing of a business is met by both short-term and long-term resources

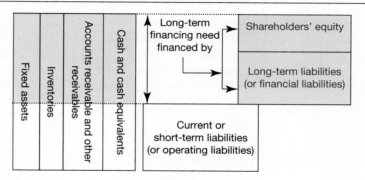

■ Temporary imbalances in the equilibrium between the various components of the operating cycle (for example due to a strong seasonality factor). Although such imbalances are generally short lived and self-correcting, they tend to reoccur on a regular basis and often require long-term funding as a way of avoiding the transaction costs that would be incurred in securing appropriate short-term funding each time the problem occurs.

The long-term financing need (Figure 12.2) is equal to: Fixed assets + Current assets − Current liabilities. It is satisfied (or covered) by two sources of funds:

■ shareholders' equity (see Chapter 11);

■ long-term (or financial) liabilities (developed later).

The relative interest of funding through shareholders' equity or long-term liabilities is an issue constantly debated in all businesses. The leverage effect[1] it creates is generally a major topic in corporate finance or financial statement analysis textbooks.[2] Table 12.3 summarizes some of the key issues looked at when choosing whether to go the equity or the liability route.

Long-term liabilities are generally divided between two categories:

■ **Loans or borrowings**: Each loan represents a lump sum liability, generally from a single source.

Table 12.3 Comparative characteristics of liabilities and shareholders' equity

Characteristic	Liabilities	Shareholders' equity
Repayment term	Repayment of principal is required	No repayment required
Flexibility	Highly flexible (duration, amount, ease of obtaining additional funds, possibility to refinance, etc.)	Not flexible and high transaction costs. Decision is not reversible
Cost of funds	Interest must be paid regardless of the economic outcome of the use of the funds. Rates are market based	No direct required remuneration. Dividends paid only if there is enough net income or accumulated previously undistributed income. Part of the remuneration may come from a market appreciation of the shares. Given shareholders are taking risks with their investment, their implicit remuneration is generally expected to be much higher than the cost of borrowed funds
Deductibility of the cost of funds	Interest expense is generally tax-deductible	Regular dividends are never tax-deductible.
Rights of the funds-providers	Debt-holders generally have no influence or control over the decisions or the management of the firm	Shareholders generally have influence and control over decisions and management
	New debt holders affect previous debt holders only because the interest expense of the new liability may overburden the earnings and increase the likelihood of bankruptcy	Additional shareholders may cause a dilution of the power of current shareholders
Use of funds	Funds obtained and specific projects may be linked explicitly (for example through specific securing or guarantee agreements such as in mortgages)	Funds obtained cannot be targeted to a specific project

■ **Bonds**: In this case, the debt is broken-up into small (generally equal) increments represented by certificates. The holder of a debt certificate (**bond**) can trade it on a financial market. Each certificate has a face value (or par value), a specific coupon rate (interest rate) that specifies the periodic interest paid to the bond bearer, and a mention of the date by which the principal must be repaid (and under what condition it will be repaid – such as either at the end of the specified life of the bond, or mentioning the possibility of an early retirement of the debt at the initiative of the borrower).

The specificities of accounting for bonds will be dealt with in section 7. Loans or borrowings can take on many different forms depending on whether or not they are secured. For example, a mortgage liability is a debt secured by real property.

4 Accounting for current liabilities

Current liabilities are liabilities that relate to the operating cycle or that will be settled within twelve months after the balance date. They include **accounts payable**, **notes payable**, employee benefits payable (which will be dealt with in section 9), income taxes payable, sales or value added taxes payable, and the current portion of long-term liabilities.

4.1 Accounts payable

An 'account payable' (or 'trade payable') represents the obligation of a business to a creditor (generally a supplier or vendor) usually arising from the purchase of goods and services on credit. Most businesses around the world show their accounts payable (the sum of all individual accounts payable) as a separate line item under current liabilities on their balance sheet.

Figure 12.3 illustrates the accounts payable mechanism. Larsson Company, a video equipment manufacturer, acquires electronic components, on credit, from Gynt AB. The components will be kept in inventory for a few days before being consumed in the manufacturing process. The purchase of these components amounts to 100 CU. It will be settled in two installments: a first payment of 90 CU after 30 days and the balance after 45 days (which will fall in period X2, and thus is not relevant for this entry). Figure 12.3 illustrates both the acquisition ❶ and the first payment ❷.

Figure 12.3 Accounts payable

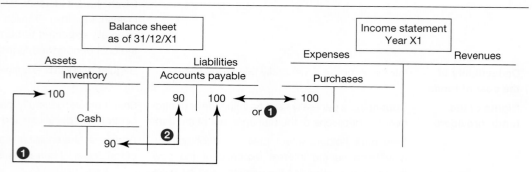

The transaction recorded as ❶ happens on the date of the purchase. It either involves incrementing the inventory if the cost of part of merchandise consumed is calculated by accumulating the requisitions for withdrawals from inventory (see Chapters 2 and 9, 'Method 1') or recognizing the transaction as a purchase (i.e., in traditional financial accounting that assumes all purchases are presumed consumed and the cost of materials consumed is obtained by deducting the net increase/decrease in inventory between 2 physical inventories) ('Method 2').

Entry ❷, recorded on the date of the first settlement, accounts for the first payment.

4.2 Notes payable

Chapter 10 introduced 'notes receivable' (bills of exchange and promissory notes) in the accounts of the seller. Notes payable are the equivalent items in the buyer's books. Figure 10.8 and the developments of Appendices 10.3 and 10.4 (Chapter 10) are applicable without complexity (as a mirror image) to notes payable.

When notes are payable within the next 12 months, they are shown in the balance sheet as current liabilities. Otherwise, they are reported as long-term liabilities (if a presentation by maturity term is adopted). An illustration of the recording of notes payable is given in Appendix 12.1.

4.3 Income taxes payable

The recording of income taxes has been presented in Chapter 6.

4.4 Sales tax and value added tax (VAT) collected

The topic value-added taxes (VAT) or sales-taxes collected is introduced and developed in Appendix 10.2 (Chapter 10). VAT and sales tax collected follow similar mechanisms. When sellers (whether retailers or enterprises involved in business to business activities) collect VAT or sales taxes, they are agents of the state or local government. Appendix 12.2 illustrates the sales tax payable accounting entries.

4.5 Current portion of long-term debt

If a business has decided to report long-term and short-term debts as separate items in the liabilities section of the balance sheet, the part of long-term debts that becomes due within a year from the closing of the books (20 CU in the example below) should be reclassified as part of current liabilities. The required entry, as displayed in Figure 12.4, is recorded when preparing the financial statements.

5 Reporting liabilities

The degree of detail provided by any firm in reporting their liabilities in both the balance sheet and the notes will assist (or hinder) the ability of the analyst or of the investor to understand the financial position of the firm, the potential dynamics of its evolution and the risks they are taking.

Figure 12.4 Transfer to current liabilities of the current portion of long-term liabilities

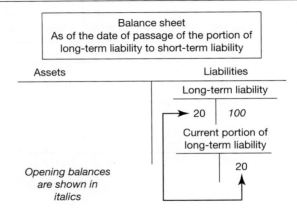

5.1 No separation between short-term and long-term liabilities on the balance sheet

When the balance sheet is presented along the distinction operating versus financial liabilities, it does not separate short-term and long-term liabilities. In that case, the annual report often provides, in the notes to the statements, a fairly detailed table listing the liabilities by date of maturity. Such a disclosure is essential since the liabilities are not structured by relative maturity dates in the balance sheet.

Real-life example Fiat

(Italy – IFRS – Source: Annual report 2008 – Car manufacturer)

(in € million)	31 December 2008	31 December 2007
SHAREHOLDERS' EQUITY AND LIABILITIES		
Shareholders' equity:	11,101	11,279
– Shareholders' equity of the Group	10,354	10,606
– Minority interest	747	673
Provisions:	8,144	8,562
– Employee benefits	3,366	3,597
– Other provisions	4,778	4,965
Debt:	21,379	17,951
– Asset-backed financing	6,663	6,820
– Other debt	14,716	11,131
Other financial liabilities	1,202	188
Trade payables	13,258	14,725
Current tax payables	331	631
Deferred tax liabilities	170	193
Other current liabilities	6,185	6,572
Liabilities held for sale	2	35
TOTAL SHAREHOLDERS' EQUITY AND LIABILITIES	61,772	60,136

The liabilities are presented by nature (i.e., separating the operating liabilities (trade accounts payable, other liabilities) from financial ones). Note 27 to the financial statements discloses the detail of liabilities by degree of maturity.

	At 31 December 2008				At 31 December 2007			
(in € million)	Due within one year	Due between one and five years	Due beyond five years	Total	Due within one year	Due between one and five years	Due beyond five years	Total
Asset-backed financing	4,647	1,845	171	6,663	4,070	2,707	43	6,820
Bonds	785	4,642	1,609	7,036	431	4,101	2,534	7,066
Borrowings from banks	3,250	2,953	163	6,366	1,559	993	170	2,722
Payables represented by securities	94	16	–	110	149	14	–	163
Other	793	162	249	1,204	809	155	216	1,180
Total Other debt	4,922	7,773	2,021	14,716	2,948	5,263	2,920	11,131
Total Debt	9,569	9,618	2,192	21,379	7,018	7,970	2,963	17,951

5.2 Short-term and long-term liabilities reported separately on the balance sheet

The most common situation is to report liabilities separately by showing the short-term liabilities distinctly from the long-term liabilities with the expression 'long-term' meaning a date of maturity of more than one year. A typical example is provided by the ArcelorMittal annual report.

Real-life example ArcelorMittal

(Luxembourg – IFRS – Source: Annual report 2008 – Steel)

This company discloses in its balance sheet the following categories of liabilities, in increasing order of maturity date:

- Short-term debt
- Other short-term liabilities (trade accounts payable, accrued expenses, income tax liabilities, liabilities held for sale)
- Short-term provisions
- Long-term debt
- Other long-term liabilities (deferred tax liabilities, deferred employee benefits)
- Long-term provisions.

Notes to the financial statements provide some information on these categories. As an example, we show below notes 14 and 21, which provide more information about two categories of liabilities in ArcelorMittal's balance sheet.

Note 14: Short-term debt

| | 31 December | |
(in US$ million)	2007	2008
Short-term bank loans and other credit facilities	3,653	4,564
Current portion of long-term debt	4,832	3,777
Revaluation of interest rate hedge instruments	–	3
Current portion of lease obligations	57	65
Total	**8,542**	**8,409**

Note 21: Accrued expenses and other liabilities

| | 31 December | |
(in US$ million)	2007	2008
Accrued payroll and employee related expenses	2,008	1,949
Other payables	1,703	1,942
Other creditors	1,535	1,320
Revaluation of derivative instruments	549	1,094
Other amounts due to public authorities	909	791
Unearned revenue and accrued payables	571	317
Total	**7,275**	**7,413**

6 Liabilities, provisions and contingent liabilities

Quasi-liabilities often render 'liabilities' reporting complex. Liabilities are the materialization of a future obligation. However, the reality and immediacy of that obligation may be subject to debate. Quasi-liabilities are obligations for which either the triggering event may not come from a transaction with a third party, or the timing of the obligation may not be clear, or the amount may not be well defined, or any combination of the three. Liabilities (in the broad sense) include:

- liabilities (strict sense)
- provisions
- accrued liabilities
- contingent liabilities.

Figure 12.5 illustrates the distinguishing characteristics of each and summarizes the differences on the basis of the certainty of three characteristics of the obligation they represent: principle creating the obligation (causality), timing, and valuation or amount of the obligation.

6.1 Provision versus liability (in the strict sense of the word)

A provision is an obligation that could eventually be reversed because some degree of estimation is involved in its amount and timing (Figure 12.5). It represents an obligation whose object is real although potential, the amount of which cannot easily be determined with precision at the time. A liability (in the strict sense of the word), however, is generally irreversible. Both its timing and principal amount are known with certainty, and can only be settled according to the terms of the contract or event that created it.

The IASB Framework (IASB 1989: § 64) explains that: 'Some liabilities can be measured only by using a substantial degree of estimation. Some entities describe these liabilities as provisions. In some countries, such provisions are not regarded as liabilities because the concept of a liability is defined narrowly so as to include only amounts that can be established without

Figure 12.5 Liabilities and related concepts

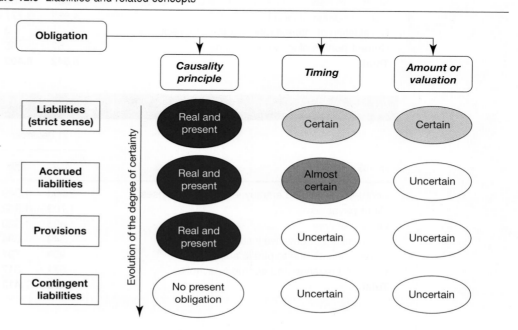

the need to make estimates.' The IASB definition of a liability favors the broader approach. Thus, according to the IASB, 'when a provision involves a real and present obligation and satisfies the rest of the definition, it is a liability even if the amount has to be estimated' (Conceptual Framework: § 64). Examples include provisions for payments to be made under existing warranties provided to customers and provisions to cover pension obligations.

For IASB (IAS 37: § 10), a provision is 'a liability of uncertain timing or amount'. A provision shall therefore be recognized 'when:

(a) an entity has a present[3] obligation (legal or constructive) as a result of a past event;

(b) it is probable that an outflow of resources embodying economic benefits will be required to settle the obligation; and

(c) a reliable estimate can be made of the amount of the obligation.

If these conditions are not met, no provision shall be recognized' (§ 14).

The debate about what does or does not constitute a provision is extremely important to understand. particularly when studying a company's reported performance. According to IAS 37 (§ 16), 'in almost all cases it will be clear whether a past event has given rise to a present obligation. In rare cases, for example in a law-suit, it may be disputed either whether certain events have occurred or whether those events result in a present obligation. In such a case, an entity determines whether a present obligation exists at the end of the reporting period by taking account of all available evidence, including, for example, the opinion of experts. The evidence considered includes any additional evidence provided by events after the reporting period. On the basis of such evidence:

(a) where it is more likely than not that a present obligation exists at the end of the reporting period, the entity recognizes a provision (if the recognition criteria are met); and

(b) where it is more likely that no present obligation exists at the end of the reporting period, the entity discloses a **contingent liability**, unless the possibility of an outflow of resources embodying economic benefits is remote (…).'

A 'provision for restructuring' is quite frequently found in annual reports. IAS 37 (§ 70) states: 'The following are examples of events that may fall under the definition of restructuring:

■ sale or termination of a line of business;

■ closure of business locations in a country or region or the relocation of business activities from one country or region to another;

■ changes in management structure, for example, eliminating a layer of management;

■ fundamental reorganizations that have a material effect on the nature and focus of the entity's operations.'

IASB has adopted a very strict position when it comes to provisions for restructuring. IAS 37 (§ 71) adds: 'A provision for restructuring costs is recognized only when the general recognition criteria for provisions set out in paragraph 14 are met'. Some detailed conditions are then defined (§ 72): 'A constructive obligation to restructure arises only when an entity:

(a) Has a detailed formal plan for the restructuring identifying at least:

(i) the business or part of a business concerned;

(ii) the principal locations affected;

(iii) the location, function, and approximate number of employees who will be compensated for terminating their services;

(iv) the expenditures that will be undertaken; and

(v) when the plan will be implemented; and

(b) Has raised a valid expectation in those affected that it will carry out the restructuring by starting to implement that plan or announcing its main features to those affected by it.'

The restructuring provision amount shall be calculated so as to reflect estimates of 'only the direct expenditures arising from the restructuring, which are those that are both (a) necessarily entailed by the restructuring; and (b) not associated with the ongoing activities of the entity' (IAS 37: § 80).

Because estimates of future costs are often difficult to establish objectively, many managers have long used 'provisions for restructuring' as a preferred tool of earnings

Real-life example ISS – International Service System

(Denmark – IFRS – Source: Annual report 2008 – Support services)

The consolidated balance sheet and notes include the following elements.

Consolidated balance sheet (excerpts)

in Danish Krone (DKK) million	As at 31.12. 2008	2007
Pensions and similar obligations	834	724
Deferred tax liabilities	2,498	2,786
Other provisions	397	326
Total long-term provisions	**3,729**	**3,836**
Other short-term provisions	435	327
Total provisions	**4,164**	**4,163**

Note 29 to the consolidated financial statements: Other provisions

(in DKK million) (2008)	Labor-related items	Self-insurance	Acquisition and integration costs	Contingent liabilities in acquisitions	Other	**Total**
Other provisions at 1 January	86	167	41	14	345	**653**
Foreign exchange adjustments	(3)	(17)	(3)	–	(13)	**(36)**
Transfers, net	2	8	(1)	–	8	**17**
Additions from acquired companies	23	–	–	31	68	**122**
Provisions for the year (included in goodwill)	–	–	68	–	–	**68**
Provisions for the year (included in the income statement)	37	103	66	–	199	**405**
Provisions for the year (dismantling costs)	–	–	–	–	30	**30**
Provisions reversed (against the income statement)	(23)	(18)	(1)	–	(42)	**(84)**
Provisions used during the year	(30)	(77)	(125)	–	(112)	**(344)**
Unwind of discount	–	–	–	–	1	**1**
Other provisions at 31 December	**92**	**166**	**45**	**45**	**484**	**832**
Current	68	70	43	13	241	**435**
Non-current	24	96	2	32	243	**397**
	92	**166**	**45**	**45**	**484**	**832**

Pensions and similar obligations, also called provision for pensions or pension liability, are developed later in section 9.

'**Deferred taxes**' were introduced in Chapter 6.

The details of '**Other provisions**' are provided in Note 29 to the consolidated financial statements (435 and 397 DKK million).

Labor-related items The provision mainly relates to obligations in Belgium, France, the Netherlands and Spain.

Self-insurance In Australia, Ireland, the USA and the United Kingdom, the group carries an insurance provision on employers' liability. Ireland and the United Kingdom are self-insured up to a yearly limit of DKK 18 million (…) for employers' liability. The USA is self-insured up to a limit of DKK 1.3 million per claim. Australia is self-insured up to a limit of DKK 1.8 million per claim. ISS Corporate has taken out a group third party liability insurance program. The ISS captive insurance company Global Insurance A/S carries part of the risk on the third party liability program with a maximum annual limit of DKK 42 million (…).

Acquisitions The provision includes obligations incurred in the normal course of acquisitions mainly related to transaction costs, redundancy payments, and [costs of] termination of [leases on] rental of properties.

Other: The provision comprises various obligations incurred in the normal course of business e.g. costs related to changes in local working and social regulations etc., provision for dismantling costs, operational issues, closure of contracts and legal cases.

Comment: As the effect of time value of money (see Appendix 12.3) is not considered to be material, provisions are not discounted.

management or income smoothing. An overestimation of the amount of the provision (for example, decided by a newly appointed management team) offers the possibility of improving future earnings when the actual expense reveals itself to be lower than anticipated (i.e., lower than had been provisioned) since the excess provision will be reversed and added to the income of the following period.

Movements in the provision accounts are generally reported in the notes to the financial statements. Since the appropriate reporting is similar to that of accounts receivable variations as described in Chapter 10, this topic will not be developed further.

6.2 Provision versus accrued liabilities

Accrued liabilities are the results of both the accrual process and the time lag between an event and its complete resolution in the course of the cycle of operations. IAS 37 states (§ 11): 'Provisions can be distinguished from other liabilities such as trade payables and accruals because there is uncertainty about the timing or amount of the future expenditure required in settlement. By contrast:

(a) Trade payables are liabilities to pay for goods or services that have been received or supplied and have been invoiced or formally agreed with the supplier; and

(b) Accruals are liabilities to pay for goods or services that have been received or supplied but have not been paid, invoiced or formally agreed with the supplier, including amounts due to employees (for example, amounts relating to accrued vacation pay). Although it is sometimes necessary to estimate the amount or timing of accruals, the uncertainty is generally much less than for provisions.

Accruals are often reported as part of trade and other payables, whereas provisions are reported separately.'

Accrued liabilities are usually recorded as part of the end-of-period entries (Chapter 4). Many annual reports do not distinguish clearly between 'liabilities' and 'accrued liabilities' and merge them under only one category in the balance sheet. However, it is clear that such a distinction could considerably help the analyst or the investor in understanding the effect of the operating cycle on the liquidity and solvency of the firm. Notes often provide much needed details.

Real-life example Sulzer

(Switzerland – IFRS – Source: Annual report 2008 – Medical technology, mechanical applications in the oil, gas and chemical industries, pumps)

Note 26 Other current and accrued liabilities		
	31 December	
in Swiss francs (CHF) million	2008	2007
Notes payable	3.1	3.9
Social security institutions	9.9	11.5
Taxes (VAT, withholding tax)	24.2	25.3
Derivative financial instruments	43.4	6.2
Other current liabilities	129.8	124.7
Total other current liabilities	**210.4**	**171.6**
Vacation and overtime claims	34.5	37.4
Salaries, wages and bonuses	67.2	69.5
Contract-related costs	123.8	126.1
Other accrued liabilities	66.0	45.5
Total accrued liabilities	**291.5**	**278.5**
Total other current and accrued liabilities	**501.9**	**450.1**

Comment: While only the 'Total other current and accrued liabilities' is reported on the balance sheet, Sulzer discloses in the notes the details of this category of liabilities, separating the current and the accrued liabilities.

Real-life example China Eastern Airlines Corporation

(China – Hong Kong GAAP/IFRS – Source: Annual report 2008 - Airline company)

Note 33 Provisions for operating lease aircraft return condition check		
in Renminbi (RMB) 000	2008	2007
At 1 January	956,910	510,621
Additional provisions	618,555	446,289
Utilization	−41,447	−
At 31 December	1,534,018	956,910
Less: current portion	−213,830	−
Long-term portion	1,320,188	956,910

Provision of operating lease aircraft return condition check represents the present value of estimated costs of major return check for aircraft under operating leases as the group has the responsibility to fulfill certain return conditions under relevant leases.

Comment: China Eastern discloses the movements in accrued aircraft overhaul expenses (provisions for operating lease aircraft return condition checks). It also provides the split between long-term and short-term provisions.

6.3 Contingent liabilities

Contingent liabilities, as shown in Figure 12.6, are the liabilities for which there is uncertainty simultaneously about causation principle, timing and amount. Contingent liabilities, as their name implies, are obligations that are contingent (conditional) on events that are not entirely under the control of the firm.

IAS 37 (§ 10) defines a contingent liability as:

(a) 'A possible obligation that arises from past events and whose existence will be confirmed only by the occurrence or non-occurrence of one or more uncertain future events not wholly within the control of the entity; or

(b) A present obligation that arises from past events but is not recognized because:

    (i) it is not probable that an outflow of resources embodying economic benefits will be required to settle the obligation; or

    (ii) the amount of the obligation cannot be measured with sufficient reliability.'

6.4 Provisions versus contingent liabilities

6.4.1 Discussion

The borderline between provisions and contingent liabilities is not always clear-cut. IAS 37 (§ 12) explains that, 'in a general sense, all provisions are contingent because they are uncertain in timing or amount'. In this context, IAS 37 explains in its paragraph 13 the distinction 'between provisions and contingent liabilities:

1. Provisions are recognized as liabilities (assuming that a reliable estimate can be made) because they are present obligations and it is probable that an outflow of resources embodying economic benefits will be required to settle the obligations; and

2. Contingent liabilities are not recognized as liabilities because they are either:

    (i) possible obligations, as it has yet to be confirmed whether the entity has a present obligation that could lead to an outflow of resources embodying economic benefits; or

    (ii) present obligations that do not meet the recognition criteria in this Standard (because either it is not probable that an outflow of resources embodying economic benefits will be required to settle the obligation, or a sufficiently reliable estimate of the amount of the obligation cannot be made).'

IAS 37 does not address the recognition issue of obligations derived from 'commitments' (such as loan repayment guarantees given by a solid parent for the benefit of helping a fledgling subsidiary secure a lower cost of financing). These commitments actually and conceptually represent an obligation that meets the same criteria as a contingent liability. In fact, most businesses report commitments in the same footnote to the financial statements in which they give the details pertaining to their 'contingent liabilities'.

6.4.2 Litigation liabilities

The provisions created in anticipation of the possible worst outcome of litigation cases are often mentioned as contingent liabilities. Since litigation takes a significant amount of time to settle, creating such a provision as close as possible in time to the triggering event is coherent with the matching principle. Litigation provisions are often mentioned as part of the contingent liabilities as exemplified by the following excerpt from the Stora Enso annual statement.

Real-life example Stora Enso

(Finland – IFRS – Source: Annual report 2008 – Production of paper)

Note 30 Commitments and contingent liabilities

Contingent liabilities

Stora Enso has undertaken significant restructuring actions in recent years which have included the divestment of companies, sale of assets and mill closures. These transactions include a risk of possible environmental or other obligations whose existence will be confirmed only by the occurrence or non-occurrence of one or more uncertain future events not wholly within the control of the Group. Stora Enso is responsible for the site of the former Pateniemi sawmill in Oulu, Finland, where there is heavy ground pollution. The Group is working with the local authorities and external parties to find a solution to the problem, though in the current economic situation, it is difficult to assess the precise outcome and thus make any accurate assessment of the group's ultimate liability. Stora Enso is party to legal proceedings that arise in the ordinary course of business and which primarily involve claims arising out of commercial law. The group is also involved in administrative proceedings relating primarily to competition law. The directors do not consider that liabilities related to such proceedings before insurance recoveries, if any, are likely to be material to the group financial condition or results of operations.

Reporting precise information about a litigation or lawsuit places the business in a conundrum: if detailed quantified information is published, such as an estimate of the possible out-of-court settlement or court verdict or award, such reporting might be construed by the opposing party as an acknowledgment of responsibility. By the same token, if there is not enough information about the case and the risks involved, users of financial information might consider themselves maligned if events turn to the disadvantage of the entity (and, in turn, these users of financial information might sue the business!).

6.4.3 Contingent liability derived from discounted notes or bills of exchange

We have seen in Chapter 10 that one way to record the discount of bills of exchange and notes receivable is to cancel the account 'notes receivable'. In that case, the discount mechanism for notes creates a contingent liability if the discount is 'with recourse' (see Chapter 10). This liability is often mentioned in a footnote. The mention of such a liability is critical in the calculation of the average days' sales ratio that must take into account the notes discounted in the denominator since the final responsibility is still borne by the company in case the discounted note is not paid in the end.

However, there is no contingent liability if the firm follows the rules of IAS 39 (IASB 2008: § 20) that require the discounted notes remain in the assets of the balance sheet, with a bank debt recorded in the liabilities of the balance sheet.

Real-life example Mitsubishi Electric

(Japan – US GAAP – Source: Annual report 2009 – Electrical and electronic equipment used in home products, and commercial and industrial systems and equipment)

Note 17 Commitments and contingent liabilities

(...) It is common practice in Japan for companies, in the ordinary course of business, to receive promissory notes in settlement of trade accounts receivable and to subsequently discount such notes at banks. At 31 March 2009, certain subsidiaries were contingently liable to trade notes discounted in the amount of ¥686 million ($7,000 thousand). Discounted notes are accounted for as sales. (...)

There is no established or normalized terminology for reporting discounted notes. For example, Toray Industries, a Japanese company, discloses in its 2009 annual report the amounts of discounted notes-related contingent liabilities as 'Contingent liabilities associated with securitization[4] of receivables'.

6.4.4 Other contingent liabilities

A variety of other contingent liabilities are found in annual reports, e.g., contingent liability as loan guarantor, contingent liability to cover product warranty obligations.

6.5 Environmental liability

More and more businesses are aware that their business activity may create environmental risks. They not only explicitly manage such risk but also want to report the potential liabilities this creates (both as a signaling move to customers and other stakeholders, and for the sake of completeness of reporting to shareholders, analysts, and investors). This 'environmental liability' is presented in Appendix 12.4.

7 Bonds

7.1 Definition

In order to attract interest-bearing funds from investors, a company may issue bonds. A bond is a certificate allowing the division of a debt between large numbers of investors (bondholders), each of whom can contribute only a small amount of the debt (the face value, or the selling price if sold at a discount or with a premium). If the face value of a bond is small, it makes this lending instrument accessible to a large public and thus may be useful to raise funds from a broad spectrum of possible lenders. In the aggregate a bond issue may represent a very large amount of borrowed funds to cover all or part of the company's financing needs. The larger the bond issue, the larger the number of bonds that can be sold individually or in blocks.

The bond or certificate shows the evidence of the claim held by the bondholder. The claim is based on a lending agreement between the provider of funds who purchases the bond (bondholder or investor) and the business (the borrower or the issuer of the bond). Each bond has a par or face value, a coupon rate (interest rate) and a maturity or redemption date. Bond issuance offers businesses an alternative to bank loans. Instead of dealing with a single (or a limited pool of) financial institution(s), the business choosing to float a bond issue goes to the open financial markets (generally through financial institutions for placement) to collect funds from a variety of sources (institutional as well as private) who value the liquidity offered by the tradability of bonds.

A company that issues bonds assumes two obligations:

1. To pay investors a specified amount of cash on an agreed upon maturity date (when the bond will be redeemed) which may be either a specified and un-modifiable date or a date which can be established later at the initiative of the borrower, generally after a period during which early retirement of the bond is not allowed. The amount that will be given to the bondholder on the date of redemption is called principal, par value, face value, or maturity value.

2. To pay investors a cash interest at periodic intervals on specified dates (generally before the maturity date) at a rate of interest defined on the date of issuance (fixed rate or conditional rates linked, for example, to the evolution of the prime rate or to the market price of some commodity).

Bonds are most of the time traded on financial markets, thus providing the lender with the possibility of making their investment liquid if needed.

There are at least two basic types of bonds:

- **Term bonds** in one bond issue mature all on the same date. All the bonds are repaid *in fine*, i.e., at the end of the maturity period. For example, 500 term bonds of 1,000 CU each with a maturity date of five years from the date of issuance represent a total maturity value of 500,000 CU that will be paid on the fifth anniversary of the issuance.

- **Serial bonds** mature in predetermined installments (but the specific bonds called in a given installment are often drawn through a lottery). For example, 500 serial bonds, with a 1,000 CU face-value each, would, in this case, for example, mature at the rate of 100,000 CU per year over a five-year period.

Zero-coupon bonds (or Zeroes) are bonds that do not pay interest during their life and for which the face value or maturity value is the result of the compounding of the specified interest rate over the maturity period of the bond. Such bonds sell for an amount that is, of course, much reduced compared to the maturity value and offer a tax advantage to the holder as no taxable interest is earned by the lender during the entire life of the bond until it matures. Such bonds are also interesting for growing firms that may be cash-strapped at some point of their development (often in the early phases) and thus need not divert cash to pay a periodic interest.

7.2 Interest, discount, and premium

Bonds are generally issued with a fixed or variable stated interest rate. The main concepts related to bonds issue will be illustrated through the example of Berwald Company. The data for this illustration are given in Table 12.4.

In this example, the bond is a term bond. Its principal will be repaid *in fine*, at the end of year X5. The selling price of a bond should be equal to the present value of the future cash flows the lender will receive, i.e., all the interest payments (during the lending period) and the reimbursement of the principal (at the end). (Time value of money and present value are developed in Appendix 12.3).

In this computation, the interest rate (also called discount rate) used is the market rate of interest at the issue date for like instruments with similar risk. Table 12.6 shows the value of the bond issue described in Table 12.4 for market interest rates of 8%, 6%, and 10%.

Table 12.5 summarizes the current cash flows (in CU), while Table 12.6 illustrates the present value of those cash flows.

In this table no issuance cost is assumed. Such cost would of course have to be covered by the funds received and the issuer of the bonds would receive less than the amount stated as the selling price in Table 12.6.

Case 1: Interest assumed in discounting is the same as in the bond issue, i.e., 8%. When the rate that investors can earn on investments of similar risk is 8%, that is the stated rate, the bonds will sell at par (face) value and yield 8%.

Table 12.4 Berwald Company – Basic data

Date of issuance	1 January X1
Term	5 years
Principal at face value (1)	500,000
Stated interest rate (2)	8%
Annual interest expense (1) × (2)	40,000
Payment of interest	Annually, 31 December
Maturity date	31 December X5

Table 12.5 Cash flows linked to the bond

	1 Jan. X1	31 Dec. X1	31 Dec. X2	31 Dec. X3	31 Dec. X4	31 Dec. X5
Interest payment		40,000	40,000	40,000	40,000	40,000
Repayment of the principal						500,000
Total	Value of bonds = Net present value of the stream of future payments shown in this row (see Table 12.6)	40,000	40,000	40,000	40,000	540,000

Table 12.6 Present value of the cash flows from Table 12.5

If the market rate on 1 January X1 is:				8%	6%	10%
	Basis	Number of years				
Present value of repayment of principal	500,000	5	(1)	340,292	373,629	310,461
Present value of interest payments	40,000/year	5	(2)	159,708	168,495	151,631
Selling price			(3) = (1) + (2)	500,000	542,124	462,092
Stated value of principal			(4)	500,000	500,000	500,000
Premium or (discount)			(5) = (3) − (4)	0	42,124	(37,908)
Effective yield on the selling price				8%	6%	10%

(1) Present value = $\dfrac{\text{Principal}}{(1 + \text{assumed discount rate})^5}$ (See Appendix 12.3 and Table 12.1A).

(2) Present value of an ordinary annuity (see Appendix 12.3 and Table 12.3A).

Case 2: Assumed discount rate is lower than the stated coupon rate. When the market rate of interest is 6% (i.e., investors can earn only 6% on bond issues or other investments of comparable level of risk), investors will bid up the price of the bonds (face value of 500,000 CU) to 542,124 CU (the fair value of the bond) because the stated rate of 8% is more favorable than the current (opportunity) market rate. In this case, the effective yield will correspond to the market rate of 6% and the bonds will sell at a premium of 42,124 CU (i.e., above face value).

Case 3: Assumed discount rate is greater than the stated coupon rate. When the market rate of interest is 10% (i.e., investors could earn 10% on bond issues or other investments of comparable level of risk), the price (fair value) of the bonds will be only 462,092 CU (even though the face value is 500,000 CU) because the stated rate of 8% is less favorable than the current (opportunity) market rate. In this case, the effective yield will correspond to the market rate of 10% and the bonds will sell at a discount of 37,908 CU (i.e., below face value) to attract investors.

The difference between what was received at the date of issue and what must be paid at maturity is a premium (if the market rate is lower than the stated rate) or a discount (if the market rate is higher than the stated rate).

7.3 Accounting for bonds

The mechanism is illustrated in Figures 12.6, 12.7 and 12.3A.

7.3.1 Bonds issued at par

Figure 12.6 Accounting for bonds issued at par

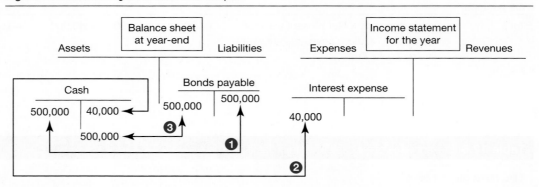

❶ On 1 January X1. At issuance: receipt of the selling price (equal to the principal of the bond).

❷ On 31 December X1 (and on 31 December for each of the four following years): payment of the interest due.

❸ At maturity (31 December X5): repayment of the principal.

7.3.2 Bonds issued at a premium

Figure 12.7 Accounting for bonds issued at a premium

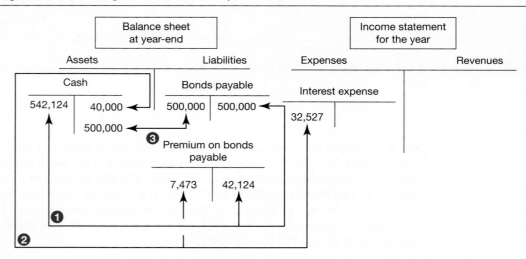

❶ On 1 January X1, at issuance date: receipt of the selling price, which is higher than the principal. (It is also possible to record the bonds in one account, including the premium).

❷ On 31 December X1 (and on 31 December for each the four following years): payment of the interest and amortization of the premium (see Table 12.7 below). In this context, the term 'amortization' does not have exactly the same meaning as the term used in Chapter 8 when discussing the amortization of intangible assets. However, both are methods of distributing a cost over a period of time in application of the matching principle.It is possible to split this entry into two different entries: payment of cash interest (40,000) and, in a second step, amortization of the premium (7,473) by reduction of the interest expense account.

❸ At maturity (31 December X5): repayment of the principal.

Amortization   A premium received by the firm issuing the bond represents the difference between future interest expenses and those that would have been incurred on the basis of the estimated future market interest rate(s). The premium needs to be offset against future interest expense (which is a mechanism called 'amortization') to follow the matching principle. Two methods of amortization are possible:

■ effective interest method
■ straight-line method.

Effective interest method   The effective interest method considers the issuance price (including the premium) as the amount to be 'amortized' (to be repaid). The periodic interest expense is determined by multiplying the amount to be amortized (book value at the beginning of each period) by the 'effective' (market) interest rate at the time the bonds were issued (6% in our example). As the issuing business entity pays a yearly interest expense (40,000 CU), which is higher than the effective interest (32,527 CU in year X1, for example, if the interest rate had been 6%), the 'excess' interest paid partly amortizes the amount of the premium. In other words, the premium amortization for each (interest) period is the difference between the interest calculated at the stated rate (8%) and the interest calculated at the effective rate (6%). Table 12.7 presents an illustration of such a calculation.

Straight-line method   The interest expense is a constant amount each year, equal to the cash interest minus the annual premium amortization (total premium divided by the number of years the bond will live): 31,575.2 CU. This figure represents the interest [40,000 CU] minus a constant part of the premium [42,124 CU / 5 years = 8,424.8 CU].

The interest patterns under the effective interest method conform more closely to economic reality. In most countries, the effective interest method must be used if the results are materially different from those of the straight-line method.

7.3.3 Bonds issued at a discount

The mechanism for an issuance at a discount is the reverse of one with a premium (see developments in Appendix 12.5).

Table 12.7 Schedule of interest and book value – Effective interest method, in the case of a premium

Year ending	Effective interest expense	Cash (interest paid)	Premium amortization expense (decrease in book value)	Book value of bonds
	(1) = 6% x [(4) of previous period]	(2)	(3) = (1) – (2)	(4)
				542,124
31 Dec. X1	32,527	40,000	–7,473	534,651
31 Dec. X2	32,079	40,000	–7,921	526,730
31 Dec. X3	31,604	40,000	–8,396	518,334
31 Dec. X4	31,100	40,000	–8,900	509,434
31 Dec. X5	30,566	40,000	–9,434	500,000
Total	157,876	200,000	–42,124	

8 Leased assets

A business may choose to enjoy the benefits of having a long-term asset at its disposal without necessarily wanting (or having the means) to own it. In this case, the user (called, in this case, the lessee) will enter into a leasing contract with the supplier or a specialized financial institution (called, in this case, the lessor).

In a leasing contract, title to the asset does not change hands. An analyst or an investor would want to know what lease agreement the business has entered into, both because the access to the assets involved is a potential source of value creation, and because the lease contract creates an obligation to pay a rent for the equipment, property or building. Leases are therefore an important element in the description of the financial situation of a firm at any point in time and must be reported to the users of financial information.

IAS 17 (IASB 2003: § 4) defines a 'lease' as 'an agreement whereby the lessor conveys to the lessee, in return for a payment or series of payments, the right to use an asset for an agreed period of time'. This Standard further distinguishes between:

■ **finance leases**, which are 'leases that transfer substantially all the risks and rewards incidental to ownership of an asset. Title may or may not eventually be transferred' (§ 4); and

■ **operating leases** which are 'lease[s] other than a finance lease' (§ 4).

In this definition,

■ Risks include the possibilities of losses from idle capacity or technological obsolescence and of variations in return due to changing economic conditions.

■ Rewards may be represented by the expectation of profitable operation over the asset's economic life and of gain from appreciation in value or realization of a residual value.

Concretely, a finance lease is essentially equivalent to the acquisition of a fixed asset with debt financing.

8.1 Accounting recording of leased assets

The distinction between the concepts of 'finance' and 'operating' leases plays a major role in the way leased assets will be reported. Figure 12.8 illustrates the issues at hand.

We will only examine here the accounting issues from the point of view of the lessee. Leases in the financial statements of lessors will not be developed and the reader interested in this topic can consult IAS 17 (§§ 36–57).

Figure 12.8 Accounting treatment of leased assets

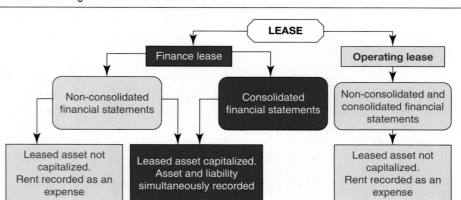

8.2 Finance and operating leases

IAS 17 (§ 10) states that 'Whether a lease is a finance lease or an operating lease depends on the substance of the transaction rather than the form of the contract. Examples of situations that individually or in combination would normally lead to a lease being classified as a finance lease are:

(a) The lease transfers ownership of the asset to the lessee by the end of the lease term.

(b) The lessee has the option to purchase the asset at a price that is expected to be sufficiently lower than the fair value at the date the option becomes exercisable for it to be reasonably certain, at the inception of the lease, that the option will be exercised.

(c) The lease term is for the major part of the economic life of the asset even if title is not transferred.

(d) At the inception of the lease the present value of the minimum lease payments amounts to at least substantially all of the fair value of the leased asset.

(e) The leased assets are of such a specialized nature that only the lessee can use them without major modifications.'

In these situations, several terms are defined in IAS 17 (§ 4):

'*Fair value* is the amount for which an asset could be exchanged, or a liability settled, between knowledgeable, willing parties in an [at] arm's length transaction'.

'*Economic life* is either:

(a) The period over which an asset is expected to be economically usable by one or more users; or

(b) The number of production or similar units expected to be obtained from the asset by one or more users'.

'The *inception* of the lease is the earlier of the date of the lease agreement and the date of commitment by the parties to the principal provisions of the lease'.

'*Minimum lease payments* are the payments over the lease term that the lessee is, or can be required, to make, excluding contingent rent, costs for services and taxes to be paid by and reimbursed to the lessor, together with:

(a) For the lessee, any amounts guaranteed by the lessee or by a party related to the lessee; or

(b) For the lessor, any residual value guaranteed to the lessor by (i) the lessee, (ii) a party related to the lessee, or (iii) a third party unrelated to the lessor that is financially capable of discharging the obligations under this guarantee.

However, if the lessee has an option to purchase the asset at a price that is expected to be sufficiently lower than the fair value at the date the option becomes exercisable for it to be reasonably certain, at the inception of the lease, that the option will be exercised, the minimum lease payments comprise the minimum payments payable over the lease term to the expected date of exercise of this purchase option and the payment required to exercise it'.

'The *lease term* is the non-cancellable period for which the lessee has contracted to lease the asset together with any further terms for which the lessee has the option to continue to lease the asset, with or without further payment, when at the inception of the lease it is reasonably certain that the lessee will exercise the option'.

When a contract meets at least one of the criteria laid-out by the IASB, it should be considered as a finance lease. The IASB criteria are different from the criteria laid out by SFAS 13 (FASB 1976) under US GAAP. In IAS 17, the key differences between financial and operational leases pertain mainly to the two following criteria: 'the major part of the economic life of the asset' criterion and the 'present value of the minimum [accumulated] lease payments amounts to at least substantially all of the fair value of the leased asset'.

The IASB favors a professional appreciation of the situation over specifying precise conditions. Any precise list of conditions could always be bypassed or interpreted in borderline cases so as to avoid reporting a useful piece of information to investors and analysts. A principles-based approach in providing guidance for reporting is generally more effective than a rules-based approach if the intent is to be as informative as possible.

In the United States, SFAS 13 lists the four conditions that create a finance lease (meeting only one of these conditions is enough, however):

1. The lease transfers ownership of the asset to the lessee by the end of the lease term.

2. The lease contains a bargain purchase option.

3. The non-cancellable lease term is 75% or more of the estimated economic life of the leased asset.

4. The present value of the minimum lease payments equals or exceeds 90% of the fair value of the leased asset.

Under condition (3), 'the major part' (IAS 17) is replaced by 75% (SFAS 13) and under condition (4), 'substantially' (IAS 17) is replaced by 90% (SFAS 13).

8.3 Capitalization of finance leased assets

IAS 17 (§ 20) recommends that finance leases be recognized as assets (the use of the leased object is to create future economic benefits) and liabilities (representing future lease payments) on the balance sheet. Such recording of finance leases is often known as the 'capitalization' of the leased asset. As shown in Figure 12.9, capitalization is generally adopted in the consolidated financial statements. However, in the non-consolidated financial statements, some countries' GAAP do not follow the IAS recommendation and do not recognize leased assets at all in the balance sheet (it is the case, to date, for France and Italy, for example). In fact, legally the property belongs to the owner throughout the duration of the lease and for that reason EU countries with accounting systems based on commercial law do not capitalize leases and consider the rental payments as expenses in the income statement. Some European countries, for example Belgium, Netherlands, Switzerland and the UK, prefer to respect the accounting principle of 'substance over form' and require that the assets held under a finance lease agreement be reported in the balance sheet, following, implicitly or explicitly, the prescription of IAS 17.

If a firm decides to capitalize leased assets, it can follow IAS 17's prescriptions (§ 20): 'At the commencement of the lease term, lessees shall recognize finance leases as assets and liabilities in their balance sheets at amounts equal to the fair value of the leased property or, if lower, the present value of the minimum lease payments, each determined at the inception of the lease. The discount rate to be used in calculating the present value of the minimum lease payments is the interest rate implicit in the lease, if this is practicable to determine; if not, the lessee's incremental [i.e., marginal] borrowing rate shall be used. Any initial direct costs of the lessee are added to the amount recognized as an asset'. This 'incremental borrowing rate' is 'the rate of interest the lessee would have to pay on a similar lease or, if that is not determinable, the rate that, at the inception of the lease, the lessee would incur to borrow over a similar term, and with a similar security, the funds necessary to purchase the asset' (§ 4).

If leased assets are capitalized, lease payments must be apportioned between finance expense and reduction of the outstanding liability. Simultaneously, the asset must be depreciated consistently with the depreciable assets that are owned by the company. 'If there is no reasonable certainty that the lessee will obtain ownership by the end of the lease term, the asset shall be fully depreciated over the shorter of the lease term and its useful life.' (IAS 17: § 27). Otherwise, the period of expected use is the useful life of the asset.

In practice, 'the sum of the depreciation expense for the asset and the finance expense for the period is rarely the same as the lease payments payable for the period, and it is, therefore, inappropriate simply to recognize the lease payments payable as an expense. Accordingly, the asset and the related liability are unlikely to be equal in amount after the commencement of the lease term' (IAS 17: § 29). In this context, it is necessary to restate the lease payment (The Lindblad Company example, below, illustrates how this is done).

8.4 Example of accounting for leased assets

The Lindblad Company leases equipment (worth 600 CU at fair market value) under a finance lease. The contract is for a five-year period. The annual lease payment amounts to 150 CU. The purchase option at the end of the lease has been established at 10 CU. Such equipment would usually, if owned outright, be depreciated over an eight-year period.

The interest rate implicit in the lease may be determined by applying the method described below (and see additional information in Appendix 12.3).

Value of the equipment	600 CU
Total payments (5 × 150 + 10)	760 CU

The value of the asset is provided by the following formula (solving for i):

$$\text{Value of the leased equipment} = \text{Lease payment} \times \sum_{t=1}^{5} \frac{1}{(1+i)^t} + \frac{\text{Purchase option}}{(1+i)^5} = 150 \times \sum_{t=1}^{5} \frac{1}{(1+i)^t} + \frac{10}{(1+i)^5}$$

In this formula, the factor

$$\sum_{t=1}^{5} \frac{1}{(1+i)^t}$$

can be replaced by the following formula

$$\frac{1-(1+i)^{-n}}{i}$$

where n represents the duration of the contract, i.e., five years.

Since the purchase value of the asset is known, one can solve the above equation for *i*. The interest rate *i* may be obtained from a statistics table (such as the one provided in Appendix 12.3) or by using some advanced handheld calculators, spreadsheet or statistics software. Our example yields an implied rate of interest $i = 8.357\%$. In the case where the implicit rate is impossible to determine mathematically, the lessee's incremental borrowing rate may be used. Table 12.8 shows the schedule of financial amortization of the implicit debt.

It is important to note that the beginning lease liability equals the value of the equipment (600 CU) and not the total payments (760 CU).

The depreciation of the equipment will follow the depreciation schedule shown in Table 12.9. Given that the useful life is eight years, the depreciation rate is 12.5% (1/8) if straight-line is used.

Figure 12.9 illustrates the accounting of the leased asset in year 1 as both an asset and a liability, using the information from both Tables 12.8 and 12.9.

Because the time schedule of the expense paid (lease payment of 150) differs from that of the reported expense (Depreciation expense + Interest expense = 75 + 50.14 = 125.14, for example in year 1), a deferred taxation situation arises (see Chapters 6 and 13).

Table 12.8 Repayment schedule of the implicit debt

Year	Beginning lease liability	Interest expense	Repayment of liability	Lease payment	Ending lease liability
	(1)	(2) = (1) × 8.357%	(3) = (4) – (2)	(4)	(5) = (1) – (3)
Year 1	600.00	50.14	99.86	150.00	500.14
Year 2	500.14	41.80	108.20	150.00	391.94
Year 3	391.94	32.75	117.24	150.00	274.70
Year 4	274.70	22.96	127.04	150.00	147.66
Year 5	147.66	12.34	137.66	150.00	10.00
Purchase	10.00		10.00	10.00	0.00
Total		160.00	600.00	760.00	

Table 12.9 Depreciation schedule of the leased equipment (assuming straight-line depreciation)

Year	Depreciable basis	Depreciation expense	Book value
Year 1	600	75	525
Year 2	525	75	450
Year 3	450	75	375
Year 4	375	75	300
Year 5	300	75	225
Year 6	225	75	150
Year 7	150	75	75
Year 8	75	75	0

Figure 12.9 Capitalization of leased equipment

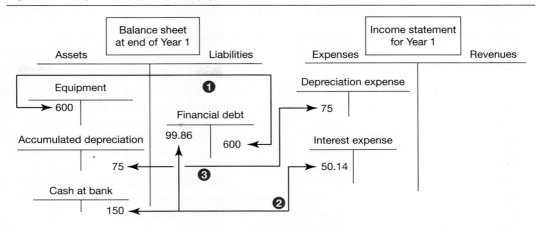

❶ The leased equipment is recorded as both an asset and a liability (for the same amount).

❷ The lease payment (150) is split between interest expense and repayment of the financial debt (figures are derived from Table 12.8).

❸ The leased asset is depreciated over 8 years (figures are derived from Table 12.9).

8.5 Operating leases

According to IAS 17 (§ 33): 'Lease payments under an operating lease shall be recognized as an expense on a straight-line basis over the lease term unless another systematic basis is more representative of the time pattern of the user's benefit'.

8.6 Sale [of an asset] and leaseback transactions

Sale and leaseback transactions are developed in Appendix 12.6.

8.7 Reporting lease agreements to the users of financial information

Since leases are a very important way through which a business acquires control over assets (alternative to outright acquisition), it is very important to agree on how the commitment created by the lease is reported.

IAS 17 (§ 31) states that lessees should disclose the following elements regarding their finance leases:

(a) 'For each class of asset, the net carrying amount at the end of the reporting period.

(b) Reconciliation between the total of future minimum lease payments at the end of the reporting period, and their present value. In addition, an entity shall disclose the total of future minimum lease payments at the end of the reporting period, and their present value, for each of the following periods: (i) not later than one year; (ii) later than one year and not later than five years; (iii) later than five years.

(c) Contingent rents recognized in income for the period.

(d) (...)

(e) A general description of the lessee's significant leasing arrangements including, but not limited to, the following: (i) the basis on which contingent rent payable are determined; (ii) the existence and terms of renewal or purchase options (...), and (iii) restrictions imposed by lease arrangements, such as those concerning dividends, additional debt, and further leasing.'

Real-life example Benihana

(USA – US GAAP – Source: Annual report 2008 – Japanese style restaurants essentially in the USA)

Note 12: Leases

We generally operate our restaurants in leased premises. We are obligated under various lease agreements for certain restaurant facilities and our corporate office, which are classified as operating leases. The typical restaurant premises lease is for a term of between 10 to 25 years with renewal options ranging from 5 to 20 years. The leases generally provide for the obligation to pay property taxes, utilities and various other use and occupancy costs. We are also obligated under various leases for office space. Under the provisions of certain of our leases, there are rent holidays and/or escalations in payments over the base lease term, percentage rent, as well as options for renewal for additional periods. The effects of the rent holidays and escalations have been reflected in rent expense on a straight-line basis over the expected lease term, which includes option periods we are reasonably assured to exercise due to the fact that we would incur an economic penalty for not doing so. Generally, the lease term commences on the date when we become legally obligated for the rent payments or as specified in the lease agreement. Recognition of rent expense begins when we have the right to control the use of the leased property, which is typically before rent payments are due under the terms of most of our leases. Percentage rent expense is generally based upon sales levels and is accrued at the point in time we determine that it is probable that the sales levels will be achieved.

Minimum payments under lease commitments are as follows (*in US$ 000*)

Fiscal year	Operating leases
2010	15,483
2011	15,417
2012	15,184
2013	15,168
2014	14,276
Thereafter	129,838
Total minimum lease payments	**205,366**

Comment: This example illustrates the required disclosure for operating leases.

9 Employee benefits and pension accounting

Employee benefits give rise to complex future obligations. IAS 19 (IASB 1998a) deals with this topic. Its paragraph 4 distinguishes between (a) short-term employee benefits (i.e., while the employee is employed), (b) **post-employment benefits**, (c) other long-term employee benefits and (d) termination benefits. It defines the first three categories as:

(a) 'Short-term employee benefits, such as wages, salaries and social security contributions, paid annual leave and paid sick leave, profit-sharing and bonuses (if payable within twelve months of the end of the period) and non-monetary benefits (such as medical care, housing, cars and free or subsidized goods or services) for current employees;

(b) Post-employment benefits such as pensions, other retirement benefits, post-employment life insurance and post-employment medical care;

(c) Other long-term employee benefits, including long-service leave or sabbatical leave, jubilee or other long-service benefits, long-term disability benefits and, if they are not payable wholly within twelve months after the end of the period, profit-sharing, bonuses and deferred compensation' (IAS 19: § 4).

Figure 12.10 summarizes, in a simplified way, the accounting issues arising from the handling of employee benefits.

Figure 12.10 Accounting for employee benefits

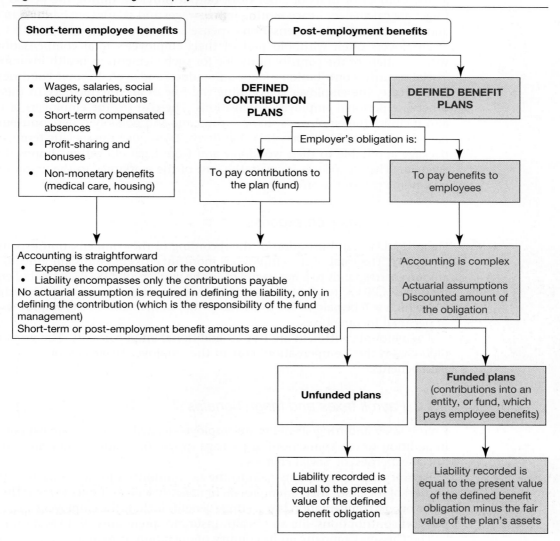

9.1 Short-term employee benefits

Accounting for short-term employee benefits, as seen earlier, is generally straightforward because no actuarial assumption is required to evaluate the obligation and its cost. A business should recognize the undiscounted amount of short-term employee benefits expected to be paid in exchange for the service rendered by employees:

■ as an expense for the amount paid whenever payment takes place;

■ as a liability (accrued expense) as the amount accrues and while it is still due (i.e., the expense of the period minus any amount already paid).

Employers compensate their employees (salaries, wages, or some other form of remuneration) in exchange for their 'labor'. Salaries are paid on a periodic basis (generally every two weeks or every month) as a fixed installment of an agreed upon total amount defined as the remuneration for the person making her or his services available to the employer for an agreed-upon annual number of hours, regardless of the level of occupation the employer will be able to provide. Wages refer to the payment (daily, weekly, biweekly or monthly) of an amount defined by an agreed hourly or piecework rate applied to the actual number of units of labor or of output provided during the period for which the wages are calculated. In accounting terms, wages and salaries are handled in the same way and are recorded as 'compensation expense'.

Employers often withhold part of their employee's total compensation to pay the worker's share of the contributions due for such elements as health insurance premiums, 'social security' contributions, labor union dues, and even, in some countries, income tax. In this case, the employer is assuming the role of an intermediary in the settlement of otherwise personal employees' obligations. The cost (to the employer) of compensation also includes the employer's share of the same and possibly other contributions (such as payroll taxes and fringe benefits) that derive from both the specific terms of the benefits package applicable to their workforce and from legal obligations imposed by regulatory agencies. These expenses increase the cost of the workforce to the employer beyond the take-home pay of the employee.

9.1.1 Compensation expense

Figure 12.11 is an illustration of the recording of the compensation expense for Larsson Company. The total of the employees' monthly gross pay-slips amounts to 300 CU. This amount corresponds to a net payment to the workers of 235 CU, a total of employee withholdings of 20 CU for contribution to the social security program and a withholding of 45 CU, which will be paid to the fiscal authorities in the name of the employees in settlement of personal income taxes.

The amounts withheld are not an additional employer cost. The gross remuneration (300 CU) is the 'compensation' cost to the employer *before* payroll taxes and employer-paid benefits.

9.1.2 Payroll taxes and fringe benefits

Payroll taxes and fringe benefits are employee-related costs that are paid by the employer in addition to the compensation package (wages or salaries). They are sometimes called 'social expenses' or 'social charges'.

Payroll taxes are amounts paid to the tax authorities for items such as the employer's portion of social security, unemployment taxes (federal and state taxes as the case may be), and workers' compensation taxes. Fringe benefits include the employer's share of employees' pension contributions, life and health insurance premiums, and vacation pay.

The Larsson Company, in its country of operation, is required (a) to pay an employer's social security contribution equal to 12% of the gross salary, and (b) to contribute to the workforce's retirement account recording an employer's contribution amounting to 20% of gross remuneration. The total compensation cost (to the employer) is thus $300 + [300 \times (12\% + 20\%)] = 396$ CU, with 300 CU as the compensation expense and 96 CU as the employee's fringe benefits expense.

The necessary entry is recorded in Figure 12.11.

9.2 Post-employment benefits

As explained in IAS 19 (IASB 1998a: § 24), 'post-employment benefits include, for example:

(a) Retirement benefits such as pensions; and

(b) Other post-employment benefits, such as post-employment life insurance [or payment of premiums to a life insurance plan] and post-employment medical care [or contribution to a health and medical care plan for the retirees and their beneficiaries].

Figure 12.11 Accounting for compensation expense

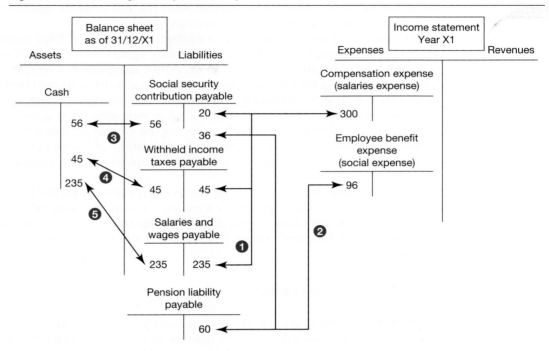

❶ Compensation expense. The net amount due to the employees is recorded in the 'salaries payable' account but the expense that will eventually be recognized in the income statement is the compensation expense.

❷ Recording of the employer's contribution.

❸, ❹, and ❺ Payment (separately) of each liability on the appropriate date when it is due. (The social security withheld from the employees (20 CU) and the social security charged to the employer (36 CU) are often paid at the same time).

The total amount of personnel expenses amounts to 300 (gross salary) + 96 (social expenses) = 396 CU.

Arrangements whereby an entity provides post-employment benefits are [referred to as] post-employment benefit plans.'

Accounting for post-employment benefits will depend on a very important distinction made regarding the nature of the benefit plan: defined contribution plans or defined benefit plans. Reporting the obligations created vary greatly between the two types of plans.

9.2.1 Defined contribution plans

A defined contribution plan is a retirement savings program under which an employer contractually commits to making certain periodic contributions (generally same periodicity as the payment of the remuneration) to a participant's retirement account (commonly managed by a third party, but can be managed by the individual) throughout the employment period, but with no guaranteed retirement benefit.

The post employment benefit received by the beneficiary is based exclusively upon the contributions made to the plan (which can be supplemented by the individual), and earnings derived from the investment, by the manager of the plan, of the cumulated contributions. When the employee leaves the firm, for whatever reason, the employer's obligation to contribute ceases. The benefit the former employee receives ceases when the account balance is depleted, regardless of the retiree's age or circumstances.

The move towards defined contribution that is developing worldwide, away from defined benefits (see below), is coherent with the difficulty in guaranteeing the actual payment of a pre-established level of benefits (pension).

The employer pays a premium or contribution to a capital fund managed by a third party that will provide the service contractually agreed with the employee(s) (payment of a capital or of an annuity). The firm needs not recognize any obligation, provision or liability. Accounting for the contribution expenses to a defined contribution plan is identical to that of short-term employee benefits such as salaries or wages.

In Europe many state-run, state-controlled or state-appointed agencies have been created specifically to be the third party, relieving the employer from any post-employment benefit obligation management beyond the obligation of payment of the contributions or to pay out the retirement benefits to the employee at the contractually agreed or defined age.

In the USA mainly, the fund can be and is often managed by the firm itself, and, even worse in our view, a large part of – or even all – the fund is routinely invested in shares of the firm itself, with little or no diversification, thus leading to an increased risk for the employees if the firm's shares lose value on the markets or the firm must declare bankruptcy.

9.2.2 Defined benefit plans

Principles A defined benefit plan is a pension plan under which an employee receives a set monthly (or quarterly) amount upon retirement, guaranteed for her or his life, or the joint lives of the member and their spouse. This benefit may include a cost-of-living clause during retirement. The amount of the periodic benefit received is based upon the participant's length of service and level of remunerations (often calculated over a number of the participant's 'best years').

In defined benefit plans, the entity itself assumes the obligation to provide, in the future, certain agreed benefits to current and former employees. This obligation needs to be measured (quantified), managed and reported in the balance sheet. However, 'accounting for defined benefit plans is complex because actuarial assumptions are required to measure the obligation and expense and there is a possibility of actuarial gains and losses. Moreover, the obligations are measured on a discounted basis because they may be settled many years after the employees render the related service' (IAS 19: § 48).

Defined benefit plans are still common in government employees' pension plans. They are used less and less frequently in all other economic sectors or activities, due to the complexity of the hypotheses required for actuarial calculations, the risks attached to the ability to actually be able to deliver the benefit, and the increasingly unpredictable fluctuations of the return on financial investments in the market.

In addition to providing retirement pay until the former employee, or his beneficiaries, decease, many businesses have included in their employment package the promise of payment of a one-time retirement bonus (at the time of retirement) that is most of the time proportional to the length of employment in the firm. Since the calculation method of the bonus is public knowledge[5] and cannot be modified without negotiation, such bonuses are considered to be defined benefits and should be recognized as an expense (and funded) throughout the period of employment since they are part of the compensation package for services rendered.

Funded versus unfunded An entity has a choice of alternatives in handling pension plans:

- *The plan may be unfunded.* In this case the business bears the sole responsibility of the obligation and pays the agreed upon benefits to the employees, either on a pay-as-you-go basis (the expense is covered as incurred – a very risky proposition either when the active workforce headcount reduces faster than the population of beneficiaries does, or when an economic downturn affects the profitability and liquidity of the firm), or by saving privately to cover the obligation and managing the fund inside the firm itself. In addition, unfunded pension plans tend to create ethical issues: when the savings created by the entity have increased in value (due to a bull market, for example) the value of the fund may vastly exceed the actuarially needed funds; the entity may be tempted to recapture the contributions it appears to have paid in excess of the need. Such situations have not been uncommon in the past. They have potentially dramatic consequences when the market turns bearish. For all these reasons, unfunded plans tend to be uncommon because of the risks they offer.

- *The plan may be funded*, either partly or completely. In this case the entity pays a premium to an entity (or fund) that is (in theory) legally and completely separate and independent from the reporting business. The premiums will be managed by the fund so as to create enough capital to allow the future payment of benefits. This type of plan is the most common. The premium expenses are equivalent to a 'forced' saving plan for the firm. Insurance companies have made a specialty of managing this type of fund as they have the actuarial expertise in establishing the level of the premiums that will guarantee the ability to honor the contractual obligation of the fund to the employer and the employees. The amount of the periodic premium paid into the fund to meet actuarial obligations may vary greatly from period to period.

In a simplified way, the amount recognized as pension liability in the balance sheet will be the net total of the following amounts:

- net present value of the pension obligation as of the reporting date;
- minus the fair value on the reporting date of the plan's assets (if the plan is funded).

In practice, the calculations required for the quantification of pension obligations are rather complex. They require the use of the services of actuaries. Such a topic is generally well covered in an intermediate accounting course.[6]

10 Financial statement analysis

The choices made regarding how to value, record and report the business future obligations to a variety of constituencies impact on the understanding of and the ability to decode the firm's situation through its financial statements. Choices made about liability reporting affect also the assets side (through the capitalization of leases) and the value of various ratios.

10.1 Capitalized leased assets

Even if the firm does not capitalize its leases (the frontier between finance and operational leases is fuzzy at times), analysts generally restate the published financial information and treat any ambiguous lease as a finance lease to create the financial statement that would have been obtained if the asset had been acquired and 100% financed by debt. In the restated income statement, the interest portion of the lease payment is classified as 'interest expense' and the depreciation expense of the lease payment is a part of the depreciation expense. Both the balance sheet and the income statement are affected by the handling of leases and thus many ratios are also affected.

10.2 Ratios

Although ratios will be covered extensively as part of Chapter 18, Table 12.10 lists some of the key ratios pertaining to liabilities. These ratios are especially important in

Table 12.10 Debt ratios

Name of the ratio	Computation	Interpretation or meaning
Debt ratio or debt to total assets ratio	Total debt/Total assets	Firm's long-term debt-paying ability The lower this ratio, the better the company's position
Debt to equity ratio	Debt[7]/Shareholders' equity or Debt/(Shareholders' equity + Debt)	
Long-term debt to equity ratio	Long-term Debt/Shareholders' equity or Long-term debt/(Shareholders' equity + Long-term debt)	Firm's degree of financial leverage
Interest coverage ratio	Operating income (before interest expense and income taxes)/Interest expense	Number of times that a firm's interest expense is covered by operation earnings Rule of thumb: minimum of 5
Inventory trade financing	Accounts payable/Inventory	How much suppliers contribute to financing the operational cycle. If the ratio is greater than 1, suppliers are contributing to the possible growth of the firm

evaluating both the risk and the return on investment a business can offer to investors. All these ratios can be affected greatly by the choices made in handling the recognition of liabilities. Provisions (which, as mentioned, can sometimes be used for income smoothing) are generally included in liabilities for the computation of **debt ratios**. Some analysts exploit the notes to the financial statements to eventually restate the provisioned amounts and the income statement or simulate the range of values the ratios could take if the provisions were either accepted at face value or restated under specified hypotheses.

These ratios are critical for a potential lender or investor who may need to evaluate the risk attached to a transaction with another firm. One critical element of the dynamics of the risk evaluation is that the larger the shareholders' equity is, the lower are the liabilities to third parties and thus the less risky the business appears to be to a lender (and conversely). The first three ratios in Table 12.10 relate to that aspect of the evaluation of the firm's risk. They reflect the weight of third-party liabilities in the long-term financial resources of the firm. The fourth ratio in Table 12.10 (interest coverage) reflects the likely capability of the firm to face its interest obligation. This ratio is often considered to be a good proxy for the ability of the firm to cover its short-term or current liabilities or obligations. The fifth ratio is an indication of the power of the entity over its suppliers and indicates whether or not suppliers contribute to more than funding inventories.

The generic definitions of the ratios presented in Table 12.10 are subject to many variations and adaptations to serve the specific needs of the analyst. Amendments can be made to either or both of the numerator or the denominator. For example, some practitioners restrict long-term liabilities in their ratio calculations to long-term interest-bearing liabilities.

Minority interests in consolidated statements (percentage of a subsidiary's shareholders' equity held by shareholders different from the parent company) add a little complexity to the calculation of the key liability-based ratios. Chapter 13 deals with these issues. A key question is to decide whether minority interests are part of liabilities or part of shareholders' equity. Both choices are possible in reporting the financial position of the firm.

Key points

- Liabilities are obligations to pay cash or to provide goods and services to third parties in the future. They represent a major source of financing in any business.
- Liabilities are classified as current versus non-current, which encompasses two presentations: operating versus financial (emphasis on operating cycle) or short-term versus long-term (emphasis on solvency).
- Weight represented by liabilities in the balance sheet as well as liabilities reporting practices are extremely variable across countries, business sectors, and firms.
- Liabilities should be distinguished from related but different concepts: (1) accrued liabilities; (2) provision; and (3) contingent liabilities on the basis of their varying degrees of certainty in (1) the principle causing the obligation, (2) its timing, and (3) its amount.
- Bonds may be issued with a premium (sold above par if the interest rate is higher than the market rate) or with a discount (sold below par, in the opposite case).

- Leasing is a very convenient and flexible medium for obtaining the right to use a fixed asset.
- Operating leases and finance leases respond to different business needs, follow different business models and need to be handled differently in the accounting and the reporting systems.
- A finance lease is equivalent to the acquisition of an asset completely financed by a loan. Most countries require that financial leases be reported in the balance sheet as both a fixed asset and a financial liability.
- Costs relating to short-term employee benefits and defined contribution plans for post-employment benefits are expenses as incurred.
- Defined benefits plans for post-employment benefits open complex issues of valuation and accounting. They mainly require provisioning (or recognizing the (ever) increasing pension liability) during the period of employment of the eligible workforce.

Review (solutions are at the back of the book)

Review 12.1 Stenborg

Topic: Repayment of a bank loan

The Stenborg Company has obtained a bank loan on 30 June X1, with the following terms and conditions:

- Amount: 100,000 CU.
- Annual interest: 10%.
- Reimbursement by ordinary annuities starting on 30 June X2 (annual payment).
- Term to maturity of the loan: five years.
- Closing date used by Stenborg in its books: 31 December.

Required

1. Compute the amount of the constant annuity (interest expense plus part of the principal) following the effective interest rate method.
2. Present the repayment schedule of the debt.
3. Show the accounting entries:
    - On the date of subscription
    - On the first closing date
    - On the first repayment date.

Review 12.2 Haeffner PLC (1)

Topic: Provisions and contingent liabilities

Haeffner PLC is an accounting firm. Some of its clients face the following situations. For each, it is assumed that a reliable estimate can be made of any outflows expected:

1. Acme Manufacturing Enterprises Ltd (AME) provides a warranty on its products at the time of sale. Under the terms of the warranty contract, AME undertakes to make good, by repair or replacement, any manufacturing defect that becomes apparent within three years from the date of sale. Based on past experience, it is probable that there will be some claims under the warranties.

2. Stone Oil Industries Co. (SOI) has been a medium-size oil producer and refiner for the past 50 years. It operates in many parts of the world. On occasions, SOI units have incurred spills of crude or refined products that have contaminated land and water. It is SOI's management philosophy that clean-up should be organized only when the firm is required to do so under the laws of the country in which the spill took place. One country in which SOI operates has, until now, not had any legislation requiring cleaning-up. SOI has been contaminating land and water in that country for several years without taking any corrective action. On 31 December X1 it becomes virtually certain that a draft law mandating retroactive cleaning-up of land and waterways already contaminated will be enacted shortly after the year-end.

3. Sudstrom AB is a large upscale retail store established in most major consumer market areas. It has built its reputation on selection and quality of its products and on a well-advertised policy of refunding purchases to dissatisfied customers without asking any questions as long as Sudstrom carries the product, even in cases where the store may not be under any legal obligation to do so.

4. On 18 December X1, the board of Zygafuss Agglomerated Enterprises Co. (ZAE) decided to close down one of its industrial divisions. By closing date (31 December) the decision had not yet been communicated to any of those affected (not even to the Works Council), and no other steps had been taken to implement the decision.

5. During X1 Mutter GmbH had provided a loan guarantee for the benefit of Scout AG, a trading partner (in which Mutter does not hold any share interest) opening the market for Mutter products in Transmoldavia (a fictitious country). Scout's financial condition at that time is considered to be sound and its economic prospects bright. Bankers have, however, requested a loan guarantee because of the short history of Scout in this market and the possible instability of the Transmoldavian market. During X2 the market in Transmoldavia experiences a serious economic downturn and Scout's financial condition deteriorates. On 30 June X2 Scout AG actually files for protection from its creditors.

Required

Analyze each of these five situations and make a recommendation for each as to the necessity of recording (and reporting), or not, an appropriate provision.

Assignments

Assignment 12.1
Multiple-choice questions

Select the right answer (one possible answer, unless otherwise stated).

1. Provisions for risks and liabilities are recorded

   (a) In the expenses
   (b) In the revenues
   (c) In the shareholders' equity and liabilities
   (d) As a contra-asset
   (e) None of these

2. An example of financial liabilities is

   (a) Income tax payable
   (b) Unearned revenues
   (c) Bank borrowings
   (d) Salaries payable
   (e) None of these

3. An example of a current liability is

   (a) Bank loan or borrowing (long-term portion)
   (b) Unearned revenues
   (c) Share capital
   (d) Retained earnings
   (e) None of these

4. An example of an item that is not a current liability is

   (a) Accrued expenses
   (b) Prepaid expenses
   (c) Salaries payable
   (d) Accounts payable
   (e) Unearned revenues
   (f) None of these

5. Warranty costs are recognized as an expense

   (a) At the time the products covered by the warranty are sold
   (b) At the time the costs are really incurred
   (c) None of these

6. When the balance sheet is presented by nature, the current portion of a long-term liability is still included in the financial liabilities section of the balance sheet

   (a) True
   (b) False

7. Notes payable represent bills of exchange or promissory notes

   (a) True
   (b) False

8. The net salary (after deduction of withholdings) is recorded as an expense

   (a) True
   (b) False

9. A contingent liability is recorded

   (a) As part of the assets
   (b) As part of the shareholders' equity and liabilities
   (c) As part of the revenues
   (d) As part of the expenses
   (e) None of these

10. A provision for restructuring can be recorded as soon as a company has decided to close a business entity

    (a) True
    (b) False

Assignment 12.2
Reporting liabilities in different sectors of activity

On the Internet, or in the library, find the annual reports of four companies from different sectors of activity in a given country or in different countries.

Required

1. How are liabilities presented in the balance sheet? What decisions on the basis of this information can investors or shareholders take? What decisions would be difficult to take on the basis of just this information?

2. Are there any notes relating to liabilities? How do they enlarge the decision analysis possibilities offered to shareholders and investors?

3. What are the accounting treatments applied to these liabilities?

4. What is the weight of liabilities as a percentage of total shareholders' equity and liabilities? What strategic implications do you derive from this ratio?

Assignment 12.3
Reporting liabilities in the same sector of activity

On the Internet, or in the library, find the annual reports of four companies essentially in identical or similar industries in a given country or in different countries.

Required

Use questions from Assignment 12.2.

Assignment 12.4
Club Méditerranée*

Topic: **Bonds, bank loans and debts**

Club Méditerranée, the French leisure company, reports the following information relating to its financial liabilities (Source: Annual report 2008, financial year ended 31 October 2008).

Consolidated balance sheet (excerpts)

(in € million)	As at 31.10. 2007	2008
EQUITY AND LIABILITIES (...)		
[Non-current] borrowings and interest-bearing liabilities (...)	408	260
[Current] borrowings and interest-bearing liabilities (...)	36	187

Note 18.2 Borrowings and other interest-bearing liabilities by category

(in € million)	As at 31.10. 2007	2008
OCEANE convertible bonds	279	142
Long-term bank borrowings	115	115
Draw downs on lines of credit	10	
Financial lease obligations	4	3
Total long-term borrowings and other interest-bearing liabilities	**408**	**260**
OCEANE convertible bonds	10	159
Current portion of long-term bank borrowings	8	8
Draw downs on lines of credit	–	–
Short-term bank loans and overdrafts	14	17
Fair value of derivative instruments	4	2
Total short-term borrowings and other interest-bearing liabilities	**36**	**187**
Total	**444**	**447**

Required

1. Reconcile the figures provided in the notes with those provided in the balance sheet.
2. What do 'convertible bonds' represent?
3. What do 'financial lease obligations' represent?
4. What do 'draw downs on lines of credit' represent?
5. What is the difference between 'current portion of long-term bank borrowings' and 'short-term bank loans'?
6. Are 'short-term bank loans' and 'overdrafts' equivalent?

Assignment 12.5
Haeffner PLC (2)

Topic: Provisions and contingent liabilities

Haeffner PLC is an accounting firm. Some of its clients face the following situations. For each, it is assumed that a reliable estimate can be made of any outflows expected:

1. On 9 December X1 the board of Shankar Inc. decided to close down its defense division, effective 1 June X2. On 20 December X1 a detailed plan for closing down the division was agreed by the board. The plan was further discussed and amended during a scheduled meeting of the works council on 21 December. In the following week, letters were sent to customers warning them to seek alternative sources of supply and redundancy notices were sent to the staff of the division who would not be offered other positions in the company. The accounting closing date of Shankar Inc. is 31 December.

2. The government introduces a number of changes in legislation, which will generate the need for Acme Amalgamated Enterprises Co. to retrain its security and quality control staff. At closing date, no retraining of staff has taken place.

3. Five people were severely injured in an industrial accident in which machinery and equipment sold by Lang Sein Enterprise Inc. was involved. The injured parties' lawyers have started legal proceedings against Lang Sein Enterprise, seeking damages. Lang Sein disputes its liability. As of the date of approval for publication of the financial statements for the year ending 31 December X1, Lang Sein's lawyers are of the opinion that the evidence will probably show that the enterprise will not be found liable. However, one year later, due to new developments in the case, the Lang Sein lawyers believe that it is probable the enterprise will be found at least partially liable.

Required

Analyze each situation and draw conclusions about the necessity to record a provision or not.

Assignment 12.6

Stora Enso*, Repsol YPF*, Cobham* and Thales*

Topic: Reporting movements in provisions

Below are excerpts from notes to consolidated financial statements of four companies reporting movements in provisions.

Stora Enso (Finland – IFRS – Source: Annual report 2008 – Production of paper)

Note 24 Other provisions

(in € million)	Environmental	Restructuring	Other obligatory	Total provisions
Carrying value at 31 December 2007	**67.4**	**262.2**	**3.6**	**333.2**
Translation difference	−8.8	−10.2	−0.2	−19.2
Companies disposed	–	−2.6	–	−2.6
Charge in income statement: Continuing operations				0.0
New provisions	15.6	228.2	1.1	244.9
Increase in existing provisions	18.9	7.8	–	26.7
Reversal of existing provisions	−9.7	−24.3	−0.3	−34.3
Charge in income statement: Discontinued operations	–	1.4	–	1.4
Payments	−2.9	−158.2	−1.6	−162.7
Carrying value at 31 December 2008	**80.5**	**304.3**	**2.6**	**387.4**

Repsol YPF (Spain – IFRS – Source: Annual report 2008 – Oil and gas)

Note 20 Provisions for contingencies and expenses

	Long-term provisions				Short-term provisions		
(in € million)	Provisions for pensions	Provisions for field dismantling costs	Other provisions	Total	Provisions for pensions	Other provisions	Total
Balance at 31 December 2007	**66**	**931**	**1,568**	**2,565**	**3**	**283**	**286**
Period provisions charged to income	2	82	627	711	2	39	41
Reversals of provisions with a credit to income	(2)	(1)	(160)	(163)	–	(7)	(7)
Provisions released due to payment	(9)	(19)	(98)	(126)	–	(233)	(233)
Changes in the scope of consolidation	(10)	(9)	(7)	(26)	(1)	(1)	(2)
Translation differences	–	49	51	100	–	10	10
Reclassifications and other changes	1	68	(420)	(351)	5	337	342
Balance at 31 December 2008	**48**	**1,101**	**1,561**	**2,710**	**9**	**428**	**437**

The 'other provisions' caption includes mainly technical reserves for insurance, provisions for environmental contingencies, provisions for litigation in progress and other provisions for future contingencies.

Cobham (United Kingdom – IFRS –- Source: Annual report 2008 – Equipment, systems and components for aerospace and defense industries)

22. Provisions

(in € million)	2008	2007
Current liabilities	75.2	29.5
Non-current liabilities	25.8	30.3
	101.0	59.8

Movements in provisions during the year

(in € million)	Contingent consideration	Warranty claims	Contract loss provisions	Aircraft maintenance provisions	Other	Total
At 1 January 2008	13.6	4.5	4.6	7.9	29.2	59.8
Reclassification (to)/from accruals	–	(0.1)	(0.4)	–	0.2	(0.3)
Additional provisions in the year	20.1	1.7	2.1	2.7	20.5	47.1
Acquired with business combinations	–	0.9	0.6	–	4.2	5.7
Utilization of provisions	(1.4)	(2.3)	(1.9)	(1.1)	(5.6)	(12.3)
Unused amounts reversed in the year	–	(0.3)	(0.5)	(1.7)	(4.1)	(6.6)
Foreign exchange adjustments	(0.2)	1.3	0.9	0.5	5.1	7.6
At 31 December 2008	32.1	5.7	5.4	8.3	49.5	101.0

Closing balances

(in £ million)	Contingent consideration	Warranty claims	Contract loss provisions	Aircraft maintenance provisions	Other	Total
Current liabilities	21.3	5.1	4.5	3.8	40.5	75.2
Non-current liabilities	10.8	0.6	0.9	4.5	9.0	25.8
	32.1	5.7	5.4	8.3	49.5	101.0

Thales (France – IFRS – Source: Annual report 2008 – Electronic systems and industrial electronics)

Note 22 Reserves for contingencies

31/12/2008 (in € million)	Opening	Changes in exchange rate and other	Increase	Reversal	Closing
Restructuring	**201.3**	**(7.9)**	**30.0**	**(115.9)**	**107.5**
Provisions on contracts:	**581.2**	**9.2**	**167.4**	**(191.4)**	**566.4**
– guarantees	208.3	(10.8)	80.3	(54.8)	223.0
– litigation	185.0	16.2	21.6	(33.7)	189.1
– estimated losses on long-term contracts	47.1	1.3	19.9	(28.0)	40.3
– other	140.8	2.5	45.6	(74.9)	114.0
Other reserves for contingencies	**243.5**	**20.8**	**87.4**	**(64.1)**	**287.6**
Total	**1,026.0**	**22.1**	**284.8**	**(371.4)**	**961.5**

For the four studied companies, all the figures mentioned in the caption 'total' or 'balance at end of period' have been recorded in the balance sheet.

Required

1. What is (are) the main formal difference(s) you can notice in the presentation of the tables between the four companies?

2. Identify and comment on the differences in the terminology used to name each table.

3. Explain each component of the movements for the four studied companies.

4. Explain the nature of each provision.

5. What difference(s) do you notice in the way these companies record reductions in provisions?

Assignment 12.7
Nilsson Company

Topic: Leasing

Nilsson Company closes its books on 31 December each year. During the past year they have taken a three-year lease on a computer web server to support the development of their e-business activities. The terms and conditions of the lease agreement are provided as Exhibit 1. The lease contract itself is summarized in Exhibit 2.

Required

1. Explain how this contract should be recorded in Nilsson's books if the company does not capitalize the lease.
2. Calculate the implicit interest rate in this lease contract. Prepare the schedule of amortization of a loan that would have the same principal, the same semi-annual reimbursements and the same residual value. Break down each semi-annual reimbursement between interest expense and principal reimbursement.
3. Illustrate the accounting entries required if the lease is capitalized.
4. Prepare the relevant information that should be placed in the notes to the financial statements if the leased equipment is not capitalized.

Note: In the case of an outright acquisition of the web server, Nilsson would have depreciated it on a straight-line basis over five years.

Exhibit 1: Everylease PLC

26 December X0
Customer: Nilsson Company
Object: File number no. 982 (Nilsson)
Characteristics of the equipment provided by Everylease PLC to Nilsson Company:

- Price of the web server (in CU)   1,500
- Date of availability   1 January X1
- Purchase residual value of the
  web server at the end of the
  contract (in CU)   10

   Schedule of payments and terms of the contract (all payments are due at the end of the relevant period): There will be six semi-annual rent payments of 280 CU each on the following dates: 30 June X1, 31 December X1, 30 June X2, 31 December X2, 30 June X3, 31 December X3.

Exhibit 2: Lease contract

The following lease agreement is between, on one hand, Everylease, Public Limited Company, with a Capital of 2,000,000 CU; Headquarters address: 15, Lost Rents Avenue, London, UK, hereafter called 'the lessor', and Nilsson Company, on the other hand, hereafter called 'the lessee'. The parties agree to the following:

1 Order and commitment to lease

The lessor has ordered from:

Micro Server Incorporated (hereafter called 'the supplier'), the equipment selected directly by the lessee from the supplier. Equipment consists of the following: Microcomputer Server Hexium V, 1,200 Mhz purchased at a price of 1,500 CU.

- The lessee has committed to take delivery of the equipment as ordered.
- The actual price in the lease will reflect the prices practiced by the supplier and the lessee acknowledges knowing what this price is going to be or accept what it will be.
- Delivery of the equipment will take place in accordance with the terms and conditions enumerated in Article 1 of the General Conditions of Lease Contracts and on the date agreed to by both supplier and lessee.

2 Lease date and duration

- The lease agreement is for an irrevocable 36-month period and will be effective as of the signing of the contract pursuant to the terms and conditions of Article 1 of the General Conditions of Lease Contracts.
- Residual value: The residual value at the end of the irrevocable lease period pursuant to Articles 5, 9 and 10 of the General Conditions of Lease Contracts granting the lessee an option to buy is set at 0.67% of the actual price of the equipment.
- If the purchase option is exercised by the lessee, the residual value will be paid by lessee to lessor on 31 December X3.

3 Schedule and amount of the rent

- The first semi-annual rent payment is due at the end of the semester during which the delivery took place as attested by the invoice of the supplier and the signed delivery notice; a copy of each shall be forwarded to lessor.
- The lease payments will be in six semi-annual payments of equal amount.

Signed   *Signed*
The lessor   The lessee

Assignment 12.8
United Internet*

Topic: Reporting for liabilities

United Internet, a German internet service provider, reports in its financial statements for the year ended 31 December 2008 the following simplified balance sheet (Source: Annual report 2008 – IFRS).

Consolidated balance sheet (excerpts)		
	As at December 31	
(in € 000)	2008	2007
ASSETS		
Current assets		
Cash and cash equivalents	55,372	59,770
Accounts receivable and other assets	119,066	123,788
Inventories	19,048	16,785
Prepaid expenses	28,791	23,020
Loans to joint ventures	0	4,007
Other assets	12,737	16,371
	235,014	243,741
Non-current assets		
Shares in associated companies / joint ventures	221,684	309,023
Other financial assets	72,785	67,867
Property, plant and equipment	86,494	77,105
Intangible assets	97,512	120,031
Goodwill	378,876	388,822
Deferred tax asset	9,632	7,437
	866,983	970,285
Total assets	1,101,997	1,214,026
LIABILITIES		
Current liabilities		
Trade accounts payable	170,743	232,421
Liabilities due to banks	16,069	2,056
Advance payments received	6,453	6,069
Accrued taxes	33,855	30,172
Deferred revenue	106,401	102,200
Other accrued liabilities	4,513	7,683
Other liabilities	61,765	60,243
	399,799	440,844
Non-current liabilities		
Convertible bonds	74	245
Liabilities due to banks	528,301	369,049
Deferred tax liabilities	17,351	19,061
Other liabilities	10,892	886
	556,618	389,241
Total liabilities	956,417	830,085

In the notes to the financial statements, the detail of liabilities due to banks is provided.

Note 32 Liabilities due to banks		
(in € 000)	2008	2007
Bank loans	528,301	369,223
less		
Current portion of liabilities to banks	0	–174
Non-current portion of liabilities to banks	**528,301**	**369,049**
Current portion of non-current liabilities to banks	0	174
Short-term loans/overdrafts	16,069	1,882
Current portion of liabilities to banks	**16,069**	**2,056**
Total	**544,370**	**371,105**

Note 36 provides a detailed description of other liabilities:

Note 36 Other liabilities		
(in € 000)	2008	2007
Liabilities to the tax office	20,929	19,222
Salary and social security liabilities	11,027	11,764
Liability from interest hedging	6,671	0
Option agreement	6,425	2,663
Marketing and selling expenses / commissions	6,133	7,387
Transaction costs for sale of shares	2,153	2,153
Legal and consulting fees, auditing fees	1,816	3,125
Indemnity commitment	0	5,000
Loans received from associated companies	0	2,983
Purchase price for acquisition of shares	0	1,836
Others	6,611	4,110
Total	**61,765**	**60,243**

Required

1. Reconcile the figures reported for liabilities in the notes and the figures given in the balance sheet.

2. Comment on each component of 'other liabilities' and explain their meaning.

Assignment 12.9
Saint Gobain*

Topic: Reporting for leasing

Saint Gobain, a France-based enterprise, is involved in the production and sales of flat glass and building materials. It reports in its financial statements for the year ended 31 December 2008 the following balance sheet excerpts (Source: Annual report 2008 – IFRS).

Consolidated balance sheet (excerpts)

	As at 31 December	
(in € million)	2008	2007
Long-term debt	10,365	8,747
Provisions for pensions and other employee benefits	2,443	1,807
Deferred tax liabilities	1,130	1,277
Other non-current liabilities and provisions	1,950	1,483
Non-current liabilities	**15,888**	**13,314**
Current portion of long-term debt	1,364	971
Current portion of other liabilities	460	547
Trade accounts payable	5,613	5,752
Current tax liabilities	263	317
Other payables	3,390	3,425
Liabilities held for sale	0	41
Short-term debt and bank overdrafts	1,887	1,504
Current liabilities	**12,977**	**12,557**

In Note 18 to the accounts, the detail of net debt is provided.

Note 18 Net debt

	As at 31 December	
(in € million)	2008	2007
Bond issues and medium term notes	7,604	8,048
Perpetual bonds and participating securities	203	203
Acquisition-related bank borrowings	2,034	
Other long-term debt including finance leases	320	358
Debt recognized at fair value under the fair value option	157	146
Fair value of interest rate hedges	47	(8)
Total long-term debt (excluding current portion)	**10,365**	**8,747**
of which long-term portion of accrued interest	1	2
Current portion of long-term debt	**1,364**	**971**
Short-term financing programs (US CP, Euro CP and *Billets de Trésorerie*)	690	
Bank overdrafts and other short-term bank borrowings	798	922
Securitization	462	591
Fair value of derivatives relating to borrowings not qualified as hedges	(63)	(9)
Short-term debt and bank overdrafts	**1,887**	**1,504**
TOTAL GROSS DEBT	**13,616**	**11,222**
Cash and cash equivalents	(1,937)	(1,294)
TOTAL NET DEBT INCLUDING ACCRUED INTEREST	**11,679**	**9,928**

In Note 25 (Commitments), several disclosures concerning lease arrangement can be found.

Obligations under finance leases

Non-current assets acquired under finance leases are recognized as an asset and a liability in the consolidated balance sheet. At 31 December 2008, €64 million of future minimum lease payments due under finance leases concerned land and buildings. Total assets under finance leases recognized in consolidated assets amounted to 201 million at 31 December 2008 (31 December 2007: €190 million).

(in € million)	As at 31 December	
	2008	2007
Future minimum lease payments		
Within 1 year	48	48
1 to 5 years	106	96
Beyond 5 years	28	33
Total	**182**	**177**
Less finance charge	(17)	(21)
Present value of future minimum lease payments	**165**	**156**

Obligations under operating leases

The group leases equipment, vehicles, and office, manufacturing and warehouse space under various non- cancellable operating leases. Lease terms generally range from 1 to 9 years. The leases contain rollover options for varying periods of time and some include clauses covering the payment of real estate taxes and insurance. In most cases, management expects that these leases will be rolled over or replaced by other leases in the normal course of business. Net rental expense was €696 million in 2008, corresponding to rental expense of €713 million – of which €437 million for property leases – less €17 million in revenue from subleases. Future minimum payments due under non-cancellable operating leases are as follows:

(in € million)	Total 2008	within 1 year	1 to 5 years	Beyond 5 years	Total 2007
	Payments due				
Operating leases					
Rental expense	3,246	641	1,507	1,098	3,090
Subletting revenue	(91)	(14)	(30)	(47)	(133)
Total	**3,155**	**627**	**1,477**	**1,051**	**2,957**

Required

1. Reconcile the figures reported for net debt in the notes and the figures given in the balance sheet.

2. Identify in the notes the figures relating to finance leases.

3. Reconcile the detail of net debt and the special information given on finance leases.

4. In the notes, what information relating to interest implicit in lease payments and to finance leases in general is not given?

Assignment 12.10
ArcelorMittal*

Topic: Debt ratios

ArcelorMittal is a global steel producer headquartered in Luxembourg. The balance sheet and income statement for the years 2005 to 2008 (Source: Annual reports 2005–2008), prepared in accordance with IFRS, are provided as follows.

Consolidated balance sheet

(in US$ million)	As at 31 December			
	2005	2006	2007	2008
ASSETS				
Current assets:				
Cash and cash equivalents	2,035	6,020	7,860	7,576
Restricted cash	100	120	245	11
Short-term investments	14	6	–	–
Assets held for sale	–	1,267	1,296	910
Trade accounts receivable and other	2,287	8,769	9,533	6,737
Inventories	5,994	19,238	21,750	24,741
Prepaid expenses and other current assets	925	3,942	4,644	4,439
Total current assets	**11,355**	**39,362**	**45,328**	**44,414**
Non-current assets:				
Goodwill and intangible assets	1,806	10,782	15,031	16,119
Property, plant and equipment	19,045	54,696	61,994	60,755
Investments in associates and joint ventures	947	3,492	5,887	8,512
Other investments	277	1,151	2,159	437
Deferred tax assets	318	1,670	1,629	751
Other assets	119	1,013	1,597	2,100
Total non-current assets	**22,512**	**72,804**	**88,297**	**88,674**
TOTAL ASSETS	**33,867**	**112,166**	**133,625**	**133,088**
LIABILITIES AND EQUITY				
Current liabilities:				
Short-term debt and current portion of long-term debt	334	4,922	8,542	8,409
Trade accounts payable and other	2,504	10,717	13,991	10,501
Short-term provisions	109	569	1,144	3,292
Liabilities held for sale	–	239	266	370
Accrued expenses and other liabilities	2,169	7,579	7,275	7,413
Income tax liabilities	483	534	991	775
Total current liabilities	**5,599**	**24,560**	**32,209**	**30,760**
Non-current liabilities:				
Long-term debt, net of current portion	7,974	21,645	22,085	25,667
Deferred tax liabilities	2,174	7,274	7,927	6,395
Deferred employee benefits	1,054	5,285	6,244	7,111
Long-term provisions	611	1,880	2,456	2,343
Other long-term obligations	998	1,331	1,169	1,582
Total non-current liabilities	**12,811**	**37,415**	**39,881**	**43,098**
Total liabilities	**18,410**	**61,975**	**72,090**	**73,858**
Commitments and contingencies (notes 22 and 24)				
EQUITY:				
Common shares	60	17	9,269	9,269
Treasury stock	(111)	(84)	(1,552)	(5,800)
Additional paid-in capital	2,239	25,566	20,309	20,575
Retained earnings	10,270	14,974	23,552	30,403
Reserves	828	1,654	5,107	751
Equity attributable to the equity holders of the parent	**13,286**	**42,127**	**56,685**	**55,198**
Minority interest	2,171	8,064	4,850	4,032
Total equity	**15,457**	**50,191**	**61,535**	**59,230**
TOTAL LIABILITIES AND EQUITY	**33,867**	**112,166**	**133,625**	**133,088**

Consolidated income statement				
	Year ended 31 December			
(in US$ million)	2005	2006	2007	2008
Sales	28,132	58,870	105,216	124,936
Cost of sales	22,341	48,411	84,953	106,110
Gross margin	**5,791**	**10,459**	**20,263**	**18,826**
Selling, general and administrative	1,062	2,960	5,433	6,590
Operating income	**4,729**	**7,499**	**14,830**	**12,236**
Other income - net	214	49	–	–
Income from investments in associates and joint ventures	86	301	985	1,653
Financing costs - net	(353)	(654)	(927)	(2,352)
Income before taxes	**4,676**	**7,195**	**14,888**	**11,537**
Income tax expense	881	1,109	3,038	1,098
Net income (including minority interest)	**3,795**	**6,086**	**11,850**	**10,439**
Net income attributable to:				
Equity holders of the parent	3,301	5,226	10,368	9,399
Minority interest	494	860	1,482	1,040
Net income (including minority interest)	**3,795**	**6,086**	**11,850**	**10,439**

Required

1. Compute for the years 2005 to 2008 the first four 'debt ratios' introduced in section 10 of this chapter: debt ratio, debt to equity ratio, long-term debt to equity ratio, and interest coverage ratio.

2. Analyze these ratios. Note that minority interests[8] are often included in equity in the computation of ratios based on this concept.

References

FASB (1976), Statement of Financial Accounting Standard No. 13: Accounting for lease, Norwalk, CT.

IASB (1989), Framework for the Preparation and Presentation of Financial Statements, London.

IASB (1998a) International Accounting Standard No. 19: Employee Benefits, London.

IASB (1998b) International Accounting Standard N°o.37: Provisions, Contingent Liabilities and Contingent Assets, London.

IASB (2003) International Accounting Standard No. 17: Leases, London.

IASB (2007) International Accounting Standard No. 1: Presentation of Financial Statements, London.

IASB (2008) International Accounting Standard No. 39: Financial Instruments: Recognition and Measurement, London.

Plender, J., Simons, M. and Tricks, H. (2005) 'Cash benefit: how big supermarkets fund expansion by using suppliers as bankers', *Financial Times*, Wednesday December 7, 2005, 13.

Stice, J., Stice, E.K. and Skousen, F. (2009) *Intermediate Accounting*, 17th edn, South-Western Cengage Learning, Mason, OH.

Vernimmen, P., Quiry, P., Le Fur, Y., Dallocchio, M. and Salvi, A. (2009) *Corporate Finance: Theory and Practice*. 2nd edn, Wiley-Blackwell, Oxford.

Further reading

Cravens, K.S. and Goad Oliver, E. (2000) 'The influence of culture on pension plans', *International Journal of Accounting* 35(4): 521–37.

Fisher, J. G., Maines, L.A., Peffer, S.A. and Sprinkle, G.B. (2005) 'An experimental investigation of employer discretion in employee performance evaluation and compensation', *The Accounting Review* 80(2): 563–83.

Garrod, N. and Sieringhaus, I. (1995) 'European Union accounting harmonization: the case of leased assets in the United Kingdom and Germany', *European Accounting Review* 4(1): 155–64.

Moneva, J.M. and Llena, F. (2000) 'Environmental disclosures in the annual reports of large companies in Spain', *European Accounting Review* 9(1): 7–29.

Additional material on the website

Go to http://www.cengage.co.uk/stolowy3 for further information, journal entries and extra assignments for each chapter.

The following appendices to this chapter are available on the dedicated website:

Appendix 12.1: Accounting for notes payable
Appendix 12.2: Accounting for sales tax
Appendix 12.3: Interest and time value of money
Appendix 12.4: Environmental liability
Appendix 12.5: Bonds issued at a discount
Appendix 12.6: Sales and leaseback transactions

Notes

1. Leverage can be illustrated by the following small example: Two firms A and B are identical in all respects, except the structure of their long-term funding. Each has, during last the accounting period, earned an income before interest of 100 CU. The market based interest rate for long-term funds they both face is 5%. Firm A's shareholders' equity is 200 CU while long-term debt amounts to 1,000 CU. The before tax return on equity for firm A is $(200 - 5\% \times 1,000)/200 = 75\%$. Meanwhile, firm B's equity is 500 CU and its long-term debt amounts to 700 CU. The return on equity before taxes for firm B is $(200 - 5\% \times 700)/500 = 33\%$.

Firm A is more leveraged than firm B in that a CU of shareholders' equity yields a higher return than an equivalent CU in firm B. Higher leverage means higher shareholders' return on equity, but too much leverage (too little shareholders' equity) may lead to interest expenses that may reduce dramatically the income (or the cash flow) from operations and thus put the firm in danger (either through higher interest rates or through insufficient cash to keep the operating cycle going).

2. See, for example, Vernimmen *et al.* (2009).
3. We chose in Figure 12.6 to use the term 'real and present' rather than simply 'present' because we feel it is more explicit regarding the causality principle.
4. The process of gathering a group of debt obligations such as receivables into a pool, and then dividing that pool into portions that can be sold as securities in the secondary market. (Adapted from www.investordictionary.com)
5. The method of calculation is either firm specific or industry specific.
6. See for example Stice *et al.* (2009).
7. 'Debt' represents long-term and short-term interest-bearing liabilities.
8. They represent the part of the net results of operations of a subsidiary attributable to interests which are not owned, directly or indirectly through subsidiaries, by the parent company (minority shareholders). This item will be presented in a more detailed manner in Chapter 13 devoted to Consolidation.

C13

Chapter 13
Business Combinations

Learning objectives

After studying this chapter, you will understand:

- What a business combination is.
- Why consolidated financial statements are useful.
- That three methods of consolidation coexist and that the choice of the appropriate one depends on the nature of the relation between the investing firm and its investee.
- What non-controlling (minority) interests and goodwill represent.
- How the consolidation process works.
- That deferred taxes may arise from specific consolidation rules and procedures that may differ from tax rules.
- How the translation of financial statements labeled in a foreign currency is recorded.
- How mergers are recorded.

Enterprises create value for their owners by utilizing and transforming resources to satisfy solvent customer demand. This means extracting more resources from the customer in exchange for the services or products provided than it took to create these and make them available to the customer.

We have seen that financial statements, and especially the income statement and the statement of cash flows, reflect the transformation process that is implemented through the operations of a firm. However, the process of value creation may require that the firm look (and be proactive) beyond the frontiers of the 'legal entity' and start developing a network of relationships in order to secure a superior ability to deliver customer satisfaction in a sustainable way, and thus a return to its investors higher than other investments in the same risk class.

Besides strategic alliances that are beyond the scope of this text, the development of such a network organization can lead a business to engage in intercorporate investments. These are the focus of this chapter.

We saw in Chapter 10 that when operations create resources (cash or equivalents) in excess of the day-to-day and normal needs, the surplus must be invested in marketable securities to protect the purchasing power of these 'excess' liquidities while waiting for the appropriate use of this resource. Such investments are short lived in general (even if, in rare cases, the financial instrument itself may be long-term, it will be, in any case, held for only a short period of time). Such investments are coherent with a position of 'wait and see' until an attractive (and strategically coherent) investment opportunity presents itself or is created. Investments in marketable securities are passive: the investing firm has no significant right or possibility, and, most importantly, no intent to influence the behavior of the business entity.

This chapter deals with active investment of the resources of the firm in financial assets (as opposed to tangible or intangible assets). We use the term active in the sense that the investing firm chooses to apply its resources to deliberately grow its value creation potential and do so with a long-term, strategic view, requiring that it takes an active role in the decision-making process of the firm in which it has invested. In this category of investments we find close-knit and loose networks, often built around a 'leader firm' specialized in production or distribution or both.

Some networks however require no direct investment. The aerospace and automotive industries, with their long established system of concentric first-, second- and third-tier suppliers are examples of such networks, but networks of small businesses are also more and more common. A general contractor in the construction industry is a traditional example of such loose network of medium to small enterprises. The idea here is to partition the risk and increase the speed of reactivity of the whole network to the needs and opportunities of both technology and markets while focusing each firm on its core competence and thus improving the efficiency of use of resources in delivering effectively the value proposition.

We focus on active financial investments that are the product of a deliberate strategy on the part of the leading (investing) firm. These can take several forms. Three generic models or approaches can easily be combined to create customized 'solutions' fitting any tactical or strategic need:

1. **The lender approach**: The simplest solution to create a preferred relationship is probably to lend resources to another corporate entity (controlled or not) in order to foster its development in a strategically targeted way so as to, for example, create a reliable supplier (possibly using a defined technology) or a reliable customer. Under the lender approach the entity does not behave as a substitute to a financial institution, but actively encourages, by providing loan funds, a third party entity to develop a certain technology, carry out a focused research program, increase quality or capacity, acquire facilities or equipment, etc. that will, *in fine*, benefit the lending entity.

2. **The joint business creation approach**: A business can also create another corporate entity either alone or in active partnership with one or several already existing firms sharing a similar interest. The new entity would be expected to be more nimble and reactive or able to deal more effectively than the investing firm(s) with regards to a core competence or core market (for example by being 'closer' to the technology, the resources, or the customers or any combination of the three), or have access to less expensive resources. The issue here becomes one of degree of strategic control held by the reporting entity (provider of capital) over the third-party entity. Two levels of strategic control (i.e., integration in the value creation process of the investing firm) lead to different types of reporting. Accountants traditionally distinguish between influence[1] and **control**.[2]

IAS 28 defines influence as having between 20% to 50% of the voting rights – the implicit assumption being that owning less than 20% of the capital of an entity does not give **significant influence** to the investor.[3]

The term control is used to describe the relationship when the investing firm has more than 50% of the capital of the new entity. In the case of control, the reporting issues and practices are identical to those evoked under the acquisition approach below.

3. **The acquisition approach**: The third approach consists in acquiring a controlling interest in – or combining with – an already existing entity (thus, hopefully, reducing the risks inherent in the creation of a new venture), either to gain access to a technique or a market segment or to grow the size of the business to enjoy greater economies of scale and/or scope. Recent examples abound in the financial press of business entities creating closer links between their activities: Rio Tinto/Alcan, BP/Amoco, Nokia/Navtech, Pernod-Ricard/Allied-Domecq, Banque Populaire/Caisse d'Epargne, Pfizer/Wyeth, Sprint/Nextel, etc. and, of course, the almost innumerable list of mergers and acquisitions in the financial sector after the financial crisis of October 2008 including BNP Paribas/Fortis and Chase/Washington Mutual.

A fourth strategy exists that has no reporting implication in that it consists in creating a network of gentleman's agreements between firms that agree to cooperate freely (and often seal their agreement to work together through contracts, but without financial investment changing hands) either because of family or friendship ties between their leaders or because they feel all members of the network will benefit from their cooperation. Since such strategy has no reporting implications beyond their being optionally mentioned in the notes to the annual report, we will not explore the issues raised by this approach.

The focus of this chapter is about reporting to shareholders the financial links created by – and, more importantly, the value creation potential of – these sometimes complex, more or less close-knit networks of firms. If the organizing firm (or 'pivot' of the network) were to only report its own economic activities, without acknowledging the value created and the value creation potential (and obligations) resulting from these preferred linkages its active financial investments have built, it would not give true and fair information to the shareholders or potential investors. The pivot firm's only visible assets might be the loans granted or the shares acquired. The nature of the business and its potential, opportunities, obligations and correlated risks would thus not be apparent from the figures reported in its balance sheet.

Consolidated financial statements create a description of the financial position of an economic entity that is the agglomeration or conglomeration of diverse and, often, distinct legal entities headed by a common management and connected by relations of intercorporate investments or lending relationships. A subsidiary, however, is generally not individually liable for the liabilities of another. Issues of degree of autonomy of each member of the '**group**' and definition of rules partitioning the wealth created by the networked entity must be addressed if one is to provide relevant financial statements to financial information users. Such issues are central to this chapter.

The fact that complex, more- or less-loosely coupled 'groups' are now often more the norm than are the pre-1970s-style 'integrated' single legal entity firms, has led countries such as the USA and Canada to even cease asking the pivot firm to report as a stand-alone entity since its balance sheet would, as a rule, be largely meaningless to a potential investor.

We first look at the method of establishment and interpretation of consolidated financial reports (sections 1–3). Sections 4–7 explore more technical points. The consolidation process follows a rigorous methodology, which will be covered in section 4. We will then address two especially sticky points in the consolidation process: deferred taxation arising from consolidation entries (due, among other reasons, to timing differences as seen in Chapter 6) and translation of financial statements established in a currency different from the one used by the reporting entity (the parent company). We will go on to cover the reporting issues resulting from a 'legal merger' in which the two or more combining entities literally disappear into a third entity.

Consolidated financial statements describe the financial position of an economic entity resulting from the existence of active intercorporate financial investments or fixed financial assets. The latter can take different forms.

1 Types of investments

The three combinatorial strategies evoked in the introduction lead to the existence of four types of financial fixed assets:

- shares in subsidiaries;
- shares in associated (also called affiliated) companies;
- shares in other investments (including joint ventures);
- loans to subsidiaries, associated companies and other investments.

We will clarify later in this chapter the difference between **subsidiary**, **associate** and interest in a **joint venture**. We have seen in Chapter 10 that IAS 39 (IASB 2008a: § 9), which addresses the issues relating to four categories of financial instruments, does not concern itself with investments in subsidiaries, associates and joint ventures because, as will be seen in section 2, these instruments will be eliminated in the consolidation process (for subsidiaries and joint ventures) or revalued according to specific rules (for associates). Such investments are recorded and reported in accordance with IAS 27 (2003a, amended 2008), IAS 28 (2003b) and IAS 31 (2003c).

2 Business combinations: principles

2.1 Definition

A **business combination** is 'a transaction or other event in which an acquirer obtains control of one or more businesses. Transactions sometimes referred to as "true mergers" or "mergers of equals" are also business combinations as that term is used in this IFRS' (IASB 2008b, IFRS 3: Appendix A, 'Defined terms').

A variety of scenarios can be followed in order to create a business combination. The following list is illustrative of some of the most commonly observed scenarios but is in no way exhaustive. Merger and acquisition specialists (financiers and lawyers alike) compete in creativity in designing approaches best tailored to each specific situation. Essentially all solutions are variations on (or, even, combinations of) the generic five scenarios that are described below:

- Acquisition of an interest in another entity: Company X obtains control over Company Y by acquiring enough shares of Y in exchange for cash or in exchange for shares of X or a combination of the two. In this case, Company Y continues to exist as a separate legal entity (and thus may still be required to produce its own financial statements) but becomes a subsidiary of X. The financial statements of Y are integrated in the consolidated financial statements of X, which becomes the meaningful reporting entity.

- Legal (or statutory) merger: Company X acquires all outstanding shares of Company Y. The latter is dissolved as a legal entity and all its assets and liabilities are merged in the accounts of Company X.

- Statutory consolidation: Company X and Company Y decide jointly to combine all their activities to become the Z Company entity. Both Company X and Company Y are dissolved as legal entities and their assets and liabilities are entirely integrated in the accounts of the Z entity.

- Creation of a holding entity: Company X and Company Y decide jointly to combine all their activities but, unlike in the previous case, neither of the combining companies is dissolved. The shareholders of each company exchange their shares against those of a newly formed holding Company H. Company H, a holding company, becomes the sole shareholder of both Company X and Company Y. These in turn become subsidiaries of H and their activities, assets and liabilities are consolidated in the accounts of the holding company (the reporting company).

■ Acquisition of assets and liabilities: Company X acquires directly all the assets of Company Y, without acquiring its shares (acquisition of assets). Company Y is essentially liquidated as it currently exists and the cash it receives in exchange for its assets is used to settle its liabilities. Company Y then either returns the surplus cash to its shareholders before dissolving itself or becomes a totally different business by investing the available funds in a new venture.

The method used to record any of the above business combinations is known as 'purchase accounting' (consolidation or merger). This method is based on the basic assumption that one of the combining entities obtains control over the other combining entity. However, in a not-so-distant past, when, in exceptional circumstances, it was not possible to identify an acquirer, the shareholders of the combining entities joining in a substantially equal arrangement to share control over the most, or effectively the most, of their net assets and operations, another accounting method had been used: the 'uniting of interests' (also known as 'pooling of interests'). The use of this method, developed in Appendix 13.1, has been forbidden in the USA since June 2001 and is now prohibited in IFRS 3 (IASB 2008b). Occurrences of its use should therefore dwindle rapidly towards extinction as only non-IFRS- or non-US-GAAP compliant countries still allow the use of this approach.

2.2 Usefulness of consolidated financial statements

A corporation owning shares of another holds power over the second. The economic entity resulting from the combination of two or more entities linked by intercorporate investments of sufficient importance to warrant effective control of one over the other is called a 'group', which is defined by IASB (IAS 27, 2003a: § 4) as 'a parent and all its subsidiaries'. In most countries (with the notable exception of Germany) a group is generally not a legal entity as such and the parent company (pivot of the combination) and each controlled corporation are separate legal entities.

In order to allow investors or shareholders to shape their opinion about the financial position and the performance potential of a group, it is essential for the management of the combined entities to develop and provide group accounts, also called consolidated accounts or consolidated financial statements.

Consolidated financial statements are needed because the accounts of the pivot company (parent or holding company) contain, as mentioned earlier, and developed below, little useful information about the performance potential and the resources and obligations of the group. Some of the reasons for the lack of representativeness of the unconsolidated accounts of the parent are listed as follows. Each is a justification for developing consolidated statements:

1. If the parent company is a 'pure' holding company (i.e., the case of a corporation whose sole purpose is to own – hold and manage – the shares of the members of the group and coordinate their activities without directly exercising any industrial, commercial or service activity itself).

   (a) The unconsolidated income statement of the holding company is very 'simple' and characterized by the following elements:

      (i) It does not include any of the 'traditional' items such as 'sales revenue', 'cost of goods sold' or 'purchases'.

(ii) Revenues are essentially comprised of 'management fees' (internal billing of 'services' to each group member company) and 'investment income' which is the sum of all dividends received.

(iii) Expenses include mainly administrative expenses (personnel expenses, depreciation of equipment) of an often very light coordination team. For example the headcount at the Saint-Gobain headquarters (a parent company based in Paris, operating essentially in the high-performance construction materials, flat glass, and packaging sectors) averages 228 people, while the whole group employs around 208,053 persons! (Source: Annual report 2008).

(b) The unconsolidated balance sheet is also somewhat unusual in its structure:

(i) It probably does not include any significant (or relevant for evaluating the financial position) amounts under accounts receivable, accounts payable, and inventories.

(ii) The value of tangible and intangible assets is often low.

(iii) However, financial investments represent an unusually high percentage of total assets. These are the shares of group companies owned by the parent company. Since, in our opinion, IAS 39 does not address the valuation of these investments, they are generally reported at their acquisition cost. Some GAAP allow or encourage reporting these investments valued at equity (i.e., for each group company, the value of the investment is obtained by multiplying the number of shares owned by the parent by the book equity per share of the subsidiary or associate).

2. If the parent company is a 'mixed' holding company (i.e., a corporation which both exercises a significant economic activity of its own and, in addition, administers a group of companies), the unconsolidated financial statements of the parent may have a more informative content than the equivalent balance sheet of a 'pure' holding, since they reflect at least the stand-alone economic activity of the parent as well as the financial result of the holding activity. Despite their somewhat greater relevance than those of a pure holding company, the unconsolidated financial statements of the parent would still be very far from giving a true and fair view of the performance potential of the group and of its risks, assets and obligations: importance of financial investments, importance of investment income and management fees hide the reality of the relationships of the group with its markets.

Given each and all of these weaknesses and insufficiencies of unconsolidated statements, it appears judicious, so as to inform investors, to require such businesses to prepare financial statements that reflect the economic activity of a group. As stated in IAS 27 (IASB 2003a: § 4): 'Consolidated financial statements are the financial statements of a group presented as those of a single economic entity'.

2.3 Nature of relations between parent company and group entities

The nature of the relation(s) existing between the parent company and the different group entities is a determinant of the way the financial statements of each of the individual group entities will be taken into account in the consolidation process to create the group financial statements.

Table 13.1 lists the definitions suggested by the IASB of the three types of group companies that result from a classification and a qualification of the subsidiarity[4] relationship that exists between a parent and another corporation. Any corporation whose relation to the 'parent' does not fall in one of the three types shown in Table 13.1 will not be considered as a group company (i.e., it will not be within the scope of consolidation) and thus will not be consolidated.

Table 13.1 Relations between a 'parent' and another group entity

	Type of relation		Type of group company
Control	'Power to govern the financial and operating policies of an entity so as to obtain benefits from its activities' (IAS 27: § 4).	Subsidiary	'Entity (…) that is controlled by another entity (known as the parent)' (IAS 27: § 4).
Significant influence	'Power to participate in the financial and operating policy decisions of the investee but it is not control or joint control over those policies' (IAS 28: § 2).	Associate	'Entity (…) over which the investor has significant influence and that is neither a subsidiary nor an interest in a joint venture' (IAS 28: § 2).
Joint control	'Contractually agreed sharing of control [between two or more legal entities] over an economic activity' (IAS 31: § 3).	Joint venture	'Contractual arrangement whereby two or more parties undertake an economic activity that is subject to joint control' (IAS 31: § 3).

2.3.1 Detailed definition of the three types of relations

Control   According to IAS 27 (IASB 2003a: § 13), 'control is presumed to exist when the parent owns directly, or indirectly through subsidiaries, more than one half of the voting power of an entity (…). Control also exists even when the parent owns one half or less of the voting power of an entity when there is:

(a) power over more than one half of the voting rights by virtue of an agreement with other investors;

(b) power to govern the financial and operating policies of the entity under a statute or an agreement;

(c) power to appoint or remove the majority of the members of the board of directors or equivalent governing body and control of the entity is by that board or body; or

(d) power to cast the majority of votes at meetings of the board of directors or equivalent governing body and control of the entity is by that board or body'.

'Control' may sometimes exist even though less than a majority of the capital is held by the parent since voting rights alone define control (as seen in Chapter 11, multiple voting rights or no voting rights may be attached to shares). What matters is the actual ability to exercise control.

Significant influence   According to IAS 28, entitled 'Investment in Associates' (IAS 2003b: § 6): 'If an investor holds, directly or indirectly through subsidiaries, twenty per cent or more of the voting power of the **investee**, it is presumed that the investor has significant influence, unless it can be demonstrated that this is not the case. Conversely, if the investor holds, directly or indirectly (…) less than twenty per cent of the voting power of the investee, it is presumed that the investor does not have significant influence, unless such influence can be clearly demonstrated'. The Standard adds: 'A substantial or majority ownership by another investor does not necessarily preclude an investor from having significant influence'.

In practice: 'The existence of significant influence by an investor is usually evidenced in one or more of the following ways:

(a) representation on the board of directors or equivalent governing body of the investee;

(b) participation in policy-making processes including participation in decisions about dividends or other distributions;

(c) material transactions between the investor and the investee;

(d) interchange of managerial personnel; or

(e) provision of essential technical information' (IAS 28: § 7).

Joint control   Joint ventures take on many different forms and structures and are described in IAS 31 (IASB 2003c). All joint ventures result from a contractual arrangement between two or more economic entities which establish **joint control** of a (most of the time newly created) third company.

2.3.2 Percentage of control and percentage of interest

The percentage of control and the percentage of interest affect the way the accounts will be consolidated and how the value created will be shared:

1. **Percentage of control** (also called percentage of voting rights) is the term used to reflect the degree of dependency in which a parent company holds its subsidiaries or associates. The higher the percentage, the higher the dependency of the group company. This percentage measures the proportion of total voting rights held by the parent in its related company and is used to determine which method of consolidation will be applied in establishing the consolidated financial statements. The three methods are **full consolidation**, **equity method**, and **proportionate consolidation** and are described below.

2. **Percentage of interest** (also called percentage of ownership or of stake) represents the claim held by the parent company over the shareholders' equity (including net income) of its subsidiaries or associates. This percentage is used in the process of consolidation of accounts and calculations to define majority and non-controlling (minority) interests.

The percentage of control held by a parent may be different from the percentage of interest it holds in a given subsidiary or associate. This is the case, for example, when there is a cascade of dependency links. Figure 13.1 illustrates a situation in which a parent company P is linked to corporation C2 both directly and indirectly by way of another corporation C1 in which the parent holds a non-controlling interest.

The *percentage of control* of the parent P over C2 is equal to only 43% and not to 83% (43% + 40%) because P does not have control over C1 (30% only) thus the 'possible influence' branch that goes through C1 gives zero control to P over C2. With 43% control by the parent and without any additional element qualifying the relationship between P and C2, we can only say that there is significant influence.

The *percentage of interest* of P in C2 however is equal to 55% [43% + (30 % × 40%), i.e., (43% + 12%)]. Even with a percentage of interest equal to 55% (which is higher than 50%), there is nonetheless not more than 'significant influence' as the insufficient percentage of control dominates (43%, which is lower than 50%).

Note that the percentage of control equals the percentage of interest in case of a direct link (30% between P and C1, 40% between C1 and C2 and 43% between P and C2 [for the direct link only]).

Figure 13.1 Percentages of control may differ from percentages of interest

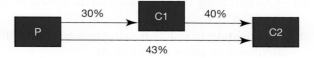

3 Reporting the acquisition of a financial interest: consolidation methods

When there is control and/or influence, consolidation is generally required. Table 13.1 introduced the three main types of control or influence relationships and to each corresponds a method of consolidation as shown in Figure 13.2.

In Figure 13.2, the dotted arrow between 'joint venture' and 'equity method' arises from IAS 31 (2003c: § 38), which states that 'as an alternative to proportionate consolidation (…), a venturer shall [can, in our opinion] recognize its interest in a jointly controlled entity using the equity method'. The text of that standard, however, adds that the IASB 'does not recommend the use of the equity method because proportionate consolidation better reflects the substance and economic reality of a venturer's interest in a jointly controlled entity, that is to say, control over the venturer's share of the future economic benefits. Nevertheless, this Standard permits the use of the equity method, as an alternative treatment, when recognizing interests in jointly controlled entities' (§ 40).

3.1 Impact of an acquisition on reporting

Each method described in Figure 13.2 will be analyzed below from a conceptual viewpoint and its mechanism illustrated both in a schematic diagram and through a quantified (running) example based on the Lentz Company acquiring an interest in Meder Co. At the end of year X1 Lentz Company acquires an interest in the Meder Company which continues to exist, and becomes its subsidiary.

We will look at six situations: first, by reporting the impact of the acquisition when no consolidation is required or mandated, and, second, when consolidation is required. We will cover this latter case, through 'simulations' of the consolidated statements in the following five alternative situations:

1. *Case 1*: An interest of 100% is acquired for a price equal to the book value of the acquired equity (full consolidation).

2. *Case 2*: An interest of only 90% is acquired (with the same assumption of price equals book value) (full consolidation).

3. *Case 3*: An interest of 100% is acquired for a price that is larger than the book value of the equity acquired (full consolidation).

4. *Case 4*: An interest of 30% is acquired for a price equal to the book value of the acquired equity (equity method).

5. *Case 5*: An interest of 50% is acquired for a price equal to the book value of the acquired equity (proportionate consolidation).

Figure 13.2 Consolidation methods

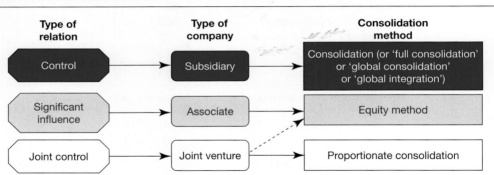

3.2 When no consolidation is required

Lentz Company is headquartered in a country where consolidation is compulsory only if the group size exceeds a certain threshold. At the time of acquisition, Lentz Company does not meet the threshold level. The price paid in cash (320 CU) is equal to the share-holders' equity (book value of the subsidiary). It corresponds to 100% of the subsidiary's shareholders' equity at the time of acquisition (share capital, retained earnings/reserves, and undistributed net income).

Table 13.2 shows the unconsolidated balance sheet of Lentz Company before and after acquisition. The only modifications of Lentz' balance sheets stem from the investment in Meder and the corresponding decrease in cash. It is important to remember that the balance sheet of Lentz Company after the acquisition is not a consolidated balance sheet, just a balance sheet that reflects a financial asset acquired.

3.3 When full consolidation is required

Figure 13.3 illustrates the basic principles of full consolidation.

The founding principle of full consolidation is that all assets and liabilities of the sub-sidiary are added to those of the parent (excluding, of course, the investment the parent holds in the subsidiary, which is eliminated in the process). Technically, if the percentage of interest of the parent is not 100%, part of the assets and liabilities (and thus of the equity) of the subsidiary belongs to 'minority shareholders' and will be identified as such in the consolidated statements (see Lentz Company, Case 2 below).

Two years later (at the end of X3), because of the growth of Lentz Company's business over the previous two years, the threshold is crossed, and providing shareholders with consolidated financial statements is now required (financial statements as of 31 December X3 to be published in early X4).

The unconsolidated (stand-alone) financial statements of both companies at the end of X3 are shown in Table 13.3.

Table 13.2 Balance sheets at acquisition

Balance sheets as of 31 December X1	Lentz before acquisition	Meder (stand-alone)	Lentz after acquisition
Assets			
Investment in Meder	0		320
Other assets (including cash)	2,000	500	1,680
Total	2,000	500	2,000
Equity and liabilities			
Share capital	600	200	600
Retained earnings/Reserves	460	100	460
Net income	30	20*	30
Liabilities	910	180	910
Total	2,000	500	2,000

*The shareholders have decided at the annual meeting that net income will not be distributed.

Figure 13.3 Full consolidation

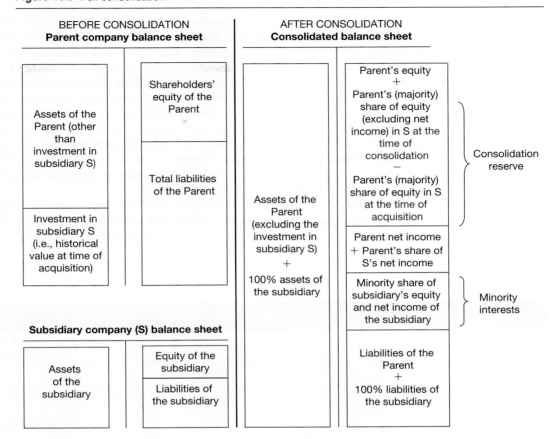

Table 13.3 Financial statements as of 31 December X3

Balance sheets as of 31 December X3	Lentz	Meder
Assets		
Investment in Meder	320	
Other assets (including cash)	1,880	600
Total	2,200	600
Equity and liabilities		
Share capital	600	200
Retained earnings/Reserves	500	300
Net income	50	40
Liabilities	1,050	60
Total	2,200	600
Income statements – Year X3	Lentz	Meder
Sales	1,000	400
Expenses	950	360
Net income after tax	50	40

3.3.1 Case 1: Consolidation – 100% of interest – full consolidation

The 'full consolidation' method consists in a series of eliminations and adjusting entries that create the consolidated financial statements. Table 13.4 illustrates the consolidated balance sheet in Case 1 and Table 13.5 illustrates the consolidated income statement.

When applying the full consolidation mechanism, as stated in IAS 27 (§ 18): 'An entity combines the financial statements of the parent and its subsidiaries line by line by adding together like items of assets, liabilities, equity, income and expenses'. However, such a combined balance sheet does not provide a 'true and fair view' of the group because it includes the investment in Meder as an asset and, in the equity, the corresponding share of equity of the subsidiary, which belongs to Lentz, the parent company. In other words, the combined balance sheet shows an investment of the group in itself. This investment must be eliminated along with the corresponding share of equity of the carrying amount of the parent's investment in each subsidiary.

This elimination is carried out as operation (a) in Table 13.4. Consequently, the consolidated equity represents only the share capital and reserves of the parent company (plus the undistributed net income of both parent and subsidiary companies).

Table 13.4 Consolidated balance sheet (full consolidation)

As of 31 December X3	Lentz (stand-alone) (1)	Meder (stand-alone) (2)	Combined (3) = (1) + (2)	Elimination entries and adjustments	(4)	Consolidated balance sheet (5) = (3) + (4)
Assets						
Investment in Meder	320		320	(a)	–320	0
Other assets (including cash)	1,880	600	2,480			2,480
Total	2,200	600	2,800		–320	2,480
Equity and liabilities						
Share capital	600	200	800	(a)	–200	600
Retained earnings/Reserves	500	300	800	(a)	–300	500
Consolidation reserve				(a)	180	180
Net income	50	40	90			90
Liabilities	1,050	60	1,110			1,110
Total	2,200	600	2,800		–320	2,480

Table 13.5 Consolidated income statement (full consolidation)

Year X3	Lentz (stand-alone)	Meder (stand-alone)	Combined	Elimination entries and adjustments	Consolidated income statement
Sales	1,000	400	1,400		1,400
Expenses	950	360	1,310		1,310
Net income	50	40	90		90

Figure 13.3 and Table 13.4 both show a 'consolidation reserve'. This reserve is the difference between:

- at the time of consolidation: the share (i.e., percentage of interest) of the subsidiary equity held by the consolidating parent (majority share of subsidiary's equity) *excluding* undistributed net income, and
- at the time of acquisition: the share (i.e., percentage of interest) of the subsidiary equity held by the consolidating parent *including* undistributed net income.

In our example, the consolidation reserve amounts to:

$$(200 + 300) \times 100\% - (200 + 100 + 20) \times 100\% = 180$$

An alternative description of the full consolidation process is to say that the investment in the subsidiary is mathematically and mechanically replaced by the book value of assets and liabilities of the subsidiary reflecting the percentage of interest of the parent. As we will see in Case 2, had the interest been less than 100%, there would have been **minority interests**, which would be shown on the equity and liabilities side of the balance sheet.

Intra-group balances and intra-group transactions (i.e., transactions between the parent and the subsidiary or between subsidiaries) should be eliminated in full. For example, if Lentz Company had held accounts receivable in the amount of 50 CU on Meder Company – which would mean the latter had recorded accounts payable to Lentz for the same amount – both balances would have been eliminated when calculating the consolidated assets and liabilities since these balances would have been of equal amount and opposite sign.

Table 13.5 illustrates the resulting consolidated income statement, which can be used to report the profit generation potential of the combined businesses.

We have assumed no intra-group trade, thus Table 13.5 shows no adjusting or eliminating entry is needed in the preparation of the consolidated income statement. The consolidated income statement is thus the result of combining mechanically the parent and subsidiary income statements with, of course, the elimination of any intra-group transactions. The elimination of intra-group trade has, in fact, no impact on net income of the group since the sales revenue recognized in one firm's stand-alone income statement is part of the costs incurred in the other's stand-alone income statement. However, it is critical to explicitly cancel-out all intra-group transactions to avoid the risk of biasing operating ratios involving sales revenue and cost of sales separately (by artificially inflating the balances).

3.3.2 Case 2: Consolidation – 90% of interest – full consolidation with existence of non-controlling interest (minority interests)

Principles   Let us now assume that Lentz Company had not acquired a 100% interest in Meder Company but had acquired only 90% of its shares. In this case, we will assume the purchase price had been established at 90% of the book value of the shareholders' equity of the acquired firm (share capital, retained earnings/reserves and undistributed current net income of Meder Company). This means that the purchase price was $(200 + 100 + 20) \times 90\% = 288$ CU, which is assumed, for the sake of simplicity, to have been paid out in cash. The (more common) case of a purchase price different from the book value of the share of equity will be dealt with in Case 3 below.

As mentioned earlier, the parent company must integrate 100% of the assets and liabilities of the subsidiary in its consolidated accounts because it holds effective economic control over the decisions of the subsidiary company. However, 10% of the Meder shareholders (the 'minority shareholders') still hold a (proportional) claim on the assets, liabilities and past and future profits of Meder Company. The consolidated statements must explicitly recognize the existence of these claims as 'non-controlling interests' (often called 'minority interests' in practice).

Non-controlling interests are defined in IAS 27 (§ 4) as: 'the equity in a subsidiary not attributable, directly or indirectly, to a parent'. Table 13.6 illustrates the calculation and reporting of minority interests in the consolidated balance sheet at the end of X3.

In this example, two elimination entries will be required to carry out the full consolidation. Entry (a) in Table 13.6 serves to eliminate the investment of Lentz in Meder (for the same reasons as those mentioned in Case 1).

The purchase price of the 90% interest in Meder was 288 CU, established as follows (remember that in this case we have assumed the purchase price was based on book values only, not on market values of assets or equity):

- 180 CU (90% of the 200 CU share capital of Meder)
- plus 90 CU (90% of the 100 CU accumulated retained earnings/reserves of Meder at the time of acquisition)
- plus 18 CU (90% of the 20 CU undistributed net income of Meder at the time of acquisition).
- = 288 CU.

The adjustment to retained earnings/reserves amounting to 270 CU corresponds to the elimination of 90% of the retained earnings/reserves of Meder at the end of X3. A consolidation reserve is thus created amounting to 162 CU, which can be calculated as follows: $[(200 + 300) \times 90\% - (200 + 100 + 20) \times 90\%] = 450 - 288 = 162$ CU.

Entry (b) establishes the claim of the minority shareholders regarding both shareholders' equity and current income. The minority rights over Meder's equity amount to 54 CU. Non-controlling interests include 20 CU (10% of share capital of 200) plus a 10% claim on the accumulated retained earnings/reserves of 300 CU and a claim of 10% over the

Table 13.6 Consolidated balance sheet (full consolidation with non-controlling interests)

	Lentz (stand-alone)	Meder (stand-alone)	Combined	Elimination entries and adjustments		Consolidated balance sheet
As of 31 December X3	(1)	(2)	(3) = (1) + (2)		(4)	(5) = (3) + (4)
Assets						
Investment in Meder	288		288	(a)	−288	0
Other assets (including cash)	1,912	600	2,512			2,512
Total	2,200*	600	2,800		−288	2,512
Equity and liabilities						
Share capital	600	200	800	(a)	−180	
				(b)	−20	600
Retained earnings/Reserves	500	300	800	(a)	−270	
				(b)	−30	500
Consolidation reserve				(a)	162	162
Net income**	50	40	90	(b)	−4	86
Non-controlling interests				(b)	54	54
Liabilities	1,050	60	1,110			1,110
Total	2,200	600	2,800		−288	2,512

*For the sake of simplicity, we have assumed that the balance sheet total of Lentz (stand-alone) is here, as it was in Case 1, equal to 2,200. The amount of 'other assets' has thus been calculated as the difference between the assets total and the carrying, historical, value of the investment in Meder.

**Here again, we assume the shareholders voted to not distribute the income of the period.

undistributed income of the period (10% of 40 CU). The non-controlling interests thus represent a total amount of 20 + 30 + 4 = 54 CU.

As in the previous case, assets and liabilities are added to create their consolidated balances (with the elimination of intra-group loans if there had been any). The consolidated share capital and retained earnings/reserves represent the share capital and retained earnings/reserves of the parent company. The non-controlling interests line item in the balance sheet acts as a mechanism to offset the mechanical 'over-incorporation' of assets and liabilities resulting from their mere addition and helps calculate, by deduction, the net claim held by the combined entity over the assets and liabilities it effectively 'owns'.

Table 13.7 presents the mechanism of establishing the consolidated income statement when there are non-controlling interests. The net income attributable to the group differs from the net income of the combined operation by the amount of the claim held by non-controlling interests over income. This claim is established by the third component of the (b) entry mentioned earlier.

Reporting non-controlling interests   Should non-controlling interests be reported as part of shareholders' equity or liabilities? They appear to be some kind of hybrid between the two. Choosing under which of the two categories to report non-controlling interests will affect some ratios calculations and might affect the conclusions of the financial analysis a user would carry on the consolidated financial statements. The answer to the question is therefore meaningful.

The way non-controlling interests are reported (either as a liability to a third party, or as a part of shareholders' equity, or even ignored altogether) stems from the beliefs – and perception – held by each company of the purpose of consolidated financial statements in reporting to shareholders and investors. Three types of beliefs systems (property, parent, and entity) lead to four reporting positions (three 'pure' positions, and a 'hybrid' one).

- *Property approach (or property concept)*: Its foundation is that consolidated financial statements are meant to describe what shareholders have invested in the company. In this case what is of foremost interest is the description of their shareholders' ownership in the subsidiary company. Thus no non-controlling interests would need to be reported.

- *Financial approach (or parent company concept)*: Its conceptual foundation is that the consolidated statements must focus mainly on informing the shareholders of the parent company because they are the ones who control the managerial decisions and orientations. In this case, minority shareholders are considered as residual (i.e., third party) and thus non-controlling interests would be considered to be part of the business' liabilities (to third parties).

- *Economic approach (or entity concept)*: Its foundation is that the consolidated financial statements are established mainly for internal decision-making purposes. Consolidated financial statements should therefore give a fair view of what the consolidated entity actually controls, i.e., assets, shareholders' equity and liabilities of the whole group,

Table 13.7 Consolidated income statement (full consolidation with non-controlling interests)

Year X3	Lentz (stand-alone)	Meder (stand-alone)	Combined	Eliminations and adjustments	Consolidated income statement
Sales	1,000	400	1,400		1,400
Expenses	950	360	1,310		1,310
Net income of consolidated entity	50	40	90		90
Non-controlling interests (10%) in subsidiary's net income				–4	–4
Net income of owners of the parent					86

without making any reference to the specificity of the legal claim of some special class of shareholders (minority or majority). Non-controlling interests would thus be reported as an unidentified or undistinguishable part of shareholders' equity.

■ *Mixed approach (or parent company extension concept)*: This fourth case is a hybrid of two previous approaches in that the minority shareholders are considered as a special and distinct class of shareholders and not dealt with as if they had been a third party. Non-controlling interests are reported as part of shareholders' equity (i.e., in line with the economic approach) but are identified as a specific item (i.e., coherent with the financial approach).

The IASB has adopted this approach (position). IAS 27 (§ 27) states that 'Non-controlling interests shall be presented in the consolidated statement of financial position within equity, separately from the equity of the owners of the parent'.

Each set of beliefs regarding the foundations of consolidated financial statements leads to a specific way of reporting non-controlling interests. These are summarized in Table 13.8.

Table 13.8 Non-controlling interests and theories of consolidation

Theory	Reporting of non-controlling interests
Property approach (Property concept)	No non-controlling interests are reported (theory implies proportionate consolidation)
Financial approach (Parent company concept)	Non-controlling interests are part of liabilities of consolidated entity
Economic approach (Entity concept)	Non-controlling interests are part of shareholders' equity
Mixed approach (Parent company extension concept)	Non-controlling interests are reported as a specific category of shareholders' equity listed after the shareholders' equity of the parent and before liabilities

Real-life example Stora Enso

(Finland – IFRS GAAP – Source: Annual report 2008 – Production of paper)

In the following tables only selected and aggregated relevant data are provided.

Consolidated balance sheet (excerpts)		
	31 December	
(in € million)	2008	2007
Equity and liabilities		
Equity attributable to parent company shareholders		
Share capital	1,342.2	1,342.2
Share premium (reclassified)	2,037.5	2,037.5
Reserve fund	238.9	238.9
Treasury shares	−10.2	−10.2
Other comprehensive income	334.0	960.4
Cumulative translation adjustment	−443.8	−115.6
Retained earnings (restated)	2,768.8	3,355.1
Net (loss) / profit for the period	−673.4	−214.7
	5,594.0	**7,593.6**
Minority interests	56.5	71.9
Total equity	**5,650.5**	**7,665.5**

Consolidated income statement (excerpts)		
	Year ended 31 December	
(in € million)	2008	2007
(...)		
(Loss)/profit before tax	**−893.8**	**20.2**
Income tax	214.8	−7.4
Net (loss)profit for the year from continuing operations	**−679.0**	**12.8**
Discontinued operations: Profit/(loss) after tax for the year	**4.3**	**−225.2**
Net (loss)profit for the year from total operations	**−674.7**	**−212.4**
Attributable to		
Equity holders of the parent company	−673.4	−214.7
Minority interest	−1.3	2.3
Net (loss)profit for the year	**−674.7**	**−212.4**

Comments:
- Stora Enso uses the 'old' term of 'minority interests'. IAS 27 now prefers the use of the term of 'non-controlling interests'.
- Stora Enso respects the requirement of IAS 27 (§ 27): Non-controlling interests are reported within equity, separately from the equity of the owners of the parent.

3.3.3 Case 3: Consolidation with 100% of interest, but the price paid to acquire the controlling interest is different from the book value of the assets that are being purchased

Principles   This hypothesis is closer to everyday life than the previous cases, which were oversimplified for pedagogical purposes. Most of the time the acquired entity's book value of net assets (i.e., equity) is, indeed, lower than the amount paid by the acquiring firm (otherwise the acquiree's shareholders would have little incentive to enter into a cession agreement). In this example, we consider that Lentz Company had acquired 100% of the outstanding shares of Meder Company in X1 (same as in Case 1), however, whereas the acquisition price paid in Case 1 had been 320 CU (equal to the book value of equity), we now make the hypothesis that Lentz had to pay 420 CU in cash on 31 December X1 to acquire a 100% interest in Meder Company. As seen before, at the time of acquisition, the book value of the shareholders' equity (including net income) of Meder Company was 320. There was therefore a premium of 100 CU paid by Lentz Company, which resulted from the difference between the price paid (420 CU) and the book value of equity of the acquired subsidiary (320 CU). This 'premium' is called 'difference arising on first consolidation'. The term 'first consolidation' refers to the fact the difference is calculated – and analyzed – only the first time the subsidiary's financial statements are integrated in consolidated financial statements, whenever such action takes place (and the difference will not change ever after). Consequently, at the time of consolidation, even if such action takes place several years after acquisition, it will be necessary to go back to archived data and extract the fair values of all the assets and liabilities at the time of acquisition. These, of course, were known at the time of the acquisition and should not be difficult to retrieve.

The premium over book value paid by the investor for the investee finds its roots in two sources, as shown in Figure 13.4. A first component of the premium comes from the difference between fair and book values of identifiable assets and liabilities: this component is

Figure 13.4 Analysis of the difference arising on first consolidation

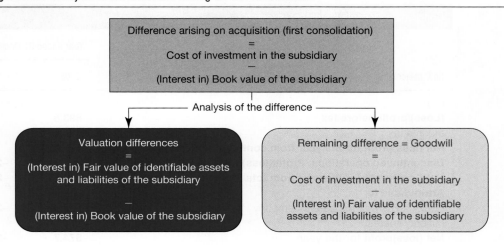

called **valuation differences**. The other component reflects the excess value embedded in the purchase price over and above the fair market value of the identifiable assets and liabilities. This second part of the premium, which is not explained by valuation differences, is called **goodwill** (as seen in Chapter 8).

Goodwill is defined in IFRS 3 (IASB 2008b: Appendix A, 'Defined terms') as 'An asset representing the future economic benefits arising from other assets acquired in a business combination that are not individually identified and separately recognized'. In the former version of IFRS 3 (dated 2004), goodwill used to be defined as the cost [of acquisition] of the business combination [i.e., the **acquiree**] over the acquirer's interest in the net fair value of the identifiable assets, liabilities and contingent liabilities [of the acquiree].

As mentioned in Chapter 8, goodwill represents such intangible 'assets' as customer loyalty, existing relationships with customers or distributors, etc. Figure 13.4 describes the analysis carried out at the time of a first consolidation.

For the sake of our example, let us assume that the fair market value of Meder's identifiable assets (tangible or intangible), net of liabilities, amounts, in X1, to 390 CU. The global gross difference (100 CU) between cost of acquisition and book value of what was acquired (computed at the time of acquisition in X1) can be broken down into two components as shown in Figure 13.4. (The same principle has been explained in Chapter 8, Figure 8.2). This difference arising on first consolidation of the acquisition of Meder by Lentz is broken down in Table 13.9.

Table 13.9 Breakdown of the difference arising on first consolidation

Purchase price	420	(1)
Book value of shareholders' equity (including net income) of subsidiary at the time of acquisition (in X1)	320	(2)
Interest in book value of shareholders' equity (including net income) of subsidiary at the time of acquisition (in X1)	320	(3) = (2) × 100%
Difference arising on first consolidation (calculated in X3 when consolidation is carried out)	100	(4) = (1) − (3)
Fair value of identifiable assets and liabilities of subsidiary (historical fair value as of X1)	390	(5)
Interest in fair value of identifiable assets and liabilities of subsidiary (historical fair value as of X1)	390	(6) = (5) × 100%
Valuation difference (reported in X3, when consolidation is carried out)	70	(7) = (6) − (3)
Goodwill (is only reported as of X3)	30	(8) = (4) − (7)

Table 13.10 presents the consolidated balance sheet that results from the acquisition of the shares of Meder Company by Lentz Company for 420 CU.

If we refer to the consolidated balance sheet (see Table 13.10), transaction (a) is similar to the one described in case 1 (elimination of investment in Meder). Let us emphasize here that the elimination entry concerns only the book value of equity of Meder (320). In a second step (transaction (b)), the difference arising on first consolidation (100) is broken up and distributed between 'other assets' for an amount of 70 CU and 'goodwill' for an amount of 30 CU. We will not cover in this text the complexity introduced by the coexistence of goodwill and non-controlling interests. The reader wishing to explore this situation is encouraged to consult advanced textbooks.[5]

Measurement of goodwill in the reporting posterior to its initial recording   The measurement of goodwill has been presented in detail in Chapter 8. IFRS 3 (§ B63) recalls that 'IAS 38 prescribes the accounting for identifiable intangible assets acquired in a business combination. The acquirer measures goodwill at the amount recognized at the acquisition date less any accumulated impairment losses'. The reasons which had originally led the firm to pay a premium over and above the fair value of the identifiable assets and liabilities of the acquired entity might have weakened, or even disappeared. If such is the case, the decrease in value of the goodwill must be recorded by acknowledging its 'impairment'. The determination of a possible impairment is carried out in accordance with IAS 36 (IASB 2004). An impairment loss cannot be reversed, contrary to the rule applicable to other intangibles (see Chapter 8).

The USA's Statement of Financial Accounting Standard (SFAS) No. 141, 'Business combinations' (FASB 2001a), and SFAS No. 142, 'Goodwill and other intangible assets' (FASB 2001b), has led the way and was

Table 13.10 Consolidated balance sheet (full consolidation with goodwill)

	Lentz (stand-alone)	Meder (stand-alone)	Combined	Elimination entries and adjustments		Consolidated balance sheet
As of 31 December X3	(1)	(2)	(3) = (1) + (2)		(4)	(5) = (3) + (4)
Assets						
Investment in Meder	420	0	420	(a)	–320	
Of which:						
Difference arising on first consolidation (based on fair values dating back to X1)	100			(b)	–100	0
Goodwill				(b)	30	30
Other assets (including cash)	1,780	600	2,380	(b)	70	2,450
Total	2,200*	600	2,800		–320	2,480
Equity and liabilities						
Share capital	600	200	800	(a)	–200	600
Retained earnings/Reserves	500	300	800	(a)	–300	500
Consolidation reserve				(a)	180	180
Net income**	50	40	90		0	90
Liabilities	1,050	60	1,110			1,110
Total	2,200	600	2,800		–320	2,480

*For the sake of simplicity, we have assumed that the balance sheet total of Lentz (stand-alone) was, here again, equal to 2,200 CU. The amount of other assets has, thus, been calculated as the difference between the assets total and the purchase price (420 CU) of the investment in Meder.
**Once more, we assume the shareholders voted to not distribute the income of the period.

largely followed by the IASB. SFAS 142, adopted in June 2001, had already abolished the previously accepted amortization over 40 years and replaced it by an impairment test. The same modification had also been adopted in Canada before 2004.

In the case of the Lentz Company all calculations have assumed, for the sake of simplicity, that the goodwill did not require any impairment.

3.4 When equity method is required

When the voting rights acquired in the subsidiary are between 20% and 50%, there is no consolidation in the strict sense seen in the previous section, but the annual financial statements of the combined entities statements will be built using the equity method.

3.4.1 Principles

The equity method consists in re-evaluating, in the consolidated accounts of the parent company, the investment in the associate (or affiliated) company over which the parent company exerts a significant influence. This method, therefore, excludes any idea of cumulating assets and liabilities. This method is not, in the strict sense, a consolidation since there is no 'integration' of the financial statements of the associate. IAS 28 (IASB 2003b: § 2) defines the equity method as: 'A method of accounting whereby the investment is initially recognized at cost and adjusted thereafter for the post-acquisition change in the investor's share of the net assets of the investee'. The IASB adds in the same paragraph: 'the profit or loss of the investor includes the investor's share of the profit or loss of the investee'. The asset value of the intercorporate investment will therefore be called 'at equity' since it will reflect the share of the shareholders' equity controlled by the 'parent'.

Figure 13.5 illustrates schematically the application of the basic principles of the equity method. In this figure the term 'consolidated' as applied to the balance sheet of the combined businesses is placed between quotation marks to emphasize the fact that it is not a true consolidation but more a revaluation.

3.4.2 Case 4: 30% of interest

Going back to the Lentz Company example, let us now assume that Lentz acquired only 30% of the outstanding shares of Meder Company. Meder Company can no longer be called a subsidiary: it is called an associated company or associate. The 'consolidated' balance sheet, i.e., in which the investment is valued at equity, is shown in Table 13.11.

Investment in the associate has been paid 96 CU [(200 + 100 + 20) × 30%]. We do not cover in this book the situation when the investment in the associate has been acquired for a price higher than the book value of the associate. In practice, the same mechanism of calculation of the goodwill would be used as the one shown in Case 3 above (full consolidation).

The consolidation reserve is the difference between the interest in the equity of the associate (excluding net income) *at the time of consolidation* and the interest in the equity of the associate (including net income) *at the time of acquisition*.

Here, given our hypotheses, this reserve is 54 [(200 + 300) × 30% – (200 + 100 + 20) × 30%]. After the acquisition is completed and the two businesses begin to cooperate or coordinate their actions, the value of the equity of the associate fluctuates independently of the cost of the acquisition by the 'parent' (hopefully increasing if the move was

Figure 13.5 Equity method

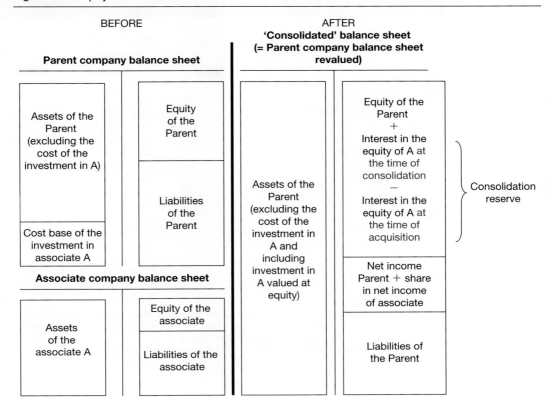

strategically justified and the expected benefits of the cooperation actually accrue to each participant in the combination).

The fact that Lentz Company owns 30% of Meder Company leads to Lentz having a claim over 30% of the income of Meder or 12 CU (40 CU × 30% = 12). The investment in Meder is now valued at 162 CU, calculated as follows [(200 + 300 + 40) × 30%].

In the equity method, the 'consolidated' income statement is equivalent, as shown in Table 13.12, to the income statement of the parent company (Lentz) with the addition of the share of net income of the associate Meder pertaining to Lentz' interest.

3.5 When proportionate consolidation is required

3.5.1 Principles

Under this method there is a simple line-by-line addition of the financial statements of the parent company (called the 'venturer') and the appropriate part (proportion) of each of the corporate entities whose shares are owned by the parent in the context of a joint control. Such a corporate entity is generally referred to as a joint venture or JV. A joint venture, by definition, has at least two parents. In this text, we concentrate on the position of only one of the parents whom we call 'Parent 1' in Figure 13.6.

IAS 31 (IASB 2003c: § 3) defines proportionate consolidation as: 'A method of accounting whereby a venturer's share of each of the assets, liabilities, income and expenses of a jointly controlled entity is combined, line by line, with similar items in the venturer's financial statements or reported as separate line items in the venturer's financial statements'.

Table 13.11 Consolidated balance sheet (equity method)

As of 31 December X3	Lentz with investment valued at cost	Lentz with investment valued at equity
Assets		
Investment in Meder	96	162*
Other assets (including cash)	2,104	2,104
Total	2,200**	2,266
Equity and liabilities		
Share capital	600	600
Retained earnings/Reserves	500	500
Consolidation reserve		54
Net income***	50	50
Share of Meder's net income resulting from Lentz owning 30% of Meder's equity		12
Liabilities	1,050	1,050
Total	2,200	2,266

* Valued at equity
**For the sake of simplicity, we have assumed that the balance sheet total of Lentz (stand-alone) was, here again, equal to 2,200 CU. The amount of other assets has, thus, been calculated as the difference between the assets total and the (historical) price of the investment in Meder.
***Once more, we assume the shareholders voted to not distribute the income of the period.

Table 13.12 Income statement (equity method)

Year X3	Lentz (stand-alone)	Adjustment due to the equity interest in Meder	Consolidated income statement
Sales	1,000		1,000
Expenses	950		950
Net income resulting from equity in Meder		12	12
Net income	50	12	62

Figure 13.6 illustrates the mechanism of this method. As shown in this figure, proportionate consolidation is a true consolidation method in that the investment in the joint venture is eliminated at the same time as is the share of parent company in the equity of the joint venture at the time of acquisition. There is, however, a major difference between proportionate consolidation and full consolidation: the assets and liabilities of the joint venture are integrated only proportionately to the interest held by the venturer in the JV, hence the absence of non-controlling interests.

3.5.2 Case 5: 50% of interest (joint control)

Let us now assume Lentz Company shares joint control over Meder Company with Marcus SA, which is an equal partner. Lentz Company acquired its 50% control over the

Figure 13.6 Proportionate consolidation

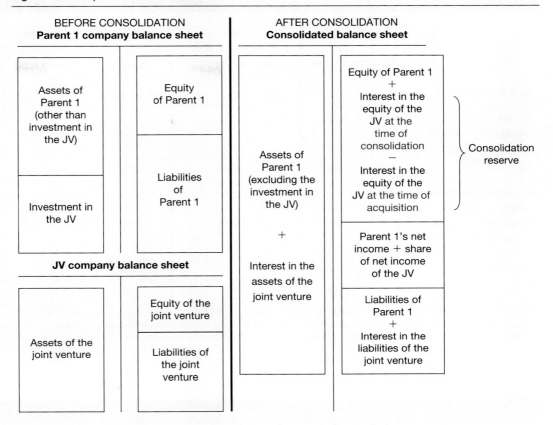

joint venture by paying 160 CU. The price of the investment, at the time of acquisition, was equal to 50% of the shareholders' equity: 160 = [(200 + 100 + 20) × 50%]. The consolidated balance sheet that resulted is illustrated in Table 13.13.

The consolidation reserve is computed as in the two previous methods: [(200 + 300) × 50% − (200 + 100 + 20) × 50%].

The consolidated income statement (Table 13.14) integrates only 50% of the income statement items of the joint venture.

3.6 Reporting which method(s) was(were) used in consolidation

Generally, the notes to the financial statements provide the list of all subsidiaries and associates that have been consolidated and specify the percentage of interest (ownership) and sometimes the percentage of control (stake or voting rights) the parent holds in each. For example, the French company Thales (defense electronics) provides in the notes to its financial statements (2008 annual report) a table showing the list of main consolidated companies (see following excerpts).

Groups' financial statements often contain a section on 'Changes in scope of consolidation', providing a list of newly consolidated and deconsolidated companies.

3.7 Impact of each of the three methods on reported group sales revenue and net income

Tables 13.15 and 13.16 provide a synthesis of the impact of each consolidation method on consolidated sales and consolidated income (share of the group). From a financial statement analysis viewpoint, understanding this impact is important.

Table 13.13 Consolidated balance sheet (proportionate consolidation)

As of 31 December X3	Lentz (stand-alone)	Meder (Lentz's interest in Meder's assets and liabilities)	Combined	Elimination entries and adjustments		Consolidated balance sheet
	(1)	(2)	(3) = (1) + (2)		(4)	(5) = (3) + (4)
Assets						
Investment in Meder	160		160	(a)	−160	0
Other assets (including cash)	2,040	300	2,340			2,340
Total	2,200*	300	2,500		−160	2,340
Equity and liabilities						
Share capital	600	100	700	(a)	−100	600
Retained earnings/Reserves	500	150	650	(a)	−150	500
Consolidation reserve				(a)	90	90
Net income	50	20	70			70
Liabilities	1,050	30	1,080			1,080
Total	2,200	300	2,500		−160	2,340

*For the sake of simplicity, we assumed that the balance sheet total of Lentz was, once again, equal to 2,200 CU. The amount of other assets has, thus, been calculated as the difference between the assets total and the (historical) price of the investment in Meder.
**Here again, we assume the shareholders voted to not distribute the income of the period.

Table 13.14 Consolidated income statement (proportionate consolidation)

Year X3	Lentz (stand-alone)	Meder (50% of stand-alone)	Combined	Elimination entries and adjustments	Consolidated income statement
Sales	1,000	200	1,200		1,200
Expenses	950	180	1,130		1,130
Net income	50	20	70		70

List of main consolidated companies (not including Thales SA, the parent company) (as of 31 December)

	% Control 2008	% Control 2007	% Control 2006	% Stake 2008	% Stake 2007	% Stake 2006
1. CONSOLIDATED SUBSIDIARIES						
African Defence Systems Pty Ltd (South Africa)	80	80	80	80	80	60
Thales Australia Ltd (Australia)	100	100	100	100	100	100
TDA Armaments SAS (France)	100	100	100	100	100	100
Thales Air Systems SA (France)	100	100	100	100	100	100
Thales ATM GmbH (Germany) (...)	100	100	100	100	100	100

List of main consolidated companies (not including Thales SA, the parent company) (as of 31 December) *(Continued)*

	% Control 2008	% Control 2007	% Control 2006	% Stake 2008	% Stake 2007	% Stake 2006
2. ACCOUNTED FOR UNDER THE PROPORTIONATE METHOD						
Air Command Systems International SAS (ACSI) (France)	50	50	50	50	50	50
Armaris (France)	–	–	50	–	–	50
Citylink Telecommunications Holding Ltd (UK)	33	33	33	33	33	33
Diehl Avionik Systeme GmbH (Germany)	49	49	49	49	49	49
Faceo (France)	–	–	50	–	–	50
(...)						
3. ACCOUNTED FOR UNDER THE EQUITY METHOD						
Aviation Communications & Surveillance Systems (USA)	30	30	30	30	30	30
Camelot Group Plc (UK)	20	20	20	20	20	20
DCNS (France)	25	25	–	25	25	–
DpiX LLC (USA)	20	20	20	20	20	20
Elettronica SpA (Italy)	33	33	33	33	33	33
(...)						

Table 13.15 Integration of a subsidiary, associate or joint venture company in the consolidated sales revenue (for the consolidated income statement)

Consolidation method [For companies consolidated using: ...]	Integration of sales revenue	Percentage (if applicable)
Full consolidation	Yes	100%
Proportionate consolidation	Yes	% of interest
Equity method	No	–

Table 13.16 Content of the consolidated income – share of the group

Consolidation method	Share of the group (to be added to the net income of the parent to create the consolidated income)
Full consolidation	100% of revenues – 100% of expenses = 100% of income – Non-controlling interests = % of interest of the group in the net income
Proportionate consolidation	% of interest in the revenues – % of interest in the expenses = % of interest of the group in the net income
Equity method	Share of income in associates (% of interest of the group × net income of associates)

4 Consolidation process

The consolidation process is a complex and rigorous sequential process that requires good organization. Preliminary steps include:

- Creating detailed record of all companies that could be included in the scope of consolidation so that all relevant information will be located in the same database or file.

- Setting up a consolidation guide, continuously updating and describing the various steps in the consolidation activities, the procedures to be followed and an allocation of responsibilities, etc.

- Issuance of a group accounting guide setting down the principles, rules and methods of valuation the group companies involved in the consolidation perimeter or scope must follow to facilitate the consolidation work. The accounting guide will also specify the types of adjustments needed when required local practice or principles are not coherent with the group's principles and methods.

- Preparation of the 'consolidation package', i.e., the work documents, files and tables that each group company must prepare following strict rules to prepare the consolidation calculations.

The consolidation process follows four standard steps:

Step 1: Identification of the economic entities to be consolidated   Decide for each firm in which the parent holds an investment whether they should be included in the scope of consolidation. Based on the finding as to control and interest, decide on the method of consolidation that will be retained for each company.

Step 2: Pre-consolidation   This step is generally carried out locally as it consists essentially of restatements of the financial statements of the subsidiary or associate, kept in accordance with local practices and GAAP, to align them with the accounting policies of the parent:

- Individual financial statements of all companies included in the scope of consolidation are restated so they present their financial position in a homogeneous way and follow the prescriptions of the group accounting guide.

- If the need exists, the restated financial statements must be converted to the functional currency used by the parent.

Step 3: Consolidation entries and operations

- Preparation of a comprehensive balance of all restated accounts.

- Elimination of intra-group operations and entries (between subsidiaries or between a subsidiary and the parent). The consolidation process retains only the operations and results arising from transactions with (third) parties external to the consolidation scope. Transactions that generate trivial or immaterial amounts are generally ignored as the potential benefit in improved reporting that would be obtained rarely balances the cost of their elimination activity.

■ Elimination of the intra-group investments (in group companies) and partition of equities and net income of each consolidated company between the group and non-controlling interests if the need arises.

Step 4: Preparation of the consolidated financial statements   The trial balance of consolidated accounts (as they stand after step 3) serves to prepare consolidated balance sheet, consolidated income statement and consolidated notes to financial statements, and sometimes both consolidated statement of cash flows and statement of changes in consolidated shareholders' equity.

The elimination of intra-group transactions (step 3) represents a very important part of the consolidation process and the key elimination entries are generally reported in the notes.

Real-life example China Eastern Airlines

(China – IFRS/Hong Kong GAAP – Source: Annual report 2008 – Airline company)

Excerpted from the notes of China Eastern Airlines related to the consolidation process.

Subsidiaries

Inter-company transactions, balances and unrealized gains on transactions between group companies are eliminated. Unrealized losses are also eliminated unless the transaction provides evidence of an impairment for the asset transferred. Accounting policies of subsidiaries have been changed where necessary to ensure consistency with the policies adopted by the group.

Associates

Unrealized gains on transactions between the group and its associates are eliminated to the extent of the group's interest in the associates. Unrealized losses are also eliminated unless the transaction provides evidence of an impairment of the asset transferred. Accounting policies of associates have been changed where necessary to ensure consistency with the policies adopted by the group.

---

5 Deferred taxation on consolidation

The consolidation operations bring together companies that may not follow the same tax calendar as the parent, or whose financial statements have been established in accordance with local tax or reporting rules that may differ from those selected in the group accounting guide or that apply to the parent. Chapter 6 showed that these differences create deferred taxation issues. Appendix 13.2 develops the specificity of deferred taxation arising on consolidation. In summary, deferred taxation may arise from:

■ Tax issues arising from restatements carried out in accordance with intra-group harmonization procedures: taxable revenues and deductible expenses, which are valued differently in individual group companies (for example, the most common differences arise from the choice of depreciation methods and the recording of leased assets).

■ Restatements incurred in order to eliminate entries that were required by tax regulations.

- The tax consequences of eliminating intra-group profit (which may not have been taxed homogeneously between countries where the various group companies operate).

6 Foreign currency translations

Once each of the individual non-consolidated (stand-alone) financial statements have been restated and harmonized in keeping with the prescriptions of the group accounting guide, and before they can be aggregated, it is essential to express all accounts in the same currency. The unique currency or 'reporting currency' used in establishing the consolidated accounts is generally the parent's reporting currency (functional currency). Foreign exchange rates therefore affect the translation of financial statements, established originally in foreign currencies, for all entities that are included in the perimeter of either a full or proportionate consolidation or the application of the equity method. The treatment of foreign currency translations is further developed in Appendix 13.3.

7 Legal mergers

A 'legal merger' between two companies may take two different forms. Either:

- The assets and liabilities of one company (the merged company) are transferred to the other company (the merging company) and the former (merged) company is dissolved.
- Or the assets and liabilities of both companies are transferred to a new company and both original companies are dissolved.

The major accounting issues pertaining to a legal merger are:

- determination of the value of each business;
- determination of the rate of exchange of shares;
- determination of the number of shares to issue;
- determination of the merger premium;
- accounting entries for recording for the merger so as to be able to produce a relevant new balance sheet.

Let us illustrate and discuss these points around an example.

Hol Company merges with Van Rennes Company. Table 13.17 presents the balance sheet of each firm before the merger (in thousands of the same CU).

Table 13.17 Balance sheets of merging and merged companies

Assets (000 omitted)	Hol	Van Rennes	Equity and liabilities (000 omitted)	Hol	Van Rennes
Assets	1,500	500	Capital	400	200
			Retained earning/Reserves	800	50
			Liabilities	300	250
Total	1,500	500	Total	1,500	500
Number of shares included in the capital:				4,000	2,000
Par value				100	100

The facts of the merger are as follows:

- Hol merges with Van Rennes, which is dissolved. The **purchase accounting** method is applied.
- However, the book values of assets do not reflect the economic (fair) values of the different Van Rennes balance sheet items, as indicated in the following table:

Van Rennes assets (excerpts)	Book value	Fair value	Difference
Assets	500	520	20 (potential gain on assets)
Other non-recorded or identifiable elements	0	30	30 (potential goodwill)

We should note that, in this example, we assume, for the sake of simplicity, that book values of Hol equal their fair values. Had we faced a different situation, we could have used these fair values to compute the 'rate of exchange of shares' (see below). However, the fair values of the acquirer are not taken into account in the preparation of the merged financial statements (this disparity of treatment is one more reason for stating clearly which firm is the acquirer and which is the acquiree).

7.1 Determination of the value of both companies

Table 13.18 shows the determination of the value of each company.

The determination of the value of each company is rather flexible if they are unlisted, while, if they are listed, the market value is used. In this example, we can assume that neither company is listed and the approach implemented is therefore possible, plausible, and accepted by both parties.

7.2 Determination of the rate of exchange of shares

The ratio of the per share values is:

$$\frac{\text{Value of a share of Van Rennes}}{\text{Value of a share of Hol}} = 150/300 = 1/2$$

The rate of exchange is thus equal to 1 share of Hol for 2 shares of Van Rennes. We can check that one Hol share has the same value as 2 Van Rennes shares: $300 \times 1 = 150 \times 2$.

Table 13.18 Value of companies

		Hol	Van Rennes
Capital (000 omitted)	(1)	400	200
Retained earnings/Reserves (000 omitted)	(2)	800	50
Shareholders' equity (000 omitted)	(3) = (1) + (2)	1,200	250
Number of shares	(4)	4,000	2,000
Book value of a share	(5) = (3)/(4) × 1,000	300	125
Potential gain on assets (000 omitted)	(6a)		20
Goodwill (000 omitted)	(6b)		30
Net assets at fair value (000 omitted)	(7) = (3) + (6a) + (6b)	1,200	300
Fair value per share	(8) = (7)/(4) × 1,000	300	150

7.3 Determination of the number of shares to issue in the merger

Hol, the merging company, should issue: 2,000 × (number of shares in Van Rennes) × 1/2 = 1,000 new shares of Hol to be awarded to the former shareholders of Van Rennes so they will retain the same value as they gave up in agreeing to the merger.

7.4 Determination of the merger premium

The capital increase is equal to 100 CU (par value) × 1,000 × (number of new shares) = 100,000 CU. The difference between net assets of Van Rennes (300,000 CU) and the capital increase is the merger premium (see Table 13.19).

Table 13.19 Determination of the merger premium

(000 omitted)	Computations	Share capital Hol	Merger premium
Capital Hol		400	
Net assets at fair value of Van Rennes	300		
Share capital increase	−100	100	
Merger premium	200		200
Total		500	200

7.5 Accounting for the merger

Table 13.20 illustrates the balance sheet after the merger.

Table 13.20 Balance sheet of Hol after the merger

(000 omitted)	Hol	Merger entries (see notes below)		Balance sheet after merger
Assets	1,500	520	(a)	2,020
Goodwill		30	(a)	30
Total	1,500	550		2,050
Capital	400	100	(b)	500
Merger premium		200	(b)	200
Retained earnings/Reserves	800			800
Liabilities	300	250	(a)	550
Total	1,500	550		2,050

(a) Integration of the net assets of the merged company at fair value:

Identifiable assets of the merged company at fair value	520
minus liabilities of the merged company	(250)
plus non identifiable difference (goodwill)	30
Total (net assets of the merged company at fair value)	300

(b) Increase of the capital of the merging company (100 + merger premium of 200).

The resulting balance sheet calls for several observations that affect the decision-making usefulness of the merged financial statements:

- A merger is a business combination and should comply with IFRS 3 (IASB 2008b: § 4) which states that 'An entity shall account for each business combination by applying the acquisition method'.

- The retained earnings and reserves of the merged company are only those of Hol Company.

- The merger premium is the difference between the fair value of the assets contributed to the merger (300) and the nominal (or par value) of the shares of capital issued by Hol (100).

- 'The consideration transferred in a business combination shall be measured at fair value, which shall be calculated as the sum of the acquisition-date fair values of the assets transferred by the acquirer, the liabilities incurred by the acquirer to former owners of the acquiree and the equity interests issued by the acquirer. (…) Examples of potential forms of consideration include cash, other assets, a business or a subsidiary of the acquirer, contingent consideration, ordinary or preference equity instruments, options, warrants and member interests of mutual entities' (IFRS 3: § 37). 'This 'cost' is the amount 'paid' by the acquirer to control the acquiree. However, in practice, and especially in the case of a merger, the acquirer is not always required to 'pay' something. It can create new shares given to the shareholders of the acquiree to obtain the control of the acquiree. In our example, the 'cost' of the business combination equals the fair value of the Hol shares issued, i.e., 300 × 1,000 = 300,000 CU. This cost is allocated to net identifiable assets of Van Rennes up to an amount of (520 − 250) = 270 thousands of CU. The unallocated difference (300 − 270 = 30 thousands of CU) is recorded in the assets as goodwill.

- 'As of the acquisition date, the acquirer shall recognize, separately from goodwill, the identifiable assets acquired, the liabilities assumed and any non-controlling interest in the acquiree' (IFRS 3: § 10).

Appendix 13.1 presents the 'pooling of interests' method and compares it to the 'purchase method'.

Key points

- Consolidated financial statements create a description of the financial position and performance of an economic entity which is the agglomeration or conglomeration of diverse and often distinct legal entities connected by relations of intercorporate investments, control or lending relationships.

- Financial investments include mainly: (1) shares in subsidiaries, (2) shares in associated companies, (3) shares in other investments, and (4) loans to subsidiaries, associated companies and other investments.

- A *subsidiary* is an entity that is controlled by another entity (known as the parent) and an *associate* is an entity in which the investor has significant influence.

- A business combination is the bringing together of separate entities into the economic entity as a result of one entity uniting with, or obtaining control over, the net assets and operations of another entity.

- Accounting for business combinations is based on two exclusive generic hypotheses: purchase and uniting of interests. The latter is now forbidden under both IFRS and US GAAP.

- The usefulness of consolidated financial statements partly arises from the lack of informativeness and relevance of the unconsolidated accounts of the parent (holding) company.

- The nature of subordination and control relationship linking group companies to the parent drives the choice of the consolidation method.

- There are three main types of relationships (control, significant influence and joint control) and to each corresponds a method of consolidation (full consolidation, equity method and proportionate consolidation).

- In full consolidation, if the percentage of interest is below 100%, non-controlling interests must be reported. They represent that part of the net results of operations and of net assets of a subsidiary attributable to interests owned by investors other than the parent (directly, or indirectly).
- If the purchase price of the acquired entity exceeds the value of the interest in its book value, the difference arises from both valuation differences on its identifiable assets and liabilities, and 'goodwill'.

- The consolidation process follows a rigorous methodology.
- Consolidation often gives rise to deferred taxation.
- The financial statements of all group companies should be expressed in the same currency. Financial statements of group entities prepared in a currency different from the reporting one should be translated into the reporting currency.
- A legal merger raises accounting issues regarding value of each business, rate of exchange of shares, number of shares to issue, merger premium, etc.

Review (solutions are at the back of the book)

Review 13.1 Mater & Filia

Topic: Consolidated balance sheet (three methods)

The balance sheet of the Mater & Filia companies, as of 31 December X1, are given in the following table (Mater Co. is the parent company, and Filia Co. is the subsidiary company).

Balance sheet as of 31 December X1 (in 000 of CU)		
	Mater	Filia
Assets		
Fixed assets (net)	1,500	550
Investment in Filia Company (1)	160	–
Inventories	930	510
Other current assets	1,210	740
Total assets	3,800	1,800
Liabilities and shareholders' equity		
Capital	500	200
Retained earnings and reserves	780	600
Net income (2)	220	150
Debts	2,300	850
Total liabilities and shareholders' equity	3,800	1,800

(1) Mater acquired 80% of the capital of Filia when the latter was first incorporated.
(2) Net income will not be distributed.

Required

Prepare the consolidated balance sheet by each of the following methods:

- Full consolidation
- Proportionate consolidation
- Equity method.

Assignments

Assignment 13.1
Multiple-choice questions

Select the right answer (one possible answer, unless otherwise stated).

1. The percentage of interest
   (a) Is used to define the dependency link
   (b) Is used to decide about the inclusion of a company in the consolidation scope
   (c) Reflects the interests that are controlled directly and indirectly
   (d) None of these

2. In the situation described in the diagram above, the percentage of control (voting rights, vote) of P in C2 is:

   (a) 10%
   (b) 20%
   (c) 30%
   (d) 27%
   (e) None of these

3. In the diagram of question 2 above, the percentage of interest (ownership, stake) is:
   (a) 10%
   (b) 20%
   (c) 30%
   (d) 27%
   (e) None of these

4. Non-controlling interests can be reported (several possible answers):
   (a) As a part of shareholders' equity
   (b) As a part of long-term liabilities
   (c) As a part of current liabilities
   (d) Between shareholders' equity and long-term liabilities
   (e) As a negative liability within financial fixed assets
   (f) None of these
   (g) All of these

5. Associate and affiliate are often considered as synonymous
   (a) True
   (b) False

6. The only possibility to hold control of a company is to own more than 50% of the voting rights of this entity
   (a) True
   (b) False

7. Non-controlling interests are reported when which method is used?
   (a) Full consolidation
   (b) Equity method
   (c) Proportionate consolidation
   (d) None of these

8. Goodwill is the difference between the purchase price (cost of investment) of shares and the book value of these shares
   (a) True
   (b) False

9. Before the adoption and implementation of SFAS 141 and IFRS 3, the study of annual reports showed that goodwill was generally amortized over 20 or 40 years
   (a) True
   (b) False

10. The equity method should be used when the percentage of control is more than 30% and less that 50%
    (a) True
    (b) False

Assignment 13.2
Mutter & Tochter

Topic: Preparation of a consolidated balance sheet

The balance sheet of the Mutter & Tochter companies, as of 31 December X1, are given in the following table (Mutter Co. is the parent and Tochter Co. is the subsidiary).

Balance sheet as at 31 December X1 (in 000 CU)				
	Mutter		Tochter	
Fixed assets (net)	22,000		16,000	
Investment in Tochter Company	10,000	(1)	–	
Inventories	34,000		10,000	
Other current assets	25,700	(2)	9,200	
Total assets	91,700		35,200	
Capital	40,000		15,000	
Retained earning/reserves	14,000		6,000	
Net income	7,000		4,000	
Debts	30,700		10,200	(3)
Total shareholders' equity and liabilities	91,700		35,200	

(1) When Mutter acquired 60% of the capital of Tochter, the shareholders' equity (capital, retained earnings/reserves and net income) of the subsidiary was valued at 16,000.

(2) Includes a loan to Tochter — 1,000

(3) Includes a debt to Mutter — 1,000

Required

Prepare the consolidated balance sheet by each of the following methods:

- Full consolidation
- Proportionate consolidation
- Equity method.

Assignment 13.3

China International Marine Container*, Honda Motors*, EVN* and Cobra-Bio*

Topic: Reporting for minority interests

The following are excerpts of the equity and liabilities section of the balance sheet of four companies (with notes when applicable).

China International Marine Containers

(China – IFRS – Source: Annual report 2008 – Production of marine containers)

Honda Motor Co.

(Japan – US GAAP – Source: Annual report 2009 – Manufacturer of automotive vehicles, motorcycles and light farming equipment)

Consolidated balance sheet (aggregated) China International Marine Containers		
	31 December	
(in RMB 000)	2008	2007
Liabilities and shareholders' equity		
Current liabilities	1,011,268	1,821,669
Non-current liabilities	6,126,019	3,871,579
Shareholders' equity		
Share capital	2,662,396	2,662,396
Capital reserve	1,118,064	3,376,580
Surplus reserve	3,577,588	3,497,045
Retained earnings	1,064,613	1,493,044
Translation differences of financial statements denominated in foreign currency	(1,269,893)	(974,163)
Total equity attributable to the shareholders of the company	13,428,901	15,913,757
Minority interests	1,505,547	1,628,544
Total equity	**14,934,448**	**17,542,301**

Consolidated balance sheet (excerpts) Honda Motor Co		
	31 March	
(in ¥ million)	2008	2009
Current liabilities	**4,672,336**	**4,237,368**
Long-term debt, excluding current portion	**1,836,652**	**1,932,637**
Other liabilities	**1,414,270**	**1,518,568**
Total liabilities	**7,923,258**	**7,688,573**
Minority interests in consolidated subsidiaries	**141,806**	**123,056**
Stockholders' equity:		
Common stock	86,067	86,067
Capital surplus	172,529	172,529
Legal reserves	39,811	43,965
Retained earnings	5,106,197	5,099,267
Accumulated other comprehensive income (loss), net	(782,198)	(1,322,828)
Treasury stock, at cost	(71,927)	(71,712)
Total stockholders' equity	**4,550,479**	**4,007,288**

EVN AG

(Austria – IFRS – Source: Annual report 2007/08 – Energy and water services)

Consolidated balance sheet (aggregated) EVN AG		
	30 September	
(in € 000)	2008	2007
Equity		
Equity attributable to EVN AG shareholders	2,975,927.3	2,788,012.5
Minority interest	232,532.3	226,720.8
Total equity	**3,208,459.6**	**3,014,733.3**
Liabilities		
Non-current liabilities	2,655,280.3	2,400,553.0
Current liabilities	772,535.8	846,639.6
Total liabilities	**3,427,816.1**	**3,247,192.6**
Total equity and liabilities	**6,636,275.7**	**6,261,925.9**

Cobra Bio-Manufacturing

(UK – IFRS – Source: Annual report 2008 – Biotechnology)

Consolidated balance sheet (aggregated) Cobra Bio-Manufacturing		
	30 September	
(in £ 000)	2008	2007
Current liabilities	**4,263**	**3,023**
Non-current liabilities	**2,467**	**2,806**
Equity		
Called up share capital	443	1,959
Share premium	10,411	9,634
Merger reserve	29,729	29,729
Other reserves	473	453
Profit and loss reserve	(38,781)	(35,506)
Total equity	**4,038**	**6,269**

Required

■ Compare and contrast the way minority interests are reported in the four companies.
■ Suggest a coherent set of arguments that support the solution that has been adopted by each firm. How robust is your set of arguments? In other words, what hypotheses could be challenged that might change the outcome in terms of reporting the minority interests?

Assignment 13.4
Bosmans and Badings

Topic: Legal merger

Bosmans Company merges with the Badings Company, which will be dissolved after the merger. The balance sheet of each company is provided here (in 000 of CU).

Balance sheets of the merging companies (in 000 of CU)		
	Bosmans	Badings
Assets		
Fixed assets	700	500
Inventories	600	400
Receivables and cash	150	200
Total	1,450	1,100
Equity and liabilities		
Capital	400	600
Retained earnings/reserves	500	280
Liabilities	550	220
Total	1,450	1,100
Number of shares	4,000	6,000
Par value	100	100

You are informed that, for some assets of Badings Company, the fair value is different from the book value, as indicated in the following table.

Assets (excerpts)	Book value	Fair value
Fixed assets	500	560
Inventories	400	390
Receivables and cash	200	170

Required

Prepare, step-by-step, the balance sheet of Bosmans after its merger with (absorption of) Badings under the following two sets of hypotheses:

- The net assets of Badings are integrated at fair value
- The net assets of Badings are integrated at book value.

Discuss the pros and cons of each method, using the data of the Bosmans-Badings merger.

References

Alexander, D., Britton, A. and Jorissen, A. (2009) *International Financial Reporting and Analysis*. 4th edn, Cengage Learning, London.

FASB (2001a) Statement of Financial Accounting Standards No. 141: 'Business Combinations', Norwalk, CT.

FASB (2001b) Statement of Financial Accounting Standards No. 142: 'Goodwill and Other Intangible Assets', Norwalk, CT.

IASB (2003a) International Accounting Standard No. 27: Consolidated and Separate Financial Statements, London.

IASB (2003b) International Accounting Standard No. 28: Investments in Associates, London.

IASB (2003c) International Accounting Standard No. 31: Interests in Joint Ventures, London.

IASB (2004) International Accounting Standard No. 36: Impairment of Assets, London.

IASB (2008a) International Accounting Standard No. 39: Financial Instruments: Recognition and Measurement, London.

IASB (2008b) International Financial Reporting Standard No. 3: Business Combinations, London.

Deloitte Global IFRS Leadership Team, IASB revises IFRS 3 and IAS 27, *IAS Plus*, Deloitte Global IFRS Leadership Team, www.iasplus.com.

Ding, Y., Richard, J. and Stolowy, H. (2008) 'Towards an understanding of the phases of goodwill accounting in four Western capitalist countries: From stakeholder model to shareholder model', *Accounting, Organizations and Society*, 33(7–8): 718–55.

Feige, P. (1997) 'How "uniform" is financial reporting in Germany? – The example of foreign currency translation', *European Accounting Review*, 6(1): 109–22.

Higson, C. (1998) 'Goodwill', *British Accounting Review*, 30(2): 141–58.

Kothavala, K. (2003) 'Proportional consolidation versus the equity method: A risk measurement perspective on reporting interests in joint ventures', *Journal of Accounting and Public Policy*, 22(6): 517–38.

Lapointe-Antunes, P., Cormier, D. and Magnan, M. (2009) 'Value relevance and timeliness of transitional goodwill-impairment losses: Evidence from Canada', *The International Journal of Accounting*, 44(1): 56–78.

Mora, A. and Rees, W. (1998) 'The early adoption of consolidated accounting in Spain', *European Accounting Review*, 7(4): 675–96.

Further reading

Al Jifri, K. and Citron, D. (2009) 'The value-relevance of financial statement recognition versus note disclosure: Evidence from goodwill accounting', *European Accounting Review*, 18(1): 123–40.

Beatty, A. and Weber, J. (2006) 'Accounting discretion in fair value estimates: An examination of SFAS 142 goodwill impairments', *Journal of Accounting Research*, 44(2): 257–88.

Busse von Colbe, W. (2004) 'New accounting for goodwill: Application of American criteria from a German perspective', in C. Leuz *et al.* (eds) *The Economics and Politics of Accounting*, pp. 201–18. Oxford University Press, Oxford.

Cooper, J. (2007) 'Debating accounting principles and policies: The case of goodwill, 1880–1921', *Accounting, Business & Financial History*, 17(2): 241–64.

Additional material on the website

Go to http://www.cengage.co.uk/stolowy3 for further information, journal entries and extra assignments for each chapter.

The following appendices to this chapter are available on the dedicated website:

Appendix 13.1 Uniting of interests and the pooling of interest method

Appendix 13.2 Deferred taxation on consolidation

Appendix 13.3 Foreign currency translations

Notes

1. *Significant influence* is the power to participate in the financial and operating policy decisions of the investee but implies not having control or joint control over those policies.
2. *Control* is the power to govern the financial and operating policies of an entity, so as to obtain benefits from its activities.

3. However, examples abound where a stake of significantly less than 20% still grants significant influence to the investor. For example, Kirk Kerkorian (through his private investment firm Tracinda Corporation), even after reducing, in December 2005, his stake in General Motors from 10% to 7.8% (a move that negatively impacted the share value on the NYSE) still held a significant influence over the strategy of GM by his public comments, his suggesting a cross-participation in the capital of Renault–Nissan and by seeking a seat on the board for a person close to him. After failing to orient GM's strategy in the direction Kerkorian recommended, Tracinda liquidated its position in GM's capital at the end of November 2006, before the deadly downward spiral that led GM to declare bankruptcy in June of 2009. The threshold of 20% may be a remnant of the past, but accountants need to have clear rules to avoid discretionary behavior in reporting (and a rule, even if imperfect, is better than no rule): under 20%, the' investment is considered just that, i.e., an investment without influence, but above 20% it is considered that the influence on the value creation of the firm is significant and must be reported as such. Most countries require that the financial statements (or the publicly accessible filings with regulatory agencies) list the major stockholders and most stock exchanges require that investors signal to the market when their investment exceeds 5% and successively higher thresholds.

4. The EU defines subsidiarity as the principle that decisions should always be taken at the lowest possible level or closest to where they will have their effect, for example in a local area rather than nationally. By extension, a well-managed group should delegate to its subsidiaries the responsibilities that allow the group to most effectively and rapidly respond to market demands and opportunities. Decisions should be made as close to the market as possible as long as they remain coherent with the higher-level strategy defined by supervisors above. We use the term here to refer to the degree of autonomy over operations, strategy and financing granted by a parent to one of its subsidiaries. The concept therefore covers issues of delegation, control and strategic autonomy.

5. See, for example, Alexander, Britton and Jorissen (2009).

C14

Chapter 14
Statement of Cash Flows Construction

Learning objectives

After studying this chapter, you will understand:

- What a statement of cash flows is.
- That such a statement is very useful from many perspectives.
- That the publication of a statement of cash flows is required in many countries, especially for listed firms.
- That the statement of cash flows classifies cash flows into three categories: operating, investing and financing.
- What the content of each of the three categories of activities described in the statement of cash flows is.
- That, although the format of the statement of cash flows is relatively harmonized in the world, there are still some differences of classification of the uses and sources of flows of cash.
- What the direct and indirect methods of computation of the operating cash flow are.
- What the potential cash flow is and what is its role in the determination of the operating cash flow.
- How to deal with non-cash investing and financing flows.

As seen in Chapters 1 and 3, 'cash is king' and the cash pump is the heart of any business. The ability to transform current assets (receivables and inventories) rapidly into cash is essential to the immediate survival of any company. Similarly, the ability to mobilize financing of the cash needs created by operations or growth is key to the firm being a going concern.

Neither the balance sheet nor the income statement provide a dynamic view of the evolution of the financial structure of a business, i.e., changes in this structure in general (on both the assets and the liabilities and equity sides), and changes in the cash position in particular.

Understanding such evolution over a period of time is of interest to both the company's management and external financial analysts. As IAS 7 puts it (IASB 1992: § 3): 'Users of an entity's financial statements are interested in how the entity generates and uses **cash** and **cash equivalents**. This is the case regardless of the nature of the entity's activities and irrespective of whether cash can be viewed as the product of the entity, as may be the case with a financial institution. Entities need cash for essentially the same reasons, however different their principal revenue-producing activities might be. They need cash to conduct their operations, to pay their obligations, and to provide returns to their investors'.

The **statement of cash flows** was developed to meet these informational needs. It used to be known as **cash flow statement** until IASB revised IAS 1 in 2007 (see IASB 2007). A rudimentary statement of cash flows was presented in Chapter 3, showing how it related to both balance sheet and income statement. This chapter develops the model of statement of cash flows adopted by the IASB, and many countries. It focuses on the construction of the statement of cash flows while Chapter 17 will deal with the analysis of the statement.

1 Structure of the statement of cash flows

According to IAS 7 (IASB 1992: § 1): 'An entity shall prepare a statement of cash flows (...) and shall present it as an integral part of its financial statements for each period for which financial statements are presented'. In some countries (the USA, the UK and France [for the consolidated financial statements], for instance), publishing a statement of cash flows is compulsory, whereas in others (France [for stand-alone or individual financial statements] and Italy, for instance), it is optional. However, with the required application since 2005 of IFRS/IAS by listed firms in Europe and some other countries, such as Australia (see more on this in Chapter 5), the publication of a statement of cash flows has become compulsory for these firms. In practice, most major listed companies had already long included a statement of cash flows in their annual report, even if it was not required.

One of the objectives of a statement of cash flows is, by definition, to provide information on those transactions that affect the cash position. The statement of cash flows reports cash generated or provided and used during a given period. It classifies cash flows into three categories of activities: operating, investing, and financing, as shown in Table 14.1.

This classification by activity, as mentioned in IAS 7 (§ 11) 'provides information that allows users to assess the impact of those activities on the financial position of the entity and the amount of its cash and cash equivalents. This information may also be used to evaluate the relationships among those activities'.

2 Usefulness of the statement of cash flows

'A statement of cash flows, when used in conjunction with the rest of the financial statements, provides information that enables users to evaluate [a] the changes in net assets of an entity, [b] its financial structure (including its liquidity and solvency) and [c] its ability

Table 14.1 Statement of cash flows structure

Net cash provided by/used in **operating** activities	A
Net cash provided by/used in **investing** activities	B
Net cash provided by/used in **financing** activities	C
Net increase/decrease in **cash and cash equivalents**	D = A + B + C
Cash and cash equivalents at beginning of year	E
Cash and cash equivalents at end of year	F = D + E

to affect the amounts and timing of cash flows in order to adapt to changing circumstances and opportunities' (IAS 7: § 4). The statement of cash flows is a useful statement in its own right, explaining the changes in the cash position over the period, just as the income statement explains the components of net income.

2.1 The importance of cash

In Chapter 1 we highlighted the fact that cash is the 'blood' of the entity and we presented the cash pump as the most basic business model of an economic entity. IAS 7 (§ 4) stresses the fact that 'cash flow information is useful in assessing the ability of the entity to generate cash and cash equivalents'. The cash position is a key indicator for management and financial analysis, both in the short-term (assessing solvency) and the long-term (measuring financing requirements). The importance of the cash position, in both absolute and relative terms, and its sign (positive or negative) may reveal the company's situation: financially healthy, vulnerable, struggling, etc. Cash is a valuable indicator in forecasting business difficulties and possible bankruptcy, as the triggering event of bankruptcy is the inability to cover, with available cash and cash equivalents, the repayment of debt which is due. Similarly the speed at which cash is consumed, generated or replenished in the course of operations is a sign of financial health of any firm.

2.2 Cash is objective

Statements of cash flows enhance the comparability of reported operating performance by different entities because they ignore accruals and eliminate the effects of using different accounting rules or procedures for the same transactions and events.

2.3 A valuable forecasting tool

The statement of cash flows is well suited for both retrospective analysis (where did funds come from and what were they used for) and forecasting (where will funds come from and are they sufficient to implement the entity's strategy, thus starting an adjustment loop if, for example, funds from operations are not sufficient). It is therefore an essential part of any business planning process and is critical in the preparation of annual budgets.

In addition, statements of cash flows enable users of financial information to assess and compare both the predictability of future cash flows and the present value of future cash flows of different entities.

2.4 Developments in international practice

There is currently a clear movement towards the adoption of a relatively uniform statement of cash flows format, replacing a variety of previously used statements such as the **funds flow statement**, also called **statement of changes in financial position**, built around a breakdown of the change in working capital (defined as the difference between equity and long-term debts on one hand, and fixed assets on the other, or the difference between current assets [including cash] and current liabilities – see Chapter 15). Some developments on this statement are presented in Appendix 14.1.

Even in countries where the local standards do not require a statement of cash flows, many companies nonetheless publish one, whether they apply IFRS/IAS in their annual report, or they are quoted on a major stock exchange, or they wish to more fully inform their investors.

3 Definition of the three categories of activities impacting cash flows

Clear partitioning of the statement of cash flows between the various 'activities' creating or consuming cash (operating, investing and financing) is vital. Each activity is defined by IAS 7 and we will follow that position. These definitions are used in international accounting practice and are coherent with the principal national standards regarding statement of cash flows (e.g., SFAS 95 in the USA [FASB 1987], FRS 1 in the UK [ASB 1991, revised 1996], Regulation CRC 99-02, art. 4260 and 4261 in France, etc.).

The classification of certain operations may sometimes prove to be difficult. For example, deciding in which activity financial expenses should be reported has been a hotly debated subject as the answer impacts on the very philosophy of what a business does. In addition, a single transaction may include cash flow components that belong to two or more distinct categories. For example, the monthly or quarterly cash repayment of an installment loan generally includes both an interest component and a partial reimbursement of the capital or principal. A similar issue arises from the payment of a lease rental agreement that had been classified as a **financial lease** (see Chapter 12). The interest element is generally classified as an operating activity, while the reimbursement of the principal is classified as a financing activity.

3.1 Operating activities

Cash flows from operating activities (often referred to as **operating cash flows**, in short, or **cash flows from operations**) are primarily derived from the main or core revenue-producing undertakings (activities) of the entity. They generally result from the transactions and other events that enter into the determination of net profit or loss. The amount of cash flows from operating activities is a key indicator of the extent to which the operations of the entity have generated sufficient cash flows to keep it afloat (in both the short- and the long-term). That implies the ability to maintain the operating capability of the entity, repay loans, pay dividends without needing recourse to external sources of financing and, possibly, make new investments for the development of the firm.

Examples of cash flows from operating activities, as given in IAS 7 (§ 14), are provided in Table 14.2 and in Appendix 14.2.

Some transactions, such as the sale of a fixed asset, may give rise to a gain or loss, which will be included in the determination of net profit or loss. However, the cash flows relating to such transactions should be included in **cash flows from investing activities** since the normal business of the entity is not to sell its fixed assets. The sale of a fixed asset is a way for the firm to obtain funds, thus avoiding the need to obtain the equivalent amount of liquid resources from lenders or shareholders.

> For example, as part of its reorganization plan in early 2003 [to get out of Chapter 11 bankruptcy protection], Kmart, a US big box retailer, planned to sell '326 stores around the country over the next three months. The plan, which the executives described as necessary for Kmart to become "a stronger company," was submitted yesterday to the federal judge overseeing Kmart's reorganization, as was a **financing plan** that includes an option to close 400 more stores'[1] (emphasis added).

Section 4 is dedicated to the methods and approaches to calculating operating cash flows.

3.2 Investing activities

Investing activities refer to the buying and selling of long-lived assets. These assets can be physical, such as land, buildings, machinery, equipment, etc., intangible, or financial, such as long-term securities, loans granted (and collecting their repayment) and equity in third parties.

The separate disclosure of cash flows arising from investing activities is important because these cash flows represent 'the extent to which expenditures have been made for resources intended to generate future income and cash flows' (IAS 7: § 16) (see examples of investing cash flows in Table 14.2 and Appendix 14.2).

3.3 Financing activities

Financing activities consist of (1) obtaining funds from existing or new shareholders and providing them with dividends; and (2) obtaining long-term loans, or long-term funds through bond issues, and managing their repayment. The separate disclosure of cash flows arising from financing activities is important because it is useful in predicting claims on future cash flows by providers of long-term capital or funds to the entity. It also helps understand how much of the cash available in a business comes from influxes of 'fresh funds' by shareholders or financial partners of the firm (see examples of financing cash flows in Table 14.2 and Appendix 14.2).

Table 14.2 summarizes the contents of each cash-related activity. As already mentioned and as will be seen later, the classification of certain items is subject to debate. Our table reflects current standard practice.

3.4 Differences in classification

Most events in the life of a business fit neatly into one of three classes: operating, investing, and financing activities. **Operating activities** reflect, in most local GAAP, one common line of thinking, namely that cash flows from operations are the result of the cash effect of transactions and other events that enter into the determination of net income, with the exception of gains or losses on sale of fixed assets (see above). Consequently, operating activities include managerial actions and decisions that are required by operations in the strictest sense (procurement, manufacturing, selling and distributing, for example), trade financing and cash management, as well as taxes and employee remuneration and profit sharing (the latter being a part of the compensation package that allows the firm to retain talent). All affect operating cash flows.

Some events are, however, difficult to assign clearly and unambiguously to one particular class of sources or uses of cash. They include the payment of interests, the distribution of dividends and the payment of taxes. As shown in Table 14.3, the IASB, unlike US GAAP, leaves the choice to the reporting entity.

Appendix 14.3 provides some developments on the contents of Table 14.3. The best reporting practice, regardless of the classification adopted, is to provide as much specific information to allow users of financial statements to make any reclassifications they judge useful and to assess the effect of the company's classification policy. Appendix 14.4 presents the model adopted in the UK and Ireland, which differs in its concepts from the IASB approach.

Table 14.2 Classification of cash flows

Activities	Cash inflows (receipts)	Cash outflows (payments)
Operating activities	■ Sale of goods and rendering of services to customers ■ Royalties, fees, commissions and other revenues ■ Interests on loans and investments	■ Purchase of goods and services ■ Salaries, fringe benefits and social expenses ■ Taxes ■ Interests on borrowings
Investing activities	■ Sale of fixed assets (intangible, tangible, financial – securities which are not cash equivalents) ■ Receipt of repayment of loans and advances	■ Purchase of long-lived assets (intangible, tangible, financial – i.e., long-term securities which are not cash equivalents) ■ Loans and advances made
Financing activities	■ Proceeds from issuing new shares ■ Proceeds from selling own shares ■ Proceeds from issuing new debt	■ Repurchase of own shares ■ Repayment of debts ■ Payment of dividends

Table 14.3 Differences in classification of five flows of cash

	Interests paid	Interests received	Dividends paid	Dividends received	Taxes paid
IASB	OPE or FIN	OPE or INV	OPE or FIN	OPE or INV	OPE or INV or FIN
USA	OPE	OPE	FIN	OPE	OPE

OPE = operating activities; INV = investing activities; FIN = financing activities

4 Calculating cash flows from operating activities

There are two ways of determining cash flows from operating activities: the **direct method** and the **indirect method**.

4.1 The direct method of calculating cash flows from operating activities

The *direct method* calculates the cash flows by grouping cash effects of transactions classes. In other words, it presents receipt and payment flows separately for each category of operating activities: selling, purchasing, securing employees labor, etc. In practice, there are two sub-categories of the direct method:

- A 'semi-direct' method, where accounting flows (sales, purchases, labor costs, etc.) are adjusted for changes in inventories and operating or trade receivables and payables to give cash flows of the period. For instance, cash received from customers equals sales revenue minus change in accounts receivable (balance of receivables at end of X2 minus equivalent balance at end of X1).

- A 'true' direct method, where cash flows are entered directly into the statement of cash flows from the accounting records of cash movements in the 'cash at bank' and 'cash in hand' accounts.

4.2 The indirect method of calculating cash flows from operating activities

The *indirect method* calculates the net cash flow from operating activities by adjusting net profit or loss (calculated on an accrual basis) for the effects of:

- Non-cash items such as depreciation, provisions, deferred taxes (see Chapter 6), unrealized foreign currency gains and losses, undistributed profits of associates, and non-controlling (minority) interests (see Chapter 13).

- Changes during the period in inventories and operating receivables and payables.

- All other items for which the cash effects are investing or financing cash flows. For instance, the gain or loss from sale of fixed assets is adjusted because it will be included in the investing activities (see later).

4.3 Reporting cash flows from operating activities

Figure 14.1 summarizes both methods.

The computation of the operating cash flow using both methods is detailed later in this chapter. Most standards (IAS 7, SFAS 95 in the USA, FRS 1 in the UK, etc.) recommend using the direct method in reporting, while allowing the use of the indirect method. Although the direct method provides information which may be useful in estimating future

Figure 14.1 Reporting cash flows from operating activities

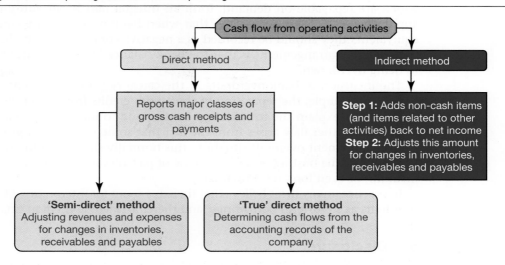

cash flows and which is not available under the indirect method, it is, however, complex and difficult to implement, especially in manufacturing firms (see end of section 7.1.2). Managers may also see it as too revealing of the detailed actual operations of their firm. The implementation of the 'semi-direct' method is also relatively complex.

Thus the vast majority of businesses – with the important exception of some Australian (e.g., Coles Group Limited) and Chinese (e.g., Shenzhen Expressway Limited) firms – report cash flows from operating activities using the indirect method, which is much simpler to implement. Unfortunately, the information thus provided by the statement of cash flows is also, as a result, much less valuable than what the direct method would have provided.

To conclude on this issue, we should stress the difference between the determination of the cash flows from operating activities and reporting of that cash flow. A given company may be able to, internally, determine the operating cash flow with a semi-direct, or even true direct method, and nevertheless decide to report the operating cash flow using the indirect method presentation. In other words, the format adopted for reporting does not allow any assumption as to which method was actually used to determine the reported operating cash flow. Many firms, however, specify in their notes which method was used.

5 Cash and cash equivalents

5.1 Definitions

According to IAS 7 (§ 6): '*Cash* comprises cash on hand and demand deposits. *Cash equivalents* are short-term, highly liquid investments that are readily convertible to known amounts of cash and which are subject to an insignificant risk of changes in value'. An investment normally qualifies as a cash equivalent only when it has a short maturity of, as the illustrations in section 5.2 will show, three months or less from the date of acquisition. Equity investments are excluded from cash equivalents unless they are, in substance, cash equivalents, for example in the case of preferred shares with a specified redemption date acquired within a short period of their maturity.

'Bank borrowings are generally considered to be financing activities' (IAS 7: § 8). However, IAS 7 (§ 8) leaves the decision of classification of bank overdrafts open. For instance, 'in some countries, [such as Germany, France, and the UK], bank overdrafts, which are repayable on demand, form an integral part of an entity cash management' approach (IAS 7: § 8). IAS 7 states that when bank overdrafts are considered to be cash equivalents they should be recorded as a negative component of cash. A characteristic of such banking arrangements is that the bank balance often fluctuates from being positive to being overdrawn.

The inclusion of bank overdrafts in the category 'cash equivalents' is not without its flaws. For example, the separation of short-term credits from other debts makes it impossible to fully explain the total change in debt and to measure accurately the leverage on the debt. Another flaw arises from the fact that some (mostly fast growing) entities have a quasi-permanent overdraft situation: this normally short-term financial instrument can be used by some businesses, as is the case of payables in fast moving retail businesses, for medium- or even long-term financing.

In practice, many firms believe that there is a room for interpreting IAS 7. They treat bank overdrafts as short-term borrowings[2] and therefore include them in financing activities.

5.2 Disclosure

'An entity shall disclose the components of cash and cash equivalents and shall present a reconciliation of the amounts in its statement of cash flows with the equivalent items reported in the statement of financial position' (IAS 7: § 45).

Real-life example Club Méditerranée

(France – IFRS – Source: Annual report 2008 – Leisure)

Notes to the financial statements

Cash and cash equivalents
    Cash and cash equivalents are held to meet the group's short-term cash needs. They include cash at bank and in hand, short-term deposits with an original maturity of less than three months and money-market funds that are readily convertible into cash. Cash equivalents are defined as short-term, highly liquid investments that are readily convertible into known amounts of cash and which are subject to an insignificant risk of changes in value.

Comment: The wording of this note is pretty much boiler plate and can be found in many annual reports.

Real-life example Aluminum Corporation of China

(China – Hong Kong GAAP – Source: Annual report 2008 – Production, sales and research of alumina and primary aluminum)

Notes to the financial statements

Cash and cash equivalents
    Cash and cash equivalents include cash in hand, deposits with banks and other cash investments with original maturities of three month or less. For the purpose of the cash flow statement, time deposits and other cash investments with original maturities of more than three months are excluded from cash and cash equivalents.

Real-life example Stora Enso

(Finland – IFRS – Source: Annual report 2008 – Production of paper)

Notes to the financial statements

Cash and cash equivalents
   Cash and cash equivalents comprise cash-in-hand, deposits held at call with banks and other liquid investments with original maturity of less than three months. Bank overdrafts are included in short-term borrowings under current liabilities.

Comment: This firm explicitly includes bank overdrafts in its financing activities, which is in line with one of the two formats allowed in IAS 7.

Real-life example Cobham

(UK – IFRS – Source: Annual report 2008 – Aerospace)

Notes to the financial statements

Cash and cash equivalents
   Bank balances and cash comprise cash held by the Group and short-term bank deposits with an original maturity of three months or less. The carrying amount of these assets approximates to their fair value.
   Cash and cash equivalents include the following for the purposes of the cash flow statement:

(£m)	2008	2007
Cash and cash equivalents per balance sheet	311.0	444.5
Bank overdrafts	(6.6)	(12.5)
Cash and cash equivalents per cash flow statement	304.4	432.0

Comment: This excerpt from the notes illustrates an application of the letter of IAS 7 (§ 45).

6 Example of a statement of cash flows

Table 14.4 presents an example of a generic statement of cash flows template for the year X2 reflecting the most common practices. The third column in Table 14.4 would not normally be found in a published statement of cash flows. It is presented, for pedagogical reasons only, to show the source of information for each line.

   Table 14.4 shows, for pedagogical purposes, both the direct and the indirect methods for the cash flows from operating activities. Of course, in practice, only one of these methods is applied in the presentation of any statement of cash flows.

   This table also displays the **potential cash flow**, which is often not included in the published versions of the statement of cash flows but is useful in understanding the basic mechanism of the indirect method. Potential cash flow is calculated by adjusting net income for non-cash items, and correcting for gains or losses on sales of fixed assets. Potential cash flow is illustrated in section 7.1, below.

Table 14.4 Example of a statement of cash flows		
		Source of the information
Cash flow from operating activities *(indirect method)*		
Net income/loss	±	IS X2
Adjustments to reconcile net income/loss to net cash provided by/used in operating activities		
Depreciation and amortization (excluding those applying to current assets [inventories and accounts receivable])	+	IS X2
Gain/loss on sale of fixed assets	±	IS X2
Potential cash flow	=	
Changes in operating assets and liabilities		
Change in accounts receivable (net amount)	±	BS X1/X2
Change in inventories (net amount)	±	BS X1/X2
Change in prepaid expenses	±	BS X1/X2
Change in accounts payable and accrued expenses	±	BS X1/X2
Net cash provided by/used in operating activities = (A)	=	
OR		
Cash flow from operating activities *(direct method)*		
Cash received from customers	+	IS X2 & BS X1/X2
Cash paid to suppliers*	−	IS X2 & BS X1/X2
Cash paid to employees*	−	IS X2 & BS X1/X2
Cash dividend received	+	IS X2 & BS X1/X2
Other operating cash receipts	+	IS X2 & BS X1/X2
Other operating cash payments	−	IS X2 & BS X1/X2
Interest paid in cash	−	IS X2 & BS X1/X2
Income taxes paid in cash	−	IS X2 & BS X1/X2
Net cash provided by/used in operating activities = (A)	=	
Cash flows from investing activities		
Purchases of long-lived assets	−	BS X1/X2 & AI X2
Proceeds from sale of long-lived assets	+	IS X2 & AI X2
Loans granted	−	BS X1/X2 & AI X2
Repayment of loans	+	BS X1/X2 & AI X2
Net cash provided by/used in investing activities = (B)	=	
Cash flows from financing activities		
Proceeds from issuance of long-term debt	+	BS X1/X2 & AI X2
Proceeds from issuance of shares	+	BS X1/X2 & AI X2
Dividends paid	−	BS X1/X2 & AI X2
Payment on long-term debt	−	BS X1/X2 & AI X2
Payment on reduction of share capital (repayment of shares)	−	BS X1/X2 & AI X2
Net cash provided by/used in financing activities = (C)	=	
Net increase in cash and cash equivalents = (A) + (B) + (C) = (D)	=	
Cash and cash equivalents at beginning of year = **(E)**		
Cash and cash equivalents at end of year = **(F) = (E) + (D)**		

IS: Income statement; BS: Balance sheet; AI: Additional information
* These two lines are often merged.

7 Construction of a statement of cash flows

Tables 14.5 and 14.6, pertaining to the published statements of the Liszt Company, a retail and wholesale commercial business, provide the raw material for the construction of a statement of cash flows.

Additional events took place during the year that are relevant for the preparation of the statement of cash flows for the year X2 (all figures in 000 CU):

■ New equipment was purchased for 175.

■ Equipment with an original cost of 20 and accumulated depreciation of 14 was sold for 9.

■ No new loan was either granted or obtained.

Table 14.5 Liszt Company – Comparative balance sheets before appropriation – years ended 31 December X2 and X1

(000 CU)	X2	X1	Changes (X2–X1)
Assets			
Fixed assets			
Tangible assets			
Equipment (gross)	615	460	155
Accumulated depreciation	–116	–70	–46
Equipment (net)	499	390	109
Financial assets (loans granted)	115	174	–59
Total fixed assets	614	564	50
Current assets			
Inventories	144	100	44
Accounts receivable	44	63	–19
Cash and marketable securities	25	15	10
Prepaid expenses*	4	7	–3
Total current assets	217	185	32
Total assets	831	749	82
Shareholders' equity and liabilities			
Shareholders' equity			
Share capital	282	200	82
Share premium	198	115	83
Retained earnings/Reserves	124	122	2
Net income of the period (before appropriation)	9	10	–1
Total shareholders' equity	613	447	166
Liabilities			
Long-term liabilities (loans received and bonds)	155	245	–90
Current liabilities			
Accounts payable	62	54	8
Income taxes payable	1	3	–2
Total current liabilities	63	57	6
Total liabilities	218	302	–84
Total shareholders' equity and liabilities	831	749	82

* Related to 'Other operating expenses'

Table 14.6 Liszt Company – Income statement –Year X2

(000 CU)	Year X2
Sales	800
Cost of merchandise sold	–570
Gross profit	230
Depreciation expense	–60
Other operating expenses	–162
Operating profit	8
Interest expense	–15
Investment income	18
Gain on sale of equipment	3
Profit before taxes	14
Income taxes	–5
Net profit	9

- 135 were raised from the issue of shares in cash (share capital of 66 plus share premium of 69).
- Convertible bonds were converted into capital for 30 (share capital for 16 and share premium for 14).
- Other bonds were repaid at face (nominal) value at maturity for 60.
- Dividends (relating to net income of X1) were paid in cash for 8.

7.1 Cash flows from operating activities

The indirect method and direct method will be used successively. Although we believe that the direct method is more relevant, from a financial statement analysis standpoint, we start our explanation with the indirect method, which is by far the most frequently reported method.

7.1.1 Indirect method

The indirect method consists of adjusting net income for non-cash expenses (such as depreciation expense) and revenues, also called non-cash items, gain/loss on sale of fixed assets and changes in receivables and payables. We will develop each of these elements, starting with the concept of **non-cash items** and potential cash flow.

Non-cash items and potential cash flow   The cash flows from operating activities cannot be obtained directly from the income statement, because the latter records accrual based revenues and expenses, not receipts (cash inflows) and payments (cash outflows). Therefore, the first step is to determine a potential cash flow. This is done by separating revenues and expenses into two categories: first, those which, by nature, will eventually generate a real cash flow (they are called **cash items** or monetary items); and second, those which will not generate a real cash flow (non-cash items or non-monetary items).

Cash items make up most of the income statement (sales, cost of merchandise sold, compensation expenses, operating expenses, etc.). Non-cash items include depreciation expense, amortization expense, depletion expense, provision expense (non-cash expenses) and reversal of provision (non-cash revenue). Figure 14.2 illustrates the fact that the income statement can be converted easily into the needed format for the calculation of the potential cash flow.

There are two ways of calculating the potential cash flow, since the sum of the expenses plus net income is, by definition, equal to the sum of revenues:

Figure 14.2 Cash and non-cash items in the income statement

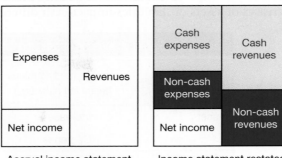

Accrual income statement | Income statement restated for the calculation of the potential cash flow

> Potential cash flow = Cash revenues − Cash expenses
>
> OR
>
> Potential cash flow = Net income + Non-cash expenses − Non-cash revenues

The first formula (Cash revenues – Cash expenses) is the one used in the direct method (see more details below).

The second formula (Net income + Non-cash expenses – Non-cash revenues) is applied in the indirect method. It highlights the difference between cash flow generated and net income: the latter must be adjusted for non-cash items in order to provide the potential cash flow.

Gain on sale of equipment   In our example (all figures in 000 CU), equipment with an original cost of 20 and accumulated depreciation of 14 was sold for 9. A gain of 3 on the sale will contribute to the period's income. It is computed in the following way:

Sale price		9
Original cost	20	
Accumulated depreciation	−14	
Book (or net) value	6	−6
Gain on sale		3

The cash inflow from the sale of equipment (here amounting to 9) is recorded as part of the cash from investing activities ('proceeds from sale of equipment').

If the gain on the sale had been considered as a part of operating activities, it would end up being recorded twice in the statement of cash flows: once under operating activities (for an amount of 3), and once in investing activities (since the gain is, by construction, included in the sale price of 9). The gain on the sale of an asset must, therefore, never be considered as belonging to operating activities. As a matter of fact, many, if not most, businesses consider gains/losses on sales of fixed assets as a non-cash item, and, thus, include them in the calculation of their potential cash flow. We adopted this position in Figure 14.4, and throughout this chapter.

Changes in inventories, receivables and payables   As we will show later in the direct method, the potential cash flow determined by adjustment of net income for non-cash items, then corrected for gains or losses on sales of fixed assets, now has to be adjusted by the amount of changes in inventories, receivables and payables. Changes in balance sheet items are calculated by a simple method: Year X2 balance minus Year X1 balance. However, increases or decreases of assets or liabilities impact cash differently, as shown below in Table 14.7.

Table 14.7 Sign of changes in assets and liabilities and impact on cash

	Change (ending minus beginning balances)	Impact on cash
Assets	Increase	–
	Decrease	+
Liabilities	Increase	+
	Decrease	–

The determination of the operating cash flow in the indirect method is shown in Figure 14.3.

Figure 14.3 From 'potential' cash flow to 'real' cash flow from operations

Potential cash flow
{
– Increase in related current assets excluding cash
+ Decrease in related current assets excluding cash

+ Increase in related liabilities
– Decrease in related liabilities
}
= Real cash flow from operations

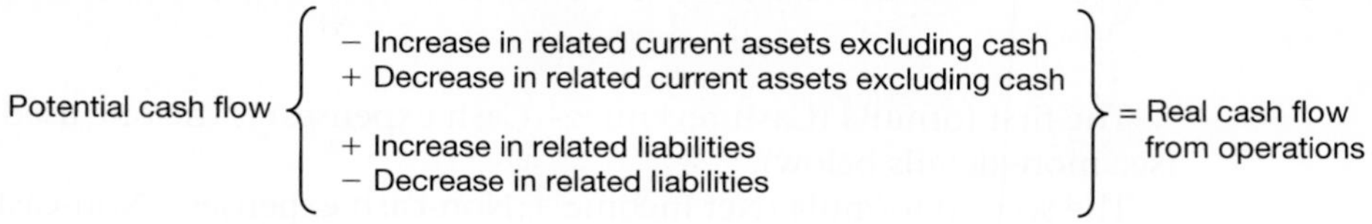

The change in inventories, accounts receivable, prepaid expenses, accounts payable and income taxes payable are taken from the 'changes' column of the comparative balance sheet (see Table 14.5). The nature of the change (positive or negative) in one of these accounts is important. If we take the example of accounts receivable, a negative figure in the comparative balance sheet indicates a decrease, and this has a positive impact on cash (it means that more customers paid-off their trade debt than new customers added to the trade receivable balance).

Summary of the indirect method   Figure 14.4 summarizes the determination of the operating cash flow with the indirect method.

Figure 14.4 Indirect method

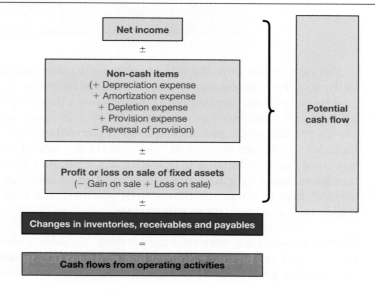

Liszt Company's schedule of cash flows from operating activities (indirect method)   The cash flows from operating activities for Liszt Company are computed in Table 14.8.

Table 14.8 Cash flows from operating activities (indirect method)		
Net income		9
Adjustments to reconcile net income/loss to net cash provided by/used in operating activities		
Depreciation expense	60	
Gain on sale of fixed assets	–3	
Potential cash flow		66
Adjustments to acknowledge changes in operating assets and liabilities		
Change in accounts receivable	19	
Change in inventories	–44	
Change in prepaid expenses	3	
Change in accounts payable	8	
Change in income taxes payable	–2	
Total adjustments	41	41
Net cash provided by/used in operating activities		50

Since the cash flows from operating activities must be the same under both methods, we will have to check after completion of the direct method that we find the same operating cash flow.

7.1.2 Direct method

We use the 'semi-direct' method defined earlier, where income statement items are adjusted for changes in inventories and operating receivables and payables to give cash flows.[3] This, in effect, transforms a *funds* flow (a transaction), calculated on an accrual basis (income statement item), into a *cash* flow. This calculation can be systematized into the equation shown as Figure 14.5.

Figure 14.5 Determination of cash flows using the semi-direct method

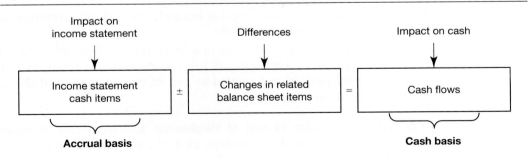

One difficulty is the correct association of related income statement and balance sheet items for inventories, receivables and payables. Another difficulty is the determination of the sign of the change in related balance sheet items. (This issue has been covered above with the indirect method – see Figure 14.3 and Table 14.7).

The determination of the operating cash flow with the direct method is shown in a simplified way in Figure 14.6, which represents a variation of Figure 14.3 (indirect method):

Figure 14.6 From income statement to 'real cash flow' (to be extended to each cash item on the income statement)

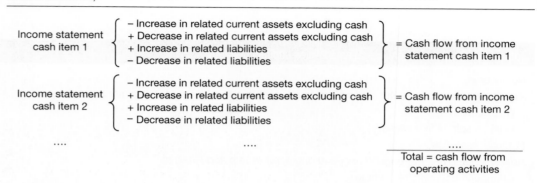

The equation in Figure 14.6 shows that each cash flow item is determined in the following way: a potential cash flow (represented by each income statement cash item) is adjusted by a change in inventories, receivables or payables to obtain the real cash flow. The equation is illustrated with the calculation of each component of the cash flow.

Cash received from customers

Income statement item	±	Change in related balance sheet item	=	Cash flow from customers
Sales revenue (accrual basis)		Change in accounts receivable		Cash received from customers
800	+	19 (decrease)	=	819

- 'Sales revenue' is obtained from the income statement. It flows through the 'accounts receivable' before becoming cash.
- The change in accounts receivable is taken from the 'changes' column of the comparative balance sheet.
- The nature of the change in accounts receivable (positive or negative) is important. A negative figure in the comparative balance sheet (X2 – X1) indicates a decrease, and this has a positive impact on cash.
- The cash inflow from sales, in this example, exceeds sales revenue by the amount of the change in accounts receivable.
- The receivable arising on the sale of a fixed asset (if there were one – which is not the case here) should be kept separate from 'trade accounts receivable'. If there had been one, it would have been included as part of the calculation of the cash flow derived from investing activities.

Cash paid-out in relation to cost of merchandise sold (cash paid to suppliers of goods for resale) This is calculated in two steps. First, the amount of purchases is reconstructed by eliminating the effect of change in inventories. As already seen in Chapter 9, the cost of merchandise sold can be computed as follows for a trading (retailer) company:

Purchases + Change in inventories (i.e., beginning minus ending) = Cost of merchandise sold

Given that in Table 14.5 the balance sheet changes are calculated by deducting Year X1 figures from Year X2 figures (i.e., ending − beginning), this formula becomes:

Purchases − Change in inventories (i.e., ending minus beginning) = Cost of merchandise sold

Purchases are consequently calculated as follows:

Purchases	=	Change in inventories (ending minus beginning)	+	Cost of merchandise sold
Purchases	=	Change in inventories	+	Cost of merchandise sold
614	=	44	+	570

The second step is now to calculate the related cash flow.

Income statement item	±	Change in related balance sheet item	=	Cash flow related to the purchase of merchandise
Purchases		Change in accounts payable		Cash paid out for purchases
−614	+	8 (increase)	=	−606

We assume here that all accounts payable relate to purchases of merchandise.

Cash paid for other operating expenses (cash paid to suppliers of other operating expenses)

Income statement item	+	Change in related balance sheet item	=	Cash flow related to other operating expenses
Other potentially cash impacting operating expenses		Change in prepaid expenses		Cash paid out for other operating expenses
−162	+	3 (decrease)	=	−159

- If there had been any accrued liabilities, or compensation expenses, fringe benefits and social expenses payable in the balance sheet, then these items would have been included in the adjustment of other operating expenses.
- Depreciation expense (and amortization expense, which does not exist in this example) has no impact on cash. These expenses are therefore not included in the direct method calculation.

Cash paid for interest   In our example, there is no accrued interest payable on the balance sheet. The cash outflow is thus equal to the interest expense: −15. In general, cash paid for interest is equal to the interest expense adjusted for the change in accrued interest payable.

Cash received from investment income   Our example does not include any accrued interest receivable on the balance sheet. The cash inflow is thus equal to the investment income (dividends received): 18.

Cash paid for income taxes This is calculated as was done for 'other operating expenses'.

Income statement item	±	Change in related balance sheet items	=	Cash flow related to taxes
Income taxes expense		Change in income taxes payable		Income taxes paid
–5	–	2 (decrease)	=	–7

Gain on sale of equipment The gain on sale of equipment is not included in the direct method. The proceeds from the sale of fixed assets are included in investing activities.

Summary of adjustments Table 14.9 shows balance sheet items (receivables and payables) related to income statement items.

Depreciation expense and amortization expense are not included in this table because they have no impact on cash. Any given income statement item may be related, at the same time, to both assets and liabilities.

Liszt Company's schedule of cash flows from operating activities (direct method) Table 14.10 shows how cash flows from operating activities are calculated.

At this stage, we can cross-check the cash flow figure obtained with the direct method (50) with the one determined previously with the indirect method. As expected we find the figures from each method to be identical.

7.1.3 Special case of manufacturing firms

Keep in mind the Liszt example is a retailing/wholesaling firm. If an analyst or an outside user of financial information wants to calculate the cash flows from operating activities created by a manufacturing firm that uses 'cost of goods sold' in its (functional) income

Table 14.9 Income statement items and related balance sheet items

Income statement items	Related current assets	Related current liabilities
Sales	Accounts receivable	Advances received from customers Revenues recorded in advance (unearned revenues)
Financial revenues	Interests receivable Accrued interests receivable	Unearned interests
Cost of merchandise sold	Inventory Advances paid to suppliers	Accounts payable
Rent expense	Prepaid rent (Expenses recorded in advance)	Rent payable Accrued rent payable
Compensation and social expenses	Prepaid compensation and social expenses (Expenses recorded in advance)	Compensation and social expenses payable Accrued salaries and social expenses payable
Other operating expenses	Prepaid other operating expenses (Expenses recorded in advance)	Other expenses payable Accrued other expenses payable
Taxes including income taxes	Prepaid taxes – prepaid income taxes (Expenses recorded in advance)	(Income) Taxes payable Accrued (income) taxes payable
Financial expenses	Prepaid interests	Interests payable Accrued interests payable

Table 14.10 Cash flows from operating activities (direct method)

Cash received from customers	819
Cash paid in relation to cost of merchandise sold	−606
Cash paid in relation to other operating expenses	−159
Cash paid on interest	−15
Cash received from investment income	18
Cash paid on income taxes	−7
Net cash provided by/used in operating activities	50

statement, the computation will be a little more complex than it was here, in the case of a retailing or a service business (the problem, of course, does not exist if the entity reports its income statement by nature, since, in that case, the total depreciation expense will be clearly identified). If the firm uses a functional income statement, the depreciation expense that will be used is likely to be only an approximation because the cost of goods sold does include part of the manufacturing depreciation expense and the other part of the manufacturing depreciation expense is attached to inventories which means less – if increase in inventory level –, or more – if decrease in inventory level – than the depreciation of the period may have been, in fact, included in the cost of goods sold.

The following equations (ignoring, for the sake of simplicity, work in process) need to be kept in mind when looking at a manufacturing entity. They illustrate the reason why the total depreciation expense is not available directly in an income statement by function:

Raw materials and components (RM) consumed = Purchases + beginning inventory of RM − ending inventory of RM

Cost of goods manufactured = Cost of RM consumed + cost of manufacturing labor + manufacturing depreciation + manufacturing overhead (i.e., supervision and support costs)

Cost of goods sold = Cost of goods manufactured + beginning inventory of finished goods − ending inventory of finished goods.

The total depreciation expense (manufacturing plus non-manufacturing depreciation expenses), which must be known to be able to use the indirect method of cash flow calculation, is not available directly from reading the income statement. An approximate value can be extracted through an analysis of the balance sheet.

The difference in accumulated depreciation between the beginning and ending balance sheets provides an approximation of the total depreciation expense of the period. It must be adjusted appropriately if the notes to the financial statements mention any acquisition or sale of fixed assets during the period: the acquisition value and date might be mentioned, but generally are not; the sale should be reported, at least in the aggregate, and mention both the revenue from the sale and the book value and relevant accumulated depreciation of the assets sold.

In a case like this, the depreciation expense that will thus be used in calculating the cash flows from operating activities using the indirect method will not be the depreciation expense reported in the functional income statement (that figure pertains only to non-manufacturing assets, since the manufacturing depreciation expense is 'buried' in the cost of goods sold and in the inventories fluctuations), but it will be the estimated depreciation expense calculated on the basis of comparing balance sheets, taking into account the comment made in the preceding paragraph.

7.2 Cash flows from investing activities

The flow of cash to be calculated is the cash flow from investing activities. The relevant data for this activity for Liszt Company are (all figures in 000 CU):

- Equipment was purchased for 175.
- Equipment with an original cost of 20 and accumulated depreciation of 14 was sold for 9.
- No new loans were granted.

For balance sheet items affected by investing activities, the following equation is key (the same equation applies to any balance sheet item). It allows the calculation of any one of the four items when the other three are known.

Beginning balance	+	Increases	−	Decreases	=	Ending balance
A	+	B	−	C	=	D

An application of this equation is illustrated below.

7.2.1 Purchase of equipment

Beginning balance	+	Increases	−	Decreases	=	Ending balance
Equipment (gross value)	+	New equipment purchased (at cost)	−	Original cost of equipment sold	=	Equipment (gross value)
460	+	175	−	20	=	615

7.2.2 Sale of equipment

As stated earlier, the selling price of the equipment (9) must be included in the statement of cash flows, since it represents a cash inflow. If the sale had been done (partially or in its entirety) on credit, the price would represent a potential cash flow and should be adjusted by the changes in the specific accounts receivable (distinct from trade accounts receivable) to give the net cash flow from that transaction.

The change in accumulated depreciation between the beginning and end of the year should be verified (but that element has no impact on the cash flow).

Beginning balance	+	Increases	−	Decreases	=	Ending balance
Accumulated depreciation	+	Depreciation expense of the period	−	Accumulated depreciation of fixed assets sold	=	Accumulated depreciation
70	+	60	−	14	=	116

7.2.3 Repayment of loans (previously) granted to third parties

In our example, no new loan was granted, but the ending balance of loans granted to third parties is lower than the beginning balance. We therefore know that some borrowers have repaid their loans. As an external user of financial information we can deduce the amounts that were reimbursed and were therefore cash inflows for Liszt Company. The equation yields the missing piece of data:

Beginning balance	+	Increases	–	Decreases	=	Ending balance
Loan	+	New loan granted	–	Repayment of loan	=	Loan
174	+	0	–	?	=	115

$174 + 0 - X = 115$ thus $X = 174 - 115 = 59$. Borrowers have repaid a total amount of 59 of the loans previously granted by Liszt Company.

7.2.4 Liszt Company schedule of cash flows from investing activities

Table 14.11 summarizes the cash flows from investing activities.

Table 14.11 Cash flows from investing activities	
Purchase of equipment	−175
Proceeds from sale of equipment	9
Repayment of loan by borrowers	59
Net cash provided by/used in investing activities	−107

7.3 Cash flows from financing activities

The relevant information available (all figures in 000 CU) is:

- 135 were raised from the issuance of new shares in cash (66 of share capital and 69 of share premium).
- Convertible bonds with a face value of 30 were converted into capital: thus creating additional share capital for 16 and an increase in share premium of 14.
- Other bonds were repaid at face value at maturity for 60.
- Dividends (relating to net income of X1) were paid in cash in the amount of 8.

7.3.1 Issuance of new share capital

The changes in share capital and share premium are due to both issuance of new shares and conversion of bonds:

Beginning balance	+	Increases	–	Decreases	=	Ending balance
Share capital	+	Issued	–	Repurchase	=	Share capital
200	+	66 + 16 = 82	–	0	=	282
Share premium	+	Issued	–	Repurchase	=	Share premium
115	+	69 + 14 = 83	–	0	=	198

These two transactions are separated in Table 14.12.

Only the cash derived from the issuance of new shares can be included in the statement of cash flows (here it is 66 + 69 = 135). The debt-conversion issue is a non-cash 'financing' activity and will be mentioned in a separate schedule as a footnote to the statement of cash flows.

Beginning balance	+	Increases	–	Decreases		=	Ending balance
				Repayment	Conversion		
Bonds	+	New issue	–			=	Bonds
245	+	0	–	(60 + 30)		=	155

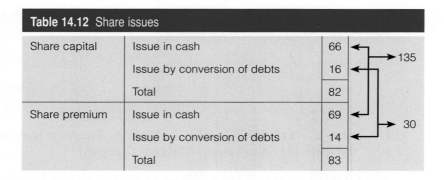

Table 14.12 Share issues

Share capital	Issue in cash	66	135
	Issue by conversion of debts	16	
	Total	82	
Share premium	Issue in cash	69	30
	Issue by conversion of debts	14	
	Total	83	

The decrease of the balance of bond debt is the result of the following two actions:

- Repayment: 60.
- Conversion into capital: 30.

7.3.2 Dividends

When the balance sheet is presented *before profit appropriation*, changes in retained earnings/reserves can be explained as follows:

Beginning balance 31/12/X1	+	Increases (Added on 31/12/X1)	−	Decreases during X2	=	Ending balance 31/12/X2
Retained earnings/ Reserves before income of X1	+	Net income of year X1	−	Dividends paid in year X2 or capitalization to Retained earnings/ Reserves	=	Retained earnings/ Reserves before income of X2
122	+	10	−	8	=	124

The dividends paid in year X2 are usually related to the net income of year X1. However, they could also represent advance payments on dividends related to net income of year X2. As the amount of dividends paid (8) fully explains the movements in retained earnings/reserves, we can infer that there was no capitalization of retained earnings/reserves during the period. (We also know from the study of share issues that the movement in capital was arising from an increase in cash and not from a transfer from retained earnings/reserves – see Chapter 11.)

Table 14.13 shows how **cash flows from financing activities** are computed.

7.4 Full statement of cash flows

Since we have calculated its three components, the statement of cash flows can now be constructed by adding the three components. For the sake of simplicity, Table 14.14 uses the indirect method. The direct method would be obtained by replacing, in Table 14.14,

Table 14.13 Cash flows from financing activities

Proceeds from issuance of shares	135
Payments on long-term debt	−60
Dividends paid	−8
Net cash provided by/used in financing activities	67

Table 14.14 Statement of cash flows of Liszt Company – year X2 (indirect method)	
Cash flows from operating activities (indirect method)	
Net income	9
Adjustments to reconcile net income to net cash provided by operating activities	
Depreciation expense	60
Gain on sale of fixed assets	–3
Potential cash flow	66
Changes in operating assets and liabilities	
Change in accounts receivable	19
Change in inventories	–44
Change in prepaid expenses	3
Change in accounts payable	8
Change in income taxes payable	–2
Total adjustments	41
Net cash provided by/used in operating activities	50
Cash flows from investing activities	
Purchase of equipment	–175
Proceeds from sale of equipment	9
Repayment of loan	59
Net cash used in investing activities	–107
Cash flows from financing activities	
Proceeds from issuance of shares	135
Payments on long-term debt	–60
Dividends paid	–8
Net cash provided by financing activities	67
Net increase in cash and cash equivalents	10
Cash and cash equivalents at beginning of year	15
Cash and cash equivalents at end of year	25
Schedule of non-cash investing and financing transactions (see section 9)	
Conversion of bonds into capital	30

the operating cash flow (obtained by the indirect method) by the details of Table 14.12, which summarized the cash flow from operating activities using the direct method.

The total cash flow (net increase in cash and cash equivalents) is equal to the sum of the flows of cash from the three activities: $50 - 107 + 67 = 10$. This figure corresponds to the changes in cash as reported in the balance sheet ($25 - 15 = 10$).

8 Reporting the statement of cash flows

Companies often report additional relevant information on events that have or could have impacted on the cash balance such as:

- non-cash investing and financing transactions;
- other [more detailed] cash flow information (for example by indicating clearly the detailed amounts of interest and taxes paid);
- business acquisitions, net of cash acquired.

Real-life example Benihana Inc.

(USA – US GAAP – Source: Annual report 2008 – Japanese style restaurants, operating mainly in the USA)

Supplemental cash flow information

(in $ 000)	29 March 2009	30 March 2008	1 April 2007
Cash paid during the fiscal year for			
Interest	801	300	447
Income taxes	1,304	7,898	5,775
Non-cash investing and financing activities			
Acquired property and equipment for which cash payments had not yet been made	5,867	6,735	4,235
Accrued but unpaid dividends on the Series B preferred stock	241	245	249
Unrealized loss on investment securities available for sale, net of tax	166	31	–
Fair value of assets acquired, other than cash	–	–	2,743
Note receivable received as part of consideration for sale of location	–	–	24

Comment: The 'cash paid during the fiscal year' information is given because the company used the indirect method to compute the cash flows from operating activities. As a result, the statement does not show interest- and tax-related cash flows separately, and so the company provides these additional details. Non-cash financing activities are not included in the statement of cash flows but disclosed separately (see section 9).

9 Non-cash investing and financing transactions

Some transactions affecting the capital and asset structure of an entity do not have any direct impact on current cash flows. They must, however, be reported, for the sake of completion (and in coherence with the no-offsetting principle). Examples of such transactions are:

- The acquisition of assets, either by assuming directly related liabilities, or by means of a finance lease (see Chapter 12).
- The acquisition of an entity exclusively by means of an equity issue.
- The conversion of debt to equity (see Chapter 11).
- The issuance of shares by capitalization of retained earnings/reserves (bonus issue) (see Chapter 11).

Under IAS 7 (§ 43), and, accordingly, under most national standards, 'investing and financing transactions that do not require the use of cash or cash equivalents shall be excluded from a statement of cash flows. Such transactions shall be disclosed elsewhere in the financial statements [generally in the notes] in a way that provides all the relevant information about these transactions' (see Benihana Inc. example in section 8).

Key points

- Users of financial statements are interested in how the entity generates and uses cash and cash equivalents.

- The statement of cash flows, also called cash flow statement, is the tool designed to give users better understanding of how a firm creates and uses cash.

- The statement of cash flows is an integral part of a firm's financial statements. In some countries, it is compulsory to publish a statement of cash flows, whereas in others, it is optional. In practice, most major listed companies include a statement of cash flows in their annual report.
- The statement of cash flows separates cash flows of a period between three activities: operating, investing, and financing.
- Cash flows from operating activities are primarily derived from the principal revenue-producing activities of the entity. Therefore, they generally result from the transactions and other events that enter into the determination of net profit or loss.
- The cash flows arising from investing activities represent both the expenditures made in order to obtain resources intended to generate future income and cash flows, and the divestments of those resources.
- The financing cash flows help predict claims on future cash flows by providers of capital to the entity. They are the net result of cash proceeds from issuing shares or debt, cash repayments of amounts borrowed and dividends paid.
- There are two ways of determining cash flows from operating activities: the detailed direct method (which discloses major classes of gross cash receipts and gross cash payments) and the aggregated indirect method (which discloses the net cash flow from operating activities by adjusting net profit or loss for the effects of several non-cash items and/or non-operating items).

Review (solutions are at the back of the book)

Review 14.1 Dvorak Company (1)

Topic: Preparation of a statement of cash flows

The balance sheets and income statements of Dvorak Company for the years X1 and X2 are presented in the following tables.

Dvorak Company Balance sheet		
ASSETS	X1	X2
Fixed assets (gross amount)	12,000	14,950
Less accumulated depreciation	−3,700	−4,300
Fixed assets (net amount)	8,300	10,650
Inventories (gross amount)	2,300	2,000
Less accumulated provision	0	0
Inventories (net amount)	2,300	2,000
Accounts receivable	1,650	2,300
Cash at bank	190	80
TOTAL ASSETS	12,440	15,030
EQUITY AND LIABILITIES	X1	X2
Share capital	3,000	3,200
Retained earnings/Reserves	3,600	3,800
Net income/loss of the period	2,780	2,560
Shareholders' equity	9,380	9,560
Financial liabilities (1)	3,000	4,350
Accounts payable	60	870
Fixed assets accounts payable	0	250
TOTAL EQUITY AND LIABILITIES	12,440	15,030
(1) Including bank overdrafts	200	950

Dvorak Company Income statement	
REVENUES	*X2*
Sales of merchandise	14,100
Other operating revenues	150
Total operating revenues	14,250
Financial revenues	300
Exceptional income (1)	450
TOTAL REVENUE	15,000
EXPENSES	*X2*
Purchases of merchandise	3,700
Change in inventory of merchandise	300
Other purchases and external expenses	550
Taxes and similar expenses	70
Personnel expenses	4,310
Depreciation expenses	1,400
Provision expenses	0
Total operating expenses	10,330
Financial expenses	580
Exceptional expenses (2)	250
Income tax	1,280
TOTAL EXPENSES	*12,440*
Net income	2,560
(1) Selling price of fixed assets disposed of	450
(2) Book value of sold fixed assets	250

The following additional information was taken from the company's record.

Additional information				
	31/12/X1	+	−	31/12/X2
Fixed assets (gross amount)	12,000	4,000	1,050	14,950
Accumulated depreciation	3,700	1,400	800	4,300
Accumulated provision	0	−	−	0
Financial liabilities (excluding overdrafts)	2,800	1,000	400	3,400
	X2			
Dividends paid	2,580			

Required

Prepare a statement of cash flows for the year X2, using the direct *and* the indirect method.

Assignments

Assignment 14.1
Multiple-choice questions

Select the right answer (one possible answer, unless otherwise stated).

1. Which of the following cannot be a main objective of a statement of cash flows?

   (a) To provide relevant information on the cash receipts and cash payments of an entity during a given period

   (b) To explain changes in cash in the same way as the income statement explains the components that comprise the net income

   (c) To provide information on the operating, financing and investing activities of an entity and the effects of those activities on cash resources

   (d) To explain the changes in working capital between opening and closing balance sheets

   (e) To report on a standard basis the cash generation and cash consumption for a period

   (f) To provide relevant information to users of the cash inflows and cash outflows of an entity during a reporting period

   (g) To provide information on the historical changes in cash and cash equivalents

2. Which of the following would not be integrated in the computation of the cash flow from operating activities?

   (a) Cash received from customers

   (b) Cash paid to suppliers

   (c) Proceeds from sale of fixed assets

   (d) Depreciation and amortization

   (e) Gain on sale of fixed assets

3. Which of the following would not be included in investing activities? (more than one answer is possible)

   (a) Repayment of a loan granted to a subsidiary

   (b) Dividends paid

   (c) Purchase cost of fixed assets

   (d) Depreciation and amortization

   (e) Gain on sale of fixed assets

4. Which of the following would not be included in financing activities? (more than one answer is possible)

   (a) Proceeds from issuance of shares

   (b) Dividends received

   (c) Repayment of debt

   (d) Issuance of share capital by capitalization of reserves

   (e) Dividends paid

5. When using the indirect method to compute the operating cash flow, which of the following items will not be included?

   (a) Change in inventory

   (b) Depreciation expense

   (c) Gain on sale of fixed assets

   (d) Cash paid to employees

   (e) Net income

6. When using the direct method to compute the operating cash flow, which of the following items will not be included?

   (a) Cash received from customers

   (b) Depreciation expense

   (c) Cash paid to suppliers

   (d) Cash paid to employees

   (e) Cash paid on other operating expenses

7. Depending on the country, interest expenses are included in either operating activities or investing activities

   (a) True

   (b) False

8. Under IAS 7, bank overdrafts are reported either as a part of cash equivalents (as negative cash) or as a part of financing activities

   (a) True

   (b) False

9. Dividends received are usually included in

   (a) Operating activities

   (b) Investing activities

   (c) Financing activities

10. Which of these stages are included in the indirect method? (more than one answer is possible)

    (a) Add any increase in inventory

    (b) Subtract any increase in accounts receivable

    (c) Add any loss on sale of fixed assets

    (d) Subtract depreciation expense

    (e) Subtract any increase in accounts payable

Assignment 14.2
Janacek Company (1)

Topic: Preparation of a statement of cash flows

The Janacek Company has a commercial activity in the beauty cream business.

Required

■ With the help of the following balance sheets, income statements and additional information, prepare a

statement of cash flows for the years X2 and X3 using the direct method.

■ Prepare a separate statement reconciling the net income and the net cash provided by/used in operating activities. This statement represents the application of the indirect method in calculating the cash flow from operating activities.

Janacek Company Balance sheet (000 CU)			
ASSETS	Year end X1	Year end X2	Year end X3
Fixed assets (gross amount)	15,000	22,000	27,400
Less accumulated depreciation	−4,900	−5,500	−6,000
Fixed assets (net amount)	10,100	16,500	21,400
Inventories (gross amount)	3,200	4,500	5,700
Less accumulated provision	0	0	−100
Inventories (net amount)	3,200	4,500	5,600
Accounts receivable	2,020	3,500	5,300
Cash at bank	1,150	250	240
TOTAL ASSETS	*16,470*	*24,750*	*32,540*
EQUITY AND LIABILITIES	Year end X1	Year end X2	Year end X3
Share capital	3,000	5,000	7,500
Retained earnings/Reserves	3,800	4,200	4,400
Net income/loss	1,728	474	246
Shareholders' equity	8,528	9,674	12,146
Financial liabilities (1)	3,900	8,500	11,500
Accounts payable	4,042	6,126	5,094
Accounts payable to suppliers of fixed assets	0	450	3,800
TOTAL EQUITY AND LIABILITIES	*16,470*	*24,750*	*32,540*
(1) Including bank overdrafts	100	1,000	2,000

Janacek Company Income statement (000 CU)			
REVENUES	X1	X2	X3
Sales of merchandise	16,000	20,900	25,500
Other operating revenues	310	220	710
Total operating revenues	16,310	21,120	26,210
Financial revenues	55	140	220
Exceptional income (1)	0	200	400
TOTAL REVENUES	16,365	21,460	26,830
EXPENSES	X1	X2	X3
Purchases of merchandise	3,500	7,100	9,000
Change in inventory of merchandise	200	−1,300	−1,200
Other purchases and external expenses	750	1,000	1,530
Taxes and similar expenses	100	200	500
Personnel compensation expenses	7,561	11,000	13,000
Depreciation expenses	800	1,000	1,500
Provision expenses	0	0	100
Total operating expenses	12,911	19,000	24,430
Financial expenses	717	1,149	1,931
Exceptional expenses (2)	145	600	100
Income tax expense	864	237	123
TOTAL EXPENSES	14,637	20,986	26,584
Net income	1,728	474	246
(1) Selling price of fixed assets	0	200	400
(2) Book value of items sold	0	600	100

It should be noted that this income statement is presented by nature.

Janacek Company Additional information							
	31/12/X1	+	−	31/12/X2	+	−	31/12/X3
Fixed assets (gross)	15,000	8,000	1000	22,000	6,500	1,100	27,400
Accumulated depreciation	4,900	1,000	400	5,500	1,500	1,000	6,000
Accumulated provision	0	−	−	0	100	−	100
Financial liabilities (excluding overdrafts)	3,800	4,000	300	7,500	3,000	1,000	9,500

	X2	X3
Dividends paid:	1,328	.274

Assignment 14.3
Smetana Company

Topic: Preparation of a statement of cash flows

Smetana Company is a manufacturing firm.

Required

- With the help of the following income statement, balance sheet, statement of retained earnings and additional information, prepare a statement of cash flows for year X2 using the direct method.
- Prepare a separate statement reconciling the net income and the net cash provided by/used in operating activities. This statement represents the application of the indirect method in calculating the cash flow from operating activities.

Smetana Company– Income statement (000 CU) –Year X2	
Sales	1,000
Cost of goods sold	−600
Gross profit	400
Depreciation expense	−60
Other operating expenses	−150
Operating profit	190
Interest expense	−18
Investment income	16
Loss on sale of equipment	−5
Profit before taxes	183
Income taxes	−60
Net profit	123

Smetana Company – Comparative balance sheets (000 CU) – Years ended 31 December X2 and X1			
	X2	X1	Changes (X2 – X1)
Assets			
Current assets			
Cash	65	20	45
Accounts receivable	55	80	−25
Prepaid expenses*	8	10	−2
Inventories	131	80	51
Total current assets	259	190	69
Fixed assets			
Financial assets (loans)	150	140	10
Tangible assets			
Equipment	700	600	100
Accumulated depreciation	−110	−80	−30
Equipment (net)	590	520	70
Total fixed assets	740	660	80
Total assets	999	850	149
Shareholders' equity and liabilities			
Liabilities			
Current liabilities			
Accounts payable	136	135	1
Income taxes payable	40	35	5
Total current liabilities	176	170	6
Long-term liabilities (bonds)	160	180	−20
Total liabilities	336	350	−14
Shareholders' equity			
Share capital	300	250	50
Share premium	150	120	30
Retained earnings/Reserves	213	130	83
Total shareholders' equity	663	500	163
Total shareholders' equity and liabilities	999	850	149

* Related to other operating expenses

Smetana Company – Statement of retained earnings (000 CU) – Year ended 31 December X2	
Retained earnings (at end of Year X1)	130
Net income of Year X2	123
Dividends paid during Year X2	−40
Retained earnings (at end of Year X2)	213

The following additional information is also relevant for the preparation of the statement of cash flows for the year X2 (all figures in 000 CU):

■ Equipment with an original cost of 50 and accumulated depreciation of 30 was sold for 15.

■ A new loan was granted. No loan was repaid.
■ 80 were raised from the issue of shares in cash (share capital of 50 plus share premium of 30).
■ Some bonds were repaid at maturity; they had a total face value of 70.

References

ASB (1991, revised 1996) Financial Reporting Standard No. 1: Cash flow statements, London.

FASB (1987) Statement of Financial Accounting Standards No. 95: Statement of cash flows, Norwalk, CT.

IASB (1992) International Accounting Standard No. 7: Statement of cash flows, London.

IASB (2007) International Accounting Standard No. 1: Presentation of Financial Statements, London.

Further reading

Boussard, D. and Colasse, B. (1992) 'Funds-flow statement and cash-flow accounting in France: evolution and significance', *European Accounting Review* 1(2): 229–54.

Broome, O.W. (2004) 'Statement of cash flows: Time for change!', *Financial Analysts Journal* 60(2): 16–22.

Cheng, C. and Hollie, D. (2008) 'Do core and non-core cash flows from operations persist differentially in predicting future cash flows?', *Review of Quantitative Finance & Accounting* 31(1): 29–53.

Cheng, C.S.A., Liu, C.S. and Schaefer, T.F. (1997) 'The value-relevance of SFAS No. 95 cash flows from operations as assessed by security market effects', *Accounting Horizons* 11(3): 1–15.

Clinch, G., Sidhu, B. and Sin, S. (2002) 'The usefulness of direct and indirect cash flow disclosures', *Review of Accounting Studies* 7(4): 383–402.

Dhar, S. (1998) 'Cash flow reporting in India – A case study', *Indian Accounting Review* 2(2): 39–52.

Haller, A. and Jakoby, S. (1995) 'Funds flow reporting in Germany: A conceptual and empirical state of the art', *European Accounting Review* 4(3): 515–34.

Jing, L., Nissim, D. and Thomas, J. (2007) 'Is cash flow king in valuations?', *Financial Analysts Journal* 63(2): 56–68.

Kim, M. and Kross, W. (2005) 'The ability of earnings to predict future operating cash flows has been increasing – not decreasing', *Journal of Accounting Research* 43(5): 753–80.

Kinnunen, J. and Koskela, M. (1999) 'Do cash flows reported by firms articulate with their income statements and balance sheets? Descriptive evidence from Finland', *European Accounting Review* 8(4): 631–54.

Krishnan, G.V. and Largay III, J.A. (2000) 'The predictive ability of direct method cash flow information', *Journal of Business Finance & Accounting* 27(1/2): 215–45.

Kwok, H. (2002) 'The effect of cash flow statement format on lenders' decisions', *The International Journal of Accounting* 37(3): 347–62.

Nissan, S. Kamata, N. and Otaka, R. (1995) 'Cash reporting in Japan', *The International Journal of Accounting* 29: 168–80.

Orpurt, S.F. and Zang, Y. (2009) 'Do direct cash flow disclosures help predict future operating cash flows and earnings?', *The Accounting Review* 84(3): 893–935.

Pae, J. (2005) 'Expected accrual models: The impact of operating cash flows and reversals of accruals.', *Review of Quantitative Finance & Accounting* 24(1): 5–22.

Rai, A. (2003) 'Reconciliation of net income to cash flow from operations: An accounting equation approach', *Journal of Accounting Education* 21(1): 17–24.

Stolowy, H. and Walser-Prochazka, S. (1992) 'The American influence in accounting: Myth or reality? The statement of cash flows example', *The International Journal of Accounting* Autumn: 185–221.

Wallace, R.S.O., Choudhury, M.S.I. and Pendlebury, M. (1997) 'Cash flow statements: An international comparison of regulatory positions', *The International Journal of Accounting* 32(1): 1–22.

Wallace, R.S.O., Choudhury, M.S.I. and Adhikari, A. (1999) 'The comprehensiveness of cash flow reporting in the United Kingdom: Some characteristics and firm-specific determinants', *The International Journal of Accounting* 34(3): 311–47.

Additional material on the website

Go to http://www.cengage.co.uk/stolowy3 for further information, journal entries and extra assignments for each chapter.

The following appendices to this chapter are available on the dedicated website:

Appendix 14.1: Funds flow statement or statement of changes in financial position

Appendix 14.2: Content of activities according to IAS 7

Appendix 14.3: Differences in classification

Appendix 14.4: The UK/Ireland model.

Notes

1. Hays, C.L., *The New York Times*, 15 January 2003, section C page 4. Available at: http://www.nytimes.com/2003/01/15/business/kmart-will-lay-off-up-to-35,000-and-close-326-stores.html.

2. When a financial institution extends an overdraft authorization to a business, it is, *de facto*, equivalent to extending a 'line of credit' which would unambiguously be considered to be part of the financing activities of the business.

3. The 'true' direct method is not presented, since it requires access to internal company information, and this is not consistent with the users' perspective adopted in this book (users do not have access to inside information).

Part 3

Financial Statement Analysis

C15

Chapter 15
Balance Sheet Analysis

Learning objectives

After studying this chapter, you will understand:

■ That financial statements analysis consists of applying a set of tools, practices, processes and procedures to decode financial statements to address the informational concerns of internal and external decision-makers regarding a business' future performance and attached risks.

■ How to analyze the informational content of the balance sheet.

■ That a balance sheet is analyzed through the statement of financial structure, which formalizes the cash equation.

■ That the statement of financial structure relates the three major component of the balance sheet structure: working capital, working capital need and net cash.

■ That the three components can take either positive or negative values.

■ That the combination of the different signs leads to six different possible scenarios of balance sheet financial structures.

■ That the decomposition of the balance sheet can be applied equally to balance sheets by nature or by term, which allows the user to analyze any financial statement of any company, regardless of the GAAP used in its reporting.

Whereas previous chapters have emphasized the decision-making potential and usefulness of reported financial information, this chapter focuses in more detail on the actual use of such information by decision-makers. Data reported to shareholders, the financial community, and all interested parties are, first and foremost, descriptive. They are not meant to be directly useable in decision-making. In order to bring their information content to light, they need to be analyzed, compared, decoded and interpreted.

Financial statements analysis consists in applying a set of tools, practices, processes and procedures to decode financial statements to address the informational concerns of internal and external decision-makers regarding a business' future performance and attached risks. It builds on understanding past financial performance or achievements as well as present financial and market condition(s) and opportunities. It uses various techniques integrating accounting and non-accounting data[1] and additional information, emphasizing comparative and relative analysis over time for one firm and between firms in a single period or over time.

Users are interested in understanding such elements as liquidity, solvency, leverage effects, and profitability of a firm as well as knowing its asset management policy, its investment policy preparing its capability to face future challenges and its ability to deliver a return to investors in order to ground decisions about the future.

Although financial statements analysis practices may vary across countries, the main techniques used (and developed in this chapter and in the next three chapters) are generally universal. They include the same three different approaches:

(a) Create comparable bases (analysis may lead information users to compare firms that are of different size):

- trend or horizontal analysis: comparison of the evolution of a specific item over time or of several items (or same item in several firms) concurrently over a similar period of time;

- common-size or vertical analysis: measurement of a particular item, in any of the financial statements, as a percentage of a reference item in the same statement, allowing the comparison of the evolution of the structure of any financial statement.

(b) Analyze the structure of each financial statement:

- balance sheet structure and cash equation (this chapter);

- income statement analysis (Chapter 16);

- statement of cash flows analysis (Chapter 17).

(c) Analyze dynamic relations between items belonging to one or different statements:

- ratio analysis: evaluation of the dynamic relation(s) between components of one or different financial statements – see Chapter 18.

After a general presentation of trend and common-size analysis, the present chapter will focus on the analysis of the balance sheet.

1 Trend analysis (also known as horizontal or chronological analysis)

Users are interested in gaining an understanding of the characteristics of the stream of future income of the firm. The analysis of the evolution over time of each (or some) constituent of its current and past income (and attached financial risks or volatility) represents a fundamental element of reflection. A measurement of the changes over the past accounting period (or over a longer period of time) of a limited number of items, or, by way of contrast, of the complete set of financial statements (balance sheet, income statement or statement of cash flows) can help the analyst or the user of the analysis understand the dynamics of the income (wealth) generation model, the dynamics of the evolution of the inner structure of any of the three statements, and thus allow for extrapolations. Such a comparison over time is known as **trend analysis**.

This comparison is carried line item by line item (in absolute values and/or in percentages) against the like value in a base year (often the previous year). However, trend analysis is not often applied to the balance sheet. It is more useful for the income statement and we will consequently develop this topic in more depth in Chapter 16. Trend analysis has some limits (see also Chapter 16) which have led to the development of common-size analysis of financial statements.

2 Common-size analysis (also known as vertical analysis)

2.1 Definition

Common-size analysis is based on the restatement of the balance sheet, income statement, and/or statement of cash flows by presenting each line item as a proportion of a base figure (conventionally indexed as 100, thus the proportion is expressed as a percentage). Such restated statements are said to have been 'common-sized' and are 'common-size statements'. In this chapter, we will focus on common-size analysis as applied to the balance sheet. The income statement will be covered in Chapter 16 and the statement of cash flows will be dealt with in Chapter 17. For the balance sheet, the base figure is generally total assets (or total equity and liabilities).

The common-size analysis provides an understanding of the relationships *between* items in the financial statements during a period. By combining vertical and horizontal analyses (trend analysis), assuming one has access to a series of financial statements, it is possible to additionally evaluate the evolution over time of such relationships, thus highlighting scissor effects (or 'squeeze effects').

The common-size balance sheet is often referred to as **balance sheet structure** or **structural balance sheet**.

2.2 Usefulness of common-size analysis

Common-size analysis, in addition to being a powerful internal analytical tool, also permits the analyst (or the manager) to compare and contrast more easily the financial statements of two and more companies in the same industrial sector or risk class.

The most frequent use of common-size financial statements, both by managers and analysts and users, is a comparison of an entity's financial data with industry norms or averages, or 'rules of thumb' about (presumably) 'good' management, such as the rule of three thirds for the equity and liabilities side of the balance sheet: one third equity, one third long-term debt and one third short-term debt. A further example is the (debatable) rule in the restaurant business which states that the cost of materials should not exceed one third of revenue.

The uses of common-size financial statements are summarized in Figure 15.1.

Figure 15.1 The use of common-size financial statements

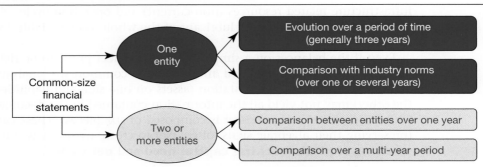

2.3 Common-size balance sheet

In the case of the balance sheet, the selected common-size basis will generally depend on the reporting format adopted. The base line seems to be, more or less, culturally based. No basis is intrinsically superior to another. A survey of common practices indicates that:

■ Total assets (or 'total equity plus total liabilities', the two are identical by definition) seem to be preferred in the majority of continental European countries, in the United States, and in Japan.

■ Shareholders' equity (total shareholders' funds) appears to be the favored base line in the UK and Ireland.

■ Long-term capital employed (shareholders' equity plus long-term debts) appears to be the most frequently used base line in India and also, but less frequently, by some Dutch companies.

Beyond country practices, what matters most in the choice of the denominator is the format in which the balance sheet is presented:

■ Single-step → Total assets
■ Multiple-step balancing with equity → Equity
■ Multiple-step balancing with long-term funding → Long-term funding

2.3.1 Traditional common-size balance sheet

The balance sheet of Procter & Gamble (in US$ million) illustrates, in Table 15.1, the application of common-sizing.

In a common-size presentation, several lines of the balance sheet can usefully be aggregated if they are not the focus of attention of the analyst. This has been the case for the shareholders' equity.

3 Balance sheet structure and cash equation

3.1 Balance sheet structure

Managers and other users rely on the balance sheet to evaluate, on a given date, the result of decisions made over the previous accounting period. The many line balances of a business' balance sheet can usefully be simplified down to their essence to sort out key issues. The balances are generally regrouped and structured (a) by distinguishing two separate 'time horizons' within each side of the balance sheet (current or short-term; and non-current or long-term), each corresponding to different types of decisions for both assets, on one hand, and shareholders' equity and liabilities, on the other; or (b) by separating infrastructure related resources (non-current) and operation-cycle related resources (current) from cash, which is the lubricant of the whole system. Table 15.2 illustrates such a simplified structure.

Even if the balances on a simplified balance sheet prove to be rich with information, (a) many details are obliterated and a detailed common-size analysis may prove useful, and (b) the traditional presentation (assets on one side and liabilities and net worth on the other) may not yield all the information contained in the document. As seen in Table 15.2, a simplified balance sheet is composed of six 'pieces'. These can be moved around (preserving their algebraic signs, of course) to create useful 'new' intermediate balances: **working capital, working capital need** and **net cash**.

Table 15.1 Procter and Gamble – Consolidated balance sheets (in US$ million) and common-size balance sheets for the years ended 30 June 2005–2008 (Source: Annual reports 2008 and 2006)

Years ended 30 June (in US$ million)	Balance sheets				Common-size balance sheets			
	2008	2007	2006	2005	2008 %	2007 %	2006 %	2005 %
CURRENT ASSETS								
Cash and cash equivalents	3,313	5,354	6,693	6,389	2.3	3.9	4.9	10.4
Investment securities	228	202	1,133	1,744	0.2	0.1	0.8	2.8
Accounts receivable	6,761	6,629	5,725	4,185	4.7	4.8	4.2	6.8
Inventories								
Materials and supplies	2,262	1,590	1,537	1,424	1.6	1.2	1.1	2.3
Work in process	765	444	623	350	0.5	0.3	0.5	0.6
Finished goods	5,389	4,785	4,131	3,232	3.7	3.5	3.0	5.3
Total inventories	8,416	6,819	6,291	5,006	5.8	4.9	4.6	8.1
Deferred income taxes	2,012	1,727	1,611	1,081	1.4	1.3	1.2	1.8
Prepaid expenses and other current assets	3,785	3,300	2,876	1,924	2.6	2.4	2.1	3.1
Total current assets	**24,515**	**24,031**	**24,329**	**20,329**	**17.0**	**17.4**	**17.9**	**33.0**
PROPERTY, PLANT AND EQUIPMENT								
Buildings	7,052	6,380	5,871	5,292	4.9	4.6	4.3	8.6
Machinery and equipment	30,145	27,492	25,140	20,397	20.9	19.9	18.5	33.2
Land	889	849	870	636	0.6	0.6	0.6	1.0
Total property, plant and equipment	38,086	34,721	31,881	26,325	26.5	25.2	23.5	42.8
Accumulated depreciation	(17,446)	(15,181)	(13,111)	(11,993)	(12.1)	(11.0)	(9.7)	(19.5)
Total property, plant and equipment	**20,640**	**19,540**	**18,770**	**14,332**	**14.3**	**14.2**	**13.8**	**23.3**
GOODWILL AND OTHER INTANGIBLE ASSETS								
Goodwill	59,767	56,552	55,306	19,816	41.5	41.0	40.8	32.2
Trademarks and other intangible assets, net	34,233	33,626	33,721	4,347	23.8	24.4	24.9	7.1
Net goodwill and other intangible assets	**94,000**	**90,178**	**89,027**	**24,163**	**65.3**	**65.3**	**65.6**	**39.3**
OTHER NONCURRENT ASSETS	**4,837**	**4,265**	**3,569**	**2,703**	**3.4**	**3.1**	**2.6**	**4.4**
TOTAL ASSETS	**143,992**	**138,014**	**135,695**	**61,527**	**100.0**	**100.0**	**100.0**	**100.0**
CURRENT LIABILITIES								
Accounts payable	6,775	5,710	4,910	3,802	4.7	4.1	3.6	6.2
Accrued and other liabilities	10,154	9,586	9,587	7,531	7.1	6.9	7.1	12.2
Taxes payable	945	3,382	3,360	2,265	0.7	2.5	2.5	3.7
Debt due within one year	13,084	12,039	2,128	11,441	9.1	8.7	1.6	18.6
Total current liabilities	**30,958**	**30,717**	**19,985**	**25,039**	**21.5**	**22.3**	**14.7**	**40.7**
Long-term debt	23,581	23,375	35,976	12,887	16.4	16.9	26.5	20.9
Deferred income taxes	11,805	12,015	12,354	1,896	8.2	8.7	9.1	3.1
Other noncurrent liabilities	8,154	5,147	4,472	3,230	5.7	3.7	3.3	5.2
TOTAL LIABILITIES	**74,498**	**71,254**	**72,787**	**43,052**	**51.7**	**51.6**	**53.6**	**70.0**
SHAREHOLDERS' EQUITY	**69,494**	**66,760**	**62,908**	**18,475**	**48.3**	**48.4**	**46.4**	**30.0**
TOTAL LIABILITIES AND SHAREHOLDERS' EQUITY	**143,992**	**138,014**	**135,695**	**61,527**	**100.0**	**100.0**	**100.0**	**100.0**

Table 15.2 Balance sheet structure: the simplified balance sheet (SBS)

Assets	Shareholders' equity and liabilities
■ Fixed (non-current) assets (FA)	■ Shareholders' equity and long-term (financial) liabilities (= Long-term capital) (LTC)
■ Current assets (except cash) (CA)	■ Current liabilities (except bank overdrafts) (CL)
■ Cash and cash equivalents (positive cash) (PC)	■ Bank overdrafts (negative cash) (BO)
Total assets	Total shareholders' equity and liabilities

3.2 Cash equation: working capital, working capital need and net cash

3.2.1 Principles

If we move the six components of a simplified balance sheet, we can identify and highlight some critical and different balances, which are very useful in both managing the firm and evaluating its income growth potential and risks (see Table 15.3).

Table 15.4 provides an illustration of these balances, which, when combined, form the **cash equation** (the relationship between the three components). When formalized as a table, the cash equation forms the **statement of financial structure**.

Table 15.3 Links between the balance sheet structure and the cash equation

Assets	=	Shareholders' equity and liabilities
FA + CA + PC	=	LTC + CL + BO
Or, without breaking the equilibrium, by moving FA to the right and BO and CL to the left, we have:		
(CA – CL) + (PC – BO)	=	(LTC – FA)
WCN + NC	=	WC
Or by moving WCN to the right, we have:		
(PC – BO)	=	(LTC – FA) – (CA – CL)
NC	=	WC – WCN

Table 15.4 Cash equation/Statement of financial structure

	Shareholders' equity and long-term (financial) liabilities (long-term capital or LTC)
(–)	Net fixed (non-current) assets, i.e., net of accumulated depreciation (FA)
(=)	**Working capital or WC**
	Current assets (except cash) (CA)
(–)	Current liabilities (except bank overdrafts) (CL)
(=)	**Working capital need (financing need arising from the operating cycle) or WCN**
	Positive cash (i.e., cash and cash equivalents) (PC)
(–)	Bank overdrafts (BO)
(=)	**Net cash (NC)**

Given that 'shareholders' equity plus liabilities' always equal total assets, Tables 15.3 and 15.4 can be summarized as the cash equation:

$$\text{Working capital} - \text{Working capital need} = \text{Net cash}$$
or
$$\text{Working capital} = \text{Working capital need} + \text{Net cash}$$
or
$$\text{Working capital need} = \text{Working capital} - \text{Net cash}$$

Working capital can be calculated in two ways (as shown in Table 15.3), each reflecting a different view of business risks:

(a) Shareholders' equity *plus* long-term liabilities *minus* fixed assets: How much excess long-term capital does the firm have over and above the funding of fixed assets (production capacity)?; or

(b) Current assets except cash (i.e., inventories plus receivables) *plus* cash *minus* current or short-term liabilities and bank overdrafts: How much long-term financing is *needed* for funding the operating cycle beyond short-term liabilities?

Since current assets and current liabilities often contain minor elements that do not pertain to ongoing operations (e.g., a receivable on a sale of fixed asset), the working capital is often cleaned up of these elements and the resulting calculation provides the **trade working capital**.

The managerial interest of the **working capital need** comes from the fact that, when looking at the future results of a business, cash is an unknown, while the evolution of fixed and current assets (excluding cash), as well as of liabilities, can be fairly well anticipated given that their amount will result from known decisions that will be made: new equipment may need to be acquired, total receivables may grow with increased sales volume, or increase/decrease if credit terms are modified, inventories may be reduced by the decision of the management to go towards a just-in-time sourcing and selling policy, etc. Working capital need is a metric that allows any analyst to anticipate how much additional cash (if any) might be needed to support the growth of the firm and thus anticipate whether the entity might need additional long-term or short-term capital. The manager, like the analyst, is very interested, for the same reasons as the latter, in knowing how much additional funding might be required to implement an action plan. Of course, the manager has more specific answers than the analyst does, but the reasoning remains the same. During 'road-shows', where managers address the financial community about their entity's financial and market performance, the managers will, most of the time, explain how they will meet the working capital need in the coming years.

Each approach in defining working capital, although it provides the very same figure in the end, communicates a different emphasis in the message.

The 'long-term financing minus net fixed assets' approach (called (a) in Figure 15.2) gives an indication of the financial solidity of the entity and its state of health: it essentially identifies how much long-term capital is available to finance the operating cycle.

The availability of long-term financing reduces the risk that would come if, by some event, short-term financing was totally removed (an undoubtedly dramatic event, but definitely possible as the 2008–2009 liquidity crisis showed). The working capital (method a) measures the likelihood the business would still be viable under these (extreme) circumstances. The question is answered by looking at what current assets would *remain available* to keep the operating cycle (or the cash pump) going, once the required assets would have been partially or completely liquidated to offset current liabilities. This approach is passive and defensive.

A second approach, we'll call it the (b) approach (see Figure 15.3), is more proactive. In this approach, the working capital is calculated by deduction of the current (short-term) financing from the current assets. Its calculations emphasize what would be needed if the unavailability of current liabilities was to obtain, assuming the manager's job is to maintain a viable operating cycle.

There are, of course many different ways to address the problem of keeping the cash pump active. Both approaches give the same end-figures, but not with the same emphasis, nor do they point to the same type of decisions to keep the firm a going concern. Clearly, if the operating cycle (cash pump) is to remain viable in the case of a (possibly total) short-term credit crunch, it is best to have some cash, receivables and inventories left to operate with, *and* enough long-term financing to support these operating resources. Whether calculated through method (a) or method (b), the working capital addresses these issues.

The (a) approach (Figure 15.2) is most commonly used in continental Europe and emphasizes the availability of long-term capital to keep the cash pump going. This approach emphasizes the ability of the firm to survive if it were to lose all short-term financial support.

The (b) approach (Figure 15.3) is the one most commonly used in North America. It highlights the capacity of the company to cover its short-term liabilities with its available

Figure 15.2 The (A) approach: WC (a) = Shareholders' equity + Long-term liabilities – Fixed assets

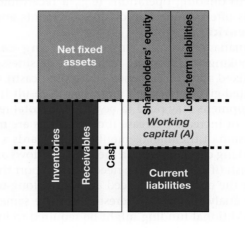

Figure 15.3 The (B) approach: WC (b) = Cash + receivables + inventories – current liabilities

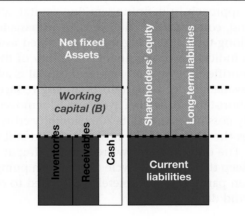

cash, receivables and inventories accounts, i.e., without needing to liquidate long-term (fixed) assets, a sale which would endanger the going concern nature of the firm.

From both approaches to the calculation of the working capital, it should be clear that there cannot be any generic normative, or rule-of-thumb value for an 'appropriate' level of working capital. The appropriate level of working capital is a function of the nature of the business, its opportunities and threats to continued growth, its relationships with suppliers and customers, and of the specific business processes or business cycle of the firm, which affect the speed and variance of the operating cycle.

The target working capital can be defined as the one that would keep the business afloat if all short-term financial supports were removed. Working capital is a useful indicator, especially when viewed dynamically over time and in comparison with other entities operating in the same or similar economic or geographic sector of activity. The smaller the magnitude of the working capital, the less long-term capital is used to guarantee the security of the going concern. The larger the working capital, the more security the firm has in weathering storms. Too little or too much are both risky: too little = risk of bankruptcy, too much = financing the operating cycle with very expensive resources, thus reducing profitability. Long-term financial resources are costly (both the cost of loans and the cost of securing shareholders' equity) while current liabilities are mostly not interest bearing, thus inexpensive. The more secure a firm is by keeping a large working capital, the more it pays in financing costs for the long-term funds that create this security. All things being equal, we can say that low risk means lower profitability, while higher liquidity risk (small or negative working capital) means higher profitability.

Originally, analysts were only looking at working capital, a static measure, ignoring the working capital need, a dynamic measure that helps plan the evolution of the funding needs created by sales growth or changes in the portfolio of products sold. Working capital was expected to always be positive and was considered to represent a measure of security and survival ability of the firm. The structure of financing was expected to remain rather stable overtime. Cash was not a critical issue. Today, the management of cash levels and of the financing structure are critical decisions. Working capital need and net cash have become the two relevant components of working capital.

Further, the existence of very large retail and distribution entities and the development of the 'new economy' (service- and information-technology-based entities) have made the existence of a negative working capital situation perfectly acceptable in a growing economy.

For example, when a retailer has an inventory that rotates at least 52 times a year, has no receivables because customers pay cash – credit card payment is essentially similar to cash payment – and obtains 45 days of effective credit from its suppliers, the working capital need will be, by construction, negative. In the retail business (unlike in a manufacturing entity), such a measure is not a sign of imminent danger (i.e., of possible inability to pay suppliers), as long as demand does not slow down. Of course if demands slows down, or even plateaus, the incoming cash (current sales revenue) may not be sufficient to cover the accumulated short-term debt or accounts payable. In that case, either inventories must be sold at a large discount, or fixed assets must be liquidated, or any combination of other alternatives must be activated to raise the needed cash, all of which endanger the going concern potential of the business.

A negative working capital computed with the (b) approach (negative working capital means suppliers are a source of funds for the firm) encourages (obligates) retailers to continuously grow, *de facto*, financed by suppliers. Thus, some retailers tend to finance long-term assets (acquisition of additional retail space or leaseholds in desirable locations, for example) through short-term (suppliers) credit. They are therefore simultaneously supporting their own growth (enlarging their scope or perimeter) and increasing their profitability while also increasing their risk in the case of a credit crunch, of a slowing down of their inventory turnover, which could be due to events such as errors in composing the mix of items offered in the store, difficulty in sourcing, increasingly long lead time for procurement from delocalized vendors, etc., or of a decline in sales (due to economic conditions affecting their customers), or whatever other reason(s).

The working capital need (working capital minus net cash) defines the financing need arising from the operating cycle. It is sometimes called **working capital requirements**.[2] The cash equation establishes a critical liaison between the constituents of the balance sheet and allows users and analysts of financial information to evaluate the position of the firm with regard to its operating cycle revenue.

3.2.2 Different scenarios of working capital need and net cash

Each of the three components of the cash equation defined above can be either positive or negative. The combination of the different signs leads to six different possible scenarios of (balance sheets) financial structures. These are illustrated in Figure 15.4 which shows the diverse combinations of working capital and working capital need.

Working capital is illustrated in medium blue ▰▰▰, while the working capital need is the difference between the current assets (minus cash) in dark blue ▰▰▰, and current liabilities in light blue ▰▰▰.

In Figure 15.5, the three components of the cash equation are shown relative to each other, following the same six cases illustrated in Figure 15.4.

Working capital was described earlier as a measure of the ability of the firm to survive if short-term credits were to be cancelled. It is therefore logical to ask the question: how long could the firm survive in such a case? Practitioners have adopted the habit of expressing the short-term capability of survival of a business in terms of numbers of days of sales revenue.

This metric highlights the survival potential of the firm in that it describes the number of sales activity days required to fund the working capital need. The essential definition of this metric is:

$$\text{Working capital need (in days of sales)} = \frac{\text{Working capital need}}{\text{Sales revenue}} \times 365$$

Appendix 15.1 presents some developments on this indicator and its usefulness.

3.3 The statement of financial structure in practice: comparative analysis of Exxon, Sinopec and Total

To illustrate the use of the statement of financial structure, we will compare three major oil and gas firms located in different countries.[3] The three firms are ExxonMobil in the United States, Sinopec in China, and Total in France.

3.3.1 Company background

ExxonMobil Exxon Corporation was incorporated in the State of New Jersey in 1882. On 30 November 1999, Mobil Corporation became a wholly-owned subsidiary of Exxon Corporation, and the enlarged entity changed its name to ExxonMobil Corporation – hereafter 'Exxon'. Headquartered in Irving, Texas, Exxon is principally traded on the NYSE. According to the Platts (a division of The McGraw-Hill Companies) 2008 Top 250 Global Energy Companies rankings, Exxon is the world's largest integrated oil and gas company.[4]

Exxon engages in the exploration, production, transportation, and sale of crude oil and natural gas. It also engages in the manufacture, transportation, and sale of petroleum products and petrochemicals, and participates in electric power generation. The company also manufactures and markets commodity petrochemicals, including olefins, aromatics, polyethylene and polypropylene plastics, and other specialty products. Exxon conducts business in almost 200 countries and territories around the globe.

Figure 15.4 Different types of financial structures of WC/WCN/NC

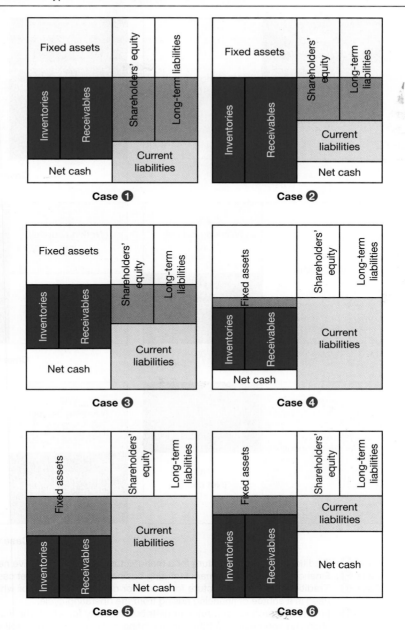

Sinopec   China Petroleum & Chemical Corporation – hereafter 'Sinopec' – was founded in 2000 and is headquartered in Beijing in the People's Republic of China. Sinopec's shares are listed in Hong Kong, New York, London, and Shanghai. Sinopec operates, through its subsidiaries, as an integrated oil and gas and chemical company in the People's Republic of China.

Sinopec is China's second largest producer and supplier of oil products, including gasoline, diesel and jet fuel, and major petrochemical products, including petrochemical intermediates, synthetic resin, monomers and polymers, and chemical fertilizer. It is also China's second largest crude oil producer. Sinopec has joint venture agreements with Mitsui Chemicals, Inc. and BP plc, and has formed a strategic alliance with McDonald's Corporation to open drive-through restaurants in the People's Republic of China.

Figure 15.5 The three components of the cash equation

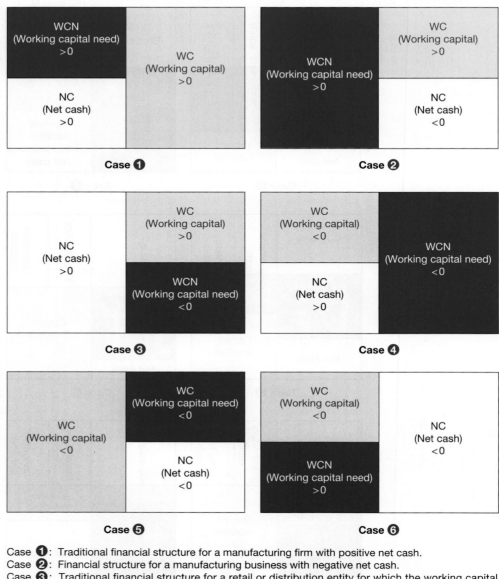

Case **❶**: Traditional financial structure for a manufacturing firm with positive net cash.
Case **❷**: Financial structure for a manufacturing business with negative net cash.
Case **❸**: Traditional financial structure for a retail or distribution entity for which the working capital need is a source of financing arising from the operating cycle.
Case **❹**: Financial structure for a retail or distribution entity for which the working capital need is a financing source arising from the operating cycle and working capital is negative indicating an excess of investment in fixed assets.
Case **❺**: An atypical and risky structure: the negative cash and the financing source arising from the operating cycle actually finance part of the fixed assets.
Case **❻**: An atypical and even riskier structure: the negative cash finances both part of the fixed assets and the financing need arising from the operating cycle.

Total   Total SA – hereafter 'Total' – was incorporated in 1924 and is based in Courbevoie, France. It is listed on stock exchanges in France, the United States, and Belgium. Together with its subsidiaries, it operates as an integrated oil and gas company in more than 130 countries.

The company operates in three segments: Upstream, Downstream, and Chemicals. The Upstream segment engages in exploration and production activities, as well as natural gas transportation and storage, liquefied natural gas and power, trading of liquefied petroleum gas, and coal operations. The Downstream segment involves refining, distribution and marketing of Total and Elf brand petroleum products, automotive and other fuels, and specialties such as LPG, aviation fuel, and lubricants. The marketing is done both through its own retail network and through other outlets. The Chemicals segment operates essentially in petrochemicals (olefins and aromatics and their derivatives polyethylene, polypropylene and styrenics) and fertilizers. Its various products are used in the automobile, transportation, packaging, construction, sports and leisure, health and beauty care, water treatment, paper, electronics, and agriculture industries.

3.3.2 Financial information

■ Table 15.5 presents the consolidated balance sheets for Exxon for the fiscal years ended 31 December 2008, 2007 and 2006. The balance sheets were prepared in accordance with US GAAP.

■ Table 15.6 presents the consolidated balance sheets for Sinopec for the fiscal years ended 31 December 2008, 2007 and 2006. The balance sheets were prepared in accordance with IFRS.

■ Table 15.7 presents the consolidated balance sheets for Total for the fiscal years ended 31 December 2008, 2007 and 2006. The balance sheets were prepared in accordance with IFRS.

3.3.3 Simplified balance sheet

In undertaking a comparison of firms' financial structures, the information reported in the firms' balance sheets is used. However, in situations where the balance sheets are prepared using different balance sheet formats – for example, as seen in our three examples, firms from different countries using different accounting practices or presentations – it is first necessary to place the information on a common basis. This process is illustrated below with the preparation of first, the simplified balance sheet, and second, the statement of financial structure.

The first step in achieving a common basis for different firms' financial information is the preparation of a simplified balance sheet (SBS). In the SBS, as was shown in Table 15.2 above, the assets side of the original balance sheet is sub-divided into three parts, whereas the liabilities and equity part of the balance sheet is split into three (or four) sub-categories. For example, as was shown in Table 15.2, the three parts of the assets section are divided into cash (or positive cash) denoted as (PC), current assets (excluding cash) (CA), and non-current assets (NCA). Whereas Table 15.2 splits the equity and liabilities into three parts, we show below an alternative presentation where the long-term capital is in turn divided between equity and long-term debts. Thus, we get four categories.

It should be noted that in preparing the SBS, the ordering of the items should be adapted to conform to the ordering used by the company in its balance sheet. For the sake of simplicity, we adopted a common order – by decreasing liquidity, the one followed by Exxon. If the balance sheet is presented by increasing order of liquidity, then the order in the template must be reversed. This example also illustrates the idea developed in Chapter 5: the format of the balance sheet has no real influence on its meaningfulness or on its analysis. This will illustrate our statement made earlier that the statement of financial structure can be adapted to any format.

In the present case, we have three different but very common formats:

■ Single-step and decreasing (typically, a US balance sheet): Exxon

■ Multiple-step (mostly used in the UK and by some Chinese firms): Sinopec

■ Single-step, increasing (often used in Continental Europe): Total.

Table 15.5 Exxon – Consolidated balance sheets for the years ended 31 December 2008, 2007 and 2006 (Prepared using US GAAP)

31 December (US$ million)	2008	2007	2006
Assets			
Current assets			
Cash and cash equivalents	31,437	33,981	28,244
Cash and cash equivalents – restricted	0	0	4,604
Marketable securities	570	519	0
Notes and accounts receivable, less estimated doubtful amounts	24,702	36,450	28,942
Inventories – Crude oil, products and merchandise	9,331	8,863	8,979
Inventories – Materials and supplies	2,315	2,226	1,735
Prepaid taxes and expenses	3,911	3,924	3,273
Total current assets	**72,266**	**85,963**	**75,777**
Investments, advances and long-term receivables	28,556	28,194	23,237
Property, plant and equipment, at cost, less accumulated depreciation and depletion	121,346	120,869	113,687
Other assets, including intangibles, net	5,884	7,056	6,314
Total assets	**228,052**	**242,082**	**219,015**
Liabilities			
Current liabilities			
Notes and loans payable (*)	2,400	2,383	1,702
Accounts payable and accrued liabilities	36,643	45,275	39,082
Income taxes payable	10,057	10,654	8,033
Total current liabilities	**49,100**	**58,312**	**48,817**
Long-term debt	7,025	7,183	6,645
Post-retirement benefits reserves	20,729	13,278	13,931
Deferred income tax liabilities	19,726	22,899	20,851
Other long-term obligations	13,949	14,366	11,123
Equity of minority and preferred shareholders in affiliated companies	4,558	4,282	3,804
Total liabilities	**115,087**	**120,320**	**105,171**
Commitments and contingencies (see note 15)			
Shareholders' equity			
Benefit plan related balances			
Common stock without par value (9,000 million shares authorized)	5,314	4,933	4,786
Earnings reinvested	265,680	228,518	195,297
Accumulated other non-owner changes in equity			
Cumulative foreign exchange translation adjustment	1,146	7,972	3,733
Post retirement benefits reserves adjustment	(11,077)	(5,983)	(6,495)
Common stock held in treasury	(148,098)	(113,678)	(83,387)
Total shareholders' equity	**112,965**	**121,762**	**113,934**
Total liabilities and shareholders' equity	**228,052**	**242,082**	**219,105**
*Bank loans	1,139	1,238	753
*Commercial paper	172	205	274
*Long-term debt due within one year	368	318	459
*Other	721	622	216

Table 15.6 Sinopec – Consolidated balance sheets for the years ended 31 December 2008, 2007 and 2006 (Prepared using IFRS)

At 31 December (in RMB million)	2008	2007	2006
Non-current assets			
Property, plant and equipment	403,265	375,142	355,757
Construction in progress	121,886	95,408	52,871
Goodwill	14,237	15,490	14,325
Interest in associates	15,595	16,865	11,898
Interest in jointly controlled entities	11,781	12,723	9,236
Investments	1,483	3,194	2,926
Deferred tax assets	12,810	10,439	7,182
Lease prepayments	10,817	8,224	2,574
Long-term prepayments and other assets	11,642	10,124	7,573
Total non-current assets	**603,516**	**547,609**	**464,342**
Current assets			
Cash and cash equivalents	6,948	7,696	7,063
Time deposits with financial institutions	752	668	635
Trade accounts receivable	12,989	22,947	15,144
Bills receivable	3,659	12,851	8,462
Inventories	95,255	116,032	94,894
Prepaid expenses and other current assets	34,924	24,922	20,292
Income tax receivable	9,784		
Total current assets	**164,311**	**185,116**	**146,490**
Current liabilities			
Short-term debts (*)	74,896	44,654	56,467
Loans from Sinopec Group Company and fellow subsidiaries	23587	15840	7013
Trade accounts payable	56,667	93,049	52,767
Bills payable	17,493	12,162	21,714
Accrued expenses and other payables	101,878	89,171	69,200
Income tax payable	16	10,479	9,211
Total current liabilities	**274,537**	**265,355**	**216,372**
Net current liabilities [current assets – current liabilities]	**(110,226)**	**(80,239)**	**(69,882)**
Total assets less current liabilities	**493,290**	**467,370**	**394,460**
Non-current liabilities			
Long-term debts	90,254	83,134	61,617
Loans from Sinopec Group Company and fellow subsidiaries	36,890	37,180	39,020
Deferred tax liabilities	5,235	5,636	6,339
Other liabilities	11589	8662	827
Total non-current liabilities	**143,968**	**134,612**	**107,803**
Total assets – total liabilities	**349,322**	**332,758**	**286,657**
Equity			
Share capital	86,702	86,702	86,702
Reserves	241,967	220,731	177,632
Total equity attributable to equity shareholders of the Company	**328,669**	**307,433**	**264,334**
Minority interests	**20,653**	**25,325**	**22,323**
Total equity	**349,322**	**332,758**	**286,657**
*Short-term loans	40,735	21,294	25,666
*Current portion of long-term loans	34,161	23,360	30,801

Table 15.7 Total – Consolidated balance sheets for the years ended 31 December 2008, 2007 and 2006 (Prepared using IFRS)

As of 31 December (in € million)	2008	2007	2006
ASSETS			
Non-current assets			
Intangible assets, net	5,341	4,650	4,705
Property, plant and equipment, net	46,142	41,467	40,576
Equity affiliates: investments and loans	14,668	15,280	13,331
Other investments	1,165	1,291	1,250
Hedging instruments of non-current financial debt	892	460	486
Other non-current assets	3,044	2,155	2,088
Total non-current assets	**71,252**	**65,303**	**62,436**
Current assets			
Inventories, net	9,621	13,851	11,746
Accounts receivable, net	15,287	19,129	17,393
Prepaid expenses and other current assets	9,642	8,006	7,247
Current financial assets	187	1,264	3,908
Cash and cash equivalents	12,321	5,988	2,493
Total current assets	**47,058**	**48,238**	**42,787**
Total assets	**118,310**	**113,541**	**105,223**
LIABILITIES AND SHAREHOLDERS' EQUITY			
Shareholders' equity			
Common shares	5,930	5,989	6,064
Paid-in surplus and retained earnings	52,947	48,797	41,460
Cumulative translation adjustment	(4,876)	(4,396)	(1,383)
Treasury shares	(5,009)	(5,532)	(5,820)
Total shareholder's equity – Group share	**48,992**	**44,858**	**40,321**
Minority interests and subsidiaries' redeemable preferred shares	**958**	**842**	**827**
Total shareholders' equity	**49,950**	**45,700**	**41,148**
Non-current liabilities			
Differed income taxes	7,973	7,933	7,139
Employee benefits	2,011	2,527	2,773
Other non-current liabilities	7,858	6,843	6,467
Total non-current liabilities	**17,842**	**17,303**	**16,379**
Non-current financial debt	**16,191**	**14,876**	**14,174**
Current liabilities			
Accounts payable	14,815	18,183	15,080
Other creditors and accrued liabilities	11,632	12,806	12,509
Current borrowings (*)	7,722	4,613	5,858
Current financial instruments	158	60	75
Total current liabilities	**34,327**	**35,662**	**33,522**
Total liabilities and shareholders' equity	**118,310**	**113,541**	**105,223**
* Current financial debt and bank overdrafts	5,586	2,530	3,348
* Current portion of non-current financial debt	2,136	2,083	2,510

The preparation of the simplified balance sheet is a preliminary step towards completing the statement of financial structure. Practically, however, it is a most difficult part of the process because the balance sheet items must be grouped properly into the sub-categories of assets, liabilities and equity. Some items in the balance sheet may be difficult to classify because they could as easily fall into either one of two possible categories. Hence any analyst must exercise judgment, and it is possible two analysts may not decide to classify borderline items in the same way. For example, one analyst might classify some categories of short-term investments as positive cash, while another would consider them as part of current assets (excluding cash) if she/he were to assume that these investments cannot, easily and rapidly, be transformed into cash. Importantly, consistent categorization of like items by the analyst is required across the compared firms. Table 15.8 presents the simplified balance sheets for Exxon, Sinopec and Total.

Table 15.8 Simplified balance sheet of Exxon, Sinopec and Total

EXXON (in US$ million)	2008	2007	2006
Cash and bank	32,007	34,500	32,848
Current assets (excluding cash)	40,259	51,463	42,929
Non-current assets	155,786	156,119	143,238
Total assets	228,052	242,082	219,015
Short-term bank loans and bank overdrafts	1,311	1,443	1,027
Current liabilities (excluding short-term bank loans and bank overdrafts)	47,789	56,869	47,790
Long-term liabilities	65,987	62,008	56,354
Equity	112,965	121,762	113,934
Total shareholders' equity, provisions and liabilities	228,052	242,082	219,105

SINOPEC (in RMB million)	2008	2007	2006
Cash and bank	7,700	8,364	7,698
Current assets (excluding cash)	156,611	176,752	138,792
Non-current assets	603,516	547,609	464,342
Total assets	767,827	732,725	610,832
Short-term bank loans and bank overdrafts	40,735	21,294	25,666
Current liabilities (excluding short-term bank loans and bank overdrafts)	233,802	244,061	190,706
Long-term liabilities	143,968	134,612	107,803
Equity	349,322	332,758	286,657
Total shareholders' equity, provisions and liabilities	767,827	732,725	610,832

TOTAL (in € million)	2008	2007	2006
Non-current assets	71,252	65,303	62,436
Current assets (excluding cash)	34,737	42,250	40,294
Cash and bank	12,321	5,988	2,493
Total assets	118,310	113,541	105,223
Equity	49,950	45,700	41,148
Long-term liabilities	34,033	32,179	30,553
Current liabilities (excluding short-term bank loans and bank overdrafts)	28,741	33,132	30,174
Short-term bank loans and bank overdrafts	5,586	2,530	3,348
Total shareholders' equity, provisions and liabilities	118,310	113,541	105,223

3.3.4 Statement of financial structure

Once the simplified balance sheet has been prepared, the creation of the statement of financial structure is relatively straightforward and mechanical. Table 15.9 presents, respectively, the statements of financial structure for Exxon, Sinopec and Total.

3.3.5 Analysis

In all three original consolidated balance sheets, we observe that the separation between non-current assets versus current assets and between non-current liabilities versus current liabilities was clearly defined, hence easing the preparation of the simplified balance sheets and statements of financial structure. Note also how Exxon has a balance sheet item entitled 'Equity of minority and preferred shareholders in affiliated companies' which it includes in long-term liabilities; similar minority interest balances in Sinopec and Total are included in their equity sections. We emphasize, however, that this difference has no influence on our financial structure analysis since both long-term liabilities and equity are similarly included (as long-term financing) in the computation of working capital. Note that to complete the statement of financial structures, we need additional information from the notes to the financial statements – these are shown at the bottom of the balance sheets. For example, in the case of Exxon, the amount in line item 'short-term bank loans and bank overdrafts' (created to represent negative cash in Table 15.8) is considered to include 'bank loans' and 'commercial paper'; for Sinopec it consists of the firm's 'short-term loans' and for Total it is the 'current financial debt and bank overdrafts'. In our comparison below, we will show that while the three companies operate in the same industry, they employ different financial structures.

As mentioned above, the three companies' balance sheets are prepared using three different formats. In addition, each balance sheet reports its results in different currencies: US Dollars (Exxon), Renminbi (Sinopec) and Euros (Total). Note, however, that these differences in both format and currency are adjusted for – or standardized – through the statements of financial structure. This standardization then allows us to appropriately examine and compare how the companies manage their financial structures.

We first present in Figure 15.6 a global view of the financial structure of each company (by reference to Figure 15.5).

There is an alternative way – shown in Table 15.10 – to present (and visualize) the financial structures as they evolve over the three years under scrutiny.

Exxon   With a growing negative WCN, Exxon's financial structure is similar to that of a retail or distribution firm (Case ❸ in Figures 15.4 and 15.5). This type of financial structure is one where the firm has the ability to retain a significant amount of payables, and has rigorous inventory and receivable control systems (with a capacity to keep these two elements at a low level). Meanwhile, Exxon is quite prudent in its investment management with all its long-term investments being financed by long-term capital (WC > 0). However, WC is decreasing steadily mainly because of the firm's aggressive plan of share repurchase. One potential 'criticism' of Exxon's structure is the high level of net cash. It might be seen by some that it would be more efficient to use this cash to repay some short or long-term debt, or to finance additional business investments. As Exxon is always looking for the acquisition of new oil reserves, it may wish to keep this extra cushion of cash to be able to act quickly. Another possible explanation is that as a world leader in its industry, Exxon might be facing a serious problem of lack of future growth opportunities, as illustrated by the stock repurchase plan.

Sinopec   At first glance Sinopec has the 'weakest' financial structure of the three firms, with all three working capital indicators being negative (see Case ❺ in Figures 15.4 and 15.5).

Table 15.9 Statement of financial structure of Exxon, Sinopec and Total

EXXON (in US$ million)	2008	2007	2006
Equity	112,965	121,762	113,934
Long-term liabilities	65,987	62,008	56,354
Non-current assets	(155,786)	(156,119)	(143,238)
Working capital	**23,166**	**27,651**	**27,050**
Current assets (excluding cash)	40,259	51,463	42,929
Current liabilities (excluding short-term bank loans and bank overdrafts)	(47,789)	(56,869)	(47,790)
Working capital need	**(7,530)**	**(5,406)**	**(4,861)**
Cash	32,007	34,500	32,848
Short-term bank loans and bank overdrafts	(1,311)	(1,443)	(1,027)
Net cash	**30,696**	**33,057**	**31,821**
SINOPEC (in RMB million)	2008	2007	2006
Equity	349,322	332,758	286,657
Long-term liabilities	143,968	134,612	107,803
Non-current assets	(603,516)	(547,609)	(464,342)
Working capital	**(110,226)**	**(80,239)**	**(69,882)**
Current assets (excluding cash)	156,611	176,752	138,792
Current liabilities (excluding short-term bank loans and bank overdrafts)	(233,802)	(244,061)	(190,706)
Working capital need	**(77,191)**	**(67,309)**	**(51,914)**
Cash	7,700	8,364	7,698
Short-term bank loans and bank overdrafts	(40,735)	(21,294)	(25,666)
Net cash	**(33,035)**	**(12,930)**	**(17,968)**
TOTAL (in € million)	2008	2007	2006
Equity	49,950	45,700	41,148
Long-term liabilities	34,033	32,179	30,553
Non-current assets	(71,252)	(65,303)	(62,436)
Working capital	**12,731**	**12,576**	**9,265**
Current assets (excluding cash)	34,737	42,250	40,294
Current liabilities (excluding short-term bank loans and bank overdrafts)	(28,741)	(33,132)	(30,174)
Working capital need	**5,996**	**9,118**	**10,120**
Cash	12,321	5,988	2,493
Short-term bank loans and bank overdrafts	(5,586)	(2,530)	(3,348)
Net cash	**6,735**	**3,458**	**(855)**

Table 15.10 Financial structure of the three companies studied (alternative presentation, where '+' means positive and '–' means negative)

	Exxon			Sinopec			Total		
	2008	2007	2006	2008	2007	2006	2008	2007	2006
Working capital	+	+	+	–	–	–	+	+	+
Working capital need	–	–	–	–	–	–	+	+	+
Net cash	+	+	+	–	–	–	+	+	–

Figure 15.6 Main financial structure of the three studied companies (using simplified balance sheets for year-end 2008)

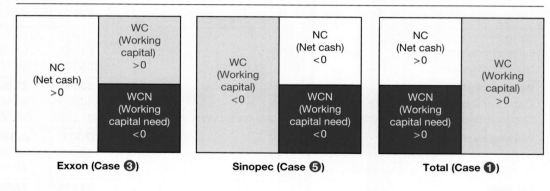

However, we need to be very cautious in this interpretation in terms of awareness of the business environment in China. If we concentrate on WC, we see Sinopec has the most dynamic balance sheet with its non-current assets increasing more than 10% each year. This increase is consistent with the recent (and ongoing) dynamism of the Chinese economy. In order to satisfy its need for financing, Sinopec is relying mainly on profit reinvestment and to a lesser extent on long-term debt. However, this strategy is not, in itself, sufficient, and hence WC has remained consistently negative for the three years 2006–2008.

How are the other sources of long-term investment generated? They come from payables (WCN < 0) and from short-term borrowings (NC < 0). In a more stable economy – one with relatively consistent but slow growth – we could conclude that this financial situation is very risky. However, owing to Sinopec's quasi-duopoly position in the industry and its well-established political connections, the firm is considered as very creditworthy in China, and has an extremely strong negotiation position vis-à-vis its suppliers (including its banks). Hence, a negative WCN is, for the time being, a sustainable solution for Sinopec. Note also that, probably due to the lack of a well-established financial market in China, very few long-term financial instruments are used. Revolving short-term bank borrowings are the typical financial source for many firms in China, even for long-term investment projects. Here again, due to its dominant position and strong political connections, it is difficult to imagine that Chinese banks would deny Sinopec the systematic renewal of its short-term financing.

At the same time, it is important to note that Sinopec's future solvency still depends fundamentally on the quality of the investments it makes. The explanations in the previous paragraph are descriptive in nature and only cover the fund supply side of the story. In the foreseeable future, if the liquidity in China becomes tighter and/or Sinopec's investment projects prove to be less profitable than previously expected, the company might experience similar painful experiences to those that many Japanese large groups faced during the 1990s.

Total   Total's financial structure corresponds to Case ❶ in Figures 15.4 and 15.5, which represents a stable financial structure of a manufacturing firm, with WC, WCN, and NC all being positive (with a minor exception of net cash being negative in 2006). This implies that Total has sufficient long-term capital to finance both its long-term investment needs (since WC > 0), and its ongoing operating activities. The trends for Total over the past three years are showing some positive signals, with a decrease in WCN, generating an increase in cash.

Key points

- Financial statement analysis processes, evaluates and interprets the data reported to shareholders and the financial community to facilitate its usability in decision-making.
- Financial statement analysis can be carried out by both managers and outsiders to the firm in order to assess a firm's past performance or achievements, present condition and future prospects.
- It uses various techniques integrating accounting data and additional information, emphasizing comparative and relative analysis over time for one firm and between firms.
- Understanding current and past performance of a business helps users of financial statements, and principally investors, derive the firm's business model and its correlated risks.
- Users are interested in understanding liquidity, solvency, leverage, and profitability of a firm, as well as understanding its asset management policies and the resulting return to investors.
- Financial statements analysis requires comparability which is obtained by: (1) trend or horizontal analysis (comparison over time of the evolution of a specific expense or revenue item or a particular asset or liability item); (2) common-size or vertical analysis (comparison of the evolution of the structure of the balance sheet).
- 'Trend analysis' measures the changes over past accounting period(s) of a limited number of items or, on the contrary, of the whole financial statements (balance sheet, income statement, and statement of cash flows). It reveals the dynamics of the income generation model.
- 'Common-size analysis' is prepared by presenting each financial statement component in terms of its percentage of a selected base figure, generally indexed as 100, such as total assets for balance sheet elements.
- The common-size analysis allows the analyst to compare and contrast more easily the financial statements of two or more companies in the same industrial sector or risk class, especially when their sizes are different.
- A firm's simplified balance sheet can be structured by identifying two separate 'time horizons' (current or short-term; and non-current or long-term), each corresponding to different types of decisions about assets, on one hand, and shareholders' equity and liabilities on the other.
- One extension of this simplified balance sheet, beyond the common-size analysis, is the cash equation establishing the relation between three major components: working capital, working capital need, and net cash.
- The relation between the three components of the cash equation can be formalized explicitly as the statement of financial structure.
- Working capital need (a dynamic measure) and working capital (a static measure) illustrate the resilience of the firm to the reduced availability of the short-term financing.

Review (solutions are at the back of the book)

Review 15.1 Dvorak Company (2)

Topic: Preparation of a statement of financial structure

Required

1. With the help of the financial statements (see review 14.1 Dvorak Company (1), in Chapter 14), prepare a simplified balance sheet with three sub-headings in the assets and three sub-headings in the equity and liabilities for the years X1 and X2 (see Table 15.2).

2. Prepare a statement showing the financial structure of the company for the years X1 and X2 (i.e., compute the working capital, working capital need and net cash).

3. Evaluate and comment on these statements.

Review 15.2 Chugoku Power Electric Company (1)*

Topic: Balance sheet structure

Chugoku Electric Power Company, Inc., was established in 1951 as one of 10 electric power companies in Japan. It maintains its head office in the city of Hiroshima and supplies electricity to the Chugoku region through an integrated structure that encompasses all stages of power supply, from generation to transmission and distribution.

The consolidated balance sheet for the period 2007–2008 follows (Source: Annual report 2008). The consolidated financial statements of Chugoku Electric Power have been prepared in accordance with the provisions set forth in the Japanese Financial Instruments and Exchange Law and its related accounting regulations, and the Electricity Utilities Industry Law and in conformity with Japanese GAAP, which are different in certain respects as to application and disclosure requirements from IFRS.

31 March (in ¥ million)	2008	2007
Assets		
Property		
Utility plant and equipment	5,350,705	5,320,797
Other plant	267,961	258,002
Construction in progress	289,226	194,940
	5,907,892	**5,773,739**
Less:		
Contributions in aid of construction	77,985	76,034
Accumulated depreciation	3,741,561	3,640,643
	3,819,546	**3,716,677**
Net property	**2,088,346**	**2,057,062**
Nuclear fuel	**133,841**	**133,772**
Investments and other assets		
Investment securities	50,895	61,025
Funds reserved for reprocessing of irradiated nuclear fuel	91,115	93,667
Investments and advances to non-consolidated subsidiaries and affiliates	86,879	89,021
Long-term loans to employees	924	1,229
Deferred tax assets	61,101	56,839
Other assets	37,868	24,357
Total investments and other assets	**328,782**	**326,138**
Current assets		
Cash and time deposits	17,073	21,722
Receivables, less allowance for doubtful accounts	73,510	73,172
Inventories, fuel and supplies	48,304	46,834
Deferred tax assets	10,437	12,830
Other current assets	10,388	9,252
Total current assets	**159,712**	**163,810**
Total assets	**2,710,681**	**2,680,782**

31 March (in ¥ million)	2008	2007
Liabilities and net assets		
Long-term liabilities		
Long-term debt	1,365,901	1,327,691
Other long-term liabilities	20,976	3,842
Employees' severance and retirement benefits	60,786	61,547
Retirement allowances for directors and corporate auditors	1,399	–
Provision for reprocessing of irradiated nuclear fuel	100,691	118,286
Provision for reprocessing of irradiated nuclear fuel without a fixed plan to reprocess	2,753	1,777
Provision for decommissioning of nuclear power generating plants	56,547	47,711
Total long-term liabilities	**1,609,053**	**1,560,854**
Current liabilities		
Long-term debt due within one year	126,737	145,453
Short-term borrowings	67,600	67,780
Accounts payable	67,064	67,085
Accrued income taxes	7,118	10,979
Accrued expenses	41,017	42,650
Allowance for bonuses to directors and corporate auditors	191	221
Other current liabilities, including other long-term liabilities due within one year	56,940	64,079
Total current liabilities	**366,667**	**398,247**
Provision for drought	–	656
Provision for depreciation of nuclear power plant	23,881	5,053
Net assets:		
Owners' equity		
Common stock	185,528	185,528
Capital surplus	17,200	17,192
Retained earnings	507,554	500,499
Treasury stock	(12,239)	(12,020)
Total owners' equity	**698,043**	**691,199**
Net unrealized holding gains on securities	7,983	19,680
Foreign currency translation adjustments	5	20
Minority interests	5,049	5,073
Total net assets	**711,080**	**715,972**
Total liabilities and net assets	**2,710,681**	**2,680,782**

Required

1. What is the format of the balance sheet?

2. Prepare a simplified balance sheet with three sub-headings in the assets and three sub-headings in the equity and liabilities (see Table 15.2).

3. Prepare the statement of financial structure (i.e., compute the working capital, working capital need and net cash).

4. Comment on your findings.

Assignments

Assignment 15.1
Multiple-choice questions

Select the right answer (one possible answer, unless otherwise stated).

1. Common-size analysis is based on the preparation of common-size financial statements, i.e., a balance sheet presented in percentage of a base figure (indexed as 100). What is generally the base used for analyzing the balance sheet?

   (a) Net income
   (b) Net sales
   (c) Total assets
   (d) Total liabilities
   (e) None of these

2. Which of the following relations is correct?

   (a) Working capital – Working capital need = Net cash
   (b) Working capital/Working capital need = Net cash
   (c) Working capital × Working capital need = Net cash
   (d) Working capital + Working capital need = Net cash

3. How is the working capital calculated?

   (a) Working capital = Shareholders' equity and long-term debts – Fixed assets
   (b) Working capital = Shareholders' equity and long-term debts + Fixed assets
   (c) Working capital = Fixed assets + Current assets
   (d) Working capital = Fixed assets – Current assets

4. How is the working capital need calculated?

   (a) Working capital need = Working capital – Current assets (except cash)
   (b) Working capital need = Current assets (except cash) – Current liabilities
   (c) Working capital need = Long-term debt – Current liabilities
   (d) Working capital need = Fixed assets – Current assets (except cash)

5. How is the net cash calculated?

   (a) Net cash = Bank borrowings + Bank overdrafts
   (b) Net cash = Bank borrowings + Bank overdrafts – Positive cash and cash equivalents
   (c) Net cash = Positive cash and cash equivalents – Bank overdrafts
   (d) Net cash = Fixed assets – Bank borrowings + Positive cash and cash equivalents

6. Which of the following types of financial structure corresponds generally to a manufacturing company with negative net cash?

   (Note: WC = Working capital, WCN = Working capital need, NC = Net cash)

   (a)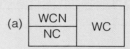

   (b)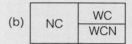

   (c)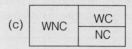

   (d)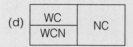

7. Which approach gives an indication of the financial short-term solidity of an entity and its state of health?

   (a) The approach that considers the equation: Working capital = Shareholders' equity + Long-term debts – Fixed assets
   (b) The approach that considers the equation: Working capital = Cash + Receivables + Inventories – Short-term liabilities

8. A positive working capital need is typical of a firm operating in the distribution sector

   (a) True
   (b) False

9. The cash equation and the three related concepts (working capital, working capital need and net cash) can be computed only if the balance sheet is presented by term (and not by nature)

   (a) True
   (b) False

10. If the balance sheet is presented by term in a decreasing format, the cash equation and the three related concepts (working capital, working capital need and net cash) cannot be computed

    (a) True
    (b) False

Assignment 15.2
Janacek Company (2)

Topic: Preparation of a statement of financial structure

The Janacek Company has a commercial activity in the beauty products and cosmetics sector.

Required

1. With the help of the balance sheet, income statement, and additional information (see Assignment 14.2 Janacek Company (1), in Chapter 14), prepare a simplified balance sheet with three sub-headings in the assets and three sub-headings in the equity and liabilities for the years X1, X2, and X3 (see Table 15.2).

2. Prepare a statement showing the financial structure of the company for the years X1, X2, and X3 (i.e., compute the working capital, working capital need and net cash).

3. Evaluate and comment on these statements.

Assignment 15.3
Club Méditerranée*

Topic: Statement of financial structure

The French group Club Méditerranée is an active service provider in the leisure and hospitality field with, in particular, its rich network of all-inclusive resort 'villages'. The balance sheets (prepared in accordance with IFRS) for the period 2005–2008 follow (source: Annual reports 2008 and 2006).

Consolidated balance sheets				
	31 October			
(in € million)	2005	2006	2007	2008
ASSETS				
Goodwill	103	103	108	32
Intangible assets	79	79	83	53
Property, plant and equipment	975	859	841	919
Non-current financial assets	66	80	86	89
Total fixed assets	**1,223**	**1,121**	**1,118**	**1,093**
Deferred tax assets	42	35	30	30
Non-current assets	**1,265**	**1,156**	**1,148**	**1,123**
Inventories	21	21	22	33
Trade receivables	66	81	86	58
Other receivables	96	108	142	116
Cash and cash equivalents	160	165	108	152
Current assets	**343**	**375**	**358**	**359**
Assets held for sale	11	92	87	45
Total assets	**1,619**	**1,623**	**1,593**	**1,527**
EQUITY AND LIABILITIES				
Share capital	77	77	77	77
Additional paid-in capital	562	562	563	563
Retained earnings/(deficit)	(179)	(185)	(201)	(206)
Net income /(loss) for the year	9	5	(10)	1
Equity attributable to shareholders	**469**	**459**	**429**	**435**
Minority interests	54	55	61	59
Equity	**523**	**514**	**490**	**494**
Pensions and other long-term benefits	26	28	27	26
Borrowings and interest-bearing liabilities	435	346	408	260
Other liabilities	30	36	43	54
Deferred tax liabilities	102	86	64	61
Non-current liabilities	**593**	**496**	**542**	**401**
Provisions	38	41	24	23
Borrowings and interest-bearing liabilities	48	109	36	187
Trade payables	160	170	184	145
Other liabilities	164	177	186	157
Customer prepayments	93	112	131	120
Current liabilities	**503**	**609**	**561**	**632**
Liabilities related to assets held for sale	–	4	–	–
Total equity and liabilities	**1,619**	**1,623**	**1,593**	**1,527**

Required

1. What is the format of the balance sheet?

2. Prepare a simplified balance sheet with three sub-headings in the assets and three sub-headings in the equity and liabilities (see Table 15.2).

3. Prepare the statement of financial structure (i.e., compute the working capital, working capital need and net cash).

4. Comment on the results and information created in your answers to questions 2 and 3.

Assignment 15.4
Vimpel Communications*

Topic: Statement of financial structure

Vimpel Communications (VimpelCom) is a leading provider of wireless telecommunications services in Russia, operating under the 'Beeline' brand, which is one of the most recognized telecom brand names in Russia.

The balance sheets for the period 2005–2008 follow (source: Annual reports 2008, 2007 and 2006). VimpelCom maintains its records and prepares its financial statements in accordance with Russian accounting and tax legislation and US GAAP.

Consolidated balance sheets (in US$ 000)				
Assets	2008	2007	2006	2005
Current assets:				
Cash and cash equivalents	914,683	1,003,711	344,494	363,646
Trade accounts receivable, net of allowance for doubtful accounts	475,667	281,396	311,991	144,197
Inventory	142,649	58,838	52,368	60,864
Deferred income taxes	82,788	98,407	115,379	85,968
Input value added tax	182,045	112,273	140,551	229,415
Due from related parties	168,196	5,405	4,853	–
Other current assets	440,479	166,887	154,920	77,335
Total current assets	**2,406,507**	**1,726,917**	**1,124,556**	**961,425**
Property and equipment, net	6,425,873	5,497,819	4,615,675	3,211,112
Telecommunications licenses and allocations of frequencies, net of accumulated amortization	764,783	915,211	924,809	826,948
Goodwill	3,476,942	1,039,816	775,223	477,495
Other intangible assets, net	882,830	262,502	257,917	196,356
Software, net	549,166	622,815	547,902	538,703
Investments in associates	493,550	5,908	1,269	–
Other non current assets	725,502	497,896	189,195	94,997
Total assets	**15,725,153**	**10,568,884**	**8,436,546**	**6,307,036**
Liabilities and shareholders' equity	2008	2007	2006	2005
Current liabilities:				
Accounts payable	896,112	697,816	670,918	545,670
Due to employees	105,795	81,118	44,513	27,654
Due to related parties	7,492	2,773	1,035	–
Accrued liabilities	288,755	186,114	96,058	33,390
Taxes payable	152,189	81,757	60,974	81,524
Customer advances, net of VAT	425,181	386,883	282,588	279,114
Customer deposits	29,557	36,728	31,787	30,533
Bank loans and other debt, current portion	1,909,221	526,512	424,103	421,467
Total current liabilities	**3,814,302**	**1,999,701**	**1,611,976**	**1,419,352**
Deferred income taxes	644,475	576,276	528,025	371,008
Bank loans, less current portion	6,533,705	2,240,097	2,065,329	1,576,699
Other non-current liabilities	122,825	52,614	30,447	10,802
Minority interest	221,040	288,410	257,859	188,626
Shareholders' equity:				
Common stock	92	92	92	92
Additional paid-in capital	1,445,426	1,413,403	1,382,522	1,370,654
Retained earnings	3,271,878	3,327,716	2,195,713	1,384,224
Accumulated other comprehensive income, net of tax	(88,941)	801,243	423,088	6,536
Treasury stock, at cost	(239,649)	(130,668)	(58,505)	(20,957)
Total shareholders' equity	**4,388,806**	**5,411,786**	**3,942,910**	**2,740,549**
Total liabilities and shareholders' equity	**15,725,153**	**10,568,884**	**8,436,546**	**6,307,036**

Required

1. What is the format of the balance sheet?

2. Prepare a simplified balance sheet with three sub-headings in the assets and three sub-headings in the equity and liabilities (see Table 15.2).

3. Prepare the statement of financial structure (i.e., compute the working capital, working capital need and net cash).

4. Comment on the results and information created in questions 2 and 3.

Assignment 15.5
Infosys Company*

Topic: Statement of financial structure

Based in India, Infosys Technologies Limited (Infosys) is a global technology services firm that defines, designs and delivers information technology-enabled business solutions to its clients.

The consolidated financial statements have been prepared by the Company's management in accordance with the requirements of Accounting Standard 21, Consolidated Financial Statements, issued by the Institute of Chartered Accountants of India. The consolidated balance sheets for the financial years ended 31 March 2009, 2008 and 2007 are provided below (source: Annual reports 2008 and 2007).

Consolidated balance sheets			
As at 31 March (in Rupees in crore[5])	2009	2008	2007
SOURCES OF FUNDS			
SHAREHOLDERS' FUNDS			
Share capital	286	286	286
Retained earnings/Reserves and surplus	17,968	13,509	10,969
MINORITY INTEREST	0	0	4
	18,254	13,795	11,259
APPLICATION OF FUNDS			
FIXED ASSETS			
Original cost	7,093	5,439	4,642
Less: Accumulated depreciation and amortization	2,416	1,986	1,836
Net book value	4,677	3,453	2,806
ADD: Capital work-in-progress	677	1,324	965
	5,354	4,777	3,771
INVESTMENTS	0	72	25
DEFERRED TAX ASSETS	126	119	92
CURRENT ASSETS, LOANS AND ADVANCES			
Sundry debtors	3,672	3,297	2,436
Cash and bank balances	9,695	6,950	5,834
Loans and advances	3,279	2,771	1,251
	16,646	13,018	9,521
LESS: CURRENT LIABILITIES AND PROVISIONS			
Current liabilities	2,004	1,722	1,469
Provisions	1,868	2,469	681
NET CURRENT ASSETS	12,774	8,827	7,371
	18,254	13,795	11,259

Required

1. What is the format of the balance sheet?

2. Prepare a simplified balance sheet with three sub-headings in the assets and three sub-headings in the equity and liabilities (see Table 15.2).

3. Prepare the statement of financial structure (i.e., compute the working capital, working capital need and net cash).

4. Comment on the results and information created in questions 2 and 3.

References

Chan, K., Chan, L.K.C., Jegadeesh, N. and Lakonishok, J. (2006) 'Earnings quality and stock returns', *Journal of Business* 79(3): 1041–82.

Ding, Y., Entwistle, G.M. and Stolowy, H. (2007) 'Identifying and coping with balance sheet differences: A comparative analysis of US, Chinese, and French oil and gas firms using the "statement of financial structure"', *Issues in Accounting Education* 22(4): 591–606.

Further reading

Cote, J.M. and Latham, C.K. (1999) 'The merchandising ratio: A comprehensive measure of working capital strategy', *Issues in Accounting Education* 14(2): 255–67.

Additional material on the website

Go to http://www.cengage.co.uk/stolowy3 for further information, journal entries and extra assignments for each chapter.

The following appendix to this chapter is available on the dedicated website:

Appendix 15.1: Working capital need in sales days

Notes

1. We distinguish data from information. A piece of data is a fact, a number, a descriptor. It has no specific meaning in and of itself. It is descriptive of something. Information is the result of a process applied to data (comparison with other pieces of data such as the construction of a ratio, calculation of the trend of the evolution over time of a given measure, replacing the piece of data in its historical or competitive context, etc.) that yields (potentially useful) metrics that can effectively be used in a decision model. These useful metrics are called information. Information has the *potential* of leading the decision-maker to modify the decision he or she would have taken before the 'new' piece of information was provided. Data do not have such potential.

2. See Chan *et al.* (2006).

3. This section is based on and updated from Ding *et al.* (2007).

4. For comparative purposes, the 2008 rankings of the top ten oil, gas and energy companies worldwide are: 1. ExxonMobil Corp, 2. Royal Dutch Shell, 3. Total SA, 4. Chevron Corp, 5. BP, 6. Rosneft Oil, 7. ENI SpA, 8. StatoilHydro, 9. Petrochina Co., 10. Gazprom OAO. Sinopec is 15th, worldwide, in 2008 and second in Asia, after Petrochina (Source: http://www.platts.com/Top250Home.aspx#).

5. 1 crore = 10 million.

C16

Chapter 16

Income Statement Analysis

Learning objectives

After studying this chapter, you will understand:

■ That the structure of the income statement of a firm is the reflection of its strategy.

■ That analysts can usefully compare this structure over time and/or with that of other firms in the same risk class to help detect changes in strategy or differences in market approaches.

■ That inter-firm comparisons and time-based analysis of a single firm rely on trend analysis and common-size analysis.

■ That decomposing the income statements in subsections based on managerial decision-making levels, i.e., creating a statement of intermediate balances, can lead to a more complete understanding of the dynamics of a business' financial performance.

■ That these tools can be applied equally to income statements 'by nature' or 'by function', which allows users to analyze the financial statements of any business, regardless of the GAAP it used in its reporting.

■ How users of financial information can use each of these tools to guide their decision-making.

In Chapter 15 we introduced the common features of financial statements analysis, i.e., common-sizing a statement or using trend analysis. We applied these to balance sheet analysis and developed the statement of financial structure. In this chapter, we move to the income statement which will be analyzed essentially with:

■ Trend or horizontal analysis (comparison over time of the evolution of a specific expense or revenue item).

■ Common-size or vertical analysis (measurement of a particular item, in the income statement, as a percentage of a reference item (generally net sales) in the same statement and/or comparison of the evolution of the structure of the income statement over time).

■ The introduction of **intermediate balances**, and mainly the calculation of the <u>value added</u> by the firm's operations and its partitioning between personnel, depreciation, remuneration of the providers of interest-bearing liabilities, taxes, and shareholders. These intermediate balances, beyond providing a valuable basis for defining the strategy of the firm, give the analyst a detailed view of how profit was created. Intermediate balances are fundamental tools for forecasting future income, once the business context that prevailed is understood and included in the analysis.

1 Trend analysis (also known as horizontal or chronological analysis) applied to the income statement

1.1 Principles and intent

Chapter 15 defined trend analysis as a comparison carried line item by line item (in absolute values and/or in percentages) against the like value in a base year (often the previous year). Trend analysis of a firm's income statements highlights any evolution of its operational strategy.

If the percentage change approach is used, the base year item amount (sales revenue, cost, etc.) is used as an index with a conventional base value of 100. Other periods are then measured against that index. For example: sales this year are 120% of last year's, cost of goods sold (COGS) is 125% of last year's and commercial expenses are 150% of last year's. This example indicates that this firm appears to have been caught in a 'scissor effect' – the COGS grew faster than revenue, thus squeezing the gross margin, and commercial expenses have been rising faster than revenue, thus reducing profit from levels observed over the previous period(s).

An analyst, before formulating any meaningful conclusion, would need to identify the actions the firm did take, which may have been imposed by market circumstances, that may explain these evolutions (changes in competition, new markets opened, change in sales mix, new products introduction, product aging, etc.). The analyst would also need to identify (for example by looking at quarterly income statements) what actions the firm took (or not) to either counter that scissor effect, or to manage it appropriately and reduce its effect.

In doing so, she/he will bring to bear additional knowledge about the market and the behavior of its players (suppliers, competitors, clients, regulators, etc.), and take into consideration what is publicly known about the current environment and strategy of the firm: Are they, for example, in the process of launching one or several new products? Is there a relative shortage of materials, or an increase in price, due to a climactic event (think, for example, about the impact of an instance of freezing weather in Florida or violent rains in Brazil on the price of orange juice, or of increased hurricane activity on oil production in the Gulf of Mexico or of political events on the oil output in the Niger delta), etc. To be meaningful beyond simple observation, trend analysis, particularly in the case of an income statement, must always be placed in the context that prevailed when the events that created it took place.

1.2 Advantages and limitations of trend analysis

This method allows the examination of short (two or three years) or long trends (evolution over 10 years for example). Long trends are not always meaningful because the business model parameters (and the perimeter or the scope) of the entity and/or the environmental and competitive conditions may have changed significantly over that period.

For example, there would be very little meaning in carrying out a trend analysis of the income statement of Vivendi Universal from 1995 to 2006: this company evolved in just over 10 years, through acquisitions and divestitures, from Générale des Eaux (water distribution and environmental services) to become Vivendi (telecommunication and environmental services) and eventually Vivendi Universal (telecommunication and entertainment products and services) before easing out of the entertainment field and becoming Vivendi SA again. Further, a series of acquisitions and divestitures, mainly from 1998 to 2006, drastically changed yearly the scope, business model and nature of the firm. However, a trend evolution of the income statement from 2006 (when it became, once again, Vivendi SA after the sale of 80% of its Universal division to General Electric to form NBC Universal) to 2009 (before 1 December, when Vivendi SA sold to General Electric the remaining 20% it held of NBC Universal) would make sense, as the new entity has, although growing rapidly by acquisitions, essentially stayed within the same business model. Business never sleeps! Perimeters are often difficult to identify. For trends to be meaningful, especially for the analysis of income statements, the business model must have been stable over the period of comparison. Trend analysis between competitors is always dubious because, even if they serve some of the same markets, their business models may be very different.

One may also argue that, regardless of the strategies chosen by the company (such as strengthening its competitive position in its current business, or opting for a radical change of business model), its ultimate goal remains to improve its profitability and the return to its shareholders. Trend analysis of the income statement is always useful in tracking the bottom line, but may not always be fruitful in explaining the evolution observed.

1.3 Example of trend analysis

Let us consider a fictitious firm, Bernstein AG, a provider of computer services (software and support) to medium and small entities. Its income statements for years X1 and X2 are compared in Table 16.1 (in millions of CU).

This simple illustration shows that the components of income have varied from one year to the next in very different proportions. Some people may consider as positive the fact that income before tax (or net operating profit before tax or NOPAT) grew by 8%.

Table 16.1 Trend analysis

	X2	X1	Amount of change	% of change (X2/X1)−1
Net sales revenue	28,500	25,000	3,500	14
Costs and expenses				
COGS (cost of goods sold)	14,700	12,000	2,700	23
Selling expenses	5,500	5,100	400	8
General and administrative expenses	5,000	5,000	0	0
Interest expenses	745	570	175	31
Interest income	−50	−90	40	−44
Income before tax	2,605	2,420	185	8
Income tax expense	1,042	847	195	23
Net income	1,563	1,573	−10	−1

But the situation has changed and, at first glance (i.e., without reference to the context), seems to have deteriorated:

(a) COGS grew faster than sales leading to a reduction of the gross margin;

(b) interest expenses were higher in X2 than they were in X1;

(c) interest income was lower; and consequently,

(d) net income declined, despite the growing volume of sales.

The fact that selling expenses grew less rapidly than sales revenue (not in itself an abnormal event as many such expenses, except for commissions, can generally be considered to be fixed costs, i.e., invariant with volume) deserves special attention in the light of the reduction of the gross margin. A series of questions need to be asked. The manager, of course, will have an easier time finding the answer to these than would an outside analyst (especially in the case of a small to medium size firm), but, nonetheless, the questions are the same and need to be addressed squarely by both:

- Did the mix of services sold drift, unwittingly or deliberately, towards lower margin ones?

- Was the customer base developed or enlarged (or has it evolved by itself) towards customers whose resources lead them to prefer off-the-shelf (ready-made and therefore lower margin) products that require fewer (high margin) post-sale services?

- Linked to the previous point, we can observe the possible meaningfulness of the reduction of interest income. If we assume this revenue is derived from investing customer cash-advances linked to developing customized software and if we further assume this return came from investing the cash at a modest annual interest rate of, say, 3%, we can work backwards to find the amount of implied invested cash. In X1, this average invested cash must have amounted to 3,000 CU (3,000 × 0.03 = 90). We can thus deduce that customized sales (on which Bernstein AG likely receives cash advances from customers) represented somewhere around at least 12% of sales revenue (the actual percentage could only be found if we knew the cycle time of production and the pattern of invoicing). But in X2, the same calculation indicates the cash advances (under the same hypotheses and methodology) amount to only 1,666 CU [1,666 × 0.03 = 50], i.e., sales assumed to be coming from high margin customized products represent in X2 a percentage of total sales revenue of not more than 6% [1,666/28,500]. If the hypotheses are correct, the firm incurred a reduction of 50% of its sales of customized products. A dramatic evolution of the trend and a complete modification of the business model.

- Have credit terms been extended (by choice) or have they deteriorated (customer behavior) between X1 and X2? If this was the case it might explain why interest expenses have grown disproportionately: a larger working capital need (current assets [excluding cash] minus current liabilities [excluding bank overdrafts]) (see Chapter 15) may have resulted from this evolution. The need was apparently covered by additional borrowings. An alternative explanation of the rise in interest expense might also be that the firm engaged in a significant capital investment campaign to prepare the future (this could be verified by looking at either or both the balance sheets and statement of cash flows for both years).

- Did the suppliers reduce their credit terms, thus creating a larger working capital need?

- Did labor expenses have to be increased in order to keep talent in the firm? (Such an event would explain part of the growth in the COGS.)

- Was there a change in market positioning of the firm's offering due to the entry of a new competitor in the market?

- The fact that selling expenses increased by only 8% while sales revenue increased by 14% means it costs the firm less in X2 than it did in X1 to create one CU of sales revenue. This increase in commercial productivity is, in itself, a good thing and needs to be replaced in the possible contexts evoked above. However, any coin has another side. We might wonder whether the management of the firm did not sacrifice selling expenses (and even possibly general and administrative expenses) in order to save, somewhat successfully in the short run, the bottom line which was threatened by the runaway COGS. As we know, because of the limitations in accounting measurement (principle of prudence), many resource consumptions (such as advertisement, R&D or personnel training – more on this in Chapter 18), conceptually regarded as investments by managers, are treated as period expenses in the income statement (see Chapter 8). Cutting these expenses offers an immediate positive effect on profitability, but doing so is likely to prove counterproductive for the long-term future of the firm.

This example shows the potential richness and also the difficulty and possible limits of trend analysis. What is important is not only to measure the evolution of any one line item over time, but also to measure its evolution relative to other elements of the financial statements and to contextual elements, or to measure the evolution of its relative weight in the determination of income. It is critical to confirm whether the causal relations creating the income (i.e., the business model) have been modified from one year to the next before appropriate conclusions can be drawn and actions taken on the basis of this analysis.

Difficulties and limits of trend analysis have led to the development of common-size analysis applied, this time, to the income statement.

2 Common-size analysis (also known as vertical analysis) of the income statement

2.1 Principle and intent

Chapter 15 defined common-size analysis as the restatement of a financial statement, here the income statement, by presenting each line item as a proportion of a base figure (conventionally indexed as 100, thus the proportion is expressed as a percentage). The base figure for the income statement is generally net sales. Common-size income statements are often referred to as **income statement structure** or **structural income statement**.

2.2 Illustration

The common-size income statements for Bernstein AG are shown in Table 16.2, revealing the evolution of the structure.

Table 16.2 confirms, for example, that the moderate (8%) increase in selling expenses we have observed in Table 16.1 (trend analysis) reveals a change in either strategy, market demand or cost control over the consumption of this resource. The drift in COGS is confirmed by the fact that it increases to 52% of sales from a previous 48%.

Common-size analysis, just like trend analysis, fails to give complete, sufficient or final answers. Each method of analysis helps raise questions that need to be explored by the decision-maker in seeking further data and information to interpret the financial data provided. Some of these additional data are of a non-accounting nature.

For example, the same increase in COGS can be due to a variety of causes in Bernstein AG's actions or reactions to market factors. Examples of causes of the increase in COGS could be:

■ Introduction of a large number of different and totally new services or products in X2.

■ Possible start-up difficulties in 'production' of new products or services.

■ Increase in the cost of complexity of new products or services (the more complex a product or service is, the more costly it is to effectively and successfully provide it to customers).

Table 16.2 Common-size analysis

	X2 %	X1 %
Net sales revenue	100	100
Costs and expenses		
COGS (cost of goods sold)	52	48
Selling expenses	19	20
General and administrative expenses	18	20
Interest expenses	3	2
Interest income	ns	ns
Income before tax	9	10
Income tax expense	4	3
Net income (as a % of sales revenue)	5	6

ns = not significant

- Changes in the mix of sales.

- Growth in sales due mainly to lower margin, maturing products or to more successful standardized products, at the expense of custom designed software.

- Possible difficulties in development efficiency, or/and a saturation of the current development capacity.

A limit to common-size analysis is that some items may be considered not material (not significant [ns] compared to the base) when, in fact, they may very well be. For example, in the common-size analysis, interest income is deemed (legitimately) not significant as a percentage of revenue (2/10ths of 1% is not a significant quantity in most cases), while we have shown in section 1.3 that the evolution of interest income might be quite meaningful in an analysis of the sales situation of Bernstein AG.

As we see here, and have said in section 1, any parameter expressed as a percentage of sales (or its growth) must be related to the contextual circumstances before it can be interpreted and exploited to anticipate future bottom line or performance of the firm.

2.3 Common-size income statement

As mentioned before, when analyzing the income statement, the base line is generally the net sales figure (i.e., net of rebates, discounts and returns). We examine separately the application of common-size analysis to income statements presented by function and by nature (see Chapter 5 for the distinction) since each income statement structure reveals different aspects of performance.

2.3.1 Common-size income statement by function

Table 16.3 illustrates the common-size consolidated income statements by function of Procter & Gamble. Absolute figures are provided in the upper part of the table, while, in the lower part of the table, each line item of the income statement is divided by the net sales of the corresponding year and is shown as a percentage of net sales revenue.

Table 16.3 Procter and Gamble – Consolidated statement of earnings (in US$ million) and common-size income statements for the years ended 30 June 2005–2009 (source: Annual reports 2009, 2008 and 2007)

(in US$ million)	2009	2008	2007	2006	2005
Net sales	79,029	81,748	74,832	68,222	56,741
Cost of products sold	38,898	39,536	35,659	33,125	27,804
Selling, general and administrative expense	24,008	25,575	24,170	21,848	18,010
Operating income	16,123	16,637	15,003	13,249	10,927
Interest expense	1,358	1,467	1,304	1,119	834
Other non-operating income, net	560	462	565	283	346
Earnings before income taxes	15,325	15,632	14,264	12,413	10,439
Income taxes	4,032	3,834	4,201	3,729	3,182
Net earnings from continuing operations	11,293	11,798	10,063	8,684	7,257
Net earnings from discontinued operations	2,143	277	277	–	–
Net earnings	13,436	12,075	10,340	8,684	7,257

In percentage of net sales	2009 %	2008 %	2007 %	2006 %	2005 %
Net sales	100.0	100.0	100.0	100.0	100.0
Cost of products sold	49.2	48.4	47.7	48.6	49.0
Selling, general and administrative expense	30.4	31.3	32.3	32.0	31.7
Operating income	20.4	20.4	20.0	19.4	19.3
Interest expense	1.7	1.8	1.7	1.6	1.5
Other non-operating income, net	0.7	0.6	0.8	0.4	0.6
Earnings before income taxes	19.4	19.1	19.1	18.2	18.4
Income taxes	5.1	4.7	5.6	5.5	5.6
Net earnings from continuing operations	14.3	14.4	13.4	12.7	12.8
Net earnings from discontinued operations	2.7	0.3	0.4	0.0	0.0
Net earnings	17.0	14.8	13.8	12.7	12.8

Common-size income statements are used to identify structural changes in a company's operating results. For example, it is quite significant to observe that earnings before income taxes represent 19.4% of revenue in 2009 while it was 18.2% in 2006. It would appear some significant modification of the business model or of the product offering took place between these years. The case of Procter & Gamble can be studied in more details in Assignment 16.3.

2.3.2 Common-size income statement by nature and statement of intermediate balances (principles)

Given that common-size statements are often used for comparing an entity with others, an income statement by nature may offer a challenge in applying common-sizing if the benchmarked firms use different by-nature formats or report by function. There is a diversity of legitimate presentations by nature, often reflecting that charts of accounts are specific to each entity. Even if common-sized, the resulting income statements do not always lead to useful inter-entities comparisons. A common or standardized presentation of the statement by nature has to be created first.

An income statement presented by nature must be restructured in order to identify the key intermediate balances (based on standardized definitions) that help describe the value creation process of the analyzed entities, which, then, become comparable. For example, some firms may use many subcontractors in their supply chain, while other may wish to control directly the resources required to create and deliver their value proposition to the markets. Intermediate balances such as **commercial margin**, **value added** and **gross operating profit** highlight similarities and differences of the business process of any number of entities.

An income statement by nature, in which all intermediate balances have been clearly identified, is called a **statement of intermediate balances**. We will now explain how such a statement is constructed to allow comparisons between firms. Once restructured, the income statement can be common-sized without any difficulty. It suffices to choose a meaningful base line that will be used to calculate the percentages.

The schematics of a statement of intermediate balances are illustrated in Figure 16.1. Such a document describes and reports the sequence of 'levels' in the step-by-step formation of the income of the period. A more detailed definition of terms used is provided after Figure 16.1.

Essentially, a statement of intermediate balances dissects the income statement into meaningful blocks of data to help in the user's financial understanding and interpretation of the firm's economic activity. The intermediate balances may be presented in absolute monetary amounts, as percentages of some relevant in-period basis (i.e., common-size analysis) or as percentages of variations from one period to another (i.e., trend analysis). This restructured income statement can prove to be particularly useful to the user when a firm carries, side by side, diverse business lines such as a manufacturing activity (manufacture of goods or services for sale) and a dealership or brokerage activity (merchandise purchased for resale).

The following paragraphs will develop the meaning and decision-making implications of the main terms (i.e., intermediate balances) used in a **restructured income statement** (that was by nature in the first place).

Commercial margin (margin on sales) The commercial margin expresses the difference between the sales revenue and the cost of merchandise sold. It is useful to separate the resale segment from other segments since this line of business often requires specific resources and is subject to different growth drivers than the main business of a manufacturing firm.

Total 'production' in the period (current period 'production') The term 'production' used in Figure 16.1 may prove to be somewhat ambiguous to some readers. It is the commonly used term, drawn from economics, and refers to the potential wealth created by the activity of the firm, before considering *how* this additional potential wealth was created.

The entity's *industrial* output during the period is the total of units it sold, valued at their sales price (i.e., the sales revenue), plus (minus) increases (decreases) in absolute value of the finished goods and work-in-progress inventories, valued at cost, plus the cost of any self-produced fixed assets.

Consumption of goods and services from third parties This term refers to all operating resources (i.e., excluding financial expenses) the firm consumed that it did not provide itself: any resource such as materials or components, energy, maintenance contracts, consulting support, work of advertising agencies, etc. comes under this heading. Labor is a resource provided by the firm and so is the consumption of the productive capacity (depreciation, amortization and depletion). To simplify, this category of resources consumed comprises all operating resources over which the firm does not exercise short-term (or long-term) control.

Figure 16.1 Structure of the income statement by intermediate balances of financial performance

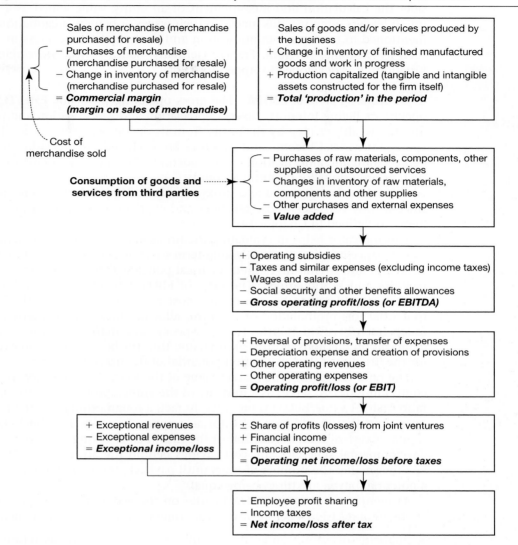

Value added   The term value added is a basic concept used in macroeconomics (Gross National Product accounting), which refers to the amount contributed by a particular entity to the national wealth. It is the creation or increase in 'value', resulting from the entity's current business activities, over and above the value of goods and services consumed by the entity that were provided by third parties. Roughly speaking, any firm's policy does, *de facto*, partition the value added it created by its market strategy between the five contributors to, or facilitators of, the ability of the firm to operate as a going concern:

- employees;
- maintenance of the productive capacity (depreciation, amortization or depletion);
- providers of interest-bearing liabilities;
- the state (taxes); and
- shareholders.

Value added is infrequently used in reporting to shareholders. Financial analysts consider the calculation and measurement of an entity value added as a basic tool. Labor union leaders often use this metric in their wages or benefits negotiations. It is frequently mentioned in business communication and in the specialized press in several countries, such as Australia, Belgium, France, Germany, South Africa, Switzerland or the United Kingdom. It is developed in Appendix 16.1.

Gross operating profit or EBITDA   The gross operating profit, or **EBITDA** (Earnings from operations Before Interests, Taxes, Depreciation and Amortization and provisions), measures the wealth created by the entity from its operations, independently of its financing strategy (financial income and expenses are excluded), depreciation policy (charges for depreciation and amortization are excluded), and other firm specific income adjustments such as provisions for doubtful accounts.

EBITDA is also looked at as a proxy measure of the cash flow generated by operations since it only considers those revenues and expenses that have an impact on cash (cash items, as defined in Chapter 14).

This indicator helps in evaluating the firm's management's short-term ability to create wealth, since it is not affected by long-term strategic decisions regarding financing (capital structure) and capital investment or fiscal policies (including choice of location of both facilities and headquarters). The ratio of EBITDA to sales (or accounting 'production') is often considered to be one of the most relevant measures of the intrinsic 'business (potential for) profitability' of the firm, allowing meaningful inter-entity comparisons, independently of the policies that are specific to a management team's choices (such as depreciation methods or provisioning) and thus the best proxy – and easiest to calculate – for the 'true' cash flow generation potential of the firm.

The ratio comparing the market value of the shares of the entity (net market value of equity) to EBITDA, serves as a measure of the vulnerability of the firm to a takeover. This ratio (market value/EBITDA) provides, in fact, a rough estimate of the number of years of operations that would be needed for an acquirer to get to a payback, i.e., to recover the capital invested in an acquisition of the firm (before taking into consideration the likely developmental synergies and cost savings behind the acquisition). The lower the ratio, i.e., the smaller the number of years until payback, the more attractive the business is to a potential buyer, all things being equal.

As mentioned above, EBITDA focuses on the economic consequences of the normal operational decisions, before any of the somewhat discretionary elements that are:

- financing decisions (an entity's financing strategy is truly discretionary, as, for example, there is no normative rule regarding leveraging of equity);
- taxes (impacted by location and, for example, by tax advantages provided for special development zones); and
- depreciation and amortization policy (muddled by tax incentives, as seen in Chapter 7).

Some companies have extended the concept of EBITDA to suit their specific needs and exclude any other cost element that is not central to operations or which could be procured through other means.

For example, entities that rely heavily on leased assets, in the construction industry or in the air transport business, often use the concept of EBITDAR, which represents the Earnings before Interest, Taxes, Depreciation, Amortization and Rent.[1] The airline easyJet, for example, reports in its annual report 2008 an intermediate balance similar to EBITDAR, which it defines as 'Earnings before interest, taxes, depreciation, amortization, dry lease and long-term wet lease costs,[2] and the share of profit after tax of associates'.

Another variation exists on the same theme for holding companies: EBITDAM, which is defined as the Earnings Before Interest, Taxes, Depreciation, Amortization and Management fees. For example, Allied Capital Corporation, a US company engaged in private equity investment and management, uses EBITDAM to assess its portfolio companies' financial performance or to value a portfolio company.

Operating profit or EBIT   Operating profit, or **EBIT** (<u>E</u>arnings from operations <u>B</u>efore <u>I</u>nterests and <u>T</u>axes), represents the result of the firm's normal and current activity without taking into account income taxes or financial and extraordinary (exceptional) elements (see Chapter 6). This intermediate balance allows a comparison of firms while ignoring their financing strategies but taking into account their depreciation policies. It is a logical metric to use for comparison when businesses in an economic sector tend to use similar policies for the depreciation of their assets.

Operating net income before taxes   Operating net income before taxes indicates economic and financial performance before consideration of extraordinary (exceptional) items and taxes. It is a measure of the basis used to calculate and forecast the wealth creation expected to occur in the coming years.

Exceptional income   Exceptional income (sometimes called **unusual income** or **non-operating income**) represents the profit or loss from activities that are not related to the firm's usual operations, and are, therefore, out of the ordinary, or exceptional. In most cases, this income or loss is related to gains or losses on the sale of one or several fixed assets. Since it is, by nature, non-recurrent, this income should be shown as a separate item on the statement of intermediate balances. It should never be hidden (by addition or subtraction) as a part of any other main section of the statement.

Net income/loss   The last line of the statement of intermediate balances is the reported net income/loss after tax, which is self-explanatory. It is also known as the 'bottom line'. This balance is useful, however, to double-check the equality between this restructured statement and the original income statement.

An income statement by nature can always be presented in a common-size format, even without the restructuring we have used to identify the intermediate balances. Of course, without restructuring, its usefulness would be greatly reduced and would apply only to that firm, as the metrics identified may not be comparable between two entities.

2.3.3 The statement of intermediate balances in practice: analysis of China Eastern Airlines

Company background   China Eastern Airlines Corporation Ltd ('China Eastern') is one of the largest Chinese air carriers. It was established in the People's Republic of China in 1995. It is headquartered in Shanghai. Although a majority of the shares are state-owned, its shares are listed in Shanghai, Hong Kong and New York. The company, together with its subsidiaries, is principally engaged in civil aviation, including the provision of passenger, cargo, mail, and other transportation services. The company is primarily focused in the provision of domestic, regional and international passenger airline services. China Eastern operates approximately 6,090 scheduled flights per week (excluding charter flights), serving a route network that covers 134 cities within China and abroad (source: Annual report 2008). During the year ended 31 December 2008, it operated a total of approximately 423 routes. As of 31 December 2008, the company accounted for approximately 19.3% of the total commercial air traffic handled by Chinese airlines. The company operates primarily from Shanghai's Hongqiao Airport and Shanghai Pudong International Airport.

Financial statements   Table 16.4 presents the China Eastern consolidated statements of income for fiscal years ended 31 December 2006 through 31 December 2008 (source: Annual reports 2008, 2007 and 2006). These follow a presentation by nature. The financial

Table 16.4 China Eastern Airlines – Consolidated statements of income for years ended 31 December 2008, 2007 and 2006

(in RMB 000)	2008	2007	2006
Revenues	41,072,557	42,533,893	37,634,132
Other operating income	405,163	487,562	424,265
Other gains	267,084	–	–
Operating expenses			
Aircraft fuel	(18,488,242)	(15,117,147)	(13,608,793)
(Loss)/gain on fair value movements of financial derivatives	(6,400,992)	83,965	(1,035,343)
Take-off and landing charges	(5,279,590)	(5,174,183)	(4,989,382)
Depreciation and amortization	(4,781,562)	(4,719,735)	(4,597,178)
Wages, salaries and benefits	(4,545,312)	(4,327,397)	(3,538,082)
Aircraft maintenance	(3,272,981)	(2,392,039)	(2,647,340)
Impairment losses	(2,976,678)	(227,456)	–
Food and beverages	(1,321,268)	(1,230,754)	(1,188,016)
Aircraft operating lease rentals	(2,734,802)	(2,850,873)	(2,954,751)
Other operating lease rentals	(369,236)	(292,844)	(276,715)
Selling and marketing expenses	(1,562,945)	(1,805,342)	(1,734,987)
Civil aviation infrastructure levies	(769,849)	(781,613)	(696,428)
Ground services and other charges	(268,873)	(224,466)	(162,104)
Office, administrative and other expenses	(4,055,679)	(3,833,938)	(3,620,718)
Total operating expenses	**(56,828,009)**	**(42,893,822)**	**(41,049,837)**
Operating (loss)/profit	**(15,083,205)**	**127,633**	**(2,991,440)**
Finance income	2,061,625	2,140,457	1,008,563
Finance costs	(2,328,147)	(1,978,550)	(1,765,981)
Share of results of associates	69,668	58,312	103,566
Share of results of jointly controlled entities	24,050	30,086	29,595
(Loss)/profit before income tax	**(15,256,009)**	**377,938**	**(3,615,697)**
Income tax	(73,916)	(23,763)	162,932
(Loss)/profit for the year	**(15,329,925)**	**354,175**	**(3,452,765)**

statements of the group have been prepared in accordance with IFRS and the disclosure requirements of the Hong Kong Companies Ordinance.

From the previous annual reports of the company, we extracted the following comparative data for 2005:

(in RMB 000)	2005
Revenues	27,454,443

From the annual reports, we extract some information on 'other operating income' and 'other gains'. The following data will allow restating some elements of the income statement.

(in RMB 000)	2008	2007	2006
Government subsidies	405,163	487,562	462,370
Net fair value (losses)/gains on financial instruments			(38,105)
Other operating income	405,163	487,562	424,265
Gains on disposal of property, plant and equipment	267,084		
Other gains	267,084		

As the income statement is presented by nature, it allows the preparation of the statement of intermediate balances (SIB) in value and in percentages (see Table 16.5).

Before analyzing the statement of intermediate balances (SIB), we must acknowledge we made the following simplifications or choices:

- The 'other operating income', which mainly contains government subsidies, are included as part of gross operating income. These subsidies are actually linked, at least in part, to the move of China Eastern operating base from Hongqiao Airport to Pudong Airport and are meant to compensate for the loss of business this government-imposed move caused.

- The 'other gains', which correspond to gain on sale of fixed assets, will be integrated in unusual income.

- Because the annual reports explain that office and administration expenses mainly include training expenses, and expenses relating to overseas sales, they have been included in the consumption from third parties.

- Impairment losses mainly correspond to goodwill impairment, impairment charge on property, plant and equipment and impairment charge on non-current assets held for sale. We have included them in unusual items.

Analysis, revenues/production   Even though the common-size SIB is based on the principle of dividing all other figures in the statement by the total production for the year, we have added to the statement a line showing the change in production for each year as compared with the previous year. It can be seen that China Eastern experienced a decrease in its activity in 2008 (this is explained, as mentioned earlier, by the move of the main operations from one airport to another, as well as by the downturn in the world economy in the second half of 2008). The 37.1% jump in production that China Eastern experienced in 2006 over 2005 has to be replaced in context: although the air transportation market is, indeed, very dynamic in China, this spectacular gain in production is largely due to a change in the perimeter of the firm (its acquisitions of China Northwest Airlines and China Yunnan Airlines). This last observation is a reminder of (1) the need to understand the context before formulating an opinion, and (2) to always compare metrics on a comparable corporate perimeter.

Consumption of resources acquired from third parties   The ratio of 'consumption from third parties' to 'total production' has increased from 84.7% in 2006 to 92.8% in 2008. Looking at the breakdown of consumption from third parties, we see that fuel cost represents the greatest expense. Fuel cost as a percentage of total production increased for China Eastern from 2006 (36.2%) to 2008 (45.0%) – one serious reason why China Eastern has to report a series of losses from operations in 2006 and 2008. Common-sizing the SIB allows the user to separate the effect of growth in the revenue (which should be adjusted for the small decrease in the load factor – a loss of about 1 to 3 points per year for an effective load factor of 62% in 2008 – source: Annual report) from the impact of the cost of fuel

Table 16.5 Statement of intermediate balances (in value and in percentage)

	In value (RMB 000)			In %		
	2008	2007	2006	2008	2007	2006
Revenues	41,072,557	42,533,893	37,634,132	100.0	100.0	100.0
Total production for the period	**41,072,557**	**42,533,893**	**37,634,132**	**100.0**	**100.0**	**100.0**
Change in production	*–3.4%*	*13.0%*	*37.1%*			
Aircraft fuel	(18,488,242)	(15,117,147)	(13,608,793)	(45.0)	(35.5)	(36.2)
Take-off and landing charges	(5,279,590)	(5,174,183)	(4,989,382)	(12.9)	(12.2)	(13.3)
Aircraft maintenance	(3,272,981)	(2,392,039)	(2,647,340)	(8.0)	(5.6)	(7.0)
Food and beverages	(1,321,268)	(1,230,754)	(1,188,016)	(3.2)	(2.9)	(3.2)
Aircraft operating lease rentals	(2,734,802)	(2,850,873)	(2,954,751)	(6.7)	(6.7)	(7.9)
Other operating lease rentals	(369,236)	(292,844)	(276,715)	(0.9)	(0.7)	(0.7)
Selling and marketing expenses	(1,562,945)	(1,805,342)	(1,734,987)	(3.8)	(4.2)	(4.6)
Ground services and other charges	(268,873)	(224,466)	(162,104)	(0.7)	(0.5)	(0.4)
Civil aviation infrastructure levies	(769,849)	(781,613)	(696,428)	(1.9)	(1.8)	(1.9)
Office, administrative and other expenses	(4,055,679)	(3,833,938)	(3,620,718)	(9.9)	(9.0)	(9.6)
Consumption from third parties	*(38,123,465)*	*(33,703,199)*	*(31,879,234)*	*(92.8)*	*(79.2)*	*(84.7)*
Value added	**2,949,092**	**8,830,694**	**5,754,898**	**7.2**	**20.8**	**15.3**
Other operating income	405,163	487,562	424,265	1.0	1.1	1.1
Wages, salaries and benefits	(4,545,312)	(4,327,397)	(3,538,082)	(11.1)	(10.2)	(9.4)
Gross operating income	**(1,191,057)**	**4,990,859**	**2,641,081**	**(2.9)**	**11.7**	**7.0**
Depreciation and amortization	(4,781,562)	(4,719,735)	(4,597,178)	(11.6)	(11.1)	(12.2)
Earnings (loss) from operations	**(5,972,619)**	**271,124**	**(1,956,097)**	**(14.5)**	**0.6**	**(5.2)**
Finance income	2,061,625	2,140,457	1,008,563	5.0	5.0	2.7
Finance costs	(2,328,147)	(1,978,550)	(1,765,981)	(5.7)	(4.7)	(4.7)
Share of results of associates	69,668	58,312	103,566	0.2	0.1	0.3
Share of results of jointly controlled entities	24,050	30,086	29,595	0.1	0.1	0.1
(Loss)/gain on fair value movements of financial derivatives	(6,400,992)	83,965	(1,035,343)	(15.6)	0.2	(2.8)
Operating net income before taxes	**(12,546,415)**	**605,394**	**(3,615,697)**	**(30.5)**	**1.4**	**(9.6)**
Gain on disposal of PPE	267,084			0.7		
Impairment losses	(2,976,678)	(227,456)		(7.2)	(0.5)	
Unusual income (loss)	**(2,709,594)**	**(227,456)**		**(6.6)**	**(0.5)**	
Income tax	(73,916)	(23,763)	162,932	(0.2)	(0.1)	0.4
(Loss)/profit for the year	**(15,329,925)**	**354,175**	**(3,452,765)**	**(37.3)**	**0.8**	**(9.2)**

purchased. Here we can see that China Eastern experienced an increase in the average cost of aviation fuel. Not surprisingly, the oil price inflation turned fuel cost into a major issue for the company (as well as for all airlines that had not hedged their purchase price of aviation fuel against fluctuations of the price of crude oil).

China Eastern reports an increase in aircraft and maintenance fees from 7.0% in 2006 to 8.0% in 2008. The reasons for such a change might be a combination of any of the following factors: an older aircraft fleet, an increase in the size of the fleet, or higher quality and safety standards of maintenance, etc. China Eastern also reports a slight decrease in the average take-off and landing fees (12.9% in 2008, versus 13.3% in 2006). Only by digging further would an analyst find the true explanation(s), which might include a reduction of the landing fees at some airports, the reduction of the number of landings at expensive airports, a shift of flights to less desirable time slots, etc.

Value added   While not widely used in North America, the value added figure shows the extent to which an entity contributes to the national wealth of the country and what amount of 'value' is to be shared between the various stakeholders. The value added figure for China Eastern sharply declined to 7.2% in 2008 (20.8% in 2007). This implies not only less value added to the national wealth of the country, but also less value available for shareholders, employees, depreciation (a function of, and a surrogate for, future investments), bankers and taxes.

Since the allocation of value added is, in the short-run, a zero-sum game, China Eastern faces strategic challenges (or opportunities) for the future. For example:

1. The recruiting needs of this growing airline are likely to demand that an increased share of value added be dedicated to salaries and remunerations.

2. The development of the fleet, or its renewal, is likely to cause total depreciation expense to increase.

3. Expansion of the fleet is costly and external funding will probably need to be secured, thus increasing the claim of bankers and bond holders on value added.

4. The part of value added available to remunerate shareholders is going to mechanically decrease.

Thus, managers must address the challenge of creating a rate of growth of the value added such that it will allow the satisfaction of every stakeholder's growth expectations, unless they are willing to make heart-wrenching (and potentially dangerous) choices between investments, growth of headcount, maintenance of competitive remuneration practices, quality financing and remuneration of shareholders.

Gross operating income   The ratio of salaries, wages and benefits to total production is not high (11.1% in 2008), even though it increased from 9.4% in 2006. China Eastern makes a gross operating loss (–2.9% in 2008), probably due, as mentioned earlier, to its high level of fuel costs, higher office and administrative expenses in its new location (implying duplication of several operations support functions) and a reduction in the load factor and thus in total production.

As discussed previously, gross operating income reflects the return derived from the core (recurring) activities of the entity. A negative gross operating income (i.e., a gross operating loss), is indeed a sign of financial distress.

Earnings from operations   For China Eastern, depreciation and amortization represent 11.6% of production in 2008 and had been declining from 2006 to 2007 (a possible sign of an aging fleet, if they used an accelerated form of depreciation). Since sales decreased heavily compared to previous years and expenses increased, China Eastern shows a significant deterioration of operating income which is a loss in 2008 of –14.5% and in 2007 of –5.2%.

Operating net income before taxes   In 2008, China Eastern ratio of interest expense to total production was high (5.7%), but the ratio of interest income showed an increase from 2006 (2.7%) to 2008 (5.0%), which was a good sign (for example: more tickets were purchased and paid for in advance or they were purchased even earlier than before).

A heavy loss on fair value movements of financial derivatives in 2008 (−15.4% in relation to total production), caused a negative operating loss before income taxes in 2008 (−30.5%) compared to a profit in 2007 (+1.4%). This huge loss in 2008 was related to a series of hedging contracts China Eastern signed with some leading world investment banks. In fact, when the oil price dropped, somewhat unexpectedly, below US$60 per barrel, these contracts obligated China Eastern to pay very high compensations to these investment banks. It is an indicator that China Eastern has not reached the necessary level of financial savvy and established the robust risk management system required in this industry before they ventured into the field of complex hedging derivatives.

Unusual income (loss)   China Eastern recorded a huge loss under this heading (−7.2%) in 2008 because of the impairment losses.

Net income (loss)   China Eastern recorded a 37.3% loss in 2008, after facing a very small profit in 2007 (0.8% of total production).

Synthesis   The preparation of an SIB confirms that focusing mainly on net income figures is not sufficient to gain a full understanding of what went on (and therefore to be able to forecast future results, and thus take appropriate actions). The other intermediate balances, such as value added and gross operating income are also, as illustrated above, important to the analyst as they are sources of questions to be discussed with management, for example during a quarterly earnings conference call. In the present case, despite the wealth of knowledge the notes and general information provided, and the numerous questions raised through the SIB analysis, we feel that, in addition, a comparison with other airline companies would have considerably enriched the analysis. Baker, Ding and Stolowy (2005) compare the statement of intermediate balances of China Eastern, Southwest Airlines (long a champion at hedging the cost of aviation fuel) and Air France (which has, within its markets, a domestic/international, short-haul/long-haul route structure relatively analogous to that of China Eastern).

Key points

- Trend analysis measures the changes, over past accounting period(s), of user-selected components of the income statement. It reveals the dynamics of the income generation model.
- Common-size analysis of the income statement is prepared by presenting its components in terms of their percentage of net sales.
- The common-size analysis allows the analyst to compare and contrast more easily the income statements (or any financial statement) of two or more companies in the same industrial sector or risk class.
- When presented by function, the income statement does not need to be restated and the computation of common-size figures is generally sufficient to analyze it.

- When presented by nature, the income statement can be subdivided in several levels of income which form the statement of intermediate balances (SIB).
- The main concepts in the SIB are: value added, gross operating income (EBITDA), and operating net income before taxes.
- Value added (net revenue minus resources consumed that are provided from third party sources) represents an amount that is to be partitioned, in a zero sum game (in the short run at least), between the workforce, depreciation (surrogate for future investments), the providers of interest-bearing debts, the government (taxes) and shareholders. The core of the strategic decisions of a firm can be narrowed down to how they allocate the value added they create between these five 'claimants'.

Review (solutions are at the back of the book)

Review 16.1 Chugoku Power Electric Company (2)*

Topic: Common-size income statements by nature

Chugoku Electric Power Company, Inc., was established in 1951 as one of 10 electric power companies in Japan. It maintains its head office in the city of Hiroshima and supplies electricity to the Chugoku region through an integrated structure that encompasses all stages of power supply, from generation to transmission and distribution. The company has 27 subsidiaries and 19 associated companies.

The income statements of the parent company for the years ended 31 March 2006–2008 are presented below (source: Annual report 2008). Consolidated figures are very close to the non-consolidated ones because the parent is the heaviest actor in the group.

The non-consolidated financial statements have been prepared in accordance with the provisions set forth in the Japanese Financial Instruments and Exchange Law and its related accounting regulations, and the Electricity Utilities Industry Law and in conformity with accounting principles generally accepted in Japan ('Japanese GAAP'), which are different in certain respects as to application and disclosure requirements from IFRS.

Non-consolidated statements of income

(in ¥ million)	2008	2007	2006
Operating revenues	1,038,438	996,007	976,835
Operating expenses			
Personnel	105,272	116,529	122,008
Fuel	268,327	214,559	178,649
Purchased power	154,991	146,861	161,771
Depreciation	130,501	128,490	136,569
Maintenance	82,105	90,001	80,747
Taxes other that income taxes	61,388	61,698	61,556
Purchased services	36,703	33,465	33,732
Other	121,316	126,176	110,001
	960,603	917,779	885,033
Operating income	77,835	78,228	91,802
Other expenses (income):			
Interest expense	30,232	28,419	27,855
Interest income	(1,639)	(1,076)	(101)
Loss on revaluation of investments in subsidiary	0	0	12,590
Other, net	(2,034)	(2,110)	(1,452)
	26,559	25,233	38,892
Income before special items and income taxes	51,276	52,995	52,910
Special item:			
Provision (reversal) for drought	(657)	112	(1,913)
Provision for depreciation of nuclear power plant	18,828	5,053	0
Provision for income taxes:			
Current	11,929	16,855	25,863
Deferred	452	(2,428)	(1,287)
Net income	20,724	33,403	30,247

Required

1. What is the format of the income statement?

2. Prepare common-size statements on the basis of the income statement, as published by the company.

3. Restate the income statement and prepare common-size intermediate balances following the format of Figure 16.1.

4. Comment on these different statements.

The item 'Other, net' in 'Other expenses (income)' can be assumed to refer to 'Financial expenses and income'.

Assignments

Assignment 16.1
Multiple-choice questions

Select the right answer (one possible answer, unless otherwise stated).

1. Which of the situations described below would mean the firm analyzed is caught in a 'scissor effect':

   (a) Its interest expense grows faster than its labor compensation expense
   (b) Its cost of goods sold declines more slowly than its sales revenue
   (c) Its sale revenue is growing faster than its personnel expenses
   (d) Its depreciation expenses and remuneration expenses vary in opposite directions

2. Common-sizing an income statement generally means expressing each line item of the statement as a percentage of:

   (a) Gross sales
   (b) Operating profit
   (c) Net sales
   (d) Net income before taxes

3. When an entity extends its geographical market to reach less dense customer bases and thus increases its sales volume, it is logical (assuming the mix of sales remains the same) that, in the short-term at least:

   (a) The cost of selling, as a percentage of sales, will increase
   (b) Cost of goods sold, as a percentage of sales revenue, will increase
   (c) The total cost of production will decrease
   (d) R&D expenses will be increased in absolute value

4. Founded in 1853, *Compagnie Générale des Eaux*, by a succession of acquisitions and divestitures, became a huge diversified conglomerate. It renamed itself Vivendi in July 2000, Vivendi Universal in December 2000 and back to Vivendi in April 2006 (still its name as of 2009). Over which of the following periods would a trend analysis of its income statement make sense:

   (a) 1853–2009
   (b) 2007–2009
   (c) 1999–2002
   (d) 2005–2007

5. In a common-size analysis of the income statement, which of the following elements are relevant for a forecast of the future income of a firm (several possible answers):

   (a) Net income before taxes as a percentage of net sales
   (b) Interest expense as a percentage of total interest bearing liabilities
   (c) Exceptional income as a percentage of net income after taxes
   (d) Operating income as a percentage of net sales revenue

6. The term EBIT means:

   (a) Earning Before Investments and Transport expenses
   (b) Earnings Before Investments and Taxes
   (c) Earnings Borne In Transit
   (d) Earnings Before Interest and Taxes

7. One element of the strategy of a firm is to decide how to share its value added between:

   (a) Customers, investors, investments (preparing the future) and taxes
   (b) Employees, taxes (government), bankers, depreciation and shareholders
   (c) Customers, employees, bankers, shareholders and government (taxes)
   (d) Shareholders and bankers (providers of long-term funds), suppliers and investors

8. The lists offered below contain elements called 'intermediate balances' and some elements of income statements that are not called intermediate balances. Which list contains only so-called intermediate balances:

   (a) Production, value added, gross operating profit (EBITDA), unusual income and net profit
   (b) Gross margin, value added, sales expenses, purchasing expenses, cost to serve the market and net income

(c) R&D expenses, cost of goods sold, value added, net income and net financial income

(d) EBIT, EBITDA, R&D expenses, net income, commercial margin, and cost of resources procured from third parties

9. If the income statement of a firm is structured by function, the calculation of value added can be carried out without any restatement.

   (a) True
   (b) False

10. If the lease of an asset is considered to be a financial lease (i.e., is capitalized), the rent paid (periodic lease payment) is considered as part of the 'resources consumed from third parties' in the calculation of the value added created by the firm.

   (a) True
   (b) False

Assignment 16.2
Janacek Company (3)

Topic: Preparation and analysis of a statement of intermediate balances

The Janacek Company has a commercial activity in the sector of beauty products and cosmetics.

Required

1. With the help of the balance sheet, income statement, and additional information (see assignment 14.2 Janacek Company (1), in Chapter 14), prepare a statement of intermediate balances for the years X1, X2, and X3.

2. Comment on this document.

Assignment 16.3
Procter & Gamble (1)

Topic: Common-size income statements by function

The common-size income statements of Procter & Gamble have been prepared for the years 2005–2009 (see Table 16.3 in this chapter).

Required

1. What financial performance intermediate balance does not appear in the income statement and would be useful to your analysis of the firm's performance and evolution?

2. What additional information would be interesting for your analysis?

3. Comment on the common-size income statements over the period.

Assignment 16.4
Creaton AG*

Topic: Common-size income statements by nature

Creaton AG is one of Germany's leading clay roofing tile manufacturers. Its name stands for a uniquely broad product range and a strong exports focus. Its brand image says ultra-modern, eco-friendly technologies and product consistency.

   The annual financial statements for the group have been prepared applying IFRS. You will find below the income statements for the periods ended 31 December 2005–2008 (source: Annual reports 2008 and 2006).

Creaton AG, Consolidated income statements

(in EUR 000)	2008	2007	2006	2005
Sales revenue	202,595	200,540	162,618	134,874
Increase/(decrease) in finished goods and work in progress	11,913	8,007	(6,167)	2,414
Other operating income	17,536	28,634	4,449	4,621
Cost of materials	(84,010)	(77,457)	(38,191)	(33,757)
Personnel expense	(48,330)	(43,624)	(36,528)	(35,459)
Scheduled depreciation/amortization	(13,738)	(13,084)	(13,167)	(12,538)
Other operating expense	(88,006)	(65,701)	(54,065)	(45,955)
Operating profit	**(2,040)**	**37,315**	**18,949**	**14,200**
Interest income	925	632	344	164
Profit/(loss) attributable to associated companies carried at equity	62	21	47	(21)
Interest expense	(2,505)	(2,547)	(2,769)	(2,515)
Earnings from ordinary activities	**(3,558)**	**35,421**	**16,571**	**11,828**
Taxes on income	(1)	(1,208)	(5,481)	(4,516)
Consolidated net income/(loss) for the year	**(3,559)**	**34,213**	**11,090**	**7,312**

Required

1. Prepare common-size statements on the basis of the income statement, as published by the company.

2. Restate the income statement and prepare common-size intermediate balances following the format of Figure 16.1.

3. Comment on these different statements.

Assignment 16.5
Infosys Company (2)*

Topic: Common-size income statements by function

Based in India, Infosys Technologies Limited (Infosys) is a global technology services firm that defines, designs and delivers information technology-enabled business solutions to its clients.

The consolidated financial statements have been prepared by the company's management in accordance with the requirements of Accounting Standard (AS) 21, Consolidated Financial Statements, issued by the Institute of Chartered Accountants of India.

Below are provided the consolidated income statements for the financial years ended 31 March, 2009, 2008, 2007, 2006 and 2005 (source: Annual reports 2009, 2008, 2007 and 2006).

Consolidated income statements

For the year ended 31 March (in Rupees crore[3])	2009	2008	2007	2006	2005
Income from software services, products and business process management	21,693	16,692	13,893	9,521	7130
Software development and business process management expenses	11,765	9,207	7,458	5,066	3,765
GROSS PROFIT	9,928	7,485	6,435	4,455	3,365
Selling and marketing expenses	1,104	916	929	600	461
General and administration expenses	1,629	1,331	1,115	764	569
OPERATING PROFIT before interest, depreciation and minority interest	7,195	5,238	4,391	3,091	2,335
Interest	0	0	0	0	0
Depreciation	761	598	514	437	287
OPERATING PROFIT before tax, minority interest and exceptional items	6,434	4,640	3,877	2,654	2,048
Other income, net	473	704	372	139	124
Provision for investments	0	0	2	1	0
NET PROFIT before tax, minority interest and exceptional items	6,907	5,344	4,247	2,792	2,172
Provision for taxation	919	685	386	313	326
NET PROFIT after tax and before minority interest and exceptional items	5,988	4,659	3,861	2,479	1,846
Income on sale of investments, net of taxes	0	0	6	0	45
NET PROFIT after tax, exceptional items and before minority interest	5,988	4,659	3,867	2,479	1,891
Minority interest	0	0	11	21	0
NET PROFIT after tax, exceptional items and minority interest	5,988	4,659	3,856	2,458	1,891

The notes to the financial statements provide details of several components of the income statement.

Software development and business process management expenses	2009	2008	2007	2006	2005
Salaries and bonus including overseas staff expenses	9,792	7,651	6,071	4,129	3,026
Contribution to provident and other funds (part of compensation expenses)	245	192	154	92	82
Staff welfare (part of compensation expenses)	72	58	46	33	22
Overseas travel expenses	609	505	461	345	252
Traveling and conveyance	0	2	0	19	9
Technical sub-contractors	396	265	289	163	109
Software packages					
For own use	320	225	203	139	116
For service delivery to clients	41	26	25	30	15
Communication expenses	94	79	69	62	55
Rent	71	49	34	25	12
Computer maintenance	25	27	23	21	16
Consumables	22	21	24	16	16
Provision for post-sales client support and warranties	39	45	13	−14	31
Miscellaneous expenses	39	62	46	6	4
	11,765	9,207	7,458	5,066	3,765

Selling and marketing expenses	2009	2008	2007	2006	2005
Salaries and bonus including overseas staff expenses	825	607	552	366	276
Contribution to provident and other funds	3	4	3	1	2
Staff welfare	4	3	3	2	1
Overseas travel expenses	110	102	106	78	56
Traveling and conveyance	5	4	8	4	11
Brand building	62	56	70	48	35
Commission and earn-out charges	11	64	101	31	25
Professional charges	22	21	24	27	18
Rent	16	15	19	16	11
Marketing expenses	20	19	26	12	11
Telephone charges	14	8	6	6	5
Printing and stationery	1	1	1	1	0
Advertisements	2	6	3	2	2
Sales promotion expenses	2	3	2	2	1
Office maintenance	0	0	1	0	1
Communication expenses	4	2	1	1	2
Insurance charges	0	0	0	0	1
Consumables	0	0	0	0	0
Software packages					
For own use	0	0	1	0	0
Computer maintenance	0	0	0	0	0
Rates and taxes	0	0	0	0	0
Miscellaneous expenses	3	1	2	3	3
	1,104	916	929	600	461

General and administration expenses	2009	2008	2007	2006	2005
Salaries and bonus including overseas staff expenses	447	350	271	169	122
Contribution to provident and other funds	17	12	12	8	8
Staff welfare	0	1	0	1	1
Telephone charges	160	133	118	85	52
Professional charges	237	189	151	102	68
Power and fuel	147	122	97	68	44
Office maintenance	168	136	108	75	45
Guesthouse maintenance	5	1	0	0	
Traveling and conveyance	92	102	95	66	41
Overseas travel expenses	29	24	23	19	12
Insurance charges	26	26	32	25	32
Printing and stationery	12	18	16	12	11
Rates and taxes	34	36	26	12	9
Donations	21	20	21	17	21
Rent	27	22	17	11	18
Advertisements	4	7	8	14	11
Professional membership and seminar participation fees	10	9	10	10	6
Repairs to building	33	23	22	16	14
Repairs to plant and machinery	22	20	15	11	8
Postage and courier	11	11	8	6	5
Books and periodicals	3	4	5	5	3
Recruitment and training	6	3	7	7	2
Provision for bad and doubtful debts	75	43	26	10	24
Provision for doubtful loans and advances	1	0	1	0	0

General and administration expenses	2009	2008	2007	2006	2005
Commission to non-whole-time directors	6	4	2	1	1
Auditors' remuneration					
Statutory audit fees	2	1	1	1	1
Certification charges	0	0	0	0	0
Others	0	0	0	0	0
Out-of-pocket expenses	0	0	0	0	0
Bank charges and commission	3	1	1	1	1
Freight charges	1	1	1	1	1
Research grants	20	4	13	1	1
Software packages					
For own use	0	0	0	1	1
Transaction processing fee and filing fee	0	0	1	0	0
Miscellaneous expenses	10	8	7	9	6
	1,629	1,331	1,115	764	569

Required

1. Prepare the common-size income statements.
2. Comment on the common-size income statements over the period.

Assignment 16.6
China Communications Construction*

Topic: Common-size income statements by function and nature

The group China Communications Construction is based in the People's Republic of China and principally engaged in infrastructure construction, infrastructure design, dredging and manufacturing of port machinery and other businesses.

We provide below:

- The consolidated income statements for the financial years ended 31 December 2008, 2007, 2006 and 2005 (source: Annual reports 2008, 2007 and 2006).
- The common-size income statements for the same period.

China Communications Construction Consolidated income statements

for the years ended 31 December 2008, 2007, 2006 and 2005

Income statement as reported (in RMB million)	2008	2007	2006	2005	2008 %	2007 %	2006 %	2005 %
Turnover	178,889	150,601	114,881	83,265	100.0	100.0	100.0	100.0
Cost of sales	(161,031)	(135,033)	(103,066)	(75,110)	(90.0)	(89.7)	(89.7)	(90.2)
Gross profit	17,858	15,568	11,815	8,155	10.0	10.3	10.3	9.8
Other gains - net	1,171	243	76	205	0.7	0.2	0.1	0.2
Selling and marketing expenses	(490)	(409)	(413)	(463)	(0.3)	(0.3)	(0.4)	(0.6)
Administrative expenses	(7,447)	(6,059)	(5,341)	(4,117)	(4.2)	(4.0)	(4.6)	(4.9)
Other income	2,212	2,226	1,338	1,001	1.2	1.5	1.2	1.2
Other expenses	(1,417)	(983)	(987)	(972)	(0.8)	(0.7)	(0.9)	(1.2)
Operating profit	11,887	10,586	6,488	3,809	6.6	7.0	5.6	4.6
Interest income	657	491	347	117	0.4	0.3	0.3	0.1
Finance costs	(2,636)	(1,545)	(1,337)	(433)	(1.5)	(1.0)	(1.2)	(0.5)
Share of loss of jointly controlled entities	(88)	(41)	(93)	(47)	(0.0)	(0.0)	(0.1)	(0.1)
Share of profit of associates	11	132	109	117	0.0	0.1	0.1	0.1
Profit before income tax	9,831	9,623	5,514	3,563	5.5	6.4	4.8	4.3
Income tax expense	(1,955)	(2,049)	(1,228)	(592)	(1.1)	(1.4)	(1.1)	(0.7)
Profit for the year	7,876	7,574	4,286	2,971	4.4	5.0	3.7	3.6

The consolidated financial statements of the group have been prepared in accordance with IFRS. The income statement is presented by function. However, in the notes to the financial statements, the group publishes a breakdown by nature of the expenses (cost of sales, distribution costs and administrative expenses) (see below).

Note 32. Expenses by nature (in RMB million)	2008	2007	2006	2005
Raw materials and consumables used	66,528	55,910	44,332	31,917
Subcontracting costs	46,806	40,163	29,126	19,165
Employee benefits	12,792	10,995	8,532	7,236
Changes in contract work-in-progress	4,597	6,301	4,980	4,101
Transportation costs	5,335	4,953	3,401	2,761
Equipment usage cost	5,848	4,854	3,574	3,442
Business tax and other transaction taxes	4,375	3,525	2,666	2,042
Rentals	3,865	3,214	2,386	2,199
Depreciation of property, plant and equipment and investment properties	3,407	2,411	2,166	1,893
Fuel	2,845	2,308	1,611	1,020
Repair and maintenance expense	2,217	1,849	1,436	906
Travel	1,235	928	858	652
Research and development costs	1,087	279	179	57
Provision for impairment of trade and other receivables	162	269	24	69
Changes in inventories of finished goods and work-in-progress	1,268	327	(105)	60
Insurance	209	182	136	89
(Reversal of)/provision for foreseeable losses on construction contracts	19	(146)	720	295
Auditors' remuneration	43	50	48	12
Amortization of lease prepayments	67	24	27	34
Advertising	29	20	20	19
Amortization of intangible assets	26	18	12	10
Provision for / (reversal of) impairment of inventories	1	18	29	(4)
Other expenses	6,207	3,049	2,662	1,715
Total cost of sales, distribution costs and administrative expenses	168,968	141,501	108,820	79,690

Required

1. With the help of note 32, restate the income statement and prepare the statement of intermediate balances, in value and in percentage of sales.

2. Analyze the income statement on the basis of the format by function

3. Analyze the income statement on the basis of the format by nature (statement of intermediate balances).

4. What is the value added of each analysis, compared to the other?

References

Baker, C.R., Ding, Y. and Stolowy, H. (2005) 'Using "statement of intermediate balances" as tool for international financial statement analysis in airline industry', *Advances in International Accounting* 18: 169–98.

Further reading

Deppe, L. (2000) 'Disclosing disaggregated information', *Journal of Accountancy* 190(3): 47–52.

Haller, A. and Stolowy, H. (1998) 'Value added in financial accounting: A comparative study of Germany and France', *Advances in International Accounting* 11: 23–51.

McLeay, S. (1983) 'Value added: A comparative study', *Accounting, Organizations & Society* 8(1): 31–56.

Pong, C. and Mitchell, F. (2005) 'Accounting for a disappearance: A contribution to the history of the value added statement in the UK', *Accounting Historians Journal* 32(2): 173–99.

van Staden, C. (2003) 'The relevance of theories of political economy to the understanding of financial reporting in South Africa: The case of value added statements', *Accounting Forum* 27(2): 224–45.

Additional material on the website

Go to http://www.cengage.co.uk/stolowy3 for further information, journal entries and extra assignments for each chapter.

The following appendix to this chapter is available on the dedicated website:

Appendix 16.1: Value added

Notes

1. See www.vernimmen.com.
2. Dry lease and wet lease have been defined in Chapter 5, Assignment 5.4 Nokia and others, as a footnote to easyJet's income statement.
3. 1 crore = 10 million.

C17

Chapter 17
Statement of Cash Flows Analysis and Earnings Quality

Learning objectives

After studying this chapter, you will understand:

- How to analyze the statement of cash flows.
- The importance of available cash flow and free cash flow in financial statement analysis.
- That several ratios can be computed to analyze the statement of cash flows.
- The definition of accounts manipulation.
- The various forms of accounts manipulation.
- The difference between cash-based or accrual-based earnings management.
- How to use the indirect method of operating cash flow construction as a tool to analyze the earnings quality of a company.

In analyzing the financial position of a firm, in the general sense, we have seen that understanding the structure of the balance sheet (see Chapter 15) was a very important step in understanding the potential of future value creation by the firm, but it had taken the statement of cash flows (see Chapter 14) to understand how the cash had evolved from the beginning to the end of the period. Analyzing the income statement (see Chapter 16) explained, step-by-step, how shareholders value grew and matched each intermediate balance to different managerial action. We saw in Chapter 14 that the statement of cash flows decomposed cash creation and use into three categories, each focused on a family of managerial decisions. In this chapter we address the analysis of the cash flow from operating activities (normally the main source of new cash for any firm in a steady state) and of the two other cash flow activities: investing and financing. We will review the two basic alternative methods of calculation of the cash from operations. The strategic information

627

needs of the firm are met by different stages in aggregating cash flows, from cash from operation to net cash. Each aggregate opens up different strategic questions, the answer to which helps prepare the firm for future opportunities.

The cash position is a 'hard number'. The same qualifier applies to each cash flow. Cash is in or it is not. Earnings, on the other side, are the result of the application of accrual rules. Earnings for a period are always approximations, at one point in time, of the anticipated long-term cash flows. Even if, in the long run, earnings streams and cash flow streams converge, managers can use some leeway, within the rules or outside the rules, to modify the timing of recognition of earnings. Whether it is the doubtful, but strongly believed-in functional-fixation hypothesis[1] (earnings figures drive the value of a share), or the sensitivity of financial markets to the firm meeting expectations of earnings (whether these were declared by managers or created by independent analysts), or the fact that many managerial compensation packages are indexed on earnings numbers, or the simple human preference for increasing numbers (in many cultures, and definitely under capitalism, more is, rightly or wrongly, generally seen as being better), all these create the temptation for managers to 'massage' their earnings numbers to meet expectations and either match the target or show the steady growth in earnings financial markets seem to like so much (investors do not welcome excessive uncertainty). Taking some liberty to orient earnings one way or another is called accounts manipulation. It is generally only a question of modifying the timing of earnings, but it could also be fraudulent. Accounts manipulation will be our second section.

The detection of accounts manipulation practices, especially through the use of the analysis of the statement of cash flows, will be the topic of our third section.

1 Analysis of the statement of cash flows

There are several possible ways in which users of financial statements can analyze a statement of cash flows.

1.1 Algebraic sign of cash flows

Generally, the cash flow from operating activities is expected to be positive.[2] In fact, many financial and business analysts believe it *should* be positive: in other words, the core activity of the entity should generate a positive cash flow. A negative cash flow from operating activities is seen, in most circumstances, as a serious indicator of potential weakness and an important indicator that bankruptcy may be looming on the horizon. It can also be considered as a strong signal that the firm either needs to find significant cost savings and/or to generate rapid revenue growth, and/or to shed some business segment that is bleeding cash, and/or sell some non-strategic assets, in order to reach the more stable situation created by a positive cash flow from operations. However, it is expected that, in the early phase of the life cycle of a business, the cash flow from operations may legitimately be negative, as the firm establishes its position in the market and has not yet reached a 'steady state', implying sufficiency for maintaining the status quo (see endnote 2).

Under normal circumstances, the cash flow from investing activities should almost always be negative, as a business is expected to invest more cash in new assets than it receives from the sale of its under-used or obsolete fixed assets. Note though that the cash flow from investing activities can be (sometimes significantly) positive in the case of divestment, i.e., the sale of a subsidiary or of a part of the firm that may represent a whole business segment. However a positive investing cash flow is generally short-lived since the funds thus raised are most of the time intended either to finance another investment (which may not take place in the same year), or to rebuild the net cash position of the firm, or to begin to reduce the debt burden (interest expenses do affect both cash flows and net earnings), or even, in rare cases, to allow payment of an exceptional dividend (this last possibility is often seen as a signal that the management team has run out of investment opportunities, not a good prognosis of the entity being a 'going concern').

The cash flow from financing activities can be positive or negative in any one year, depending on specific circumstances and on the sign of the two previous cash flows.

1.2 From excess cash flow to free cash flow

Cash flows were analyzed in Chapter 14 as cash from operating activities, cash from investing activities and cash from financing activities. This decomposition was static as it was describing only what had happened. 'Cash is king' remains the motto of any firm. Cash is the way through which the strategy of the firm can be implemented. It is therefore useful to create a new decomposition following the strategic choices of the firm: we will successively examine **excess cash flow**, **available cash flow** and **free cash flow**. Table 17.1 illustrates how managers and analysts go from one cash flow strategic descriptor to the next, and end up with the 'change in cash position'.

1.2.1 Excess cash flow

In addition to the traditional statement of cash flows, some companies also report **excess cash flow** (sometimes called, we think erroneously, **free cash flow**). It is defined as 'cash flow from operating activities *minus* the absolute value of the *minimum* cash flow from investing activities required to maintain the competitive position of the firm'.

This minimum cash flow from investing activities is difficult to define by an outsider to the firm. Thus the common proxy used by analysts to calculate excess cash flow is generally 'cash flow from operating activities minus [purchases of fixed assets minus proceeds from sales of fixed assets]', thus assuming that business management did actually take the appropriate decisions to keep the business competitive. However, any cash flow dedicated to development-oriented investing is, *de facto*, included in this proxy measure, making it less useful than the true concept would be if it was obtainable.

Analysts tend to use direct contact with senior management in order to estimate which part of the investing activity pertains to maintenance of competitiveness and which part pertains to developing it. The management perspectives section in the annual report often contains information relevant, although not explicitly, to the determination of the amounts and nature of investments for development and growth. This excess cash flow conceptually represents the amount available for development (internal or external through acquisitions of third party businesses) *and* for supporting financing activities (such as dividends payment, debt reimbursement, or purchase of treasury shares).

The choices of possible strategic moves by a firm (development investments or financing decisions) are guided by both the availability of such excess cash flow and the potential to raise more financing cash from external sources, and possibly, internal sources (divestments).

1.2.2 Available cash flow

The **available cash flow** is the sum of the cash flow from operating activities and the net cash flow from all investing activities (i.e., maintenance of the competiveness level *and* development).

Since, in a well-managed successful business, both the (total) net cash flow and the cash flow from operating activities are normally positive when the available cash flow is positive, the financing cash flow can be negative, without endangering the ongoing nature of the business. For example, a positive available cash flow balance can be used to engage in a policy, for example, of repayment of the firm's interest-bearing debt, of acquisition of treasury shares, and/or of distribution of dividends. When, however, the available cash flow is negative, the business will need to compensate for this situation by creating a positive financing cash flow. This would be achieved, for example, by issuing new shares or by contracting new debt. The observed (retrospective) available cash flow and its anticipated evolution form, therefore, a very important tool for understanding the likely future financing policy of a business, as well as its long-term developmental and survival potential.

1.2.3 Free cash flow

Many managers and analysts consider that an annual payment of dividends is a recurring obligation for the firm and thus they consider it to be a part of maintaining the competitive position of the entity (although counter-examples do exist: to wit, Microsoft Corporation never paid any dividend between its creation in 1975 and March 2003). Managers and analysts alike define free cash flow as 'available cash flow minus dividends paid'.

The free cash flow is seen by many financial statement users as more useful than the available cash flow because, since the payment of a dividend is most of the time a requirement for keeping the support of shareholders, the free cash flow represents the only amount of cash truly unencumbered and available for a possible reimbursement of debt, or the purchase of treasury shares or the identification of new development opportunities that may have been self censored before. Table 17.1 summarizes the links between the three cash flow visions.

Table 17.1 Excess, available and free cash flows

Net cash provided by operating activities	100
Acquisitions of fixed assets	–30
Proceeds from sale of fixed assets	10
Excess cash flow	**80**
Acquisition of shares of other businesses	–20
Available cash flow	**60**
Dividends paid	–15
Free cash flow	**45**
Other financing cash flows	–40
Net increase in cash and cash equivalents	5

1.2.4 Underlying hypothesis

Excess cash flow, available cash flow and free cash flow assume that the investing activity is supposed to be financed first by cash from operating activities, and therefore, that the financing strategy is the consequence of any insufficiency in cash from operating activities. Such a hypothesis is pretty robust in a reasonably non-inflationary economy.

1.2.5 Illustration of the calculation process of available and free cash flows

Going back to the Liszt company example, developed in Chapter 14, section 7, we can determine the available and free cash flows (see Table 17.2).

Table 17.2 Liszt Company – Available and free cash flows	
Net cash provided by operating activities	50
Net cash used in investing activities	–107
Available cash flow	**–57**
Dividends paid	–8
Free cash flow	**–65**
Other financing cash flows	75
Net increase in cash and cash equivalents	10

Given that the available cash flow is negative and Liszt pays dividends, it is logical that the free cash flow follows the same direction. This means the operating cash flow is not sufficient to finance the investing strategy of the firm, and it should therefore both reconsider its dividends policy downwards (a strong signal of distress in most cases, thus avoided by most management teams) and obtain new sources of financing (issuing new shares was the answer in this example) to balance its cash flows.

1.3 Analyzing the statement of cash flows

Users of financial information need answers to legitimate questions such as:

- What is the relationship between cash flows and sales?
- What is the relationship between cash flows and earnings?
- What is the ability of the firm to reimburse its liabilities?

Several ratios help address these questions.

1.3.1 Cash flow as percentage of sales

Cash flow from operating activities/Sales revenue

By comparing the operating cash flow to net sales over several years, the 'transformation of sales into cash' can be measured and evaluated. For Liszt Company, this ratio is (50/800) = 6.25% in the year examined. Liszt Co. is not quite a 'cash machine'. Microsoft, however, although its cash generation has deteriorated slowly (a sign of the increasing maturity of its current markets?), remains a cash machine, with a ratio of cash flow from operating activities to sales revenue at 32% in 2009, down from 35% in 2008 and 2007. Microsoft is far from the cash machine it was, for example, in 2002 with a ratio of 50%, but still quite impressive. Knowing the evolution of this ratio over time gives a good understanding of the prospects of the firm. For example, it is clear that even if Microsoft's sales increased by almost 14% from 2007 to 2009, its additions to cash due to operating activities only increased by 6%. However, a total cash flow from operating activities of $19 billion remains impressive and opens huge opportunities to rejuvenate the portfolio of activities of the firm, but its current slow growth of cash flow from operations is seen by many as an indicator of the difficulty Microsoft faces in creating new cash-cows with its new products. To put Microsoft's situation in perspective, Apple, despite its media success, reported in 2009 a ratio of cash from operating activities to sales of only 28%.

1.3.2 Operating cash ratio or cash flow yield

> Operating cash flow/Net income

For Liszt, the **operating cash ratio** or **cash flow yield** is equal to (50/9) = 5.56, which indicates a very good yield. For Microsoft this ratio in 2009 was 19.0/14.6= 1.30. This ratio partly reflects the impact of depreciation policy of the business since one of the differences between income and operating cash flow derives from non-cash items, depreciation expense being the most important element of that category. (The other difference relates to changes in inventories, accounts receivable and accounts payable.) In comparing two identical firms except for their using different depreciation policies, it is a useful ratio in determining when the cash advantage of accelerated depreciation over straight-line will cease. Knowledge of the depreciation policy of the firm is an essential element in the ability to use this ratio effectively.

1.3.3 Cash liquidity ratio

> Operating cash flow/Average current liabilities

This ratio indicates the company's ability to repay its current liabilities using its operating cash flows. For the Liszt company, the ratio is 50/[(63 + 57)/2] = 83.3%.

In 2009 that ratio stands at 19.0 / [(29.9 + 28.5)/2] or 66.6% for Microsoft.

1.3.4 Cash leverage ratio

> Operating cash flow/Average total liabilities

This ratio indicates the company's ability to repay its total liabilities using its operating cash flows. For the Liszt company, it is 50/[(218 + 302)/2] = 19.2%. For Microsoft that ratio stood, in 2009, at 19.0/[(38.3 + 36.5)/2] or more than 50%.

1.3.5 Other ratios

Investment ratio

> $$\frac{\text{Capital expenditures}}{(\text{Depreciation expense} + \text{Proceeds from sales of long-term assets})}$$

The **investment ratio** indicates the ability of the business to maintain its competitive potential (depreciation expense is a proxy for the loss of productive capability of long-term assets). A growing firm will have a ratio greater than 1.

Cash flow adequacy

> Cash flow from operations/(Long-term capital expenditures + dividends + scheduled debt reimbursements)

When the ratio is greater than 1, it is an indication that the firm is self-sufficient in its ability to maintain its productive capability. If the ratio is less than 1, it indicates a financing need that will be met by bringing in new cash from shareholders or lenders or by selling some assets.

1.3.6 Structure of each of the cash flows

In order to examine the contents of each activity, it is possible to divide each cash flow by the total cash flow of the activity. For example, the proceeds from issuance of shares can be divided by the financing cash flows, over several years if required, to understand how much the business relies on issuing new shares for its financing and the evolution of that policy. It is also important for a user of financial statements to know the relative percentage each cash flow source contributes to the total net cash increase.

2 Accounts manipulation and quality of financial statements

2.1 Principles

A major part of financial statement analysis is based on figures including net income (the 'bottom line') or other intermediate levels of measurement of earnings (such as gross margin or value added). It is therefore important to evaluate the formal quality of such figures, in other words the **quality of earnings**.[3] This quality is influenced by three factors:

- accounting methods (choice of and change in);
- accounting estimates and judgments;
- classification of exceptional (or extraordinary) items in the income statement.

These three factors, joined together, have given rise to a practice known broadly as **accounts manipulation** which encompasses **earnings management** (including **income smoothing** and **'big bath' accounting**) and **creative accounting**.

Copeland (1968: p. 101) defines manipulation as some ability to increase or decrease reported net income at will. At the same time, he implicitly acknowledges that the notion of manipulation may result from at least three types of behavioral patterns: 'income maximizers', 'income minimizers', and 'income smoothers'.

However, we believe that accounts manipulation has a broader meaning than what Copeland describes. It also includes income statement classificatory practices, presented by Barnea *et al.* (1975, 1976) and Ronen and Sadan (1975), and also those related to the balance sheet, which are far less well described in the literature (Black *et al.*, 1998). These practices represent a more important phenomenon now than when Copeland published his seminal article.

Such accounts manipulation practices are based on a common functional fixation view of share price determination, which states that accounting numbers contribute to the determination of share prices, although the neoclassic finance theory assumes that financial markets are essentially efficient and generally would 'see through' accounts manipulation engaged in by listed firms. Meanwhile, unlisted firms are not subject to the scrutiny of market analysts but they are operating in a very different institutional environment than that of listed companies and may manipulate their accounts for some other reasons, such as minimizing tax payment or 'dressing up' the accounts to facilitate obtaining a loan and/or a lower interest rate. In any case, accounts manipulation may affect both cash flow and risks perceived by analysts through the impact of any manipulation on the value of ratios.

We distinguish different streams of accounts manipulation, based on the fundamental principle that the aim of providing financial information is the reduction of the cost at which long-term capital (including equity and interest-bearing liabilities) is obtained for the firm's endeavors. This reduction is related to the perception of the firm's risk by investors, both lenders and shareholders. The first ones will demand a higher interest rate if they perceive a risk of not being repaid or of seeing the interest payment obligation unmet, while the second ones want to be compensated for the risk level they assume (they can lose all their investment if the firm is poorly managed), over and above the 'risk free' rate they could earn by investing in government securities in strong economies.

Risk for a firm is seen as being the result of at least two components:

- The firm-specific level of risk is technically measured, for listed companies, by the so-called *beta*[4] factor, which measures the relation of the firm's earnings with that of a market-wide portfolio. This measure reflects the quality of the decisions made by management in the past to prepare the firm to extract superior returns from opportunities in their market, compared to the return of others operating in the same market.
- The structural risk revealed by the equilibrium between debt and equity.

The objectives of accounts manipulation are to alter at least one of the above and thus affect the variance of earnings per share and the debt/equity ratio.

Earnings per share can be modified in two ways:

- First, by adding or removing revenues or expenses (modification of net income), and
- Second, by listing an item 'before' or 'after' the profit definition used to calculate the earnings per share (classificatory manipulations, such as excluding or including some items as either extraordinary or not).

Regarding the nature of practices, the literature has mainly discussed manipulations that are legitimate interpretations of standards, for instance, decisions on the level of accruals. But manipulation can also be of dubious legitimacy and deliberate, i.e., transactions can be designed in order to allow a preferred accounting treatment yielding the result desired. For instance, a leasing contract might be written in such a way that the leased equipment does not need to be capitalized, thus affecting the reporting of the lease expense (see Chapter 12).

2.2 The different forms of accounts manipulation

Stolowy and Breton (2004) identify four forms of accounts manipulation.

2.2.1 Earnings management

In this family of manipulation practices, management somewhat artificially manages earnings to achieve or meet some pre-established level of 'expected' earnings (e.g., analysts' expectations or forecasts, management's prior estimates, or continuation of some earnings trend) (Fern *et al.*, 1994). This can be done by modifying, in the short-term, some 'discretionary' expenses such as advertising, training costs, replenishing inventories to a normal level of service, or even R&D, to achieve the desired target income number, possibly at the expense of sacrificing the future of the firm.

2.2.2 Income smoothing

Income smoothing is mainly a reduction of the variance of the profit measure. More specifically, income smoothing has the clear objective of producing a steadily growing stream of profits by shifting the date on which some components of costs or revenues are recognized. It implies practicing earnings management, repeatedly, year after year. This form of manipulation can be, for example, the result of creating and canceling provisions (which means that, at some point, profit was large enough to allow these – possibly unjustified – provisions), or through the appropriate choice of the date of recognition of profit on long-term contracts, or through the *ad hoc* sale of inventories or long-lived assets which were undervalued. For example, this was the case for a (now defunct) firm that sold TV rights from the large inventory of (old) films it had obtained through an earlier acquisition and which were had little value on the acquisition date because there was little demand for TV content at that time. Incidentally, the firm was using this mechanism to boost the value of its shares and thus was able to easily acquire many other enterprises (which were either very profitable, cash rich, or with large accumulated tax deductible losses[5]) by floating new shares in exchange for the equity of their target (with no cash changing hands).

2.2.3 Big bath accounting

Intuitively, big bath accounting is easy to understand. When a new CEO is appointed, she or he may wish to 'clean up' the accounts (a) to start on a sound base that will facilitate obtaining, more easily, an improved income figure over that obtained under the predecessor, or (b) so as to create provisions, which will later be used to create some form of income smoothing. Such practices, consisting of drastically reducing earnings when the 'new' leadership takes over, are believed to be reassuring to shareholders in that they facilitate the creation of a future stream of positive income. (The functional fixation hypothesis is definitely not dead in the minds of the general public!). As Moore (1973: p. 100) explained, new management has a tendency to be very pessimistic about the value of certain assets or about the future profitability of currently engaged contracts. They often adjust downward, sometimes more than necessary, the value of these questionable assets or underestimate the profitability of ongoing contracts by taking the losses now and keeping the (unlikely in their eyes) possibility of profit as a possible happy surprise if it ever happens. This type of behavior is colloquially known as 'taking a bath'.

2.2.4 Creative accounting

Creative accounting is an expression that has been developed by both practitioners and commentators (journalists) of financial markets activities. Creative accounting means using accounting standards inappropriately, with the aim of misleading investors by presenting them with what they want to see, like a nice steadily increasing profit figure (the functional fixation hypothesis once again!). Creative accounting has been studied by authors like Griffiths (1986, 1995) and Smith (1996), an investment analyst, who refers to an 'accounting sleight of hand'. Mathews and Perera (1996: p. 260) include activities such as 'fiddling the books', 'cosmetic reporting' and 'window dressing the accounts' under the heading of creative accounting. Griffiths (1986) starts, in his introduction, from the assumption that: 'Every company in the country is fiddling its profits. Every set of accounts is based on books, which have been gently cooked or completely roasted'. Creative accounting has been used with various meanings and brings some confusion into the field of accounts manipulation. It mainly includes earnings management (without any reference to income smoothing) and focuses a lot on classificatory manipulations (either related to income statement or to balance sheet).

2.3 Practices

Numerous practices are available, and use different 'manipulatable' variables. There follows a non-comprehensive list of such practices. This is not a hit parade and the order in which practices are listed is not particularly significant and only corresponds to the order of chapters in this book:

- Income recognition timing (see Chapter 6).

- Changes in accounting policies (this includes many possibilities and could be considered as a generic activity – see Chapter 6).
- Accounting treatment of government grants (liability or revenue? – see Chapter 6).
- Long-term contracts: percentage of completion versus completed contract method (see Chapter 6).
- Treatment of unusual gains and losses (exceptional versus operating or extraordinary versus ordinary: classificatory manipulation; to anticipate or postpone: inter-temporal manipulation – see Chapter 6).
- Change from accelerated to straight-line depreciation (see Chapter 7).
- Capitalization (or not) of interest costs (see Chapter 7).
- R&D costs: capitalized or expensed? Expenses deferred or anticipated? (see Chapter 8).
- Discretionary accounting decisions (expenses split over several years or deferred expenses, in countries allowing this practice – see Chapter 8).
- Change in inventory valuation method (FIFO, WAC – see Chapter 9).
- Evaluation of provisions (inventories, doubtful accounts, long-term and marketable securities, loan loss, risks – see Chapters 9, 10 and 12).
- Capitalization of leases (see Chapter 12).
- Pension costs (see Chapter 12).
- Purchase versus pooling decision (see Chapter 13). Pooling was frequently used in the past although this possibility is no longer relevant, given the suppression of the possibility of using the pooling method in many countries. If an analyst carries out any historical research, he or she may encounter its occurrence.
- Merger recorded at fair value or at book value (see Chapter 13).
- Calculation of the difference arising on first consolidation (see Chapter 13).

2.4 Difference between cash-based or accrual-based earnings management

Another angle used to classify the different manipulations is to check their impacts on cash flow during the given reporting period.

2.4.1 Cash-based manipulations

Managers have much discretion when they make some business-related decisions. Normally, we assume that they are making these decisions *only* based on the strategies adopted by the board of directors of the company and on their understanding of internal and external business factors. However, they may also take advantage of this discretion and use (or abuse) these options for some non-business related causes: for example, they may try to improve the present profitability and/or financial position to the detriment of the future by: stopping (or reducing) some resource consumptions (such as advertisement, R&D or personnel training), selling prematurely some assets to realize the latent gains, or making their products more attractive to customers through abnormally generous future guarantees (the cost of servicing the guarantee obligation will occur much later and the managers may, in addition, not fully provision the corresponding ill-defined risk). In some other contexts, they may also understate the current profitability and/or financial position and defer the 'good elements' for recognition in the future by using the same techniques, but in the opposite way. These manipulations are often closely embedded or hidden into normal business decisions made by managers. They are therefore extremely difficult to detect by outsiders (shareholders, auditors, potential investors, analysts or regulators).

2.4.2 Accrual-based manipulations

These are operations related to the traditional definition of accrual accounting. Here are several examples of typical manipulation for moving the profit from future to present:

1. Reducing the depreciation and provision below the necessary level.

2. Extending or shortening the depreciable life for new acquisitions of a class of assets compared to the previous practice. This may even be done with existing assets as illustrated by the case of EDF, a giant French electrical utility, that changed the depreciable life of its nuclear power plants from 20 years to 40 years, arguing with regulatory and tax authorities that the technology had not been well understood early on and that experience showed that the expected useful life had been under-estimated (see Chapter 7).

3. Reversals of un-used provisions: canceling the provisions in the balance sheet (increasing the provision for potential assets impairment or decreasing the provision for 'risks and charges') and reducing some expenses in the current income statement.

4. Assets revaluation: increasing the value of assets and putting the difference into other comprehensive income (accumulated in equity under the heading of revaluation surplus, see IAS 16, § 39).

5. Inflated sales: inflating the sales by shipping and invoicing more goods than the customer requested and booking them into receivables until the customer either returns the excess shipment (at the seller's expense) or demand a serious rebate thus reducing future gross margin.

6. Inflated inventory: production exceeds expected sales, thus inventory grows and 'immobilizes' part of the period manufacturing and procurement fixed cost in the inventory, thus reducing the cost of goods sold in the income statement.

7. Capitalization: eliminating an expense in the current income statement by capitalizing it as an asset. The depreciation expense of that asset will be much lower in the current income statement that the expense would have been (e.g., R&D capitalization).

In the same vein, a company may postpone the profit from present to future by using the above-mentioned mechanisms but in the opposite way. These accrual-based manipulations (i.e., non-cash, or having no impact on cash) will cause a large deviation between accrual-based accounting earnings and cash flows in the same period. The accrual to cash gap will be further analyzed in section 3.

2.5 Can accounts manipulation remove the usefulness of financial statements?

Some analysts believe that financial statements have no value because of so many possibilities of carrying out such manipulations (many anecdotes abound to support the reality of their existence). We do not agree with such a radical (and pessimistic) conclusion.

When prepared in accordance with GAAP, financial statements are always useful. The user must, however, be aware of the limitations placed on their reliability. The notes to financial statements are a very good source of information that can be used to cross-check and validate the reported figures and to restate, if needed, the financial statements so as to perform comparative analyses. Moreover, the consistency accounting principle (see Chapter 4) often works as a good limitation to manipulations. One should also never forget that most of the manipulations, principally those based on 'cooking the books' with such actions as constituting inappropriate provisions, will, inevitably, have an opposite effect at the time of their reversal. This is also an efficient source of limitation to the temptation a manager may feel in order to 'look better'. Alas, by the time the subterfuge is discovered, the author of the manipulation may have already moved on … or been promoted.

In addition to limits created by IFRS or any GAAP, the role of auditors is, among other things, to help verify that no manipulative practice took place during the period covered by the financial statements. We should also point out the responsibility of all directors (executive and non-executive members of the board) in conforming to standards and the increasing liability that rests on them, especially since the governance regulations that followed the Enron scandal, for the content of the companies' reports (see Chapter 18).

Last, but certainly not least important, common sense on the part of the financial information user should help detect earnings manipulations: it is completely improbable that a business, large or small, can deliver, year after year, a steady growth of its earnings. 'Investor beware' should be the rule: if it is too good to be true, it probably is not true.[6]

3 Using the indirect method of operating cash flow as a tool to analyze the earnings quality of a company

The indirect method of calculation of the cash flow from operating activities (see Figure 14.4 in Chapter 14) describes how one can link accrual-based net income to the net cash surplus the company obtained for the same period, under cash-based accounting.

In a normal business situation and over several periods, a positive and significant correlation between net income and operating cash flow for the same period and convergence of their cumulated value would be logical. When, instead of converging the two quantities drift apart, we can assert the earnings are of low quality.

The explanation of the possible drift between net operating income and cash flow from operating activities (i.e., the root causes of low earnings quality) can be found in the three groups of adjustments used to progress from income to cash flow from operations (non-cash items, gain/loss on sale of fixed assets and changes in inventories/receivables/payables).

Non-cash items impact positively and negatively on the net income of the period but have, by definition, no influence on the cash position at the end of the period. If a company uses any of accrual-based earnings manipulations developed in sections 2.3 and 2.4.2, the income stream and the cash flow stream will be incoherent. For example, in 2001, the French company Vivendi Universal recorded a net loss of €13.5 billion while reporting a positive cash flow from operating activities of €4.5 billion. The reason for the incoherence was an abnormally high amount of depreciation and amortization (€19 billion) caused by the write-off of overvalued goodwill.

Gains or losses from the sale of the firm's assets are often cash-based. They are, however, not related to the core business of the company and will not be recurring. For example, in the interim report of the first six months of 2007, the Chinese home appliance maker, Hisense Kelon Electrical Holdings Co. Ltd, reported a half-year profit of 96 million RMB. However, a close analysis revealed that 92 million RMB, or nearly 96%, came from the disposal of land and buildings.

Changes in inventories/receivables/payables, as seen in section 2.4.2 and often referred to as 'working capital need management' may signal likely errors in management that may lead to abnormal divergence between income and cash. For example, a firm may report a high net income but a low cash flow from operating activities. This might be due to possibly abnormally increased inventories or receivables and/or surprisingly decreased payables. In the best case, the firm did not manage its working capital need efficiently and/or lost the bargaining power it held with its suppliers or customers (not a sign of long-term earnings quality, either); in the worst case, it 'cooked' its earnings by booking anticipated sales and/or artificially reduced COGS (once again, not a good sign of long-term earnings quality). For example, when the world's third largest rail infrastructure engineering firm, China Railway Group Ltd, went public in November 2007, it reported for the six first months of 2007, a profit of 1.5 billion RMB but a negative cash flow from operating activities of 4.4 billion RMB. An analysis of the application of the indirect method in the calculation of the cash flow revealed that cash had been reduced by 12 billion RMB because of inventory increases and by 1.3 billion RMB because of accounts receivables increases, while the increase of payables only brought 5.5 billion RMB of extra cash. In such a dubious situation, investors may seriously doubt the future earnings quality of the firm as reported by the managerial team in place at the time.

The analysis above shows that the indirect method of operating cash flow can be a very powerful tool in detecting some earnings management practices and in better assessing the earnings quality of the firm. In summary, if a business relies largely on some non-cash, non-core or non-recurring items to boost its profit of the current year, the financial statement user can legitimately place a big question mark on the sustainability of the firm's performance in the future.

The use of the indirect method of cash flow calculation to detect manipulations has, like any tools, some limits. Some earnings management practices cannot be detected by using this approach: expense capitalization not only makes the expense 'disappear' from the current year's income statement (except for the related amortization expense, which may be hard to detect in the total amortization expense), but, since it is now recognized as an asset acquisition, that 'expense' has been shifted from the calculation of the cash outflow from operating activities to the cash outflow due to/from investing activities.

Key points

- The algebraic sign of the operating, investing and financing cash flows is, in itself, often full of useful information.
- The available cash flow is defined as the addition of the cash generated by operations and the cash flow generated by/used to finance the investing activity of the firm.
- Free cash flow is the difference between available cash flow and dividends paid. The same term is sometimes used to refer to the difference between cash flow from operations and the minimum level of cash used to maintain competitiveness of the firm (including dividends paid).
- Several ratios capture the dynamics of the statement of cash flows. The most commonly analyzed ratios include the 'cash flow as percentage of sales' and 'cash flow yield' (operating cash flow/net income).

- The 'quality of earnings' is influenced by (1) accounting methods changes; (2) accounting estimates, especially of required provisions; and (3) classification of exceptional (or extraordinary) items in the income statement.
- 'Accounts manipulation' is the result of earnings management including income smoothing and 'big bath' accounting, as well as a series of actions called creative accounting.
- Earnings management can be cash-based or accrual-based.
- The indirect method of calculation of the cash flow from operations can be used as a tool to analyze the earnings quality of a business and detect some of the deceptive income manipulations practices a management team may have engaged in.

Review (solutions are at the back of the book)

Review 17.1 Mitsubishi Electric*

Topic: Understanding and analyzing a statement of cash flows

Mitsubishi Electric Corporation is a multinational concern headquartered in Tokyo, Japan. It develops, manufactures and distributes a broad range of electrical equipment in fields as diverse as home appliances and space electronics.

The company's 2009 total sales revenue is broken down between its principal lines of business (or business segments) as shown in the following table:

Business segments sales revenue (2009)	¥ (millions)	%
Energy and electric systems	1,043,633	25.1
Industrial automation systems	851,688	20.5
Information and communication systems	582,146	14.0
Electronic devices	166,969	4.0
Home appliances	915,710	22.0
Others	596,091	14.3
Subtotal	**4,156,237**	**100.0**
Eliminations [of intra-segment transactions]	(491,118)	
Consolidated total	**3,665,119**	

The financial statements are reported in conformity with the US GAAP. The following table presents the statement of cash flows of the group for the period 2007–2009 (source: Annual reports 2009 and 2008).

Consolidated statements of cash flows

(in ¥ million)	2009	2008	2007
Cash flows from operating activities			
Net income	12,167	157,977	123,080
Adjustments to reconcile net income to net cash provided by operating activities:			
Depreciation	148,018	136,283	130,130
Impairment losses of property, plant and equipment	28,704	3,043	11,384
Loss from sales and disposal of property, plant and equipment, net	1,832	2,544	6,206
Deferred income taxes	20,137	5,442	9,553
Loss (gain) from sales of securities and other, net	(605)	(2,161)	(4,214)
Devaluation losses of securities and other, net	18,556	1,132	1,917
Equity in earnings of affiliated companies	67,715	(10,675)	(18,507)
Decrease (increase) in trade receivables	108,729	(29,936)	(35,474)
Decrease (increase) in inventories	(37,726)	(16,531)	(15,954)
Decrease (increase) in other assets	(8,800)	(4,579)	964
Increase (decrease) in trade payables	(133,954)	26,890	19,252
Increase (decrease) in accrued expenses and retirement and severance benefits	(43,192)	(8,312)	(33,753)
Increase (decrease) in other liabilities	(39,080)	(12,582)	78,135
Other, net	38,638	10,334	1,911
Net cash provided by operating activities	**181,139**	**258,869**	**274,630**
Cash flows from investing activities			
Capital expenditure	(141,434)	(144,623)	(140,557)
Proceeds from sale of property, plant and equipment	4,340	3,293	4,782
Purchase of short-term investments and investment securities	(86,749)	(42,174)	(24,115)
Proceeds from sale of short-term investments and investment securities	13,693	32,191	28,163
Decrease (increase) in loans receivable	146	21,405	(18,973)
Other, net	(4,935)	(2,442)	(4,899)
Net cash used in investing activities	**(214,939)**	**(132,350)**	**(155,599)**
Cash flows from financing activities			
Proceeds from long-term debt	102,940	63,620	32,200
Repayment of long-term debt	(112,021)	(107,017)	(154,250)
Increase (decrease) in short-term debt, net	122,024	(50,530)	50,496
Dividends paid	(27,904)	(25,758)	(19,317)

(in Yen million)	2009	2008	2007
Purchase of treasury stock	(205)	(139)	(132)
Reissuance of treasury stock	59	68	162
Other, net	–	–	2,107
Net cash provided by (used in) financing activities	**84,893**	**(119,756)**	**(88,734)**
Effect of exchange rate changes on cash and cash equivalents	(26,788)	(15,092)	7,829
Net increase (decrease) in cash and cash equivalents	24,305	(8,329)	38,126
Cash and cash equivalents at beginning of year	334,311	342,640	304,514
Cash and cash equivalents at end of year	**358,616**	**334,311**	**342,640**

From the balance sheet and income statement, we have extracted the following information:

(in ¥ million)	2009	2008	2007
Sales revenue	3,665,119	4,049,818	3,855,745
Net earnings	12,167	157,977	123,080
Current liabilities	1,413,015	1,505,901	1,529,838
Total liabilities	2,432,183	2,393,860	2,332,661

Required

Step one: Understanding

1. Which method (direct or indirect) was used to compute the operating cash flow?

2. Compute the potential cash flow (see this concept in Chapter 14).

3. Why does the statement use the expression 'decrease (increase)' to describe changes in trade receivables, inventories and prepaid expenses while it uses the expression 'increase (decrease)' when referring to changes in trade payables and other liabilities?

4. How are short-term investments reported? What could have been another legitimate possibility? Comment on why they chose the method they did over another.

5. Short-term debt can be considered equivalent to 'bank overdrafts'. Comment on the way they are reported in the above statements. What would have been another possibility?

Step two: Analyzing

6. Analyze the statement of cash flows over the period.

Review 17.2 Bartok Company (1)

Topic: Comparative financial analysis – statement of cash flows

You receive information extracted from the financial statements of three companies.

	Company 1	Company 2	Company 3
Increase in capital	800	–	700
Purchase of tangible fixed assets	900	900	1,400
Purchase of financial assets	700	–	400
Increase in long-term debts	100	1 500	1,100
Repayment of long-term debts	–	300	–
Potential cash flow*	1,000	400	100
Dividends paid	200	600	–

*Net income adjusted for non-cash items.

Required

1. From the information, prepare the statement of cash flows.

2. Comment on the resulting statements.

Assignments

Assignment 17.1
Multiple-choice questions

Select the right answer (one possible answer, unless otherwise stated).

1. Generally, the operating cash flow is expected to be negative
   (a) True
   (b) False

2. How is the available cash flow calculated?
   (a) Cash flow from operating activities (assumed to be positive) + Cash flow from investing activities (assumed to be negative)
   (b) Cash flow from investing activities + Cash flow from financing activities
   (c) Cash flow from operating activities + Cash flow from financing activities
   (d) Cash flow from operating activities – Dividends paid

3. How is free cash flow calculated?
   (a) Cash flow from operating activities + Cash flow from investing activities
   (b) Available cash flow + Cash flow from financing activities
   (c) Available cash flow – Dividends paid
   (d) Available cash flow – Cash flow from financing activities

4. Which of the following ratios is the cash liquidity ratio?
   (a) Operating cash flow/Average current assets
   (b) Financing cash flow/Average current liabilities
   (c) Financing cash flow/Average current assets
   (d) Operating cash flow/Average current liabilities

5. What ratio is used to calculate the 'cash flow yield'?
   (a) Operating cash flow/Net sales
   (b) Operating cash flow/Interest paid
   (c) Operating cash flow/Net income
   (d) Operating cash flow/Average current liabilities

6. Which type of accounts manipulation mainly consists of a reduction in the variance of the profit?
   (a) Creative accounting
   (b) Earnings management
   (c) Income smoothing
   (d) Big bath accounting

7. Which factor(s) influence(s) the quality of earnings?
   (a) Accounting methods.
   (b) Accounting estimates.
   (c) Classification of exceptional items in the income statement
   (d) All of these

8. Cash-based earnings management is easier to detect than accrual-based earnings management
   (a) True
   (b) False

9. Which statements below are not true? (several possible answers)
   (a) The non-operating income from assets disposals is normally non-recurring in the future
   (b) It is difficult to manipulate net income since it is accrual-based
   (c) A sharp increase of receivables during the period may reveal that the company has a weakened negotiation power vis-à-vis its customers
   (d) When operating cash flow is much lower than net income, we may expect a higher growth from the company in the future

10. Which manipulation cannot be detected by comparing net income and operating cash flow?
    (a) R&D capitalization
    (b) Increasing profit by selling some lands
    (c) Reducing profit by exaggerating depreciation/amortization expenses
    (d) Inflating sales by booking some fake sales (without cash inflows)

Assignment 17.2
Janacek Company (4)

Topic: Statement of cash flows analysis

The Janacek Company has a commercial activity in the sector of beauty products and cosmetics.

Required

Analyze the statement of cash flows prepared in assignment 14.2 Janacek Company (1), in Chapter 14.

Assignment 17.3
Ericsson*

Topic: Statement of cash flows analysis

The company is a provider of telecommunications equipment and related services to mobile and fixed network operators globally. Over 1,000 networks in 140 countries utilize their network equipment and 40 percent of all mobile calls are made through their systems. They are one of the few companies worldwide that can offer end-to-end solutions for all major mobile communication standards. Through the Sony Ericsson Mobile Communications joint venture they offer a range of mobile devices, including those supporting multimedia applications and other services allowing richer communication.

Ericsson operates in three segments:

- Networks, which involves communications infrastructure and related deployment services.
- Professional services, which includes managed services, services for network systems integration, consulting and education and customer support services.
- Multimedia, which involves networked media and messaging, enterprise applications, revenue management, service delivery platforms (SDP) and mobile platforms.

The recent evolution of sales by business segments is the following:

Ericsson (in SEK billion)	2008	2007	2006	2005
Networks	142,050	128,985	127,518	114,134
Professional services	48,978	42,892	36,813	26,324
Multimedia	17,902	15,903	13,877	10,496
Unallocated	–	–	1,613	2,268
Total	208,930	187,780	179,821	153,222

Ericsson (in % of total)	2008	2007	2006	2005
Networks	68	69	71	74
Professional services	23	23	20	17
Multimedia	9	8	8	7
Unallocated	0	0	1	1
Total	**100**	**100**	**100**	**100**

Below is the statement of cash flows for the years 2008, 2007, 2006 and 2005 (source: Ericsson, Annual reports 2008, 2007, 2006, 2005). The Ericsson financial statements comply with IFRS.

Consolidated statements of cash flows

January–December (in SEK million)	2008	2007	2006	2005
Operating activities				
Net income	11,667	22,135	26,436	24,460
Adjustments to reconcile net income to cash	14,318	7,172	6,060	10,700
	25,985	29,307	32,496	35,160
Changes in operating net assets				
Inventories	–3,927	–445	–2,553	–3,668
Customer finance, current and non-current	549	365	1,186	–641
Trade receivables	–11,434	–7,467	–10,563	–5,874
Provisions and post-employment benefits	3,830	–4,401	–3,729	–15,574
Other operating assets and liabilities, net	8,997	1,851	1,652	7,266
	–1,985	–10,097	–14,007	–18,491
Cash flow from operating activities (1)	**24,000**	**19,210**	**18,489**	**16,669**
Investing activities				
Investments in property, plant and equipment	–4,133	–4,319	–3,827	–3,365
Sales of property, plant and equipment	1,373	152	185	362
Acquisitions of subsidiaries and other operations	–74	–26,292	–18,078	–1,210
Divestments of subsidiaries and other operations	1,910	84	3,086	30
Product development	–1,409	–1,053	–1,353	–1,174
Other investing activities	944	396	–1,070	13
Short-term investments	–7,155	3,499	6,180	6,375
Cash flow from investing activities (2)	**–8,544**	**–27,533**	**–14,877**	**1,031**
Cash flow before financing activities	**15,456**	**–8,323**	**3,612**	**17,700**
Financing activities				
Proceeds from issuance of borrowings	5,245	15,587	1,290	657
Repayment of borrowings	–4,216	–1,291	–9,510	–2,784
Sale of own stock and options exercised	3	94	124	174
Dividends paid	–8,240	–8,132	–7,343	–4,133
Cash flow from financing activities (3)	**–7,208**	**6,258**	**–15,439**	**–6,086**
Effect of exchange rate changes on cash (4)	1,255	406	58	–288
Net change in cash [(1) + (2) + (3) +(4)]	9,503	–1,659	–11,769	11,326
Cash and cash equivalents, beginning of period	28,310	29,969	41,738	30,412
Cash and cash equivalents, end of period	**37,813**	**28,310**	**29,969**	**41,738**

Required

Step one: Understanding

1. Which method is used for computing the cash flow from operating activities?

2. What does the 'Changes in operating net assets' represent?

3. Compute the potential cash flow (see this concept in Chapter 14).

4. What does the 'Cash flow before financing activities' represent?

Step two: Analyzing

5. Prepare an analysis of the statement of cash flows.

Assignment 17.4
Sinopec*

Topic: Statement of cash flows analysis

China Petroleum & Chemical Corporation (known as 'Sinopec'), introduced in Chapter 15, is an integrated energy and chemical company. The principal operations of Sinopec Corp. and its subsidiaries include:

- Exploring for and developing, producing and trading crude oil and natural gas
- Processing crude oil into refined oil products, producing refined oil products and trading, transporting, distributing and marketing refined oil products
- Producing, distributing and trading petrochemical products.

The significant accounting policies adopted by the group are in compliance with the China Accounting Standards for Business Enterprises.

Below are the statements of cash flows of the group for the years ended 31 December 2005 to 2008 (source: Annual reports 2006–2008).

(in RMB million)	2008	2007	2006	2005
Cash flows from operating activities				
Cash received from sale of goods and rendering of services	1,717,060	1,400,348	1,239,086	965,505
Rentals received	491	370	384	387
Grants received	53,705	–	5,161	9,415
Other cash received relating to operating activities	4,738	2,793	3,700	3,572
Sub-total of cash inflows	1,775,994	1,403,511	1,248,331	978,879
Cash paid for goods and services	(1,544,176)	(1,135,587)	(1,030,412)	(790,429)
Cash paid for operating leases	(7,717)	(6,764)	(6,075)	(5,629)
Cash paid to and for employees	(27,773)	(22,255)	(20,414)	(18,710)
Value added tax paid	(35,538)	(41,011)	(31,580)	(27,928)
Income tax paid	(21,072)	(27,674)	(19,586)	(20,998)
Taxes paid other than value added tax and income tax	(48,246)	(30,965)	(27,332)	(17,288)
Other cash paid relating to operating activities	(16,589)	(15,005)	(14,062)	(12,934)
Sub-total of cash outflows	(1,701,111)	(1,279,261)	(1,149,461)	(893,916)
Net cash inflow from operating activities	**74,883**	**124,250**	**98,870**	**84,963**
Cash flows from investing activities				
Cash received from disposal of investments	1,366	1,441	569	417
Dividends received	3,682	2,657	647	668
Net cash received from disposal of fixed assets and intangible assets	602	446	358	510
Cash received on maturity of time deposits with financial institutions	1,358	3,340	1,337	1,462
Other cash received relating to investing activities	446	404	540	386
Sub-total of cash inflows	7,454	8,288	3,451	3,443
Cash paid for acquisition of fixed assets and intangible assets	(108,575)	(110,638)	(77,375)	(65,031)
Cash paid for acquisition of fixed assets and intangible assets of jointly controlled entities	–	–	–	(2,474)
Cash paid for acquisition of investments	(3,089)	(1,581)	(3,761)	(3,605)
Cash paid for acquisition of time deposits with financial institutions	(1,442)	(3,373)	(916)	(565)
Cash paid for acquisition of subsidiaries and minority interests, net	(598)	(7,468)	(21,971)	(3,128)
Cash paid for acquisition of subsidiaries	–	–	–	(4,324)
Sub-total of cash outflows	(113,704)	(123,060)	(104,023)	(79,127)
Net cash outflow from investing activities	**(106,250)**	**(114,772)**	**(100,572)**	**(75,684)**
Cash flows from financing activities				
Cash received from contribution from minority shareholders of subsidiaries	1,137	1,223	1,255	129
Cash received from issuance of convertible bonds, net of issuing expenses	29,850	11,368	–	9,875
Cash received from issuance of corporate bonds	15,000	35,000	22,689	550,557
Cash received from borrowings	1,147,279	768,039	772,954	3,954
Sub-total of cash inflows	1,193,266	815,630	796,898	564,515
Cash repayments of corporate bonds	(10,000)	(12,000)	(21,000)	–
Cash repayments of borrowings	(1,125,333)	(788,793)	(761,389)	(557,432)
Cash paid for dividends, profits distribution or interest	(23,651)	(20,843)	(19,761)	(17,365)
Dividends paid to minority shareholders of subsidiaries	(1,404)	(593)	(722)	(1,611)
Distributions to Sinopec Group Company	(2,180)	(2,182)	–	–
Sub-total of cash outflows	(1,162,568)	(824,411)	(802,872)	(576,408)
Net cash inflow/(outflow) from financing activities	**30,698**	**(8,781)**	**(5,974)**	**(11,893)**
Effects of changes in foreign exchange rate	(79)	(64)	(25)	(22)
Net (decrease)/increase in cash and cash equivalents	**(748)**	**633**	**(7,701)**	**(2,636)**

The notes to the financial statements include some 'supplemental information to the statement of cash flows'.

Note – Reconciliation of net profit to cash flows from operating activities

(in RMB million)	2008	2007	2006	2005
Net profit	26,115	58,721	52,086	39,558
Add: Impairment losses on assets	16,617	6,975	1,004	–
Impairment losses on fixed assets	–	–	–	1,851
Impairment losses on long-term investments	–	–	–	77
Provision/(reversal of) for allowance for doubtful accounts	–	–	–	(144)
Provision for diminution in value of inventories	–	–	–	82
Depreciation of fixed assets	45,012	42,216	33,713	30,845
Amortization of intangible assets	841	1,129	614	986
Dry hole costs	4,236	6,060	3,960	2,992
Net gain on disposal of fixed assets	(248)	(766)	1,647	2,202
Fair value (gain)/loss	(3,969)	3,211	–	–
Financial expenses	8,723	4,890	5,780	5,266
Investment income	(980)	(5,756)	(3,769)	(890)
(Increase)/decrease in deferred tax assets	(2,377)	(3,293)	(966)	(1,733)
Decrease in deferred tax liabilities	(337)	(871)	(90)	–
Decrease/ (increase) in inventories	12,336	(24,324)	(2,993)	(25,078)
Decrease/ (increase) in operating receivables	12,284	(12,928)	(2,540)	(2,256)
(Decrease)/increase in operating payables	(43,370)	48,986	9,527	28,303
Minority interests	–	–	897	2,902
Net cash flow from operating activities	74,883	124,250	98,870	84,963

From the consolidated financial statements, the following additional data was collected:

RMB millions	2008	2007	2006	2005
Income from principal operations (sales)	1,420,321	1,173,869	1,034,816	799,115
Net profit	26,115	58,721	52,983	39,558
Current liabilities	234,050	222,190	212,776	167,792
Total liabilities	363,075	344,065	320,921	275,566

Required

Step one: Understanding

1. What is the method used to compute the cash flow from operating activities?

2. What does the note represent? How useful is it to users of financial information?

3. Compute the potential cash flow (see this concept in Chapter 14).

4. What inconsistency do you notice between the note and the additional information?

Step two: Analyzing

5. Analyze the statement of cash flows over the period. You can use the additional information provided in the above table (source: Annual reports 2006 –2008).

Assignment 17.5
Procter & Gamble (2)

Topic: Statement of cash flows analysis

Procter & Gamble Co., is an American multinational corporation that manufactures a wide range of consumer goods, such as laundry and homecare (Ariel, Mr Clean), feminine protection (Always), healthcare, food and beverages, beauty care (Head & Shoulders), and baby care (Pampers).[7] The following consolidated statement of cash flows are found in its 2009, 2008 and 2007 annual reports.

Consolidated statements of cash flows

Years ended 30 June (in US$ million)	2009	2008	2007	2006	2005
Cash and cash equivalents, beginning of year	3,313	5,354	6,693	6,389	4,232
Operating activities					
Net earnings	13,436	12,075	10,340	8,684	6,923
Depreciation and amortization	3,082	3,166	3,130	2,627	1,884
Share-based compensation expense	516	555	668	585	524
Deferred income taxes	596	1,214	253	(112)	564
Gain on sale of businesses	(2,377)	(284)	(153)	–	–
Change in accounts receivable	415	432	(729)	(524)	(86)
Change in inventories	721	(1,050)	(389)	383	(644)
Change in accounts payable, accrued and other liabilities	(742)	297	(278)	230	(101)
Change in other operating assets and liabilities	(758)	(1,270)	(151)	(508)	(498)
Other	30	(127)	719	10	113
Total operating activities	14,919	15,008	13,410	11,375	8,679
Investing activities					
Capital expenditures	(3,238)	(3,046)	(2,945)	(2,667)	(2,181)
Proceeds from asset sales	1,087	928	281	882	517
Acquisitions, net of cash acquired	(368)	(381)	(492)	171	(572)
Change in investments	166	(50)	673	884	(100)
Total investing activities	(2,353)	(2,549)	(2,483)	(730)	(2,336)
Financing activities					
Dividends to shareholders	(5,044)	(4,655)	(4,209)	(3,703)	(2,731)
Change in short-term debt	(2,420)	2,650	9,006	(8,627)	2,016
Additions to long-term debt	4,926	7,088	4,758	22,545	3,108
Reductions of long-term debt	(2,587)	(11,747)	(17,929)	(5,282)	(2,013)
Treasury purchases	(6,370)	(10,047)	(5,578)	(16,830)	(5,026)
Impact of stock options and other	681	1,867	1,499	1,319	521
Total financing activities	(10,814)	(14,844)	(12,453)	(10,578)	(4,125)
Effect of exchange rate changes on cash and cash equivalents	(284)	344	187	237	(61)
Change in cash and cash equivalents	1,468	(2,041)	(1,339)	304	2,157
Cash and cash equivalents, end of year	4,781	3,313	5,354	6,693	6,389

Required

Step one: Understanding

1. What is unusual about this statement as regards its presentation of cash and cash equivalents at the beginning and the end of year?

2. Which method is used for computing the cash flow from operating activities?

3. Why are the operating cash flows larger than the net income each year?

Step two: Analyzing

4. With the help of the additional data provided in the following table (source: Annual reports 2007–2009), prepare an analysis of the statement of cash flows.

(in US$ million)	2009	2008	2007	2006	2005
Cash payments for					
Interest	1,226	1,373	1,330	1,045	783
Income taxes	3,248	3,499	4,116	2,869	2,644
Assets acquired through non-cash capital leases	8	13	41	363	68
Gillette acquisition funded by share issuance	–	–	–	53,371	–
Divestiture of coffee business in exchange for shares of P&G stock	2,466	–	–	–	–
Sales	79,029	81,748	74,832	68,222	56,741
Net earnings	13,436	12,075	10,340	8,684	6,923
Current liabilities	30,901	30,958	30,717	19,985	25,039
Total liabilities	71,734	74,498	71,254	72,787	44,050

Assignment 17.6

International Marine Containers (Group) Ltd. (CIMC)*

Topic: Statement of cash flows and earnings quality

China International Marine Containers (Group) Ltd (CIMC) defines its mission as being its customers' partner for modern transportation. It manufactures and sells transportation equipment, such as containers, road transport vehicles and airport ground-handling equipment. It also provides logistical support to its clients. CIMC is the leading firm of transportation equipment manufacturing and services based in China.[8] CIMC was founded in January 1980 in Shenzhen. CIMC went public in 1993 and has been listed in Shenzhen Stock Exchange since 1994. The main shareholders are COSCO and China Merchants Holdings.

The income statement (with common-size analysis) and the computation of operating cash flow based on the indirect method from CIMC's interim report from 1 January to 30 June 2007 are provided below.

Additional data extracted from CIMC's interim report from 1 January to 30 June 2007 include:

1. In the segment reporting its sales, CIMC states that 24.49% are to North America, 36.42% to Europe, 38.64% to Asia and 0.45% to other parts of the world.

2. Note 42 on 'financial expenses', reports a loss of 81 million RMB in foreign exchange during the first half of 2007 (only 4 million for the same period in 2006); more than 100 million RMB net interest expenses during the first half of 2007 (only 11 million for the same period in 2006).

3. Note 44 on 'gains from changes in fair values', reports 124 million RMB for the unrealized gains of trading securities during the first half of 2007 (only 39 million for the same period in 2006).

4. Note 45 on 'investment income', reports 164 million RMB for the realized gains of trading securities during the first half of 2007 (109 million for the same period in 2006).

Additional data:

1. From 1 January to 30 June 2007, the Chinese Yuan or RMB appreciated 2.53% against US dollar.

2. From 1 January to 30 June 2007, the leading Shanghai and Shenzhen 300 Shares Index increased 84.82%.

3. According to the format of statement of cash flows proposed by the China Ministry of Finance, the cash outflow for financial expenses is classified within financing activities.

Required

1. In the income statement, compare the performance between 2006 and 2007 and comment.

2. By linking the net profit to the operating cash flow, comment on the earnings quality for the observation period.

Income statement

	Jan.–June 2007 RMB	Jan.–June 2006 RMB	Jan.– June 2007 %	Jan.–June 2006 %
Turnover	23,388,134,138	15,028,733,308	100.0	100.0
Cost of operations	(20,749,698,661)	(13,079,972,536)	(88.7)	(87.0)
Business tax and surcharges	(5,321,598)	(6,657,843)	(0.0)	(0.0)
Operation expenses	(608,491,294)	(462,033,991)	(2.6)	(3.1)
General and administrative expenses	(792,825,403)	(394,807,738)	(3.4)	(2.6)
Financial expenses	(193,179,840)	(22,318,606)	(0.8)	(0.1)
Loss of impairment on assets	(51,844,930)	208,915,235	(0.2)	1.4
Gains from changes in fair values	204,555,282	39,543,161	0.9	0.3
Investment income*	251,985,973	127,743,101	1.1	0.8
Operating profit	1,443,313,667	1,439,144,091	6.2	9.6
Non-operating income	6,592,038	162,697,319	0.0	1.1
Non-operating expenses**	(4,438,147)	(4,582,129)	(0.0)	(0.0)
Total profit	1,445,467,558	1,597,259,281	6.2	10.6
Income taxes	(87,338,346)	(94,006,362)	(0.4)	(0.6)
Net profit	1,358,129,212	1,503,252,919	5.8	10.0
Profit attributable to equity holders of the Company	1,323,066,535	1,385,998,080	5.7	9.2
Minority interest	35,062,677	117,254,839	0.1	0.8
*Including: share of profit of associates and jointly controlled entities	38,650,103	8,426,342	0.2	0.1
**Including: loss on disposal of non-current assets	496,337	1,789,919	0.0	0.0

Supplementary information to consolidated statement of cash flows

	Jan.– June 2007 RMB	Jan.– June 2006 RMB
Reconciliation of net profit to cash flows from operating activities		
Net profit	**1,358,129,212**	**1,503,252,919**
Provision for asset impairment	51,844,930	(208,915,235)
Depreciation of fixed assets	184,613,347	163,378,769
Amortization of intangible assets	57,156,563	8,363,106
Increase in long-term prepaid expenses	15,105,505	5,694,079
Losses on disposal of fixed assets, intangible assets and long-term assets	289,034	1,656,736
Gains from changes in fair values (deduct: gains)	(204,555,282)	(39,543,161)
Financial expenses	280,404,292	45,119,294
Losses arising from investments (deduct: gains)	(251,985,973)	(127,743,101)
Decrease in deferred tax assets and liabilities (deduct: increase)	(16,382,410)	18,180,137
Decrease in inventories (deduct: increase)	(2,038,454,739)	(1,743,154,439)
Decrease in operating receivables (deduct: increase)	(4,768,053,427)	(2,223,439,185)
Increase in operating payables	3,645,637,896	2,918,538,421
Net cash flow from operating activities	**(1,686,251,053)**	**321,388,340**

References

Barnea, A., Ronen, J. and Sadan, S. (1975) 'The implementation of accounting objectives: An application to extraordinary items', *The Accounting Review,* January: 58–68.

Barnea, A., Ronen, J. and Sadan, S. (1976) 'Classificatory smoothing of income with extraordinary items', *The Accounting Review* January: 110–22.

Black, E.L., Sellers, K.F. and Manly, T.S. (1998) 'Earnings management using asset sales: An international study of countries allowing noncurrent asset revaluation', *Journal of Business Finance & Accounting* 25(9/10): 1287–1317.

Copeland, R.M. (1968) 'Income smoothing', *Journal of Accounting Research, Empirical Research in Accounting, Selected Studies*, 6(Supplement): 101–16.

Fern, R.H., Brown, B. and Dickey, S.W. (1994) 'An empirical test of politically-motivated income smoothing in the oil refining industry', *Journal of Applied Business Research* 10(1) Winter: 92–99.

Griffiths, I. (1986) *Creative Accounting,* Irwin, London.

Griffiths, I. (1995) *New Creative Accounting*, Macmillan, London.

Mathews, M.R. and Perera, M.H.B. (1996) *Accounting Theory and Development*, Melbourne: Nelson/ITPC.

Moore, M.L. (1973) 'Management changes and discretionary accounting decisions', *Journal of Accounting Research* (Spring): 100–107.

Ronen, J. and Sadan, S. (1975) 'Classificatory smoothing: Alternative income models', *Journal of Accounting Research* (Spring): 133–49.

Smith, T. (1996) *Accounting for growth – Stripping the camouflage from company accounts* (2nd edn), Century Business, London.

Stolowy, H. and Breton, G. (2004) 'Accounts manipulation: A literature review and proposed conceptual framework', *Review of Accounting and Finance* 3(1): 5–65.

Further reading

Adhikari, A. and Duru, A. (2006) 'Voluntary disclosure of free cash flow information', *Accounting Horizons* 20(4): 311–32.

Broome, O.W. (2004) 'Statement of cash flows: Time for change!', *Financial Analysts Journal* 60(2): 16–22.

Cheng, C.S.A., Liu, C.S. and Schaefer, T.F. (1997) 'The value-relevance of SFAS No. 95 cash flows from operations as assessed by security market effects', Accounting Horizons, 11(3): 1–15.

Clinch, G., Sidhu, B. and Sin, S. (2002) 'The usefulness of direct and indirect cash flow disclosures', *Review of Accounting Studies* 7(4): 383–402.

Garcia Osma, B. (2008) 'Board independence and real earnings management: The case of R&D expenditure', *Corporate Governance: An International Review* 16(2): 116–31.

Jeanjean, T. and Stolowy, H. (2008) 'Do accounting standards matter: A exploratory analysis of earnings management before and after IFRS adoption', *Journal of Accounting and Public Policy* 27(6): 480–94.

Krishnan, G.V. and Largay III, J.A. (2000) 'The predictive ability of direct method cash flow information', *Journal of Business Finance & Accounting* 27(1/2): 215–45.

Kwok, H. (2002) 'The effect of cash flow statement format on lenders' decisions', *The International Journal of Accounting* 37(3): 347–62.

Markarian, G., Pozza, L. and Prencipe, A. (2008) 'Capitalization of R&D costs and earnings management: Evidence from Italian listed companies', *The International Journal of Accounting* 43(3): 246–67.

Additional material on the website

Go to http://www.cengage.co.uk/stolowy3 for further information, journal entries and extra assignments for each chapter.

Notes

1. The functional fixation hypothesis (linked to technical analysis, i.e. assumes that past performance is a good predictor of future performance) is challenged by many theories, including the Capital Asset Pricing Model (CAPM) developed by Nobel Prize in Economics winner Bill Sharpe and the 'Random Walk Theory' of Burton G. Malkiel. Both are central references in any market finance course, but are outside the scope of this book.

2. Known exceptions are start-up companies, and especially biotech or dot.com firms that require a large discretionary investment in operating facilities up-front and build their business slowly. When speaking of many dot.com firms before the year 2000 crash or of many weakened airlines such as TWA (which disappeared in 2000) or United Airlines from 2003 to early 2006, or General Motors for much of the period between 2005 and 2009 (and probably beyond), their negative cash flow from operating activities (expressed on a per month basis) is referred to in the economic press as their 'cash burn rate'. Such firms either have a large stash of cash available (and then one can calculate how many months they can be expected to survive unless some serious reorganization takes place) or will require a constant influx of cash from either shareholders or financial institutions, or from selling assets, or, as happened in the automotive industry in the US, an influx of 'bail-out' cash from the government, making it the largest single shareholder. The question of the survival of such firms hinges on their ability to turn around a 'cash burn' situation into one with a positive cash flow from operating activities.

3. We take here 'earnings quality' to mean that it describes fairly and accurately (truly and fairly) the situation of the firm. Financial market analysts sometimes use the same expression but, in that case, they refer to the fact the earnings variance over time is proportionately small, thus that earnings are easily predictable by simple extrapolation and, most of the time, that the trend of earnings over time is ascending. We limit our analysis here to the formal quality (accurate descriptiveness) of the reported figures.

4. The *beta (β)* is defined as the ratio of the covariance between a firm's earnings and those of all firms in the reference market divided by the variance of the firm's earnings. It is a measure describing the relation of the returns of a firm with that of the financial market as a whole. In the capital asset pricing model (CAPM), it measures the part of the firm's earnings statistical variance that cannot be mitigated by diversification. A firm with a beta of zero sees it earnings evolve in a totally uncorrelated way to those the market at large; a positive beta means the firms earnings go up when those of the firms in the market go up; a beta of one means the firm's earnings follow those of the market, while a negative beta means the firm's earnings are evolving against the market movements. Beta is therefore a measure of the relative risk of the company's shares compared to that of the market. It relates the variance of earnings of a company with the average variance of earnings of the market.

5. Remember that losses can be used to offset taxable profits generally three years back and five years forward (or a number of years specific to each country).

6. See, for example, Smith, R., Lipin, S. and Naj, A.K. for a candid and in-depth description of 'How General Electric Damps Fluctuations in its Annual Earnings (*Wall Street Journal*, 2 November 1994). General Electric was long known for the slow, steady and reliable growth of its earnings, but, as that article illustrated, it was partly done 'with mirrors'.

7. The group possesses many other brands besides the brands quoted.

8. Source: http://www.cimc.com/web/769/.

C18

Chapter 18
Ratio Analysis, Financial Analysis and Beyond

Learning objectives

After studying this chapter, you will understand:

- Value creation for shareholders is the 'normal' purpose of a business entity. Thus, measurement of 'how much' value was created and 'how' this value was created remains the main focus of all financial information users.

- Ratios, by bringing together data from a variety of sources, help highlight relationships in the business model of the firm and thus address part of the 'how' question.

- Ratios, generally rich in useful information, should nonetheless be used with caution since the presumed relationship between the components has to be meaningful to help the decision-maker.

- Financial statement analysis, beyond what was presented in Chapters 15 to 17, must be supplemented by data from many diverse available sources providing relevant information and data on the firm, its competitors, their markets and their economic environment.

- The measurement of income over a period is not sufficient information to meet the needs of shareholders, a key stakeholder.

- Managers, financiers and consultants have developed, over the years, many alternative or complementary metrics describing the value created for the shareholders.

- The most elemental metric of shareholder value creation is earnings per share, an indicator simple in concept but often complex to calculate.

- That earnings per share is completed by return on total assets and return on long-term sources of funds (equity plus interest-bearing liabilities)

- The decomposition of the return on long-term funds (return on capital employed or ROCE) can be used effectively to analyze elements of the strategy of competitors, or formulate one's own strategy.

- What are residual income (RI), and its more modern version, called EVA® (economic value added).

- Why many consider RI or EVA as more relevant measures of 'value creation' for shareholders than ROCE.

- That EVA and RI lead the way to a family of other metrics of shareholders' value creation such as market value added (MVA) and cash flow return on investment (CFROI).

- Breaking down the entity's business model into homogeneous sub-models or segments, helps improve the predictability of the future streams of economic benefits.

- Models, called scoring models, may be used to detect an increased risk of corporate failure (i.e., the end of the process of creating value for shareholders).

- All measures of value creation are meaningless unless there is solid governance and ethical behavior in the firm.

Value creation for shareholders is the 'normal' purpose of a business entity. Some argue that shareholder value creation is not a purpose, but merely a constraint that must be met to preserve shareholders' willingness to keep reinvesting their earnings back into the business and show enough satisfaction with the management team (the board of directors represents shareholders and appoints the key officers), to indicate their estimation of the risk and return levels are acceptable, thus leading other fund providers to support the firm at an acceptable cost. Whether a constraint or a purpose, value creation from the point of view of the providers of 'capital at risk' must be measured and managed (equity can be lost if the firm declares bankruptcy).

This chapter focuses on the two key questions that structure the work of all financial analysts: 'how much' value creation (in the past, now, and in the future) and, its corollary 'how' the value creation was, is or will be achieved. The 'how much' question is addressed, quantitatively, by the income statement, but from the point of view of a shareholder, who is always free to sell his or her shares and reinvest the proceeds in another venture, which might provide a higher return and/or less risk, it means 'how much return on my investment, given the level of risk I am willing to take' and to that question the income statement does not give a sufficient answer.

The last three chapters focused on the decision usefulness of each of the three key statements in answering elements of the 'how' question. In the discussion of accounts manipulation (Chapter 17) we saw that figures can be fiddled with, sometimes within the limits allowed by GAAP, or, unfortunately, sometimes in unethical ways. Measures might need to be supplemented by oversight, regulated or not.

If we want to fully answer the question 'how', the information content of the three financial statements must be analyzed, compared, decoded and interpreted, not just statement by statement, but in an integrated way. The business model is described and explained in more detail if we cross data and information *between* statements and if we place these in their context (i.e., integrating data that may not be directly financial).

Ratio analysis, covered in section 1, is based on several sources of information, internal and external (see section 2 for external sources). It is a way of relating parameters from within and between the three statements, plus, often, additional data from the notes and external (often non-financial) sources to provide a more thorough understanding of the relationships between parameters defining the business model. The understanding of the business model must be compared to that of other firms. Only from comparison with others can a forecast be formulated about the ability to improve, in the future, the amount of shareholders value created.

The accounting measurement of past value created for shareholders is net income, provided as part of the income statement. That does not provide a fully satisfactory answer to most shareholders, as the income statement is only descriptive of the past and shareholders are interested in the future: the value of a share is essentially the net present value of future cash flows. We saw in Chapters 14 and 17 that understanding how the entity created and used its cash is a key source of information about the ability of the firm to continue creating value in the future. Cash flow is king for shareholders.

Measures of shareholders' value creation, beyond net earnings, must include measures of return (see section 3). This means, *a minima*, earnings per share, but also return on long-term capital employed or ROCE (a metric that addresses both the 'how much' and the 'how' questions), and the derivatives of residual income (also dual answer metrics), the best known of which is Stern Stewart's economic value added® or **EVA**® and its cousins, MVA or CFROI and others. The disclosure of segmental information is a key element for financial analysts (see section 4).

In case of failure of the firm, our two questions are moot. Risk of failure is an issue of interest to both shareholders and managers (see section 5). Shareholders want to know whether the firm they own is a going concern or if they are likely to lose their investment. Managers need to evaluate the likelihood of survival of key suppliers, of key customers, or of key competitors, otherwise any answer to the 'how' question that was built on analyzing the past is useless. If a value-chain partner in the business model fails, all relationships will have to be rebuilt. No one knows, beforehand, how the new relationships will be operating and shareholders dislike too much uncertainty. An intersection of the fields of finance and accounting has led to the creation of predictive models helping managers or financial users to see signals of possible dangers before it is too late to react.

Finally, the litmus test of the true quality of our answers to the two questions is whether the business model is built and operated with strong and ethical **governance**. We will conclude the chapter with a review of the issues affecting governance and its regulation (see section 6).

1 Ratio analysis: searching for answers to the 'how' question

1.1 Definition

A ratio is the quotient of two quantities, the numerator and the denominator. It assumes there is a meaningful relationship between the two elements of the quotient. The causal relationship between numerator and denominator helps understand the 'how' based on past data. The evolution of the relation helps predict the 'how much' for the future.

In financial analysis, quantities used in all ratio calculations come either from any of the financial statements (often comparing data from different statements – such as working capital need per monetary unit of sales revenue), or from financial data compared to descriptors of the business' activity (such as **sales revenue per employee**, average sale price per unit sold, revenue by % of market share, etc.).

The methods of computation and the interpretation of the meaning of any given ratio are more or less homogeneous between countries. Ratio analysis is probably the most widely used analytical technique for interpreting financial statements for the benefit of decision-makers and managers. However, caution should be exercised in using such tools.

1.2 Conditions of use of ratio analysis

A ratio *assumes* (reflects) that *a meaningful relationship exists* between two or more quantities descriptive of the business model of the firm analyzed. A causal interpretation of the variation over time of a ratio may weigh differently a variation of the numerator alone, of the denominator alone, or of both simultaneously.

It is also essential to verify both the logic of the relation between variables assumed in the formula, and the coherence or homogeneity of the quantities that are being related in the ratio. The user must, particularly, consider whether the variables used:

■ correspond to the same perimeter of analysis (possibly as the result of mergers, acquisition, closures or divestment, etc.);

■ result from similar accounting or classification rules: for example weighted average costing versus first-in first-out costing of inventory flows – see Chapter 9;

■ reflect the same operating assumptions (for example: possibility of a divergence of views about the useful life of a tangible or intangible asset, or of the reality of its impairment, or different strategies of sourcing between years or between firms compared);

■ are expressed in coherent units if applicable;

■ have been calculated in similar inflationary environments (or that inflationary effects have been neutralized);

■ reflect the true underlying behavior of the relevant parameters. For example, if there was a strong seasonality in demand, the average inventory calculated by summing opening and closing inventories and dividing by 2 may not reflect the impact on working capital need of the maximum inventory that was held during the peak of the season.

When using comparative or cross-sectional ratio analysis, it is important to remember that the assumed causal relationship behind a certain value of a ratio may not have the same meaning in two different entities. For example, Toyota Motor Company relies more heavily on outsourcing of key car components than Volkswagen. Relationships between car manufacturers and their dealers vary, from country to country, as to who owns the inventory on the dealer's lot, or, even, in its showroom. Thus inventory related ratios need to be interpreted only in the light of the specific strategy of each firm. It is also critical to consider that business practices between countries may be very different. We can take the example of supplier credit terms, or of the role of financial institutions as providers of long-term capital – to wit: in Chapter 15, the comparison of three energy producers showed that Sinopec had ratios relating to working capital that were 'surprising' for an industrial going concern in a 'western economy', but were perfectly legitimate in the Chinese environment.

Essentially, it is important to remember that ratios are best used to raise questions, and, thus, provide a powerful screening tool. No ratio alone tells the whole story. Several ratios must be used simultaneously to capture the richness of the business model. Ratios rarely allow direct interpretation. Ratio calculations are generally the first step in an investigative research to get to some of the root causes of the situation described by the financial statements.

Some suggestions follow for an appropriate use of ratios in financial analysis.

■ Base the analysis on appropriate comparisons (like risk factors, like industry, like markets, like size, etc.).

■ Avoid 'information overload' that would likely result from computing seemingly different ratios, which, in reality, have the same informational content because, for example, they are the inverse of one another or its complement to 1. For example:

 – Equity/(equity + long-term debt) is the complement to 1 of the ratio long-term debt/(equity + long-term debt).

 – The financial leverage ratio may be computed in two different, but essentially equivalent, ways: long-term debt/equity or long-term debt/(equity + long-term debt).

 – The **average collection period** ([average accounts receivable/net sales] × 365) is the inverse of the accounts receivable turnover (net sales/average accounts receivable) times 365. The same reasoning could be applied to **inventory turnover**, using cost of goods sold (COGS) as the numerator rather than net sales revenue and accounts payable in lieu of accounts receivable, of course.

- Some ratios are often referred to by somewhat standardized 'names' valid in many countries. For example, all analysts in English-speaking environments know that the '**current ratio**' is defined as (current assets/current liabilities – it has an equivalent name in all non English-speaking countries) or that the '**quick ratio**' is defined as (cash equivalents plus receivables)/current liabilities. However, many firms define their own in-house name for many ratios and give it a seemingly proprietary name, often undecipherable into an understandable formula by an outsider. It is, therefore, essential (especially given the mobility of personnel between firms) to make sure that all parties in a discussion of ratios interpret each metric to *really* mean the same thing, and understand it to be constructed in the same way (same formula). It may often prove best practice to provide the explicit definition (calculation formula) of the ratio next to the values reported, so as to avoid any ambiguity or misunderstanding.

- The analyst should have an idea of what she or he is looking for before calculating ratios. A few key ratios might be sufficient to put the analyst on the path that will lead her or him to the problem issues if there are any. Only then is it useful, if necessary, to engage in drilling down in the facts for a more detailed and focused understanding.

- A wisely selected number of relevant ratios will create a good picture of the prospects, performance and financial position of a firm. Ratios should not be used in a 'fishing expedition' using a trawler and a wide net with a fine mesh.

- Be selective: avoid calculating too many ratios. Sometimes too many trees can hide the forest (the pattern or the business model) or the 'magnificent tree' you needed or wanted to see (the ratio that could indicate whether or not there might be a serious problem needing to be addressed, or which issue is critical).

- Ratios should only be used as fact-based evidence supporting one's pre-existing hunches, intuition or viewpoint. The best way to use ratio analysis is to apply a 'sandwich approach' (or a 'peeling the onion, one layer at a time' approach), i.e., one general layer of inquiry based on intuition (or doubts) backed-up, or informed, by one layer of ratios as fact-based evidence, followed by another layer of redirected intuition backed-up or informed by a new layer of ratios, etc.

- Be aware of the limits of ratios due to the timing of financial statements. The balance sheet gives figures valid on a given date, while the income statement or the statement of cash flows give figures that summarize a period. A ratio based on crossing data from different statements may be misleading, in particular in the case of a seasonal or cyclical activity. One solution to account for seasonality or rapid growth or decline of volumes, in the case of balance sheet components, consists, for example, in averaging figures: (a) from quarterly statements, if they are available, in a case of suspected seasonality (and, ideally, using four rolling quarters to smooth out seasonality and visualize any trend) or (b) at least, averaging beginning and ending balance sheet figures.

- Be aware that the validity of any ratio is limited by the quality of financial statements on which it is based (revisit Chapter 17 for a dose of sound humility).

- Be aware of the difficulty of interpreting negative ratios (because either the numerator or the denominator is negative – for instance, a loss or negative net income). Notice that, even if it sounds silly, a company with net losses and a negative equity does offer a seemingly very high return on equity! The algebraic sign of a longitudinal ratio (evolution of an item over time) is meaningful and should be mentioned in any analysis, but, in that case, the absolute value of the ratio might be difficult to interpret without reference to some context. For example, a decline in sales revenue of 5%, normally bad news, might be considered good news if, simultaneously, the market share increased – i.e., the market shrank faster than the revenue, but it is also bad news if no alternate market is currently being developed, or there is no hope of seeing the market pick up again.

■ Do not look for a standardized list of universally applicable ratios. Frustrating though it might feel, such a 'ready-to-use' list cannot and should not exist. There are hundreds of possible different ratios, due to the large number of items found in the financial statements and, consequently, the almost unlimited possibility of combinations. Not all possible combinations are meaningful. The ratios listed below, in section 1.4, are *examples* of some of the most frequently used and discussed ratios. This list is not intended to be comprehensive, nor does it represent a sufficient or necessary set of ratios. These indicators may not be appropriate in a given strategic context or competitive environment, or for a specific entity or industry. Ratios often are economic-sector-specific, firm-specific and always are time-specific. The analyst should first understand the business the firm is engaged in (i.e., its markets, strategy and business processes) before choosing the ratios that will prove to be relevant, rather than doing the opposite. Although, sometimes, in all truthfulness, a few fundamental ratios may help the analyst identify some key additional questions that will allow her or him to understand the business.

■ Ratios defined in a given country should only be used with great caution as a benchmark in analyzing financial statements of another country. Ratio interpretation is dependent, among many other things, on accounting principles followed in business practices and in local business culture (although the generalization of IFRS/IAS adoption will somewhat reduce differences over time. For instance:

(a) Some ratios describing liquidity and solvency require a given presentation of the balance sheet increasing liquidity or decreasing liquidity (see Chapter 5), which may not be current reporting practice in that market. In countries where the balance sheet does not distinguish elements by term, the concepts of liquidity and solvency may prove to be more difficult to measure directly, without restatement, using some of the classic ratios.

(b) Diversity of practices in terms of accounts receivable credit terms in different parts of the world: a 90-day customer credit term might be good business practice in Greece but an indication of an abnormal relation with the customer in Denmark or Finland. It is not unusual in the US to hear furniture stores promote a policy of 12 months of 'free (customer) credit', while such a practice would be considered unusual and, possibly unethical or illegal, in France.

(c) Practices concerning liabilities may also differ in the financing of long-term investments: US firms traditionally procure most of their long-term funding through financial markets, German firms procure most of their long-term funding through bank loans, while for many Chinese companies, long-term funding comes from securing revolving short-term bank borrowings.

■ Financial statement analysis is based on judgment calls and contextual interpretation on the part of the analyst. Never overestimate the explanatory power of any ratio. Always place ratio analysis within a more comprehensive analysis of the whole set of financial statements and of the business.

1.3 Comparisons of ratios

There are three possible different types of comparisons in the creation of ratios. They are mentioned in Figure 18.1.

1.3.1 Time-series comparisons (or longitudinal ratio analysis)

Ratios are computed yearly or more frequently and use data of a given period of time. When available, it is always a good idea to use quarterly data to be able to use sliding

Figure 18.1 Ratio comparisons

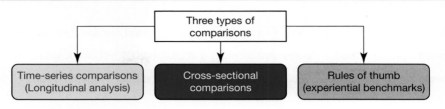

periods such as defining a running year as four quarters, dropping the oldest quarter and adding the new one, each time a new quarterly data set is available. The ratios reflecting one year of activity are then compared to the historical ratios of the business for previous periods of equivalent duration. Although the length of the period over which the evolution of ratio should be analyzed is not standardized, practice seems to imply that calculating and comparing ratios over a three-year sliding period generally provides enough relevant and useful information to decision-makers, without running into the risk of a dramatic evolution of either business context or business processes.

Real-life example Michelin

(France – IFRS – Source: Annual reports 2008 and 2007 – Tires)

	2008	2007	2006
Operating profit/sales	5.1%	7.8%	6.8%

It appears that, in 2008, Michelin has experienced a 34% deterioration of its operating profit, while, in 2007, it had seen an improvement over 2006. Further inquiry is required to understand the meaning of what happened. Neither a causal explanation nor a recommended action will rise directly from the data. The analysts of Michelin should take into consideration the fact that in 2008 the automotive market collapsed (between 10 and 25% depending on markets and segments) and, for example, The Goodyear Tire and Rubber Company, a US competitor, saw its operating profit decline by 57% over the same period, while Continental AG, a German competitor, saw its profit from ordinary activities fall from +21% of sales revenue in 2007 to –20% in 2008. Unless analysts or managers have a clear understanding of the reasons for the deterioration in 2008 and its context, they know nothing by just looking at the value of the ratios. Once managers (and analysts observing their actions) know why the situation evolved, in this case downwards, they will be able to create, or maintain, the conditions needed to ensure improvement, thus bucking the trend.

1.3.2 Cross-sectional comparisons

Ratios can be compared to equivalent ratios of other entities, a competitor for instance, or against industry averages. One limit of industry comparisons stems from the fact that there is no such thing as an 'average business process' or an 'average strategy'. Furthermore, the business process and activities of compared firms (or even of different country subsidiaries of one multinational corporation) rarely offer a homogeneous or consistent basis for comparison. Another issue is the difficulty in obtaining the relevant ratios for competitors or businesses in the same economic sector.

Real-life example

Nokia (Finland – IFRS – Source: Annual reports 2008 and 2007 – Telephone and communication)

Ericsson (Sweden – IFRS – Source: Annual reports 2008 and 2007 – Network solutions)

Motorola (USA – US GAAP – Source: Annual reports 2008 and 2007 – Telephone and communication)

Average days of inventory available: (Average inventory level/COGS) × 365	Nokia	Ericsson	Motorola
2008	29	67	46
2007	26	70	41
2006	20	70	33

Ericsson appears to be an outlier in this telecommunication equipment economic sector (in any sector, a fast turnover of inventories is generally considered preferable to a slower one). However, Ericsson's strategy and business scope are different from those of either Nokia or Motorola. Nokia is focused on handsets plus network construction (in partnership with Siemens). Ericsson has essentially transferred the handset business to Sony and focuses on infrastructure engineering and sales. Motorola is less involved in infrastructure and focuses, through its three divisions, on terminals, whether they be handsets, business terminals (such as bar code readers or cable TV sets), or military, fire and police telecommunication equipment. The only way to interpret the days of sales available for each firm is to replace the metric in the context of the firm's specific strategy.

For example, Ericsson's main activity is in large infrastructure contracts. Thus, many of these contracts lead to customer down payments. Despite an apparently slow turnover of inventory, it ends up that this inventory is largely financed by the down payments or advance payments of customers and, thus, the 'cash to cash' cycle (see the cash pump in Chapter 1) of Ericsson is better than that of either Nokia or Motorola. Never trust a ratio on its 'face value', replace it in context and associate it to other ratios. Table 10.4 in Chapter 10 offered another illustration of the difficulty of within-industry comparisons or of designing a meaningful sample (in that case about the ratio of accounts receivable over total assets).

1.3.3 Rules of thumb (experiential benchmarks)

Ratios can be compared to selected references. These can be either measures derived from competitors (such as comparing to the 'best in class' – with all the problems implied by the concept), or rules of thumb based on industry-wide 'experience'. Many consulting firms, such as Alsbridge in the US or Cegos in France, earn a large part of their revenue by selling a benchmarking service of ratios by industry and firm size. For example one often speaks of the rule of the three-thirds for a 'sound' structure of equity and liabilities in the balance sheet: this rule implies shareholders' equity 'should' represent one third of total assets, long-term liabilities another third, and short-term liabilities the final third.

Such references for interpreting ratios can prove to be difficult to use effectively for any of the following reasons, and probably even many more:

■ If the ratio is compared to industry-wide statistics or norms, all problems already raised about cross-sectional comparisons apply. For example, the rule that used to say that the working capital was supposed to be positive is continuously challenged (appropriately) in distribution and retail activities (or, as we have seen in the case of Sinopec in Chapter 15, when the relevant banking system operates on different bases than 'traditional'). Another rule of three-thirds applies to the restaurant business in which one often hears that, in order to be 'normally' profitable, the price ought to be three times the cost of the raw materials. But even if this is often true, the same so-called rule of thumb probably cannot apply at the same time to fast-food establishments or institutional kitchens (here the rule of thumb is considered to be [price should be 'twice' the cost of materials] – but, what about a branch of a fast-food chain on the Champs Elysées in Paris, versus a branch of the same chain in a popular suburb – the rent expense per square meter is probably not comparable between the two!) Or gastronomic restaurants where the rule of thumb is closer to price equals four to six times cost of raw materials and can even reach a tenfold mark-up. The location of the restaurant may also have a great impact on the relevant benchmark: labor cost or rent per square meter in a capital city may be vastly different from that in rural areas.

- If the ratio is based on a 'rule of thumb' built over the years without any reasoned basis, the meaningfulness of any analysis based on this ratio should be subjected to critical doubt. For example, one often hears something like 'a healthy firm in industry X is one that generates at least €150,000 of revenue per person employed'. However, such a rule (or belief) does not take into account the fact that entities, even in the same industry, differ vastly in their degree of value-addition, or in the intrinsic role of labor in the generation of revenue. For example an aircraft manufacturer may focus only on design and engineering, final assembly and after sales service, while a competitor's strategy is built around the same activities, plus the manufacturing of most of the key components of the airframe. Not only labor content may be different, but the importance and price of components or raw materials quality and price may also differ. Seemingly similar raw materials in a three-star restaurant are probably more expensive than they are in a neighborhood diner and both headcount and labor costs are probably vastly different between the two. Military-grade and space industry-grade microchips cost about 800 times more per unit than their equivalent for civilian applications (essentially because of difference in volumes, different tolerance limits, and extreme performance expectations); brokers might have to handle a huge amount of trade to be able to cover the cost of their headcount. Software or computer games manufacturers incur most of their costs in the design phase, not in the manufacturing and distribution phase of their products, but synergies exist for the larger designers that are not accessible to the smaller manufacturers. Oil refiners might see their raw material cost represent 90% of their costs, while an oil-based fine chemistry firm, although also considered part of the same broad industry might see its cost of oil (as raw material) represent not more than 30% of its total costs, etc.

1.4 Some key ratios

Ratios are organized in four categories, each addressing questions and issues expressed by shareholders or decision-makers (sub-sets of the 'how' and 'how much' questions): (1) evaluation of short-term liquidity and solvency; (2) evaluation of long-term solvency and financial leverage; (3) evaluation of profitability and generation of profitability; and (4) measures of shareholders' return.

Table 18.1 lists some key ratios, and the reader is reminded to remain very cautious in using such a list. The ratios mentioned may not all be appropriate, or the best suited ones, for any given situation. This list is a 'tool box' and the user must first identify the nature and issues of the business evaluated before selecting the appropriate tools from the box.

There are hundreds of possible different ratios, since the number of combinations of all the items on the financial statements, plus the possibility of relating these to non-financial

Table 18.1 Some key ratios[1]

Name of the ratios	Computation	Comments
Short-term liquidity ratios (firm's ability to finance its day-to-day operations and to pay its liabilities as they fall due)		
Current ratio (or working capital ratio)	Current assets[a]/Current liabilities (creditors: amounts falling due within one year)[b]	Firm's ability to pay its current liabilities from its current assets Rule of thumb: 2:1 as an 'ideal'
Quick ratio (or quick asset or acid-test or liquidity)	(Cash + marketable securities + accounts receivable)/Current liabilities	Firm's ability to pay its current liabilities from its current assets excluding the sale of inventories
Cash ratio	(Cash + marketable securities)/Current liabilities	Firm's ability to pay its current liabilities from its cash and cash equivalents
Average collection period	[{(Accounts receivable Year 2 + Accounts receivable Year 1)/2} × 365]/Sales	Average length of time to collect accounts receivable
Average payment period	[{(Accounts payable Year 2 + Accounts payable Year 1)/2} × 365]/Purchases of goods and services	Average length of time to pay accounts payable
Inventory turnover	Cost of sales/[(Inventories Year 2 + inventories Year 1)/2]	Number of times that a firm sells or turns over its inventories per year
Long-term solvency ratios (firm's ability to pay its long-term liabilities)		
Debt ratio	Total debt/Total assets	Firm's debt-paying ability or degree of leverage (the lower these ratios, the 'stronger' the firm's position)
Debt to equity ratio	Debt[c]/Shareholders' equity or Debt/(Shareholders' equity + Debt)	
Debt to tangible net worth	Debt/(Shareholders' equity − intangible assets)	
Long-term debt to equity ratio	Long-term debt/Shareholders' equity or Long-term debt/(Shareholders' equity + Long-term debt)	Firm's long-term debt-paying ability The lower this ratio, the 'stronger' the firm's position Firm's degree of financial leverage
Interest coverage ratio	Operating income (before interest expense and income taxes)/Interest expense	Number of times that a firm's interest expense is covered by operation earnings Rule of thumb: minimum of 5
Profitability ratios (measure of the firm's performance)		
Return on shareholders' equity (ROE)	Net income/Average equity[d] or Income before interest and tax/Average equity	Return to shareholders
Return on investment (ROI) (return on capital employed or ROCE)	Net income/(Average long-term liabilities + equity) = Net income/Capital employed or Earnings before interest and tax (EBIT)/capital employed	Measure of the income earned on the invested capital
Gross profit rate (gross profit margin)	Gross profit/Sales	Percentage of each sales currency unit not absorbed by the cost of sales

Table 18.1 *(Continued)*

Name of the ratios	Computation	Comments
Return on sales (net profit margin)	Net income/Sales	Percentage of each sales currency unit that contributes to net income
Asset turnover	Sales/[(Assets Year 2 + assets Year 1)/2]	Firm's ability to generate sales relative to its investment in assets
Return on assets (ROA)	Net income/[(Assets Year 2 + assets Year 1)/2]	Firm's ability to use its assets to create profits
Sales per employee	Sales/Number of employees	Measure of the sales productivity of the workforce
Market price and dividend ratios (capital markets' perception of the firm's share)		
Earnings per share	Net income/average shares outstanding	Measure of share performance
Price/earnings ratio (P/E or PER)	Market price per share/earnings per share	Amount that investors are willing to pay for each currency unit of a firm's earnings – market confidence in a firm
Market to book ratio	Market price per share/Book value per share	Amount that investors are willing to pay for each currency unit of a firm's net assets
Dividend yield ratio	Cash dividends per share/Market price per share	Cash return on the investment in a firm
Dividend pay-out ratio	Cash dividends per share/Earnings per share	Proportion of earnings paid out in the form of dividends

a Current assets include cash.
b Current liabilities include bank overdrafts.
c Debt represents long-term and short-term interest-bearing liabilities.
d Average equity = (Beginning shareholders' equity + Ending shareholders' equity)/2.

activity descriptors, is almost limitless. As a consequence, ratios are frequently classified in subgroups which reflect a particular aspect of financial performance or position.

1.5 Additional remarks about ratios computation

Table 18.1 includes the '**average payment period**' (accounts payable/purchases × 365). It is not always easy for an outside analyst to calculate such a ratio, however useful it might be in measuring the cash-to-cash cycle: the value of purchases is, for example, not provided in an income statement by function, and, in that situation, is rarely provided in the notes either. However, in the case of businesses presenting their income statement by nature, this ratio is easily and frequently computed. It is also a ratio that is pretty systematically calculated in any internal financial analysis, as it is a key element of the management of the speed of the operating cash cycle.

When net income is used in ratios, it is sometimes replaced by the earnings before interest and taxation (EBIT) because doing so takes away the financing policy effect as well as the income tax effects, thus facilitating cross-sectional and longitudinal comparisons.

1.6 Pyramids of ratios

Ratios can be linked or decomposed in useful ways to gain further understanding of the answers to the 'how' question. Two pyramids of ratios are shown in Figures 18.2 and 18.3.

1.6.1 Pyramid of ROE-related ratios and strategy

Developing a ratio into sub-ratios may allow the manager, and an analyst alike, to understand better the business model and the trade offs that are open to the firm's management.

Figure 18.2 illustrates how the ROE (return on equity) can be broken into ROA (return on assets) and financial leverage. ROA can, in turn, be broken up into return on sales multiplied by asset turnover. The latter two allow users to analyze the strategy of the firm (an antecedent to the current and future ROE) independently of its use of leveraging its equity. **Return on sales** and **asset turnover** can be used to create a two-dimensional map of ROA as shown in Figure 18.3.

Figure 18.2 The pyramid of ROE-related ratios

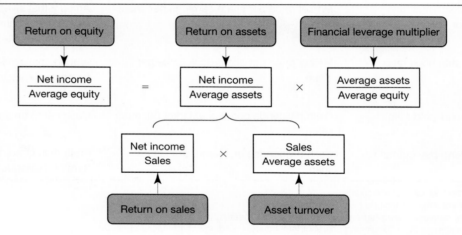

In Figure 18.3 we can see that very different strategies can lead to the same **return on assets**, even in the same industry: one firm with a relatively high operating margin (profit/sales revenue) of 6% and a slow turnover of assets of 2, enjoys a ROA of 12%. This might be a High Street store with a very deep selection of diverse products (which, thus, lead to an inventory that does not turn rapidly). Another firm, which could be a Big Box store,

Figure 18.3 Iso-curves of ROA

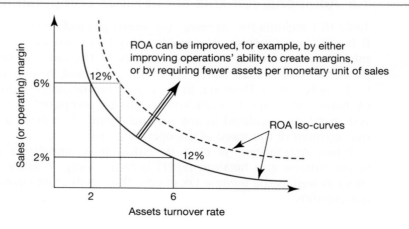

commands a low operating margin of 2%; it strives for a high turnover of assets of 6 by offering a narrow selection of high demand standard products; it, too, enjoys an ROA of 12%. The locus of all the equal values of ROA resulting from combining sales margin and assets turnover is called an iso-curve.

We can see that either firm can improve their ROA by modifying either (or both) of the two decision variables. There is a real improvement in the situation of the firm only if it can move to a 'higher' iso-curve.

The two firms may have the same ROA but their current strategies are very different and managers and analysts need to understand what firm-specific actions can be taken to move the ROA to a higher iso-curve. It might be easier for the High Street store to increase its asset turnover to 3 without endangering its operating margin of 6%, for a resulting ROA of 18%, than it is for the Big Box store to improve its margin to 3% or its asset turnover to 9 to reach the same ROA of 18%. Both management teams continuously strive to stay on the same iso-curve, or move to a higher one, by defining and implementing a strategy around the trade off between assets turnover and operating margin.

The situation described in Figure 18.3 also allows each firm to identify what it must do if the world changes around them: for example, if the High Street store sees its margin eroding (due to competition or foreign exchange evolution, the only way they can preserve their ROA is by improving their asset turnover.

1.6.2 The DuPont formula, the grandmother of all pyramids of ratios

Donaldson Brown, in the 1920s, developed a pyramid of ratios and financial parameters, as a management tool, for DuPont de Nemours. DuPont was a huge conglomerate and its headquarters needed to find a way to communicate to all division heads both the need to improve ROCE, i.e., return on long-term capital employed, on which managers were measured and rewarded, but also the identification of the action-levers each could activate, in relative autonomy, to achieve the result intended. The 'DuPont formula' is illustrated in Figure 18.4. Since ROCE does not take into consideration the financing

Figure 18.4 The so-called 'DuPont formula'

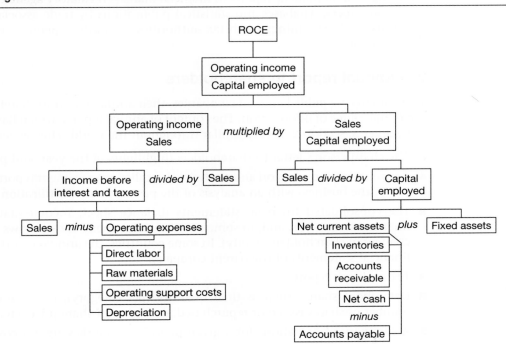

strategy or the leverage effect (shareholders' equity and long-term debt are merged under the term 'capital employed'), it is a metric that is thus applicable to any size firm and almost any subset of any business entity, including, as intended originally, divisions in larger organizations.

The set of linked elements, forming a basis for many ratio calculations, known as the 'DuPont formula', allowed (allows) any manager to know how her or his action (or those of the team they managed) impact(ed) the ROCE of their business unit and all divisional ROCEs could (can) be consolidated to obtain the group-wide ROCE. The power of this 'analytical and managerial' modeling tool is such that it is still used in many firms around the world today, in various amended forms, as an internal managerial tool. Most analysts use the template it represents to structure their initial analysis. Much of the data required is directly available from the annual reports.

1.6.3 Financial footprint: creating a model of the 'business model'

The financial data of a business, with their key ratios, can be used to create a simulation model, or more simply be used to create a 'financial footprint', i.e., a potentially dynamic model of how the ROA or ROE are derived from elemental actions (isolated or coordinated). If used as a simulation tool, the footprint allows managers and analysts to evaluate the potential impact of (sensitivity to) some external events and of key decisions on the resulting ROA or ROE. An example of a financial footprint is illustrated in Figure 18.5.

Additional remarks on ratios computation are presented in Appendix 18.1.

2 Sources of information about business entities

As mentioned earlier, ratios must be replaced in the context in which the data they use was created. Public sources of financial, operational and strategic data and information about business entities are plentiful and often are free of charge. They all give a partial view of the whole and must be used conjointly, as much as possible: annual statements reporting to shareholders, reports to financial markets regulatory agencies, business magazines and papers, databases and statistical publications by trade associations or consulting firms, and legal filings (with tax authorities or courts depending on the regulatory environment).

2.1 Annual report to shareholders

When analyzing publicly traded companies, their annual report to shareholders represents the prime source of information. The content of annual reports, which has been introduced in Chapter 5, section 2, is very similar throughout the world. They generally contain:

- The chairperson's letter to shareholders (highlights of the year, and perspectives).

- A management discussion and analysis, also called management report (segmental analysis of the business with an analysis of the past and the identification of perspectives).

- The consolidated financial statements (balance sheet, income statement, notes to financial statements, and, in some countries, statement of cash flows and statement of changes in shareholders' equity). In some countries, the annual report also includes the financial statements of the parent company.

- The auditor's report.

- Data about shares, such as their quantity (per category), issuance of stock options, number of shares issued or repurchased, evolution of share price, etc.

- A summary of operations for a given period of time (key figures covering a five-year period in general).

Figure 18.5 Financial footprint (An Excel version of this document is available on the book's dedicated website)

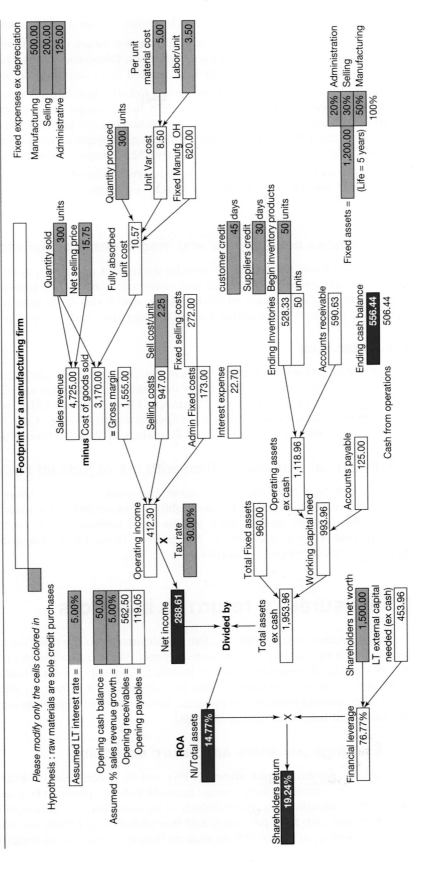

Annual reports can be obtained in an electronic format in different ways:

- Access to the company's website and the section 'financials' or 'investors relations' either through www.yahoo.com or www.google.com. Yahoo.com offers a particularly interesting finance section where core analyses of quoted firms can often be accessed at no cost.

- Access to the financial market regulator's website, in countries where this regulator provides an access to annual reports filed by listed companies: e.g., in China through the stock exchanges in Shanghai (http://www.sse.com.cn) or in Shenzhen (http://www.szse.cn/), in France through www.amf-france.org, in Spain at www.cnmv.es, or in the US at www.sec.gov and its Edgar database: www.SECFilings.com *or* www.edgar-online.com).

- Access to a commercial database, such as www.infinancials.com, which contains a collection of annual reports, including archives, covering major listed companies all over the world.

2.2 Business newspapers and magazines, specialized magazines

All countries have business and financial magazines and newspapers reporting news and current events about the financial and economic world. They represent a wealth of contextual, strategic and financial information, which can be helpful for financial analysts. Appendix 18.2 provides examples of such magazines and newspapers.

2.3 Databases

Private organizations sell subscriptions to databases which include financial statements of companies worldwide. The four main international databases are: Global (Standard and Poor's), Infinancials, Worldscope (Thomson Financial) and Osiris or Orbis (Bureau Van Dijk). Other databases are available for specific countries (e.g., Compustat North America [Standard and Poor's, for the USA and Canada, or Diane for France [Bureau van Dijk]).

2.4 Financial statements filed with tax or judicial authorities

In some countries (it is the case in most European countries), there is an obligation for certain entities (in general all limited liability companies) to file their financial statements with a government agency, such as the fiscal administration or the judiciary, which, in turn, makes these available to the public. These filing obligations are described in Appendix 18.3 for several countries.

3 Measures of return to investors

The performance of an entity, i.e., the simple answer to the question 'how much', both in terms of past net income and in terms of potential or future prospects of value creation, is not all that the shareholders want to monitor. They want to see whether they earn enough to keep their money invested in this firm at that level of risk, or whether they ought to move it to another business investment. Two families of indicators are used here: earnings per share and return on capital invested.

3.1 Earnings per share and return on equity

The ratio of **earnings per share (EPS)** and its distant cousin, **return on equity**, are still critically important for financial markets as they appear to be used as a common metric for the evaluation, by shareholders, of most businesses, although operating cash flow per share, net cash flow per share, and free cash flow per share seem to be used more and more frequently, in lieu of EPS, in making financial investment decisions. As we have seen repeatedly in the previous chapters, the definition of 'earnings' for any given period can be quite complex. Many countries, essentially those with active financial markets, have felt the need to clarify the process of calculation of EPS by issuing specific accounting standards, or reporting regulations, so that the markets can operate efficiently, with every user understanding this piece of data to mean the same thing.

Earnings per share is defined as the ratio of net income after taxes (and after preferred dividends if there are any)[2] to the average number of shares during the period for which the income has been calculated. As we have seen, the calculation of earnings (income) for the numerator as well as the definition of the denominator can be complex. For example, how does one reflect the coexistence of ordinary, convertible preferred and treasury shares? Many countries have issued statements or standards aimed at clarifying how earnings, denominator shares numbers and, consequently, earnings per share, ought to be calculated for public reporting. Examples of such regulations are FRS 14 in the UK (ASB 1998) and SFAS 128 in the US (FASB 1997). At the international level, IASB revised IAS 33 in 2003. It supersedes previously existing regulations in countries where IFRS were adopted as the rule of the land.

A particularly bothersome difficulty comes from the existence of 'share equivalents' such as stock options, stock warrants, or convertible instruments such as convertible bonds, which can be turned into shares any time the conditions specified when they were issued are met. The 'fully diluted earnings per share' is calculated by using, as the denominator, the maximum number of shares possible if all these conditional agreements unfolded and led to the issuance of more shares. This figure thus reveals the risk that the EPS would be much lower than currently calculated if all holders of options or warrants or convertible instruments were to effectively convert their rights into shares.

For example, let us assume a high-tech firm with a capital of one million CU (100,000 shares with a 10 CU par) has issued stock options to attract and retain managerial and creative talent. Options amount to a potential of 200,000 additional shares. Let us assume that today, for the most recent period of activity, the EPS was 2 CU per share (i.e., total earnings were 200,000 CU, thus EPS = 2 = 200,000 CU/100,000 shares). If total earnings were to increase by 50% to 300,000 CU in the next year, *and* all options were exercised, the original shareholders would see, to their great dismay, the EPS figure fall to only 1 CU:

$$\frac{200,000 \times 1.5}{100,000 + 200,000} = 1$$

Each Standard prescribes principles for the determination and presentation of earnings per share that improve comparisons of performance between entities in one period, and between different periods for the same entity.

All regulations adopted apply to publicly-traded companies and specifically to their consolidated financial statements. However, these rules and recommendations are common sense and may usefully be applied to not-publicly-traded companies and to unconsolidated financial statements.

IAS 33 makes a distinction between basic and diluted earnings per share. Numerous companies compute adjusted earnings after the impact of both operating and non-operating exceptional items and amortization/impairment of goodwill in order to provide a better understanding of the underlying performance of the company on a normalized basis. By doing so, four different measures of earnings per share may be computed:

- basic EPS
- diluted EPS
- adjusted basic EPS
- adjusted diluted EPS.

3.1.1 Basic earnings per share

IAS 33 (§ 10) defines basic earnings per share as:

> Profit or loss for the period attributable to ordinary equity holders of the parent entity
> ──
> Weighted average number of ordinary shares outstanding during the period

In this definition, the profit is computed after deduction of any preference dividends. The time-weighted average number of ordinary shares outstanding during the period is computed according to one of the two methods shown in Table 18.2.

'The time-weighting factor is the number of days that the shares are outstanding as a proportion of the total number of days in the period' (IAS 33: § 20). Moreover, as shown in Table 18.2, there are two different ways to compute the time-weighted average number of outstanding shares. However both give the same result.

3.1.2 Diluted earnings per share

Principles As indicated in IAS 33 (§ 31), 'for the purpose of calculating diluted earnings per share, an entity shall adjust profit or loss attributable to ordinary equity holders of the parent entity, and the weighted average number of shares outstanding, for the effects

Table 18.2 Time-weighted average number of shares

		Shares issued (1)	Treasury shares (2)	Shares outstanding	
1 January X1	Balance at beginning of year	3,100	400	2,700	= (1) − (2)
30 April X1	Issue of new shares for cash	900	–	3,600	
1 November X1	Purchase of treasury shares for cash	–	600	3,000	
31 December X1	Balance at end of year	4,000	1,000	3,000	= (1) − (2)

		Balance (1)	Number of months shares were held (2)	Weighted balance (1) × (2)/12
Method 1	1 January X1 – 30 April X1	2,700	4	900
	1 May X1 – 30 October X1	3,600	6	1,800
	1 November X1 – 31 December X1	3,000	2	500
	Time-weighted average number of shares			3,200
Method 2	1 January X1 – 31 December X1	2,700	12	2,700
	30 April X1 – 31 December X1	900	8	600
	1 November X1 – 31 December X1	−600	2	−100
	Time-weighted average number of shares			3,200

of all dilutive potential ordinary shares'. The term 'potential ordinary share', as seen in Chapter 11, refers to a variety of financial instruments or other contracts that may entitle its holder to ordinary shares.

The amount of profit or loss pertaining to ordinary shares must be adjusted (§ 33) by the following 'after-tax elements:

(a) any dividends or other items related to dilutive potential ordinary shares deducted in arriving at profit or loss attributable to ordinary equity holders (…);

(b) any interest recognized in the period related to dilutive potential ordinary shares; and

(c) any other changes in income or expense that would result from the conversion of the dilutive potential ordinary shares'.

In other words, the profit or loss of the period is increased (decreased) by the amount of dividends, interest and other income or expense that would be saved (added) on the conversion of the dilutive potential ordinary shares into ordinary shares. Table 18.3 presents an example of computation of diluted earnings per share based on the conversion of bonds.

In our example, the shareholders, in order to obtain bond financing at a lower than market rate took the risk of seeing their EPS diluted by 2.5% in order to attract fixed-rate lenders. The latter trade off a lower-than-market guaranteed return against the potential of a higher but riskier return if the shares price evolves favorably, i.e., the actual return turns out to exceed 5% after the two years guaranteed life as a bond. Of course, if the market cost of fixed-rate funding evolves favorably for current shareholders (i.e., becomes lower than 5%, net of transactions costs), refinancing of the bonds may become an attractive

Table 18.3 Computation of the diluted earnings per share

Reported net income (in CU) (net of all interest expenses)	(1)	5,000
Number of ordinary shares outstanding	(2)	2,500
Basic earnings per share (CU per share)	(3) = (1)/(2)	2
Number of convertible bonds (face value 5 CU, coupon rate 5%, duration 10 years)	(4)	200
Conditions of conversion (at the initiative of the company after 2 years): 10 bonds for 4 shares	(5)	0.4
Number of potential new shares issued from the conversion	(6) = (4) × (5)	80
Interest expense for the current full year relating to the liability component of the convertible bond (it would not be incurred if the conversion were to take place, so we'll have to add it back to (1))	(7) = 200 × 5 × 0.05	50
Current and deferred tax shield relating to that interest expense (tax rate assumed at 40%). We lose the tax deductibility of interests since interest expense would no longer exist from this source; this would reduce net reported income by that much.	(8)	20
Adjusted net profit (reflects the hypothetical complete conversion of the bonds)	(9) = (1) + (7) − (8)	5,030
Number of ordinary shares used to compute diluted earnings per share	(10) = (2) + (6)	2,580
Diluted earnings per share after assumed conversion	(11) = (9)/(10)	1.95
Effect of the potential dilution (1.95 − 2.00)/2.00 = −2.5%		2.5%

alternative. Shareholders may then decide (if the covenants covering the bonds allow it) either to call the bonds and reimburse the lenders, or to force the conversion into shares. In any case they have locked-in the dilution risk at a maximum of 2.5%. On their side, the lenders have locked in their return at a minimum of 5%, in case the share price does not rise as expected and yield more than 5%.

Options, warrants and their equivalents are also covered in IAS 33. 'For the purpose of calculating diluted earnings per share, an entity shall assume the exercise of dilutive options and warrants of the entity. The assumed proceeds from these instruments shall be regarded as having been received from the issue of ordinary shares at the average market price of ordinary shares during the period. The difference between the number of ordinary shares issued and the number of ordinary shares that would have been issued at the average market price of ordinary shares during the period shall be treated as an issue of ordinary shares for no consideration' (IAS 33: § 45).

'Options and warrants are dilutive when they would result in the issue of ordinary shares for less than the average market price of ordinary shares during the period. The amount of the dilution is the average market price of ordinary shares during the period minus the issue price. Therefore, to calculate diluted earnings per share, potential ordinary shares are treated as consisting of both the following:

(a) A contract to issue a certain number of the ordinary shares at their average market price during the period. Such ordinary shares are assumed to be fairly priced and to be neither dilutive nor anti-dilutive. They are ignored in the calculation of diluted earnings per share.

(b) A contract to issue the remaining ordinary shares for no consideration. Such ordinary shares generate no proceeds and have no effect on profit or loss attributable to ordinary shares outstanding. Therefore, such shares are dilutive and are added to the number of ordinary shares outstanding in the calculation of diluted earnings per share' (IAS 33: § 46).

Real-life example Irish Continental Group

(Ireland – UK/Irish GAAP – Source: Annual report 2008 – Shipping, transport and leisure group principally engaged in the transport of passengers and cars [Irish Ferries], freight and containers)

Note 12 to the annual report provides a detailed computation of earnings per share.

Basic earnings per share		2008	2007
Basic earnings per share is calculated as follows:			
Numerator: Profit attributable to shareholders (€m)	(1)	40.5	38.3
Denominator: Weighted average number of shares in issue (number)	(2)	24,586	23,794
Basic earnings per share (€cent)	(3) = (1)/(2) × 100000	164.7	161.0

Diluted earnings per share		2008	2007
Diluted earnings per share is calculated as follows:			
Numerator: Profit attributable to shareholders (€m)	(4)	40.5	38.3
Denominator: Weighted average number of shares in issue, including options exercisable at the date of this report (number)	(5)	24,880	24,101
Diluted earnings per share (€cent)	(6) = (4)/(5) × 100000	162.8	158.9

3.1.3 Price earnings ratio

The comparison of the market price of a share to its corresponding earnings per share is called the P/E ratio (**price earnings ratio**), PER or 'multiple'. The formula is:

> P/E ratio = Price of the share/earnings per share

It is a ratio used for evaluating the level of expectations of the market regarding the shares of that firm: it can be interpreted as the arithmetic number of years of earnings (ignoring both growth and time-value of money) it will take for an investor to recover the price he or she would pay on that day for the share. Price reflects current investor demand for a company share, and this demand is based on expectations of future cash flows, thus, for a given level of earnings per share, a high P/E ratio means shareholders expect much more future growth of earnings on the part of the firm than they do for a firm with a lower P/E ratio. The reciprocal of the PE ratio is known as the 'earnings yield'.

3.2 Measures of return on capital invested: residual income and economic value added

3.2.1 Principles

Shareholders want to measure whether the firm in which they have invested earns them a fair return, a fair surplus over and above the risks they are taking by investing. The idea behind these methods of value creation measurement is that the profit reported in the accounting statements only accounts for the cost of interest-bearing liabilities (essentially long-term funds and their current portion), when, in fact, shareholders also have provided long-term funds and do expect a return on their investment (higher even than that of borrowed funds, because shareholders assume much more risk than banks or bond lenders do).

We have throughout the book and particularly in Chapter 1 emphasized the need to separate the firm's decisions from those made by individual shareholders. A shareholder may acquire, or have acquired, on the financial market or through a direct transaction, shares of the firm at a price per share that is likely to be different from (greater than, in most cases) the book value of equity divided by the number of shares. The explanation of the difference between the market value of a share and its book value is the subject of market finance, a topic not covered here. A shareholder is interested in the yield of his or her shares on the basis of their acquisition price. This yield results from both dividends received and potential capital gains (reflections of expected future earnings per share). In measuring whether a firm has created value during a period of time, we will ignore share yield and only consider the return on the book value of equity (the only one managers actually have the power to modify).

3.2.2 Residual income

The original idea behind 'residual income' is that the 'real' profit of the firm (surplus of resources received over resources consumed) should be defined as the income after taking into account the *cost of all sources of funds*, including a fair (even if nominal) remuneration for the shareholders, not just the financial costs due to interest-bearing liabilities.

Shareholders demand excess return over and above the risk free rate (essentially the rate earned on government bonds of major economies). This excess return is a function of the risk-factors of the firm and is often referred to as the 'risk premium'.

Let us assume in a short example that, for the risk class in which Acme Co. operates, shareholders feel (collectively) that an excess return of 10% over and above the risk-free rate (assumed to be 5%) would be an acceptable return on their book equity. In this case, the shareholders implicitly expect a return of 15%. Assume further that Acme Co. earned an after-tax income of 1,000 CU and has a book-value of equity of 10,000 CU. Its residual income is 1,000 − (10,000 × 0.15) = − 500 CU. Acme Co., which showed a positive accounting profit, is in fact not returning enough, during that period, to meet the shareholders' expectations. Many businesses actually do show a negative residual income, at least during some periods of their life.

Residual income is an old concept: it was introduced by R. Hamilton in 1777 in Volume 1 of his self-published work *An Introduction to Merchandize*, published in Edinburgh (Mepham, 1983). Despite its use having been 'rejuvenated' after World War II, for example at General Electric, under the auspices of the now-defunct accounting firm Arthur Andersen, residual income 'suffers' from accepting GAAP-defined accounting income 'at face value'. As we have seen, any GAAP, in any country, and even IFRS are the result of compromises and derive from the application of, among others, the prudence principle: they may, therefore, create what some consider an 'overly prudent' bias in the determination of net income, the numerator in ROE and one key element in the calculation of residual income.

3.2.3 Economic value added

Although Peter Drucker discussed the weaknesses of accounting-based residual income, and laid down the foundations of what became EVA, as early as his 1964 book *Managing for Results*, it is Stern Stewart and Co, a New York-based financial advisory firm, that claims the rights to EVA® in the book *The Quest for Value*, authored by G. Bennett Stewart III, published in 1991 by Harper Collins.

Their position is that many accounting elements used in the determination of income do not reflect a long-term view and thus the accounting bottom line does not reflect the ('true') point of view of the shareholders (interested more in the future than in the past, and particularly interested in the ability of the entity to remain a going concern). In total they suggest some 150 adjustments to the income figure to free themselves from the constraints of prudence-based GAAP. Two examples of such adjustments concern R&D and advertising or marketing expenses, which are period expenses under most GAAP (see Chapter 8) while, in an EVA-recalculated income, these two consumptions of resources are considered as investments necessary to prepare the future of the firm. Under such an hypothesis, all of R&D expenses and advertising or marketing expenses are capitalized (thus modifying shareholders book equity accordingly), and amortized over the expected duration during which they will bring benefits to the firm, thus modifying the 'income figure' used in the, now adjusted, residual income calculation. The derivation of EVA® from cash flow from operations, cascading through a succession of other metrics of business performance, is illustrated in Figure 18.6. Other consulting firms have coined their own proprietary, slightly different, approaches.

Stern Stuart and Co. extended their model to recognize the difference between book equity and market equity. It led to MVA (market value added) (see Figure 18.7).

MVA reflects the perception by financial markets of the capability of the firm to create value. It measures the excess market valuation of the shares, beyond the requisite reward of long-term capital investment at that level of risk. It uses the revised book value of equity after all the accounting adjustments Stern Stuart and Co recommend.

> MVA = market capitalization of the firm − (revised book value of equity + interest-bearing liabilities)

MVA reflects the opinion of the financial market about past performance and, according to some authors, provides an estimation of its capability to create value in the future. The concept is graphically illustrated in Figure 18.7 and the link between MVA and EVA is illustrated in Figure 18.8.

Figure 18.6 Cascading from cash flow from operations to EVA[®][3]

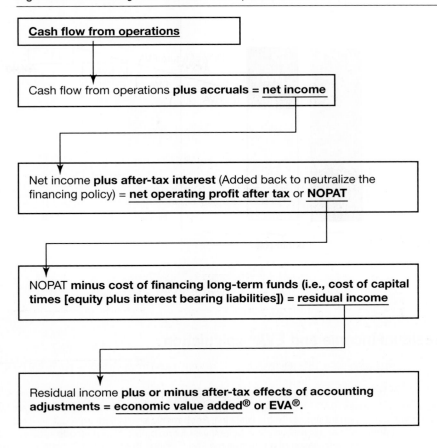

Cash flow from operations

Cash flow from operations **plus accruals = net income**

Net income **plus after-tax interest** (Added back to neutralize the financing policy) = **net operating profit after tax** or **NOPAT**

NOPAT **minus cost of financing long-term funds (i.e., cost of capital times [equity plus interest bearing liabilities]) = residual income**

Residual income **plus or minus after-tax effects of accounting adjustments = economic value added[®] or EVA[®].**

Figure 18.7 The concept of MVA (market value added)

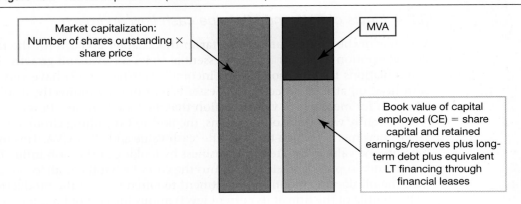

Market capitalization: Number of shares outstanding × share price

MVA

Book value of capital employed (CE) = share capital and retained earnings/reserves plus long-term debt plus equivalent LT financing through financial leases

Figure 18.8 illustrates the fact that, essentially, MVA can also be defined as the net present value (NPV) of future EVA[®] streams, thus reconciling the two approaches. However, while EVA[®] measures the excess value created during one period, MVA cannot distinguish between estimation by the market of the value created in the past (or from the undervaluation of the book value of assets) from that created this current period or in the future, thus the definitional link, although logical, may be spurious at best.

Figure 18.8 MVA and EVA related

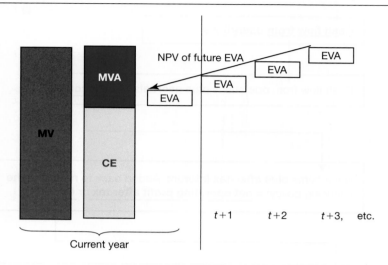

Example of residual income and EVA® calculation

(assuming a shareholders' expectation of a 15% return – i.e., risk free rate plus firm-specific risk premium) (See Table 18.4)

EVA®, residual income or any other method in the same family such as MVA, try to provide what their authors feel is a 'better' answer to the question 'Did a business *really* create value?' than does accounting and traditional financial analysis. As usual, no method provides a complete or perfect answer to the question. Each metric sheds light on a different aspect of financial performance, especially as it pertains to an estimation of the potential for future profits. New methods appear continuously that try to compensate for the weaknesses or limitation of a previous method (Ferling, 1993; Boston Consulting Group, 1996).

3.2.4 Limits of EVA and MVA: the cash flow approach

Very few of the items examined so far in this chapter account for the fact that the cash flow generation ability of a firm is essential to its survival and growth. Since accounting manipulations that are possible on income (see Chapter 17) have very little impact on cash flow, or, at least, affect it to a lesser extent or only indirectly, it would seem logical to search for measures of value creation that are based on cash flows.

Coherently with these observations, the Boston Consulting Group (BCG) introduced in 1996 a new metric, which they call the 'cash value added' or CVA. This metric attempts to measure the value generated by a business by looking at the cash influx (after-tax income before interest plus depreciation) minus the cost of what they call 'economic depreciation' (i.e., the minimum amount of investment required to keep the production and commercial potential of the firm at its current level) minus the cost of long-term funds (equity and interest-bearing liabilities). Such a measure appears to be more appropriate than many of the other synthetic metrics of shareholder value creation for helping the manager-decider in his or her decision to invest to grow the firm (by adding capacity, carrying out research or by upgrading its value proposition and thus extracting a possible price premium).

A ratio of CVA to the market value of the shareholders' equity invested shows the 'cash flow return on investment' or CFROI (also a BCG creation). An aggressively investing firm that chooses the 'right' sectors to invest in (i.e., those in which the firm can generate excess cash flow over what is needed to maintain the firm at its current level of market acceptance

Table 18.4 Example of economic value added*

Income statement

Sales revenue	6,500
COGS	3,500
Gross margin (after depreciation expense)	3,000
R&D expenses	500
Selling, general and administrative expenses	600
EBIT	1,900
Interest expenses on long-term (LT) liabilities (interest rate = 5%)	200
Taxable income	1,700
Tax expense (assumed to be at 33% of taxable income)	561
Net income after tax	1,139

Balance sheet

Fixed assets (net)	8,500
Current assets	5,500
Current liabilities	4,500
Long-term liabilities	4,000
Total shareholders' equity (capital provided, on which shareholders expect a return of 15% per year)	5,500

Residual income calculation (We assume all long-term capital costs the same as shareholders' funds so as not to presume the leveraging policy of the firm, especially if we want to extrapolate to the future)

Profit after tax and before interest 1,139 + 200 (1–0.33) =	1,273
Cost of long-term capital (5,500 + 4,000) × 15%	1,425
Residual income (RI)	**−152**

The residual income indicates the firm was short by 152 CU of creating wealth over and beyond the cost of long-term capital (chosen here to be the minimum return expected by shareholders).

If we consider the leverage policy to be a given, we can use the weighted average cost of capital (10.79% = [4,000 × 5% + 5,500 × 15%]/9,500) instead of the higher cost of shareholders' equity. In that case we find another value for residual income of +248 CU (i.e., 1,273 – (9,500 × 10.79%) = +248). The difference between the two versions of RI indicates the benefit of leveraging long-term capital at a lower rate than the cost of equity capital. The firm saves 400 CU by leveraging. The residual income calculated in our second case (248 CU), is a pool of funds the management team can choose to affect 'freely' to paying extra dividends, to awarding bonuses to employees, or to invest in R&D, in quality, in volume or in market development. However, this is conditional on keeping the long-term lenders happy, while the figure of RI = −152 was more descriptive of the situation before leveraging, and thus more meaningful for future decisions.

EVA calculation

Profit after tax and before interest (See RI calculations)	1,273
After-tax reintegration of R&D* expenses (considered to be an investment) [500) × (1–0.33) = 335]	+335
After-tax amortization of capitalized R&D* (assumed over 3 years)	−111
Adjusted income base	1,497
Long-term capital employed (equity plus long-term debt)	9,500
Adjustment for R&D* before tax = (500 capitalized – 1/3 of amortization)	335
Adjusted long-term capital employed	9,835
Cost of capital (9,835 × 15%) *(Rate of 15% is assumed to be applicable to any long-term funds, for the same reasons as above)*	1,475
EVA® (1,497 – 1,475)	**+ 22**

*The R&D expense is considered to be an investment. Consequently, the profit is increased and the shareholders' equity (included in the long-term capital) must also be adjusted by the same amount corresponding to the change in profit. (See capitalization of R&D, in Chapter 8).

and market satisfaction capabilities) will be rewarded with a 'good' value of this indicator, while the management team that invested in the 'wrong' sector will be shown to be poor performers by this metric. These tools allow the shareholder, or the supervisor or the manager, to evaluate, *ex post*, the quality of the managerial decisions. Although designed to analyze the past, CVA and CFROI can, of course, also be used, through simulations, in the analysis of future action plans, business plans and budgets, i.e., in deciding about the future.

4 Segment reporting

Segmenting the activities of a business means breaking down the entity into self-contained homogeneous business model components, or segments. Segmenting may be by markets, by customer profiles, by families of products or services, by families of technologies, by geographical areas, by type of currency exposure, by type of dependency on a given raw material, etc. Reporting financial information by segment may, namely, assist the financial statements users in:

- better understanding the entity's co-existing operating models and, thus, better interpreting past performance as a leading indicator of future performance;

- better assessing the entity's risks and returns, opportunities and threats, which may be vastly different in separate segments;

- making more informed judgments about the entity as a whole;

- estimating whether, in their opinion, the firm is extracting enough synergies from its complexity, or should be broken up and sold 'by apartments'.

Segments often yield differing profitability rates, experience different opportunities for growth, present unequal future prospects and risks. Segment reporting is essential for both the management team of the firm (especially in the context of resource allocation) and for shareholders (owning shares of a multi-segmented business may be a form of diversification of their risk). The principles and practices of segment reporting are documented through IFRS 8 (IASB 2006) [which has superseded IAS 14 (IASB 1997)], and SFAS 131 (FASB 1997) in the USA. These standards, requiring reporting of segment information, apply mainly to publicly traded companies and especially to their consolidated financial statements. However, they promote good management and can, without any difficulty, and with great potential informational benefits, be applied to not-publicly-traded companies and to non-consolidated financial statements.

4.1 Definitions

IFRS 8 (§ 5) defines an 'operating segment' as 'a component of an entity:

(a) that engages in business activities from which it may earn revenues and incur expenses (including revenues and expenses relating to transactions with other components of the same entity);

(b) whose operating results are regularly reviewed by the entity's chief operating decision-maker to make decisions about resources to be allocated to the segment and assess its performance; and

(c) for which discrete financial information is available'.

4.2 Disclosure

IFRS 8 refers to the concept of 'reportable segments' by indicating that (§ 11) 'an entity shall report separately information about each operating segment that (...) exceeds the quantitative thresholds [defined] in paragraph 13':

'An entity shall report separately information about an operating segment that meets any of the following quantitative thresholds:

(a) Its reported revenue, including both sales to external customers and intersegment sales or transfers, is 10 per cent or more of the combined revenue, internal and external, of all operating segments.

(b) The absolute amount of its reported profit or loss is 10 per cent or more of the greater, in absolute amount, of (i) the combined reported profit of all operating segments that did not report a loss and (ii) the combined reported loss of all operating segments that reported a loss.

(c) Its assets are 10 per cent or more of the combined assets of all operating segments.

Operating segments that do not meet any of the quantitative thresholds may [nonetheless] be considered reportable, and separately disclosed, if management believes that information about the segment would be useful to users of the financial statements' (IFRS 8 § 13).

In practice, 'an entity shall disclose information to enable users of its financial statements to evaluate the nature and financial effects of the business activities in which it engages and the economic environments in which it operates' (IFRS 8: § 20). 'To give effect to the principle in paragraph 20, an entity shall disclose the following for each period for which a statement of comprehensive income [i.e., an income statement] is presented:

(a) general information as described in paragraph 22;

(b) information about reported segment profit or loss, including specified revenues and expenses included in reported segment profit or loss, segment assets, segment liabilities and the basis of measurement, as described in paragraphs 23–27; and

(c) reconciliations of the totals of segment revenues, reported segment profit or loss, segment assets, segment liabilities and other material segment items to corresponding entity amounts as described in paragraph 28' (IFRS 8: § 21).

IFRS 8 (§ 22): states: 'An entity shall disclose the following general information:

(a) factors used to identify the entity's reportable segments, including the basis of organization (for example, whether management has chosen to organize the entity around differences in products and services, geographical areas, regulatory environments, or a combination of factors and whether operating segments have been aggregated); and

(b) types of products and services from which each reportable segment derives its revenues'.

IFRS 8 has adopted the so-called 'management approach' in the sense that:

(a) entities report segments that correspond to internal management reports;

(b) entities report segment information that are more consistent with other parts of their annual reports;

(c) some entities report more segments than others.

IFRS 8 has abandoned the division, which was required under IAS 14, between primary and secondary reporting formats. According to that Standard, each entity had to choose to report both a primary and, within this first classification, a secondary segment report-ing format: for example, market-, or product-, or service-based **business segments** as primary information, and geographical segments as secondary information (or the opposite).

IFRS example   Table 18.5, provided in IFRS 8 (§ IG3), illustrates a suggested format for disclosing information about reportable segment profit or loss, assets and liabilities.

Table 18.5 Suggested form of reporting of segment activity

(in CU)	Car parts	Motor vessels	Software	Electronics	Finance	All other	Totals
Revenues from external customers	3,000	5,000	9,500	12,000	5,000	1,000	35,500
Intersegment revenues	–	–	3,000	1,500		–	4,500
Interest revenue	450	800	1,000	1,500	–	–	3,750
Interest expense	350	600	700	1,100	–	–	2,750
Net interest revenue	–	–	–	–	1,000	–	1,000
Depreciation and amortization	200	100	50	1,500	1,100	–	2,950
Reportable segment profit	200	70	900	2,300	500	100	4,070
Other material non-cash items: Impairment of assets	–	200	–	–	–	–	200
Reportable segment assets	2,000	5,000	3,000	12,000	57,000	2,000	81,000
Expenditures for reportable segment non-current assets	300	700	500	800	600	–	2,900
Reportable segment liabilities	1,050	3,000	1,800	8,000	30,000	–	43,850

Real-life example Toray Industries

(Japan – Japanese GAAP – Source: Annual report 2009 – Manufacturer of synthetic fibers and textiles)

The company reports its activity in six business segments (Table 18.6) and three geographical areas (Table 18.7).

Table 18.6 Reporting by business segment – 2009 (in ¥ million)

Year ended 31 March 2009	Fibers and textiles	Plastics and chemicals	IT related products	Carbon fiber composite materials	Environment and engineering	Life science and other businesses	Total	Elimination and corporate	Consolidated total
Sales to outside customers	568,996	377,644	229,421	70,390	160,207	64,903	1,471,561	–	1,471,561
Intersegment sales	649	25,816	8,249	703	54,786	18,180	108,383	–108,383	–
Total sales	**569,645**	**403,460**	**237,670**	**71,093**	**214,993**	**83,083**	**1,579,944**	**–108,383**	**1,471,561**
Operating income	7,664	4,072	9,822	8,398	3,303	3,185	36,444	–438	36,006
Total assets	418,622	373,904	295,691	227,328	184,456	101,508	1,601,509	–77,906	1,523,603
Depreciation and amortization	23,547	22,541	18,813	13,588	3,122	4,170	85,781	–2,017	83,764
Loss on impairment of fixed assets	2,968	968	7,954	247	46	79	12,262	–	12,262
Capital expenditures	13,811	23,571	15,908	37,843	1,350	3,085	95,568	–3,219	92,349

Table 18.7 Reporting by geographic segment – 2009 (in ¥ million)						
Year ended 31 March 2009	Japan	Asia	North America, Europe and other areas	Total	Eliminations and corporate	Consolidated total
Sales to outside customers	1,016,046	302,547	152,968	1,471,561	–	1,471,561
Intersegment sales	103,000	66,501	12,079	181,580	–181,580	–
Total sales	**1,119,046**	**369,048**	**165,047**	**1,653,141**	**–181,580**	**1,471,561**
Operating income	18,179	7,211	10,381	35,771	235	36,006
Total assets	1,077,924	269,185	207,682	1,554,791	–31,188	1,523,603

The reader will notice that Toray Industries, although, in fact, providing both a primary and secondary segmentation of their accounts, did not provide a matrix that would allow the user to know the presence of one primary segment in a geographical area. Reporting to the outside users such information would undoubtedly give too much knowledge about the firm, at a low cost of acquisition, to competitors, suppliers or customers. It would be strategically unwise to reveal too much, even if, internally, that structuring of the data is likely to be readily available.

5 Scoring models

As we said earlier, the questions 'how much' and 'how' are moot if the firm under scrutiny ceases to be viable. It is therefore of prime importance for managers and financial information users to try to evaluate the probability that an entity might no longer be a going concern.

5.1 Principles

One main preoccupation of analysts is, therefore, to identify the likelihood of a business failing. Several authors (for example, Altman, 1968; Sands *et al.*, 1983; or Fulmer *et al.*, 1984) have developed models, called **scoring models**, generally based on a linear multivariate regression analysis (or using linear discriminant analysis) of several ratios and/or elements of the financial statements that create a unique 'score' for a firm at one point in time. If the score is (or drifts) above or below certain experiential thresholds, the likelihood of the business failing is declared to be high or low.

5.2 Example: Altman's Z score

Altman's model is probably the original model of failure likelihood measurement and has become a classic of this genre. The original 'Z score', based on a limited sample of large manufacturing firms that had filed for bankruptcy, was created by the following equation where the coefficients had been determined by analyzing the data from the firms in the sample:

$$Z = 1.2 \times (\text{working capital/total assets}) + 1.4 \times (\text{shareholders' equity/total assets})$$
$$+ 3.3 \times (\text{earnings before income taxes/total assets}) +$$
$$0.6 \times (\text{market value of equity/book value of debt}) + 1.0 \times (\text{sales/total assets})$$

To evaluate a firm's likelihood of bankruptcy (after, of course, verifying the firm analyzed is generally similar to those in the original sample), an analyst would compare the firm's Z score with the empirically determined thresholds shown below.

- If Z < 1.81, high probability of bankruptcy
- If 1.81 ≤ Z ≤ 2.99, one cannot tell (zone of ignorance)
- If Z > 2.99, low probability of bankruptcy.

The Z score approach, with appropriate adjustments of the coefficients to relevant samples and to economic environment, has proven to be relatively successful in the real world. Most applications confirm the findings of the original research, which showed the model correctly predicting 72% of bankruptcies two years prior to the event.

The values of the coefficients and of the thresholds have to be specified for each homogeneous group of businesses (size, industry, etc.). The coefficients for the Z score are not standardized, but most of the ratios combined in the Z score seem to be valid for all manufacturing industries.[5]

Financial analysts rely heavily on scoring models and other models to help them anticipate dramatic events in the life of the entity. For more details on scoring models, see Appendix 18.4.

6 Governance

As defined in Chapter 1, accounting is the set of processes and procedures that create figures that reflect and depict the economic activity of an economic entity. Figures created by accounting result from a certain number of well-defined practices, developed throughout this book, which must be run in accordance with the accounting principles that were introduced in Chapter 4. Yet, as we have seen, a lot of leeway is still granted by all GAAP in coding, classifying and reporting economic events. Particularly difficult questions are those of revenue and cost recognition and timing, or the creation of provisions.

The figures handled by the accounting system are the products of human endeavor. Managers are risk takers: the reward to shareholders and the reasoned risk management practiced by the entity's board and the firm executives are linked. Ethical (or unethical) behavior, risk management practices and the way to use the entity's resources in the business process affect the truthfulness and usefulness of the figures reported in an economic entity's accounts.

6.1 Enterprise governance defined

Unfortunately, despite frequent references to governance in the general media, the concept is not a new topic. Adam Smith in his 'Wealth of Nations' (1776) already mentioned the agency situation, albeit in a pessimistic tone, which creates the need for governance: 'Being managers of other people's money but their own, it cannot well be expected that they should watch over it with the same anxious vigilance with which ... [they] frequently watch over their own. Negligence and profusion,[6] therefore must always prevail more or less in the management of the affairs of a company'.

Managers, and CEOs, and executive managers more directly than others, have received a mandate from shareholders to be their agent (thus the term 'agency') in creating wealth with the resources they have handed over to the firm.

In 1992, Sir Adrian Cadbury defined governance as 'the system for direction and control of the corporation'.[7] In 1999, the same author, in a work for the World Bank gave a broader definition of governance: 'Corporate governance is ... holding the balance between economic and social goals, and between individual and communal goals. The governance framework is there to encourage the efficient use of resources and equally to require accountability for the stewardship of these resources. The aim is to align as nearly as possible the interests of individuals, corporations and society. The incentive to corporations is to achieve their corporate aims and to attract investments. The incentive for states is to strengthen their economics and discourage fraud and mismanagement'.[8]

Although we acknowledge the societal aspects of business entities and the need for societal governance, we will adopt a narrower definition of the term in the context of this section: 'Enterprise governance is the set of responsibilities and practices exercised by the board and executive management, with the goal of:

1. providing strategic direction;

2. ensuring that objectives are achieved;

3. ascertaining that risks are managed appropriately; and

4. verifying that the organization's resources are used responsibly'.[9]

Enterprise governance, for the scope of this text, focuses mainly on the latter two parts of this definition. There are subsets or prerequisites of a larger question: is the image of the economic situation and value creation, past, present and future of the business entity, true and fair?

6.2 Corporate governance and internal controls, accountability and assurance

Corporate governance builds on what used to be called 'internal control systems'. It includes all systems, practices and procedures designed to ensure conformance, both during the implementation of strategy and when reporting its outcome, with pre-defined principles and regulations and to create accountability assurance.

6.3 Business governance and value creation

Business governance addresses the question of responsible and strategically appropriate usage of resources of the firm, within a pre-defined, acceptable risk-taking policy. The purpose of business governance is to find whether the management team has actually fulfilled its agency obligation and created value.

We have seen that value creation can be measured by a variety of instruments. All the measures we examined are somehow accounting-based and thus suffer from a 'retrospective view' bias, even if the methods underlying each measure can be used in simulations and budgets. True value creation, in the logic of a going concern entity, is when cash flows and profits generated (and reported) are effectively used to ensure the long-term development of the firm, i.e., to create the conditions for on-going success. In this context, investments in R&D, market development and capacity growth as well as 'risk management' become the major responsibilities of executive management. Identification of opportunities, development of competence, strategic orientation of R&D, risk evaluation and preparing for the occurrence of these risks become the key activities for preparing the firm for the future.

According to a 2007 PricewaterhouseCoopers survey, an integrated approach to governance, regulation and compliance (GRC) can enhance reputational value (by 23%), employee retention value (by 10%) and increase revenue (by 8%) (PwC, 2007a). See also PwC (2007b) for a detailed approach to managing governance.

6.4 Business governance metrics

The strategic vision of the executive management team is difficult to evaluate or measure. It is the role of the board of directors to exercise oversight to make sure opportunities and risks are appropriately apprehended and managed.

Three families of measures exist to report on value creation, each addressing a different question:

1. *What is the current profitability of this business?* What is the ability of this business to generate positive and durable cash flows from the currently installed asset base? Examples of measures employed to answer this question include EPS, gross margin, free cash flow, **return on capital employed** (ROCE), EVA®, and plenty more.

2. *What is the value today of this business entity?* Examples of measures used here, in the absence of a market value, of course, are price to earning ratio multiples, shareholders' equity multiples or discounted future cash flows.

3. *By how much has this business and management team increased the value from time t to t+1?* (Value is defined by one of the measures cited above, or, for listed firms, by the market value of shareholders' equity). The measure most frequently used to address this question is the 'total shareholders' return' or TSR:

$$TSR = [(Value_{t+1} - Value_t) + Dividends]/Value_t$$

6.5 Regulating enterprise governance

After the fairly recent series of spectacular bankruptcies or scandals, including Chrysler, General Motors, Enron, Parmalat, Tyco, Vivendi-Universal or WorldCom on the industrial side and the financial bankruptcies of the likes of AIG, Lehman Brothers, Wachovia Bank, Fortis Bank, Washington Mutual, the total collapse of the Icelandic banking system, or the financial scandals of Bernie Madoff's *'Ponzi Scheme'* or the unreported risk-taking by the Galleon Hedge Fund, to name a few, investors have begun doubting the validity of reported company accounts and the effectiveness of the oversight exercised by both the board of directors (or its equivalent if the firm uses another format for oversight) and external auditors. Governments and regulators around the world have promulgated appropriate legislation or regulations to prevent further occurrences of such scandals, which threaten all firms by casting a shadow over the fairness of information and thus the fairness of access to funds through financial markets. From the first thorough regulation of governance by the Sarbanes-Oxley Act in the US (2002), to the World Bank 2002 governance recommendations for developing economies, to the UAE (United Arab Emirates) making, as of April 2010, mandatory the implementation of corporate governance regulations in all UAE-based businesses (largely inspired by the Sarbanes-Oxley Act and incorporating the World Bank recommendations), almost all countries have designed their own set of regulations.

One well-known and exemplary such piece of legislation is the already mentioned Sarbanes-Oxley Act in the United States (applicable only to US firms or to firms quoted on a US stock exchange). It is a complex piece of legislation but contains three key provisions that are directly relevant to the usefulness of reported accounts.

- Section 302: CEOs and CFOs must personally certify and guarantee the accuracy of quarterly and annual financial statements.

- Section 404: Businesses must (1) clearly communicate the current managerial responsibilities for establishing and maintaining appropriate internal controls pertaining to the protection of assets and the establishment of financial statements, and (2) make public an assessment of the effectiveness of these internal controls (this second aspect is subject to an external audit report).

- Section 409: The firm is required to disclose in real time (within two days) any significant event that affects its financial position. Examples of such events would be the loss of a major customer, a change in the evaluation score issued by one of the financial-risk rating agencies or a modification to the benefit package that may result from labor negotiations.

These requirements are clearly quite strict. They can, however, if one so desires, be satisfied only to the letter, in a mechanical way (i.e., putting the emphasis on creating an 'audit trail' and only formally creating a responsibility chain, but with no accountability). They fail, in our view, to address some of the real issues that are behind the scandals that have cast a pall over financial reporting: greed and personal ambition, leading to excessive risk-taking and its under-reporting, to accounting and information technology malpractice to cover one's own tracks (most of the banking failures or financial scandals in the US took place post Sarbanes-Oxley).

Enron and other scandal-ridden firms had regularly and systematically abused the possibility of off-balance sheet commitments. They had under-reported (or reported in unclear ways) their off-balance sheet commitments (thus potentially creating real liabilities). The scandal of the derivatives, and particularly that of Credit Default Swaps, in 2008, which brought down mighty banks was, despite regulators efforts, the result in large part of imprudent off-balance sheet commitments. Off-balance sheet commitments are not always fraudulent, but they always need to be understood to visualize the actual financial position of the firm and the risks they imply. This is why, throughout this text we have emphasized the notes are an integral and important part of financial statements.

Transparency is one of the main accounting principles but the complexity of today's business transactions makes it sometimes difficult to be fully transparent, even when no ill will is intended.

6.6 The causes of violations of the good governance principles

In 2003 the International Federation of Accountants (IFAC) mandated a research team to study governance frameworks in light of recent reporting scandals. Twenty-seven cases were studied around the world. The researchers distinguished two categories of issues: corporate governance on one hand, and strategy definition and implementation issues on the other.

Under corporate governance they listed the following sources of possible 'causes' for violation of the principle of true and fair view:

- The role of the chief executive (dominant, charismatic, authoritarian and not inclined to being challenged, focused on external growth though mergers and acquisitions (M&A), lack of clear strategy, etc.)

- The role of the board of directors (unable to challenge or direct the CEO because its members are too friendly with, or linked in one way or another with, the CEO or with key senior executive managers)

- Executive remuneration plans (non-congruent incentive or bonus programs, over-aggressive targets leading to earnings management to obtain the bonus).

- Ethics, culture and tone at the top (poor ethical standards among senior executives, slowness in acknowledging and responding to difficulties in implementation of the strategy, particularly those pertaining to M&A).

- Internal controls (weak internal controls over the usage of assets and resources, including human resources).

The combination of these negative traits leads to earnings management, ethical violations and generally leads to compromising with the truth.

6.7 Regulating ethics

The Sarbanes-Oxley Act (SOX) and its country-specific equivalents attempt to create better oversight of these problems, but the spirit of the law is too often compromised in favor of respecting only its letter. Legislation like the Sarbanes-Oxley Act has not been sufficient, as the collapses of financial institutions in 2008 illustrated, to prevent all attempts at incomplete or 'fraudulent' reporting of off-balance sheet commitments (morality is a question of society), but without such regulations, there might have been more such attempts. For example, the Ford Motor Company, which used to keep off-balance sheet the Ford Credit risks linked to car leases (in 2000 the off-balance sheet risk of leases was four times larger than reported long-term liabilities), now fully reports this risk as an on-balance sheet fully provisioned item. The three sections of SOX we highlighted above are essential to creating a good climate in the organization. However no one can say, for example, whether a target or objective is too demanding or not, too risky or not, whether a leader is too charismatic or not or whether a strategy is well formulated or not. It boils down to a question of morals and culture. As Peter Drucker is often quoted to have said: 'There is no such things as business ethics ... There is just ethics; and we all have to practice them every day in everything we do'.

Values in an organization begin with senior management and their oversight by a qualified and independent board of directors, truly representing the interests of shareholders. Shareholders have the responsibility to elect board members who will really be stand-up people. Respect of the agency mandate received by both board members and senior executives from the shareholders sets the condition for relevant financial accounts.

6.8 Corporate social responsibility

Without going into details on this subject (whole books are devoted to the theme), we would like to cite some good questions suggested by Djordjija Petkoski of the World Bank Institute (2004)[10] that are relevant to evaluating the long term future of a business:

- What kind of impact does the firm, in its sector, can have on poverty [health and education]?
- How is wealth created distributed? (Between profit reward to shareholders, remuneration to workers and suppliers, customers, the state, etc.)
- What kinds of activities constitute best practice in this area?
- Is the business aware of its impact?
- Is it doing something about it?
- If not, what are the issues the business needs to face, that have been faced effectively by others in the sector?

All businesses should behave as citizens of the world if they want to really serve their constituency of stakeholders in the long run.

Key points

- Financial statement analysis processes, evaluates and interprets the data reported to shareholders and the financial community to facilitate its usability in decision-making.
- Managers and outsiders of the firm both must carry out financial statement analysis to answer the questions: Has the firm created value for shareholders? How did they do it and is it a renewable achievement?
- Users of financial information are interested in understanding liquidity, solvency, leverage, and profitability of a firm, as well as understanding its asset management policies and the resulting return to investors.
- A ratio is the quotient of two quantities, the numerator and the denominator, showing (assuming) there is a relationship between them.
- Ratio analysis helps describe the business model in a set of causal relationships and their evolution.
- Ratios must be used cautiously as the numerator and denominator must be coherent within the business model and correspond to the same time period. Further, not all items in the financial statements are meaningfully related.
- Three types of comparison increase the information content of ratios: (1) time-series comparisons; (2) cross-sectional comparisons; and (3) comparisons against a competitive or rule of thumb-based benchmark.

- A financial analyst supplements the accounting data by additional information from a variety of sources.
- Earnings per share and return on capital invested help shareholders decide whether or not to keep their money invested in this firm.
- The 'economic value added' measures the (adjusted) excess value (i.e., strategically available resources) generated by a business, after the cost of obtaining long-term capital has been covered (which includes shareholders' expected remuneration).
- Segmenting the activity of a business means breaking down its business model into homogeneous sub-models or segments to help improve the predictability of future streams of economic benefits.
- Financial analysts strive to identify the risk of a business failing, i.e., going bankrupt. Scoring models establish, for each firm, a synthetic index or 'score' which, when benchmarked, indicates whether a firm should be considered as healthy or in difficulty.
- The power of financial analysis is limited by the ethical behavior of managers and board members. Governance is an issue many countries attempt to regulate with some success.

Review (solutions are at the back of the book)

Review 18.1 Bizerte Home Furniture Company

Topic: Comprehensive financial statement analysis

The headquarters and plant of Bizerte Home Furniture Company (BHF) are located in the tax-advantaged industrial zone of Bizerte, Tunisia. BHF manufactures a complete line of high-quality home furniture and sofas for distribution through relatively exclusive retail stores strategically located within selected high-end marketing areas. These wholesale customers, all over the Mediterranean basin, comprise specialized independent home furnishing retailers, regional specialized chains, as well as department stores. The retailers carry products from a few different brands other than BHF in their showrooms. They promote locally the BHF products and those of competitors, take orders, and provide delivery service. BHF does not engage in retail sales itself, but promotes its brand in the various markets where its presence is significant through its distributors.

Unlike Tunisian furniture importers, who, often, either offered long delays for delivery, or had to carry a large inventory of finished products, BHF had invested both in a modular approach to furniture and sofas design and in sophisticated flexible manufacturing equipment. BHF had a significant inventory of imported kiln-dried woods in various grades, of various veneers and carried a wide selection of fabrics and foams. This inventory allowed BHF to manufacture 70% of its products to order for rapid delivery (less than two weeks ex-works, on average) and 30% for stock for immediate delivery when an order was received from a retailer.

The critical success factors of any furniture product line are, of course, design, brand name and quality. But visibility and availability are the most critical of all variables. Retailers carry a large inventory of a manufacturer's product in their showroom only if the supplier finances most of the inventory. Credit terms granted by BHF (and its competitors) are therefore crucial to the continued success of their brand.

In May 2010, Leila Smaoui, credit analyst for the Bizerte Home Furniture Company, was revisiting, as she did yearly, the credit situation of all customer accounts. The economic slowdown had seriously affected the overall furniture market. BHF's sales had been down almost 25% for the first quarter of the year over the same quarter a year earlier and the last quarter of 2009 had not been particularly good with an overall shipment decline of 5% over the same quarter a year earlier.

The situation of two retailers, representing, together in 2010, about 10% of BHF's Tunisian sales and 4% of its overall sales, seemed to raise urgent questions as to whether BHF should continue supplying them and extending supplier credit: Galleria Group SA, based in Tunis, and Le Grand Marché, based in Sfax.

Galleria Group was a young upscale retailer of quality home furnishings. It operated in three locations, one in downtown Tunis, one in Hammamet (over two-thirds of the sales of the Galleria store in this resort town were from contract sales to hotels) and the third, opened in late 2008, in Les Berges du Lac (new upscale, very large and rapidly growing, suburban development of Tunis with a planned mix of retail stores, light industry and services, business headquarters and offices, private residences and hotels). The BHF brand represented about 60% of the Galleria Group sales revenue. The Galleria sales manager insisted that his sales force require a 20% cash deposit to confirm an order and the rest of the payment would either be paid cash upon delivery (this applied to 75% of the sales) or the remainder of the invoice would be paid in up to six-month installment terms.

Galleria had been a customer of BHF Company since the opening of its first store in downtown Tunis about 7 years ago. It had, until recently, handled its relations with BHF in a most satisfactory manner.

Le Grand Marché (LGM), although long-established, was a comparatively new customer of BHF, having opened an account only in 2006. A sizeable furniture store in Sfax, Le Grand Marché was well known regionally for its extensive lines of home furnishings, serving the needs of a wide range of clienteles, institutional as well as up-market and down-market individual residential customers. Its institutional customers were essentially the many hotels in the nearby resort island of Djerba. BHF products represented only about 40% of its total sales. Its payment history to BHF had been satisfactory through early 2009 and then many overdue invoices had accumulated. LGM required only 10% down payment from their customers when they placed an order. The remainder was generally paid in equal installments over two months after delivery. However, lately, more and more customers had asked for, and obtained, extensions of one to two months of additional credit

Sales by BHF to both these wholesale accounts were on the standard commercial terms for the industry in Tunisia: a discount of 1% if the invoice was paid within 10 days of receipt, or net invoiced price due no later than 30 days after delivery. The CFO of BHF, Souad Mahmoudi, and Leila Smaoui in agreement with the sales manager, had previously established a 130,000 Tunisian Dinars (TND) credit limit on Galleria Group and a 105,000 TND limit on Le Grand Marché. Whether these limits were still appropriate was one of the questions Leila was debating.

Given BHF's own needs for liquidity and growth to occupy the fixed capacity of the plant, Souad Mahmoudi had asked Leila Smaoui to stay on top of the financial status of all customers. Leila was reviewing all situations annually on the basis of financial statements provided, at her request, by the customers, and would switch to a semi-annual analysis if she felt the situation of a client was deteriorating such as when the balance of overdue invoices exceeded 10% of the credit limit. Both Galleria Group and Le Grand Marché had hit and exceeded their limit.

In early May 2010, Leila Smaoui received the unaudited 2009–10 annual reports of Galleria and Le Grand Marché (both firms closed their annual accounts on the last Saturday before March 31). These statements, and the equivalent documents for the two preceding years, are provided as Exhibits 1– 4.

In the early months of 2010, demand for home furniture had remained weak. Although the drop in retail sales had not been as dramatic as in the second half of 2008 and first half of 2009, retail stores had placed fewer orders than anticipated, especially on new product lines, and had reduced their reorders of more classic products. BHF's sales force had mentioned that store showrooms were quite full, all over the network of distributors. The traditional end-of-year sale had not cleared the showrooms as it usually did to make room for the new collection. The dilemma for BHF was to find the balance between maintaining sales to distributors (which required extending credit) and keeping the receivables within acceptable limits, both in terms of balance and risk.

Required

1. Analyze the financial statements of Galleria and Le Grand Marché to understand how each reacted to the downturn in the market. Base your analysis on facts logically derived from the financial statements, such as selected ratios, longitudinal analyses, or any other relevant information contained in the case. Explain your selection of the metrics used in your analysis.

2. What recommendation(s) would you suggest to the management of BHF regarding these two clients, and especially whether it is appropriate to extend their credit limit and continue to ship to each or either?

Exhibit 1 – Galleria – Income statement

Year ending 31 March (in TND 000)	2008	2009	2010
Gross sales	22,000	18,000	18,100
Minus returns and allowances	−1,980	−2,160	−1,448
Net sales	**20,020**	**15,840**	**16,652**
Cost of goods sold	−10,010	−8,712	−9,658
Gross profit or gross margin	**10,010**	**7,128**	**6,994**
Operating expenses	−7,800	−6,345	−7,710
Operating profit	**2,210**	**783**	**−716**
Interest expense or income (net)	−294	−321	−381
Earnings before taxes	**1,916**	**462**	**−1,097**
Income taxes	479	−116	0
Net profit or loss	**1,437**	**347**	**−1,097**
Additional information			
Dividends paid (in year following)	*210*	*210*	*0*

Exhibit 2 – Galleria – Balance sheet

(in TND 000)	31/3/08	31/3/09	31/3/10
Cash	85	40	50
Accounts receivable net	2,600	3,100	3,300
Inventory	4,430	3,600	3,650
Total current assets	**7,115**	**6,740**	**7,000**
Land	300	900	900
Building, fixtures and equipment	5,200	5,800	6,613
Minus accumulated depreciation	800	1,200	1,650
Net Building, fixtures and equipment	4,400	4,600	4,963
Deferred charges	200	120	20
Total assets	**12,015**	**12,360**	**12,883**
Accounts payable	2,900	3,478	3,720
Salaries and fringe payable	40	165	165
Estimated income tax due	479	116	0
Current part of LTD	155	360	220
Down payments from customers	440	250	50
Total current liabilities	**4,014**	**4,369**	**4,155**
Long-term loans	4,000	4,200	4,800
Common stock	900	900	900
Additional paid-in capital	100	100	100
Retained earnings	1,564	2,791	2,928
Income of the year	1,437	347	−1,097
Total liabilities and net worth	**12,015**	**12,360**	**12,883**

Exhibit 3 – Le Grand Marché – Income statement

Year ending 31 March (in TND 000)	2008	2009	2010
Gross sales	64,125	60,265	52,970
Minus returns and allowances	5,825	5,600	5,841
Net sales	**58,300**	**54,665**	**47,129**
Cost of goods sold	36,105	34,851	32,388
Gross profit or gross margin	**22,195**	**19,814**	**14,741**
Operating expenses	18,080	16,995	18,765
Operating profit or loss	**4,115**	**2,819**	**–4,024**
Income tax expense	1,029	705	0
Net profit after taxes	**3,086**	**2,114**	**–4,024**
Additional information			
Dividends paid (in year following)	*725*	*600*	*25*

Exhibit 4 – Le Grand Marché –Balance sheet

(in TND 000)	31/3/08	31/3/09	31/3/10
Cash	165	140	75
Accounts receivable	4,900	6,825	5,678
Inventory	4,612	3,541	2,493
Prepaid and deferred expenses	140	145	155
Total current assets	**9,817**	**10,651**	**8,401**
Fixed assets net	1,139	1,200	1,160
Leasehold improvements net	4,480	3,712	3,050
Total assets	**15,436**	**15,563**	**12,611**
Accounts payable	10,305	9,612	10,699
Customer down payments	630	60	45
Total current liabilities	**10,935**	**9,672**	**10,744**
Common stock	1,220	1,220	1,220
Retained earnings	195	2,556	4,671
Income of the period	3,086	2,114	–4,024
Total liabilities and net worth	**15,436**	**15,563**	**12,611**

Assignments

Assignment 18.1
Multiple choice questions

Select the right answer (one possible answer, unless otherwise stated).

1. Which of the following statements is *not* correct?

   (a) A ratio reflects a business model relationship between two or more quantities

   (b) When using comparative ratio analysis, it is important to remember that the causal relationship behind a certain value of a ratio may not apply similarly to two different entities

   (c) Ratio analysis is rarely used for interpreting financial statements

   (d) A ratio calculation is generally the first step in an investigative research to get to the root cause of the situation described by the financial statements

2. In which type of comparisons are the ratios of one year compared to the historical ratios of the company?

   (a) Comparisons against a competitive benchmark.
   (b) Comparisons against rules of thumb based on industry-wide experience.
   (c) Time-series comparisons.
   (d) Cross-sectional comparisons.

3. How is the cash ratio calculated?

   (a) (Cash + Marketable securities + Accounts receivable)/Current liabilities
   (b) Cash dividends per share/Earnings per share
   (c) Cash/Marketable securities
   (d) (Cash + Marketable securities)/Current liabilities

4. How is the price earnings ratio (PER) calculated?

   (a) Market price per share/Book value per share
   (b) Market price per share/Earnings per share
   (c) Cash dividends per share/Market price per share
   (d) Cash dividends per share/Earnings per share

5. How is the interest coverage ratio calculated?

   (a) Operating income (before interest expense and income taxes)/Interest expense
   (b) Net income/Interest expense
   (c) Shareholders' equity/Interest expense
   (d) Long-term debts/Interest expense

6. The economic value added represents the creation or increase in 'value', resulting from the entity's current business activities, over and above the value of goods and services, consumed by the entity, that were provided by third parties

   (a) True
   (b) False

7. In what way(s) might reporting financial information by segment help the financial statements users?

   (a) It may help them better understand the entity's operating model and thus better interpret past performance as a leading indicator of future performance.
   (b) It may help them better assess the entity's risks and returns, opportunities and threats.
   (c) It may help them make more informed judgments about the entity as a whole.
   (d) All of these.

8. IFRS 8 distinguishes business segments and geographical segments.

   (a) True
   (b) False

9. According to IFRS 8, which factor(s) should be considered in identifying segments?

   (a) Similarity of economic conditions.
   (b) Relationships between operations in different geographical areas.
   (c) Special risks associated with operations in a particular area.
   (d) All of these.

10. According to IFRS 8, which of the following need *not* be reported for a business segment?

    (a) Segment revenue from external customers.
    (b) Total carrying amount of segment assets.
    (c) Total depreciation and amortization of segment assets included in the segment income.
    (d) Total cost incurred to acquire segment tangible and intangible assets.

Assignment 18.2
ULMA Construccion Polska SA*

Topic: Ratio analysis

ULMA Construccion Polska SA, formerly Bauma SA, is a Poland-based company that is primarily involved in the development, production and sale of construction products. The company offers vertical and horizontal formwork systems, engineering systems, props and shoring systems, as well as scaffolding systems.

The financial statements have been prepared in accordance with IFRS. From the annual reports 2008 and 2007, we extracted the balance sheet and income statement (see below).

Consolidated balance sheet

(in PLN (Polish Zloty) 000)	31 December 2008	31 December 2007	31 December 2006
ASSETS			
I. Fixed assets			
1. Tangible fixed assets	404,719	287,997	180,724
2. Intangible assets	641	796	860
3. Interests in associated entities	2,302	119	0
4. Other fixed assets	4,454	4,509	0
Total fixed assets	412,116	293,421	181,584
II. Working assets			
1. Stocks	16,044	21,302	15,288
2. Trade and other receivables	55,618	52,776	44,196
3. Income tax receivables	2,889	552	0
4. Cash and cash equivalents	6,059	29,838	2,251
Total working assets	80,610	104,468	61,735
Total assets	**492,726**	**397,889**	**243,319**
EQUITY AND LIABILITIES			
I. Equity			
1. Share capital	10,511	10,511	9,781
2. Paid-up capital – surplus of sale of shares over nominal value	114,990	114,990	25,776
3. Foreign exchange gains/loss due to consolidation	(3,939)	(699)	(403)
4. Retained earnings, of which:	142,348	116,495	65,614
Net profit for the financial year	*25,853*	*50,881*	*32,928*
Total equity	263,910	241,297	100,768
II. Liabilities			
1. Long-term liabilities			
a. Loans	146,128	82,710	86,420
b. Liabilities under deferred income tax	2,093	714	3,356
c. Long-term liabilities under pension benefits	74	43	28
d. Long-term liabilities under financial leasing	96	280	294
Total long-term liabilities	148,391	83,747	90,098
2. Short-term liabilities			
a. Loans	40,878	10,562	17,227
b. Short-term liabilities under pension benefits	9	0	0
c. Short-term liabilities under financial leasing	166	155	3,533
d. Liabilities under current income tax	0	4	122
e. Trade and other liabilities	39,372	62,124	31,571
Total short-term liabilities	80,425	72,845	52,453
Total liabilities	228,816	156,592	142,551
Total equity and liabilities	**492,726**	**397,889**	**243,319**

Income statement

(Common-size income statements added)	12 months ended on 31 December					
	2008	2007	2006	2008	2007	2006
	PLN 000	PLN 000	PLN 000	%	%	%
Sales revenues	241,505	222,567	154,255	100.0	100.0	100.0
Costs of sold products, goods and materials	(178,319)	(136,792)	(90,549)	(73.8)	(61.5)	(58.7)
I. Gross profit on sales	**63,186**	**85,775**	**63,706**	**26.2**	**38.5**	**41.3**
Costs of sale and marketing	(4,750)	(7,441)	(7,850)	(2.0)	(3.3)	(5.1)
Overheads	(10,605)	(10,034)	(9,795)	(4.4)	(4.5)	(6.3)
Other net costs	(6,884)	(1,707)	(127)	(2.9)	(0.8)	(0.1)
II. Profit on operations	**40,947**	**66,593**	**45,934**	**17.0**	**29.9**	**29.8**
Financial income	431	1,549	24	0.2	0.7	0.0
Financial expense	(11,099)	(6,010)	(4,896)	(4.6)	(2.7)	(3.2)
Net financial expense	(10,668)	(4,461)	(4,872)	(4.4)	(2.0)	(3.2)
Share in profit (loss) of associated companies	185	0	0	0.1	0.0	0.0
III. Gross profit	**30,464**	**62,132**	**41,062**	**12.6**	**27.9**	**26.6**
Income tax	(4,611)	(11,251)	(8,134)	(1.9)	(5.1)	(5.3)
IV. Net profit for the financial year	**25,853**	**50,881**	**32,928**	**10.7**	**22.9**	**21.3**

Required

1. Analyze the common-size income statements.
2. Compute the following ratios:
   - Current ratio
   - Average collection period (in days)
   - Long-term debt to equity ratio
   - Return on sales (in %).
3. Analyze these ratios.

Assignment 18.3
Microsoft Corporation*

Topic: Earnings per share

Microsoft Corporation is engaged in developing, manufacturing, licensing, and supporting a range of software products and services for different types of computing devices. The company's common stock is traded on the NASDAQ. The annual report 2009 (for the year ended 30 June) contains the following information: 'Basic earnings per share is computed on the basis of the weighted average number of shares of common stock outstanding during the period. Diluted earnings per share is computed on the basis of the weighted average number of shares of common stock plus the effect of dilutive potential common shares outstanding during the period using the treasury stock method. Dilutive potential common shares include outstanding stock options, stock awards, and shared performance stock awards'.

The weighted average outstanding shares of common stock, in 2009 was 8,945 million and dilutive effect of stock-based awards was 51 million. The income statement shows net income to be US $14,569 million.

Required

Prepare a statement showing the computation of basic and diluted earnings per share for the year 2009.

Assignment 18.4
TeleChoice International Limited*

Topic: Reliability of the predictive content of financial information

Incorporated in Singapore on 28 April 1998 and listed on the Main-Board of the Singapore Exchange Securities Trading Limited (SGX-ST) on 25 June 2004, TeleChoice International Limited ('TeleChoice') is a leading provider of telecommunications services and solutions. TeleChoice is a subsidiary of Singapore Technologies Telemedia Pte Ltd, a leading info-communications company with operations in Asia-Pacific, the Americas and Europe.

TeleChoice offers a comprehensive suite of services and solutions for the telecommunications industry:

- Distribution services: distribution, retail and fulfillment services relating to mobile handsets, accessories and other telecommunications equipment.
- Telecommunications services: value-added voice and data services, such as SunPage iDD *[Internet Digital*

Data] and Budget MobileCall, PushMail, Mobile Data Network Services.

■ Network engineering services: network provision, including network planning, project and resource management, network implementation and optimization, and managed outsourcing services.

Headquartered in Singapore, TeleChoice has operations around the Asia-Pacific region, including Indonesia, Malaysia and Thailand. As of 2004 its three-year compounded annual growth rate placed TeleChoice amongst the Fastest Growing Singapore 50. In 2005 it was recognized as one of Singapore's top 100 companies by highest overseas revenue.

Its self-declared 'commitment to good corporate governance and high standards of corporate disclosure', TeleChoice was ranked in 2005 amongst the top 10% of SGX-ST listed companies covered under The Business Times Corporate Transparency Index.

TeleChoice's major customers and principals include StarHub Ltd and PT Indosat Tbk, and Motorola, Nokia, and Sony Ericsson respectively.

Required

1. Analyze the financial performance of TeleChoice over the years 2003–2005, using the three years of financial data provided (Exhibits 1–3) and the additional information available in the exhibits.

2. Illustrate, from the financial statements for 2003–2005, the selected points made by the management in the conference call to investors shown as Exhibit 4.

Hint: You may or may not find that some statements made about recent evolution of financial performance may be somewhat optimistic or may not be supported by the data – be as fact-based as possible.

Exhibit 5 provides some key ratios for the relevant period. Exhibit 6 provides the evolution of the share price from 2003 to 2009 as background information. Using the statements for 2006 (Exhibits 7–9), illustrate (with fact-based statements) whether or not the vision described by management in March 2006, actually did materialize.

Exhibit 1 – TeleChoice International – Income statement

(in S$ 000)	2005	2004	2003
Revenue	569,931	530,102	320,295
Cost of sales	−524,952	−488,248	−285,955
Gross margin (GM)	44,979	41,854	34,340
GM as % of revenue	7.9%	7.9%	10.7%
Other income	2,161	1,074	779
Selling and marketing expenses	−8,967	−10,010	−8,863
Administrative expenses	−16,467	−11,441	−8,238
Other expenses	−258	−222	195
Profit from operations	21,448	21,255	18,213
Finance cost	−34	−133	−93
Share of profit in joint ventures	102	105	0
Profit before tax	21,516	21,227	18,120
PBT as % of revenue	3.8%	4.0%	5.7%
Tax expense	−4,342	−4,140	−3,389
Net income	**17,174**	**17,087**	**14,731**
Attributable to:			
Equity holders of the parent	17,654	16,969	14,215
% of revenue	3.1%	3.2%	0
Minority interest	−480	118	516

Exhibit 2 – TeleChoice International – Balance sheet

(in S$ 000)	2005	2004	2003
Non-current assets			
Investment in jointly controlled entity	1,371	1,038	0
Property, plant and equipment	2,792	1,959	1,371
Intangible assets	689	145	89
Deferred tax assets	425	263	549
Total non-current assets	5,277	3,405	2,009
Current assets			
Inventories	18,896	24,492	23,591
Work in progress	2,537	1,759	251
Trade receivables	13,928	20,526	10,946
Other receivables, deposits and prepaid	15,317	13,926	7,015
Amounts due from:-			
related corporations	21,788	20,215	20,087
holding companies	36	69	66
related minority shareholder of subs	3,930	9,951	4,034
Cash and cash equivalents	44,626	29,300	16,453
Total current assets	121,058	120,238	82,443
Total assets	126,335	123,643	84,452
Current liabilities			
Trade payables	46,902	57,723	41,252
Other payables and accruals	16,582	14,298	9,581
Amounts owed to:			
Related corporations	1,375	611	50
Holding companies	232	538	1,905
Minority shareholders	0	0	735
Current tax payable	4,458	3,566	3,238
Deferred income	1,228	1,390	1,044
Total current liabilities	70,777	78,126	57,805
Net current assets	50,281	42,112	24,638
Deferred tax liabilities	209	118	553
Long-term capital required	55,349	45,399	26,094
Share capital	8,906	8,840	8,000
Retained earnings (reserves)	45,949	36,242	18,094
Minority interest	494	317	0
Shareholders' equity	55,349	45,399	26,094

Exhibit 3 – TeleChoice International – Statement of cash flows

(in S$ 000)	2005	2004	2003
Cash flow from operations			
Profit before tax	21,516	21,227	18,120
Depreciation	1,343	866	1,609
Amortization of intangibles	228	81	83
Loss/gain on disposal of assets	78	12	−45
Impairment of assets	0	0	251
Value of employees services in exchange for stock options	333	350	0
Goodwill on consolidation	0	−28	0
Loss/gain on sale of subsidiary	0	138	-38
Goodwill on acquisition	−84	0	0
Interest income	−611	−191	−271
Interest expense	34	133	93
Share of profit of joint operations	−102	−105	0
Accretion of deferred income	−1,390	−1,044	−1,023
Cash from operating profit before changes in working capital (WC)	21,345	21,439	18,779
Changes in working capital	6,055	−9,566	-8222
Cash generated from operations	27,400	11,873	10,557
Income tax paid	−3,829	-3,436	−1,724
Interest received	611	193	293
Net cash from operations	24,182	8,630	9,126
Cash flow from investing			
Purchase of PPE assets	−2,045	−1,520	−932
Purchases of intangibles	−165	−147	−118
Proceeds from disposal of PPE	23	0	60
Acquisition additional interest in subsidiaries	0	−340	−657
Acquisition/addition to joint venture	−478	−519	
Cash inflow from acquisition/disposal of subsidiary	125	0	286
Loan to joint venture	242	−458	
Net cash from investing	−2,298	−2,984	−1,361
Cash flow from financing activities			
Non-trade balances w/ related corporations	1,672	5,568	28,974
Proceeds of IPO or capital contribution by minority	0	10,745	80
Return of capital by STMD & STSP			−27,775
Proceeds from share option scheme	684	0	
Interest paid	−34	−134	−95
Dividends paid	−8,903	−8,840	−12,140
Net cash flow from financing	−6,581	7,339	−10,956
Net increase in cash and cash equivalent	15,303	12,985	−3,191
Opening cash and equivalent	29,300	16,453	19,492
Effect of exchange rate differences	23	−138	152
Ending cash and cash equivalent	44,626	29,300	16,453

Exhibit 4 – TeleChoice International – Selected elements of the transcript of a Q&A session on 20 March 2006 between management and investors

Q1.1 *May I know what is the current order book for the Mobile Network and Engineering Services segment?*

The current outstanding order book for Network Engineering Services stands at approximately S$20M (FY05: S$44.2M).

Q1.2 *Will there be any further write-offs for the Australian and Indonesia handset distribution business?*

Based on the current information available, we do not foresee further write-offs on account of Distribution Services operations for Australia and Indonesia.

Q2.1 *Could you elaborate on some of the production gains and operating efficiencies the company is maximizing currently?*

(...) To maximize productivity and operating efficiencies, we constantly cross-leverage on expertise and resources across our business divisions, and minimize the duplication of cost-centres and resources wherever possible.

Q2.4 *I noticed selling and marketing expenses for FY05 have decreased while administrative expenses for FY05 have increased. (...)*

Included in the administrative expenses is a one-time S$3.8 million of bad debts written off for Distribution Services operations in Indonesia, due to currency devaluation.

Q3.1 *Earnings guidance for the current year 2006 and growth potential in the next 3 years for the company*

For FY06, the business outlook for TeleChoice is expected to remain positive and we expect to maintain our operating performance for FY06.

We are confident of our longer-term growth opportunities, and will continue to seek to acquire synergistic businesses and to grow organically in the region, and to maximize productivity gains and operating efficiencies.

(...) We will continue to leverage on the strength of our business model and the growth strategies for our three business segments in growing our business going forward.

Q4.3 *What are the main challenges facing Telechoice?*

TeleChoice has successfully transformed from a predominantly mobile handset distribution business into a leading provider of innovative telecommunications services and solutions.

Going forward, we plan to grow our higher margin Telecommunications Services and Network Engineering Services businesses, as well as strengthen and broaden our Distribution Services offerings. We will seek to expand our businesses regionally through acquisitions and strategic alliances.

Q5.1 *I have been a small investor in your company and am extremely pleased with the generous dividend payout over the last two years, generating a 10 % return per annum with no loss of capital value. I am just curious as to what your thoughts are on why the share price does not follow your company's performance and your long-term strategies to grow the company to create shareholder value.*

(...)

Our track record on dividends is as follows:

1. For FY04, we paid an interim net dividend of 2 cents per share.
2. For FY05, we paid an interim net dividend of 2 cents per share. We have also announced a proposed final (one-tier, tax exempt) dividend of 0.5 cents per share, and special (one tier, tax-exempt) dividend of 2 cents per share for FY05.

The declaration of dividends is determined by our directors, taking into account the group's earnings, cash flows and capital requirements.

(...) TeleChoice has been profitable since inception. We have consistently achieved ROE of over 30%, and strong cash balances. The group generated $24.2 M of net cash from operations in FY05. Our strong cash position of $44.6 M allows us to continue to take advantage of growth opportunities in all our three business segments, as well as deliver good returns to our shareholders.

Perhaps one reason for the current share price is investors' perception that we remain predominantly a handset distribution company.

TeleChoice offers a comprehensive suite of services and solutions for the telecommunications industry (...).

(Continued)

Exhibit 4 *(continued)*

Q6.2 *Substantial part of revenue comes from StarHub. What arrangement does the company have with StarHub? What are the details of the arrangement? Can this be sustained over the long term?*

Our parent, Singapore Technologies Telemedia Pte Ltd (through its subsidiary STT Communications Ltd) is the single largest shareholder in both TeleChoice and StarHub. Our transactions with StarHub Ltd and its subsidiaries are conducted on an arm's-length basis (…).

We treasure our relationship with StarHub Ltd as our top-tier customer and business partner. As is the case for our other key customers and business partners, we firmly believe in and are committed to further strengthening the relationship (…), by continually innovating and enhancing the value of our service offerings for StarHub Ltd.

Q6.3 *Has [the] company considered going into Store Value IDD [Internet Digital Data] and local cards and renting of Travel Phone at airports?*

We recently announced the strengthening and re-alignment of Telecommunications Services to better position for opportunities arising from the convergence of voice and data services. We have been aggressively expanding Telecommunications Services' suite of products and services which now includes value-added voice and data, pre-paid BMC, international roaming using call-back services, PushMail and mobile data network.

Q6.4 *As regards the recent acquisition of Tiny Planet, any plans for development and future expansion of Planet? How can Planet value add to the group?*

(…) We acquired a strategic 40% stake in Planet in August 2005. After completing the further acquisition of a 30% stake in Planet on 10 March 2006, we now hold a 70% stake in Planet.

The acquisition of Planet enables us to strengthen our Distribution Services offerings. (…)

Q7.1 *I would like to ask management about the future growth and direction of the company's earnings.*

For FY06, the business outlook for TeleChoice is expected to remain positive and we expect to maintain our operating performance in FY06. We are confident of our longer-term growth prospects, and will continue to seek to acquire synergistic businesses and to grow organically in the region, and to maximise productivity gains and operating efficiencies.

Exhibit 5 – TeleChoice International – Financial ratios

(in S$)	FY2005 Dec.	FY2004 Dec.	FY2003 Dec.
Adjusted EPS ($) (Earnings/latest number of shares)	0.03965	0.03889	0.03192
Adjusted NAV ($) (Shareholders' equity/latest number of shares)	0.1232	0.1012	0.0586
Price earnings ratio (Price/Adjusted EPS)	7.82	7.97	9.71
Price/revenue (Price × current number of shares/revenue)	0.242	0.258	0.008
Net earnings margin (%) (Net earnings/revenue)	3.098	3.267	4.438
Revenue growth (%) ([Current revenue – last year revenue]/last year revenue)	7.513	65.504	15.496
Net earnings growth (%) ([Current profit – last year profit]/last year profit)	1.934	21.836	8.969
Return on assets (%) (Net income/total assets)	13.974	14.007	16.837
Return on equity (%) (Net income/equity)	32.183	38.417	54.476
Current ratio (Current assets/current liabilities)	1.170	1.539	1.426

Notes
1. Adjusted fundamental data is data that is adjusted for share splits, bonus issues, share consolidations, rights issues and other changes in share capital (such as placement shares). The latest number of shares is used to calculate these adjusted ratios and is applied right across all the full year results. ShareInvestor updates the total number of shares in issue on a best effort basis.
2. Share splits, bonus issues, share consolidations and rights issues are updated on the ex-date whereas other changes in share capital are updated within seven working days of the release of the company's latest results announcement.
3. Please also note that the column headings for the financial ratios are different from that of the balance sheets and P&L. This is because the financial ratios are only applicable to full year results and not to quarterly results.

Exhibit 6 – TeleChoice International – Stock price

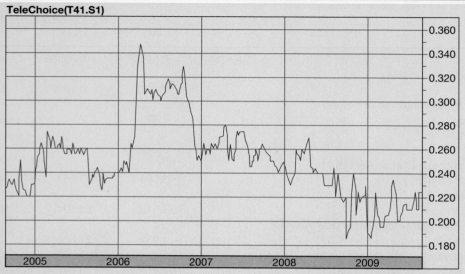

Source: Shareinvestor

Exhibit 7 – TeleChoice International – Consolidated balance sheet

(in S$ 000)	2006	2005
Non-current assets		
Property, plant and equipment	2,698	2,792
Intangible assets	1,918	689
Jointly controlled entity	1,767	1,371
Deferred tax assets	527	425
	6,910	5,277
Current assets		
Inventories	17,824	18,896
Work in progress	1,050	2,537
Trade and other receivables	48,726	53,672
Cash and cash equivalents	28,941	44,626
	96,541	119,731
Total assets	103,451	125,008
Equity attributable to equity holders of the company		
Share capital	20,439	8,906
Reserves	36,057	45,949
	56,496	54,855
Minority interests	0	494
Total equity	56,496	55,349
Non-current liabilities		
Financial liabilities	14	0
Deferred tax liabilities	197	209
Current liabilities		
Trade and other payables	38,775	63,019
Financial liabilities	603	0
Current tax payable	5,214	4,458
Provision for warranties	487	745
Deferred income	1,665	1,228
	46,744	69,450
Total liabilities	46,955	69,659
Total equity and liabilities	103,451	125,008

Exhibit 8 – TeleChoice International – Consolidated income statement

(in S$ 000)	2006	2005
Revenue	459,757	569,931
Cost of sales	–418,229	–524,952
Gross profit	41,528	44,979
Other income	3,197	2,161
Sales and marketing expenses	–7,491	–8,967
Administrative expenses	–14,076	–16,467
Other expenses	–930	–258
Finance costs	–10	–34
Share of profit of jointly controlled entity (net of tax)	114	102
Profit before income tax	22,332	21,516
Income tax expense	–5,442	–4,342
Profit for the year	16,890	17,174
Attributable to:		
Equity holders of the company	17,216	17,654
Minority interests	–326	–480
Profit for the year	16,890	17,174
Earnings per share (cents)		
Basic	3.84	3.98
Diluted	3.82	3.97

Exhibit 9 – TeleChoice International – Consolidated statement of cash flows

(in S$ 000)	2006	2005
Operating activities		
Profit before income tax	22,332	21,516
Adjustments for:		
Accretion of deferred income	–978	–1,390
Amortization of intangible assets	669	228
Depreciation of property, plant and equipment	1,565	1,343
Interest expense	10	34
Interest income	–740	–611
Loss on disposal of property, plant and equipment	14	78
Negative goodwill recognized on acquisition of additional interest in subs.	0	–84
Provision for warranties	74	376
Value of employee services received for issue of share option.	79	333
Share of profit of jointly controlled entity	–114	–102
	22,911	21,721
Changes in working capital:		
Inventories and work in progress	2,402	5,702
Trade and other receivables	4,931	10,717
Trade and other payables	–23,943	–10,740
Cash generated from operations	6,301	27,400
Income taxes paid	–3,595	–3,829
Interest received	740	611
Cash flows from operating activities	3,446	24,182
Investing activities		
Balances with related corporations (non-trade)	0	2,009
Acquisitions of additional equity interests in subsidiaries	–960	0
Additional investment in jointly controlled entity	0	–478
Acquisition of business	–1,087	0
(Loan to)/repayment from jointly controlled entity	–263	242
Net cash inflow from acquisition of subsidiary	0	125
Proceeds from disposal of property, plant and equipment	19	23
Purchase of intangible assets and PP&E	–1,491	–2,210
Cash flows from investing activities	–3782	–289
Financing activities		
Balances with related corporations (non-trade)	–219	–337
Dividends paid	–16,776	–8,903
Interest paid	–10	–34
Proceeds from trust receipts (unsecured) –	561	0
Proceeds from issue of shares from share options	1,010	684
Cash flows from financing activities	–15,434	–8,590
Net (decrease)/increase in cash and cash equivalents	–15,770	15,303
Cash and cash equivalents at beginning of the year	44,626	29,300
Exchange rate effect on balances held in foreign currency	85	23
Cash and cash equivalents at end of the year	**28,941**	**44,626**

References

Altman, E.I. (1968) 'Financial ratios, discriminant analysis and the prediction of corporate bankruptcy', *The Journal of Finance* 23(4): 589–609.

ASB (1998) Financial Reporting Standard No. 14: Earnings per share, London.

Biddle, G.C., Bowen, R.M. and Wallace, J.S. (1999) 'Evidence on EVA®', *Journal of Applied Corporate Finance* 12(2): 69–79.

Boston Consulting Group (1996), *Shareholder Value Metrics*, Boston, MA: The Boston Consulting Group, Inc.

Eidleman, G.J. (1995) 'Z scores – a guide to failure prediction', *The CPA Journal* 65(2): 52–3.

FASB (1997) Statement of Financial Accounting Standard No. 128: Earnings per share, Norwalk, CT.

FASB (1997) Statement of Financial Accounting Standard No. 131: Disclosures about segments of an enterprise and related information, Norwalk, CT.

Ferling, R.L. (1993) 'Quality in 3D: EVA, CVA, and employees', *Financial Executive*, 9(4): 51.

Fulmer, J.G. Jr., Moon, J.E., Gavin, T.A. and Erwin, M. J. (1984), 'A Bankruptcy Classification Model For Small Firms', *Journal of Commercial Bank Lending*, July: 25–37.

IASB (1997) International Accounting Standard No. 14: Segment Reporting, London.

IASB (2003) International Accounting Standard No. 33: Earnings Per Share, London.

IASB (2006) International Accounting Standard No. 8: Operating Segments, London.

Lebas, M. (ed.) (1999) *Management Accounting Glossary*, ECM, Paris, and CIMA, London.

Mepham, M.J. (1983) 'Robert Hamilton's contribution to accounting', *The Accounting Review* 58(1): 43–57.

PricewaterhouseCoopers (2007a) *Smarter risk decisions*, available at http://www.pwc.com/gx/en/risk-management/reinventing-risk.jhtml.risk decisions: reinventing risk

PricewaterhouseCoopers (2007b) *The art of effective business: Making it work*, available at http://www.pwc.co.uk/pdf/art_of_effective_business.pdf.

Sands, E.G., Springate, G.LV. and Var, T. (1983) 'Predicting business failures'. *CGA Magazine*, May: 24–7.

Smith, A. (2003) *The Wealth of Nations (1776)* new edn, Bantam Classics, NY.

Further reading

Alford, A., Jones, J., Leftwich, R. and Zmijewski, M. (1993) 'The relative informativeness of accounting disclosures in different countries', *Journal of Accounting Research*, 31(Sup.): 183–223.

Cote, J.M. and Latham, C.K. (1999) 'The merchandising ratio: A comprehensive measure of working capital strategy', *Issues in Accounting Education* 14(2): 255–67.

Deppe, L. (2000) 'Disclosing disaggregated information', *Journal of Accountancy* 190(3): 47–52.

Haller, A. and Park, P. (1994) 'Regulation and practice of segmental reporting in Germany', *European Accounting Review* 3(3): 563–80.

Hendrikse, J. and Hendrikse, L. (2004) *Business Governance Handbook*, Juta & Co., Cape Town, SA.

Lainez, J.A. and Callao, S. (2000) 'The effect of accounting diversity on international financial analysis: empirical evidence', *International Journal of Accounting*, 35(1): 65–83.

Northrup, C.L. (2006) *Profitable Sarbanes-Oxley Compliance: Attain Improved Shareholder Value and Bottom-Line Results*, J. Ross Publishing, Fort Lauderdale, FL.

Prather-Kinsey, J. and Meek, G. K. (2004) 'The effect of revised IAS 14 on segment reporting by IAS companies', *European Accounting Review* 13(2): 213–34.

Prencipe, A. (2004) 'Proprietary costs and determinants of voluntary segment disclosure: Evidence from Italian listed companies', *European Accounting Review* 13(2): 319–40.

Street, D.L., Nichols, N.B. and Gray, S.J. (2000) 'Segment disclosures under SFAS No. 131: Has business segment reporting improved?', *Accounting Horizons* 14(3): 259–85.

Additional material on the website

Go to http://www.cengage.co.uk/stolowy3 for further information, journal entries and extra assignments for each chapter.

The following appendices to this chapter are available on the dedicated website:

Appendix 18.1: Complementary remarks on ratios computation

Appendix 18.2: Business newspapers and magazines – specialized magazines

Appendix 18.3: Filing of financial statements

Appendix 18.4: Scoring models

Notes

1. Assumed to be calculated for one year – should a different duration prove to be useful, replace 'year', where appropriate, by 'period'.
2. The relevance of extraordinary items in the determination of the income integrated in the EPS computation has been discussed and the practice differs a lot.
3. Adapted from Biddle, Bowen and Wallace (1999).
4. Adapted from Lebas (ed.) (1999) *Management Accounting Glossary*.
5. For a quick introduction to Altman's Z score, see: 'Z scores – a guide to failure prediction' by Gregory J. Eidleman, *The CPA Journal*, Feb. 1995 (The CPA Journal online).
6. In the 18th century, the word profusion meant 'wasting' or 'squandering' of resources.
7. The Report on the Financial Aspects of Corporate Governance, 1992.
8. Sir Adrian Cadbury: 'Corporate governance: a framework for implementation', World Bank.
9. Information Systems Audit and Control Foundation, 2001.
10. 'Governance for young leaders: Understanding corporate governance', 23 March 2004.

Solutions to Review Questions and Problems

Review 1.1 Multiple-choice questions

1. (a), (c), (d) and in certain countries (b).

The statement of changes in shareholders' equity, which presents the changes in the 'net worth' (as described in the introduction to the chapter) has not been included in this list. It is, however, a compulsory financial statement in some countries. This statement will be explored further in Chapter 11.

2. False.

Many transactions have no impact on cash, either because the impact is postponed to a later date (as in the case of a sale on account) or because there never will be a direct cash impact as is the case, as we will see later in Chapters 2 and 7, for the recognition of the loss of value of physical assets or the consumption of the productive capacity of a fixed asset (depreciation).

3. False.

Financial accounting does not always have clear or complete documents supporting the exact value at which a transaction should be recorded. That value is often subjective. For example, the risk of uncollectibility on a credit sale may be estimated statistically (on the basis of past records) but cannot be known exactly for each transaction before final settlement or an incident actually occurs.

4. (b)

Bookkeeping means 'formal recording of transactions'. It is therefore part of financial accounting since recording of transactions is compulsory. Management accounting also uses the same recorded data for its own analyses.

Review 1.2 Discussion questions

1. Why do decision-makers use accounting information and for what purpose? Decision-makers use accounting information for decisions regarding resource allocation. This allocation concerns management for internal purposes

so as to increase the wealth creation of the firm. It concerns shareholders who may want to reconsider investing their wealth in this or that firm. Decision-makers also use accounting to monitor the achievements of subordinate managers since accounting records their actions and the consequences of these.

2. Why have standards of reporting emerged that constrain the way events are recorded in accounting? To a large extent reporting standards have emerged to reduce the transaction cost borne by both producers and users of financial information. If the producer knows the recommended or preferred way to record an event, there is no need for the accountant to search for the most suitable way to do so. If the user receives data that come from a standardized coding method (whether rules-based or principles-based) and agreed methods of aggregation and transformation, all users can interpret the same piece of data to mean the same thing. Further, it improves the possibility of inter-firm comparisons without removing the possibility, for the user, of recoding the data in a preferred format. The topic of financial reporting standards will be further developed in Chapter 5.

3. What distinguishes financial accounting and reporting from managerial accounting? The answer to this question is covered in Table 1.9.

Review 2.1 Vivaldi Company (1)

Topic: Transactions and the business equation

1. Basic business equation

	Assets					=	Liabilities			+	Shareholders' equity (SE)		
	Cash	Accounts receivable	Merchandise inventory	Equipment	− Accumulated depreciation		Taxes payable	Salaries payable	Accounts payable		Retained earnings variation	Share capital	Details of SE transactions
(A)	+60			+40								+100	Initial investment
(B)									+40		−40		Purchases of merchandise
(C)									+7		−7		External expense
(D)		+120									+120		Sales of merchandise
(E)								+45			−45		Personnel expenses
(F)							+20				−20		Tax expenses
(G)	+60	−60											
(H)	−35								−35				
(I)	−30							+30					
(J)					−4						−4		Depreciation expenses
(K)			+10								+10		Change in inventory
Ending balance	55	60	10	40	−4	=	20	15	12	+	14	100	

Assets total: (161)

Liabilities + Shareholders' equity total: (161)

2. Preparation of the year-end balance sheet (as of 31 December X1)

Assets		Equity and liabilities	
Fixed assets (equipment)	40	Capital	100
Equipment depreciation	−4	Net income	14
Fixed assets (net value)	36	Accounts payable (40 + 7 − 35)	12
Merchandise inventory	10	Salaries and social expenses payable	15
Accounts receivable (120 − 60)	60	(30 + 15 − 30)	20
Cash at bank (60 + 60 − 35 − 30)	55	Taxes payable	
Total	161	Total	161

3. Preparation of the income statement (for the year X1)

Expenses		Revenues	
Purchases of merchandise	40	Sales of merchandise	120
Change in inventory of merchandise	−10		
Other purchases and external expenses	7		
Taxes	20		
Personnel expenses (30 + 15)	45		
Depreciation expenses	4		
Net income	14		
Total	120	Total	120

Comments

■ The balance sheet is itself an account, which is comprised of the balances of all balance sheet subsidiary accounts. The net income (profit or loss) is itself the balance of the balance sheet account.

■ The income statement is the account that records the balances of all the expense and revenue accounts. Net income (profit or loss) is the balance of the income statement.

■ The income of the period is the same, by construction, in the balance sheet and the income statement. In the balance sheet, it is also the net potential addition to retained earnings, subject to appropriation by shareholders. These will decide at the annual general assembly how much of the yearly net income should be paid out as dividends to shareholders, and how much (the complement to one) should be retained and added to the retained earnings.

Review 2.2 Vivaldi Company (2)

Topic: Transactions and impact on the financial statements

Balance sheet as of 31 December X1

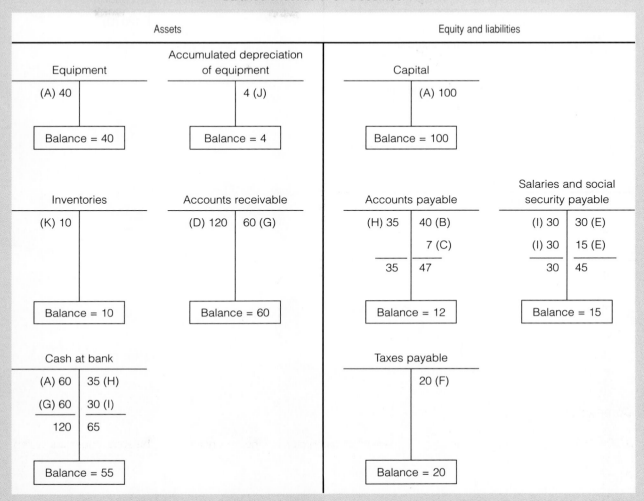

Assets	Equity and liabilities

Equipment

(A) 40	

Balance = 40

Accumulated depreciation of equipment

	4 (J)

Balance = 4

Capital

	(A) 100

Balance = 100

Inventories

(K) 10	

Balance = 10

Accounts receivable

(D) 120	60 (G)

Balance = 60

Accounts payable

(H) 35	40 (B)
	7 (C)
35	47

Balance = 12

Salaries and social security payable

(I) 30	30 (E)
(I) 30	15 (E)
30	45

Balance = 15

Cash at bank

(A) 60	35 (H)
(G) 60	30 (I)
120	65

Balance = 55

Taxes payable

	20 (F)

Balance = 20

Income statement for the year X1

Expenses		Revenues	
Purchases of merchandise		**Sales of merchandise**	
(B) 40			120 (D)
Change in inventory of merchandise			
	10 (K)		
Other purchases and external expenses			
(C) 7			
Taxes			
(F) 20			
Personnel expenses			
(E) 30			
(E) 15			
Depreciation expense			
(J) 4			

Review 2.3 Albinoni

Topic: Transactions and the business equation

Perpetual inventory

	Assets					=	Liabilities			Shareholders' equity (SE)		
	Cash +	Accounts receivable +	Merchandise inventory +	Equipment +	Accumulated depreciation	=	Financial debt +	Accounts payable +	Net income of the period +	Share capital +	Details of SE transactions
(1)	30			80			200			110	Initial investment
(2)	200						200				
(3)	−40								−40		Taxes
(4)		80	50					50			Legal fees
(5)	−10								−10		Personnel expenses
(6)	−30								−30		Sales
(7)	20		−40						100		Cost of merchandise sold
									−40		
(8)	−30							−30			
(9)	70	−70									
(10)					−20				−20		Depreciation expense
(11)											
Ending balance	210 +	10 +	10 +	80 +	−20	=	200 +	20 +	−40 +	110 +	

(290) assets = (290) liabilities + shareholders' equity

Periodic inventory

| | Assets | | | | | = | Liabilities | | + | Shareholders' equity (SE) | | |
	Cash	+ Accounts receivable	+ Merchandise inventory	+ Equipment	+ Accumulated depreciation	=	Financial debt	+ Accounts payable	+	Net income of the period	+ Share capital	Details of SE transactions
(1)	30			80							110	Initial investment
(2)	200						200					
(3)	-40									-40		Taxes
(4)								50		-50		Purchase of merchandise
(5)	-10									-10		Legal fees
(6)	-30									-30		Personnel expenses
(7)	20	80								100		Sales
(8)	-30							-30				
(9)	70	-70										
(10)					-20					-20		Depreciation expense
(11)			10							10		Change in inventory
Ending balance	210	+ 10	+ 10	+ 80	+ -20	=	200	+ 20	+	+ -40	+ 110	

290 (Assets)   290 (Liabilities + SE)

Review 3.1 Beethoven Company (1)

Topic: Link between balance sheet, income statement and statement of cash flows [Income statement by nature]

Income statement (000 CU) for year X2				
Operating expenses			**Operating revenues**	
Purchases of raw materials	510		Sales	1,600
Change in inventory of merchandise (B – E)	20			
External charges	250			
Miscellaneous taxes	120			
Personnel expenses	430			
Depreciation expense	40			
Financial charges	0		**Financial income**	0
Exceptional charges	0		**Exceptional income**	0
Sub total	1,370		Sub total	1,600
Income tax	92			
Net income	*138*			
Total	1,600		Total	1,600

Balance sheet (000 CU) at the end of year X2				
Fixed assets			**Shareholders' equity**	
Manufacturing equipment (net)	1,060		Capital	710
Manufacturing assets (gross) = 800 + 300			Reserves	444
Minus accumulated depreciation = 40			Net income/loss	138
			Sub total	1,292
			Liabilities	
Current assets			Financial debts	30
Merchandise inventory	130		Bank overdraft	0
Accounts receivable	200		Accounts payable	110
Cash at bank	134		Income tax payable	92
Total	1,524		Total	1,524

Cash flow budget (000 CU) for the year X2	
Cash flows from operating activities	
Cash from sales	1,400
Cash from receivables (see preceding balance sheet)	400
Purchases for the year	−400
Accounts payable (see preceding balance sheet)	−120
Payment of previous year's income tax payable	−144
Miscellaneous taxes	−120
Personnel expenses	−430
Advertising expenses	−250
Financial expenses	0
Net cash flows from operating activities (1)	*336*
Cash flows from investing activities	
Investments	−300
Other (sale of fixed assets)	0
Net cash flows used in investing activities (2)	*−300*
Cash flows from financing activities	
Other (capital)	0
Repayment of debts	−80
Dividends paid	−72
Net cash flows used in financing activities (3)	*−152*
Net increase (decrease) in cash and cash equivalents (4) = (1) + (2) + (3)	*−116*
Opening balance (5)	250
Ending balance (6) = (4) + (5)	134

Review 3.2 Beethoven Company (2)

Topic: Link between balance sheet, income statement and statement of cash flows [Income statement by function]

Income statement (000 CU)	
Sales	1,600
Purchases of merchandises	−510
Change in inventory of merchandise (B − E)	−20
Cost of goods sold	−530
Gross margin	1,070
External charges	−250
Personnel expense (selling)	−300
Selling expenses	−550
Miscellaneous taxes	−120
Personnel expense (administration)	−130
General and administrative expense	−250
Depreciation expense	−40
Operating profit	230
Financial charges	0
Income before income tax	230
Income tax	−92
Net income	*138*

The balance sheet and statement of cash flows are identical to the statements presented in Review 3.1 Beethoven (1).

Review 3.3 Grieg Company (1)

Topic: The accounting process: from the journal to the financial statements (purchases of merchandise are recorded first in inventory)

Merchandise 'transits' through the inventory account – a balance sheet account – before being consumed and recognized as merchandise sold. Ending inventory is what is left after consumption, i.e., withdrawals, required to meet customers demand.

Journal entries

1	BS (A+)		Cash at bank		10,000	
		BS (L+)		Shareholders' equity		10,000
2	BS (A+)		Equipment		1,200	
		BS (A–)		Cash at bank		1,200
3	BS (A+)		Merchandise inventory		9,000	
		BS (L+)		Accounts payable		9,000
4	BS (A+)		Cash at bank		500	
		BS (L+)		Debt		500
5	IS (E+)		Cost of goods sold		7,000	
		BS (A–)		Merchandise inventory		7,000
5	BS (A+)		Cash at bank		6,000	
	BS (A+)		Accounts receivable		5,000	
		IS (R+)		Sales		11,000
6	BS (A+)		Cash at bank		4,000	
		BS (A–)		Accounts receivable		4,000
7	BS (L–)		Accounts payable		8,000	
		BS (A–)		Cash at bank		8,000
8	IS (E+)		Depreciation expense		120	
		BS (A–)		Accumulated depreciation, Equipment		120
					50,820	50,820

General ledger

```
              Assets accounts                              Equity and liabilities accounts

                 Equipment                                           Capital

       (2) 1,200          |                                 |          10,000 (1)
   ─────────────────────  |                                 |  ───────────────────────
   D balance = 1,200      |                                 |          C Balance = 10,000

           Accumulated depreciation                                   Debt

                          |  120 (8)                        |          500 (4)
   ─────────────────────  |  ──────────────                 |  ───────────────────────
                          |  C balance = 120                |          C balance = 500

           Merchandise inventory                            Accounts payable

       (3) 9,000          |  7,000 (5)                 (7) 8,000       |  9,000 (3)
   ─────────────────────  |  ──────────────            ──────────────  |  ───────────────
   D balance = 2,000      |                                            |  C balance = 1,000

           Accounts receivable

       (5) 5,000          |  4,000 (6)
   ─────────────────────  |  ──────────────
   D balance = 1,000      |

               Cash at bank

       (1) 10,000         |  1,200 (2)
       (4)     500        |  8,000 (7)
       (5)   6,000        |
       (6)   4,000        |
   ─────────────────────  |
   D balance = 11,300     |


              Expenses accounts                              Revenues accounts

           Cost of goods sold                                       Sales

       (5) 7,000          |                                 |          11,000 (5)
   ─────────────────────  |                                 |  ───────────────────────
   D balance = 7,000      |                                 |          C balance = 11,000

           Depreciation expense

       (8) 120            |
   ─────────────────────  |
   D balance = 120        |
```

Comment

- The accounts have been divided into four main categories: assets, equity and liabilities, expenses and revenues.

Trial balance

	Entries of the period		Ending balance	
	D	C	D	C
Equipment	1,200		1,200	
Accumulated depreciation		120		120
Merchandise inventory	9,000	7,000	2,000	
Accounts receivable	5,000	4,000	1,000	
Cash at bank	20,500	9,200	11,300	
Share capital		10,000		10,000
Accounts payable	8,000	9,000		1,000
Debt		500		500
Cost of goods sold	7,000		7,000	
Depreciation expense	120		120	
Sales		11,000		11,000
Total	*50,820*	*50,820*	*22,620*	*22,620*

Balance sheet and income statement

Balance sheet at 31 January X1			
ASSETS		LIABILITIES	
Fixed assets		**Shareholders' equity**	
Equipment	1,200	Share capital	10,000
Accumulated depreciation	−120	*Income for the month*	*3,880*
Net amount	1,080		
Current assets		**Debts**	
Merchandise inventory	2,000	Debt	500
Accounts receivable	1,000	Accounts payable	1,000
Cash at bank	11,300		
Total assets	*15,380*	*Total liabilities*	*15,380*

Income statement for the month ended 31 January X1	
REVENUES	
Sales	11,000
Total revenues (1)	11,000
EXPENSES	
Cost of merchandise sold	7,000
Depreciation expense	120
Total expenses (2)	7,120
Net income (1) − (2)	3,880

Comment

■ The net income as calculated in the income statement is the same as the one reported in the balance sheet (or required to balance the balance sheet).

Review 3.4 Grieg Company (2)

Topic: The accounting process: from the journal to the financial statements (purchases of merchandise are first recorded in the income statement)

Purchases are, initially, presumed fully consumed. They are thus considered to be an expense in their totality on the date of recording of the purchase. Physical stock-taking of the existing inventory at the end of the period allows the accountant to adjust the already expensed purchases by the variation in inventory to obtain, by subtraction or addition, the cost of merchandise sold that was incurred to meet customers demand during the period.

Journal entries

1	BS (A+)		Cash at bank	10,000	
		BS (L+)	Shareholders equity		10,000
2	BS (A+)		Equipment	1,200	
		BS (A–)	Cash at bank		1,200
3	IS (E+)		Purchase of merchandise for resale	9,000	
		BS (L+)	Accounts payable		9,000
4	BS (A+)		Cash at bank	500	
		BS (L+)	Debt		500
5	BS (A+)		Cash at bank	6,000	
	BS (A+)		Accounts receivable	5,000	
		IS (R+)	Sales		11,000
6	BS (A+)		Cash at bank	4,000	
		BS (A–)	Accounts receivable		4,000
7	BS (L–)		Accounts payable	8,000	
		BS (A–)	Cash at bank		8,000
8	IS (E+)		Depreciation expense	120	
		BS (A–)	Accumulated depreciation, Equipment		120
9	BS (A+)		Merchandise inventory	2,000	
		IS (E–)	Change in inventories		2,000
				45,820	45,820

General ledger

Assets accounts	Equity and liabilities accounts

Equipment

(2) 1,200	
D balance = 1,200	

Accumulated depreciation

	120 (8)
	C balance = 120

Merchandise inventory

(9) 2,000	
D balance = 2000	

Accounts receivable

(5) 5,000	4,000
D balance = 1,000	

Cash at bank

(1) 10,000	1,200 (2)
(4) 500	8,000 (7)
(5) 6,000	
(6) 4,000	
D balance = 11,300	

Share capital

	10,000 (1)
	C balance = 10,000

Debt

	500 (4)
	C balance = 500

Accounts payable

(7) 8,000	9,000 (3)
	C Balance = 1,000

Expense accounts	Revenue accounts

Purchase of merchandise

(3) 9,000	
D balance = 9,000	

Change in inventories

	2,000 (9)
	C balance = 2,000

Depreciation expense

(8) 120	
D balance = 120	

Sales

	11,000 (5)
	C balance = 11,000

Comment

■ The accounts have been divided into four main categories: assets, equity and liabilities, expenses and revenues.

Trial balance

	Entries of the period		Ending balance	
	D	C	D	C
Equipment	1,200		1,200	
Accumulated depreciation		120		120
Merchandise inventory	2,000		2,000	
Accounts receivable	5,000	4,000	1,000	
Cash at bank	20,500	9,200	11,300	
Share capital		10,000		10,000
Debt		500		500
Accounts payable	8,000	9,000		1,000
Purchase of merchandise	9,000		9,000	
Change in inventories		2,000		2,000
Depreciation expense	120		120	
Sales		11,000		11,000
Total	45,820	45,820	24,620	24,620

Balance sheet and income statement

Balance sheet at 31 January X1

ASSETS		LIABILITIES	
Fixed assets		**Shareholders equity**	
Equipment	1,200	Share capital	10,000
Accumulated	−120	*Income for the month*	*3,880*
depreciation			
Net amount	1,080		
Current assets		**Debts**	
Merchandise inventory	2,000	Debt	500
Accounts receivable	1,000	Accounts payable	1,000
Cash at bank	11,300		
Total assets	15,380	Total liabilities	15,380

Income statement for the month ended 31 January X1

REVENUES	
Sales	11,000
Total revenues (1)	11,000
EXPENSES	
Purchase of merchandise	9,000
Change in inventories	−2,000
Depreciation expense	120
Total expenses (2)	7,120
Net income (1) − (2)	3,880

Comments

■ The net income as calculated in the income statement is the same as the one reported in the balance sheet (or required to balance the balance sheet).

- The comparison of Review Problems Grieg (1) and Grieg (2), confirms (see Chapters 2 and 9) that the 'cost of merchandise sold' is, indeed equal to the total 'Purchases + Change in inventories'.

Review 4.1 Adam

Topic: Accounting principles and end-of-period entries

Note: in all tables in this review problem, figures shown in **bold** refer to modified figures; figures shown in *italics* refer to impact of the entry.

Company 1

Accounting principles involved: Prudence (conservatism) and 'lower of cost or market'.
Accounting entry: ç

- In the balance sheet: decrease of assets (provision for depreciation).
- In the income statement (not displayed): increase in expenses (provision expense).

Company 1 – Modified balance sheet				
Assets			Shareholders' equity and liabilities	
Fixed assets	300,000		*Shareholders' equity*	
Less accumulated depreciation *(–40,000)*	**–200,000**		Share capital and retained earnings/reserves	330,000
Fixed assets (net)	100,000		Net income of the period *(–40,000)*	**–20,000**
Current assets			*Liabilities*	40,000
Inventories	120,000			
Accounts receivable	130,000			
Total assets	350,000		**Total shareholders' equity and liabilities**	350,000

Company 2

Accounting principle involved: Prudence (conservatism).
Accounting entry:

- In the balance sheet: decrease in assets (provision for depreciation of the receivables).
- In the income statement (not displayed, but the impact is, *in fine*, on net income): increase in expenses (provision expense).

Company 2 – Modified balance sheet				
Assets			Shareholders' equity and liabilities	
Fixed assets	250,000		*Shareholders' equity*	
Less accumulated depreciation	–130,000		Share capital and retained earnings/reserves	300,000
Fixed assets (net)	120,000		Net income *(–60,000)*	**–10,000**
Current assets			*Liabilities*	20,000
Inventories	100,000			
Accounts receivable *(–60,000)*	**90,000**			
Total assets	310,000		**Total shareholders' equity and liabilities**	310,000

Review 5.1 Orkla*

Topic: Constructing a balance sheet

1. Reconstruct the balance sheet in a vertical, single-step and increasing format (Check figure: total assets on the balance sheet = 104,926).

Balance sheet, as of 31 December 2008 (in millions of NOK)	
ASSETS	**2008**
Property, plant and equipment	26,368
Intangible assets	16,317
Deferred tax assets	984
Investments in associates	17,112
Other non-current financial assets	1,219
Non-current assets	**62,000**
Assets in discontinued operations	3,148
Inventories	9,564
Receivables	14,331
Share portfolio etc.	11,445
Cash and cash equivalents	4,438
Current assets	**42,926**
Total assets	**104,926**
EQUITY AND LIABILITIES	**2008**
Paid-in equity	1,993
Retained earnings	45,390
Minority interests	2,686
Equity	**50,069**
Deferred tax	2,872
Provisions and liabilities	2,361
Non-current interest-bearing liabilities	29,598
Non-current liabilities	**34,831**
Liabilities in discontinued operations	665
Current interest-bearing liabilities	3,654
Income tax payable	1,005
Other current liabilities	14,702
Current liabilities	**20,026**
Equity and liabilities	**104,926**

2. Given the terminology used, was the original balance sheet organized by nature or by term?

The balance sheet is organized by term, as we find a clear distinction between long-term (non-current) and short-term (current) liabilities.

Review 5.2 Holcim*

Topic: Constructing an income statement

1. Prepare the income statement in a multiple-step format (Check figure: bottom line = 2,226).

Income statement, as of 31 December 2008 (in millions of CHF)	
Million CHF	2008
Net sales	**25,157**
Production cost of goods sold	(14,116)
Gross profit	**11,041**
Distribution and selling expenses	(5,921)
Administration expenses	(1,760)
Operating profit	**3,360**
Other income	19
Share of profit of associates	229
Financial income	271
Financial expenses	(990)
Net income before taxes	**2,889**
Income taxes	(663)
Net income	**2,226**
Attributable to:	
Equity holders of Holcim Ltd	1,782
Minority interest	444

2. Given the terminology used, was the original income statement organized by nature or by function?

The income statement is presented by function as we find listed items such as 'production cost of goods sold', 'distribution and selling expenses' and 'administration expenses'.

Review 6.1 Schultz Accountancy Firm (1)

Topic: Revenue recognition

(a) Media commissions should be recognized when the related advertisement or commercial appears before the public. The accounting treatment followed by this ad agency is not correct.

(b) Revenue from artistic performances, banquets, and other special events is recognized when the event takes place. When a subscription to a number of events is sold, the fee is allocated to each event, on a basis that reflects the extent to which services are performed at each event. The policy adopted by Altrium Auditorium is not correct, unless the events are distributed 1/4 and 3/4 over time, which does not appear to be the case on the basis of the problem data.

(c) Revenue is recognized when delivery is made and cash is received by the seller or its agent. The accounting treatment is correct.

(d) Revenue recognition depends on the uncertainty of the collection of the membership fee. The fee is recognized as revenue when no significant uncertainty about collection exists. In the present case, since the fee permits only membership (and must be paid before the member gains access to other services that will be paid separately), the club should not defer the recognition on a straight-line basis but should recognize it when it is paid, not by allocation over the months of the membership.

Review 6.2 Schall Company

Topic: Deferred taxation

1. Compute the deferred taxation, assuming that the pre-tax income before recording the royalty fee expense is the same in X2 as it was in X1.

   The impact on income tax calculations is as follows when no deferred tax account is to be used:

Financial statements			Income tax return		
	Year X1	Year X2		Year X1	Year X2
Pre-tax income before recording the royalty fee expense	110	110	Pre-tax income before recording the royalty fee expense	110	110
Royalty fee expense recorded on cash basis	−10	0	Deduction of fee expense (tax rules)	−10	0
Pre-tax income after recording the fee expense	100	110			
Add back fee expense (which will be recognized over 2 years)	10	0			
Recognition of the fee expense split over 2 years	−5	−5			
Pre-tax reported income	105	105	Taxable income	100	110
Income tax expense (from income tax return)	−40	−44	Income tax expense	40	44
Reported net income after tax	65	61			

In countries that authorize or require deferred taxation, the left-hand side of the table is not allowed because it mixes pre-tax income (coming from accounting for reporting calculations) and income tax, which is the result of a fiscal calculation.

The following table illustrates what needs to be done if the use of deferred taxes is required.

2. Record the deferred taxation at the end of X1 and at the end of X2.

Theoretical tax expense based on financial reporting			Actual tax expense based on tax return		
	Year X1	Year X2		Year X1	Year X2
Reported pre-tax income	105	105			
'Theoretical' income tax expense (40% of reported pre-tax income)	42	42	Income tax expense (40% of taxable income) – see previous table	40	44
Reported net income	63	63			

The reconciliation between the 'theoretical' tax expense reported and the actual tax expense incurred is handled by creating, in the balance sheet, a deferred tax account. A tax liability of 2 is recognized in X1 – a tax expense of 42 was recognized in X1, but only 40 were added to taxes payable. This liability will be reversed in X2 when the tax expense recognized will be 42 but the taxes owed will be 44. The mechanism is illustrated in the T-accounts flows shown below.

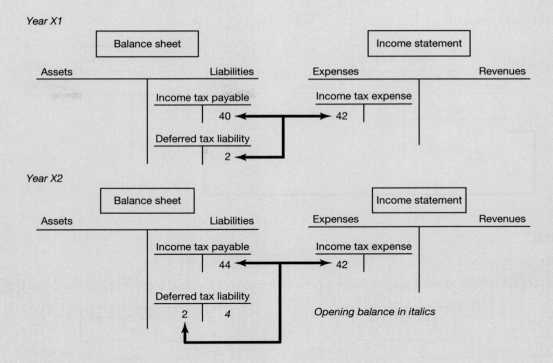

Year X1

Balance sheet | Income statement

Assets | Liabilities | Expenses | Revenues

Income tax payable | Income tax expense
40 | 42

Deferred tax liability
2

Year X2

Balance sheet | Income statement

Assets | Liabilities | Expenses | Revenues

Income tax payable | Income tax expense
44 | 42

Deferred tax liability
2 | 4

Opening balance in italics

Review 7.1 Gibbons

Topic: Determining the cost of acquisition

1. Computation of the acquisition cost of the machine

Retail price		1,500
Discount	20%	–300
Net invoiced cost		1,200
Freight expenses		150
Installation expenses		100
Total acquisition cost		1,450

The repair expenses are not considered as a component of the machine's acquisition cost because those expenses were not necessary to obtain the machine. Because these repair expenses were the result of an error, they would not have been, normally, incurred in bringing the machine to an operational status. They represent a period cost and must be recognized as incurred and not become part of the depreciable basis.

2. Accounting entries

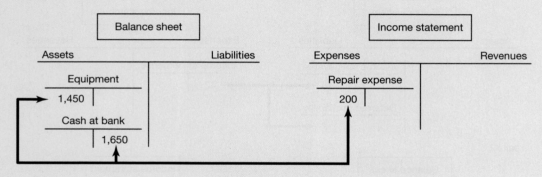

Review 8.1 Turina

Topic: Various intangibles

The answers to the three questions are described in the schematics of T-accounts below (all figures in 000 CU).

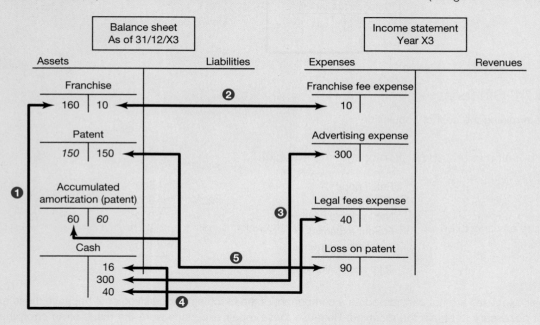

Question 1

❶ Recording of the acquisition of the franchise as an intangible asset.

❷ Franchise fee expense: (160 / 8 years) × ½ (to recognize the acquisition happened in mid year, i.e., we should only recognize 6 months of consumption of the productive capacity of the franchise). In the case of a franchise, a direct amortization (through the 'franchise fee expense' account) is possible. The 'franchise fee expense' is then equivalent to an amortization expense.

Question 2

❸ Advertising expense is not considered as an intangible asset (application of the prudence or conservatism principle).

Question 3

❹ The legal fees are recorded as incurred.

❺ The patent and accumulated amortization accounts are cancelled and a loss of 90 is recorded.

Review 8.2 De Falla

Topic: Accounting for R&D

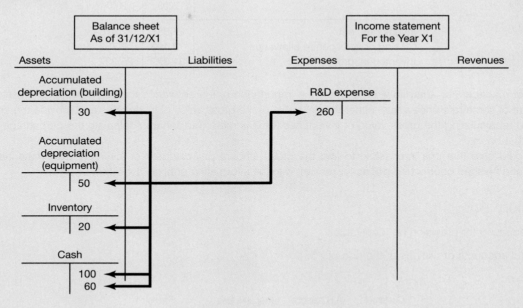

All the expenses listed in the question can be included in the R&D expense of the period and thus will reduce profit in the income statement for that amount. We assumed for the sake of simplicity that wages and salaries, as well as general and administrative expenses, were paid in cash. A set of 'payables' accounts could as easily have been used instead of 'cash'. In application of the prudence or conservatism principles, R&D cannot, normally, be capitalized, i.e., transformed into an asset to be amortized over the years during which benefits from the research expense will be derived. If the R&D expenses could have been traced to a customer-specific contract (thus becoming more 'development' than 'research'), these expenses could have been capitalized (i.e., not expensed immediately) and recognized over the life of the contract, on the basis of percentage of completion for example.

Review 9.1 Ericsson*

Topic: Reporting for inventory

1. What are 'obsolescence allowances' usually called?

   They are usually called 'provision for depreciation of inventories' or 'valuation allowance for depreciation of inventories'.

2. What do the 'additions' in these allowances represent?

   They represent the provision expense for loss of value (depreciation) of inventories, charged against income of each year.

3. What does the term 'utilization' in note 13, subsection on 'movements in obsolescence allowances', refer to?

   It represents the reversal of provisions when the allowance is no longer necessary, for instance because inventories have been consumed, sold or otherwise disposed of.

4. What restatement is necessary to obtain the gross amount of inventories?

The amounts reported in the balance sheet for inventories (27,836 in 2008 and 22,475 in 2007) are net amounts, i.e., net of all allowances (increases and decreases). This interpretation is confirmed by the use, in note 13, of the caption 'inventories, net'. The movements of the provision (allowances) are shown separately in a second half of the note. The gross amount of inventories could be obtained by adding back the 'obsolescence allowance' to the net amount, as illustrated in the following table.

	2008	2007
Inventories, net	27,836	22,475
Closing obsolescence allowance	3,493	2,752
Inventories, gross	31,329	25,227

Whether managers or analysts want to know the importance of the allowance for loss of value or inventories as a percentage of some reference value, either the net value or the gross value of inventories can provide the answer. We suggested recalculating the gross value of inventories, as it is more traditional to calculate the percentage of loss of value on that basis.

We should note that it is impossible to find the gross amount per category of inventory (raw materials, work in progress and finished goods, and goods for resale), with the information publicly available.

Review 10.1 Berg

Topic: Accounting for provision on receivables

1. Doubtful accounts provisions at the end of X3.

Customer	A/R balance	Probable loss	Provision
Alban	200	25%	200 × 25% = 50
Adam	300	40%	300 × 40% = 120
Total	500		170

2. Entries at the end of X3.

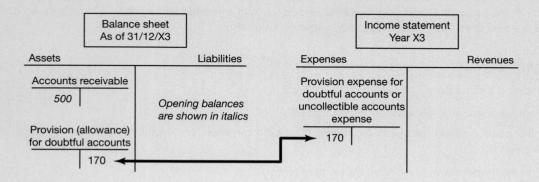

3. Doubtful accounts provisions at the end of X4.

Customer	Accounts receivable	Probable loss	Provision
Alban	200	70%	200 × 70% = 140 – 50 (provision year X3) = 90
Adam	300	–	Payment for 50. Reversal of provision (120)

4. Entries at the end of X4.

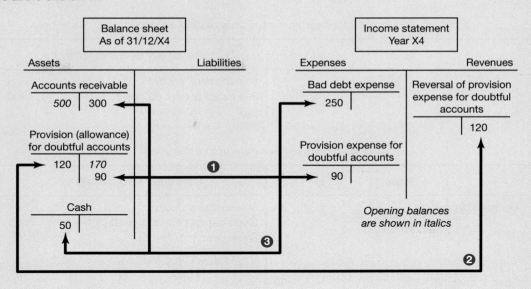

Review 11.1 Copland Company

Topic: Share issuance in cash

In the following answers all 000 are omitted.

1. Accounting entries

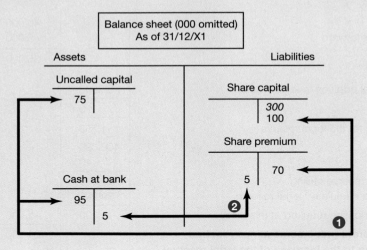

Detail of computation ❶
Cash at bank is calculated as follows: 95,000 = (100 × 25% + 70) × 1,000
Uncalled capital is equal to 75,000 = (100 × 75%) × 1,000.

2. Balance sheet excerpts

Balance sheet excerpt before new share issuance (000 omitted)	
Assets	**Shareholders' equity and liabilities**
(...)	*Shareholders' equity* Share capital (incl. 300 paid) 300 (...)

Balance sheet excerpt after new share issuance (000 omitted)	
Assets	**Shareholders' equity and liabilities**
Uncalled capital 75	*Shareholders' equity* Share capital (incl. 325 paid) (300 + 100) 400 Share premium (70 – 5) 65
(...) Cash at bank (95 – 5) 90	(...)

Review 11.2 Menotti Company

Topic: Profit appropriation

1. Prepare a table detailing the profit appropriation calculations (including the per share dividend for each class of shares).

Net income		40,000
Losses brought forward		–5,000
Sub-total		35,000
Legal reserve		
Basis for annual addition to legal reserve	35,000	
Rate	5%	
Amount usable for the legal reserve	1,750	
Share capital	400,000	
Rate	10%	
Required legal reserve ceiling	40,000	
Current existing cumulated legal reserve	39,000	
Maximum contribution required at this time	1,000	–1,000
Distributable profit (net income minus required appropriation to the increase of the legal reserve)		34,000
Regulated reserve		–2,000
Optional reserve		–10,000
Preference dividend (Class A shares)		
Number of shares	1,000	
Par value (in CU)	100	
Rate of minimum dividend	5%	
Amount of dividend to preferred shares	5,000	–5,000
Ordinary dividends (Class A and B shares)		
Number of shares	4,000	
Amount per share (in CU)	4	
Amount	16,000	–16,000
Profit brought forward to retained earnings		1,000

Notes

- Since the legal reserve only requires an increment of 1,000 CU to reach the level of 10% of the capital at par, the amount appropriated to that purpose is limited (and will be nil for the next period).
- Legally, the increment of the regulated reserve is not truly compulsory. The creation of such a reserve is generally linked to a tax advantage. If the firm were to renounce the tax break, the regulated reserve would not have to be incremented. This is the reason why the distributable profit is calculated before the provision to increment the regulated reserve.
- All shares are entitled to receive the ordinary dividend.
- The dividends per share are as follows:
  - Preference shares (class A): 5 (preference dividend) + 4 (ordinary dividend) = 9 CU
  - Ordinary shares (class B): 4 CU (ordinary dividend).

2. Prepare the appropriation accounting entries.

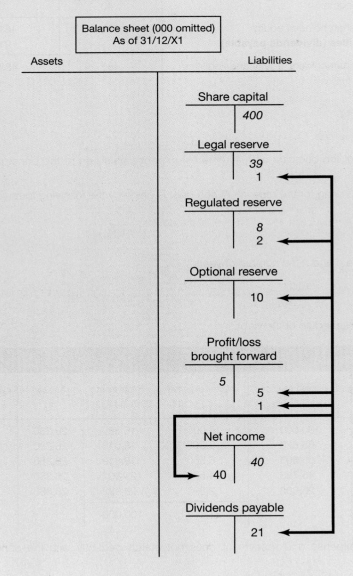

Balance sheet (000 omitted)
As of 31/12/X1

Assets   Liabilities

Share capital
                        400

Legal reserve
                        39
                         1

Regulated reserve
                         8
                         2

Optional reserve
                        10

Profit/loss
brought forward
          5
                         5
                         1

Net income
                        40
          40

Dividends payable
                        21

3. Prepare a table detailing the shareholders' equity and liabilities before and after appropriation.

000 omitted	Before appropriation	After appropriation
Shareholders' equity		
Share capital	400	400
Reserves		
Legal reserve	39	40
Regulated reserve	8	10
Optional reserve		10
Profit/loss brought forward (retained earnings)	−5	1
Net income	40	0
Total shareholders' equity	482	461
Liabilities (dividends payable)		21
Total shareholders' equity and liabilities	482	482

Review 12.1 Stenborg

Topic: Repayment of a bank loan

1. Compute the amount of the constant annuity (interest expense plus part of the principal) following the effective interest rate method.

The constant annuity allowing for the repayment of a debt is given by the following formula:

$$\text{Annual cash flow} = \text{Amount of the debt} \times \frac{i}{1 - (1 + i)^{-n}}$$

Where i is the interest rate and n the number of years.

$$\text{Annual cash flow} = 100{,}000 \times \frac{0.10}{1 - (1.10)^{-5}} = 100.000 \times \frac{0.10}{0.379078677} = 100{,}000 \times 0.263797481 = 26{,}380 \text{ CU units (rounded)}$$

2. Present the repayment schedule of the debt.

	Repayment schedule				
Years	Beginning balance (1) = (5) previous	Interest expense (2) = (1) × 10%	Repayment (3) = (4) − (2)	Annuity (4)	Ending balance (5) = (1) − (4)
30/6/X1	100,000	10,000	16,380	26,380	83,620
30/6/X2	83,620	8,362	18,018	26,380	65,602
30/6/X3	65,603	6,560	19,819	26,380	45,784
30/6/X4	45,783	4,578	21,801	26,380	23,982
30/6/X5	23,982	2,398	23,982	26,380	0
		31,898	100,000		

The addition of interest expense and repayment does not match perfectly with the annuity (26,380 CU) due to rounding.

3. Show the accounting entries: on the date of subscription, on closing date, on the first repayment date.

Year X1

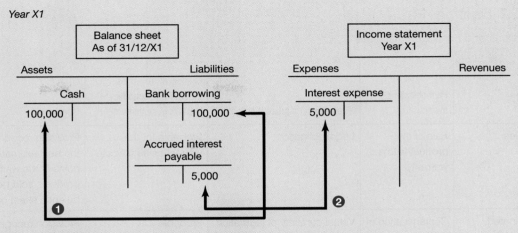

1 On 30 June X1, subscription of the debt. Receipt of the principal.

2 On the closing date (31 December X1), accrual of the interest relating to X1 (10,000 × 6 months from July to December = 5,000).

Year X2

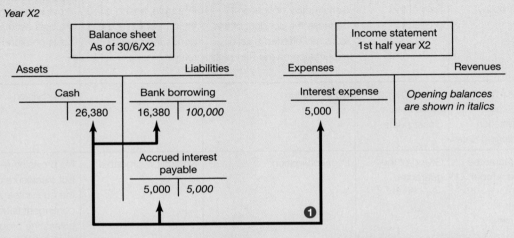

1 At the first maturity date (30 June X2), repayment of the principal according to the schedule (16,380 CU), cancellation of the accrued interest payable (5,000 CU) and recording of the second part of the interest (10,000 CU × 6 months from January to June = 5,000 CU).

Review 12.2 Haeffner PLC (1)[1]

Topic: Provisions and contingent liabilities

Situations	Past obligating event...	...resulting in a present obligation	Outflow of resources embodying economic benefits in settlement	Conclusion
1. Warranties	Sale of the product with a warranty	Legal obligation	Probable for the warranties as a whole	Provision recognized for the best estimate of the costs of the warranty for products sold before the balance sheet date
2. Contaminated land – legislation virtually certain to be enacted	Contamination of the land	Virtual certainty of legislation requiring clean-up	Probable	Provision recognized for the best estimate of the costs of the clean-up
3. Refunds policy	Sale of the product	Constructive obligation because the conduct of the store has created a valid expectation on the part of its customers	Probable, based on the proportion of the goods returned for refund	Provision recognized for the best estimate of the costs of refunds
4. Closure of a division – no implementation before closing date	No obligating event before closing date	No obligation	–	No provision
5. Single guarantee At 31 December X1	Giving of the guarantee	Legal obligation	No outflow probable	No provision recognized but disclosure of the guarantee as a contingent liability unless the probability of any outflow is regarded as remote
At 31 December X2	Giving of the guarantee	Legal obligation	Probable	Provision recognized for the best estimate of the obligation

Review 13.1 Mater & Filia

Topic: Consolidated balance sheet (three methods)

The requirement of application of the three consolidation methods is rather artificial here. In reality, only one of the three methods should be used and the method that is appropriate is defined by the percentage of control. Here, full consolidation is the only legitimate consolidation method, given the percentage of control – 80% – Mater holds in Filia.

However this review problem has the pedagogical objective of showing the differences between the three methods, even if the context is rather artificial.

Full consolidation

	Mater	Filia	Combined statements	Elimination of investment	Minority interest	Consolidated balance sheet
				Elimination entries and adjustments		
Fixed assets (net)	1,500	550	2,050			2,050
Investment in Filia Company	160	–	160	–160		0
Inventories	930	510	1,440			1,440
Other current assets	1,210	740	1,950			1,950
Total assets	**3,800**	**1,800**	**5,600**	**–160**	**0**	**5,440**
Group interests						
Share capital	500	200	700	–160	–40	500
Retained earning/reserves	780	600	1,380	–480	–120	780
Consolidation reserve				480		480
Net income	220	150	370		–30	340
Minority interests						
Share capital of Filia					40	40
Retained earnings/reserves of Filia					120	120
Net income of Filia					30	30
Liabilities	2,300	850	3,150			3,150
Total equity and liabilities	**3,800**	**1,800**	**5,600**	**–160**	**0**	**5,440**

In the elimination of the investment in Filia, the investment (at cost) is canceled and the share of reserves of Filia belonging to the parent company, Mater, is transferred to the consolidation reserve. The minority interests are materialized by the transfer to that caption of the share of minority shareholders over the share capital, reserves, and net income of Filia.

Proportionate consolidation and equity method compared to full consolidation

Consolidated balance sheet as at 31 December X1 (000 CU)
Comparison of the three methods

	Full consolidation	Proportionate consolidation	Equity method
Fixed assets (net)	2,050	1,940	1,500
Investment in Filia Company	0	0	0
Investment valued at equity	–	–	760
Inventories	1,440	1,338	930
Other current assets	1,950	1,802	1,210
Total assets	**5,440**	**5,080**	**4,400**
Group interests (shareholders' equity)			
Share capital	500	500	500
Retained earnings/reserves	780	780	780
Consolidation reserve	480	480	480
Net income	340	340	340
Minority interests			
Share capital of Filia	40	0	0
Retained earnings/reserves of Filia	120	0	0
Net income of Filia	30	0	0
Liabilities	3,150	2,980	2,300
Total equity and liabilities	**5,440**	**5,080**	**4,400**

In the **proportionate consolidation**, all assets and liabilities would be the result of the combination, line by line, of the Mater Company items + 80% of the corresponding Filia items. For instance, for fixed assets, 1,500 + 550 × 80% = 1,500 + 440 = 1,940. However, the group interests (shareholders' equity) would be the same as with full consolidation.

In the **equity method**, there is no integration. Consequently, the assets (with the exception of investment) and liabilities of the consolidated entity would only be those of the parent (Mater) balance sheet. The share capital and reserves would also only be those of the parent company. However, the investment in Filia (160 originally) would be revalued. The current value is: [Shareholders' equity of Filia (including current net income)] × (percentage of interest) = (200 + 600 + 150) × 80% = 760. The difference between this value and the acquisition price (760 – 160 = 600) would be split between the consolidation reserve (480 which would represent the share of the reserves of Filia which did not exist at the time of acquisition: 600 × 80%) and net income (120 which would represent the share of the current net income of Filia: 150 × 80%).

Notice that the total amount of the group shareholders' equity is the same, whichever method is used.

Review 14.1 Dvorak Company

Topic: Preparation of a statement of cash flows

The solution using the indirect method of calculation of cash flow from operating activities is used first.

Statement of cash flows	
	X2
Cash flows from operating activities (indirect method)	
Net income/loss [per income statement]	2,560
Adjustments to reconcile net income/loss to net cash provided by/used in operating activities	
Depreciation [non-cash expenses, thus need to be added back] (and provision expense, if there had been any [with the exception of provision movements on current assets])	1,400
Gain/loss on sale of fixed assets [exceptional income 450 minus net book value of assets sold 250 equals a profit of 200 – already included in the sales price in investing activities]	–200
Potential cash flow	3,760
Changes in operating assets and liabilities	
Change in inventories [net amounts]	300
Change in accounts receivable [net amounts]	–650
Change in accounts payable	810
Net cash provided by/used in operating activities (1)	4,220
Cash flows from investing activities	
Purchase of fixed assets	–4,000
Change in fixed assets payable	250
Cash paid on purchase of fixed assets	–3,750
Proceeds from sales of fixed assets	450
Net cash provided by/used in investing activities (2)	–3,300
Cash flows from financing activities	
Dividends paid	–2,580
Proceeds from issuance of share capital	200
Proceeds from issuance of financial liabilities	1,000
Repayment of financial liabilities	–400
Net cash provided by/used in financing activities (3)	–1,780
Net increase/decrease in cash and cash equivalents (4) = (1) + (2) + (3)	–860
Cash and cash equivalents at beginning of year (5)	–10
Cash and cash equivalents at end of year (6) = (5) + (4)	–870
Cash and cash equivalents at end of year (as reported in the balance sheet: 80 in positive cash and 950 in bank overdraft, i.e., negative cash) (7) Control: (7) = (6)	–870

The cash flow from operating activities computed using the direct method is provided below.

Cash flows from operating activities (direct method)	
Sales of merchandise	14,100
Change in accounts receivable (net amounts)	–650
Cash received from customers	13,450
Purchases of merchandise	–3,700
Change in accounts payable	810
Cash paid to suppliers	–2,890
Other operating revenues [assumed to be in cash]	150
Financial revenues [assumed to be in cash]	300
Other purchases and external expenses [assumed to be in cash]	–550
Taxes and similar expenses [assumed to be in cash]	–70
Personnel expenses [although personnel are paid weekly, bi-weekly or monthly, this expense is generally considered to be a cash payment]	–4,310
Financial expenses [assumed to be in cash]	–580
Income tax [assumed to have been paid during the period, i.e., in cash – otherwise we would have calculated the cash outflow using the same approach as was used for the calculation of the payments to suppliers]	–1,280
Net cash provided by/used in operating activities	4,220

In the statement of cash flows, bank overdrafts were assumed to represent an integral part of the cash management strategy of Dvorak Co. As a consequence, overdrafts were excluded from the financing activities and included in the 'cash and cash equivalents', as negative cash.

Another solution in calculating the cash provided by/used in financing activities would be perfectly acceptable. This would not involve, of course, any change of the final cash figure reported, but a change in classification in the statement of cash flows, and thus, possibly, a change in the perception by the reader/analyst of the cash flow processes used by Dvorak Co.: it would consist of including the 'change in bank overdrafts' as part of the financing activities. In that case, the cash and cash equivalents would only comprise the 'cash at bank'. The following table describes this second solution.

Cash flow from financing activities (1) [from previous tables]	4,220
Cash flow from investing activities (2) [from previous tables]	–3,300
Cash flows from financing activities	
Dividends paid	–2,580
Proceeds from issuance of share capital	200
Proceeds from issuance of financial liabilities	1,000
Repayment of financial liabilities	–400
Change in bank overdrafts*	750
Net cash provided by financing activities* (3)	–1,030
Net increase/decrease in cash [and cash equivalents if there were any – not the case here] (4) = (1) + (2) + (3)	–110
Cash [and cash equivalents] at beginning of year (5)	190
Cash [and cash equivalents] at end of year (6) = (5) + (4)	80
Cash [and cash equivalents] at end of year [as reported in the balance sheet] (7) Control: (7) = (6)	80

* Lines which are different from the previous solution.

Review 15.1 Dvorak Company (2)

Topic: Preparation of a statement of financial structure

1. With the help of the financial statements, prepare a simplified balance sheet with three sub-headings in the assets and three sub-headings in the equity and liabilities for the years X1 and X2.

	Amounts		Structure	
	X1	X2	X1	X2
Fixed assets	8,300	10,650	66.7%	70.9%
Current assets	3,950	4,300	31.8%	28.6%
Cash	190	80	1.5%	0.5%
Total assets	**12,440**	**15,030**	**100.0%**	**100.0%**
Equity and long-term liabilities	12,180	12,960	97.9%	86.2%
Current liabilities	60	1,120	0.5%	7.5%
Bank overdrafts	200	950	1.6%	6.3%
Total liabilities	**12,440**	**15,030**	**100.0%**	**100.0%**

2. Prepare a statement showing the financial structure of the company for the years X1 and X2 (i.e., compute the working capital, working capital need and net cash).

The balance sheet structure was described, on a 'common-size basis', in the table showing the answer to question 1.

Statement of financial structure	X1	X2
Equity and long-term liabilities	12,180	12,960
Fixed assets	−8,300	−10,650
Working capital	**3,880**	**2,310**
Current assets	3,950	4,300
Current liabilities	−60	−1,120
Working capital need	**3,890**	**3,180**
Cash	190	80
Bank overdrafts	−200	−950
Net cash	**−10**	**−870**
Control: Working capital less working capital need = net cash	−10	−870
Synthesis	X1	X2
Working capital	3,880	2,310
Working capital need	3,890	3,180
Net cash	−10	−870

3. Evaluate and comment these statements.

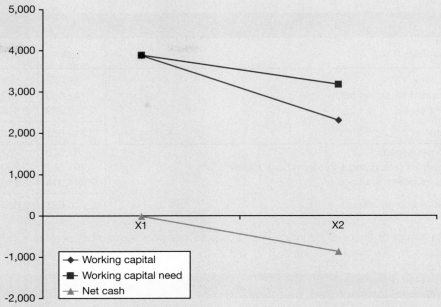

Plotting net cash is not really necessary in the graph since net cash is nothing more than the difference between the first two lines above it. However, showing net cash emphasizes the negative net cash at the end of the period.

The financial structure in both years corresponds to scenario ❷ in Figure 15.5: working capital does not fully finance the working capital need and, consequently, net cash (and cash equivalents) is negative. However, the situation further deteriorates in X2, despite the decrease in working capital need. In fact, the negative cash increases because of an even higher decrease in working capital, due to an increase in fixed assets.

Review 15.2 Chugoku Power Electric Company (1)*

Topic: Balance sheet structure

1. What is the format of the balance sheet?

The reader should first refer to Chapter 5. The format is:

- Vertical.
- Single-step, because the balance sheet is balanced with the equation: assets = liabilities + equity (called 'net assets' in this case).
- By term, because long-term and short-term liabilities are clearly distinguished. The existence of the caption 'long-term debt due within one year' in the current liabilities is an evidence of the presentation by term.
- The ordering of assets on the one hand, and liabilities and equity on the other, is unusual: whereas the assets are presented in an increasing order of liquidity, liabilities and equity are displayed in a decreasing order.

2. Prepare a simplified balance sheet with three sub-headings in the assets and three sub-headings in the equity and liabilities.

Simplified balance sheet		
31 March (in millions of Yen)	2008	2007
Cash and bank	17,073	21,722
Current assets (excluding cash)	142,639	142,088
Non-current assets	2,550,969	2,516,972
Total assets	2,710,681	2,680,782
Short-term bank loans	67,600	67,780
Current liabilities (excluding short-term bank loans)	299,067	330,467
Equity and long-term liabilities	2,344,014	2,282,535
Total liabilities and net assets	2,710,681	2,680,782

3. Prepare the statement of financial structure (i.e., compute the working capital, working capital need and net cash).

Statement of financial structure		
31 March (in millions of Yen)	2008	2007
Equity and long-term liabilities	2,344,014	2,282,535
Non-current assets	(2,550,969)	(2,516,972)
Working capital	**(206,955)**	**(234,437)**
Current assets (excluding cash)	142,639	142,088
Current liabilities (excluding short-term bank loans)	(299,067)	(330,467)
Working capital need	**(156,428)**	**(188,379)**
Cash and bank	17,073	21,722
Short-term bank loans	(67,600)	(67,780)
Net cash	**(50,527)**	**(46,058)**

4. Comment on your findings.

The diagram below illustrates the evolution of working capital and working capital need. Net cash need not be shown specifically as it is merely the difference between the two lines describing the evolution of working capital and working capital need.

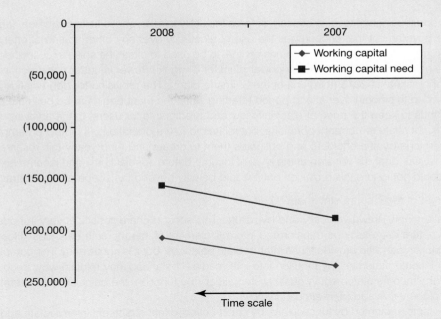

As the order of years is anti-chronological in the tables and the figure, the analyst should be careful with the way these documents are read and should start from the right.

A practical suggestion is to recommend that the analyst of any financial statement always first draws an arrow indicating the direction of the time scale specific to each document to be sure to read data and graphs in the appropriate way: firms report in almost equal proportions in a chronological way, i.e., time increases from left to right, and an anti-chronological way, i.e., time increases from right to left.

The financial structure corresponds to that of scenario ❺ in Figure 15.5. It is a surprising situation for a utility company. This situation appears to be similar to that of Sinopec described in section 3.3. As for this company, the financial structure, with all three working capital indicators being negative, could be considered at first glance as a sign of 'weakness' of the firm and a cloud over the going concern status of the firm. However, we need to be very cautious in any such interpretation without complete understanding of the business environment in Japan.

Review 16.1 Chugoku Power Electric Company (2)*

Topic: Common-size income statements by nature

The reader must pay attention to the signs of 'other expenses (income)': positive sign for expenses and negative sign for income. We will refer in our analysis to Chugoku Power Electric Company as Chugoku Power.

Preamble: This case analysis will be *very simplified.* Chugoku Power is a very large and complex utility company serving over 8 million people. It uses a variety of sources of energy to create electricity: coal (mainly gasified), diesel fuel, liquefied natural gas, nuclear and waterfall (for hydroelectric power). We will consider it uses only one source of energy so as to simplify the analysis. That simplification may lead to deductions that might appear to be at odds with reality to an insider. Our purpose with this case is not to fully analyze Chugoku Power, but to use that firm's financial statement to illustrate the methodology of analysis of an income statement. Some of our approximations may be wildly off the mark, but the methodology followed remains rigorous.

One line in the income statement deserves a special commentary. Provision for depreciation of nuclear power plant is a deduction that appears after the calculation of the 'operating net income before tax' in the income statement. It is a special expense that is related to the Electric Utility Industry Law and an ordinance from the Ministry of Economy, Trade and Industry of Japan. Both came in effect in 2006. The principle behind this mandated deduction is based on the observation that, upon commencement of the commercial activities of a nuclear power plant, (1) the utility company incurs a spike in expenses way out of line with costs incurred during the plateau phase of operation of a nuclear power plant; and (2) much of the nuclear equipment must be depreciated rapidly upon going online. If this spike in costs were allowed to be recognized as incurred, the operating costs would either force heavy losses for utility companies at that time (not an attractive prospect for shareholders when a utility is encouraged to develop nuclear power plants to fight the greenhouse effect and thus needs to raise capital), or force the utility to raise prices to its customers (again not an attractive prospect for a government that encourages the use of electricity over any other source of energy). Thus the law creates a reserve fund, before the new plant comes on line, to be used to offset the spike in cost when the next nuclear power plant will be going online. A new nuclear power plant for Chugoku Power is under construction at the time of the case and will be operational in 2013 (third unit of the Shimane plant). The provision for depreciation of nuclear power plant is a process used to smooth over a long period (starting when the plant begins to be built) the cost of producing nuclear kWh, and thus to keep the price of electricity low and predictable for users. In the analysis we will ignore this provision as it does not relate to current operations, but relates to future operations. It simply preempts the freedom of appropriation of earnings by shareholders and obligates them to create and fund yearly this reserve out of operating income before taxes. Our analysis will stop at the level of income before special items and income taxes. A much more detailed analysis could not ignore this provision but it would be way beyond the scope of this illustrative exercise.[2]

1. What is the format of the income statement?

The income statement is drawn vertically and by nature. This second characteristic is very important because only a statement by nature can easily be transformed into a 'statement of intermediate balances'. However, the income statement by function can also provide these intermediate balances, but it is not as easy. The complexity of the transformation of an income statement by function into intermediate balances may explain why, in countries where the presentation of the income statement is quasi systematically by function, the calculation of intermediate balances, especially that of the value added, is almost unknown.

Income statements presented by function are, by construction, offering different intermediate aggregate measures which are the various steps of margins, none of which can be related to the concept of value added we evoked above. These successive steps in the constitution of income provide useful information regarding discounts, gross margin, commercial margin (gross margin minus cost of selling), operating margin, etc.

2. Prepare common-size statements on the basis of the income statement, as published by the company.

In answering this question (as is the case for any question), it is important to know why we do what we do, and what signals will create 'information'. Remember: a figure, whether an absolute amount or a percentage, is just a piece of data, i.e., it is inert. It becomes 'information', often after manipulation and confrontation with other data, once it is – or has been transformed into – a new signal or metric that has *the potential of changing* the decision of the user of these financial statements.

The purpose of common-sizing an income statement (or any of the financial statements) in the case of one entity, as is the case here, is to analyze the common-size structure of the income statement over three years (it could have been a longer period) in order to detect 'anomalies', i.e., elements that are counter intuitive to the pre-existing perceived business model, which, therefore, become information. The 'benchmark' for detecting anomalies or surprises is, for each year, the previous year's figure. Anomalies or surprises are observed deviations from a 'straw man' (logical but simplistic) model of either the expected structure of the statement, or of the expected evolution of the structure of the statement over time on the basis of the model one holds of the operation of the business. This is why a contextual analysis of the firm under scrutiny (here a power generation and distribution firm) is always a first step. A succinct contextual analysis was provided in the text of this problem and in the preamble above, but it would need to be enriched and better documented from various sources, in this case as well as, mostly, in the real world, where no one will ever formulate the problem for the analyst.

For example, if volume of sales increases, as is the case for Chugoku Power, as least when expressed in yens, over the three years we analyze, we do not expect certain elements of the income statement to evolve proportionately (i.e., remain at the same percentage level from year to year).

A naïve expectation (a straw man hypothesis) would be that consumption of fuel varies proportionately to the volume of kWh produced, i.e., the percentage represented by fuel cost out of sales revenue (if prices are constant) should remain more or less constant over the years, *unless there are efficiency gains*.

Further, prices of fuels do vary, especially in the period under scrutiny here. Since a power company is a regulated entity in most countries (and that is definitely the case in Japan), Chugoku Power may not be allowed to pass on to the customer the full price increase/decrease it encounters or may only be able to do so with a significant lag. A cursory review of the annual report shows that in Japan, the price per kWh is expected to decline or remain constant over the long run – the price per kWh began going down in 1997 and has rarely even stabilized since. The surprise (i.e., the information that leads to further questions and to possible revision of decisions) would be that the fuel cost would remain a constant proportion to sales revenue: on one hand, at best, the selling price per kWh is constant, on the other the price of energy fuel varies. The fact the two quantities do not vary in concert is a normal expectation.

However, it is the way the two quantities do diverge that will be the informational content the analyst is looking for. Our analysis, especially in question 4, will focus on these 'surprises' or 'anomalies' to enrich the information user with fact-based information and knowledge.

Another important point when we conduct such a common-size time-series analysis is for the analyst to verify that the analysis compares things that are comparable. A company is alive: it is evolving constantly over time, changing its business plan, entering into some new business segments, buying some business units in other sectors or spinning out some existing business. Therefore, the 'anomalies' we observe over time may result not from any performance or efficiency improvements or deteriorations, but from the already-mentioned structural changes. For example, the decline in maintenance cost from 2007 to 2008 from 9% of sales revenue to 7.9% of sales revenue is an anomaly. If the analyst digs further, she or he will discover that Chugoku Power was able to close down in 2007 two aging thermal plants that required an abnormal amount of maintenance to keep them running. Gains in efficiency (capacity is fixed) in other plants filled the gap left by these closures. It is clear that an interrogation always finds an answer, either in the annual report, or in the press or by contacting the firm directly. But the question cannot be asked if there was no triggering signal that said something has changed in the business model.

Note that in the case of a cross sectional analysis (several businesses in the same risk-class and/or in the same economic sector), common-size analysis leads to (a) the ability to compare different strategies between firms, and (b), if several years are provided for all firms in the sample, to visualize how strategies changed over time for each firm and which ones appear to be more 'effective' (however the analyst defines the term 'effective', it must be defined *before hand*).

Common-size income statements

Percentages	2008	2007	2006
	Time scale is right to left		
Operating revenues	100.0%	100.0%	100.0%
Operating expenses			
Personnel	10.1%	11.7%	12.5%
Fuel	25.8%	21.5%	18.3%
Purchased power	14.9%	14.7%	16.6%
Depreciation	12.6%	12.9%	14.0%
Maintenance	7.9%	9.0%	8.3%
Taxes other that income taxes	5.9%	6.2%	6.3%
Purchased services	3.5%	3.4%	3.5%
Other	11.7%	12.7%	11.3%
	92.5%	92.1%	90.6%
Operating income	7.5%	7.9%	9.4%
Other expenses (income):			
Interest expense	2.9%	2.9%	2.9%
Interest income	(0.2%)	(0.1%)	(0.0%)
Loss on revaluation of investments in subsidiary	0.0%	0.0%	1.3%
Other, net	(0.2%)	(0.2%)	(0.1%)
	2.6%	2.5%	4.0%
Income before special items and income taxes	4.9%	5.3%	5.4%
Special item:			
Provision (reversal) for drought	(0.1%)	0.0%	(0.2%)
Provision for depreciation of nuclear power plant	1.8%	0.5%	0.0%
Provision for income taxes:			
Current	1.1%	1.7%	2.6%
Deferred	0.0%	(0.2%)	(0.1%)
Net income	2.0%	3.4%	3.1%

3. Restate the income statement and prepare common-size intermediate balances following the format of Figure 16.1.

Statement of intermediate balances						
	(in millions of yen)			(in percentage)		
	2008	2007	2006	2008	2007	2006
Operating revenues	1,038,438	996,007	976,835	100.0%	100.0%	100.0%
Total production for the period	**1,038,438**	**996,007**	**976,835**	**100.0%**	**100.0%**	**100.0%**
Change in production year on year	*4.3%*	*2.0%*				
Fuel	268,327	214,559	178,649	25.8%	21.5%	18.3%
Purchased power	154,991	146,861	161,771	14.9%	14.7%	16.6%
Maintenance	82,105	90,001	80,747	7.9%	9.0%	8.3%
Purchased services	36,703	33,465	33,732	3.5%	3.4%	3.5%
Consumption from third parties	**542,126**	**484,886**	**454,899**	**52.2%**	**48.7%**	**46.6%**
Value added	**496,312**	**511,121**	**521,936**	**47.8%**	**51.3%**	**53.4%**
Taxes other that income taxes	61,388	61,698	61,556	5.9%	6.2%	6.3%
Personnel	105,272	116,529	122,008	10.1%	11.7%	12.5%
Gross operating profit	**329,652**	**332,894**	**338,372**	**31.7%**	**33.4%**	**34.6%**
Depreciation	130,501	128,490	136,569	12.6%	12.9%	14.0%
Other	121,316	126,176	110,001	11.7%	12.7%	11.3%
Operating profit	**77,835**	**78,228**	**91,802**	**7.5%**	**7.9%**	**9.4%**
Interest expense	30,232	28,419	27,855	2.9%	2.9%	2.9%
Interest income	(1,639)	(1,076)	(101)	(0.2%)	(0.1%)	(0.0%)
Loss on revaluation of investments in subsidiary	0	0	12,590	0.0%	0.0%	1.3%
Other, net	(2,034)	(2,110)	(1,452)	(0.2%)	(0.2%)	(0.1%)
Operating net income before taxes	**51,276**	**52,995**	**52,910**	**4.9%**	**5.3%**	**5.4%**
Provision (reversal) for drought	(657)	112	(1,913)	(0.1%)	0.0%	(0.2%)
Provision for depreciation of nuclear power plant	(18,828)	(5,053)	0	(1.8%)	(0.5%)	0.0%
Exceptional result	**(18,171)**	**(5,165)**	**1,913**	**(1.7%)**	**(0.5%)**	**0.2%**
Provision for income taxes:	12,381	14,427	24,576	1.2%	1.4%	2.5%
Net income/loss after tax	**20,724**	**33,403**	**30,247**	**2.0%**	**3.4%**	**3.1%**

4. Comment on these different statements.

Note: the comments below are only suggested answers and form a set of illustrations of the use of the methodology developed in the chapter, so as to gain knowledge about the situation of Chugoku Power. Another analyst might very well come up with different hypotheses, different views of the business model of a power plant, or of the economic environment in Japan, or of the energy markets in 2006–2008 and therefore end up with different conclusions. That would be normal: unless an analyst has an inside source, she or he must rely on publicly available data, always incomplete and subject to interpretation. However, any analyst would have used a methodology very similar to the one we illustrate below.

With regard to the different intermediate financial performance balances, many are the same as those reported in the non-restated income statement (earnings before taxes, exceptional result, net income after tax). The added 'information' concerns mainly the upper part of the statement (value added, consumption from third parties and gross operating profit).

A statement of intermediate balances is interesting and useful largely because it offers an actionable decomposition of operating profit, (a) by separating what is fully under the control of managers from what is procured from outside sources, and (b) presenting the elements of the income statement in a format that allows each manager to see what she or he can do to increase net income after tax. The analyst can now, on the basis of the tables above, and in light of the comments already made, start 'analyzing', in a fact-based way, the situation of Chugoku Power to gain a better understanding of what happened over the three years and thus be able to better anticipate the coming years.

1. Despite the growth in operating revenues, the added value rate decreased over the period (from 53.4% in 2006 to 47.8% in 2008). It may be an indication of a modification in the production business model such as, on a 'benign' scale, more reliance on outsourcing of maintenance, possibly explaining the decline of internal maintenance in 2008 over 2007 from 9% of sales to 7.9% of sales and the concurrent increase in purchased services from 3.4% to 3.5% of sales. On a more 'significant' scale, the evolution of the price of fuel is, of course, pretty meaningful (see below). So is the closure of two plants and the shift towards a different fuel mix (data not mentioned in the case, extracted from the full annual report). The structure of the business model has changed.

2. Fuel cost represents a major explanation of the reduction of value added as a percentage of sales. Since maintenance and purchased services are unlikely to be varying (if at all) with sales, if Chugoku Power could pass on to its customers the fuel price variations it faces, value added should (in the fuel price-increase environment of 2006–2008) either remain constant as a percentage of sales or improve (increase due to gains in efficiency, created for example by using more combined cycle gasification of coal or co-generation turbines – both technologies, to make it simple, use the energy twice by using high pressure and low pressure turbines). The fact the value added balance declines over the period from 53.4% to 47.8% is either a signal (new information) – or a confirmation – that Chugoku Power has been unable to modify its selling prices at the same rate as its fuel prices increased.

To go further we need to index the cost of fuel. A quick search on the Web of the price of diesel fuel yielded a graph, provided by the US Energy Information Administration, of the evolution of the price of diesel fuel. Diesel fuel will be accepted as a proxy for power plant fuel because the relative prices of oil, gas, coal and nuclear fuel are likely to evolve relatively in parallel, as their prices are arbitraged on the basis of their BTU content (where BTU = British Thermal Units). A more detailed analysis would of course look at the evolution of the mix of fuels used (provided in the annual report) and the actual evolution of their prices (provided, for example, in publications like the *Financial Times* or the *Singapore Straight Times*). We chose to assume one single source of fuel, just to illustrate the methodology, not to be right. The evolution of the price of diesel fuel (as estimated on the New York market – its biggest market, even before Rotterdam) is provided in the graph below:

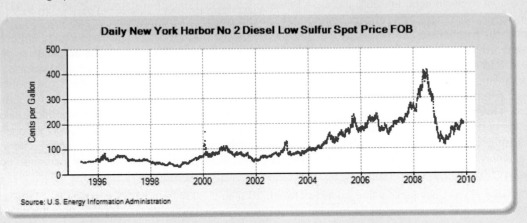

Source: U.S. Energy Information Administration

We can assume, when reading this graph, that the *average price* of diesel fuel, and therefore of all other fuels, by BTU equivalency, was pretty steady in 2006–2007, despite severe punctual fluctuations (which we choose to ignore for the sake of simplicity), at around $200 a barrel, but there appears to be an increase of 25% to an average of about $250 a barrel in 2008. We can assume this 25% price increase does apply to all fuels across the board (even if we *do know* the arbitraging is not perfect) and thus to the fuel used by Chugoku Power. Therefore, we can see that the price of fuel consumed should have been more or less proportional to the growth in sales in 2006 and 2007, thus showing a constant proportion of fuel consumed to sales revenue. Such is not the case: fuel moved from 18.3% of sales in 2006 to 21.5% of sales in 2007, raising interrogations as to the deteriorating efficiency of the power plants at Chugoku Power, as sales grew by only 2% (non-inflation adjusted). An explanation may be found in the two aging plants plant closed after 2007, or in difficulties in introducing efficiencies through the use of combined cycles in the process of gasification of coal, or the generalization of co-generation. Please note that the answer is not what is important, what is crucial is to have formulated a question by creating a straw man (here: stability of the fuel consumption and stability of the price in 2006–2007), creating an index of the key variable and calculating the 'theoretical' metric derived from the model and then comparing that metric with the real world figures. The possibility that the two aging plants were put to full use before their closure can be supported (1) by the observation that purchases of outside electricity (to meet peak demand in excess of capacity) declined from 2006 to 2007 (16.6% of sales in 2006 versus 14.7% of sales in 2007, despite a growth in total production (sales); and (2) by the analysis of the 2008 figures that follows.

If the price of fuel had remained constant in 2008 over 2007 (i.e., fuel costs had been 21.5% of sales in 2008 as they were in 2007), the consumption of fuel in 2008 should have been (any productivity issue aside) ¥M1,038,438 × 21.5% = ¥M223,264. If we apply the estimated average price increase of fuel in 2008 over 2007 at 25%, as mentioned above, we should have expected fuel cost in 2008 to be around ¥M223,264 × 1.25 = ¥M279,080. Since we observe that the *actual cost* of fuel consumed in 2008 is ¥M268,327 (a 4% downwards deviation from 'expected'), we can conclude that whatever loss in productivity that may have occurred in 2007 over 2006 was stopped, as 2008 shows a slightly better productivity than that of 2007, after accounting for increases in fuel prices. The 'surprise' of seeing the cost of fuel as a percentage of sales move from 18.3% to 25.8% of sales revenue over the three years has been decomposed into a price increase of fuel (not totally controllable in the short-term by managers), and a degradation of efficiency of production in 2007 (over 2006) that was controlled and even slightly reversed in 2008.

This leads to another surprise (or confirmation, depending on what background information is known), linked to the evolution of the value added intermediate balance: the evolution of the maintenance cost, which fell from 9% in 2007 to 7.9% in 2008. In 2008, the productivity issues have indeed stabilized, because the two gas guzzling aging plants have been closed and more modern plants have boosted their production. The rapid decrease in maintenance cost has been mentioned and explained earlier. Is Chugoku Power taking a big risk by reducing the support effort and reducing maintenance? Probably not, but a breakdown of production by technologies would certainly help shed some light on the risks Chugoku Power takes or does not take. More conjectures, more questions for the analyst to ask management when they meet.

3. The same hypothesis of the 25% price increase of fuel oil in 2008 over 2007 leads us to analyze also the issue of the selling price evolution of the kWh sold by Chugoku Power. If the producer had been able to pass on its resource cost to customers, the 25% increase in fuel price should have translated in 2008 into a 9%[3] increase in selling price (all other costs, except fuel and purchased power, should be more or less fixed in a power production firm). If we inflate 2007 sales by 9%, we should get the minimum sales revenue Chugoku Power should have reported in 2008: ¥996,007 × 1.09 = ¥1,085,647 in sales revenue. We observe the actual sales of 2008 are ¥1,038,438 (a figure which is lower by 4.5%). We are confirmed in our view that Chugoku Power was unable to pass on any part of its incurred fuel cost increase to its customers; but the key point is that since prices per kWh remained constant, the volume of production must have increased (+2% in 2007 and +4.3% in 2008): a 6.3%[4] increase in kWh is a significant increase. Did such an increase create stress in the production/distribution system or was the capacity found by spreading the increases over the day and over the week (using rate driven behavior, for example to encourage, through lower rates, the use of electricity late at night for water heaters and heat accumulators) or by judicious purchases of additional power (purchases of external power increased from 14.7% of sales in 2007 to 14.9% in 2008).

4. The decrease in the balance of value added between 2007 and 2008 from 51.3% of sales to 47.8% appears to have been fairly well compensated for by savings before the operating profit line, as we will see below.

5. The management took some actions to preserve income.

   ■ A reduction of the weight of the personnel expenses: down from 12.5% in 2006 to 10.1% in 2008 (i.e., a 13.7% reduction of personnel expense in absolute amount over the three years (1− [/¥105,272/¥122,008]), including a 9% reduction in 2008 alone, over 2007 (1− [¥105,272/¥116,529]). This reduction is most surprising as labor cost, in a power plant, is expected to be a fixed expense (its amount does not vary significantly with output – up or down), but we have to realize that personnel in a power company are not just in production but also in maintenance of the distribution system, in reading meters, in accounting and billing, etc. We observe that maintenance and personnel both declined as a percentage of growing sales and we can legitimately feel impressed: a competitor (or a water distribution firm, for benchmarking purposes) might wish to know what processes were introduced to have such gains of productivity in services outside of production. These cost reductions may have preserved some profitability in the short-run, but we would need to know more about the nature of the actions to feel totally reassured that Chugoku Power is not endangering future prospects in order to salvage today.

■ Maintenance expenses declined, not surprisingly, in 2008 over 2007, from 9% of sales to 7.9% of sales, after only a modest increase (from 8.3% of sales in 2006 to 9% of sales in 2007) in 2007 over 2006. As mentioned earlier, this is linked to the closure of two plants and possibly more outsourcing.

■ The choices made by management were not totally sufficient as operating profit declines both in absolute terms and as a percentage of sales revenue (from 34.6% of sales in 2006 to 31.7% in 2008), but if prices of fuel had not increased by 25% in 2008, the cost of fuel and purchased power would only have been (268,327 + 154,991)/1.25 = ¥M338,654 or a reduction of 423,318 – 338,654 = ¥M84,663 or 8% of sales. Had the increase in price not taken place, the value added would have been, in 2008, 47.8% + 8% = 55.8% of sales, i.e., an improvement over 2007. Thus, the actions of management have limited the damage of the maelstrom of the fuel price increases.

■ Depreciation expenses decline as percentage of sales as is to be expected, since usage and time cause a decrease in the value of the productive potential, that is a fixed expense (if straight-line is used) unless new investments are carried out. If we look at the absolute value of depreciation over the three years, we can see it declined as expected in 2007 over 2006 but increased in 2008 over 2007. We know, since two plants were closed in 2007 (and can seek details from managers), this increase indicates investment(s) in new productive facilities (actually more improvement of existing capacity rather than pure capacity increase). It is a good sign for the future.

■ Other operating expenses increased from 11.3% of sales in 2006 to 11.7% in 2008 (with a peak at 12.5% in 2007). This is totally counter-intuitive: these expenses, although not detailed, should be constant over time or, maybe, vary with something like headcount or labor costs (which both declined over the three years). More questions unanswered.

■ Although that item is not quite directly under the authority of the management team, one can observe that non income-related taxes decline regularly over the three years as percentage of sales revenue. This is not surprising since their absolute amount remains pretty constant throughout the three years while sales increase. The decline as a percentage of sales is no reason for rejoicing: it is the result of a mechanical effect. Non income-related taxes are generally either property taxes (based on the value of assets) or business taxes (generally based on headcount), or a combination (addition) of both (an analyst familiar with the Japanese tax environment would know the exact tax base supporting these figures – we just make hypotheses that are plausible but which can be changed at will). The fact these taxes remain pretty much constant year to year is, therefore, a surprise. Why did they remain constant? We have identified that headcount and personnel expenses were going down, in addition there was also an increased recourse to outsourcing: labor expenses are probably going down more slowly than headcount expenses, because workers are likely to have received pay increases, plus co-generation and combined cycles require more qualified personnel than those personnel eliminated through the two closures. Chugoku Power did invest in additional assets, as shown above, and confirmed by looking at the increase in depreciation expense absolute values. The stability of the non income-related taxes is an indication that management's reduction of headcount was compensated by capital-intensive increase in automation (this is probably true as co-generation and combined cycles are technologies that are very capital intensive and use few personnel, even if highly qualified), thus balancing out the non income-related taxes reduction and increases.[5]

6. Interest expense remained steady at 2.9% of sales revenue through the three-year period. That is most surprising since there is no logical explanation to support interest expenses varying proportionately with sales volume. The serious increase in interest expense (larger rate of increase than the rate of increase of revenue) is likely to be the result of the solution adopted to finance the negative working capital need we have observed previously (see Review 15.2 Chugoku Power Electric Company). This is an unfavorable signal, as it indicates that, despite management's ability to find actions to largely offset the impact of the decrease of the value added balance on the operating profit line, the financial situation appears to have more than offset these efforts and ended-up creating a 3.2% [(51,276 – 52,995)/52,995] decrease in the absolute value of earnings before taxes and exceptional events (a signal made even more clear by the use of common-sizing, as the operating profit before taxes went down from 5.3% of sales in 2007 to 4.9% in 2008). We have some questions that have no logical or obvious answers without going through an analysis of the statement of cash flows. Analyzing one isolated statement, out of the three plus

the notes that constitute the core of an annual report, always leads to questions that force the analyst to go to the other statements for more complete answers.

7. Many analysts may see the steady increase in interest income as not significant: after all, it went from 0% in 2006, to 0.1%, to 0.2% in 2008. One might be tempted to dismiss this set of data, as its diminutive amount pales in the light of, for example, the percentage of sales revenue represented by fuel, purchases of power, or labor costs. However interest income means Chugoku Power increased its financial investments: the increase in interest income, in absolute value, is +52% in 2008 over 2007. Where can such excess cash come from? It might be down payments by customers for future deliveries (utility customers, in most countries, must deposit a refundable advance with their power supplier before they can receive service). The increase in interest income may be a signal that the number of customers have increased; but if customer numbers had increased by over 50% (the proportion of increase of the interest income), sales should have gone up by more than the observed 4.3% in 2008 over 2007 (keep in mind there was no price increase per kWh sold). More questions are lining up for the analyst to seek answers to by digging further into all financial statement of Chugoku Power.

We have shown, in this very superficial analysis (superficial because it focuses on a single financial statement and because of the simplifying hypotheses we made and explained in the preamble), how the methods we have applied do lead to a cascading series of questions. Few can receive an answer from just within the income statement. As we said earlier in the chapter, financial analysis is the beginning of a serious inquiry into the nature and policies of an entity. It can start with any one of the financial statements, but will always lead to exploring all three, together with the relevant notes, and, if available, the managerial comments and perspectives made by the senior managers that are part of the annual report.

By asking a fairly long list of questions, we have documented that Chugoku Power is caught in a scissor effect: it cannot increase its prices fast enough to follow the rise in the cost of fuel; it cannot reduce operational costs in the short term enough to compensate for the rise in the cost of fuel (these are mainly fixed outside of energy): Chugoku Power's only way out appears to be to invest in fuel-price-independent and non labor-intensive technologies; thus, their development of co-generation, combined cycles and the construction of a third unit for their Shimane nuclear power plant is logical; volume in kWh is increasing and the new technologies are the only ways to meet demand and keep lowering kWh prices. Not an 'easy' situation for the next few years, however. If all the questions we raised were answered, the analyst could understand better what management can do to get out of the scissor effect situation, and/or tell investors what to expect in terms of future earnings. Those answers will come from an analysis of the full annual report and broadly based data about Chugoku Power and its environment.

Review 17.1 Mitsubishi Electric*

Topic: Understanding and analyzing a statement of cash flows

1. Which method (direct or indirect) was used to compute the operating cash flow?

The method used to compute the operating cash flow is the indirect method, which starts from the net income and adjusts it by adding back non-cash expenses and gain on sale of fixed assets, subtracting non-cash revenues and loss on sale of fixed assets, and integrating the changes in inventories, receivables, and payables.

2. Compute the potential cash flow.

The potential cash flow is the net income adjusted with non-cash items. In this example, non-cash items are depreciation, impairment losses of property, plant and equipment, the deferred income taxes, devaluation losses of securities and other, net, and equity in earnings of affiliated companies. Net income is also adjusted with gain and loss of elements of investing activities: loss from sales and disposal of property, plant and equipment, net, and loss (gain) from sales of securities and other, net.

We provide below, as a check, the computation of the potential cash flow but also compute the operating cash flow.

(in Yen millions)	2009	2008	2007
Net income	12,167	157,977	123,080
Depreciation	148,018	136,283	130,130
Impairment losses of property, plant and equipment	28,704	3,043	11,384
Loss from sales and disposal of property, plant and equipment, net	1,832	2,544	6,206
Deferred income taxes	20,137	5,442	9,553
Loss (gain) from sales of securities and other, net	(605)	(2,161)	(4,214)
Devaluation losses of securities and other, net	18,556	1,132	1,917
Equity in earnings of affiliated companies	67,715	(10,675)	(18,507)
Potential cash flow	**296,524**	**293,585**	**259,549**
Changes in inventory, receivables and payables	(115,385)	(34,716)	15,081
Operating cash flow	181,139	258,869	274,630

3. Why does the statement use the expression 'decrease (increase)' to describe changes in trade receivables, inventories and prepaid expenses while it uses the expression 'increase (decrease)' when referring to changes in trade payables and other liabilities?

The statement indicates the changes having a positive impact on cash with a + sign and the changes having a negative impact with a – sign (or brackets).

For the changes in inventories, trade receivables, and prepaid expenses (which are assets), an increase implies less cash (minus sign) was received or generated than the accrual revenues would lead one to expect, and a decrease implies more cash (plus sign) was received or generated than the accrual revenues would lead one to expect. Conversely, for the changes in trade payables and other liabilities, an increase is synonymous with more cash (plus sign) being kept (reduced cash outflow) than the accrual cost of goods sold would lead one to expect and a decrease leads to less cash (minus sign) being kept (increased cash outflow) than the accrual cost of goods sold would lead one to expect.

4. How are short-term investments reported? What could have been another legitimate possibility? Comment as to why they chose the method they did over another?

Mitsubishi Electric reports short-term investments as part of their investing activities. Alternatively, these short-term investments could have been considered as cash equivalents, 'short-term, highly liquid investments, that are readily convertible to known amounts of cash and which are subject to an insignificant risk of changes in value' (IAS 7: § 6) and thus not reported as such, at the end of the statement of cash flows.

5. Short-term debt can be considered equivalent to 'bank overdrafts'. Comment on the way they are reported in the above statements. What would have been another possibility?

Short-term debt represents a debt for the company (liability towards banks). Mitsubishi Electric reports these as part of their financing activities. They could have been included as negative cash in 'cash and cash equivalents'.

6. Analyze the statement of cash flows over the period.

Before any analysis, the general structure of the statement of cash flows must be produced:

(in Yen millions)	2009	2008	2007
Net cash provided by operating activities (1)	181,139	258,869	274,630
Net cash used in investing activities (2)	(214,939)	(132,350)	(155,599)
Available cash flow (3) = (1) + (2)	(33,800)	126,519	119,031
Dividends paid (4)	(27,904)	(25,758)	(19,317)
Free cash flow (5) = (3) + (4)	(61,704)	100,761	99,714
Other financing cash flows (6)	112,797	(93,998)	(69,417)
Effect of exchange rates (7)	(26,788)	(15,092)	7,829
Change in cash and cash equivalents (8) = (5) + (6) + (7)	24,305	(8,329)	38,126

The data provided in the text of the review problem indicates Mitsubishi Electric showed sales increased from 2007 to 2008 and decreased from 2008 to 2009. The evolution of net income followed the same pattern (increase followed by a decrease). However, the change in cash and cash equivalents shows an exactly inverse pattern: negative in 2009 and 2007 but positive in 2008. Let us explain why.

The available cash flow is positive in 2007 and 2008 but negative in 2009, which shows deterioration. The operating cash flow is in fact sufficient to finance the investing cash flow in both 2007 and 2008. In 2009, however, Mitsubishi Electric is caught in a scissor effect: decrease in the operating cash flow on one hand and, on the other, investing cash flow even more 'negative', i.e., reflecting a significant increase in new investments over the pattern it had followed in the previous years. The positive available cash in 2007 and 2008 allows the company to have a negative financing cash flow every year. In other words, the company has enough available cash flow to repay some of its debts (see below). However, in 2009, the available cash flow being negative, the company needs to have a positive financing cash flow, particularly as it decided to increase the amount of dividends paid.

Operating activities

The operating cash flow has decreased significantly over the period. A key reason for this decline may be that despite the increase in the potential cash flow (see question 2) the change in inventories, receivables and payables has an even more negative impact on the operating cash flow. Looking at the statement of cash flows, we see that major impact comes from the change in trade payables.

This deterioration appears in the computation of the two following ratios.

	2009	2008	2007
Operating cash flow to sales	4.9%	6.4%	7.1%
Cash flow yield (operating cash flow/net earnings)	14.9	1.6	2.2

Investing activities

Cash used in investing activities becomes more 'negative' over the period, i.e., Mitsubishi Electric uses more cash to invest than in previous years. One might have expected this increase in the investing cash flow (62.4% in absolute value 2009 over 2008) to be incurred in order to develop capacity, markets or research, but one key explanation is much more pedestrian (yearly capital expenditures remain pretty much constant over the three years): these investments come from the purchase of short-term investments and investment securities, which almost double each year (from ¥M 24,115 in 2007 to ¥M 86,749 in 2009) while the proceeds from the sales of such short-term investments decline between 2007 (when, with an amount ¥M 28,163, they were actually greater than the purchases standing at ¥M 24,115) and 2009 when the purchases exceed the sales by a factor of approximately 6.3 (86,749/13,693).

When a firm invests cash in short-term securities, it is often to protect the purchasing power of its cash, not to develop the capabilities of the firm. Unless the management report explains the purpose or reason for this cash 'savings' (any 'productive' reason such as a planned acquisition, a buffer in the crisis, a postponed – but not cancelled – productive investment, etc.), the shareholders are legitimately entitled to ask the question: 'Could I not find, privately, a higher rate of return at that level of risk outside of Mitsubishi Electric?' If the answer is positive, the dividend policy the annual general assembly might vote would probably call for a much higher increase in the modestly growing dividend amount than the one reported in 2009. The dividend increase in 2009 represents an 8.3% increase over 2008, while in 2008, the dividend amount had increased by 33.3% over 2007.

Financing activities

The financing cash flow is positive in 2007 and 2008 and negative in 2009, which shows that Mitsubishi Electric was able to reduce its debt at the beginning of the period under review. However, in 2009, we notice a sharp increase in short-term debts in 2009 and when we relate liabilities to the operating cash flow, the two following ratios provide an 'unfavorable' evolution:

	2009	2008	2007
Cash liquidity ratio (operating cash flow/average current liabilities)	12.4%	17.1%	35.9%
Cash leverage ratio (operating cash flows/average total liabilities)	7.5%	11.0%	23.5%

Given these apparently unfavorable signals, one could legitimately question the logic of the growth in short-term debt in 2009 over 2008, concurrently with an increase in short-term investments.

One possible rationalization of the choices revealed by figures could come from the fact that Mitsubishi Electric is involved, to a large extent, in long-term contracts with its customers. The three segments Energy and Electric Systems, Industrial Automation Systems, and Information and Communication Systems represent almost 60% of sales revenue in 2009. Sales, in all three of these segments, are carried out mostly through long-term contracts. It is likely Mitsubishi Electric received large down payments from customers (a short-term liability in almost all cases), and needed to invest that cash before it was needed in manufacturing the products customers have ordered.

If this hypothesis is true (and a simple reading of the management comment and perspectives of the annual report will give the analyst a confirmation or a refutation), the situation of Mitsubishi Electric would appear under a more favorable light than it appeared to be when we hypothesized, earlier, that it had too much liquidity that should be distributed. The fact that by 'peeling one more layer of the onion', i.e., by juxtaposing several successive elements of our ever deeper analysis we may change a previous fact-based interpretation, is a perfect illustration of the fact an analyst gets a deeper understanding and can raise more questions about the firm analyzed as she or he progresses in the analysis.

Conclusion

We have shown that each part of the analysis gives progressively evolving theories of what went on in the firm. Sales increased over the three years; cash and cash equivalents remained pretty much steady from year to year. The yearly investing and financing strategy of the firm changed depending on the cash flow from operating activities: development, reimbursement of long-term debt, dividend increase, etc. In the end it appears that the firm is probably on an excellent footing if, as we have surmised, it shows an increase in the down payments on long-term contracts in 2009 as opposed to the situation in 2008, which showed a decline in down payments over 2007. Based on our progressive analysis, business prospects look good for Mitsubishi Electric: the share value of Mitsubishi Electric had grown steadily until the end of 2007, 2008 saw a division of its value almost by five, results and share price evolution in the year 2009 seems to point towards a perception by the markets of a recovery in the firm's business (in coherence with our analysis to date – but with wild swings in price fluctuation as is to be expected for a 'recovering' firm). Whether such a rally will be sustained is beyond the scope of financial analysis of a statement of cash flows.

Review 17.2 Bartok Company (1)

Topic: Comparative financial analysis – statement of cash flows

1. From the information, prepare the statement of cash flows.

As an introduction, it should be stressed that the proposed exercise is intentionally simplified, and does not include the handling of any changes in inventory, receivables or payables.

	Company 1	Company 2	Company 3
Cash flows from operating activities			
Potential cash flow	1,000	400	100
Net cash provided by operating activities	*1,000*	*400*	*100*
Cash flows from investing activities			
Purchase of tangible fixed assets	–900	–900	–1,400
Purchase of financial assets	–700	0	–400
Net cash used in investing activities	*–1,600*	*–900*	*–1,800*
Cash flows from financing activities			
Dividends paid	–200	–600	0
Proceeds from share issuance	800	0	700
New debt	100	1,500	1,100
Repayment of long-term debts	0	–300	0
Net cash provided by financing activities	*700*	*600*	*1,800*
Increase in cash and cash equivalents	100	100	100

1. Comment on the resulting statements.

   It may be useful to draw up the following table summarizing the above information:

	Company 1	Company 2	Company 3
Net cash provided by operating activities (OCF)	1,000	400	100
Net cash used in investing activities (ICF)	–1,600	–900	–1,800
Available cash flow (ACF)	–600	–500	–1,700
Net cash provided by financing activities (FCF)	700	600	1,800
Change in cash	100	100	100

All three companies have experienced the same change in cash, although their cash structures are very different.

Company 1

- It has the highest OCF of the three companies. This is a good sign.
- Its ICF is negative, as is almost always the case, since it represents investments.
- The ACF is negative, which means that the company will need financing to restore financial equilibrium. It does this through its FCF.

Company 2

- Its OCF is lower than that of Company 1. This is not as good, but not yet a real cause for concern.
- The ICF is negative but not as low as that of Company 1. This is apparently logical, since Company 2's investments are not as high.
- This is reflected in the ACF, which is almost identical to that of Company 1.
- Once again, financing is necessary, hence the positive FCF.

Company 3

■ The OCF is very low; this is an early warning of future difficulties.
■ At the same time, the ICF is enormous, with the company making particularly large investments.
■ The ACF is dramatically negative.
■ The only solution is to use external financing, and this is reflected in the FCF.

After commenting on the main items in the statement of cash flows, the contents of each function may be examined. For example, it might be interesting to point out that in its search for financing, Company 3 uses loans but also, although to a lesser extent, calls on its shareholders.

Review 18.1 Bizerte Home Furniture Company

Topic: Financial statement analysis

This case offers a wide open application of financial statement analysis of both distributors singly and comparatively, as well as a basis for decision-making by Leila Smaoui of BHF. The main issue is to assist her in evaluating the going concern status of two of BHF customers and deciding whether or not trade credit should be extended. The remarks that follow are not the only way the case could be analyzed. As usual in a case analysis, it is the methodology and the questions raised that are important, not the answers nor the conclusion.

The analysis will be carried out in four steps:

1. What happened to each retailer in the past three periods. Four dimensions will be explored (one key element of the case is in choosing the metrics that will be monitored – the table below is only an *example* of what can be looked at – many other metrics could be looked at usefully as well):

   (a) operational measures pertaining to revenues and earnings;

   (b) operational metrics pertaining to working capital need;

   (c) elements of description regarding long-lived assets; and

   (d) elements relating to the financing strategy.

2. Derivation of forecasts of what might lie ahead, for each firm.

3. Comparative analysis of the two firms' situations as described in steps 1 and 2 to see if more can be learned from a comparative analysis and, eventually, if available, from incorporating extra accounting data such as the evolution of the downstream and upstream markets, interest rates evolution, availability of credit, etc.

4. Formulate a recommendation to Leila Smaoui regarding her two customers.

All figures are in 000 TND, unless otherwise specified.

Galleria Step 1

What is the current situation? In order to see the evolution of the situation at Galleria as the market deteriorated, we will look at ratios or metrics for each of the four groups mentioned above (see Table R.1).

Table R.1 Selected ratio values for Galleria

	Year 08	Year 09	Year 10
		Time scale →	
Profit related measures			
Net revenue growth (year on year)		−20.88%	5.13%
% of customer returns and allowances	9.00%	12.00%	8.00%
Gross margin as % of sales	50.00%	45.00%	42.00%
Operating expenses as % of gross margin	77.92%	89.02%	110.24%
Profit margin as % of sales	11.04%	4.94%	−4.30%
Profit growth (year on year)		−75.89%	−416.64%
Working capital need evolution			
Days in receivables (day sales outstanding or DSO)		66	70
Inventory turnover (in days)		146	152
Days in payables		134	136
Trade working capital need (in 000 TND)	3,016	2,332	2,795
Cash advances evolution (year on year)		−190	−200
Fixed assets evolution			
Expected life of BF&E (building, fixtures and equipment) (in years)		14.5	14.7
Net investment in new BF&E (000 TND)		600	813
Tangible assets intensity	4.26	2.88	2.84
Ratio of loan increases to asset increases		59%	118%
Financing evolution			
Shareholders equity as % of total assets	33.30%	33.48%	21.97%
LTD % of total assets	33.29%	33.98%	37.26%
Net variation of LT loans year on year (000 TND)		355	960
Interest expense as % of sales	1.33%	1.78%	2.10%
Effective average interest rate	7.07%	7.04%	7.59%
Marginal interest rate on new loans		13.89%	11.53%

From the first group of measures it is clear that Galleria managed to turn around, in 2010, the erosion of its revenue and generate growth, even managing to reduce, simultaneously, the percentage of customer returns. However, this growth of sales was obtained by dramatically increasing operating expenses (an increase of 21.5% from 2009 to 2010: [(7,710/6,345)−1]/100) and thus extended the downturn of the profit margin and entered into losses. Operating expenses include, among other expenses, the remuneration of the sales force and depreciation.

Further supporting the new growth is an investment of 813 in new furniture and fixtures (Gross building, furniture and fixtures, in the balance sheet, increased from 5,800 in 2009 to 6,613 in 2010). In all likelihood, this investment is due to a refurbishment of the stores in Tunis and/or Les Berges du Lac, and/or a development of the Hammamet store where the hospitality industry may offer a stabilizing effect, as the mainly foreign clientele might not have led to as dramatic a reduction of occupancy or development as the crisis might have created in private and institutional sales in the Tunis area. However, a possibly worrisome signal can be observed in the continued decline of customer advance payments: it might be an indication customers, institutional or private, buy what is in stock, are willing to wait or let Galleria take the risk of procurement (an element that may favor BHF over other suppliers to Galleria, because it is a local producer which can deliver rapidly).

The increase in operating expenses is the main explanation for the deterioration of profit. Depreciation as a percentage of gross asset declined marginally: although the depreciation expense is not provided in the income statement by function, it can be estimated a minima (because no sales of assets were reported) by taking the growth in accumulated depreciation in the balance sheet; we can estimate the depreciation expense in 2008 to be 400 in 2009 (1,200 − 800 = 400) and 450 in 2010 (1,650 − 1,200 = 450), i.e., a ratio of depreciation expense to gross value of depreciable assets (building, furniture and fixture only, i.e., not including land which is never depreciable) drops from 6.89% (400/5,800) to 6.80% (450/6,613) in 2010. If we assume a linear depreciation, we can estimate the expected life of the assets: 100/6.89 = 14.5 years in 2009, and 100/6.8 = 14.7 years in 2010, thus confirming that some assets were added or, at least relooked or rejuvenated (a major 'repair' is always added to the depreciable base).

The working capital need management situation is most surprising for a retailer. The trade working capital need is positive for all three years and even increases in 2010 over 2009. As Chapter 15 indicated, a negative working capital need is expected for a retailer (as will be the case for Le Grand Marché in 2008 and 2010). The fact the receivables days (DSO) have increased from 66 to 70 days (calculated by using the average receivables over two consecutive years) is a very worrisome signal.

The very fact DSO increased is mitigated by the fact receivables, in absolute value, stay pretty much even between 2009 and 2010. The credit policy of the firm is not followed by its sales force and/or enforced by the finance department. Remember the payment policy, described in the text, was 20% down and cash on delivery payments were 75% of sales. Up front cash payments are down. In addition the figure for DSO in Table R.1 is optimistic: if 75% of sales are paid cash as mentioned in the case, the days of receivables should be recalculated on the (residual) credit sales, which we can assume, for the sake of simplicity, are 25% of 80% of sales (since a down payment of 20% is expected), thus the revised credit terms: ([(1/({80% of the part remaining to be paid upon delivery – i.e., 25% of sales, since 75% of sales are supposed to be cash on delivery for the 80% remaining to be collected}/average receivables)] × 365) appear to be 328 days in 2009, i.e., [(((2,600+3,100)/2)/(80% × 0.25 × 15,840)) × 365] and 351 days in 2010, i.e., much more than the expected 180 days (or 6 months as mentioned in the text).

Even if we neutralize the down payment (assume 100% – instead of 80% – of credit sales are collected after delivery and no down payment had been provided), the days of credit are still 263 days in 2009[6] and 281 days in 2010, i.e., once again much more than the expected norm. Galleria thus has a serious problem in getting its sales force to follow its normal credit policies and its finance group to enforce collection. Is there a problem of governance? When a customer is past overdue, it might make sense to stop shipping, but that would assume the sales people and the finance people do speak to each other. Another whole story opens up there! Sales revenue may have increased in 2010 mainly because credit terms were extended, probably even to individuals, 'beyond reason'. The sales growth may therefore be somewhat artificial.

Inventory stands at 146 and 152 days in 2009 and 2010. This is a very high level of inventory for a retailer, even of furniture. It seems difficult to justify such a level of inventory, especially when 60% of the sales revenue comes from products that can be obtained almost just in time, or close to it, from a supplier (BHF) whose facilities are not far (65 km from the plant to downtown Tunis and a little over 130 km to Hammamet). Meanwhile, the days payable are increasing slightly (134 days to 136 days). BHF is worried about its receivables from Galleria as BHF may have been treated favorably in the past (it is logical to suppose one treats one's largest supplier well and pays on time as much as possible) and they may feel they will be treated, now, like every other supplier (i.e., payment is delayed without a clear date as to when the payment will be received). The dramatic change Galleria may have experienced leads to tension with suppliers, and thus the need for this analysis, possibly leading BHF to consider limiting their sales to Galleria.

On the investment side, Galleria did invest, as mentioned before, in new furniture and fixtures. That may be a good sign for the future, but the firm could hardly afford to do so, given its situation (especially its over-investment in working capital need). While the investment in 2009 was only partially financed by increased loans, the investments in 2010 are 100% financed by loans and actually the extra borrowing beyond the investment needs may have been used to finance either the inventory or the receivables. A strange situation to say the least: why borrow when so much cash is immobilized in seemingly unnecessary inventories and abnormal receivables?

The financing situation is source of satisfaction: Galleria seems to meet almost to the letter the rule of the three thirds for its liabilities and shareholders' equity side of the balance sheet (even if it does not make much sense for a retailer which should be largely financed by its suppliers). On the other hand the marginal interest rates that Galleria had to pay for the new loans in 2009 and 2010 is clearly higher than the average interest rate of the previous years; encouraging sign: the marginal rate (calculated by assuming the basic old loan paid the effective interest rate of the previous year and thus finding the 'theoretical' interest on the base loans, the new loans being the cause of the increase in the interest expense) obtained in 2010 (11.53%) is lower than the one obtained in 2009 (13.89%).

The real evaluation of the situation regarding loan financing would come from benchmarking with the market: in 2009 and 2010 rates were lowered, worldwide, to boost local economies. The bank may have seen Galleria as a bad risk in 2009 (and may have taken some real guarantees on the loan) since the marginal rate in 2009 was over 13% for an average rate, based on all previous loans, of just over 7%. The situation in 2010 appears to have improved since the marginal long-term loan rate is around 11%, but by how much did the market rate decline in 2010 over 2009?

Galleria Step 2

Galleria's hope is that the operating expenses can be either stabilized or reduced without slowing down the positive trend of sales growth. The main hope is in managing the working capital need to match 'normal behavior' and thus free immobilized long-term funds. What would Galleria look like if it had received, as planned, 20% of its sales as down payments, and 75% of total sales were paid cash on delivery for the remaining amount due?

Let us assume a continued sales growth at the same rate as the one observed in 2010 over 2009. Sales revenue would become 19,028 in 2011 (i.e., 18,100 × 1.0513). Receivables would be (19,028 × 0.8 × 0.25) * 0.5 (i.e., 6 months) = 1,903, thus freeing 1,397 in cash (3,300 − 1,903).

If the inventory were reduced to two weeks of sales (almost no inventory is needed for BHF furniture), thus leaving a need for say between 4 and 5 weeks of inventory from other suppliers, i.e., the inventory would amount to about 470 (i.e., estimated 2011 sales = 19,028 × 1.0513 = 19,028 in gross sales; net sales: 19,028 × (1–0.08) = 17,506 in net sales assuming the same return rate of 8% as observed in 2010; cost of goods sold is assumed to be 55% of net sales, i.e., 17,506 × 0.55 = 10,465; of these 60% are provided by BHF, and thus need, at most, one week of inventory i.e., [(10,465 × 60%)/52] = 121; for the other suppliers the inventory required is [(10,465 × 40%)/12] = 349, if we assume one month of inventory), thus freeing 3,180 (3.650 − 470[7]).

In total Galleria could free, in a short time, about 4,577 (i.e., 1,397 + 3,180 = 4,577). It could use this freed cash to reimburse the interest-bearing loans by that amount. Current, i.e., 2010, interest bearing debt equals 4,800 + 220 = 5,020. If we use the freed up 4,577 cash to reimburse part of that debt, the remaining interest-bearing debt becomes 5,020 − 4,577 = 443. If we assume that the average interest rate remains the same as has been calculated in 2010, i.e., at 7.59%, the new interest expense would be 443 × 0.0759 = 33 versus the 381 reported in 2010, thus savings of about 347 that would be added to profit.

The 'new' (steady state) income statement would look something like Table R.2.

Table R.2 A possible steady state income statement for Galleria in 2011		
(in 000 TND)	Year 2011	
Gross sales	19,028	(18,100 * 1.0513)
Minus returns and allowances	1,522	8%
Net sales	**17,506**	
Cost of goods sold	10,465	From 'normal year' 2009: 55%
Gross profit or gross margin	**7,040**	
Operating expenses	7,710	Idem 2010
Operating profit	**(670)**	
Interest expense or income (net)	33	See text above
Profit (or loss) after interest	**(703)**	
Income tax	0	N/A
Net profit or loss	**(703)**	

Galleria would not yet be profitable but the loss would be reduced by 30%. Alternatively, it is easy to imagine that part of the freed 4,577 could have been used to grow the market (advertising, promotion, etc). The loss is only 4% of gross sales. One could imagine that a growth in gross margin by about 720 (no need to recalculate the new interest expense, an approximation is sufficient) would bring Galleria back into the black. Such an increase in gross margin requires a growth of the net sales by 720/0.45 = 1,600, i.e., a growth of 8.4% (i.e., 1,600/19,028) over and above the already included growth of 5.13% for a total net growth of 2011 over 2010 by [(1.0513 × 1.084)–1] = 14%, not an impossible objective (especially if we aim for it over two years instead of all in one year) in a growing economy. Tunisia has both a healthy internal market plus export sales should start picking up with the recovery of Europe, bringing more income to the country. BHF should not be worried whether its payables will be paid. The cash pump of Galleria should get back to operating normally within two years at the most and, eventually, Galleria could easily return to normal credit conditions.

If we had prepared our simulation on the basis of only two weeks of inventory for the products coming from non-BHF suppliers instead of the one month we used here, Galleria's income statement for 2011 would be in the black. We will not provide the calculation as we have already gone through many iterations. Galleria is not a high-risk firm if it brings its receivables and inventories in line with more normal conditions, which had already been experienced in 2009 and are thus achievable again.

Le Grand Marché Step 1

This analysis will only provide the same indicators, when available, as used for Galleria and we limit our comments to the key points regarding this retailer. These ratios are shown in Table R.3.

Table R.3 Key ratio values for Le Grand Marché

	Year 08	Year 09	Year 10
Profit related measures			
Net revenue growth (year on year)		−6.02%	−12.10%
% of customer returns and allowances	9.08%	9.29%	11.03%
Gross margin as % of sales	38%	36%	31%
Operating expenses as % of gross margin	31%	31%	40%
Profit margin as % of sales	5.29%	3.87%	−8.54%
Profit growth (year on year)		−31%	−290%
Working capital need evolution			
Days in receivables (day sales outstanding or DSO)		39	48
Inventory turnover (in days)		43	34
Days in payables		104	114
Trade working capital need (in 000 TND)	−1,283	839	−2,418
Cash advances evolution (year on year)		−570	−15
Fixed assets evolution			
Expected life of BF&E (in years)		?	?
Net investment in new BF&E (000TND)		?	?
Tangible assets intensity	10.4	11.1	11.2
Financing evolution			
Shareholders equity as % of total assets	29.2%	37.8%	14.8%

The first thing an analyst would notice is the downward spiral of both revenue and profit, to a situation in 2010 which appears to be dramatic: the loss of 2010 wipes out almost entirely the accumulated retained earnings. Incidentally, with only 195 of retained earnings in 2008, Le Grand Marché (LGM) must clearly have had, despite being a 'long-established' firm, profitability problems for a long while.

One key point is that Le Grand Marché has no long-term debt and, except for 2009, uses its suppliers effectively to help fund the working capital need.

Another point worth noting is that Le Grand Marché does not seem to own either the land or the buildings in which it operates (unlike Galleria, and thus needing a lot less long-term funding) and, in all likelihood, rents its facilities (although the income statement is, at best, lacking in details). The largest long-lived asset is represented by the leasehold improvements. Because no details are provided on accumulated depreciation or depreciation expense, the age of the fixed assets (or their expected life) cannot be calculated.

Even if customers are said to ask for longer delays for payment, the DSO remains well within acceptable limits (the policy is 60 days and the actual in 2010 is only 48 days, even though it is up from 39 days). The inventory, at 43 and 34 days for 2009 and 2010 respectively, illustrates the fact Le Grand Marché has reduced its inventory faster than its sales were declining (incidentally we confirm here that the 4 to 5 weeks inventory we have assumed for an 'ideal' Galleria in the previous section was not out of line).

The dramatic downturn in profitability appears to have four distinct sources:

- First and foremost, the decline in sales, which, unlike in Galleria's case, seems to be a longer-term trend (Galleria saw its net sales decline in 2009 over 2008 by over 20% but was able to stop and reverse the hemorrhage in 2010 (net sales grew by 5.13% in 2010 over 2009), but at what cost?). No action taken by Le Grand Marché seems to have stopped the drain on revenue (with net sales declining each year: –6% in 2009 and –12% in 2010 over the previous year) and we know that past years, before 2008, were, in all likelihood, not very profitable either.
- More customer returns (9.3% in 2009 up to 11% in 2010).
- A 7-point loss over three years (38% in 2008 to 31% in 2010) in gross margin due to an increase in the value of COGS as a percentage of net sales. It would be interesting for Leila Smaoui to find out whether this is due to price increases by suppliers (BHF is not the major supplier so it only knows its own pricing policy), or to a reduction in selling prices by LGM, or to a change in the mix of sales towards lower margin products. The latter case would not be a good sign for the future of the relationship between LGM and GHF, since GHF is rather upscale and would expect the retailer to take a larger margin on better designed and manufactured products, appealing to upscale customers and institutional clients, and available *quasi* immediately to the end-customer.
- An inexplicable increase in operating expenses or Opex (rent, depreciation and salaries are likely to be the most important expenses in this category, although commercial expenses might be significant too). Why the operating expenses in 2010 are back at about their level of 2008 is quite surprising, especially since sales have declined in the meantime by 17%. Since Opex were reduced strictly proportionally to sales revenue in 2009, why do they climb back up in 2010? That should be a big source of interrogation for Leila Smaoui. Nothing in the financial statements provides a clue as to an answer. Net leasehold improvements seem to decline regularly by about 700,000 TND each period, thus indicating the likelihood that no new investment has been incurred. A cash flow statement would be most useful in this situation, but none is provided and is probably not required for an unlisted business.

Le Grand Marché Step 2

Even if the operating expenses could have been reduced by 1.7 million TND, back to their 2009 level, income for the most recent period would still have been a loss of 2.3 million TND. There is no information in the financial statements to support any idea as to what LGM is doing to stop the spiral of death. The only (faint) hope is that the Opex increase in 2010 is due to an aggressive marketing or promotional campaign and/or to the hiring of highly-skilled sales personnel, so that 2011 could be seeing a stop to the sales decline. But even if that were the case, to get back to the 2009 operating profitability level would mean that over 6,800 in additional gross margin, to make up the over 4,024 loss of 2010 and create the over 2,800 (rounded figure) of operating profit of 2009, could be obtained (all other costs being assumed steady), or a 41% increase in sales: if the needed gross margin is 6,800, given the gross margin ratio is 31% of sales in 2010, the corresponding sales increase is 6,800/0.31= 21,740 and 21,740/52,970 = 41% , i.e., 52,970 + 21.740 = 74,900, i.e., 10,000 more than the 2008 level of sales. It will take at least several years for LGM to get back in the black, if that is at all possible!

Comparison Step 3

The comparison is fairly simple to carry out. Galleria is, as we have shown, salvageable if they manage to get rid of their long-term debt by freeing liquidity through a realignment of both receivables and inventories with their intended policy. They have a growing market. Whether the management has the authority and the vision to do so is the key question. Le Grand Marché seems to be on a relatively unstoppable decline, in a market that may not be as expandable as the one around Tunis, and any return to profitability can only be in the fairly long-term.

Conclusion and recommendation Step 4

If our analysis is correct (and we have made a lot of hypotheses another analyst may choose notto make), of the two BHF clients we looked at in detail (fortunately BHF has other clients), Galleria seems to be a business-to-business customer 'with a future', while Le Grand Marché seems to be a 'potential loser'.

Galleria needs some sound advice, and, as a key supplier, BHF may be in the position to reason with the management of Galleria for them to implement some of the recommendations we evoked in the analysis above. If Galleria's management is responsive, it would seem logical for BHF to continue to support their distributor and help them grow by maintaining the credit level actually provided and continuing shipping. However, BHF needs to be aware that, if Galleria liquidates its excess inventory (which inevitably will include some BHF products) at a 'fire sale' price, it might tarnish BHF's image and also reduce potential shipments from BHF to Galleria for a while. Maybe BHF could consider buying back the excess inventory of its products held by Galleria to avoid signaling to the market that prices currently obtained by BHF products are 'too high'.

Le Grand Marché is a potential loser and the greatest care should be brought to analyzing the firm in more detail: a statement of cash flows, plus an explanation of the growth of Opex, plus a strategic plan for their getting back in the black are the minimum additional sets of data BHF needs before it can formulate a fully informed decision about LGM. If these documents are not provided by LGM to Leila Smaoui, the position BHF should take is likely to be a tough one. LGM should be kept under a tight leash: its credit line with BHF should be reduced; payments terms should be imposed and enforced. The risk analysis here is to find the difficult balance between the risk of BHF not being paid for what is shipped to LGM, and the risk of losing a distributor and its volume of sales. Unless BHF has another potential new distributor in the area, it can prove to be very expensive to find a new reliable distributor that will absorb the same volume of production as LGM does.

Notes

1. These review answers are based on the appendix to IAS 37.
2. The preceding paragraph results from our interpretation of a seven-line paragraph in Note 2 to the financial statements 'significant accounting policies' and a few vague allusions to the law and the firm's strategy in the review of operations and the strategy sections of the annual report.
3. [21.5% (fuel as percentage of sales in 2007) + 14.7% (cost of purchased power as percentage of sales in 2007)] × 0.25 = 9%.
4. $1.02 \times 1.043 = 1.063$.
5. If you feel, by now, that whoever wrote this note knows more about power production than you would ever care to know, you are probably right. The point is an analyst must familiarize her or himself first with the whole ecosystem in which the analyzed firm operates. Look at professional analysts, each one follows very few economic sectors (sometimes one or two key firms in a sector, if they are large and complex firms), but knows absolutely everything that can be known about the sector and the firms they follow.
6. For 2009, the figure is the result of the following calculation: $[(((2,600 + 3,100)/2)/(100\% \times 0.25 \times 15,840)) \times 365)]$.
7. $470 = 121 + 349$.

Glossary of Key Terms

Accelerated depreciation	Depreciation method allowing the recognition of a large amount of depreciation in the first year of an asset's life and progressively smaller amounts each year as the years pass. Several methods of accelerated depreciation exist.
Account payable	Obligation of a business to a creditor (generally a supplier) usually arising from the purchase of goods and services on credit.
Accounting	System of measurement ('to count') and reporting ('to account for') of economic events for the purpose of decision-making.
Accounting changes	Changes in accounting policies, changes in accounting estimates and prior-period errors.
Accounting cycle	See Cash pump.
Accounting period	The measurement of income is carried in contiguous yet clearly separated time slices. The duration of a 'time slice' is an accounting period. This duration is at most a year, and is more and more frequently shorter than a year.
Accounting principles	Coherent set of behavioral rules and guidelines that range from pure concepts to very operational guidelines about practice.
Accounting standards	See Financial reporting standards
Accounts receivable	The amount corresponding to the delay granted to the customer to pay for the goods or services delivered.
Accrual basis	'An entity shall prepare its financial statements, except for cash flow information, under the accrual basis of accounting' (IAS 1, IASB 2007: § 27). Under this method, transactions and events are recognized when they occur (and not when cash or its equivalent is received or paid) and they are recorded in the accounting records and reported in the financial statements of the periods to which they relate.
Accrual principle	Revenue (expense) is recorded in the income statement at the time of the transaction that causes it, and not at the time of the cash inflow (or outflow, for an expense). It is paired with the 'matching principle'.
Accrued expense	Expense consumed during the accounting period and recognized in the income statement on the closing date, although all documentation pertaining to the transaction has not been obtained or the settlement in cash has not occurred. Its recognition in the income statement leads to the creation of a liability in the balance sheet.
Accrued revenue	Revenue earned during the accounting period and recognized in the income statement on the closing date, although all documentation pertaining to the transaction has not been issued or the settlement in cash has not occurred. Its recognition in the income statement leads to the creation of an asset in the balance sheet.
Acquiree	Legal and independent business entity of which an investor (or acquirer) acquires an interest (synonym: investee).
Acquisition cost	'Amount of cash or cash equivalents paid or the fair value of the other consideration given to acquire an asset at the time of its acquisition or construction' (IAS 16, IASB 2003: § 6).
Adjusting entries	Year-end adjustments related to the influence of time on revenue and expense recognition so that revenues and expenses are attached to the accounting period to which they pertain. These adjustments include accrual of unrecorded revenues, unearned revenues, accrual of unrecorded expenses, and prepaid expenses.
Annual accounts	Synonym: (yearly) financial statements.

Annual report	Document published annually by listed companies (as well as some non-listed but large companies). It includes elements on business reporting (key financial information, management report …) and financial reporting as required by local authorities (financial statements comprising at least the opening and closing balance sheets, and the income statement and the statement of cash flows for the period, plus notes to these documents).
Asset	'Resource (a) controlled by an entity as a result of past events and (b) from which future economic benefits are expected to flow to the entity' (Conceptual framework, IASB 1989: § 49 and IAS 38, IASB 2004: § 8).
Asset turnover	Sales revenue of a period/Average assets during that period.
Associate	'Entity (…) over which the investor has significant influence and that is neither a subsidiary nor an interest in a joint venture' (IAS 28, IASB 2003: § 2).
Authorized capital	Maximum amount of capital (at par) that the charter states a corporation can issue, when needed.
Available cash flow	Addition of the cash flow from operating activities and the cash flow from investing activities.
Available-for-sale financial assets	Financial assets other than 'financial assets at fair value through profit or loss', 'held-to-maturity investments', and 'loans and receivables'. They are valued at fair value directly through equity.
Average collection period	[{(Accounts receivable Year 2 + Accounts receivable Year 1)/2} × 365]/Sales revenue
Average days of sales in receivables (DSO-Days Sales Outstanding), or Average collection period	Ratio providing the average duration of credit terms offered to customer: (Average accounts receivable/Net sales) × 365 days.
Average payment period	[{(Accounts payable Year 2 + Accounts payable Year 1)/2} × 365]/Purchases of goods and services (calculated if the income statement is structured by function as follows: [{(Accounts payable Year 2 + Accounts payable Year 1)/2} × 365]/[Cost of goods sold adjusted by the variation in inventory]).
Bad debt expense	Expense corresponding to the (partial or complete) write-off of a specifically identified uncollectible receivable.
Balance sheet	■ Set of two lists with equality of the valuation total of the items composing each list: resources on one side (also called assets) and obligations to external parties on the other side (liabilities to creditors and the residual, known as shareholders' equity, due to shareholders or owners). ■ 'Snapshot' of the financial position of the firm at a given point in time, hence its other (and official) name of 'Statement of financial position'. 'The elements directly related to the measurement of financial position are assets, liabilities and equity' (Conceptual framework, IASB 1989: § 49).
Basic business equation (balance sheet equation)	Equation representing the balance sheet: Resources (or assets) = obligations to third parties (liabilities) *plus* equity (shareholders' claims).
Bill of exchange	See Notes receivable.
Bonds	A bond is a certificate allowing the division of a lender-funded debt between a large number of investors (bondholders), each of whom can contribute only a small part of the amount of the debt financing (the face value, or the selling price if sold at a discount [i.e., below face value] or with a premium [i.e., above face value]).

Book value	Difference between an asset's acquisition cost (i.e., its gross value) and the balance of its accumulated depreciation.
Borrowing costs	'Interest and other costs incurred by an entity in connection with the borrowing of funds' (IAS 23, IASB 1993 amended 2007: § 5).
Business	'An integrated set of activities and assets that is capable of being conducted and managed for the purpose of providing a return in the form of dividends, lower costs or other economic benefits directly to investors or other owners, members or participants' (IASB Glossary).
Business combination	'A transaction or other event in which an acquirer obtains control of one or more businesses. Transactions sometimes referred to as "true mergers" or "mergers of equals" are also business combinations as that term is used in this IFRS' (IFRS 3, IASB 2008: Appendix A, 'Defined terms').
By function (income statement)	Income statement in which items are classified by reference to the function (i.e., purpose) of expenses. The expenses are classified according to their role in the determination of income (e.g., cost of goods sold, commercial, distribution or administrative expenses).
By nature (balance sheet)	Balance sheet in which items are classified by reference to the operating cycle.
By nature (income statement)	Income statement in which items are classified by reference to the nature of expenses (for example, purchases of materials, transportation costs, taxes other than income tax, salaries and social expenses, depreciation, etc.).
By term (balance sheet)	Balance sheet in which items are classified by reference to their realization/settlement being within twelve months after the reporting period or after more than twelve months after the reporting period.
Capital	Total amount of the par value of shares or stock certificates multiplied by the number of shares issued. Capital is the evidence of the contribution (at par) of the shareholders to the formation of the initial resources of the firm.
Capital expenditure	Expenses incurred for the purpose of generating future economic benefits.
Capitalization of borrowing costs	Inclusion of borrowing costs in the cost of the 'construction' of a long-lived asset.
Capitalization of reserves or retained earnings (bonus issue)	Incorporation of retained earnings or reserves into the share capital, generally giving rise to the issuance of additional (free) shares to existing stockholders.
Carry-forward (or carry-back)	Mechanism which allows a business to carry a net operating loss forward (or back) a certain number of years and offset it against future profits (or receive refunds for income taxes paid in the past).
Cash	'Cash on hand' [coins, banknotes and currency available] and demand deposits' [deposits in bank accounts that are available on demand]' (IAS 7, IASB 1992: § 6).
Cash account	Cash in hand, cash on hand, or cash at bank.
Cash equation	Working capital − Working capital need = Net cash
Cash equivalents	'Short-term, highly liquid investments that are readily convertible to known amounts of cash and which are subject to an insignificant risk of changes in value' (IAS 7, IASB 1992: § 6).
Cash flow adequacy	Cash flow from operations/(Long-term capital expenditures + dividends + scheduled debt reimbursements).

Cash flow as percentage of sales	Operating cash flow/Sales revenue.
Cash flow statement	See Statement of cash flows.
Cash flow yield	Operating cash flow/Net income (for the same period).
Cash flows from financing activities	Cash flows related to providers of long-term funds to the firm: capital for shareholders and loans or bonds for other sources of long-term funding to the enterprise.
Cash flows from investing activities	Cash flows representing 'the extent to which expenditures [or revenue] have been made for [with regards to] resources intended to generate future income and cash flows' (IAS 7, IASB 1992: § 16).
Cash flows from operating activities	Cash flows primarily deriving from the main or core revenue-producing activities of the entity.
Cash items	Items of the income statement which, by nature, will eventually generate a real cash flow.
Cash leverage ratio	Operating cash flow of a period/Average total liabilities (i.e., [opening + closing total liabilities balances]/2).
Cash liquidity ratio	Operating cash flow/Average current liabilities (i.e. [opening + closing current or short-term liabilities balances]/2).
Cash pump	Descriptive term used to refer to the operating cycle or the cash-to-cash cycle. It is composed of several stages, each of which consumes cash. Some of these stages are: procurement of resources, holding of resources in inventory if applicable, transformation process, holding of finished goods in inventory if applicable, selling, delivering, and collecting cash.
Cash ratio	(Cash + Marketable securities)/Current liabilities.
Change in inventory	Difference between: ■ beginning and ending inventory of raw materials or merchandises. ■ ending and beginning inventory of finished products.
Chart of accounts	Logically organized list of all recognized accounts used in recording transactions in a firm. A chart of accounts generally assigns a unique code to each account.
Closing entries	The act of closing a revenue or expense account by transferring its balance from the income statement to the balance sheet.
Commercial margin	Difference between sales revenue from merchandise sold and cost of merchandise sold.
Common-size or vertical analysis	Representation of the structure of a financial statement by using a base number in that document and expressing all other items on the document as percentages of the base item. If the same is done for several consecutive periods, it visualizes the changes in the structure over time.
Component of a tangible asset	Physically identifiable part of an item of property, plant and equipment with a separable cost that is significant in relation to the total cost of the item. For example, in a truck, tires, engine, autonomous refrigeration equipment, and body and chassis may be recognized as different components of the truck (they can be procured separately from the ensemble) and can be depreciated on different useful lives.
Comprehensive income	■ 'Total comprehensive income' = 'the change in equity during a period resulting from transactions and other events, other than those changes resulting from transactions with owners in their capacity as owners'. ■ 'Other comprehensive income' = 'Items of income and expense (including reclassification adjustments) that are not recognized in profit or loss as required or permitted by other IFRSs)' (IASB Glossary).

Conservatism	'Inclusion of a degree of caution in the exercise of the judgments needed in making the estimates required under conditions of uncertainty, such that assets, [revenues] or income are not overstated and liabilities or expenses are not understated' (Conceptual framework, IASB 1989: § 37).
Consistency of presentation	Financial statements must be presented over time in similar fashion, and using equivalent descriptors or parameters.
Consolidation	Process by which the financial statements of two or more entities are combined into one for reporting purposes. There exist three methods of consolidation: full consolidation, equity method and proportionate consolidation.
Construction contract	See Long-term contract.
Contingent liability	'(a) Possible obligation that arises from past events and whose existence will be confirmed only by the occurrence or non-occurrence of one or more uncertain future events not wholly within the control of the entity or (b) a present obligation that arises from past events but is not recognized because (i) it is not probable that an outflow of resources embodying economic benefits will be required to settle the obligation; or (ii) the amount of the obligation cannot be measured with sufficient reliability' (IAS 37, IASB 1998: § 10).
Control	'Power to govern the financial and operating policies of an entity so as to obtain benefits from its activities' (IAS 27, IASB 2003: § 4).
Copyright	Provides the holder with exclusive rights to the publication, production, and sale of the rights for an intellectual creation, be it a musical, artistic, literary, or dramatic work (and often, by extension, software).
Cost of goods sold (COGS)	Valuation, at cost, of the goods or services transferred to customers against a consideration, which is recognized as revenue.
Cost of inventories	'All costs of purchases, costs of conversion and other costs incurred in bringing the inventories to their present condition and location' (IAS 2, IASB 2003: § 10).
Credit	Right-hand side of a T-account.
Current investments	Investments that are, by their nature, readily realizable (into cash) and are intended to be held for not more than one year.
Current liability	'A liability shall be classified as current when it satisfies any of the following criteria: (a) it is expected to be settled in the entity's normal operating cycle; (b) it is held primarily for the purpose of being traded; (c) it is due to be settled within twelve months after the reporting period; or (d) the entity does not have an unconditional right to defer settlement of the liability for at least twelve months after the reporting period. An entity shall classify all other liabilities as non-current' (IAS 1, IASB 2007: § 69).
Current ratio	Current assets/Current liabilities.
Debit	Left-hand side of a T-account.
Debt ratio or Debt to total assets ratio	Total debt/Total assets.
Debt to equity ratio	Debt/Shareholders' equity or Debt/(Shareholders' equity + Debt) or Long-term debt/ Shareholders' equity
Debt to tangible net worth	Debt/(Shareholders' equity − intangible assets).
Declining balance method	Depreciation method which recognizes greater amounts of depreciation in the early years of an asset's life and smaller amounts in the later years.

Deferred taxation accounting	Recognition of the tax consequences of the temporary differences by including its tax effect as income tax expense on the income statement and as an asset or a liability (called a deferred tax asset or a deferred tax liability) in the balance sheet.
Depletion	The process of allocating the cost of 'acquiring' a source of non-renewable natural resources over the period during which it will provide usable resources.
Depreciable amount	'Cost of an asset, or other amount substituted for cost in the financial statements, less its residual value' (IAS 16, IASB 2003: § 6).
Depreciation	'Systematic allocation of the depreciable amount of an asset over its useful life' (IAS 16, IASB 2003: § 6). Process of allocating the cost of acquiring a tangible or fixed asset (with the exception of land) over the period during which economic benefits will be received by the firm, i.e., process of adjusting (downwards) the net value of an asset by recognizing it is consumed in a way that does not completely eliminate the resource. The depreciation allowance or expense recognizes the fact the potential of any asset is consumed through usage or passage of time.
Depreciation expense	The cost of consuming a fixed asset over a specific, clearly defined, period of time. It reflects the consumption, in the course of the firm's activities, of the future benefit-creation potential of this asset.
Derivative	Any financial instrument derived from securities or physical markets such as futures, options, warrants and convertible bonds.
Development	'Application of research findings or other knowledge to a plan or design for the production of new or substantially improved materials, devices, products, processes, systems or services before the start of commercial production or use' (IAS 38, IASB 2004: § 8).
Direct method	Computation of the 'net cash flow from operating activities' by grouping cash effects of homogeneous transactions classes.
Discontinued operation	'Component of an entity that either has been disposed of, or is classified as held for sale and: (a) represents a separate major line of business or geographical area of operations; (b) is part of a single coordinated plan to dispose of a separate major line of business or geographical area of operations; or (c) is a subsidiary acquired exclusively with a view to resale' (IFRS 5, IASB 2004: § 32).
Discounting (of a note receivable)	Endorsement of a note receivable for the benefit of a third party (generally a bank), which, in exchange, transfers to the company the cash value of the note minus a discounting fee.
Discounting fee	Represents (1) the interest for the period separating the date of discounting and the maturity date, (2) an administrative fee, and most often, (3) a risk premium.
Dividend	Distribution of the earnings of the business to its shareholders.
Dividend pay-out ratio	Cash dividends per share/Earnings per share.
Dividend yield ratio	Cash dividends per share/Market price per share.
Double entry accounting	Each transaction impacts the basic business equation in at least two ways that always keep the equation balanced. In other words, each individual accounting transaction has at least two sides, which are always balanced.
Double entry bookkeeping	See Double entry accounting.
Doubtful or disputed accounts	Accounts receivable partly or totally uncollectible.
Earnings	Result of the difference between the resources created by the economic activity of the business (revenues) and the resources consumed in operating the firm and creating the revenues (expenses).

Earnings per share (EPS)	Ratio of net income after taxes (and after preferred dividends if there are any) to average number of shares during the period for which the income has been calculated.
EBIT	Earnings from operations Before Interests and Taxes.
EBITDA	Earnings from operations Before Interests, Taxes, Depreciation, Amortization and provisions.
EBITDAM	Earnings Before Interest, Taxes, Depreciation, Amortization and Management fees.
EBITDAR	Earnings Before Interest, Taxes, Depreciation, Amortization and Rent, where Rent refers to the periodic lease payment incurred in order for the firm to have medium to long-term control over assets that are essential to the ability of the firm to carry out its business.
Economic value added	See EVA®.
End-of-period entries	Any such entries that are necessary, in an accrual accounting process, to give a true and fair view of both the financial position at the end of an accounting period and the income statement for the accounting period. These entries will be carried out every time one closes the books (yearly, half-yearly, quarterly, monthly, etc.).
Entity concept	Regardless of the legal form of the economic entity, economic transactions carried by the entity must be recorded separately from the personal transactions of actors involved in or with the entity.
Equity	■ Claim, right or interest one has over some 'net worth'. ■ 'Residual interest [of the investors] in the assets of the entity after deducting all its liabilities' (Conceptual framework, IASB 1989: § 49).
Equity method	'Method of accounting whereby the investment is initially recognized at cost and adjusted thereafter for the post-acquisition change in the investor's share of the net assets of the investee. The profit or loss of the investor includes the investor's share of the profit or loss of the investee' (IAS 28, IASB 2003: § 2).
EVA®	Residual income corrected (positively or negatively) for the after-tax effects of several accounting adjustments.
Exceptional items	Items in the income statement pertaining to actions, decisions, and events that are occasional and unusual.
Excess cash flow	Cash flow from operating activities *minus* the absolute value of the *minimum* cash flow from investing activities required to maintain the competitive position of the firm. It is often approximated, for lack of better publicly available information, by cash flow from operating activities minus [purchases of fixed assets minus proceeds from sales of fixed assets].
Expenses	'Decreases in economic benefits during the accounting period in the form of outflows or depletion of assets or incurrence of liabilities that result in decreases in equity, other than those relating to distributions to equity participants' (Conceptual framework, IASB 1989: § 70).
Extraordinary items	See Exceptional items.
Fair value	'Amount [on a given date] for which an asset could be exchanged, or a liability settled, between knowledgeable, willing parties in an [at] arm's length transaction' (IAS 39, IASB 2008: § 9).
Faithful presentation	'To be reliable, information must represent faithfully the transactions and other events it either purports to represent or could reasonably be expected to represent' (Conceptual framework, IASB 1989: § 33).
Finance leases	'Lease [contract] that transfers substantially all the risks and rewards incidental to ownership of an asset [to an entity that will operate or use said asset for its own revenue generating business]. Title may or may not eventually be transferred' (IAS 17, IASB 2003: § 4).

Financial accounting

Process of description of the various events that take place in the life of a firm. It allows for the periodic creation of synthetic reports called financial statements.

Financial asset

'Any asset that is (a) cash; (b) an equity instrument of another entity; (c) a contractual right: (i) to receive cash or another financial asset from another entity; or (ii) to exchange financial assets or financial liabilities with another entity under conditions that are potentially favorable to the entity; or (d) a contract that will or may be settled in the entity's own equity instruments and is: (i) a non-derivative for which the entity is or may be obliged to receive a variable number of the entity's own equity instruments; or (ii) a derivative that will or may be settled other than by the exchange of a fixed amount of cash or another financial asset for a fixed number of the entity's own equity instruments. For this purpose the entity's own equity instruments do not include instruments that are themselves contracts for the future receipt or delivery of the entity's own equity instruments' (IAS 32, IASB 2008: § 11).

Financial asset at fair value through profit or loss

'Financial asset (...) that (...) is classified as held for trading' or, upon initial recognition, (...) is designated by the entity as at fair value through profit or loss (IAS 39, IASB 2008: § 9). The value of this financial asset in the balance sheet will be its fair market value as of the balance sheet day, thus creating a profit or a loss between the fair value and the cost of acquisition.

Financial asset classified as held for trading

Financial asset '(i) acquired or incurred principally for the purpose of selling or repurchasing it in the near term; (ii) on initial recognition, (...) part of a portfolio of identified financial instruments that are managed together and for which there is evidence of a recent actual pattern of short-term profit-taking; or (iii) (...) derivative (except for a derivative that is a financial guarantee contract or a designated and effective hedging instrument) (IAS 39, IASB 2008: § 9). Its value in the balance sheet is reported at 'fair value'.

Financial instrument

'Financial instrument is any contract that gives rise to a financial asset of one entity and a financial liability or equity instrument of another entity' (IAS 32, IASB 2008: § 11).

Financial leverage

Practice consisting of using preferably borrowed funds, rather than shareholders' funds, to finance investments: as long as the ROI is greater than the net cost of borrowed funds, this practice will increase the return on equity.

Financial reporting

To report, in a somewhat aggregated way, the (economic) performance of the firm to essential external users such as shareholders, bankers, creditors, customers, unions, tax authorities, etc.

Financial reporting standards

Also named 'Accounting standards'. Authoritative statements of how particular types of transaction and other events should be reflected in financial statements. These standards include specific principles, bases, conventions, rules, and practices necessary to prepare the financial statements. They are prepared by national or supranational not-for-profit agencies. The main issuers of standards are the IASB (IFRS) for most of the world and the FASB (SFAS) for the United States.

Financial statements

'A complete set of financial statements comprises: (a) a statement of financial position as at the end of the period [balance sheet]; (b) a statement of comprehensive income [including an income statement] for the period; (c) a statement of changes in equity for the period; (d) a statement of cash flows for the period; (e) notes, comprising a summary of significant accounting policies and other explanatory information; and (f) a statement of financial position as at the beginning of the earliest comparative period when an entity applies an accounting policy retrospectively or makes a retrospective restatement of items in its financial statements, or when it reclassifies items in its financial statements' (IAS 1, IASB 2007: § 10).

Finished goods

Completed products ready for sale.

First-in, first-out (FIFO)

Goods withdrawn are valued batch by batch in the order in which they entered inventory.

Franchise	Contractual agreement that allows, for a fee and within a limited geographical territory, the holder (franchisee), with or without direct support from the franchisor, to sell certain products or services, to use certain trademarks, or to do other specific things identified in the franchise agreement without loss of ownership over these by the franchisor.
Free cash flow	Available cash flow of a period minus dividends paid pertaining to that period.
Full consolidation	Mechanism where 'an entity combines the financial statements of the parent and its subsidiaries line by line by adding together like items of assets, liabilities, equity, income and expenses' (IAS 27, IASB 2003: § 18).
Function	See 'by function'.
GAAP	Generally Accepted Accounting Principles.
General ledger	Grouping of all subsidiary (i.e., detailed) accounts.
Going concern	Assumption that a business entity has a long life expectancy. This concept separates a business from a project (which has a definite completion or termination date).
Goodwill	'An asset representing the future economic benefits arising from other assets acquired in a business combination that are not individually identified and separately recognized' (IFRS 3, IASB 2008: Appendix A, 'Defined terms'). 'Cost [of acquisition] of the business combination [i.e., the acquiree] over the acquirer's interest in the net fair value of the identifiable assets, liabilities and contingent liabilities [of the acquiree]' (former definition, IAS 38: IASB 2004, § 11).
Governance	Enterprise governance is the set of responsibilities and practices exercised by the board and executive management, with the goal of growing shareholders' equity by: 1. providing strategic direction; 2. ensuring that objectives are achieved; 3. ascertaining that risks are managed appropriately; and 4. verifying that the organization's resources are used responsibly.
Grants related to assets	'Government grants whose primary condition is that an entity qualifying for them should purchase, construct or otherwise acquire long-term assets' (IAS 20, IASB 1994: § 3).
Gross profit or gross margin	Difference between the revenue from sales and the cost of goods or services sold.
Gross profit rate	Gross profit/Sales.
Group	'A parent and all its subsidiaries' (IAS 27, IASB 2003: § 4).
Held-to-maturity investments	'Non-derivative financial assets with fixed or determinable payments and fixed maturity that an entity has the positive intention and ability to hold to maturity (…)' (IAS 39, IASB 2008: § 9). They are valued in the balance sheet at cost. Such investments are kept until maturity because they may be part of the laddering of future cash inflows needed for known future, fixed date outflows.
Historical cost	Valuation of resources at the cost at which they were acquired, without ever adjusting it (except in application of the lower of cost or market principle).
Horizontal format (balance sheet or income statement)	Two lists of accounts balances side by side (with equal totals).
IASB	International Accounting Standards Board: independent, private sector body, formed in 1973, under the name of International Accounting Standards Committee (IASC), and restructured in 2001 when the name was changed to IASB. Its main objective is to promote convergence of accounting standards and principles that are used by businesses and other organizations for financial reporting around the world.

Impairment loss	'Amount by which the carrying amount of an asset exceeds its recoverable amount' (IAS 16, IASB 2003: § 6). It must be acknowledged as an expense of the period when recognized in order for the firm to remain in line with the principle of 'lower of cost or market'.
Income from operating activities	Income from the core business of an entity – it is part of a flow of income that is expected to be recurring (i.e., excluding extraordinary or exceptional elements).
Income statement	■ Record of what happened during the period that caused the observed income (profit or loss). ■ 'Film' of the activity of the business during a given period. ■ Statement reporting the detail of the shareholders' value created during a given period.
Indirect method	Computation of the net cash flow from operating activities by adjusting net profit or loss for the effects of changes during the period in inventories and operating receivables and payables, and non-cash items such as depreciation and provisions.
Information	Signal, generally resulting from the transformation of data or other information, that has the potential to change the decision of a person receiving the signal.
Intangible asset	'An identifiable non-monetary asset without physical substance' (IAS 38, IASB 2004: § 8). An example of such asset would be a copyright or an acquired brand name.
Interest	Cost a borrower must pay (equivalent to a rent) to have the right to use someone else's monies (the lender's monies) in the course of running her/his business.
Interest coverage ratio	Operating income (before interest expense and income taxes)/Interest expense.
Inventories	'Assets: (a) held for sale in the ordinary course of business; (b) in the process of production for such sale; or (c) in the form of materials or supplies to be consumed in the production process or in the rendering of services' (IAS 2, IASB 2003: § 6).
Inventory trade financing	Accounts payable/Inventory.
Inventory turnover	Number of times the inventory 'turns' during the accounting period. For finished products, it is calculated as the ratio obtained by dividing the cost of goods sold over a period by the average inventory value of finished goods over the period. By extension, and for simplicity reasons and lack of publicly available information, that ratio often includes all inventories in the denominator. Dividing 365 by the inventory turnover ratio transforms it into a number of days held in inventory.
Investee	Legal and independent business entity in which an investor is acquiring an interest. Synonym: acquiree.
Investment ratio	Capital expenditures/(Depreciation plus sales of long-term assets).
Joint control	'Contractually agreed sharing of control [between two or more legal entities] over a [third] economic activity' (IAS 31, IASB 2003: § 3).
Joint venture	'Contractual arrangement whereby two or more parties undertake an economic activity that is subject to joint control' (IAS 31, IASB 2003: § 3).
Journal	Day-to-day chronological register of accounting data describing economic transactions.
Last-in, first-out (LIFO)	Method of valuation of goods withdrawn from inventory, in which withdrawals are valued at the unit cost of the batch they belong to using the batches (till exhaustion of the batch) in the reverse order from the one they followed when entering inventory.
Lease	'Agreement whereby the lessor conveys to the lessee in return for a payment or series of payments the right to use an asset for an agreed period of time' (IAS 17, IASB 2003: § 4).
Ledger	Grouping of accounts having homogeneous characteristics such as reflecting similar types of transactions.

Legal forms of organization	The most common legal forms of organization are: (1) Sole proprietorship; (2) partnership; and (3) limited [liability] company.
Liability	'Present obligation of the entity arising from past events, the settlement of which is expected to result in an outflow from the entity of resources embodying economic benefits' (Conceptual framework, IASB 1989: § 49).
Limited liability company	Incorporated business where liability assumed by the investors does not extend beyond their investment.
Loans and receivables	'Non-derivative financial assets with fixed or determinable payments that are not quoted in an active market (…)' (IAS 39, IASB 2008: § 9). They are valued in the balance sheet at cost.
Long-term contract	Contract linking two parties that span several accounting periods for the purpose of delivering, by one party to the other, an asset at a given date (or on several dates) or provision of a defined service for the duration of the contract against a pre-agreed flow of considerations.
Long-term debt to equity ratio	Long-term debt/Shareholders' equity or Long-term debt/(Shareholders' equity + Debt).
Long-term funding or long term capital employed	Shareholders' equity + Long-term debt.
Long-term or long-lived	Qualifier of an activity or a resource that will create benefits or obligations over a period exceeding 12 months.
Lower of cost or market	Principle of valuation of resources or liabilities under which an item is valued at its historical cost, or at market value if the latter is lower than the cost.
Managerial accounting	It deals with a rather detailed account of how resources are acquired, managed and used in the various business processes constituting the firm and is thus of particular interest to managers inside the firm.
Mark to market	The fair valuation of an investment with an active quoted market price.
Mark to model	The fair valuation of an investment without an active quoted market price as obtained from a selected (and publicly described) valuation model or method.
Market to book ratio	Market price per share/Book value per share.
Matching principle	'Simultaneous or combined recognition of revenues and expenses that result directly and jointly from the same transactions or other [linked] events' (Conceptual Framework, IASB 1989: § 95).
Materiality and aggregation	'Omissions or misstatements of items are material if they could, individually or collectively, influence the economic decisions of users taken on the basis of the financial statements' (IAS 1, IASB 2007: § 7). 'An entity shall present separately each material class of similar items. An entity shall present separately items of a dissimilar nature or function unless they are immaterial' (IAS 1, IASB 2007: § 29).
Measurement	'Process of determining the monetary amounts at which the elements of the financial statements are to be recognized and carried in the balance sheet and income statement' (Conceptual framework, IASB 1989: § 99).
Merchandise	Goods purchased for resale without transformation.
Minority interests	See non-controlling interests.
Monetary assets	'Money held and assets to be received in fixed or determinable amounts of money' (IAS 38, IASB 2004: § 8).

Movements (changes) in tangible assets	Statement providing a reconciliation of the gross and net carrying amount of tangible assets at the beginning and end of the period by listing acquisitions and disposals.
Multiple-step format (balance sheet)	List of subsets of the main categories of assets and liabilities. Identification of useful subtotals by subtracting relevant other sub-categories of assets or liabilities.
Multiple-step format (income statement)	Revenue and expense categories are paired so as to highlight the components of total net income.
Nature	See 'by nature'.
Net assets	Assets minus liabilities (same as net worth).
Net cash	Difference between cash and cash equivalents (assets) and liabilities accounts corresponding to negative cash (such as bank overdrafts).
Net income	Remainder after all relevant expenses have been deducted from revenues. Measure of the wealth created by an economic entity (increased shareholders' equity) during an accounting period.
Net value	See Book value.
Net worth	Difference between total assets and liabilities (same as net assets).
No offsetting	'An entity shall not offset assets and liabilities or income and expenses, unless [explicitly] required or permitted by an IFRS' (IAS 1, IASB 2007: § 32).
Nominal or par value	Face value of a share (or a bond).
Non-cash items	Items of the income statement which, by nature, will never generate a real cash flow (depreciation expense, provision expense...).
Non-controlling interests	'The equity in a subsidiary not attributable, directly or indirectly, to a parent' (IAS 27, IASB 2003: § 4).
Non-operating items	See Exceptional items.
Notes payable	Accounts payable (promise by the customer, recognized in the books of the customer, to pay the supplier) represented by a note issued by the customer and accepted by the supplier or issued by the supplier and accepted by the customer.
Notes receivable	Accounts receivable (recognition, in the books of the supplier, of a claim the supplier holds over a customer, for their future payment of supplier-provided goods or services) represented by a note issued by the seller and accepted by the customer or issued by the customer (promissory note). Such notes can be sold to a third party.
Notes to the financial statements	The notes 'shall: (a) present information about the basis of preparation of the financial statements and the specific accounting policies used in accordance with paragraphs 117–124 [which deal with 'Disclosure of accounting policies']; (b) disclose the information required by IFRSs that is not presented elsewhere in the financial statements; and (c) provide information that is not presented elsewhere in the financial statements, but is relevant to an understanding of any of them' (IAS 1, IASB 2007: § 112).
Obligation	'Duty or responsibility to act or perform in a certain way' (Conceptual Framework, IASB 1989: § 60).
Off balance sheet items	Items not listed in the balance sheet of the company.
Operating cash ratio	see Cash flow yield
Operating leases	'Lease[s] other than a finance lease' (IAS 17, IASB 2003: § 4).

Operating segment	'A component of an entity: (a) that engages in business activities from which it may earn revenues and incur expenses (including revenues and expenses relating to transactions with other components of the same entity); (b) whose operating results are regularly reviewed by the entity's chief operating decision-maker to make decisions about resources to be allocated to the segment and assess its performance,;and (c) for which discrete financial information is available' (IFRS 8, IASB 2006: § 5).
Organization costs (incorporation or set-up costs)	Costs incurred during the process of establishing or incorporating a business.
Partnership	Legal form of organization of a business, often not incorporated, where associates or partners are fully responsible for all the consequences of the actions of the entire business.
Patent	Document granted by a government or an official authority bestowing on the inventor of a product or manufacturing process the exclusive right to use or sell the invention or rights to it.
Periodic inventory system	Periodic (annual) physical counting to establish the quantities of each item existing in the ending inventory. This system implies that the cost of goods sold is found by deduction.
Permanent difference	Difference between taxable income and pre-tax income linked to recognition or non-recognition.
Perpetual inventory system	Continuous recording of changes in inventory (each entry leads to an update and each withdrawal is valued at the current Weighted Average cost or appropriate FIFO cost). The cost of goods sold is the sum of the cost of all withdrawals. The value of the theoretical ending inventory is found by deduction, before being confronted (and adjusted if necessary) with a physical count of the existing inventory.
Post-employment benefits	Obligations an employer has towards its personnel after they leave the firm. Such obligations to an individual accrue with the passage of time in employment. It becomes definitive immediately if the post-employment benefit program is external to the firm. When the firm administers internally the payment of these benefits, the obligation becomes definitive once the duration of employment of the individual in that firm exceeds a pre-determined threshold and the individual's rights are 'vested'. The cost of funding these benefit plans is a part of the labor compensation expense. Such benefits include: pensions, other retirement benefits, post-employment life insurance and post-employment medical care.
Posting	Process of transferring entries from the journal to a ledger.
Potential cash flow	Cash flow from operating activities calculated solely on the basis of cash items.
Preferred shares	Shares granting a higher or guaranteed dividend or a priority dividend.
Prepaid expense	An asset representing the acquisition of a service for which an invoice has been received but which has not yet been consumed. This is for example the case of the payment of an insurance premium. The expense will be recognized in the income statement by reducing the prepaid expense (as an asset) proportionately to the consumption of the service (usually proportional to passage of time).
Price/earnings ratio	Market price per share/earnings per share.
Profit and loss account (or statement)	Also referred to as P&L, this is an alternative name for the income statement.
Profit appropriation	Decision taken by the shareholders to distribute dividends and/or to retain earnings.

Proportionate consolidation	'Method of accounting whereby a venturer's share of each of the assets, liabilities, income and expenses of a jointly controlled entity is combined line by line with similar items in the venturer's financial statements or reported as separate line items in the venturer's financial statements' (IAS 31, IASB 2003: § 3).
Provision	'Liability of uncertain timing or amount' (IAS 37, IASB 1998: § 10).
Quick ratio	(Cash + marketable securities + accounts receivable)/Current liabilities.
R&D intensity	R&D expenses/sales revenue.
R&D per employee	R&D expenses/number of employees.
Ratio analysis	Measure of the assumed relation between two or more components of financial statements.
Raw materials	Goods or untransformed resources incorporated in the production process that become integrally and physically part of the sellable object resulting from the transformation process. Raw materials are distinct in purpose from supplies and energy, for example, which could be the same resources as raw materials but which are consumed in order to facilitate the transformation process creating the product that will eventually be sold.
Receivables turnover	Ratio measuring the number of times receivables turned over during the year: Net sales/ Average accounts receivable.
Recognition of intangible assets	'An intangible asset shall be recognized if, and only if: (a) it is probable that the expected future economic benefits that are attributable to the asset will flow to the entity; and (b) the cost of the asset can be measured reliably' (IAS 38, IASB 2004: § 21).
Recourse	If the discounting of a note is *without recourse*, the note is sold with complete transfer to the buyer of the note of the default risk of the drawer. If it is made *with recourse*, i.e., it is a conditional sale: if the drawer defaults on the maturity date, the discounting financial institution will demand full reimbursement of the note plus fees from the seller of the note who sold it for discounting in the first place.
Relevance	Information is relevant when it has the potential to influence the economic decisions of users by helping them evaluate past, present or future events and either confirm or amend past evaluations.
Reliability	Information should be 'reliable, in that financial statements: 1. represent faithfully the financial position, financial performance and cash flows of the entity; 2. reflect the economic substance of transactions, other events and conditions, and not merely the legal form; 3. are neutral, i.e., free from bias; 4. are prudent; and 5. are complete in all material respects' (IAS 8, IASB 2003: § 10).
Research	'Original and planned investigation undertaken with the prospect of gaining new scientific or technical knowledge and understanding' (IAS 38, IASB 2004: § 8).
Reserves (different types)	Earnings set aside on a yearly basis either due to regulatory rules, to statutory rules or to discretionary decisions made by the general assembly of shareholders for a specific purpose. Examples of reserves are: legal reserve, statutory reserves, regulated reserves, optional (voluntary) reserves, revaluation reserves. Reserves are part of shareholders' equity.
Residual income (RI)	Income after taking into account the *cost of all sources of funds*, including a fair (even if nominal) remuneration for the shareholders, not just the financial costs due to interest-bearing liabilities.
Residual value	'Estimated amount that an entity would currently obtain from disposal of the asset, after deducting the estimated costs of disposal if the asset were already of the age and in the condition expected at the end of its useful life' (IAS 16, IASB 2003: § 6).

Retained earnings	Part of the value created through the firm's operations that shareholders have chosen not to take out of the firm. It is a *de facto* increase in their contribution to the ongoing activity of the firm. They are part of shareholders' equity and could be distributed as dividends if the shareholders decided to do so, for example if earnings of a period were insufficient to maintain a level of dividend expected by shareholders.
Return on assets (ROA)	Net income/[(Assets Year 2 + Assets Year 1)/2].
Return on capital employed (ROCE)	Earnings before interest and tax (EBIT)/Capital employed (where Capital employed is: Average long-term liabilities + Average equity).
Return on equity	Net income/Average equity.
Return on investment (ROI)	Net income /Capital employed (where Capital employed is: Average long-term liabilities + Average equity).
Return on sales (net profit margin)	Net income/Sales.
Return on shareholders' equity (ROE)	Net income/Average equity.
Revenue	'Gross inflow of economic benefits during the period arising in the course of the ordinary activities of an entity when those inflows result in increases in equity, other than increases relating to contributions from equity participants' (IAS 18, IASB 1993: § 7).
Revenue expenditure	Expenses caused by the short-term usage – or maintenance – of the revenue generating potential of an asset (examples: minor spare parts, oil and cooling fluids, maintenance expenses, minor repairs expenses).
Revenue recognition	Recording the impact of a transaction on the revenue component of the income statement.
Revenues	'Gross inflow of economic benefits during the period arising in the course of the ordinary activities of an entity when those inflows result in increases in equity, other than increases relating to contributions from equity participants' (IAS 18, 1993: § 7).
Sales return	Reversal of a sale when a customer is not satisfied for any reason with the product that was delivered (such as non-conformity of delivery with order, defects, etc.). The sales transaction is reversed and the goods must be re-entered into inventory after control of their quality, or otherwise disposed of through a 'fire sale', or shipping to a specialized outlet store.
Sales revenue per employee	Sales/Number of employees.
Scoring models	Model generally based on a linear multivariate regression analysis (or using linear discriminant analysis) of several ratios and/or elements of the financial statements that create a unique 'score' for a firm at one point in time. If the score is (or drifts) above or below certain experiential thresholds, the likelihood of the business failing is declared to be high or low.
Semi-finished goods	Items that are finished with regard to one stage of production but are nonetheless not sellable in that condition. They will generally be integrated into a finished product at a later date.
Share capital	Historical value (at par) of the contributions to the firm all shareholders have made in the beginning and during the life of the firm by making external resources available to the firm and giving up control over these resources (cash, effort or ideas, physical assets, etc.).
Share dividend (also stock dividend)	Dividends paid out by giving shares of the firm (or portion of shares) to the shareholders in lieu of cash. The issue of share dividends can be in lieu of dividends for all shareholders or as a possibility offered to an individual shareholder to opt and forego her or his right to a dividend and increase the number of shares she/he holds.
Share premium	Difference between the issue price and the par value of a share.

Significant influence	'Power to participate in the financial and operating policy decisions of the investee but it is not control or joint control over those policies' (IAS 28, IASB 2003: § 2).
Single-step format (balance sheet)	Balance sheet presented with assets, on the one hand, and shareholders' equity and liabilities on the other. No mix of assets and shareholders' equity and liabilities is performed.
Single-step format (income statement)	Simplified version of the income statement. Expenses and revenues are each considered as one category.
Specific identification method	Method of inventory-movements valuation in which the cost on withdrawal from inventory of items that are not ordinarily interchangeable or fungible, is absolutely identical, item by item, to the one they had when entering in inventory.
Stakeholders	Any party that has a 'stake' in the outcome and output resulting from the activity of an entity. They include a variety of parties: investors, employees, customers, suppliers, government, etc.
Statement of cash flows	'The statement of cash flows shall report cash flows during the period classified by operating, investing and financing activities' (IAS 7, IASB 1992: § 10). Financial statement providing information about the historical changes in cash and cash equivalents of an entity and classifying cash flows during the period in three sections: operating, investing and financing activities.
Statement of financial position	Official name, under IFRS, for balance sheet.
Statement of financial structure	Statement formalizing the cash equation which relates three main concepts: working capital, working capital need and net cash.
Statement of intermediate balances	Statement highlighting the key sequential intermediate balances that describe the value (income) creation process such as commercial margin, value added and gross operating profit.
Stock options plan	Motivational device in which the corporation grants employees the right to acquire a specified personalized number of shares of the corporation at a predetermined invariant price and for a specified time window.
Straight-line method	The asset is depreciated evenly over its useful life.
Subscribed or issued capital	Part of the capital authorized that the shareholders have agreed to purchase and pay when called to do so.
Subsidiary	'Entity (…) that is controlled by another entity (known as the parent)' (IAS 27, IASB 2003: § 4).
Substance over form	'If information is to represent faithfully the transactions and other events that it purports to represent, it is necessary that they are accounted for and presented in accordance with their substance and economic reality and not merely their legal form' (Conceptual framework, IASB 1989: § 35). The capitalization of financial leases is an example of the application of this principle.
Tangible assets (also called 'tangible fixed assets', 'property, plant and equipment', 'plant assets', or 'operational assets')	'Tangible items that: (a) are held for use in the production or supply of goods or services, for rental to others, or for administrative purposes; and (b) are expected to be used during more than one period' (IAS 16, IASB 2003: § 6).
Taxable income	Difference between taxable revenue and deductible (or tax deductible) expenses or costs.
Temporary difference	Difference between taxable income and pre-tax income linked to the timing of recognition of revenues or expenses.
Term	See 'by term'.

Trademark (or trade name or brand name) — Distinctive identification (symbol, logo, design, word, slogan, emblem, etc.) of a manufactured product or of a service that distinguishes it from similar products or services provided by other parties.

Transaction types — Sale of goods, rendering of services, interest, royalties, dividends.

Treasury shares (own shares) — Shares of a company acquired by itself.

Trend or horizontal analysis — Comparison over time of the evolution of a specific expense or revenue item or a particular asset or liability item.

Trial balance — List of the debit and credit footings for each account in the general ledger.

True and fair view — Objective of financial statements not defined in the accounting standards.

Unearned revenue — A liability recognizing that a customer has paid before the product or service has been delivered. A prepayment or a down payment leading to the recognition of a liability called unearned revenue, balancing the cash received. It is generally considered as part of short-term liabilities. The liability will be drawn down as the service is rendered, or the goods are delivered, or as a percentage of the completion of the contract.

Unit of measurement — Financial accounting only records transactions expressed in financial units.

Useful life — 'Either: (a) the period of time over which an asset is expected to be available for use by an entity; or (b) the number of production [output] or similar units expected to be obtained from the asset by an entity' (IAS 16, IASB 2003: § 6).

Users (of financial information) — Managers and stakeholders.

Value added — Creation or increase in value, resulting from the entity's current professional activities, over and above that of goods and services provided by third parties and consumed by the firm.

Vertical format (balance sheet or income statement) — Continuous list of account balances.

Weighted average cost method (WAC) — Method of valuation of goods withdrawn from inventory. Under this method, goods are considered to be totally fungible. Withdrawn units are valued at the average cost per unit of available goods. The average is updated after each new addition to inventory, or once a month.

Work in process (WIP) — Products still in the manufacturing process at the close of the day and services rendered but not invoiced.

Work in progress (WIP) — In a long-term contract, the accumulated costs incurred to date not yet billed to the customer. It is an asset.

Working capital — Shareholders' equity plus long-term (financial) debt minus fixed (non-current) assets or, alternatively, currents assets (including cash) minus current liabilities (including bank overdrafts).

Working capital need — Current assets (excluding net cash) minus current liabilities (excluding bank overdrafts).

Index: Financial Accounting & Reporting Global Perspective (Stolowy, Lebas and Ding)